T0134712

Lecture Notes in Business Information Processing 415

Series Editors

More information about this series at http://www.springer.com/series/7911

Samira Cherfi · Anna Perini ·
Selmin Nurcan (Eds.)

Research Challenges in Information Science

15th International Conference, RCIS 2021
Limassol, Cyprus, May 11–14, 2021
Proceedings

Editors
Samira Cherfi
Conservatoire National des Arts et Métiers
Paris, France

Anna Perini
Fondazione Bruno Kessler
Trento, Italy

Selmin Nurcan
University Paris 1 Panthéon-Sorbonne
Paris, France

ISSN 1865-1348 ISSN 1865-1356 (electronic)
Lecture Notes in Business Information Processing
ISBN 978-3-030-75017-6 ISBN 978-3-030-75018-3 (eBook)
https://doi.org/10.1007/978-3-030-75018-3

This Springer imprint is published by the registered company Springer Nature Switzerland AG
The registered company address is: Gewerbestrasse 11, 6330 Cham, Switzerland

Preface

It is our great pleasure to welcome you to the proceedings of the 15th International Conference on Research Challenges in Information Science (RCIS 2021). RCIS brings together scientists, researchers, engineers, and practitioners from the whole spectrum of information science and provides opportunities for knowledge sharing and dissemination.

RCIS 2021 was originally planned to take place in Limassol, Cyprus, during May 11–14, 2021. The Organizing Committee decided to turn it into an online conference due to the persistence of the COVID-19 pandemic. The scope of RCIS 2021 is summarized by the following eight thematic areas: (i) Information Systems and their Engineering, (ii) User-Oriented Approaches, (iii) Data and Information Management, (iv) Business Process Management, (v), Domain-Specific Information Systems Engineering, (vi) Data Science, (vii) Information Infrastructures, and (viii) Reflective Research and Practice.

The special theme we proposed for RCIS 2021 is "Information Science and global crisis". Global crises, such as the pandemic we are currently experiencing, natural disasters, wars, and international political crises, are challenging Information Science to help build effective management solutions, to learn from previous experience how to prevent them, and to support humans in performing core activities, such as education and communication. The diversity of causes, the quality of the collected data, and the complexity of the underlying mechanisms are among the relevant research challenges.

Our two keynote speakers provided their perspectives on the role of Information Science at the time of the global pandemic we are experiencing. Neil Maiden (City, University of London) gave a keynote entitled "Augmenting creativity to resolve global challenges: An information systems approach", which focused on the power of cumulative creative thinking for designing effective solutions to complex problems, such as those we are facing during the COVID-19 pandemic. Science journalism about COVID-19 vaccines and their rollout has been considered as an example.

Jennifer Horkoff (Chalmers University of Technology and the University of Gothenburg, Sweden), in her keynote entitled "Requirements Engineering for Social Crises", proposed a reflection on the role of requirements engineering, not only to capture functional and non-functional requirements of a software system but also more intangible social needs such as security, privacy, or job satisfaction. Examples from the "RE Cares" initiative and from COVID contact tracing apps were discussed.

This is the second edition of RCIS that has proceedings published by Springer through their Lecture Notes in Business Information Processing (LNBIP) series. These proceedings include the papers in all the tracks of RCIS 2021, and therefore constitute a comprehensive account on the conference.

The main track received 116 abstracts, which materialized into 109 submissions. The Program Committee co-chairs desk rejected 10 papers which were out of scope, resulting in 99 papers that were peer reviewed. Each paper was reviewed by at least three Program Committee members; these reviews served to initiate an online discussion moderated by one Program Board member, who concluded the discussion by writing a meta-review and a suggestion for full acceptance, conditional acceptance with gatekeeping, invitation for the Posters and Demos track or for the Research Projects track, or rejection. The Program Committee co-chairs discussed each paper and took the final decisions, largely in line with the Program Board advice, leading to 35 accepted papers in the main track. The breakdown by category is follows: technical solution - 17 accepted out of 53 reviewed, scientific evaluation - 7 out of 18, industrial experience - 5 out of 12, and work in progress - 6 out of 16.

The Posters and Demos track, chaired by Giovanni Meroni and Dominik Bork, attracted 6 submissions, 4 of which were accepted. Furthermore, 9 additional papers were accepted from those papers invited from the main conference track, leading to a total of 13 posters and demos. The Research Projects RCIS track, chaired by Denisse Muñante and Anthony Simonofski, received 13 submissions, out of which 8 were accepted. An additional paper was accepted from those papers invited from the main conference track, leading to a total of 9 research projects . The Doctoral Consortium track, chaired by Xavier Franch and Renata Guizzardi, with the support of Blagovesta Kostova in the role of student co-chair attracted 6 submissions, 4 of which were accepted. The Tutorials track, chaired by Sergio España and Patricia Martín-Rodilla, received 4 proposals, 3 of which were accepted. RCIS 2021 would not have been possible without the engagement and support of many individuals. As editors of this volume, we would like to thank the RCIS Steering Committee members for their availability and guidance. We are grateful to the members of the Program Board and of the Program Committee, and to the additional reviewers for their timely and thorough reviews of the submissions and for their efforts in the online discussions. A special thank you goes to those who acted as gatekeepers for the conditionally accepted papers. We would like to thank our social media chairs Itzel Morales Ramírez and Vítor E. Silva Souza, who guaranteed visibility through Twitter. We are deeply indebted to George A. Papadopoulos, the general co-chair responsible for the local organization, for his continuous logistics and operation efforts. We would also like to thank the RCIS 2021 proceedings chair, Raihana Ferdous, who carefully managed the proceedings preparation process, and Christine Reiss from Springer for assisting in the production of these proceedings. Finally, we are thankful to all the authors and attendants who contributed to the program, sharing their work, findings, and feedback with the community to continue to advance the field of Information Science.

March 2021

Samira Cherfi
Anna Perini
Selmin Nurcan

Organization

General Chairs

Selmin Nurcan	Université Paris 1 Panthéon Sorbonne, France
George Papadopoulos	University of Cyprus, Cyprus

Program Committee Chairs

Samira Cherfi	CEDRIC-Conservatoire National des Arts et Métiers, France
Anna Perini	Fondazione Bruno Kessler, Italy

Posters and Demos Chairs

Dominik Bork	TU Wien, Austria
Giovanni Meroni	Politecnico di Milano, Italy

Doctoral Consortium Chairs

Xavier Franch	Universitat Politécnica de Catalunya, Spain
Renata Guizzardi	University of Twente, Netherlands
Blagovesta Kostova	Ecole Polytechnique Fédérale de Lausanne, Switzerland

Tutorial Chairs

Patricia Martín-Rodilla	Institute of Heritage Sciences, Spanish National Research Council, Spain
Sergio España Cubillo	Utrecht University, Netherlands

Research Project Chairs

Denisse Muñante	Télécom SudParis, France
Anthony Simonofski	University of Namur and KU Leuven, Belgium

Proceedings Chair

Raihana Ferdous	Fondazione Bruno Kessler, Italy

Social Media Chairs

Itzel Morales Ramírez	Instituto de Ingeniería de la UNAM, Mexico
Vítor E. Silva Souza	Federal University of Espírito Santo, Brazil

Steering Committee

Said Assar	Institut Mines-Telecom Business School, France
Marko Bajec	University of Ljubljana, Slovenia
Pericles Loucopoulos	Institute of Digital Innovation and Research, Ireland
Haralambos Mouratidis	University of Brighton, UK
Selmin Nurcan	Université Paris 1 Panthéon Sorbonne, France
Óscar Pastor	Universitat Politécnica de Valéncia, Spain
Jolita Ralyté	University of Geneva, Switzerland
Colette Rolland	Université Paris 1 Panthéon-Sorbonne, France
Jelena Zdravkovic	Stockholm University, Sweden

Program Board

Raian Ali	Hamad Bin Khalifa University, Qatar
Said Assar	Institut Mines-Telecom Business School, France
Marko Bajec	University of Ljubljana, Slovenia
Xavier Franch	Polytechnic University of Catalunya, Spain
Jennifer Horkoff	Chalmers University and University of Gothenburg, Sweden
Evangelia Kavakli	University of the Aegean, Greece
Pericles Loucopoulos	Harokopio University of Athens, Greece
Haralambos Mouratidis	University of Brighton, UK
Andreas Opdahl	University of Bergen, Norway
Óscar Pastor	Universitat Politécnica de Valéncia, Spain
Jolita Ralyté	University of Geneva, Switzerland
Colette Rolland	Université Paris 1 Panthéon Sorbonne, France
Camille Salinesi	Université Paris 1 Panthéon Sorbonne, France
Monique Snoeks	Katholieke Universiteit Leuven, Belgium
Jelena Zdravkovic	Stockholm University, Sweden

Main Track Program Committee

Nour Ali	Brunel University London, UK
Carina Alves	UFPE, Brazil
Daniel Amyot	University of Ottawa, Canada
Joao Araujo	Universidade NOVA de Lisboa, Portugal
Fatma Başak Aydemir	Boğaziçi University, Turkey
Dominik Bork	TU Wien, Austria
Mario Cortes-Cornax	Université Grenoble Alpes, France
Fabiano Dalpiaz	Utrecht University, Netherlands
Maya Daneva	University of Twente, Netherlands
Rebecca Deneckere	Centre de Recherche en Informatique, France
Chiara Difrancescomarino	Fondazione Bruno Kessler, Italy
Tania Di Mascio	University of L'Aquila, Italy
Sophie Dupuy-Chessa	Université Grenoble Alpes, France

Sergio Espana Cubillo	Utrecht University, Netherlands
Raihana Ferdous	Fondazione Bruno Kessler, Italy
Hans-Georg Fill	University of Fribourg, Switzerland
Andrew Fish	University of Brighton, UK
Agnès Front	Université Grenoble Alpes, France
Mohamad Gharib	University of Florence, Italy
Cesar Gonzalez-Perez	Institute of Heritage Sciences, Spanish National Research Council, Spain
Renata Guizzardi	University of Twente, Netherlands
Fayçal Hamdi	CEDRIC - Conservatoire National des Arts et Métiers, France
Felix Härer	University of Fribourg, Switzerland
Truong Ho Quang	University of Gothenburg and Chalmers University of Technology, Sweden
Mirjana Ivanovic	University of Novi Sad, Serbia
Amin Jalali	Stockholm University, Sweden
Haruhiko Kaiya	Kanagawa University, Japan
Christos Kalloniatis	University of the Aegean, Greece
Maria Karyda	University of the Aegean, Greece
Marite Kirikova	Riga Technical University, Latvia
Elena Kornyshova	Conservatoire des Arts et Métiers, France
Blagovesta Kostova	Ecole Polytechnique Fédérale de Lausanne, France
Konstantinos Kotis	University of the Aegean, Greece
Tong Li	Beijing University of Technology, China
Lidia Lopez	Universitat Politécnica de Catalunya, Spain
Andrea Marrella	Sapienza University of Rome, Italy
Patricia Martín-Rodilla	University of A Coruña, Spain
Massimo Mecella	Sapienza University of Rome, Italy
Giovanni Meroni	Politecnico di Milano, Italy
Denisse Muñante	Télécom SudParis, France
John Mylopoulos	University of Toronto, Canada
Kathia Oliveira	Université Polytechnique Hauts-de-France, France
Barbara Pernici	Politecnico di Milano, Italy
Geert Poels	Ghent University, Belgium
Gil Regev	Ecole Polytechnique Fédérale de Lausanne, Switzerland
Marcela Ruiz	Zurich University of Applied Sciences, Switzerland
Mattia Salnitri	Politecnico di Milano, Italy
Maribel Yasmina Santos	University of Minho, Portugal
Rainer Schmidt	Munich University of Applied Sciences, Germany
Florence Sedes	Université Toulouse III - Paul Sabatier, France
Estefanía Serral	Katholieke Universiteit Leuven, Belgium
Anthony Simonofski	Katholieke Universiteit Leuven, Belgium
Pnina Soffer	University of Haifa, Israel
Dimitris Spiliotopoulos	University of Houston, USA
Paola Spoletini	Kennesaw State University, USA

Angelo Susi	Fondazione Bruno Kessler, Italy
Eric-Oluf Svee	Stockholm University, Sweden
Nicolas Travers	Léonard de Vinci Pôle Universitaire, France
Yves Wautelet	Katholieke Universiteit Leuven, Belgium
Hans Weigand	Tilburg University, Netherlands

Posters and Demos Program Committee

Raian Ali	Hamad Bin Khalifa University, Qatar
Claudia P. Ayala	Universitat Politécnica de Catalunya, Spain
Judith Barrios Albornoz	University of Los Andes, Colombia
Cinzia Cappiello	Politecnico di Milano, Italy
Jose Luis de la Vara	University of Castilla-La Mancha, Spain
Abdelaziz Khadraoui	University of Geneva, Switzerland
Manuele Kirsch-Pinheiro	Université Paris 1 Panthéon Sorbonne, France
Elena Kornyshova	CNAM, France
Emanuele Laurenzi	FHNW, Switzerland
Dejan Lavbi	University of Ljubljana, Slovenia
Vik Pant	University of Toronto, Canada
Francisca Pérez	Universidad San Jorge, Spain
Iris Reinhartz-Berger	University of Haifa, Israel
Marcela Ruiz	Zurich University of Applied Sciences, Switzerland
Estefanía Serral	Katholieke Universiteit Leuven, Belgium
Manuel Wimmer	Johannes Kepler University Linz, Austria
Jelena Zdravkovic	Stockholm University, Sweden

Doctoral Consortium Program Committee

Maya Daneva	University of Twente, Netherlands
Geert Poels	Ghent University, Belgium
Jolita Ralyté	University of Geneva, Switzerland
Marcela Ruíz	Zurich University of Applied Sciences, Switzerland
Paola Spoletini	Kennesaw State University, USA
Angelo Susi	Fondazione Bruno Kessler, Italy

Additional Reviewers

Simone Agostinelli
Workneh Ayele
Oussama Ayoub
Jérôme Fink
Ramin Firouzi
Fáber Danilo Giraldo Velásquez
Stelios Kapetanakis
Herve Leblanc
Armel Lefebvre
Katerina Mavroeidi
Fabian Muff
Argyri Pattakou
Nikolaos Polatidis
Benedikt Reitemeyer
Katerina Vgena

Abstracts of Keynote Talks

Requirements Engineering for Social Crises

Jennifer Horkoff

Chalmers|University of Gothenburg, Gothenburg, Sweden
jennifer.horkoff@gu.se

Requirements Engineering (RE) develops concepts and methods to help systematically understand a problem, breaking it down into actionable items or desired qualities. Although we often think of RE in a technical role, deriving concrete requirement statements or models for software or system engineering, RE has long been positioned to bridge the social and the technical worlds [12]. We aim to understand the complex problems of people, their organizations and ecosystems, and define them in a way that is actionable by technology.

For years, work in RE has focused on non-functional requirement (NFR) or system qualities [2]. This allows us to not only capture how well a system must accomplish its functions, but to capture more intangible social needs such as security, privacy, or job satisfaction – needs which are important, but often hard to operationalize. Past work has focused on early RE, gaining a deeper understanding of system needs from a social perspective [11]. In previous projects, my colleagues and I have worked on capturing the social needs of philanthropic organizations using NFRs as "softgoals", leading to technical recommendations [7].

Further work has looked at RE from this social perspective, aiming to avoid crises. For example, RE for sustainability, creating methods to consider sustainability system impacts early in the requirements analysis process [5]. Similar work has been conducted from an RE perspective aiming to increase system safety using traceability techniques [10], to reduce security attacks from a social perspective [9], or to consider trust in technology adoption [8].

Along this line, in the last four years, RE researchers have grouped together to introduce the "RE Cares" event to the IEEE International RE Conferenc [3, 4]. Each year, the team finds a philanthropic problem, and invites RE experts to work with this problem, before and during the RE conference, to help them better understand their issues, develop a requirement specification, and begin work on system prototypes. Example problems include disaster management, transportation for tourists with special needs, cyber security for small businesses, and systems to help track and manage gun violence prevention tactics.

Recent events and the rise of technology pervasiveness make this line of work even more relevant. As the RCIS 2021 theme description states: "Global crisis, as the pandemic we are experiencing in these days, natural disasters, wars and international political crisis, are challenging Information Science to help building effective management solutions..." We can find examples of applications addressing social crises which are technically sound, but fail or cause harm because they did not take into account social needs. We can look to the recent example of COVID contact tracing apps, particularly the privacy concerns which led to the low uptake of the Italian Immuni app [1].

In terms of advancing technology, the rise in Artificial Intelligence and Machine Learning (ML) has the potential to bring new social crises. We note that critical decisions are automated in ways we can not understand (transparency), making decisions which may work against certain groups (bias). These qualities are NFRs in a traditional RE sense, but the meaning and prominence of such NFRs may change with the rise of ML [6]. As part of this talk, I describe ongoing work applying RE techniques to ML, with a focus on understanding NFRs in this new and important context.

Much future work can continue in the direction of RE for AI, keeping in mind the social perspective. For example, RE knowledge and techniques can be used to help to determine the boundaries between AI and human operation – when to automate or when to involve human expertise. Further work can go beyond crises brought by AI systems and look more generally at the potential social impact of trends and events, and how an RE mindset can be used to help mitigate negative consequences through successful applications of technology.

References

1. Amante, A.: Italy launches covid-19 contact-tracing app amid privacy concerns. Reuters, June 2020. https://reut.rs/2XlRD6H
2. Chung, L., Nixon, B.A., Yu, E., Mylopoulos, J.: Non-functional Requirements in Software Engineering, vol. 5. Springer Science & Business Media, New York (2012). https://doi.org/10.1007/978-1-4615-5269-7
3. Dekhtyar, A., et al.: From RE cares to SE cares: software engineering for social good, one venue at a time. In: Proceedings of the ACM/IEEE 42nd International Conference on Software Engineering: Software Engineering in Society, pp. 49–52 (2020)
4. Dekhtyar, A., et al.: Requirements engineering (re) for social good: Re cares [requirements]. IEEE Softw. **36**(1) 86–94 (2019)
5. Duboc, L., et al.: Requirements engineering for sustainability: an awareness framework for designing software systems for a better tomorrow. Requir. Eng. **25**(4), 469–492 (2020). https://doi.org/10.1007/s00766-020-00336-y
6. Horkoff, J.: Non-functional requirements for machine learning: challenges and new directions. In: 2019 IEEE 27th International Requirements Engineering Conf. (RE). pp. 386–391. IEEE (2019)
7. Horkoff, J., Yu, E.: Interactive goal model analysis for early requirements engineering. Requir. Eng. **21**(1), 29–61 (2016). https://doi.org/10.1007/s00766-014-0209-8
8. Horkoff, J., Yu, E., Liu, L.: Analyzing trust in technology strategies (2006)
9. Li, T., Horkoff, J., Mylopoulos, J.: Holistic security requirements analysis for sociotechnical systems. Softw. Syst. Model. **17**(4), 1253–1285 (2018). https://doi.org/10.1007/s10270-016-0560-y
10. Steghöfer, J.P., Knauss, E., Horkoff, J., Wohlrab, R.: Challenges of scaled agile for safety-critical systems. In: Franch, X., Männistö, T., Martínez-Fernández, S., (eds.) PROFES 2019. LNCS, vol. 11915, pp. 350–366. Springer, Cham (2019). https://doi.org/10.1007/978-3-030-35333-9_26

11. Yu, E.S.: Towards modelling and reasoning support for early-phase requirements engineering. In: Proceedings of the ISRE 1997: 3rd IEEE International Symposium on Requirements Engineering, pp. 226–235. IEEE (1997)
12. Zave, P., Jackson, M.: Four dark corners of requirements engineering. ACM Trans. Softw. Eng. Methodol. (TOSEM) **6**(1), 1–30 (1997)

Augmenting Creativity to Resolve Global Challenges: An Information Systems Approach

Neil Maiden

Business School, City, University of London
neil.maiden.1@city.ac.uk

Today's global challenges, such as the COVID19 pandemic, populist politics and the climate crisis, are complex and wicked problems. Established ways of thinking rarely solve these problems effectively. Instead, effective solutions are often found in alternative new ideas that challenge these ways of thinking, and that often result from the cumulative creative thinking of many individuals and groups. However, many people who could contribute to solving global challenges lack the necessary creativity knowledge, skills and self-belief to generate new and useful ideas regularly. Simple-to-use information systems that augment people's creative thinking capabilities are one means of filling the skills gap [1, 2]. This keynote will demonstrate the role of creative thinking during the COVID pandemic, describe how this new breed of information system can help, and demonstrate a concrete use of one such system in science journalism about COVID vaccines and their rollout.

References

1. Lockerbie, J., Maiden, N.: Modelling the quality of life goals of people living with dementia. Inf. Syst. 101578 (2020)
2. Maiden, N., et al.: Digital creativity support for original journalism. Commun. ACM **63**(8), 46–53 (2020)

Contents

Business and Industrial Processes

Information Security and Risk Management

Data and Information Management

Domain Specific Information Systems Engineering

User-Centred Approaches

Data Science and Decision Support

Information Systems and Their Engineering

Poster and Demo

Doctoral Consortium

Tutorials and Research Projects

Business and Industrial Processes

Robotic Process Automation in the Automotive Industry - Lessons Learned from an Exploratory Case Study

Judith Wewerka[1,2](✉) and Manfred Reichert[1]

[1] Institute of Databases and Information Systems, Ulm University, Ulm, Germany
{judith.wewerka,manfred.reichert}@uni-ulm.de
[2] Research and Development, BMW Group, Munich, Germany

Abstract. Robotic Process Automation (RPA) is the rule-based automation of business processes by software bots mimicking human interactions. The aims of this paper are to provide insights into three RPA use cases from the automotive domain as well as to derive the main challenges to be tackled when introducing RPA in this domain. By means of an exploratory case study, the three use cases are selected from real RPA projects. A systematic method for analyzing the cases is applied. The results are structured along the stages of the lifecycle model of software development. We provide information on every lifecycle stage and discuss the respective lessons learned. In detail, we derive five challenges that should be tackled for any successful RPA implementation in the automotive domain: (1) identifying the right process to automate, (2) understanding the factors influencing user acceptance, (3) explaining RPA to the users, (4) designing human bot interaction, and (5) providing software development guidelines for RPA implementation.

Keywords: Robotic Process Automation · RPA · Exploratory case study · Use case · Automotive industry

1 Introduction

To stay competitive in their market, companies need to organize their business processes in an efficient and cost-effective manner [11]. They, therefore, demand for an increasing degree of process automation. A promising approach is provided by Robotic Process Automation (RPA), which aims to automate business processes or parts of them by software robots (bots for short) mimicking human interactions. Thus, an increasing number of companies have been running RPA initiatives [2].

Scientifically, RPA has been investigated in various directions, e.g., systematic literature reviews [6,17], case studies in areas like shared services [10,22] and telecommunications [16,23], methods fostering RPA implementation [4,7], and attempts to quantify RPA effects [20]. However, there exists little research on introducing RPA in the automotive industry. Consequently, lessons

S. Cherfi et al. (Eds.): RCIS 2021, LNBIP 415, pp. 3–19, 2021.
https://doi.org/10.1007/978-3-030-75018-3_1

learned resulting from RPA application in this domain have not been extensively reported in literature yet. This raises the question whether and–if yes–how RPA projects in automotive industry can be successfully completed.

The purpose of this paper is to gain a better understanding of RPA projects. Moreover, we want to highlight the challenges that need to be tackled to enable a successful RPA implementation. We conduct an exploratory case study in the automotive industry to find out what is happening, to gain novel insights into real world projects, and to generate ideas for new research [21].

The remainder of the paper is organized as follows: Sect. 2 summarizes existing RPA case studies and the lessons learned in their context. Section 3 describes the method we applied for this case study research. The results are presented in Sect. 4, followed by a cross-case analysis and a systematic derivation of the challenges in automotive industry in Sect. 5.

2 Related Work

We summarize results from existing RPA case studies with a focus on the lessons learned for a successful RPA implementation. To the best of our knowledge, no case study exists that has been conducted in the automotive domain. Therefore, we focus on giving an overview of RPA case studies in general. These lessons learned are used in Sect. 5 to classify our results.

In [8], RPA in business process outsourcing is introduced with the goal to create and validate premium advice notes. Overall, 14 processes are automated with 120.000 cases per month resulting in cost savings of 30%. Eight lessons learned are emphasized: (1) RPA needs a sponsor, (2) a culture of business innovation and technology accelerates RPA adoption, (3) RPA should sit in the business, (4) processes should be standardized and stabilized before automation, (5) RPA must comply with enterprise architecture policies, (6) internal RPA capability should be built, (7) bots should be multi-skilled, and (8) internal communication is highly important for RPA projects.

The RPA journey of an energy supplier is presented in [9]. One process is automated to resolve infeasible customer meter readings. In total, 25 processes are automated with 1 million cases per month. The lessons learned that are reported in [8] are picked up and expanded with further aspects: the composition of the RPA teams should evolve over time, continuous prototyping becomes necessary to expand RPA to new business contexts, RPA should complement enterprise information systems, and components should be reused to scale quickly and to reduce development costs.

The RPA journey of a shared service company automating the generation of the financial close is described in [10]. Overall, 44 processes are automated saving 45 Full Time Equivalents (FTEs). The lessons learned are to pick the right RPA approach (i.e., to differentiate between screen automation and process automation), to redesign work prior to implementation, and to prepare the employees. [22] presents another RPA journey in shared service highlighting sub-processes that may be subject to RPA, e.g., copy data from an Excel sheet to a human resource management system. Finally, [22] emphasizes that RPA benefits are immense, but results (e.g., faster processes or FTE savings) cannot be always guaranteed.

An RPA journey of a telecommunication company is presented in [16]. Two processes are discussed, i.e., bundle support tools for the field service technician on one hand and proactive problem solving on the other. During the RPA journey, 800 FTEs are saved. As lessons learned, RPA should be designed and implemented in an agile way, RPA impact on staff members should be carefully managed, and technical and organizational interrelations should be investigated from the beginning. Another RPA journey in telecommunications is described in [23]: 15 processes are automated with around 500.000 cases per month. RPA is considered as one tool working hand in hand with process elimination, process improvement, and other business process tools. As the two main lessons learned, bots require more explicit instructions than humans and some risks need to be taken to successfully introduce RPA.

How to automate the generation of a payment receipt with a business process outsourcing provider is described in [1]. The as-is and to-be processes are described, and it is shown how RPA increases productivity, e.g., the group using the RPA bot could handle 21% more cases than the one without bot. Another RPA use case in the same domain is presented in [5]–the automated processes update employee payment details and create employment relationships. The lessons learned include preparing the IT department and developing RPA capabilities, addressing fears about losing jobs, selecting processes carefully, and measuring process improvements.

In [3], RPA is applied to digital forensics in two use cases: keyword search on forensic platforms and import evidence files to a forensic platform. As main lesson learned, special forensic software cannot be properly automated with available RPA software solutions.

The case study presented in [12] emphasizes the benefits of RPA for mastering data management. Companies are accompanied to show the qualitative benefits achieved with RPA, including improved data quality, reduced human errors, increased productivity, and decreased costs. As particular lesson learned it is mentioned to overcome the lack of understanding RPA technology.

In [24], an RPA system supporting corporate service providers is presented. Both the as-is and the to-be processes are described, and RPA is evaluated quantitatively. Concrete numbers to productivity improvements (over 1,000%) are provided and managerial impacts are derived. No lessons learned are given.

Finally, [18] investigates RPA use cases in procurement to explore practical implications and the impact on the procurement functions. The use cases are further analyzed regarding challenges during RPA implementation, e.g., employees fear to change their working habits, or the procurement function needs to be mature. Details on the concrete cases are missing.

3 Methodology

This section presents the method we applied to conduct the RPA case study in the automotive domain. A case study in software engineering is "an empirical enquiry that draws on multiple sources of evidence to investigate one instance (or a small number of instances) of a contemporary software engineering phenomenon within its real-life context" [14] to improve the software engineering process and the resulting product, i.e., the RPA bot in the context of this work [14]. We combine the methodologies presented in [14,21,25] and obtain the following method: first, the case study is designed, research questions are derived, and use cases are selected (cf. Sect. 3.1). Second, the data collection method is defined (cf. Sect. 3.2). Third, the data analysis method is selected (cf. Sect. 3.3).

3.1 Case Study Design

Introducing RPA in the automotive domain has been little studied in the literature and, hence, concrete RPA applications, i.e., use cases, are still rare. Existing case studies, e.g., [1], focus on the benefits, risks, and results of RPA. The aim of the study presented in this paper is to explore RPA use cases in the automotive industry along the software lifecycle model [13]. Furthermore, the challenges to be tackled for each lifecycle stage are derived [4,7]:

- The *Analysis Stage* focuses on understanding and analyzing the as-is process, which is the candidate to be automated with RPA.
- The *Product Design Stage* defines the to-be process that shall be executed by the bot.
- The *Coding and Testing Stage* implements the RPA bot according to the design defined in the previous stage. The bot is tested to determine whether it behaves correctly.
- The *Operation Stage* deploys, maintains, and operates the RPA bot. Moreover, it measures its performance.

Research Question Definition. In [20], we discovered that RPA projects in the automotive industry do not always achieve the positive benefits promised in the literature. Therefore, our general research question is "What challenges are raised in each lifecycle stage?". In detail, different aspects in each stage are questioned to answer the general research question. For the *analysis stage* we consider the following aspects: (1) How does the as-is process look like? (2) What problems exist with the as-is process?, and (3) What are the goals of the RPA project? The *product design stage*, in turn, addresses the two aspects: (1) How does the to-be process look like? and (2) Is the process standardized, i.e., can the number of process variants be kept small? For the *coding and testing stage* we consider the following aspects: (1) How long does coding and testing of the RPA bot take? and (2) What problems arise in this stage? Finally, the *operation stage* addresses four aspects, namely: (1) When is the bot released? (2) How is the bot communicated to the users? (3) How much time is needed for maintenance?, and (4) What are the lessons learned in the RPA project?

Case Selection. In order to select appropriate cases to identify general challenges of RPA implementation in the automotive domain, we consider the following criteria [21]: availability of information, variation of cases, and repeatability. In this context, it is noteworthy that one of the authors deals with the selection of processes in RPA projects in automotive engineering. Over a period of one and a half years, she decided in 42 cases whether or not the suggested process should be automated with RPA (cf. Fig. 1). 31 of them were rejected as they were unsuitable for RPA (19), did not save enough FTEs (8), or for other reasons (4). Hence, 11 processes were automated with RPA, of which two each failed during coding and testing, respectively. Two processes are still in the testing stage, five were successfully completed. Thereof two are retired and three are actively used. Information was available for all 42 processes as one of the author is part of the RPA team. To ensure the variation of cases, we want to explore one process that failed after testing, one successfully completed, and one being active. Finally, the repeatability criteria results in the selection of the processes called Process 1 (Ordering), Process 2 (Construction Report Creation), and Process 3 (Report Generation).

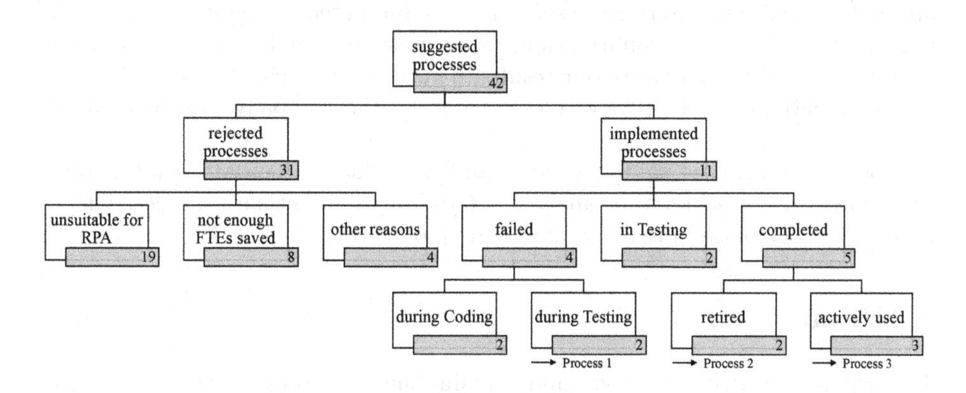

Fig. 1. Processes suggested for automation with RPA.

3.2 Data Collection Method

The data is collected from primary and secondary data sources to ensure data triangulation [21]. We conducted semi-structured interviews with the main actors involved in RPA projects. Each interview lasted around one hour. The interviews were recorded and transcribed. The basis for the interview are the general research question, the aspects defined above, and our observations during the RPA projects. The interview guideline is, therefore, structured as follows:

1. Analysis: process before automation, problems with manual process, and RPA expectations.
2. Product Design: process standardization and process after automation.

3. Coding and Testing: duration and problems.
4. Operation: release date, communication of RPA, problems during usage, effort for maintenance, and lessons learned.
5. Additional comments.

Secondary data originated from (1) the observations we made during process analyses and (2) archival data (e.g., meeting minutes, technical documents, management documents, and reports). In addition, these data were used to validate the statements made during the interviews. Note that the combination of primary and secondary data fosters internal validity of the collected data [21].

3.3 Data Analysis Method

All gathered data are analyzed in a structured way to draw conclusions [25] and to answer our research question. First of all, the three cases are treated separately. Problems and challenges are reported for each lifecycle stage and are summarized as lessons learned. Afterwards a cross-case synthesis is performed to generalize the lessons learned from the three cases [21]. The general challenges are derived from the interview results and are presented to the participants for confirmation. After this confirmation, we compare our challenges with findings from the literature to classify our results in current research.

Confidentiality and privacy rules set out by the company are followed all time.

Special attention is paid to validity and reliability of the data analysis [21]. Internal validity is achieved by analyzing data from different data sources. Therefore, eventually biased interview data can be objectified.

4 Results

This section describes, analyses, and explains the three selected cases, i.e., Process 1 (Ordering), Process 2 (Construction Report Creation), and Process 3 (Report Generation), separately along the aforementioned lifecycle stages [21].

4.1 Process 1 - Ordering

Analysis. Figure 2 visualizes Process 1 before RPA implementation using the Business Process Model and Notation (BPMN). If engineers need a part, they send the order to an employee checking for its completeness. If the order is incomplete, the engineer is notified accordingly to provide the missing details. Otherwise, the employee logs into the order system, copies and pastes the order details from the e-mail into the system, saves and submits the order, and notifies the engineer about the creation of the order. As problems of this as-is process the system is very slow and, therefore, takes a long time to completion. Additionally, the task is a simple copy and paste task. Hence, the management supported the implementation of the bot to relieve the employees from this tedious task.

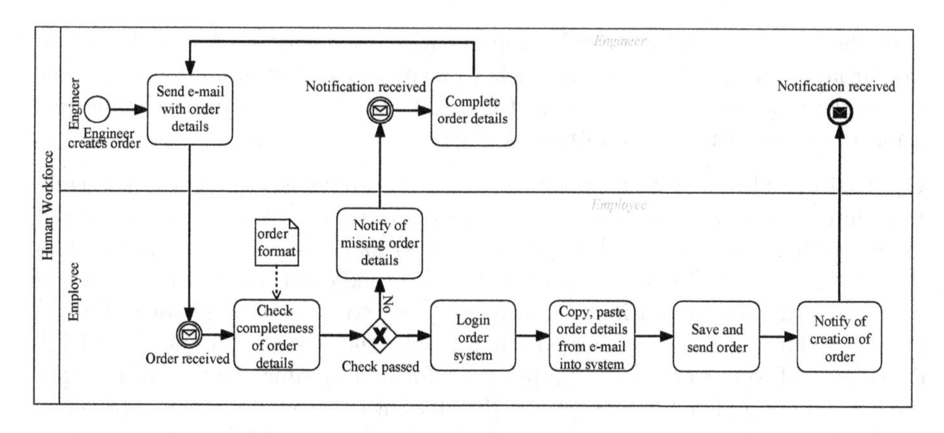

Fig. 2. BPMN Model of Process 1 (Ordering) before RPA implementation.

Product Design. The process has not been standardized prior to RPA implementation. For the engineer the procedure remains the same. For the employee, in turn, an additional check becomes necessary: if the received order is suitable for the RPA bot, it is forwarded to the bot, which then performs the subsequent process steps. Afterwards, the employee is informed, and then needs to submit the order and notify the engineer (cf. Fig. 3). If the bot fails, the employee receives a generic error message not providing any details. Therefore, the results from the bot are not the same as if done manually, as one cannot see exactly what error has occurred where.

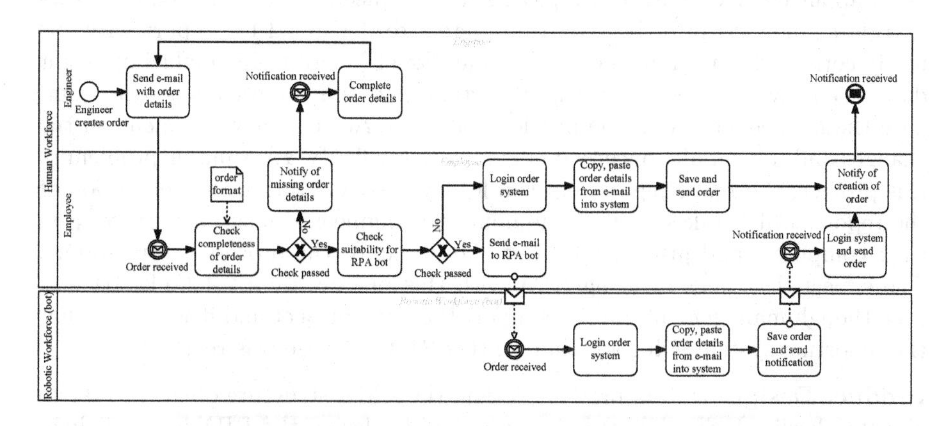

Fig. 3. BPMN Model of Process 1 (Ordering) after RPA implementation.

Coding/Testing. Coding the RPA bot took the RPA developer 1.5 months, followed by 2 months spent on testing. As major problem during coding, selectors (i.e., attributes of a graphical user interface element to tell the bot how to interact with the interface) did not work properly with the order system and a lot of workarounds with keyboard shortcuts became necessary. Obtaining the necessary access rights for the bot turned out to be difficult. The IT department did not want a bot operating in their order system.

Operation. The operation stage started with problems, as moving the code from integration to production did not work properly. Problems undiscovered in the testing stage occurred, e.g., selectors no longer worked. Employees who should test the bot did not use it after it had turned out that the process differs from the manual one and input documents need to be generated solely for the bot. Therefore, the users preferred staying with the manual process. The RPA developer still spent around 1–2 h per week for maintaining the bot. In the end, the bot did not go live but was retired after testing due to the sketched problems. In addition, management changed and the new management no longer supported the project.

Lessons Learned. As the most important lesson learned from this RPA project significantly more efforts and time need to be spent in process analysis and documentation. The selected process should be standardized and mature. Furthermore, the process should be precisely documented to facilitate the coding of the RPA bot. Another lesson learned concerns user acceptance: In the given project users did not accept the bot and preferred to execute the process manually.

4.2 Process 2 - Construction Report Creation

Analysis. Process 2 describes the generation of reports informing other engineers about changed data (cf. Fig. 4). After engineers have corrected construction data, they log into the reporting system to download the report with the newly corrected data. Further, they run an Excel Macro to highlight important data, then save the report on the filesystem, and runs another macro to compare the new version with the previous one. Afterwards, they comment on the changes and inform all concerned engineers accordingly. As a major problem of this process, the reporting system is a legacy system. During the generation of the report, which takes around one hour, the engineers can no longer work on their computers and just have to wait. Additionally, the process is error-prone. The expected savings of using RPA with this process were 2.4 FTEs. Hence, even though management did not support the RPA project and it was clear that the reporting system will soon change, this RPA use case was realized.

Product Design. During product design, the folder structure of the filesystem was standardized. Special attention was paid to design the RPA bot to deliver exactly the same result as if performing the process manually. This resulted in the process depicted in Fig. 5: The engineers correct data and log into the reporting system. However, instead of downloading the report right away, they assign the task to the RPA bot. The next day, they can find all prepared documents in the filesystem and focus on commenting and communicating the changes. Twice a day, the RPA bot logs into the reporting system and downloads all assigned

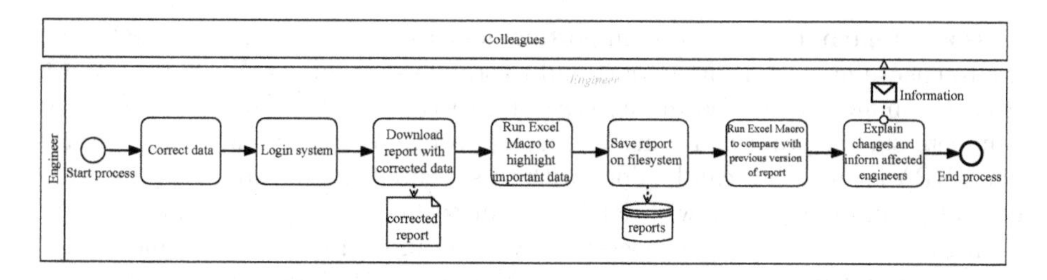

Fig. 4. BPMN Model of Process 2 (Construction Report Creation) before RPA implementation.

reports, runs the Excel Macro to highlight important data, and saves the reports on the filesystem. On the latter, a second Excel Macro is run to compare the new report with its previous version and to save the prepared files on the filesystem. The two processes are decoupled, except for the report database used by both the bot and the engineer.

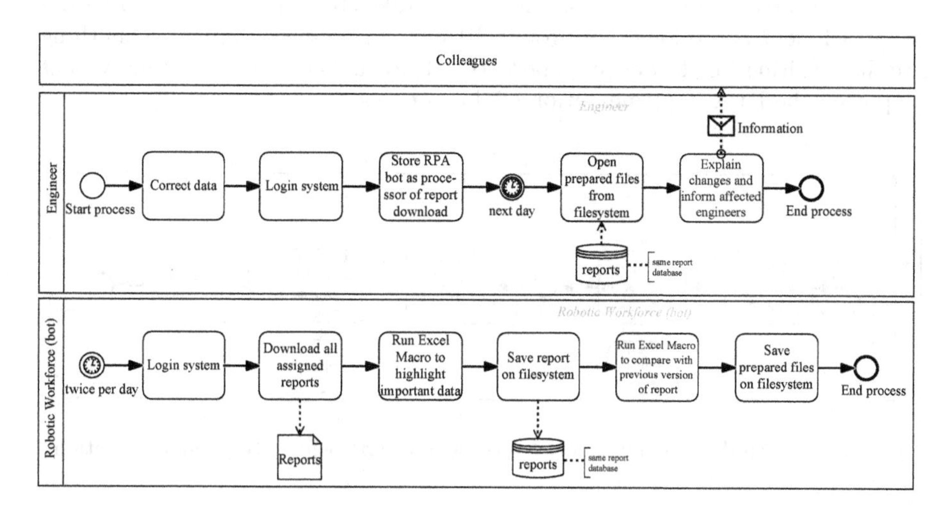

Fig. 5. BPMN Model of Process 2 (Construction Report Creation) after RPA implementation.

Coding/Testing. Coding the RPA bot took the RPA developer 2 weeks, afterwards 2 weeks were spent for testing. No major problems occurred. The bot went live in April 2019. The reporting system was changed one year later, the documents are now generated via server and the bot is no longer needed.

Operation. After going live, the employees who had to use the bot received training, a detailed description of how to use the bot, and a live demonstration. During usage of the bot, no problems occurred for users. Concerning maintenance, the RPA developer spent around one hour per week.

Lessons Learned. The most important lessons learned from this RPA case are to ensure management support and to standardize inputs. Without support from the management, as in the case of Process 2, it is hard to successfully complete such a project. To ensure the support, it is important to understand what RPA is and what can be done with this technology. According to the RPA developer, most problems with RPA are caused by errors of the employee, e.g., typing errors. Therefore, he suggests only using input from IT tools and design the human bot interaction accordingly. Overall, the RPA developer emphasizes the huge potential for RPA in future, but wishes more support for the RPA developers concerning guidelines and best practices of RPA implementation.

4.3 Process 3 - Report Generation

Analysis. In Process 3, reports are generated by logging into the report system and creating the desired specifications (cf. Fig. 6). Every Sunday, the engineer receives an automated e-mail from the reporting system. By clicking on the attachment, the report is generated and the engineer can save it on the filesystem. As major problem of this process, the time it takes to generate the report from the attachment is too long. For around 10 min the engineer cannot do anything else than waiting for the desired report to be loaded. Therefore, the management supported the RPA implementation of this process.

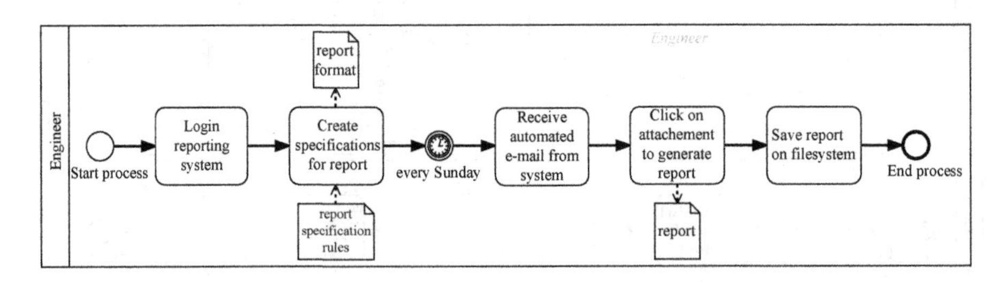

Fig. 6. BPMN Model of Process 3 (Report Generation) before RPA implementation.

Product Design. The product design stage started with standardizing the process and, in particular, the filesystem. The engineers were asked whether a weekly report is sufficiently up-to-date, which they agreed on, especially as the results remain the same as for the manual process. After RPA implementation, the process works as follows (cf. Fig. 7): the engineers log into the system, specify the reports they need, and configure the e-mail client such that the bot receives the automated e-mails from the system. For this purpose, every Sunday the bot receives these e-mails, clicks on the attachments, and generates the report. Afterwards, an Excel Macro is executed for comparing the current reports with the one-week old ones and the reports are saved on the filesystem. Consequently, the engineers can always find a weekly up-to-date report on the filesystem. The two workforces work decoupled from one another. However, the report is shared among them. If engineers need it, they load it from the filesystem where the bot has saved the report before.

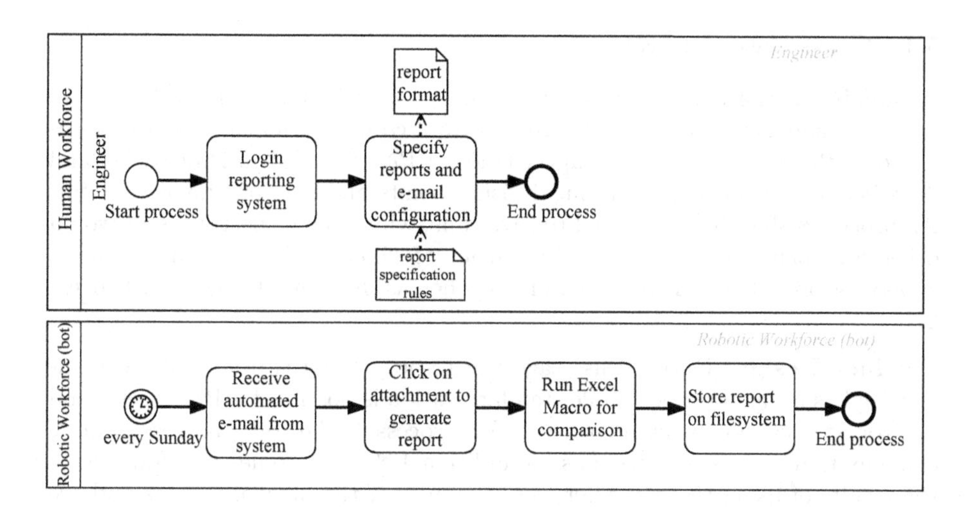

Fig. 7. BPMN Model of Process 3 (Report Generation) after RPA implementation.

Coding/Testing. After two months, the bot was coded and tested by the RPA developer. During this period, no problems occurred. Especially, the bot only required reading access rights for the report system and writing access to the filesystem managed by the department.

Operation. The bot has been live since May 2019 and will be outdated in about 2 years when a new reporting system will be built. Despite the maintenance effort of 2 h per week, the bot is a great success.

Lessons Learned. Again, the lesson learned in this case is to use standardized input, ideally provided by an IT tool, and to design the human bot interaction accordingly. The developer believes that he has implemented the most appropriate process for RPA. Subsequently proposed processes were not suited for an automation using RPA. Therefore, it is challenging to identify the right process to automate. In general, RPA is difficult to understand for colleagues believing in the automation of everything. The department is quite disillusioned and has no ideas what else could be automated by RPA. Additionally, the developer adds that RPA can still be optimized for maintenance, e.g., to receive information about the bot via e-mail. Finally, the bot developer wishes support in terms of guidelines for RPA development.

5 Cross-Case Analysis and Derivation of Challenges

This section discusses the results of all three cases along the bot lifecycle and elaborates on the main challenges of applying RPA in the automotive domain.

These challenges are compared with the ones reported in RPA literature (cf. Sect. 2). Finally, threats to validity and limitations of the study are discussed.

5.1 Cross-Case Analysis

Analysis. In the analysis stage, the as-is process is analyzed, problems are detected, and goals of the RPA project are recorded. Compared to Processes 2 and 3, Process 1 is rather complex before RPA automation. Processes 2 and 3 are sequential processes without decision points and only one involved actor. All processes shall be automated to save time, which the respective actor would otherwise spend on waiting for the output of different systems. Management support is provided for Processes 1 and 3, whereas this is not the case for Process 2.

Product Design. During this stage the to-be process is designed and standardized as far as possible. While standardization is possible for Processes 2 and 3, Process 1 cannot be standardized. For Process 1, the to-be process is more complex than the as-is process as an additional check becomes necessary. Still, the results of using the bot differ from the ones of the manual process and are less understandable for the employee. The other two processes require less work than before and the robotic workforce is decoupled from the one of humans. For Processes 2 and 3, special attention is paid to ensure that the results of the bot and the manual process are the same.

Coding/Testing. The coding and testing stage is analyzed with respect to the problems and efforts. Coding and testing are accomplished the fastest for Process 2, after one month the bot is ready and no major issues arise. The implementation of process 3 takes two months with no major problems. Finally, coding and testing of Process 1 takes 3.5 months. Two problems hinder a faster implementation: the selectors do not work properly in the system and getting the access rights granted for the bot is difficult.

Operation. In the operation stage, ongoing maintenance efforts as well as lessons learned are documented. For all three projects maintenance efforts are around 1–2 h per week.

Lessons Learned. Lessons learned for the three use cases are:

1. Identify the right process to automate and spend sufficient time and efforts into process analysis and documentation. (Processes 1 and 3)
2. Understand the factors influencing user acceptance of RPA. (Process 1)
3. Explain RPA and the benefits of this technology. (Processes 2 and 3)
4. Properly design the interaction between human and RPA bot. (Processes 2 and 3)
5. Provide software development guidelines for RPA. (Processes 2 and 3)

Table 1 summarizes our main findings and compares the three cases.

Table 1. Overview of the three use cases.

Lifecycle stage	Aspect	Process 1	Process 2	Process 3
Analysis	As-is process	Complex, decision points, multiple actors involved	linear, one actor involved	linear, one actor involved
	Reason for automation	Time savings	Time savings, error reductions	Time savings
	Management support	Yes	No	Yes
Product Design	Standardization	No	Yes	Yes
	To-be process	Additional check, more complex	Less work	Less work
	Human-Bot-Interaction	Interaction via e-mail and user input	User assigns task to bot, gets result the next day	Specify once the report and receive it up-to-date every week
	Manual vs. Bot Result	Different	Same	Same
Coding/ Testing	Time effort	3.5 months	1 month	2 months
	Problems	With selectors and access right for bot	No	No
Operation	Maintenance effort	1–2/week	1 h/week	2 h/week
	Lessons Learned	Identify the right processes to automate, understand factors influencing user acceptance	Design the human bot interaction, explain RPA and its merits, provide software development guidelines	Design the human bot interaction, explain RPA and its merits, provide software development guidelines, identify the right process to automate
Evaluation		Failed before go-live, money and FTEs spent	2.4 FTEs saved, 13 months of usage	1.2 FTEs saved, used for 15 months, will be used for 2 years

5.2 Derivation of Challenges

The five lessons learned are compared with findings from literature. Further, we highlight future research possibilities to overcome the challenges.

The challenge to **identify the right processes for automation** is addressed in [5,8,10]. [5] emphasizes that the processes need to be carefully selected and recommends the choice of rule-based processes, which usually require a lot of time and resources. [8] suggests selecting standardized and stabilized processes as candidates for RPA. [10] points out that RPA is one process automation approach among others (e.g., screen scraping) and, therefore, processes for RPA need to be chosen with care. However, to the best of our knowledge, there is no comprehensive overview of existing process selection methods. Apart from an overview of these methods, an assessment regarding applicability in the automotive domain is desirable. Future research should, therefore, focus on providing an overview and assessment of process selection methods for RPA.

The challenge to **understand the factors influencing RPA user acceptance** is covered partly in [5,8,18]. [5] suggests addressing concerns about job losses early on such that the employees are more comfortable using the software bots. Similarly, [18] encounters the challenge of convincing employees to change their work habit. [8] indicates that a culture of business innovation and technology fosters RPA adoption. Nonetheless, these are only some aspects, which probably influence user acceptance of RPA. A more general approach that covers the variety of factors influencing RPA user acceptance needs to be developed. Based on the identified factors, further RPA software improvements can be achieved.

How to **explain RPA and its merits** is discussed in [10,12,16]. [10] suggests preparing the employees accordingly, whereas [16] emphasizes the need to manage the impact of RPA carefully. In any case, a transparent communication with the concerned employees becomes necessary from the beginning. In [12], the same challenge is discussed, namely, the lack of RPA understanding, with the recommendation to provide background knowledge to the employees. Future work should, therefore, provide new ways of explaining RPA to employees. To the best of our knowledge, there are no sophisticated communication concepts for explaining RPA and its advantages to the concerned employees. Special attention needs to be paid to adapt these concepts to highly skilled engineers.

The challenge to **design the interactions between the employee and the bot** could be linked to user acceptance, e.g., the interactions should be designed in a way such that the change of work habit becomes minimal [18]. [23] states that robots need more explicit instructions than humans. This is one aspect to be considered in the interaction design. However, many more aspects should be considered to provide guidance for a good user interface design in RPA. Future work should develop an evaluation model to assess the interaction between employee and RPA bot. The results could then be used to derive recommendations for the user interface design resolving the discovered challenge.

Finally, the challenge of **how to implement RPA solutions** has been tackled by only few works. [9] states that components should be reused to enable faster bot implementation, [16] emphasizes the need for an agile RPA development. Details, models or recommendation for an RPA development constitute another aspect of future work. Finally, the software development guidelines should be tailored to the requirements of an engineer as well.

In a nutshell, the challenges we discovered in the automotive domain have been at least partly addressed in the literature that deals with RPA implementations in other domains.

5.3 Threats to Validity and Limitations

With the presented exploratory case study, we gathered experiences with RPA projects in a real environment. However, there are several threats to validity and limitations of our research.

As a first limitation, the case study is solely conducted in one domain, i.e., automotive engineering, covering three different projects. Nevertheless, we believe that the obtained results are generalizable to other domains and projects for the following two reasons: 1) In the literature, we can find RPA case studies in different areas deriving similar challenges and 2) we have insights into additional RPA projects from the automotive industry (cf. Fig. 1), which confirm this. Unfortunately, we cannot provide more information on these additional studies due to confidentiality reasons. To ensure external validity and confirm the generalization of our results, new case studies in other domains and companies need to be conducted as well.

Second, one may argue that the discovered challenges are not RPA-specific, but might be observed in other software projects as well. We briefly sketch differences between RPA and traditional software projects [15]: The goal of RPA is to create bots that run independently and human only hand over the task. Contrariwise, traditional software is designed to support the human in executing tasks. Further, RPA bots are mostly implemented by domain experts [22], whereas the implementation of traditional software is done by software engineers from the IT department. Therefore, RPA projects have to be addressed in another way than traditional software projects.

6 Summary and Outlook

The presented exploratory case study provides insights into concrete RPA projects from the automotive industry. The discovered challenges, i.e., to identify the appropriate processes for RPA, to understand the factors influencing user acceptance, to explain RPA to employees, to design human bot interaction, and to provide RPA software development guidelines, will be further addressed by us to ensure a successful application of RPA in practice.

To be more precise, we are working on a framework addressing these challenges holistically. For example, the challenge to understand the factors influencing user acceptance is addressed in [19], which develops a model for assessing RPA user acceptance as well as the factors influencing it. These factors are used to derive recommendations for designing and implementing RPA bots with increased user acceptance among employees using the bots in their daily work.

Further case studies and studies are necessary to enhance these results, confirm findings, and ensure external validity. The same case study method should be used by further research to discuss RPA use cases and to generate comparable results.

References

1. Aguirre, S., Rodriguez, A.: Automation of a business process using robotic process automation (RPA): a case study. In: Figueroa-García, J.C., López-Santana, E.R., Villa-Ramírez, J.L., Ferro-Escobar, R. (eds.) WEA 2017. CCIS, vol. 742, pp. 65–71. Springer, Cham (2017). https://doi.org/10.1007/978-3-319-66963-2_7
2. Asatiani, A., Penttinen, E.: Turning robotic process automation into commercial success - Case OpusCapita. J. Inf. Technol. Teach. Cases **6**(2), 67–74 (2016). https://doi.org/10.1057/jittc.2016.5
3. Asquith, A., Horsman, G.: Let the robots do it! - taking a look at robotic process automation and its potential application in digital forensics. Forensic Sci. Int. Reports **1**, 100007 (2019). https://doi.org/10.1016/j.fsir.2019.100007
4. Chacón-Montero, J., Jiménez-Ramírez, A., Enríquez, J.G.: Towards a method for automated testing in robotic process automation projects. In: 14th International Workshop on Automation Software Test, pp. 42–47. IEEE Press (2019). https://doi.org/10.1109/AST.2019.00012
5. Hallikainen, P., Bekkhus, R., Pan, S.L.: How OpusCapita used internal RPA capabilities to offer services to clients. MIS Q. Exec. **17**(1), 41–52 (2018)
6. Ivančić, L., Vugec, D.S., Vukšić, V.B.: Robotic process automation : systematic literature review. Int. Conf. Bus. Process. Manag. **361**, 280–295 (2019)
7. Jiménez-Ramírez, A., Chacón-Montero, J., Wojdynsky, T., González Enríquez, J.: Automated testing in robotic process automation projects. J. Softw. Evol. Process. pp. 1–11 (2020). https://onlinelibrary.wiley.com/doi/epdf/10.1002/smr.2259
8. Lacity, M., Willcocks, L., Craig, A.: Robotic process automation at xchanging. Outsourcing Unit Work. Res. Pap. Ser. **15**(3), 1–26 (2015)
9. Lacity, M., Willcocks, L., Craig, A.: Robotic process automation: mature capabilities in the energy sector. Outsourcing Unit Work. Pap. Ser. **15**(6), 1–19 (2015)
10. Lacity, M., Willcocks, L., Craig, A.: Robotizing global financial shared services at royal DSM. Outsourcing Unit Work. Res. Pap. Ser. **16**(2), 1–26 (2016)
11. Lohrmann, M., Reichert, M.: Effective application of process improvement patterns to business processes. Softw. Syst. Model. **15**(2), 353–375 (2014). https://doi.org/10.1007/s10270-014-0443-z
12. Radke, A.M., Dang, M.T., Tan, A.: Using robotic process automation (RPA) to enhance item master data maintenance process. LogForum **16**(1), 129–140 (2020)
13. Royce, W.W.: Managing the development of large software systems: concepts and techniques. In: 9th International Conference on Software Engineering, pp. 328–338 (1987)
14. Runeson, P., Höst, M., Rainer, A., Regnell, B.: Case Study Research in Software Engineering: Guidelines and Examples (2012). https://doi.org/10.1002/9781118181034
15. Rutschi, C., Dibbern, J.: Towards a framework of implementing software robots: transforming human-executed routines into machines. Data Base Adv. Inform. Syst. **51**(1), 104–128 (2020). https://doi.org/10.1145/3380799.3380808
16. Schmitz, M., Dietze, C., Czarnecki, C.: Enabling digital transformation through robotic process automation at Deutsche Telekom. In: Urbach, N., Röglinger, M. (eds.) Digitalization Cases, Management for Professionals, pp. 15–33 (2019). https://doi.org/10.1007/978-3-319-95273-4
17. Syed, R., et al.: Robotic process automation: contemporary themes and challenges. Comput. Ind. **115**, 103162 (2020). https://doi.org/10.1016/j.compind.2019.103162

18. Viale, L., Zouari, D.: Impact of digitalization on procurement: the case of robotic process automation. Supply Chain Forum An Int. J. **21**, 1–11 (2020). https://doi.org/10.1080/16258312.2020.1776089
19. Wewerka, J., Dax, S., Reichert, M.: A user acceptance model for robotic process automation. In: IEEE International Enterprise Distributed Object Computing Conference (2020). https://doi.org/10.1109/EDOC49727.2020.00021
20. Wewerka, J., Reichert, M.: Towards quantifying the effects of robotic process automation. In: IEEE International Enterprise Distributed Object Computing Workshop on Front Process Aware System (2020). https://doi.org/10.1109/EDOCW49879.2020.00015
21. Wieringa, R.J.: Design Science Methodology for Information Systems and Software Engineering. Springer, Heidelberg (2014). https://doi.org/10.1007/978-3-662-43839-8
22. Willcocks, L., Lacity, M.: Robotic process automation: the next transformation lever for shared services. Outsourcing Unit Work. Res. Pap. Ser. **15**(7), 1–35 (2015)
23. Willcocks, L., Lacity, M.: Robotic process automation at telefónica O2. MIS Q. Exec. **15**(1), 21–35 (2016)
24. William, W., William, L.: Improving corporate secretary productivity using robotic process automation. In: International Conference on Technologies and Applications of Artificial Intelligence, pp. 1–5 (2019). https://doi.org/10.1109/TAAI48200.2019.8959872
25. Yin, R.K., et al.: Case Study Research: Design and Methods (2003)

A Framework for Comparative Analysis of Intention Mining Approaches

Rébecca Déneckère[1](✉), Elena Kornyshova[2], and Charlotte Hug[1]

[1] CRI, Université Paris 1 Panthéon Sorbonne, Paris, France
rebecca.deneckere@univ-paris1.fr
[2] CEDRIC, Conservatoire National des Arts et Métiers, Paris, France
elena.kornyshova@cnam.fr

Abstract. Intention Mining has the purpose to manipulate of large volumes of data, integrate information from different sources and formats and extract useful insights as facts from this data in order to discover users' intentions. It is used in different fields: Robotics, Network forensics, Security, Bioinformatics, Learning, Map Visualization, Game, etc. There is actually a large variety of intention mining techniques applied to different domains as information retrieval, security, robotics, etc. However, no systematic review had been conducted on this recent research domain. There is a need to understand what is Intention Mining, what is its purpose, what are the existing techniques and tools to mine intentions. In this paper, we propose a comparison framework to structure and to describe the domain °of Intention Mining for a further complete systematic literature review of this field. We validate our comparison framework by applying it to five relevant approaches in the domain.

Keywords: Intention · Intention mining · Comparison framework

1 Introduction

The concept of intention is becoming increasingly important in different areas of computer science as information retrieval, network forensics, security, robotics and bioinformatics, among others, to understand the goals of the users of the systems. [1] defines an intention as "a determination to act in a certain way; a concept considered as the product of attention directed to an object or knowledge". Psychology specifies "Our common sense psychological scheme admits of intentions as states of mind; and it also allows us to characterize actions as done intentionally, or with a certain intention" [2]. These intentions can be clearly and explicitly stated or they can be implicitly expressed in natural language in different kind of sources as documents, queries, logs, etc. Many approaches tackle the problem of identifying intentions by using mining techniques.

This research domain is quite new, and the term *Intention Mining* (IM) has different meanings according to the communities. The proposed IM techniques and their aims are quite different from one domain to another. Moreover, *Intention Mining* is not the only term used to designate this activity as it has many synonyms: an "intention" may be an

S. Cherfi et al. (Eds.): RCIS 2021, LNBIP 415, pp. 20–37, 2021.
https://doi.org/10.1007/978-3-030-75018-3_2

"intent", a "goal", an "objective", etc.; mining may signify "discovery", "analysis", etc. It is then necessary to conduct a literature review on what is IM and how it is defined by the different research communities in Computer Science context. There are techniques aiming at discovering intentions behind web queries to improve the recommended web pages or services [3, 4]; others propose techniques to identify intentions in home videos to provide adapted home video services [5], while others propose to discover intentions hidden behind user activities defined in logs to understand users ways of working [6], etc. There is an obvious lack of overview of the existing IM techniques as they are defined in different areas.

Our future goal is to conduct a systematic literature review (SLR) on IM. To our knowledge, no proper systematic literature review has been conducted on Intention Mining. [7] propose a state of the art of intention recognition but it is not a systematic literature review. [8] proposes a review of intention process mining but restrict itself to the discovery of goal-oriented processes. Moreover, these works do not use a structured framework to analyse and compare the existing approaches.

To provide a detailed and structured overview of the IM approaches and to clarify IM elements and categories, we have elaborated a comparison framework composed of four dimensions: object, usage, method and tool. This structure was inspired from [9–12]. In this paper, we detail the comparison framework containing a set of criteria to differentiate and compare these different approaches and apply it to the most referenced papers of our study in order to check its feasibility. A detailed comparison framework is useful (i) for our future research, to carry out the SLR to compare the existing literature on IM and to define open issues, (ii) for a user, to be able to quickly compare the existing IM approaches and select the one best fitting its case, and (iii) for a new IM approach, to position it with regards to the existing literature.

The paper is organized as follows. Section 2 describes our research process. Section 3 presents the comparison framework to analyse the IM approaches. In Sect. 4, we apply the proposed framework to the 5 most referenced IM approaches and we conclude and define our research perspectives in Sect. 5.

2 Research Process

Our goal in this paper is to establish a comparison framework that will serve as a scope for the future systematic literature review. Our research process is presented on Fig. 1.

Define Research Questions. The research goal is to identify a set of characteristics allowing to compare works on intention mining. The existing literature on existing comparison frameworks (applied to the field of software engineering [9], process engineering [10], decisional methods [11], method engineering [12], etc.) was analyzed in order to identify the research questions covering the main dimensions usually used to compare different approaches as approaches objects (*What is IM?*), approaches goals (*Why IM?*), approaches methods (*How is done IM?*), and, finally, approaches associated tools (*By which means is done IM?*). Thus, the defined research questions are:

- RQ1: What is intention mining? How IM is defined in the research papers or community, what does it consist in?

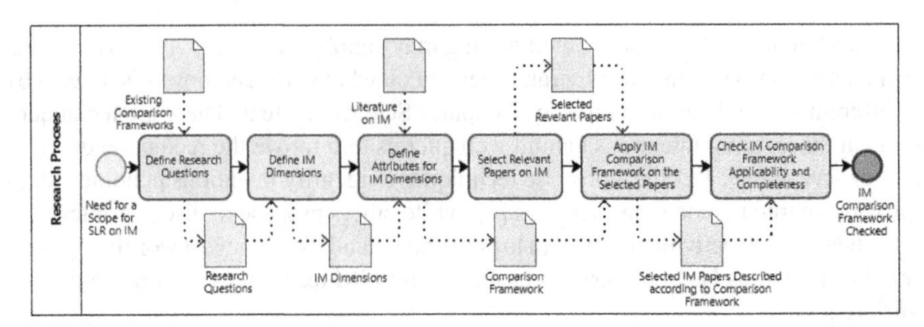

Fig. 1. Research process used to develop the intention mining comparison framework.

- RQ2: Why using intention mining? What is the purpose of IM in the research papers or community?
- RQ3: How is intention mining achieved? What are the existing IM techniques?
- RQ4: By which means is the intention mining method put in practice? What are the tools and algorithms that support the mining of intentions?

Define IM Dimensions. Based on these research questions, we have identified four IM dimensions of our comparison framework: Object dimension, Usage dimension, Method Dimension, and Tool Dimension (all detailed in the following section).

Define Attributes for IM Dimensions. The next step was to read the literature on IM. For this purpose, we used papers on IM appearing in Google Scholar. At this step, it was firstly important to identify various characteristics allowing to differentiate IM approaches. For instance, several approaches mention only intentions extraction [13], whereas other ones establish intentions models [6, 14]. Thus, we identified the characteristic (an attribute in our comparison framework) *Structuredness*. Once different attributes identified, we grouped them into the four previously established dimensions according to their nature to structure the Comparison Framework.

Select Relevant Papers on IM. To select relevant papers, we have used the ongoing work related to SRL. Our main research query used the following combination of key words: (user OR actor) AND (goal OR intention OR intent OR objective) AND (discovery OR mining OR analysis). We have identified 238 research papers from the research bases IEEE, Springer, ACM, Science Direct with the following inclusion criteria: papers should be in French or in English, title or abstract should be related to IM. Then we applied some exclusion criteria (papers should be journal or conference papers, be present in DBLP (except for 2020 papers), and restrictions related to the citation number: if dated before 2010, we excluded papers cited less than 100 times, if dated between 2010 and 2017, we removed papers cited less than 10 times). We have finally obtained 145 papers. We have extracted the citation number from Google Scholar (access on January 2021) for each of these papers and selected the three most referenced papers [15, 16], and [3] having correspondingly 364, 347, and 306 citations. As these papers were published before 2010, we have also selected one most cited paper for 2010–2015 ([4] with 151 citations) and one most cited paper for 2016–2020 ([17] with 78 citations) to validate our comparison framework with more recent studies on IM.

Apply IM Comparison Framework on the Selected Papers. At this step, we characterized the five IM papers with the attributes of the IM Comparison Framework. The details are given in Sect. 4.

Check IM Comparison Framework Applicability and Completeness. The goal of this step was to verify if each selected IM approach could be characterized using the proposed framework (its *applicability*) and if was complete (its *completeness*).

To find potentially useful papers in scientific bases, we followed the SLR methodology. In IEEE, ACM and Science Direct, we searched till around 625 hits. In Google scholar and Springer, where the search had to be cut into little pieces, 24 queries (corresponding to 24 possible combinations of keywords) were done. In Google scholar, we stopped after 100 hits for each query. In Springer, we checked all retrieved papers. This way of working does not exclude that we missed some interesting papers, especially old ones. That implies our second validity threat: the analysis of several missed papers could have provided some additional details for the IM comparison framework attributes.

3 Comparison Framework

Classification frameworks, such as the one presented in [9–12] are a useful way to introduce a domain and discuss literature in a systematic way. They help characterizing methods techniques and tools, comparing them, demonstrating the originality of given approaches with respect to the rest of the literature, finding gaps in the literature, etc.

As Fig. 2 shows, we propose a classification framework that emphasizes 4 main dimensions of Intention Mining, related to the research questions: the object, the usage, the method, and the tool. More precisely:

- The Object dimension raises the question *What is intention mining?* It refers to the structure of the intentions, their taxonomy and formalism.
- The Usage dimension raises the question *Why using intention mining?* It provides an insight on the different types of objective of intention mining, the domains of application, the source and target of the existing approaches.
- By providing details on intention mining approaches, the Method dimension raises the question *How is intention mining achieved?* For instance, the method dimension characterizes an intention mining approach by indicating the theoretical grounding of the method, whether it exploits classification techniques or ontologies.
- The Tool dimension provides details on support offered to enact the method. The question here is *By which means is the intention mining method put in practice?* Looking at this dimension of an intention mining method indicates the algorithms on which it relies, and the tools that it uses or implements.

The distinction between methods and tools is not obvious; it can be understood with the cooking metaphor: if methods correspond to recipes, tools are kitchen instruments.

Each dimension is specified as a set of attributes with a name and a domain. For instance, the object dimension has 3 attributes: "structuredness" indicates whether the

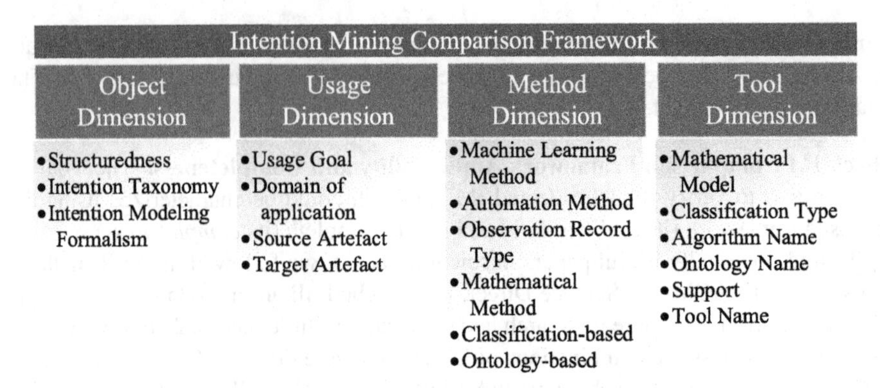

Fig. 2. Intention mining comparison framework.

output is an individual intention or a model, "intention taxonomy" and "intention modeling formalism" indicate how mined intentions are further specified, by classification in taxonomy or by using a specific formalism. Each dimension of the intention mining classification framework is described in a sub-section below.

3.1 The Object Dimension

Table 1 details the object dimension of intention mining that has 3 attributes: *structuredness* defines if the aim is to mine individual intentions (a mining technique can of course still generate collections of individual intentions), or in relationship with other intentions (in which case, the output are intention models); the *intention taxonomy* attribute characterizes the fundamental nature of the mined intentions (several taxonomies can be used in combination, hence the SET OF ENUM type); last the *intention modeling formalism* attribute indicates which notation is used to formalize individual intentions or collections of intentions.

Table 1. Details of the object dimension.

Attributes	Values
Structuredness	ENUM (Individual, Model)
Intention taxonomy	SET OF (ENUM (Action/Semantic; Soft/Hard; Uni-token/Multi-token; Informational/Ambiguous/Navigational/Transactional; Explicit/Implicit; Objective/Subjective; Research/Purchase; Collective/Individual))
Intention modelling formalism	ENUM (Map, I*, Kaos, linguistic, Schemata)

Structuredness. The Object of an IM approach may be to point out intentions either individually, or under the form of structured collections. Each intention can itself be made explicit, e.g. in natural language, or stay implicit as introduced by [18]. For instance, it may be sufficient to find the class of an intention, rather than providing its name or other details [13]. On the other extreme, it is possible to specify intention models, i.e. specifications that conform to a formal notation [6, 14]. At the level of collections of intentions, models define dependencies between intentions, such as refinement, abstraction, complementarity, alternatives, positive and negative contributions, etc. At the individual level, models reveal the underlying structure of intentions, for instance their linguistic structure, their formal condition of realization, etc.

Intention Taxonomy. Several definitions and taxonomies of intentions are proposed in the IM literature. [19] define *action* intentions and *semantic* intentions. The first group represents "basic actions performed on a computer", the second includes intentions corresponding to "what the user wants to achieve at high level, which may involve several basic actions on a computer to accomplish it". Whereas *hard* goals can be associated with verification conditions that determine when the goal is achieved, there is no way to determined when *soft* goals are achieved in a clear-cut and definitive way [20]. As an example "protect asset A from any harm" is a typical soft goal: a lot can be done to satisfy it, but whatever is done to protect the asset, nobody can absolutely guarantee that no harm will ever happen to it. [20] presents a taxonomy of web engine user's intents that emphasizes three main categories: *navigational*, *informational*, and *transactional*. The purpose of a navigational intent is to "reach a particular site". A web engine user who has an informational intent seeks to "acquire some information assumed to be present on one or more web pages". Last, the aim of transactional intents is to "perform some web-mediated activity". This taxonomy is adapted in [21], which generalizes navigational and transactional intents using a concept of non-informational intention, and introduces a concept of ambiguous intention. An even more general taxonomy is the one proposed by [22], which contains 135 high-level intentions grouped in 30 clusters. For [23] an intention is either *objective* when it is about getting factual information, *subjective* when the user wants to collect personal opinions or social when it's not about getting information but creating interactions with others. For [24], intent is of two commercial types: *research* and *purchase*. [25] consider the taxonomy of intentions based on *implicit* or *explicit* geolocation. [26] considers two other kinds of intentions: *collective* ones and *individual* ones. The collective intentions, often defined as a "commitment of an individual to participate in joint action, and involves an implicit or explicit agreement between the participants to engage in that joint action" are called we-intention, whereas individual intentions are called i-intentions [27].

Intention Modeling Formalism. Besides identifying individual intentions, the object of intention mining approaches may be to generate intentional models specified using a formal notation. Focusing on the IS engineering literature, we distinguish KAOS, i* and MAP. The *KAOS* formalism [28] specifies "goals" arranged in a hierarchy, from higher-level goals down to operational goals, i.e. goals that can be operationalized by a system function. Two kinds of dependencies can be specified using KAOS: AND refinement, and OR refinement. The driving principle is that the satisfaction condition of a given higher level goal is semantically equivalent to the conjunction (respectively the disjunction) of the satisfaction condition of the goals that refine it with an AND (respectively OR) refinement link. KAOS models are hierarchy of goals that can be used to elicit, specify, analyze, negotiate, complete, verify, bundle and trace systems requirements. Besides introducing the distinction between "hard goals" and "soft goals", the *i** framework [29] focuses on the links and dependencies between goals and other concepts such as actors, tasks, resources, etc. and extends the and/or decomposition links with a typology of semantic links such as means/ends, decomposition, dependency, and so-called "contribution links": makes, breaks, hurts, helps, etc. The *MAP* formalism [30] combines the concepts of "intention" and "strategy" in collections of models (called "maps") organized hierarchically with refinement links. [31] indicates that explicit intentions can be specified with a single word (uni-token) or several words (multi-token). This is further formalized by [32] that uses a linguistic approach inspired by Chomsky's case grammar to specify the semantic roles of words used in intention names. Another example of individual intention modelling comes from the Schemata method [33] that proposes to model the salient features of individual intentions from a cognitive psychology perspective. Intentions specified with Schemata are for instance mined in [34] to specify intentions in so-called "intention maps" that associate to any web engine query the collection of intentions that motivate it.

3.2 The Usage Dimension

The usage of intention mining approaches can be defined with 4 attributes: the objective of the mined material, the domain of application in which intention mining is used, the source and target users. The domain of these attributes is further defined in Table 2.

Table 2. Details of the usage dimension.

Attributes	Values
Usage goal	ENUM (Discovery, Recommendation, Conformance, Enhancement)
Domain of application	ENUM (Information Retrieval, Robotics, Video, Network forensics, Security, Bioinformatics, Learning, Business Process Modelling, Requirements Engineering, Virtual Consumption, Map Visualization, Game, Database, e-Government, Healthcare, …)
Source artefact	ENUM (Individual, Group)
Target artefact	ENUM (Individual, Group)

Usage Goal. Intentions *discovery* allows understanding people's intents behind their actions, when executing a query with a search engine [35]. The idea of using intention mining in the context of *recommendation* is that better guidance can be provided if a better knowledge of people's intentions is acquired [44]. This can be useful to provide personalization, adapted services or products. Conformance and enhancement are two other approaches defined in the Process Mining area [36]. Intention *conformance* aims at controlling whether mined intentions match with their pre-defined specifications. For instance, intention conformance can be used to check that a prescribed model is actually enacted, or measuring the gap between the prescribed models and observing people's behavior. The idea of *enhancement* is to complete (by refinement, abstraction, or addition) intention models, or improve them in some other way, e.g. with respect to their consistency, feasibility, etc.

Domain of Application. There are many domains of application for IM. Our literature review allowed us to identify: *web engines and information retrieval* [19, 21, 31], which represent the majority of the papers we found, including *online video search* [5, 37]; *network forensics* [38, 39] and *security* [40], *bioinformatics* [41, 42], *business process engineering* [43], *method enactment* [44], *system usage analysis* [45], *learning* [46], *requirements engineering* [32] and *method engineering* [47]. The literature review also included research in *robotics* [16, 48, 49]. Not only we believe this list is not exhaustive, but we have no doubt many more applications will emerge in the future.

Source and Target Artefact. Analysing the aforementioned approaches reveals that the source and target of intention mining can be considered either as *individual* or as a *group*. Intentions can be mined for only one individual (individual sources). In this case, the mined intentions only represent the point of view of one user (obtained from his/her sources). If intentions are mined from many users (group sources), they will represent the point of view of a group of users or "crowd" (obtained from all the logs of the users). The same reasoning can be applied for the target of intention mining. Intentions can be addressed to only one user (individual target) or to many users (group target) depending on the nature of the activity or the objective of the approach.

3.3 The Method Dimension

As shown in Table 3, the Method dimension of intention mining can be further refined with the following attributes: Machine learning, to characterize the use of machine learning techniques; Automation method, that indicates the degree of automation used in the method; Observation record type, that indicates what is the input of the method; Mathematical method, that characterizes the theoretical foundation of the mining technique; and Classification-based and Ontology-based, which indicate whether the method exploits a classification technique and ontology.

Machine Learning. *Supervised* learning is a machine learning technique that consists in inferring a function from labeled training data [50]. *Unsupervised* learning operates on unlabeled data - input where the desired output is unknown [61]. In the context of intention mining, this can be achieved through cluster analysis for instance. *Semi-supervised* learning falls between supervised and unsupervised learning [15].

Automation Method. The automation method attribute characterizes the fact that a method is *manual* (every step of the approach requires a human action) [24], *automatic* (the approach can be fully executed without any intervention) [3, 4, 16] or *semi-automatic* (some steps are manual, others are automatic) [15, 17].

Table 3. Details of the method dimension.

Attributes	Values
Machine learning	ENUM (Supervised, Unsupervised, Semi-supervised, NULL)
Automation method	ENUM (Manual, Semi-automatic, Automatic)
Observation record type	ENUM (Log, Contextualized trace)
Mathematical method	ENUM (Probabilistic, Statistic, Deterministic, Fuzzy, NULL)
Classification-based	BOOLEAN
Ontology-based	BOOLEAN

Observation Record Type. Intention mining methods use observations recorded as *logs* or *contextualized traces.* Logs or Traces are temporal sequences of observed events [51]. Existing methods mostly focus on computer logs produced by the users of the systems (as activity, user, timestamp or properties of the used objects) [52]. Enriched log-files contain annotations made by the user while or after performing activities. They are useful in the context of supervised learning methods. Cambridge Dictionary defines a trace[1] as "a sign that something has happened or existed", here the focus is on what we expect to observe. Contextual traces record specific actions performed in a specific context; they embed the user activities in the context of their enactment [51]. For instance, software traces can be used to record specific user input, then provided to developers for debugging. [24] use enriched logs containing query, scroll, mouse movements and key press events.

Mathematical Method. Several intention mining methods rely on a mathematical analysis. Their theoretical foundations are: probabilistic, statistic or deterministic. *Deterministic* data do not involve any random variable [53]. When input data are deterministic, then the parameters of the mathematical model are known, and the relationships between variables are strictly functional. In other words, mining techniques based on deterministic models rely on the fundamental assumption that any given input always produces the same output. In *probability* theory, a stochastic process represents an evolution, discrete or continuous, of random variables [53]. Statistical or probabilistic models can be used to deal with stochastic processes. A *statistical* model is a set of probability distribution functions or probability density functions [53]. It involves random variables and assumes that the parameters of a model can be well-estimated using statistical properties of the observed data (as parametric random process). In intention mining approaches that are based on statistical models, the outputs are precisely determined through known statistical relationships between intentions and observations. In the context of intention mining, probabilistic models are analyzed to identify what intentions most probably hide behind the observed behaviors.

[1] Cambridge Advanced Learner's Dictionary & Thesaurus http://dictionary.cambridge.org/dictionary/british/.

Classification and Ontology Based. The added value of ontologies over classifications is that they specify (a) relationships between intentions and other concepts, and (b) reasoning mechanisms.

3.4 The Tool Dimension

Intention mining approaches can be further characterized in terms of the techniques and tools needed to put them into practice. As Table 4 shows, the Tool Dimension of the intention mining classification framework has 5 attributes.

Table 4. Details of the tool dimension.

Attributes	Values
Mathematical model	ENUM (Bayesian Model, Hidden Markov Model, Conditional Random Field, NULL)
Classification type	ENUM (manual, automatic)
Algorithm name	STRING
Ontology name	STRING
Support	ENUM (sensor, robot, microphone, internet navigation, NULL, etc.)
Tool name	STRING

Mathematical Models. Mathematical models are abstract formal representations used to support reasoning. As we know, two main mathematical models are used in intention mining methods: the Bayesian model [18, 19] and Markov Models [49, 54]. *Bayesian* networks are graphical models that represent random variables and their conditional probabilities via a directed acyclic graph. *Hidden Markov Models* (HMM) are a variant of stochastic Markov chain that represent hidden sequences of states. HMM generalize finite-state automata by evaluating both the probability of transitions between states and probability distributions of observations in those states. The framework *Conditional Random Field* is also used in [24, 55] to define probabilistic models and some works also use other probabilistic models, specially designed for the problem at hand [56, 57].

Classification Type. Classification is of first importance in the proposed approaches as the content is often classified to determine the category to which a document or a query belongs. There are a lot of different approaches combining different techniques, like Support Vector Machine [18, 23, 24], Naive Bayes [18, 19], Expectation–maximization [49, 58], Complete-link clustering and Cosine similarity [59]. [14] introduce an improved version of the algorithms proposed by [60], agglomerative clustering using a distance metric based on dynamic time warping (DTW) [61], 1R, J48 and Expectation–Maximization [62]. Sometimes is used Click Intent Model (a hierarchical semantic clustering model) [63], Web Query Classification based on User Intent [64] or even clicks graphs [15].

Algorithm Name. Many algorithms formalize the different stages of IM methods. Among others we can cite for text analysis: TD/IDF [19], Porter Algorithm [31], GBRAM (Goal-Based Requirements Analysis Method) [65], or Markov random walk algorithm and OKAPI BM 25 [3]. Text analysis is one of the first steps of the proposed approaches as queries and document content have to be understandable by algorithms.

Ontology Name. Two ontologies are mainly used in intention mining methods: ConceptNet [18, 66] and WordNet [19, 66]. *ConceptNet* [74] is an ontological system for lexical knowledge and common sense knowledge representation and processing. The ConceptNet knowledge base is a semantic network consisting of over 1.6 million assertions encompassing the spatial, physical, social, temporal, and psychological aspects of everyday life. *WordNet* [67] is a lexical database. It groups English words into sets of synonyms, provides short and general definitions, and records various semantic relations between words, such as antonymy, hypernymy and hyponymy. Some ontology-based methods, such as [21], do not use these ontologies, but other ones, like the *Open Directory Project* [68], which categorizes websites. *ASPIC*, a biomedical knowledge base was used in [41] and [69] used the *Library of Congress Subject Headings* as ontology. [61] and others used *Freebase* to create a corpus, so did [3] with *Wikipedia.*

Support. Most of the IM approaches use input logs or user clicks in an Internet navigation [3, 4, 15]. Others approaches include specific devices to support their tool (in [16], a microphone is used to catch human speech to be interpreted by a robot).

Tool Name. Many tools are exploited or proposed to implement intention-mining methods. For instance, [70] and [71] uses the *LIBSVM* tool [72] that implements the Support Vector Machine algorithm. [18] uses the *Natural Language Tool Kit* to manipulate natural language data, and the *WEKA data mining toolkit* for intentions classification. WEKA is widely used for classification [23, 24, 62]. *Mallet* is used by [24] to implement the Conditional Random Field classification algorithm. In [62], a query is transformed into WSMX goals (Web Services Execution Environment) using a system called *Ontopath.* [43] uses the commercial tool *Disco* [73] to mine processes specified using the BPMN formalism. Of course, some other authors developed a tool from scratch [41, 45].

4 Comparison Framework Application

As explained above, we have pre-selected 5 papers to validate the IM comparison framework. [15] use click graphs to better classify users query intents by semi-supervised learning. That allows to avoid to enrich feature representation. [16] aims at detecting affective intents in speech in case of human-robot interaction. Their goal is to learn robots to identify praise, prohibition, comfort, attention, and neutral speech. In [3], the authors present an approach to classify query intents of users by mining the content of Wikipedia. They associate an intent probability to Wikipedia articles and categories to provide a better classification. In the approach described in [4], a new way to capture users' intentions is proposed to improve Internet image search engines. The main idea is to include images in addition to the classic keywords query and to refine search results

Table 5. IM comparison framework application to the selected IM approaches.

	[15]	[16]	[3]	[4]	[17]
Object dimension					
Structuredness	Individual	Individual	Individual	Individual	Cluster
Intention taxonomy	Query intent	"Approval, prohibition, attention, comfort, neutral"	Query intent	Keyword	User intent
Intention modelling formalism	Linguistic	Linguistic	Linguistic	Linguistic	Linguistic
Usage dimension					
Usage Goal	Discovery of Click Graphs	Discovery of emotional intent	Discovery of category	Recommendation of images	Discovery
Domain of application	Information retrieval	Robot speech	Information retrieval	Internet search image	Information retrieval
Source Artefact	Group	Individual	Group	Individual	Group
Target Artefact	Group	Individual	Individual	Individual	Individual
Method dimension					
Machine learning method	Semi-supervised	–	–	–	Semi-supervised
Automation method	Semi-automatic	Automatic	Automatic	Automatic	Semi-automatic (manual labelling)
Observation record type	Query/clickthrough data	Sentence	'Search query log/category graph/article graph	Query keywords/query image	Search query log

(*continued*)

Table 5. (*continued*)

	[15]	[16]	[3]	[4]	[17]
Mathematical method	–	–	Probabilistic	Probabilistic	Probabilistic
Classification-based	1	1	1	1	1
Ontology-based	0	0	1	0	0
Tool dimension					
Mathematical model	–	Gaussian model	Markov random walk	Word probability model	–
Classification type	Content based classification (maximum entropy classifier)	EM algorithm/Kurtosis-based approach	Intent classifier	one-class SVM classifier	Intent detection classifier
Algorithm name	"Algorithm 1"/"Algorithm 2"	–	"Algo 1"/"ESA"/"Intent predictor"	–	"Algorithm 1"/"Algorithm 2"
Ontology name	–	–	Wikipedia articles and categories link	–	–
Support	Internet navigation	Microphone	Internet navigation	Internet navigation	Internet navigation

depending on the clicked image. [17] introduce Capsule Neural Networks to detect user intents when labeled utterances are not available. The proposed approach allows to avoid to label utterances as intents and thus reduce time and labor consumption.

We described the selected IM approaches using the suggested comparison framework (See Table 5). As a result, we were able to check its validity accordingly to two criteria: applicability and completeness. With the first validation criterion, each approach was characterized with regards to the most part of comparison attributes. According to the second criterion, following the application, we found a new attribute - that we called Support – to add to the Tool dimension. Indeed, it is useful to characterize different IM approaches by different kinds of used supports, like specific devices for instance. Based on these findings, we consider that the given comparison framework could be used as a scope for the further systematic literature review. Its application will allow to identify possible values for the framework attributes; thus, it will be possible to provide hints of guidance through the IM approaches selection and to carry out the detailed comparison of the IM approaches based on statistical analysis. In addition, a cross-referenced analysis will allow to identify open issues for future research on IM.

5 Conclusion

This paper proposes a framework to classify intention mining works. Inspired by other classification frameworks, our proposal examines IM in four different views, answering the four main questions about IM called dimensions: "What is IM?", "Why IM?", "How is done IM", and "By which means is done IM?". Each dimension corresponds to a set of classification attributes, found in the existing literature. We validated our framework by testing it on five existing and good referenced works and concluded that the given framework will be useful to conduct the systematic literature review on IM.

Our next step is to complete our systematic literature review on IM, characterizing all our selected papers within this framework in order to provide a detailed overview of the existing IM works and to define open issues.

References

1. Merriam-Webster: Definition of Intention. http://www.merriam-webster.com/dictionary/intention. Accessed 10 Nov 2020
2. Bratman, M.: Intention, Plans, and Practical Reason. Harvard University Press, Cambridge (1987)
3. Hu, J., Wang, G., Lochovsky, F., Sun, J., Chen, Z.: Understanding user's query intent with Wikipedia. In: Proceedings of the 18th international conference on World Wide Web, pp. 471–480. Association for Computing Machinery, New York, NY, USA (2009)
4. Tang, X., Liu, K., Cui, J., Wen, F., Wang, X.: IntentSearch: capturing user intention for one-click internet image search. IEEE Trans. Pattern Anal. Mach. Intell. **34**, 1342–1353 (2012)
5. Mei, T., Hua, X.-S., Zhou, H.-Q., Li, S.: Modeling and mining of users' capture intention for home videos. IEEE Trans. Multimed. **9**, 66–77 (2007)
6. Khodabandelou, G., Hug, C., Deneckère, R., Salinesi, C.: Supervised intentional process models discovery using hidden Markov models. In: IEEE 7th International Conference on Research Challenges in Information Science (RCIS), pp. 1–11 (2013)

7. Moshfeghi, Y., Joemon, J.: On cognition, emotion, and interaction aspects of search tasks with different search intentions. In: Proceedings of the 22nd International Conference on World Wide Web, WWW 2013, May, 2013, Rio de Janeiro, Brazil, pp. 931–942. ACM (2009)
8. Dai, H., Zhao, L., Nie, Z., Wen, J.-R., Wang, L., Li, Y.: Detecting online commercial intention (OCI). In: Proceedings of the 15th international conference on World Wide Web, WWW 2006, Edinburgh, Scotland, UK, 23–26 May 2006, pp. 829–837. ACM (2006)
9. Jarke, M., Mylopoulos, J., Schmidt, J.M., Vassilou, Y.: DAIDA: conceptual modeling and knowledge based support of information systems development process. Techn. Sci. Inf. **9**(2), 122–133 (1990)
10. Rolland, C.: A comprehensive view of process engineering. In: 10th Conference on Advanced Information Systems Engineering, Pisa, Italy (1998)
11. Kornyshova, E., Salinesi, C.: MCDM Techniques selection approaches: state of the art. In: IEEE Symposium on Computational Intelligence in Multicriteria Decision Making, USA (2007)
12. Deneckere, R., Iacovelli, A., Kornyshova, E., Souveyet, C.: From method fragments to method services. In: Exploring Modeling Methods for Systems Analysis and Design (EMMSAD 2008), pp. 80–96, Montpellier, France (2008)
13. Azin, A., Clarke, C., Agichtein, E., Guo, Q.: Estimating ad click through rate through query intent analysis. In: IEEE/WIC/ACM International Conference on Web Intelligence (2009)
14. Chapelle, O., Ji, S., Liao, C., Velipasaoglu, E., Lai, L., Wu, S.-L.: Intent-based diversification of web search results: metrics and algorithms. Inf. Retrieval **14**, 572–592 (2011)
15. Xiao L., Gunawardana, A., Acero, A.: Unsupervised semantic intent discovery from call log acoustics. In: IEEE International Conference on Acoustics, Speech, and Signal Processing (ICASSP 2005), 2005, pp. I/45-I/48, vol. 1 (2005)
16. Breazeal, C., Aryananda, L.: Recognition of affective communicative intent in robot-directed speech. Auton. Robots. **12**, 83–104 (2002)
17. Xia, C., Zhang, C., Yan, X., Chang, Y., Yu, P.S.: Zero-shot user intent detection via capsule neural networks. In: EMNLP 2018 (2018)
18. Strohmaier, M., Kröll, M.: Acquiring knowledge about human goals from search query logs. Inf. Process. Manag. **48**, 63–82 (2012)
19. Chen, Z., Lin, F., Liu, Y., Ma, W.-Y., Wenyin, L.: User intention modeling in web applications using data mining. In: Conference World Wide Web (2002)
20. Broder, A.: A taxonomy of web search. In: ACM Sigir Forum, pp. 3–10. ACM (2002)
21. Baeza-Yates, R., Calderón-Benavides, L., González-Caro, C.: The intention behind web queries. In: String Processing and Information Retrieval, pp. 98–109 (2006)
22. Chulef, A.S., Read, S.J., Walsh, D.A.: A Hierarchical Taxonomy of Human Goals. Motivation and Emotion. **25**, 191–232 (2001)
23. Chen, L., Zhang, D., Mark, L.: Understanding user intent in community question answering. Proceedings of the 21st international conference companion on World Wide Web. pp. 823–828. ACM (2012)
24. Guo, Q., Agichtein, E.: Ready to buy or just browsing?: Detecting web searcher goals from interaction data. In: 33rd International ACM SIGIR Conference on Research and Development in Information Retrieval – SIGIR 2010, p. 130. ACM Press, Geneva, Switzerland (2010)
25. Yi, X., Raghavan, H., Leggetter, C.: Discovering users' specific geo intention in web search. In: Proceedings of the 18th International Conference on World Wide Web, pp. 481–490. ACM, New York, NY, USA (2009)
26. Shen, A.X., Lee, M.K., Cheung, C.M., Chen, H.: An investigation into contribution I-Intention and We-Intention in open web-based encyclopedia: Roles of joint commitment and mutual agreement. In: ICIS 2009 Proceedings, vol. 7 (2009)
27. Tuomela, R.: We-intentions revisited. Philos. Stud. **125**, 327–369 (2005)

28. Dardenne, A., van Lamsweerde, A., Fickas, S.: Goal-directed requirements acquisition. Sci. Comput. Program. **20**, 3–50 (1993)
29. Yu, E.S.-K.: Modelling strategic relationships for process reengineering (1996)
30. Rolland, C., Prakash, N., Benjamen, A.: A multi-model view of process modelling. Requirements Eng. **4**, 169–187 (1999)
31. Hashemi, R., Bahrami, A., LaPlant, J., Thurber, K.: Discovery of intent through the analysis of visited sites. In: 2008 International Conference on Information & Knowledge Engineering, pp. 417–422. CSREA Press, Las Vegas, Nevada (2008)
32. Prat, N.: Goal formalisation and classification for requirements engineering. In: Proceedings the 3rd International Workshop on Requirements Engineering (1997)
33. Rumelhart, D.E.: Schemata: The Building Blocks of Cognition. Lawrence Erlbaum, Hillsdale (1980)
34. Park, K., Lee, T., Jung, S., Lim, H., Nam, S.: Extracting search intentions from web search logs. In: 2010 2nd International Conference on Information Technology Convergence and Services (ITCS), pp. 1–6 (2010)
35. Kaabi, R.S., Souveyet, C.: Capturing intentional services with business process maps. In: Proceedings of the 1st International conference in Research Challenges in Information Science (2007)
36. van der Aalst, W.: Process Mining. Springer, Berlin, Heidelberg (2011)
37. Hanjalic, A., Kofler, C., Larson, M.: Intent and its discontents: the user at the wheel of the online video search engine. In: 20th ACM international conference on Multimedia, pp. 1239–1248. Association for Computing Machinery, New York, NY, USA (2012)
38. Jantan, A., Rasmi, Mhd, Ibrahim, Mhd.I., Rahman, A.H.A.: A similarity model to estimate attack strategy based on intentions analysis for network forensics. In: Thampi, S.M., Zomaya, A.Y., Strufe, T., Alcaraz Calero, J.M., Thomas, T. (eds.) SNDS 2012. CCIS, vol. 335, pp. 336–346. Springer, Heidelberg (2012). https://doi.org/10.1007/978-3-642-34135-9_34
39. Rasmi, M., Jantan, A.: Attack Intention Analysis Model for Network Forensics. In: Software Engineering and Computer Systems. pp. 403–411. Springer Berlin Heidelberg (2011)
40. Shirley, J., Evans, D.: The user is not the enemy: fighting malware by tracking user intentions. In: Proceedings of the 2008 workshop on New Security Paradigms, pp. 33–45. ACM (2009)
41. Sutherland, K., McLeod, K., Ferguson, G., Burger, A.: Knowledge-driven enhancements for task composition in bioinformatics. BMC Bioinf. **10**, S12 (2009)
42. Shanechi, M.M., Wornell, G.W., Williams, Z., Brown, E.N.: A parallel point-process filter for estimation of goal-directed movements from neural signals. In: 2010 IEEE International Conference on Acoustics Speech and Signal Processing (ICASSP), pp. 521–524. IEEE (2010)
43. Outmazgin, N., Soffer, P.: Business process workarounds: what can and cannot be detected by process mining. In: Nurcan, S., Proper, H.A., Soffer, P., Krogstie, J., Schmidt, R., Halpin, T., Bider, I. (eds.) BPMDS/EMMSAD -2013. LNBIP, vol. 147, pp. 48–62. Springer, Heidelberg (2013). https://doi.org/10.1007/978-3-642-38484-4_5
44. Epure, E.V., Hug, C., Deneckere, R., Brinkkemper, S., others: What shall I do next? Intention mining for flexible process enactment. In: Proceedings of 26th International Conference on Advanced Information Systems Engineering (CAiSE), pp. 473–487 (2014)
45. Krüger, F., Yordanova, K., Kirste, T.: Tool support for probabilistic intention recognition using plan synthesis. In: Paternò, F., de Ruyter, B., Markopoulos, P., Santoro, C., van Loenen, E., Luyten, K. (eds.) Ambient Intelligence, pp. 439–444. Springer, Berlin Heidelberg (2012)
46. Niekum, S., Barto, A.G.: Clustering via Dirichlet process mixture models for portable skill discovery. In: Advances in Neural Information Processing Systems. Weinberger (2011)
47. Deneckère, R., Hug, C., Khodabandelou, G., Salinesi, C.: Intentional process mining: discovering and modeling the goals behind processes using supervised learning. Int. J. Inf. Syst. Model. Design **5**, 22–47 (2014)

48. Aarno, D., Kragic, D.: Layered HMM for motion intention recognition. In: 2006 IEEE/RSJ International Conference on Intelligent Robots and Systems, IROS 2006, 9–15 October 2006, Beijing, China, pp. 5130–5135 (2006)
49. Bascetta, L., et al.: Towards safe human-robot interaction in robotic cells: an approach based on visual tracking and intention estimation. In: 2011 IEEE/RSJ International Conference on Intelligent Robots and Systems, IROS 2011, San Francisco, CA, USA, September, 2011, pp. 2971–2978. IEEE (2011)
50. Mohri, M., Rostamizadeh, A., Talwalkar, A.: Foundations of Machine Learning. The MIT Press, Cambridge (2012)
51. Laflaquière, J., Settouti, L.S., Prié, Y., Mille, A.: Trace-based framework for experience management and engineering. In: Gabrys, B., Howlett, R.J., Jain, L.C. (eds.) KES 2006. LNCS (LNAI), vol. 4251, pp. 1171–1178. Springer, Heidelberg (2006). https://doi.org/10.1007/11892960_141
52. Clauzel, D., Sehaba, K., Prie, Y.: Modelling and visualising traces for reflexivity in synchronous collaborative systems. In: International Conference on Intelligent Networking and Collaborative Systems, 2009. INCOS 2009, pp. 16–23 (2009)
53. Milton, J.S., Arnold, J.C.: Introduction to Probability and Statistics: Principles and Applications for Engineering and the Computing Sciences. McGraw-Hill Inc., New York (2002)
54. Sadikov, E., Madhavan, J., Wang, L., Halevy, A.Y.: Clustering query refinements by user intent. In Proceedings of the 19th International Conference on World Wide Web, WWW 2010, Raleigh, North Carolina, USA, 26–30 April 2010, pp. 841–850. ACM (2010)
55. Shen, Y., Yan, J., Yan, S., Ji, L., Liu, N., Chen, Z.: Sparse hidden-dynamics conditional random fields for user intent understanding. In Proceedings of the 20th International Conference on World Wide Web, WWW 2011, Hyderabad, India, March 28–April 1, 2011, pp. 7–16. ACM (2011)
56. Liu, N., Yan, J., Fan, W., Yang, Q., Chen, Z.: Identifying vertical search intention of query through social tagging propagation. In: 18th International Conference on World Wide Web, WWW 2009, Madrid, Spain, 20–24 April 2009, pp. 1209–1210. ACM (2009)
57. Xi, X., Wang, Y.-Y., Acero, A.: Learning query intent from regularized click graphs. In: SIGIR Conference on Research and Development in Information Retrieval (2008)
58. Zhu, C., Cheng, Q., Sheng, W.: Human intention recognition in smart assisted living systems using a hierarchical hidden Markov model. In: IEEE International Conference on Automation Science and Engineering, CASE 2008, pp. 253–258. IEEE (2008)
59. Yamamoto, T., Sakai, T., Iwata, M., Yu, C., Wen, J.-R., Tanaka, K.: The wisdom of advertisers: mining subgoals via query clustering. In: Proceedings of the 21st ACM International Conference on Information and Knowledge Management, pp. 505–514. ACM (2012)
60. Agrawal, R., Gollapudi, S., Halverson, A., Ieong, S.: Diversifying search results. In: Proceedings of the Second ACM International Conference on Web Search and Data Mining, pp. 5–14. ACM, New York, NY, USA (2009)
61. Cheung, J.C.K., Li, X.: Sequence clustering and labeling for unsupervised query intent discovery. In: Proceedings of the Fifth ACM International Conference on Web Search and Data Mining, pp. 383–392 (2012)
62. Ciesielski V., Lalani A.: Data mining of web access logs from an academic web site. In: Design and Application of Hybrid Intelligent Systems, pp. 1034–1043. IOS Press, Amsterdam, The Netherlands (2003)
63. Hakkani-Tür, D., Celikyilmaz, A., Heck, L., Tur, G.: A weakly-supervised approach for discovering new user intents from search query logs (2013)
64. Jansen, B.J., Booth, D.L., Spink, A.: Determining the informational, navigational, and transactional intent of Web queries. Inf. Process. Manag. **44**, 1251–1266 (2008)
65. Anton, A.I., Earp, J.B., Reese, A.: Analyzing website privacy requirements using a privacy goal taxonomy. IEEE Joint Int. Conf. Requir. Eng. **2002**, 23–31 (2002)

66. Krenge, J., Petrushyna, Z., Kravcik, M., Klamma, R.: Identification of learning goals in forum-based communities. In: 11th IEEE International Conference on Advanced Learning Technologies (ICALT), pp. 307–309. IEEE (2011)
67. Miller, G.A., Beckwith, R., Fellbaum, C., Gross, D., Miller, K.J.: Introduction to wordnet: an on-line lexical database*. Int. J. Lexicogr. **3**, 235–244 (1990)
68. DMOZ. http://www.dmoz.org/. Accessed Nov 2020
69. Shen, Y., Li, Y., Xu, Y., Iannella, R., Algarni, A.: An ontology-based mining approach for user search intent discovery, 9 (2011)
70. González-Caro, C., Baeza-Yates, R.: A multi-faceted approach to query intent classification. In: Grossi, R., Sebastiani, F., Silvestri, F. (eds.) String Processing and Information Retrieval, pp. 368–379. Springer, Heidelberg (2011)
71. Herrera, M.R., de Moura, E.S., Cristo, M., Silva, T.P., da Silva, A.S.: Exploring features for the automatic identification of user goals in web search. Inf. Process. Manag. **46**, 131–142 (2010)
72. Chang, C.-C., Lin, C.-J.: LIBSVM: a library for support vector machines. ACM Trans. Intell. Syst. Technol. **2**, 27:1–27:27 (2011)
73. Fluxicon. http://www.fluxicon.com/disco/. Accessed Nov 2020
74. Liu, H., Singh, P.: ConceptNet & Mdash: a practical commonsense reasoning tool-kit. BT Technol. J. **22**, 211–226 (2004)

Exploring the Challenge of Automated Segmentation in Robotic Process Automation

Simone Agostinelli(✉), Andrea Marrella, and Massimo Mecella

Sapienza Universitá di Roma, Rome, Italy
{agostinelli,marrella,mecella}@diag.uniroma1.it

Abstract. Robotic Process Automation (RPA) is an emerging technology that allows organizations to automate intensive repetitive tasks (or simply *routines*) previously performed by a human user on the User Interface (UI) of web or desktop applications. RPA tools are able to capture in dedicated UI logs the execution of several routines and then emulate their enactment in place of the user by means of a software (SW) robot. A UI log can record information about many routines, whose actions are mixed in some order that reflects the particular order of their execution by the user, making their automated identification far from being trivial. The issue to automatically understand which user actions contribute to a specific routine inside the UI log is also known as *segmentation*. In this paper, we leverage a concrete use case to explore the issue of segmentation of UI logs, identifying all its potential variants and presenting an up-to-date overview that discusses to what extent such variants are supported by existing literature approaches. Moreover, we offer points of reference for future research based on the findings of this paper.

1 Introduction

Robotic Process Automation (RPA) is an automation technology in the field of Business Process Management (BPM) that creates *software (SW) robots* to replicate rule-based and repetitive tasks (or simply *routines*) performed by human users in their applications' user interfaces (UIs). A typical routine that can be automated by a SW robot using a RPA tool is transferring data from one system to another via their respective UIs, e.g., copying records from a spreadsheet application into a web-based enterprise information system [21]. In recent years, much progress has been made both in terms of research and technical development on RPA, resulting in many deployments for industrial-oriented services [4,17,19,28]. Moreover, the market of RPA solutions has developed rapidly and today includes more than 50 vendors developing tools that provide SW robots with advanced functionalities for automating office tasks in operations like accounting and customer service [5]. Nonetheless, when considering state-of-the-art RPA technology, it becomes apparent that the current generation of RPA tools is driven by predefined rules and manual configurations made by expert users rather than automated techniques [2,10].

S. Cherfi et al. (Eds.): RCIS 2021, LNBIP 415, pp. 38–54, 2021.
https://doi.org/10.1007/978-3-030-75018-3_3

In fact, as reported in [16], in the early stages of the RPA life-cycle it is required the support of skilled human experts to: *(i)* identify the candidate routines to automate by means of interviews and observation of workers conducting their daily work, *(ii)* record the interactions that take place during routines' enactment on the UI of software applications into dedicated *UI logs*, and *(iii)* manually specify their conceptual and technical structure (often in form of flowchart diagrams) for defining the behavior of SW robots.

This approach is not effective in case of UI logs that keep track of many routines executions, since the designer should have a global vision of all possible variants of the routines to define the appropriate behaviours of SW robots, which becomes complicated when the number of variants increases. Indeed, in presence of UI logs that collect information about several routines, the recorded actions are mixed in some order that reflects the particular order of their execution by the user, making the identification of candidate routines in a UI log a time-consuming and error-prone task. The challenge to understand which user actions contribute to which routines inside a UI log is known as *segmentation* [2,21].

This paper aims to explore the challenge of automated segmentation in RPA through the evaluation of two research questions: *(i)* what are the variants of a segmentation solution needed to properly deal with different kinds of UI log? *(ii)* to what extent such variants are supported by literature approaches?

To answer these research questions, we first leverage a concrete RPA use case in the administrative sector to explain the segmentation issue (Sect. 2). After having described the relevant background on UI logs (Sect. 3), we discuss how a segmentation technique should behave in presence of three different (and relevant) forms of UI logs, which may consist of: *(i)* several executions of the same routine, *(ii)* several executions of many routines without the possibility to have user actions in common, and *(iii)* several executions of many routines with the possibility to have user actions in common (Sect. 4). Then, we investigate how and if such forms of UI logs are tackled by the current state-of-the-art segmentation approaches (Sect. 5). Finally, we provide future directions for automated segmentation in RPA based on the findings of our study (Sect. 6).

2 A RPA Use Case

In this section, we describe a RPA use case derived by a real-life scenario at Department of Computer, Control and Management Engineering (DIAG) of Sapienza Universitá di Roma. The scenario concerns the filling of the travel authorization request form made by personnel of DIAG for travel requiring prior approval. The request applicant must fill a well-structured Excel spreadsheet (cf. Fig. 1(a)) providing some personal information, such as her/his bio-data and the email address, together with further information related to the travel, including the destination, the starting/ending date/time, the means of transport to be used, the travel purpose, and the envisioned amount of travel expenses, associated with the possibility to request an anticipation of the expenses already incurred (e.g., to request in advance a visa). When ready, the spreadsheet is

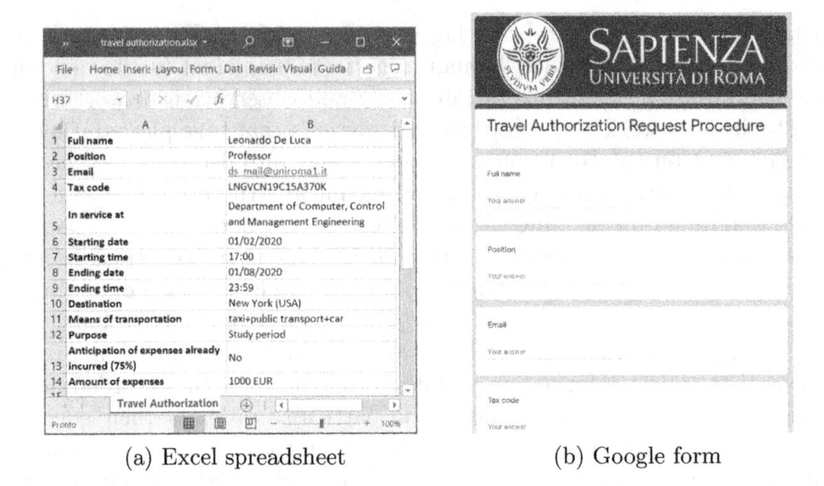

(a) Excel spreadsheet (b) Google form

Fig. 1. UIs involved in the use case

sent via email to an employee of the Administration Office of DIAG, which is in charge of approving and elaborating the request. Concretely, for each row in the spreadsheet, the employee manually copies every cell in that row and pastes that into the corresponding text field in a dedicated Google form (cf. Fig. 1(b)), accessible just by the Administration staff. Once the data transfer for a given travel authorization request has been completed, the employee presses the "Submit" button to submit the data into an internal database.

In addition, if the request applicant declares that s/he would like to use her/his personal car as one of the means of transport for the travel, then s/he has to fill a dedicated web form required for activating a special insurance for the part of the travel that will be performed with the car. This further request will be delivered to the Administration staff via email, and the employee in charge of processing it can either approve or reject such request. At the end, the applicant will be automatically notified via email of the approval/rejection of the request.

The above procedure, which involves two main routines (in the following, we will denote them as R1 and R2), is performed manually by an employee of the Administration Office of DIAG, and it should be repeated for any new travel request. Routines such as these ones are good candidates to be encoded with executable scripts and enacted by means of a SW robot within a commercial RPA tool. However, unless there is complete a-priori knowledge of the specific routines that are enacted on the UI and of their concrete composition, their automated identification from an UI log is challenging, since the associated user actions may be scattered across the log, interleaved with other actions that are not part of the routine under analysis, and potentially shared by many routines.

For the sake of understandability, we show in Figs. 2 and 3 the interaction models of R1 and R2 required to represent the structure of the routines of

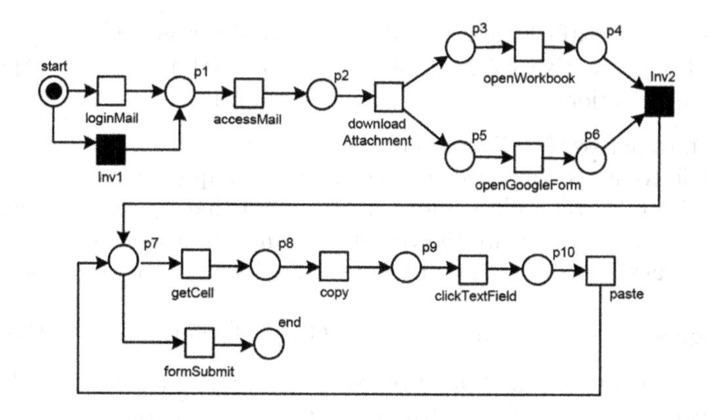

Fig. 2. Interaction model for R1

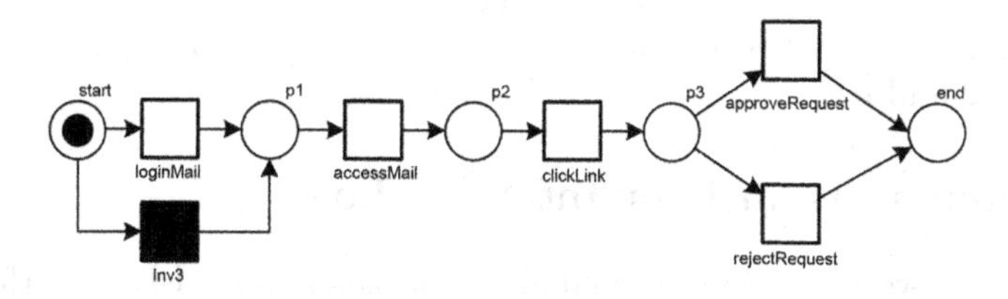

Fig. 3. Interaction model for R2

interest, depicted as Petri nets.[1] For example, analyzing the Petri net in Fig. 2, it becomes clear that a proper execution of R1 requires a path on the UI made by the following user actions:[2]

- loginMail, to access the client email;
- accessMail, to access the specific email with the travel request;
- downloadAttachment, to download the Excel file including the travel request;
- openWorkbook, to open the Excel spreadsheet;
- openGoogleForm, to access the Google Form to be filled;
- getCell, to select the cell in the i-th row of the Excel spreadsheet;
- copy, to copy the content of the selected cell;
- clickTextField, to select the specific text field of the Google form where the content of the cell should be pasted;
- paste, to paste the content of the cell into a text field of the Google form;
- formSubmit, to finally submit the Google form to the internal database.

As shown in Fig. 2, the user actions openWorkbook and openGoogleForm can be performed in any order. Moreover, the sequence of actions

[1] The research literature is rich of notations for expressing human-computer dialogs as interaction models. Among them, Petri nets guarantee a good trade-off between expressiveness and understandability of the models [26].

[2] Note that the user actions recorded in a UI log can have a finer granularity than the high-level ones used here just with the purpose of describing the routine's behaviour.

⟨getCell, copy, clickTextField, paste⟩ will be repeated for any travel information to be moved from the Excel spreadsheet to the Google form. On the other hand, the path of user actions in the UI to properly enact R2 is as follows:

- loginMail, to access the client email;
- accessMail, to access the specific email with the request for travel insurance;
- clickLink, to click the link included in the email that opens the Google form with the request to activate the travel insurance on a web browser;
- approveRequest, to press the button on the Google form that approves the request;
- rejectRequest, to press the button on the Google form that rejects the request;

Note that the execution of approveRequest and rejectRequest is exclusive, cf. the Petri net in Fig. 3. Then, in the interaction models of R1 and R2, there are transitions that do not represent user actions but are needed to correctly represent the structure of such models. These transitions, drawn with a black-filled rectangle, are said to be "invisible", and are not recorded in the UI logs (cf. Inv1, Inv2 and Inv3).

3 Preliminaries on User Interface Logs

In this section, we provide some preliminary notions about User Interface (UI) logs, needed to understand the rest of the paper. A single UI log in its raw form consists of a long sequence of user actions recorded during one user session.[3] Such actions include all the steps required to accomplish one or more relevant routines using the UI of one or many sw application/s. For instance, in Fig. 4, we show a snapshot of a UI log captured using a dedicated action logger[4] during the execution of R1 and R2. The employed action logger enables to record the *events* happened on the UI, enriched with several data fields describing their "anatomy". For a given event, such fields are useful to keep track the name and the timestamp of the user action performed on the UI, the involved sw application, the human/sw resource that performed the action, etc.

For the sake of understandability, we assume here that any user action associated to each event recorded in the UI log is mapped at most with one (and only one) Petri net transition, and that the collection of labels associated to the Petri net transitions is defined over the same alphabet as the user actions in the UI log,[5] i.e., the alphabet of user actions in the UI log is a *superset* of that used for defining the labels of Petri net transitions. In the running example, we can recognize in R1 and R2 a universe of user actions of interest $Z =$ {loginMail, accessMail, downloadAttachment, openWorkbook, openGoogleForm, getCell, copy, clickTextField, paste, formSubmit, clickLink, approveRequest, rejectRequest}.

[3] We interpret a user session as a group of interactions that a single user takes within a given time frame on the UI of a specific computer system.

[4] The working of the action logger is described in [1]. The tool is available at: https://github.com/bpm-diag/smartRPA.

[5] In [22], it is shown how these assumptions can be removed.

	A	B	C	D	E	F	G	H	I	J
1	timestamp	user	category	application	event type	event src path	clipboard content	workbook	worksheet	cell content
2	2020-04-06 13:47	Simone	Mail	Outlook	loginMail					
3	2020-04-06 13:47	Simone	Mail	Outlook	accessMail					
4	2020-04-06 13:47	Simone	Mail	Outlook	downloadAttachment					
5	2020-04-06 13:47	Simone	MicrosoftOffice	Microsoft Excel	openWorkbook	C:\Users\Simone\Desktop\richiesta missione ac		richiesta missione.xlsx	Foglio1	
6	2020-04-06 13:47	Simone	MicrosoftOffice	Microsoft Excel	openWindow	C:\Users\Simone\Desktop		richiesta missione.xlsx	Foglio1	
7	2020-04-06 13:47	Simone	MicrosoftOffice	Microsoft Excel	afterCalculate					
8	2020-04-06 13:47	Simone	MicrosoftOffice	Microsoft Excel	resizeWindow	C:\Users\Simone\Desktop		richiesta missione.xlsx	Foglio1	
9	2020-04-06 13:47	Simone	Browser	Chrome	openGoogleForm					
10	2020-04-06 13:47	Simone	MicrosoftOffice	Microsoft Excel	getCell			richiesta missione.xlsx	Foglio1	Simone Agostinelli
11	2020-04-06 13:47	Simone	Clipboard	Clipboard	copy		Simone Agostinelli			
12	2020-04-06 13:47	Simone	Browser	Chrome	clickTextField					
13	2020-04-06 13:48	Simone	Mail	Outlook	clickLink					
14	2020-04-06 13:48	Simone	Browser	Chrome	paste		Simone Agostinelli			
15	2020-04-06 13:48	Simone	Browser	Chrome	changeField					
16	2020-04-06 13:48	Simone	Browser	Chrome	approveRequest					
17	2020-04-06 13:48	Simone	MicrosoftOffice	Microsoft Excel	getCell			richiesta missione.xlsx	Foglio1	Dottorando
18	2020-04-06 13:48	Simone	Clipboard	Clipboard	copy		Dottorando			
19	2020-04-06 13:48	Simone	MicrosoftOffice	Microsoft Excel	resizeWindow	C:\Users\Simone\Desktop		richiesta missione.xlsx	Foglio1	
20	2020-04-06 13:48	Simone	Browser	Chrome	clickTextField					
21	2020-04-06 13:48	Simone	Browser	Chrome	paste		Dottorando			

Fig. 4. Snapshot of a UI log captured during the executions of R1 and R2 (Color figure online)

As shown in Fig. 4, a UI log is not specifically recorded to capture pre-identified routines. A UI log may contain multiple and interleaved executions of one/many routine/s (cf. the blue/red boxes that group the user actions belonging to R1 and R2, respectively), as well as redundant behavior and noise. We consider as *redundant* any action that is unnecessary repeated during the execution of a routine, e.g., a text value that is first pasted in a wrong field and then is moved in the right place through a corrective action on the UI. On the other hand, we consider as *noise* all those actions that do not contribute to the achievement of any routine target, e.g., a window that is resized. In Fig. 4, the sequences of user actions that are not surrounded by a blue/red box can be safely labeled as noise.

Segmentation techniques aim to extract from a UI log all those user actions of a routine R, filtering out redundant actions and noise. Any sequence of actions in the UI log that can be replayed from the initial to the final marking of the Petri net-based interaction model of R is said to be a *routine trace* of R. For example, a valid routine trace of R1 is ⟨loginMail, accessMail, downloadAttachment, openWorkbook, openGoogleForm, getCell, copy, clickTextField, paste, formSubmit⟩. The interaction model of R1 suggests that valid routine traces are also those ones where: *(i)* loginMail is skipped (if the user is already logged in the client email); *(ii)* the pair of actions ⟨openWorkbook, openGoogleForm⟩ is performed in reverse order; *(iii)* the sequence of actions ⟨getCell, copy, clickTextField, paste⟩ is executed several time before submitting the Google form. On the other hand, two main routine traces can be extracted from R2: ⟨loginMail, accessMail, clickLink, acceptRequest⟩ and ⟨loginMail, accessMail, clickLink, rejectRequest⟩, again with the possibility to skip loginMail, i.e., the access to the client email.

4 Identifying the Segmentation Cases

Given a UI log that consists of events including user actions with the same granularity[6] and potentially belonging to different routines, in the RPA domain *segmentation* is the task of clustering parts of the log together which belong to the same routine. In a nutshell, the challenge is to automatically understand which user actions contribute to which routines, and organize such user actions in well bounded routine traces [2,21].

As shown in Sect. 3, in general a UI log stores information about several routines enacted in an interleaved fashion, with the possibility that a specific user action is shared by different routines. Furthermore, actions providing redundant behavior or not belonging to any of the routine under observation may be recorded in the log, generating noise that should be filtered out by a segmentation technique. Based on the above considerations, and on a concrete analysis of real UI logs recorded during the enactment of the routines presented in Sect. 2, we have identified three main forms of UI logs, which can be categorized according to the fact that: *(i)* any user action in the log exclusively belongs to a specific routine (Case 1); *(ii)* the log records the execution of many routines that do not have any user action in common (Case 2); *(iii)* the log records the execution of many routines, and the possibility exists that some performed user actions are shared by many routines at the same time (Case 3). In the following, we analyze the characteristics of the three cases and of their variants. For the sake of understandability, we use a numerical subscript ij associated to any user action to indicate that it belongs to the $j - th$ execution of the $i - th$ routine under study. Of course, this information is not recorded in the UI log, and discovering it (i.e., the identification of the subscripts) is one of the "implicit" effects of segmentation when routine traces are built.

Case 1. This is the case when a UI log captures many executions of the same routine. Of course, in this scenario it is not possible to distinguish between shared and non-shared user actions by different routines, since the UI log keeps track only of executions associated to a single routine. Two main variants exist:

- **Case 1.1.** Starting from the use case in Sect. 2, let us consider the case of a UI log that records a sequence of user actions resulting from many non-interleaved executions of R1 (cf. Fig. 5(a)). We have also the presence of some user actions that potentially belong *at the same time* to many executions of the routine itself. This is the case of loginMail, which can be performed exactly once at the beginning of a user session and can be "shared" by many executions of the same routine. Applying a segmentation technique to the above UI log would trivially produce a segmented UI log where the (already well bounded) executions of R1 are organized as different routine traces: the

[6] The UI logs created by generic action loggers usually consist of low-level events associated one-by-one to a recorded user action on the UI (e.g., mouse clicks, etc.). We will discuss the abstraction issue in Sect. 5, where state-of-the-art techniques are shown that enable to flatten the content of a log to a same granularity level.

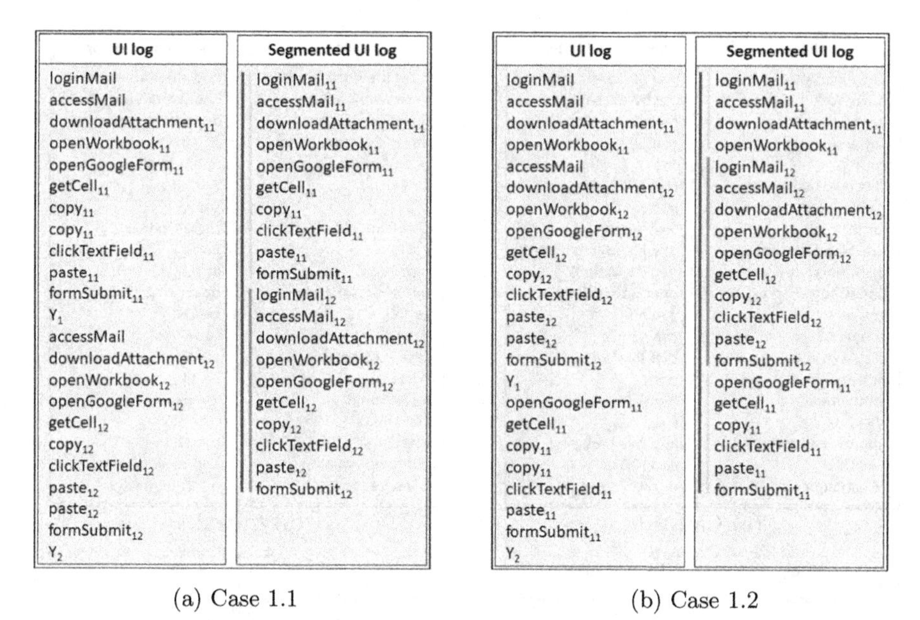

(a) Case 1.1

(b) Case 1.2

Fig. 5. Variants for Case 1 (Color figure online)

yellow and orange vertical lines outline the routine traces, while the red line outlines the routine segment of R1.

- **Case 1.2**. The same segmented UI log is obtained when the executions of R1 are recorded in an interleaved fashion in the original UI log (cf. Fig. 5(b)). Here, the segmentation task is more challenging, because the user actions of different executions of the same routine are interleaved among each others, and it is not known a-priori to which execution they belong.

Both variants of Case 1 are affected by *noise* or *redundant* actions. The logs contain elements of noise, i.e., user actions $\mathbf{Y}_{k \in \{1,n\}} \in Z$ (remind that Z is the universe of user actions allowed by a UI log, as introduced in Sect. 3) that are not allowed by R1, and redundant actions like copy and paste that are unnecessary repeated multiple times. Noise and redundant actions need to be filtered out during the segmentation task because they do not contribute to the achievement of the routine's target. For the sake of space, in the following analysis we do not consider anymore the presence of noise and redundant actions, since their handling is similar for all the cases.

Case 2. In this case, a UI log captures many executions of different routines, with the assumption that the interaction models of such routines include only transitions associated to user actions that are exclusive for that routines. To comply with the latter constraint, let us suppose that in both interaction models of R1 and R2 the transitions loginMail and accessMail are not required. Four main variants of Case 2 can be identified:

UI log	Segmented UI log
downloadAttachment$_{11}$	downloadAttachment$_{11}$
openWorkbook$_{11}$	openWorkbook$_{11}$
openGoogleForm$_{11}$	openGoogleForm$_{11}$
getCell$_{11}$	getCell$_{11}$
copy$_{11}$	copy$_{11}$
clickTextField$_{11}$	clickTextField$_{11}$
paste$_{11}$	paste$_{11}$
formSubmit$_{11}$	formSubmit$_{11}$
downloadAttachment$_{12}$	downloadAttachment$_{12}$
openWorkbook$_{12}$	openWorkbook$_{12}$
openGoogleForm$_{12}$	openGoogleForm$_{12}$
getCell$_{12}$	getCell$_{12}$
copy$_{12}$	copy$_{12}$
clickTextField$_{12}$	clickTextField$_{12}$
paste$_{12}$	paste$_{12}$
formSubmit$_{12}$	formSubmit$_{12}$
clickLink$_{21}$	clickLink$_{21}$
approveRequest$_{21}$	approveRequest$_{21}$
clickLink$_{22}$	clickLink$_{22}$
rejectRequest$_{22}$	rejectRequest$_{22}$

(a) Case 2.1

UI log	Segmented UI log
downloadAttachment$_{11}$	downloadAttachment$_{11}$
openWorkbook$_{11}$	openWorkbook$_{11}$
openGoogleForm$_{11}$	openGoogleForm$_{11}$
downloadAttachment$_{12}$	downloadAttachment$_{12}$
openWorkbook$_{12}$	openWorkbook$_{12}$
getCell$_{11}$	getCell$_{11}$
copy$_{11}$	copy$_{11}$
clickTextField$_{11}$	clickTextField$_{11}$
paste$_{11}$	paste$_{11}$
formSubmit$_{11}$	formSubmit$_{11}$
openGoogleForm$_{12}$	openGoogleForm$_{12}$
getCell$_{12}$	getCell$_{12}$
copy$_{12}$	copy$_{12}$
clickTextField$_{12}$	clickTextField$_{12}$
paste$_{12}$	paste$_{12}$
formSubmit$_{12}$	formSubmit$_{12}$
clickLink$_{21}$	clickLink$_{21}$
clickLink$_{22}$	clickLink$_{22}$
approveRequest$_{21}$	approveRequest$_{21}$
rejectRequest$_{22}$	rejectRequest$_{22}$

(b) Case 2.2

UI log	Segmented UI log
downloadAttachment$_{11}$	downloadAttachment$_{11}$
openWorkbook$_{11}$	openWorkbook$_{11}$
openGoogleForm$_{11}$	openGoogleForm$_{11}$
getCell$_{11}$	getCell$_{11}$
copy$_{11}$	copy$_{11}$
clickTextField$_{11}$	clickTextField$_{11}$
paste$_{11}$	paste$_{11}$
formSubmit$_{11}$	formSubmit$_{11}$
clickLink$_{21}$	clickLink$_{21}$
approveRequest$_{21}$	approveRequest$_{21}$
downloadAttachment$_{12}$	downloadAttachment$_{12}$
openWorkbook$_{12}$	openWorkbook$_{12}$
openGoogleForm$_{12}$	openGoogleForm$_{12}$
getCell$_{12}$	getCell$_{12}$
copy$_{12}$	copy$_{12}$
clickTextField$_{12}$	clickTextField$_{12}$
paste$_{12}$	paste$_{12}$
formSubmit$_{12}$	formSubmit$_{12}$
clickLink$_{22}$	clickLink$_{22}$
rejectRequest$_{22}$	rejectRequest$_{22}$

(c) Case 2.3

UI log	Segmented UI log
downloadAttachment$_{11}$	downloadAttachment$_{11}$
openWorkbook$_{11}$	openWorkbook$_{11}$
openGoogleForm$_{11}$	openGoogleForm$_{11}$
downloadAttachment$_{12}$	downloadAttachment$_{12}$
openWorkbook$_{12}$	openWorkbook$_{12}$
getCell$_{11}$	getCell$_{11}$
copy$_{11}$	copy$_{11}$
clickTextField$_{11}$	clickTextField$_{11}$
paste$_{11}$	paste$_{11}$
formSubmit$_{11}$	formSubmit$_{11}$
clickLink$_{21}$	clickLink$_{21}$
openGoogleForm$_{12}$	openGoogleForm$_{12}$
getCell$_{12}$	getCell$_{12}$
copy$_{12}$	copy$_{12}$
clickTextField$_{12}$	clickTextField$_{12}$
paste$_{12}$	paste$_{12}$
formSubmit$_{12}$	formSubmit$_{12}$
clickLink$_{22}$	clickLink$_{22}$
approveRequest$_{21}$	approveRequest$_{21}$
rejectRequest$_{22}$	rejectRequest$_{22}$

(d) Case 2.4

Fig. 6. Variants for Case 2 (Color figure online)

- **Case 2.1**. Let us consider the UI log in Fig. 6(a). The output of the segmentation task would consist of a segmented log where the (already well bounded) executions of R1 and R2 are organized as different routine traces: *(i)* the yellow and orange vertical lines outline the routine traces of R1, *(ii)* the light blue and grey vertical lines outline the routine traces of R2, while *(iii)* the outer red and blue lines outline the routine segments of R1 and R2. In the following, the coloring scheme will be kept the same.
- **Case 2.2**. Similarly to what already seen in Case 1.2, it may happen that many executions of the same routine are interleaved among each other (cf.

Fig. 6(b)), e.g., the first execution of R1 is interleaved with the second execution of R1, the first execution of R2 is interleaved with the second execution of R2, and so on.
- **Case 2.3**. Another variant is when the UI log records in an interleaved fashion many different routines but not the routine executions (cf. Fig. 6(c)), e.g., the first execution of R2 follows the first execution of R1, the second execution of R2 follows the second execution of R1, and so on.
- **Case 2.4**. The complexity of the segmentation task becomes more challenging in presence of both interleaved routines and routine executions (cf. Fig. 6(d)), e.g., the first execution of R1 is interleaved with the second execution of R1; the second execution of R1 is interleaved with the first execution of R2; the first execution of R2 is interleaved with the second execution of R2.

Case 3. In this case, a UI log captures many executions of different routines, and there exist user actions that are shared by such routines. This case perfectly reflects what happens in the use case of Sect. 2. In particular, loginMail and accessMail are shared by R1 and R2, as they are included in the interaction models of both routines. Four variants can be distinguished:

- **Case 3.1**. Let us consider the UI log depicted in Fig. 7(a). loginMail is *potentially involved* in the enactment of any execution of R1 and R2, while accessMail is *required by all* executions of R1 and R2, but it is not clear the association between the single executions of accessMail and the routine executions they belong to. The complexity of the segmentation task here lies in understanding to which routine traces the execution of loginMail and accessMail belong to. The outcome of the segmentation task will be a segmented log where the executions of R1 and R2 are organized as different routine traces according to the coloring scheme explained in Case 2.1.
- **Case 3.2**. This is the case when the UI log records interleaved executions of the same routine in presence of shared user actions (cf. Fig. 7(b)), e.g., the first execution of R1 is interleaved with the second execution of R1, and the first execution of R2 is interleaved with the second execution of R2.
- **Case 3.3**. Another variant is when the UI log records in an interleaved fashion many different routines but not the routine executions in presence of shared user actions (cf. Fig. 7(c)), e.g.: the first execution of R2 follows the first execution of R1 and the second execution of R2 follows the second execution of R1.
- **Case 3.4**. The segmentation task becomes more challenging in presence of more complex UI logs consisting of both interleaved routines and routine executions with shared user actions (cf. Fig. 7(d)), e.g., the first execution of R1 is interleaved with the second execution of R1, the second execution of R1 is interleaved with the first execution of R2, and the first execution of R2 is interleaved with the second execution of R2.

The above three cases and their variants have in common that all the user actions are stored within a single UI log. It may happen that the same routine

UI log	Segmented UI log
loginMail	loginMail$_{11}$
accessMail	accessMail$_{11}$
downloadAttachment$_{11}$	downloadAttachment$_{11}$
openWorkbook$_{11}$	openWorkbook$_{11}$
openGoogleForm$_{11}$	openGoogleForm$_{11}$
getCell$_{11}$	getCell$_{11}$
copy$_{11}$	copy$_{11}$
clickTextField$_{11}$	clickTextField$_{11}$
paste$_{11}$	paste$_{11}$
formSubmit$_{11}$	formSubmit$_{11}$
accessMail	loginMail$_{12}$
downloadAttachment$_{12}$	accessMail$_{12}$
openWorkbook$_{12}$	downloadAttachment$_{12}$
openGoogleForm$_{12}$	openWorkbook$_{12}$
getCell$_{12}$	openGoogleForm$_{12}$
copy$_{12}$	getCell$_{12}$
clickTextField$_{12}$	copy$_{12}$
paste$_{12}$	clickTextField$_{12}$
formSubmit$_{12}$	paste$_{12}$
accessMail	formSubmit$_{12}$
clickLink$_{21}$	loginMail$_{21}$
approveRequest$_{21}$	accessMail$_{21}$
accessMail	clickLink$_{21}$
clickLink$_{22}$	approveRequest$_{21}$
rejectRequest$_{22}$	loginMail$_{22}$
	accessMail$_{22}$
	clickLink$_{22}$
	rejectRequest$_{22}$

(a) Case 3.1

UI log	Segmented UI log
loginMail	loginMail$_{11}$
accessMail	accessMail$_{11}$
downloadAttachment$_{11}$	downloadAttachment$_{11}$
openWorkbook$_{11}$	openWorkbook$_{11}$
openGoogleForm$_{11}$	openGoogleForm$_{11}$
accessMail	loginMail$_{12}$
openWorkbook$_{12}$	accessMail$_{12}$
openGoogleForm$_{12}$	openWorkbook$_{12}$
getCell$_{11}$	openGoogleForm$_{12}$
copy$_{11}$	getCell$_{11}$
clickTextField$_{11}$	copy$_{11}$
paste$_{11}$	clickTextField$_{11}$
formSubmit$_{11}$	paste$_{11}$
downloadAttachment$_{12}$	formSubmit$_{11}$
getCell$_{12}$	downloadAttachment$_{12}$
copy$_{12}$	getCell$_{12}$
clickTextField$_{12}$	copy$_{12}$
paste$_{12}$	clickTextField$_{12}$
formSubmit$_{12}$	paste$_{12}$
accessMail	formSubmit$_{12}$
accessMail	loginMail$_{21}$
clickLink$_{21}$	accessMail$_{21}$
approveRequest$_{21}$	loginMail$_{22}$
clickLink$_{22}$	accessMail$_{22}$
rejectRequest$_{22}$	clickLink$_{21}$
	approveRequest$_{21}$
	clickLink$_{22}$
	rejectRequest$_{22}$

(b) Case 3.2

UI log	Segmented UI log
loginMail	loginMail$_{11}$
accessMail	accessMail$_{11}$
downloadAttachment$_{11}$	downloadAttachment$_{11}$
openWorkbook$_{11}$	openWorkbook$_{11}$
openGoogleForm$_{11}$	openGoogleForm$_{11}$
getCell$_{11}$	getCell$_{11}$
copy$_{11}$	copy$_{11}$
clickTextField$_{11}$	clickTextField$_{11}$
paste$_{11}$	paste$_{11}$
formSubmit$_{11}$	formSubmit$_{11}$
accessMail	loginMail$_{21}$
clickLink$_{21}$	accessMail$_{21}$
approveRequest$_{21}$	clickLink$_{21}$
accessMail	approveRequest$_{21}$
downloadAttachment$_{12}$	loginMail$_{12}$
openWorkbook$_{12}$	accessMail$_{12}$
openGoogleForm$_{12}$	downloadAttachment$_{12}$
getCell$_{12}$	openWorkbook$_{12}$
copy$_{12}$	openGoogleForm$_{12}$
clickTextField$_{12}$	getCell$_{12}$
paste$_{12}$	copy$_{12}$
formSubmit$_{12}$	clickTextField$_{12}$
accessMail	paste$_{12}$
clickLink$_{22}$	formSubmit$_{12}$
rejectRequest$_{22}$	loginMail$_{22}$
	accessMail$_{22}$
	clickLink$_{22}$
	rejectRequest$_{22}$

(c) Case 3.3

UI log	Segmented UI log
loginMail	loginMail$_{11}$
accessMail	accessMail$_{11}$
downloadAttachment$_{11}$	downloadAttachment$_{11}$
openWorkbook$_{11}$	openWorkbook$_{11}$
openGoogleForm$_{11}$	openGoogleForm$_{11}$
accessMail	loginMail$_{12}$
openWorkbook$_{12}$	accessMail$_{12}$
openGoogleForm$_{12}$	openWorkbook$_{12}$
getCell$_{11}$	openGoogleForm$_{12}$
copy$_{11}$	getCell$_{11}$
clickTextField$_{11}$	copy$_{11}$
paste$_{11}$	clickTextField$_{11}$
formSubmit$_{11}$	paste$_{11}$
accessMail	formSubmit$_{11}$
downloadAttachment$_{12}$	loginMail$_{21}$
getCell$_{12}$	accessMail$_{21}$
copy$_{12}$	downloadAttachment$_{12}$
clickTextField$_{12}$	getCell$_{12}$
paste$_{12}$	copy$_{12}$
formSubmit$_{12}$	clickTextField$_{12}$
accessMail	paste$_{12}$
clickLink$_{21}$	formSubmit$_{12}$
approveRequest$_{21}$	loginMail$_{22}$
clickLink$_{22}$	accessMail$_{22}$
rejectRequest$_{22}$	clickLink$_{21}$
	approveRequest$_{21}$
	clickLink$_{22}$
	rejectRequest$_{22}$

(d) Case 3.4

Fig. 7. Variants for Case 3 (Color figure online)

Table 1. Literature approaches to tackle segmentation variants

Papers	Case 1		Case 2				Case 3			
	1.1	1.2	2.1	2.2	2.3	2.4	3.1	3.2	3.3	3.4
Agostinelli *et al.* [3]	✓	✓	✓	✓	✓	✓	∼	∼		
Baier *et al.* [7]	✓		✓							
Bayomie *et al.* [8]	✓									
Bosco *et al.* [9]	✓		✓							
Kumar *et al.* [18]	✓		✓							
Leno *et al.* [20]	✓	∼	✓	∼	∼	∼				
Liu [23]	✓		✓	∼	∼	∼				
Fazzinga *et al.* [12]	✓		✓				✓			
Ferreira *et al.* [13]	✓		✓							
Mannhardt *et al.* [24]	✓		✓							
Măruşter *et al.* [27]	✓									
Srivastava *et al.* [29]	✓		✓							

is spread across multiple UI logs, in particular when there are multiple users that are involved in the execution of the routine on different computer systems. This case can be tackled by "merging" the UI logs where the routine execution is distributed into a single UI log, reducing the segmentation issue to one of the already analyzed cases. It is worth noticing that although the classification of cases and variants was illustrated with only two routines (interleaving or not), the classification is defined in a generic way and applies to any number of routines.

5 Assessing the Segmentation Approaches

In the field of RPA, segmentation is an issue still not so explored, since the current practice adopted by commercial RPA tools for identifying the routine steps often consists of detailed observations of workers conducting their daily work. Such observations are then "converted" in explicit flowchart diagrams [16], which are manually modeled by expert RPA analysts to depict all the potential behaviours (i.e., the traces) of a specific routine. In this setting, as the routine traces have been already (implicitly) identified, segmentation can be neglected.

On the other hand, following a similar trend that has been occurring in the BPM domain [25], the research on RPA is moving towards the application of intelligent techniques to automate all the steps of a RPA project, as proven by many recent works in this direction (see below). In this context, segmentation can be considered as one of the "hot" key research effort to investigate [2,21].

Table 1 summarizes the current literature techniques that could be leveraged to tackle the different variants of the segmentation issue. We will use ✓ to denote the full ability of an approach to deal with a specific UI log variant, while $\sim$ denotes that the approach is only partially able to deal with a specific UI log variant (i.e., under certain conditions). In the following, we discuss to what extent such variants can be supported by existing literature approaches, grouping them by means of their research area. It is worth noticing that the assessment of the literature approaches is based on what was reported in the associated papers.

Concerning RPA-related techniques, Bosco et al. [9] provide a method that exploits rule mining and data transformation techniques, able to discover routines that are fully deterministic and thus amenable for automation directly from UI logs. This approach is effective in case of UI logs that keep track of well-bounded routine executions (Case 1.1 and Case 2.1), and becomes inadequate when the UI log records information about several routines whose actions are potentially interleaved. In this direction, Leno et al. [20] propose a technique to identify execution traces of a specific routine relying on the automated synthesis of a control-flow graph, describing the observed directly-follow relations between the user actions. The technique in [20] is able to achieve cases 1.1, 1.2 and 2.1, and partially cases 2.2, 2.3 and 2.4, but (for the latter) it loses in accuracy in presence of recurrent noise and interleaved routine executions. The main limitation of the above techniques is tackled in [3]. Here, a supervised segmentation algorithm able to achieve all variants of cases 1, 2 and (partially) 3 has been proposed, except when there are interleaved executions of shared user actions of many routines. In that case, the risk exists that a shared user action is associated to a wrong routine execution (i.e., Case 3.3 and Case 3.4 are not covered). However, to make the algorithm works, it is required to know a-priori the structure of the interaction models of the routines to identify in the UI log.

Even if more focused on traditional business processes in BPM rather than on RPA routines, Bayomie et al. [8] address the problem of correlating uncorrelated event logs in process mining in which they assume the model of the routine is known. Since event logs allow to store traces of one process model only, as a consequence this technique is able to achieve Case 1.1 only. In the field of process discovery, Măruşter et al. [27] propose an empirical method for inducing rule sets from event logs containing execution of one process only. Therefore, as in [8], this method is able to achieve Case 1.1 only, thus making the technique ineffective in presence of interleaved and shared user actions. A more robust approach, developed by Fazzinga et al. [12], employs predefined behavioural models to establish which process activities belong to which process model. The technique works well when there are no interleaved user actions belonging to one or more routines, since it is not able to discriminate which event instance (but just the event type) belongs to which process model. This makes [12] effective to tackle Case 1.1, Case 2.1 and Case 3.1. Closely related to [12], there is the work of Liu [23]. The author proposes a probabilistic approach to learn workflow models from interleaved event logs, dealing with noises in the log data. Since each workflow is assigned with a disjoint set of operations, it means the proposed approach is able to achieve both cases 1.1 and 2.1, but partially cases 2.2, 2.3 and 2.4 (the approach can lose accuracy in assigning operations to workflows).

Differently from the previous works, Time-Aware Partitioning (TAP) techniques cut event logs on the basis of the temporal distance between two events [18,29]. The main limitation of TAP approaches is that they rely only on the time gap between events without considering any process/routine context. For this reason, such techniques are not able to handle neither interleaved user actions of different routine executions nor interleaved user actions of different routines. As a consequence, TAP techniques are able to achieve cases 1.1 and 2.1.

There exist other approaches whose the target is not to exactly resolve the segmentation issue. Many research works exist that analyze UI logs at different levels of abstraction and that can be potentially useful to realize segmentation techniques. With the term *"abstraction"* we mean that groups of user actions to be interpreted as executions of high-level activities. Baier et al. [7] propose a method to find a global one-to-one mapping between the user actions that appear in the UI log and the high-level activities of a given interaction model. This method leverages constraint-satisfaction techniques to reduce the set of candidate mappings. Similarly, Ferreira et al. [13], starting from a state-machine model describing the routine of interest in terms of high-level activities, employ heuristic techniques to find a mapping from a "micro-sequence" of user actions to the "macro-sequence" of activities in the state-machine model. Finally, Mannhardt et al. [24] present a technique that map low-level event types to multiple high-level activities (while the event instances, i.e., with a specific timestamp in the log, can be coupled with a single high-level activity). However, segmentation techniques in RPA must enable to associate low-level event instances (corresponding to user actions) to multiple routines, making abstractions techniques ineffective to tackle all those cases where is the presence of interleaving user actions of the same (or different) routine(s). As a consequence, all abstraction techniques are effective to achieve Case 1.1 and Case 2.1 only.

6 Conclusion

In this work, we have leveraged a real-life use case in the administrative sector to explore the issue of automated segmentation in RPA, detecting its potential variants and discussing to what extent the literature approaches are able to support such variants. The analysis of the related work has pointed out that the majority of literature approaches are able to properly extract routine traces from unsegmented UI logs when the routine executions are not interleaved from each others, which is far from being a realistic assumption. Only few works [3,12,20,23] have demonstrated the full or partial ability to untangle unsegmented UI logs consisting of many interleaved routine executions, but with any routine providing its own, separate universe of user actions. However, we did not find any literature work able to properly deal with user actions potentially shared by many routine executions in the UI log. This is a relevant limitation, since it is quite common that a user interaction with the UI corresponds to the executions of many routine steps at once.

Moreover, it is worth noticing the majority of the literature works rely on the so-called *supervised* assumption, which consists of some a-priori knowledge of the structure of routines. Of course this knowledge may ease the task of segmenting a UI log. But, as a side effect, it may strongly constrain the discovery of routine traces only to the "paths" allowed by the routines' structure, thus neglecting that some valid yet infrequent variants of a routine may exist in the UI log. For this reason, we think that an important first step towards the development of a more complete segmentation technique is to shift from the current model-based approaches to learning-based ones. In this direction, two main strategies seem feasible to relax the above supervised assumption: *(i)* to investigate *sequential pattern mining* techniques [11] to examine frequent sequences of user actions having common data attributes; *(ii)* to employ clustering techniques to aggregate user actions into clusters, where any cluster represents a particular routine and each associated sequence of user actions a routine trace [14,15].

Finally, we want to underline that process discovery techniques [6] can also play a relevant role to tackle the segmentation issue, as demonstrated by some literature works [8,12,23] discussed in Sect. 5. However, the issue is that the majority of discovery techniques work with event logs containing behaviours related to the execution of a single process model only. And, more importantly, event logs are already segmented into traces, i.e., with clear starting and ending points that delimitate any recorded process execution. Conversely, a UI log consists of a long sequence of user actions belonging to different routines and without any clear starting/ending point. Thus, a UI log is more similar to a unique (long) trace consisting of thousands of fine-grained user actions. With a UI log as input, the application of traditional discovery algorithms seems unsuited to discover routine traces and associate them to some routine models, even if more research is needed in this area.

Acknowledgments. This work has been supported by the "Dipartimento di Eccellenza" grant, the H2020 project DataCloud and the Sapienza grant BPbots.

References

1. Agostinelli, S., Lupia, M., Marrella, A., Mecella, M.: Automated generation of executable RPA scripts from user interface logs. In: Asatiani, A., et al. (eds.) BPM 2020. LNBIP, vol. 393, pp. 116–131. Springer, Cham (2020). https://doi.org/10.1007/978-3-030-58779-6_8
2. Agostinelli, S., Marrella, A., Mecella, M.: Research challenges for intelligent robotic process automation. In: Di Francescomarino, C., Dijkman, R., Zdun, U. (eds.) BPM 2019. LNBIP, vol. 362, pp. 12–18. Springer, Cham (2019). https://doi.org/10.1007/978-3-030-37453-2_2
3. Agostinelli, S., Marrella, A., Mecella, M.: Automated segmentation of user interface logs. In: Robotic Process Automation. Management, Technology, Applications. De Gruyter (2021)
4. Aguirre, S., Rodriguez, A.: Automation of a business process using Robotic Process Automation (RPA): a case study. In: Figueroa-García, J.C., López-Santana, E.R., Villa-Ramírez, J.L., Ferro-Escobar, R. (eds.) WEA 2017. CCIS, vol. 742, pp. 65–71. Springer, Cham (2017). https://doi.org/10.1007/978-3-319-66963-2_7

5. AI-Multiple: All 55 RPA software tools & vendors of 2021: sortable list (2021). https://blog.aimultiple.com/rpa-tools/
6. Augusto, A., et al.: Automated discovery of process models from event logs: review and benchmark. IEEE Trans. Knowl. Data Eng. **31**(4), 686–705 (2019)
7. Baier, T., Rogge-Solti, A., Mendling, J., Weske, M.: Matching of events and activities: an approach based on behavioral constraint satisfaction. In: 30th ACM Symposium on Applied Computing, pp. 1225–1230 (2015)
8. Bayomie, D., Di Ciccio, C., La Rosa, M., Mendling, J.: A probabilistic approach to event-case correlation for process mining. In: Laender, A.H.F., Pernici, B., Lim, E.-P., de Oliveira, J.P.M. (eds.) ER 2019. LNCS, vol. 11788, pp. 136–152. Springer, Cham (2019). https://doi.org/10.1007/978-3-030-33223-5_12
9. Bosco, A., Augusto, A., Dumas, M., La Rosa, M., Fortino, G.: Discovering automatable routines from user interaction logs. In: Hildebrandt, T., van Dongen, B.F., Röglinger, M., Mendling, J. (eds.) BPM 2019. LNBIP, vol. 360, pp. 144–162. Springer, Cham (2019). https://doi.org/10.1007/978-3-030-26643-1_9
10. Chakraborti, T., et al.: From robotic process automation to intelligent process automation: emerging trends. In: 18th International Conference on Business Process Management (RPA Forum), pp. 215–228 (2020)
11. Dong, G., Pei, J.: Sequence Data Mining. Advances in Database Systems, vol. 33. Springer, Boston (2007). https://doi.org/10.1007/978-0-387-69937-0
12. Fazzinga, B., Flesca, S., Furfaro, F., Masciari, E., Pontieri, L.: Efficiently interpreting traces of low level events in business process logs. Inf. Syst. **73**, 1–24 (2018)
13. Ferreira, D.R., Szimanski, F., Ralha, C.G.: Improving process models by mining mappings of low-level events to high-level activities. J. Intell. Inf. Syst. **43**(2), 379–407 (2014). https://doi.org/10.1007/s10844-014-0327-2
14. Folino, F., Guarascio, M., Pontieri, L.: Mining predictive process models out of low-level multidimensional logs. In: Jarke, M., et al. (eds.) CAiSE 2014. LNCS, vol. 8484, pp. 533–547. Springer, Cham (2014). https://doi.org/10.1007/978-3-319-07881-6_36
15. Günther, C.W., Rozinat, A., van der Aalst, W.M.P.: Activity mining by global trace segmentation. In: Rinderle-Ma, S., Sadiq, S., Leymann, F. (eds.) BPM 2009. LNBIP, vol. 43, pp. 128–139. Springer, Heidelberg (2010). https://doi.org/10.1007/978-3-642-12186-9_13
16. Jimenez-Ramirez, A., Reijers, H.A., Barba, I., Del Valle, C.: A method to improve the early stages of the robotic process automation lifecycle. In: Giorgini, P., Weber, B. (eds.) CAiSE 2019. LNCS, vol. 11483, pp. 446–461. Springer, Cham (2019). https://doi.org/10.1007/978-3-030-21290-2_28
17. Kokina, J., Blanchette, S.: Early evidence of digital labor in accounting: innovation with robotic process automation. Int. J. Account. Inf. Syst. **35**, 100431 (2019)
18. Kumar, A., Salo, J., Li, H.: Stages of user engagement on social commerce platforms: analysis with the navigational clickstream data. Int. J. Electron. Commer. **23**(2), 179–211 (2019)
19. Lacity, M., Willcocks, L.: Robotic process automation at telefónica O2. MIS Q. Exec. **15** (2016)
20. Leno, V., Augusto, A., Dumas, M., La Rosa, M., Maggi, F.M., Polyvyanyy, A.: Identifying candidate routines for robotic process automation from unsegmented UI logs. In: 2nd International Conference on Process Mining, pp. 153–160 (2020)
21. Leno, V., Polyvyanyy, A., Dumas, M., La Rosa, M., Maggi, F.M.: Robotic process mining: vision and challenges. Bus. Inf. Syst. Eng. 1–14 (2020). https://doi.org/10.1007/s12599-020-00641-4

22. de Leoni, M., Marrella, A.: Aligning real process executions and prescriptive process models through automated planning. Expert Syst. Appl. **82**, 162–183 (2017)
23. Liu, X.: Unraveling and learning workflow models from interleaved event logs. In: 2014 IEEE International Conference on Web Services, pp. 193–200 (2014)
24. Mannhardt, F., de Leoni, M., Reijers, H.A., van der Aalst, W.M., Toussaint, P.J.: Guided process discovery - a pattern-based approach. Inf. Syst. **76**, 1–18 (2018)
25. Marrella, A.: Automated planning for business process management. J. Data Semant. **8**(2), 79–98 (2019)
26. Marrella, A., Catarci, T.: Measuring the learnability of interactive systems using a Petri Net based approach. In: 2018 Conference on Designing Interactive Systems, pp. 1309–1319 (2018)
27. Măruşter, L., Weijters, A.T., Van Der Aalst, W.M., Van Den Bosch, A.: A Rule-based approach for process discovery: dealing with noise and imbalance in process logs. Data Min. Knowl. Disc. **13**(1), 67–87 (2006)
28. Schmitz, M., Dietze, C., Czarnecki, C.: Enabling digital transformation through robotic process automation at Deutsche Telekom. In: Urbach, N., Röglinger, M. (eds.) Digitalization Cases. MP, pp. 15–33. Springer, Cham (2019). https://doi.org/10.1007/978-3-319-95273-4_2
29. Srivastava, J., Cooley, R., Deshpande, M., Tan, P.: Web usage mining: discovery and applications of usage patterns from web data. SIGKDD Exp. **1**(2), 12–23 (2000)

Adapting the CRISP-DM Data Mining Process: A Case Study in the Financial Services Domain

Veronika Plotnikova(✉), Marlon Dumas, and Fredrik Milani

Institute of Computer Science, University of Tartu, Narva mnt 18, 51009 Tartu, Estonia
{veronika.plotnikova,marlon.dumas,fredrik.milani}@ut.ee

Abstract. Data mining techniques have gained widespread adoption over the past decades, particularly in the financial services domain. To achieve sustained benefits from these techniques, organizations have adopted standardized processes for managing data mining projects, most notably CRISP-DM. Research has shown that these standardized processes are often not used as prescribed, but instead, they are extended and adapted to address a variety of requirements. To improve the understanding of how standardized data mining processes are extended and adapted in practice, this paper reports on a case study in a financial services organization, aimed at identifying perceived gaps in the CRISP-DM process and characterizing how CRISP-DM is adapted to address these gaps. The case study was conducted based on documentation from a portfolio of data mining projects, complemented by semi-structured interviews with project participants. The results reveal 18 perceived gaps in CRISP-DM alongside their perceived impact and mechanisms employed to address these gaps. The identified gaps are grouped into six categories. The study provides practitioners with a structured set of gaps to be considered when applying CRISP-DM or similar processes in financial services. Also, number of the identified gaps are generic and applicable to other sectors with similar concerns (e.g. privacy), such as telecom, e-commerce.

Keywords: Data mining · CRISP-DM · Case study

1 Introduction

The use of data mining to support decision making has grown considerably in the past decades. This growth is especially notable in the service industries, such as the financial sector, where the use of data mining has generally become an enterprise-wide practice [1]. In order to ensure that data mining projects consistently deliver their intended outcomes, organisations use standardised processes, such as KDD, SEMMA, and CRISP-DM[1], for managing data mining projects.

[1] KDD - Knowledge Discovery in Databases; SEMMA - Sample, Explore, Modify, Model, and Assess; CRISP-DM - Cross-Industry Process for Data Mining.

S. Cherfi et al. (Eds.): RCIS 2021, LNBIP 415, pp. 55–71, 2021.
https://doi.org/10.1007/978-3-030-75018-3_4

These processes are industry agnostic and, thus, do not necessarily fulfil all requirements of specific industry sectors. Therefore, efforts have been made to adapt standard data mining processes for domain-specific requirements [2–4]. Although the financial services industry was early to employ data mining techniques, no approach has been proposed to address the specific requirements for data mining processes of this sector [5]. Yet, business actors in this sector adapt and extend existing data mining processes to fit requirements of their data mining projects [5]. This observation suggests that practitioners in the financial sector encounter needs that standardized data mining processes do not satisfy.

In this setting, this research aims to identify perceived gaps in CRISP-DM within the financial sector, to characterize the perceived impact of these gaps, and the mechanisms practitioners deploy to address such gaps. To this end, we conduct a case study in a financial services company where CRISP-DM is recommended and widely used, but not mandated. We studied a collection of data mining projects based on documentation and semi-structured interviews with project stakeholders. We discovered and documented 18 perceived gaps within and across all phases of the CRISP-DM lifecycle, their perceived impact and how practitioners addressed them. Our findings could support experts in applying CRISP-DM or similar standardized processes for data mining projects.

The rest of this paper is structured as follows. Section 2 introduces CRISP-DM and related work. This is followed by the presentation of the case study design (Sect. 3) and results (Sect. 4). Section 5 discusses the findings and threats to validity. Finally, Sect. 6 draws conclusions and future work directions.

2 Theoretical Background

Several data mining processes have been proposed by researchers and practitioners, including KDD and CRISP-DM, with the latter regarded as a 'de facto' industry standard [6]. CRISP-DM consists of six phases executed in iterations [6]. The first phase is business understanding including problem definition, scoping, and planning. Phase 2 (data understanding) involves initial data collection, data quality assurance, data exploration, and potential detection and formulation of hypotheses. It is followed by Phase 3 (data preparation), where the final dataset from the raw data is constructed. In Phase 4 (modelling phase) model building techniques are selected and applied. Next, in Phase 5 (model evaluation), findings are assessed and decisions are taken on the basis of these findings. Finally, in the deployment phase, the models are put into use.

CRISP-DM is often adapted to accommodate domain-specific requirements [7]. For example, Niaksu [2] extended CRISP-DM to accommodate requirements of the healthcare domain, such as non-standard datasets, data interoperability, and privacy constraints. Solarte [3] adapted CRISP-DM to address aspects specific for data mining in the industrial engineering domain. These adaptations concern, for instance, defining project roles and stakeholders, analysis of additional data requirements, and selection of data mining techniques according to organisational goals and data requirements. Meanwhile, Marban et al. [4] propose adaptations specifically targeting the industrial engineering domain by introducing new tasks, steps, and deliverables.

In [5], we conducted a systematic review of adaptations of CRISP-DM in the financial domain. This review identified three types of adaptations: modification, extension, and integration. Modification refers to the situation where adjustments are made at the level of sub-phases, tasks or deliverables. Extension refers to significant changes, including new elements, which affect multiple phases of the process. Lastly, integration refers to the combination of a standardized process (e.g. CRISP-DM) with approaches originating from other domains.

3 Case Study Design

A case study is an empirical research method aimed at investigating a specific reality within its real-life context [8]. This method is suitable when the defining boundaries between what is studied and its context are unclear [9], which is the case in our research. The case study was conducted according to a detailed protocol[2]. The protocol provides details of the case study design and associated artifacts, including interview questions, steps taken to validate these questions, the procedure used to code the interview responses, etc.

The first step in the case study is to define its objective and research questions. We decomposed our research objectives into three components: perceived gaps, their respective impact, and the adopted workarounds. Accordingly, we defined three research questions: (1) What gaps in CRISP-DM practitioners perceive in the financial services industry? (RQ1); (2) Why do practitioners perceive these gaps, i.e. what is the perceived impact of the identified gaps? (RQ2); (3) How is CRISP-DM adapted to address these gaps (RQ3).

The second step was to define the organisational context and scope of the case study. We sought an organisation that: (1) operates within the financial service industry, (2) has systematically engaged with data mining over the last 3 years, (3) uses CRISP-DM for their data mining projects, and (4) grants access to domain experts and documentation. In line with these requirements, we conducted the case study in the data mining department of a bank operating in Northern Europe. This department acts as a centralised data mining function (Centre of Excellence), responsible for execution of data mining projects across the organisation. The department's portfolio of projects spans over several years and covers several regions and business lines.

We selected a representative subset of projects (Table 1), covering four project types. The first is Business Delivery, i.e., the development of models for different banking products or complex algorithms for analysis of a bank's customers, such as private customers micro-segmentation. The second type is Model Rebuild. These projects share the commonality of rebuilding, retraining, and re-deploying existing models and algorithms. The third is "Proof of Concept" (POC), which explores the use of new analytics techniques, namely process mining, for discovering improvement opportunities in lending processes. The fourth, last category

[2] The protocol is available at: https://figshare.com/s/33c42eda3b19784e8b21.

is Capability Development, i.e., projects aimed at the development of competencies and tools for repeatable usage in other data mining projects. The selected project in this category concerns exploration of advanced graph analytics methods and development of a visualisation algorithm library. All projects adhered to key phases of CRISP-DM.

Table 1. Projects characteristics.

No.	Project definition	Geography	Project type	Time span	No. of interviews	Participants
1	Product propensity model	1	Business-driven	2018	2	Data Scientist, Project Manager
2	Retail customers micro-segmentation	2,3,4	Business-driven	2017–2019	2	Data Scientist, Project Manager
3	Product propensity model	2,3,4	Business-driven	2018	1	Data Scientist
4	Lending process mining	2,3,4	POC	2019	1	Data Scientist
5	Payments categorization model	2,3,4	Model rebuild	2019	1	Data Scientist
6	Graph analytics library	1	Capabilities development	2019	1	Data Scientist

The third step of the case study was data collection. We approached this step in a two-pronged manner. First, we collected documentation about each project. Second, we conducted semi-structured interviews with data scientists and project managers involved in their execution. The interview questions were derived from the research questions and literature review. The interviews were transcribed (total of 115 pages) and encoded following the method proposed by [10]. The first level coding scheme was derived and refined in iterations. It resulted in combining a set of initial codes (based on reviews and research questions) and codes elicited during coding process. Second level coding, also obtained by an iterative approach, was based on themes that emerged from the analysis. The final coding scheme is available in the case study protocol referenced above.

4 Case Study Results

In this section, we present the results of our case study. We have structured the results according to the main components of ITIL framework (Information Technology Infrastructure Library). ITIL is industry-agnostic and an accepted approach for management of IT services widely adopted across different business domains [11]. It consists of three main elements: process inputs and outputs, process controls, and process enablers. We view data mining projects as instances of IT delivery and, thereby, encompassed by the scope of ITIL. Therefore, the results for each of the five phases of CRISP-DM correspond to the main process according to ITIL, which we present first. Next, aspects concerning process controls and enablers related to CRISP-DM lifecycle are described.

4.1 Phase 1: Business Understanding (BU)

The business understanding (BU) phase focuses on identifying business objectives and requirements of the project. Our study shows a significant interdependency between BU and the other phases. All interviewees noted "numerous" iterations and reversals back to the BU phase during the project. One participant expressed that BU *"...had a lot of back and forth with business. It is basically spread over the whole duration of the project"*. Another participant highlighted that although such iterations are time-consuming, they enable adequate elicitation and management of business requirements.

The number and degree of iterations vary across projects. Projects with multiple stakeholders reported higher degree of iterations. As noted, *"...the CRISP-DM process, when it is applied to use cases which are unsupervised, especially when there is some kind of segmentation exercise with a lot of different interested business counterparties, it is little bit more difficult to apply [...] because there's [sic] lots of going back to the business discussion, and scoping and Business Understanding part"*. More complex data mining solutions, such as project 2 that required layers of multidimensional calculations, reported more extensive iterations. Exploratory projects (e.g. project 4), required iterations when the obtained results were first applied by end-users. The introduction of new data types, and the discovery of previously unknown data limitations, necessitated reverting to the BU phase for continuous updating and understanding of the requirements, making it essentially intertwined with the data understanding.

Projects that deliver a model as a product (projects 1, 3) reported less iterations, but the BU phase was both demanding and crucial for delivery of the right product. One participant underscored BU's significance when defining it as *"one of the most important [...] just a little mistake on the focus and not understanding well what you are targeting [...] you have to start all over again"*. Another interviewee emphasized the necessity of the BU phase and its iterations as *"you don't really exactly know the scope [...] you might have an idea and you need to present that, but then it can go back and forth a couple of times before you even know the actual population and what kind of products are we looking at...*". Unexpected iterations are also necessitated by the introduction of new regulations and compliance requirements (projects 2, 3).

To summarize, CRISP-DM does not fully reflect the interdependence between BU and the other phases. The main gap (RQ1) of BU is the lack of specific tasks and activities to capture, validate, and refine business requirements. This can cause a (RQ2) mismatch between a business' needs and the outputs of data mining projects. Furthermore, it can lead to missed insights and incorrect inferences. Practitioners commonly address this gap (RQ3) by iterating back to the BU phase in order to align the project outputs with the business needs, regularly eliciting new requirements, and validating existing ones.

4.2 Phases 2–3: Data Understanding (DU) and Preparation (DP)

The Data Understanding (DU) and Data Preparation (DP) phases concentrate on data collection, dataset construction, and data exploration. Here, the interviewees highlighted a recurrent need to iterate between DU and DP, as well as between DU, DP and BU. This need was more emphasized in complex project (project 2) and in both POC projects (4, 6). In one of these projects (project 4), the three phases DU, DP and BU, had been merged altogether. The participants indicated that the reason for iterating between DU, DP, and BU is that business requirements (identified in BU) often give rise to new data requirements or refinement of existing ones, and reciprocally, insights derived during DU give rise to observations that are relevant from a business perspective and thus affect the BU phase. Also, data limitations identified during DP may require stakeholders to refine the questions raised during BU.

Data quality issues were continuously detected when working with new data types, methods, techniques, and tools. Such issues required referring back to the DU phase. Furthermore, modelling, analysis, and interpretation of results prompted replacing certain data points or enhancing the initial dataset with new ones. Such changes required an iterative process between DU and other phases. In project 5, though it aimed at rebuilding and releasing updated version of already deployed model, data scientists had to redo the entire process, as interviewee expressed, *"I would say that from one side, we have this Data Understanding from first version, but due to different data preparation tools planned to use, it kind of required pretty much to start from scratch.... it's kind of requires completely different data sources...* ".

We also observed an important adjustment in regard to data privacy. CRISP-DM includes privacy as a sub-activity to the "Assess Situation" task in the context of project requirements elicitation. GDPR[3] strictly regulates personal data processing. Institutions can use privacy preserving technologies to reduce efforts and secure compliance. However, if such solutions are lacking, the data mining projects have to include assessment of data falling under GDPR and consider how to act (anonymize or remove). The interviewees underscored the

[3] A recently introduced EU legislation to safeguard customer data.

impact of GDPR requirements throughout entire data mining lifecycle (discussed in 4.6 *Lifecycle Gaps, Data Mining Process Enablers*).

Our findings indicate that DU and DP phases have inter-dependencies, data requirement elicitation, and privacy compliance gaps (RQ1). In CRISP-DM, the inter-dependencies between DU/DP and other phases are not addressed, and it does not provide specific tasks for capturing, validating, and refining data requirements throughout data mining lifecycle. Tasks to ensure compliant data processing are also lacking. Such gaps prolong the projects execution (RQ2), and practitioners mitigate them with extensive iterations between the phases. In some cases, DU/DP and BU phases are practically merged into one. The iterations between these phases are also used to address new data requirements, in particular, in regard to data privacy, and to validate existing ones (RQ3).

4.3 Phase 3: Modelling

The Modelling phase focuses on constructing the model after selecting suitable method and technique. The case study showed that this phase was not limited to prototyping only, as stipulated by CRISP-DM. Rather, models (especially, in projects 1, 2, 4) were developed in iterations, mostly between the modelling and the other phases, such as DU/DP, BU, and Deployment. These iterations were born of the need to improve the models. For instance, the requirements discovered during the BU and deployment phases influenced both which technique to use and model design. One interviewee expressed that *"...there is one quite new dependency or requirement for our side, this is actually latency, because we need to classify or scoring part should happen very fast. ...even here in the Modelling phase, we kinda consider [...] at least kept in mind this latency thing... "*.

For models to be accepted, their outcomes have to satisfy pre-defined performance criteria as measured with evaluation metrics. In contrast to standard CRISP-DM, we observed that model performance metrics and requirements have been adjusted and adapted to business stakeholders' requirements, such as acceptable level of false positives, accuracy, and other criteria, to make model fit real business settings and needs. Projects with complex modelling tasks (projects 1, 3, 5) adopted a distinct step-up modelling approach. These projects were characterized by first creating a baseline model (benchmark) followed by a set of experiments to identify the best approach to improve the models, i.e., satisfy specific performance metrics, *"... I think we just started off the model, any model just to get start, to get some sort of results to incorporate that in a pipeline [...] once we got one model up and running, then we started to incorporate several other models just to make any comparisons. [...] So, that's what we tried to, a lot of different models and, and we, we wanted [...] the model to be suitable for amount of data that we had, the skewed data, the number of rows and the number of the attributes. And since the data was very skewed and we didn't have that many targets, so to say...then we didn't want that many features and that's, that limited our dataset and in turn that limited which model we would use [...] So we compare these models also by different measures, and the one we ended up with stood out quite significantly."* Also, the Modelling phase explicitly incorporated elements of software development approaches resembling agile processes (project 1), specifically a Test-Driven Development approach (project 6), *"[...] we tried to then develop the actual function, and it could only pass that test if the criteria was met. So, it was a test-based or test driven implementation what we did [...] So even in the code we have all the test cases available....".*

Practitioners commented on the restrictive notion that the outcome of the Modelling phase should be a model. They discussed situations where the results of the modelling phase were various interpretations of the model and different analytical metrics (projects 2, 4, 6). To this end, interviewees reported on both applying actual modelling techniques and executing algorithm-based data processing (e.g. using Natural Language Processing techniques) or experimenting with various process representations (project 4). For one of the POC projects, it was noted, *"[...] it can be quite questionable what we consider as the modelling here ... process map, or the more formal process model in the process model language but as next steps in more advanced process mining projects, there could also be, additional models, for prediction and detection and so on. So, the process mining project can end up as a quite big project where many different types of modelling are involved."* Thus, the Modelling phase can be defined as "multi-modelling" with the set of unsupervised and supervised modelling outcomes.

In summary, the Modelling phase of CRISP-DM does not cater to needs of developing, improving, and refining models in data mining lifecycle. Furthermore, explicit guidelines how to iterate between phases, in particular, the BU, DU/DP, and Deployment, are lacking. Refinement of existing requirements and capturing new requirements, which originate from the Modelling phase and other phases, is not supported. Finally, CRISP-DM is restrictive with respect to modelling outcomes, not catering to "multi-modelling", unsupervised modelling, and specialized modelling techniques (RQ1). These gaps can prolong data mining projects execution and increase the risk of mismatch between business need and outcome (RQ2). Commonly, practitioners address these gaps by employing an iterative and metric-driven modelling process, frequent iterations with other phases, and calibration with requirements from other phases. Also, tasks and activities are introduced to deliver various analytical outcomes ("multi-modelling") and to accommodate use of various techniques (RQ3).

4.4 Phase 4: Evaluation

The Evaluation phase is concerned with quality assessment and confirming that the business objectives of the projects are met. Majority of interviewed practitioners underscored the importance of validating and testing the models in a real usage scenario setting. While CRISP-DM prescribes assessing if the models meets business objectives, the "how" is not discussed. As noted, *"Crisp-DM should be updated specifically on the step of Evaluation to include how to test the model in business industry. I mean taking into account real scenarios, and there should be a list of steps in there. Which actually we have figured, figured out these steps [. . .] in an empirical way."* CRISP-DM prescribes a two-step validation. The first is a technical model validation which is conducted in the Modelling phase and considers metrics such as accuracy. The second step assesses if the models meet the business objectives which is conducted in the Evaluation phase. However, practitioners conducted these validations concurrently (projects 1–4). Stakeholders evaluated the models by considering the technical aspects, such as accuracy, and if the models are meaningful in a business setting, as noted, *"important thing is that we like to think the evaluation through and really measure the thing that we want to measure and, and also not rely on only one measure, but can see the results from different angles."*

For unsupervised models (project 2, 4), we noted that the evaluation was primarily subjective. The consideration was given to how meaningful the results were for the business, how they could be interpreted, and to what extent actions could be taken based on the results. Thus, suitability and model usage, i.e., business sensibility, were the basis for model evaluation. As one participant noted that *"it is difficult to define some sort of quality measure for this kind of unsupervised result other than, well, actionability and future usage because we could have a quality measures for the clustering itself that just means that the clustering, cluster is distinct, but they don't mean that clusters are actionable for business and there can be non-distinct groups which on the other hand are interesting for business. So, there was, in this case it's kind of [...] technical quality measures are not necessarily suitable for a practical, practical quality."*

Our findings show that the Evaluation phase of CRISP-DM does not specify how models can be assessed to determine if they meet the business objectives. In particular, there are gaps related to assessing and interpreting the models in their business context. Also, the separation of technical and business evaluation, as outlined by CRISP-DM, can be problematic (RQ1). These gaps can lead to poor model performance in real settings and reduce actionability (RQ2). Practitioners address these deficiencies by piloting models in actual business settings (RQ3).

4.5 Phase 5: Deployment

The Deployment phase is concerned with implementing data mining project outcomes to ensure they are available and serve business needs of end-users. In CRISP-DM, deployment tasks and activities are first considered in this phase. However, we observed the necessity to address deployment strategy and elicitation of deployment requirements earlier (project 1, 3, 5). As one participant noted, *"when we develop a model, we think about what's important to us..and the business side, it could be interested in to see the results in a different way, or to include different columns or some things... So I understood after that process that one should have the Deployment phase already on your mind when [making] up the model, also, more or less from the very start,.....and to see the actual data that the business will pick up, and in the way they will pick it up....".*

In addition, CRISP-DM does not address specification of deployment requirements well. Therefore, practitioners adapt reference process, especially to elicit requirements towards the format of the deployed solution and its end-usage in business contexts (projects 1, 2, 4). As noted, *"the results were meant to be used on a daily basis by frontline people ... so, in this sense there are different levels of results that are needed ...there have to be some very simple KPIs and some very simple visualizations that don't need this more advanced process knowledge and understandable for everyone. So, that was something that we didn't know at the beginning that actually we need to report it not only to the Business Development department and process managers, but also to really frontline people ...".* Thus, the deployment phase can involve calibrating requirements to adapt models for their ongoing end-usage.

We also observed that the practitioners adopted a different deployment process compared to CRISP-DM, which focuses on the deployment plan rather than implementation. Also, participants reported using a wider range of deployment formats. For instance, projects based on unsupervised models might not require deployment at all as their purpose is discovery of features and interpreting said features within the context of a specific business problem (project 4). In contrast, algorithm library was reported as deployed solution in project 6.

Our main finding from the Deployment phase is that CRISP-DM stipulates the elicitation of deployment requirements too late. The often-needed calibration of deployment requirements elicited in earlier phases of CRISP-DM, is not covered. Also, this phase, as stipulated by CRISP-DM, assumes a restrictive stance and is not open to different deployment strategies. Lastly, CRISP-DM focuses on producing a deployment plan, but does not address implementation itself (RQ1). These gaps can prolong project execution, and increase the risk of a mismatch between the project outcome and the intended end-usage, i.e., the business need (RQ2). Practitioners address these gaps by considering deployment scenarios and eliciting deployment requirements early on, as well as extending the Deployment phase to include implementation tasks (RQ3).

4.6 Lifecycle Gaps

We also identified gaps that concern the whole CRISP-DM lifecycle rather than a specific phase thereof. Below, we present these gaps, organized according to two key pillars of the ITIL framework: process controls and enablers.

Data Mining Process Controls. ITIL identifies five process controls: process documentation, process owners, policy, objectives, and feedback. Furthermore, in the context of IT delivery projects, it specifies process owners, process quality measurement, and reporting as key controls [13]. In our case study, practitioners highlighted three main aspects of data mining project controls – governance, quality, and compliance – which are in line with ITIL.

Our analysis shows that the practitioners have adopted elements of agile practices into their data mining life cycles. This is explicit in recent projects where 2-week sprints have been used, requirements are captured in epics, teams have daily stand-ups, sprint planning, and retrospectives. Practitioners also noted that CRISP-DM does not support the agility required for some data mining projects. As one practitioner stated, there is a *"...flaw in this methodology. It [...] tells you that it's dynamic, but it does not tell you what to do, [...] when do you have to go back to step 1, and how to do it faster".*

Another aspect mentioned in relation to governance, is roles and responsibilities of both internal and external stakeholders. The importance of stakeholder management was emphasized. When stakeholders were not identified early on, *"[...] there was a lot of additional tasks... and secondly, each part [...] could have different stakeholders."* The stakeholders' understanding of the business problem and what the team delivering data mining projects can achieve, matter. For instance, in project 4, it was noted that *"...it can be two ways like either we present to the stakeholder a solution for a potential problem they could have, meaning we have to, to sell an idea. Or the other way around, they already have a problem that they have identified very clearly, and then they come looking for a solution, that we will provide. So I think as stakeholders understand more what we do it's more than the second one because they know we can help as they data scientists."* External stakeholders (customers) are not included in the validation of the data mining solutions. Nevertheless, they can, potentially, contribute to improving the quality of the results, as was expressed, *"... the end customer, the client [...] The only thing we can measure currently is if they accept or not accept a product or service, but there will be a very interesting [to] involve, ... to have them ask why they took a consumer loan or why didn't they, and in what way? [...] get a lot more information about the end user. [...] just to understand what, what is the actual driver. We can only read black and white on data, but we don't know if something else motivates them to do certain choices."*

Another aspect observed is that of quality. In particular, we noted the evolution of adopting quality assurance mechanisms in the data mining process. These measures are expressed as the implementation of a formal peer-review process that is integrated in the project execution. Such quality assurances are visible as checkpoints – both in the daily work routines, and via review-based checklists. These quality assurance measures serve to validate five key aspects of data mining projects: (1) privacy-compliant data processing, (2) project scope, business goals, and data mining target, (3) input dataset quality, (4) modelling method application, and (5) code quality (software development controls).

Lastly, participants highlighted compliance, in particular in regard to GDPR, as an example of external requirements that impact data mining projects. GDPR has introduced a set of privacy-compliance requirements , limited the usage of certain data types and how final results can be used. For instance, in project 5, the company required customers to express GDPR consent, resulting in a limited number of customers using the data mining-based solution.

Data Mining Process Enablers. The data mining process enablers, in this context, refer to capabilities required for the organisation to be able to execute data mining projects. These enablers concern aspects that support projects that follow, to different extent, the CRISP-DM process. The capabilities discussed are related to data, data mining code, tools, infrastructure, technology, and organisational factors.

Data quality, understood as reliability, persistence, and stability, was reported as crucial for all projects. Practitioners expressed that more important than tools is *"... it's about the data because you have great tools, but if the quality of the data is not good enough, then, it doesn't matter, so to me this is like the most important thing".* Another practitioner stated that *"[...] the thing people often are referring to is if they have like a lot of nulls maybe, or like missing fields in the data. So that would be one side of the quality, but that's just according to me lack of data, that wouldn't be [...] really a concern in my mind. Quality of data would be that it's reliable and that the sources are stable and not changing. So that would be quite important, and I guess you just have to incorporate a lot of sanity checks in order to trust the sources. "*

We also observed a consensus that data should be made readily available for (self-service) usage and as underscored by one interviewee, "good databases are the key". Data consistency and completeness across various data sources is another critical aspect reported in, for instance, project 4 (specialized process mining project). In this case, setting up correct workflow registration in source systems was a prerequisite to obtain acceptable data. In addition, it was emphasized that self-reported data was subject to biases and interpretations, thus it may be less reliable and, therefore, should be used with caution. The practitioners also referred to the quality of data mining project code. Its importance was chiefly noted for projects 5 and 6, in the context of scalability and optimization.

Available tools and infrastructure that ensure adequate prototyping, scaling, and deployment are regarded as pre-requisite capabilities for all projects. Limitations to operate with large datasets and difficulties in applying methods and algorithms were cited as consequences of tools and infrastructure limitations in projects 2 and 4. *"[...] we had a lot of impediments on the technology side, in the sense that we were using quite big amount of data, and we were doing the analysis on local computer so there were some restrictions or issues with data size, sometimes the data size actually didn't allow to compute clustering quality measures.. this data size also put restrictions on the algorithms that You can use, for example, it was not possible to use many different clustering methods because they just do not scale so we were somewhat limited in choice of algorithms.... ".*

Furthermore, a critical requirement mentioned in regard to tools and infrastructure, was the ability to support automated, repeatable, and reproducible data mining deployments, *"I would say it's important that we have, that entire pipeline, the infrastructure for the entire pipeline would be prioritized. So, so like going from start to end, maybe in a very thin or narrow manner in the sense that we might not have that many different systems or programs to use, but that we can deploy going also fast to, to market."* Also, interviewees reported that available tools, platforms, and infrastructure had an impact on the choice of model design and language used. For instance, for project 6 *"....the main concern was to create a library that is usable inside our team [...] And we even considered a different programming language like Scala, as it could be more efficient. But since most of the end users, which are basically our team members were Python programmers, we decided to go for Python library [...]... of course we could just do Python, but we wanted the solution to be also scalable for, for large graphs. And that's why we chose Spark ... that depended on the ... business requirements, and business requirements indicated that we need to work on large datasets... ".*

Finally, organisational factors, such as data-driven decision-making culture and maturity have been referred to as crucial elements enabling adoption of data mining solutions in business practice (project 2). Interviewees referred to 'push-pull' paradigm whereby stakeholders actively 'pushed' for solution initially, and with active participation have converted to 'pull'. Further, education of stakeholders to support data-driven decision-making culture thus transforming organisation towards 'pull' paradigm has been emphasized and reported.

To summarize, we found that the CRISP-DM life cycle has gaps related to governance, quality assurance, and external compliance management. Also, CRISP-DM has deficiencies associated with data quality management and stakeholder management (RQ1). These gaps prolong project execution, increase a risk of mismatch between project outputs and business needs, and negatively impact business value realization (RQ2). We found that these gaps are filled by adopting agile software development practices, specifically Test-Driven Development (TDD), Scrum ceremonies and Scrum boards, via regular interaction with business stakeholders across all CRISP-DM phases, and via integration of regulatory compliance requirements into the data mining process (RQ3).

5 Discussion and Threats to Validity

In this section, we discuss the gaps identified both in the phases and entire CRISP-DM data mining lifecycle (Fig. 1 below). We group them, based on their characteristics, into six distinct categories and, for each category, discuss the gaps (RQ1), perceived impact (RQ2), and how practitioners adapt CRISP-DM to mitigate the gaps (RQ3). We conclude this section with threats to validity.

The first category of gaps, *Inter-dependency Gaps (1, 3, 6)*, concerns the lack of iterations between different CRISP-DM phases. As practitioners noted, these gaps lead to missed insights, skewed interpretations, and an increased risk of incorrect inferences. If the *Inter-dependency gaps* are not addressed, an increased effort in the form of re-work and repeated activity cycles is required, resulting in prolonged project execution. Practitioners address this gap by making numerous iterations between the CRISP-DM phases or merging them.

The *Requirement Gaps (2, 4, 7, 8, 13)* relate to the lack of tasks for validation and modification of existing requirements and elicitation of new ones, and they are present in all CRISP-DM phases except for the Evaluation phase. Such deficiencies increase the risk of a mismatch between the outputs of the data mining project and the business needs. Practitioners reduce their impact by adding validation and calibration steps and by iteratively eliciting new requirements. Practitioners also adopt software development support tools, methods and incorporate elements from agile practices in their data mining projects.

The *Inter-dependency* and *Requirements Gaps* constitute the lion share of the gaps. These gaps stem from the largely sequential structure of CRISP-DM. Although iterations between the phases are possible, the procedural structure of CRISP-DM prescribes a linear approach where each phase is dependent on deliverables from the previous phase.

The third category, *Universality Gaps (9, 10, 14)* concerns a lack of support for various analytical outcomes, unsupervised and specialized techniques, as well as deployment formats. This category has been discovered for the Modelling and Deployment phases. Our results indicate that the standard CRISP-DM is, at times, overly specialized. In the case of the Modelling phase, it is restrictive in supporting standard, supervised, modelling techniques and associated data mining outcomes. For deployment, CRISP-DM does not provide tasks for implementation and associated technical requirements. These gaps lead to an increased risk of mismatch between data mining outcomes and business needs. Practitioners address these gaps by adding tasks to support unsupervised, specialized models' development and the delivery of various non-modelling analytical outcomes ('multi-modelling') as well as different deployment formats.

Further, we discovered *Validation Gap (11)* and *Actionability Gap (12)*, which concern the Evaluation and Deployment phases respectively. These gaps refer to a lack of support for piloting models in real-life settings. Thus, if models are not validated in practical settings, they are likely to exhibit poor performance when deployed. Also, CRISP-DM does not address elicitation of scenarios for model application. The lack of a model usage strategy, and an insufficient understanding of the models' application settings, leads to limited or incorrect usage of the models, or result in models not being used at all ('producing models to the shelf' scenario). These gaps were filled by extensively using pilots in real-life settings, as well as addressing the actionability of the created analytical and model assets. The gaps of Universality, Validation, and Actionability stem from CRISP-DM's over-emphasis on classical data mining and supervised machine learning modelling. Data mining itself is regarded as mostly a modelling exercise, rather than addressing business problems or opportunities using data.

The sixth category of gaps, *Privacy and Regulatory Compliance Gaps (5, 15)*, deals with externally imposed restrictions. These gaps are related to the DU, DP, and Deployment phases. CRISP-DM does not, generally, cater for privacy and compliance and, in particular, lacks tasks to address the processing of customer data. The impact of these gaps can result in non-compliance. Thus, practitioners have established standardized privacy risk assessments, adopted compliance procedures, and checklists. These gaps stem from the fact that CRISP-DM was developed over two decades ago, when a different regulatory environment existed.

We also identified *Process Gaps (16, 17, 18)* which do not concern a specific phase but, rather, the entire data mining life cycle. These gaps encompass data mining process controls, quality assurance, and critical process enablers required for the effective execution of data mining projects. We note that CRISP-DM does not address projects governance aspects such as work organisation, stakeholders, roles, and responsibilities. Further, procedures for quality assurance are not provided for, and required key capabilities, i.e., for data, code, tools, infrastructure and organisational factors, are not taken into consideration. These gaps can reduce data mining project effectiveness and inhibit their business value realization. Practitioners mitigate them by incorporating quality assurance peer-reviews into the execution of data mining projects. Process gaps

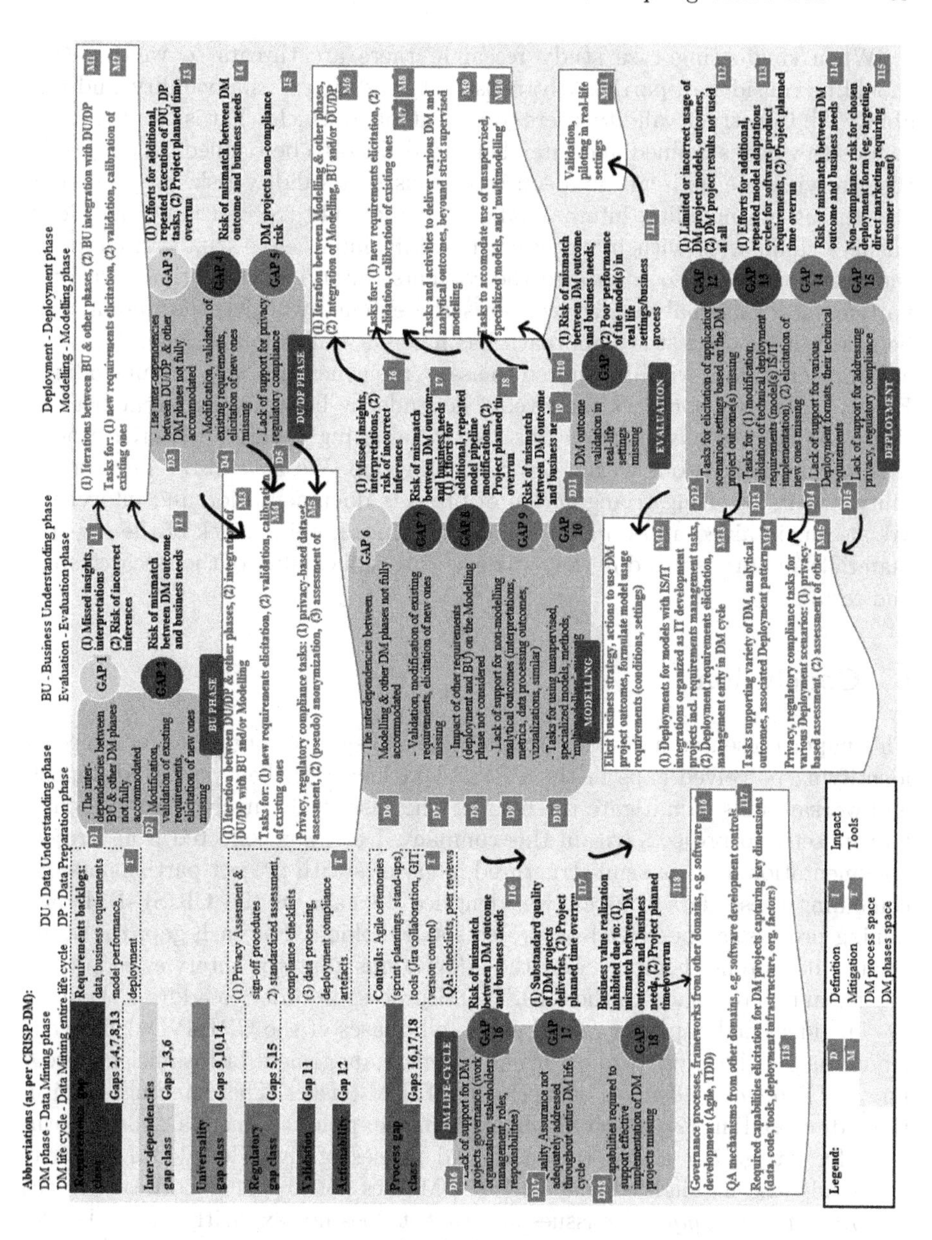

Fig. 1. Identified gaps mindmap

appear as CRISP-DM only partially incorporates project management activities, and does not take broader organisational and technical aspects for project management into consideration. Thus, process controls and enablers needed to support multiple data mining projects on organizational level continuously are not addressed.

When conducting case study research, there are threats to validity that should be considered, particularly, construct validity, external validity, and reliability [8]. Construct validity refers to the extent to which what is studied corresponds to what is defined and intended and defined to be studied. In our study, the interview method can be a source of construct validity risk. We mitigated this threat by including internal validity checkpoints (reconfirming questions, answers summaries with interviewee) to verify interviewee's understanding of the questions. We also confirmed the contents (interview transcripts) with the participants. External validity concerns the extent by which the findings can be generalized. Case study approach has inherent limitation of generalizability, and further studies will be required to assert the generalizability of our findings. Finally, reliability concerns the level of dependency between the researcher and study results. We have tackled this risk by adopting iterative research process with regular validations within our research group. We have also reduced reliability threats by using triangulation of projects documentation and interviews. We also maintained appropriate chain of evidence keeping track of the research materials and process and in that way ensuring replicability of the research steps and results.

6 Conclusion

This paper presented a case study in a financial services organization aimed at identifying perceived gaps in the CRISP-DM lifecycle, their perceived impact, and workarounds to mitigate these gaps. The case study involved a representative subset of 6 projects within this company. Data was collected from project documentation and via semi-structured interviews with project participants. By combining these data sources, we identified 18 gaps in the CRISP-DM data mining process, as perceived by projects stakeholders. For each gap, the study elicited its potential impact and the adaptations that the interviewed project participants have made to the CRISP-DM process in order to address them.

The identified gaps are spread across all phases of the CRISP-DM lifecycle. About half of the gaps relate to *Requirements* management or insufficient recognition of *Inter-dependencies* between CRISP-DM phases. These findings confirm those discussed in [12], which highlighted that, in practice, there are many pathways for navigating across the tasks and phases of the CRISP-DM lifecycle. Our study also highlighted that CRISP-DM does not explicitly address *Privacy and Regulatory Compliance* issues and that it does not explicitly tackle *Validation and Actionability* concerns. Finally, we found a category of gaps (*Process Gaps*) arising from the fact that CRISP-DM does not fully consider the wider organisational and technical context of a data mining project.

The study also identified five adaptations: (1) inclusion of explicit iterations between phases or merging of phases, (2) addition of tasks to address requirements elicitation and management concerns, (3) addition of 'piloting' tasks for validation, (4) combination of CRISP-DM with IT development project management practices, and (5) addition of quality assurance mechanisms. A direction for future work is to define an extension of CRISP-DM that addresses the identified gaps, taking as a basis the adaptations identified in this study as well as insights from adaptations of CRISP-DM in other domains. We also foresee that the gaps in the *Process* class could be addressed by combining CRISP-DM with the ITIL framework. Another direction for future work is to conduct similar case studies in other organisations, both within the financial sector and in other services sectors, such as telecom, where similar concerns (privacy, compliance, risk management) arise.

References

1. Forbes Homepage (2017). https://www.forbes.com/sites/louiscolumbus/2017/12/24/53-of-companies-are-adopting-big-data-analytics. Accessed 30 Jan 2021
2. Niaksu, O.: CRISP data mining methodology extension for medical domain. Baltic J. Mod. Comput. **3**(2), 92 (2015)
3. Solarte, J.: A proposed data mining methodology and its application to industrial engineering. Ph.D. thesis, University of Tennessee (2002)
4. Marbán, Ó., Mariscal, G., Menasalvas, E., Segovia, J.: An engineering approach to data mining projects. In: Yin, H., Tino, P., Corchado, E., Byrne, W., Yao, X. (eds.) IDEAL 2007. LNCS, vol. 4881, pp. 578–588. Springer, Heidelberg (2007). https://doi.org/10.1007/978-3-540-77226-2_59
5. Plotnikova, V., Dumas, M., Milani, F.P.: Data mining methodologies in the banking domain: a systematic literature review. In: Pańkowska, M., Sandkuhl, K. (eds.) BIR 2019. LNBIP, vol. 365, pp. 104–118. Springer, Cham (2019). https://doi.org/10.1007/978-3-030-31143-8_8
6. Marban, O., Mariscal, G., Segovia, J.: A data mining and knowledge discovery process model. In: Julio, P., Adem, K. (eds.) Data Mining and Knowledge Discovery in Real Life Applications, pp. 438–453. Paris, I-Tech, Vienna (2009)
7. Plotnikova, V., Dumas, M., Milani, F.P.: Adaptations of data mining methodologies: a systematic literature review. PeerJ Comput. Sci. **6**, e267, (2020)
8. Runeson, P., Host, M., Rainer, A., Regnell, B.: Case Study Research in Software Engineering: Guidelines and Examples. Wiley, Hoboken (2012)
9. Yin, R.K.: Case Study Research and Applications: Design and Methods. Sage Publications, Los Angeles (2017)
10. Saldana, J.: The Coding Manual for Qualitative Researchers. Sage Publications, Los Angeles (2015)
11. McNaughton, B., Ray, P., Lewis, L: Designing an evaluation framework for IT service management. Inf. Manag. **47**(4), 219–225 (2010)
12. Martinez-Plumed, F., et al.: CRISP-DM twenty years later: from data mining processes to data science trajectories. IEEE Trans. Knowl. Data Eng. (2019)
13. AXELOS Limited: ITIL® Foundation, ITIL 4 Edition. TSO (The Stationery Office) (2019)

A Method for Modeling Process Performance Indicators Variability Integrated to Customizable Processes Models

Diego Diaz[1](✉), Mario Cortes-Cornax[1], Agnès Front[1], Cyril Labbe[1], and David Faure[1,2]

[1] Univ. Grenoble Alpes, CNRS, Grenoble INP, LIG, 38000 Grenoble, France
{diego.diaz,mario.cortes-cornax,agnes.front, cyril.labbe}@univ-grenoble-alpes.fr
[2] Groupe INCOM & COSI+, Grenoble, France
dfaure@incom-sa.fr

Abstract. Process Performance Indicators (PPIs) are quantifiable metrics to evaluate the business process performance providing essential information for decision-making as regards to efficiency and effectiveness. Nowadays, customizable process models and PPIs are usually modeled separately, especially when dealing with PPIs variability. Likewise, modeling PPI variants with no explicit link with the related customizable process generates redundant models, making adjustment and maintenance difficult. The use of appropriate methods and tools is needed to enable the integration and support of PPIs variability in customizable process models. In this paper, we propose a method based on the Process Performance Indicator Calculation Tree (PPICT), which allows to model the PPIs variability linked to customizable processes modeled on the Business Process Feature Model (BPFM) approach. The Process Performance Indicator Calculation (PPIC) method supports PPIs variability modeling through five design stages, which concerns the PPICT design, the integration of PPICT-BMFM and the configuration of required PPIs aligned with process activities. The PPIC method is supported by a metamodel and a graphical notation. This method has been implemented in a prototype using the ADOxx platform. A partial user-centered evaluation of the PPICT use was carried out in a real utility distribution case to model PPIs variability linked to a customizable process model.

Keywords: Process performance indicators · Process families · Variability

1 Introduction

Models that support variability and customization of Business Processes (BP), i.e., process variants, have been widely studied [1, 2]. However, the variability of Process Performance Indicators (PPIs) has not been addressed in the same way [3, 4]. PPIs are quantifiable metrics that allow an evaluation of the efficiency and effectiveness of business processes. PPIs can be measured directly by generating data through the process

S. Cherfi et al. (Eds.): RCIS 2021, LNBIP 415, pp. 72–87, 2021.
https://doi.org/10.1007/978-3-030-75018-3_5

flow [5]. Decision-makers identify PPIs to get the necessary information to compare current process performances with a required objective and thus determine fundamental actions to reach proposed goals [6]. In the context of customizable processes, organizations adapt their business processes and thus their PPIs according to customers' requirements, policies or audit entities evaluations criteria. The business process variability makes PPIs definition and calculation difficult since processes and PPIs are tightly related. The performance evaluation of business processes is focused on the definition of performance requirements, e.g., a set of PPIs [7]. The design of PPIs is a time-consuming and error prone task, highly dependent on the expert know-how, which makes it difficult to integrate the modeling of customizable processes [5]. PPIs management, in the context of customizable processes, is not only delimited to the evaluation phase of business process variants, but also includes PPIs redefinition that must be carried out throughout the whole lifecycle of BP [8]. Therefore, a method that helps and promotes PPIs modeling and reusability is necessary to evaluate the performance of customizable process models.

Works related to Business Process Model Families (BPMFs) [9] and the identification of the variability of PPIs [8] respond in part to our need. For instance, the Business Process Feature Model (BPFM) is an approach to model process families, i.e., customizable processes. BPFM extends the Feature Models, which is a classic representation of software product lines variability [10, 11]. Customizable process models capture a family of process model variants in a way that the individual variants can be derived via transformations, e.g., adding, or deleting fragments [1]. However, customizable process models such as BPFM do not support PPIs variability. Likewise, the approaches modeling PPI variability such as PPINOT [5] are not integrated with customizable processes, as they treat PPIs variability in the context of a predefined process model.

In previous work, we presented the Process Performance Indicator Calculation Tree (PPICT) [12] in order to model the PPIs variability linked to customizable process models following some construction rules. The integration with the customizable process models, using the BPFM approach, was not formalized nor included in an overall method supported by a tool. Relying on our experience in a real industrial case, we propose the Process Performance Indicator Calculation (PPIC) method, which is based on the PPICT to integrate PPIs variability to customizable processes models. The contribution in this paper is threefold: I) a method of five design stages to facilitate the design and use of the PPICT, II) a metamodel to formalize the PPICT and its corresponding graphical notation, and, III) a prototype supporting the method. The method is illustrated in the context of public services distributors. Software publishers such as INCOM[1], provide these processes and PPIs to distributors. Processes that are evaluated differently by public services stakeholders as decision-makers and utility regulatory entities [13].

The rest of the paper is structured as follows. Section 2 presents in detail problems related to the modeling of PPIs variability with customizable process models. Section 3 presents our method to integrate PPIs variability modeling within BPFM. Section 4 formalizes the PPICT through a metamodel. The PPIC method validation though a user-centered evaluation is shown in Sect. 5. Section 6 discusses related works. Finally, Sect. 7 concludes, summarizes, and presents the considered perspectives.

[1] www.incom-sa.fr.

2 Modeling PPIs Variability in Customizable Process Models

Our first objective in this paper is to formalize and tool up the PPICT, which allows to integrate the PPIs variability modeling with customizable process models. The PPIs variability modeling is also called PPIs families modeling [12]. The PPICT of the Fig. 1 (b), models a family of PPIs used to evaluate a reference process dealing with the creation of contracts for utility distributors. This family of PPIs has been developed and validated in collaboration with PPIs expert developers of INCOM, a French software publisher that works for 250 public services distributors. Every distributor evaluates its own processes under different criteria, in part because these processes are variants of INCOM's reference processes. Indeed, customers can customize their software solution depending on their needs. The customizable process model Create Contract, Fig. 1 (a) is modeled using the aforementioned Business Process Feature Model (BPFM), which provides a global representation of all process variants [14]. Using a similar approach, the PPIs variability integrated to customizable process models, is represented using the so-called Process Performance Indicator Calculation Tree (PPICT) [12]. The PPICT provides a global representation of the PPIs variability definitions and calculations in a given domain through the systematic modeling of variability and common points. The PPICT defines the available PPIs members of a family of PPIs, as well as dependencies between them. A PPI in the PPICT corresponds to a query that results in an aggregation of several tuples. The "query view" of the PPICT is explained in [12] and illustrated in the next section.

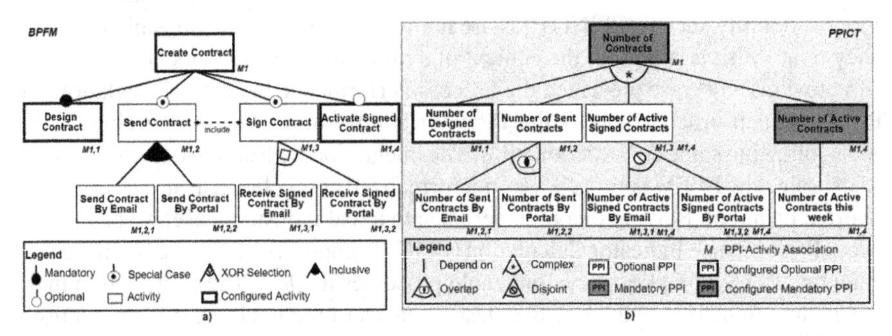

Fig. 1. (a) Customizable process model using BPFM, (b) PPICT based on the family *Number of Contracts*

To model the PPIs variability integrated to customizable process models, we rely on the graphical notation described in Sect. 4. The PPICT organizes a set of PPIs as a tree, where the tree's root identifies a PPIs family, cf. Fig. 1 (b). Each PPI of the internal tree's structure is a *Reference PPI*, i.e., each PPI that is not a tree leaf is a reference PPI including the root. Regarding PPIs-leaf, they are variants of a higher-level PPI, called *Variant PPI*. Thus, all PPIs of the internal structure except for the PPI-root are also variants of a higher-level PPI, i.e., the only PPIs that have a single role are the PPIs-leaf with variant role and the PPI-root with the reference role, cf. Fig. 1 (b). A reference PPI is a PPI that serves as the basis for calculating its variant PPIs, e.g.,

Figure 1 (b) shows that the Number of Contracts is the reference PPI of the Number of Actives Contracts. Additionally, the resulting tuples of a reference PPI contain all resulting tuples of its variant PPIs, i.e., all resulting tuples of variant PPIs are subsets of resulting tuples of its reference PPI. A variant PPI is a PPI derived from its reference PPI. This means that a variant PPI has only one reference PPI that meets this condition. Moreover, the PPICT allows to include some PPIs definitions such as, Optional PPI, Mandatory PPI, Configured Optional PPI and Configured Mandatory PPI. Likewise, the PPICT allows to integrate connections between reference PPIs and variant PPIs, which are called Overload Constraint, Disjoint Constraint, Complex Constraint and Depend on Constraint.

To integrate the PPIs variability model to the BPFM, PPICT proposes the PPI-Activity association (M), which defines that an activity can have zero or several associated PPIs and that a PPI must have at least one associated activity to be calculated: for example, the Number of Contracts PPI, Fig. 1 (b) is linked to the Create Contract activity, Fig. 1 (a). In this paper, we propose a five-stage method to facilitate the construction and use of the PPICT formalizing the PPIs variability modeling linked to customizable process models supported by a metamodel and a graphical notation.

3 PPIC Method

This section presents the Process Performance Indicator Calculation (PPIC) method, which has been partially implemented in a prototype developed on ADOxx platform. This platform allows to guide users in the development and instantiation of a metamodel. The PPIC method extends the BPFM method [14] by integrating design stages to model and calculate PPIs within customizable process models. The PPIC method is divided in 5 steps: I) the construction of the PPICT, II) the PPIs design, III) the BPFM and PPICT association, IV) the configuration of PPIs, and, V) the configuration checking concerning the business process variant. These 5 steps are described below and illustrated in Fig. 2. An example relying on a simplified INCOM's industrial case is systematically given for every step. The example is based on the Create Contract Process presented in the previous section.

Step 1, PPICT Design: refers to the manual addition of all PPIs family members using the PPICT graphical notation. PPICT Design allows to represent PPIs variability by adding PPIs depending on stakeholders' requirements. This stage must be carried out by a competence center, which includes domain experts, BP designers and decision makers to build the PPIs family.

Example: in this step, we design the PPICT in the following ways: I) by adding the PPI root into the PPIs family tree to evaluate a BP family, or, II) by adding new PPIs variants of existing PPIs according to stakeholders' requirements. In our example, the PPIs have the form Number of, as decided by the competence center. A PPICT like the one illustrated in Fig. 3 is the output of this stage and which has been implemented in our prototype.

Step 2, PPIs Design: specifies that all PPIs family members must be designed according to stakeholders' definitions and design criteria as detailed in the *PPI class* in Sect. 4. This stage must be carried out by a competence center, which includes experts in domains,

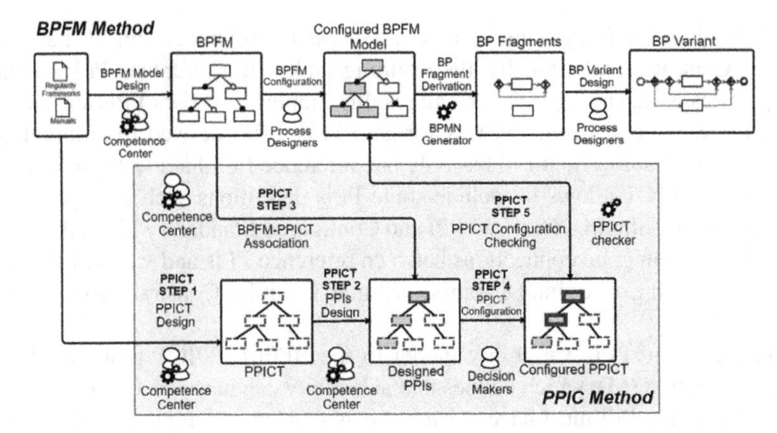

Fig. 2. PPIC method's steps

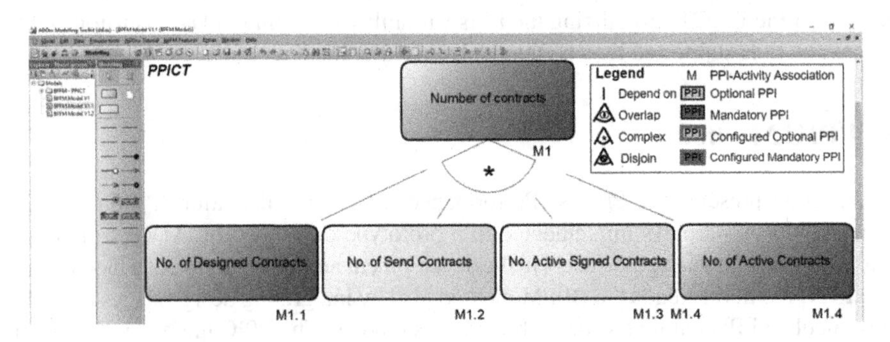

Fig. 3. PPICT (numbers of contracts PPIs family model)

BP designers and PPIs calculation experts to implement all PPIs family members as a query, e.g., as a SQL query.

Example: at this stage, PPIs are designed according to PPI class attributes detailed in Sect. 4. For instance, the Root reference PPI Number of Contracts is a mandatory PPI with a measure type Number, a measure aggregation count and a measure representation Value. A PPICT like the one illustrated in Fig. 4 (b) using SQL queries, is the output of this stage.

Step 3, BPFM-PPICT Association: allows the BPFM and PPICT association. This stage uses the PPI-Activity Mapping constraint of the PPICT relying on BPFM Model to associate reference PPIs and variant PPIs to process activities. This stage must be done manually using PPICT's PPI-Activity Mapping constraint described in [12].

Example: Fig. 4 (a) shows all activities of the Create Contract family, which are described using BPFM notation [14]. Figure 4 (b) shows all PPIs designed to evaluate the Create Contract process Family. The mappings PPI-Activity are shown here. They are done relying on each activity or group of activities that are linked to the data model of a software application, i.e., activities that generate data during their execution. For this, we integrate the process flow execution record present by default in some software

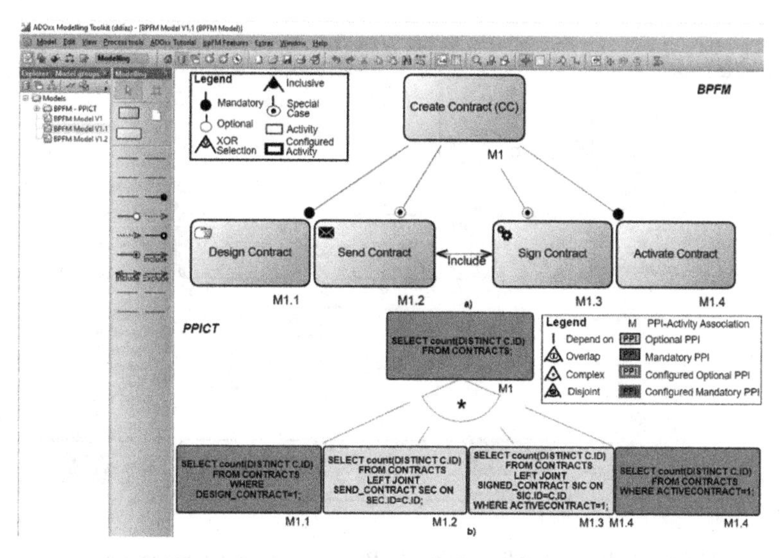

Fig. 4. Mapping PPI-activity: (a) BPFM; (b) PPICT using SQL queries

applications such as the INCOM's one. This record contains all tables and attributes used by each activity.

Step 4, PPICT Configuration: defines the PPICT configuration, i.e., the PPIs family members configured by the client. The configuration of a PPI depends on I) mandatory indicators required by regulatory entities, and, II) stakeholders' specifications to evaluate their BP variants. PPICT Configuration allows to define which PPIs family members must be included into the BP variant considering on business regulations and decision makers criteria. This step is done semi-automatically, since mandatory PPIs are automatically configured, unlike optional PPIs that must be configured manually.

Example: at this stage, decision makers configure PPIs that they believe are convenient to evaluate their process variants according to stakeholders' definitions and criteria, cf. Fig. 5 (b). Decision makers can choose any optional PPI. It does not mean these PPIs are going to be deployed, since we must check PPI-Activity match using the BP variant that has been configured.

Step 5, PPICT Configuration Checking: aligns the PPICT configuration with the BPFM configuration, i.e., check if PPICT configuration matches with BPFM configuration. PPICT Configuration Checking allows to check which members of the configured PPIs family do not match with the BP configuration. Thus, the competence center must change configured PPIs to include them into BP variant or change the BP configuration. This alignment check can be done automatically. If there is any misalignment between the PPICT and the BPFM configurations, it is necessary to return to the previous steps.

Example: at this stage, the match between PPICT and BPFM model configurations is checked. If any configured PPI is mapped to any unconfigured activity, the competence center must reconfigure BPFM or PPICT to align configured members of each family. After the reconfiguration Fig. 5 (a) and (b) shows a correct alignment BPFM-PPICT implemented in our prototype.

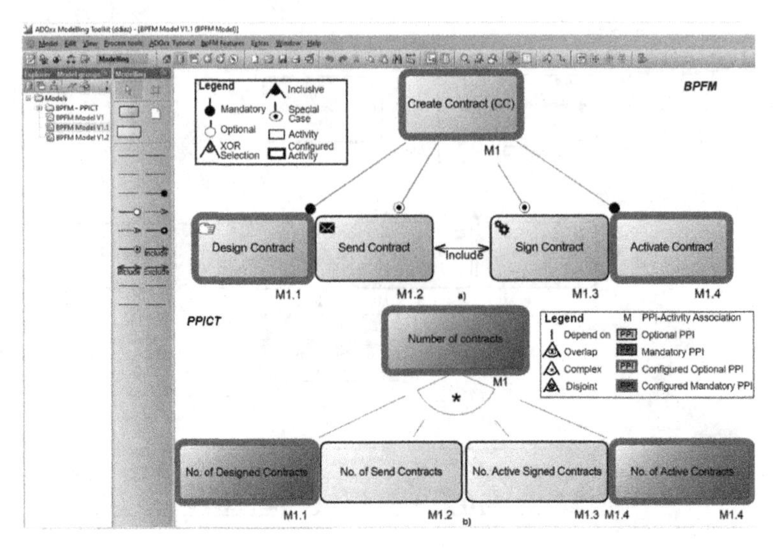

Fig. 5. (a) BPFM configuration, (b) PPICT conforming configuration

Analysts could stay in a design phase without reaching the process deployment and execution, i.e., until step 5. In this case, PPICT would be useful to analyze the feasibility of PPIs studying their alignment with the process activities in the BP family.

4 The PPICT Metamodel

This section discusses the PPICT metamodel, which extends the BPFM metamodel within the PPIs variability modeling and supports the five steps presented in the previous section. This extension is carried out according to the BP configuration and business criteria defined by stakeholders. We divide the PPICT metamodel into the following classes:

PPI class: allows to model and define all PPIs of the PPICT providing necessary information to calculate them. Every PPI must be easily identified by stakeholders, for this a short name attribute and a long name attribute are included in this class, e.g., as long name we can have *Number of Active Signed Contracts* and as short name NASC. Moreover, the selection of a PPI may imply the inclusion or exclusion of another PPI according to evaluation rules established by stakeholders. Additionally, all PPIs have a *Measure Type* that determines how they can be calculated depending on the result that the client is looking for. We define each measure type as follows:

- *Number* specifies the PPI calculation according to the number of tuples that validate a predicate, e.g., 83 Contracts are Actives.
- *Percentage* specifies the PPI calculation according to the percentage of tuples that validate a predicate, e.g., 60% of Contracts are Actives.
- *Proportion* specifies the PPI calculation according to the proportion between tuples and a target value, e.g., (3/5) 3 out of 5 Contracts are Actives.

- *Delay* specifies the PPI calculation according to the difference between creation dates of tuples, e.g., 3 Delay Days in Activating Contracts ($Date_{today} - Date_{deadline}$).
- *Respect Rate* specifies the PPI calculation according to the proportion of the difference between two dates and a target value, e.g., (3/2), 3 Current Delay Days in Activating Contracts compared to 2 Maximum Delay Days Allowed by Law ($Date_{today} - Date_{deadline}$)/*Value*.

Furthermore, every PPI has a *Measure Representation* to visualize resulting tuples in different ways depending on the type of information that the decision-maker wants to analyze, cf. Fig. 6. We define each measure representation as follows:

- *Value* representation is a type of representation that allows to visualize a set of resulting tuples as a value, e.g, 83, 60%, 5/3, 3 or 3/2.
- *Listing* representation is a type of representation that allows to visualize a set of resulting tuples as a listing. It requires to include additional projections to analyze complementary information linked to resulting tuples, e.g., *Contract Creation Date, Contract Activation Date, Contract holder, Holder's phone, among others.*
- *Geographical* representation is a type of representation that allows to visualize a set of resulting tuples geographically. It requires to group the geographical tuples, e.g., *by City, by Type of Contract, among others.*
- *Chart* representation is a type of representation that allows to visualize a set of resulting tuples as a Chart. It requires to group tuples regardless of their type, e.g., *by Year, by Type of public service, among others.*

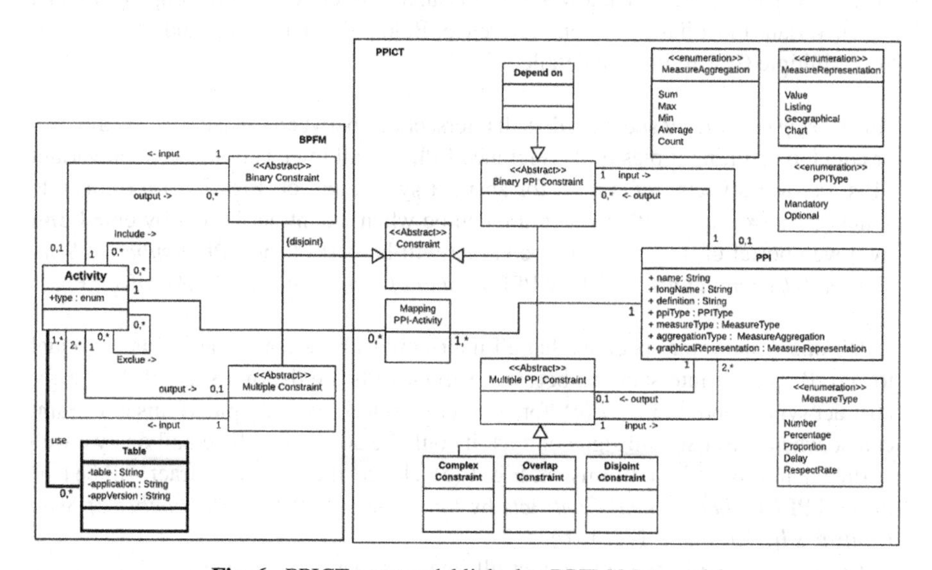

Fig. 6. PPICT metamodel linked to BPFM Metamodel

Likewise, every PPI has the attribute *Measure Aggregation* to aggregate resulting tuples in different ways, e.g., *Sum, Count, Avg, Min* and *Max*. It depends on the type of performance indicator that the decision maker wants to analyze, cf. Fig. 6.

Constraints Class: the PPICT constraints are divided into 3 groups [12]: binary constraint, multiple constraint, and PPI-activity mapping constraint. These Constraints represent (I) dependencies between reference PPIs and variant PPIs, and, (II) associations between PPIs and activities. According to [12] a PPI can be the reference for several individual variants, but a variant has only one reference.

Concerning the binary relation between PPIs, each individual variant PPI added to the tree must be connected to its reference PPI using a binary constraint. Below the definition and an example of the PPICT binary constraint:

- A *Depend-on* Constraint specifies that all resulting tuples of the connected variant PPIs are a subset or equal to resulting tuples of its reference PPI (cf. Fig. 6 for abstract syntax and cf. Fig. 7 (a). for concrete syntax). For example, a contract that was activated this week will be part of the PPI *Number of Active Contracts this week,* but it will be also a part of the PPI reference *Number of Active Contracts* cf. Fig. 1 (b).

Every group of variant PPIs added to the tree must be connected to its reference PPI as multiple relationship. We use the PPICT Multiple Constraints presented in previous works [12], which specify the dependency between a reference PPI and a group of variants PPIs. Nevertheless, these Multiple Constraints were not considered a *Complex Constraint*, which we can describe as a combination between the existing constraints, *Overlap* and *Disjoint* proposed by [12]. That is why, we include the complex constraint to the PPICT in this paper. We know that a PPI can be the reference of a group of variants, but each variant must have only one reference. Below the definitions and examples of PPICT Multiple Constraints are detailed:

- An *Overlap Constraint* specifies that all intersections between variant PPIs are a subset or equal to resulting tuples of its reference PPI, i.e., all intersections between variant PPIs are overlap sets. (cf. Fig. 6 for abstract syntax and cf. Fig. 7 (b) for concrete syntax). An example of this constraint can be when a contract is sent by email **and** by a web portal cf. Fig. 1 (a), this contract will be part of the PPI *Number of Send Contracts by Email* **and** part of the PPI *Number of Send Contracts by Portal,* cf. Fig. 1 (b).
- A *Disjoint Constraint* specifies that all intersections between variant PPIs are equal to zero Ø, i.e., all intersections between variant PPIs are disjoint sets (cf. Fig. 6 for abstract syntax and cf. Fig. 7 (c). for concrete syntax). An example of this constraint can be when a user should sign contract, it could be done either by email **or** by a web portal but not by both platforms, cf. Fig. 1 (a). Hence, the signed contract will be part of the PPI *Number of Send Contracts by Email* **or** part of the PPI *Number of Send Contracts by Portal,* cf. Fig. 1 (b).
- A *Complex Constraint* specifies that all intersections between variant PPIs can be equal to zero Ø or not, i.e., intersections between variant PPIs can be disjoint sets or not (cf. Fig. 6 for abstract syntax and cf. Fig. 7 (d) for concrete syntax). For instance, a contract can be designed and sent but waiting to be activated, cf. Fig. 1 (a). Hence,

this contract will be part of the PPIs *Number of Designed Contracts* and *Number of Send Contracts* but will not be part of the PPI *Number of Active Contracts,* cf. Fig. 1 (b).

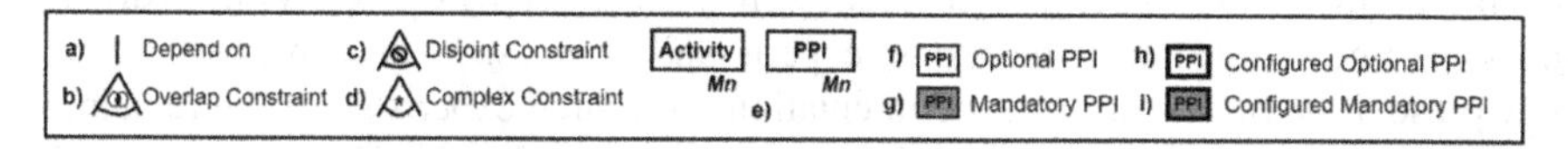

Fig. 7. PPICT concrete syntax

Additionally, a PPI can be configured optionally or not, according to the business context or decision makers requirements. Below the PPI Type is defined:

- An *Optional PPI* specifies that the PPI can be optionally configured. However, if the PPI is configured all its ascending PPIs will also be configured. (cf. Fig. 6 for abstract syntax and cf. Fig. 7 (f) for concrete syntax).
- A *Mandatory PPI* specifies that the PPI must be configured as well as all its ascending PPIs. (cf. Fig. 6 for abstract syntax and cf. Fig. 7 (g) for concrete syntax).
- A *Configured Optional PPI* specifies that an *Optional PPI* has been selected to be deploy for a given process variant. (cf. Fig. 6 for abstract syntax and cf. Fig. 7 (h) for concrete syntax).
- A *Configured Mandatory PPI* specifies that a *Mandatory PPI* has been selected to be deploy for a given process variant. (cf. Fig. 6 for abstract syntax and cf. Fig. 7 (i) for concrete syntax).

Mapping PPI-Activity Class: since PPICT is an extension of the BPFM approach, it is necessary to link the PPIs families modeling and the BP families modeling. For this, we propose the PPI-Activity association, which defines that an activity can have zero or several associated PPIs and that a PPI must have at least one associated activity to be calculated, (cf. Fig. 6 for abstract syntax and cf. Fig. 7 (e) for concrete syntax).

Table Class: all PPIs must be calculated under a specific context, according to the tables used by each activity. For this, we propose to enrich the BPFM metamodel, cf. Fig. 6 with a class that has the list of tables used by each activity. This relation Activity-Tables is usually registered in the process flow execution record presents by default in some software applications. Since every single activity may generate essential data for the PPIs calculation. The PPICT metamodel assume that the relation Activity-Tables is known and can be used to evaluate the process performance.

Note that we present here a simplified version of our PPICT metamodel, where options such as target, threshold, and worst PPIs values, as well as time conditions or state conditions are not modeled.

5 PPIC Method Validation Though a User-Centered Evaluation

An experimental protocol[2] was built relying on the THEDRE method and its decision tree MATUI [15], since this method allows to lead researches in human-centered computer science and guide researchers. We have selected this decision tree MATUI to guarantee the traceability of experimental works that were carried out. Moreover, we have divided this experimentation into two groups: experts and novices. In this analysis, we will only present the results of our experimentation with three experts since the remaining experiments had to be reprogrammed due to the current COVID-19 health crisis. The experiment description about chosen tools and produced data was essential to develop a relevant experimental protocol. Therefore, sharing a common vision between internal and external actors, i.e., researches and experts, was crucial to build the experimental material.

We have set the experimental protocol targets to achieve concerning developments, experiments, and communications, e.g., (I) involve indicator developers in the modeling of PPIs according to customizable processes, (II) explore how users express their PPIs definitions, and (III) identify users' modeling methodologies and PPIs calculation practices. Likewise, we have fixed the following Hypotheses (H) to evaluate during the experimental protocol execution:

- H1: Experts do not have a formalized method to calculate the PPIs.
- H2: PPIs are impacted by the process variability and cause uncertainty on the PPIs calculation.
- H3: Experts differentiate the main concepts of the PPCIT.
- H4: Experts take ownership of the PPCIT and understand the relationship and constraints between PPIs.
- H5: PPICT allows experts to place new PPIs in the tree structure.
- H6: Experts fill all PPI's attributes.
- H7: Existing PPIs allow experts to create new ones.
- H8: Understanding the data structure owing to the PPICT.

Regarding the experimental protocol results, experts were able to validate the PPIC method according to the PPIs variability modeling language proposed. During experiments, each hypothesis proposed some exercises based on a PPIs family scenario supported by interview guides and workbooks. Thus, experts expressed their points of view individually on either improvements or questions. Below, a synthesis about the eight hypotheses is presented:

- H1 validation: Experts do not have formal methods for calculating PPIs, but they do have practices used independently based on their experiences. Two experts apply software development methods to PPIs calculation.
- H2 validation: All experts said that *"processes variability leads to uncertainty over PPIs"* and they agree that there is a lack of reliability in PPIs calculation because they do not have tools and methods for modeling PPIs variability, e.g., tools allowing

[2] https://drive.google.com/drive/folders/1fvjgJsUu3uzbte8DL_Q5eehP4nyICiHS?usp=sharing.

users to model and calculate relationships between PPIs. Experts define the impact of process variability in different ways applying their knowledge of the trade. They said that *"the standardization of a software product is very complex"*.
- H3 validation: Experts said that *"it is indeed possible to divide the definitions of an invariable PPI and a variable PPI"*. An expert prefers simpler definitions like "*Father PPI*" and "*Son PPI*" as well as "*registrations*" instead of tuples.
- H4 validation: Several possible improvements were mentioned by the experts. For example, one of them proposed the possibility to guide user to select the correct reference PPI when new variant PPIs are added. This expert also said that *"this automatic guide to add new variant PPI can be possible through a search system allowing the indexing of the tables and fields used for each PPI"*. This improvement is very relevant for a PPICT having many modeled PPIs, that is why it can be implemented in future versions of the PPICT.
- H5 validation: Experts appreciated the notation and considered it understandable. However, an expert said that *"certain concepts need to be improved such as the constraint depends on by adding an arrow to indicate the direction of the variant"*. Another expert said that *"it was difficult to place new PPIs when the labels were too long"*. The expert proposes to suggest the possible reference PPI of a new variant PPI using the labels through a search function.
- H6 validation: An expert said that *"it is much easier to add certain missing attributes to the PPIs located at the bottom of the PPICT because in general these PPIs have more information than those of the higher level"*.
- H7 validation: All experts concluded that *"the more information we have in the PPICT, the easier it is to add new PPI"*.
- H8 validation: Two experts said that *"even if some PPIs were more complicated to calculate than others, the PPICT is a tool easy to use to build PPIs and it can be used by beginners or experts concerning PPI calculation"*.

These experimental results and research targets were checked such as methodological hypotheses and clarity of concepts to determine the experiments to come and PPIC method improvements. The scientific knowledge attained helped us to define the limits and advantages of our contribution, e.g., a limit is the impossibility of suggesting automatically existing reference PPIs for new variant PPIs. The prototype allowed a successful validation of the PPICT formalization facilitating the PPIs variability modeling linked to a customizable process model of our utility distributors study case.

6 Related Works

Process performance indicators are usually used to analyze the performance of business processes [7]. However, the application of PPIs in customizable process models complicates the PPIs variability modeling and management [12]. Hence, it is necessary to define new mechanisms to help PPIs developers to identify and organize the essential information to model variables performance indicator in customizable process models. Current software publishers' needs have been motivated by the measurement of customizable process models performances. The association between process variability and performance indicators variability implies that PPIs of a non-variable process, should be redefined [8].

Regarding the performance measurement of non-customizable process models, research efforts have carried out many approaches that propose languages and architectures for monitoring and defining PPIs such as [16] or [17]. However, these approaches do not consider neither customizable process models nor the PPIs variability. Others works such as [18] have extended the Business Process Model Notation to define business process goals and performance measures, but without considering any type of variability. Regarding expressiveness of PPIs modeling, [18] has proposed a graphical notation for Business Activity Monitoring without including PPIs definitions related to data. Moreover, [19] propose an execution measurement model for business processes based on an existing software measurement ontology. But they do not consider the definition of domain-specific and user-defined PPIs. Likewise, it is also worth mentioning the standard Case Management Model and Notation for decision modelling [20], which considers the process-related measures calculation but only for non-customizable process models.

PPIs are generally defined in an informal way, e.g., in natural language, what leads to problems of ambiguity, coherence and traceability in relation to process models [21], e.g., missing information in the definition of a PPI. Likewise, PPIs are usually defined from a process variant or instance losing the perspective of the customizable process model. This entails that if a process variant evolves, PPIs definitions in the customizable process model will not be updated accordingly. On one side, the deployment of a performance management solution takes time and resources, what limits the PPIs evolutions and increases the cost for organizations [5]. On the other side, the significant gap that exists between PPIs implementation languages and natural language may cause errors in PPIs evolutions. Additionally, PPIs developers must detect and remove manually the ambiguities generated by natural language in order to calculate PPIs properly [22]. This is an error-prone task since PPIs developers often do not share the same PPIs definition as decision-makers, due to the nature of their jobs, because developers are closer to technology, while decision-makers are closer to management [5].

Customizable processes models managing either the variability by restriction or by extension have not integrated the PPIs variability modeling [1, 8]. For example, models managing variability by restriction, also called configurable process models [23], contain every possible behavior from all process variants. Thus, during the process customization the model's behavior is restricted by skipped or blocked some activities. Moreover, models managing variability by extension do not contain all possible behavior from all process variants. Instead, it represents the most common behavior in process variants and during the customization the model's behavior is extended for a specific context, e.g., new activities may be inserted to create a dedicated variant [1].

To model the PPIs variability linked to customizable processes models. We rely on the Business Process Feature Model (BPFM) [14], which includes the refinement of process variants even if the process has been customized as analyzed on [12]. This approach also considers the deployment context information adapting execution paths for every process variant. Moreover, BPFM is implemented in the ADOxx platform[3], whereby this

[3] www.adoxx.org.

approach enables to guide users to make customization decisions and prevent behavioral anomalies for every process variant. Additionally, this approach has been validated considering several Public Administration scenarios through the European Project Budget Report case study endorsed by the Learn PAd Project[4].

Classical architectures such as Data Warehouse, Business Intelligence, Business Activity Monitoring [18] or Modeling Performance Indicators [16] allow to model and calculate indicators dealing with the importance of enforcing objectives defined by business strategies and metrics. Nevertheless, in the case of customizable process models, the information extraction from business data is insufficient, especially when different PPI definitions depend on flexible evaluation criteria and process variants. The PPIs variability allows an advanced definition of variable performance indicator independently of the language used to model the BP [8]. The PPINOT approach [5] proposes a language for defining and modeling PPIs together with business processes. It enhances the PPIs modeling as well as the visual representation of business process-PPI links through a metamodel. PPINOT allows also to express PPIs definitions, which were impossible to model in previous approaches as analyzed in [21]. However, the PPINOT approach does not consider neither customizable process models nor the PPIs variability. In summary, the works of [8] and [5] do not allow to model and define relations between PPIs variability and customizable process models.

Our previous work [12] proposed the Performance Indicator Calculation Tree (PPICT), which models the PPIs variability as a tree to facilitate the PPIs definitions integrated to customizable process models. PPICT relies on BPFM constraints and proposes the term family of PPIs following the same pattern of family of processes [1]. PPICT defines a family of PPIs as a paradigm for calculating PPIs using a set of processes that form a common structure, which serves as a basis for calculating derived PPIs according to process variants and PPIs definitions.

From the study of the state of the art, we conclude that when an organization explores its data sources and uses it as part of new process, there are no design stages for customizable process models-PPIs variability links. For this reason, we propose a method that formalizes the PPICT and extends BPFM method to model and facilitate the definitions of PPI variants in the context of customizable process models.

7 Conclusion and Open Issues

Nowadays, customizable process models and PPIs are usually modeled separately, especially when dealing with PPIs variability. Since the support of process variability complicates the PPIs definition and calculation. Modeling PPI variants with no explicit link with the related customizable process generates redundant models, making adjustment and maintenance difficult. In previous work, we presented the Process Performance Indicator Calculation Tree (PPICT) [12] in order to model the PPIs variability linked to customizable process models. However, the integration with customizable process models, using the BPFM approach, had not yet been formalized nor included in an overall method supported by a tool. This paper proposes the PPIC method based on the PPICT

[4] www.learnpad.eu.

to integrate PPIs variability to customizable process models. Our contribution lies in three main axes: (I) a method of five design stages to facilitate the design and use of the PPICT, (II) a metamodel to formalize the PPICT and its corresponding graphical notation, and, (III) a prototype supporting this method developed on ADOxx Platform. The PPIC method is illustrated in a real utility distributor case and has been validated by PPI calculation experts. The validation was carried out though a user-centered evaluation, which allows to use the PPICT to model a PPIs family linked to a BP family. Additionally, the PPIC method complements the related works of customizable process models by broadening the spectrum not only of the processes variants to be measured, but also of the measures themselves through the PPIs variability modeling. Today, the prototype does not allow to execute SQL queries to calculate PPIs. The latter feature is planned to be implemented rapidly, after completing the experimentations. A deepening track would be the integration with queries execution tools as business intelligence systems to implement all PPIs family members. Another interesting improvement would be the modeling of the PPIs variability in BP families that use non-relational storage systems, e.g., by extending the PPICT notation and links between PPIs and data being data-model agnostic.

References

1. La Rosa, M., Van Der Aalst, W.M.P., Dumas, M., Milani, F.P.: Business process variability modeling: a survey. ACM Comput. Surv. (CSUR) **50**, 2 (2017)
2. Milani, F., Dumas, M., Ahmed, N., Matulevičius, R.: Modelling families of business process variants: A decomposition driven method. Inf. Syst. **56**, 55–72 (2016)
3. Domínguez, E., Pérez, B., Rubio, Á.L., Zapata, M.A.: A taxonomy for key performance indicators management. Comput. Stand. Interfaces **64**, 24–40 (2019)
4. Estrada-Torres, B.: Improve performance management in flexible business processes. In: Proceedings of the 21st International Systems and Software Product Line Conference-Volume B, pp. 145–149 (2017)
5. del Río Ortega, A., Resinas, M., Durán, A., Bernárdez, B., Ruiz-Cortés, A., Toro, M.: Visual PPINOT: a graphical notation for process performance indicators. Bus. Inf. Syst. Eng. **61**, 137–161 (2019)
6. Peral, J., Maté, A., Marco, M.: Application of data mining techniques to identify relevant key performance indicators. Comput. Stand. Interfaces **54**, 76–85 (2017)
7. Estrada Torres, B., Torres, V., del Río Ortega, A., Resinas Arias de Reyna, M., Pelechano, V., Ruiz Cortés, A.: Defining PPIs for process variants based on change patterns. In: JCIS 2016: XII Jornadas de Ciencia e Ingeniería de Servicios (2016)
8. Estrada-Torres, B., del-Río-Ortega, A., Resinas, M., Ruiz-Cortés, A.: Identifying variability in process performance indicators. In: La Rosa, M., Loos, P., Pastor, O. (eds.) BPM 2016. LNBIP, vol. 260, pp. 91–107. Springer, Cham (2016). https://doi.org/10.1007/978-3-319-45468-9_6
9. La Rosa, M., Dumas, M., Ter Hofstede, A.H.M., Mendling, J.: Configurable multi-perspective business process models. Inf. Syst. **36**, 313–340 (2011)
10. Gröner, G., et al.: Validation of families of business processes. In: Mouratidis, H., Rolland, C. (eds.) CAiSE 2011. LNCS, vol. 6741, pp. 551–565. Springer, Heidelberg (2011). https://doi.org/10.1007/978-3-642-21640-4_41
11. Villota, A., Mazo, R., Salinesi, C.: The high-level variability language: an ontological approach. In: Proceedings of the 23rd International Systems and Software Product Line Conference-Volume B, pp. 162–169 (2019)

12. Diaz, D.: Integrating PPI variability in the context of customizable processes by extending the business process feature model. In: 2020 IEEE 24th International Enterprise Distributed Object Computing Workshop (EDOCW), pp. 80–85. IEEE (2020)
13. Diaz, D., Cortes-Cornax, M., Labbé, C., Faure, D.: Modélisation de la variabilité des indicateurs dans le cadre des administrations de services publics (2019)
14. Cognini, R., Corradini, F., Polini, A., Re, B.: Business process feature model: an approach to deal with variability of business processes. In: Karagiannis, D., Mayr, H., Mylopoulos, J. (eds.) Domain-Specific Conceptual Modeling, pp. 171–194. Springer, Heidelberg (2016)
15. Mandran, N., Dupuy-Chessa, S.: Supporting experimental methods in information system research. In: 2018 12th International Conference on Research Challenges in Information Science (RCIS), pp. 1–12. IEEE (2018)
16. Popova, V., Sharpanskykh, A.: Modeling organizational performance indicators. Inf. Syst. **35**, 505–527 (2010)
17. Saldivar, J., Vairetti, C., Rodríguez, C., Daniel, F., Casati, F., Alarcón, R.: Analysis and improvement of business process models using spreadsheets. Inf. Syst. **57**, 1–19 (2016)
18. Friedenstab, J.-P., Janiesch, C., Matzner, M., Muller, O.: Extending BPMN for business activity monitoring. In: 2012 45th Hawaii International Conference on System Sciences, pp. 4158–4167. IEEE (2012)
19. Delgado, A., Weber, B., Ruiz, F., de Guzmán, I.G.-R., Piattini, M.: An integrated approach based on execution measures for the continuous improvement of business processes realized by services. Inf. Softw. Technol. **56**, 134–162 (2014)
20. OMG: Case Management Model and Notation (CMMN). 1.1 (2016)
21. Del-RíO-Ortega, A., Resinas, M., Cabanillas, C., Ruiz-Cortés, A.: On the definition and design-time analysis of process performance indicators. Inf. Syst. **38**, 470–490 (2013)
22. van der Aa, H., et al.: Narrowing the business-IT gap in process performance measurement. In: Nurcan, S., Soffer, P., Bajec, M., Eder, J. (eds.) CAiSE 2016. LNCS, vol. 9694, pp. 543–557. Springer, Cham (2016). https://doi.org/10.1007/978-3-319-39696-5_33
23. Reichert, M., Hallerbach, A., Bauer, T.: Lifecycle management of business process variants. In: vom Brocke, J., Rosemann, M. (eds.) Handbook on Business Process Management 1 International Handbooks on Information Systems, pp. 251–278. Springer, Berlin, Heidelberg (2015). https://doi.org/10.1007/978-3-642-45100-3_11

Information Security and Risk Management

Novel Perspectives and Applications of Knowledge Graph Embeddings: From Link Prediction to Risk Assessment and Explainability

Hegler C. Tissot(✉)

University of Pennsylvania, Philadelphia, PA, USA
hegler@seas.upenn.edu
https://hextrato.com

Abstract. Knowledge graph representation is an important embedding technology that supports a variety of machine learning related applications. By learning the distributed representation of multi-relational data, knowledge embedding models are supposed to efficiently deal with the semantic relatedness of their constituents. However, failing in the fundamental task of creating an appropriate form to represent knowledge harms any attempt of designing subsequent machine learning tasks. Several knowledge embedding methods have been proposed in the last decade. Although there is a consensus on the idea that enhanced approaches are more efficient, more complex projections in the hyperspace that indeed favor link prediction (or knowledge graph completion) can result in a loss of semantic similarity. We propose a new evaluation task that aims at performing risk assessment on domain-specific categorized multi-relational datasets, designed as a classification problem based on the resulting embeddings. We assess the quality of embedding representations based on the synergy of the resulting clusters of target subjects. We show that more sophisticated embedding approaches do not necessarily favor embedding quality, and the traditional link prediction validation protocol is a weak metric to measure the quality of embedding representation. Finally, we present insights about using the synergy analysis to provide risk assessment explainability based on the probability distribution of feature-value pairs within embedded clusters.

Keywords: Knowledge graphs · Link prediction · Risk assessment

1 Introduction

Decision support system applications based on knowledge graphs (KGs) have been reported in different scenarios, such as entity linking [20], drug-to-drug similarity measurements [22], and recommender systems [32]. Graph-based knowledge representation uses a set of symbolic *(head, relation, tail)* triplets (or facts)

S. Cherfi et al. (Eds.): RCIS 2021, LNBIP 415, pp. 91–106, 2021.
https://doi.org/10.1007/978-3-030-75018-3_6

to represent the various entities (nodes) and their relationships (edges) from a multi-relational dataset. Each entity represents one of various types of an abstract concept of the world and each relation is a predicate that represents a fact involving two entities. There is a consensus that the heterogeneous nature of the data sources, where facts are usually extracted from to create a KG, makes the latter typically inaccurate. Although containing a huge number of triplets, most open-domain KGs are usually taken as incomplete, covering only a small subset of the true domain knowledge they are supposed to represent.

Knowledge embedding representation (KER) approaches have been proposed as an effective way to map the symbolic entities and relations into a continuous vector space, enforcing the embedding compatibility while preserving semantic information. Embedding vectors are easier to manipulate than the original symbolic entities and relations, and their popularity has led to the development of refined techniques to increase their quality [2]. KER aims to efficiently measure semantic correlations in knowledge bases by projecting entities and relations into a dense low-dimensional space, significantly improving performance on knowledge inference and alleviating sparsity issues, and it is usually presented as an efficient tool to complete knowledge bases (Link Prediction – LP) without requiring extra knowledge [33]. LP aims at predicting new relationships between entities by automatically recovering missing facts based on the observed ones. However, to our knowledge, there has been not much effort on evaluating the embedding representation quality resulting from KG embedding approaches. A preliminary study aims to contrast the effectiveness of hyperparameter choices when using the resulting embedding representation in subsequent machine learning classification tasks, instead of just relying on KG completion [5].

In this work, we propose a new evaluation task that aims at performing risk assessment on domain-specific categorized multi-relational datasets. We redesign the KER evaluation as a risk assessment task to validate the ability of knowledge embedding approaches to retain the semantic relatedness of KG constituents, i.e., quantifying the degree to which two components are associated with each other. We measure the synergy of feature-value pairs within clusters of resulting embeddings in order evaluate the ability of KER approaches on capturing the semantic similarity among target subjects. We provide evidence that simpler approaches perform better than more sophisticated embedding formulations when targeting embedding quality rather than trying to improve knowledge completion. Finally, we present insights on how to use the synergy analysis over the resulting embeddings to provide risk assessment explainability based on the probability distribution of feature-value pairs within the resulting embeddings.

2 Knowledge Embedding Representation

Multi-relational data is usually presented in the form of a KG. Entities (nodes) and relations (edges) provide a structured representation of the knowledge about a specific domain, and a reasoning ability that can be used for inference. In a KG, structured information is encoded in the form of triples *(h, r, t)* (also known as *subject, predicate, object*), where h and t are the *head* and *tail* entities and r represents the *relation* between h and t. Although containing a huge number of triplets, most open-domain KGs are taken as incomplete, covering only a small subset of the true knowledge that they are supposed to represent, whereas in domain-specific KGs, incompleteness results from missing values and cardinality-related inconsistencies that are usually produced by automatic information extraction processes from unstructured data sources (e.g., clinical notes).

Learning knowledge embedding representation enables a range of tasks including KG completion [4,26], entity classification [19] and relation extraction [27]. Within this technique, entities and relations are embedded onto a low-dimensional vector space to capture the semantic relatedness behind observed facts and operate on the latent feature representation of the triple constituents. However, embedding quality is an aspect that has not been much explored alongside the KER evaluation process.

Translational embedding approaches use relatively simple assumptions to achieve accurate and scalable results on embedding KGs. Overall, these models try to learn vectors for each constituent *(h, r, t)*, so that every relation r is a translation between h and t in the embedding space, and the pair of embedded entities h and t can be approximately connected by r with low error. Embedding methods operate on the latent feature representation of the constituents and on their semantic relatedness, by defining a distinct relation-based scoring function $f_r(h,t)$ to measure the plausibility of the triplet *(h, r, t)*. $f_r(h,t)$ implies a transformation on the pair of entities which characterizes the relation r. The final embedding representation is learned using an algorithm that optimizes a margin-based objective function or ranking criterion over a training set.

TransE [4] is a baseline translational embedding approach known by its flaws at dealing with *one-to-many*, *many-to-one* and *many-to-many* relations when applied to open-domain data [31]. Other methods extended TransE by varying the way they assign different representations to each entity and each relation to achieve better link prediction performance. For example, TransH [26], TransR [15], and TransD [11] use projection matrices to pre-project each h into a relation-specific vector space. Therefore, they use separate distinct vector spaces to embed entities and relations, each entity can have distinct distributed representations when involved in different relations, which allows entities to play different roles in different relations. However, this makes it hard to compare the similarity of two distinct entities without taking relations into account.

Other KER approaches have been proposed, with a common goal to improve low-dimensional KG representation targeting specific evaluation tasks. However, they differ in the theoretical problem concerned or the solution approach as reflected in their scoring functions, including adapted scoring functions to allow more flexible translations (e.g., TransM [7] and TransA [28]), Gaussian embeddings to model semantic uncertainty (e.g., KG2E [10] and TransG [29]), tensor factorization (RESCAL [18]), compositional vector representation (HolE [17]), complex spaces (ComplEx [25]), transitive relation embeddings (TRE [34]), and neural neighborhood-aware embeddings (LENA [12]). Although these models achieve great results on the benchmark open-domain datasets, their implementations are scattered and unsystematic, and their codes for model validation and reproducibility are often time-consuming, making them difficulty to be used in further development, and adopting them for real-world applications [9].

In domain-specific KGs, multi-relational data can be categorized, i.e., each entity is presented with its corresponding type and relations are also restricted by domain and range. Type-based constraints can support latent variable models, by integrating prior knowledge about entity and relation types, significantly improving these models in the link prediction tasks, especially when a low model complexity is enforced [13]. In categorized KGs, each entity e is associated with a category (or type) $c \in \mathcal{T}$, and each triple is presented in the form $(c_h : h,\ r,\ c_t : t)$, where c_h and c_t represent the types of h and t. For example, in the triple `(Patient:P01, hasGender, Gender:male)`, the relation *hasGender* is constrained by the domain *Patient* and the range *Gender*.

There are multiple suggested ways to apply type-based constraints in training latent variable models: (a) entities belonging to the same semantic type can be placed close together in the embedding space with the use of geometric constraints such as manifold regularization [8]; (b) entities can be projected onto type-specific vector spaces, analogous to the relation-specific projections [30]; (c) type information can also be used to measure semantic similarity, which has been used to calculate prior probabilities in a Bayesian learning process, alongside creating a set of multiple semantic vectors for each entity [16]; and (d) type-independent hyperspaces can be used to accommodate entities that belong to the same type, constraining the selection of negative samples and favoring LP accuracy by restricting the set of entities ranked during evaluation [24].

The LP evaluation task has originally emerged from the idea that KGs are usually incomplete. Several embedding approaches have been proposed for predicting the missing links in the KGs [32]. During the evaluation process, a typical question answering task aims at completing a triple (h, r, t) with h or t missing, by predicting t given $(h, r, ?)$ or predicting h given $(?, r, t)$, where '?' denotes the missing element. Rather than giving the best answer, LP mimics a recommendation system by ranking the plausibility of a set of candidate entities based on a similarity score. Overall results are usually presented by reporting: a) Mean Rank (MR); b) Mean Reciprocal Rank (MRR) of correct entities; and c) the proportion of correct entities in top-N ranked entities (Hits@N, with N usually equals 10). A LP model should achieve lower MR or higher MRR and Hits@N. MRR calculates the average reciprocal rank of all the entities (relations), and it is less sensitive to outliers comparatively with MR.

3 Materials and Methods

In opposite to a general open-domain KG that contains common sense information, a vertical KG is based on more complex domain-specific categorized multi-relational data, mostly suitable for specific industry applications. Whereas open-domain KGs are wider in terms of breadth, deeper and sparser, domain-specific graphs usually have low level of granularity (higher level of detail) and they are more dense [14]. In addition, the former can be composed of multiple independent sub-graphs, whereas this is usually hard to observe in the latter due to the intra-relational structured data sources they are extracted from.

We aim to use KER learned for categorized multi-relational data in a decision support pipeline. Therefore, instead of trying to complete a KG, we look at the risk assessment task, targeting the probability of a given entity h having (r) a label t that makes a triple in form (h,r,t) true when the resulting probability exceeds a threshold l ($P(h, r, t) > l$), where l is a tuning hyperparameter. Thus, to evaluate the quality of embedding representation, we designed risk prediction as a classification task based on the distribution probability of nearby neighbors in the entity vector space having the target label.

3.1 Datasets

Focused on domain-specific data, we conducted experiments on three publicly available datasets (Mushroom, Epilepsy and CHSI) and on private dataset (Pregnancy) from the clinical domain – data controllers have granted us permission to use and perform analysis on a de-identified version of this dataset. A description for each dataset and the corresponding pre-processing tasks are given below.[1] Overall dataset statistics are shown in Table 1.

Table 1. Benchmark datasets statistics. 'Classes' represents the number of target classification labels (independent target labels are used in *Pregnancy*, whereas target labels are mutually exclusive in *Epilepsy* and *CHSI*. 'Subjects' is the number of entities in the target type (in all datasets consistently represented by the type of *head* entity). 'Triples' in the test set are given by randomly selecting subjects (not triples) from the original KG, except for *Pregnancy*, in which test set was split based on the year each pregnancy started (2010–2014 for training, and 2015 for test); subjects in the test set are never seen in the training set.

		# Subjects				# Triples	
Datasets	Classes	Train	Test	# Entities	# Relations	Train	Test
Mushroom	1	7,537	879	8,485	22	163,593	19,079
Epilepsy	5	10,354	1,146	27,473	178	1,843,012	203,988
CHSI	10	2,828	313	7,034	679	1,059,838	117,720
Pregnancy	3	20,200	4,676	31,472	99	1,270,529	288,270

Mushroom[2] is a publicly available dataset deposited on the UCI Machine Learning Repository that classifies hypothetical samples corresponding to distinct species of mushrooms into edible or poisonous based on 22 categorical attributes describing shape, surface, color, odor, gill, stalk, veil, ring, population

[1] https://github.com/hextrato/KRAL-benchmark.

[2] https://archive.ics.uci.edu/ml/datasets/mushroom.

and habitat characteristics. This dataset was originally used to perform logical rules and further considered as a relatively easy task for machine learning approaches, some reaching accuracy of 100%. Triples are presented in the form of *many-to-one* relations only, and it was used in previous LP evaluation tasks for categorized multi-relational data [5,24].

Epilepsy[3] (Epileptic Seizure Recognition) is also available on the UCI Machine Learning Repository. It presents 178 continuous variables collected for a recording of brain activity for 23.6 s, aiming to assign each of the 11,500 instances (500 individuals × 23 s) to one of five possible classes (1–5), in which subjects in class 1 are taken as having epileptic seizure, and subjects falling in classes 2, 3, 4, and 5 are those who did not have epileptic seizure. Although most authors have done binary classification, namely class 1 (Epileptic seizure) against the others, we kept the risk assessment task focused on all the five independent target classes. All continuous variables have values varying from −1885 to +2047 and they were heuristically normalized into positive and negative ranges of 30 values ($[-30, 0[, [0, 30[, [30, 60[, [60, 90[, ...$) in order to simplify the KG symbolic representation.

CHSI (Community Health Status Indicators)[4] is a dataset designed to support combating obesity, heart disease, and cancer as a component of the Community Health Data Initiative. It provides key health indicators, comprising over 200 measures for 3141 United States counties that enable a more comprehensive understanding on the behavioral factors such as obesity, tobacco use, diet, physical activity, alcohol and drug use, sexual behavior and others substantially contribute to deaths, like the ones due to heart disease and cancer. There is not any specific target label in this dataset. Thereat, for evaluation purposes only, in the context of this work, we designed the evaluation task as a prediction of average life expectancy (ALE) in each county, with target labels varying from 70 to 79+-years-old (10 possible classes).

Pregnancy combines structured and unstructured data extracted from an Electronic Health Record (EHR) system regarding 24,876 pregnancies occurring from 2010 to 2015, comprising demographic and clinical history before (e.g., history of medication, allergies, infections, and other clinical conditions) and during pregnancy (e.g., prescriptions, procedures, and diagnoses). Although the dataset was originally created to perform risk assessment of miscarriage, we added two additional target risk labels: *Hyperemesis gravidarum*, and high risk pregnancy. This is a dataset predominantly composed of *many-to-many* relations (83.7%), expect for the *one-to-many* demographic relations. Data from 2010 to 2014 was used to learn the embedding representation, and risk analysis is performed ever the 2015's patient set (test set).

[3] https://archive.ics.uci.edu/ml/datasets/Epileptic+Seizure+Recognition.
[4] https://healthdata.gov/dataset/community-health-status-indicators-chsi-combat-obesity-heart-disease-and-cancer.

3.2 Method Outline

Although embedding representation approaches are traditionally evaluated using the LP task, we believe LP does not directly impact quality of entity embeddings, and result models are biased, only favoring the LP task accuracy instead. Therefore, our evaluation protocol was designed accordingly to the following phases (further implementation details are given in the subsequent subsection):

1. Firstly, we learn embedding representation for the training set. Triples corresponding to the target classification labels are NOT used during the embedding process to avoid biasing further clustering analysis. MRR score was initially used during training to select the best model.
2. Alternatively, we added a cluster synergy score (KSyn, see 'Implementation Details' section), performed when evaluating embedding representation in conjunction with MRR. KSyn aims to evaluate the ability of each model to capture entity similarities among subjects in each target cluster. We used K-Nearest Neighbor (KNN) algorithm [1] and we tested multiple numbers of clusters (K) to find the best radius to be taken into account when performing synergy analysis.
3. Resulting entity and relation embeddings from the training set are frozen and the test triples are appended to the KG. A second short embedding round is performed to properly accommodate the test subjects in the vector space (only entities from the test set not yet seen during training have their embedding representation learned during this phase).
4. Finally, we extract the vector representation of each subject entity (split into training and test subjects). For each subject in the test set, we calculate the probability distribution of its neighbors (training subjects) regarding each target classification label. The probability of each test subject belonging to any of the target classes is recorded and subsequently used to perform accuracy analysis, looking for the best threshold to optimize ROC (AUPRC due the unbalanced nature of target labels) and F scores.

3.3 Implementation Details

We used an embedding approach proposed for domain-specific categorized multi-relational datasets [24] that utilizes type-dependent vector spaces as a basis for all our experiments. Additionally, we added a feature to activate a relation-based projection that mimics other enhanced translational approaches, such as TransH and TransR.[5]

Type-dependent vector spaces restrict domain and range for each relation and are effective to optimize the selection of negative samples during training instead of random sampling from the whole set of possible entities, lessening the probability of constructing a poor-quality negative triple, and being more efficient and sped up, with reduced impact from uninformative constituents. In

[5] https://github.com/hextrato/KRAL.

addition, only entities belonging to the same type are scored for comparison in the loss function during the validation step.

Formally, given a training set S of categorized triples $(c_h : h,\ r,\ c_t : t)$, embedding vectors for entities and relations are learned, so that each categorized entity $c{:}e$ is represented by an embedding vector $\mathbf{e_c} \in \mathbb{R}^K$, and each relation r is represented by an embedding vector $\mathbf{r} \in \mathbb{R}^K$. A score function f_r (Eq. 1) represents a L2-norm dissimilarity, such that the score $f_r(h_{c_h}, t_{c_t})$ of a plausible typed triple $(c_h : h, r, c_t : t)$ is smaller than the score $f_r(h'_{c_h}, t'_{c_t})$ of an implausible typed triple $(c_h : h', r, c_t : t')$. Then, the optimal KER is learned by minimizing a margin-based (γ) loss function $\mathcal{L}$ (Eq. 2) adapted from TransE, where γ is the margin parameter, $\mathcal{S}$ is the set of correct triples, $\mathcal{S}'$ is the set of incorrect triples $(c_h : h', r, c_t : t) \cup (c_h : h, r, c_t : t')$, and $[x]_+ = max(0, x)$.

$$f_r(h_{c_h}, t_{c_t}) = \|h_{c_h} + r - t_{c_t}\|_{l_2} \tag{1}$$

$$\mathcal{L} = \sum_{\substack{(c_h:h,r,c_t:t)\in\mathcal{S} \\ (c_h:h',r,c_t:t')\in\mathcal{S}'}} [\gamma + f_r(h_{c_h}, t_{c_t}) - f_r(h'_{c_h}, t'_{c_t})]_+ \tag{2}$$

Alternatively, we used a relation-based projection matrix $M_r \in \mathbb{R}^{K\times K}$ to mimic translational approaches that attempt to enhance TransE (Eq. 3).

$$f'_r(h_{c_h}, t_{c_t}) = \|M_r \times h_{c_h} + r - t_{c_t}\|_{l_2} \tag{3}$$

A regularization constraint is used during training to restrict the magnitude of embedding vectors and prevent loss-minimization by inappropriately increasing the embedding norms for each entity e, usually given by $|\mathbf{e}| \leq q$, where q is given by Eq. 4 [24]. Although there is no proven evidence that q improves embedding performance over a fixed magnitude threshold ($|\mathbf{e}| \leq 1$), we found this adaptive constraint favors the embedding vectors to spread the range of latent values in $[-1, +1]$ for each dimension.

$$q = \max(1, \frac{\sqrt{k}}{2}) \tag{4}$$

The primordial assumption when dealing with any kind of ML model is the ability of such resulting model on generalizing. Embedding models are weak regarding to this aspect. Previous KER approaches usually perform a single learning round, including training, validation, and test sets simultaneously, the latter supposedly for testing the generalization ability. However, validation and test sets are required to be designed with entities and relations that appear at least once in the training set.

Instead, we consider the test set should not be seen during the initial training to avoid biasing the resulting model. Therefore, our training protocol introduces substantial changes comparatively to the usual routine for learning KER. We start by using triples from the KG training set only to perform up to 500 training cycles when learning the initial vector representation for entities and relations

– during initial experiments we consistently observed models achieved best performance in early training cycles (≈200-300) for categorized datasets. We tested multiple number of dimensions $k \in \{8, 16, 32, 64, 128, 256\}$ and we used an adaptive adjustable learning rate (η) and learning margin (γ) to monitor performance. η is made smaller (from 0.1 to 0.01) once the performance of the model plateaus, whereas γ is made bigger ($\frac{q}{8}$ to $\frac{2 \times q}{3}$). We tuned hyperparameter by selecting the best performance on a 10-folder cross validation performance based on a combination of MRR and KSyn (see below), and we report the results of each model on the corresponding test set.[6] Subsequently, we mimic TransE-like enhanced models. We pick-up the best model during training and we perform additional 500 training steps, now using a relation-based projection matrix (Eq. 3).

Cluster Synergy (KSyn). When learning KER, we performed a validation step every 20 training cycles looking at simultaneously improving of two metrics: (a) MRR and cluster synergy (KSyn). From the latter we expect to capture the ability of a given embedding representation to approximate similar entities. The resulting embedding representation for the subject entities are clustered using KNN algorithm with multiple variations of $K \in \{16, 32, 48, 64, 96, 128\}$ – the bigger K is, the smaller the average cluster radius become. For each cluster, we look at each pair $(r,\ c_t : t)$ that correspond to a feature value for a given subject $c_h{:}h$. If the probability of $(r,\ c_t : t)$ occurring in a cluster u (i.e. $P_u(r,\ c_t : t)$) is bigger than the overall probability of the same feature-value pair occurring in the entire training dataset $P(r,\ c_t : t)$, we consider the difference $P_u(r,\ c_t : t) - P(r,\ c_t : t)$ as the contribution of the feature-value pair to synergy of cluster u. KSyn of a given cluster u is the average of all positive contributions from each possible feature-value pair within that cluster, whereas KSyn of the resulting embedding model is the average KSyn of all clusters. The average radius m from the best cluster setup is saved to be further used in the final classification task.

Differently from previous KER approaches that use training and test triples simultaneously during training, we consider our approach is more realistic when adding the test set only in a subsequent learning step. In addition, subjects from the test set are totally distinct from those used during training. We perform a second embedding training round aiming to accommodate the test subjects in the vector space. Only entities from the test set not yet seen during training have their embedding representation learned during this phase, whereas embedding representation for entities used during the first training phase are kept frozen.

Finally, we use the embedding representation from all training and test subjects to perform risk assessment as a classification task. The best average cluster radius m learned from the KSyn validation is used as a radius threshold when calculating the probabilistic distribution of target labels in each embedding cluster (each one centered by a test subject). For each target label l, we calculate the probability of l for each test subject s. Thus, each test subject is taken as the

[6] We used a Linux x86 64-bits Intel® Xeon® CPU E5-2630 v4 @ 2.20 GHz as a computing infrastructure for our experiments.

center of a cluster u_s with radius m. Then we use the resulting embeddings from the training subject neighbors within a maximum L2-norm distance m from s, and we calculate the probability of label l happening in cluster u_s. The probability scores in the range [0,1] of each label l for each test subjects are then analyzed regarding AUPRC and F-score to find the best classification threshold.

4 Results and Discussion

We presents our results in four distinct perspectives: (a) we contrast low- *vs.* high-dimensional spaces and we show how the number of dimensions can influence the ability of embedding approaches to capture the semantic relatedness of graph constituents; (b) we present our findings on how LP and cluster quality metrics can be complementary when simultaneously used to both model generalization and embedding quality; (c) we provide evidence that simpler approaches perform better than more sophisticated embedding formulations when targeting embedding quality rather than trying to improve link prediction; and (d) we demonstrate how cluster synergy analysis can be used to provide explainability for a resulting embedding model.

Low- *vs.* High-Dimensional Spaces. In higher dimensional spaces, a density estimator can misbehave when there is no smooth low-dimensional manifold capturing the distribution [3]. Although higher dimensional spaces can provide more space to accommodate entities, this does not necessarily favor the similarity of nearby entities, as evidenced in [5]. We tested the effect of both lower and higher k-dimensional spaces ($8 \leq k \leq 256$), and we present the final classification results (AUPRC) on the test set for each dataset in each k-dimensional space in Table 2. None of the datasets was able to consistently improve classification performance alongside increasing the number of dimensions in the vector space. Oppositely, the number of required k dimensions that best fit the embedding representation seems to be somehow related to the complexity (shape and size) of the dataset and classification tasks. For example, 'Mushroom' and 'Epilepsy' are the datasets devoid of any *many-to-many* relations, thus requiring lower embedding dimensionality.

Link Prediction *vs.* Embedding Quality. MRR and Hits@N are correlated metrics traditionally used as embedding evaluation scores. However, the more MRR can be improved the better embedding quality it is not necessarily entailed. This becomes more evident when we look at the way embedding approaches try to improve overall model accuracy by adding relation-based projections and how they are affected by hyperparameters (learning rate η and learning margin γ). Figure 1 shows how MRR and the proposed KSyn scores evolve along the training process. Each chart presents the two-phase 500-cycle learning process, each phase following Eqs. 1 and 3 (in Sect. 3.3) respectively:

(1) In the first learning phase, η varies from 0.1 to 0.01 in the first 300 cycles, and it is kept fixed at 0.01 so on, whereas γ is fixed at $(q/8)$ along the first 200 learning cycles, when it is then progressively increased up to $(q \times 1.5)$ in the cycle

Table 2. Average AUPRC scores for each dataset on each k-dimensional space on the risk assessment task - average of scores resulting from each classification label - best score in bold for each dataset.

	Datasets			
k-dim	Mushroom	Epilepsy	CHSI	Pregnancy
8	0.9991	**0.5475**	0.3592	0.1506
16	**0.9993**	0.5254	0.3799	0.1628
32	0.9979	0.5195	0.3852	0.1492
64	0.9984	0.4911	0.3844	**0.1651**
128	0.9993	0.4499	**0.4019**	0.1586
256	0.9992	0.4100	0.3978	0.1575

500 (see Eq. 4). Although embedding quality (KSyn) is not necessarily worsen during the last 200 learning cycles, higher values for γ can negatively affect MRR, which seems consistent to results found in [6].

(2) In the second learning phase, a relation-based projection matrix is added to the best model (chosen by selecting the best combination of MRR and KSyn) for additional 500 learning cycles. There is a considerable improvement in the MRR metric in the first cycles (<50), when no further improvement is shown, and models become stable regarding MRR. However, the MRR improvement implies decay in the KSyn score. We believe relation-based projection matrices do not favor embedding quality and make embedding approaches biased by the traditional LP evaluation protocol. One possible reason for this outcome is that non-similar entities separated by opposite hyper-hemispheres (opposite sides of any dimension within the hyperspace), even if they are very close to each other, can be pre-projected to opposite directions by the relation matrix before having the relation vector added to their latent composition.

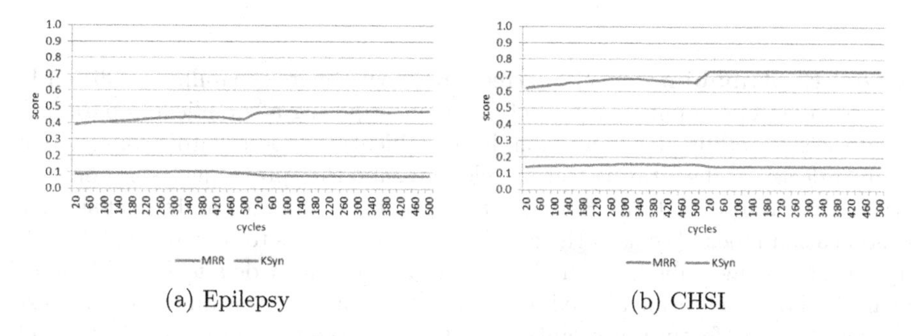

(a) Epilepsy (b) CHSI

Fig. 1. MRR *vs* KSyn on two benchmark datasets – although MRR slightly improves when a relation-base projection matrix is added in the second learning phase, there is a decay in the KSyn score indicating loss of embedding quality.

Simple *vs.* Complex Embedding Approaches. In Table 3, we present the F1-scores for the risk assessment problem designed as a classification task. We compare three distinct learning approaches: (a) firstly, embedding models are learned based on the MRR metric only; (b) then we used a combination of MRR and KSyn metrics to perform evaluation and select the best model during training; (c) finally, we added a relation-based projection matrix on the top of the best model. Although MRR does not directly reflect the resulting embedding quality and synergy for similar clustered entities, it is still a good evaluation metric to be used alongside the process of learning KER. However, when we pairwise MRR with a way of enforcing embedding synergy (MRR+KSyn Linear), the resulting models are more suitable for a classification tasks that directly relying on the embedding representation and the probabilistic distribution of target labels within the entity neighbors in the vector space. Finally, although previous approaches have been exploring more complex ways of learning KER (MRR+KSyn Matrix), we found strong evidence that the LP diverts attention from the fact the overall embedding representation model is expected to carry on a semantically relatedness among similar entities, favoring the knowledge completion task only, thus badly performing when evaluated on tasks the rely on the embedding quality, such as risk assessment.

Table 3. Resulting F1-scores for the risk assessment task regarding each embedding learning validation strategy.

Dataset	Learning validation strategy		
	MRR (only) (Linear)	MRR + KSyn (Linear)	MRR + KSyn (Matrix)
Mushroom	0.9986	**0.9988**	0.8679
Epilepsy	0.5799	**0.5828**	0.4973
CHSI	0.3718	**0.4794**	0.3644
Pregnancy	0.2964	**0.3053**	0.2293

Model Explainability. Decision trees are known by its capability to efficiently deal with large, complicated datasets without imposing a complicated parametric structure, and break down a complex classification process into a collection of simpler decisions, facilitating feature selection, and thus providing a solution that is easier to interpret [21,23]. However, they are model-oriented and target specific classification labels. We used the cluster synergy analysis to provide explainability for a resulting embedding model: (a) first, we can provide a feature-relevance analysis that is performed based on the resulting model regarding a specific test set, i.e., the way features are ranked is sensible to the test subjects (Fig. 2); and (b) to each test subject we can perform feature-relevance analysis and provide the individual explainability to each test case. Figure 3 compares feature-value relevance from two samples of mushroom (poisonous *vs.* edible) in the test set.

Relevant feature-value pairs differ between each other sample, and also differ comparatively to the resulting feature relevance regarding the overall test set, when comparing Figs. 2 and 3.

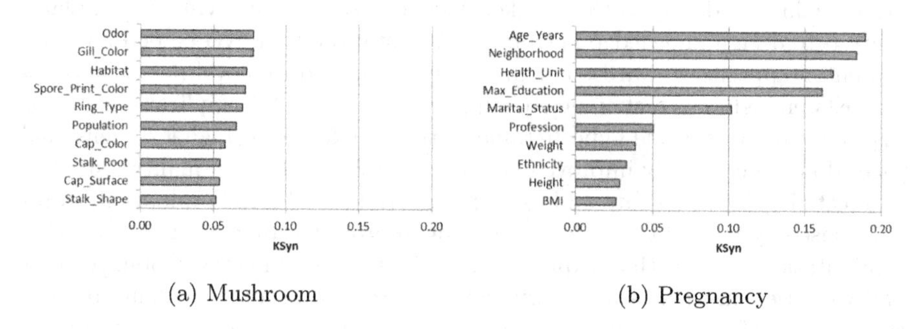

(a) Mushroom (b) Pregnancy

Fig. 2. Feature relevance analysis for the resulting embedding model regarding the test set over the training set.

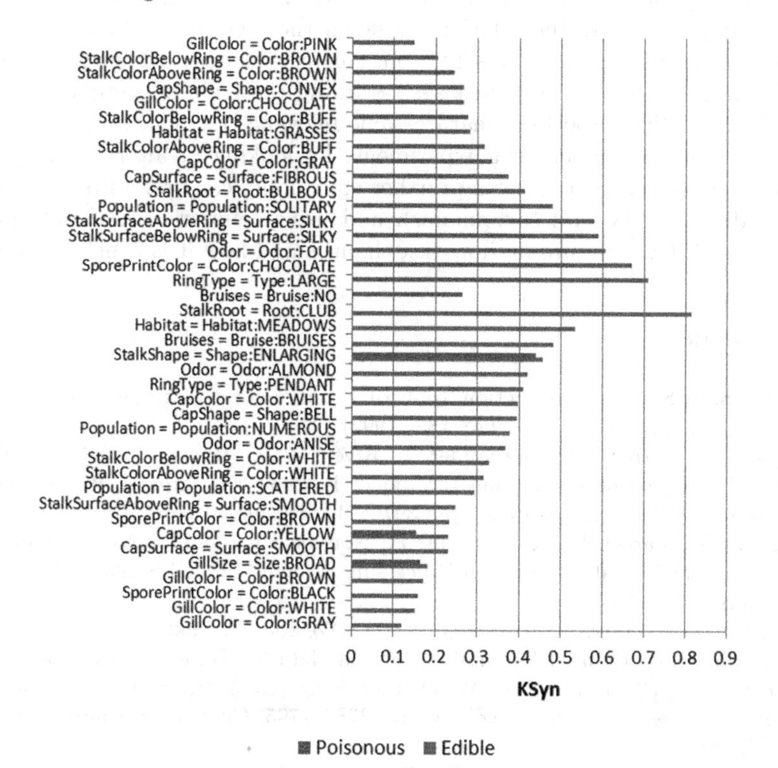

Fig. 3. Risk assessment explainability analysis – KSyn of each pair (feature, value) for two mushroom samples; relevant feature-values pair are different comparing two mushroom samples (poisonous *vs.* edible).

5 Conclusions

While deep learning methods have led to many breakthroughs in practical ML applications, there is still a lack on how to develop systems that can 'understand' and 'explain' the decisions they make. A critical step in achieving ML explainability is to design knowledge meaning representations, and KG embeddings are a potential approach towards that direction. We introduce novel perspectives of using KG embeddings techniques to support subsequent ML applications in this sense and we review some hyperparameter tuning effects: (a) higher dimensional spaces do not necessarily improve embedding performance and quality, but they are affected by learning rate and margin; (b) traditional KER evaluation protocol is biased by the LP task, i.e., embedding approaches are expected to provide representation models that express the semantically similarity among similar nearby entities; instead, whereas trying to improve LP accuracy, enhanced models fail on satisfying the intra-cluster semantic similarity of entity vectors; and finally, (c) we introduce a cluster synergy analysis to support model explainability that enables tracking input entities back into the training gold standard sets and understanding the relations between these entities – from the resulting knowledge embedding representation, cluster synergy analysis provides the overall feature-relevance for a test set regarding the training samples, and the ability to individually perform feature-value relevance to each test subject.

We plan to expand current experiments by looking at alternative ways of dealing with test cases, evaluating further embedding constraints (e.g., regularization, disjoint sets, and taxonomies), and using temporal-based datasets to draw the high-level picture on how risk changes and how it is timely affected.

References

1. Altman, N.S.: An introduction to kernel and nearest-neighbor nonparametric regression. Am. Stat. **46**(3), 175–185 (1992)
2. Ayala, D., Borrego, A., Hernández, I., Rivero, C.R., Ruiz, D.: AYNEC: all you need for evaluating completion techniques in knowledge graphs. In: Hitzler, P., et al. (eds.) The Semantic Web, pp. 397–411. Springer, Cham (2019)
3. Bengio, Y., Larochelle, H., Vincent, P.: Non-local manifold parzen windows. In: Advances in Neural Information Processing Systems 18 (NIPS 2005). MIT Press, Cambridge (2005)
4. Bordes, A., Usunier, N., Garcia-Duran, A., Weston, J., Yakhnenko, O.: Translating embeddings for modeling multi-relational data. In: Burges, C.J.C., Bottou, L., Welling, M., Ghahramani, Z., Weinberger, K.Q. (eds.) Advances in Neural Information Processing Systems, vol. 26, pp. 2787–2795. Curran Associates, Inc., Red Hook (2013)
5. Chung, M.W.H., Liu, J., Tissot, H.: Clinical knowledge graph embedding representation bridging the gap between electronic health records and prediction models. In: Wani, M.A., Khoshgoftaar, T.M., Wang, D., Wang, H., Seliya, N. (eds.) 18th IEEE International Conference On Machine Learning And Applications, ICMLA 2019, Boca Raton, FL, USA, 16–19 December 2019, pp. 1448–1453. IEEE (2019)

6. Chung, M.W.H., Tissot, H.: Evaluating the effectiveness of margin parameter when learning knowledge embedding representation for domain-specific multi-relational categorized data. In: StarAI 2020 - Ninth International Workshop on Statistical Relational AI. AAAI, February 2020
7. Fan, M., Zhou, Q., Chang, E., Zheng, T.F.: Transition-based knowledge graph embedding with relational mapping properties. In: Proceedings of the 28th Pacific Asia Conference on Language, Information and Computing (2014)
8. Guo, S., Wang, Q., Wang, B., Wang, L., Guo, L.: SSE: semantically smooth embedding for knowledge graphs. IEEE Trans. Knowl. Data Eng. **29**(4), 884–897 (2017)
9. Han, X., et al.: OpenKE: An open toolkit for knowledge embedding. In: Proceedings of the 2018 Conference on Empirical Methods in Natural Language Processing: System Demonstrations, pp. 139–144. Association for Computational Linguistics (2018)
10. He, S., Liu, K., Ji, G., Zhao, J.: Learning to represent knowledge graphs with gaussian embedding. In: Proceedings of the 24th ACM International on Conference on Information and Knowledge Management (CIKM 2015), pp. 623–632. ACM, New York (2015)
11. Ji, G., He, S., Xu, L., Liu, K., Zhao, J.: Knowledge graph embedding via dynamic mapping matrix. In: Proceedings of the 53rd Annual Meeting of the Association for Computational Linguistics and the 7th International Joint Conference on Natural Language Processing of the Asian Federation of Natural Language Processing (ACL 2015), 26–31 July 2015, Beijing, China, Volume 1: Long Papers, pp. 687–696 (2015)
12. Kong, F., Zhang, R., Mao, Y., Deng, T.: LENA: locality-expanded neural embedding for knowledge base completion. In: Proceedings of the AAAI Conference on Artificial Intelligence, vol. 33(01), 2895–2902 (2019)
13. Krompaß, D., Baier, S., Tresp, V.: Type-constrained representation learning in knowledge graphs. In: Proceedings of the 13th International Semantic Web Conference (ISWC) (2015)
14. Lin, Jinjiao., Zhao, Yanze., Huang, Weiyuan., Liu, Chunfang, Pu, Haitao: Domain knowledge graph-based research progress of knowledge representation. Neural Comput. Appl. **33**(2), 681–690 (2020). https://doi.org/10.1007/s00521-020-05057-5
15. Lin, Y., Liu, Z., Sun, M., Liu, Y., Zhu, X.: Learning entity and relation embeddings for knowledge graph completion. In: Proceedings of the Twenty-Ninth AAAI Conference on Artificial Intelligence (AAAI 2015), pp. 2181–2187. AAAI Press (2015)
16. Ma, S., Ding, J., Jia, W., Wang, K., Guo, M.: TransT: type-based multiple embedding representations for knowledge graph completion. In: The European Conference on Machine Learning and Principles and Practice of Knowledge Discovery in Databases (2017)
17. Nickel, M., Rosasco, L., Poggio, T.: Holographic embeddings of knowledge graphs. In: Proceedings of the Thirtieth AAAI Conference on Artificial Intelligence (AAAI 2016), pp. 1955–1961. AAAI Press (2016)
18. Nickel, M., Tresp, V., Kriegel, H.P.: A three-way model for collective learning on multi-relational data. In: Proceedings of the 28th International Conference on International Conference on Machine Learning (ICML 2011), pp. 809–816. Omnipress, USA (2011)
19. Nickel, M., Tresp, V., Kriegel, H.P.: Factorizing YAGO: scalable machine learning for linked data. In: Proceedings of the 21st International Conference on World Wide Web (WWW 2012), pp. 271–280. ACM, New York (2012)

20. Rotmensch, M., Halpern, Y., Tlimat, A., Horng, S., Sontag, D.: Learning a health knowledge graph from electronic medical records. Sci. Rep. **7**(1), 5994 (2017)
21. Safavian, S.R., Landgrebe, D.: A survey of decision tree classifier methodology. IEEE Trans. Syst. Man Cybern. **21**(3), 660–674 (1991)
22. Shen, Y., Yuan, K., Dai, J., Tang, B., Yang, M., Lei, K.: KGDDS: a system for drug-drug similarity measure in therapeutic substitution based on knowledge graph curation. J. Med. Syst. **43**(4), 92 (2019)
23. Song, Y.Y., Lu, Y.: Decision tree methods: applications for classification and prediction. Shanghai Arch. Psychiatry **27**(2), 130–135 (2015)
24. Tissot, H.: Using ontology-based constraints to improve accuracy on learning domain-specific entity and relationship embedding representation for knowledge resolution. In: Proceedings of the 10th International Joint Conference on Knowledge Discovery, Knowledge Engineering and Knowledge Management, IC3K 2018, Volume 1: KDIR, Seville, Spain, 18–20 September 2018, pp. 70–79 (2018)
25. Trouillon, T., Welbl, J., Riedel, S., Gaussier, E., Bouchard, G.: Complex embeddings for simple link prediction. In: Proceedings of the 34 Annual International Conference on Machine Learning (ICML) (2016)
26. Wang, Z., Zhang, J., Feng, J., Chen, Z.: Knowledge graph embedding by translating on hyperplanes. In: Brodley, C.E., Stone, P. (eds.) Proceedings of the Twenty-Eighth AAAI Conference on Artificial Intelligence, pp. 1112–1119. AAAI Press (2014)
27. Weston, J., Bordes, A., Yakhnenko, O., Usunier, N.: Connecting language and knowledge bases with embedding models for relation extraction. In: Proceedings of the 2013 Conference on Empirical Methods in Natural Language Processing, Seattle, Washington, USA, pp. 1366–1371. Association for Computational Linguistics, October 2013
28. Xiao, H., Huang, M., Hao, Y., Zhu, X.: TransA: an adaptive approach for knowledge graph embedding. CoRR (2015)
29. Xiao, H., Huang, M., Zhu, X.: TransG: a generative model for knowledge graph embedding. In: Proceedings of the 54th Annual Meeting of the Association for Computational Linguistics (Volume 1: Long Papers), pp. 2316–2325. Association for Computational Linguistics (2016)
30. Xie, R., Liu, Z., Sun, M.: Representation learning of knowledge graphs with hierarchical types. In: Proceedings of the Twenty-Fifth International Joint Conference on Artificial Intelligence (IJCAI 2016), pp. 2965–2971. AAAI Press (2016)
31. Xiong, S., Huang, W., Duan, P.: Knowledge graph embedding via relation paths and dynamic mapping matrix. In: Woo, C., Lu, J., Li, Z., Ling, T.W., Li, G., Lee, M.L. (eds.) Advances in Conceptual Modeling, pp. 106–118. Springer, Cham (2018)
32. Zhang, Y., Wang, J., Luo, J.: Knowledge graph embedding based collaborative filtering. IEEE Access **8**, 134553–134562 (2020)
33. Zhiyuan, L., Maosong, S., Yankai, L., Ruobing, X.: Knowledge representation learning: a review. J. Comput. Res. Dev. **53**(2), 247 (2016)
34. Zhou, Z., Liu, S., Xu, G., Zhang, W.: On completing sparse knowledge base with transitive relation embedding. In: Proceedings of the AAAI Conference on Artificial Intelligence, vol. 33(01), pp. 3125–3132 (2019)

How FAIR are Security Core Ontologies? A Systematic Mapping Study

Ítalo Oliveira(✉), Mattia Fumagalli, Tiago Prince Sales, and Giancarlo Guizzardi

Conceptual and Cognitive Modeling Research Group (CORE), Free University of Bozen-Bolzano, Bolzano, Italy
{idasilvaoliveira,mattia.fumagalli,tiago.princesales, giancarlo.guizzardi}@unibz.it

Abstract. Recently, ontology-based approaches to security, in particular to information security, have been recognized as a relevant challenge and as an area of research interest of its own. As the number of ontologies about security grows for supporting different applications, semantic interoperability issues emerge. Relatively little attention has been paid to the ontological analysis of the concept of security understood as a broad application-independent security ontology. *Core* (or *reference*) ontologies of security cover this issue to some extent, enabling multiple applications crossing domains of security (information systems, economics, public health, crime *etc.*). In this paper, we investigate the current state-of-the-art on *Security Core Ontologies.* We select, analyze, and categorize studies on this topic, supporting a future ontological analysis of security, which could ground a well-founded security core ontology. Notably, we show that: most existing ontologies are not publicly findable/accessible; foundational ontologies are under-explored in this field of research; there seems to be no common ontology of security. From these findings, we make the case for the need of a FAIR Core Security Ontology.

Keywords: Security core ontology · Security reference ontology · Systematic mapping study · FAIR principles

1 Introduction

Security concerns are pervasive in society across different contexts, such as economics, public health, criminology, aviation, information systems and cybersecurity, as well as international affairs. In recent years, multiple ontologies about security have been developed with the main goal of supporting different kinds of applications, such as the simulation of threats and risk management. Covering multiple application areas, *security ontologies* deal with many kinds of core and cross-domain concepts such as risk, asset, threat, and vulnerability [15]. An example of the current worries about security and, in particular, information security is the open letter addressed to the United Nation by the World Wide

S. Cherfi et al. (Eds.): RCIS 2021, LNBIP 415, pp. 107–123, 2021.
https://doi.org/10.1007/978-3-030-75018-3_7

Web Foundation[1]. As the interest in security and related applications grows, the need for a rigorous analysis of the already existing resources and related concepts increases, with the main goal of enabling ontologies for information structures design and reuse. However, because of the different applications, the multiplicity of existing security ontologies dealing with different aspects of this domain brings back the issues of *semantic interoperability*, *domain understanding* and *data and model reusability*, suggesting the need for a common view, i.e., an explicit agreement about the semantics of the concepts therein. Core ontologies are intended to provide a solution to these problems, addressing to some extent the question of the general ontology of a given domain.

To better understand and organize the state-of-the-art on core ontologies of security, we carry out a systematic mapping study by following the guidelines of Petersen et al. [19]. Our contribution is a mapping of the literature about this type of ontology, selecting and categorizing the papers, then identifying research gaps. In particular, we are interested in investigating how much the existing Security Core Ontologies abide by the FAIR principles [13], i.e., how *Findable*, *Accessible*, *Interoperable* and *Reusable* are they?

This output is expected to be the basis of future research towards an ontological analysis of security, the development of a common ontology of security, and the development of an ontology-based security modeling language. The enterprise of building a general security ontology is a well-known open challenge in the field [4]. Indeed, the need for security ontology (rather than just taxonomy of security terms) was already recognized nearly two decades ago [5].

This paper is structured as follows. Section 2 establishes some definitions according to the literature; Sect. 3 presents related work; Sect. 4 describes the process we followed in our mapping study; Sect. 5 presents the outcomes of our analysis; Sect. 6 briefly discuss some results; and Sect. 7 concludes the paper by discussing the main conclusions and prospects for future work.

2 Terminological Remarks on Ontology

The term "ontology" is semantically overloaded. In philosophy, ontology is concerned with "what there is", i.e., with the nature and characteristics of the categories of entities that are assumed to exist by some theory [20]. In Computer Science, "ontology" has several different meanings [21], but one often cited definition is that "an ontology is a formal, explicit specification of a shared conceptualisation" [26]. Obviously each term in the *definiens* requires further elaboration; for that we refer the reader to [10]. The notion of conceptualization is useful here because it allows a broader view of ontology: the things forming a conceptualization of a given domain are used to articulate abstractions of a certain state of affairs in reality [10]; a conceptualization is a sort of abstract model of some phenomenon in the world, identifying the relevant concepts and relations of that phenomenon [26]. So, a definition that is not far from the original philosophical one after all. Adopting this view, we then are going to consider ontology

[1] See https://webfoundation.org/2020/09/un-trust-and-security-letter/.

as whatever expresses such a conceptualization for security in a general level, regardless of the language in which this conceptualization is expressed, i.e., this might be (a) a *conceptual model*, made in a conceptual modeling language (e.g., UML) or just stated in natural language, describing the entities and relations in the domain; (b) a *formal specification* of this conceptual model (for example, in a form of a set of description logic axioms); (c) the *executable information artifact* of this specification (a *Web Ontology Language* file, for example). These three meanings are interrelated and of interest here, because we are aiming at surveying works that present core security ontologies in any of these senses.

Ontologies have different scopes or domain granularities. The broader their scope, the more generic their concepts. A *foundational ontology*, aka "upper ontology" or "top-level ontology", intends to establish a view of the most general aspect of reality, such as events, processes, identity, part-whole relation, individuation, change, dependence, causality *etc.*. Examples include the Descriptive Ontology for Linguistic and Cognitive Engineering (DOLCE), the Basic Formal Ontology (BFO), and the Unified Foundational Ontology (UFO). Foundational Ontologies offer key support in the development of high-quality core and domain ontologies, improving their consistency and interoperability [9]. *Core reference ontologies* are built to grasp the central concepts and relations of a given domain, possibly integrating several domain ontologies and being applicable in multiple scenarios [21]. The terms "core ontology", "reference ontology" and "core reference ontology" or even "common ontology" often denote the same type of artifact [28]. In our context here, this kind of ontology, implicitly or explicitly, deals with the security-related concepts and relations across numerous domains of applications. Both foundational ontologies and core ontologies are application-independent, but the former are domain-independent as well.

3 Related Work

To the best of our knowledge, the first systematic literature review on security ontologies was published by Blanco et al. [3]. The authors highlight that building ontologies in the information security domain is an important research challenge. They identified that most works were focused on specific application domains, and were still at the early stages of development, lacking the available source files of the security ontologies. They concluded that the security community at that time needed yet a complete security ontology able to provide reusability, communication, and knowledge sharing. More than a decade has passed since the publication of that study, so we can verify whether some of its conclusions still hold.

A review made by Sicilia et al. [24], focused on information security ontologies that were published between 2014 and June 2015, which is a rather narrow period of analysis. Arbanas and Čubrilo [2] review and categorize information security ontologies in the same way as Blanco et al. [4]. The former covers the period between 2004 and 2014, and it does not follow a systematic methodology. The latter is a systematic literature review, more aligned with our investigation, though it was made ten years ago; [4] noticed at that time that the majority of security ontologies were focused on formalizing concrete domains to solve a specific problem.

Sikos [25] collects and describes OWL ontologies in cybersecurity, including what he calls "Upper Ontologies for Cybersecurity", which is analogous to what we call core reference security ontologies. Implementations of security ontologies in other languages were not part of that analysis.

Meriah and Rabai [16] proposes a new classification of information security ontologies: (a) ontology-based security standards and (b) ontology-based security risk assessment. The goal of their analysis is specifically to support security stakeholders choice of the appropriate ontology in the context of security compliance and risk assessment in an enterprise.

Ellerm and Morales-Trujillo [6] did a mapping study on security modeling in the context of Enterprise Architecture; they conclude there exists a necessity for reference models, security standards and regulations in the context of micromobility to enable an accurate and effective representation through modeling languages. Here, among other things, we make a case for a similar conclusion about security in a broader context (i.e., beyond micromobility).

As we see, these useful reviews have some limitations, some of which we intend to address in this work. More importantly, we notice *there is hitherto no mapping study exclusively on security core ontologies.* A reference ontology of security (in the sense discussed in Sect. 2 but also in the same sense of [7] for legal relations, [22] for Value and Risk, and [18] for Service) that is applicable to several security sub-domains has yet to be proposed.

4 Methodology

Our procedure is linear and follows the guidelines of Petersen et al. for systematic mapping studies in software engineering [19]:

i) **Research Questions:** We define and justify a set of input research questions, which give us the review scope, including inclusion-exclusion criteria;
ii) **Search Procedures:** We carry out the searches, defining the total amount of papers;
iii) **Screening of the Studies:** We screen them to define solely the relevant papers;
iv) **Classification Scheme:** We analyze certain parts of the relevant papers (keywords, abstract, introduction *etc.*) aiming to formulate categories for classifying the papers;
v) **Results:** We finally gather the data, then producing a landscape of reference ontologies of security - described in the results Sect. 5.

Notice that, in this paper, when we talk about the object of our investigation, we use the terms "work", "paper", "study" and "research" interchangeably.

4.1 Research Questions

Our study is driven by the following research questions that define its scope:

RQ1: *Which security core ontologies exist in the literature?*
RQ2: *Which languages have been used to represent the core ontologies of security?*
RQ3: *Are the specifications of the security core ontologies publicly available? If so, in which source (URL)?*
RQ4: *Which foundational ontologies have been used in the design of security core ontologies?*
RQ5: *Which terms appear most often in the core ontologies of security?*

RQ2 and **RQ4** directly speaks to the topic of *interoperability* [11]; **RQ3** to *findability*; *accessibility* is indirectly assessed through findability, as the absence of the latter blocks the possibility of the former; analogously, *reusability* is indirectly assessed through *interoperoperality* and, hence, **RQ4** (with respect to the need for having rich meta-data about domain-related terms [13]) but it is also related to **RQ2**, as the use of standard languages can foster the reusability of models; **RQ1** defines the space of models of our analysis and **RQ5** the space of concepts. Through **RQ5** we also take the first steps toward a common conceptualization of the domain of security.

Given the listed RQs, we define explicit inclusion and exclusion criteria. The final collection of papers is defined by the studies that, *simultaneously*, suffice every inclusion criterion, *and* that do *not* satisfy any exclusion criteria.

Inclusion Criteria

1. Studies whose goals include introducing an ontology in at least one of the three senses we defined in Sect. 2: conceptual models expressed in any form, formal specifications, and executable information artifacts - each describing a general conceptualization of the security domain.
2. Studies presenting a security ontology that can be seen, at least partially, as a core reference ontology, that is, an application-independent ontology describing the general concepts and relations of the domain [21], and thus, could be reused for different types of application.
3. Studies published in the last twenty years, that is, between 2000 and 2020 (included).[2]

Exclusion Criteria

1. Studies presenting application-based or microdomains ontologies of security - for example, an ontology method to solve the heterogeneity issues in a layered cloud platform [27].
2. Studies available solely in abstracts or slide presentations.

[2] Indeed, our searches suggests there is almost no ontology-based study about security before 2000.

3. Publications not available in English.
4. Works about "ontological security", defined in *international relations studies* as "the need to experience oneself as a whole, continuous person in time - as being rather than constantly changing - in order to realize a sense of agency" [17].
5. Studies on security ontology as a philosophical issue. Though they should be useful for future ontological analysis of security-related notions, our work here is focused on core ontology of security as information artifacts.

4.2 Search Procedures

Considering the RQs, in November 2020, we made several queries to the following databases, according to the search strings shown below in the exact described form: Web of Science, DBLP, ACM Digital Library, Science Direct, IEEE Xplore, Google Scholar, and Scopus. Here, the comma denotes different queries.

To formulate the search strings we assume a sort of "gold standard" based on our previous knowledge about studies that must be retrieved (such as [29,39,41,50]) plus the reference of the related works (such as [4]). The goal of these search strings is to capture as many studies as possible that present some security ontology in the general level required by our scope (see especially inclusion criterion 2). At the same time, the search strings should not retrieve an overwhelming amount of papers; that is one of the reason why they are different according to the database.

Though some papers appear in multiple databases, large databases end up hiding some relevant papers because of the number of results. This is why we use different search strings in different databases: in general, we make broader searches on smaller databases, like DBLP, and we make narrower searches on bigger databases, like Google Scholar. Moreover, we have experimented and cross-checked several search string options in multiple databases before finally deciding the ones that follow.

For each database all queries were made using *the most general field of search*, except when otherwise specified. The number of results retrieved from each database and query is written with parentheses below. We used the *Harzing's Publish or Perish software*[3] to make the queries to Scopus since this software allows a convenient visualization of results. The other queries were made directly to the respective databases. Notice that in DBLP we use the term "ontolog" to capture variations like "ontological", "ontologies" and "ontology", according to the search algorithm of this database.

DBLP (263) = security ontolog (258), core reference ontology (2), common security ontology (2), security core ontology (1)

Science Direct (113) = "core security ontology" OR "security ontology" OR "core reference ontology"

[3] https://harzing.com/resources/publish-or-perish.

IEEE Xplore, ACM Digital Library (55, 67) = "core reference ontology" OR "common security ontology" OR "security core ontology" OR "core security ontology" OR "security conceptual model" OR "security modeling language" OR "conceptual model of security" OR "core ontology of security" OR "common ontology of security" OR "general security ontology" (15, 30), "security knowledge" AND "ontology" (40, 37)

Google Scholar (591) = "common security ontology" OR "security core ontology" OR "core security ontology" OR "security conceptual model" OR "security modeling language" OR "conceptual model of security" OR "core ontology of security" OR "common ontology of security" OR "general security ontology"

Through *Harzing's Publish or Perish software*, we used the "Keywords" search (the most general search) for all queries over Scopus, except for the last two, whose searches were made over "Title words" - constrained to the periods 2010–2015 and 2016–2020.

Scopus, Web of Science (322, 294) = "core reference ontology" OR "common security ontology" OR "security core ontology" OR "core security ontology" OR "security conceptual model" OR "security modeling language" OR "conceptual model of security" OR "core ontology of security" OR "common ontology of security" (53, 160) OR "general security ontology" (4, 1) OR ("security knowledge" AND "ontology") (63, 36) OR security ontology (202, 97)[a]

[a]We have added double quotation marks for exact phrase search in this last query on Web of Science. Otherwise more than 1400 papers are returned.

The first author was the main responsible for executing this phase, though discussion and revision were made with the other coauthors.

4.3 Screening of the Studies

The previous phase of our mapping study found thousands of papers, as seen in the last subsection. To select those relevant for us, according to the aforementioned inclusion-exclusion criteria, we proceeded to read key parts of the text as much as necessary to decide whether (or not) each study satisfies each criterion. These parts include, in the following order, the title, keywords, and abstract, and if those were not sufficient, the introduction and conclusion, and, finally, if needed, the other sections. Moreover, we compared the results of our queries to works classified as security ontology with general purpose by other reviews [4,24] both to select relevant works and to validate our queries. During this process, we realized that some selected studies just mention ontologies of other primary studies in order to achieve their own purposes - hence, except when the former presents progress in the ontology itself, we keep only the primary study, whose main purpose was the introduction of the ontology.

This whole process was made by the first author, then the outcome was checked by co-authors of this paper, then the first author proceeded a double checking to guarantee the relevance of the selected papers according to the inclusion-exclusion criteria. After the conclusion of this phase, the amount of relevant studies was reduced to 57. They were added to "My Library" on the Google Scholar profile of the first author for storage and metadata extraction.

4.4 Classification Scheme

After this procedure, we propose the classification schemes listed below, which are related to the RQs. The classification procedure was executed by the first author, then the outcome was checked and discussed by the co-authors, then the first authors proceeded a double checking.

- **Implementation language (RQ1, RQ2):** The language used to express the ontology, in particular for execution. In case no executable implementation (like OWL) exists, we mention only the conceptual modeling language, such as *Unified Modeling Language* (UML), the logic language (say, description logic), or natural language. We also use the term "UML-like" to refer to a non-specified diagrammatic language that looks like UML class diagrams.
- **Artifact availability (RQ3):** In case the security model had been implemented, is it publicly available? If so, in which source can it be found? We have searched for the implemented model both inside the paper and on internet in general, aiming at finding the latest version of the source and of the file.
- **Foundational ontology (RQ4):** Whether or not the security ontology is based on some upper ontology, like BFO, DOLCE and UFO.
- **Concept words (RQ5):** We consider the term denoting security core concepts appearing in the selected studies, in order to describe their relative frequency. The goal is to support the identification of the most important concepts for a security common ontology.

5 Results

RQ1: Which security core ontologies exist in the literature? Our final data set of studies reporting core reference security ontologies, published between 2000 and 2020, ended up with 57 items. Their distribution in time is shown by Fig. 1. We notice there is no study published between the beginning of 2000 and the end of 2002. The list of the selected studies is attached at the end of the paper, but Table 1 already shows the collected studies presenting some security core ontology while classifying them by their representation language.

RQ2: Which languages have been used to represent the core ontologies of security? Using the data from Table 1, we plotted the pie chart shown in Fig. 2, which clearly shows the preference for OWL as the representation language of core security ontologies. This is not a surprise, considering that OWL 2 is a standard recommended by W3C since October of 2009.

Table 1. The 57 selected studies presenting core security ontologies grouped by their language of implementation (See RQ1, RQ2)

Language	Study
OWL	[29,32,41–46,49,50,53,54,57–59,61,70–73,81,82] [34,36–38,52,60,69,75,77,79,80,85]
UML	[40,48,51,63,65–67,74]
Natural language	[33,39,55,64,68,76]
UML-like	[47,56,83]
RDF	[35,78]
Description Logic	[30,62]
AS^3 Logic	[84]
XML	[31]

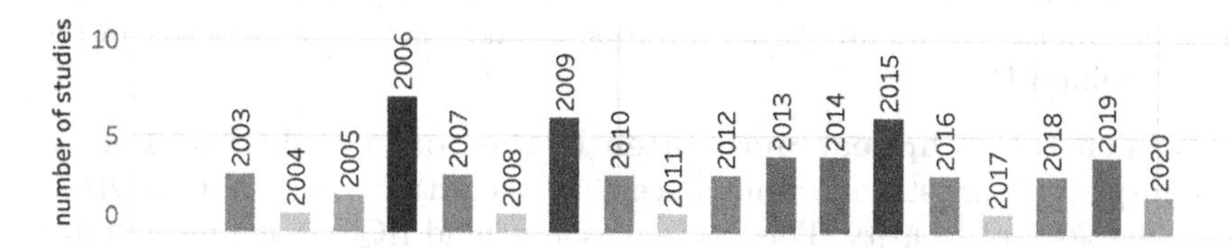

Fig. 1. 57 studies presenting core reference security ontologies grouped by year

AS3 logic	DL	NL	OWL	RDF	UML	UML-like	XML
1,75%	3,51%	10,53%	59,65%	3,51%	14,04%	5,26%	1,75%

Fig. 2. Proportions of representation languages in studies shown on Table 1

RQ3: Are the specifications of the security core ontologies publicly available? If so, in which source (URL)? After searching for the file containing the ontology both within the papers and on the internet, we were only able to find 6 of them, namely [41][4], [49][5], [53][6], [54][7], [35][8], [69][9]. We found some links, even when they were not included in their respective papers, in a dedicated catalog for security ontologies[10].

RQ4: Which foundational ontologies have been used in the design of security core ontologies? Among the 57 selected studies, only four have made

[4] Source: https://github.com/ferruciof/Files.
[5] Source: http://semionet.rnet.ryerson.ca/ontologies/sio.owl.
[6] Source: http://securitytoolbox.appspot.com/stac.
[7] Source: https://www.ida.liu.se/divisions/adit/security/projects/secont/.
[8] Source: https://sourceforge.net/projects/vulneranet/files/Wiki/.
[9] Source: https://github.com/brunomozza/IoTSecurityOntology.
[10] http://lov4iot.appspot.com/?p=lov4iot-security.

use of some foundational ontology, which represents 7% of the total: [37] uses BFO, and [64,70,71] use DOLCE. We briefly present them below.

Massacci et al. [64] present an extended ontology for security requirements based on DOLCE that unifies concepts from the Problem Frames and Secure i* methodologies, and security concepts such as asset and threat.

Oltramari et al. [71] propose an OWL-based ontological framework that is constituted by a domain ontology of cyber operations (OSCO), which is based on DOLCE and extended with a security-related middle-level ontology (SECCO). The authors later extend this framework with the Human Factors Ontology (HUFO) [70] to support predictive cybersecurity risk assessment. Considering human factors, HUFO includes individual characteristics, situational characteristics, and relationships that influence the trust given to an individual.

Lastly, Casola et al. [37] present a "first step towards an ISO-based Information Security Domain Ontology" to support information security management systems. They show a high-level ontology for modeling complex relations among domains, and a low-level, domain-specific ontology, for modeling the ISO 27000 family of standards. To assure higher interoperability, they have made use of the principles behind BFO.

RQ5: Which terms appear most often in the core ontologies of security? Grasping the most important concepts of security is essential to devise a common ontology of security. This is the reason behind RQ5. A frequency table would be helpful to approach the issue. However, the results for RQ3 show few available files, which could be used for precise counting. To deal with that we count the frequency of the most general terms when *explicitly stated inside the ontology described in the very paper.* We also normalize some terms, for example avoiding plural, in order to reflect the frequency of the concept rather than the frequency of the word itself. The result is shown by Table 2, which shows the relative frequency of terms in the sense that it reliably presents the most common terms, though the exact counting can harmlessly vary.

Table 2. Relative frequency of most common concept terms

Concept Term	⩾ #	Concept Term	⩾ #
Vulnerability	24	Risk	9
Asset	23	Attacker	7
Threat	21	Control	7
Countermeasure	12	Stakeholder	6
Attack	9	Consequence	6

Among the 57 selected studies, each work presents a security ontology and each term appears only once in each ontology if it appears at all. Then we can conclude there exists no concept shared by all selected ontologies. This suggests a general lack of agreement between those security ontologies. At this point, we may wonder whether some of the selected ontologies have been more adopted than others. Since the number of citations (in Google Scholar) offers an approach to this question, we notice [33] with more than 6500 citations stands out from any other work. Studies with the number of citations between 100 up to 300 citations are [39,46,50,54,58,65,80].

6 The Need for a FAIR Core Security Ontology

The interest in security ontologies has been growing in the last fifteen years. Most likely because of the rapid growth of Web apps and the popularization of the internet, which remarkably increased information security concerns. However, these ontologies are not easily *findable* since only circa 10% of them are publicly available. Indeed, the lack of availability of security ontologies was noted by [3] in 2008, so this scenario has not changed signifcantly so far.

Moreover, the use of foundational ontologies for grounding core security ontologies is still very incipient. The lack of a foundational ontology supporting the construction of a domain ontology is not a problem *per se*. However, studies have shown that foundational ontologies significantly contribute to prevent and to detect bad ontology design [23], improving the quality and interoperability of domain and core ontologies [14]. Indeed, modeling domain and core ontologies without making explicit the underlying ontological commitments of the conceptualization gives rise to semantic interoperability problems. In fact, there is a strong connection between the ability of articulating domain-specific notions in terms of formal ontological categories in conceptual models, and the *interoperability* of these artifacts [11].

Semantic interoperability is also hindered by the sole use of languages such as OWL, which merely address logical issues neglecting truly ontological ones [9,11]. Once meaning negotiation and semantic interoperability issues have been established by the usage of an ontologically well-founded modeling language, knowledge representation languages such as OWL can be employed for ontology implementation if necessary [9].

Still regarding interoperability, in our set of selected papers, only four ontologies grounded on a foundational ontology were identified, three of which are based on DOLCE. As demonstrated in [22], risk (and, hence, risk management, including risk control measures) is an inherently relational phenomenon. This makes DOLCE an odd choice for grounding a reference ontology in this area, given that it does not support relational aspects (relational qualities and bundles thereof) (see [12]). In contrast, UFO comprises a rich theory of relations that has successfully been used to address related phenomena such as risk, value [22], and trust [1].

In assessing *reusability*, we focus here on two aspects, namely, whether the ontologies *meet domain-relevant community standards* and whether they *provide rich metadata* [13]. Regarding the former, one positive aspect is the fact that most of the ontologies found in our study are represented using international standard languages (e.g., OWL - which is a W3C standard - and UML - which is a OMG *de facto* standard - together account for 73,69% of all the models as per Fig. 1). This at least affords syntactic reusability as well as some predictability in terms of automated inference (in the case of OWL models). However, from a semantic point of view, reusability requires a safe interpretation of the elements being reused in terms of the correct domain categories. In this sense, rich metadata grounded in well-understood ontological categories is as important for safe reusability as it is for safe interoperability. Here, the same limitations identified for the latter (e.g., the use of ontologically-poor languages such as OWL and UML [9], and the lack of use of foundational ontologies) can also be identified as a hindrance to the former.

In summary, our study highlights the need for advancing on the proposal of Core Security Ontologies that are *Findable, Accessible, Interoperable and Reusable, i.e., FAIR* [13].

7 Conclusion

In this paper, we presented a systematic mapping study about the literature on core reference security ontologies, considering the last twenty years of research. We started an analysis to understand this research scenario, the implementation languages that have been used, the availability of the ontology files, the domains, and the role of foundational ontologies in security ontologies. Our mapping study has made clear an important research gap in security ontology field: there seems to be no domain-independent core security ontology in the same general sense of [7] for Legal Relations, [22] for Value and Risk, and [18] for Service . Moreover, foundational ontologies are very underutilized in the field (interoperability). Another gap is the lack of public availability of the actual security core ontologies as artifacts (findability), which makes their analysis and (re)use difficult.

As future work, we intend to use the results of this systematic review as support for the development of a well-founded security ontology grounded on the Unified Foundation Ontology [8] and as an extension of the Common Ontology of Value and Risk [22], following *FAIR* principles [13].

Acknowledgement. This work is supported by Accenture Israel Cyber R&D Lab. (*RiskGraph* project).

References

1. Amaral, G., Sales, T.P., Guizzardi, G., Porello, D.: Towards a reference ontology of trust. In: Panetto, H., Debruyne, C., Hepp, M., Lewis, D., Ardagna, C.A., Meersman, R. (eds.) OTM 2019. LNCS, vol. 11877, pp. 3–21. Springer, Cham (2019). https://doi.org/10.1007/978-3-030-33246-4_1
2. Arbanas, K., et al.: Inf. Organiz. Sci. **39**(2), 107–136 (2015)
3. Blanco, C., et al.: A systematic review and comparison of security ontologies. In: 3rd International Conference on Availability, Reliability and Security, pp. 813–820. IEEE (2008)

4. Blanco, C., et al.: Basis for an integrated security ontology according to a systematic review of existing proposals. Comput. Stand. Interfaces **33**(4), 372–388 (2011)
5. Donner, M.: Toward a security ontology. IEEE Secur. Priv. **3**, 6–7 (2003)
6. Ellerm, A., et al.: Modelling security aspects with archimate: a systematic mapping study. In: Euromicro Conference on Software Engineering and Advanced Applications, pp. 577–584. IEEE (2020)
7. Griffo, C.: Ufo-l: A core ontology of legal concepts built from a legal relations perspective. Doctoral Consortium Contributions, IC3K-KEOD (2015)
8. Guizzardi, G.: Ontological foundations for structural conceptual models. CTIT, Centre for Telematics and Information Technology (2005)
9. Guizzardi, G.: The role of foundational ontologies for conceptual modeling and domain ontology representation. In: 2006 7th International Baltic Conference on Databases and Information Systems, pp. 17–25. IEEE (2006)
10. Guizzardi, G.: On ontology, ontologies, conceptualizations, modeling languages, and (meta) models. Frontiers Artif. Intell. Appl. **155**, 18 (2007)
11. Guizzardi, G.: Ontology, ontologies and the "I" of FAIR. Data Intell. **2**(1–2), 181–191 (2020)
12. Guizzardi, G., et al.: Towards ontological foundations for conceptual modeling: the unified foundational ontology (UFO) story. Appl. Ontol. **10**(3–4), 259–271 (2015)
13. Jacobsen, A., et al.: FAIR principles: interpretations and implementation considerations. Data Intell. **2**(1–2), 10–29 (2020)
14. Keet, C.M.: The use of foundational ontologies in ontology development: an empirical assessment. In: Antoniou, G., Grobelnik, M., Simperl, E., Parsia, B., Plexousakis, D., De Leenheer, P., Pan, J. (eds.) ESWC 2011. LNCS, vol. 6643, pp. 321–335. Springer, Heidelberg (2011). https://doi.org/10.1007/978-3-642-21034-1_22
15. Kovalenko, O., et al.: Knowledge model and ontology for security services. In: International Conference on System Analysis & Intelligent Computing, pp. 1–4. IEEE (2018)
16. Meriah, I., et al.: Analysing information security risk ontologies. Int. J. Syst. Softw. Secur. Prot. **11**(1), 1–16 (2020)
17. Mitzen, J.: Ontological security in world politics: state identity and the security dilemma. Eur. J. Int. Relat. **12**(3), 341–370 (2006)
18. Nardi, J.C., et al.: A commitment-based reference ontology for services. Inf. Syst. **54**, 263–288 (2015)
19. Petersen, K., et al.: Systematic mapping studies in software engineering. In: 12th International Conference Evaluation and Assessment in Software Engineering (EASE) 12, pp. 1–10 (2008)
20. Quine, W.V.: On what there is. Rev. Metaphys. **2**(5), 21–38 (1948)
21. Roussey, C., Pinet, F., Kang, M.A., Corcho, O.: An introduction to ontologies and ontology engineering. In: Ontologies in Urban Development Projects. Advanced Information and Knowledge Processing, vol. 1, pp. 9–39. Springer, London (2011). https://doi.org/10.1007/978-0-85729-724-2_2
22. Sales, T.P., Baião, F., Guizzardi, G., Almeida, J.P.A., Guarino, N., Mylopoulos, J.: The common ontology of value and risk. In: Trujillo, J.C., et al. (eds.) ER 2018. LNCS, vol. 11157, pp. 121–135. Springer, Cham (2018). https://doi.org/10.1007/978-3-030-00847-5_11
23. Schulz, S.: The role of foundational ontologies for preventing bad ontology design. In: 4th Joint Ontology Workshops (JOWO), vol. 2205. CEUR-WS (2018)

24. Sicilia, M.-A., García-Barriocanal, E., Bermejo-Higuera, J., Sánchez-Alonso, S.: What are information security ontologies useful for? In: Garoufallou, E., Hartley, R.J., Gaitanou, P. (eds.) MTSR 2015. CCIS, vol. 544, pp. 51–61. Springer, Cham (2015). https://doi.org/10.1007/978-3-319-24129-6_5
25. Sikos, L.F.: OWL ontologies in cybersecurity: conceptual modeling of cyber-knowledge. In: Sikos, L.F. (ed.) AI in Cybersecurity. ISRL, vol. 151, pp. 1–17. Springer, Cham (2019). https://doi.org/10.1007/978-3-319-98842-9_1
26. Studer, R., et al.: Knowledge engineering: principles and methods. Data Knowl. Eng. **25**(1–2), 161–197 (1998)
27. Tao, M., et al.: Multi-layer cloud architectural model and ontology-based security service framework for IoT-based smart homes. Fut. Gen. Comput. Syst. **78**, 1040–1051 (2018)
28. Zemmouchi-Ghomari, L., et al.: Reference ontology. In: International Conference on Signal Image Technology and Internet Based Systems, pp. 485–491. IEEE (2009)

Selected Studies

29. Agrawal, V.: Towards the ontology of ISO/IEC 27005: 2011 risk management standard. In: International Symposium on Human Aspects of Information Security & Assurance, pp. 101–111 (2016)
30. do Amaral, F.N., et al.: An ontology-based approach to the formalization of information security policies. In: International Enterprise Distributed Object Computing Conference Workshops. IEEE (2006)
31. Wang, A., et al.: An ontological approach to computer system security. Inf. Secur. J. A Glob. Perspect. **19**(2), 61–73 (2010)
32. Arogundade, O.T., et al.: Towards an ontological approach to information system security and safety requirement modeling and reuse. Inf. Secur. J. A Glob. Perspect. **21**(3), 137–149 (2012)
33. Avizienis, A., et al.: Basic concepts and taxonomy of dependable and secure computing. IEEE Trans. Dependable Secure Comput. **1**(1), 11–33 (2004)
34. Beji, S., et al.: Security ontology proposal for mobile applications. In: 10th International Conference on Mobile Data Management: Systems, Services and Middleware. IEEE (2009)
35. Blanco, F.J., et al.: Vulnerapedia: security knowledge management with an ontology. In: International Conference on Agents and Artificial Intelligence, pp. 485–490 (2012)
36. Boualem, S.A., et al.: Maintenance & information security ontology. In: International Conference on Control, Decision and Information Technologies, pp. 312–317. IEEE (2017)
37. Casola, V., et al.: A first step towards an ISO-based information security domain ontology. In: International Conference on Enabling Technologies: Infrastructure for Collaborative Enterprises, pp. 334–339. IEEE (2019)
38. Chen, B., et al.: Research on ontology-based network security knowledge map. In: International Conference on Cloud Computing, Big Data and Blockchain, pp. 1–7. IEEE (2018)
39. Cherdantseva, Y., et al.: A reference model of information assurance & security. In: International Conference on Availability, Reliability and Security, pp. 546–555. IEEE (2013)

40. Chowdhury, M.J.M.: Security risk modelling using secureUML. In: 16th International Conference on Computer and Information Technology, pp. 420–425. IEEE (2014)
41. de Franco Rosa, F., Jino, M., Bonacin, R.: Towards an ontology of security assessment: a core model proposal. In: Latifi, S. (ed.) Information Technology – New Generations. AISC, vol. 738, pp. 75–80. Springer, Cham (2018). https://doi.org/10.1007/978-3-319-77028-4_12
42. dos Santos Moreira, E., Andréia Fondazzi Martimiano, L., José dos Santos Brandão, A., César Bernardes, M.: Ontologies for information security management and governance. Inf. Manag. Comput. Secur. **16**(2), 150–165 (2008). https://doi.org/10.1108/09685220810879627
43. Dritsas, S., Gymnopoulos, L., Karyda, M., Balopoulos, T., Kokolakis, S., Lambrinoudakis, C., Gritzalis, S.: Employing ontologies for the development of security critical applications. In: Funabashi, M., Grzech, A. (eds.) I3E 2005. IIFIP, vol. 189, pp. 187–201. Springer, Boston, MA (2005). https://doi.org/10.1007/0-387-29773-1_13
44. Ekelhart, A., Fenz, S., Klemen, M.D., Tjoa, A.M., Weippl, E.R.: Ontology-based business knowledge for simulating threats to corporate assets. In: Reimer, U., Karagiannis, D. (eds.) PAKM 2006. LNCS (LNAI), vol. 4333, pp. 37–48. Springer, Heidelberg (2006). https://doi.org/10.1007/11944935_4
45. Ekelhart, A., Fenz, S., Klemen, M.D., Weippl, E.R.: Security ontology: simulating threats to corporate assets. In: Bagchi, A., Atluri, V. (eds.) ICISS 2006. LNCS, vol. 4332, pp. 249–259. Springer, Heidelberg (2006). https://doi.org/10.1007/11961635_17
46. Ekelhart, A., et al.: Security ontologies: improving quantitative risk analysis. In: Annual Hawaii International Conference on System Sciences, pp. 156a–156a. IEEE (2007)
47. Ekelhart, A., et al.: Extending the UML statecharts notation to model security aspects. IEEE Trans. Softw. Eng. **41**(7), 661–690 (2015)
48. Elahi, G., Yu, E., Zannone, N.: A modeling ontology for integrating vulnerabilities into security requirements conceptual foundations. In: Laender, A.H.F., Castano, S., Dayal, U., Casati, F., de Oliveira, J.P.M. (eds.) ER 2009. LNCS, vol. 5829, pp. 99–114. Springer, Heidelberg (2009). https://doi.org/10.1007/978-3-642-04840-1_10
49. Fani, H., et al.: An ontology for describing security events. In: SEKE, pp. 455–460 (2015)
50. Fenz, S., et al.: Formalizing information security knowledge. In: International Symposium on Information, Computer, and Communications Security, pp. 183–194 (2009)
51. Fernandez, E.B., et al.: A security reference architecture for cloud systems. In: WICSA 2014 Companion Volume, pp. 1–5 (2014)
52. Guan, H., Yang, H., Wang, J.: An ontology-based approach to security pattern selection. International Journal of Automation and Computing **13**(2), 168–182 (2016). https://doi.org/10.1007/s11633-016-0950-1
53. Gyrard, A., et al.: The STAC (security toolbox: attacks & countermeasures) ontology. In: International Conference on World Wide Web, pp. 165–166 (2013)
54. Herzog, A., et al.: An ontology of information security. Int. J. Inf. Secur. Priv. **1**(4), 1–23 (2007)
55. Jonsson, E.: Towards an integrated conceptual model of security and dependability. In: International Conference on Availability, Reliability and Security. IEEE (2006)

56. Kang, W., et al.: A security ontology with MDA for software development. In: International Conference on Cyber-Enabled Distributed Computing and Knowledge Discovery, pp. 67–74 (2013)
57. Karyda, M., et al.: An ontology for secure e-government applications. In: International Conference on Availability, Reliability and Security, p. 5. IEEE (2006)
58. Kim, A., Luo, J., Kang, M.: Security ontology for annotating resources. In: Meersman, R., Tari, Z. (eds.) OTM 2005. LNCS, vol. 3761, pp. 1483–1499. Springer, Heidelberg (2005). https://doi.org/10.1007/11575801_34
59. Kim, B.J., et al.: Analytical study of cognitive layered approach for understanding security requirements using problem domain ontology. In: Asia-Pacific Software Engineering Conference, pp. 97–104. IEEE (2016)
60. Kim, B.J., et al.: Understanding and recommending security requirements from problem domain ontology: a cognitive three-layered approach. J. Syst. Soft. **169**, (2020)
61. Korger, A., Baumeister, J.: The SECCO ontology for the retrieval and generation of security concepts. In: Case-Based Reasoning Research and Development (2018)
62. Li, T., et al.: An ontology-based learning approach for automatically classifying security requirements. J. Syst. Soft. **165**, (2020)
63. Lund, M.S., et al.: UML profile for security assessment. Technical report STF A **3066** (2003)
64. Massacci, F., Mylopoulos, J., Paci, F., Tun, T.T., Yu, Y.: An extended ontology for security requirements. In: Salinesi, C., Pastor, O. (eds.) CAiSE 2011. LNBIP, vol. 83, pp. 622–636. Springer, Heidelberg (2011). https://doi.org/10.1007/978-3-642-22056-2_64
65. Mayer, N.: Model-based management of information system security risk. Ph.D. thesis, University of Namur (2009)
66. Mayer, N., Aubert, J., Grandry, E., Feltus, C., Goettelmann, E., Wieringa, R.: An integrated conceptual model for information system security risk management supported by enterprise architecture management. Softw. Syst. Model. **18**(3), 2285–2312 (2018). https://doi.org/10.1007/s10270-018-0661-x
67. Milicevic, D., Goeken, M.: Ontology-based evaluation of ISO 27001. In: Cellary, W., Estevez, E. (eds.) I3E 2010. IAICT, vol. 341, pp. 93–102. Springer, Heidelberg (2010). https://doi.org/10.1007/978-3-642-16283-1_13
68. Mouratidis, H., Giorgini, P., Manson, G.: An ontology for modelling security: the tropos approach. In: Palade, V., Howlett, R.J., Jain, L. (eds.) KES 2003. LNCS (LNAI), vol. 2773, pp. 1387–1394. Springer, Heidelberg (2003). https://doi.org/10.1007/978-3-540-45224-9_187
69. Mozzaquatro, B.A., et al.: Towards a reference ontology for security in the internet of things. In: International Workshops on Measurements & Networking, pp. 1–6. IEEE (2015)
70. Oltramari, A., et al.: Towards a human factors ontology for cyber security. In: STIDS, pp. 26–33 (2015)
71. Oltramari, A., et al.: Building an ontology of cyber security. In: Conference on Semantic Technology for Intelligence, Defense, and Security, vol. 1304, pp. 54–61 (2014)
72. Parkin, S.E., et al.: An information security ontology incorporating human-behavioural implications. In: Proceedings of SIN'09, pp. 46–55 (2009)
73. Pereira, T.S.M., et al.: An ontology approach in designing security information systems to support organizational security risk knowledge. In: KEOD, pp. 461–466 (2012)

74. Pereira, D.P., et al.: A stamp-based ontology approach to support safety and security analyses. J. Inf. Secur. Appl. **47**, 302–319 (2019)
75. Ramanauskaitė, S., et al.: Security ontology for adaptive mapping of security standards. Int. J. Comput. Commun. & Control **8**(6), 813–825 (2013)
76. Schumacher, M.: Toward a security core ontology. Security Engineering with Patterns. LNCS, vol. 2754, pp. 87–96. Springer, Heidelberg (2003). https://doi.org/10.1007/978-3-540-45180-8_6
77. Souag, A., Salinesi, C., Mazo, R., Comyn-Wattiau, I.: A security ontology for security requirements elicitation. In: Piessens, F., Caballero, J., Bielova, N. (eds.) ESSoS 2015. LNCS, vol. 8978, pp. 157–177. Springer, Cham (2015). https://doi.org/10.1007/978-3-319-15618-7_13
78. Takahashi, T., et al.: Reference ontology for cybersecurity operational information. Comput. J. **58**(10), 2297–2312 (2015)
79. Tsoumas, B., Papagiannakopoulos, P., Dritsas, S., Gritzalis, D.: Security-by-ontology: a knowledge-centric approach. In: Fischer-Hübner, S., Rannenberg, K., Yngström, L., Lindskog, S. (eds.) SEC 2006. IIFIP, vol. 201, pp. 99–110. Springer, Boston, MA (2006). https://doi.org/10.1007/0-387-33406-8_9
80. Tsoumas, B., et al.: Towards an ontology-based security management. In: International Conference on Advanced Information Networking and Applications, vol. 1, pp. 985–992 (2006)
81. Vale, A.P., et al.: An ontology for security patterns. In: 38th International Conference of the Chilean Computer Science Society, pp. 1–8. IEEE (2019)
82. Vorobiev, A., Bekmamedova, N.: An ontological approach applied to information security and trust. Australasian Conference on Information Systems, p. 114 (2007)
83. Vorobiev, A., et al.: An ontology-driven approach applied to information security. J. Res. Pract. Inf. Technol. **42**(1), 61 (2010)
84. Yau, S.S., Yao, Y., Buduru, A.B.: An adaptable distributed trust management framework for large-scale secure service-based systems. Computing **96**(10), 925–949 (2013). https://doi.org/10.1007/s00607-013-0354-9
85. Zheng-qiu, H., et al.: Semantic security policy for web service. In: International Symposium Parallel and Distributed Processing with Applications, pp. 258–262. IEEE (2009)

PHIN: A Privacy Protected Heterogeneous IoT Network

Sanonda Datta Gupta(✉), Aubree Nygaard, Stephen Kaplan, Vijayanta Jain, and Sepideh Ghanavati

School of Computing and Information Science, University of Maine, Orono, ME, USA
{sanonda.gupta,aubree.nygaard,stephen.kaplan,vijayanta.jain, sepideh.ghanavati}@maine.edu

Abstract. The increasing growth of the Internet of Things (IoT) escalates a broad range of privacy concerns, such as inconsistencies between an IoT application and its privacy policy, or inference of personally identifiable information (PII) of users without their knowledge. To address these challenges, we propose and develop a privacy protection framework called PHIN, for a heterogeneous IoT network, which aims to evaluate privacy risks associated with a new IoT device before it is deployed within a network. We define a methodology and set of metrics to identify and calculate the level of privacy risk of an IoT device and to provide two-layered privacy notices. We also develop a privacy taxonomy and data practice mapping schemas by analyzing 75 randomly selected privacy policies from 12 different categories to help us identify and extract IoT data practices. We conceptually analyze our framework with four smart home IoT devices from four different categories. The result of the evaluation shows the effectiveness of PHIN in helping users understand privacy risks associated with a new IoT device and make an informed decision prior to its installation.

Keywords: Personally identifiable information · Heterogeneous IoT · Privacy notice · Privacy risk analysis

1 Introduction

The Internet of Things (IoT) is composed of interconnected smart devices that can transfer real-time data among each other and with the physical world. It is estimated that by 2025, more than 40 billion IoT devices will be deployed, generating 79.4 zettabytes of data annually [2]. This rapid growth of deployment and level of inter-connectivity between devices raises many privacy risks, such as inference of personally identifiable information (PII) by common third-parties [22] and lack of consistency between the functionality of an IoT device and its privacy policy. For example, IoT devices may collect data not directly relevant to their functionalities, leading to potential inconsistencies between the device's

S. Cherfi et al. (Eds.): RCIS 2021, LNBIP 415, pp. 124–141, 2021.
https://doi.org/10.1007/978-3-030-75018-3_8

data collection practices and its privacy policy [27]. In heterogeneous networks, the potential for common third-parties to infer consumers' PII presents additional privacy risks [22]. For example, Fig. 1 shows an excerpt from the iRobot privacy policy [4] which states that third-parties associated with iRobot have control over the device's data collection practices, and the collected data might be shared according to the third-parties' privacy practices. An iRobot may share PII with the same third-party as other devices connected to the same network. The third-party could, then, infer new information by consolidating data collected by iRobot and other devices.

iRobot permits third-parties to develop apps and tools which interact with our Robots, including, e.g., Amazon Alexa and Google Assistant. If you choose to utilize a third-party app or service, we will permit the third-party to collect information from your Robot. Please note that iRobot does not control the data collection and use practices of these third-parties.

Fig. 1. An excerpt of iRobot Privacy Policy [4]

IoT devices such as smart thermostats and smart light-bulbs have limited capabilities in terms of interacting with consumers, but they are highly connected and may share data among each other and with third-parties. Due to their limited user interface, IoT devices are more likely to notify consumers about their data practices through long privacy policies or terms of services that are written in complex legal jargon [10] than through other mediums. These documents, however, are time-consuming to read and difficult for consumers to understand [19,27]. Hence, providing detailed and effective privacy notices to consumers is one of the major privacy concerns in the IoT.

In recent years, much work has been done to address some of the aforementioned concerns by evaluating the inference of PII [15,20,26], analyzing violations and discrepancies in privacy policies [16,17,24,28–30,32,35], providing design mechanisms for privacy notices [11,21,27] or having question and answering systems to inform users about privacy practices [14,25] described in privacy policies.

While previous research have taken initial steps toward protecting users' data privacy in the IoT, they either focus on analyzing the effectiveness of existing privacy mechanisms or evaluating privacy concerns of a single IoT device [15,20]. Currently, to the best of our knowledge, there is no framework that provides a comprehensive analysis of the privacy risks involved in deploying a new IoT device within a heterogeneous IoT network and informs users about those risks. To address this research gap, we propose a new privacy protection framework, called **P**rotected **H**eterogeneous **I**oT **N**etwork (PHIN), that aims to identify privacy risks associated with adding a new IoT device to the network and notifying the user about those risks [13]. In this paper, we propose PHIN by considering a smart home as an example of a heterogeneous IoT network. Based on the existence of discrepancies in privacy policies [16,17,35] and inference of PII in a single IoT device [15,20,26] demonstrated in previous research, in our framework, we define three privacy risk groups. These are: i) risks related to inconsistencies between the data collected by a new IoT device and the data collection practices specified in its privacy policy, ii) inference risks of PII by common third-parties among IoT devices, and iii) lack of compatibility of a new IoT device's data practices with users' privacy preferences. In this paper, we only focus on identifying the first two types of privacy risks (i.e. (i) and (ii)). Also, we only consider mobile-based IoT devices since they are the preferred channel to access the IoT due to their ease of development [3].

PHIN supports the following functionalities: i) identifying privacy risks from three different perspectives, ii) assigning a privacy risk group to a new IoT device by analyzing the identified privacy risks, and iii) generating a two-layered notice for users with respect to the identified risks. To support these functionalities, we developed a privacy taxonomy, called IoT-DPA (data practices analyzer), by analyzing 75 IoT privacy policies from 12 different categories. To evaluate the effectiveness of PHIN's functionalities, we conceptually analyze our framework with four IoT applications from four different categories: smart health, smart security, smart vacuum cleaners, and smart cooking. Our analysis shows that PHIN can identify potential privacy risks, assign a risk level, and generate a detailed privacy notice for users to help them make an informed decision before deploying a new IoT device within the network.

The rest of the paper is organized as follows: Sect. 2 discusses the related work. In Sect. 3 and Sect. 4, we detail the overview of PHIN, our IoT-DPA (data practices analyzer) taxonomy, and our data practices mapping schemas. Section 5 describes how PHIN analyzes privacy risks. In Sect. 6, we show the conceptual evaluation of our framework and outline the future work. We conclude the paper in Sect. 7.

2 Related Work

As mentioned above, PHIN aim to identify inconsistencies between an IoT application and its privacy policy, risk of inference of PII, and generating a two-layered privacy notice for the user with respect to the identified risks. Therefore, in this section, we present closely related work in the following categories which are related to functionalities of PHIN: i) analyzing privacy practice consistency [6,8,9,17,29,33,35], ii) identifying risk of inference of PII [15,20,26], and iii) generating privacy notice [11,18,27,34].

Analyzing Privacy Practice Consistency. Much research has been done to identify inconsistencies between privacy policies and mobile applications [6,8,9, 17,29,33,35]. Yu et al. [33] propose the *PPChecker* approach which evaluates 1,197 mobile applications and shows that more than 23.6% of them consist of (1) incorrect privacy policies: the policy states that an application does not collect a specific type of PII, but it actually does, or (2) inconsistent privacy policies: there are conflicts between the application's policy and those of third-party libraries. Zimmeck et al. [35] analyzed 17,991 mobile applications' privacy policies with their requirements and show that 17% of them share information with third-parties without mentioning it in their policies. We extend these efforts in identifying inconsistencies to IoT applications.

Identifying Risk of Inference of PII. Some work focus on examining how the PIIs can be inferred by mobile applications or wearable devices [15,20,26]. Liu et al. [15] develop an approach to detect driving activities through wrist-mounted inertial sensors. They show that through a wearable device, it is possible to separate steering movements from other movements such as drinking or eating. An approach called *PowerSpy* [20] illustrates that an attacker can predict a user's location through monitoring device battery activity, which is a function of cell network signal strength. In our work, instead of considering risks of inference of PII for a single IoT device, we aim to identify such risks between a new IoT device and all other devices deployed in the same network.

Generating Privacy Notices. Providing effective privacy notices as recommended by FTC [12] is one of the significant privacy challenges in the era of IoT. Schaub et al. [27] propose guidelines for providing effective privacy notices. To understand consumers' privacy preferences, Zeng et al. [34] interviewed fifteen users and observed that the end-users are mostly concerned about third-party access to their data. To understand privacy and security concerns of smart devices in AirBnBs, Mare et al. [18] interviewed 82 hosts and 554 guests. Their results indicate that users are primarily concerned about information collected by smart devices without their knowledge. To increase awareness and accountability of privacy and data collection practices, Emami et al. [11] propose a prototype of security and privacy labels for IoT devices. The prototype includes fields for collected information, third-parties with whom the device shares the collected information, and the purpose of such collection. However, the label is limited to providing notice about a single IoT device and does not focus on its functionalities when the device is in a heterogeneous IoT network. In our framework, we aim to show a detailed report on the privacy risks of adding a new device within a network of other deployed devices.

Although much research has been done to address some of the privacy concerns in the IoT, very few focus on identifying the risks in a heterogeneous IoT network where many devices share their collected or generated data with common third-parties. To address this research gap, we concentrate primarily on evaluating privacy risks associated with an IoT device in a heterogeneous network and develop a framework which analyzes these risks with respect to the device's privacy policy, other deployed devices, and users' privacy preferences.

3 An Overview of the PHIN Framework

Our privacy protection framework, PHIN, aims to notify users about privacy risks of a new IoT device before its deployment within a heterogeneous network in three risks groups: (i) risks of inconsistencies between a new IoT device and its privacy policy, (ii) inference risks of PII by common third-parties among IoT devices, and (iii) lack of compatibility of a new IoT device's privacy policy with user's privacy preferences. As mentioned in Sect. 1, we identify these three risk groups based on previous research on discrepancies in privacy policies [16,17,35] and inference of PII in a single IoT device [15,20,26].

To evaluate and identify privacy risks related to these risk groups, first, we need to extract sensitive information collected by the new and deployed IoT applications. Then, we need to check if there is any inconsistency between the new IoT application and its privacy policy. Next, we check if there are any common third-parties between the new IoT application and other deployed devices, and we analyze the inference risks of PII associated with the common third-parties. Finally, based on the results of these analyses, we generate a detailed two-layered privacy notice for the user. To achieve these tasks, PHIN includes four major components: (1) Information Extractor (IE), (2) Privacy Checker, (3) Privacy Risk Analyzer (PRA), and (4) Notice Generator [13]. Figure 2 shows the high-level overview of PHIN. We briefly discuss the functionalities of each component in this section and provide details of PHIN's privacy risk analysis approach in Sect. 5.

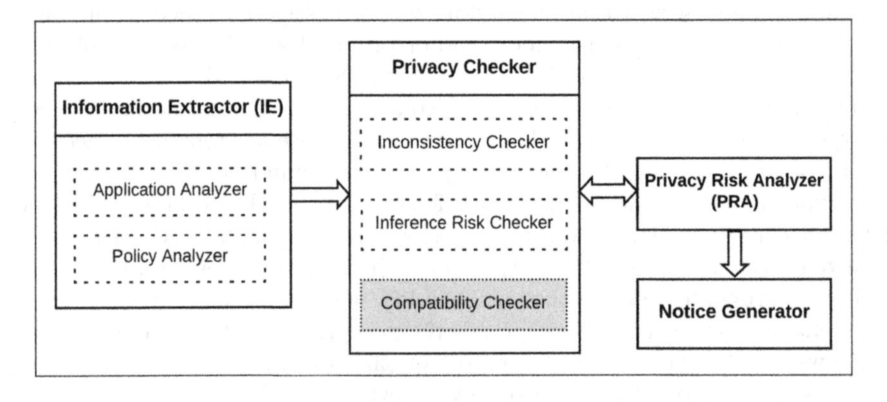

Fig. 2. High-level overview of PHIN framework

Information Extractor (IE). This component has two sub-components: "Application Analyzer" and "Policy Analyzer". The "Application Analyzer" extracts sensitive data collected and processed by the new IoT device through analyzing the application's source code and then classifies them into categories of *Sensitive Data Types* which we define in Sect. 4. The "Policy Analyzer" analyzes privacy policies of the new and already deployed IoT devices and extracts collected information and third-parties with whom the collected information is shared. These collected information and third-parties are then labelled with a category of *Policy Phrases* and *Third-Party Categories*, respectively. We further classify *Policy Phrases* into eight high-level categories of information which we call *Policy Phrase Categories*. Details of these categories are described in Sect. 4. The IE, then, passes the extracted *Sensitive Data Types* and *Policy Phrases* of the new IoT device to the "Privacy Checker"'s Inconsistency Checker to identify inconsistencies between the device and its privacy policy. The IE also passes the extracted *Third-Party Categories* and *Policy Phrase Categories* to the "Privacy Checker"'s Inference Risk Checker to identify inference risk of PII between two IoT devices due to existence of common third-parties. We consider *Policy Phrase Categories* instead of *Policy Phrases* for this purpose since, if two devices collect different information from the same high-level information category, common third-parties may be able to infer PII about the user. Consider the following scenario: A user Alice, who is a Canadian citizen, uses two IoT devices. One device collects "citizenship" and another collects "zipcode" as part of their required information. Although the collected pieces of information are different, they both belong to the "Demographic" information category. These two devices share information with the same third-party company. If the third-party knows that Alice is Canadian and also knows Alice's approximate location, there is a risk that the third-party may infer Alice as the user of these devices.

Privacy Checker. This component serves as inconsistency, inference risk, and compatibility checkers in the PHIN framework. As shown in Fig. 2, the "Privacy Checker" includes three sub-components. Each of these sub-components takes inputs from the "Information Extractor" and maps them to each other as described in Sect. 5 to identify privacy risks associated with the three above mentioned risk groups. In this paper, we only focus on the "Inconsistency Checker" and "Inference Risk Checker", and we do not consider the "Compatibility Checker".

Privacy Risk Analyzer (PRA). The objective of this component is to assign a privacy risk level to the new IoT device based on the results of the three sub-components of the "Privacy Checker". Every time a sub-component of the "Privacy Checker" completes the analysis, PRA updates the risk level of the new IoT device. Therefore, PRA is bidirectionally linked to the "Privacy Checker" component as shown in the Fig. 2. The risk level is set to *low* when both of the following cases take place: (1) if there is an inconsistency within a certain threshold or no inconsistency between the new IoT device and its privacy policy and (2) the new IoT device is the only device in the network. The PRA assigns the risk level to *medium*, if there are inconsistencies between the IoT device and its privacy policy, or there is a risk of inferring PII within a certain threshold. The risk level is *high*, if the inconsistency between the new IoT device and its privacy policy, or the risk of inferring PII exceeds a certain threshold. Figure 5 shows the summary of privacy risk levels. We define the threshold in Subsect. 5.5.

Notice Generator. This component is responsible for generating a detailed privacy notice based on the result of the PRA. The generated notice has two layers. The first layer shows the result of the "Privacy Checker"'s sub-components and the risk level assigned to the device by the PRA. The second layer shows details of the results and other information mentioned in a privacy policy such as purpose(s) of data collection, data retention period, consumers' control mechanisms, and a link to the application's privacy policy.

4 The IoT-DPA Taxonomy and Data Practices Mapping Schemas

In this section, we first describe our *IoT-DPA* (Data Practice Analyzer) taxonomy which we developed to evaluate privacy policies and identify the topic of each segment in a privacy policy. Next, we explain four data practice mapping schemas for *Policy Phrases*, *Policy Phrase Categories*, *Third-Party Categories* and *Sensitive Data Types* which help us categorize the information extracted from the IoT devices in the network and their corresponding privacy policies by "Information Extractor" component of PHIN. To create our taxonomy and these four schemas, we manually analyzed 75 IoT privacy policies randomly selected from the top 100 most popular IoT devices[1] from 12 different categories[2] and the Android public documentation[3].

4.1 The IoT-DPA (Data Practices Analyzer) Taxonomy

We developed the *IoT-DPA* taxonomy by following the guidelines provided by Nickerson et al. [23]. We defined our *meta-characteristics* as *data practices which exist in the IoT privacy policies.* We considered both subjective and objective end conditions as mentioned in [23]. Table 1 shows the dimensions of our taxonomy and their definitions. To define these dimensions, we conducted two empirical to conceptual iterations and three conceptual to empirical iterations on 75 IoT privacy policies. The *IoT-DPA* helps categorizing different parts of a privacy policy and to create our data practice mapping schemas.

Table 1. Our IoT-DPA taxonomy to identify data practices in IoT privacy policies

Dimensions	Definition
Data collection	What and how the information is collected
Third-party sharing	Which third-party and how the collected data is being shared
Data retention	How long the collected information is stored
Purpose	What is the purpose of the collection
Access control	How do users have access and control over their shared data

[1] The most popular IoT devices: http://iotlineup.com/.
[2] The list of analyzed IoT privacy policies: https://tinyurl.com/y3pbhlf8.
[3] https://developer.android.com/docs.

4.2 Policy Phrases and Policy Phrase Categories Mapping Schemas

During our analysis of the 75 privacy policies, we found that some of them use different terminology for the same information. For example, some privacy policies mention "telephone number", whereas others mention "phone number" as collected information. We follow and extend the approach proposed by Bokaei [7] and create a mapping schema as follows: We map "telephone number" and "phone number" to a more generic form "contact number". We call such generic form a *Policy Phrase*. This mapping helps us handle cases such as synonyms and hypo-/hypernyms in privacy policies. We obtained a set of 79 *Policy Phrases* from 75 analyzed privacy policies. Figure 3(b) shows an example of such mapping. Here, the "Geo Location" is mapped to a more generic category "Location".

Since IoT devices collect different information based on their functionalities, we further categorized *Policy Phrases* into *Policy Phrase Categories* which are: Demographic, Identity, Health, Environmental, Biometric, Technical, Activity, and Network Information. In Fig. 3(b), "Location" and "Temperature" are mapped to "Environmental" category. *Policy Phrase* and *Policy Phrase Categories* mapping schemas are available for further research[4].

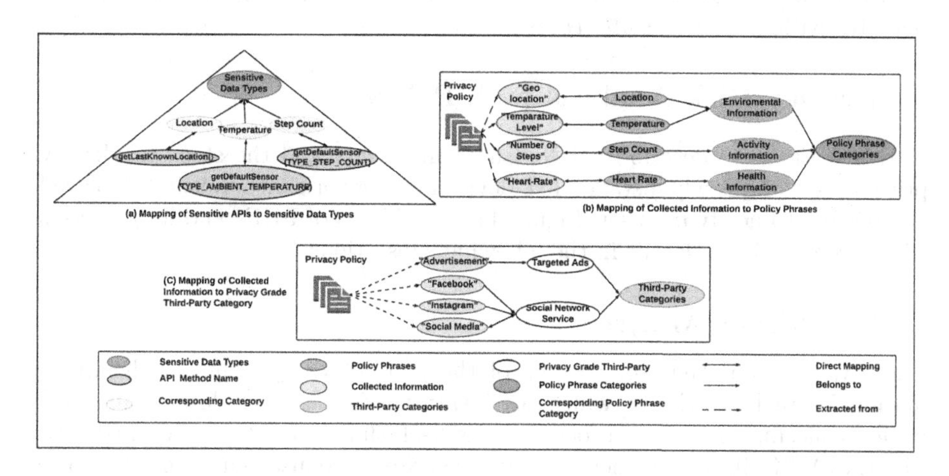

Fig. 3. Examples of mapping (a) Sensitive data types, (b) Policy phrases and policy phrase categories, and (c) Third-party categories

4.3 The Third-Party Categories Mapping Schema

According to privacy regulations such as the EU General Data Protection Regulation (GDPR) [5] and California Consumer Privacy Act (CCPA) [1], companies must list the names of third-parties or third-party categories with whom they

[4] Policy Phrase and Policy Phrase Categories Schemas: https://tinyurl.com/y5ty2a8d.

share collected information. However, based on our manual analysis of 75 privacy policies, we found that 78% of privacy policies mention generic categories of third-parties (e.g., Analytics) while 22% of them provide specific names of third-parties (e.g., Google Analytics). As a result, we only consider third-party categories rather than the specific ones as mentioned in *Privacy Grade*[5]. We then map specific third-party names to these categories. In Fig. 3(c), "Facebook" and "Instagram" are names of specific third-parties which are mapped to the corresponding *Third-Party Category* "Social Media Network".

4.4 The Sensitive Data Types Mapping Schema

To derive *Sensitive Data Types*, we identify the methods used in the application source code to collect consumers' sensitive personal information. In this paper, we only consider mobile-based IoT applications. To access users' sensitive personal data (such as health data), mobile applications are required to ask permission from the user. We define the APIs that require permission as sensitive APIs. We collect Android APIs, strings, and class names from Android public documentation. We then map the sensitive APIs to their categories. For example, the `getDefaultSensor(TYPE_AMBIENT_TEMPERATURE)` API is mapped to the corresponding category "Temperature" (see Fig. 3(a)). We call the categories of sensitive APIs *Sensitive Data Types*[6].

5 Privacy Risk Analysis with PHIN

In this section, we describe PHIN's sub-components and the steps to identify privacy risks of a newly installed IoT device in a network with multiple deployed devices and to notify the user. Figure 4 shows details of PHIN and its processes which we explain in details in the following subsections.

5.1 Application Analyzer

The "Application Analyzer" is one of the two sub-components of the Information Extractor (IE), in which we identify what type of data a new IoT device collects, shares, or processes. Figure 4 shows its steps. We first collect the APK file of the new IoT device. Next, we use our in-house static analysis tool, *PDroid*[7] to search for Android sensitive APIs used in the application with their class names or a string as a parameter. For example, `getDefaultSensor()` returns different values based on a defined string parameter. `getDefaultSensor(TYPE_AMBIENT_TEMPERATURE)` returns environmental temperature whereas `getDefaultSensor(TYPE_STEP_COUNT)` returns numbers of steps taken by the user. Once we extract sensitive APIs, we map them to our *Sensitive Data Types*. For example, in Fig. 3(a), `getDefaultSensor(TYPE_STEP_COUNT)` is mapped to its corresponding *Sensitive Data Types* "Step Counts".

[5] http://privacygrade.org/third_party_libraries.

[6] Sensitive API to *Sensitive Data Types* Mapping: https://tinyurl.com/y5ty2a8d.

[7] GitHub Link: https://www.github.com/vijayantajain/PDroid.

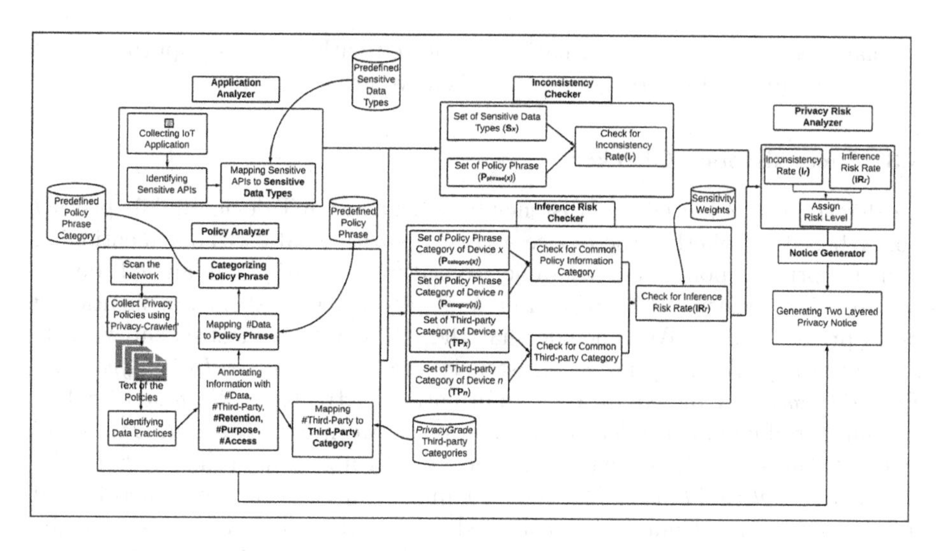

Fig. 4. The PHIN's privacy risk analysis and notice generation processes

5.2 Policy Analyzer

In IE's second sub-component, "Policy Analyzer", we analyze privacy policies of the new and already deployed IoT devices, extract the collected information and third-parties and then categorize them based on the *Policy Phrases*, *Policy Phrase Categories* and *Third-Party Categories*. Figure 4 illustrates the details. We first collect the names of the deployed IoT devices within a network by scanning the network. Next, we extract their privacy policies with the help of our "Privacy-Crawler"[8]. The "Privacy-Crawler" segments the heading and the policies' text from a given HTML file by leveraging a machine-learning-based-segmenter [31]. Once we get the text of privacy policies, we use the *IoT-DPA* taxonomy to identify the data practices. We annotate a privacy policy with the following five labels: #Data, #Third-party, #Retention, #Purpose, and #Access which correspond to dimensions of the taxonomy shown in Table 1.

In the next step, we map the parts annotated with #Data to *Policy Phrases*. Figure 3(b) shows an example of mapping #Data to *Policy Phrases*. For example, "Geo Location" is the information mentioned in a privacy policy labelled with #Data. We map "Geo Location" to its corresponding *Policy Phrase* "Location". Once we complete the mapping, we further categorize them by using the *Policy Phrase Categories* mapping schema. For example, in Fig. 3, *Policy Phrase* "Location" and "Temperature" are further categorized with the corresponding *Policy Phrase Category* "Environmental Information".

Finally, we map the information annotated with #Third-party to our *Third-Party Categories*. In Fig. 3(c), for example, "Facebook" and "Social Media" are annotated with #Third-party. We map them to the *Third-Party Category*

[8] https://github.com/SKaplanOfficial/Privacy-Crawler.

"Social Media Network". Information annotated with #access, #purpose, and #retention are used to provide a comprehensive privacy notice.

5.3 Inconsistency Checker

We determine a potential inconsistency between a new IoT device and its privacy policy based on whether the device accesses sensitive data without mentioning it in its privacy policy. For example, consider a scenario that an IoT device accesses five sensitive data of a user and only three of them are mentioned in its privacy policy. We conclude that the IoT device is inconsistent with its privacy policy. To check for inconsistencies, we use *Sensitive Data Types* and *Policy Phrases* extracted by the "Information Extractor". We first calculate the number of common collected information between *Sensitive Data Types* and *Policy Phrases* as well as the total number of information in both *Sensitive Data Types* and *Policy Phrases.* We then compute the ratio of common collected information to total number of collected information. This ratio gives us the **percentage** of consistency between the new IoT device and its privacy policy. If the two sets have the same number of collected information, it means that the privacy policy is consistent with the application. According to our above scenario, the calculated ratio is 0.60 (the new application is 60% consistent with its privacy policy). Finally, we subtract this ratio from 1, which gives us the Inconsistency Rate (I_r) between the new IoT device with its privacy policy (0.40 or 40% for our given example). We calculate the Inconsistency Rate, as explained, with Eq. 1. Here, S_x is the set of *Sensitive Data Types* of a new IoT application x and $P_{phrase(x)}$ is the set of *Policy Phrases* of a new IoT's privacy policy. $N(S_x \cap P_{phrase(x)})$ is the number of common information between the application and its privacy policy. $N(S_x \cup P_{phrase(x)})$ is the total number of information.

$$I_r = 1 - \frac{N(S_x \cap P_{phrase(x)})}{N(S_x \cup P_{phrase(x)})} \tag{1}$$

5.4 Inference Risk Checker

To check the inference risk of PII, we consider common third-party categories with whom IoT devices share their collected data (i.e. *Third-Party Categories*) and the *Policy Phrase Categories.* We assume that the risk of inferring PII increases with the higher number of common third-parties among IoT devices. As mentioned in Sect. 3, if two devices collect different information from the same information category, common third-parties may be able to infer PII about the user. Hence, we use *Policy Phrase Categories* instead of *Policy Phrases.*

$$IR_{r(x,n)} = w_1 * \overbrace{\frac{N(P_{category(x)} \cap P_{category(n)})}{N(P_{category(x)} \cup P_{category(n)})}}^{\text{common Policy Phrase Categories}} + w_2 * \overbrace{\frac{N(TP_x \cap TP_n)}{N(TP_x \cup TP_n)}}^{\text{common Third-Party Categories}} \tag{2}$$

To calculate the inference risk, first, we compute the ratio of the number of common *Policy Phrase Categories* to the total number of all *Policy Phrase Categories* between a new IoT device and a deployed device. This ratio gives us the **percentage** of common *Policy Phrase Categories* that is collected by two IoT devices. Next, we compute the ratio of the number of common *Third-Party Categories* to total number of all *Third-Party Categories* between a new IoT device and a deployed device. This ratio gives us the **percentage** of common *Third-Party Categories* that is used by the two IoT devices. Finally, we calculate the inference risk rate (IR_r) between the two IoT devices by adding the weighted percentage of common *Policy Phrase Categories* and common *Third-Party Categories* as shown in Eq. 2. Here, $IR_{r(x,n)}$ is the inference risk rate between a new IoT device x and n^{th} deployed IoT device, where n= $1, 2, 3....$ $P_{category(x)}$ and $P_{category(n)}$ are *Policy Phrase Categories* of a new IoT device x and n^{th} deployed IoT device. TP_x and TP_n are *Third-Party Categories* of a new IoT device x and n^{th} deployed IoT device. In this paper, we give equal importance to *Policy Phrase Categories* and *Third-Party Categories.* Thus, we multiply them with w_1 and w_2, which are sensitivity weights with values set to 0.5. However, depending on devices and scenarios, these weights can be adjusted.

$$IR_{r(max)} = max(IR_{r(x,1)}, IR_{r(x,2)},,, IR_{r(x,n)}); \tag{3}$$

Finally, we calculate inference risk rate (IR_r) between the new device x and all the deployed devices within the network. We consider the maximum value of the inference risk rate between the new device x and other deployed devices $IR_{r(max)}$ since it denotes the highest risk of inferring PII if the user installs a new device within their network. We choose $IR_{r(max)}$ by selecting *maximum* value of IR_r as shown in Eq. 3.

5.5 Privacy Risk Analyzer (PRA)

After calculating the I_r and $IR_{r(max)}$ of the new device x, we assign the risk level. Based on the results of the previous sub-components, the PRA assigns a risk level of *low*, *medium* or *high.* Figure 5 shows the overview of the risk levels.

Risk Levels	Inconsistency Rate (Ir)	Maximum Inference Risk Rate (IRr(max))
Low	Ir = 0	IRr(max) = 0
Medium	0 < Ir < 0.50	0 < IRr(max) < 0.50
High	0.50 ≤ Ir ≤ 1	0.50 ≤ IRr(max) ≤ 1

Fig. 5. The overview of privacy risk levels in the PRA

– *Low:* The PRA assigns a risk level *low* to the new device if the results of both I_r and $IR_{r(max)}$ are 0. The risk level *low* can be assigned if *both* of the following cases take place: i) there is inconsistency within a certain threshold or no inconsistency between the new device and its privacy policy and ii) the new IoT device is the only device in the network.

– *Medium:* The PRA assigns a risk level *medium* if any of the two conditions is met: i) $0 < I_R < 0.50$, or ii) $0 < IR_{r(max)} < 0.50$.

– *High:* The PRA classifies a device as *High* risk if any of the two conditions is met: i) $0.5 \leq I_r \leq 1.0$, or ii) $0.5 \leq IR_{r(max)} \leq 1.0$.

5.6 Generating a Notice

After assigning a privacy risk level, we generate a two-layered notice for the user. This comprehensive notice includes the assigned risk level and other data practices' details such as user access control and data retention period. "Layer 1" includes a brief report of the following information: Device No., Device name, Provider's name, Inconsistency with the privacy policy, Common third-party categories, Inference risk of PII, and Risk level. "Layer 2" includes the detailed results of the privacy risk analysis along with details of other data practices' presented in a privacy policy such as purpose and retention period which are captured by IoT-DPA taxonomy, and a link to the device's privacy policy. Fig. 6 shows an example of the two-layered notice created by PHIN.

Privacy Notice- Layer 1	Detail Report
Device Name	Withings Blood Pressure Monitor
Provider	Withings
Inconsistency with Privacy Policy	Present
Common Third-Party with Deployed Devices	Present
Inference Risk of PII	Present
Risk Level	HIGH

Privacy Notice- Layer 2	Back Layer 1
Inconsistency with the Application's Privacy Policy is 36%	
Maximum Risk of Inferring Personally Identifiable Information is 66 %	
Purpose: Providing Product Survices	
Retention Period: Unspecified	
Access and Control: Access personal data via your account or customer support department.	
Privacy Policy: *https://www.withings.com/us/en/legal/privacy-policy*	

Fig. 6. An example of two layered privacy notice proposed by PHIN

6 Evaluation and Discussion

In this section, we conceptually evaluate the PHIN framework by assessing four IoT applications, all from different categories, deployed in a single network. We then discuss the current limitations of PHIN and our future plans to address them.

6.1 Analysis of PHIN Framework

We follow the methodology described in Sect. 5 and conceptually analyze functionalities of PHIN with the following IoT devices: Withings Blood Pressure Monitor (new IoT device), Arlo Home Security Camera (deployed IoT device 1), Dyson V11 Absolute (deployed IoT device 2), and Anova Precision Cooker (deployed IoT device 3)[9].

In the first step, in the IE, we identified and extracted the *Sensitive Data Types* from the APK file of the new IoT device (i.e. Withings Blood Pressure Monitor) with the help of our previously developed static analysis tool *PDroid.* We also identified and extracted *Policy Phrases*, *Policy Phrase Categories*, and *Third-Party Categories* from the new and deployed IoT devices' privacy policies. We show partial extracted information from the IoT devices in Table 2. The full dataset of our evaluation is publicly available[10].

Table 2. Partial extracted information from the new and deployed IoT devices

Extracted information	Withings	Arlo home	Dyson V11	Anova
P_{phrase}	{Location, Temperature, Blood Pressure}	{Age, Video, IP Address}	{Product Feature, Payment, Browser History}	{Location, IP Address, address}
$P_{category}$	Identity, Demographic	{Activity, Environment, Network}	{Activity, Environment,Network}	{Environment, Demographic, Technical}
$TP_{category}$	Marketing, Beacons, Cookies	{Marketing, Utility, Cookies, Beacons}	{Marketing, Utility, Social Network Service}	{Marketing, Payment, Social Network Service}
$S_{withings}$	{Location, Blood Pressure, Heart Rate}	–	–	–

In the next step, we calculated the inconsistency rate I_r between the Withings device and its privacy policy using Eq. 1. Here, S_x is the set of *Sensitive Data Types* collected by the Withings device and $P_{phrase(x)}$ is the set of *Policy Phrases*

[9] https://www.withings.com/us/en/legal/privacy-policy; https://www.arlo.com/en-us/about/privacy-policy/; https://privacy.dyson.com/en/globalprivacypolicy.aspx; https://anovaculinary.com/privacy/.

[10] PHIN's Evaluation Dataset: https://tinyurl.com/yyu2r58r.

extracted by "IE" (x = Withings Blood Pressure Monitor). As shown in the first sheet of our dataset, there are seven common information categories between the Withings device and its privacy policy, and there are 11 total information categories. Based on Eq. 1, the inconsistency rate (I_r) is 0.36 or 36% (see Sheet: Withing Blood Pressure Monitor).

Next, in the "Inference Risk Checker", we calculated the inference risk of PII between the Withings device and the other three deployed IoT devices. We follow the steps described in Subsect. 5.4. First, we calculate the inference risk rate $IR_{r(x,1)}$, $IR_{r(x,2)}$, and $IR_{r(x,3)}$ based on the common *Third-Party Categories* and common *Policy Phrase Categories* between the Withings device and the other three deployed IoT devices. Then, we selected the maximum value of the inference risk of PII $IR_{r(max)}$ among the calculated inference risk rates. For example, as shown in our dataset, there are four common *Policy Phrase Categories* between Withings and Arlo Home, and seven total number of *Policy Phrase Categories* between these two devices. They also have three common *Third-Party Categories* and four total number of *Third-Party Categories.* Based on the Eq. 2, the inference risk rate between these two devices $IR_{r(x,1)}$ is calculated as follows: 0.57 * 0.5 + 0.75 * 0.5 = 0.66 or 66%. Similarly, we calculated $IR_{r(x,2)}$ and $IR_{r(x,3)}$. Finally, based on the Eq. 3, we selected the maximum inference risk rate $IR_{r(max)}$ which is 66% (see Table 3).

Table 3. The evaluation of the PHIN; x = Withings Blood Pressure, i= 1, 2, 3.

Values	Deployed device 1	Deployed device 2	Deployed device 3
$IR_{r(x,i)}$	0.66	0.46	0.58
$IR_{r(max)}$	0.66		
I_r	0.36		

After we calculated the I_r and $IR_r(max)$, in "Privacy Risk Analyzer", we assign the risk level by comparing the values with the given thresholds shown in Fig. 5. According to Table 3, the risk level of the new IoT device, the Withings Blood Pressure Monitor, is *High.* Finally, in "Notice Generator", we generated a two-layered privacy notice where layer 1 shows the privacy risk report analyzed by PHIN and layer 2 shows a detailed risk report with additional information. Figure 6 illustrates this two-layered privacy notice.

6.2 Future Work

Our approach includes four limitations which we plan to resolve in future work:

1. Currently, we consider sensitive APIs which are mentioned in Android Public Documentation. However, since IoT applications have different functionalities, often Android APIs are not enough and developers are likely to use APIs outside of the Android ecosystem (e.g.,Google APIs). To make our API dataset

more robust, we plan to collect APIs from Google APIs[11] which contains a wide range of sensor APIs for developing different IoT applications.

2. As mentioned in Sect. 5, at present, we give equal importance to both common third-party categories and common information categories. The weights can change based on the types of sensitive information collected. For example, health information is more sensitive than demographic information. In future, we plan to conduct a user study to understand the sensitivity level of the types of information categories and users' concern for sharing the information with third-parties. Based on this user study, we will adjust the sensitivity weights.

3. Currently, PHIN identifies privacy risks from two different perspectives: i) identifying inconsistency between the new IoT device and its privacy policy and ii) checking inference risk of PII by common third-parties. In future work, we plan to include a third perspective, which is users' privacy preferences. We will provide an input interface to the user so that they can give their privacy preferences, and PHIN will evaluate the preference against an IoT device's privacy policy and identify potential privacy risks.

4. In this paper, we only conceptually analyzed the functionalities of PHIN with a small heterogeneous network with four IoT devices. As shown in Subsect. 6.1, PHIN can effectively analyze IoT devices and identify potential privacy risks. In future, we will implement all the components of the framework and conduct a comprehensive evaluation of PHIN with a larger heterogeneous IoT network.

7 Conclusion

In this paper, we proposed a privacy protection framework, PHIN, for heterogeneous IoT networks. PHIN focuses on identifying inconsistencies between a new IoT device and its privacy policy, analyzing inference risks of PII by third-parties, and notifying users about the privacy risks of deploying the device in a network. To support the functionalities of the framework and to help identify and extract IoT data practices explained in privacy policies, we developed a privacy taxonomy and data practice mapping schemas by analyzing 75 privacy policies from 12 different categories. We also conceptually evaluated PHIN with four IoT applications, from different categories, deployed in a single network. Our analysis shows that PHIN can help users understand privacy risks and make educated decisions before deploying a new IoT device in a network.

References

1. California Consumers' Privacy Act. https://oag.ca.gov/privacy/ccpa
2. International Data Corporation Forecast. https://tinyurl.com/y694wg2v
3. IoT-based mobile applications and their impact on user experience. https://tinyurl.com/hpwpjnre

[11] https://developers.google.com/apis-explorer/.

4. iRobot Privacy Policy. https://tinyurl.com/w6ghop6. Accessed May 2020
5. The EU GDPR - Article 14. https://eugdpr.org. Accessed May 2020
6. Bhatia, J., Breaux, T.E.A.: Privacy risk in cybersecurity data sharing. In: Proceedings of the ACM on Workshop on ISCS, pp. 57–64 (2016)
7. Bokaie, H.M.: Information retrieval and semantic inference from natural language privacy policies. Ph.D. thesis, The University of Texas at San Antonio (2019)
8. Breaux, T.D., Hibshi, H., Rao, A.: Eddy, a formal language for specifying and analyzing data flow specifications for conflicting privacy requirements. Requirements Eng. **19**(3), 281–307 (2013). https://doi.org/10.1007/s00766-013-0190-7
9. Breaux, T.D., Smullen, D., Hibshi, H.: Detecting repurposing and over-collection in multi-party privacy requirements specifications. In: 2015 IEEE 23rd International Requirements Engineering Conference (RE), pp. 166–175. IEEE (2015)
10. Cate, F.H.: The limits of notice and choice. IEEE Secur. Privacy **8**, 59–62 (2010)
11. Emami-Naeini, P., Agarwal, Y., Cranor, L.F., Hibshi, H.: Ask the experts: what should be on an IoT privacy and security label? In: 2020 IEEE Symposium on Security and Privacy (SP)
12. FTC: Internet of Things: Privacy & Security in a Connected World (2015)
13. Gupta, S.D., Ghanavati, S.: Towards a heterogeneous IoT privacy architecture. In: The 35th ACM/SIGAPP SAC - IoT Track (2020)
14. Harkous, H., Fawaz, K., Lebret, R., Schaub, F., Shin, K.G., Aberer, K.: Polisis: automated analysis and presentation of privacy policies using deep learning. In: 27th {USENIX} Security Symposium ({USENIX} Security 2018), pp. 531–548 (2018)
15. Liu, L., et al.: Toward detection of unsafe driving with wearables. In: Proceedings of the 2015 Workshop on WS, pp. 27–32. ACM
16. Liu, X., Leng, Y., Yang, W., Wang, W., Zhai, C., Xie, T.: A large-scale empirical study on android runtime-permission rationale messages. In: 2018 IEEE Symposium on Visual Languages and Human-Centric Computing, pp. 137–146 (2018)
17. Maitra, S., Suh, B., Ghanavati, S.: Privacy consistency analyzer for android applications. In: 5th International Workshop (ESPRE), pp. 28–33 (2018)
18. Mare, S., Roesner, F., Kohno, T.: Smart devices in airbnbs: considering privacy and security for both guests and hosts, vol. 2020, pp. 436–458. Sciendo (2020)
19. McDonald, A.M., Cranor, L.F.: The cost of reading privacy policies. Isjlp **4**, 543 (2008)
20. Michalevsky, Y., Schulman, A.E.A.: Powerspy: location tracking using mobile device power analysis. In: 24th {USENIX} Security Symposium, pp. 785–800 (2015)
21. Naeini, P., et al.: Privacy expectations and preferences in an IoT world. In: 13th SOUPS' 2017
22. National Science & Technology Council: National Privacy Research Strategy (2016) https://www.nitrd.gov/PUBS/NationalPrivacyResearchStrategy.pdf
23. Nickerson, R.C., Varshney, U., Muntermann, J.: A method for taxonomy development and its application in information systems. Eur. J. Inf. Syst. **22**, 336–359 (2013)
24. Okoyomon, E., et al.: On the ridiculousness of notice and consent: contradictions in app privacy policies (2019)
25. Rosen, S., Qian, Z., Mao, Z.M.: Appprofiler: a flexible method of exposing privacy-related behavior in android applications to end users. In: Proceedings of the Third ACM Conference on Data and Application Security and Privacy, pp. 221–232 (2013)

26. Safi, M., Reyes, I., Egelman, S.: Inference of user demographics and habits from seemingly benign smartphone sensors
27. Schaub, F., et al.: A design space for effective privacy notices. In: 11th Symposium On Usable Privacy and Security, pp. 1–17 (2015)
28. Slavin, R., et al.: PVdetector: a detector of privacy-policy violations for android apps. In: IEEE/ACM International Conference on Mobile Software Engineering & Systems, pp. 299–300 (2016)
29. Slavin R., et al.: Toward a framework for detecting privacy policy violations in android application code. In: Proceedings of the 38th International Conference on SE, pp. 25–36 (2016)
30. Smullen, D., et al.: Modeling, analyzing, and consistency checking privacy requirements using eddy. In: Proceedings of the Symposium and Bootcamp on the Science of Security
31. Vanderbeck, S., Bockhorst, J., Oldfather, C.: A machine learning approach to identifying sections in legal briefs. In: MAICS, pp. 16–22 (2011)
32. Yee, G.O.M.: An approach for protecting privacy in the IoT, pp. 2710–2723 (2016)
33. Yu, L., Lou, X., et al.: Can we trust the privacy policies of android apps? In: 46th Annual IEEE/IFIP International Conference on (DSN), pp. 538–549. IEEE (2016)
34. Zeng, E., et al.: End user security and privacy concerns with smart homes. In: SOUPS
35. Zimmeck, S., Story, P., Smullen, D., et al.: Maps: scaling privacy compliance analysis to a million apps. In: Proceedings on Privacy Enhancing Technologies 2019(3), pp. 66–86 (2019)

PriGen: Towards Automated Translation of Android Applications' Code to Privacy Captions

Vijayanta Jain[1(✉)], Sanonda Datta Gupta[1], Sepideh Ghanavati[1], and Sai Teja Peddinti[2]

[1] School of Computing and Information Science, University of Maine, Orono, ME, USA
{vijayanta.jain,sanonda.gupta,sepideh.ghanavati}@maine.edu
[2] Google Inc., Mountain View, USA
psaiteja@google.com

Abstract. Mobile applications are required to give privacy notices to the users when they collect or share personal information. Creating consistent and concise privacy notices can be a challenging task for developers. Previous work has attempted to help developers create privacy notices through a questionnaire or predefined templates. In this paper, we propose a novel approach and a framework, called PriGen, that extends these prior work. PriGen uses static analysis to identify Android applications' code segments which process personal information (i.e. *permission-requiring code segments*) and then leverages a Neural Machine Translation model to translate them into *privacy captions*. We present the initial analysis of our translation task for ~300,000 code segments.

Keywords: Privacy · Android applications · Neural Machine Translation

1 Introduction

Privacy notices are defined as an application's artifact that inform the users about the collection and processing of their personal information. Since mobile applications may use sensitive personal information for their core functionalities as well as for advertisements and performance assessments [17], the Federal Trade Commission recommends companies to inform users about their data practices and give them choices [5]. Currently, three distinguished mechanisms exist for providing privacy notices for mobile applications: (i) a privacy policy, (ii) an application description, and (iii) a permission rationale. Although these mechanisms seem adequate, the generated notices might be inconsistent, generic, or incomplete [12,15,22,25] and they might remain static when the code changes.

In recent years, much effort has been done to identify inconsistencies between mobile applications and their privacy notices [6,12,15,18,21,25]. Other research attempts to create privacy policies, notices, or permission-based descriptions by

S. Cherfi et al. (Eds.): RCIS 2021, LNBIP 415, pp. 142–151, 2021.
https://doi.org/10.1007/978-3-030-75018-3_9

using a questionnaire [13,19,20], and/or by evaluating the code behavior [23,24]. While the above work are promising and have shown initial success, they either rely on applications' descriptions, which might not fully describe the code's behavior and lead to inconsistencies [13,20], or they rely on predefined templates [23], which may result in generic notices without including any specific rationale for using personal information. More importantly, these approaches do not provide traceability between the source code and the generated privacy statements which can result in inconsistencies when the source code changes.

To address these challenges and to help developers provide privacy notices with rationales that match applications' source code, even when a change occurs, we propose a framework called *PriGen* (pronounced *pry-gen*). PriGen provides a set of deep learning models, methodologies, and tools to help developers generate privacy captions directly from an application's source code. We define *privacy captions* as concise sentences that accurately describe an application's privacy practices. The generated privacy captions can serve four distinct purposes: First, they can be revised and included in different privacy notice formats; second, they can be used as privacy engineering guidelines for developers to help them improve their code; third, they can be used in discussions between developers, legal and policy experts, and business executives while creating privacy notices; and fourth, they can be used for internal and external audits as evidence of application's privacy-preserving practices. The purposes described above provide an overview of how our framework presents additional advantages over other related work (a detailed comparison with related work is described in Sect. 2).

We posit that generating privacy captions from code is a language translation problem, where the source language is an extracted *permission-requiring* code segment (PRCS) (i.e. a type of method which processes personal information), and the target language is a privacy caption that describes the code segment. A PRCS can include multiple methods that are nodes of a call graph. This is because the first method in the call graph (first hop) that processes personal information can share that information with other methods (second, third, or further hops) which also process them. In this paper, we only consider the first hop (a single method) that calls a *permission-requiring* API. PriGen extends the current effort in generating comments and commit messages from source code [3,8,9,14] with Neural Machine Translation (NMT) models [4] to privacy engineering domain for generating privacy captions.

In this paper, we describe PriGen's components which consist of a static analysis approach with its tool, *PDroid*[1], our novel methodology to generate privacy captions, a PRCS dataset, and a trained Code2Seq model (Sect. 3.2). We also present our preliminary results for generating privacy captions and discuss challenges and future work (Sect. 4.1). To show initial results, we downloaded ~80,000 Android applications from the Androzoo collection [2], created a dataset of ~300,000 PRCS, and finally trained Code2Seq[2] [3], an NMT model to generate captions. We leverage Code2Seq for our captioning task because this

[1] https://www.github.com/vijayantajain/PDroid.
[2] https://github.com/tech-srl/code2seq.

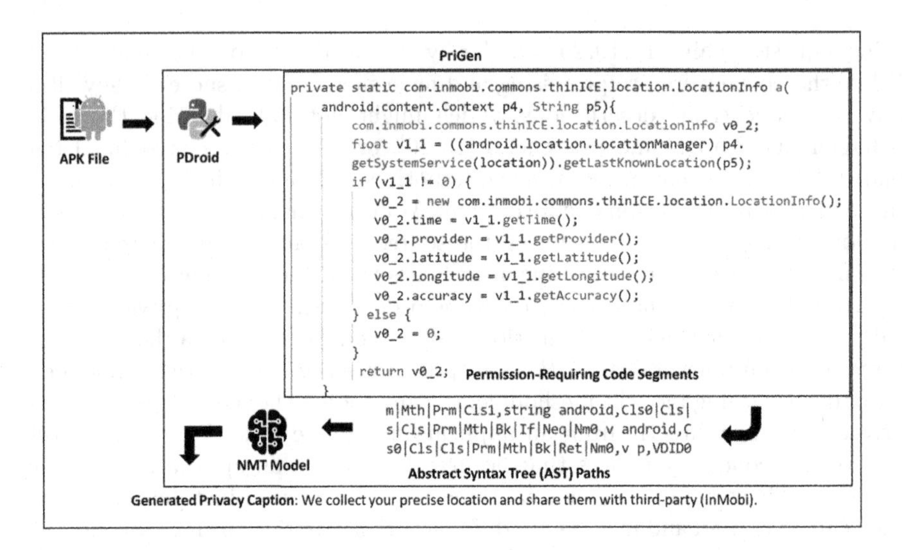

Fig. 1. A high-level overview of the PriGen framework

model provides one of the best scores for the BLEU metric, the source code for the model is open-sourced, and it is easy to experiment with other datasets. Our preliminary results show that, using an NMT model, we can generate accurate and readable captions for a PRCS with 4–5 lines of code.

2 Related Work

Privacy Consistency Analysis: Much research focuses on identifying inconsistencies between an application's source code and its privacy notices [6,12,15,25]. Zimmeck et al. [25] evaluate over a million Android applications and show an average of 2.89 inconsistencies between an application and its privacy policy. Gorla et al. [6] and Liu et al. [12] identify mismatches between Android applications' behavior and their descriptions or permission rationales. While these work are promising, they do not provide any support to resolve the inconsistencies. Our work differs from these approaches in that PriGen helps *resolve* inconsistencies by offering traceability between code and privacy captions (and therefore privacy notices) to determine where changes need to happen (either in code or in the notices).

Generating Privacy Notices: Other approaches attempt to improve the understanding of applications' privacy practices by generating permission explaining sentences [13] or template-based privacy policies [20]. PAGE [20] and AppProfiler [19] generate privacy policies from a set of questions without considering the source code. CLAP mines similar applications' descriptions, identifies reasons behind the required permissions, and summarizes them to generate permission explaining sentences [13]. AutoPPG [23], a closely related work, creates a privacy policy by analyzing the code and using the predefined `subject form object [condition]` format to create privacy statements. This approach provides generic privacy statements that do not contain any rationale. PriGen differs from AutoPPG [23] in that it generates captions that provide rationales for using personal information. This is because the NMT model of PriGen is trained on a dataset of PRCS, which contains multiple hops, and includes human-annotated privacy captions with rationales. Figure 1 shows a PRCS with a privacy caption that the NMT model generates. PriGen generates multiple captions for an Android application which developers can combine to create a single privacy notice such as *"We collect location to find nearby cabs and to share it with third-parties"*. This is a more comprehensive caption as compared to what AutoPPG can generate *"We would use your location (including, latitude and longitude)"* [23]. PrivacyFlashPro [24], another closely related work, is a tool that combines code analysis with a questionnaire to generate legally compliant privacy policies for iOS applications. PriGen differs from PrivacyFlashPro since it provides traceability, i.e., it shows which code segments are translated to which privacy captions. This kind of traceability not only supports consistency between an application's source code and its privacy notice but also enhances internal and external legal or policy audits.

Translating Code to Natural Language Sentences: NMT models have been widely used in software engineering research to generate comments for the source code [3,7,9] or commit messages for the changes in a code [8,14]. These works use an encoder-decoder architecture where an encoder creates an internal representation of the code segment and the decoder translates this representation into natural language statement. Alon et al. [3] propose Code2Seq, an NMT model based on the encoder-decoder architecture to generate code captions. To translate a code segment, this work first generates the abstract syntax tree (AST) of the code and then extracts the paths between the leaf nodes of the tree (i.e. the terminal nodes). These paths between the terminal nodes are used to represent a code segment and as input to the model which are then translated to a caption. We show in Fig. 1 an example of how after extracting the source code, we extract the AST paths that the NMT model inputs and then translates it into a caption. We extract the AST paths using the pre-processing script provided with the Code2Seq repository[3]. LeClair et al. [9] propose to use Convolutional Graph Neural Networks(ConvGNN) to translate code into natural language and achieve better BLEU-4 and ROUGE-LCS scores than Code2Seq. We plan to use ConvGNN model in our future work.

3 The PriGen Framework

3.1 Overview of PriGen

PriGen framework includes two functionalities: (1) Extracting the PRCS data from an Android application and (2) Generating privacy captions with their

[3] https://github.com/tech-srl/code2seq/blob/master/preprocess.sh.

rationale. For this, it first takes an Android Application Package (APK) file, and by using PDroid, our static analysis tool, it identifies and extracts the *Permission-Requiring* Code Segments (PRCS). Next, it preprocesses the PRCS by generating their Abstract Syntax Tree (AST) paths. Finally, it uses a trained NMT model to predict a privacy caption for each code segment from its AST paths. Figure 1 shows a high-level overview of PriGen.

3.2 Creating the Permission-Requiring Code Segments Dataset

We create a PRCS dataset from ~80,000 APK files which we downloaded from the Androzoo Collection [2]. For this, we (a) identify and extract the PRCS using our static analysis tool PDroid; and (b) create privacy descriptions for the PRCS.

Identifying and Extracting the PRCS: To protect the users' privacy, access to users' personal information is governed by system APIs and permissions in Android. If an Android application wants to access users' personal information, it must call a system API and declare the necessary permissions in `AndroidManifest.xml` file. We call the system APIs which require permissions, *permission-requiring* APIs. We leverage a static analysis approach to first identify the *permission-requiring* APIs and then extract the methods that call these APIs (i.e. first hop in a PRCS). In future, we will extract multiple hops.

To identify *permission-requiring* APIs, we manually search the Android Developer Documentation[4] and extract the API name, its class name, its description string, and the personal information accessed. We save this information in a JSON file. We also consider deprecated APIs from the documentation, since some Android applications might be built for older Android SDKs. In this work, we only include 69 APIs that require permissions related to Internet, Network, and Location permission groups. We will develop a thorough mapping of all APIs and permissions, in future.

Next, we developed PDroid, a static analysis tool, using Androguard [1] to *automate* the rest of the process which includes the analysis of an APK file to identify and extract the PRCS. PDroid uses the JSON file created above to automatically locate all the *permission-requiring* APIs that are used in an APK file. Then, using Androguard's call graph analysis, it identifies all the methods that call at least one *permission-requiring* API and extracts their source code. Using PDroid, we automated the process of identifying and extracting ~300,000 PRCS from the ~80K downloaded APK files.

Creating Privacy Captions for the PRCS: After extracting the PRCS, we create a privacy caption for each PRCS. Since manually creating such sentences for a large dataset is not feasible, we propose a semi-automated approach using Human-in-the-Loop framework. For this, we first generate *code* captions

[4] https://developer.android.com/reference/.

of a PRCS using a pre-trained Code2Seq [3] model, and then concatenate these captions with the API descriptions for those *permission-requiring* APIs that are called in the PRCS to create privacy captions. A code caption tells us *"what does this code do?"*, whereas the API description describes *"the nature of the personal information accessed"*. Combining the two should approximately help us answer *"how does this code process the personal information?"*. After concatenation, we evaluate the statements for accuracy and coherence and then, manually modify them to improve their quality. In this work, we only focus on the code captioning step and the Human-in-the-Loop step is left for future work.

To this end, we have trained Code2Seq [3] on Funcom dataset [10] and generated code captions for the PRCS. We choose Funcom as our code captioning dataset, instead of Code2Seq's own Java Large dataset [3], because the captions in Funcom dataset are much longer than in Java Large and the dataset is still considerably large with ∼2 million examples. We train Code2Seq model with the following configuration parameters[5]: Embedding Size - 512, RNN Size - 512, and Decoder Size - 512, and Max Target Parts - 37.

4 Results and Discussion

We quantitatively evaluate our model (i.e. Code2Seq trained on Funcom) with cumulative BLEU-4 [16] and ROUGE LCS [11] scores and compare them with existing results. The scores and the comparison demonstrates the competitive performance of our model at generating code captions. BLEU and ROUGE metrics are commonly used in almost all NMT work and they both measure the similarity between the predicted sentence and the reference sentence. BLEU is a precision-based metric which calculates the number of words (unigram) or pair of words (n-gram) that occur both in the predicted and the reference sentences, and the *cumulative* BLEU score is the weighted geometric mean of all grams from 1 to n. ROUGE is a recall-based metric that also computes n-gram matches but additionally includes recall and F1 scores. ROUGE Longest Common Subsequence (LCS) computes these metrics using the longest sub-sequence of words occurring in predicted and reference sentences. These scores are calculated using a validation set containing 10% samples of Funcom. We achieved a cumulative BLEU-4 score of 18.9 and ROUGE LCS scores for precision, recall, and F1 of 47.71, 44.46, and 44.49 respectively. Comparing our results with ConvGNN [9], we find that our model performed reasonably well. ConvGNN approach achieved a BLEU score of 19.93 which is close to ours. Our ROUGE-F1 score is lower by almost 10 points because of the difference in the two models' architecture. ConvGNN architecture additionally leverages the graph structure of AST paths which improves the scores for the code captioning task. In this work, we used Code2Seq because of the availability of source code but we will use ConvGNN architecture for translation in our future work.

[5] https://github.com/tech-srl/code2seq/blob/master/config.py.

```
public boolean startLocationProvider(org.osmdroid.
views.overlay.mylocation.IMyLocationConsumer p9){
    this.mMyLocationConsumer = p9;
    int v7 = 0;
    java.util.Iterator v6 = this.mLocationManager.
    getProviders(1).iterator();
    while (v6.hasNext()) {
        String v1_1 = ((String) v6.next());
        if ((gps.equals(v1_1)) || (network.equals
        (v1_1))) {
            v7 = 1;
            this.mLocationManager.
            requestLocationUpdates(v1_1, this.
            mLocationUpdateMinTime, this.
            mLocationUpdateMinDistance, this);
        }
    }
    return v7;
}
```

Predicted Code Caption: set the location of the location

```
private void stopListening()
{
    if (this.listening) {
        this.locationManager.
        removeUpdates(this.myLocationListener);
        this.locationProvider = 0;
        this.listening = 0;
    }
    return;
}
```

Predicted Code Caption: removes all the location listeners from this object

Fig. 2. An example of two PRCS with their code captions predicted by the trained code2seq model.

We also conducted a preliminary qualitative analysis of captions generated from code samples in the PRCS dataset. The goal of this preliminary analysis was to inspect the accuracy and readability of the generated captions. For this, we randomly selected 50 code samples from the dataset and then extracted their AST paths and used them as input to the trained Code2Seq model to generate their captions (Sect. 2 explains the working of Code2Seq). The first two authors then manually analyzed the predicted code captions for accuracy and readability. For accuracy, we read each caption and then evaluated if it can accurately describe the code segment (a binary response). For readability, we looked for grammatical correctness and lack of repetition of words and phrases. We found that the predicted code captions were accurate and readable for code segments with 4–5 lines of code (LOC), which is a promising result. However, for longer code segments (i.e. LOC > 5), the captions were vague and often contained repetitive words. The Fig. 2 shows two exemplary PRCS samples from our evaluation set and their captions that were generated by the process described above. For the PRCS on the right, our model predicts a readable code caption that clearly describes what the code segment does with "location listeners". Whereas the predicted code caption for the PRCS on the left does not describe the code segment, does not have any semantic meaning, and repeats the word "location" twice. In future and after we train the NMT model on the PRCS dataset, we plan to conduct a formal and more rigorous qualitative evaluation of the model with a larger number of samples to ensure the accuracy and readability of the captions.

4.1 Current Challenges

We plan to resolve the following challenges in future:

1. The captions predicted by our model are accurate and readable for code segments with 4–5 LOC. To be able to translate longer code segments, our plan is to explore other NMT architectures, such as ConvGNN. We will also manually modify the generated captions for about 30,000 PRCS which will be used to re-train our NMT model.
2. Code reuse is a common practice in software engineering and developers often use code segments obtained from the internet to develop applications. Because of this practice, there are several PRCS that are similar in our dataset which can cause an NMT model to be biased. In future, we will use software similarity to identify and remove duplicate samples.
3. The PRCS dataset contains several obfuscated methods which means that the original identifier names are replaced with generic ones. The NMT model cannot generate meaningful code captions for obfuscated code. To address this challenge, we will remove obfuscated code segments from our dataset, since developers, will use the PriGen's model on their un-obfuscated code.

5 Conclusion

In this paper, we presented a novel approach to help developers create consistent and concise privacy captions from Android applications' source code. We described how by using static analysis, we can identify code segments that process personal information and by using NMT models, we can translate these code segments into privacy captions. We also trained an NMT model on a code captioning dataset and used the model to generate captions for the PRCS. We evaluated the quality of the captions and found promising results. We also discussed the current challenges that we will address in the future.

References

1. Androguard. https://androguard.readthedocs.io/en/latest/
2. Allix, K., Bissyandé, T.F., Klein, J., Le Traon, Y.: AndroZoo: collecting millions of android apps for the research community. In: Proceedings of the 13th International Conference on Mining Software Repositories MSR 2016, pp. 468–471. ACM (2016)
3. Alon, U., Brody, S., Levy, O., Yahav, E.: code2seq: Generating sequences from structured representations of code. In: International Conference on Learning Representations (2019)
4. Bahdanau, D., Cho, K., Bengio, Y.: Neural machine translation by jointly learning to align and translate (2014). arXiv preprint: arXiv:1409.0473
5. Commission, F.T., et al.: Mobile Privacy Disclosures: Building Trust Through Transparency. Federal Trade Commission, USA (2013)

6. Gorla, A., Tavecchia, I., Gross, F., Zeller, A.: Checking app behavior against app descriptions. In: Proceedings of the 36th International Conference on Software Engineering, pp. 1025–1035 (2014)
7. Iyer, S., Konstas, I., Cheung, A., Zettlemoyer, L.: Summarizing source code using a neural attention model. In: Proceedings of the 54th Annual Meeting of the ACL, pp. 2073–2083 (2016)
8. Jiang, S., Armaly, A., McMillan, C.: Automatically generating commit messages from diffs using neural machine translation. In: 2017 32nd IEEE/ACM International Conference on Automated Software Engineering (ASE), pp. 135–146 (2017)
9. LeClair, A., Haque, S., Wu, L., McMillan, C.: Improved code summarization via a graph neural network (2020). arXiv preprint: arXiv:2004.02843
10. LeClair, A., McMillan, C.: Recommendations for datasets for source code summarization (2019). arXiv preprint: arXiv:1904.02660
11. Lin, C.Y.: Rouge: a package for automatic evaluation of summaries. In: Text Summarization Branches Out, pp. 74–81 (2004)
12. Liu, X., Leng, Y., Yang, W., Wang, W., Zhai, C., Xie, T.: A large-scale empirical study on android runtime-permission rationale messages. In: The Symposium on Visual Languages and Human-Centric Computing, pp. 137–146. IEEE (2018)
13. Liu, X., Leng, Y., Yang, W., Zhai, C., Xie, T.: Mining android app descriptions for permission requirements recommendation. In: The 26th International Requirements Engineering Conference, pp. 147–158. IEEE (2018)
14. Loyola, P., Marrese-Taylor, E., Matsuo, Y.: A neural architecture for generating natural language descriptions from source code changes (2017). arXiv preprint: arXiv:1704.04856
15. Okoyomon, E., et al.: On the ridiculousness of notice and consent: contradictions in app privacy policies (2019)
16. Papineni, K., Roukos, S., Ward, T., Zhu, W.J.: BLEU: a method for automatic evaluation of machine translation. In: Proceedings of the 40th Annual Meeting on Association for Computational Linguistics, pp. 311–318. ACL (2002)
17. Peddinti, S.T., Bilogrevic, I., Taft, N., Pelikan, M., Erlingsson, Ú., Anthonysamy, P., Hogben, G.: Reducing permission requests in mobile apps. In: Proceedings of the Internet Measurement Conference, pp. 259–266 (2019)
18. Reyes, I., et al.: "won't somebody think of the children?" Examining COPPA compliance at scale. Proc. PETS **2018**(3), 63–83 (2018)
19. Rosen, S., Qian, Z., Mao, Z.M.: Appprofiler: a flexible method of exposing privacy-related behavior in android applications to end users. In: Proceedings of the Third ACM Conference on Data and Application Security and Privacy, pp. 221–232 (2013)
20. Rowan, M., Dehlinger, J.: Encouraging privacy by design concepts with privacy policy auto-generation in eclipse (page). In: Proceedings of the 2014 Workshop on Eclipse Technology eXchange, pp. 9–14 (2014)
21. Slavin, R., et al.: PVDetector: a detector of privacy-policy violations for android apps. In: IEEE/ACM International Conference of MOBILESoft, pp. 299–300 (2016)
22. Sun, R., Xue, M.: Quality assessment of online automated privacy policy generators: an empirical study. In: Proceedings of the Evaluation and Assessment in Software Engineering, pp. 270–275 (2020)
23. Yu, L., Zhang, T., Luo, X., Xue, L., Chang, H.: Toward automatically generating privacy policy for android apps. IEEE Trans. Inf. Forensics Secur. **12**(4), 865–880 (2016)

24. Zimmeck, S., Goldstein, R., Baraka, D.: Privacyflash pro: automating privacy policy generation for mobile apps. In: 28th Network and Distributed System Security Symposium (NDSS 2021). NDSS 2021, Internet Society, Online, February 2021
25. Zimmeck, S., et al.: Maps: scaling privacy compliance analysis to a million apps. Proc. PETs **2019**(3), 66–86 (2019)

CompLicy: Evaluating the GDPR Alignment of Privacy Policies - A Study on Web Platforms

Evangelia Vanezi(✉), George Zampa, Christos Mettouris, Alexandros Yeratziotis, and George A. Papadopoulos

Department of Computer Science, University of Cyprus, Nicosia, Cyprus
{evanez01,gzampa01,mettour,ayerat01,george}@cs.ucy.ac.cy

Abstract. The European Union General Data Protection Regulation (GDPR) came into effect on May 25, 2018, imposing new rights and obligations for the collection and processing of EU citizens personal data. Inevitably, privacy policies of systems handling such data are required to be adapted accordingly. Specific rights and provisions are now required to be communicated to the users, as specified in GDPR Articles 12-14. This work aims to provide insights on whether privacy policies are aligned to the GDPR in this regard, i.e., including the needed information, formulated in sets of terms, by studying the paradigm of web platforms. We present: (1) a defined set of 89 terms, in 7 groups that need to be included within a systems' privacy policy, resulting from a study of the GDPR and from an examination and analysis of real-life web platforms privacy policies; (2) the CompLicy tool, which as a first step crawls a given web platform, to infer whether a privacy policy page exists and, if it does, subsequently parses it, identifying GDPR terms and groups within, and finally, providing results for the inclusion of the necessary GDPR information within the aforementioned policy; (3) the evaluation of 148 existing web platforms, from 5 different sectors: (i) banking, (ii) e-commerce, (iii) education, (iv) travelling, and (v) social media, presenting the results.

Keywords: GDPR compliance · Privacy policies · Web platforms

1 Introduction

Privacy, constituting one of the fundamental rights of the European Union (EU) [3] was recently established in a legal framework through the EU General Data Protection Regulation (GDPR) [4], that came into effect on May 25, 2018. Privacy is becoming a critical issue as the usage of systems collecting and processing user personal data[1] is increasing. Based on recent statistics[2], it is

[1] According to GDPR, personal data are defined as information that relates to an identified or identifiable individual.

[2] https://www.statista.com/statistics/278414/number-of-worldwide-social-network-users/.

S. Cherfi et al. (Eds.): RCIS 2021, LNBIP 415, pp. 152–168, 2021.
https://doi.org/10.1007/978-3-030-75018-3_10

estimated that by 2025, 4.41 billion people will be owning social media accounts. In addition, the number of digital buyers worldwide is increasing each year. In 2020, an estimated 2.05 billion people purchased goods or services online, estimated to increase to 2.14 billions for 2021[3]. On top of that, in 2020, the usage of online educational sites has increased substantially due to the COVID-19 worldwide crisis, imposing a digital online education scheme. Large numbers of learners are impacted by this change[4]. Using such systems, users provide their personal data, which are being stored and processed in several ways. Privacy policies are included into systems, to describe the rights and obligations of the involved parties, i.e., the system and its users, in regards to personal data collection, storage, and processing. As such, all systems that are processing personal data of individuals need to include a properly formed privacy policy, providing all needed information to the users.

With the application of the GDPR, privacy policies were imposed to change and adapt their contents. Specific rights and provisions are now required to be communicated to the users, as specified in GDPR Articles 12-14. As defined, "the controller shall take appropriate measures to provide any mandatory information and communication relating to processing to the data subject", and "the controller shall provide the data subject with information necessary to ensure fair and transparent processing", including the different user rights defined within Articles 12-23 of the GDPR. Our aim is to study whether the privacy policies of software systems are following the GDPR in this regard, i.e., including and communicating the needed information to the users. The tool developed, is aiming to provide a higher level check of the inclusion of the needed GDPR information, formulated in sets of terms, within privacy policies. Extensive manual auditing or more sophisticated methodologies, e.g., exploiting Artificial Intelligence or Natural Language Processing, could be complementary, in order to examine and analyse the text in a deeper level of detail. In addition, our work does not check whether the actual system implementation (i.e., the code), complies with the content of its privacy policy, nor with the GDPR.

Towards our aim, we focus on the case study of web platforms. Web platforms were selected as they comprise a huge portion of the market, being also easily accessible in an open-manner for both users, and researchers. According to statistics[5], by 2019, 1.72 billion websites were published on the web. Our target group includes both users and software engineers. Long before the GDPR, it was shown that users do not usually read the privacy policies, but when they do, it is difficult to comprehend [8]. Even after the definition of articles mandating the clear and understandable form of privacy policies, their readability and usability is still under investigation [6,9]. Our work aims to help users understand whether a system's privacy policy follows the GDPR guidelines by providing a summary of the included and excluded terms. On the other hand, software

[3] https://www.statista.com/statistics/251666/number-of-digital-buyers-worldwide/.

[4] https://www.statista.com/chart/21224/learners-impacted-by-national-school-closures/, https://en.unesco.org/covid19/educationresponse.

[5] https://www.statista.com/chart/19058/how-many-websites-are-there/.

system engineering methodologies do not explicitly capture privacy requirements or privacy policies. Software engineers mostly use the vocabulary of data security to approach privacy challenges, which limits their perceptions of privacy mainly to third-party threats coming from outside [5]. In addition, software engineers are not familiar with legal content. Our work can also provide assistance to engineers in monitoring privacy compliance in a system design, by indicating the needed, included and missing rights and provisions from within the privacy policy text, serving as a guideline for the functionalities that are expected to be implemented into the actual system.

Towards reaching our aims we present: (1) a defined set of 89 terms, in 7 groups that need to be included within a system's privacy policy, resulting from a study of the GDPR and from an examination and analysis of real-life web platforms privacy policies; (2) a tool developed (CompLicy), which as a first step crawls a given web platform, to infer whether a privacy policy page exists and, if it does, subsequently parses it, identifying GDPR terms and groups within, and finally, providing results for the inclusion of the necessary GDPR information within the aforementioned policy; (3) the evaluation of 148 existing web platforms, from 5 different sectors: (i) banking, (ii) e-commerce, (iii) education, (iv) travelling, and (v) social media, presenting the results of their alignment to the GDPR. In specifics, the evaluation examines the existence of the following GDPR provisions and rights: "*Lawfulness of Processing*", "*Right to Erasure*", "*Right of Access by the Data Subject*", "*Right to Data Portability*", "*Right to Rectification*", "*Right to Restriction of Processing*", and "*Right to Object*".

The rest of the paper is structured as follows: Sect. 2 presents an overview of the related work and background. Section 3 discusses our methodology towards creating a list of terms to be included in web platforms privacy policies, and the final list, while Sect. 4 presents the design and implementation of the crawler and parser tool (CompLicy) for automatically locating and analysing a privacy policy of a given website. Subsequently, Sect. 5 presents an evaluation of 148 websites, from 5 different sectors, and their results. Finally, Sect. 6 concludes this paper with a discussion of the conclusions and future work.

2 Background and Related Work

The GDPR [4] was enacted by the EU in an attempt to address the issue of personal data privacy. It came into effect on May 25, 2018, imposing new rights and obligations for the collection and processing of EU residents personal data, i.e., even when the system is not located within the EU. In [13] the application of GDPR articles and provisions is studied, in the design and development of web platforms. The GDPR-compliant implementation of a case study platform is demonstrated, and a set of guidelines based on the methodology followed is extracted. The work discusses all the GDPR articles judged as relevant, and additionally explains all other GDPR articles, reasoning why they were not included in the specific implementation. In [9], the authors perform an investigation on how privacy policies can be both GDPR-compliant and usable. They synthesise

GDPR requirements into a checklist and derive a list of usability design guidelines for privacy notifications. They then provide a usable and GDPR-compliant privacy policy template for the benefit of policy writers.

In [7], a large number of privacy policies was collected and analysed in regards to their versions prior and after the GDPR establishment. The authors created an automated tool for this analysis, and were focused on the change occurring for the users experience when interacting with such privacy policies. Their conclusions were that, between March and July 2018, with May being the main point, more than 45% of the examined policies had changed. Furthermore, it was shown that GDPR was mainly affecting EU policies, rather than policies of organisations outside the EU. The authors of [1] try to address the issue of privacy policies being too long and complex with poor readability and comprehensibility to users. They propose an automated privacy policy extraction system, implemented on Android smartphones. This work's main focus is addressing users' concerns and the *transparency* requirement of the GDPR. With the same aim, [10], propose a machine learning based approach to summarise long privacy policies into short and condensed notes, and [11] presents a privacy policy summarisation tool.

In [12] the authors provide automated support for checking completeness of a privacy policy in regards to the GDPR. In order to do so, metadata from privacy policies are extracted, and a set of completeness criteria based on a conceptual model is used for recognising issues. Additionally, [2] aims at automating legal evaluation of privacy policies, under the GDPR, using artificial intelligence. In their study, they present the preliminary results of the evaluation of a number of privacy policies.

Our tool aims both at providing a summarisation of the included GDPR terms to users, and in helping software engineers keep track of GDPR functionality implemented in their web systems. We focus on web platforms, creating a list of GDPR terms to be included in their policies. We then apply an automated method including a crawler to locate privacy policy pages, and a parser to analyse the policy text from within the source code. We examine web platforms' privacy policies from 5 different sectors.

3 GDPR Privacy Policy Terms List

This section presents the procedure followed for creating a *list of GDPR privacy policy terms*. As a first step, we created an initial list based on the GDPR, extracting the specific provisions and user rights terms, that should be included within a web platform privacy policy. Next, we expanded our list based on our investigation and observation of existing web platforms privacy policies.

3.1 Analysing the GDPR

The first step of our methodology included studying the 99 articles and 173 recitals of the GDPR [4], as well as the related literature and legal documentation, to conclude to a list of rights and provisions that should be clearly stated within a web platform privacy policy. Below we discuss the 7 provisions and rights, judged as relevant to web platforms based on our work of [13], in which we designed and developed the required GDPR functionality on a web platform real case study. We refer the reader to that work, for explanations on why the rest of the articles were not judged as relevant:

1. "*Lawfulness, fairness and transparency*", is one of the provisions defined in Article 5 of the regulation, as "*Personal data shall be processed lawfully, fairly and in a transparent manner in relation to the data subject*". For a processing to be lawful, the system must establish one of the *lawful bases* defined in Article 6 "*Lawfulness of Processing*". In the context of a web platform, we consider the lawful bases of *consent* and *performance of a contract*, and that the platform must first ensure one of them, before proceeding with any processing of personal data. The selected *lawful basis* should be clearly presented within the privacy policy text.
2. The "*Right of Access by the Data Subject*" defined in GDPR Article 15, states that the user has the right to be informed whether their data are being processed, and to access a copy of their personal data stored and processed in the system, i.e., the web platform.
3. The "*Right to Rectification*" defined in GDPR Article 16, states that the user "*shall have the right to obtain from the controller without undue delay the rectification of inaccurate personal data*" and "*have the right to have incomplete personal data completed*". In web platforms, a user should be able to edit their personal data at any given time.
4. The "*Right to Erasure*", defined in Article 17 of the regulation, states that the users "*have the right to obtain from the controller the erasure of personal data without undue delay*", thus in a web platform managing user accounts, one should be able to delete a part or all of their information or their account.
5. The "*Right to Restriction of Processing*", of GDPR Article 18 states that users can ask for their personal data to stop being processed for an amount of time until they decide to resume the processing. In such a case, a web platform should stop processing but not delete the respective data.
6. The "*Right to Data Portability*" defined in GDPR Article 20, states that the users "*have the right to receive their personal data, in a structured, commonly used and machine-readable format and have the right to transmit those data to another controller*". Hence, a web platform user should be able to request and obtain a package including all the respective data, in such a format as requested by the regulation.
7. Finally, the "*Right to object*", defined in Article 21 states that the user has the right to object to the processing of their personal data. Like so, one's data should not be processed in case of an objection, until it is resolved.
   All the previously described rights of the users should be clearly stated in the privacy policy text.

As a result of the above study, we created an initial *list of GDPR privacy policy terms*, as presented in Table 1.

Table 1. Initial list of GDPR privacy policy terms

1	Lawfulness of Processing	5	Right to Restriction of Processing
2	Right of Access by the Data Subject	6	Right to Data Portability
3	Right to Rectification	7	Right to Object
4	Right to Erasure		

3.2 Examining Web Platforms

As a second step towards creating our *list of GDPR terms for privacy policies*, we examined a number of web platforms. We observed the structure of their privacy policies, and how the GDPR terms of our initial list are placed and included within these policies. We then observed differences and similarities between the terms expressing the same right in different platforms but also in comparison to the GDPR official terms as collected in the first step (see Sect. 3.1). A set of such different variations for each term was collected, extending the existing list. Examples of such variations, are shown below:

Example 1 (Terms Variations).
- "*Right to Erasure*": "The Right to Request Deletion", "Right To be Forgotten"
- "*Right to restriction of processing*": "Requests the Restriction of Their Use"
- "*Right to Rectification*": "Right to Correction", "Right to Correct", "The Right to Correct and Update"

Additionally, we infused the list with some more variations by interchanging the sequence of the words, or replacing basic words with similar ones, as shown in the following example:

Example 2 (Terms Variations).
- "*Right to Object to Processing*": "Processing Objection"
- "*Right Of Access*": "Access Personal Data"

3.3 The Final Set

We resulted in a set comprised of 89 terms. We then divided the terms into groups based on the 7 initial list terms collected from the GDPR during the first step. In this way, we consider that, if any of the terms of a group is found within a policy, the whole group is considered as included. The list includes a set of exact strings to be searched within privacy policies. This implies a limitation on the tool, as, if a GDPR term variation included in a policy is not exactly the same to any of the variations of the current list, it will not be recognised. However, the list is open for future editing and expansion. Improving and enhancing the list is envisioned as a continuous iterative process. After each iteration of evaluation of a set of platforms, a manual auditing is planned and terms that were not included, but shown to be needed, added to the list. In case the GDPR will be updated, or new regulations need to be added, the list is flexible enough to be adapted to accommodate them. At the moment the list includes only English language GDPR terms. The final *list of GDPR privacy policy terms* in groups, is presented in Table 2 below.

Table 2. List of GDPR privacy policy terms

`Lawfulness of Processing (5 terms)`	`Right to Restriction of Processing`
Lawfulness of Processing	Restriction of Processing
Consent	Restrict Your data
Contract	Right to Restrict
Right to Withdraw Consent	Right to demand processing restrictions
Withdraw consent	Right to restriction of processing
	Request the Restriction of Their Use
	Request the Restriction of Data Use
	Request the Restriction of Personal Data Use
	Right of data subjects to be informed about the restriction
	Right to propose other restriction
`Right of Access by the Data Subject`	`Right to Data Portability`
Right Of Access	Right to Data Portability
Right To Access	Right of Portability
Access Personal Data	Right to Portability
Access Your Personal Data	Right to Transmit Those Data
Access your data	Right to Transmit Personal Data
Access Your Personal Information	Right to Transmit My Data
Access Personal Information	The Right to Transmit Those Data
Right to Lodge a Complaint	Right to Transmit Data
Right to complaint	Transmit Your Data
Right to File a Complaint	Transmit Your Personal Data
Right to Obtain a Copy	Right to Transmit Personal Data
Request a Copy of your Information	Request the transfer of your personal data
Request a Copy of your personal Information	Request the transfer your personal data
Request a Copy of your data	Request the transfer personal data
Request a Copy of your personal data	Request the transfer data
Request access to a copy of your personal data	Right to Receive the Personal Data
Right to Information	Right to Receive your Personal Data
Right to request and receive information	Right to Receive Personal Data

(*continued*)

Table 2. (*continued*)

Request access	Right to Receive a Subset of the Personal Data
	Right to receive a copy of your personal information
`Right to Rectification`	`Right to Object`
Right To Rectification	Right to Object
Right to have incomplete personal data	Right to Object at any time to Processing of Personal data
Right to complete incomplete personal data	Right to Object at any time to Processing
Right to Request Proper Rectification	Right to Object to Processing
Right to Request Rectification	Processing Objection
Rectify Your Data	Object to processing
The Right to Correct and Update	`Right to Erasure`
The Right to Correct	Right to Erasure
The Right to Update	Right of Erasure
Update or Correct your Information	Right to Request Deletion
Update your Information	Right To be Forgotten
Correct your Information	Erase your Information
Right to request the correction	Request erasure
Right to request correction	Erase the Personal data
Right to request update	Erase your Personal data
Right to Correction	To Erase Your Data
Right to Correct	Erase any personal data
Rectify	Erase personal data

4 The CompLicy Tool

In order to provide insights on whether privacy policies are aligned to the GDPR, by studying web platforms, we designed and developed the CompLicy[6] tool that uses the results of the previous steps of this work as the foundation to automatically locate and evaluate such platforms' privacy policies. First, the tool crawls a given web platform, starting from the given homepage URL, to infer whether a privacy policy page exists and, if it does, subsequently parses it, identifying GDPR terms and groups within based on our *list of GDPR privacy policy terms*, and finally, provides results for the compliance of the aforementioned policy with the GDPR, by displaying which terms out of the list were located within the policy, and which groups are thus represented.

Crawler. As a preliminary step for implementing the crawler, we manually examined the source code of a set of web platforms. We additionally examined

[6] "*CompLicy*" is a portmanteau, i.e., a made-up word, coined from the combination of the words "*Compli*ance" and "Po*licy*".

their front-ends. In both source codes and front-end interfaces, we observed: (1) how the navigation was done from each platform homepage towards the privacy policy page, (2) the key-words included in the respective privacy policy URLs, and (3) the different variations of names for the specific page in the menu or other interface parts of the web platforms. Based on these observations, we created a list of respective key phrases, that would help the crawler in locating and recognising a privacy policy page. In the case of examining the URLs, the key-phrases extracted were part of them. For example, in the case of a web platform of which the privacy policy page URL is *http://<an-example-page>/data-processing/*, the key-phrase extracted would be "*data-processing*". The final key-phrases set is the following: {*data-processing, data-privacy, privacy, policy, privacy-policy, legal, privacy-policy-link, privacy_check, guidelines*}.

4.1 System Design

Architecture. Figure 1 presents the architecture of the tool. The *User*, through the *graphical user interface (GUI)*, gives as input the URL of the web platform (*platform link)* to be examined, which is subsequently passed on to the *Crawler*. The web *Crawler* (or spider) is aimed to realise a systematic navigation into the website directed by the URL. In order to do so, it also receives as input the text file with the key-phrases, i.e., the *list of terms for crawling.* The *Crawler* then searches within the given website, to locate the privacy policy page, and if found, subsequently passing the *privacy policy page source code* to the *Parser* which in turn receives also as input the *list of GDPR privacy policy terms* in the format of a text file, searches and recognises the list terms within the privacy policy text and returns the *results* to the GUI. The GUI also inputs the list of GDPR terms as categorised in the groups, printing both the list and the results, and presenting them to the user. Figure 2 presents a more detailed version of the system architecture.

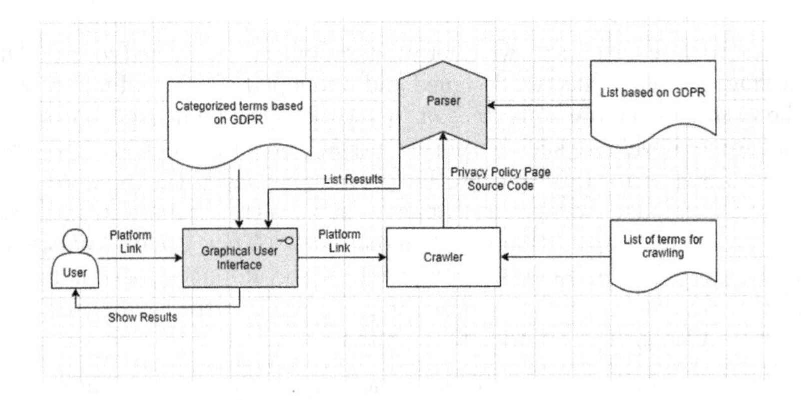

Fig. 1. Tool architecture

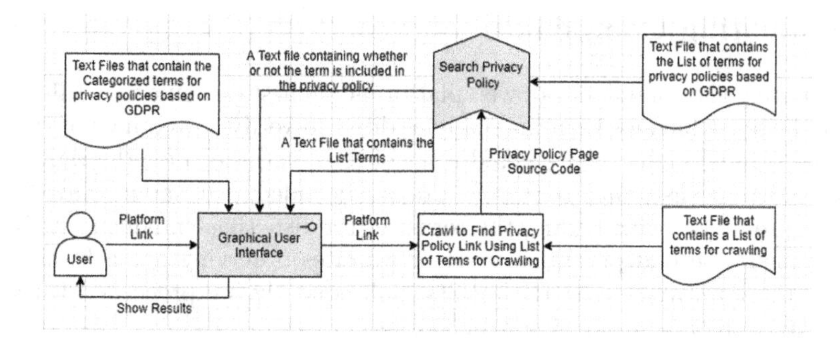

Fig. 2. Tool detailed architecture

4.2 System Implementation

Tools. The system was implemented using the Python programming language, in the PyCharm integrated development environment (IDE). The Qt Designer and the PyQt5 library were used for designing and implementing the GUI.

User Interface. Figure 3 presents the tool GUI. Users can provide a URL at the text box located at the top left side of the screen, and press the "*start*" button to initiate the crawling and parsing procedure, which when completed, the results will be presented in two tables as shown. The top table presents the complete *list of GDPR privacy policy terms*, accompanied with a "yes" or "no" answer, depending on whether the term was included within the policy or not, and the total number of terms located. The bottom table presents the 7 groups, accompanied by a mapping to the top list terms, and a 1-point scoring system for each group if at least one of its terms was included in the policy text. Finally, the total score of the privacy policy is presented in the format of points score and percentage.

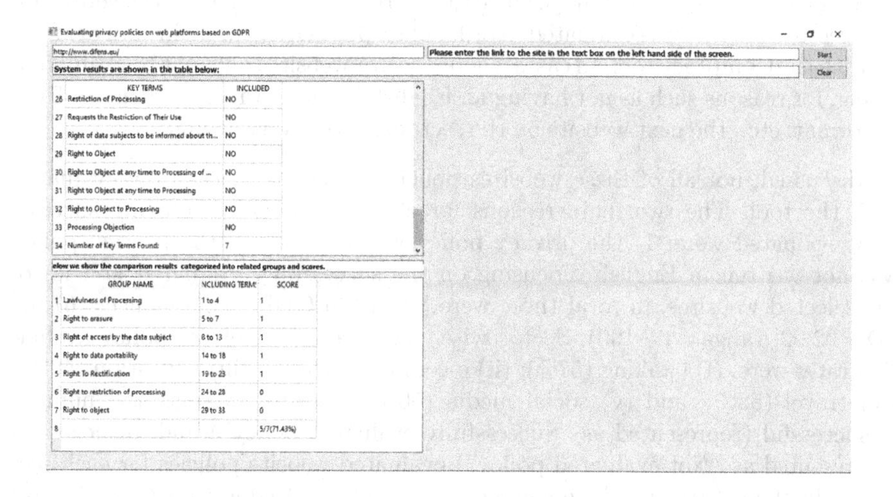

	KEY TERMS	INCLUDED
26	Restriction of Processing	NO
27	Requests the Restriction of Their Use	NO
28	Right of data subjects to be informed about th...	NO
29	Right to Object	NO
30	Right to Object at any time to Processing of ...	NO
31	Right to Object at any time to Processing	NO
32	Right to Object to Processing	NO
33	Processing Objection	NO
34	Number of Key Terms Found:	7

	GROUP NAME	NCLUDING TERM	SCORE
1	Lawfulness of Processing	1 to 4	1
2	Right to erasure	5 to 7	1
3	Right of acces by the data subject	8 to 13	1
4	Right to data portability	14 to 18	1
5	Right To Rectification	19 to 23	1
6	Right to restriction of processing	24 to 28	0
7	Right to object	29 to 33	0
8			5/7(71.43%)

Fig. 3. Graphical user interface

5 Evaluating Compliance

For evaluating the compliance of web platforms, we first examined a preliminary set of websites, which we then manually audited to verify correctness of results. From the manual audit, we gathered a set of term variations for the rights and provisions of our list, that were not already included, but should have been. We then proceeded with adding the terms in the list, thus enhancing it. Next, we examined a second preliminary set of websites observing again by manual auditing the improvement in the results. Subsequently, we proceeded with the evaluation of the actual set of web platforms.

5.1 Dataset

A total of 148 websites were considered in the dataset, i.e., given as input to the tool, from five different sectors: (i) banking; (ii) e-commerce; (iii) education; (iv) travelling; and (v) social media. As described in the introduction (Sect. 1), the increasing usage of web platforms of these sectors, as well as the importance of the data processed and the actions carried out within, mandate for privacy protection. We have collected the URLs of the biggest and most popular websites of each respective sector. The procedure for selecting the sector-based websites was founded on three main stages. These included the following:

1. Stage 1 – Online review per sector. Desk research was conducted on the five different sectors.
2. Stage 2 – Define sector shortlist. Results from Stage 1 aided in identifying the more popular websites with larger user bases within each sector. An important requirement for the website to be eligible for selection was the existence of an English version of it. With the aim to approach the number of 20 websites being evaluated for each sector, the sector shortlist included a higher number of websites ($n \geq 20$ websites per sector).
3. Stage 3 – Test sector shortlists. Once the shortlists were defined, each website on a sector-shortlist was evaluated in order of its popularity (as defined in Stage 2) with the CompLicy tool. In cases where a sector website could not be evaluated, e.g. for reasons such as not having an English version, privacy policies in PDF format, etc., the next website on the sector shortlist was evaluated.

As discussed, not all of these websites policies' could be successfully evaluated with the tool. The two main reasons for a website policy not being successfully evaluated were: 1) the privacy policy was in PDF; 2) the privacy policy was not written in English. Focusing on the successfully evaluated policies of the selected websites, in total these were 80 (mean GDPR compliance = 67.67, SD = 22.92, range = 14–100). Sector wise, the successful website policy evaluation rates were: (i) banking (57%); (ii) e-commerce (54%); (iii) education (59%); (iv) travel (52%); and (v) social media (50%). Figure 4 presents the number of successful (represented as "Successfully evaluated policy") and unsuccessful (represented as "Not evaluated policy") evaluated website policies for each sector, i) banking (n = 21); (ii) e-commerce (n = 39); (iii) education (n = 27); (iv) travel (n = 21); and (v) social media (n = 40).

Figure 5 presents the mean GDPR compliance score for the privacy policies of the successfully evaluated websites with the tool. Sector wise, the following scores were recorded: (i) banking (mean GDPR compliance = 75); (ii) e-commerce (mean GDPR compliance = 70.75); (iii) education (mean GDPR compliance = 52.68); (iv) travel (mean GDPR compliance = 72.73); and (v) social media (mean GDPR compliance = 69.29). It is not surprising that privacy policies of websites in the banking sector scored the highest in terms of GDPR compliance with 75%, yet one might expect an even higher compliance rate. Standing out however is the compliance score of websites in the education sector with 52.68%. This can be regarded as poor and does require further investigation, considering the large adoption of e-learning in 2020 and respectively large numbers of students using educational web environments.

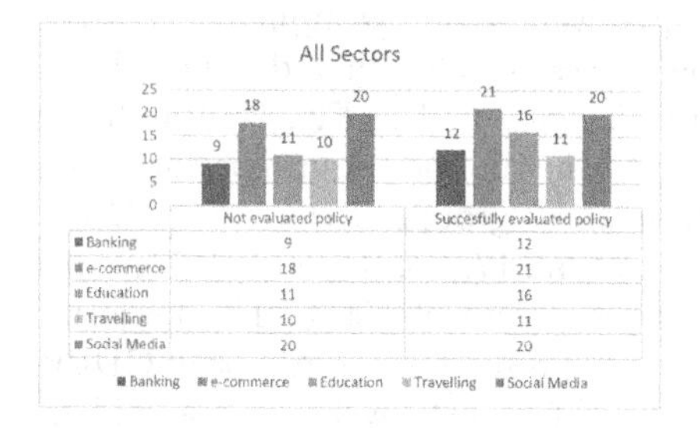

Fig. 4. Summarising successful and unsuccessful evaluation attempts according to sector websites'

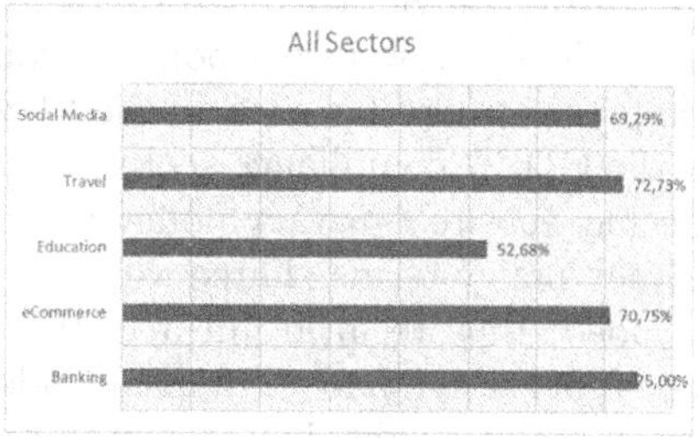

Fig. 5. Summarising average score of GDPR compliance according to sector websites'

5.2 Results

For all the results following, we will be using the following abbreviations for the 7 groups: Lawfulness of Processing (LP), Right to erasure (RE), Right of access by the data subject (RA), Right to data portability (RDP), Right To Rectification (RR), Right to restriction of processing (RR2), Right to object (RO). Data and results are available at: http://www.cs.ucy.ac.cy/seit/resources/RCIS21.zip

Banking Sector. A total of 21 websites were given as input to the tool. From these, 12 websites policies' could be successfully evaluated. The GDPR compliance score for each of the 12 websites is presented in Fig. 6. In addition to the GDPR compliance score, also evident is the number of groups that each specific website's privacy policy includes from the 7 groups of the list of GDPR privacy policy terms. Only one website (i.e., no.3), had all 7 groups included, thus resulting in a GDPR compliance score of 100%. The majority (i.e., 7 websites), had 6 groups included. Figure 7 presents the 7 groups of GDPR provisions and rights included within the list, and for the 12 websites it is evident how many in total included each respective provision and right. RO and LP were the most included, appearing in 11 websites, whereas RR and RDP were the least included, appearing in 7 websites.

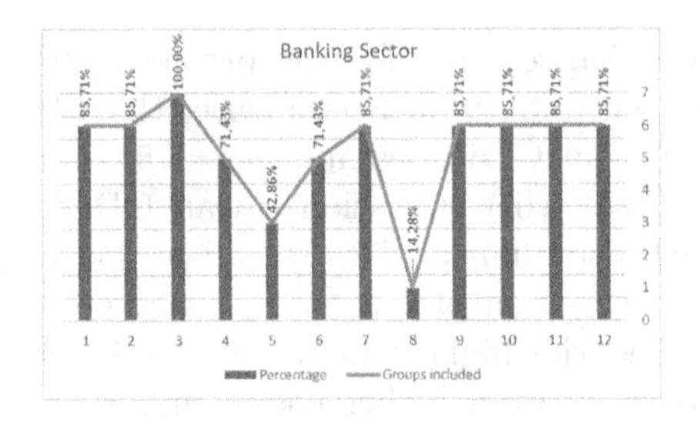

Fig. 6. Summarising average score of GDPR compliance and respective groups included in the privacy policy for successfully evaluated banking sector websites'

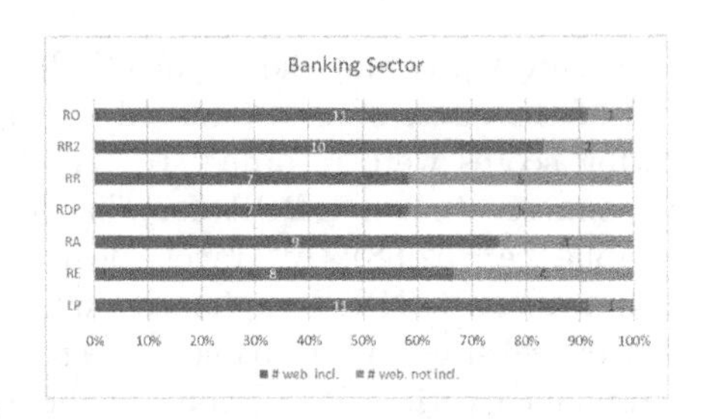

Fig. 7. Summarising the total inclusion of each group within the privacy policies of the successfully evaluated banking sector websites'

e-Commerce Sector. A total of 39 websites were given as input to the tool. From these, 21 websites policies' could be successfully evaluated. The GDPR compliance score for each of the 21 websites is presented in Fig. 8. In addition to the GDPR compliance score, also evident is the number of groups that each specific website's privacy policy includes from the 7 groups of the list of GDPR privacy policy terms. Three websites (i.e., no.14, no.17, no.21), had all 7 groups included, thus resulting in a GDPR compliance score of 100%. The majority (i.e., 6 websites), had 5 groups included. Figure 9 presents the 7 groups of GDPR provisions and rights included within the list, and for the 21 websites it is evident how many in total included each respective provision and right. Similarly to the banking sector websites, RO and LP were the most included, appearing in 19 and 21 websites respectively, whereas RR was the least included, appearing in only 6 websites.

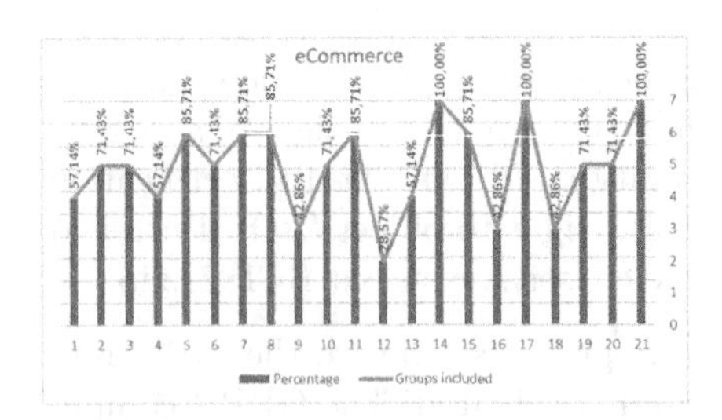

Fig. 8. Summarising average score of GDPR compliance and respective groups included in the privacy policy for successfully evaluated e-commerce sector websites'

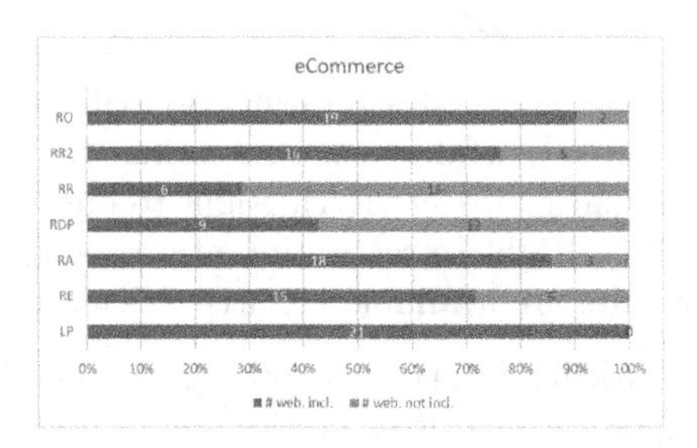

Fig. 9. Summarising the total inclusion of each group within the privacy policies of the successfully evaluated e-commerce sector websites'

Educational Sector. A total of 27 websites were given as input to the tool. From these, 16 websites policies' could be successfully evaluated. The GDPR compliance score for each of the 16 websites is presented in Fig. 10. In addition to the GDPR compliance score, also evident is the number of groups that each specific website's privacy policy includes from the 7 groups of the list of GDPR privacy policy terms. Only two websites (i.e., no.3, no.15), had all 7 groups included, thus resulting in a GDPR compliance score of 100%. The majority (i.e., 6 websites), had only 2 groups included, which is concerning, considering the large number of students sharing personal information on such websites. Figure 11 presents the 7 groups of GDPR provisions and rights included within the list, and for the 16 websites it is evident how many in total included each respective provision and right. RO and LP were again the most included, appearing in 14 and 16 websites respectively, whereas RR was also once again the least included, appearing in only 2 websites.

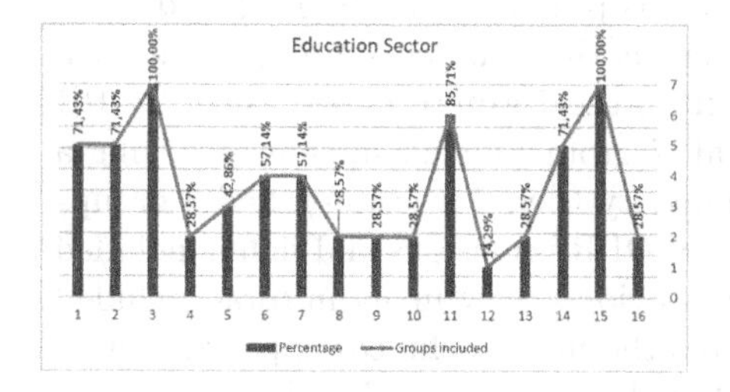

Fig. 10. Summarising average score of GDPR compliance and respective groups included in the privacy policy for successfully evaluated education sector websites'

Fig. 11. Summarising the total inclusion of each group within the privacy policies of the successfully evaluated education sector websites'

Travelling Sector. A total of 21 websites were given as input to the tool, focused on booking flights, other travel activities, or accommodation. From these, 11 websites policies' could be successfully evaluated. The GDPR compliance score for each of the 11 websites is presented in Fig. 12. In addition to the GDPR compliance score, also evident is the number of groups that each specific website's privacy policy includes from the 7 groups of the list of GDPR privacy policy terms. No website had all 7 groups included, thus achieving a GDPR compliance score of 100% was not possible for a travel sector website. The majority however (i.e., 5 websites), had 6 groups included. Figure 13 presents the 7 groups of GDPR provisions and rights included within the list, and for the 11 websites it is evident how many in total included each respective provision and right. RO, LP and RR2 were the most included, appearing in 11 websites, whereas RR was also once again the least included, appearing in only 4 websites.

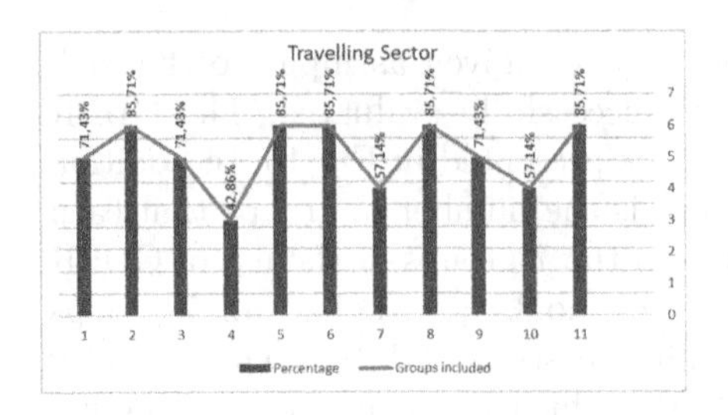

Fig. 12. Summarising average score of GDPR compliance and respective groups included in the privacy policy for successfully evaluated travelling sector websites'

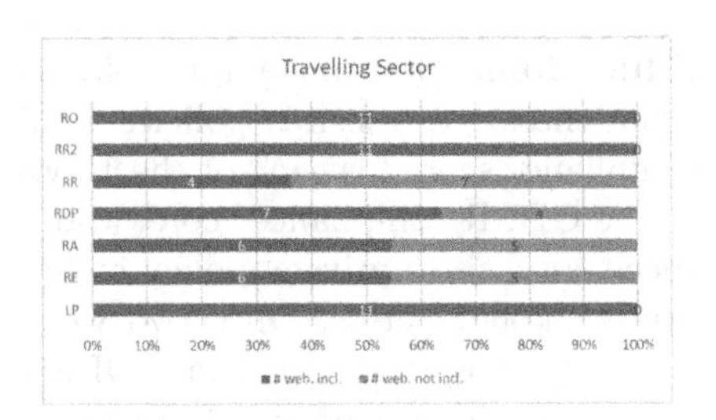

Fig. 13. Summarising the total inclusion of each group within the privacy policies of the successfully evaluated travelling sector websites'

Social Media Sector. A total of 40 websites were given as input to the tool. From these, 20 websites policies' could be successfully evaluated. The GDPR compliance score for each of the 20 websites is presented in Fig. 14. In addition to the GDPR compliance score, also evident is the number of groups that each specific website's privacy policy includes from the 7 groups of the list of GDPR privacy policy terms. Two websites had all 7 groups included, thus achieving a GDPR compliance score of 100%. The majority (i.e., 7 websites), had 4 groups included. Figure 15 presents the 7 groups of GDPR provisions and rights included within the list, and for the 20 websites it is evident how many in total included each respective provision and right. LP was the most included, appearing in 20 websites, whereas RDP was the least included, appearing in 5 websites.

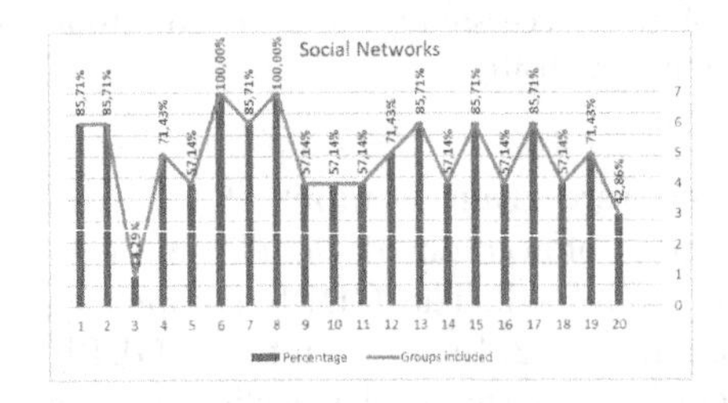

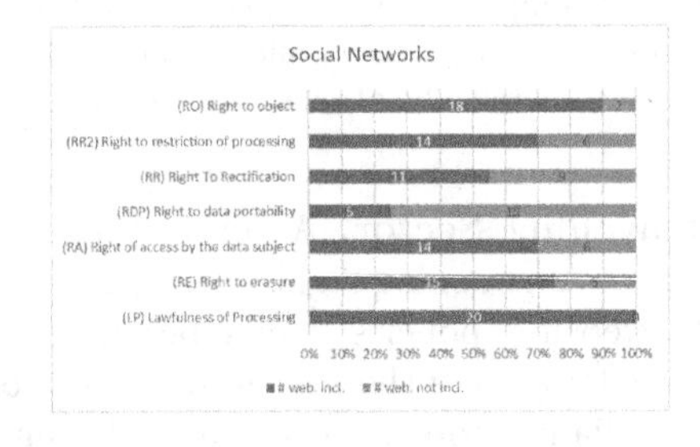

Fig. 14. Summarising average score of GDPR compliance and respective groups included in the privacy policy for successfully evaluated social media sector websites'

Fig. 15. Summarising the total inclusion of each group within the privacy policies of the successfully evaluated social media sector websites'

Websites in the banking sector scored the highest (75%), while websites in the education sector scored the lowest (52,68%). In all five sectors, "Lawfulness of Processing" was amongst the most included, appearing in all websites except in the educational and banking sectors appearing in 14 out of the 16, and 11 out of the 12 total websites evaluated respectively. On the contrary, the "Right to Rectification" was the least included in all sectors, with the exception of the social media sector, where the "Right to Data Portability" was the least included.

6 Conclusions

Recognising the importance of *privacy*, and the mandatory nature of the GDPR, in this work we aim to give insight on whether software systems privacy policies have been aligned to comply with the GDPR. In this context we focus on web platforms, and present a list of GDPR terms that need to be included within privacy policies, and the CompLicy tool which locates a given web platform privacy policy and subsequently parses it, identifying GDPR terms and groups within, providing results for its compliance. Based on their increasing usage and popularity, and their importance, we focus on web platforms of the following sectors: (i) banking; (ii) e-commerce; (iii) education; (iv) travel; and (v) social media. We evaluate a set of 148 such platforms and present the results obtained.

We observe that websites in the banking sector scored the highest, while websites in the education sector the lowest. A more thorough investigation can be conducted focusing on the education sector, especially with the increased usage due to COVID-19. Future work should also investigate the reason for the least included provisions for each sector, as shown by the results ("Right to Rectification" in 4 sectors, "Right to Data Portability" in social media). We also observe that there is still a respectful percentage of policies not being fully aligned with the GDPR. Incorporating a privacy design step explicitly within the software engineering methodologies could assist developers. We are also planning the enhancement of our list of terms increasing the accuracy of our tool. As future work, we envision to enhance the tool with PDF scanning ability to capture more websites privacy policies. New languages can also be added by translating the existing terms in English.

References

1. Chang, C., Li, H., Zhang, Y., Du, S., Cao, H., Zhu, H.: Automated and personalized privacy policy extraction under GDPR consideration. In: Biagioni, E.S., Zheng, Y., Cheng, S. (eds.) WASA 2019. LNCS, vol. 11604, pp. 43–54. Springer, Cham (2019). https://doi.org/10.1007/978-3-030-23597-0_4
2. Contissa, G., et al.: CLAUDETTE meets GDPR: Automating the evaluation of privacy policies using artificial intelligence. SSRN 3208596 (2018)
3. European Parliament and Council of the European Union: Charter of fundamental rights of the European union. Official Journal of the European Union (2012)
4. European Parliament and Council of the European Union: General data protection regulation. Official Journal of the European Union (2015)
5. Hadar, I., et al.: Privacy by designers: software developers' privacy mindset. Empirical Softw. Eng. **23**(1), 259–289 (2018)
6. Krumay, B., Klar, J.: Readability of privacy policies. In: Singhal, A., Vaidya, J. (eds.) DBSec 2020. LNCS, vol. 12122, pp. 388–399. Springer, Cham (2020). https://doi.org/10.1007/978-3-030-49669-2_22

7. Linden, T., Khandelwal, R., Harkous, H., Fawaz, K.: The privacy policy landscape after the GDPR. Priv. Enhanc. Technol. **2020**(1), 47–64 (2020)
8. McDonald, A.M., Reeder, R.W., Kelley, P.G., Cranor, L.F.: A comparative study of online privacy policies and formats. In: Goldberg, I., Atallah, M.J. (eds.) PETS 2009. LNCS, vol. 5672, pp. 37–55. Springer, Heidelberg (2009). https://doi.org/10.1007/978-3-642-03168-7_3
9. Renaud, K., Shepherd, L.A.: How to make privacy policies both GDPR-compliant and usable. In: International Conference on Cyber Situational Awareness, Data Analytics and Assessment, pp. 1–8. IEEE (2018)
10. Tesfay, W.B., Hofmann, P., Nakamura, T., Kiyomoto, S., Serna, J.: I read but don't agree: Privacy policy benchmarking using machine learning and the EU GDPR. In: The Web Conference, pp. 163–166 (2018)
11. Tesfay, W.B., Hofmann, P., Nakamura, T., Kiyomoto, S., Serna, J.: PrivacyGuide: towards an implementation of the EU GDPR on internet privacy policy evaluation. In: International Workshop on Security and Privacy Analytics. pp. 15–21 (2018)
12. Torre, D., Abualhaija, S., Sabetzadeh, M., Briand, L., Baetens, K., Goes, P., Forastier, S.: An AI-assisted approach for checking the completeness of privacy policies against GDPR. In: International Requirements Engineering Conference, pp. 136–146. IEEE (2020)
13. Vanezi, E., et al.: GDPR Compliance in the Design of the INFORM e-learning platform: a case study. In: International Conference on Research Challenges in Information Science, pp. 1–12. IEEE (2019)

Data and Information Management

WEIR-P: An Information Extraction Pipeline for the Wastewater Domain

Nanée Chahinian[1(✉)], Thierry Bonnabaud La Bruyère[1], Francesca Frontini[2,3], Carole Delenne[1,4], Marin Julien[1], Rachel Panckhurst[5], Mathieu Roche[6], Lucile Sautot[6], Laurent Deruelle[7], and Maguelonne Teisseire[6]

[1] HSM, Univ. Montpellier, CNRS, IRD, Montpellier, France
nanee.chahinian@ird.fr
[2] Istituto di Linguistica Computazionale "A. Zampolli" - CNR, Pisa, Italy
[3] CLARIN ERIC, Utrecht, The Netherlands
[4] Inria Lemon, CRISAM - Inria Sophia Antipolis – Méditerranée, Montpellier, France
[5] Dipralang, UPVM, Montpellier, France
[6] TETIS, AgroParisTech, CIRAD, CNRS, INRAE, Montpellier, France
[7] Berger Levrault, Perols, France

Abstract. We present the MeDO project, aimed at developing resources for text mining and information extraction in the wastewater domain. We developed a specific Natural Language Processing (NLP) pipeline named WEIR-P (WastewatEr InfoRmation extraction Platform) which identifies the entities and relations to be extracted from texts, pertaining to information, wastewater treatment, accidents and works, organizations, spatio-temporal information, measures and water quality. We present and evaluate the first version of the NLP system which was developed to automate the extraction of the aforementioned annotation from texts and its integration with existing domain knowledge. The preliminary results obtained on the Montpellier corpus are encouraging and show how a mix of supervised and rule-based techniques can be used to extract useful information and reconstruct the various phases of the extension of a given wastewater network. While the NLP and Information Extraction (IE) methods used are state of the art, the novelty of our work lies in their adaptation to the domain, and in particular in the wastewater management conceptual model, which defines the relations between entities. French resources are less developed in the NLP community than English ones. The datasets obtained in this project are another original aspect of this work.

Keywords: Wastewater · Text mining · Information extraction · NLP · NER · Domain adapted systems

Supported by the Occitanie-Pyrénées-Méditerrannée Region under grant 2017-006570/DF-000014.

S. Cherfi et al. (Eds.): RCIS 2021, LNBIP 415, pp. 171–188, 2021.
https://doi.org/10.1007/978-3-030-75018-3_11

1 Introduction

Water networks are part of the urban infrastructure and with increasing urbanization, city managers have had to constantly extend water access and sanitation services to new peripheral areas or to new incomers [3]. Originally these networks were installed, operated, and repaired by their owners [24]. However, as concessions were increasingly granted to private companies and new tenders requested regularly by public authorities, archives were sometimes misplaced and event logs were lost. Thus, part of the networks' operational history was thought to be permanently erased. However, the advent of Web big data and text-mining techniques may offer the possibility of recovering some of this knowledge by crawling secondary information sources, i.e. documents available on the Web. Thus, insight might be gained on the wastewater collection scheme, the treatment processes, the network's geometry and events (accidents, shortages) which may have affected these facilities and amenities. This is the primary aim of the "Megadata, Linked Data and Data Mining for Wastewater Networks" (MeDo) project, funded by the Occitanie Region, in France, and carried out in collaboration between hydrologists, computational linguists and computer scientists.

Text mining is used in the field of water sciences but it is often implemented for perception analysis [1,18], indicator categorization [22] or ecosystem management [10,14]. To the best of our knowledge this work is the first attempt at using Natural Language Processing (NLP) and Text-Mining techniques for wastewater network management in cities.

The creation of domain adapted systems for Information Extraction (IE) has been an important area of research in NLP. The outcomes of many projects have led to creating systems capable of identifying relevant information from scientific literature as well as technical and non technical documents. A pioneering domain was that of biology; see [2] for an overview of initial projects and [11] for a more recent contribution. More specifically, a fertile field of research has emerged at the intersection between NLP and Geographic Information Retrieval (GIR). Cf. [30] and [19] for a domain overview and a list of relevant projects; [16] for Digital Humanities initiatives and [13] for the Matriciel project in French.

The NLP pipelines used to mine these specialised corpora are generally composed of a mix of supervised and unsupervised or rule-based NLP algorithms; crucially the collaboration with domain experts is essential since the state of the art tools need to be re-trained and tested using corpora with specific annotation and often require structured domain knowledge as input. Generally such systems are trained and tested on English; however in many cases multilingual pipelines, and therefore resources, have been created.

The use of general semantic resources e.g. EuroWordNet[1] or dedicated thesaurii Agrovoc[2] for the French language is not adapted to address the wastewater domain. Agrovoc is a terminology, where concepts are described and translated

[1] https://archive.illc.uva.nl//EuroWordNet/.
[2] http://www.fao.org/agrovoc/about.

into various languages. In this sense it is used to standardize and control the use of domain vocabulary. WordNets are lexical resources, that can be used for NLP; EuroWordNet has been extended for specific domains. In both cases, to produce or adapt terminologies or computational lexicons for a new domain one would have to apply NLP techniques to extract and filter terms and lexemes from texts, and use a pre-processing pipeline along the lines of what we propose. The originality of our approach is based on the combination of well-known tools (e.g. spaCy, Heideltime) and the integration of expertise for highlighting semantic information related to the wastewater domain along with the selection of relevant documents using machine learning. Our global pipeline called WEIR-P combines Information Retrieval (IR) and Information Extraction (IE) techniques adapted for the French language and the wastewater domain.

Indeed, not only are there no domain specific terminological and lexical resources ready to use, but crucially also in terms of modelling, important work had to be done to identify which elements had to be annotated in the text, in order to extract the relevant information. In particular, two important contributions of this work are the implementation of NER methods for extracting original entities (Network element, Treatment, Network type, Accident, etc.) with new textual data manually labeled and the construction of relations based on spatial, temporal and thematic entities for discovering new knowledge which is an original research direction. Finally French resources (i.e. corpora, specialized terminology, etc.) are less developed in the NLP community with many English datasets available. The datasets obtained in this project (i.e. labeled corpus, terminology dedicated to wastewater domain) are another original aspect of this work.

The **research methodology** we followed is quite similar to the DSRP model presented by [23]. The **problem identification and motivation** is linked to previous research projects [5]. The **Objectives of the solution** are to develop a user-friendly tool that would help non-IT researchers and wastewater network managers transform unstructured text data from the Web into structured data and merge them with their business databases. The **Design and Development** step relied heavily on NLP, IR and IE literature. The new French data standard for drinking water and sewerage networks issued halfway into the project [12] was used as a reference for the business data model. Two case studies were designed in two cities (Montpellier-France and Abidjan-Ivory Coast). **Demonstrations** were carried out during the meetings of the project's steering committee. The **Evaluation** is two fold. It was partly carried out during the bi-annual meetings of the steering committee. A restitution workshop is also planned with members of the Aqua-Valley French Competitiveness Water Cluster. As for the **Communication**, in addition to scholarly publications such as this one, a wastewater awareness workshop was carried out in a primary school in March 2021.

In this paper we shall describe the general architecture of the system, as well as the linguistic resources used for domain adaptation and the evaluation of the various steps of the NLP pipeline. The structure of the paper is as follows: description of the data model (Sect. 2), of the system's architecture (Sect. 3) and its evaluation (Sect. 4); finally the description of the resources produced (Sect. 5) and some conclusions (Sect. 6).

2 The Data Model and the Corpus

The MeDo project aims to use textual data – available on the Web or produced by institutions – for learning about the geometry and history of wastewater networks, by combining different data-mining techniques and multiplying analysed sources.

In order to achieve this, a system for document processing has been designed, which when in production will allow a hydrologist or a wastewater network manager to retrieve relevant documents for a given network, process them to extract potentially new information, assess this information by using interactive visualization and add it to a pre-existing knowledge base.

Although textual sources may be directly imported into the system, the default pipeline begins with a Web-scraping phase retrieving documents from the Internet. The system has been built within the context of a French regional project, and is currently developed and tested for French documents. However, its architecture allows for easy adaptation to other languages, including English.

Relevant information may come from technical documents, such as reports by municipalities or private companies, but also from the general public, for instance from newspaper articles and social media posts containing descriptions of accidents in the network, or announcements of works. The goal of the system is to allow for the identification and retrieval of relevant documents from the Web, their linguistic processing and the extraction of domain information.

The case study presented hereafter is on the city of Montpellier in France. Our corpus is composed of 1,557 HTML and PDF documents. The documents were collected in July 2018 using a set of Google queries with a combination of keywords. Given the absence of guidelines for the annotation and extraction of information for wastewater management we proceeded to create our own annotation model with the help of hydrologists [7]. As is generally the case, the MeDo domain specific annotation scheme has been created extending the commonly used Named Entities (NEs) tagsets, which are defined in the guidelines of well known annotation campaigns such as MUC-5 and following [9], with domain specific entities, or tags. Our current model contains a set of entities:

- three of them are specific to the network: **Network type**, **Network element** and **Network characteristics**. Words such as "réseau pluvial" (stormwater network), "collecteur principal" (sewer main) or "gravitaire" (gravity fed) fall into these categories;
- one is related to the **Wastewater treatment** and may be used either for the plant and its components or the treatment process. This category includes for instance words like "station d'épuration" (wastewater treatment plant), "digestion anaérobie" (anaerobic digestion);

- two entities are used for the type of event reported in the document: **Accident**, **Works** i.e. "pollution", "inondation" (inundation/flooding), "raccordement au réseau" (connection to the network);
- one label describes the public or private **Organizations** such as "commune" (City council), "Entreprise" (company);
- dates and locations are marked using two labels: **Temporal**, **Spatial**;
- all quantitative data of relevance are marked as **Measurements**;
- a category **Indicator** is used to annotate any information which specifies or adds to the information provided by other categories;
- finally, two more "generic" entities are used for all words related to **Water quality** i.e. "eau brute" (raw water supply), nitrates and the **non-technical or legal aspects of wastewater management** i.e. "délégation de service public" (Public service delegation), "directive cadre sur l'eau" (Water framework Directive).

The manual annotation of these entities is complex and requires expert knowledge to be carried out correctly. A test on **inter-annotator agreement** was carried out with two experts, who had in-depth knowledge of the annotations guidelines, and non experts - students who received one-hour training before annotating. The former were asked to annotate all categories, the latter were limited to the domain specific ones. Results (see Table 1) are encouraging, given the number and technical nature of categories. It is known that Fleiss' Kappa is not appropriate for multi-entity textual annotation [27]; we therefore evaluate agreement in terms of F-measure values, reporting the results for each typology of annotators. Non experts performed slightly more poorly, which is understandable; typically, they tended to miss more annotations; however, when they did annotate a portion of text, they tended to choose the right category, which seems to indicate that the chosen annotation model is sound. For two domain categories (Water Quality and Accident), which are quite rare in the corpus, agreement remains low. The annotation guide was modified following this experiment to further clarify the annotation guidelines. The documents annotated by the students were not used to train the NER modules.

Given these results, the **Wastewater Domain Gold Standard Corpus** was carefully checked and verified by hydrologists. It consists of 23 manually annotated documents: 3 calls for tenders, 6 announcements from the city's website and 12 newspaper articles, 1 technical document and 1 tweet. They amount to 1,387 sentences and 4,505 entities. The annotation was carried out using the BRAT system[3].

Figure 1 shows an example of an annotated sentence. An extended Gold Standard containing 80 documents with 649,593 words and 29,585 entities was later complied for further tests. It is available on DataSuds dataverse [6].

Once the entities have been identified, it is necessary to define the possible **relations** which may connect them. These are defined in the **Wastewater**

[3] https://brat.nlplab.org/.

Table 1. Agreement per category, calculated using F-Measure.

Category	Expert	Non expert
Network element	0.875	0.688
Works	0.875	0.719
Treatment	0.750	0.703
Network type	0.750	0.719
Indicator	0.875	0.484
Network management	0.750	0.609
Network characteristics	0.875	0.656
Water quality	0.375	0.422
Accident	0.250	0.328
Measure	0.875	0.680
Spatial	0.875	–
Temporal	0.875	–
Organization	0.875	–
Overall	0.875	0.719

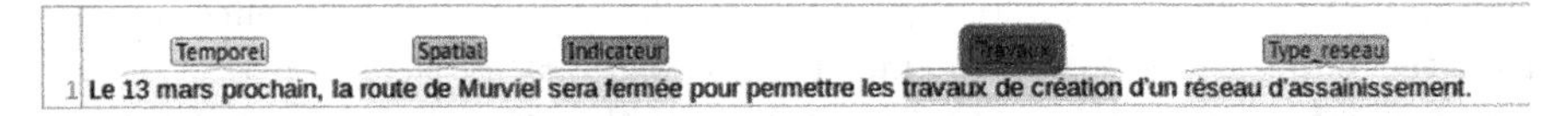

Fig. 1. A portion of the corpus manually annotated for Named Entities. English: On March 13, the road to Murviel will be closed to allow works to create a wastewater network.

Management Conceptual Model (see Fig. 2) which was developed in collaboration with hydrologists.

Based on the possible abstract relations between the entity classes in the model, entity instances found in texts are thus linked with relations: an event of type *Works* is *spatially* and *temporally* localised and specified by the *type of intervention* (implementing a new wastewater network).

3 The WEIR-P System: Architecture

To automatically extract items of information such as the ones previously described, an information extraction system has been created. The NLP pipeline is similar to those generally used for this type of task (see references in Sect. 1), but had to be adapted for our specific needs. In particular it was necessary to create a system which is able to retrieve relevant sources within a specific geographical area, to manage different types of documents, to detect and correlate specific information in texts and finally to relate such information with existing knowledge on a given wastewater system. For this reason a pluri-disciplinary approach was required.

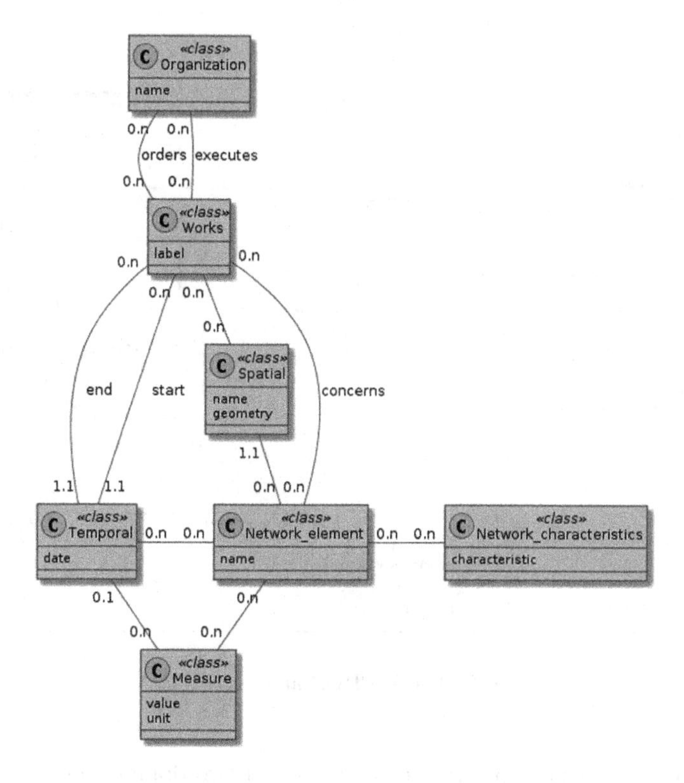

Fig. 2. The wastewater conceptual model.

The global architecture of the WEIR-P system is depicted in Fig. 3. The main steps of the proposed methodology are:

1. Collection of documents;
2. Named-Entity recognition;
3. Semantic relation extraction;
4. Mapping and data visualization.

In this article, we mainly focus on the text mining part of the MeDo project and on the domain adaptation of existing tools for the wastewater domain. It concerns the 1st, 2nd and 3rd steps of the global architecture of the WEIR-P tool (see Fig. 3, Parts A and B). We also briefly present the visualization carried out at document level. The visualization of the network elements on a wastewater map after data fusion will not be presented in this paper.

3.1 Step One - Document Pre-processing and Classification

This step is composed of different sub-steps. The document retrieval algorithm requires the user to specify a geographical area of interest (typically a city or a municipality) as input. The system scrapes documents from the Web using a set

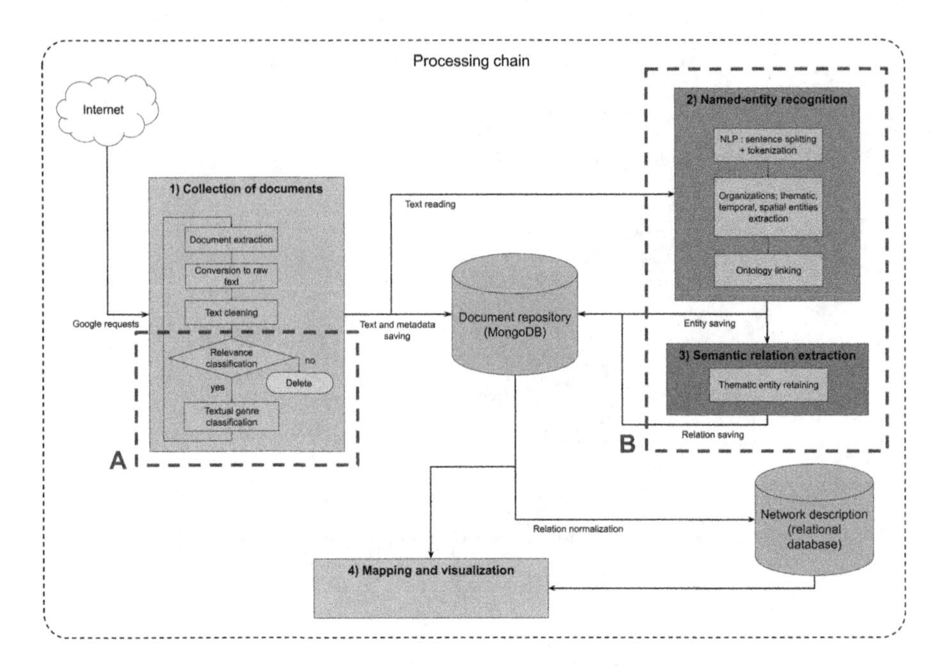

Fig. 3. The WEIR-P architecture.

of Google queries which specify a combination of two domain-related keywords and a place name.

In the corpus creation phase the texts retrieved from the internet are transformed to plain text using various out-of-the-box Python libraries (such as *BeautifulSoup* or *pdf2txt*); some text cleaning is also necessary, in order to restore broken lines and remove boilerplate text using regular expressions. Finally, all the relevant metadata are recorded and the text collection is entered in the database. Once the corpus has been successfully created, a classification for relevance is carried out using Machine Learning techniques which are detailed in Sect. 4.1. The pre-processing steps are similar to those followed for text classification using more complex learning methods [29].

This is a necessary step since the crawling algorithm, which is carried out using a coarse filtering system, will retrieve many irrelevant documents which need to be excluded by using a finer-grain classification. For instance query for documents containing words such as "Montpellier", "eau" (water), "reseau" (network), may sometimes retrieve commercial sites for home plumbing repairs.

3.2 Step Two - Named-Entity Recognition and Classification (NERC)

The goal of the second step is the annotation of Named Entities (NE) in the texts corresponding to the 13 entities or tags defined in Sect. 2.

The texts are first pre-processed by a basic NLP module which performs sentence splitting and tokenisation and PoS tagging, using the TreeTagger module for French [26]. Subsequently, an **ensemble NERC module** is used, which combines the output of three systems: spaCy [15], CoreNLP [20] and Heideltime [28], which is specifically used for temporal entities.

The system was benchmarked as follows:

1. first spaCy and CoreNLP were trained on a sub-set of the gold standard corpus in order to obtain domain adapted models; to improve the results for locations, gazetteers of place names (geographical features, locations, addresses) were extracted and used as additional training features from existing geographical bases.
2. then both spaCy and CoreNLP were tested to assess their performance on each class (except temporal entities).
3. Heideltime was tested without training on temporal entities without domain adaptation, and proved to be the best system for this type of entities.

Based on this, the final NERC algorithm runs as follows: first each text is separately annotated with all three systems and the results are compared. For all entities except temporal, in case of conflict between spaCy and CoreNLP, the best performing system for that category is given the priority. For temporal entities the Heideltime annotation is applied, if needed by overriding previous conflicting annotation by the other systems.

Results of the evaluation for NERC, as well as the details of the benchmarking for each category are provided in Sect. 4.2.

The NERC module is followed by an **Entity Linking module**, which is used to connect spatial entities such as addresses and locations to existing geographical knowledge bases, in order to produce a cartographic representation of the extracted information. The Geonames[4], BAN[5] and Nominatem[6] geographical databases and corresponding APIs are currently used.

The Entity Linking algorithm is quite basic, since filtering on city or location greatly reduces ambiguity for place names, and will not be further discussed nor evaluated in this paper.

3.3 Step Three - Semantic Relation Extraction

The objective of the third step is to connect the spatial, temporal and thematic entities discovered in Step Two.

The relation extraction is applied to ensure that the spatial, temporal and network information is accurately linked to the type of event (Works, Accidents), and that network elements and characteristics are correctly linked to each other and the network type, so that they can be used to enrich the knowledge base.

[4] https://www.geonames.org.
[5] https://adresse.data.gouv.fr/.
[6] https://nominatim.org/.

The relation extraction is performed using basic rules. Generally, for this step, we use a more specific textual context (i.e. sentences or paragraphs) than the classification task related to the first step of the MeDo project. To resolve ambiguities in more complex cases we resort to semantics and use syntactic dependencies extracted using a spaCy out-of-the-box dependency parser for French. Preliminary evaluation results are provided in Sect. 4.3.

3.4 Step Four - Mapping and Visualization

Step four aims to offer the possibility of visualizing the results of the previous treatments. It consists of two sub-steps and only the first one which deals with visualization at document level will be presented in this paper. A graphical user interface was developed to enable users to run the annotation pipeline (Steps 1-2-3) on a selected location (e.g. a city), to inspect the extracted entities and relations, and to decide whether to inject the new knowledge in the system. The interface has been developed using FLASK[7] for the web framework and celery[8] to offset the calculations related to NERC and relation extraction. The d3js library[9] is used to represent the network as a graph where the nodes are coloured according to the NE category (e.g. Temporal, Spatial, Works) and the edges according to the type of relation (e.g. "Has_Temporal", "Has_Spatial"). The Leaflet library[10] is used to map the extracted spatial entities.

The GUI is composed of a standard sign-in module, an administration panel, two monitoring menus to view the progression of tasks and the corresponding notifications and six menus that are more specifically related to the annotation platform. The Corpus menu allows registered users to compile corpora either directly from the Web, or by uploading a zipped file containing pdf documents. Users may also upload zipped files of previously annotated texts. The "Processing" menu allows users to run the classifications described in Sect. 3.1 and the NE and relation extractions described in Sect. 3.2 either simultaneously or sequentially.

Once these steps are completed, the user has the possibility of visualising the results for each individual document in the "Results" menu (Fig. 4). The text and extracted NEs are displayed on the upper part of the screen using the set colour scheme presented in the legend. The semantic relations are displayed as a graph in the lower part of the screen. The export button allows users to create and download a zipped file containing: the document in original and text formats; a pdf of the annotated document and a text file containing the annotations in Brat format (.ann); the graph of relations in svg format; the metadata as a JSON file.

The statistics related to the entire corpus (e.g. number and types of documents, number of words, number and types of entities and relations, number of documents per website, etc.) are visualized in the "Corpus Statistics" menu

[7] https://palletsprojects.com/p/flask/.
[8] http://www.celeryproject.org/.
[9] https://d3js.org/.
[10] https://leafletjs.com/.

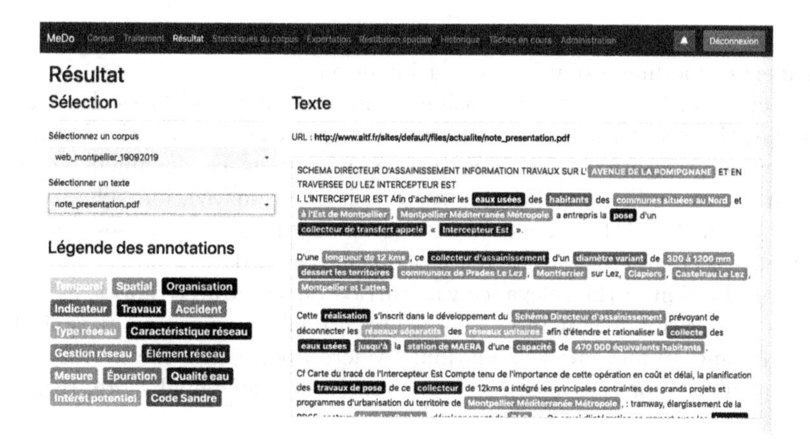

Fig. 4. Screenshot of the results menu. English: WASTEWATER MASTER PLAN INFORMATION REGARDING WORKS ON AVENUE DE LA POMPIGNANE AND ACROSS THE LEZ RIVER. EASTERN INTERCEPTOR. 1. THE EASTERN INTERCEPTOR. In order to convey the wastewater of the inhabitants of the municipalities located north and east of Montpellier, Montpellier Méditerranée Métropole undertook the installation of a sewer main called "Eastern Interceptor". With a length of 12 km, this sewer main with diameters varying between 300 to 1200 mm serves the municipal areas of Prades-le-Lez, Montferrier-sur-Lez, Clapiers, Castelnau-le-Lez, Montpellier and Lattes. This project is part of the Wastewater Master Plan, which provides for the disconnection of the separate networks from the combined sewers in order to extend and rationalise wastewater collection up to the MAERA plant with a capacity of 470,000 equivalent inhabitants. Cf Map of the Eastern Interceptor. Given the importance of this operation in terms of cost and time, the planning of the installation works for this 12 km sewer main took into account the main constraints of the major urbanization projects and programmes in the Montpellier Méditerranée Métropole area: tramway, widening of

and exported in pdf format and a map of the extracted spatial entities is displayed in the "Spatial rendering" menu. Finally, the export menu allows users to download a zipped file containing all the documents composing the corpus, the corresponding annotation files in Brat format and a JSON file of the metadata.

4 Evaluation

We describe the evaluation set-up and results of the domain adapted NERC and relation extraction modules.

4.1 Text Classification Systems

In order to learn the classification model, a training corpus was produced using a subset of the Montpellier corpus. Relevant documents should contain information either about network configuration (location, flow type, design rules, material) or incidents (flooding, pollution, water intrusion).

The classifier has been trained using a multinomial Naive Bayes classification method, with a scikit-learn Python library. For each classification the features are bags-of-words, weighted by TF-IDF (term frequency-inverse document frequency [25]). One thousand stopwords were used with no lemmatization. The relevance training corpus has 441 elements (3,512 words), split into two classes ("Relevant Document/Keep" and "Not relevant document/Discard").

The evaluation of the relevance was carried out separately and is calculated in terms of precision, recall and F-score. The evaluation presented in Table 2 was obtained using 10-fold cross validation; "Macro" represents the average of the values calculated for each class; "Micro" represents the global score, regardless of classes.

Table 2. Evaluation of textual relevance.

	Precision	Recall	F-score
Micro	0.925	0.925	0.925
Macro	0.928	0.931	0.921

The precision, recall and F-score are high (>0.90): the proposed method is able to detect the relevant documents correctly.

4.2 NERC

Evaluation was carried out using the MUC-5 specification on the annotated corpus described in paragraph Sect. 2. We provide here the evaluation result of the best model for each entity type. As it can be seen in Table 3, we can achieve the best results for all of the classes except one (*Network Type*) by combination of two models, the first of which has precedence in case of conflict.

The current results are encouraging for a subset of categories, however they still require improvement for other ones, for which the trained models seem to perform not as well. In some cases, the lower results are probably caused by the fact that some categories, such as *Accident*, are poorly represented in our corpus. In other cases, such as for *Indicator*, the problem may be linked to heterogeneity of this category, which includes modifiers such as adverbs and adjectives related to various types of information (temporal, spatial, domain specific...).

Table 3. Results for each category of entities, using the best performing systems. [e] indicates the use of an ensemble model, where the first system has priority.

Entity	Occurrences	Precision	Recall	F-score	Model
Network_type	360	70.41	68.54	69.46	corenlp
Treatment	342	66.51	62.77	64.59	[e]corenlp-spaCy
Network_element	367	61.86	65.20	63.49	[e]spaCy-corenlp
Works	310	59.74	67.29	63.29	[e]spaCy-corenlp
Spatial	1001	58.05	67.75	62.52	[e]spaCy-corenlp
Measure	882	59.07	65.42	62.08	[e]corenlp-spaCy
Temporal	219	42.53	74.50	54.15	[e]heidel-corenlp
Water_quality	136	51.85	53.85	52.83	[e]corenlp-spaCy
Network_characteristics	196	55.00	47.06	50.72	[e]spaCy-corenlp
Network_management	255	40.47	42.83	41.61	[e]corenlp-spaCy
Indicator	592	35.90	33.26	34.53	[e]corenlp-spaCy
Organization	129	44.23	27.06	33.58	[e]corenlp-spaCy
Accident	26	34.78	20.00	25.40	[e]corenlp-spaCy

4.3 Relation Extraction

As we have seen, the Relation Extraction (RE) module is rule based and adds semantic links between the various entities in order to identify units of knowledge. In order to eliminate any noise caused by possible NERC errors, and thus to evaluate RE performances in isolation, a sub-set of the gold standard was automatically annotated with relations; the output contains 2,913 relations. Seven documents corresponding to a sampling rate of 30% were randomly selected for expert evaluation. At this stage only precision was evaluated, and experts checked automatically extracted relations between entities, assessing and labelling them as correct or incorrect. Missing relations were not taken into account. The rate of correctly detected relations is relatively high (precision = 0.83). Errors mostly occur when Named Entities, *i.e.* spatial ones, are juxtaposed. Linkage results are also impacted by errors in Named Entity recognition and text conversion, *i.e.* missing punctuation marks which modify the sentence structure and impact dependency rules.

5 Use Case and Discussion

The WEIR-P information extraction pipeline offers users the possibility of rapidly acquiring information on the wastewater network of a city. The pipeline is a time-saver namely because the automatic Web-scraping phase, using a preset list of keywords, enables the user to multi-task, while the relevance check reduces the number of documents the user has to go over. In addition, the entity recognition module improves visual foraging and reduces reading time as a highlighted text will be more likely to be attended to and remembered than a plain text [8]. Note that it takes 5 hrs to run 393 queries, under a minute to determine the relevance of a corpus containing 1,040 documents, and 5 hrs and 17 mins to extract 147,423 entities on 534 documents classified as relevant. In comparison, the average silent reading rate of an adult is 238 words per minute [4]. It would thus take an average adult 10 days, 8 hrs and 9 mins non stop to merely read the 1,040 documents.

The platform is an interesting aid as it can reconstruct events. Thus, hotspots can be identified through the "Accident" or "Works" labels or simply by analysing the frequency of occurrence of street or district names. A fully automated process is being implemented in the new version of the pipeline to carry out this task. Indeed, this type of information may also be useful to wastewater network managers who have just been granted concessions by public authorities in a new city and are not yet familiar with the network's history. Two representatives of the private sector leaders in Computer-aided Maintenance Management Systems (CMMS)/Enterprise Asset Management (EAM) and water and wastewater treatment services, are part of the project's steering committee and have been following the pipeline's development. Both expressed high interest in the pipeline's ability to recover dates and link them with network equipment as it would help plan maintenance operations. This feature was also highlighted by a representative of the public service in charge of wastewater management. We performed a test on the city of Montpellier and were able to recover 233 occurrences of the word "pose" (to lay, to place in French), 559 of "mise en place" (implementation), 512 of "extension" and 375 occurrences of "réhabilitation" in the "Works" category. This type of information may also be recovered using digital archives uploaded manually by the user into the pipeline in pdf or txt format. The implementation of the platform would not be costly to local stakeholders as small material and human resources are needed to run it. The day to day life of the institutions and their regular business practices would not be affected as it would be mostly used for asset management i.e. for decision making at mid-management level. However, as with any new tool, training and time will be necessary to take in the change in practice.

As with many emerging tools, there is of course room for improvement. The evaluation results show that the current version of the system still presents various shortcomings that will be addressed in an improved version of the pipeline. In terms of information content, quantitative data (geometry, hydraulic performance) is mentioned less than events (i.e. works or accidents) in our documents (3,333 occurrences *vs.* 11,936 in the Montpellier Corpus). Also, the granularity of the spatial data is based on the type of document: street or district names are often mentioned in both technical reports and newspaper articles, however real-world coordinates are seldom found in the latter. Thus the WEIR-P pipeline may be a good tool to complete existing network databases and GIS systems. This would imply using data fusion techniques to combine and merge sometimes conflicting information. In order to improve on the current system, a larger manually annotated corpus may be necessary. The genre adaptation of NERC, exploiting the results of the text classification, will also be implemented.

A Sample-based generalization strategy [31] is implemented to ensure the genericity of the tool. Since WEIR-P relies heavily on Statistical learning, new samples from other French cities are currently being used for training. Validation is being carried out on other French speaking countries. The first tests on the city of Abidjan (Ivory Coast) are encouraging. The NER module is able to correctly label the network elements and the relation linking module will undergo further training in order to take into account local language uses.

6 Conclusions and Perspectives

We have presented a global model of the information extraction from documents related to wastewater management and a platform which implements it. The preliminary results obtained on the Montpellier corpus are encouraging and show how a mix of supervised and rule-based techniques can be used to extract useful information and reconstruct the various phases of the extension of a given wastewater management network. The pipeline may also be used to recover the dates when given pieces of equipment were laid. This feature is deemed very useful by managers who need to plan ahead maintenance operations for old assets with missing implementation dates. The genericity of the tool we have developed is being assessed through tests on other cities in France and in French Speaking countries. Indeed, some countries in North and West Africa, namely Morocco and Ivory Coast use Special Technical Specifications (STS) guidelines that are strongly inspired by the French ones. A quick analysis of the guidelines used in Quebec [21] shows that the technical vocabulary used to designate the network elements are also similar to the French ones. However, local language uses may vary. For instance the expression "assainissement d'un quartier" (sanitation of a neighbourhood) refers to sanitation/wastewater network laying for the French media and to cleaning of illegal occupation of public space for the Abidjanese. Thus, some adaptation work might be necessary to remove ambiguities.

The system still requires slight improvements as the information extraction pipeline produces some noise. Manual inspection by an expert of the extracted results may therefore be necessary and could be carried out using the visualization and spatial representation modules which enable users to easily assess the extracted data and further improve the models. In order to improve on the current system, a larger manually annotated corpus may be necessary. We also plan to use alternative classification algorithms such as One-class SVM that has been successfully adapted for reduced training samples [17] and perform semantic relation extraction based on document textual genre.

We believe that the domain modelling work carried out within MeDo will be useful to others working in the same domain, on French as well as on other languages. Since the NLP systems used in the NERC module of our pipeline support multiple languages, we assume that their adaptation should be a straightforward procedure.

References

1. Altaweel, M., Bone, C.: Applying content analysis for investigating the reporting of water issues. Comput. Environ. Urban Syst. **36**(6), 599–613 (2012). https://doi.org/10.1016/j.compenvurbsys.2012.03.004
2. Ananiadou, S., Pyysalo, S., Tsujii, J., Kell, D.B.: Event extraction for systems biology by text mining the literature. Trends Biotechnol. **28**(7), 381–390 (2010). https://doi.org/10.1016/j.tibtech.2010.04.005
3. Araya, F., Faust, K., Kaminsky, J.A.: Understanding hosting communities as a stakeholder in the provision of water and wastewater services to displaced persons. Sustain. Cities Soc. **57** 102114 (2020). https://doi.org/10.1016/j.scs.2020.102114
4. Brysbaert, M.: How many words do we read per minute? A review and meta-analysis of reading rate. J. Mem. Lang. **10**, 31–71 (2019). https://doi.org/10.1016/j.jml.2019.104047
5. Chahinian, N., Delenne, C., Commandre, B., Derras, M., Deruelle, L., Bailly, J.S.: Automatic mapping of urban wastewater networks based on manhole cover locations. Comput. Environ. Urban Syst. **78**, (2019). https://doi.org/10.1016/j.compenvurbsys.2019.101370. https://hal.archives-ouvertes.fr/hal-02275903
6. Chahinian, N., et al.: Gold Standard du projet MeDo. DataSuds, V1 (2020). https://doi.org/10.23708/H0VXH0
7. Chahinian, N., et al.: Guide d'annotation du projet MeDo. DataSuds, V1 (2020). https://doi.org/10.23708/DAAKF1
8. Chi, E.H., Gumbrecht, M., Hong, L.: Visual foraging of highlighted text: an eye-tracking study. In: Jacko, J.A. (ed.) HCI 2007. LNCS, vol. 4552, pp. 589–598. Springer, Heidelberg (2007). https://doi.org/10.1007/978-3-540-73110-8_64
9. Chinchor, N., Sundheim, B.: Muc-5 evaluation metrics. In: Fifth Message Understanding Conference (MUC-5): Proceedings of a Conference Held in Baltimore, Maryland, 25–27 August 1993, pp. 25–27 (1993)
10. Cookey, P.E., Darnsawasdi, R., Ratanachai, C.: Text mining analysis of institutional fit of Lake Basin water governance. Ecol. Ind. **72**, 640–658 (2017). https://doi.org/10.1016/j.ecolind.2016.08.057
11. Copara, J., Knafou, J., Naderi, N., Moro, C., Ruch, P., Teodoro, D.: Contextualized French Language Models for Biomedical Named Entity Recognition. Actes de la 6e conférence conjointe Journées d'Études sur la Parole (JEP, 33e édition), Traitement Automatique des Langues Naturelles (TALN, 27e édition), Rencontre des Étudiants Chercheurs en Informatique pour le Traitement Automatique des Langues (RÉCITAL, 22e édition). Atelier DÉfi Fouille de Textes, pp. 36–48. ATALA et AFCP, Nancy, France (2020)
12. COVADIS: Standard de données réseaux d'AEP & d'assainissement, version 1.2 (2019). http://www.geoinformations.developpement-durable.gouv.fr/
13. Dominguès, C., Jolivet, L., Brando, C., Cargill, M.: Place and Sentiment-based Life story Analysis. Revue française des sciences de l'information et de la communication (17), 0–22 (2019). https://doi.org/10.4000/rfsic.7228
14. Ekstrom, J.A., Lau, G.T.: Exploratory text mining of ocean law to measure overlapping agency and jurisdictional authority. In: Proceedings of the 2008 International Conference on Digital Government Research, pp. 53–62. dg.o '08, Digital Government Society of North America (2008)
15. Explosion: spaCy (2019). https://spacy.io/
16. Gregory, I.N., Hardie, A.: Visual GISting: bringing together corpus linguistics and Geographical Information Systems. Literary Linguist. Comput. **26**(3), 297–314 (2011). https://doi.org/10.1093/llc/fqr022

17. Guerbai, Y., Chibani, Y., Hadjadji, B.: The effective use of the one-class SVM classifier for handwritten signature verification based on writer-independent parameters. Pattern Recogn. **48**(1), 103–113 (2015). https://doi.org/10.1016/j.patcog.2014.07.016
18. Hori, S.: An exploratory analysis of the text mining of news articles about water and society. In: Brebbia, C.A. (ed.) WIT Transactions on The Built Environment, vol. 1, pp. 501–508. WIT Press (2015). https://doi.org/10.2495/SD150441
19. Kergosien, E., et al.: Automatic Identification of Research Fields in Scientific Papers. In: Calzolari, N., et al. (eds.) Proceedings of the Eleventh International Conference on Language Resources and Evaluation (LREC 2018), pp. 1902–1907. European Language Resources Association (ELRA), Miyazaki, Japan, 7–12 May 2018 (2018)
20. Manning, C.D., Surdeanu, M., Bauer, J., Finkel, J., Bethard, S.J., McClosky, D.: The Stanford CoreNLP natural language processing toolkit. In: Association for Computational Linguistics (ACL) System Demonstrations, pp. 55–60 (2014). http://www.aclweb.org/anthology/P/P14/P14-5010
21. Ministère du Développement Durable de l'Envionnement et de la lutte contre les changements climatiques: Description des ouvrages municipaux d'assainissement des eaux usées (DOMAEU) - Guide de rédaction. Technical report, Direction générale des politiques de l'eau, Direction des eaux usées (2018), https://www.environnement.gouv.qc.ca/eau/eaux-usees/ouvrages-municipaux/domaeu-guide-redaction.pdf
22. Park, K., Okudan-Kremer, G.: Text mining-based categorization and user perspective analysis of environmental sustainability indicators for manufacturing and service systems. Ecol. Ind. **72**, 803–820 (2017). https://doi.org/10.1016/j.ecolind.2016.08.027
23. Peffers, K., et al.: The design science research process: A model for producing and presenting information systems research. In: Proceedings of First International Conference on Design Science Research in Information Systems and Technology DESRIST (2006)
24. Rogers, C., et al.: Condition assessment of the surface and buried infrastructure/-a proposal for integration. Tunn. Undergr. Space Technol. **28**, 202–211 (2012). https://doi.org/10.1016/j.tust.2011.10.012
25. Salton, G., McGill, M.J.: Introduction to Modern Information Retrieval. McGraw-Hill Inc., New York (1986)
26. Schmid, H.: Treetagger, a language independent part-of-speech tagger. Institut für Maschinelle Sprachverarbeitung, Universität Stuttgart **43**, 28 (1995)
27. Shardlow, M., et al.: A new corpus to support text mining for the curation of metabolites in the ChEBI database. In: Proceedings of the Eleventh International Conference on Language Resources and Evaluation (LREC 2018), pp. 280–285. European Language Resources Association (ELRA), Miyazaki, Japan, May 2018. https://www.aclweb.org/anthology/L18-1042
28. Strötgen, J., Gertz, M.: Heideltime: high quality rule-based extraction and normalization of temporal expressions. In: Proceedings of the 5th International Workshop on Semantic Evaluation, pp. 321–324. Association for Computational Linguistics (2010)
29. Venkata Sailaja, N., Padmasree, L., Mangathayaru, N.: Incremental learning for text categorization using rough set boundary based optimized Support Vector Neural Network. Data Technol. Appl. **54**(5), 585–601 (2020). https://doi.org/10.1108/DTA-03-2020-0071

30. Wang, W., Stewart, K.: Spatiotemporal and semantic information extraction from Web news reports about natural hazards. Comput. Environ. Urban Syst. **50**, 30–40 (2015). https://doi.org/10.1016/j.compenvurbsys.2014.11.001
31. Wieringa, R., Daneva, M.: Six strategies for generalizing software engineering theories. Sci. Comput. Program. **101**, 136–152 (2015). https://doi.org/10.1016/j.scico.2014.11.013

Recommendations for Data-Driven Degradation Estimation with Case Studies from Manufacturing and Dry-Bulk Shipping

Nils Finke[1,2], Marisa Mohr[1,3(✉)], Alexander Lontke[3,4], Marwin Züfle[4], Samuel Kounev[4], and Ralf Möller[1]

[1] University of Lübeck, Institute of Information Systems, Lübeck, Germany
{finke,mohr}@ifis.uni-luebeck.de
[2] Oldendorff Carriers GmbH & Co. KG., Lübeck, Germany
[3] inovex GmbH, Hamburg, Germany
[4] University of Würzburg, Department of Computer Science, Würzburg, Germany

Abstract. Predictive planning of maintenance windows reduces the risk of unwanted production or operational downtimes and helps to keep machines, vessels, or any system in optimal condition. The quality of such a data-driven model for the prediction of remaining useful lifetime is largely determined by the data used to train it. Training data with qualitative information, such as labeled data, is extremely rare, so classical similarity models cannot be applied. Instead, degradation models extrapolate future conditions from historical behaviour by regression. Research offers numerous methods for predicting the remaining useful lifetime by degradation regression. However, the implementation of existing approaches poses significant challenges to users due to a lack of comparability and best practices. This paper provides a general approach for composing existing process steps such as health stage classification, frequency analysis, feature extraction, or regression models for the estimation of degradation. To challenge effectiveness and relations between the steps, we run several experiments in two comprehensive case studies, one from manufacturing and one from dry-bulk shipping. We conclude with recommendations for composing a data-driven degradation estimation process.

Keywords: Remaining useful lifetime · Bearing · Vessel performance

1 Introduction

Data-driven products and machine learning methods offer large benefits for production engineering companies. Predictive maintenance can reduce the risk of unwanted production and operational downtime and help keep machines, vessels, and systems in optimal condition. A key challenge of this is the estimation of

N. Finke and M. Mohr—contributed equally to this work.

S. Cherfi et al. (Eds.): RCIS 2021, LNBIP 415, pp. 189–204, 2021.
https://doi.org/10.1007/978-3-030-75018-3_12

remaining useful lifetime (RUL), that is, predicting the time to failure. However, the development of such products requires a large initial investment in the model definition and training data acquisition. The latter is especially important, as the prediction quality of a machine learning model is largely determined by the data used for training. Labeled data or large amounts of observed run-to-failure data are extremely rare. Of course, one could deliberately degrade machines to capture more failure patterns, but that is at least financially irresponsible.

One way to model RUL without having labeled or entire failure data from similar machines is to use degradation models. Degradation models estimate the RUL only indirectly by relating the degradation of parts of the product itself to the failure mechanisms. Degradation analysis allows the analyst to extrapolate to an assumed failure time based on measurement of time series performance or sensor data directly related to the suspected failure of the machine under consideration. An initial evaluation of appropriate data that give an indicator of degradation presents an initial challenge. However, after initial investment, one also benefits from a prediction of intermediate states up to the failure itself.

Research provides numerous methods for modelling degradation and RUL. To decide on an appropriate approach, there are few or insufficient comparisons of existing methods. To help deciding on a solution for real-world challenges, one needs a mechanism to compare existing methods. To demonstrate feasibility, one is interested to setup a basic solution before improving the overall approach.

In this paper, we present a general data-driven approach for predicting RUL that considers comparability of existing approaches in the best possible sense. This approach includes four steps: health stage (HS) classification, frequency analysis, feature extraction, and the prediction itself performed by regression. By means of the approach, we focus on four general research questions that arise in the search for an appropriate modelling method:

1. Can HS classification improve the accuracy of prediction?
2. Does the frequency spectrum of a time series provide more useful information than the raw data, i.e., time spectrum, itself?
3. Which feature sets are appropriate for the estimation of degradation?
4. Which data-driven regression method yields the highest accuracy?

For general validity and comparability, we present two comprehensive case studies in different industries, namely manufacturing and dry-bulk shipping. The aim of this work is not to achieve the best possible predictive accuracy. Instead, we investigate the interaction of the steps and conclude with recommendations for the composition of a data-driven degradation estimation process.

2 Remaining Useful Lifetime Prediction

In this section we place our work in the context of RUL prediction, and present related work.

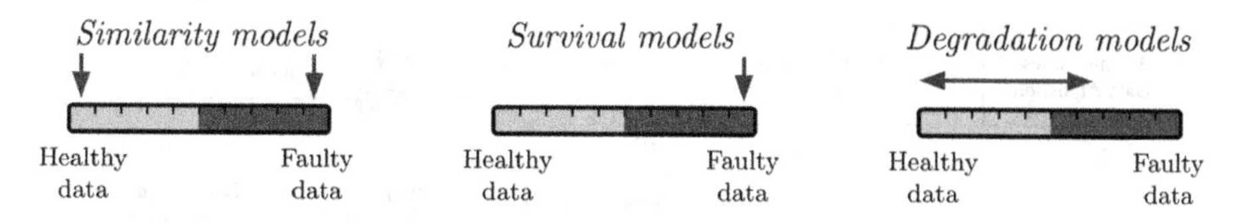

Fig. 1. Three families of models for the prediction of RUL.

2.1 Modelling the Remaining Useful Lifetime

Depending on the type of measurement data, three different model families are applied. The different families of data-driven models for predicting RUL are visualised in Fig. 1, with arrows indicating the types of training data available. *Similarity models* use run-to-failure data from similar machines, starting during healthy operation and ending close to failure or maintenance. RUL is directly estimated from historical labeled training data by applying a pattern matching of trends or conditional indicator values. *Survival models* are used when the user does not have a complete history of run-to-failure data but instead has data about the life span of related components. Probability distributions are determined based on the behaviour of related components and used to estimate RUL. *Degradation models* estimate the degradation process without requiring faulty data. Historical behaviour of a machine condition indicator is used to extrapolate the damage progression to indirectly determine RUL.

In real-world challenges complete run-to-failure data are rarely available, we focus on degradation models. We use data-driven statistical methods being suitable when little domain knowledge is available or generalised models are desired.

2.2 Related Work

Research provides many approaches for the estimation of degradation processes. In regular operation healthy data outweighs degradation data, so data-driven prediction is often challenged by imbalance. To address imbalance, an additional preprocessing step, such as HS classification can be used. To distinguish between healthy and faulty data, different classification indicators from kurtosis to self-organising maps are applied before model training, e.g., in [8,12,14,15,20,24]. To gain other information further preprocessing by frequency analysis are performed before extracting features for degradation regression. Examples range from classical discrete Fourier transform (DFT), short-time Fourier transform (STFT) to Hilbert-Huang transform [4,6,9,11,14,21]. Since most classical data-driven models cannot directly process time series, the extraction of additional scalar-valued features from time series is necessary before these algorithms can be applied.

Feature extraction performed using feature engineering methods range from classical statistical measurements such as root mean square and kurtosis [2,6,20] to information-theoretic entropies [5,11,21,25]. Other authors provide feature learning methods based on isomap [4], autoencoder [9] or convolutional neural

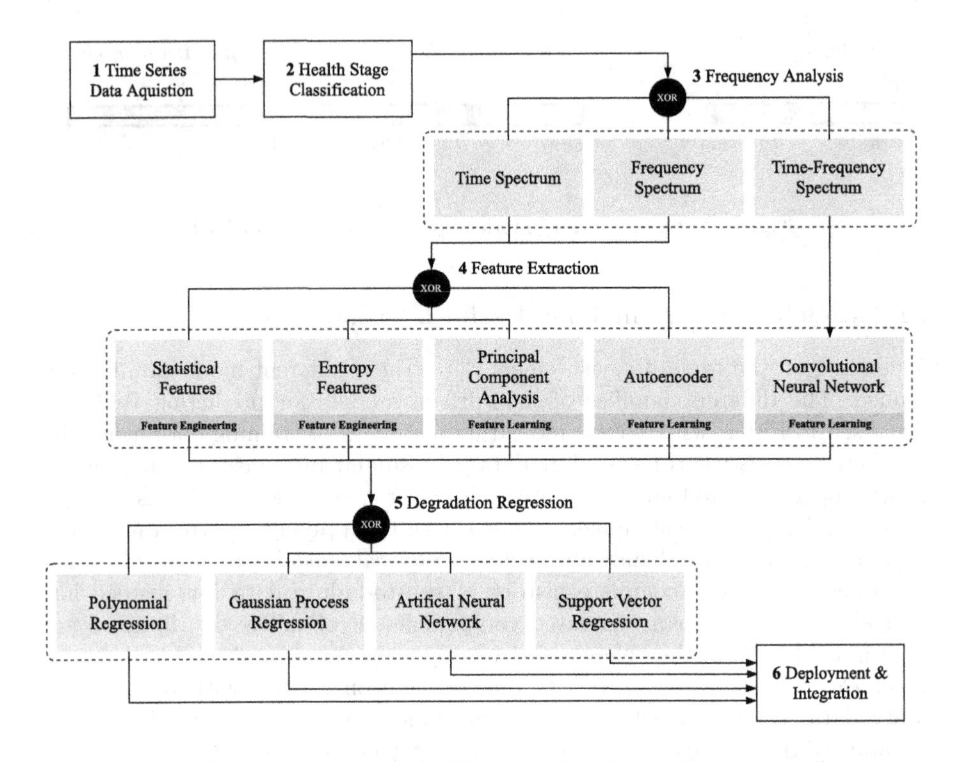

Fig. 2. Six technical steps of RUL prediction (2 and 3 are optional).

networks (CNN) [14]. Data-driven models for degradation estimation are implemented, e.g., by polynomial regression (PR) [13,23], support vector regression (SVR) [10], or artificial neural networks (ANN) for regression [21].

Besides on preprocessing steps, prediction accuracy depends on the choice of features and the regression algorithm used. Comparisons are either available for feature sets based on different selection indicators [23,25] or for data-driven methods for RUL regression [7,19]. However, none of the comparisons take into account the interaction of preprocessing steps, feature extraction, and regression algorithms at once. In two comprehensive case studies, we strengthen the understanding and effectiveness of the different steps as well as their interactions.

3 A Data-Driven Approach for Degradation Estimation

We present a general approach for comparison of the different steps for the estimation of degradation. In general, the degradation estimation process consists of six technical steps, i.e., time series data acquisition, HS classification, frequency analysis, feature or indicator extraction, degradation estimation by regression, and deployment and integration as presented in Fig. 2. We focus on steps 2 to 5, as data acquisition, and appropriate deployment, and integration of the predictive model depend on both domain and user's system infrastructure.

Next, we follow Fig. 2 by addressing the steps before discussing them as part of two case studies to answer the introduced research questions.

3.1 Health Stage Classification

The second step in the overall process visualised in Fig. 2 is considered optional. Caused by the fact that healthy data outweighs degradation data in regular operation, data-driven prediction of the degradation process can be impeded or even biased by healthy data. In order to distinguish between healthy and faulty stages in a time series, the point in time when the degradation starts has to be identified. The boundary of the two stages is called the first prediction time (FPT). For simplicity, in this work we include an approach by Li et al. [12], where kurtosis is used as such a classification indicator. The FPT corresponds to the time when the kurtosis of a sliding window over the time series exceeds the interval $\mu \pm 2\sigma$ for the second time, where μ is the mean and σ is the standard deviation at the beginning of the time series. After the identification of FPT, observations in data classified as healthy are omitted from both training and prediction of degradation. The prediction by the regression model is initiated when data is classified as unhealthy. To answer our first research question, we evaluate in Sect. 4 whether this additional step can improve the accuracy of the estimation of degradation by adding the HS classifier.

3.2 Frequency Analysis

The third step in the overall process visualised in Fig. 2 is the analysis of the frequency range of a time series that can provide further insights into the degradation process. In this step we distinguish between time spectrum, frequency spectrum and time-frequency spectrum analysis. By *time spectrum*, we denote the raw time series on which no frequency analysis is performed. By *frequency spectrum*, we denote a time series that is transformed by discrete Fourier transform (DFT). DFT transforms a finite sequence of equally-spaced observed data points $(x_0, ..., x_T)$ into another sequence $(X_0, X_1, \ldots, X_T)$ that is a complex-valued function of frequency. The fast Fourier transform (FFT) is an efficient algorithm for computing DFT. Showing a trend, degradation time series are inherently non-stationary, i.e., the mean is not constant over time. To analyse the frequency spectrum of non-stationary time series, short-time Fourier transform (STFT) is used. To assume stationarity, the STFT uses a window function to select short time periods with constant mean. Several frequency spectra are calculated per window by DFT. By *time-frequency spectrum*, we denote a time series on which STFT is performed. Note that in the next step of the overall process, not every feature extraction method can be applied on every frequency analysis method. Implementation details follow in Sect. 4.

3.3 Feature Extraction

A model cannot represent information that it does not have. The extraction of features in step four visualised in Fig. 2 refers to the creation of new

Table 1. List of statistical features.

Mean	$\bar{x} = \frac{1}{T}\sum_{i=1}^{T} x_i$	Skewness	$\frac{\frac{1}{T}\sum_{i=1}^{T}(x_i-\bar{x})^3}{(\frac{1}{T}\sum_{i=1}^{T}(x_i-\bar{x})^2)^{\frac{3}{2}}}$
Max	$\max\{x_1, ..., x_T\}$	Kurtosis	$\frac{\frac{1}{T}\sum_{i=1}^{T}(x_i-\bar{x})^4}{(\frac{1}{T}\sum_{i=1}^{T}(x_i-\bar{x})^2)^2}$
Min	$\min\{x_1, ..., x_T\}$	Peak factor	$\frac{max(x)}{\sqrt{\frac{1}{T}\sum_{i=1}^{T} x_i^2}}$
Root mean square	$\sqrt{\frac{1}{n}\sum_{i=1}^{T} x_i^2}$	Change coefficient	$\frac{\bar{x}}{\sqrt{\frac{1}{T}\sum_{i=1}^{T} x_i^2}}$
Peak to peak value	$\max(x) - \min(x)$	Clearence factor	$\frac{max(x)}{\frac{1}{T}\sum_{i=1}^{T}(x_i)^2}$
Variance	$\frac{1}{T}\sum_{i=1}^{T}(x_i - \bar{x})^2$	Absolute Energy	$\sum_{i=1}^{T} x_i^2$

information that was previously not available. Techniques for feature extraction can be classified into two groups, namely feature engineering and feature learning.

Feature Engineering is the older discipline of the two. New features are created by processing domain-specific knowledge or by transforming data. Techniques for feature engineering origin from at least two research areas. The first way to extract features is by means of statistical analysis. A list of the *statistical features* for a univariate time series $x \in \mathbb{R}^T$ used in this work is given in Table 1. Another way of extracting features is by using information-theoretic measurements, called *entropies*. The concept of entropy was first introduced by Claude Elwood Shannon in 1948 and has since been used to quantify the complexity of data in numerous other fields. (Shannon) entropy is defined as the expected number of bits needed to encode a message that is $H = -\sum_{z \in Z} p_z \log_2(p_z)$, where Z is the set of possible symbols used in a message, p_z is the probability of $z \in Z$ appearing in a message. The number of bits required is in direct relation to the complexity (and entropy) of the message, meaning few or many bits reflect a low or high entropy, respectively. To use entropies as features for time series, observations are encoded as sequences of symbolic abstractions. As far as current research is concerned, there are two general approaches of symbolisation [17]. Classical symbolisation approaches use data range partitioning and thresholds for symbol assignment such as the well-known Symbolic Aggregate approXimation (SAX). The ordinal pattern symbolisation approach, describing the up and downs in a time series, is based on an approach by Bandt and Pompe [3]. Combining the ordinal pattern symbolisation approach with Shannon entropy leads to a special case called permutation entropy. All listed features can be applied directly to time and frequency spectrum.

Feature Learning compared to feature engineering, solve optimisation problems to learn features from a set of time series. Learned features can reveal task-specific patterns that are not obvious to humans, including non-linear patterns. There are numerous ways to learn features as principal component analysis, autoencoders, and convolutional neural networks.

The *principal component analysis (PCA)* is a well-known method converting a set of observations of possibly correlated variables $X \in \mathbb{R}^{n \times p}$ into a set of values of linearly uncorrelated variables $X' \in \mathbb{R}^{n \times p}$. Using eigenvalue analysis, an orthogonal transformation that preserves greatest variance in data yields in new p basis vectors, also called principal components. Keeping only the first r principal components gives the truncated transformation $X'_r = XW_r$, where $W \in \mathbb{R}^{p \times r}$ is a matrix whose columns are the eigenvectors of $X^T X$ sorted in descending order of the r highest corresponding eigenvalues, and a new lower-dimensional representation of the data.

A relatively new method for reducing dimensionality are *autoencoders*, a branch of ANNs. The architecture consists of two connected ANNs compressing the input variable into a reduced dimensional space, also called encoder, and re-creating the input data, also called decoder. Each node of the hidden "bottleneck" layer of compressed information can be treated as a feature in subsequent learning tasks, just as the selected principle components. The autoencoder as well as PCA can be applied directly to the time and frequency spectrum.

A *convolutional neural network (CNN)* is another type of ANNs typically used for image recognition, but also for signal processing. The architecture of a classical CNN consists of one or more convolutional layers followed by a pooling layer. In a convolutional layer, a matrix, also called filter kernel, is moved stepwise over the input data calculating the inner product of both. The result is called feature map. Accordingly, neighbouring neurons in the convolutional layer correspond to overlapping regions such as similar frequencies in signals. In a pooling layer, superfluous information is discarded and a more abstract lower-dimensional representation of the relevant information is obtained by combining neighbouring elements of the map, e.g., by calculating the maximum. To feed the matrix output of the convolution layer and the pooling layer into a final fully connected layer, it must first be unrolled (flattened). The flatten layer is then treated as a feature. The CNN has to be applied to the time-frequency spectrum. Implementation details for all feature extraction methods are listed in Sect. 4.

3.4 Degradation Regression

Regression models, as one of the most popular data-driven techniques for RUL prediction, fit available degradation data by regression functions and extrapolate the future progression. We consider the following regression models: multiple linear regression, Gaussian process regression, artificial neural network regression, and support vector regression.

Multiple linear regression (MLR) is a statistical technique that fits an observed dependent variable by several independent variables using the method of least squares. More precisely, the coefficients of a linear function $y_t = x_{t1}w_1 + x_{t2}w_2 + \cdots + x_{tK}w_K + \varepsilon_t = \mathbf{x}_t^\top \boldsymbol{w} + \varepsilon_t, t = 1, 2, \ldots, T$, are estimated, where y is the response variable, x_K are the predictors, and w the coefficients of the model.

In a traditional regression model, we infer a single function, $Y = f(X)$. In *Gaussian process regression (GPR)*, we place a Gaussian process over $f(X)$. A Gaussian process (GP) is a collection of random variables, of which any finite subset of random variables is Gaussian distributed. It is completely specified by its mean $\mu = m(x) = \mathrm{E}[f(x)]$ and its covariance or kernel function $k(x, x') = \mathrm{E}[(f(x) - m(x))(f(x') - m(x'))]$. As such, GP describes a distribution over possible Gaussian density functions. The chosen kernel k (e.g. periodic, linear, radial basis function) that describes the general shapes of the functions, defines a prior distribution of $f(X)$. This similarly equals selecting the degree of a polynomial function for regression. Placing the Gaussian prior over $f(X)$ yields a posterior joint distribution being used to determine the future process.

An *artificial neuronal network (ANN)* can pretend to be any type of regression model. The output of an ANN is based on the activation function between input and output layer. As an ANN is mainly used for classification, sigmoid function is used as a popular activation function, whereas when using ANN to solve a linear regression problem, the activation function is chosen as linear equation $y = w_0 + w_1x_1 + \cdots w_nx_n$.

Support vector regression (SVR) is based on similar principles as support vector machine (SVM) for classification, identifying the optimal support vectors of a hyperplane that separates the data into their respective classes. Instead of separating classes, SVR fits a hyperplane describing the training data best. To solve the optimisation problem of finding the best hyperplane, the coefficient vector of the hyperplane is minimised – in contrast to ordinary least squares fitting where the squared error is minimised. Instead the squared error term is handled in the constraints allowing a certain error range ϵ, i.e., min $\frac{1}{2}||w||^2$ s.t. $|y_i - w_ix_i| < \epsilon$.

4 Case Studies

We present two case studies from two different branches of industry. We introduce the case studies and follow with general experimental settings before evaluating our proposed approach in each case study.

4.1 Introduction and Data

In the first case study, we address degradation of mechanical bearings in manufacturing. In the second case study, we consider performance degradation of vessels in dry-bulk shipping. In the first case study we focus on one specific machine part, whilst in the second case study we address not only one specific part, but an entire system.

Bearing Degradation in Manufacturing. The research project Collaborative Smart Contracting Platform for digital value-creation Networks (KOSMoS) provides a cross-company platform for a secure and semi-transparent exchange of production data[1]. The system establishes the optimal conditions for transparent

[1] https://www.kosmos-bmbf.de/.

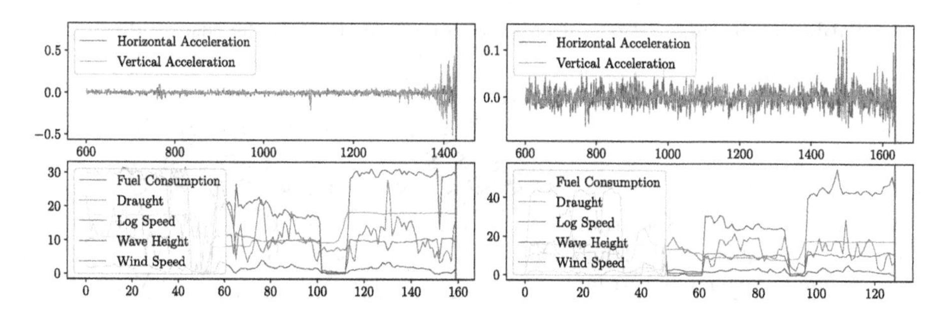

Fig. 3. Horizontal and vertical acceleration (vibration) of bearings b_{14} (top left) and b_{32} (top right). Fuel consumption, draught, speed, wave height and wind speed for two vessels (bottom left and right). The red line indicates end of useful lifetime. (Color figure online)

documentation of the maintenance processes of a machine and thus supports, for example, the planning of service deployments. In addition, machine downtimes can be avoided by combining transparent documentation of maintenance history and production data in predictive maintenance models [16]. A common challenge for the KOSMoS consortium partners from industry is the RUL prediction of mechanical *bearings*, a degrading machine part, which is installed in almost every machine, and thus has significant relevance for maintenance.

The dataset used for the case study is the well-known bearing dataset provided by FEMTO-ST institute within PRONOSTIA, an experimental platform dedicated to the testing and validation of bearing failure detection, diagnostic, and prognostic approaches [18]. The FEMTO bearing dataset contains run-to-failure tests of 17 bearings each with time series data of vibration acceleration along the horizontal and vertical dimension as well as temperature. Temperature is not present in every run, thus, we exclude it in our experiments.

Details can be found in [18]. The observed data are divided into a training and a test set with six and eleven bearings, respectively. Figure 3 visualises the horizontal and vertical vibration acceleration over time for two bearings in the training set. Degradation itself corresponds directly to increasing vibrations.

Vessel Performance Degradation in Dry-Bulk Shipping. Seaborne transportation is considered to be the most energy-efficient type of transportation due the amount of cargo carried on one single *vessel*. Nonetheless, the CO_2 emission made up form shipping is substantial when considering the overall global emission. The amount of fuel burned for vessel propulsion stands in direct relation to the emission and is one major cost driver of the vessels operational costs. Thus, from an environmental and commercial perspective it is key to reduce the amount of fuel burned. An increase in the fuel consumption can be interpreted as a decrease of a vessel performance and thus a decrease of its RUL. One of the main reasons for increasing fuel consumption is hull fouling, requiring vessel owners to periodically perform hull cleaning and propeller polishing [1].

Table 2. All combinations of preprocessing steps used in the case studies.

	Statistical Features	Entropy Features	PCA	Autoencoder	Statistical+ PCA	Statistical+ Autoencoder	CNN
Time Spectrum	A	B	C	D	E	F	–
Frequency Spectrum	G	H	I	J	K	L	–
Time-Frequency Spectrum	–	–	–	–	–	–	M

To determine the effect of hull fouling on the fuel consumption, the relation of other variables impacting consumption such as weather, speed and vessel load need to be considered. Figure 3 gives an intuition of the relation of some of the variables considered to determine performance degradation due to hull fouling. Fuel consumption (blue) decreases/increases with changing speed (green) and changing draught (orange) due to different load of the vessel. Further, to retain vessel speed resistance effects like wind and waves need to be overcome, in turn as well impacting consumption. Waves and wind might positively impact propulsion (and thus consumption) depending on their direction. Please note, that for simplicity we here do not present all variables used. For this case study, we mainly follow the suggestions made by Adland et al. [1] and would like to emphasise to read on for better understanding of the variables. For the sake of completeness, we just name all variables used: air temperature, mean draught, draught forward, draught aft, fuel consumption, log speed, trim, speed over ground, wave height, wave direction, water salinity, water temperature, wind speed, wind direction. Our dataset consists of sensor data of 15 vessels splitted into sets of 12 vessels for training and 3 vessels for testing. Data are ranging from beginning of 2016 to end of 2020 with a time interval of five minutes between each observation of the variables. The point in time of the hull cleaning and propeller polishing operation is used as target variable.

4.2 Experimental Settings

We perform experiments for each case study, whereas each experiment results from the combinations of the components introduced in Sect. 3. Note that technically not all combinations of components from the frequency analysis and feature extraction step are possible, thus, we denote them explicitly as follows. We choose $Z_{i,j}$ to be an experiment, where $Z \in \{A, \ldots, M\}$ denotes a combination of preprocessing steps listed in Table 2, $i \in \{\text{true}, \text{false}\}$ denotes if the HS classifier is used, and $j \in \{\text{MLR, GPR, ANN, SVR}\}$ denotes the selected regression model for prediction. In total, we conduct 104 experiments.

All approaches are compared based on the overall performance accuracy of each individual approach. To determine performance accuracy, we use root mean square error (RMSE) and Pearson correlation coefficient (PCC) between the observed and the estimated process of degradation. RMSE is defined by $\text{RMSE}(x, y) = (\frac{1}{n}\sum_{i=1}^{T}(y_i - x_i)^2)^{1/2}$, where $x = (x_1, ..., x_T)$ and $y = (y_1, ..., y_T)$ are time series and T is the length of both time series. PCC measures the linear correlation of two time series x and y, and is defined by $\text{PCC}(x, y) = (\sum_{i=1}^{T} x_i y_i - n\bar{x}\bar{y})/((T-1)s_x s_y)$ where $\bar{x}$, $\bar{y}$ and s_x, s_y are the mean and the sample standard deviation of each respective time series. PCC describes the similarity of the behaviour of two time series, i.e., PCC indicates whether a learned model is able to correctly identify the degradation pattern (in case, PCC is close to 1). Note, PCC should be considered together with RMSE.

For the purpose of reproducibility, we list the implementation details as follows. Outliers are removed based on Z-Score before data is normalised with Min-Max-Scaler by scikit-learn. In case of different parameters or results, we write $(x_{\text{case 1}}|x_{\text{case 2}})$. FFT and STFT are implemented with SciPy. For STFT, the Hann window function is used with a window length of (256|30) and an overlap of (128|15). Statistical and entropy features are provided by tsfresh. For the calculation of Shannon entropy we use the classical symbolisation of the time series by SAX from pyts. For the calculation of permutation entropy we use the ordinal symbolisation by tsfresh with delay $\tau = 10$ and order $d = 5$. PCA is implemented using scikit-learn with encoding size 25. The autoencoder, CNN and ANN are implemented using Keras. The autoencoder architecture for feature learning consists of two encoding layers of size 160 and 80, followed by the coding layer of size 25 and two decoding layers of size 80 and 160. The CNN architecture for feature learning consists of 2 convolutional layers of dimension 6×6, each followed by a pooling layer of dimension 2×2 and a batch normalisation before the flattening layer is used for feature representation. The ANN architecture for the regression task consists of two hidden layers and an output layer, each of them with 512 hidden units. The activation function is chosen as rectified linear unit, i.e., $\text{ReLu}(x) = \max(0, x)$. To avoid overfitting, the dropout rate is set to 0.5. The autoencoder, CNN, and ANN are trained using Adam optimizer with learning rate 0.001 and loss function as mean squared error. MLR, GPR and SVR are implemented by scikit-learn with default settings. For health stage classification only one of the available variables is used, namely horizontal vibration for bearing and log speed for the vessel dataset. Observations in each dataset are recorded until end of useful lifetime. Thus, the difference between the observation time and the end of the recording denotes its RUL (see red line in Fig. 3). RUL for the bearing dataset is in seconds, whilst RUL for the vessel dataset is in days.

4.3 Results

Each experiment is trained on a training dataset so that the RUL of an unseen sequence from the test dataset can be predicted before the results are then evaluated using RMSE and PCC. The experimental code and results can be found on GitHub[2]. Figure 4 shows violin plots for each experiment. We remind again that

[2] https://github.com/inovex/RCIS2021-degradation-estimation-bearing-vessels.

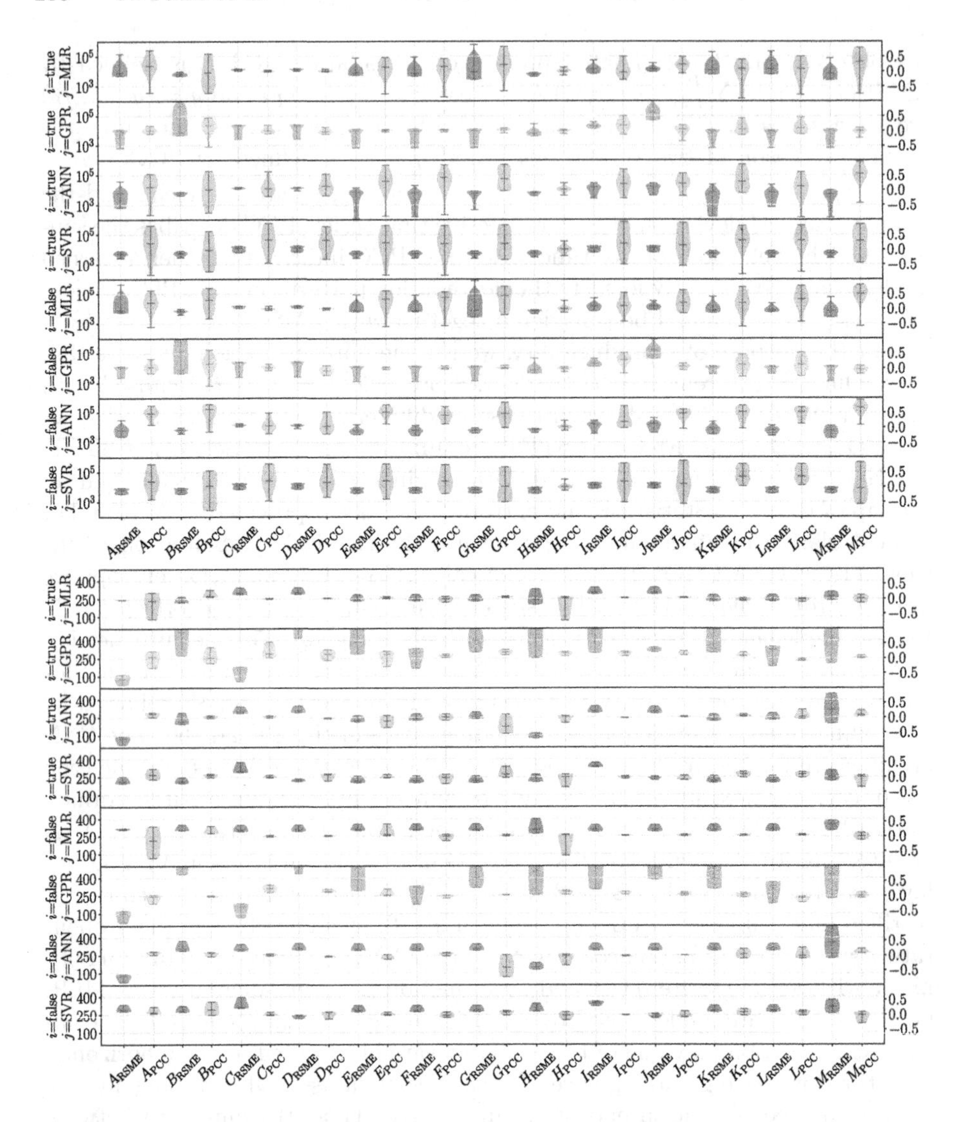

Fig. 4. Violin plots for RMSE (dark) and PCC (light) for bearing (top) and vessel (bottom) data for each experiment. Note, bearing results are log-scaled for readability. (Color figure online)

our aim is not to achieve the best prediction accuracy, but to evaluate the influence of each step in the prediction process. To answer the first research question, whether HS classification can improve the accuracy of the prediction, we compare RMSE and PCC of experiments $\{A, \ldots, M\}_{\text{true},j}$ vs. $\{A, \ldots, M\}_{\text{false},j}$ for every regression model $j = \{\text{MLR, GPR, ANN, SVR}\}$. Experiments show that RMSE decreases if the HS classifier is applied in (59|100)%, (78|97)%, (64|92)%, and (74|92)% of the predictions, respectively. Thus, in general, an improvement is observed. This does not imply that the total RMSE over all bearings or vessels must also decrease. Indeed, for *bearing* data it even increases for $\{K, L, M\}_{\mathrm{true,MLR}}$ and $\{B, J\}_{\mathrm{true,GPR}}$, which can be taken from Fig. 4 (top, blue and orange). In case of *vessel* data, it increases for $\{A\}_{\mathrm{true,ANN}}$ and $\{I\}_{\mathrm{true,SVR}}$, which can be taken from Fig. 4 (bottom, green and red). Compared to RMSE, PCC increases in (41|59)%, (63|28)%, (34|41)%, and (69|38)% of the predictions, which indicates an overall improvement. Nevertheless, there is a deterioration of the average PCC in both case studies when using MLR. Hence, it should be checked individually whether there is an improvement in the functional relationship.

To answer the second research question, whether frequency analysis can provide additional information, we compare RMSE and PCC of experiments $A_{i,j}$ vs. $G_{i,j}$, $B_{i,j}$ vs. $H_{i,j}$, $C_{i,j}$ vs. $I_{i,j}$, $D_{i,j}$ vs. $J_{i,j}$, $E_{i,j}$ vs. $K_{i,j}$ and $F_{i,j}$ vs. $L_{i,j}$ for all i, j. The average RMSE and average PCC shows that only in the case of $B_{i,j}$ vs. $H_{i,j}$ an improvement is achieved, i.e., a reduction of the RMSE and an increase of the PCC. More specifically, we find that the feature calculation on the frequency spectra leads to a reduction of RMSE only in (42|21)%, (50|58)%, (47|8)%, (38|50)%, (52|50)% and (55|42)% of the predictions, which is close to random guessing. It is further to point out that $D_{\mathrm{true,GPR}}$ and $E_{\mathrm{true,MLR}}$ lead to an increase in RMSE in 100% of the predictions for bearing data, while in the case of vessel data they decrease in 100% of predictions. Therefore, we do not recommend blind use of frequency analysis, but rather use it wisely. Note, that we did not investigate whether combining features on the raw time spectrum in combination with features on the frequency spectrum gives better results. We leave this for future work in the context of feature selection.

To answer the third research question, which feature set is most appropriate, we compare RMSE and PCC of experiments $\{A, G\}_{i,j}$ vs. $\{B, H\}_{i,j}$ vs. $\{C, I\}_{i,j}$ vs. $\{D, J\}_{i,j}$ vs. $\{E, K\}_{i,j}$ vs. $\{F, L\}_{i,j}$ vs. $\mathrm{M}_{i,j}$ for $i = \{\text{true, false}\}$ and every j. For *bearing* data, the average RMSE per feature extraction method across all 8 experiments (with and without HS classification and 4 regression methods) are 20.299, 93.429, 15.797, 50.555, 10.952, 8.449, and 15.986, respectively, suggesting that CNN as particularly effective or entropy feature particularly ineffective. However, when considering the effectiveness of the features in the context of different regression models, experiments $\{A, G\}_{i,j}$, $\{E, K\}_{i,j}$, $\{F, L\}_{i,j}$, and $\mathrm{M}_{i,j}$ perform worst with MLR, and $\{B, H\}_{i,j}$, $\{C, I\}_{i,j}$, and $\{D, J\}_{i,j}$ perform worst with GPR. Disregarding these two regression methods, average RMSEs are 6.962, 6.265, 13.603, 13.513, 7.082, 6.721, and 6.238. Learned features perform on average more than twice as bad as engineered features. Feature Learning on engineered features, such as performing PCA or autoencoder on statistical features, is more efficient. In general, there is no free lunch, i.e., not every feature set is suitable for every regression model [22]. Across all methods, CNN performs best, followed by entropy features, which only fail in the context of GPR. Comparing the model complexities of the two feature extraction methods, it is even more remarkable that the relatively simple entropy features perform so well. For further evaluation, a time and space comparison is necessary, which we leave for future work. For *vessel* data, the average RMSEs per feature extraction method across all 8 experiments is 240, 323, 324, 430, 338, 277, and 335, suggesting that statistical features as particularly effective or autoencoder particularly ineffective. In contrast to bearing data, no outliers are evident across the feature extraction method, except for $\{B, D, J\}_{i,\text{GPR}}$, which is related to the regression model.

To answer the fourth research question, which regression method yields the highest accuracy, we compare RMSE and PCC of experiments $\{A, \ldots, M\}_{i,\text{MLR}}$ vs. $\{A, \ldots, M\}_{i,\text{GPR}}$ vs. $\{A, \ldots, M\}_{i,\text{ANN}}$ vs. $\{A, \ldots, M\}_{i,\text{SVR}}$ for all i. Regarding all experiments, the average RMSEs for each different regression model $j = \{\text{MLR, GPR, ANN, SVR}\}$ are $(22.677|295), (87.091|459)$, $(9.578|267)$, and $(8.041|272)$, respectively, with a standard deviation of $(19.166|33), (202.102|304)$, $(3.663|83)$, and $(3.042|48)$, respectively. In case of *bearing* data, if the two worst preprocessing steps for each regression model are removed from the analysis, i.e., by omitting $\{A, G\}_{i,\text{MLR}}, \{B, J\}_{i,\text{GPR}}, \{I, J\}_{i,\text{ANN}}$, and $\{C, D\}_{i,\text{SVR}}$ for all i, the average RMSEs can be reduced by 29%, 86%, 11%, and 10%, respectively. As a result, GPR has a higher average RMSE than MLR. Also in the case of *vessel* data, GPR has some remarkably poor predictions, in particular on learned features by the autoencoder. The average PCCs are $(0.13|0.01)$, $(0.05|0.07)$, $(0.28|0.01)$ and $(0.21|0.03)$, respectively, which is not close to 1 but still implies a positive relationship. In the case of the vessel data, there is more or less no functional relationship identifiable, which should definitely be improved. GPR in particular turns out to be unsuitable in both cases at first glance, which must be examined with regard to the outlier predictions. All in all, ANN and SVR prove to be particularly stable, which, together with the results of the third research question, indicates good ability to generalise.

5 Open Challenges, Limits and Recommendations

Since with this paper we provide recommendations for composing several methods and not a deployment-ready out-of-the-box framework, open challenges exist. There are still numerous other methods for HS classification, frequency analysis, feature extraction and regression. We have limited ourselves here to the most popular ones. As the focus of this work was not to achieve the best possible performance, but to investigate the relation of different components, the application of regularisation, feature selection methods, a corresponding hyperparameter tuning, as well as the optimisation of network architectures are left for future work. Learning non-linear relationships, as by locally linear embeddings, isometric mappings or kernel PCA can also further improve the results.

We conclude this paper with recommendations for composing data-driven prediction processes for degradation estimation based on the conducted experiments. Limits in the application depend on the individual use case that is to be implemented. Help can be found on GitHub[3]. Note that finding suitable degrading data directly related to the RUL of a machine part or complex system is not trivial. It requires initial analyses of the data and its correlations. The functional relationship have to be investigated or, if necessary, transformed by appropriate

[3] https://github.com/inovex/RCIS2021-degradation-estimation-bearing-vessels.

preprocessing such as creation of indicators. Along the research questions we recommend as follows.

1. *HS classifier*: We advise integrating a HS classifier within the degradation estimation process, as in the vast majority of cases both RMSE and PCC are improved. Note that there are other HS classifiers that may be more appropriate for your individual problem.
2. *Frequency analysis*: We do not recommend predicting the degradation solely by features calculated on frequency spectra. This does not mean that such features cannot add value in combinations with others.
3. *Feature set*: While CNN and entropy features are most suited for bearing data, classical statistical features are for vessel data. For getting started, we recommend using feature engineering before putting a lot of effort into feature learning and tuning its hyperparameters. The feature extraction method can be easily replaced in the process later. A good prediction depends on both, the choice of features, as well as the choice of a model.
4. *Regression model*: GPR may be used with caution and only be applied to appropriate data. Furthermore, we recommend more complex models than MLR. Not surprisingly, ANN and SVR perform best, with ANN being able to better represent the functional relationship. SVR is known for good generalisation ability, which is also shown here.

Acknowledgement. Parts of the content of this paper are taken from the research project KOSMoS. This research and development project is funded by the Federal Ministry of Education and Research (BMBF) in the programme "Innovations for the production, services and work of tomorrow" (funding code 02P17D026) and is supervised by the Projektträger Karlsruhe (PTKA). We also thank Oldendorff Carriers GmbH & Co. KG., Lübeck, Germany for providing data for the case study. The responsibility for the content of this publication is with the authors.

References

1. Adland, R., Cariou, P., Jia, H., Wolff, F.C.: The energy efficiency effects of periodic ship hull cleaning. J. Clean. Prod. **178**, 1–13 (2018)
2. Ahmad, W., Khan, S.A., Islam, M.M.M., Kim, J.M.: A reliable technique for remaining useful life estimation of rolling element bearings using dynamic regression models. Reliab. Eng. Syst. Saf. **184**, 67–76 (2019)
3. Bandt, C., Pompe, B.: Permutation entropy: a natural complexity measure for time series. Phys. Rev. Lett. **88**(17), 174102 (2002)
4. Benkedjouh, T., Medjaher, K., Zerhouni, N., Rechak, S.: Remaining useful life estimation based on nonlinear feature reduction and support vector regression. Eng. Appl. Artif. Intell. **26**(7), 1751–1760 (2013)
5. Boskoski, P., Gasperin, M., Petelin, D., Juricic, D.: Bearing fault prognostics using Rényi entropy based features and Gaussian process models. Mech. Syst. Signal Process. **52**, 327–337 (2015)
6. Du, S., Lv, J., Xi, L.: Degradation process prediction for rotational machinery based on hybrid intelligent model. Robot. Comput. Integr. Manuf. **28**(2), 190–207 (2012)

7. Goebel, K., Saha, B., Saxena, A.: A comparison of three data-driven techniques for prognostics. In: 62nd Meeting of the Society For MFPT (2008)
8. Hong, S., Zhou, Z., Zio, E., Wang, W.: An adaptive method for health trend prediction of rotating bearings. Digit. Signal Process. **35**, 117–123 (2014)
9. Jia, F., Lei, Y., Lin, J., Zhou, X., Lu, N.: Deep neural networks: a promising tool for fault characteristic mining and intelligent diagnosis of rotating machinery with massive data. Mech. Syst. Signal Process. **72–73**, 303–315 (2016)
10. Kim, H.E., Tan, A.C., Mathew, J., Kim, E.Y.H., Choi, B.K.: Machine prognostics based on health state estimation using SVM. Asset condition, information systems and decision models (2012)
11. Kim, J.H.C., Nam H., D.A.: Remaining useful life prediction of rolling element bearings using degradation feature based on amplitude decrease at specific frequencies. Struct. Health Monit. **17**, 1095–1109 (2017)
12. Li, X., Zhang, W., Ding, Q.: Deep learning-based remaining useful life estimation of bearings using multi-scale feature extraction. Reliab. Eng. Syst. Saf. **182**, 208–218 (2019)
13. Loukopoulos, P., et al.: Abrupt fault remaining useful life estimation using measurements from a reciprocating compressor valve failure. MSSP **121**, 359–372 (2019)
14. Mao, W., He, J., Tang, J., Li, Y.: Predicting remaining useful life of rolling bearings based on deep feature representation and long short-term memory neural network. Adv. Mech. Eng. **10**(12), 1594–1608 (2018)
15. Mao, W., He, J., Zuo, M.J.: Predicting remaining useful life of rolling bearings based on deep feature representation and transfer learning. IEEE Trans. Instrum. Meas. **69**(4), 1594–1608 (2020)
16. Mohr, M., Becker, C., Möller, R., Richter, M.: Towards collaborative predictive maintenance leveraging private cross-company data. In: INFORMATIK 2020. Gesellschaft für Informatik, Bonn (2021)
17. Mohr, M., Wilhelm, F., Hartwig, M., Möller, R., Keller, K.: New approaches in ordinal pattern representations for multivariate time series. In: Proceedings of the 33rd International Florida Artificial Intelligence Research Society Conference (2020)
18. Nectoux, P., et al.: Pronostia: an experimental platform for bearings accelerated degradation tests. In: Conference on Prognostics and Health Management. (2012)
19. Ozkat, E.: The comparison of machine learning algorithms in estimation of remaining useful lifetime. In: Proceedings of 9th International BTKS (2019)
20. Pan, Z., Meng, Z., Chen, Z., Gao, W., Shi, Y.: A two-stage method based on extreme learning machine for predicting the remaining useful life of rolling-element bearings. Mech. Syst. Signal Process. **144**, 106899 (2020)
21. Wang, F., Wang, F., et al.: Remaining life prediction method for rolling bearing based on the long short-term memory network. Neural Process. Lett. **50**(3), 2437–2454 (2019). https://doi.org/10.1007/s11063-019-10016-w
22. Wolpert, D., Macready, W.: No free lunch theorems for optimization. IEEE Trans. Evol. Comput. **1**(1), 67–82 (1997)
23. Wu, J., Wu, C., Cao, S., Or, S.W., Deng, C., Shao, X.: Degradation data-driven time-to-failure prognostics approach for rolling element bearings in electrical machines. IEEE Trans. Ind. Electron. **66**(1), 529–539 (2019)
24. Xue, X., Li, C., Cao, S., Sun, J., Liu, L.: Fault diagnosis of rolling element bearings with a two-step scheme based on permutation entropy and random forests. Entropy **21**(1), 96 (2019)
25. Zhang, B., Zhang, L., Xu, J.: Degradation feature selection for remaining useful life prediction of rolling element bearings. Qual. Reliab. Eng. Int. **32**(2), 547–554 (2016)

Detection of Event Precursors in Social Networks: A Graphlet-Based Method

Hiba Abou Jamra(✉), Marinette Savonnet, and Éric Leclercq

Laboratoire d'Informatique de Bourgogne - EA 7534 Univ. Bourgogne Franche-Comté, Dijon, France
Hiba_Abou-Jamra@etu.u-bourgogne.fr,
{Marinette.Savonnet,Eric.Leclercq}@u-bourgogne.fr
https://lib.u-bourgogne.fr

Abstract. The increasing availability of data from online social networks attracts researchers' interest, who seek to build algorithms and machine learning models to analyze users' interactions and behaviors. Different methods have been developed to detect remarkable precursors preceding events, using text mining and Machine Learning techniques on documents, or using network topology with graph patterns.

Our approach aims at analyzing social networks data, through a graphlets enumeration algorithm, to identify event precursors and to study their contribution to the event. We test the proposed method on two different types of social network data sets: real-world events (Lubrizol fire, EU law discussion), and general events (Facebook and MathOverflow). We also contextualize the results by studying the position (orbit) of important nodes in the graphlets, which are assumed as event precursors. After analysis of the results, we show that some graphlets can be considered precursors of events.

Keywords: Graphlets · Event precursors · Social networks

1 Introduction

Online social networks (OSN) play an essential role in individuals' and businesses' daily lives. Due to social interactions between individuals in these networks, scientists have an opportunity to observe and analyze increasing amounts of data to extract value and knowledge.

Disease outbreaks, environmental and industrial crises present challenges to researchers in different domains such as economy, finance, earth sciences, epidemiology, and information science. Detection of weak signals can be a key for anticipating changes in advance and avoid letting them cause surprise [10]. OSN enhance the emergence of echo chambers where ideas are amplified and can conduct to a digital crisis. To limit negative publicity (known as "bad buzz"), organizations should be vigilant to weak signals. Detection of significant patterns or motifs helps to understand the network dynamics and identify or predict complicated situations. Network topological properties such as density, assortativity, and degree centrality help to understand the network's global structure.

S. Cherfi et al. (Eds.): RCIS 2021, LNBIP 415, pp. 205–220, 2021.
https://doi.org/10.1007/978-3-030-75018-3_13

This article introduces an approach to help experts detect weak signals by topological analysis of the Twitter network.

Our main contributions are 1) identification of graphlets as event precursors; 2) evaluation of the identified graphlets about their participation in the event; 3) contextualization of the results to help experts in interpretation; 4) evaluation of the proposed method using existing real data sets obtained from the Cocktail project and well-known data sets used as a benchmark. Cocktail is an interdisciplinary project aiming to develop a platform that will enable organizations to build a communication strategy, anticipate a crisis via a communication response, and adapt their industrial offers.

The rest of this article is organized as follows: Sect. 2 introduces some background on weak signals, event precursors, and describes similar works. In Sect. 3, after a brief reminder on graphlets concept, we explain and illustrate the proposed method starting from time series of social networks data to event precursors identification, and the study of the correlation between precursor graphlets and the event of interest. Section 4 introduces the experimental part: it describes the main characteristics of the used data sets. In Sect. 5, we test the proposed approach on real events based on industrial and environmental crises, along with experiments on benchmark network models to evaluate and verify this approach. Finally, conclusions and future perspectives are presented in Sect. 6.

2 Related Work

In a digital society, detection of weak signals has become necessary for decision-makers in industrial and commercial policy and communication strategy while projecting future scenarios. Weak signals can be the precursors of future events. The detection of these signals can either transform them towards a trend or an event in the future or stop their evolution for controlling and preventing future crises. Ansoff [2] was the first to propose the concept of a weak signal for strategic planning through environmental analysis. He defines weak signals as the first symptoms of strategic discontinuities that act as early warning information of low intensity, which can be the initiator of an important trend or event. Table 1 presents terms and definitions qualifying weak signals by social scientists. Event precursors and weak signals are two concepts with strong proximity. Generally speaking, a precursor is in a relationship with the event of interest. It is any behavior, situation, or group of events that is a leading indicator of future incidents or consequential events [6]. In the following, we present several studies related to our work. We can classify these studies into three categories: 1) text mining and Natural Language Processing (NLP); 2) Machine Learning (ML) for identification and forecasting; and 3) motifs or patterns.

Many text mining and NLP approaches have been proposed, where Web documents are analyzed through a quantitative analysis of keywords. Yoon et al. [24] have proposed two indicators: the degree of visibility based on keyword frequency and the degree of diffusion based on document frequency and considering their rates of increase in time. A keyword that has low visibility and

Table 1. Weak signals definitions and terms

Source	Definitions and terms
Ansoff 1975 [2]	Incomplete information, imprecise, fragmentary
Godet 1994 [8]	Low intensity, low visibility
Coffman 1997 [5]	Initiator of an important event, of a future trend
Hiltunen 2010 [10]	Low utility, meaningless when analyzed individually
Welz 2012 [23]	But can make sense if seen as a set of information

a low diffusion level is considered a weak signal. Other studies leaned on these two indicators by adding a context to a list of keywords and used, for example, topic modeling such as LDA (Latent Dirichlet Allocation) [14,15] and clustering algorithms such as k-Means or k-Medoids [16].

Ning et al. [17] developed a model of multiple instance learning algorithms, based on supervised learning techniques, to formulate the precursor identification and the forecasting issue. The model consists of assigning a probability to collected news articles associated with targeted events (protests in their study). The greater probability is, the more the news article is considered as a precursor containing information about this event's cause. Another study by Ackley et al. [1] adopted supervised learning techniques (Random Forest and Sequential Backward Selection algorithms) in the commercial aviation operation domain to analyze and track critical parameters leading to safety events in the approach and landing phases.

Furthermore, some researchers were interested in identifying specific patterns in networks, known as motifs, which could be considered as event precursors. Baiesi et al. [3] presented a method that studies correlations within graphs of upcoming earthquakes using tools of network theory. They measured the distance between network nodes along with the clustering coefficient, which reflected intentionally basic mechanisms of seismic movements and earthquake formation/propagation. After applying statistical tools on the network topology, they found that simple motifs such as special triangles constitute an interesting type of precursors for significant events. Later on, several approaches studied the identification and the role of motifs in critical events such as crime analysis [7] and ongoing attacks detection [13].

These works aimed to identify weak signals relying on text mining techniques and network theory tools. The last one leads us to our hypothesis that graphlets, which are particular motifs, can be precursors of events. But to the best of our knowledge, there has not been a graphlet-based solution to detect event precursors in social networks and assess their relationship with the event of interest. We present our proposed approach in the upcoming section.

3 Graphlets as Potential Event Precursors

The most known characteristics of weak signals are usually hard to quantify, so we prefer to rely on the notion of event precursors of small intensity to obtain a more precise definition, by considering an event as an activity peak and a precursor as a signal of lower importance or intensity, being in a correlation with the event.

Conventional methods based on simple statistical techniques are not able to identify event precursors easily. Instead, they are helpful to identify events such as the family of ARIMA, EDM, HDC algorithms [20]. We choose to explore another approach based on the assumption that networks' topology plays an essential role in information propagation, hence in the formation of an event, so we assume that graphlets found in social networks can be considered as potential event precursors, just as cliques are for communities. They have proven their worth in numerous contexts in network research [12].

In this section, we investigate the following questions: Can graphlets be identified as event precursors? Can these precursors be qualified as weak signals prior to the event of interest? Before going into details, we present the essential notion of graphlets. We describe how to prepare and transform data to enumerate graphlets in a temporal graph built from interactions between users and discover the potential event precursors' graphlets.

3.1 Graphlets in a Nutshell

Graphlets, first introduced by Pržulj [19], are particular types of motifs in a network, and thanks to their predefined sizes and shapes, they are easy to interpret by experts in the domain, such as social scientists or political scientists. A graphlet is a connected induced non-isomorphic subgraph (2 to 5 nodes) chosen from the nodes of a large graph. 30 graphlets from G_0 to G_{29} with up to 5 nodes are possible: the G_0 graphlet of size 2, two graphlets of size 3 which are G_1 and G_2, 6 graphlets of size 4, and 21 graphlets of size 5. Orbits, or positions, represent the equivalence classes of graphlets [18]. They are the positions to which nodes belong in the 30 graphlets; nodes belonging to the same orbit are interchangeable. For example, the star-shaped G_4 graphlet 6 7 consists of two positions; one of them is central (orbit 7) occupied by one node, and the other is peripheral (orbit 6) and shared between the remaining three nodes that are interchangeable.

There exist several algorithms to enumerate graphlets and orbits of a graph. A survey was made by Ribeiro et al. in 2019 [21], in which they provided an overview of the existing algorithms for subgraph counting, classified these algorithms, and highlighted their main advantages and limitations. They explored the methods for counting subgraphs from three perspectives: 1) exact counting algorithms (*e.g., ESU/FANMOD, RAGE, Orca*); 2) approximate counting algorithms (*e.g., ESA, RAND-ESU*); 3) parallel processing algorithms (*e.g., DM-ESU, GPU-Orca*). The survey provides valuable insight from a practical point of view of the algorithms and their existing implementations with a trade-off between accuracy and execution time.

To choose the most convenient algorithm for counting graphlets and orbits in the studied graph structures, we have defined 3 essential criteria: 1) exact counting of graphlets that are up to five nodes, to maintain the interpretability of the results; 2) orbits counting for the study of nodes positions within each graphlet; 3) availability of source code. We rely on the Orca algorithm proposed by Hočevar and Demšar in 2014 [11], which is an exact counting algorithm, coming from an analytic approach based on matrix representation, and works by setting up a system of linear equations per node of the input graph that relate different orbit frequencies. It counts small subgraphs up to 5 nodes and focuses on orbits counting. Considering e as the number of edges and d the maximum degree of nodes, its time complexity is of $\mathcal{O}(ed)$ for four-node graphlets and $\mathcal{O}(ed^2)$ for five-node graphlets. We performed an experimental analysis to evaluate Orca's implementation complexity. With up to 15 000 edges in a graph, the calculation time is less than 5 s, but it reaches 6 h with up to 160 000 edges. Figure 1 shows execution time based on the number of edges.

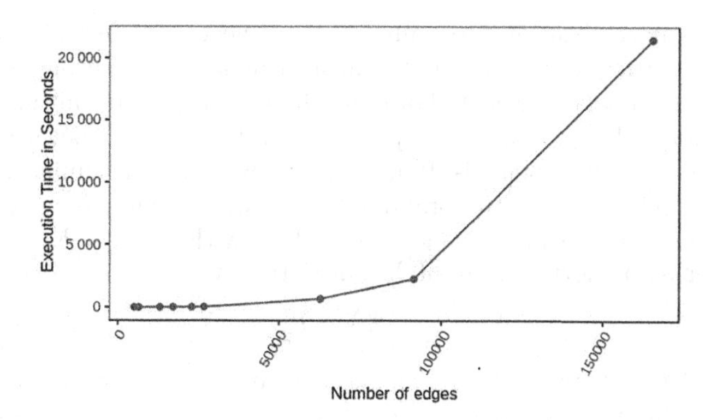

Fig. 1. Experimental evaluation of Orca's complexity

3.2 Proposed Method

We propose a graphlet-based analysis method that facilitates the results' interpretation. Once the potential precursors have been revealed, it is still necessary to validate the fact that they are weak signals, determine their link with the studied event, and then allow experts to understand their role. We prove experimentally that these graphlets can be event precursors. We present our method consisting of six steps, depicted in Fig. 2.

0. The first step is to build a time series from social networks data. Once raw data is collected, for example, tweets in JSON format, some interactions of

interest are selected (e.g., retweet, quote, mention), and a graph structure is generated as a tuple with three components representing interactions between entities at a given date (e.g., (user1,user2,124354432))). A time series X is created from the number of interactions selected between all pairs of nodes. It is a sequence of n elements $X = (x_i)_{1 \leq i \leq n} = (x_1, x_2, \ldots, x_n)$.
A method to remove the seasonal part from the original time series is then applied [4]. We consider an event as an activity peak resulting from a variation in the interactions between entities, and the peak is identified either manually or by event detection algorithms. Before and during the event, the time series is divided into snapshots S^t according to the duration or importance of the event (e.g., a day, 12 h, 6 h, 1 h), in a way to have sub time series of the original series: $S^t = (x_i)_{t \leq i < t+d}$ with d the constant duration of a snapshot, and the constraint that all the S^t form a partition of the original series X.

1. Enumeration of graphlets for each snapshot determines a topological signature before and during the event. Snapshots S^t are represented as components of a numerical vector $(G_0^t, G_1^t, \ldots, G_{29}^t)$, G_x^t is the number of graphlets of type x in the snapshot S^t. We rely on the Orca algorithm[1], it provides an acceptable runtime as all snapshots contain at most a few thousand edges (see Fig. 1).
2. We apply a normalization procedure on these vectors to re-scale their values to a particular magnitude for further measuring and calculations. This step is of significant importance as it should not hide small signals but instead make them comparable to others. The procedure relies on a framework proposed by D.Goldin and P.Kanellakis [9] in which they study the similarity between two queries relating to a temporal database. Two real numbers a and b define a transformation $T_{a,b}$ on X by joining each x_i with $a \times x_i + b$.
$\overline{X}$ represents the normal form of X calculated by:

$$\overline{X} = T_{\sigma,\mu}^{-1}(X) = T_{\frac{1}{\sigma},-\frac{\mu}{\sigma}}(X)$$

in which $\mu(\overline{X}) = 0$ and $\sigma(\overline{X}) = 1$, μ is the mean and σ the standard deviation. Therefore, the mean of each graphlet type G_x for all snapshots is calculated as:

$$\mu(G_x) = \frac{1}{s}\sum_{t=1}^{s}(G_x^t) \quad \forall x \in \{0, \ldots, 29\}, s \text{ is the number of snapshots}$$

Then the standard deviation is calculated as:

$$\sigma(G_x) = \sqrt{\frac{\sum_{t=1}^{s}(G_x^t - \mu(G_x))^2}{s-1}} \quad \forall x \in \{0, \ldots, 29\}$$

By applying this normalization procedure for each of the snapshots S^t, each component of its vector G_x^t is normalized by:

$$\overline{G_x^t} = \frac{(G_x^t) - \mu(G_x)}{\sigma(G_x)}$$

[1] https://rdrr.io/github/alan-turing-institute/network-comparison/src/R/orca_interface.R.

3. From the normalized values obtained, the evolution of all the vector components is studied via the calculation of their velocity and acceleration, with the purpose to highlight the graphlets that come out quickly before the other types. The calculation of these attributes is as follows:
   - Velocity: $\overline{V_x^t} = \overline{G_x^{t+1}} - \overline{G_x^t}\ \ \forall x \in \{0,\ldots 29\}$
   - Acceleration:

$$\overline{A_x^t} = \frac{\Delta V_x}{\Delta t} = \overline{V_x^{t+1}} - \overline{V_x^t}\ \ \forall x \in \{0,\ldots 29\}, \Delta t = 1 \text{ between snapshots}$$

4. We observe the obtained results in steps 2 and 3 to capture significant variations in their values before the activity peak. We choose the k graphlets with the highest velocity and acceleration values as potential precursors of events.
5. This step aims to validate the potential precursors' graphlets by eliminating those irrelevant (false positives) and maintaining the pertinent ones supposed as weak signals (true positives). Although keeping some false positives can help social scientists to examine the information behind critical situations. It is composed of two stages: 1) we evaluate cross-correlation between each precursors' graphlet time series and the original interactions time series, and 2) for correlated graphlets, we quantify their contribution to the global evolution of graphlets to confirm if they are weak signals or not.

   Cross-correlation[2] is used to validate the intrinsic properties of the method. It is a linear measure of similarities between two time series X and Y, which helps evaluate the relationship between two series over time [22]. An offset/lag h is associated with this measure, knowing that if $h < 0$ then X could predict Y, and if $h > 0$ then Y could predict X.

   Weak signals selection is a simple ratio calculation that measures the correlated graphlets' contribution to the global evolution of graphlets for the studied period. From the correlated graphlets found, the total number of a graphlet type x in all snapshots is divided by the total number of graphlets for all snapshots, as follows:

$$R(G_x) = \frac{\sum_{t=1}^{s}(G_x^t)}{T(G)}$$

   and $T(G) = \sum_{t=1}^{s}(\sum_{x=0}^{29}(G_x^t))$, with s the number of snapshots. The resulted ratios R, are sorted in ascending order, to verify if the identified correlated graphlets remain at the top of the list; if so, they are qualified as weak signals, the other graphlets are eliminated.

6. This step aims to provide adequate analysis elements to domain experts to interpret the previous steps' obtained results and respond to potentially critical situations. For each orbit (i.e. the position, or the node's role in the graphlet) of graphlets considered as weak signals, we count how many times nodes of the initial graph appear in these graphlets.

[2] Implemented with the R package *tseries*: https://www.rdocumentation.org/packages/tseries/versions/0.1-2/topics/ccf.

To restrict the information to study and facilitate the interpretation, we consider only the most influential nodes, hence the PageRank algorithm is used to help to identify these nodes in the graph.

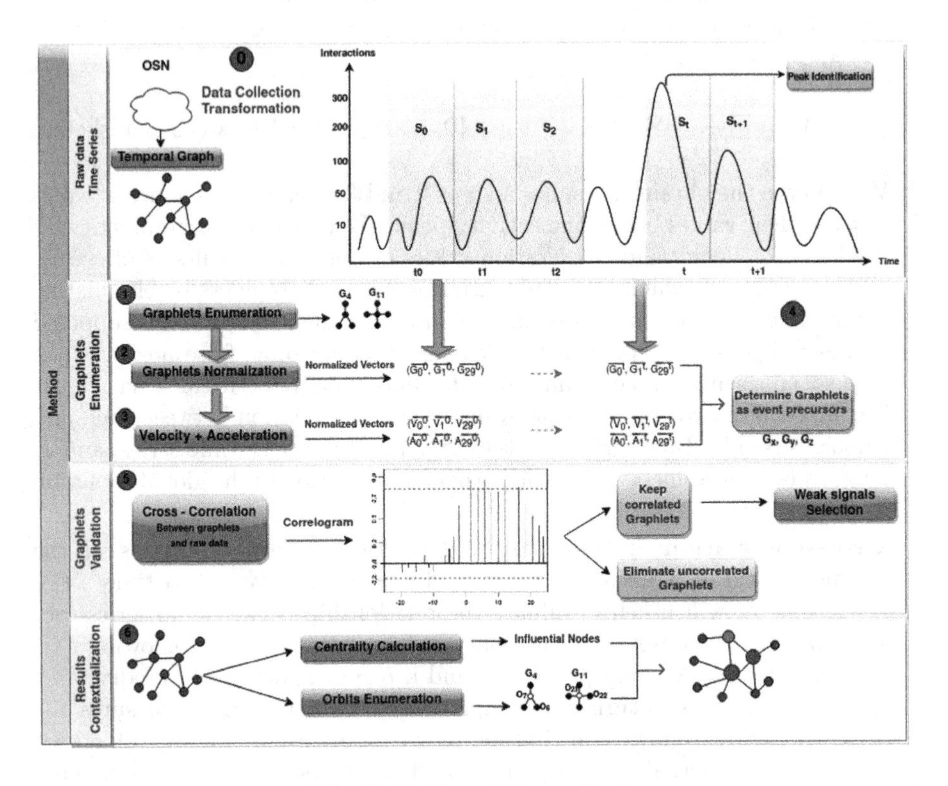

Fig. 2. Outline of the method

4 Data Description

We describe in this section the data sets used for our experiments. To this end, the selected data sets include a sequence of temporal interactions between users. Two first data sets represent real case scenarios, and the other two sets[3] are social benchmark networks used to confirm our method.

Twitter - Lubrizol fire: This network contains tweets published after a fire broke out at the Lubrizol factory in Rouen-France. From the raw Twitter data, the corpus contains tweets between midnight of October 28, 2019, and midnight of October 30, 2019. The reduced corpus consists of 18,914 tweets, 12,187 of these tweets are original, and 1,984 include mentions which are the interaction type studied in this example.

[3] https://snap.stanford.edu/data/#socnets.

Twitter - European CAP Law: This dataset contains tweets published in conjunction with the European Council meeting held on October 20, 2020, that lead to the announcement of the Common Agricultural Policy Law (CAP). The dataset comprises tweets collected from midnight of October 17, 2020, to midnight of October 20. It consists of 4,679 tweets, from which 807 are original, and 3,872 include mentions and retweets, which are the interaction type we study in this experiment.

MathOverflow Network: This network contains temporal user interactions from the Stack-Exchange site "Math-Overflow" consisting of three interaction types: 1) answering a question; 2) commenting on another user's question; 3) commenting on another user's answer. The used data set is extracted from the original sample, and consists of 1,400 relations from October 27, 2010, till October 30, 2010.

Facebook Network: This is a network representing a subset of posts to other user's walls on Facebook. The raw data sample is collected from October 2004 to January 2009, and we minimize the set to include the detailed relations between 05 January 2009, and 07 January 2009, consisting of up to 8,790 interactions between users.

5 Experiments, Results and Discussion

In this section, we present experiments that aim to validate the proposed method by detecting graphlets that are supposed to be weak signals, supplemented by contextualization elements so that experts can trigger actions. We apply experiments on four different data sets, two of them are the subject of critical situations in industry and agriculture, and the remaining ones belong to random events. The Cocktail platform collected the first two data sets, domain experts provided the accounts and keywords needed for the collection. The two other data sets were used to validate the approach.

5.1 Industrial Crisis: Twitter - Lubrizol Fire

The first experiment of the proposed approach was carried out on the Twitter Lubrizol network. Our event of interest is the unexpected visit of President Macron to Rouen, October 30, 2019, around 6 p.m. Therefore, the study period is reduced to two days before the event (28 and 29), along with the event's day (30). After step 0, we obtain a temporal graph that contains 2,231 nodes and 3,821 edges[4].

We choose to work with snapshots of one hour, to capture the biggest number of graphlet types, especially those with complex shapes, which will help with a finer interpretation of the results. The graphlets number is calculated for each snapshot and the resulting values are normalized. Next, velocity and acceleration are measured for the normalized graphlet values. After analysis of the three

[4] The difference between the number of tweets in Sect. 4 and the number of nodes and edges is since several tweets can produce the same interaction.

computed attributes, we notice an increase in certain graphlets' number and velocity on October 30 starting at 4 p.m., like G_2, G_5, G_8 and G_{27}. Therefore, we consider these graphlet types as potential event precursors. Table 2 presents graphlets number, velocity, and acceleration results for certain graphlet types, for the snapshots corresponding to three hours before the event. It compares the evolution of the attributes mentioned above between the graphlets that evolved starting at 4 p.m. (supposed precursors), and other graphlets that did not show remarkable variations for the same snapshots. The notable changes in attributes' values are highlighted in blue.

We notice that other graphlet types like G_4 and G_{11}, start increasing from 6 p.m, which is the snapshot of the activity peak, and hence they are aligned with the event.

Table 2. Enumeration results of some graphlets before the event. The highlighted values correspond to the potential precursor's graphlets

	S^t: 30/10 3p.m-4p.m			S^{t+1}: 30/10 4p.m-5p.m			S^{t+2}: 30/10 5p.m-6p.m		
Graphlet	$\overline{G^t_x}$	$\overline{V^t_x}$	$\overline{A^t_x}$	$\overline{G^t_x}$	$\overline{V^t_x}$	$\overline{A^t_x}$	$\overline{G^t_x}$	$\overline{V^t_x}$	$\overline{A^t_x}$
G2	-0,1592	0,1869	0,3738	3,0657	3,2248	3,0379	3,4863	0,4206	-2,8042
G5	-0,1881	0,1417	0,1102	2,9505	3,1387	2,9970	3,7116	0,7610	-2,3776
G8	-0,2796	0	0	3,4544	3,7340	3,7340	5,0102	1,5558	-2,1781
G27	-0,2364	0	0	5,2868	5,5233	5,5233	4,3715	-0,9152	-6,4385
G17	-0,1817	0	0,0012	0,0212	0,2030	0,2030	0,5591	0,5379	0,3348
G22	-0,1623	0	0,0006	0,0355	0,1979	0,1979	0,1083	0,0727	-0,1252

Next, we validate the potential precursors and select the ones supposed to be weak signals. We apply cross-correlation between the initial time series and the ones belonging to precursor graphlets. The time series of G_2, G_5, G_8 and G_{27} present correlations with a positive lag h of one and two hours with the initial time series, having significant values equal to 0.8, which indicates that the number of interactions in the initial series follows with a lag of 1 or 2 h the number of graphlets. The calculated ratios highlight the weak presence of these correlated graphlets in the rise of mentions number, compared with other strong graphlets like G_{11}, hence G_2, G_5, G_8 and G_{27} are considered weak signals. Figure 3 represents some of the considered weak signals' time series, compared to the initial mentions time series.

A fine-grained experiment is carried out to contextualize the obtained results in the previous steps: we calculate the number of times an influential node is in an orbit of a selected graphlet. We find users like `manon_leterq` and `massinfabien` journalists, and `76actu` the local information site, having a rise in the number of

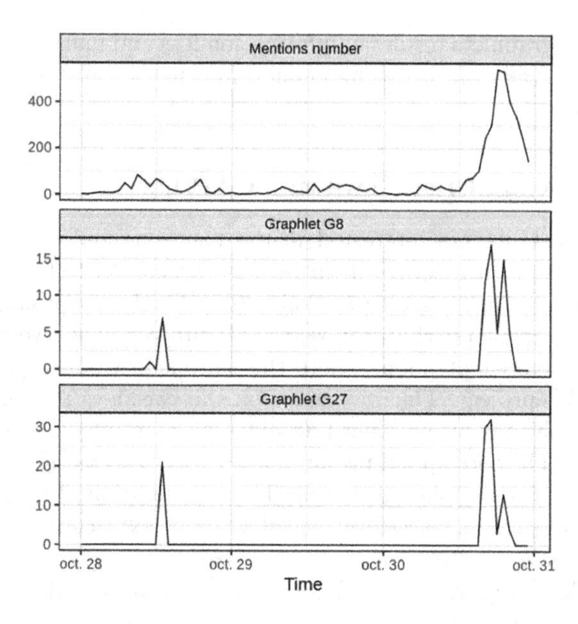

Fig. 3. Initial mentions time series vs. G_8 and G_{27} graphlets time series, considered weak signals

orbits of the selected graphlets, starting at 4 p.m (two hours before the event). Table 3 presents an extract of the number of times the above influential users appear in the orbits of graphlets G_2 (O_3) and G_{27} (O_{68} and O_{69}). The remarkable increase in values is highlighted in blue. We did the same calculations with a user chosen randomly OTT_44380; the results show that he appears a little in the graphlets' orbits.

Table 3. Extract of influential users and their orbits enumeration results for some of the precursor graphlets

	S^t: 30/10 3p.m-4p.m			S^{t+1}: 30/10 4p.m-5p.m			S^{t+2}: 30/10 5p.m-6p.m		
User	O3	O68	O69	O3	O68	O69	O3	O68	O69
OTT_44380	0	0	0	0	0	0	7	18	3
manon_leterq	0	0	0	12	72	0	20	68	0
76actu	0	0	0	31	18	49	30	5	70
massinfabien	0	0	0	10	63	0	6	32	0

We repeat the same experiment on different time windows. In the 6-hours snapshot, we were able to extract the same graphlets; on the contrary, we could not confirm the exact time of their appearance due to the window's large size. A finer study on 30 and 15 min snapshots (containing fewer edges) led to a partial vanishing of complex graphlets like G_8 and G_{27} over time. The absence of these complex graphlets results in information loss and makes decision-making more difficult. We rely on providing enough information to the experts to take preventive actions.

5.2 Environmental Crisis: Twitter - CAP Law

In this experiment, we are interested in the mentions and retweets published after European Council meetings held in late October 2020 for negotiation on the post-2020 Common Agricultural Policy (CAP) reform package, which later initiated an agreement on the proposed CAP project. The event corresponds to the 20th of October at noon, where the European Council took a position towards the CAP project. Thus, we focus on the two days preceding the event (18 and 19) and the day of the event (20). The initial graph contains 2,535 nodes and 7,897 edges. The corresponding time series of the interactions is created and divided into snapshots of one hour each. The enumeration of graphlets and the calculation of velocity and acceleration allow us to extract the most pertinent graphlets G_{15}, G_{18}, G_{21}, and G_{28} as potential event precursors, due to the rise of their values between one and three hours before the event. Other graphlet types such as G_9 arise in parallel with the event.

The cross-correlation applied to precursor graphlets shows on the one hand that G_{15} and G_{21} present a positive correlation of two and three hours lags, respectively, with the initial time series, having values equal to 0.7 and 0.6 respectively (see Fig. 4). G_{18} also shows a positive correlation of one hour lag with a value equal to 0.7.

On the other hand, G_{28} did not present a positive correlation with the initial time series, hence it is not a weak signal. Furthermore, ratios are calculated for the correlated graphlets. These graphlets have low ratios compared with other graphlets types, so they are considered weak signals.

In the last step, orbits in graphlets are enumerated for the identified influential users. The results show that, for instance, a user like `pcanfin` (Chair of the environment committee of the European Parliament) appears for the first time at 10 a.m of the event day, in orbit O_{51} of graphlet G_{21}, and at 11 a.m in orbit O_{34} of graphlet G_{15}. Another user, `TheProgressives` (representing Socialists and Democrats Group in the European Parliament), appears at 10 a.m in the orbits of G_{15}, G_{18} and G_{21}, but shows up strongly at 11 a.m in orbits O_{34} and O_{51}. Then the number of orbits of these users starts decreasing towards the event. These users interacted against the law a few hours before the announcement of the council's decision, and their positions in these graphlets (closed connected structure) above can reveal their role in a strongly connected community of users that might share the same political opinion in terms of reactions to the ongoing situation.

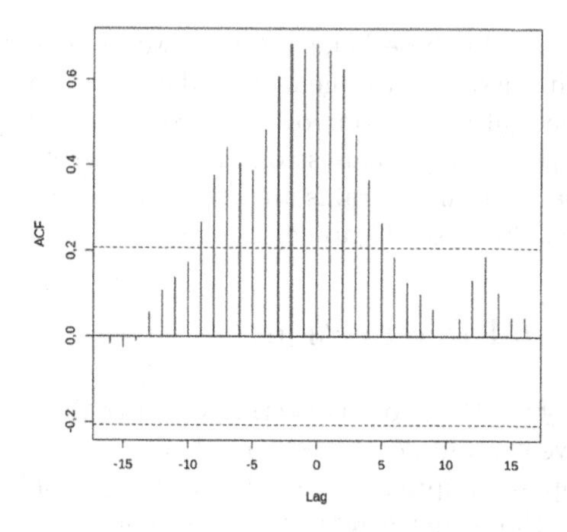

Fig. 4. Correlation of G_{15} with the initial mentions-retweet time series

5.3 Random Events: MathOverflow and Facebook

The objective of these two experiments is to verify and validate the proposed method in terms of reproducibility and results interpretation. Our method is applied to the benchmark network models MathOverflow and Facebook interactions. The event is unknown here, so we select a peak activity in the corresponding time series of each network and consider it as the event of study, to evaluate the previously obtained results for Twitter network data. We also work by snapshots of one hour.

The peak selected from the MathOverflow time series (the graph contains 414 nodes and 966 edges) belongs to activity on October 29, 2010, at 11 p.m. Enumeration results show remarkable variations in certain graphlets numbers on October 29 starting at 10 p.m. We find graphlets G_3, G_9 and G_{10} increasing first follows them the G_2 at 11 p.m., time of the peak activity. After that time, the calculated numbers start decreasing accordingly. The correlation study was not able to find positive correlations between the time series of these graphlets and the initial time series before the peak. Moreover, the enumeration of orbits in the last step was not entirely relevant since the nodes belong to anonymous users, hence the results cannot be reflected into real scenarios for analysis.

Furthermore, the Facebook data set was studied by snapshots of one hour to ease the discovery of significant precursors before the selected peak activity in the related time series (the graph contains 6,726 nodes and 6,677 edges). The peak corresponds to an event on January 07, 2009, starting at 6 a.m. We notice a prominent rise in numbers of G_2 and G_6 in the evening before the peak activity, at 6 p.m.

Just as the Mathoverflow dataset, these identified graphlets can not be considered as event precursors as they did not show significant correlation results with the initial time series.

The obtained results in these benchmark networks lead us to the interpretation synthesis that these are too generalist data sets, and we can track no targeted event in the real world. Moreover, we could not identify weak signals, since most of the graphlets participate strongly in the rise of interactions between users. Data and experimental programs are available under https://github.com/hibaaboujamra/EventPrecursorsGraphlets.

6 Conclusion and Perspectives

We have studied the hypothesis of discovering whether the graphlets are precursors for occurring events, and developed a method to evaluate and confirm this hypothesis. The proposed approach allows identifying graphlets as precursors of events and targeting those that constitute weak signals.

We performed quantitative and qualitative analyses using graph enumeration and correlation measures. The experimental results confirm that our method was able to identify event precursors and target those that can be weak signals two hours before an event.

Moreover, the last step of contextualization provides rich elements to domain experts for further analysis and interpretation of the results to react accordingly in case of critical situations.

In future works, we want to extend the experiments to other types of networks as the hashtags co-occurrence, for example, and larger networks, and automate all the method's steps. We observed experimentally that graphlets are good precursors of events, hence we attach currently to establish proof of causality between these graphlets and the event, through statistical methods like the causal inference or the Granger causality. Further investigations will consider iterating our method to eliminate nodes continuously from graphs to decrease certain graphlets' predominance and allocate the space to discover other graphlet types as event precursors to obtain a hierarchical graphlet decomposition.

Acknowledgments. This work is supported by the program "Investissements d'Avenir", ISITE-BFC project (ANR contract 15-IDEX-0003), https://projet-cocktail.fr/.

References

1. Ackley, J.L., Puranik, T.G., Mavris, D.: A supervised learning approach for safety event precursor identification in commercial aviation. In: AIAA Aviation Forum, p. 2880 (2020)
2. Ansoff, H.I.: Managing strategic surprise by response to weak signals. Calif. Manage. Rev. **18**(2), 21–33 (1975)
3. Baiesi, M.: Scaling and precursor motifs in earthquake networks. Phys. A **360**(2), 534–542 (2006)

4. Brownlee, J.: Introduction to time series forecasting with python: how to prepare data and develop models to predict the future. Machine Learning Mastery (2017)
5. Coffman, B.: Weak signal research, part I: Introduction. J. Trans. Manag. **2**(1) (1997)
6. Corcoran, W.R.: Defining and analyzing precursors. In: Accident precursor analysis and management: Reducing technological risk through diligence, pp. 79–88. National Academy Press Washington, DC (2004)
7. Davies, T., Marchione, E.: Event networks and the identification of crime pattern motifs. PloS one **10**(11), e0143638 (2015)
8. Godet, M.: From anticipation to action: a handbook of strategic prospective. UNESCO publishing (1994)
9. Goldin, D.Q., Kanellakis, P.C.: On similarity queries for time-series data: constraint specification and implementation. In: Montanari, U., Rossi, F. (eds.) CP 1995. LNCS, vol. 976, pp. 137–153. Springer, Heidelberg (1995). https://doi.org/10.1007/3-540-60299-2_9
10. Hiltunen, E.: Weak Signals in Organisational Futures. Aalto University School of Economics, Aalto (2010)
11. Hočevar, T., Demšar, J.: A combinatorial approach to Graphlet counting. Bioinf. **30**(4), 559–565 (2014). https://doi.org/10.1093/bioinformatics/btt717
12. Hulovatyy, Y., Chen, H., Milenković, T.: Exploring the structure and function of temporal networks with dynamic graphlets. Bioinformatics **31**(12), i171–i180 (2015)
13. Juszczyszyn, K., Kołaczek, G.: Motif-based attack detection in network communication graphs. In: De Decker, B., Lapon, J., Naessens, V., Uhl, A. (eds.) CMS 2011. LNCS, vol. 7025, pp. 206–213. Springer, Heidelberg (2011). https://doi.org/10.1007/978-3-642-24712-5_19
14. Krigsholm, R.: Applying text mining for identifying future signals of land administration. Land **8**(12), 181 (2019). https://doi.org/10.3390/land8120181
15. Maitre, J., Ménard, M., Chiron, G., Bouju, A., Sidère, N.: A meaningful information extraction system for interactive analysis of documents. In: International Conference on Document Analysis and Recognition (ICDAR), pp. 92–99. IEEE (2019)
16. Moreira, A.L.M., Hayashi, T.W.N., Coelho, G.P., da Silva, A.E.A.: A clustering method for weak signals to support anticipative intelligence. Int. J. Artif. Intell. Expert Syst. (IJAE) **6**(1), 1–14 (2015)
17. Ning, Y., Muthiah, S., Rangwala, H., Ramakrishnan, N.: Modeling precursors for event forecasting via nested multi-instance learning. In: ACM SIGKDD International Conference on Knowledge Discovery and Data Mining, pp. 1095–1104 (2016)
18. Pržulj, N.: Biological network comparison using GraphLet degree distribution. Bioinformatics **23**(2), e177–e183 (2007)
19. Pržulj, N., Corneil, D.G., Jurisica, I.: Modeling interactome: scale-free or geometric? Bioinform. **20**(18), 3508–3515 (2004)
20. Ray, S., McEvoy, D.S., Aaron, S., Hickman, T.T., Wright, A.: Using statistical anomaly detection models to find clinical decision support malfunctions. J. Am. Med. Inform. Assoc. **25**(7), 862–871 (2018)
21. Ribeiro, P., Paredes, P., Silva, M.E., Aparicio, D., Silva, F.: A survey on subgraph counting: concepts, algorithms and applications to network motifs and graphlets. arXiv preprint arXiv:1910.13011 (2019)
22. Ripley, B.D., Venables, W.: Modern applied statistics with S. Springer (2002)

23. Welz, K., Brecht, L., Pengl, A., Kauffeldt, J.V., Schallmo, D.R.: Weak signals detection: criteria for social media monitoring tools. In: ISPIM Innovation Symposium, p. 1. The International Society for Professional Innovation Management (ISPIM) (2012)
24. Yoon, J.: Detecting weak signals for long-term business opportunities using text mining of web news. Expert Syst. Appl. **39**(16), 12543–12550 (2012)

Developing and Operating Artificial Intelligence Models in Trustworthy Autonomous Systems

Silverio Martínez-Fernández[1(✉)], Xavier Franch[1], Andreas Jedlitschka[2], Marc Oriol[1], and Adam Trendowicz[2]

[1] Universitat Politècnica de Catalunya - BarcelonaTech, Barcelona, Spain
{silverio.martinez,xavier.franch,marc.oriol}@upc.edu
[2] Fraunhofer IESE, Kaiserslautern, Germany
{andreas.jedlitschka,adam.trendowicz}@iese.fraunhofer.de

Abstract. Companies dealing with Artificial Intelligence (AI) models in Autonomous Systems (AS) face several problems, such as users' lack of trust in adverse or unknown conditions, gaps between software engineering and AI model development, and operation in a continuously changing operational environment. This work-in-progress paper aims to close the gap between the development and operation of trustworthy AI-based AS by defining an approach that coordinates both activities. We synthesize the main challenges of AI-based AS in industrial settings. We reflect on the research efforts required to overcome these challenges and propose a novel, holistic DevOps approach to put it into practice. We elaborate on four research directions: (a) increased users' trust by monitoring operational AI-based AS and identifying self-adaptation needs in critical situations; (b) integrated agile process for the development and evolution of AI models and AS; (c) continuous deployment of different context-specific instances of AI models in a distributed setting of AS; and (d) holistic DevOps-based lifecycle for AI-based AS.

Keywords: DevOps · Autonomous Systems · AI · Trustworthiness

1 Introduction

Nowadays, Autonomous Systems (AS) are prevalent in many domains: from smart mobility (autonomous driving) and Industry 4.0 (autonomous factory robots) to smart health (autonomous diagnosis systems). One crucial enabler of this success is the emergence of sophisticated Artificial Intelligence (AI) techniques boosting the ability of AS to operate and self-adapt in increasingly complex and dynamic environments.

Recently, there have been multiple research efforts to understand diverse AS quality attributes (e.g., trustworthiness, safety) with learning-enabled components and how to certify them. Examples range from the use of declarations of conformity from AI service providers for examination by their consumers [1],

S. Cherfi et al. (Eds.): RCIS 2021, LNBIP 415, pp. 221–229, 2021.
https://doi.org/10.1007/978-3-030-75018-3_14

to the creation of new standards like SOTIF to consider AS in which learning-enabled components make decisions [2]. This is due to the assumption that the behaviour of such learning-enabled components cannot be guaranteed by neither current software development processes nor by validation and verification approaches [3], but they are a starting point [4]. Certainly, despite being software systems, AI-based AS have different properties than traditional software systems [4]. In this way, recent research has focused on software engineering best practices for AI-based systems [5], and specifically for AS [6].

In this paper, we elaborate on a novel approach pushing forward the idea that AI-based AS will benefit from an integrated development and operation approach driven by the concept of trustworthiness.

2 Challenges of Developing and Operating AI-Based AS

The potential benefits that AI-based AS can provide to their stakeholders, such as data-driven evolution and autonomous behavior [7], have their counterpart in several major challenges that act as impediments to their adoption.

Increase Users' Trust in AI-Based AS. AS could become prevalent in many aspects of people's life. Correspondingly, trustworthiness on AI is a prerequisite for the uptake of AI-based AS, so that users allow its integration into their life. Indeed, the European Commission is working on a regulatory framework leading to a unique "ecosystem of trust" [7]. Users' trust in AI-based AS is threatened by two reasons. On the one hand, key qualities of AI models (e.g., functional safety, security, reliability, or fairness of decisions) must be guaranteed in all possible (often unanticipated) scenarios. Trustworthiness is a highly complex concept and its achievement poses a number of challenges both during development and operation of AI-based AS. In AI development, it is key to address data quality since the very beginning, in order to build trust into the AI system. At operation, a trustworthy AI system must behave as expected, particularly in unanticipated situations and in case of malfunctioning of any kind, it does not behave in any unwanted, especially harmful, ways. On the other hand, users' trust requires informing users about how the decisions are derived by the AI models. For instance, understanding the reasons behind predictions is a determinant in achieving trust, which is fundamental if one plans to take action based on a prediction, or when choosing whether to deploy a new model [8]. Despite the widespread adoption of AI technologies, organizations find AI models to be black-boxes and non-transparent [8,9].

Align Software Engineering (SE) and AI Model Development Processes. Traditional software development lifecycle methodologies fall short when managing AI models, as AI lifecycle management has a number of differences from traditional software development lifecycle [4] (e.g., requirements-driven vs. data-driven) [9]. Furthermore, as reported by Atlassian and Microsoft [10], it is important to explore the role of humans from different areas (e.g., software and AI model development) in a complex modern industrial environment where AI-based systems are developed. Therefore, an integration of software and AI processes becomes necessary for AI-based AS [11,12]. In addition, this integration shall support continuously adapting AI models based on evolving users' needs and changing environments (i.e., to cope with concept drift) [13].

Context-Dependent AS and AI Model Version Control and Deployment. Learning-enabled components of AI-based AS are trained and tested with various combinations of parameters, using different data sets, customized to personalized environments, and even solved by diverse algorithms and solutions. AI model deployment challenges in industrial settings include training-serving skew, difficulties in designing the serving infrastructure, and difficulties with training at the edge [14]. These challenges have motivated the concepts of AIOps and MLOps in the grey literature, and best practices like versioning [5]. However, solutions or frameworks supporting the management of multiple instances of AI models deployed in different context-aware environments are scarce. Context is the missing piece in the AI lifecycle [15].

Closing the Gap Between the Development and Operation Phases of the AI-Based AS. Nguyen-Duc et al. [16] summarize the engineering challenges for developing and operating AI systems into seven categories: requirements, data management, model design and implementation, model configuration, model testing, evaluation and deployment, and processes and practice. Kästner et al. argue on the need of improving the educational skills covering the whole software and AI lifecycle [17]. Proposals to adopt DevOps have also been presented for AS, such as in autonomous vehicles [18]. These AI-based AS have some characteristics that differentiate them from other types of software systems, e.g., AI models are usually deployed as part of embedded systems, which require additional techniques for continuous deployment, such as Over-the-Air updates [18]. However, as aforementioned, none of the these approaches have a focus on trustworthiness nor context-specific AI model deployment. Hence, we consider that the development and operation of trustworthy AI-based AS require a holistic approach including enabling iterative cycles for reliably training, adapting, maintaining, and operating the AI model in AS.

3 Research Directions

In this section, we discuss four research directions to address the previous challenges about development and operation approaches for AI-based AS.

Direction 1: Increasing Users' Trust in AI-Based AS by Means of Transparent Real-Time Monitoring of AI Models Trustworthiness. An AS requires self-adaptation to rapidly and effectively protect their critical capabilities from disruption caused by adverse events and conditions. Hence, this direction focuses on continuous self-monitoring in operation based on a set of indicators aggregated into a *trustworthiness score* (TWS). The TWS is a high-level indicator summarizing the level of trustworthiness of an AI model. It is a mean to consider evolving users' needs and changing operational environments and can be used to guide the self-adaptation of AI models in operations, following the commonly used MAPE-K loop [19]. The high-level TWS is broken down into specific and measurable aspects of AI models at operation (not fully covered in software quality measurement standards [20]): security, dependability, integrity, and reliability. This vision on the computation of indicators of AI trustworthiness is shared by Green [21] and emerging standard groups [22]. In our case, TWS aspects are measured from contextual data collected by AS (e.g., via sensors) and monitoring the AI models (e.g., accuracy). The TWS triggers an action when outliers are predicted or identified. Then, the AS self-adapts.

These types of 'scores' are attractive for practitioners to transparently communicate and understand the real-time the status of AI models and alert the development team (or even the end-user) in case of potential threats/risks. Indeed, some companies have proposed scores for other qualities, such as Google is quantifying testing issues to decrease machine learning technical debt [23]. Furthermore, a Gartner report considers tracking AI-based systems to enable transparency as a critical lesson learned from early AI projects: "If [an AI practitioner] predicts that something will fail, the immediate question someone asks is 'Why is it going to fail?' [...] having the transparency will help him explain how he came to that conclusion" [24].

Direction 2: Integrating the Development and Evolution of AI Models and AS. Reinforcing the adaptation capabilities of AI models during their development requires highly iterative engineering processes, including the data science and AI model development processes of building, evaluating, deploying, and maintaining AI models, and software systems based upon them. An AI-based AS has two main assets: the AS, and the AI model(s) embedded in a learning-enabled component. Often, due to the methodological gap between the AI model development process and software engineering, these two assets are developed in two parallel, but independent cycles. In other words, there is a need for a seamless integration of these processes.

In addition, for two decades, agile principles have been successfully applied for the rapid and flexible development of high-quality software products [25], whereas AI model development has been guided by relatively abstract and inflexible processes [13]. It is time to break these silos. Therefore, this direction proposes an integrated process with coordinated communication between the AI model development and SE teams to develop and evolve AI models for AS. This integrated process both adopts the principles of agile software development and integrates them with existing and well-known AI model development processes, such as the Cross-industry Standard Process for Data Mining [26,27]. This is a complex task requiring the integration of different activities, roles, and multiple existing methodologies. Initial efforts in this direction are the Team Data Science Process from Microsoft [28] and tool support like IBM Watson Studio [29].

Direction 3: Providing Intelligent and Context-Aware Techniques to Deploy Updated AI Models in AS Instances. With key data from operation, AI models are continuously evolving to address trust-related threats/risks. Even when AS have the same characteristics (e.g., two autonomous vehicles of the same type), their stakeholders (e.g., owners/passengers with diverse driving style, mood) and environments (e.g., weather, traffic) vary. This is why learning-enabled components of AS need to continuously adapt or even evolve to their users and contexts. Thus, the number of instances may evolve from only one instance (e.g., in an Industry 4.0 machine infrastructure) to thousands of instances (e.g., autonomous vehicles in a smart city). A critical challenge is that often there are no clearly distinguishable components or parts of an AI model that can be analyzed regarding commonalities and variabilities.

This direction aims to facilitate a context-specific deployment of AI models in diverse AS. From the SE perspective, available research on managing software product lines might be reused to manage variabilities and commonalities among contexts in which AS are operating in and consequently among the data they collect evolve on [30]. From the data science and AI perspective, the research on transfer learning [31] and active learning [32] provide valuable strategies for sharing knowledge between various contexts and incrementally evolving AI models.

Direction 4: Bringing Together the Development and Operation of AI Models in Trustworthy AS into a Holistic Lifecycle with Tool Support. The SE community is currently researching the application of SE for AI-based systems [5]. However, challenges regarding maintenance and deployment of AI models still remain [14,17]. For instance, a survey conducted by SAS revealed that less than 50% of AI models get deployed and for those that do, it takes more than three months to complete the deployment [33]. In this context, it becomes necessary "to accelerate getting AI/ML models into production" [34].

To keep the development and operation of AI models interconnected, this direction proposes an effective DevOps holistic lifecycle for the production of trustworthy AI-based AS. Since companies typically cannot afford drastic changes of their methodology, a plug-and-play process components are of high importance. This direction includes the development of AI-specific, independent, and loosely coupled software components (ready to be integrated into companies' development and operational environments) for the three directions we presented above.

4 A DevOps Approach to Develop and Operate AI Models in AS

To address the four research directions, we propose an integrated approach bringing the concept of DevOps to AI models of AS. DevOps "integrates the two worlds of development and operation, using automated development, deployment, and infrastructure monitoring" [35]. It is an organizational shift in which cross-functional teams work on continuous operational feature deliveries [35].

Additionally, in development, the approach also aims to close the gap between data science/AI model development and SE, as shown in Fig. 1. Currently, frameworks are mainly based on the AI models lifecycle in isolation, and have not

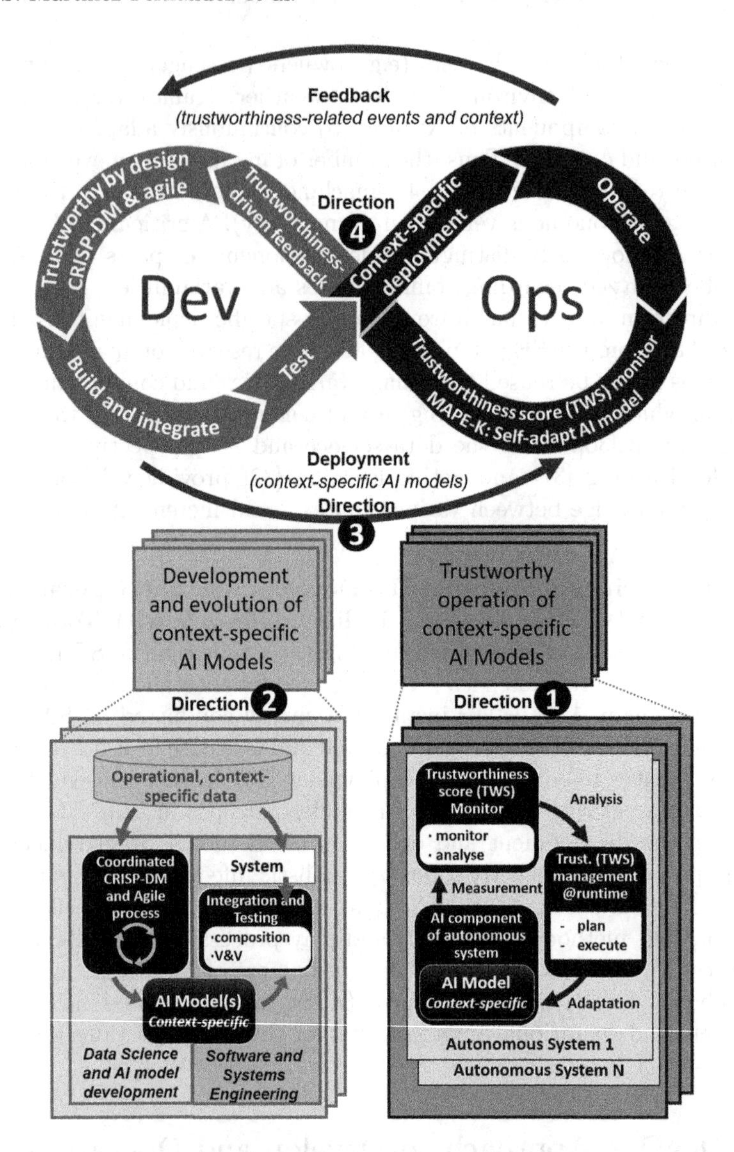

Fig. 1. Integrated approach for the development and operation of AI-based AS.

addressed the issue of integrating the AI pipeline in the DevOps cycle. The proposed approach addresses the inherent challenges of managing multiple instances of models deployed in a distributed set of autonomous systems, such as deploying multiple models in a distributed and heterogeneous environment; and collecting data from multiple sources to assess the behaviour of those models. As depicted in Fig. 1, we propose two cycles running in parallel:

1. *An operation cycle (Ops) in the form of a MAPE-K loop* [19] *ensuring trustworthy behaviour of context-specific AI models by means of continuous*

self-adaptation capabilities and resilience approaches (Direction 1 in Fig. 1). It enables AI-based AS to rapidly and effectively protect their critical capabilities from disruption caused by adverse events and conditions (e.g., enable an actuator to avoid a collision in an autonomous vehicle). Therefore, it is crucial to continuously monitor the behaviour of the AS (in particular, with respect to trustworthiness, including security, dependability, integrity, and reliability threats caused by the AI model) in new situations such as e.g., energy supply problems, malfunctioning of some component, plan for new or improved functionalities, and finally adapt their individual operation behaviour during execution.

2. An integrated AI Development cycle (Dev) that adopts agile practices for the iterative development and evolution of context-specific AI models (Direction 2 in Fig. 1). It includes continuous improvement of the AI models based on operational data and enriched by experts' knowledge. The development, maintenance and evolution of AI-based AS relies on the collaboration of AI model development and software engineering teams. The engineers involved in the maintenance of AI models in the AS are supported by (1) the TWS from operation that may require updating AI models, (2) key data collected regarding the trustworthiness of the AS and its environment, and (3) tools to prepare and enrich the collected data. The software and system engineering team integrate the AI models into the AS and implement the infrastructure to monitor the trust-related risks of the AS during its operation to ensure the trustworthiness of the entire AS.

These two cycles are integrated into a holistic DevOps approach for trustworthy AI-based AS (Direction 4 in Fig. 1), which acts as a bridge between the *Dev* and *Ops* cycles as follows. First, *Dev* deploys the AS with its incorporated context-specific AI models (Direction 3 in Fig. 1). AI models are deployed in a distributed context-specific AS. Such deployment requires specific activities, such as context identification of the AS to deploy the correct context-specific AI model instance, Over-The-Air updates to enact the deployments, and validation of AI models within the running context against predefined capabilities and bounds for data gathering or executing axioms. Second, during *Ops*, a continuous cycle gathers trustworthiness-related events and context-specific feedback data from AI models at operation and sends them to development (feedback arrow of Fig. 1). Key quality objectives for trustworthy AS are identified, e.g., effectiveness and efficiency of the AI model or environmental and social effects. The monitoring infrastructure provides feedback to manage potential risks in operation (self-adaptation of Direction 1) and in development (evolution of the AI model of Direction 2). Then, the approach starts over again, and *Dev* uses the feedback to evolve the AI models and deploy them back in existing instances and eventually in the system functionalities.

5 Concluding Remarks

We identified the challenges that need to be overcome to develop and operate trustworthy AI-based AS. We discussed four research directions to address such challenges. Finally, we present a holistic DevOps approach bringing together the development and operation of AI models in AS, aiming to increase users' trust.

Several factors may hinder the successful application of these research directions. First, the need to ensure the reliability of the TWS for different purposes and scenarios, e.g., need for customizable TWS, as well as recognizing that some aspects are challenging to be measured (e.g., ethics). Second, many companies already have pipelines to create AI-based AS based on a unique perspective (either data science or system engineering) and may be unwilling to adopt a unified approach. Third, even though being minimal, the iterative feedback cycles trigger discussions about ethics because users might be monitored (even though complying with their agreement for data collection and current legislation), and processing huge amounts of data leaves a "carbon footprint".

Future work consists of exploring how the elements of this integrated approach can be exploited or customised to support existing AI-based AS.

Acknowledgment. This work has been partially supported by the Beatriz Galindo programme (BGP18/00075) and the Catalan Research Agency (AGAUR, contract 2017 SGR 1694).

References

1. Arnold, M., Bellamy, R.K., et al.: FactSheets: increasing trust in AI services through supplier's declarations of conformity. IBM J. Res. Dev. **63**(4/5), 6-1 (2019)
2. Gharib, M., Lollini, P., et al.: On the safety of automotive systems incorporating machine learning based components. In: DSN-W, pp. 271–274 (2018)
3. Borg, M., Englund, C., et al.: Safely entering the deep: a review of verification and validation for machine learning and a challenge elicitation in the automotive industry. J. Autom. Softw. Eng. **1**(1), 1 (2019)
4. Ozkaya, I.: What is really different in engineering AI-enabled systems? IEEE Softw. **37**(4), 3–6 (2020)
5. Serban, A., van der Blom, K., Hoos, H., Visser, J.: Adoption and effects of software engineering best practices in machine learning. arXiv:2007.14130 (2020)
6. Aniculaesei, A., Grieser, J., et al.: Toward a holistic software systems engineering approach for dependable autonomous systems. In: SEFAIAS, pp. 23–30 (2018)
7. European Commission: On Artificial Intelligence - a European approach to excellence and trust. https://ec.europa.eu
8. Ribeiro, M.T., Singh, S., Guestrin, C.: Why should I trust you? Explaining the predictions of any classifier. In: ACM SIGKDD, pp. 1135–1144 (2016)
9. Akkiraju, R., et al.: Characterizing machine learning processes: a maturity framework. In: Fahland, D., Ghidini, C., Becker, J., Dumas, M. (eds.) BPM 2020. LNCS, vol. 12168, pp. 17–31. Springer, Cham (2020). https://doi.org/10.1007/978-3-030-58666-9_2
10. Kim, M., Zimmermann, T., DeLine, R., Begel, A.: Data scientists in software teams: state of the art and challenges. TSE **44**(11), 1024–1038 (2017)
11. Heck, P.: Software Engineering for Machine Learning Applications. https://fontysblogt.nl/software-engineering-for-machine-learning-applications/
12. Santhanam, P., Farchi, E., Pankratius, V.: Engineering reliable deep learning systems. arXiv:1910.12582 (2019)
13. Saltz, J., Crowston, K., et al.: Comparing data science project management methodologies via a controlled experiment. In: HICSS (2017)

14. Lwakatare, L.E., Raj, A., Crnkovic, I., Bosch, J., Olsson, H.H.: Large-scale machine learning systems in real-world industrial settings: a review of challenges and solutions. Inf. Softw. Technol. **127**, 106368 (2020)
15. Garcia, R., Sreekanti, V., et al.: Context: the missing piece in the machine learning lifecycle. In: KDD CMI Workshop, vol. 114 (2018)
16. Nguyen-Duc, A., Sundbø, I., et al.: A multiple case study of artificial intelligent system development in industry. In: EASE, pp. 1–10 (2020)
17. Kästner, C., Kang, E.: Teaching software engineering for AI-enabled systems. arXiv preprint arXiv:2001.06691 (2020)
18. Banijamali, A., Jamshidi, P., Kuvaja, P., Oivo, M.: Kuksa: a cloud-native architecture for enabling continuous delivery in the automotive domain. In: Franch, X., Männistö, T., Martínez-Fernández, S. (eds.) PROFES 2019. LNCS, vol. 11915, pp. 455–472. Springer, Cham (2019). https://doi.org/10.1007/978-3-030-35333-9_32
19. IBM: An architectural blueprint for autonomic computing. IBM White Paper, vol. 31, no. 2003, pp. 1–6 (2006)
20. Siebert, J., et al.: Towards guidelines for assessing qualities of machine learning systems. In: Shepperd, M., Brito e Abreu, F., Rodrigues da Silva, A., Pérez-Castillo, R. (eds.) QUATIC 2020. CCIS, vol. 1266, pp. 17–31. Springer, Cham (2020). https://doi.org/10.1007/978-3-030-58793-2_2
21. Trustworthy AI: explainability, safety and verifiability. https://www.ericsson.com/en/blog/2020/12/trustworthy-ai
22. Achieving trustworthy AI with standards. https://etech.iec.ch/issue/2020-03/achieving-trustworthy-ai-with-standards
23. Breck, E., Cai, S., Nielsen, E., Salib, M., Sculley, D.: The ML test score: a rubric for ML production readiness and technical debt reduction. In: Big Data, pp. 1123–1132 (2017)
24. Gartner: Lessons From AI Pioneers. https://www.gartner.com/smarterwithgartner/lessons-from-artificial-intelligence-pioneers/. Accessed 15 Oct 2020
25. Gustavsson, T.: Benefits of agile project management in a non-software development context: a literature review. PM World J. 114–124 (2016)
26. Shearer, C.: The CRISP-DM model: the new blueprint for data mining. J. Data Warehous. **5**(4), 13–22 (2000)
27. Studer, S., Bui, T.B., et al.: Towards CRISP-ML (Q): a machine learning process model with quality assurance methodology. arXiv:2003.05155 (2020)
28. Microsoft: What is the Team Data Science Process?. https://docs.microsoft.com/en-us/azure/machine-learning/team-data-science-process
29. IBM Watson Studio. https://www.ibm.com/cloud/watson-studio
30. Capilla, R., Fuentes, L., Lochau, M.: Software variability in dynamic environments. J. Syst. Softw. **156**, 62–64 (2019)
31. Torrey, L., Shavlik, J.: Transfer learning. In: Handbook of Research on Machine Learning Applications and Trends, pp. 242–264. IGI Global (2010)
32. Settles, B., Brachman, R.J.: Active learning. In: Synthesis Lectures on AI and ML. Morgan Claypool (2012)
33. SAS: Get the most from your AI investment by operationalizing analytics. https://www.sas.com/content/dam/SAS/documents/marketing-whitepapers-ebooks/sas-whitepapers/en/operationalizing-analytics-110983.pdf
34. Enterprise AI/Machine Learning: Lessons Learned. https://towardsdatascience.com/enterprise-ai-machine-learning-lessons-learned-4f39ae026c5d
35. Ebert, C., Gallardo, G., Hernantes, J., Serrano, N.: DevOps. IEEE Softw. **33**(3), 94–100 (2016)

Matching Conservation-Restoration Trajectories: An Ontology-Based Approach

Alaa Zreik(✉) and Zoubida Kedad

University of Versailles Saint-Quentin-En-Yvelines, 45 Avenue des Etats-Unis, 78000 Versailles, France
alaa.zreik@ens.uvsq.fr, zoubida.kedad@uvsq.fr

Abstract. The context of our work is a project at the French National Library (BnF), which aims at designing a decision support system for conservation experts. The goal of this system is to analyze the conservation history of documents in order to enable reliable predictions on their physical state. The present work is the first step towards such system. We propose a representation of a document conservation history as a conservation-restoration trajectory, and we specify its different types of events. We also propose a trajectory matching process which computes a similarity score between two conservation-restoration trajectories taking into account the terminological heterogeneity of the events. We introduce an ontological model validated by domain experts which will be used during the pairwise comparison of events in two trajectories. Finally, we present experiments showing the effectiveness of our approach.

Keywords: Trajectory matching · Ontology · Semantic trajectory · Semantic similarity

1 Introduction

The context of our work is an on-going project at the BnF, the French National Library, which aims at designing a decision support system for conservation and restoration experts in order to help them in defining their conservation policies. The goal of this project is to minimize the number of documents which physical state might deteriorate to the point that they become no longer available to the readers. The early identification of the documents which are likely to deteriorate would be beneficial to the experts to prioritize the ones which have to undergo some conservation processes in order to prevent further major degradations.

One possible way to provide decision support to conservation experts is to give them insight into the multiple data sources at the BnF, which store information of various nature about the documents. These information could be related to the processes in their conservation history, their possible degradations and the records of the readers' requests for these documents. The ultimate goal of

S. Cherfi et al. (Eds.): RCIS 2021, LNBIP 415, pp. 230–246, 2021.
https://doi.org/10.1007/978-3-030-75018-3_15

this project is to integrate these various heterogeneous data sources and analyse the conservation history of documents along with other relevant information in order to enable the generation of reliable predictions of the state of a given document. The first step towards this decision support system is to define a representation for document conservation data and provide a meaningful way of comparing these representations to enable future analysis tasks such as clustering and pattern extraction.

This is the focus of the present work. We propose to represent these data as conservation-restoration trajectories, consisting of a sequence of conservation-restoration events, which could be for example a conservation treatment performed on a document, or a degradation observed on a document. We formalize this conservation-restoration trajectory and we specify the different types of events composing it. These types of events are derived from a thorough study of the available heterogeneous data sources. Having defined the representation of conservation-restoration trajectories, we propose a trajectory matching process which computes a similarity score between two trajectories taking into account the terminological heterogeneity existing in the events composing them. To this end, we introduce an ontological model validated by domain experts which will be used during the pairwise comparison of the events in two trajectories. Our matching process enables the identification of matching events beyond the identical ones, and a more accurate comparison of trajectories. We have performed some experiments illustrating the quality of the results.

This paper is organised as follows. In Sect. 2, we present a statement of our problem. In Sect. 3, we introduce our representation of a document's conservation-restoration trajectory. Section 4 is devoted to event similarity and presents our algorithm for ontology-based event similarity evaluation. In Sect. 5, we present our approach for evaluating trajectory similarity based on event similarity. Section 6 presents the experiments conducted to illustrate the quality of the matching results. Section 7 presents the related works, and finally, Sect. 8 provides a conclusion and future works.

2 Problem Statement

The first problem addressed in this paper is to identify in the available sources the relevant conservation data related to documents and to propose a representation of these data. In our work, we consider that the conservation data related to a given document can be viewed as a semantic trajectory consisting of a sequence of events. Consider a set of documents $Doc = \{doc_1, doc_2..., doc_n\}$. For each document doc_i, we aim to associate a conservation-restoration trajectory of events Tr_i that represent its conservation history. This trajectory should integrate all the relevant events from the available databases. Each conservation-restoration trajectory is of the form $Tr_i = [e_1, ...e_k]$. The problem is to identify the different types of events relevant to characterize the conservation history of a document. Once a representation of the relevant data is defined, its use for analysis purposes requires the comparison of distinct trajectories. One key issue in our context is to perform such comparison considering the heterogeneity in the terminology used to describe conservation events in distinct data sources. This leads us to the second problem tackled in this paper, which can be stated as follows: how to evaluate the similarity between two conservation-restoration trajectories corresponding to distinct documents? To this end, we provide two similarity functions:

- $Sim_e(e_i, e_j)$, which evaluates the similarity between two events e_i and e_j,
- $Sim_s(Tr_i, Tr_j)$, which calculates the similarity between two trajectories Tr_i and Tr_j representing the conservation histories of the documents doc_i and doc_j respectively.

The events on the documents at the BnF may have been recorded several decades ago. Obviously, the names and types of the events involved in a sequence can be highly different according to the time they have been recorded. Moreover, the lack of a uniform and standardized vocabulary makes the terminology used in naming the events very heterogeneous. Evaluating the similarity between events and trajectories has to take into account the possible semantic relationships between events. For example, a conservation event recorded for a document twenty years ago may have a different name to an event recorded this month, but these two events might still be very similar, which could only be identified by a human expert. In our approach, we assume that the domain knowledge specific to the conservation and restoration field is available and formalized as an ontology O. Our problem is to inject the knowledge provided by O in the similarity functions Sim_e and Sim_s. This way, the analysis will incorporate the available conservation knowledge. In the following sections, we will introduce the representation used for conservation-restoration trajectories, then we will present our proposal to evaluate both the similarity between events and between trajectories.

3 Representing Conservation Trajectories

The data sources at the BnF are created and maintained by different departments, and these sources provide data covering different, possibly overlapping aspects of document restoration and conservation. For example, the collections department databases provide data describing the communication of the documents to the readers following their requests, and the observed degradations on these documents, while the conservation department database stores data about the conservation and restoration processes performed on the documents to keep them in a good physical state. All the databases have a different structure, different terminologies and attributes. We have first identified in the schemas of the databases all the attributes representing information describing either the physical state of the documents or any information that can have an influence on its physical state. We have identified three types of information. The first one is related to the conservation-restoration processes that have been performed on the documents. The second one is related to the degradations observed on the physical state or the documents. Finally, the third category of information is related to the number of requests made by readers to access the documents. An exploration of the databases showed that there were about 150 different conservation-restoration processes which could be performed on a document, and 250 different types of degradations observed by experts on the documents composing their collections. In order to analyse conservation data, each document will be represented as a conservation-restoration trajectory consisting of a sequence of events which have happened during the life of the document. These events can be either a conservation process performed on a document, or a degradation observed on a document, which are both characterized by a specific designation, but it can also be related to the number of readers having accessed the document. This can obviously have an effect on its physical state. Therefore, we also consider a specific kind of event capturing the level of access to this document by the readers. We are not interested in the exact number of times a document has been requested, we would like instead to characterize the extent to which a document has been requested. We can do so by assigning three distinct values to the communication event: low (≤ 4), average (between 4 and 8) and high (≥ 8), these values have been provided by the domain experts. In our work, a conservation-restoration trajectory is defined as follows:

Definition 1. *Conservation-Restoration Trajectory. A conservation-restoration trajectory is a sequence of the conservation events of this document ordered by their time. The sequence of events corresponding to a document* doc_i *is denoted* Tr_i*. It is such that* $Tr_i = [e_1, ...e_k]$*, where each* e_i *is an event described by a triple* $< type_i, name_i, time_i >$*.* $Type_i$ *represents the type of the event,* $name_i$ *represents the designation of the event and* $time_i$ *represents the time at which the event occurred. The possible values for* $type_i$ *are P, D or C, corresponding respectively to a conservation process, a degradation or a communication event.*

The value of $name_i$ in a trajectory depends on the type of the corresponding event. If $type_i$ = P, then the value of $name_i$ is the designation of the specific conservation process performed on the document. If $type_i$ = D, then the value of $name_i$ is the name of the degradation observed on the document, and finally, if $type_i$ = C, the value of $name_i$ is the level of communication of the document, defined as low, average or high. Obviously, the events are ordered in the sequence according to the ascending order of $time_i$. Figure 1 shows an example of history of events for a given document consisting of several readers requests, followed by an "*Acidification*" degradation observed on the document, then two conservation processes "*Deacidification*" and "*Mechanical Binding*" and finally a request from a reader. We can see at the bottom of this figure how this history of events is represented as a trajectory Tr according to our definition. Tr is composed of a communication event for which the name value is "average", representing the six requests from the readers in the beginning of the history, then a degradation event, "*Acidification*", followed by two conservation processes, "*Deacidification*" and "*Mechanical Binding*", and finally a communication event for which the name value is "low", corresponding in the example to the request of Reader 7.

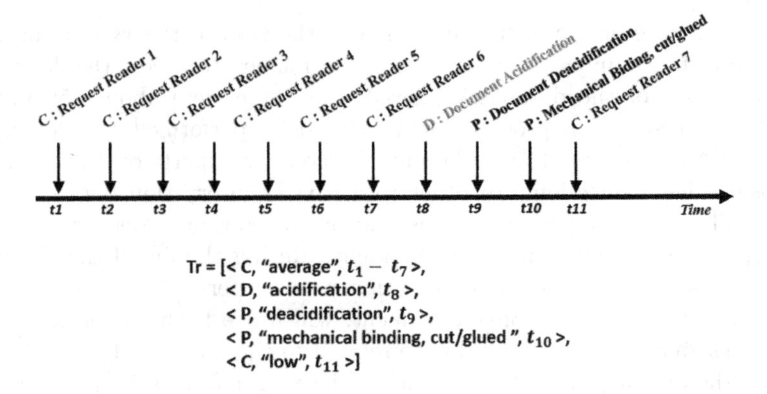

Fig. 1. Example of history of events for a document and the corresponding trajectory

4 Evaluating the Similarity Between Events

Having defined a representation for the documents conservation-restoration trajectories as sequences of events, the analysis of conservation data will require evaluating the similarity between each pair of trajectories, which in turn requires the matching of pairs of events, taking into account the terminological heterogeneity of their description. We present in this section our process for matching two events e_i and e_j belonging to two distinct trajectories. If the two compared events have different types, then they are not considered as matching events. If the two compared events have the same type, and if this type is either P or D, corresponding respectively to a conservation process or a degradation, then their names are compared to determine if they match or not. If these names are identical then obviously the events are matching ones. But if the names are different, this does not mean that the events do not match. Indeed, the terminologies used in the description of either the degradations or the conservation processes may differ, or expressed at different levels of detail according to the source they have been extracted from. In order to overcome this heterogeneity, we propose to use a Conceptual Reference Model during event comparison. Figure 2 shows an excerpt of the CRM_{BnF} ontology, initiated in close collaboration with domain experts at the BnF and its relations to three existing ontologies, CIDOC-CRM [11], CRM_{CR} [1] and CRM_{SCI} [3], which nodes are represented in green color and dotted lines. These relations will be discussed in the related works section. Each concept in the ontology corresponds to either one of the 150 existing conservation-restoration processes or to one of the 250 observed types of degradations. This ontology is expressed using the languages proposed by the W3C[1] Consortium, RDF/S[2] and OWL[3].

[1] https://www.w3.org/2001/sw/wiki/Main_Page.
[2] https://www.w3.org/RDF/.
[3] https://www.w3.org/OWL/.

Figure 2 shows the representation of a subset of both the conservation processes and the degradations related to documents at the BnF. We have identified twenty subclasses for the "BnF : $Conservation\ Process$" class; two of them, "BnF : $Short\ Maintenance$" and "BnF : $Consolidation$", are represented in the figure. We have identified twenty-two subclasses for the "BnF : $Degradation$" class, one of them, "BnF : $Headband$", is represented in the figure.

The greater the distance between the node and the root, the more precise the name of the conservation process or the degradation corresponding to this node.

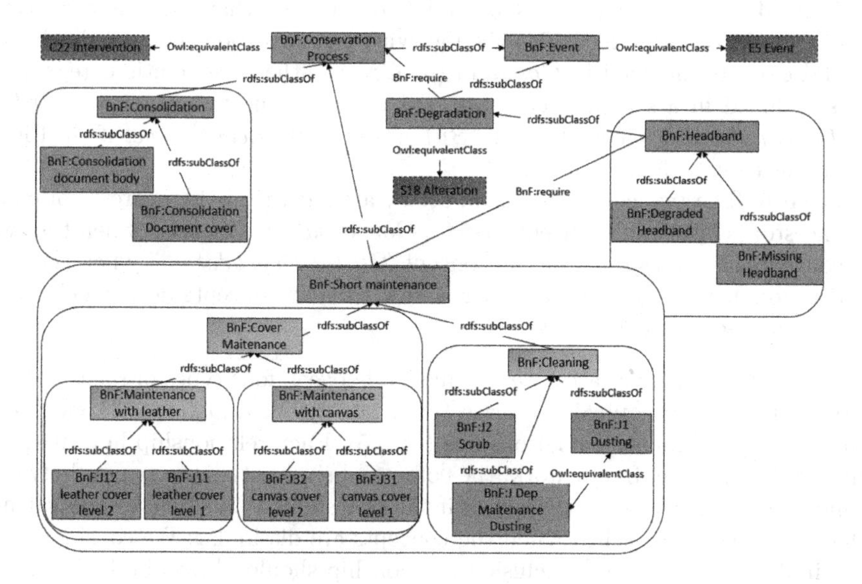

Fig. 2. Excerpt of the CRM_{BnF} ontology

The ontology was created to provide a unified vocabulary for the events in a conservation history and to help identify the similar ones beyond their terminological heterogeneity. The subclasses of the "BnF : $conservation\ Process$" class represent the most generic conservation processes; we refer to these as semantic categories. They play an important role during the identification of similar events. In the same way, we consider that the twenty-two direct subclasses identified for the "BnF : $Degradation$" class are also semantic categories. The comparison of two events e_i and e_j is performed by computing a similarity score using the domain ontology, considering the concepts corresponding to their names $name_i$ and $name_j$ respectively in the ontology. Let us denote Co_i and Co_j these two concepts. The similarity score is computed considering the relative position of Co_i and Co_j. We distinguish between five distinct cases:

- **Case 1:** The two concepts Co_i and Co_j are identical, then the two events e_i and e_j correspond both to the same concept in the ontology.

- **Case 2:** The two concepts Co_i and Co_j are such that there is a path P_{ij} between them where all the edges in the path correspond to *owl : equivalent Class* properties. For example, the two concepts "*BnF : J Dep Maintenance Dusting*" and "*BnF : J1 Dusting*" in Fig. 2 fit this case.
- **Case 3:** The two concepts Co_i and Co_j are such that there is either a path P_{ij}=[(Co_i, P_1, Co_1), (Co_1, P_2, Co_2), ...(Co_k, P_{k+1}, Co_j)] or a path P_{ji}=[(Co_j, P_1, Co_1), (Co_1, P_2, Co_2), ...(Co_k, P_{k+1}, Co_i)] where for all the edges in the path, the property P_x is the *rdfs : subclassOf* property for $1 < x < k + 1$. In this case, the two events e_i and e_j are of the same nature, but one of them is more specific than the other.
- **Case 4:** The two concepts Co_i and Co_j are such that there is a concept Co_k in the ontology for which the following two conditions hold: (i) both Co_i and Co_j are included in Co_k, and (ii) Co_k is either a semantic category or is included in a semantic category. For example, the two concepts "*BnF : J31 canvas cover level* 1" and "*BnF : J32 canvas cover level* 2" in Fig. 2 fit this case.
- **Case 5:** The two concepts Co_i and Co_j are such that the nearest common ancestor is either the concept "*BnF : Conservation Process*" when the two concepts have a *type=P* or the concept "*BnF : Degradation*" when the two concepts have a *type=D*. In other words, the two concepts do not belong to the same semantic category.

According to the above cases, we distinguish between four types of relationships between the events: equivalence (case 1 and case 2), inclusion (case 3), closeness (case 4) and dissimilarity relationships (case 5). Each relationship have its specific similarity score. In our work, the computed similarity score ranges between 0 and 1. The highest score is reached if the concepts are identical or equivalent. The lowest score is reached when the concepts are dissimilar. We consider that the similarity score for the inclusion relationship should always be higher than the similarity score of the closeness relationship. Furthermore, when there is an inclusion or a closeness relationship between two concepts, we consider that the path length between the two concepts should be reflected in the similarity score: the shorter the path, the higher the score. The similarity score corresponding to each of them is defined as follows:

Definition 2. *Similarity Score.*

- ***Equivalence.*** *The similarity score for two equivalent events is equal to 1.*
- ***Inclusion.*** *The similarity score for two concepts Co_i and Co_j such that Co_i is included in Co_j is comprised in the range $[\alpha, 1[$ and defined as follows:*

$$1 - (1 - \alpha) \times \frac{|P_{ij}|}{depth(CRM_{BnF})}$$

where $|P_{ij}|$ is the length of the path P_{ij} between Co_i and Co_j, and the depth function return the length of the longest inclusion path in CRM_{BnF}, i.e. the longest path with rdfs : subclassOf properties.

- ***Closenesss.*** *The similarity score for two concepts Co_i and Co_j both included in a third concept Co_k is comprised in the range $]0, \alpha[$ and defined as follows:*
$$\alpha - \alpha \times \frac{(|P_{ik}| + |P_{jk}|)/2}{depth(CRM_{BnF})}$$
- ***Dissimilarity.*** *If this relationship holds between two events, the similarity score is equal to 0.*

Note that α is an arbitrary value which purpose is only to represent the total order relation defined between the scores corresponding to equivalence, inclusion, closeness and dissimilarity relationships. The similarity score between two events will be used to define the similarity between conservation-restoration trajectories presented in the following section.

5 Conservation Trajectories Similarity

Evaluating the similarity between trajectories has been addressed by different streams of works, such as semantic trajectories analysis, which involves the evaluation of the similarity between the elements of the trajectory, generally associated with a location, or in the context of string comparisons, where the sequence is a string composed of characters and where distance functions have been proposed to evaluate string similarity. In all of these works, the proposed measures to calculate trajectory similarity have distinct characteristics, as discussed in the survey presented in [14]. The requirements for a similarity measure suitable for our context where trajectories represent histories of conservation events are the followings. First, the measure should not depend on the event's position, i.e. its index. Two similar events from two trajectories can match regardless of their positions. Another requirement is that the measure should depend on the event's order. For example, if there is a match between two events e_x and e_y from two distinct trajectories, then any following match between the events $e_{x'}$ and $e_{y'}$ is possible only if $x' > x$ and $y' > y$. The third requirement is that the measure should be independent from the event's time. Two similar events from two trajectories can be matched regardless of their time feature. Finally, the measure should rely on a single match for each event, which means that there is at most one match for a given event. One of the measures which is suitable to the matching requirements identified for conservation-restoration trajectories is the Longest Common SubSequence (LCSS) [13]. We choose this measure to be the basis of the conservation-restoration trajectory similarity evaluation. The LCSS measure is a partial match measure. It calculates the longest common subsequence of two compared trajectories. When applied on spatial trajectories, LCSS considers two points of two different trajectories to be a match if the distance between the two locations is less than a given threshold ϵ and for every match it increase the longest common subsequence by one. We present hereafter the definition of LCSS as stated in [14].

Definition 3. *Longest Common SubSequence (LCSS)*

$$S_{LCSS}(Tr_1, Tr_2) = \begin{cases} \emptyset, & \text{if } l_1 = 0 \text{ or } l_2 = 0 \\ S_{LCSS}(Rest(Tr_1), Rest(Tr_2)) + 1, & \text{if } d(H(Tr_1), H(Tr_2)) \leq \epsilon \\ max\{S_{LCSS}(Tr_1, Rest(Tr_2)), S_{LCSS}(Rest(Tr_1), Tr_2)\}, & \text{otherwise} \end{cases} \quad (1)$$

With l_1 and l_2 representing the length of Tr_1 and Tr_2 respectively. The H function returns the first event in the trajectory, and the Rest function returns the trajectory without its first event.

The LCSS measure can be also used with semantic trajectories by matching the identical events, and by increasing the longest common subsequence by one for each matching pair. However, LCSS can also be extended to take into account events that are similar according to our ontology-based similarity score. In our work, we introduce the Longest Common Events SubSequence $LCESS$, an extended definition of $LCSS$, which uses the similarity between events defined in the previous section. $LCESS$ is an ontology-based measure that calculates the maximum possible matches between two semantic trajectories. It is defined as follows:

Definition 4. *Longest Common Events SubSequence (LCESS)*

$$LCESS(Tr_1, Tr_2) = \begin{cases} \emptyset, & \text{if } l_1 = 0 \text{ or } l_2 = 0 \\ LCESS(Rest(Tr_1), Rest(Tr_2)) + 1, & \text{if } Sim_e(H(Tr_1), H(Tr_2)) = 1 \\ max\{LCESS(Tr_1, Rest(Tr_2)), LCESS(Rest(Tr_1), Tr_2), & \\ LCESS(Rest(Tr_1), Rest(Tr_2)) + Sim_e(H(Tr_1), H(Tr_2))\} & \text{if } 0 < Sim_e(H(Tr_1), H(Tr_2)) < 1 \\ max\{LCESS(Tr_1, Rest(Tr_2)), LCESS(Rest(Tr_1), Tr_2)\} & \text{otherwise} \end{cases} \quad (2)$$

When matching two events e_i and e_j from two trajectories, there are three possible cases:

- $Sim_e(e_i, e_j) = 1$. The two events are equivalent, they are considered as matching events.
- $Sim_e(e_i, e_j) \in]0, 1[$. The relationship between the two events is either inclusion or closeness. In this case, they are considered as matching events if there are no other matching event with a higher similarity score.
- $Sim_e(e_i, e_j) = 0$. The two events are dissimilar and they are not matching events.

By using $LCSS$ on sequences of events, only identical elements can be matched. Therefore, the main difference between $LCSS$ and $LCESS$ is that the latter takes into consideration the relationships between the concepts corresponding to the events names in the ontology. For each match, $LCESS$ increases the total score by the similarity score between the two matching events. Note that in this work, our goal is to refine the matching between trajectories and propose a measure which enables to identify more matching elements beyond the identical ones, but it is possible to further refine this measure, for example by taking into account the length of the trajectories. Figure 3 shows an example of using both $LCSS$ and $LCESS$ on two conservation-restoration trajectories of two documents doc_i and doc_j. Using $LCSS$, only equivalent and identical events are considered as matching ones, and the longest common subsequence is equal to 1. Using $LCESS$, the similarity score is increased as new matching pairs of events are identified. This will result in a longest common events subsequence of length equal to $1+SIM_e(Short\ Maintenance, Cleaning) +SIM_e(Canvas\ cover\ level\ 1, Leather\ cover\ level\ 2)$. The relationship between the "*Short maintenance*" and the "*Cleaning*" events is an inclusion relationship, and the path length between them is equal to one. Assume that the depth of CRM_{BnF} is equal to 6. The similarity score between the two events is therefore equal to 0.93. The relationship between the "*Canvas cover level* 1" and the "*Leather cover level* 2" events is a closeness relationship, as the nearest common ancestor between the concepts corresponding to the event names is the "BnF : *Cover Maintenance*" as shown in Fig. 2. The distance between the two events and their ancestor is equal to 2, therefore, the similarity score between the two events is equal to 0.4, and the $LCESS$ similarity between the two trajectories is equal to 2.33.

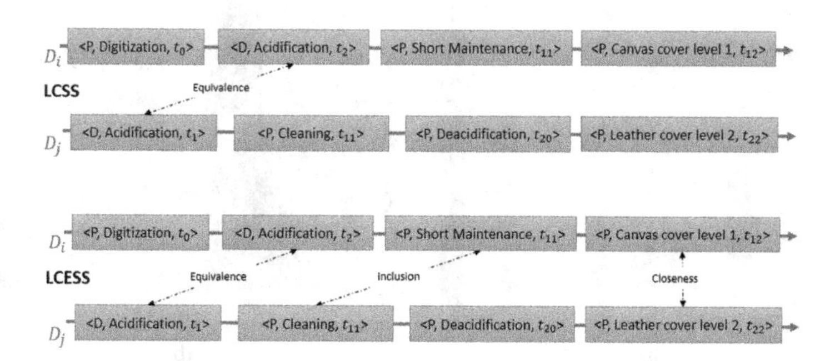

Fig. 3. LCSS vs LCESS for matching conservation-restoration trajectories

6 Experiments

The experiments presented in this section consist of three parts. The first one is related to event matching, where we show the effectiveness of the use of the ontology for searching matching events. The second part of the experiments is related to the trajectory similarity. The third part shows the effectiveness of the ontology and the similarity measure using a set of clusters generated manually by domain experts as a gold standard. In the experiments, we have used real conservation and communication datasets from the BnF, with 7,317,558 conservation events between 2003 and 2020 for 1,946,760 documents. In our datasets, the maximum trajectory length is 1397 events, the minimum length is 1 event, and the average length is 3.75 events. In the three parts of the experiments, we have set α to 0.6.

Event Matching. This part of the experiments aims to show how the use of the ontology during event matching improves the results. We run our approach three times on 100 randomly selected trajectories each time. Figure 4 (a) shows a comparison between the number of pairs of matching events found after running the three tests with and without the use of the ontology. The first test was done on 100 trajectories containing 120 events in total. The results are shown in Fig. 4 (a), showing that 1242 matching events are retrieved without the use of the ontology, while 1663 are retrieved using the ontology. This represents an increase of 33.89%. The second test was done on 100 trajectories containing 173 events in total. Without using the ontology, 1481 pairs of matching events are found. Using the ontology, this number rises to 2034, showing an increase of 37.33%. The third test was done on 100 trajectories containing 295 events in total. Without using the ontology 2473 matching events are detected, and using the ontology, the number of retrieved matching events is 3288, which represents an increase of 32.95%. These tests show a good increase of the number of matching events using the ontology, with an average of 34.72%.

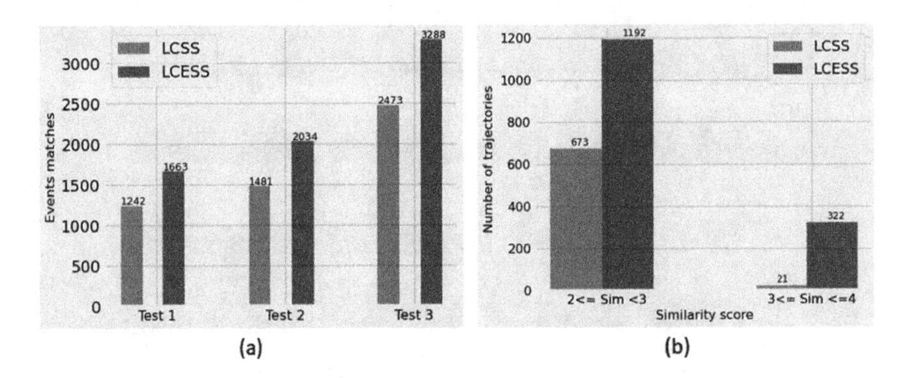

Fig. 4. Ontology-Bbsed event matching (a) and Trajectory similarity (b)

Trajectories Similarity. To show the impact of using the ontology in the evaluation of the similarity between trajectories, we have randomly selected a trajectory Tr and compared it with a set $TrSet$ of 10000 randomly selected trajectories. We have calculated the similarities between Tr and all the trajectories in the set $TrSet$ without using the ontology i.e., using the $LCSS$ measure. We have then selected those having a similarity greater than half of the length of Tr. We have performed the same experiment using the ontology i.e., $LCESS$ measure. Finally, we compare the number of trajectories having a similarity greater than half of the length of Tr using the two measures. Figure 4 (b) shows the number of trajectories which are similar to the input trajectory before and after the use of the CRM_{BnF}. The input of the experiment was a random trajectory $Tr = [<C, \text{"}High\text{"}, t_0 - t_2>, <P, \text{"}Manual\ Binding\text{"}, t_4>, <P, \text{"}1/2\ Cover\text{"}, t_6>, <C, \text{"}Low\text{"}, t_9 - t_{10}>]$ with a length equal to 4. The output shows the number of trajectories which have a similarity between 2 and 4 with Tr. The number of trajectories having a similarity greater than 2 without using the ontology was equal to 694. The number increased to 1504 using the ontology, which is an increase of 116.71%. The total similarity average without using the ontology is 0.8 and increases to 0.95.

Quality of the Matching Algorithm. This experiment aims to show the effectiveness of using CRM_{BnF} and the LCESS measure by comparing the computed similarity to a gold standard. In our case, this gold standard is a set of similarities between trajectories set by the conservation experts at the BnF. We started the experiment by selecting a random set of trajectories to be clustered manually by the conservation experts. We selected a set of 20 trajectories and provided them to the experts. They clustered 14 trajectories into 3 clusters; the 6 remaining trajectories were not assigned to any cluster as they were not similar to any other trajectory according to the experts. Let us denote the resulting clusters by Cl_1, Cl_2 and Cl_3. They contain respectively 5, 4 and 5 trajectories. For the set of considered trajectories, we will compute event similarity with and without the use of CRM_{BnF}, and compare the results. The use of the ontology should significantly increase the number of matching events inside the clusters defined by the experts. The number of matches between events from different clusters should not vary significantly. We distinguish between two situations during event matching, the compared events could either belong to trajectories from the same cluster or to trajectories from different clusters. For each cluster, we compute the number of intra-cluster matches between events. For the cluster Cl_i, this number is equal to the number of event matches between all the pairs of trajectories that belong to cluster Cl_i. We also compute the number of inter-cluster matches between two clusters Cl_i and Cl_j. This number is equal to the number of pairs of matching events (e_i, e_j) such that e_i is an event of a trajectory in Cl_i and e_j is an event of a trajectory in Cl_j.

We define these two numbers as follows. In the definitions, we denote EM the function which returns, for two trajectories, the number of matching events between them.

- Number of intra-cluster matches of the cluster Cl_x:
  $Intra(Cl_x) = \sum EM(tr_i, tr_j)$ where tr_i and $tr_j \in Cl_x$ for $1 < i < n$, $1 < j < n$ and $i \neq j$, and where n is the total number of trajectories in the cluster Cl_x.
- Number of inter-cluster matches between two clusters Cl_x and Cl_y:
  $Inter(Cl_x, Cl_y) = \sum EM(tr_i, tr_j)$ where $tr_i \in Cl_x$ and $tr_j \in C_y$ for $1 < i < n$, $1 < j < m$ and $i \neq j$, where n and m are the number of trajectories in the clusters Cl_x and Cl_y respectively.

Fig. 5 (a) shows the number of intra-cluster and inter-cluster event matches for the clusters defined by the experts using LCSS. The number of intra-cluster matches for the clusters Cl_1, Cl_2 and Cl_3 is equal respectively to 11, 10 and 13. The number of inter-cluster event matches are as follows: $Inter(Cl_1, Cl_2)$ is equal to 17, $Inter(Cl_1, Cl_3)$ is equal to 8 and $Inter(Cl_2, Cl_3)$ is equal to 21.

The goal of LCESS is to increase the similarity between the trajectories assigned to the same cluster by the experts, i.e. the similar ones, which requires the increase of the number of event matches between them. Therefore, the use of LCESS should notably increase the number of intra-cluster event matches. We show the effectiveness of using the LCESS measure and the ontology by representing the increasing percentage of the two types of event matches. Figure 5 (b) shows the new numbers using LCESS. The number of intra-cluster event matches of Cl_1, Cl_2 and Cl_3 is equal to 21, 17 and 25 respectively. The number of inter-cluster event matches are as follows: $Inter(Cl_1, Cl_2)$ is equal to 18, $Inter(Cl_1, Cl_3)$ is equal to 8 and $Inter(Cl_2, Cl_3)$ is equal to 27. The total number of inter-cluster event matches is computed as follows: $Inter(Cl_1, Cl_2) + Inter(Cl_1, Cl_3) + Inter(Cl_2, Cl_3)$. It was equal to 46 and was increased by 7 new matches, which represents an increase of 15.2%. The total number of inter-cluster event matches is computed as follows: $Intra(Cl_1) + Intra(Cl_2) + Intra(Cl_3)$. It was equal to 34 and was increased by 29 new matches, which represents and increase of 85.2%. As we can see, the use of the ontology results in a high increase of the number of intra-cluster event matches, which in turn increases the similarity between the trajectories in the same cluster. The inter-cluster event matches has increased by 15%, which is not significant, especially compared to the increase of the number of intra-cluster matches. This result also shows the validity of the ontology and the identified relations between concepts, as they represent the actual existing relationships between conservation events and thus enable accurate similarity evaluation between conservation-restoration trajectories. The results show the usefulness of the similarity measure based on the ontology where the similarity values between the trajectories that are similar in the expert's opinion increase significantly compared to those that are not similar.

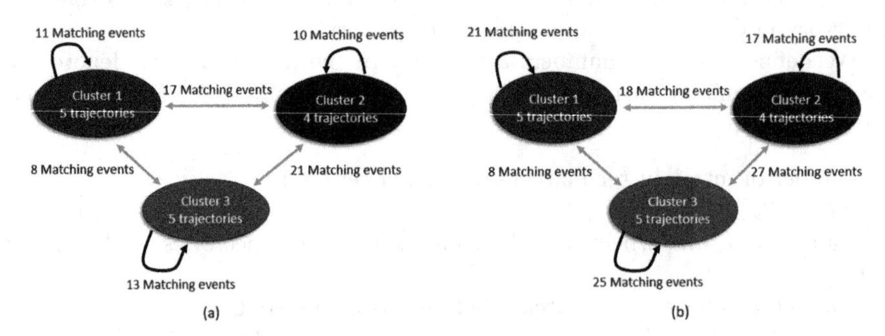

Fig. 5. Numbers of Inter-Cluster and Intra-Cluster Event Matches Using LCSS (a) and LCESS (b)

7 Related Works

Semantic trajectory representation, matching and analysis has been extensively addressed in many different fields, such as healthcare, maritime traffic and enriched spatial trajectories. In the healthcare field, [12] represents each patient by a temporal trajectory where the events are healthcare actions on the patient. [6] proposes the representation of semantic knowledge on paths by adding additional semantic layers, and [7] analyses the maritime traffic and use the raw data such as the speed and the position to create a semantic layer of two types of nodes called way-points and traversals. [2] also transforms the geotagged data into semantic trajectories and represents the semantic trajectories by sequences of location types such as restaurant or park.

Similarity measures have been proposed in many fields to compare trajectories. These include spatial trajectory distance measures, semantic trajectory similarity measures and string matching algorithms. In the calculation of the distance between spatial trajectories, each point represents a geographical location. In a semantic trajectory, each point can be either an event or a semantic node. In string matching, each point is a character. Many distance measures have been proposed for spatial trajectories or semantic ones [8].

[14] classifies the trajectory distance measures depending on the considered data type according to two criteria: (i) the discrete or continuous nature of the data, and (ii) the existence of a temporal dimension for the data. The first category corresponds to discrete trajectories and does not depend on the time dimension. The compared trajectories contain a finite number of points. Examples of measures in this category are the Euclidean Distance (**ED**), the Longest Common SubSequence (**LCSS**) [13] and the Edit Distance on Real sequence (**EDR**) [9]. These two measures are related, the LCSS calculates the length of the longest common sub-sequence, and the edit distance calculates the number of changes needed between the common sequences. We have selected LCSS as the basis for our similarity measure because we are more interested in the common events between the conservation trajectories. Indeed, this is the way experts assess the similarity between event sequences characterising documents at the BnF. The second category corresponds to discrete and spatial-temporal trajectories, where the time dimension is taken into account to calculate the similarity. Some trajectory similarity measures in this category use both the temporal and the spatial data to calculate the similarity; other measures calculate two similarity values, one of them depends on the spatial information and the other one depends on the time dimension. One of the measures in this category is the Spatio-Temporal LCSS (**STLCSS**) introduced by [16] and used in [15]. The other two categories are the measures dealing with continuous data, with or without considering the time dimension. For this type of trajectories, the shape between locations matters. A shape can be for example a road between two locations in spatial trajectories. The measures in these categories require the spatial coordinates of the points in the trajectory, they are therefore not suitable for our context.

The approach presented in [12] searches the matches between the healthcare events to represent a group of trajectories, called a "cohort", by a generated trajectory which is the most similar to all the others. The pairs of matching events contain identical events only, and their similarity score depends on the time and the length of the trajectories. This similarity computation is therefore not applicable to our sequences of events. [17] defines nine features to characterise the event sequence similarity measures and assesses the suitability of these measures to a given context. [5] discusses the existing works on text similarity and identifies three families of approaches: string-based, corpus-based and knowledge-based similarities. [4] divides string similarity measures into four classes: character-based, q-grams, token-based and mixed measures. We did not use these measures as they do not fit our requirements. For example, in the character-based class, the longest common sub-string is similar to the LCSS, but it does not allow different characters (events in our case) between the common sub-sequences. The other classes contain measures that depend on the length of the sub-sequences (q in the q-grams) or match only the identical sequences (token-based measures).

Another stream of works related to our proposal is the design of ontologies for cultural heritage data [1,3,10,11]. Some works have dealt with the unification of the terminologies used in the field of conservation-restoration. One of these works is the CIDOC-CRM ontology citech15cidoc and its extensions CRM_{CR} citech15bannour2018crm and CRM_{SCI} citech15doerr2013scientific. The BnF : *event* concept in our ontology is equivalent to the $E5$ *Event* concept in CIDOC-CRM. Extensions of CIDOC-CRM have been proposed in many areas related to cultural heritage. CRM_{CR} is an extension proposed for cultural objects in museums. The *Intervention* concept in this ontology is equivalent to the BnF : *Conservation Process* in CRM_{BnF}. CRM_{SCI} is another extension of CIDOC-CRM for the field of scientific observations. The *Alteration* concept in this ontology is equivalent to the BnF : *Degradation* concept in CRM_{BnF}. These ontologies do not cover the specific terminology used at the BnF.

8 Conclusion

In this paper, we have proposed a representation of documents conservation data as conservation-restoration trajectories. We have introduced an ontological model encompassing the main conservation and restoration concepts, and we have proposed a process to evaluate the similarity between two given events using this ontological model. We have also proposed an adaptation of an existing trajectory similarity measure to take into account our ontology-based event similarity measure. The experiments have shown that our approach improves the precision of the matching process. This work shows the ontological model's usefulness for expert knowledge representation and trajectory similarity computation. Future works will include further enrichment of the proposed ontological model by introducing more relevant properties, and extending the proposed similarity measures exploiting these properties. Another line of work would be to introduce reasoning capabilities to our similarity computation, which would enable us to take into account not only the knowledge explicitly provided in the model but also the one which could be derived through inference. Finally, this work is the first contribution towards a decision support system for conservation experts at the BnF. As future works, we will also use the trajectory representation and the similarity measures introduced in this paper as the basis to design the analysis tasks suitable for this context and to build an adequate predictive model.

Acknowledgement. The authors would like to thank Arnaud Bacour, Célia Cabane and Philippe Vallas from the Bibliothèque nationale de France (BnF) for their useful feedback, their collaboration in creating and validating the ontology and for the many helpful discussions. This work is supported by the DALGOCOL project funded by the French Heritage Science Foundation (Fondation des Sciences du Patrimoine).

References

1. Bannour, I., et al.: CRM CR-a CIDOC-CRM extension for supporting semantic interoperability in the conservation and restoration domain. In: 2018 3rd Digital Heritage International Congress (DigitalHERITAGE) Held Jointly with 2018 24th International Conference on Virtual Systems & Multimedia (VSMM 2018), pp. 1–8. IEEE (2018)
2. Cai, G., Lee, K., Lee, I.: Mining mobility patterns from geotagged photos through semantic trajectory clustering. Cybern. Syst. **49**(4), 234–256 (2018)
3. Doerr, M., Hiebel, G., Kritsotaki, Y.: The scientific observation model an extension of CIDOC-CRM to support scientific observation. In: 29th CRM-SIG Meeting, Heraklion, Greece (2013)
4. Gali, N., Mariescu-Istodor, R., Fränti, P.: Similarity measures for title matching. In: 2016 23rd International Conference on Pattern Recognition (ICPR), pp. 1548–1553 (2016)
5. Gomaa, W.H., Fahmy, A.A., et al.: A survey of text similarity approaches. Int. J. Comput. Appl. **68**(13), 13–18 (2013)
6. Karatzoglou, A.: Semantic trajectories and predicting future semantic locations. Ph.D. thesis, Karlsruhe Institute of Technology, Germany (2019)
7. Kontopoulos, I., Varlamis, I., Tserpes, K.: Uncovering hidden concepts from AIS data: a network abstraction of maritime traffic for anomaly detection. In: Tserpes, K., Renso, C., Matwin, S. (eds.) MASTER 2019. LNCS (LNAI), vol. 11889, pp. 6–20. Springer, Cham (2020). https://doi.org/10.1007/978-3-030-38081-6_2
8. Lhermitte, S., Verbesselt, J., Verstraeten, W.W., Coppin, P.: A comparison of time series similarity measures for classification and change detection of ecosystem dynamics. Remote Sens. Environ. **115**(12), 3129–3152 (2011)
9. Miller, F.P., Vandome, A.F., McBrewster, J.: Levenshtein Distance: Information Theory, Computer Science, String (Computer Science), String Metric, Damerau?Levenshtein Distance, Spell Checker. Alpha Press, Hamming Distance (2009)
10. Moraitou, E., Aliprantis, J., Caridakis, G.: Semantic preventive conservation of cultural heritage collections. In: SW4CH@ ESWC (2018)
11. Oldman, D., Labs, C.: The CIDOC conceptual reference model (CIDOC-CRM): Primer (2014)
12. Omidvar-Tehrani, B., Amer-Yahia, S., Lakshmanan, L.V.: Cohort representation and exploration. In: 2018 IEEE 5th International Conference on Data Science and Advanced Analytics (DSAA), pp. 169–178. IEEE (2018)
13. Paterson, M.S., Dancik, V.: Longest common subsequences. Technical report, GBR (1994)

14. Su, H., Liu, S., Zheng, B., Zhou, X., Zheng, K.: A survey of trajectory distance measures and performance evaluation. VLDB J. **29**(1), 3–32 (2020)
15. Su, H., Zheng, K., Huang, J., Wang, H., Zhou, X.: Calibrating trajectory data for spatio-temporal similarity analysis. VLDB J. **24**(1), 93–116 (2015)
16. Vlachos, M., Kollios, G., Gunopulos, D.: Discovering similar multidimensional trajectories. In: Proceedings 18th International Conference on Data Engineering, pp. 673–684. IEEE (2002)
17. Vrotsou, K., Forsell, C.: A qualitative study of similarity measures in event-based data. In: Smith, M.J., Salvendy, G. (eds.) Human Interface 2011. LNCS, vol. 6771, pp. 170–179. Springer, Heidelberg (2011). https://doi.org/10.1007/978-3-642-21793-7_21

Domain Specific Information Systems Engineering

A Transactional Approach to Enforce Resource Availabilities: Application to the Cloud

Zakaria Maamar[1], Mohamed Sellami[2], and Fatma Masmoudi[3,4](✉)

[1] College of Technological Innovation, Zayed University, Dubai, UAE
[2] Samovar, Télécom SudParis, Institut Polytechnique de Paris, Paris, France
[3] Department of Information Systems, College of Computer Engineering and Sciences, Prince Sattam Bin Abdulaziz University, Alkharj 11942, Saudi Arabia
f.masmoudi@psau.edu.sa
[4] ReDCAD Laboratory, University of Sfax, Sfax, Tunisia

Abstract. This paper looks into the availability of resources, exemplified with the cloud, in an open and dynamic environment like the Internet. A growing number of users consume resources to complete their operations requiring a better way to manage these resources in order to avoid conflicts, for example. Resource availability is defined using a set of consumption properties (limited, limited-but-renewable, and non-shareable) and is enforced at run-time using a set of transactional properties (pivot, retriable, and compensatable). In this paper, a CloudSim-based system simulates how mixing consumption and transactional properties allows to capture users' needs and requirements in terms of what cloud resources they need, for how long, and to what extent they tolerate the unavailability of these resources.

Keywords: Cloud · CloudSim · Consumption · Resource · Transaction

1 Introduction

In an open and dynamic environment like the Internet, ensuring resource availability to future consumers requires mechanisms that would permit to avoid conflicting demands and unnecessary costs, for example. Resources could be of types computing (e.g., CPU), storage (e.g., HD), and network (e.g., router). In this paper, we map such mechanisms onto consumption properties that we specialize into limited, limited-but-renewable, and non-shareable. The benefits of such properties in the context of business processes are already discussed in our previous work [9,12]. Here we examine how to **enforce** consumption properties at run-time so, that, situations like delay in resource consumption, excessive resource consumption, and permanent (lock) resource consumption are addressed.

The situations above could be the result of events (e.g., urgent upgrades to counter cyber attacks and urgent demands to execute last-minute requests) that

S. Cherfi et al. (Eds.): RCIS 2021, LNBIP 415, pp. 249–264, 2021.
https://doi.org/10.1007/978-3-030-75018-3_16

disrupt the agreed-upon consumption planning of resources. Disruption means suspending ongoing operations, initiating others, and resuming the suspended ones without being subject to penalties, for example. How to handle these sudden changes with minimal impact on committed resources and how to get resources ready for such changes since some are not always available and not even ready to accommodate these changes? These are questions that we address in this paper by considering transactional properties [10] that would enforce resources' consumption properties and hence, their availabilities.

In the ICT literature, transactional properties are of types pivot, compensatable, and retriable, and are commonly used in many domains such as cloud computing [2], databases [7], business processes [11], Web services [13], and Internet-of-Things (IoT) [14]. These properties allow application engineers to define the "acceptable" execution behaviors of applications such as tolerating the failure of an application and insisting on the success of another application. Our objective is to identify the relevant transactional properties that would go along with satisfying the requirements of each consumption property. For instance, a limited resource could be an obstacle to a retriable transaction, should the resource become unavailable after a certain number of necessary consumption retrials. Could we mix limited and retriable to enforce resource availability is one of the questions raised in this paper.

We apply the mix of transactional properties and consumption properties to cloud resources. Cloud is attracting the attention of the ICT community who sees a lot of benefits in adopting Everything-as-a-Service operation model when they need to secure on-demand resourcfes (e.g., infrastructure, platform, and software) for their applications [8,15]. These applications could be built upon business processes making tasks consume cloud resources, IoT making things consume cloud resources, service-oriented applications making Web services consume cloud resources, to cite just some. Our approach to enforce resources' consumption properties is independent on who will consume (task *versus* thing *versus* Web service) these resources, which is one of our contributions. Additional contributions include defining consumption properties using dedicated cycles, analyzing the disruptions that could undermine the completion of resource consumption, mixing consumption and transactional properties, and demonstrating this mix in the context of cloud using CloudSim. The rest of this paper is organized as follows. Section 2 discusses resources' consumption properties and cycles. Section 3 introduces disruptions that might occur during resource consumption and their impacts on these resources. Section 4 introduces transactional properties and their mix with consumption properties to define "acceptable" consumption cycles when disruptions occur. Section 5 presents first, our transactional approach to enforce resources' consumption properties and then, some technical details about the use of CloudSim to simulate this approach. Section 6 presents some related work. Conclusions and future work are included in Sect. 7.

2 Consumption Properties and Cycles of Resources

Building upon our previous work on social coordination of BPs [12], we consider 5 consumption properties for resources: unlimited (ul), shareable (s), limited (l), limited-but-renewable (lr), and non-shareable (ns); needles to describe the first two. First, limited means that the consumption of a resource is restricted to a particular capacity and/or period of time. Second, limited-but-renewable means that the consumption of a resource continues to happen since the (initial) agreed-upon capacity has been increased and/or the (initial) agreed-upon period of time has been extended. Finally, non-shareable means that the concurrent consumption of a resource must be coordinated (e.g., one at a time). Unless stated a resource is by default unlimited and/or shareable.

Figure 1 is a resource's state diagram whose design allows to establish its consumption cycles per property (cc_{cp}). On the one hand, the states (s_i) are: not-made-available (the resource is neither created nor produced, yet), made-available (the resource is either created or produced), not-consumed (the resource waits to be bound by a consumer), locked (the resource is reserved for a consumer in preparation for its consumption), unlocked (the resource is released by a consumer after its consumption), consumed (the resource is bound by a consumer due to the consumer's ongoing performance), withdrawn (the resource ceases to exit after unbinding all consumers that were consuming this resource), and, finally, done (the resource is unbound by a consumer after completing the consumption). On the other hand, the transitions ($trans_j$) connecting the states include start, waiting-to-be-bound, consumption-approval, consumption-update, lock, release, consumption-rejection, consumption-completion, renewable-approval, and no-longer-useful.

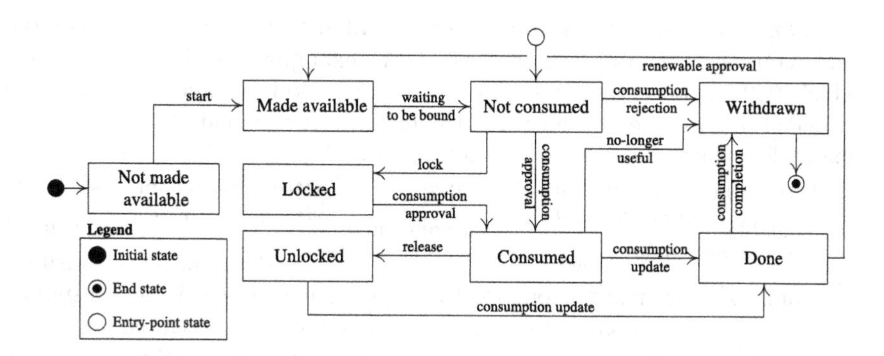

Fig. 1. Resource's consumption cycle as a state diagram (adopted from [12])

We formally define resource and resource's consumption cycle as follows.

Definition 1. *A resource r is defined by the tuple* $< id, name, capacity, period, cp, CC_{cp} >$ *where: id is the identifier of the resource; name is the name of the resource; capacity (set to null when not-applicable) is a set of Name-Value* *pairs describing the "availability" of the resource; period (set to null when not-applicable) is a temporal constraint describing the "availability" of the resource; and cp is the consumption property of the resource; and* $CC_{cp} = \{cc_{cp}\}$ *is the set of all consumption cycles (as per Definition 2) associated with the consumption property of the resource.*

Definition 2. *A resource' consumption cycle* cc_{cp} *for a consumption property cp is defined by the tuple* $< S, T, S_{active} >$ *representing the state diagram of the resource, i.e.,* $cc_{cp} = s_i \stackrel{trans_i}{\longrightarrow} s_{i+1} \stackrel{trans_{i+1}}{\longrightarrow} s_{i+2} \dots s_{j-1} \stackrel{trans_{j-1}}{\longrightarrow} s_j$ *where: S is the set of states* $\{s_i\}$*; T is the set of transitions* $\{trans_i\}$*; and* $S_{active} \subset S$ *is the set of states that have been enabled since the activation of a consumption cycle. At initialization time,* $S_{active} = \{$not-made-available$\}$.

Below are 3 illustrative consumption cycles using the public cloud provider, Amazon Web Services (*AWS*), to exemplify resources.

1. Unlimited resource has 1 consumption cycle. $r.cc_{\mathsf{ul}}$: not-made-available $\stackrel{start}{\longrightarrow}$ made available $\stackrel{waiting-to-be-bound}{\longrightarrow}$ not-consumed $\stackrel{consumption-approval}{\longrightarrow}$ consumed $\stackrel{no-longer-useful}{\longrightarrow}$ withdrawn. An example is a cloud object storage like *AWS* S3 bucket that remains available until a decision to delete it is made.
2. Limited-but-renewable resource has 2 consumption cycles. First, $r.cc_{\mathsf{lr}_1}$: not-made-available $\stackrel{start}{\longrightarrow}$ made available $\stackrel{waiting-to-be-bound}{\longrightarrow}$ not-consumed $\stackrel{consumption-approval}{\longrightarrow}$ consumed $\stackrel{consumption-update}{\longrightarrow}$ done $\stackrel{renewable-approval}{\longrightarrow}$ made available. The transition from done to made available allows a resource to be regenerated for another round of consumption. Second, $r.cc_{\mathsf{lr}_2}$: not-made-available $\stackrel{start}{\longrightarrow}$ made available $\stackrel{waiting-to-be-bound}{\longrightarrow}$ not-consumed $\stackrel{consumption-approval}{\longrightarrow}$ consumed $\stackrel{consumption-update}{\longrightarrow}$ done $\stackrel{consumption-completion}{\longrightarrow}$ withdrawn. The transition from done to withdrawn is satisfied when the resource renewal is no longer requested. An example is a virtual server like *AWS* EC2 instance that runs for a specific period of time that could be extended upon request. Otherwise, the instance is terminated.
3. Shareable resource has 2 consumption cycles.
   - First time consumption of resource ($r.cc_{\mathsf{s}}$): not-made-available $\stackrel{start}{\longrightarrow}$ made available $\stackrel{waiting-to-be-bound}{\longrightarrow}$ not-consumed $\stackrel{consumption-approval}{\longrightarrow}$ consumed $\stackrel{consumption-update}{\longrightarrow}$ done $\stackrel{consumption-completion}{\longrightarrow}$ withdrawn. The transition from not-consumed to consumed is satisfied if two or several consumers that require the same resource are simultaneously activated. And the transition from done to withdrawn is satisfied if no pending consumer consuming this resource exists.
   - Then, and as long as there is an ongoing consumption of resource ($r.cc_{\mathsf{s}}$): not-consumed $\stackrel{consumption-approval}{\longrightarrow}$ consumed $\stackrel{consumption-update}{\longrightarrow}$ done $\stackrel{consumption-completion}{\longrightarrow}$ withdrawn. The transition from not-consumed to consumed is satisfied if additional new consumers require the resource after the first consumption. And, the transition from done to withdrawn is satisfied if no pending consumer consuming the resource exists.

An example is an *AWS* subnet whose owner makes it available to other *AWS* accounts. When all parties are done, the subnet is deleted.

3 Impact of Disruptions on Consumption Cycles

This section introduces disruption types and then, examines their impacts on resources' consumption cycles.

3.1 Types of Disruptions

We identify 2 types of disruptions: making room for extra consumption cycles (for simplicity, one extra cycle) and making room for service (e.g., resource upgrade and fixing). Both types result into the development of consumption sub-cycles.

Example of suspending a consumption cycle to make room for an extra cycle in the context of a limited resource is as follows. An EC2 instance is enabled for a limited time-period for a consumer. However, this consumption is suspended because of a *pressing demand* from another consumer whose demand now constitutes the disruption. Resuming the suspended consumption cycle would, only, occur outside this time period, which is not possible confirming the suspension of this cycle.

Example of suspending a consumption cycle to make room for service in the context of a limited-but-renewable resource is as follows. A database instance like Amazon RDS is *suddenly* suspended during an allocated time period to make room for increasing the storage size. Reason of the increase is the unexpected submission of a large amount of new data to store constituting the disruption. After the update, the ongoing resource consumption is allowed to complete/proceed but no extra consumption is authorized, should a renewal be requested outside this time period.

3.2 Disruptive Consumption Sub-cycles

To capture the impact of disruption types on the completion of consumption cycles, we revise Fig. 1 that is a resource's consumption cycle. As a result of this first revision, a new state, suspended, and 2 new transitions, suspension and conditional resumption, are added to this diagram as per Fig. 2 (in all figures, dashed lines are reversed for representing disruptions). These transitions connect consumed and suspended states together signaling that an active consumption cycle would be put on-hold and then, **probably** resumed, should the resumption conditions[1] become satisfied with the ultimate goal of reaching withdrawn (final) state. A disruption occurring during the consumption of a resource r would suspend this resource's regular consumption cycle $r.cc_{\mathsf{cp}}$ forcing it to transition from consumed state to suspended state. In conjunction with this transition, a resource

[1] Conditions vary according to the resource's type and consumption property. They could be availability for limited resources and access rights for non-shareable resources.

becomes associated with a consumption sub-cycle[2] known as disruptive $r.csc_{\mathsf{cp}}$ on top of the regular consumption cycle $r.cc_{\mathsf{cp}}$. Resuming this cycle is subject to satisfying some conditions; i.e., suspended $\stackrel{conditional-resumption}{\longrightarrow}$ consumed.

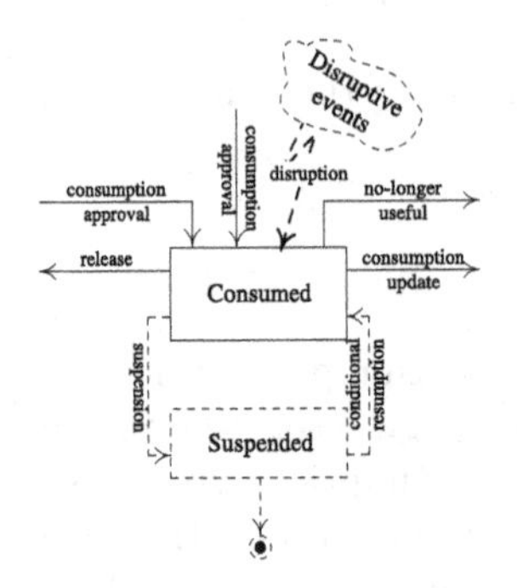

Fig. 2. First revision of a consumption cycle

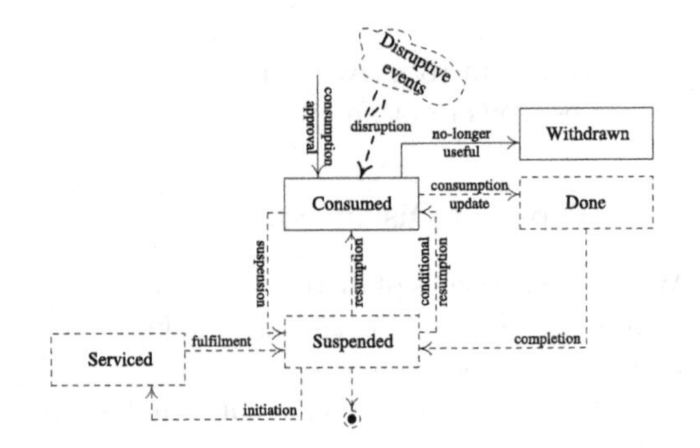

Fig. 3. Second revision of a consumption cycle

The states and transitions in a disruptive consumption sub-cycle depend on the disruption types: make room for extra consumption or make room for service. To capture these types, we revise Fig. 2 where a new state, serviced, and 4 new transitions, resumption, initiation, fulfilment, and completion, are created to form 2 separate consumption sub-cycles, one per type (Fig. 3 with focus on dashed lines). It is worth noting that when a consumption sub-cycle is launched (i.e., either suspended $\stackrel{resumption}{\longrightarrow}$ consumed because of extra consumption or suspended $\stackrel{initiation}{\longrightarrow}$ serviced because of service), the regular consumption cycle is put on-hold and remains in suspended state until this sub-cycle notifies it through either completion transition connecting done and suspended states or fulfillment transition connecting serviced and suspended states.

With respect to Fig. 3, we illustrate hereafter how a consumption cycle intertwines with a consumption sub-cycle related to either service or extra consumption. When a disruption occurs, it causes the suspension of the resource consumption cycle ($r.cc_{\mathsf{cp}}$ in suspended state) and the initiation of a consumption sub-cycle $r.csc_{\mathsf{cp}}$. Once this sub-cycle ends, $r.cc_{\mathsf{cp}}$ resumes as follows:

1. *conditional resumption* **holds**, $r.cc_{\mathsf{cp}}$ completes successfully: suspended $\stackrel{conditional-resumption}{\longrightarrow}$ consumed $\stackrel{no-longer-useful}{\longrightarrow}$ withdrawn.
2. *conditional resumption* **does not hold**, $r.cc_{\mathsf{cp}}$ fails to complete and hence, remains in suspended. What to do in this case is elaborated in Sect. 5.

For illustration purposes, below are details about 2 extra consumption cycles for an unlimited resource facing disruption.

[2] Consumption cycle/Consumption sub-cycle is similar to Process/Thread.

1. IF (($r.csc_{\mathsf{ul}}$ ends **successfully**) AND (conditional resumption **holds**)) THEN $r.cc_{\mathsf{ul}_1}$: not-made-available $\overset{start}{\longrightarrow}$ made available $\overset{waiting-to-be-bound}{\longrightarrow}$ not-consumed $\overset{consumption-approval}{\longrightarrow}$ consumed $\overset{suspension}{\longrightarrow}$ suspended $\overset{conditional-resumption}{\longrightarrow}$ consumed $\overset{no-longer-useful}{\longrightarrow}$ withdrawn.
2. IF (($r.csc_{\mathsf{ul}}$ ends **successfully**) AND (conditional resumption **does not hold**)) THEN $r.cc_{\mathsf{ul}_2}$: not-made-available $\overset{start}{\longrightarrow}$ made available $\overset{waiting-to-be-bound}{\longrightarrow}$ not-consumed $\overset{consumption-approval}{\longrightarrow}$ consumed $\overset{suspension}{\longrightarrow}$ suspended.

The way $r.cc_{\mathsf{ul}}$ progresses over time depends on both the outcome of completing a consumption sub-cycle ($r.csc_{\mathsf{cp}}$) and the potential satisfaction of resumption conditions that are strictly dependent on the consumption property's type. Since here we are dealing with an unlimited resource, the consumption cycle ($r.cc_{\mathsf{ul}}$) **will always resume** its completion by transiting back from suspended to consumed states and so on until withdrawn state is reached.

4 Mixing Transactional and Consumption Properties

Section 3.1 identified disruption types that could "slow down" the completion of resources' consumption cycles having negative consequences on consumers when they miss deadlines or overspend on resources, for example. In this part of the paper we discuss how these consequences could be "accepted" to some consumers despite the disruption/suspension. To this end, we analyze consumption cycles' (certain) states and transitions from a transactional perspective. These states and transitions are depicted throughout Fig. 1, 2 and Fig. 3. The question we raise is: could the final states of pivot, compensatable, and retriable properties be mapped onto the states and/or transitions of the resources' consumption cycles? If no, how to extend these cycles to achieve the mapping?

4.1 Transactional Properties

To begin with, we define pivot, compensatable, and retriable properties in compliance with the existing literature [10]. Pivot means that once an execution successfully completes, its effects remain unchanged forever and cannot be undone. Additionally, this execution cannot be retried following failure. Compensatable means that a successful execution's effects can be semantically undone. Finally, retriable means that an execution is guaranteed to successfully complete after several finite activations. It is worth noting that compensatable and retriable properties can be combined. Figure 4 presents the execution's life cycles of the 3 transactional properties with focus on the final states.

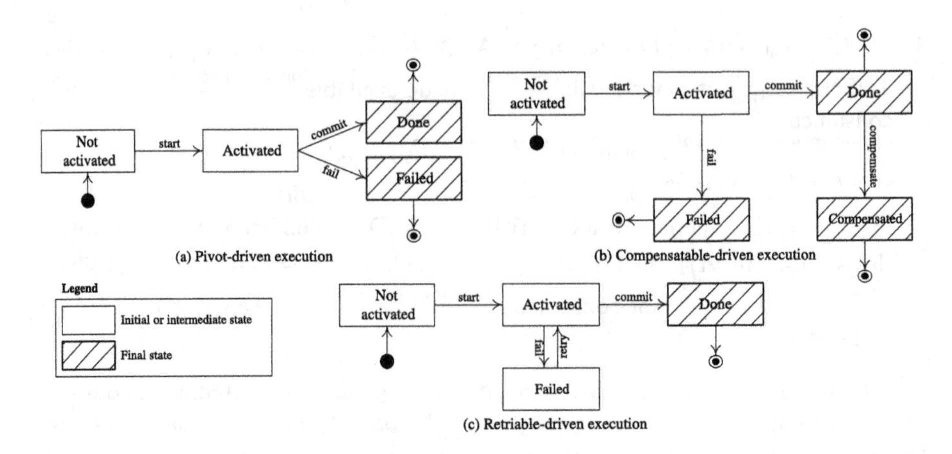

Fig. 4. Execution's life cycle per transactional property

4.2 Transaction-Driven Consumption Cycles

Next, we analyze the consumption cycles associated with the consumption properties from a transactional perspective. Depending on the final states in a transactional property's life cycle (Fig. 4), the objective is to *(i)* make these states correspond to what we refer to as acceptable states and acceptable transitions in a resource's consumption cycle and *(ii)* eventually revise the resource's state diagram by adding/dropping states and/or transitions, should the correspondence fail. For instance, done and failed are final states in a pivot-driven execution life cycle (Fig. 4-(a)). Do these 2 final states have counter-parts in a resource's consumption cycle with respect to a particular consumption property? Due to lack of space, we proceed with limited, only.

Extracted from Fig. 1 and mixed with Fig. 3, Fig. 5 illustrates this property's consumption cycle with the option of handling disruptions.

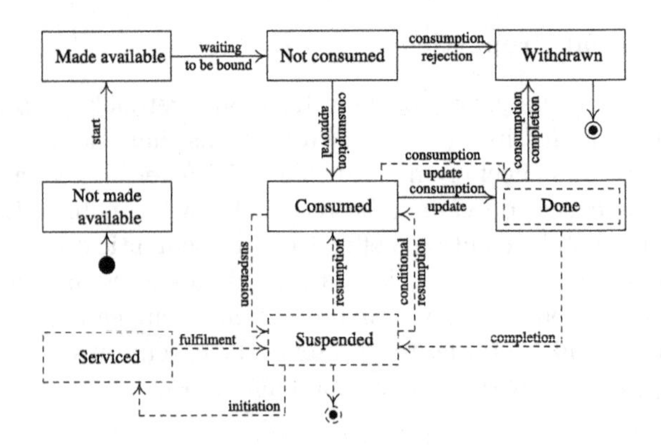

Fig. 5. Limited property's consumption cycle with disruption handling

- Pivot's (p) final states are done^{p} and failed^{p}. Mapping these 2 states onto Fig. 5's states and transitions would lead to:
  1. done^{p}:$\mathsf{withdrawn}^{l}$ signaling that a consumption cycle has successfully terminated whether a disruption happened or not.
  2. failed^{p}:$\mathsf{suspended}^{l}$ signaling that a consumption cycle has not resumed because of disruption. However, this remains acceptable to the consumer in compliance with pivot's failed state.
- Compensatable's (c) final states are done, compensated, and failed. Mapping these 3 states onto Fig. 5's states and transitions would lead to:
  1. done^{c}:$\mathsf{withdrawn}^{l}$ signals that a consumption cycle has successfully terminated whether a disruption happened or not.
  2. failed^{c}:$\mathsf{suspended}^{l}$ signals that a consumption cycle has not resumed because of disruption. However this remains acceptable to the consumer in compliance with compensatable's failed state.
  3. $\mathsf{compensated}^{c}$:$?^{l}$ signals that a resource's state diagram does not have a state for handling compensation. Compensating a resource after consumption would mean either making the resource available again or regenerating the resource again. Since the resource is limited in the current case, we map $\mathsf{compensated}^{c}$ onto $\mathsf{made\text{-}available}^{l}$ and add a conditional transition from $\mathsf{withdrawn}^{l}$ to $\mathsf{made\text{-}available}^{l}$ since $\mathsf{compensated}^{l}$ could happen after done^{c}:$\mathsf{withdrawn}^{l}$. This transition is conditioned by the resource's availability.
- Retriable's (r) final state is done. Mapping this state onto Fig. 5's states and transitions would lead to:
  1. done^{r}:$\mathsf{withdrawn}^{l}$ signals that a consumption cycle has terminated whether a disruption happened or not.
  2. $?^{r}$:$\mathsf{suspended}^{l}$ signals that the retriable-driven execution life cycle does not have a state for handling suspension like a resource's consumption cycle does. Therefore, should a consumer assign retriable as a transactional property for this resource's consumption cycle, then the transition from suspended state to final state should be removed from this cycle (Fig. 5).

Figure 6 is the outcome of mixing transactional and consumption properties and the consequence of this mapping on a resource's state diagram. Enforcing an unlimited resource consumption heavily depends on this figure. More details are given in the next section.

5 Enforcement of Resources' Consumption Properties

This section presents our transactional approach to enforce the consumption properties of resources (Sect. 5.1) and the simulation we initiated to demonstrate its feasibility using CloudSim (Sect. 5.2).

5.1 Approach's Modules and Chronology of Operations

Figure 7 illustrates the different modules upon which our transactional approach to enforce resources' consumption properties is built. Enforcing means how to ensure that the outcomes of mixing transactional properties with consumption properties are achieved as per Sect. 4; i.e., how to interpret the final states of a resource's transaction-driven consumption cycle considering both the transactional property and the consumption property (e.g., Fig. 6 with failed^c:$\mathsf{suspended}^l$ as outcome). The enforcement approach includes $\mathsf{design\text{-}time}^d$ and $\mathsf{run\text{-}time}^r$ stages and runs over 5 stopovers.

The design-time stage includes 3 stopovers. In stopover (1^d), providers assign consumption properties to their resources, as they see fit and with respect to these resources' types (e.g., software *versus* platform *versus* infrastructure in the context of cloud and off-line *versus* on-line). The resources are described[3] in a dedicated repository that contains the necessary details for the *assignment module* to produce these resources' consumption cycles according to the assigned consumption properties. In these cycles, potential disruption types in term of making room for either service or extra consumption are highlighted like shown in Fig. 3. In stopover (2^d), consumers select the appropriate transactional properties for the resources that they plan to consume. This selection reflects their acceptance of the outcome of completing a consumption cycle that could be either success, failure, or compensation when this cycle becomes effective at run-time. Like in stopover (1^d), the same repository provides the necessary details about resources to the *selection module* so, that, it produces executions' life cycles for the selected transactional properties (Fig. 4). In the final stopover (3^d), a resource's consumption cycle and an execution's life cycle are both submitted to the *mixing module* to produce what we referred to earlier as a resource's

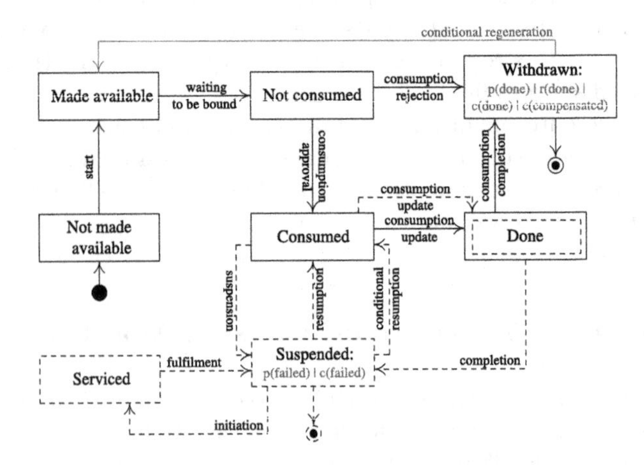

Fig. 6. Disruption handling in a transaction-driven limited consumption-cycle

[3] Our approach does not depend on any specific resource description-model.

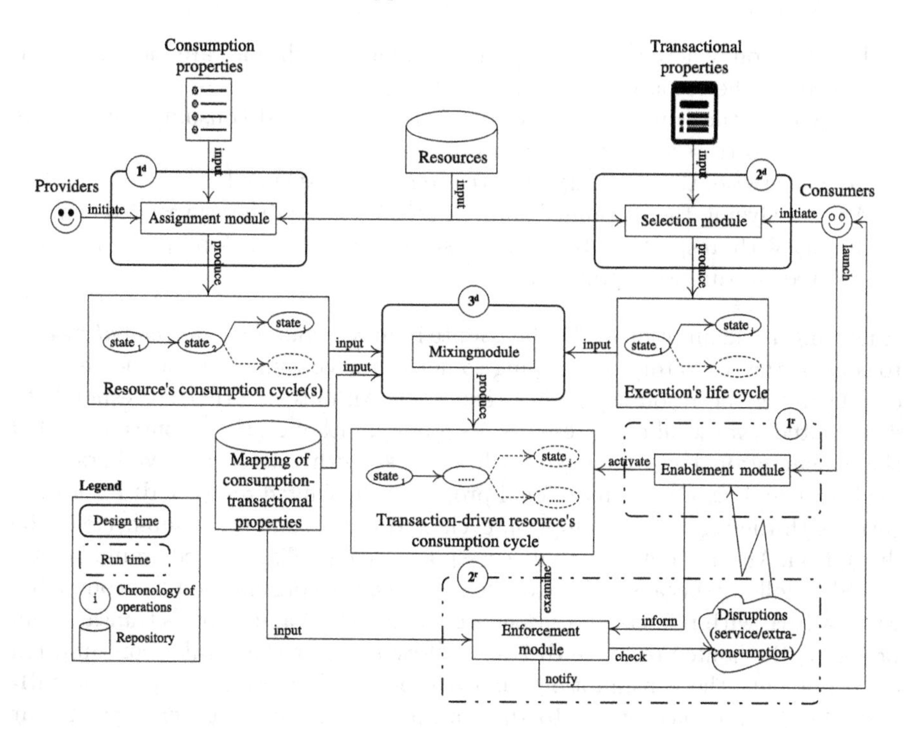

Fig. 7. Transactional approach to enforce resources' consumption properties

transaction-driven consumption cycle (e.g., Fig. 6). The mixing is done based on a set of $\text{state}^{\mathsf{transactional}}$:$\text{state}^{\mathsf{consumption}}$ mappings that are stored in the repository of mapping of consumption-transactional properties (Sect. 4).

The run-time stage includes 2 stopovers. In stopover (1^r) a consumer triggers the consumption of a resource through the *enablement module*. This one activates the resource's transaction-driven consumption cycle by ensuring that the necessary states are taken and the necessary transitions are fired. When a disruption arises, the *enablement module* receives a request to handle this disruption in terms of suspending the consumption cycle, raising a disruption flag, identifying the type of disruption whether making room for extra consumption or making room for service, activating a consumption sub-cycle with respect to this disruption's type, completing this sub-cycle by making it take the necessary states till suspended state along with firing the necessary transitions, and finally letting the *enforcement module* take over the rest of operations (stopover (2^r)) that consist of:

1. Checking the resource status after the consumption sub-cycle completes. This status is strictly dependent on the resource's consumption property such as whether the resource has expired since it is limited, the resource has still some capacity left since it is limited-but-renewable, the resource has been unlocked since it is non-shareable, etc.

2. Deciding on whether the resumption/unlock conditions are satisfied with respect to the resource status.
   (a) Should the conditions be satisfied, the suspended consumption cycle is allowed to resume till completion.
   (b) Otherwise, the consumption cycle remains suspended.
3. And, analyzing the consumption cycle's final state (either suspended or withdrawn) with respect to both the assigned transactional property and the selected consumption property.

Analyzing a consumption cycle's final state requires from the *enforcement module* to consult the repository of mapping to notify the consumer about the outcome of consuming the resource she has requested. An outcome that corresponds to done^{p}:withdrawn^{l} would be presented as follows: although the resource is limited the consumption has completed with **success** with reference to withdrawn as final state and pivot as transactional property; the limited resource **did allow** to cover both the regular consumption cycle and the consumption sub-cycle of the disruption. Another outcome that corresponds to failed^{p}:suspended^{l} would be presented as follows: because the resource is limited the consumption has completed with **failure** with reference to suspended as final state and pivot as transactional property; the limited resource **did not allow** to cover the regular consumption cycle but only the consumption sub-cycle of the disruption. Despite the **failure**, this remains acceptable to the consumer since she considered pivot that has **failed** as an acceptable final state. Should the consumer insist on **success, only**, then she should select retriable as transactional property.

5.2 CloudSim for the Approach Simulation

Using CloudSim [4], we are in the process of developing a cloud environment for simulating our approach to enforce resources' consumption properties. CloudSim is a Java-based generalized and extensible simulation framework that consists of a set of core classes describing cloud components such as Virtual Machines (VM), hosts, data centers, and brokers. CloudSim also allows provisioning hosts to VMs upon the receipt of users' requests for completing jobs. These jobs known as cloudlets could take on states such as CREATED, INEXEC, and SUCCESS allowing to track their execution progress.

Our development is going through the following stages. First, we extended Cloudlet and CloudSim classes in order to accommodate some of our work requirements like consumption property and disruption. To this end, we added suitable attributes (e.g., UPDATED) and methods (e.g., endC) to these 2 classes, respectively. Then, we integrated Easy FSM Java Library (ankzz.github.io/easyfsm) into CloudSim to create consumption cycles as finite state machines (Sect. 2). We also mapped a cloudlet's states onto a consumption cycle's states for the needs of synchronization. For instance, when a cloudlet takes on CREATED and then, READY, the consumption cycle of the resource assigned to this cloudlet transitions from not-made-available to made-available. For each consumption property, we developed a Java class that instantiates the cloud environment's necessary components and mappings.

We begin the simulation by submitting requests of creating cloudlets (Fig. 8 (b)) to a data-center's broker that binds these cloudlets to VMs (Fig. 8 (a)) thanks to bindCloudletToVm event. In Fig. 9, we show an unlimited VM instance's consumption cycle mapped onto a cloudlet's states allowing to track the progress of this cloudlet with regard to this VM that it consumes. In term of disruption, we considered the request of urgent upgrade that would impact a VM instance defined as unlimited time-period and pivot in the sense that the user tolerates either success or failure. This means interrupting the VM's consumption cycle as per Fig. 10. Following an initial consumption that lasts 30 s, the consumption cycle is suspended to make room for the disruptive consumption cycle. The completion of this cycle lasts 50 s giving the regular consumption cycle the opportunity to resume within the time limit of 2 min. Should the remaining 120 s be enough for the regular consumption cycle to complete, success is declared. Otherwise, failure is declared. Either success or failure is fine with the user in compliance with the definition of pivot.

```
// VM description
int vmid = 0;
long size = 10000; // image size (MB)
int ram = 512; // vm memory (MB)
long bw = 1000;
int pesNumber = 1; // number of cpus
String vmm = "Xen"; // VMM name
```

(a)

```
// Cloudlet properties
int id = 0;
long length = 4000;
long fileSize = 300;
long outputSize = 300;
UtilizationModel utilizationModel = new UtilizationModelFull();
```

(b)

Fig. 8. VM's and cloudlet's parameters

```
Markers  Properties  Servers  Data Source Explorer  Snippets  Console
<terminated> TestConsUnlimited [Java Application] C:\Program Files\Java\jdk-14.0.1\bin\javaw.exe (30 janv. 2021 à 16:31:36 – 16:31:37)
Simulation completed.

================================ OUTPUT ================================
Cloudlet ID              Cloudlet STATUS            Cons. cycle STATE <TRANSITION>
0              Created                          NOT_MADE_AVAILABLE
0              Ready                            <START> MADE_AVAILABLE
0              Queued                           <WAITING_TO_BE_BOUND> NOT_CONSUMED
0              InExec                           <CONSUMPTION_APPROAVAL>  CONSUMED
0              Success                           <NO_LONGER_USEFUL>  WITHDRAWN
TestConsUnlimited finished!
```

Fig. 9. CloudSim console for an unlimited resource

6 Related Work

To the best of our knowledge, there are not many works that mix consumption properties and transactional properties for resource availability. To address

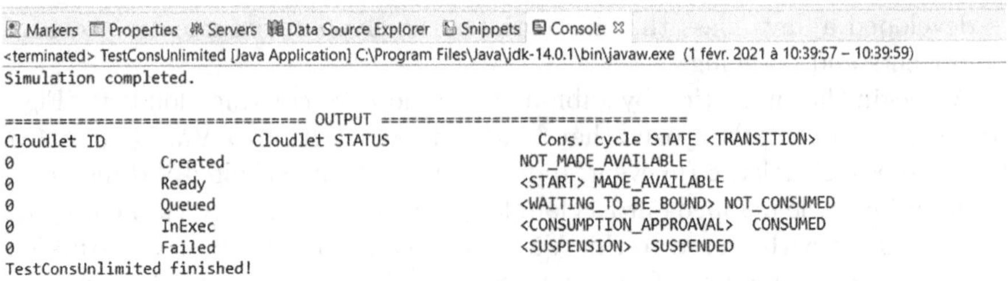

```
Markers  Properties  Servers  Data Source Explorer  Snippets  Console
<terminated> TestConsUnlimited [Java Application] C:\Program Files\Java\jdk-14.0.1\bin\javaw.exe (1 févr. 2021 à 10:39:57 – 10:39:59)
Simulation completed.

================================ OUTPUT ================================
Cloudlet ID          Cloudlet STATUS          Cons. cycle STATE <TRANSITION>
0            Created                         NOT_MADE_AVAILABLE
0            Ready                           <START> MADE_AVAILABLE
0            Queued                          <WAITING_TO_BE_BOUND> NOT_CONSUMED
0            InExec                          <CONSUMPTION_APPROAVAL>  CONSUMED
0            Failed                          <SUSPENSION>  SUSPENDED
TestConsUnlimited finished!
```

Fig. 10. CloudSim console for an unlimited resource that is disrupted

this limitation, we examined different topics ranging from general definition of resources to management of resource conflicts in business workflows and resource interruption in the cloud [1–3,6]. A simple definition of resource management is "*... the process by which businesses manage their various resources effectively. Those resources can be intangible - people and time - and tangible - equipment, materials, and finances. It involves planning so that the right resources are assigned to the right tasks. Managing resources involves schedules and budgets for people, projects, equipment, and supplies*"[4].

Although the work of Cades et al. is not related to ICT [3], their findings suggest some good insights into the impact of interruptions on task performance. Indeed, in our work some interruptions due to specific disruptions could have a positive impact on resources when these ones need to be protected from attacks, for example. They could also have a negative impact on resources when these ones are shared with others, for example. Cades et al. report that there is one body of research that considers disruptive effects as negative when completion time of a task is slowed down, while others suggest that interruptions can actually aid task performance in certain contexts. The nature of tasks to perform and types of interruptions to deal with determine how disruptive an interruption will be or whether an interruption will be disruptive at all.

In [2], Bellaaj et al. adopt transactional properties to achieve the reliability of elastic cloud resources. They first, consider elasticity as the ability to dynamically reconfigure cloud resources to respond to changes and second, focus on obstacles that could turn into failures, should necessary actions be not taken like complying with transactional properties' definitions. Reliability of an elastic cloud resource means that the resource should be in a valid state after executing an elasticity reconfiguration action. The objective is to ensure that this reconfiguration either completes successfully or fails and then, its undesirable effects must be undone. By analogy with Bellaaj et al.'s work our disruption types could be obstacles that impact the consumption and not elasticity of (cloud) resources. Our transactional properties also permit to confirm when disruption is either accepted or tolerated, which is not the case of Bellaaj et al.'s work.

In [6], Fernández el al. present a framework to model and simulate the supply process monitoring to detect and predict disruptions. These disruptions produce

[4] www.shopify.com/encyclopedia/resource-management.

negative effects and hence, affected schedules should be fixed, for example. The authors developed a Web service that organizations could use to develop discrete event-based simulation models of monitoring processes so these organizations can evaluate their readiness to detect and anticipate disruptions. By analogy with Fernández el al.'s work, our disruptions have, depending on their nature, either negative or positive effects on resources and enforcing these effects happen through a set of transactional properties. Moreover our consumption properties would nicely fit into Fernández el al.'s framework since resources like trucks could be non-shareable and transport licences could be limited but renewable.

As stated in the first paragraph, our work is at the crossroads of many ICT domains that would allow enforcing resource availability using a mix of consumption and transactional properties. This enforcement responds to events that could disrupt completing a particular resource consumption.

7 Conclusion

This paper presented an approach to enforce run-time resource availabilities during their consumption. Disruptions could impact this consumption leading sometimes to the unavailability of resources. The enforcement took place using transactional properties that allowed to declare when a resource unavailability is either acceptable or unacceptable to consumers of resources. Our approach allows first, resource providers to define resources' availabilities using consumption properties (limited, limited-but-renewable, and non-shareable) and second, resource consumers to define the acceptable outcomes of consuming resources using transactional properties (pivot, retriable, and compensatable), and finally, to enforce resource availability at run-time by automatically generating transaction-driven resources' consumption cycles. A CloudSim-based system that simulates our approach is presented in the paper showing how consumption cycles progress. In term of future work, we would like to extend the experiments further by completing the implementation of the system and considering real cloud resources. We would also like to formally define the different transaction-driven consumption cycles of resources and use model checking, [5], to verify the compliance of these cycles with transactional properties.

References

1. Agarwal, A., Prasad, A., Rustogi, R., Mishra, S.: Detection and mitigation of fraudulent resource consumption attacks in cloud using deep learning approach. J. Inf. Secur. Appl. **56** (2021)
2. Bellaaj, F., Brabra, H., Sellami, M., Gaaloul, W., Bhiri, S.: A transactional approach for reliable elastic cloud resources. In: Proceedings of SCC 2019, Milan, Italy (2019)
3. Cades, D., Werner, N., Trafton, J., Boehm-Davis, D., Monk, C.: Dealing with interruptions can be complex, but does interruption complexity matter: a mental resources approach to quantifying disruptions. In: Proceedings of the Human Factors and Ergonomics Society, 1 (2008)

4. Calheiros, R., Ranjan, R., Beloglazov, A., De Rose, C., Buyya, R.: CloudSim: a toolkit for modeling and simulation of cloud computing environments and evaluation of resource provisioning algorithms. Software: Pract. Exper. **41**(1) (2011)
5. Clarke, E., Emerson, E.: Design and synthesis of synchronization skeletons using branching time temporal logic. In: 25 Years of Model Checking - History, Achievements, Perspectives, vol. 5000 (2008)
6. Fernández, E., Bogado, V., Salomone, E., Chiotti, O.: Framework for modelling and simulating the supply process monitoring to detect and predict disruptive events. Comput. Ind. **80** (2016)
7. Frank, L., Ulslev Pedersen, R.: Integrated distributed/mobile logistics management. Trans. LDKS 5 (2012)
8. Graiet, M., Mammar, A., Boubaker, S., Gaaloul, W.: Towards correct cloud resource allocation in business processes. IEEE Trans. Serv. Comput. **10**(1) (2017)
9. Kallel, S., et al.: Restriction-based fragmentation of business processes over the cloud. Concurr. Comput. Pract. Exper. Wiley, (2019, forthcoming)
10. Little, M.: Transactions and web services. CACM **46**(10) (2003)
11. Ma, J., Cao, J., Zhang, Y.: Efficiently supporting secure and reliable collaboration in scientific workflows. JCSS **76**(6) (2010)
12. Maamar, Z., Faci, N., Sakr, S., Boukhebouze, M., Barnawi, A.: Network-based social coordination of business processes. IS, 58 (2016)
13. Maamar, Z., Narendra, N., Benslimane, D., Sattanathan, S.: Policies for context-driven transactional web services. In: Proceedings of CAiSE 2007, Trondheim, Norway (2007)
14. Maamar, Z., Sellami, M., Narendra, N., Guidara, I., Ugljanin, E., Banihashemi, B.: Towards an approach for validating the Internet-of-Transactional-Things. In: Proceedings of AINA 2020, Caserta, Italy (online) (2020)
15. Motahari-Nezhad, H., Stephenson, B., Singha, S.: Outsourcing business to cloud computing services: opportunities and challenges. IT Professional **11**(2) (2009)

A WebGIS Interface Requirements Modeling Language

Roberto Veloso, João Araujo(✉), and Armanda Rodrigues

NOVA LINCS, FCT, Universidade Nova de Lisboa, Lisbon, Portugal
r.veloso@campus.fct.unl.pt, {joao.araujo,a.rodrigues}@fct.unl.pt

Abstract. WebGIS applications have become popular due to technological advances in location and sensor technology, with diverse examples with different objectives becoming available. However, there is a lack of requirements elicitation approaches for WebGIS applications, restricting the communication between stakeholders, compromising the systematization of development, and the overall quality of the resulting systems. In this paper, we present the WebGIS Interface Requirements Modeling Language (WebGIS IRML), developed to support communication between stakeholders and developers, addressing user interface requirements during the development process of a WebGIS application. WebGIS IRML is supported by a requirements model editor, which was developed using Model-Driven Development (MDD) techniques. We also describe an experiment which was performed to evaluate the language, involving 30 participants (mostly IT Engineers), to measure the ease of understanding of the language models resulting from the use of the language in the editor and capture the feedback of participants about it. Generally, the results were quite positive, encouraging the use of the language for WebGIS development.

1 Introduction

The mass availability of APIs with maps and GPS devices, with easy accessibility and reduced costs, has led to a huge generation of web apps supported by a geographic map environment [1]. As Smartphones, tablets and other devices can currently provide real-time location of a user on the globe, Geographic Information Systems (GIS) applications for the Web have had an exponential growth. WebGIS applications are needed in diverse domains such as governmental, environmental, geographical, territorial, among others, and new application domains are being proposed, involving thousands of users and developers, with diverse training and experiences.

Often, the very different origins and skills of these users and developers hinder the requirements gathering process, during the initial phase of WebGIS development. Eventually, due to communication difficulties, divergencies arise between what was intended by the stakeholders and what is produced by the developers. Deficiencies in eliciting requirements lead to high costs in software development at a more advanced stage of design [5]. This is true for the systems in general and for WebGIS in particular. These systems will certainly evolve as time progresses and new technologies emerge, but there is still a shortage of requirements modeling languages that can explicity express the

S. Cherfi et al. (Eds.): RCIS 2021, LNBIP 415, pp. 265–273, 2021.
https://doi.org/10.1007/978-3-030-75018-3_17

fundamental concepts that are common to WebGIS. Mainly, the requirements modeling of WebGIS interfaces is a fundamental step in the success of WebGIS apps as a way to bridge the gap of communication among stakeholders, from domain experts to developers. Thus, a specific requirements modeling language is required to specify the interface requirements for WebGIS applications, not only for interested parties to be able to express what they really want, but also to facilitate the transmission of information to the development team. A WebGIS requirements language will also allow a more systematic and rigorous development, both in the specification of requirements and also in the development WebGIS applications, facilitating the future evolution of the developed system as well its maintenance processes.

The objective of this paper is to describe the WebGIS Interface Requirements Modeling Language (WebGIS IRML), which consists of a set of concepts that are common to WebGIS interfaces, but which may be initially difficult to correctly express among diverse stakeholders. To accomplish this, we define the language concepts and their relationships through a metamodel and present a language editor, which supports the production of the WebGIS interface requirements models. The focus here is on specifying the desired properties that a WebGIS Interface should offer, including the identification of its functionalities. However, the specification details of each functionality can be accomplished using any requirements language (e.g., use case descriptions). The work is still in progress, thus, this paper is a progress report.

Therefore, the main contribution of this work is to improve communication among stakeholders by providing a domain specific modelling language to specify the wanted features of WebGIS interfaces. The resulting model obtained by applying the language will serve as an artifact to validate WebGIS interface requirements by the stakeholders.

This paper is organized as follows. Section 2 describes background information on the research developed. Section 3 discusses some related work. Section 4 describes the WebGIS IRML, presenting the meta-model with its metaclasses and an example with an instantiation of the Metamodel, in a real-life WebGIS application case study. Section 5 briefly describes the language evaluation, including its result, based on the feedback of 30 volunteers. Finally, Sect. 6 discusses some conclusions and future work.

2 Background

GIS are information systems designed to capture, model, store, recover, share, manipulate, analyze, and present georeferenced data [2]. GIS allow users to execute queries, analyze and edit spatial information, using a map interface. This, as applied to various data domains, provides the ability to manage strategies, politics, and planning [5]. Urban planning, sub terrain cables, forest fires and flight trackers, are some examples of application domains where the geographic dimension is of major importance, and thus can take advantage of GIS development.

WebGIS appeared together with geographic web services [4] provided by technologies such as Google Maps, Bing Maps and Open Layers. WebGIS applications involve elements such as the base map, overlaying georeferenced data and the availability of Web tools and data resources that support interaction with the WebGIS application, from distributed sources. Generally, approaches for supporting the specification of requirements WebGIS interfaces are lacking. These will be the focus of this work.

Requirements engineering is the process of eliciting, analyzing, documenting, validating and managing services (functionalities) and constraints of a system [5]. Requirements can be modeled using different general languages like UML or goal-oriented languages. However, with domain specific modeling languages (DSML) [7], we can explicitly model systems of a particular domain, facilitating the communication between domain experts, users and developers.

DSMLs are often used in the context of model-driven development (MDD) [8] where models are the primary artefacts and, through a series of transformations, we can generate code from models. A model is an artifact formulated in a modeling language representing a system and is specified through a metamodel. A metamodel defines the concepts and relations between concepts of a domain specific language. This means that a metamodel defines the set of operations, properties and characteristics that form a system, and by metamodel, a model is instantiated.

In this paper, we propose the WebGIS IRML language, which was designed following DSML and MDD principles and techniques, and describe its metamodel, the basis of the proposed editor, which enables the construction of well-formed WebGIS interface requirements models. With this, we aim to improve the communication among the stakeholders, by providing clear specifications of WebGIS applications interfaces and avoiding the risk of project failure.

3 Related Work

Regarding works related to modeling for the specific domain of WebGIS, a proposal for a metamodel for the design of a context-sensitive WebGIS interface, from an MDA view (model-based architectures), is described in [9]. The authors propose that, in emergency conditions, context-sensitive WebGIS applications must be developed, addressing the behavior and performance required in that context. The authors validate their work through the implementation of a case study on the catastrophic floods of 2002 in Austria, concluding that a system adapted to the context of emergency situations could have saved lives and prevented further damage.

On WebGIS domain-specific languages, a project from the University of Salerno, Italy, stands out, suggesting a visual language based on WebML, for WebGIS design. The authors of this proposal [10] believe that, given the importance of these systems in contexts ranging from urban planning to marketing and prevention of natural disasters, a Web modeling language would be a strong help in development processes which include non-specialized entities. This approach seeks to model relevant interactions and common navigation operations for WebGIS applications. It is a project that focuses on the design of the interactive part of WebGIS applications.

4 WebGIS IRML

The main goal of the WebGIS IRML is to define interface requirements models of WebGIS applications. To specify those requirements, nine concepts, common to WebGIS, were included in the language. The identification of these concepts, and the relationships between them, resulted from the analysis of the user interfaces of various existing WebGIS applications performed by the first author in his thesis [12]. The resulting concepts model the major properties of WebGIS interfaces and are listed (and described) in Table 1 as metaclasses.

Table 1. Concepts of WebGIS IRML

Concepts	
Name	Definition
Terminal	This metaclass indicates the type of terminal desired for the installation and operation of WebGIS application. (e.g., Desktop, Smartphone, Tablet)
Domain	This metaclass indicates the domain in which the WebGIS application focuses, that is, the set of concepts identified and desired for the application
Concept	This metaclass indicates the main data that is supposed to be obtained from the chosen domain of the WebGIS application. It defines the main concepts of the domain
Map	This metaclass indicates the base web map to be used on application (e.g., OpenStreetMap or GoogleMap). The base map will be the one that will serve as the background to data layers that will be used in the context of the application and integrated into the map visualization
Map layer	This metaclass concerns the data layers to be integrated with the base map
Builtin	This metaclass represents general functionalities of the application. These functionalities may be related with the map, terminal, etc. (e.g., a marker on map)
Event	This metaclass identifies events that support the application execution (e.g., Click or Scroll) These events can trigger the launch of other functionalities of the application
Function	This metaclass, as the builtin metaclass, is pointed to the application in general. It is objectively to activate system behaviors. These behaviors can be related with functionalities, events, resources, map and terminal
Resource	This metaclass, concerns repositories, where the system's maps or other necessary data to the good system operation will be stored

4.1 The Metamodel and Notation

Considering the already known concepts of the domain and the relations that link these concepts, we propose a simplified metamodel of the WebGIS IRML. The full metamodel was specified using the Ecore metamodeling language. In the metamodel, shown in Fig. 1, the Map concept is central and represents the base map of the future application; it is connected to most of the other relevant concepts (Terminal, Event, Map Layer, Function, Builtin). Terminal is also key to the metamodel, linked to several other metaclasses. The relation between Terminal and Event allows the user to define events launched on the application, which are external to the GIS. The figure also displays a relation between Terminal and Map, where the application can only include one map element. MapLayers are associated with Map and Concept. Finally, Builtins and Functions need (data) Resources to execute. Figure 2 shows the corresponding visual notation used for these concepts and applied in the developed editing tool.

Figure 3 is a screenshot of the WebGIS IRML editor, showing the canvas to build the model in the center, the pallet to choose the model elements on the right-hand side, the directory of the project files on the left hand side and several functions on top (here the "Validate" function is selected, which validates the model syntax.

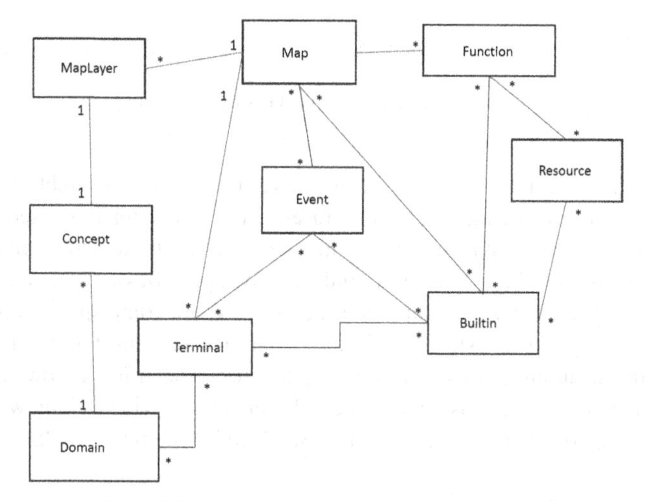

Fig. 1. Metamodel of WebGIS IRML (simplified)

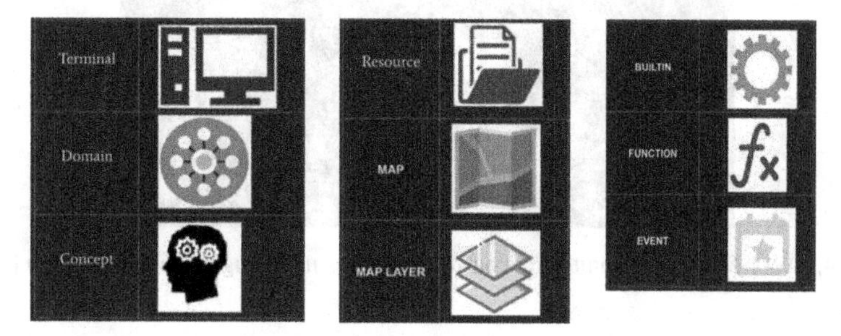

Fig. 2. Notation for WebGIS IRML

4.2 Using the Language

After the development of the language and editor, for validation purposes, we used a previous implemented case study [11] to model a real interface of an existing WebGIS application. The aim of this was to verify if the language was sufficiently complete to

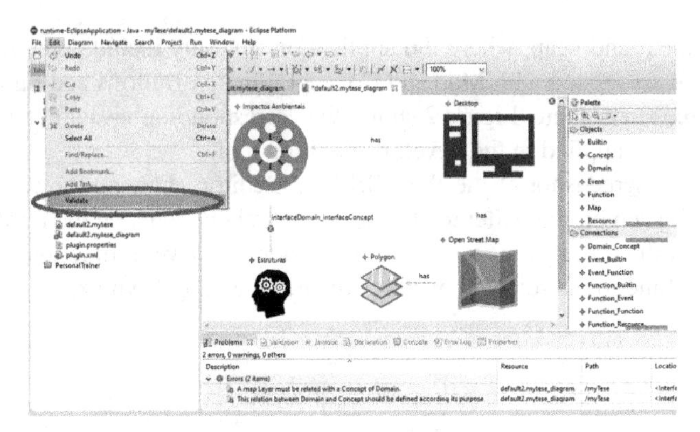

Fig. 3. Screenshot of WebGIS IRML editor

address all needed interface requirements for this application. This WebGIS application has the purpose of monitoring coastal structures in Portugal's territory (see Fig. 4).

The figure shows a coastal structure whose sections are modelled as blue polygons, in the form of a GIS data layer. An additional data layer provides several yellow markers, which represent points of view, that is the locations where some specialized staff took specific photos of the coastal structure. The red marker represents the real-time position of the user, in the moment this figure was generated. The InfoWindow in the center appears when the user clicks inside the blue polygon, and provides, along with the name of the local area (Ericeira), three functions. "See Info", "See photos", "See videos".

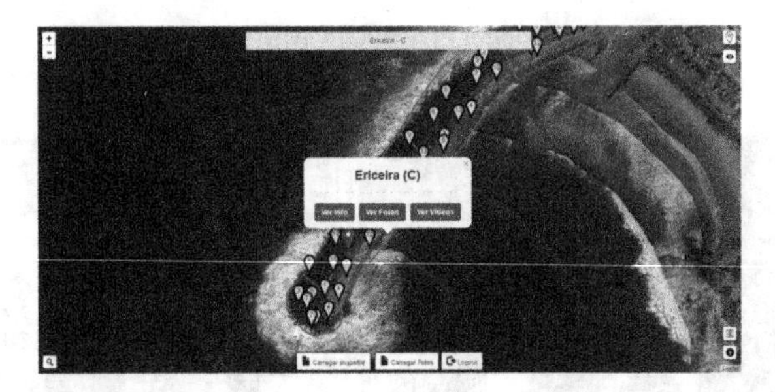

Fig. 4. Application for monitoring coastal structures in Portugal's territory (from [11])

In Fig. 5, the complete model is presented, instantiated under the metamodel rules and the requirements of this case study. We start by modeling the Terminal, a Desktop, which is related to two Builtins: Location Awareness and Menu. In Fig. 5 we observe the Domain *Estruturas Costeiras* (Coastal Structures). The data obtained from the Domain, represented as Concepts of the Domain, are *Pontões* (Structures), and *Pontos de Visibilidade* (Points of View). These Concepts of the Domain are, in the application, abstracted to map layers. The structures are represented, on the map, as Polygons and the points of view become Markers. These map layers will be layered on the base Map (Open Street Map). Also, we observe that the base map calls a Function, which handles the

API license key, that provides the developer with permission to build the WebGIS application. Going down on the image, we detect five Builtins used on the map: Polygons, Markers, Clusters, Zoom and Pan Crop. The builtin Clusters is only activated upon the event Zoom Out. Moreover, we verify that an InfoWindow is launched by the Event Click on a Polygon. It provides three functions: Query Info, Query Photos and Query Videos. Moreover, the Builtin Clusters launch an Event: Groupment on the Builtin: Markers. The figure shows 3 functions provided by the InfoWindow, they use the Resource: estruturas-Database (structuresDatabase), which stores all the necessary data of the application. The Resource *structuresDatabase* handles another Function, Edit Data, which is launched on the Builtin Menu.

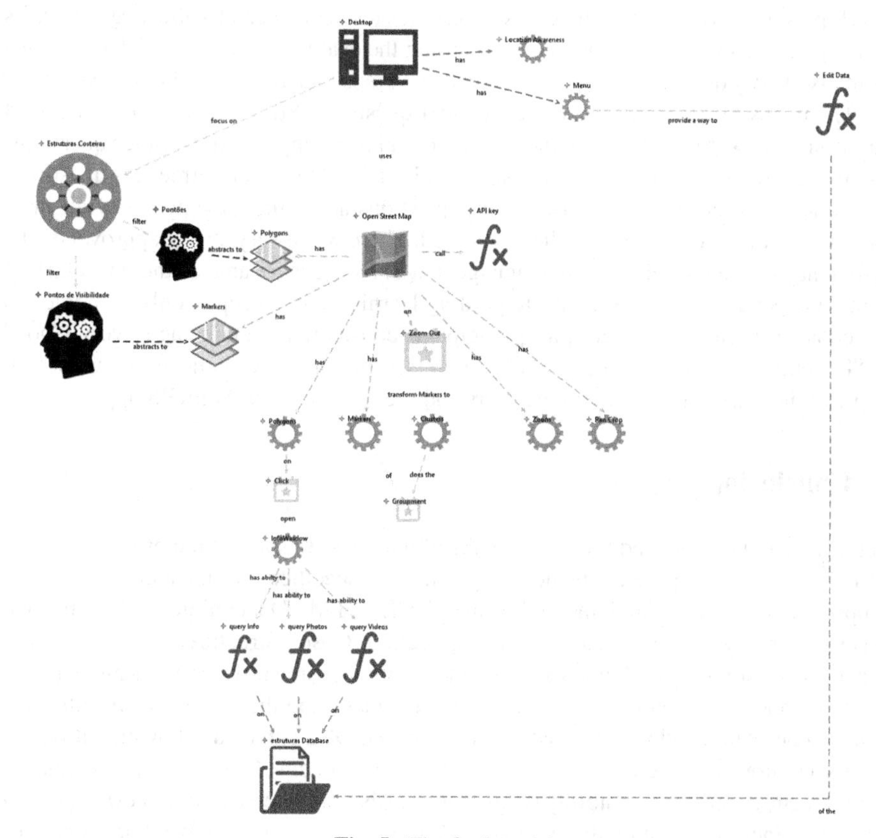

Fig. 5. The final model

5 Preliminary Evaluation

After the modeling of the requirements of the case study, 30 volunteers were invited to evaluate the model and the language. The aim of the evaluation was to check if the language and its notation were easy to understand through the execution of a set of tasks posed to the participants. We also asked them to answer some questions regarding their perception on the ease of use of the language. The evaluation was divided in 4 parts. In the 1st part the volunteers would answer questions about their experience on the use and development of WebGIS applications and DSLs. In the 2nd part, they evaluated the notation of the WebGIS IRML and the concepts of the language in the context of the case study. They were asked to answer 8 questions about the case study model where their performance was measured (3rd part). Finally, in the 4th part, the questions were about the language in general, its concepts, as well as the expressiveness of the icons used to represent the concepts. The results were quite positive. Most participants in the experiment revealed, before carrying out the evaluation, having had contact, as users or developers, with WebGIS applications. There was also evidence of knowledge on DSLs and experience in their development. Regarding the evaluation of the model, the results were also very positive. All multiple-choice questions had an approval rate $>80\%$.

There was more variation on the free text questions. Still, the pass rate for 3 of 4 questions was $>75\%$. Regarding the time used for answering multiple-choice questions, the average response time for all questions is less than 20 s. In the free text questions, an average answer was <60 s. Regarding questions about the language, they all liked the notation of the elements and the icons used. There was a very strong approval on the sufficiency of the concepts of the language, but this is questionable as there is a lack of domain experts in the experiment. Regarding learning the concepts, only 3 people did not consider it easy. In general, all participants considered the language "Very Good" or "Excellent". There was a positive general perception, so we believe this work will improve the interaction between the users and the developers of WebGIS apps.

6 Conclusions

In this paper, we presented the main results of a process to support the proposal of new WebGIS interface requirements modeling language, specified through a metamodel and supported by an editor implemented using DSML and MDD techniques. The language was validated by modeling one existing application (Costal Structures). The evaluation consisted of asking 30 participants to execute comprehension tasks, measuring their performance and asking their feedback about the language and the editor. The results were quite encouraging, and we believe that the proposed DSL can be used by practitioners.

As a future work, we will enrich the language with model elements to capture quality requirements, such as accessibility requirements. Also, we intend to further evaluate with PASEV[1] practitioners. Finally, we plan to automatically generate WebGIS interfaces from the model specifications using model-driven engineering techniques.

Acknowledgements. We thank NOVA LINCS UID/CEC/04516/2019 and PASEV PTDC/ART-PER/28584/2017 project for supporting this work.

[1] PASEV project: https://pasev.hcommons.org/.

References

1. Lammes, S., Wilmott C.: Mapping the city, playing the city: location-based apps as navigational interfaces. Convergence J. Res. New Media Technol. (2016)
2. Worboys, M., Duckham, M.: GIS: A Computing Perspective, 2nd edn. CRC Press, Boca Raton (2004)
3. Clarke, K.: Advances in geographic information systems. Comput. Environ. Urban Syst. **10**(3–4), 175–184 (1986)
4. Fu, P., Sun, J.: Web GIS: Principles and Applications. Esri Press, Redlands (2010)
5. Sommerville, I.: Software Engineering, 10th edn. Pearson, London (2015)
6. Geraci, A., Katki, F., McMonegal, L., Meyer, B., Porteous, H.: IEEE standard computer dictionary. A compilation of IEEE standard computer glossaries (1991)
7. Kelly, S., Tolvanen, J.: Domain-Specific Modeling: Enabling Full Code Generation. Wiley, Hoboken (2008)
8. Kühne, T.: What is a model? In: Bezivin, J., Heckel, R. (eds.) Language Engineering for Model-Driven Software Development. Dagstuhl Seminar Proceedings 04101 (2005)
9. Angelaccio, M., Krek, A., D'Ambrogio, A.: A model-driven approach for designing adaptive web GIS interfaces. In: Popovich, V.V., Claramunt, C., Schrenk, M., Korolenko, K.V. (eds.) Information Fusion and GIS. Lecture Notes in Geoinformation and Cartography, pp. 137–148. Springer, Berlin (2009). https://doi.org/10.1007/978-3-642-00304-2_9
10. Martino, S.D., Ferrucci, F., Paolino, L., Sebillo, M., Vitiello, G., Avagliano, G.: A WebML-based visual language for the development of web GIS applications. In: Visual Languages and Human-Centric Computing (VL/HCC) (2007)
11. Maia, A., Rodrigues, A., Lemos, R., Capitão, R., Fortes, C.: Developing a responsive web platform for the systematic monitoring of coastal structures. In: Ragia, L., Laurini, R., Rocha, J.G. (eds.) GISTAM 2017. CCIS, vol. 936, pp. 176–197. Springer, Cham (2019). https://doi.org/10.1007/978-3-030-06010-7_11
12. Veloso, R.: An interface requirements modeling language for WebGIS. MSc dissertation, Universidade Nova de Lsiboa, November 2019

CoV2K: A Knowledge Base of SARS-CoV-2 Variant Impacts

Ruba Al Khalaf, Tommaso Alfonsi, Stefano Ceri, and Anna Bernasconi(✉)

Department of Electronics, Information and Bioengineering, Politecnico di Milano, Via Ponzio 34/5, 20133 Milan, Italy
{ruba.al,tommaso.alfonsi,stefano.ceri,anna.bernasconi}@polimi.it

Abstract. In spite of the current relevance of the topic, there is no universally recognized knowledge base about SARS-CoV-2 variants; viral sequences deposited at recognized repositories are still very few, and the process of tracking new variants is not coordinated. CoV2K is a manually curated knowledge base providing an organized collection of information about SARS-CoV-2 variants, extracted from the scientific literature; it features a taxonomy of variant impacts, organized according to three main categories (protein stability, epidemiology, and immunology) and including levels for these effects (higher, lower, null) resulting from a coherent interpretation of research articles.

CoV2K is integrated with ViruSurf, hosted at Politecnico di Milano; ViruSurf is globally the largest database of curated viral sequences and variants, integrated from deposition repositories such as COG-UK, GenBank, and GISAID. Thanks to such integration, variants documented in CoV2K can be analyzed and searched over large volumes of nucleotide and amino acid sequences, e.g., for co-occurrence and impact agreement; the paper sketches some of the data analysis tests that are currently under development.

Keywords: SARS-CoV-2 · Variant impact · COVID-19 · Knowledge base · Data integration · Statistical testing

1 Introduction

The global COVID-19 pandemic, caused by the SARS-CoV-2 viral infection, has impacted everyone's lives, with more than 100 million confirmed cases, including more than 2.2 million deaths worldwide, as reported by the World Health Organization on January 31st, 2021 (https://covid19.who.int/). Achieving genetic diversity is an essential aspect for the continuation of SARS-CoV-2 (similarly to other RNA viruses), because it brings viral survival, fitness, and pathogenesis [12]. Therefore, collecting information about genetic variation in SARS-CoV-2 becomes overly necessary, e.g., for studying its relationship with effects on the COVID-19 pandemic [2].

S. Cherfi et al. (Eds.): RCIS 2021, LNBIP 415, pp. 274–282, 2021.
https://doi.org/10.1007/978-3-030-75018-3_18

To accomplish this goal, we started to build CoV2K, a knowledge base fuelled by information extracted from published papers and preprints. Unlike in other domains and contexts, automatic text mining methods are not applicable for building CoV2K, because there is not enough good quality material to instruct effective mining methods; therefore, we are building the knowledge base manually, following a systematic procedure.

In organizing the knowledge base, we designed categories that well-represent the impact of virus' variants on viral characteristics, arranged according to three main categories (protein stability, epidemiology, immunology) and including levels for these effects (higher, lower, null). The knowledge base is connected to a massive amount of publicly available data from heterogeneous sources (RefSeq, COG-UK, GenBank, NMDC, and GISAID); this connection is supported thanks to the ViruSurf database [6], a recently developed, integrated and curated resource, hosted by Politecnico di Milano. Furthermore, the knowledge base is connected to the VirusViz service (http://gmql.eu/virusviz/), which allows user-provided data to be analyzed and visualized.

The availability of CoV2K and its connection with ViruSurf and VirusViz opens opportunities for new discoveries, which can be achieved through statistical testing, e.g., about multiple variants co-occurrence and its spreading at given times within populations of particular geographical regions. Thus, it becomes possible to connect knowledge about variants published at a given time to the past and future diffusion of variants within publicly available sequences.

This paper is intended as a progress report and is organized as follows: Sect. 2 overviews how information is acquired and organized within the knowledge base; Sect. 3 describes its connection with the ViruSurf database; Sect. 4 elicits the expected data analysis activities exploiting statistical testing within parametric sub-populations; Sect. 5 finally concludes.

2 Knowledge Base Construction

2.1 Data Acquisition

The data acquisition protocol is designed for building a comprehensive and well-organized knowledge base, considering both peer-reviewed articles and preprints, with peer-reviewed articles as the most valuable sources. We selected Google Scholar, PubMed, GISAID/COG-UK reports, MedRxiv, and BioRxiv as our data sources; we then selected search keywords, used individually or in pairs/triplets, of:

- virus terms (SARS-CoV-2, Coronavirus, 2019-nCoV, COVID-19, Spike, lineage, RBD, ...);
- known clinical impacts (transmission, fatality rate, monoclonal antibodies, phenotype, severe outcome, ...);
- known variants and/or lineages (variant of interest/VOC, D614G, N501Y, B.1.1.7, UK lineage, Brazilian variant, ...).

Then, we filtered the outcome according to the relevance to the research's topic. We daily perform data searches, noting that the COG-UK report is updated on a bi-weekly basis[1].

CoV2K structure is composed of three sections. The first section represents the variant characterization, including the protein encoded by the gene (called product), the type of variant (i.e., substitution, insertion or deletion), the amino acid variation (composed of a reference sequence, its position on the reference genome, and an alternative sequence), as well as the identifier of the reference genome used in the study. The second section, which is better defined next, describes the variant's impact (i.e., how the virus behaviour is influenced by the presence of that variant). The third section links the variant to the source of information, defined by the manuscript's author, the DOI, and type of publication. We next define the second section in details.

2.2 Taxonomy of Effects

According to epidemiological studies and definitions, we organize variant effects into three categories, as follows:

Protein Stability. In this category, we organize all the variants that could lead to a change in the produced protein's stability (see R203K and G204R in Table 1, as examples). These are reported in structure-related studies focusing on the "stability" of viral proteins. Several genetic variations are non-synonymous, thus altering the amino acid composition of viral proteins, which will produce a protein with different degrees of stability [5].

Epidemiology. This category is important to understand SARS-CoV-2 evolutionary epidemiology, viral kinetics and dynamics related studies. It includes:

- *Viral transmission*, the virus capability to pass from a host to another host [10]. See P323L, D614G, and N501Y in Table 1.
- *Infectivity*, the capability of a transmitted virus to actually establish infection [8]. See V367F and D614G in Table 1.
- *Disease severity*, an assessment of systematic symptoms caused by the virus [15]. See D614G in Table 1.
- *Fatality rate*, the proportion of persons who die after the viral infection over the number of confirmed infected people [8]. See Q57H and P323L in Table 1.

Immunology. This category is concerned with immune response and virus-host interactions related studies, including any immune system process that happened in response to a virus-host interaction [10]. This category is important in the vaccine and therapeutic development studies, and it includes three sub-categories:

[1] Last accessed report (January 31st, 2021) before submission deadline: https://www.cogconsortium.uk/wp-content/uploads/2021/01/Report-2_COG-UK_SARS-CoV-2-Mutations.pdf.

Table 1. Example CoV2K variants with the related effect and level, captured on the specified literature publication of different type (publ. = published; prep = preprint).

Variant signature					Impact		Publication		
Product	Type	Orig.	Position	Alt.	Effect	Level	Author	DOI	Type
N	SUB	R	203	K	Protein stability	L	Parvez et al.	https://doi.org/10.1016/j.compbiolchem.2020.107413	Publ
N	SUB	G	204	R	Protein stability	L	Parvez et al.	https://doi.org/10.1016/j.compbiolchem.2020.107413	Publ
NS3	SUB	Q	57	H	Fatality rate	L	Oulas et al.	https://doi.org/10.1371/journal.pone.0238665	Publ
NSP12	SUB	P	323	L	Viral transmission	H	Wang et al.	https://doi.org/10.21203/rs.3.rs-49671/v1	Prep
NSP12	SUB	P	323	L	Fatality rate	H	Toyoshima et al.	https://doi.org/10.1038/s10038-020-0808-9	Publ
Spike	SUB	V	367	F	Infectivity	H	Junxian et al.	https://doi.org/10.1101/2020.03.15.991844	Prep
Spike	SUB	D	614	G	Infectivity	H	Korber et al.	https://doi.org/10.1016/j.cell.2020.06.043	Publ
Spike	SUB	D	614	G	Viral transmission	H	Zhang et al.	https://doi.org/10.1038/s41467-020-19808-4	Publ
Spike	SUB	D	614	G	Viral transmission	H	Volz et al.	https://doi.org/10.1016/j.cell.2020.11.020	Publ
Spike	SUB	D	614	G	Disease severity	N	Volz et al.	https://doi.org/10.1016/j.cell.2020.11.020	Publ
Spike	SUB	N	501	Y	Viral transmission	H	Teruel et al.	https://doi.org/10.1101/2020.12.16.423118	Prep
Spike	SUB	N	501	Y	Binding affinity host rec	H	Santos et al.	https://doi.org/10.1101/2020.12.29.424708	Prep
Spike	SUB	N	439	K	Sensitivity to conv. sera	L	Qianqian et al.	https://doi.org/10.1016/j.cell.2020.07.012	Publ
Spike	SUB	N	439	K	Sensitivity to mAbs	L	Qianqian et al.	https://doi.org/10.1016/j.cell.2020.07.012	Publ

- *Sensitivity to convalescent sera*: as in other infections, the convalescent serum from recovered individuals might be used for prevention and treatment of COVID-19 (thus providing passive immunization [1]), as it is assumed that convalescent plasma donors may have developed an effective immune response to the offending pathogen. See N439K in Table 1.
- *Sensitivity to neutralizing mAbs*, measuring the sensitivity of the variants towards monoclonal antibodies – the mechanism in which a subset of antibodies blocks the viral infection is called neutralization. This kind of sensitivity has a crucial role in vaccine development. See N439K in Table 1.

- *Binding affinity to host receptor.* SARS-CoV-2 is entering the host cells by binding its receptor-binding domain (RBD), in the spike protein, to a cell receptor called angiotensin-converting enzyme 2 (ACE2). Modifying the binding affinity could lead to a change in the efficacy of cell entering. Hence, binding affinity potentially affects cell infectivity and immune evasion [14]. See N501Y in Table 1.

Subcategories may be associated to higher, lower and null levels:

- Higher (H): the variant's presence leads to an increase of a specific effect.
- Lower (L): the variant's presence leads to a decrease of a specific effect.
- Null (N): the variant's presence does not change a specific effect (after testing).

All categories and sub-categories are flexible and will be extended according to the newly studied variants and their timely reported impact. Table 1 represents an excerpt of the current state of the knowledge base, with a few examples of variants' impacts.

3 Integration with Sequence Data

ViruSurf is a large integrated database of viral sequences of SARS-CoV-2 (and similar viruses), hosted at http://gmql.eu/virusurf/; it stores all the sequences that have been deposited to GenBank and COG-UK, whereas a similar database, hosted at http://gmql.eu/virusurf_gisaid/, stores only a subset of the data and metadata from the GISAID repository, which however includes amino acid variants, the most important information from the knowledge base perspective. An incremental pipeline can be frequently initiated (e.g. on a weekly or bi-weekly basis) in order to add new deposited sequences to the ViruSurf databases; the pipeline applies a variant calling algorithm extracting mutations on both the nucleotide and the amino acid levels, and includes a search for overlapping sequences, since many sequences deposited in GenBank and COG-UK overlap with those deposited in GISAID. As of January 31st, 2021 the databases contain about 500K non-overlapping sequences, with a significant monthly growth rate (15–25%).

Figure 1 represents the logical schema of ViruSurf databases. While the complete ViruSurf schema can be appreciated in [6] based on the Viral Conceptual Model [4], we here report the essential aspects: it is centered on the SEQUENCE table, connected to SEQUENCINGPROJECT, VIRUS, HOSTSAMPLE/HOSTSPECIES, and EXPERIMENTTYPE. The "analytical" perspective of the schema contains information about ANNOTATIONS (characterization of sub-parts of the sequence), NUCLEOTIDEVARIANTS and AMINOACIDVARIANTS.

The new knowledge base concepts are centered upon two entities, the KBAAVARIANT and the KBNUCVARIANT, respectively including all the amino acid and nucleotide-level variants captured from our data acquisition process (Sect. 2).

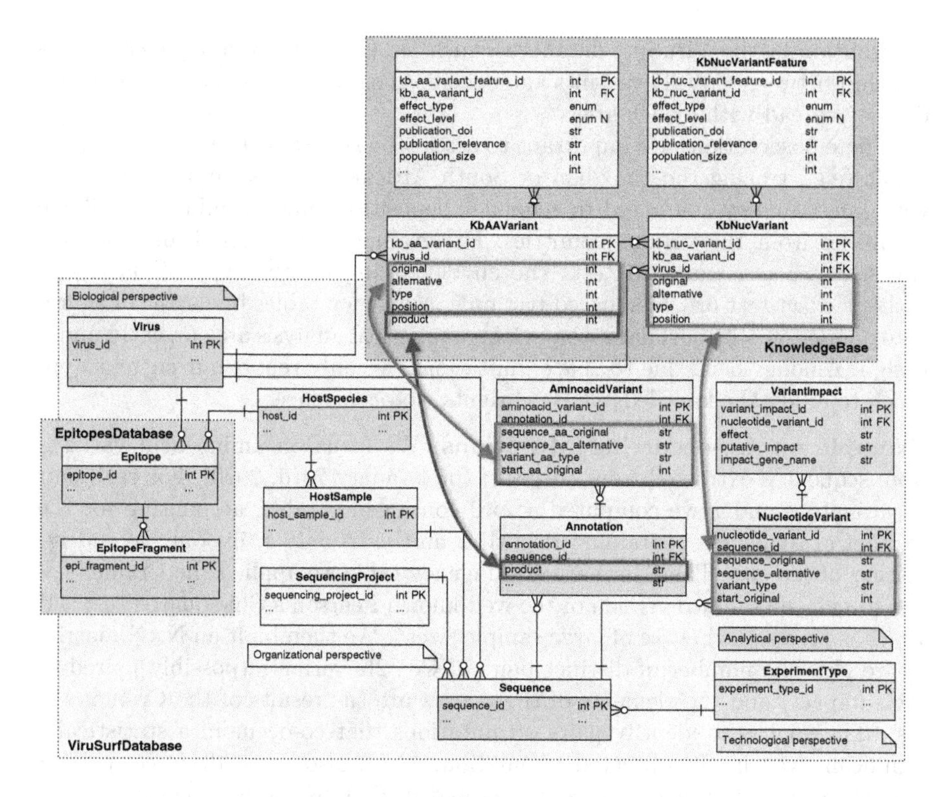

Fig. 1. Schema of the knowledge base connected to the ViruSurf database

Two one-to-many relationships connect each variant instance to its possibly many effects, respectively described in KbAAVariantFeature and KbNucVariantFeature.

The connection of the knowledge base to the database requires building bridges from the variant characterization attributes of the knowledge base to the variants in the database. The matching with the ViruSurf tables is depicted in Fig. 1: the products need to match with the annotation table, as shown by the purple arrow/boxes; the variant signatures (original, alternative, type, and position) need to match with the corresponding four fields highlighted by pink arrows/boxes.

4 Data Analysis

Basic summary statistics about the CoV2K variants' distribution and their impact can be used to describe CoV2K data, answering questions such as: (i) What is the CoV2K variants' density in a specific gene? (ii) Are there conflicts in specific variant's impact's level (e.g., a variant reporting both H and L levels)? Other simple statistics may relate CoV2K variants to their time and space distribution in the ViruSurf databases, such as: (iii) is there a significant relationship between CoV2K variants and specific geographical areas? (iv) How fast do they spread within such areas?

These observations are important to assess the status of the COVID-19 pandemic (e.g., tracing the Brazilian or South African variants) and can be done with limited delay compared to sequence deposition time in publicly available databases from the various countries. For evaluating the significance of such statistics we use standard tests chosen depending on the type of data, e.g. Fisher's exact test or Chi-squared test on contingency tables by means of aggregate queries on ViruSurf databases. Other statistical analysis are currently under design. Among them, due to space limitations, we only report our current approach to study the knowledge base variants' co-occurrence.

Example on Co-occurring Mutations. We focus on amino acid variants from sequences extracted from ViruSurf (on January 23rd, 2020). For each pair of variants x and y we computed a 2×2 contingency table, accounting for the number of sequences containing i) both x and y, ii) only x, iii) only y, and iv) neither of the two. Then, for each contingency table we applied the Cramer's V test [9], i.e., a modified version of the well-known Pearson's Chi-squared test [11] which is preferable in case of large sample sizes[2]. We then built an N×N matrix, where N is the number of distinct pairs of CoV2K variants (possibly paired to their impact) and the elements of the matrix are the results of the Cramer's V test. The goal is to identify pairs of mutations that co-occur in a statistically significant way in the observed population, which also agree/disagree in their impact, as reported in literature and stored in CoV2K; here we considered all publicly available sequences, but we plan to allow the choice of specific sub-populations.

	NS3_Q57H:fr:l	NSP12_P323L:fr:h	NSP12_P323L:vt:h	N_G204R:ps:l	N_R203K:ps:l	Spike_D614G:vt:h	Spike_N501Y:in:h	Spike_P681H	Spike_S982A
NS3_Q57H:fr:l	x								
NSP12_P323L:fr:h	0.14	x							
NSP12_P323L:vt:h	0.14	x	x						
N_G204R:ps:l	0.38	0.17	0.17	x					
N_R203K:ps:l	0.38	0.17	0.17	0.99	x				
Spike_D614G:vt:h	0.14	0.83	0.83	0.18	0.18	x			
Spike_N501Y:in:h	0.12	0.068	0.068	0.33	0.33	0.064	x		
Spike_P681H	0.13	0.068	0.068	0.32	0.32	0.066	0.92	x	
Spike_S982A	0.13	0.06	0.06	0.34	0.34	0.069	0.95	0.94	x

Fig. 2. Result matrix of co-occurrence analysis. Each row/column label represents a variant:effect(first letters):level(L/H).

Figure 2 reports an excerpt of our results. Empty cells are not computed as they are symmetrical to the lower triangular matrix; the symbol × indicates

[2] The strength of association ranges from 0 (no association) to 1 (perfect association); the value 0.1 is considered a good significance threshold for the relationship between two variables, see http://www.acastat.com/statbook/chisqassoc.htm.

positions for the same variants. An explanatory color scheme was used to explain Cramer's V test results:

- `Black` captures pairs that are not significant (lower than 0.1), e.g., the black rectangle indicates that D614G in the Spike does not significantly co-occur with the last three variants of the table.
- `Blue` captures pairs that are significant (higher than 0.1), e.g., the three values marked by a blue triangle in the figure.
- `Green` captures pairs that, in addition to being significant, agree on the same effect and its level (e.g., the Spike protein D614G with the NSP12 protein P323L, and the two N protein substitutions at 203 and 204 positions).
- `Red` captures pairs that, in addition to being significant, agree on the effect but report an opposite level. This is the case of NS3 protein Q57H variant – which is reported as *decreasing* the fatality rate – significantly co-occurring with the NSP12 protein P323L variant – which is instead reported as *increasing* the fatality rate.

Note that the last three rows of the table represent some of the variants that define the B.1.1.7 lineage[3], which correspond to the "UK strain" that raised worldwide attention since December 2020. The Cramer's V test results of these three variants against all the other ones are very similar (see the last three rows of the matrix); the co-occurrence of the three variants is also well documented by the UK strain definition [13].

As the matrix entries proved effective in confirming properties, we may use them also for prediction: by looking at entries within the blue triangle and considering that N501Y is reported as increasing the infectivity of the virus, we could predict the same effect also for P681H and S982A. Such mechanism prompts further investigations of other variant pairs that could be similarly constructed. Referring instead to variants that are not yet described in CoV2K, co-occurrence with variants with a known effect may prompt targeted lab experiments.

5 Conclusion

We reported our initial design of a knowledge base of SARS-CoV-2 variants, whose strength lies both in a well-structured procedure for acquiring and organizing data and in the integration with the ViruSurf databases; the interplay between a large amount of up-to-date sequence information and manually curated consolidated knowledge is very promising, as confirmed by our preliminary data analysis results. In the future, we will refine the breadth and complexity of statistical tests, and fine tune them by means of bias correction methods (e.g., [3]) and by choosing thresholds appropriate for large samples (e.g., [7]).

The effectiveness of CoV2K will be evaluated with the help of domain experts that will also inspire more complex analyses to increase its benefits. CoV2K

[3] https://virological.org/t/preliminary-genomic-characterisation-of-an-emergent-sars-cov-2-lineage-in-the-uk-defined-by-a-novel-set-of-spike-mutations/563.

is by now only a taxonomy, but we will consider building a richer semantic representation of its elements, thereby helping automate reasoning and statistical tests.

Acknowledgment. This research is funded by the ERC Advanced Grant 693174 GeCo (data-driven Genomic Computing).

References

1. Abraham, J.: Passive antibody therapy in COVID-19. Nat. Rev. Immunol. **20**(7), 401–403 (2020)
2. Bernasconi, A., Canakoglu, A., Masseroli, M., Pinoli, P., Ceri, S.: A review on viral data sources and search systems for perspective mitigation of COVID-19. Briefings Bioinform. **22**(2), 664–675 (2021). https://doi.org/10.1093/bib/bbaa359
3. Bergsma, W.: A bias-correction for Cramér's V and Tschuprow's T. J. Korean Stat. Soc. **42**(3), 323–328 (2013)
4. Bernasconi, A., Canakoglu, A., Pinoli, P., Ceri, S.: Empowering virus sequence research through conceptual modeling. In: Dobbie, G., Frank, U., Kappel, G., Liddle, S.W., Mayr, H.C. (eds.) Conceptual Modeling, pp. 388–402. Springer International Publishing, Cham (2020). https://doi.org/10.1007/978-3-030-62522-1_29
5. Brinda, K., Vishveshwara, S.: A network representation of protein structures: implications for protein stability. Biophys. J. **89**(6), 4159–4170 (2005)
6. Canakoglu, A., Pinoli, P., Bernasconi, A., Alfonsi, T., Melidis, D.P., Ceri, S.: ViruSurf: an integrated database to investigate viral sequences. Nucleic Acids Res. **49**(D1), D817–D824 (2021)
7. Cao, H., Hripcsak, G., Markatou, M.: A statistical methodology for analyzing co-occurrence data from a large sample. J. Biomed. Inform. **40**(3), 343–352 (2007)
8. Centers for Disease Control and Prevention: Principles of epidemiology in public health practice; an introduction to applied epidemiology and biostatistics. Atlanta, GA: US Dept. of Health and Human Services, Centers for Disease (2006). https://www.cdc.gov/csels/dsepd/ss1978/ss1978.pdf. Accessed 31 Jan 2021
9. Cramér, H.: Mathematical Methods of Statistics. vol. 43. Princeton University Press (1946)
10. He, Y., et al.: CIDO, a community-based ontology for coronavirus disease knowledge and data integration, sharing, and analysis. Sci. Data **7**(1), 1–5 (2020)
11. Pearson, K.: X. On the criterion that a given system of deviations from the probable in the case of a correlated system of variables is such that it can be reasonably supposed to have arisen from random sampling. The London, Edinburgh, Dublin Philos. Mag. J. Sci. **50**(302), 157–175 (1900)
12. Rahimi, A., Mirzazadeh, A., Tavakolpour, S.: Genetics and genomics of SARS-CoV-2: a review of the literature with the special focus on genetic diversity and SARS-CoV-2 genome detection. Genomics (2020)
13. Rambaut, A., et al.: A dynamic nomenclature proposal for SARS-CoV-2 lineages to assist genomic epidemiology. Nat. Microbiol. **5**(11), 1403–1407 (2020)
14. Shang, J., et al.: Cell entry mechanisms of SARS-CoV-2. Proc. Natl. Acad. Sci. **117**(21), 11727–11734 (2020)
15. Wu, J.T., et al.: Estimating clinical severity of COVID-19 from the transmission dynamics in Wuhan. China. Nat. Med. **26**(4), 506–510 (2020)

A Language-Based Approach for Predicting Alzheimer Disease Severity

Randa Ben Ammar(✉) and Yassine Ben Ayed

Multimedia Information System and Advanced Computing Laboratory,
Sfax University, Sfax, Tunisia

Abstract. Alzheimer's disease (AD) is the most leading symptom of neurodegenerative dementia; AD is defined now as one of the most costly chronic diseases. For that automatic diagnosis and control of Alzheimer's disease may have a significant effect on society along with patient well-being. The Mini Mental State Examination (MMSE) is a prominent method for identifying whether a person might have dementia and about the dementia severity respectively. These methods are time-consuming and require well-educated personnel to administer.

This study investigates another method for predicting MMSE score based on the language deterioration of people, using linguistic information from speech samples of picture description task.

We use a regression model over a set of 169 patients with different degrees of dementia; we achieve a Mean Absolute Error (MAE) of 3.6 for MMSE. When focusing on selecting the best features, we improve the MAE to 0.55. Obtained results indicate that the proposed taxonomy of the linguistic features could operate as a cheap dementia test, probably also in non-clinical situations.

Keywords: Alzheimer disease · Mini Mental State Examination (MMSE) · Machine learning · Prediction of clinical scores

1 Introduction

Alzheimer's disease was initially described by the German psychiatrist Alois Alzheimer, in 1906 [1]. The first patient treated was Auguste Deter, a 51-year-old woman, who suffers from memory loss, speaking problems, and impaired comprehension. Following her care, Dr. Alzheimer reported that the patient's condition met the definition of what was then called dementia, manifesting in many abnormal symptoms with memory, language, and behavior as agitation and confusion. He followed her care for five years, until her death in 1906. The disease was first discussed in the medical literature in 1907 and named after Alzheimer in 1910.

Although memory impairment is the main symptom of Alzheimer's disease, language deficit is a core symptom. In fact, the first parts of the brain cortex that decline with the disease are the parts that lead with linguistic abilities.

Many studies have accomplished promising diagnosing accuracies in classifying people with AD from Healthy Control (HC); however, they were based on different types of features extracted from the speech samples or the transcripted text of the speech.

S. Cherfi et al. (Eds.): RCIS 2021, LNBIP 415, pp. 283–294, 2021.
https://doi.org/10.1007/978-3-030-75018-3_19

In this study, we will focus on language impairment related features, in order to verify their efficiency in MMSE score prediction. The standard clinical protocol for dementia diagnosis is based on cognitive assessments the most widely used of which is the Mini Mental State Examination test. In five categories it tests the extent of cognitive impairment: orientation, registration, attention, memory, and language.

The MMSE test consists of 11 questions with a top score of 30 points (normal cognitive status), and where a score of 0 indicates a severe cognitive decline [2]. As this process is time-consuming and could be annoying for the patients, we propose in this paper another method for predicting MMSE score based on a set of linguistic features extracted from a patient's spontaneous speech.

In this study, we will focus on language impairment related features that will be extracted following a language disorder proposed taxonomy. The extracted features are then forwarded to machine learning classifiers, in order to verify their efficiency in predicting AD severity.

The paper is subdivided as follow. In the second section, we will introduce some related work in automatic AD detection. In the third section, we will formally define our experiment and the collection of linguistic features. Finally, will discuss our result and pave the way for future research.

2 Related Work

Like memory loss, which was regarded as the key symptom of Alzheimer's disease [3], language failure is a central symptom. The linguistic impairment associated with AD is actually identified from the first Alzheimer's disease clinical observation [4] and various research have identified language problems at all stages of the disease, and at varying degrees [5, 6]. Hence promising research and development for early detection of AD through speech processing is underway [7, 8].

In the following paragraphs, relevant studies will be summarized in order to examine the efficiency of language disorder in detecting AD; next some research that focused on the predicting of clinical score will be discussed. Following these studies, we will discuss a taxonomy related to speech disfluencies not for classifying AD from healthy controls, but for the prediction of the clinical score of each patient.

Fraser et al. [3] have accurately distinguished between patients with AD and healthy controls using a combination of machine-learning classification and automated quantification of language from a picture description task's speech samples. They presented a machine learning-based approach to classifying patients according to patterns in speech and language production, data was derived from DementiaBank [9]. They use four-factor analysis of linguistic measures: semantic impairment, acoustic abnormality, syntactic impairment, and information impairment. The extracted features were used into the implementations of Support Vector Machine SVM machine learning classifiers; results were promising, and 78% of speech samples could be correctly classified.

Another experiment by Orimaye et al. [10] explored promising diagnostic models using syntactic and lexical features from verbal utterances to perform binary classification of AD and healthy patients. The obtained result following the regression analysis and ML evaluations shows that the disease group used less complex sentences and makes more grammatical errors than the healthy elderly group. The best result was obtained with Support Vector Machines (SVM) classifier with an F-score of 74%. Their experiment confirms that syntactic and lexical features could be pertinent features for predicting AD and related Dementias.

Jarrold et al. [11] analyzed the acoustic features and Part Of Speech tagger (POS) features from a structured interview spoken by 9 patients with mild AD and compared to 9 healthy controls. The Multi-layer perceptron classifier results confirm that acoustic and linguistic measures are good biomarkers for early diagnosis of AD, with an accuracy value of 88%. Their experiments confirmed that Healthy controls subject would produce fewer pronouns, verbs, and adjectives and more nouns than AD patients.

Other studies have focused on predicting the clinical score for patient with and without dementia. Al-hameed et al. [12] predicted MMSE scores with acoustic information using the DementiaBank, Their model yielded a Mean Absolute Error (MAE) of 5.7 in predicting MMSE. However, they employed 811 acoustic features derived from speech samples including, fundamental frequency, Mel Frequency Cepstral Coefficients (MFCC), filter bank energy, and voice quality features such as Harmonic to Noise Ratio (HNR).

Yancheva et al. [13] used a combination of acoustic and manually extracted linguistic features derived from the DementiaBank dataset, to predict MMSE scores. However, they employed lexicosyntactic and semantic features derived from manual transcription, using a two-sample t-test and the Minimum Redundancy Maximum-Relevance (MRMR) for feature selection; the linguistic features were the relevant features selected among a set of 477 features. They obtain an MAE of 7.3 when utilizing all features and 3.8 when using only some selected features.

Luz et al. [14] used an automatic extraction process for acoustic features selection; Acoustic feature extraction was performed on the speech segments using the openS-MILE (Speech and Music Interpretation by Large-space Extraction) software; different features set were used such as emobase [14], Computational Paralinguistics Evaluation (ComParE) [15], Geneva Minimalistic Acoustic Parameter Set (GeMAPS) [16], and Multi-Resolution Cochleagram MRCG [17]. The regression results are reported as Root Mean Squared Error (RMSE) scores, they obtained an average of 5.2 with linear regression models.

Our work differs from that of Luz et al. [14], in terms of using only linguistic features (no acoustic features are required), and investigating a novel taxonomy related to language disorder for predicting clinical score.

In our previous study [18], we have used the machine learning models for the early diagnosis of Alzheimer's disease, based on features indicative of the linguistic disorder. Results show that the performance of the proposed approach is satisfactory; in fact, more than 91% accuracy has been achieved.

Contrary to our previous research [18], in this paper, we consider the linguistic disorder to help to predict the array of the different states that can be seen in AD.

3 Materials and Methods

3.1 Dataset

The used data in this study are derived from DementiaBank. The dataset consists of speech samples of a description of the Boston Cookie Theft picture task. In this task, patients were given a picture of a complex kitchen scene, and an examiner told them to describe everything they could see going in the picture. Each verbal interview was recorded along with manual transcriptions, following the TalkBank CHAT (Codes for the Human Analysis of Transcripts) protocol [19]. Hence, in this study, we extract the transcribed patient speech samples from the CHAT files and then pre-process the transcribed files for feature extraction.

3.2 Participant

The patients in the DementiaBank dataset have been classified into Healthy Control, Dementia, and Unknown patient groups. A Mini-Mental State Examination score was affected to every patient.

A total of 544 audio files were recorded from the three groups during an annual visit for the participants. The study continued for seven visits, however, the number of participants dramatically decreased per visit, so only recordings from the first four visits will be considered in our experiment.

In the experiments, the used materials are about 242 speech samples for the Alzheimer disease group derived from 169 patients with AD with an approximate age range of 49–90 years.

3.3 Extracted Feature

This section describes the feature extraction process adopted for the prognosis of AD. The collected data is being combined for the first time and has never been used for a computational study.

We consider a number of 61 features to capture a wide range of linguistic phenomena. Here we provide a brief description of the different feature types; according to the language impairment taxonomy described in the first section, features will be classified into 7 categories: Temporal disfluencies include 8 features, Verbal disfluencies include 17 features, Intelligibility analysis regroup 6 features, Lexico-syntactic diversity contain 16 features, Vocabulary richness contain 5 features, word and utterance rate with 8 features, the age of the patient has been added also as a personal attribute to the feature set.

The proposed set of features will be extracted using the CLAN program [20] (Table 1).

Table 1. Extracted features

Features category	Extracted features	Definition/How to measure
Temporal disfluencies	Duration	The total duration of speech
	Pauses, P Pauses	The total number of pauses, and the percentage of pauses
	Prolongation, P Prolongation	Vowel length is the perceived duration of a vowel sound. Vowel lengthening greater than 180 ms is coded with the CHAT program
	The filler words	The total number of filler words such as 'ahm' and 'ehm'
	Interposed word	The interposition of a short comment word such as "yeah" or "mhm"
	Question words	The total number of question words (who, where)
Verbal disfluencies	WWR, P WWR	Whole words Repetition (WWR), and the proportion of repetition words defined as the total number of repetitions divided by the totals number of words
	WWRU	Whole words repetition unit (WWRU) defined as the number of time words were repeated
	Mean RUs	The mean repetition unit is defined as the ratio of WWR divided by WWRU
	Phrase repetitions, P Phrase repetitions	Total number and proportion of phrase repetitions (similar to the WWR)
	Word revisions, P Word revisions	Number(rate) and proportion of whole words revisions
	Phrase revisions, P Phrase revisions	Number and proportion of phrases revisions
	SLD, P SLD	The number and proportion of stuttering-like disfluencies (SLD) like prolongation, non-word or blocks will be counted

(*continued*)

Table 1. (*continued*)

Features category	Extracted features	Definition/How to measure
	TD,P TD	The number and proportion of Typical disfluencies (TD) like pause, repeated words or phrases will be counted
	Total SLD-TD, P Total SLD-TD	Defined as the total TD and SLD, and the ratio of TD + SLD divided by the total number of words in each record
	Weighted SLD	It is calculated by adding part- and single-syllable (ss) word repetitions per 100 syllables (pw + ss) and multiplying by the mean number of repetition units (Mean RUs), and finally adding to the above total twice the number of stuttering-like disfluencies (SLD) The resulting equation is: $[(pw + ss) \times ru] + (2 \times SLD)$
Intelligibility analysis	Total Utterances Errors (TUE)	Number of utterances coded as errors
	Total Word Errors (TWE)	Number of words that are coded as errors
	Unintelligible word	Number of incomprehensible words
	Unintelligible utterances	Number of unintelligible utterances
	Words/TWE	Ratio of total words divided by the total number of words errors
	Utterances/TUE	Ratio of total utterances divided by the total number of utterances errors
Lexico-syntactic diversity	Prepositions	Number of prepositions
	Adjectives	Total adjectives
	Adverbs	Total adverbs
	Conjunction	Number of conjunctions
	Determiners	Number of determiners
	Pronouns	Number of pronouns
	Nouns	Total nouns

(*continued*)

Table 1. (*continued*)

Features category	Extracted features	Definition/How to measure
	Plurals	Pronouns as "we, us, they, them, their" are counted
	Verbs, Verbs/Utt	Total verbs and number of verbs per utterance
	Auxiliaries	Number of auxiliaries
	3S,1S3S	Identical forms for first and third-person singular
	PAST, PASTP, PRESP	the Past, Past participle (PASTP), Present participle (PRESP) tense will be counted
Vocabulary richness	FREQ types	Total word types do not include repetitions and revisions
	FREQ tokens	Total word tokens do not include repetitions and revisions
	FREQ TTR	Type-Token Ratio (TTR) provides a comparison to the total vocabulary used in dialogue (V) to the total word count (N) of the dialogue
	Idea density	Measure of propositional idea density
	Lexical richness	A mathematical model of how TTR varies with the token size
Word and utterance rate	Utterances	Total utterances with and without repetition
	Words	Total words with and without repetition
	MLU utterances	Number of utterances used to compute MLU (the Mean length of utterance)
	MLU words	MLU in words
	MLU morphemes	MLU in morphemes
	Utterances/Min	Total utterances per minute
	Words/Min	Total words per minute
	Words/utterances	Totals words per utterances

4 Result

As we mentioned above the main objective of this study is the prediction of MMSE score through spontaneous speech. We proposed 7 types of language-related disorders of AD patients; from this taxonomy, we extracted 61 features.

Extracted features will be used firstly on all speech samples, then in order to enhance our result data records will be divided within visit. The records of the first four visits will be exploited.

For our study, we have trained linear regression model. In general, regression models are constructed in order to predict the variance of a phenomenon (dependent variable) using a combination of explanatory factors (variables independent).

Linear regression is called multiple when the model is composed of at least two independent variables. Conversely, a simple linear regression model contains only one independent variable.

The relationship between a dependent variable and an independent variable in a simple linear regression could be calculated as follow.

$$Y = \beta_0 + \beta_1 X$$

With Y is the dependent variable (predicted value of independent variables X).

β_0 is the intercept (predicted value Y when X equal to zero).

For multiple linear regressions, multiple independent variables are used:

$$Y = \beta_0 + \beta_1 X_1 + \beta_2 X_2 + \cdots + \beta_n X_n$$

With $X_1, X_2 \ldots X_n$ are the independent variables.

$\beta_1, \beta_2, \ldots, \beta_n$ are the regression coefficient.

The result was determined using a 10-fold cross-validation. The evaluation metrics used are root mean square error (RMSE), the mean absolute error (MAE), and the mean square error (MSE).

The RMSE defined as: $RMSE = \sqrt{\frac{1}{N} \sum_{j=1}^{N} (y_j - \bar{y}_j)^2}$

The MAE defined as: $MAE = \frac{1}{N} \sum_{j=1}^{N} \left| y_j - \bar{y}_j \right|$

The MSE defined as: $MSE = \frac{1}{N} \sum_{j=1}^{N} (y_j - \bar{y}_j)^2$

Table 2 shows the RMSErelated to the prediction of the MMSE compared to the ones of the other approaches that have used the Dementiabank data.

The RMSE, MAE, and MSE results using the proposed taxonomy are displayed in Table 2. For comparison, previous studies were displayed too.

To our knowledge, the proposed taxonomy and collected features were being combined for the first time and have never been used for the computational study. In fact, our study determined more characteristic and representative features compared to Yancheva [13] and Al-Hameed [12].

Also, there is a clear amelioration comparing to previous works due mainly to the richness of the proposed taxonomy. However, Yancheva et al. [13] reported an MAE of 7.3, whereas Al-Hameed et al. [12] reported an MAE of 5.7, for Luz et al. [14] reported

Table 2. Results of MMSE

Author	RMSE	MAE	MSE
Yancheva et al. [13]	–	7.3	–
Al-Hameed et al. [12]	–	5.7	–
Luz et al. [14]	5.2	–	–
Our proposed method	**4.5**	**3.6**	**20.7**

an RMSE value of 5.2%. In our work, the linear regression model obtained the best result with an RMSE value of 4.5 and MAE value of 3.6.

As Alzheimer's disease is a neurodegenerative disease that cannot be stopped or cured, we will use the proposed taxonomy for predicting MMSE score within visit.

To enhance our results and discover the most features that contributed to the performance of our models we have applied mutual information [21] as a Feature Selection (FS) technique.

The mutual information of two random variables is a quantity measuring the statistical dependence of these variables. The mutual information of a pair (X, Y) of variables represents their degree of dependence in the probabilistic sense. This method ranks the attributes according to their importance. The top-ranked features will be manually selected as the best subset features.

This study aims to use language-related features as biomarkers for early predicting AD severity, a feature vector with 61 features was trained and processed with the features selection method.

Table 3. Result of MMSE within visit

Visit	MAE without FS	MAE with FS
Visit 1	3.16	0.68
Visit 2	3.9	0.91
Visit 3	1.1	1.5
Visit 4	4.5	0.55

To illustrate the longitudinal changes in cognitive and linguistic ability, Table 2 shows the result of decline of MMSE with and without the top most correlated features for the subset of subjects with AD. This demonstrates the MMSE score declining over four annual visits, along the proposed taxonomy.

For the mutual information method, we evaluated the model performance for subsets consisting of the n "best ranked" features.

In order to determine the suitable number of features, a test was performed according to the performance of the linear regression model (the number was reduced to 6 features for Visit 1, 5 features for Visit 2, 7 features were selected among Visit 3, and 5 features for Visit 4).

From Table 3, results show that the feature selection have improved the MAE values.The feature selected among visit 1 are FREQ TTR,Verbs, Pauses, Utterances, Utterances/TUE and lexical richness. These features lead to an MAE value of 0.68.

Figure 1 show the improvement of the predicted results among visit 1 with the best selected features.

Among the second visit the MAE value reach 0.91. Patient in the second visit use to produce more utterances and unintelligible words (the FREQ tokens, PASTP, Utterances/Min, Unintelligible utterances, Unintelligible word have the highest score).

The value of MAE augmented in the third visit to 1.5. Patients are more likely to produce more words, utterances and morphemes. Subjects with AD use more lexico-syntactic features such adjective, Plurals, 1S3S, and PRESP.

The best value of MAE was reached with the fourth visit. The five highest features score was: Words/Min, Idea density, PAST, Phrase revisions, and unintelligible utterances.

One of the advantages of our study is that the proposed taxonomy of language impairment of patient with AD has led to promising results. As the language disorder could be detected years before the diagnosis of AD [4], our results prove that features extracted from the verbal utterance of patients with AD could be good markers for predicting MMSE score.

We also show that focusing on subsets of subjects with a (visit dividing) improves the result of our model, lowering MAE to 1.1 (without FS) or equivalently lowering MAE to 0.5 using the top pertinent features.

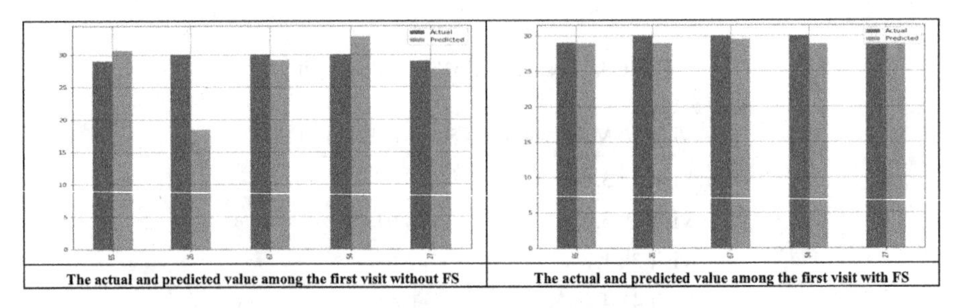

Fig. 1. Predicting MMSE score with and without feature selection

Also, the features suggested in this work are language independent, therefore there is a possibility to accomplish multilingual; extracted features could be adapted for studies in different languages.

In future work, we propose to extend the research by using more significant acoustic features that could significantly improve the result in predicting clinical score. Furthermore, the research could be extended by adding patient with Mild Cognitive Impairment MCI. As MCI has often been considered to be the predominant symptomatic phase of AD, for that enhancing the study with MCI patient will be more suitable of the early diagnosis of disease.

Conclusions

Although memory impairment is the main symptom of Alzheimer's disease, language deficit is a core symptom. In fact, the first parts of the brain cortex that decline with the disease are the parts that lead with linguistic abilities.

In this study, we have suggested taxonomy for language impairment in Alzheimer disease. Following the proposed taxonomy, a set of features was derived from the transcriptions of Alzheimer's patients and healthy elderly controls. The proposed taxonomy has showed great result in predicting clinical score of patient with and without AD.

Hopefully this will illustrate research limitations and shed light on avenues for clinical applicability and direction for future study.

Although automated MMSE score prediction will improve the screening process for AD by reducing the cost and time involved and improving reliability, future research would be more efficient by using acoustic features.

References

1. Alzheimer, A.: Über eigenartige Krankheitsfälle des späteren Alters. Zeitschrift für die gesamte Neurologie und Psychiatrie **4**(1), 356–385 (1911)
2. Folstein, M.F., Folstein, S.E., McHugh, P.R.: Mini-mental state: a practical method for grading the cognitive state of patients for the clinician. J. Psychiatr. Res. **12**(3), 189–198 (1975)
3. Fraser, K.C., Meltzer, J.A., Rudzicz, F.: Linguistic features differentiate Alzheimer's from controls in narrative speech. J. Alzheimer's Dis. **49**(2), 407–422 (2015)
4. Mickes, L., et al.: Progressive impairment on neuropsychological tasks in a longitudinal study of preclinical Alzheimer's disease. Neuropsychology **21**(6), 696–705 (2007)
5. Ankri, J.: Prévalence, incidence et facteurs de risque de la maladie d'Alzheimer. Gérontologie et société **32**(1), 129–141 (2009)
6. Chen, J., Zhu, J., Ye, J.: An attention-based hybrid network for automatic detection of Alzheimer's disease from narrative speech. In: Proceedings of Interspeech, pp. 4085–4089, January 2019
7. Ammar, R.B., Ayed, Y.B.: Speech processing for early Alzheimer disease diagnosis: machine learning based approach. In: 2018 IEEE/ACS 15th International Conference on Computer Systems and Applications (AICCSA), pp. 1–8. IEEE, October 2018
8. Ammar, R., Ayed, Y.: Evaluation of acoustic features for early diagnosis of Alzheimer disease. In: Abraham, A., Siarry, P., Ma, K., Kaklauskas, A. (eds.) ISDA 2019. AISC, vol. 1181, pp. 172–181. Springer, Cham (2021). https://doi.org/10.1007/978-3-030-49342-4_17
9. Becker, J.T., Boiler, F., Lopez, O.L., Saxton, J., McGonigle, K.L.: The natural history of Alzheimer's disease: description of study cohort and accuracy of diagnosis. Arch. Neurol. **51**(6), 585–594 (1994)
10. Orimaye, S.O., Wong, J.S.M., Golden, K.J.: Learning predictive linguistic features for Alzheimer's disease and related dementias using verbal utterances. In: Proceedings of the Workshop on Computational Linguistics and Clinical Psychology: From Linguistic Signal to Clinical Reality, pp. 78–87, June 2014
11. Jarrold, W., et al.: Depression and self-focused language in structured interviews with older men. Psychol. Rep. **109**(2), 686–700 (2011)
12. Al-Hameed, S., Benaissa, M., Christensen, H.: Detecting and predicting Alzheimer's disease severity in longitudinal acoustic data. In: Proceedings of the International Conference on Bioinformatics Research and Applications 2017, pp. 57–61, December 2017

13. Yancheva, M., Fraser, K.C., Rudzicz, F.: Using linguistic features longitudinally to predict clinical scores for Alzheimer's disease and related dementias. In: Proceedings of SLPAT 2015: 6th Workshop on Speech and Language Processing for Assistive Technologies, pp. 134–139, September 2015
14. Luz, S., Haider, F., de la Fuente, S., Fromm, D., MacWhinney, B.: Alzheimer's dementia recognition through spontaneous speech: the ADReSS challenge. arXiv preprint arXiv:2004.06833 (2020)
15. Eyben, F., Weninger, F., Gross, F., Schuller, B.: Recent developments in openSMILE, the Munich open-source multimedia feature extractor. In: Proceedings of the 21st ACM International Conference on Multimedia, pp. 835–838, October 2013
16. Eyben, F., et al.: The Geneva Minimalistic Acoustic Parameter Set (GeMAPS) for voice research and affective computing. IEEE Trans. Affect. Comput. **7**(2), 190–202 (2015)
17. Chen, J., Wang, Y., Wang, D.: A feature study for classification-based speech separation at low signal-to-noise ratios. IEEE/ACM Trans. Audio Speech Lang. Process. **22**(12), 1993–2002 (2014)
18. Ammar, R.B., Ayed, Y.B.: Language-related features for early detection of Alzheimer disease. In: Proceedings of the 24th International Conference on Knowledge-Based and Intelligent Information and Engineering Systems (KES2020), pp. 763–770, September 2020
19. MacWhinney, B.: The CHILDES project (2014). https://childes.psy.edu./manuals/chat.pdf
20. MacWhinney, B.: Tools for analyzing talk part 2: the CLAN program (2017). https://dali.talkbank.org/clan/
21. Ross, B.C.: Mutual information between discrete and continuous data sets. PLoS ONE **9**(2), e87357 (2014)

Towards a Digital Maturity Balance Model for Public Organizations

Mateja Nerima and Jolita Ralyté(✉)

Institute of Information Service Science, University of Geneva,
Battelle bat. A. Route de Drize 7, 1227 Carouge, Switzerland
jolita.ralyte@unige.ch

Abstract. The phenomenon of digital transformation is currently affecting almost all sectors of activity. Both private and public organizations face the challenge of the rapid growth of digitization. Measuring the digital maturity of an organization is a crucial step in the digitization process. The characteristics and challenges of digital transformation are specific to each sector of activity and even to each type of organization. Therefore, each of them may require a specific digital maturity model. In this work, we pay particular attention to the public sector and develop a digital maturity balance model for public organizations. The model is built on two axes: digital maturity and importance ratio, and aims to measure the balance between them. Each maturity dimension is assessed taking into account the importance ratio of this dimension in the organization.

Keywords: Digital transformation · Digital maturity model · Public organization

1 Introduction

The phenomenon of digital transformation is currently affecting almost all sectors of activity. Both private and public organizations face the challenge of the rapid growth of digitization. A study conducted by PWC in 2016 on the digitization of 300 Swiss companies [1] highlights that 76% of them had come to the same prediction: within the next five years, markets in all sectors are expected to change radically as a result of digitization. Public organizations are not an exception of this trend: in the same study, the public sector holds the second place in terms of digitization, just after telecommunication and media companies. According to Westerman et al. [2], digital transformation is a necessary process to achieve the Digital Mastery, which leads to better profits, production and performance.

Digital transformation is essential not only to improve existing business structures, but also to prevent them from becoming obsolete. The process consists in assessing the situation, i.e. the digital maturity of the organization, defining transformation goals and requirements, planning the transformation process and implementing it. In this paper we are particularly interested in the first step – the assessment of digital maturity. However, the aim of digital transformation being to reach a satisfactory degree of digital maturity, in accordance with the changes and challenges posed by the digitization of the sector

S. Cherfi et al. (Eds.): RCIS 2021, LNBIP 415, pp. 295–310, 2021.
https://doi.org/10.1007/978-3-030-75018-3_20

in which the organization operates [3], it should be noted that the same measures are useful not only at the beginning of the transformation process but also at its later steps to assess the effectiveness of the digitization strategy and to recalibrate it as soon as it is necessary [4].

To carry out maturity measurements, specific tools are necessary, they are usually called maturity models. The characteristics and challenges of digital transformation are specific to each activity sector and even each type of organization. Therefore, each of them may require a specific digital maturity model. In our work we pay a particular attention to the public sector, and argue that public organizations need dedicated tools. Our analysis of the state of the art in the domain reveals that there is no digital maturity model specifically dedicated to public enterprises and that the existing models are not well adapted or require adaptation. Therefore, the goal of this work is to develop a digital maturity model for public organizations. More precisely, to take into account the diversity of public organizations in terms of activity and size, but also to deviate from existing models, we aim to develop a *digital maturity balance model* in which each maturity dimension would be assessed taking into consideration the importance ratio of this dimension in the organization.

The paper is organized as follows: in the next section we introduce the background of our work and summarize the state of the art. In Sects. 3 and 4 we describe respectively the development and evaluation of our model and tool. Finally, in Sect. 5 we discuss the results and draw the conclusions.

2 Background and Related Literature

Digital maturity is defined as the degree of digitization achieved by an entity, through the adequate integration of its digitized processes into its structure [1]. There are several tools to measure the level of digitization, the most widespread being Digital Maturity Models (DMM) [5]. Such a model is most often represented in the form of a structured list of criteria with their assessment method [6], and can include improvement measures. The assessment of criteria is expected to disclose the current and/or desirable maturity level of the organization, while the improvement measures help to increase the level of maturity. According to [7], the typical purposes of use of maturity models are: descriptive, prescriptive and comparative. A prescriptive maturity model allows to assess the as-is state of digitization of an organization, while the prescriptive one provides guidelines for improving it: analyzing the situation, identifying priority sectors and their desirable maturity levels and setting up the digitization strategy. Comparative models are used for benchmarking between similar organizations or organizational units. A maturity model integrating the three aforementioned purposes into a single model would provide a holistic framework for improvement.

In practice, organizations use digital maturity models for determining and prioritizing their digital transformation objectives, and estimating the means and resources required to achieve them [7]. Several studies suggest that determining maturity level prior to the digitization reduces both the development time and effort in IT projects [8, 9].

Digital maturity models can have various scopes of application. They can be intended for relatively general use (e.g. COBIT 5 PAM [10] or Deloitte DMM [11]), or target a specific type of process, such as verification and validation (e.g. MB-V2M2 [12]), or data governance (Stanford DGMM [13]). They can also be dedicated to a particular geographical region (e.g. Wallonia DMM [14]) for considering its specificities. Digital maturity models for e-government (e.g. [15, 16]) are designed to measure the digitization of the official structures of a state and/or public services that emanate from them.

Valdés et al. [17] propose an e-government maturity model (E-gov-MM) which they also recommend to apply in public agencies, and illustrate the application in 30 public agencies in Chile. Eves and McGuire [18] argue that public sector needs a dedicated maturity model for assessing public digital services and propose a framework (MM for DS) for developing it. Indeed, public agencies are different from governments. They offer services to the public sector but are not part of the political structure of a state. Also, they are different from private companies mainly in their general lifespan, stability and less profit-oriented activities. There are digital maturity models specifically intended for private companies, as well as models dedicated to e-government. Therefore, we consider that the ones taking in account the specificities of public agencies should exist as well.

The offer of maturity models with multiple fields of application is very large. For our study it was necessary to select the most adequate ones. Our selection was driven by the state-of-the-art papers [19] and [6], as well as online search. We have selected twenty maturity models (see Table 1) on the basis of the type of measurement offered (digital, capability, etc.) and their field of application. Among them, ten are considered as general digital maturity models (General DMM), five are specifically dedicated to measuring maturity of e-governments and public organizations (E-Government MM), and the five remaining models allow to measure the maturity of specific aspects of digitization of the organization (Specific MM). In the perspective to build a digital maturity model dedicated to public organizations, we have examined their structure (criteria and assessment methods) and purpose (the main function and the targeted type of organization).

Table 1. Selected Maturity Models (MM)

General DMM		E-Government MM	Specific MM
COBIT 5 PAM [10]	Business-IT AMM [22]	Layne and Lee [15]	IGMM [26]
Deloitte DMM [11]	CMM for RDM [23]	PSPR [16]	CMMI V2 [27]
Wallonia DMM [14]	MB-V2M2 [12]	E-Gov-MM [17]	MDD MM [28]
IT CMF [20]	Stanford DGMM [13]	Gartner DGMM [25]	ECM3 [29]
IT Service CMM [21]	DAM MM [24]	MM for DS [18]	BPMM [30]

In the category *General DMM*, COBIT 5 PAM [10], Deloitte DMM [11] and Wallonia DMM [14] have as scope the whole organization. While COBIT 5 PAM and Deloitte DMM are advertised as international industry standard models, Wallonia DMM is a regional digital maturity self-diagnosis tool. The next two models, namely IT CMF [20] and IT Service CMM [21] deal with capability maturity measurement of all components of a company related to its IT functions or services. As its name indicates, Business-IT

AMM [22] is dedicated to measure the maturity of business and IT alignment of an organization. The scope of the last four models in this category is focused on a particular area. CMM for RDM) [23], developed at the School of Information Studies of the Syracuse University, supports the assessment of the maturity of key processes in research data management. MB-V2M2 [12] is a digital maturity model dedicated to asses and improve verification and validation processes in software development organizations. Stanford Data Governance Maturity Model – Stanford DGMM [13] focusses on both foundational and project aspects of data governance.

The most sited model in the *E-Government MM* category is by Layne and Lee [15]. An extension of this model, named Public Sector Process Rebuilding (PSPR) maturity model is proposed by Andersen and Erikson [16] to support digitization of the core governmental activities. In addition to the aforementioned E-gov-MM [17], Gartner's DGMM [24] also aims to help governmental organizations to improve the quality of digital government services for citizens. Finally, only the MM for DS [18] is fully dedicated to the public sector, but this model is still under development.

Finally, the last category, that we call *Specific MM*, includes models that are partially related to digital maturity of an organization. For example, IGMM [26] aims to evaluate the maturity of the information governance while ECN3 [29] assess the maturity of enterprise content management. CMMI V2 [27] is certainly the most known capability maturity model from which many of the aforementioned models took inspiration, especially by reusing its five-level structure. MDD MM [28] is dedicated to assess the maturity of software development teams using model-driven development approach. Finally, BPMM [30] is a well-known and a widely used model for measuring the maturity of enterprise business processes and for guiding their improvement.

Due to the lack of space, we cannot detail the structure and content of these models here. Note that they have been thoroughly analyzed to develop the first skeleton of our model as explained in the next section.

3 Development of the Model

To build our digital maturity balance model for public organizations we followed a four-stage exploratory approach as shown in Fig. 1.

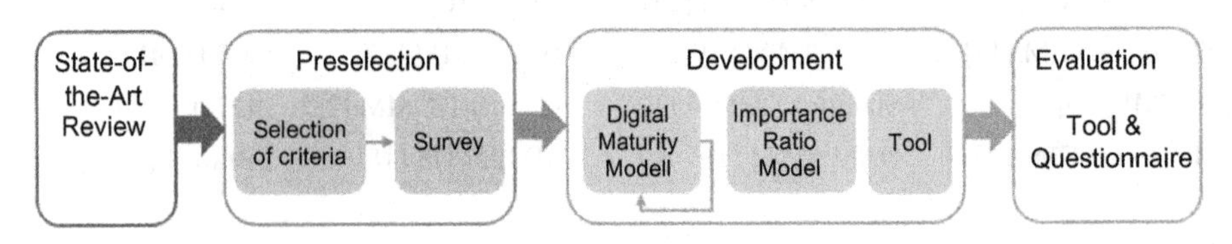

Fig. 1. Research method

Stage 1. State-of-the Art Review: We have selected and analyzed 20 maturity models with the aim to use them as a background for the development of our model.

Stage 2. Preselection: The analysis of the selected maturity models allowed us to define the first set of digital maturity criteria, which we evaluated via an online survey.

Stage 3. Development: This step consisted in building two core models, namely digital maturity and importance ratio, and developing an online self-assessment tool based on these models.

Stage 4. Evaluation: Participants, selected from public organizations, were invited to test the self-assessment tool and complete a questionnaire.

In the following we present the stages 2–4, the first one is already discussed in the previous section.

3.1 Preselection of the Measurement Criteria

The second stage of our work consisted in two steps: (1) the analysis of existing models with the aim to determine which categories and criteria are the most widespread and relevant, and (2) the gathering of opinions from organizations potentially interested in digital maturity measurement.

To build the initial list of criteria for measuring digital maturity, we analyzed and compared 20 maturity models (presented in Sect. 2). The majority of analyzed models are based on several evaluation criteria, often grouped into categories, or even sub-categories and distributed in several maturity levels, five in most cases. We first selected categories appearing in at least two models. Then, we analyzed, selected and sorted the criteria the most pertinent in these categories. Note that a criterion appearing in different model is not necessarily placed in the same category. Only the criteria that appeared several times in different models were retained. The result of the preselection is presented in Table 2.

The aim of our work being to develop a model as close as possible to the real needs of public organizations, we conducted a survey to collect the opinions of potential users. The survey took form of a questionnaire, which was sent to 50 public organizations in Switzerland (mostly Geneva area) raging from medium to big size (e.g. Geneva botanical garden, Geneva home care institution, Federal Railroad, Swiss Post). The questionnaire included a set of questions aimed at assessing the usage of digital maturity models in these companies, the need for a new maturity model specifically aimed at public organizations and the potential involvement of these organizations in the development of such model. The core of the questionnaire was formulated to evaluate the importance of the aforementioned criteria in assessing the digital maturity of a public organization. The respondents were also invited to complete the list of criteria if they considered that certain relevant criteria were missing.

Of the 50 requests to participate in the study, 15 responses were obtained within about two months (February–March 2020). The exceptional situation of spring 2020 can partly explain the relatively low number of participations.

To the questions *"Is your organization already using a digital maturity model? If yes, which one?"* 7 of the 15 organizations answered yes, most of them indicated using Cobit or Gartner DGMM (Cobit 28.57%, Gartner 42.86%, Other 28.57%). For the three following questions we have used a five-level Likert scale (from 1 – strongly disagree

Table 2. Preselected digital maturity categories and criteria

Category	Criteria
Data	Acquisition, Dissemination, Management, Quality, Representation
IT Governance	Service Delivery, Service Planning
Information	Findability, Metadata, Content, Reuse
Leadership	In Governance, Processes
Organization	Competency, Knowledge Management, Configuration Management
Performance	In Policy, Processes, Responsibility
Platform	Development, Registers
Process	Integration, Performance, Workflow
Project	Management, Monitoring, Processes
Skills	Hiring, Training, Roles Definition
Strategy	Finance, Innovation, Management, Vision
Support	Quality criteria, Practice guidelines, Standards, Metrics
System	Security, Usability
Technology	Applications, Analytics, Network, Security, Architecture, Change management

Table 3. Partial results from the survey

Question	Results
Do you agree that a maturity model specifically aimed at public enterprises is necessary?	3.93/5
Do you agree that it is necessity to involve public enterprises in the development process of such model?	4.4/5
Do you agree that it make sense to build such model based on existing models?	4.14/5

to 5 – strongly agree). The results of the survey given in Table 3 clearly indicate that there is a need to develop a new digital maturity model dedicated to public organizations. Besides, the development of the model in close collaboration with public organizations as potential users is desirable and could take inspiration from existing models.

With the next question "*Which criteria do you consider as important in assessing the digital maturity of a public enterprise?*" the participants had to select among the categories of criteria as listed in Table 2. Table 4 shows the number of selections per category in decreasing order. Five categories of criteria, namely *Data, IT Governance, Organization, Process* and *Strategy* stand out from the others by the number of votes obtained. They constitute the basis for the further development of our model.

Table 4. Rating of digital maturity criteria from the survey

Category	Selections	Category	Selections	Category	Selections
Data	14 (93.33%)	Information	11 (73.33%)	Project	8 (53.33%)
IT Governance	13 (86.67%)	Leadership	10 (66.67%)	Support	8 (53.33%)
Organization	13 (86.67%)	Skills	10 (66.67%)	System	8 (53.33%)
Process	13 (86.67%)	Performance	9 (60%)	Platform	7 (46.67%)
Strategy	13 (86.67%)	Technology	9 (60%)		

Finally, the question *"What relevant criteria do you think are missing?"* received seven proposals, namely *Digital Sobriety, Culture, Digital Responsibility, Ergonomics, Digital Maturity of Management, Business Continuity Plan* and *Strategic Plan*, which are considered in the next phase of the development.

3.2 Development of the Digital Maturity Balance Model and Tool

Public organizations range from very small (e.g. Tourist information office) to very large (e.g. University), and operate in various public service domains (e.g. transportation, health, education, culture). Therefore, the digital maturity would not necessarily make the same sense from one organization to another. For example, an organization with very few employees but a lot of data to manage would have better time to focus on the digital transformation of the data dimension (management, storage, security, etc.), rather than the organizational dimension (human resources, infrastructure, etc.). For this reason, we have decided to focus on balancing digital maturity instead of its direct assessment. We are building a digital maturity balance model in which each maturity dimension is assessed taking into consideration the importance ratio of this dimension in the organization. Therefore, building such model consists in (1) defining the method to assess digital maturity, (2) defining the method to measure the importance ratio of each digital maturity dimension, and (3) developing a self-assessment tool combining the both methods.

Building the Digital Maturity Model. This step required several iterations. To build the first version of the model we started with the five dimensions (i.e. *Data, IT Governance, Strategy, Organization* and *Process*) and their criteria selected in the previous stage. Then, we integrated the criteria suggested by the respondents of the survey. The *Digital Sobriety* and *Digital Responsibility* criteria have been placed in the *Strategy* dimension as both can fit into an overall improvement plan for the organization's IT operations and activities. The criterion *Culture* has been classified under *Organization* meaning *Organizational Culture*. *Ergonomics* was assigned to the *IT Governance* dimension because of its direct link with IT systems. The *Digital Maturity of Management* has been renamed to *Leadership* and placed in the *Organization* dimension. The *Strategic Plan* criterion has been renamed to *Strategic Alignment* to insist on the difference with the *Strategy* dimension, and then placed in the *IT Governance* dimension because it represents a way of measuring whether IT systems are aligned with the various strategic plans. The *Business Continuity Plan* has been split into *Strategic Alignment* (already placed) and *Business Agility* criteria, which has been added to the *Process* dimension as it allows to assess the flexibility and adaptability of processes to the changes in the organization. During the third iteration, we refined the five maturity dimensions by extending them with additional criteria extracted from the literature review and from additional sources (e.g. [31]). For example, the *Mobility, Safety* and *Recycling* criteria have been added to the *Data* dimension. *IT Governance* dimension has been complemented by several criteria: *Enterprise Architecture, Project Management, Risk Management, Security System, Resource Management, Performance, Value Creation* and *Integration* criteria. The final collection of criteria is shown in Table 5.

Table 5. Selected maturity dimensions and criteria

Data	IT Governance	Strategy	Organization	Process
Acquisition	Service Delivery	Digital	Skills	Integration
Dissemination	Service Planning	Finance	Knowledge Mgt.	Performance
Management	Ergonomics	Innovation	Config. Mgt.	Workflow
Quality	Strategic	Management	Culture	Agility
Representation	Alignment	Vision	Leadership	Interoperability
Mobility	Architecture	Digital Sobriety	Training	Quality
Security	Project Mgt.	Digital Resp.	Task Management	Security
Archiving	Risk Management	Portfolio	Design	Communication
Access	Security System	Stakeholder Mgt.	Infrastructure	Online Presence
Reuse	Resource Mgt.	Policy	Change Mgt.	Client Operations
	Performance		Resource Mgt.	
	Value Creation		Communication	
	Integration			

The next step was to complete the measurement system with metrics and their values. One or more metrics have been defined for each criterion; they are listed in Table 6. The meaning of the values is quite obvious. For example, *Data Acquisition Means* has values *{None, Computer-aided, Autonomous}*, where *Computer-aided* indicates the usage of a generic digital tool requiring human interaction, while *Autonomous* means that data collection is totally or partially automated. The values *Document* and *Protocol,* used for several metrics, represent a documentation in terms of guidelines, rules, models, recommendations, etc. *Specific tool* indicates the usage of a domain-specific tool. Some criteria have two or more metrics. For example, *Digital Strategy* has two metrics*: Development {None, Protocol, Computer-aided, Specific tool}* and *Update {None, Fixed, Agile}*, the first measuring the support for the strategy development while the second indicates how the update of the strategy is held. Here, the value *Fixed* means that the company has a fixed plan, while *Agile* means that the evolution of the strategy depends on the situation and needs.

Table 6. The digital maturity measurement system

Criterion	Metric	Values
Data Dimension		
Acquisition	Means	None, Computer-aided, Autonomous
Dissemination	Means	None, Computer-aided, Autonomous
Management	Protocol	None, Document, Computer-aided, Specific tool
Quality	Control	None, Computer-aided, Autonomous
Representation	Model	None, Document, Computer-aided, Specific tool
Mobility	Protocol	None, Document, Computer-aided, Specific tool
Security	System	None, Protocol, Computer-aided, Autonomous
Archiving	System	None, Computer-aided, Autonomous
Access Management	System	None, Computer-aided, Advanced
Reuse	System	None, Computer-aided, Autonomous
IT Governance Dimension		
Service Delivery	Procedure	None, On request, Systematic
Service Planning	Protocol	None, Document, Computer-aided, Specific tool
Ergonomics	Control	None, Fixed, Agile
Strategic Alignment	Level	None, Low, Medium, High
	Update	None, On request, Systematic
Enterprise Architecture	Support	None, Document, Computer-aided, Specific tool
	Method	None, Simple, Advanced
	Update	None, Fixed, Agile
Project Management	Support	None, Document, Computer-aided, Specific tool
Risk Management	Protocol	None, Document, Computer-aided, Specific tool
Security Management	System	None, Physical, Computer-aided, Specific tool
Resource Management	System	None, Document, Computer-aided, Specific tool
Performance Measurement	System	None, Physical, Computer-aided, Autonomous
Value Creation	Support	None, Document, Computer-aided, Specific tool
Strategy Dimension		
Digital	Development	None, Protocol, Computer-aided, Specific tool
	Update	None, Fixed, Agile
Finance	Development	None, Protocol, Computer-aided, Specific tool
	Update	None, Fixed, Agile
Innovation	Development	None, Protocol, Computer-aided, Specific tool
	Update	None, Fixed, Agile
Management	Development	None, Protocol, Computer-aided, Specific tool
	Update	None, Fixed, Agile
Vision	Alignment	None, Partial, Full
	Diffusion	None, Physical, Computer-aided, Specific tool
Digital Sobriety	Integration	None, Partial, Full
Digital Responsibility	Update	None, Fixed, Agile
	Diffusion	None, Physical, Computer-aided, Specific tool
Portfolio (project)	Support	None, Document, Computer-aided, Specific tool
Stakeholder Mgt.	Protocol	None, Outline, Detailed
	System	None, Document, Computer-aided, Specific tool

(*continued*)

Table 6. *(continued)*

Criterion	Metric	Values
Policy	System	None, Document, Computer-aided, Specific tool
	Update	None, Fixed, Agile
Organization Dimension		
Skills	Offering	None, Document, Computer-aided, Specific tool
Knowledge Management	System	None, Document, Computer-aided, Specific tool
Configuration Management	System	None, Document, Computer-aided, Specific tool
Culture	Diffusion	None, Document, Computer-aided, Specific tool
Leadership	Diffusion	None, Document, Computer-aided, Specific tool
	Update	None, Fixed, Agile
Training	Form	None, Document, Coaching, E-learning
	Update	None, Fixed, Agile
Task Management	System	None, Document, Computer-aided, Specific tool
Design	Homogeneity	None, Heterogenous, Homogenous
	Diffusion	None, Document, Computer-aided, Specific tool
Infrastructure	Form	None, Document, Computer-aided, Specific tool
	Update	None, Fixed, Agile
Change Management	Means	None, Document, Computer-aided, Specific tool
	Update	None, Fixed, Agile
Resource Management	Means	None, Document, Computer-aided, Specific tool
	Update	None, Fixed, Agile
Communication internal	System	None, Physical, Computer-aided, Specific tool
Process Dimension		
Integration	Means	None, Protocol, Computer-aided, Specific tool
Performance Assessment	Means	None, Protocol, Computer-aided, Specific tool
Workflow Management	Means	None, Protocol, Computer-aided, Specific tool
Agility	Level	None, Weak, Medium High
Interoperability	Level	None, Weak, Medium, Full
	Means	None, Protocol, Computer-aided, Specific tool
Quality Assessment	System	None, Protocol, Computer-aided, Autonomous
Security Management	System	None, Protocol, Computer-aided, Autonomous
Communication external	System	Physical, Computer-aided, Specific tools
Online Presence	Type	None, Informative, Interactive
Client Operations	Form	Physical, Computer-aided, Specific tools

Each value was allocated a number of points depending on its importance. For example, for *Data Acquisition Means* the values are: None = 0, Computer-aided = 1, Autonomous = 2. As the total number of points varies from one dimension to another, we have adjusted the average value of each dimension on 10 points. So, the average value per digital maturity dimension d_i can be calculated as:

$$d_i = \frac{\left(\sum_{j=1}^{n} m_j * p_j\right)}{n} * 10$$

Here, n is the number of metrics m defined in the dimension d_i, p_j is the value (the number of points) allocated to the metric m_j.

Building the Importance Ratio Model. To assess the importance ratio of digital maturity dimensions in the organization we define a set of attributes (see Table 7) that have impact on one or several digital maturity dimensions. For example, the ratio of the *Data* dimension increases with the size of the organization, the volume and length of retention of the data managed and the size of the unit dedicated to data management including the dedicated budget. Whether or not IT is the core activity of the organization also has an influence on the *Data* dimension. Therefore, the attributes allowing to measure the ratio of *Data* dimension in the organization are: *Organization size* (measured in terms of the number of employees), *Data volume, Duration of date storage, IT as core activity*, and *Data management unit* (measured in terms of importance).

The *IT governance* dimension takes on more weight if the organization is large, its core activity is IT related, most of the activities are digitalized, the main information services are complex, there is a department dedicated to the governance of information systems or a significant portion of finances is dedicated to it. The dependence on other organizational structures (e.g. partners, units, subsidiaries) also has impact on *IT governance*. Therefore, the attributes to measure the ratio of IT governance are: *Organization size, IT as core activity, Digitalized activity, Complexity of services, Dependence on other structures.*

Naturally, the ratio of the *Organization* dimension depends on the size of the organization and on the dependence on other organizational structures. Additional attribute is the *Number of departments.*

The importance of the *Strategy* dimension is also related to the size of the organization in terms of people and departments, and to the dependence on other organizational structures. Other parameters are the existence of departments dedicated to innovation and strategy, and therefore the part of the budget invested in developing the organization's strategy.

Finally, the weight of the *Process* dimension depends on the variety of the organization's activities and the relationship it has with its customers and collaborators in terms of products and services. The corresponding attributes are: *Main offer, Diversity of activities, Contact with public.* All attributes, their values and related dimensions are listed in Table 7. Please note, that the collection of these attributes is still under development; more iterations are necessary. However, the current set allow us to test the general idea of our approach.

Table 7. Attributes to measure the importance ratio of digital dimensions

Attribute	Values	Related dimensions
Organization size	1–2000 + employees	Data, IT Governance, Strategy, Organization
IT as core activity	No, Yes	Data, IT Governance
Main offer	Only administration, Partly administration, Balanced, Partly product/service, Only product/service	Process
Contact with public	No, Yes	Process
Duration of data storage	Short, Medium, Long	Data
Data volume	Small, Medium, Big, Very big	Data
Digitalized activity	0%–100%	IT Governance
Complexity of services	Basic, Simple, Complex	IT Governance
Dependence on other structures	Attached, Partly attached, Independent	IT Governance, Strategy, Organization
Number of departments	1–20+	Strategy, Organization
Innovation unit	None, Team, Service, Department	Strategy
Diversity of activities	Small, Medium, Large	Process
Data management unit	None, Team, Service, Department	Data
IT Governance unit	None, Team, Service, Department	IT Governance
Strategy unit	None, Team, Service, Department	Strategy
Process management	None, Team, Service, Department	Process
Financial breakdown	0–20, 2–40, 41–60, 61–80, 81–100%	All dimensions

Concerning the weighting of attributes, each value of an attribute was allocated a number of points. For example, for *Data volume* the values are: Small = 0, Medium = 1, Big = 2, Very big = 3.

Since all dimensions do not have the same number of attributes (Data and Strategy have 6 attributes, IT Governance has 7, Organization and Process have 5) it is necessary to adjust them, on the average number, which is 6. Therefore, the average ratio value per digital maturity dimension d_i can be calculated as:

$$d_i = \frac{\left(\sum_{j=1}^{n} a_j * p_j\right)}{n} * 6$$

Here, n is the number of attributes a defined for the dimension d_i, p_j is the value (the number of points) allocated to the metric a_j.

Self-assessment Tool. To make our model operational we developed a self-assessment tool in the form of an online questionnaire. The questions allow to assess the digital maturity criteria and the digital ratio attributes. Figure 2 illustrates the final score obtained by one of the organizations participating in the validation.

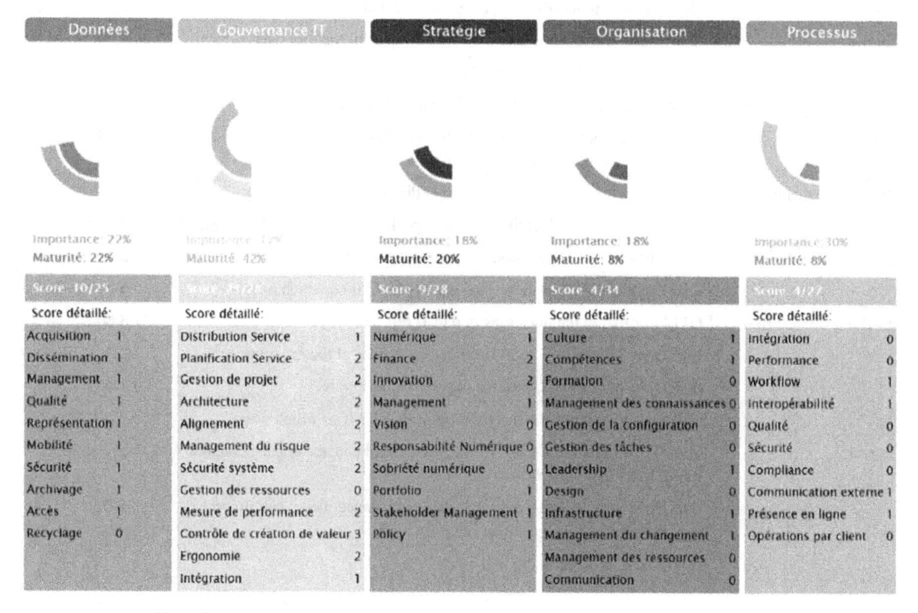

Fig. 2. Example of the result obtained with a self-assessment tool

4 Evaluation

To evaluate our model and tool we sent out invitations to the 15 organizations that participated in the first survey, 7 of them accepted to participate again. Participants received the access to the online self-assessment tool and were invited to test it. After the test they had to fill out an online questionnaire. The questionnaire was divided in three parts: *Tool*, *Model* and *General*. The *Tool* section included questions about the self-assessment tool: its utility, applicability, facility of use and clarity of results. The *Model* part aimed to evaluate the digital maturity balance model as a whole and each of its parts (part I – digital maturity, part II – importance ratio of digital dimensions) individually. It included questions on the completeness and pertinence of criteria and attributes used in this model. Finally, the *General* part included questions on the applicability of the model and the tool, and invited the respondents to provide additional comments and suggestions. A five-level Likert scale (from 1 – strongly disagree to 5 – strongly agree) have been used for most of the questions. Questions 10 and 14 required a Yes or No answer and provided space for additional comments. Table 8 reports on the received results.

Table 8. Results of the evaluation

Group	Question	Result
Tool	Q1 Do you agree that such self-assessment tool is relevant to measure digital maturity of public organization?	3.57
	Q2 Is the way to use the self-assessment tool clear?	3.57
	Q3 Are the descriptions provided for each part of the tool clear?	4.00
	Q4 Are the questions of the tool clear?	3.33
	Q5 Is the display of results suitable and understandable?	4.33
Model	Q6 Is the model for measuring the balance between the importance of each dimension and its maturity score suitable for public enterprises?	3.84
Part I digital maturity	Q7 Overall, are the questions in part I (digital maturity) relevant?	3.86
	Q8 Do the results reflect the level of digital maturity of the organization?	3.71
	Q9 Is the number of questions in part I appropriate?	2.14
	Q10 Are there any questions missing in part I? If so which ones?	5 no, 2 yes
Part II importance ratio	Q11 Overall, are the questions in part II relevant?	3.86
	Q12 Does the results of part II reflect the profile of the organization?	2.5
	Q13 Is the number of questions in part II appropriate?	1.86
	Q14 Are there any questions missing in Part II? If so which ones?	5 no, 2 yes
General	Q15 Do you think that the self-assessment tool can accompany concrete and useful steps in an organization?	3.71
	Q16 Do you think that the digital maturity balance model can support concrete and useful steps in an organization?	4.29
	Q17 Please, provide additional comments	

The question Q10 received comments from 2 respondents. One of them indicated the difficulty of understanding some questions and suggested adding more explicit definitions. The other suggested adding questions on financing capacities, including the concepts of investment, exploitation and external funds. Concerning the comments provided to the question Q14, one stressed that it was difficult to get the business reality glued to the current questions, while the other suggested adding the question *Who defines the digital strategy (ISD, CEO, a board of directors or other)?*

Two respondents left additional comments (Q17) mainly stressing on the need to clarify a few terms. One of them regretted that the presentation of the results does allow to visualize the level of maturity to be reached. Both encouraged the continuation of the study.

To conclude, the data and recommendations gathered during this evaluation step are particularly important for several reasons as they (1) come from people working in public organizations, targets of our work, (2) testify to the relevance of a such model, and (3) provide valuable material to further elaborate our model and tool.

5 Conclusion

In this paper we present our exploratory development of a digital maturity balance model for public organizations. The model is built on two axes: (1) digital maturity and

(2) importance ratio, and aims to measure the balance between them. To evaluate digital maturity, we build a model including a set of criteria regrouped into five digital maturity dimensions: Data, IT Governance, Strategy, Organization and Process. The model to assess the importance ratio of these dimensions includes a set of attributes describing different organizational aspects related to digitization. The development of both models is based on a review of the related literature and a survey of potential users. While the first model already undergoes several iterations the second only had one and needs further exploration. The evaluation of our digital maturity balance model and its self-assessment tool let us draw the following conclusions and define the road map for future work:

- The use of the model and of the self-assessment tool was found to be useful and relevant, but the development of both still needs additional iterations.
- The terminology used in the self-assessment tool needs to be clarified, and definitions should be provided for the main concepts.
- The digital maturity model (part I of the tool) is reflecting rather well the digital maturity of an organization. The next iteration should focus on refining the criteria and their values.
- The importance ratio model (part II of the tool), even if it is considered relevant, does not yet fully correspond to the reality of a public organization. Further investigation, development and evaluation is needed.

References

1. Greif, H., Küuhnis, N., Warnking, P.: Digital transformation: how mature are Swiss SMEs? A joint publication from PwC Switzerland, Google Switzerland GmbH and digitalswitzerland (2016). https://www.pwc.ch/en/publications/2016/pwc_digital_transform_how_mature_are_swiss_smes_survey_16_en.pdf
2. Westerman, G., Bonnet, D., Mcafee, A.: Leading Digital – Turning Technology into Business Transformation. Harvard Business Review Press, Boston (2014)
3. Kane, G.C., Palmer, D., Phillips, A.N., Kiron, D., Buckley, N.: Achieving Digital Maturity. Deloitte University Press, New York (2017)
4. Matt, C., Hess, T., Benlian, A.: Digital transformation strategies. Bus. Inf. Syst. Eng. **57**, 339–343 (2015)
5. Kohlegger, M., Maier, R., Thalmann, S.: Understanding maturity models results of a structured content analysis. In: Proceedings of the 9th International Conference on Knowledge Management (I-KNOW 2009), Graz, Austria, pp. 51–61 (2009)
6. Wendler, R.: The maturity of maturity model research: a systematic mapping study. Inf. Softw. Technol. **54**(12), 1317–1339 (2012)
7. Pöoppelbuß, J., Röglinger, M.: What makes a useful maturity model? A framework of general design principles for maturity models and its demonstration in business process management. In: Proceedings of ECIS 2011, 28. AIS eLibrary (2011). https://aisel.aisnet.org/ecis2011/28/
8. Clark, B.K.: The effects of software process maturity on software development effort. Ph.D. thesis, University of Southern California (1997)
9. Krishnan, M.S., Slaighter, S.: Effects of process maturity on quality, cycle time, and effort in software product development. Manag. Sci. **46**(4), 451–466 (2000). Catonsville, USA

10. COBIT 5 Supplementary Guide for the COBIT 5 Process Assessment Model (PAM). (2012). http://campus.itpreneurs.com/itpreneurs/LPEngine/Cobit/Foundation/English/GOV1230E/Unique%20Elements/COBIT%205%20Process%20Assessment%20Model.pdf
11. Data Governance Maturity Model. Office of Management and Enterprise Services (2011). https://www2.deloitte.com/content/dam/Deloitte/global/Documents/Technology-Media-Telecommunications/deloitte-digital-maturity-model.pdf
12. Jacobs, J.C., Trienekens, J.J.M.: Towards a metrics based verification and validation maturity model. In: Proceedings of STEP 2002. IEEE Xplore (2002)
13. Firican, G.: Data governance maturity models - Stanford. Lights on Data (2018). https://www.lightsondata.com/data-governance-maturity-models-stanford/, deloitte-digital-maturity-model.pdf
14. Outils de diagnostic de maturité numérique Digital Wallonia. https://www.digitalwallonia.be/fr/publications/diagnostic
15. Layne, K., Lee, J.: Developing fully functional E-government: a four stage model. Gov. Inf. Q. **18**(2), 122–136 (2001)
16. Andersen, K.V., Henriksen, H.Z.: E-government maturity models: extension of the Layne and Lee model. Gov. Inf. Q. **23**(2), 236–248 (2006)
17. Valdés, G., Solar, M., Astudillo, H., Iribarren, M., Concha, G., Visconti, M.: Conception, development and implementation of an e-Government maturity model in public agencies. Gov. Inf. Q. **28**(2), 176–187 (2011)
18. Eaves, D., McGuire, B.: Part 2: Proposing A Maturity Model for Digital Services (2018). https://medium.com/digitalhks/part-2-proposing-a-maturity-model-for-digital-services-9b1d429699e7
19. Proença, D., Borbinha, J.: Maturity models for information systems - a state of the art. Proc. Comput. Sci. **100**, 1042–1049 (2016)
20. The IT Capability Maturity Framework. One single and holistic IT Framework. https://ivi.ie/it-capability-maturity-framework/
21. Clerc, V., Niessink, F.: IT Service CMM, A Pocket Guide. Van Haren Publishing, 's-Hertogenbosch (2004)
22. Luftman, J.N.: Assessing business-IT alignment maturity. Commun. Assoc. Inf. Syst. **4**(14) (2000)
23. Qin, J., Crowston, K., Kirkland, A.: A capability maturity model for research data management, 82 p. School of Information Studies, Syracuse University, Syracuse, NY (2014)
24. What is the DAM Maturity Model? http://dammaturitymodel.org
25. 5 Levels of Digital Government Maturity. Smarter With Gartner (2017). https://www.gartner.com/smarterwithgartner/5-levels-of-digital-government-maturity/
26. ARMA International Information Governance Maturity Model. Library of Virginia archives. https://www.lva.virginia.gov/agencies/records/psrc/documents/Principles.pdf
27. CMMI V2.0. https://cmmiinstitute.com/cmmi
28. Rios, E., Bozheva, T., Bediaga, A., Guilloreau, N.: MDD maturity model: a roadmap for introducing model-driven development. In: Rensink, A., Warmer, J. (eds.) ECMDA-FA 2006. LNCS, vol. 4066, pp. 78–89. Springer, Heidelberg (2006). https://doi.org/10.1007/11787044_7
29. Pelz-Sharpe, A., Durga, A., Smigiel, D., Hartman, E., Byrne, T.: ECM3 Maturity Model. Version 1.0. Wipro (2009). https://ecmmaturity.files.wordpress.com/2009/02/ec3m-v01_0.pdf
30. Business Process Maturity Model Specification Version 1.0 (2008). https://www.omg.org/spec/BPMM/About-BPMM/
31. Board Briefing on IT Governance, 2nd edn. IT Governance Institute (2003). https://www.oecd.org/site/ictworkshops/year/2006/37599342.pdf

User-Centred Approaches

CCOnto: The Character Computing Ontology

Alia El Bolock[1,2(✉)], Nada Elaraby[1], Cornelia Herbert[2], and Slim Abdennadher[1]

[1] German University in Cairo, Cairo, Egypt
{alia.elbolock,nada.elaraby,slim.abdennadher}@guc.edu.eg
[2] Ulm University, Ulm, Germany
cornelia.herbert@uni-ulm.de

Abstract. Especially in light of the COVID-19 pandemic which is influencing human behavior, it is clear that there is a rising need for joining psychology and computer science to provide technology interventions for people suffering from negative feelings and behavior change. Behavior is driven by an individual's character and the situation they are in, according to Character Computing and the Character-Behavior-Situation (CBS) triad. Accordingly, we developed the first full ontology modeling the CBS triad with the aim of providing domain experts with an intelligent interface for modeling, testing, and unifying hypotheses on the interactions between character, behavior, and situation. The ontology consists of a core module modeling character-based interactions and use-case and domain-specific modules. It was developed by computer scientists and psychology domain experts following an iterative process. The main contributions of this paper include updating the earlier prototypical version of the ontology-based on feedback from psychology experts and existing literature, adding more tools to it for enabling domain expert interaction, and providing the final ontology. Steps taken towards evaluating and validating the ontology are outlined.

Keywords: Character Computing · Behavior · Personality · Psychology · Human-based computing

1 Introduction

Behavior and well-being have always been a major domain of interest. The current COVID-19 pandemic has, however, drastically increased the awareness of well-being and mental health. The demand for technology solutions during the pandemic is higher than ever before. It is the sole means for providing education, basic communication, and guidance for people suffering from negative feelings and behavior change. This calls for seamless integration between input from psychologists and computer scientists for developing technology solutions that help people understand and change their behavior. As proposed by Character

S. Cherfi et al. (Eds.): RCIS 2021, LNBIP 415, pp. 313–329, 2021.
https://doi.org/10.1007/978-3-030-75018-3_21

Computing [6], the behavior is driven by many factors defining an individual, denoted character. An individual's character consists of trait markers (personality, socio-demographics, and culture) and state markers (affect, mood, health, well-being, and cognition). The character interacts with the specific situation an individual is in, and together they influence behavior, denoted the Character-Behavior-Situation (CBS) triad [12,21,22]. Thus, sticking to the COVID-19 pandemic, the CBS triad would be used to represent the change in psychological well-being (behavior) of two different individuals during the lockdown (situation) given their different personalities, e.g., extroverted and introverted, their culture, and health status (character). Character Computing aims to develop applications that harness the relations within the CBS for detecting character states and traits and resulting behaviors and affecting them. A huge amount of inter-disciplinary knowledge about all factors representing an individual's character, behavior, and the situation is needed to achieve said goal. Accordingly, applying an ontology-based approach to modeling the CBS triad would be of great benefit by providing a unification of the shared terminology, a shared formal definitions of the concepts and their relations, and enabling advanced reasoning rule-based inference. The rules for the interaction between the three components of the CBS triad need to be input based on psychology theories that constantly need to be adapted based on observations, calling for the ease of involvement of psychology domain experts. Many ontologies related to behavior and its affecting factors already exist, e.g., [1,5,31,35]. However, since no single ontology contains all CBS concepts, a consolidation and subsequent extension of the existing ontologies is required.

In this paper, we present CCOnto, the first integrated ontology modeling the CBS triad of the inter-disciplinary domain of Character Computing (for an earlier prototypical version, see [15]). The ontology models human character and its interaction with behavior and situation to provide domain experts with an intelligent interface for modeling, testing, and unifying rule-based hypotheses on the interaction between the three. The presented ontology is part of a joint project to develop an inter-disciplinary and inter-cultural Character Computing platform developed by and for computer scientists and psychologists. The platform serves the joint development of psychologically-driven computer applications to detect and change situation-based behavior affected by character traits and states and vice versa. The ontology prototype presented in [15] underwent rigorous edits based on psychology domain experts' feedback and existing literature to finally reach the current version of the ontology. The main contributions of this work include presenting the final version of CCOnto with a focus on its validation and evaluation. We show how the ontology is used in an application for evaluating sleep and healthy eating habits during the novel Coronavirus pandemic based on user-input data. Not only does CCOnto provide a formal foundation for understanding and sharing knowledge about human character and its interactions, but it also serves as a knowledge base of unified, reusable data about character and its effect on behavior in a given situation. Accordingly, it can be leveraged in building psychologically-driven adaptive or interactive systems within the framework of Character Computing (see [13]).

The remainder of this paper is organized as follows: Sect. 2 introduces the CBS triad, gives an overview of existing related ontologies, and presents the running example. In Sect. 3, we present the approach used for developing CCOnto. The ontology implementation details are described in Sect. 4 and the ontology validation and evaluation methods are presented in Sect. 5.2. The conclusions and future work are presented in Sect. 6.

2 Preliminaries

2.1 The CBS Triad

Character Computing is an interdisciplinary branch of research that deals with designing systems and interfaces that can observe, sense, predict, adapt to, affect, understand, or simulate how different persons behave in specific situations based on their character. Its goal is to provide a holistic psychologically-driven model of the interaction between human character and behavior in a specific situation. Character is defined as all trait and state markers distinguishing an individual. Traits are the more stable attributes that can hardly be changed over a short period of time, e.g., personality, affect, socio-demographics, and general health. States are more variable attributes and can change from a short period of time to another, e.g., emotions, well-being, health, cognitive state. Most of the states have trait counterparts, e.g., affect (trait) and emotions (state) or general and current health. Character components are not mutually exclusive and help shape and change each other. Each of the character states and traits has many models representing them and their interaction with other components. For the purposes of this work, we represent personality through the Five Factor Model (FFM) [8] and emotions based on the Two-Factor Theory [36], and through affective processes [20]. We support continuous (valence and arousal) [33] and discrete emotions (Eckman's six basic emotions) [11]. We represent one of the six well-being dimensions, namely, physical well-being [23]. The CBS triad is a model representing the interaction between the three factors. At any given time, any two of the triad edges can be used to explain the third. This highlights that character not only determines who we are but how we are, i.e., how we behave. Accordingly, one can only achieve a Character Computing model by modeling the interactions of the CBS triad and its component. This is why the CBS triad needs to be at the center of the developed ontology.

2.2 Related Work

Several approaches have been proposed for using ontologies when representing and modeling the complex interactions between human behavior, personality, and emotions. For example, EmOCA, an emotion ontology, can be used to reason about philia and phobia based on emotion expression in a context-aware manner [4]. EmotionsOnto is another emotions ontology for developing affective applications and detecting emotions [26]. The Emotions ontology (EMO) presented in [19,20] represents emotions and all related affective phenomena, and it should enable self-reporting or articulation of emotional states and responses. In [17], an ontology of psychological user profiles (mainly personality traits and facets) is presented. A web application for detecting personality using linguistic feature analysis based on ontologies of personality and other techniques are presented in [37]. LifeOn is an "ubiquitous lifelong learner model ontology" (with a highlight on learner personality) for adaptive learning systems [32]. An ontology for insider threat risk detection and mitigation through individual (personality, affect, ideology, and other similar attributes) and organizational socio-technical factors is presented in [18]. The HeLiS ontology [28,39] models the concepts representing the food and physical activity domains. Through modeling detailed food properties and physical activity properties, HeLiS supported the construction of intelligent interfaces for domain experts to support a healthy lifestyle and was extended to representing behavior change in this aspect [9]. Another ontology for representing the psychological barriers preventing behavior change and thus enabling overcoming them is presented in [2]. All the discussed ontologies cover some of the CBS components. However, to fully represent the CBS triad and all its interactions, we need an ontology that subsumes all relevant existing ontologies and builds on them. The main relevance of CCOnto with respect to the existing related work lies in the fact that it is the first ontology modeling the domain of Character Computing, simultaneously supporting different models of character traits and states (e.g., personality and affect).

2.3 Running Example

As a motivating example, we consider Sam, a university student during the first COVID-19 lockdown. Sam has to continue her studies online and should be on lockdown. The course instructor Jack is following up on Sam's progress via an app that is tracking her daily behavior routine. The app should help Jack determine which students to take care of as they are probably falling behind and which to challenge as they are thriving and keeping up with their studies. For example, part of the app focuses on the behavior prior to sleep. We know that, unlike her regular self before the lockdown, Sam has picked up a regular exercise routine, is sleeping regularly, and that, among other traits, she is an introvert. The app would notify Jack that given Sam's behavior change, personality traits, and current living situation, she is less anxious than her regular self as she usually suffers from trait anxiety. Thus, Sam does not require special help to follow her studies but can rather be motivated to do more and thrive, given the situation.

3 CCOnto at a Glance

The development of an ontology like CCOnto requires having an interdisciplinary view, where psychologists are included as domain experts throughout all development phases. The process of developing CCOnto was based on the METHONTOLOGY methodology [16] and following the recent best practice recommendations presented in [25].

3.1 CCOnto Architecture

The recommended best practice ontology development features include modularity, ontology reuse, continuous collaboration, and agile development based on iterative rapid prototyping. During the development of CCOnto, it has become clear that the domain in question is too big to be represented as a single ontology. That is, the ontology was **modularized** into three smaller ontologies, as shown in Fig. 1. The CCOnto-Core ontology represents the generic core concepts of the CBS triad (T-Box and some A-Box individuals included in reused ontologies). The CCOnto-Domain ontologies extend CCOnto-Core with specific knowledge for different domains of interests, e.g., focusing on certain character traits, states, or behavior aspects. CCOnto-Domain ontologies include the rules for the interactions within the specific domain (extended T-Box + SWRL Rules). Finally, different app-specific ontology modules can be added depending on the use-case, as instances of CCOnto-App. CCOnto-App ontologies extend CCOnto-Domain with application-specific information to enable utilizing the ontology as a backbone of the application (extended T-Box + SWRL + A-Box). In this paper, we focus on the details of CCOnto-Core.[1] To illustrate the use of CCOnto and its full potential, we also discuss one full version of CCOnto by including a specific instance of CCOnto-Domain and CCOnto-App. The included focus domain is that of physical well-being (CCOnto-PhW), which is mainly represented through the HeLiS ontology [28]. We extend the ontology further with one app-specific module (CCOnto-Sleep) for the CCleep app by adding parts of the HDO ontology [27]. Throughout this paper, we will focus on the full version of CCOnto consisting of the three modules.[2]

Existing ontologies available in the Open Biological and Biomedical Ontology (OBO) Foundry [38] and other ontology repositories are **reused** to increase sharability and achieve an ontology network.

The METHONDOLOGY ontology development methodology is chosen as it is an **agile** ontology engineering process enabling iterative ontology development and evaluation of the ontology milestones by both knowledge engineers and domain experts. By using Protégé for ontology authoring, we enable **rapid prototyping** of the different ontology phases and subsequent updates and changes based on evaluation and validation outcomes, as well as, the feedback and need of the domain experts. For instance, there are major changes from the initial ontology prototype [15], including removing the personality facets and the enumerated person types. These changes were done, as it became apparent that not

[1] https://github.com/CharacterComputingResearch/CCOnto/blob/main/CCOnto.owl.

[2] https://github.com/CharacterComputingResearch/CCOnto/blob/main/CCOnto-Full-PhW-Sleep.owl.

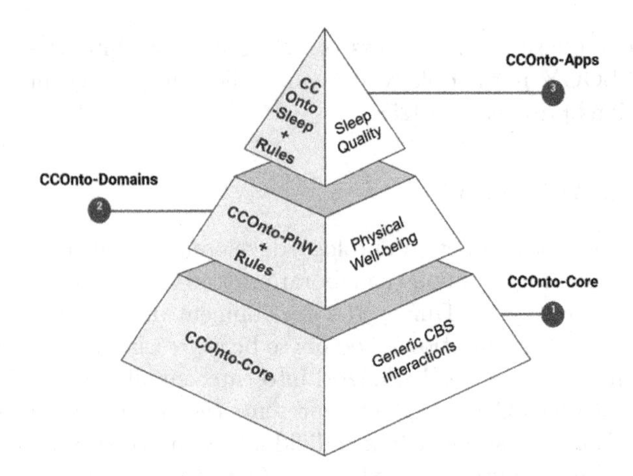

Fig. 1. The three modules of CCOnto.

all use-cases would require these detailed personalities and person distinctions. The modularization of the ontology resulted in closed-off ontology modules. For example, only person types related to a specific use case or personality facets or traits from other personality models are added in lower level modules as needed.

To enable the **continuous collaboratio**n between the domain experts and knowledge engineers the ontology versions are shared on GitHub and all milestones and deliverables are documented and privately shared between the involved researchers. The published ontology versions are always fully documented to enable sharability and reuse.

3.2 Development Methodology

The METHONTOLOGY methodology consists of 5 development steps: specification, conceptualization, formalization, implementation, and maintenance.

The **specification** of the scope and need for the ontology was done by the whole character computing research team consisting of Psychologists and Computer Scientists. The purpose of the CCOnto is two-fold. While the developed ontology provides a formal foundation for understanding and sharing knowledge about human character and its interactions, it is not the sole purpose of the ontology. The ontology serves as a unified knowledge base of reusable labeled data about the interactions within the CBS triad for different use-cases. The ontology can be integrated into different systems such as mobile or web applications or complex frameworks and systems. The knowledge required for modeling CCOnto and its concepts and properties is based on the Character Computing model. This includes knowledge based on different existing models representing the included concepts, such as trait-based personality models and models or emotion. Potential ontology users include (1) psychologists for testing their theories, (2) character computing researchers to give insights into the interaction

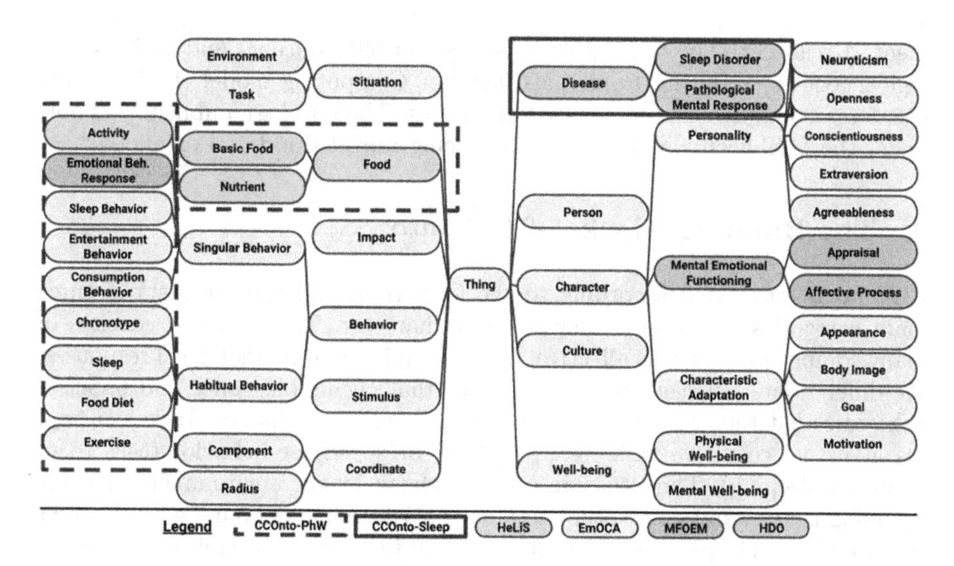

Fig. 2. An overview of entities within the full CCOnto (new concepts are in gray and the integrated concepts are color coded according to the legend). Unlabeled arrows represent is A relations. Classes added to CCOnto-Core for CCOnto-PhW and CCOnto-Sleep are highlighted using dashed and solid lines, respectively.

of character traits, states, situations, and behavior, and (3) developers using the ontology as a basis for their interactive applications.

The **conceptualization** phase included knowledge acquisition and ontology integration resulting in the conceptual model of CCOnto, shown in Fig. 2. The knowledge acquisition process involved the psychology experts of the team and bas based on foundations from the literature. After agreeing of the pool of terms to be included in the ontology, we team agreed on the ontological commitments detailing the meaning of each of the included terms. Based on the literature review, we reused concepts from existing ontologies representing the different included psychological models and processes. This is to maximize consistency, enable inter-operability for the researchers, and include various different models that are all building blocks of the CBS triad. The main concepts included from existing ontologies are (i) different aspects of wellness, such as physical activity and human consumption of basic food [28], (ii) specific health information such as sleep disorders [27], (iii) different emotional aspects and representations [20] and their interaction with personality and context [4], and (iv) basic psychological concepts needed in the model [3]. The entities of the ontologies are reused and extended to fit the scope of the Character Computing ontology to maximize consistency and enable inter-operability for the researchers.

The conceptual model of CCOnto is then **formalized** to define the constraints and properties of the individual entities. The formalized model is then **implemented** in OWL 2 using Protégé 5.2. The DL expressivity of the full ontology is SHOIF(D) and utilizes SPARQL, DLQuery, and the Pellet (incremental) reasoner. The full ontology consists of 691 concepts and 10764 OWL logical axioms, resulting from the Character Computing model [12,13,21,22], the domain experts, and the reused ontologies. The ontology publicly available under the MIT license and is constantly being **maintained** and extended.[3]

4 The Building-Blocks of CCOnto

CCOnto is structured according to the CBS triad and thus consists of three main categories: situation, behavior, and character. The behavior consists of many components, such as affective, motor, cognitive, or physiological responses. We differentiate between singular behavior that occurs only once and habitual behaviors that repeat over time and thus are considered habits. Tasks can represent actual cognitive tasks (e.g., memory or speed) or behavior tasks (e.g., eating or sleeping). The situation can be defined by the environment, the surrounding people, and many other actors [34]. Behaviors are bound with different situations e.g., sleeping behavior in a sleeping task. We distinguish between (i) one-time tasks, which in turn have performance scores as a behavior measure, and (ii) recurring tasks or activities, which have a habit "meter" as a behavior measure. The person is the central concept of the ontology relating all the others together. One can think of it in terms of a person with character x performing task y (situation) and has a score z (behavior). The x, in turn, consists of many components $x_1, x_2, \ldots, x_n$ representing the different character states and traits, e.g., personality, affect, emotion, culture, etc. Based on the different character attributes, persons can be further categorized into different subsets, as will be discussed below. Character attributes that have both trait and state counterparts (e.g., emotions and health), are represented through the same concepts (classes) and only distinguish between them through different properties (representing the stable and variable counterparts). Figure 2 shows the main upper-level classes (3-levels) of the full CCOnto, highlighting the classes integrated from EmOCA [4], Emotions Ontology (EM) [20], HeLiS [28], and Human Disease Ontology (HDO) [27]. We integrated all used concepts that are already available in the APA Psychology Terms [3] ontology, which provides a taxonomy with annotations for common Psychology-related terms), to ensure interoperability. In some cases, the upper-level classes are integrated from an ontology but re-engineered and restructured for the purposes of CCOnto.

4.1 Ontology Classes

We give an overview of the main class hierarchy, including the constructs that make up character attributes (e.g. personality and affect), behavior, and the situation. A representative sample of the third level sub-classes relevant to the presented running example and CCOnto-PhW-Sleep is included. `Character`

[3] https://github.com/CharacterComputingResearch/CCOnto and https://met.guc.edu.eg/CharacterComputing/home.html.

consists of states and traits that have been divided into three main clusters, namely `characteristic adaptation`, `mental emotionalfunctioning`, and `personality`. Characteristic adaptations are character components that can adapt by time and highly affect human behavior, such as `appearance` or a `goal`. Mental emotional functioning includes affective processes and appraisals included from the emotions ontology. For instance, an `affective process` represents specific emotions, moods, subjective emotional feelings, and bodily feelings. Personality consists of the five FFM traits. Each of them has sub-classes representing high and low values. High and low, however are categorical, and their boundaries can be decided by the ontology user depending on the preferred paradigm. We represent the `behavior` of an individual in a specific tasks as scores and differentiate between `singular` and `habitual behaviors`. Singular behaviors include `appraisal process`, `emotional behavioral process` (EM), `physical activity` (HeLiS), `entertainment behavior` like watching TV, or a `sleep behavior` representing one night's sleep. Emotional behavioral processes include emotional bodily movements, facial expressions, speaking, and physiological responses. Habits include `diet` (HeLiS) and `sleep hygiene`. A `situation` is represented as performing a specific task, e.g. a `sleep task` or a`cognitive task`. A `coordinate` (EmOCA) is a quantitative representation of emotion using a `radius` and a `coordiante` (`valence` and `arousal`). The coordinate-based representation of emotions can be mapped to the above mentioned affective processes. Both representations are supported to allow flexibility to affect reporting. C9-c and C9-d are complementing concepts incorporated from EmOCA. Based on a stimulus, each of a person's traits has an impact that pertains to a coordinate, i.e., emotion. `Culture` consists of different factors. For the time being we consider `religion` and `ethnic identity`. `Food` (HeLiS) is one main determinant of well-being-related behavior and is thus included for the purposes of the running example of this paper. Food can be represented via `nutrients` and `basic food` groups. `Well-being` has six aspects. For the purposes of this paper, we consider `emotional` and `physical well-being`. Like for food, `disease` is included to represent the two diseases of interest to the discussed use-case. We add `sleep disorders` and `pathological mental responses` as they affect and indicate sleep quality and other physical well-being behaviors. A person `a` can be in the situation of performing task `t1` and also performing another task `t2`. A person can have different character states and traits that represent him/her and can exhibit certain behaviors. Persons can be given labels based on their characteristics or behavioral tendencies to give inferences about their behavior. The `environment` can be considered an aspect of a situation. It represents the current surrounding conditions of a person and other involved entities.

4.2 Ontology Properties

The relationships and interactions between the character attributes are represented through properties. All main properties relating to components of character, behavior, and situation are shown in Fig. 2. `has impact`, `pertains to`, `is defined by` and `has trait` have been integrated from the EmOCA ontology. The behavior of the first three properties is the same as in the original ontology, which serves to represent emotions as they result from stimuli and are impacted by the big five personality traits. To differentiate between stable trait-like emotions i.e., affect and variable state-like emotions we have the `has affect` and `has emotion` which both map a person to an emotion (discrete or continuous). The `related to` property is added to relate specific emotional behavioral processes to affective processes. It is important to note that this property does not assume any causality. The following object properties have been integrated from the HeLiS ontology: `contains`, `has activity`, and `has nutrient`, alongside some data properties, including `activity duration`, `amount of calories`, `has MET value`, `has unit kCal value`. We added `has occurrent part`, `has output`, and `is output of` from EMO. For sleep evaluation, we added `has sleep` and the sub-properties (1) `has sleepiness`, for assigning a person to sleepiness. For example, if a person is suffering from daytime sleepiness, we will have: `person and has sleepiness value daytime sleepiness`, (2) `has sleep quality` and `has sleep hygiene`, for determining the sleep quality and hygiene, respectively, (3) `has chronotype`, for distinguishing whether the individual is a morning person or an evening person, (4) `consume`, indicating which foods the person consumed (used to reason about sleep quality as well, e.g., think of drinking caffeine before going to sleep.), (5) `suffer from`, to indicate the sleep diseases a person suffers from, and (7) `bedtime`, `sleep duration` and `wakeuptime`. `has behavior` assigns persons to behavior classes. For example, if a person has a daytime nap, we will have `Person and has Behavior some daytime nap`. One important property for ontologies and, thus, the CCOnto ontology, is the `has part` property. This property serves to provide the conceptualization of the topology character and its attributes. The `has part` is used to identify the constituents of character, personality and each of the traits, e.g. "Extroversion hasPart only (ExcitementSeeking or Gregariousness or Assertiveness or ActivityLevel or Cheerfulness or Friendliness)". Finally, a person has `has culture` and `has birthdate` properties mapping to (one or many) `culture` individual(s) and a date of birth (`xsd:int`).

4.3 Reasoning and Rules

CCOnto is of interest for Character Computing researchers and developers of applications that harness the interaction between behavior and character in specific situations to provide better user experiences. CCOnto can be used for applications that go beyond this basic information representation and retrieval by directly giving meaningful user feedback about behavior and character when coupled with expert rules. Accordingly, depending on the domain of interest, CCOnto is coupled with SWRL rules by the domain experts to predict certain behaviors. This enables testing different hypothesis for the interaction between the components of the CBS triad against a specific dataset or to validate empirical results (as outlined in [13,22]). It also allows us to define rules based on previous findings to predict task scores from character attributes, and vice versa.

The ontology can be used with any number of character attributes, behaviors and situations, i.e., not all of them need to be defined or included for any given application. This enables researchers to use the ontology to input data only for the attributes or models they are interested in or have data for. Finally, multiple models (e.g., two personality theories) can be tested against each other.

5 Ontology Validation and Evaluation

5.1 Validating CCOnto

We validated the full version of CCOnto extended with knowledge about the physical well-being domain and applied to sleep quality and personality prediction. Accordingly, we apply CCOnto to the running example and checking whether it can provide answers to the related queries. We use the competency questions (CQs) developed for the full version of CCOnto as guidance for the query generation and thus the validation process. While some of the CQs are generic and related to CCOnto-Core, the main focus of the CQs discussed in this paper are use-case-specific. The CQs were defined early on in the ontology development process. However, like the ontology itself, the CQs underwent many updates throughout the development iterations. A subset of the used CQs can be found in Table 1. The represented CQs are not exhaustive but rather serve as samples of the different covered question types. Some CQs have been combined together in one question for representation within the paper. For example, Q10 and Q11 each consist of multiple CQs for mapping each behavior with sleep and personality values, respectively. Q4 can, for example, can return that appraisal of being disliked may cause an emotion process of sadness or anger and of negative valence. A sample of information to be queried through Q10 is: given someone experiencing 1) a negative emotion and thus exhibiting certain behavior like 2) excessive eating at late hours, which might 3) hinder the sleeping process, he or she can experience daytime sleepiness during working.

5.2 Evaluating CCOnto

Ontology evaluation approaches can be divided into four categories [30]: error checking, metric evaluation, modularization, and fitness for a domain or task.

Modularization. As discussed in Sect. 3, the ontology is already developed in a fully modular manner and can be extended into different domain- and app-specific ontologies based on the concepts of Character Computing.

Error Checking. We evaluate the ontology from a logic-based point of view [40], to ensure there are no inconsistencies or unsatisfiable classes. We validated the ontology using Protégé and Pellet (incremental). Then, we used the OntOlogy Pitfall Scanner (OOPS!)[4], which is an ontology evaluation tool for detecting

[4] http://oops.linkeddata.es/index.jsp.

Table 1. A representative sample of CQs for validating the full CCOnto.

General CQs (CCOnto-Core)	
Q1	What are the types of human behavior (singular and habitual)?
Q2	What are character attributes (mental emotional, personality, characteristic)?
Q3	How do affective processes relate to valence (pos./neg.) and arousal
Q4	What are effects of affective processes in terms of behaviors (specifically, emotional behavioral processes)?
Q5	Which mental processes trigger which emotions
Usecase-specific CQs (CCOnto-PhW-Sleep)	
Q7	What are types of activities (quantitatively and categorically)?
Q8	Which are consumption, emotional, entertainment, sleep behaviors?
Q9	What are the different categories and nutritional values of food
Q10	What are the effects of different behaviors (food consumption, exercise, and emotional state) on sleep?
Q11	What are the effects of personality traits on different behaviors (sleep, food consumption, exercise, and emotional state), and vice versa?

common ontology development pitfalls via an evaluation report. The main critical issue was due to the multiple definitions of the range of the `performs` property that related a person with performed tasks and activities. Accordingly, the property was replaced with two separate ones for each range (`performs_action` and `performs_task`) to avoid the unintended intersection. Some properties were missing explicit domain and range definitions, which were added. The license declaration was reported missing; however, it is added in the GitHub repository where the ontology is published. Some equivalent classes from HeLiS and MFOEM were reported as not explicitly declared. Other minor common pitfall resulting from the same reused ontologies are "same label classes" and "merging different concepts in the same class". Finally, the scanner suggested that `performed task` and `performed activity` might be equivalent, which does not apply and thus was not changed. Other minor issues included missing explicit declarations of inverse relations, which are not applicable for all used relations.

Metric Evaluation. The ontology is compared against the concepts needed to describe the CBS triad and its three building blocks included in the Character Computing model. Domain experts found the ontology to accurately represent all the included concepts representing its current scope. Some concepts have not yet been fully integrated into the ontology and are thus not evaluated, e.g., for now, only physical well-being is included, and not all six aspects of well-being.

Fitness for a Specific Task - CCleep. To test the fitness of CCOnto as a basis for behavior-related applications, the full ontology is evaluated through an application. Different characters respond differently to crisis situations. The in-depth details of the implemented application, CCleep, are not within the scope of this paper, but we present it as a proof of concept for utilizing CCOnto for behavior-related applications. Sleep is a well-being factor that has a huge impact on our behavior, emotions, and performance. CCleep relies on CCOnto to reason about sleep quality and its relation to personality, emotions, and other physical well-being factors based on a set of rules from literature and domain experts.

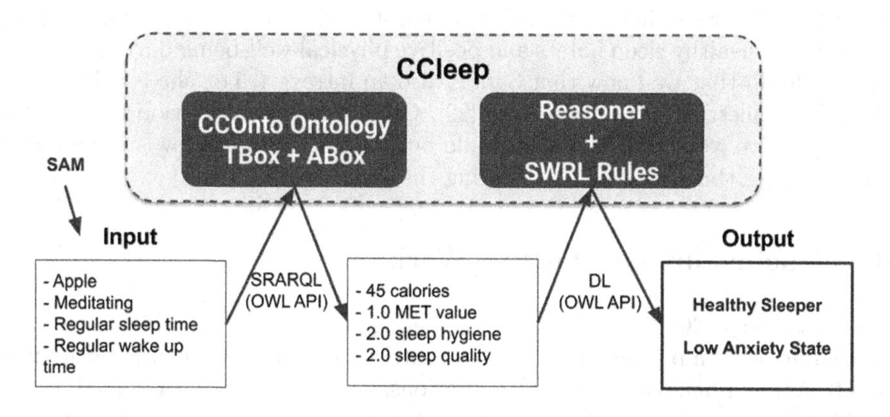

Fig. 3. CCleep input/output for the running example.

CCSleep is a Java-based web application[5] with OWLAPI and a MongoDB database. As language plays a huge role in character interactions and self-expression, CCleep supports English and Arabic self-reporting. For the time being, all application-relevant labels of CCOnto have been translated into Arabic. While a lot of applications for collecting sleep behavior and correlating it with multiple character components already exists, e.g., [14], this is the first

[5] https://charactercomputingsleep.herokuapp.com/introServlet.

ontology-based one. The application collects self-report behavior data (e.g., consumed food, performed activities, emotions, etc.) for the two hours prior to sleep and infers sleep quality and personality traits. For example, as shown in Fig. 3 imagine Sam chooses the following: apples, meditating, regular sleep time, regular wake-up time. The application then creates SPARQL queries to CCOnto about (1) the number of calories of each consumed food, (2) the MET values of each performed activity, (3) evaluation of the other chosen behavior in terms of sleep hygiene and quality scores. The scores resulting from the SPARQL query are used to calculate the total consumed calories, total MET, and total sleep hygiene and quality scores. The evaluation of the sleep hygiene and quality scores, i.e., the score in the sleep task, are evaluated based on agreed-upon findings from previous research [7,24]. For Sam, for example, an apple has 45 cal, and meditating has `metvalues 1.0` and receives `sleepHygieneScore 2` and `SleepQulaityScore 2`. A DL Query is sent to CCOnto with Sam's total scores. Based on the input, the reasoner uses the OWL restrictions to infer the final sleep evaluation and personality traits matching the reported pre-sleep behaviors. People who have good sleep hygiene, avoid caffeine, alcohol drinking, smoking, people who exercise, have regular sleep time schedules, and have light snacks in case of hunger before going to bed.

People with good sleep hygiene and quality are considered to be healthy sleepers [7,24], and thus Sam is inferred to be a healthy sleeper. People who have healthy sleep habits show high conscientiousness and low neuroticism, and vice versa [10]. Sam, however, has high neuroticism and thus high trait anxiety but exhibits healthy sleep habits and positive physical well-being during the pandemic. Recall that we know that Sam is also an introvert, i.e., she is calmer and thrives in constrained environments [29]. Given Sam's introversion and newly-found positive well-being, CCleep would output that Sam has low state anxiety and is calmer than her usual self during the lockdown.

6 Conclusions and Future Work

We presented CCOnto, an ontology modeling the CBS triad, which is central to Character Computing. It models the interactions between character (states and traits) and behavior in specific situations. CCOnto serves as a unified model enabling scientists to interact with the ontology, test hypotheses against experimental data, modify the ontology and its rules, and build applications that harness these interactions. CCleep is a proof-of-concept application to show CCOnto's potential as a predictive model for applications.

CCOnto can be extended by adding more models representing the already worked out character attributes, as well as working out the still abstract ones. A challenge will be in the non-tangible ones like goals and motivations, which are usually not assessed by quantitative questionnaires like personality or affect. More attributes for specifying behavior and situations should be added. We need to consider the cyclic relation between behavior and character in the short and long term. The reasoning capabilities available to ontologies should be combined with fuzzy logic or probabilistic methods, to be able to better model the inherently vague and non-deterministic concepts of the CBS triad. CCOnto is to be integrated into other applications (validated by both Computer Scientists and Psychologists). CCOnto is being integrated with existing upper ontologies to ensure maximum reusability.

References

1. Abaalkhail, R., Guthier, B., Alharthi, R., El Saddik, A.: Survey on ontologies for affective states and their influences. Semant. Web **9**(4), 441–458 (2018)
2. Alfaifi, Y., Grasso, F., Tamma, V.: An ontology of psychological barriers to support behaviour change. In: Proceedings of the 2018 International Conference on Digital Health, pp. 11–15 (2018)
3. Walker, A., Alexander Garcia, I.G.: Psychology ontology. In: BioPortal (2014). https://bioportal.bioontology.org/ontologies/APAONTO
4. Berthelon, F., Sander, P.: Emotion ontology for context awareness. In: 2013 IEEE 4th International Conference on Cognitive Infocommunications (CogInfoCom), pp. 59–64. IEEE (2013)
5. Blanch, A., et al.: Ontologies about human behavior. Eur. Psychol. **22**, 187 (2017)
6. El Bolock, Alia, Abdelrahman, Yomna, Abdennadher, Slim (eds.): Character Computing. HIS, Springer, Cham (2020). https://doi.org/10.1007/978-3-030-15954-2. https://books.google.com.eg/books?id=VZXHDwAAQBAJ
7. Brown, F.C., Buboltz Jr., W.C., Soper, B.: Relationship of sleep hygiene awareness, sleep hygiene practices, and sleep quality in university students. Behav. Med. **28**, 33–38 (2002)
8. Costa Jr, P.T., McCrae, R.R.: The Revised NEO Personality Inventory (NEO-PI-R). Sage Publications, Inc., London (2008)
9. Dragoni, M., Tamma, V.A.: Extending helis: from chronic diseases to behavior change. In: SWH@ ISWC, pp. 9–19 (2019)
10. Duggan, K.A., Friedman, H.S., McDevitt, E.A., Mednick, SC.: Personality and healthy sleep: the importance of conscientiousness and neuroticism. PloS one **9**(3), e90628 (2014)
11. Ekman, P., Cordaro, D.: What is meant by calling emotions basic. Emot. Rev. **3**(4), 364–370 (2011)
12. El Bolock, A.: What is character computing? In: El Bolock, A., Abdelrahman, Y., Abdennadher, S. (eds.) Character Computing. HIS, pp. 1–16. Springer, Cham (2020). https://doi.org/10.1007/978-3-030-15954-2_1
13. El Bolock, A., Abdennadher, S., Herbert, C.: Applications of character computing from psychology to computer science. In: El Bolock, A., Abdelrahman, Y., Abdennadher, S. (eds.) Character Computing. HIS, pp. 53–71. Springer, Cham (2020). https://doi.org/10.1007/978-3-030-15954-2_4
14. ElBolock, A., Amr, R., Abdennadher, S.: Non-obtrusive sleep detection for character computing profiling. In: Karwowski, W., Ahram, T. (eds.) IHSI 2018. AISC, vol. 722, pp. 249–254. Springer, Cham (2018). https://doi.org/10.1007/978-3-319-73888-8_39
15. El Bolock, A., Herbert, C., Abdennadher, S.: Cconto: towards an ontology-based model for character computing. In: 14th International Conference on Research Challenges in Information Science, RCIS 2020, Limassol, Cyprus, 23–25 September 2020. IEEE (2020)

16. Fernández-López, M., Gómez-Pérez, A., Juristo, N.: Methontology: from ontological art towards ontological engineering (1997)
17. García-Vélez, R., Galán-Mena, J., López-Nores, M., Robles-Bykbaev, V.: Creating an ontological networks to support the inference of personality traits and facets. In: 2018 IEEE XXV International Conference on Electronics, Electrical Engineering and Computing (INTERCON), pp. 1–4. IEEE (2018)
18. Greitzer, F.L., et al.: Developing an ontology for individual and organizational sociotechnical indicators of insider threat risk. In: STIDS, pp. 19–27 (2016)
19. Hastings, J., Brass, A., Caine, C., et al.: Evaluating the emotion ontology through use in the self-reporting of emotional responses at an academic conference. J. Biomed. Semant. **5**, 38 (2014). https://doi.org/10.1186/2041-1480-5-38
20. Hastings, J., Ceusters, W., Smith, B., Mulligan, K.: The emotion ontology: enabling interdisciplinary research in the affective sciences. In: Beigl, M., et al. (eds.) CONTEXT 2011. LNCS (LNAI), vol. 6967, pp. 119–123. Springer, Heidelberg (2011). https://doi.org/10.1007/978-3-642-24279-3_14
21. Herbert, C.: An experimental-psychological approach for the development of character computing. In: El Bolock, A., Abdelrahman, Y., Abdennadher, S. (eds.) Character Computing. HIS, pp. 17–38. Springer, Cham (2020). https://doi.org/10.1007/978-3-030-15954-2_2
22. Herbert, C., El Bolock, A., Abdennadher, S.: A psychologically driven, user-centered approach to character modeling. In: El Bolock, A., Abdelrahman, Y., Abdennadher, S. (eds.) Character Computing. HIS, pp. 39–51. Springer, Cham (2020). https://doi.org/10.1007/978-3-030-15954-2_3
23. Hettler, B.: Six dimensions of wellness model (1976)
24. Irish, L.A., Kline, C.E., Gunn, H.E., Buysse, D.J., Hall, M.H.: The role of sleep hygiene in promoting public health: a review of empirical evidence. Sleep Med. Rev. **22**, 23–36 (2015)
25. Kotis, K.I., Vouros, G.A., Spiliotopoulos, D.: Ontology engineering methodologies for the evolution of living and reused ontologies: status, trends, findings and recommendations. Knowl. Eng. Rev. **35**, e34 (2020)
26. López Gil, J.M., García González, R., Gil Iranzo, R.M., Collazos Ordóñez, C.A.: Emotionsonto: an ontology for developing affective applications. J. Univ. Comput. Sci. **13**(20), 1813–1828 (2014)
27. Lynn, M., Schriml, E.M.: The Disease Ontology: fostering interoperability between biological and clinical human disease-related data. Mammalian Genome **26**, pp. 584–589 (2015)
28. Dragoni, M., Bailoni, T., Maimone, R., Eccher, C.: HeLiS: an ontology for supporting healthy lifestyles. In: Vrandečić, D., Bontcheva, K., Suárez-Figueroa, M.C., Presutti, V., Celino, I., Sabou, M., Kaffee, L.-A., Simperl, E. (eds.) ISWC 2018. LNCS, vol. 11137, pp. 53–69. Springer, Cham (2018). https://doi.org/10.1007/978-3-030-00668-6_4
29. McCrae, R.R.: The five-factor model of personality traits: Consensus and controversy. The Cambridge handbook of personality psychology, pp. 148–161 (2009)
30. McDaniel, M., Storey, V.C.: Evaluating domain ontologies: clarification, classification, and challenges. ACM Comput. Surv. (CSUR) **52**(4), 1–44 (2019)
31. Norris, E., Finnerty, A.N., Hastings, J., Stokes, G., Michie, S.: A scoping review of ontologies related to human behaviour change. Nat. Hum. Behav. **3**(2), 164 (2019)
32. Nurjanah, D.: Lifeon, a ubiquitous lifelong learner model ontology supporting adaptive learning. In: 2018 IEEE Global Engineering Education Conference (EDUCON), pp. 866–871. IEEE (2018)

33. Olson, D., Russell, C.S., Sprenkle, D.H.: Circumplex Model: Systemic Assessment and Treatment of Families. Routledge, London (2014)
34. Rauthmann, J.F., et al.: The situational eight diamonds: a taxonomy of major dimensions of situation characteristics. J. Pers. Soc. Psychol. **107**(4), 677 (2014)
35. Rodríguez, N.D., Cuéllar, M.P., Lilius, J., Calvo-Flores, M.D.: A survey on ontologies for human behavior recognition. ACM Comput. Surv. (CSUR) **46**(4), 1–33 (2014)
36. Schachter, S., Singer, J.: Cognitive, social, and physiological determinants of emotional state. Psychol. Rev. **69**(5), 379 (1962)
37. Sewwandi, D., Perera, K., Sandaruwan, S., Lakchani, O., Nugaliyadde, A., Thelijjagoda, S.: Linguistic features based personality recognition using social media data. In: 2017 6th National Conference on Technology and Management (NCTM), pp. 63–68. IEEE (2017)
38. Smith, B., et al.: The obo foundry: coordinated evolution of ontologies to support biomedical data integration. Nat. Biotechnol. **25**(11), 1251–1255 (2007)
39. Bailoni, T., Dragoni, M., Eccher, C., Guerini, M., Maimone, R.: Healthy lifestyle support: the PerKApp ontology. In: Dragoni, M., Poveda-Villalón, M., Jimenez-Ruiz, E. (eds.) OWLED/ORE -2016. LNCS, vol. 10161, pp. 15–23. Springer, Cham (2017). https://doi.org/10.1007/978-3-319-54627-8_2
40. Tartir, S., Arpinar, I.B., Sheth, A.P.: Ontological evaluation and validation. In: Poli, R., Healy, M., Kameas, A. (eds.) Theory and Applications of Ontology: Computer Applications. Springer, Dordrecht. https://doi.org/10.1007/978-90-481-8847-5_5

Assessment of Malicious Tweets Impact on Stock Market Prices

Tatsuki Ishikawa , Imen Ben Sassi(✉), and Sadok Ben Yahia

Tallinn University of Technology, Akadeemia tee 15a, Tallinn 12618, Estonia
{imen.ben,sadok.ben}@taltech.ee

Abstract. Accurate stock market prediction is of paramount importance for traders. Professional ones typically derive financial market decision-making from fundamental and technical indicators. However, stock markets are very often influenced by external human factors, like sentiment information that can be contained in online social networks. As a result, micro-blogs are more and more exploited to predict prices and traded volumes of stocks in financial markets. Nevertheless, it has been shown that a large volume of the content shared on micro-blogs is published by malicious entities, especially spambots. In this paper, we introduce a novel deep learning-based approach for financial time series forecasting based on social media. Through the Generative Adversarial Network (GAN) model, we gauge the impact of malicious tweets, posted by spambots, on financial markets, mainly the closing price. We compute the performance of the proposed approach using real-world data of stock prices and tweets related to the Facebook Inc company. Carried out experiments show that the proposed approach outperforms the two baselines, LSTM, and SVR, using different evaluation metrics. In addition, the obtained results prove that spambot tweets potentially grasp investors' attention and induce the decision to buy and sell.

Keywords: Stock market prediction · Neural networks · GAN · Sentiment analysis · Malicious tweets · Spambots

1 Introduction

The stock market prediction has been always an interesting subject for both scientific researchers and finance practitioners. With the development of social media and the expansion of information sources, companies' stock information is no longer limited to numerical financial market data and integrates financial news articles with sentiment polarities. These additional factors affect the stock market prices, positively or negatively, then must be considered to improve the quality of stock market prediction. Various research works have proposed models to extract sentiment scores from micro-blogs and provided evidences of their ability to predict stock prices and traded volumes [3]. With the advent of social media, our society is more interconnected. Thus, the quantity and throughput of information exchange has been rocket dramatically by which they could obtain

S. Cherfi et al. (Eds.): RCIS 2021, LNBIP 415, pp. 330–346, 2021.
https://doi.org/10.1007/978-3-030-75018-3_22

the latest information before the traditional news media such as a newspaper and television. However, since its lack of concerning validity and accuracy, mistakenly or purposely fake information generated by fake, spam, and automated accounts can be spread out [4]. Those malicious accounts have contributed to multiple public discussions about critical subjects like politics, terrorism to daily ones like products, and celebrity life. In politics, they have proved that bots have played a significant role in numerous elections, like the French and US elections [18], the Indonesian election [11], the Swedish election [8], to cite but a few. Speaking of the financial loss concerning fake news, there is a widely known case such that a post, mentioning Barack Obama's injury because of the explosions in the White House, in 2013 rapidly caused a stock market collapse that burned 136 billion dollars[1]. Later, it turned out that the US International Press Officer's Twitter account has been hacked to spread out this rumor. Recently, the authors, in [6], have proved financial malicious content in stock micro-blogs, which raises critical concerns over the reliability of this public information.

In this paper, we assume that it is beneficial to assess the impact of unreliable article posted on one of the widely spreading micro-blogs, Twitter. We propose a novel Deep Learning approach, based on the Generative Adversarial Network (GAN) model, for stock market prediction by analyzing fundamental and technical indicators as internal factors and social media posts as external ones. Experiments are designed and conducted based on stock prices and tweets related to the Facebook Inc company. The major contributions of this research are the following.

- We combine stock market and social media data generated by both spambots and genuine users to study the impact of spambot tweets on financial markets.
- We compare several sentiment analysis tools to measure their performance in stock market prediction.
- We collect a new dataset, of 80 days of the Facebook Inc stock data between $2017-05-19$ and $2017-09-12$, for later comparison.
- We propose an alternative model for financial time series forecasting.
- We compare the proposed model with a Neural Network model and a Regression model based on several error evaluation metrics. Our method outperforms its competitors on several metrics.

We organize the remainder of this paper as follows. We start by highlighting the techniques introduced by former works for stock market prediction in Sect. 2. We briefly summarize GANs in Sect. 3. In Sect. 4, we thoroughly describe our proposed approach. Next, Sect. 5 shows the experimental results of the introduced approach and discusses our most relevant findings considering the existing studies. Finally, Sect. 6 summarizes our work with a discussion of plans for future research directions.

[1] https://www.cnbc.com/id/100646197.

2 Scrutiny of the Related Work

We devote this section to survey related work dedicated to machine learning-based stock market prediction approaches and to the estimation of the impact of malicious content on stock market prices.

2.1 Stock Market Prediction

Several research works have been carried out to predict the movement of stock market prices by applying statistical methods on the historical stock prices known as technical analysis. The base technical analysis is defined by functions that return estimations for stock prices regarding a historical length of time. Recently, many machine learning and deep learning algorithms, like Support Vector Machines (SVM) [10], Random Forest (RF) [20], and Neural Networks (NN) [15], have been applied to predict stock prices. However, with the technological development, some additional human factors have played a key role in the movement of financial markets. People are posting everyday news and comments on online social networks (OSN). The sentiment analysis of OSN posts can clarify the correlation between the movement of market prices and the human sentiment factor. In recent years, researchers have automatically analyzed numerical and textual financial data that provide from heterogeneous sources to predict stock prices. In Deng et al. [7], time-series data (namely price and volume), numerical dynamic features, and sentiment features were combined as an input feature for the prediction model. The used model is defined by a multiple kernel learning framework to predict the stock price for three Internet companies in Japan, namely Sharp, Panasonic, and Sony. The technical indicators, used as a part of the input feature, include the Rate of Change, the Moving Average Convergence Divergence (MACD), and the BIAS. The authors have extracted time-series data from Google Finance Website, however, the news data were obtained from Engadget, where the textual data is analyzed with the SentiWordNet lexicon to get sentiment scores.

In [2], the authors have predicted opening stock prices of 10 companies in the same industry in Nikkei 225 using the Long Short Term Memory (LSTM) model. The model uses three inputs, i.e., numerical data, bag-of-words, and paragraph vector representation of textual data. The experimental results show that the distributed representations of textual information are better than the numerical data based on bag-of-words methods. Besides, the LSTM model outperformed the simple Recurrent Neural Network (RNN) model, which is gauged by market simulation. In [17], the authors have collected their datasets from two sources: news sentiment and historical prices. In terms of historical prices, ticker data for four companies including AAPL, GOOGL, AMZN, and FB were collected. Concerning the news sentiments, news data derived from the Reuters platform with sentiment polarity and stock symbol were collected. The authors have trained four models, namely, RNN, Depp Neural Network (DNN), SVM, and Support Vector Regression (SVR). The authors, in [14], have applied the ForGAN model with either LSTM or Gated Recurrent Units (GRUs) in both the generator and discriminator to forecast a one-step-ahead value in three time-series data. They set the G-regression model, which has an identical structure with the generator, to compare the result of the regression problem. The results give evidence that ForGAN has a high capability of learning probability distributions and shows the effectiveness of adversarial training for forecasting tasks.

The authors in [12] have selected the stock markets in 11 markets, including KSE, LSE, TWTR, NOK, and collected the news and tweets related to these stock markets for 2 years as external features. Sentiment analysis has been performed based on the Stanford Natural Language Processing (NLP) tool to identify tweent and news text polarity. The authors have compared the performance of different machine learning classifiers to predict 10 days in future price values. They concluded that the combination of sentiment factor from both OSNs and financial news, and the reduction of spam tweets may improve the overall results. Another stock market prediction system has been built in [15], which takes an input of numerically represented data such as price and sentiment data. The authors have used a dataset of Hong Kong Stock Exchange (HKSEs), especially the Hang Seng Index (HSI), and applied the LSTM model since it can learn the sequential information. In conclusion, the LSTM model has outperformed the base model, SVM. The effectiveness of news sentiment has been investigated by calculating the ratio of accuracy change.

2.2 Malicious Content Impact on Financial Market

Misinformation and fake content shared by malicious entities have a significant impact on society, the economy, as well as micro, small, and medium-sized enterprises. The authors in [19] have analyzed the effect of fake news on two companies, Tesla, an automotive company, and Galena Biopharma, a pharmaceutical company. Tesla experienced a significant drop in its stock in a day a fake video posted on Twitter. Moreover, Galena experienced an artificial inflation in its stock when they posted a promotion article in some reputable online outlets including Seeking Alpha and Motley Fool. In this case, Galena used fake news as a way to enact a pump and dump scheme, while Tesla is the victim of fake news. The authors in [13] have scrutinized the direct impact of fake news and real ones in terms of abnormal trading volume. They found that of the 37% rise in abnormal trading volume, 15.5% occurs on the day the article is published, 12.1% the following day, and 10.1% two days later. In addition, they noticed that, in small firms that have more retail investor trading, the effect on abnormal trading volume declines strongly. This impact is six times larger for small firms than for large firms (80.9% increase versus 8.2%). Cresci et al. in [6], have revealed that large-scale speculative campaign, which is also referred as Cashtag Piggybacking, is perpetrated by coordinated groups of bots. This campaign aims to promote the low-value stock, which is traded in OTCMKTS, by exploiting the popularity of high-value ones. To conclude, fake news and malicious tweets published by spambots aim at deceiving retail investors and also to trade small companies to gain profit in the short term. Hence, we assume that it is beneficial to assess the impact of unreliable articles posted by spambots on Twitter, one of the widely spreading microblogs.

Before detailing the steps of our prediction approach, we give, in the following, an overview of GANs.

3 Generative Adversarial Network

Recently, GANs [9] have been applied to several problems in the field of sequential data and have achieved remarkable results. A GAN is a type of Deep Neural Network architecture that comprises two networks, called *Generator* and *Discriminator* [9]. The purpose of the generator network is to generate new data from a randomly generated vector of numbers, called *latent space*, whereas the purpose of the discriminator network is to differentiate whether a sample is from the model distribution or the data distribution.

3.1 Objective Function

In order to measure the similarity between the data generated by the generator and the real data, we use objective functions. Both networks, the Generator and the Discriminator, have their objective functions, which need to be minimized during the training step. Equation 1 represents the final objective function of GANs [1].

$$\min_{G}\max_{D} \mathrm{V(D,G)} = \mathrm{E}_{x\sim p_{data}(x)}[\log D(x)] + \mathrm{E}_{z\sim p_z(z)}[\log(1 - D(G(z))] \quad (1)$$

First, we sample a noise vector z from a probability distribution $p_z(z)$. The generator $G(z)$ takes z as input and generates a sample with a distribution following the original data distribution $p_{data}(x)$. At the same time, the discriminator $D(x)$ is optimized to differentiate between the generated data and the real one. In the first part of Eq. 1, $\mathrm{E}_{x\sim p_{data}(x)}[\log D(x)]$ represents how good real data is recognized as real one and the second part, $\mathrm{E}_{z\sim p_z(z)}[\log(1 - D(G(z))]$ represents how good generated data is recognized as a generated one.

3.2 GANs for Time-Series Data

Time series data prediction includes weather forecasting and financial risk management. Its goal is to predict future quantity or event of interest. Mathematically, the future value x_{t+1} is recovered from the sequential events $x_{t,t-1,\dots,0}$, so we are predicting $p(x_{t+1}|x_t...x_0)$. In order to predict interesting feature at time t+1, the GAN model can be applied. GANs are composed of a generator network and a discriminator network having as main components of an Artificial Neural Network (ANN), a Convolutional Neural Network (CNN), a RNN or a LSTM [1]. The discriminator needs to have fully connected layers with a classifier in order to classify whether an input is derived from the real sample distribution or the generated sample distribution. For predicting time-series data, RNN especially LSTM is used to capture sequential information.

4 Stock Market Prediction Based on Generative Adversarial Network

This section describes the steps performed in our proposed approach for the assessment of the impact of malicious tweets on stock market prediction.

4.1 Data Collection

Unlike the traditional way which considers only one source of information, our system is designed to allow us to integrate several sources of information. In our experiments, we use two sources of information, which come from social media and the stock market.

Facebook Inc Stock Data. The adjusting closing stock price P_{Adj} of the American social media company, Facebook Inc, is our target variable to be predicted. 80 days of the Facebook stock data, between 2017-05-19 and 2017-09-12, were extracted with pandas DataReader in Python Pandas software library. Table 1 shows the first five rows of the collected Facebook stock data. In columns, High, Low, Open, Close, Volume and Adj Close indicate the highest price of the stock in a day, lowest price, opening price, closing price, volume traded and adjusting price respectively.

Table 1. An excerpt from the collected Facebook dataset

Date	Stock price					
	High	Low	Open	Close	Volume	Adj Close
2017-05-19	149.39	147.96	148.45	148.06	16,187,900	148.06
2017-05-22	148.59	147.69	148.08	148.24	12,586,700	148.24
2017-05-23	148.81	147.25	148.52	148.07	12,817,800	148.07
2017-05-24	150.23	148.42	148.51	150.04	17,862,400	150.04
2017-05-25	152.59	149.95	150.30	151.96	19,891,400	151.96

Figure 1 plots the adjusted closing price of Facebook. The graph can be decomposed into 3 terms. The first one shows a horizontal movement in the dates between the $1st$ of June and the $1st$ of July. In the next term, between the $1st$ of July and the $1st$ of August, a very sharp spike is observed. Finally, the last term, from the $1st$ of August to the last date of the graph, shows a horizontal movement.

Social Media Data. For sentiment analysis, we use the Twitter dataset collected by Cresci et al. [6]. This dataset contains about $9M$ tweets, posted by

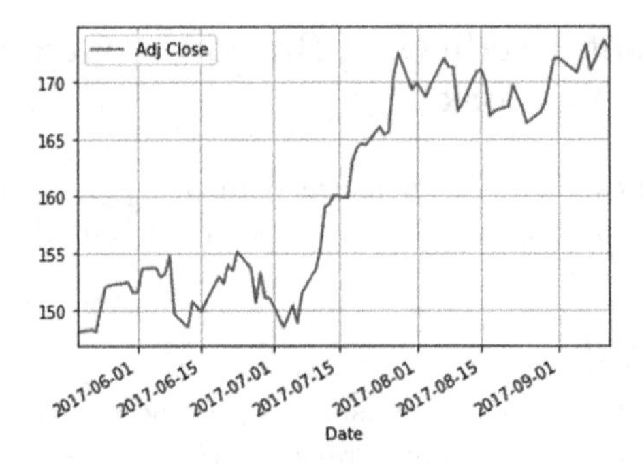

Fig. 1. Facebook adjusting close price between 2017-05-19 and 2017-09-12

about 2.5M distinct users, mentioning stocks (cashtags) about 30,032 companies traded on the 5 most important US markets, and shared between May and September 2017. This Twitter dataset is selected as the source of social media data since users data are enriched with bot classification labels obtained using a Digital DNA detection system [5]. Additionally, since we are focusing on Facebook stock exchange, we filtered the English Tweets related to Facebook with a cashtag, such as #FB and #Facebook. By and large, we obtained 162,911 Facebook-related tweets in total.

4.2 Sentiment Analysis

Sentiment analysis field pays attention to the study of people's opinions, sentiments, evaluations, appraisals, attitudes, and emotions towards entities such as products, services, organizations, individuals, issues, events, and topics [16]. There are two types of sentiment analysis approaches, namely, Machine Learning-based and Lexicon-based approaches. In this paper, we are interested in the latter approaches and namely on the five following sentiment analysis tools.

SentiWordNet[2]: Build via a semi-supervised method and contains opinion terms extracted from WordNet database. Each set of terms, sharing the same meaning in SentiWordNet (synsets), is associated with two numerical scores ranging from 0 to 1, indicating the synset's positive and negative bias. We use the NLTK POS tagging to compute the score of an overall sentence.

VADER[3] (Valence Aware Dictionary for Sentiment Reasoning): A lexicon-based model, which uses balance-based lexicon. The latter is sensitive to both polarity and intensity of sentiment in social media microblogs. Thus, it preforms exceptionally well in the social media domain.

[2] https://github.com/aesuli/SentiWordNet.
[3] https://github.com/cjhutto/vaderSentiment.

TextBlob[4]**:** A Python library for processing textual data. It provides a simple API for diving into common NLP tasks such as part-of-speech tagging, noun phrase extraction, sentiment analysis, classification, translation, and more.

AFINN[5]**:** A lexicon-based method derived from ANEW (Affective Norms for English Words) where its lexicon is a list of English terms manually rated for valence with an integer between −5 and 5.

SO-CAL[6] **(Sentiment Orientation Calculator):** Uses dictionaries of words annotated with their semantic orientation. Since the dictionary construction affects the overall accuracy of results, word dictionaries are made manually by hand-tagging on a scale ranging from −5 to 5.

4.3 Feature Selection

Two types of features namely, technical/fundamental features and sentiment features are used on our prediction approach.

Technical and Fundamental Features. In order to make a prediction model for the stock closing price of Facebook, 16 input features are collected. These features are listed in Table 2. From the viewpoint of the technical analysis, 7 features from Opening Price to Closing Price predicted by AutoRegressive Integrated Moving Average (ARIMA) are collected. Besides, we also extract 6 additional features, which are competitors of Facebook as an online advertising platform and a social media platform. Moreover, 3 market indices including the price of Dow Jone Industrial Average (DJIA), S&P 500 index (SPX), and NASDAQ 100 Index (NDX), are collected.

Table 2. Technical and fundamental features

Features	
Opening Price	Polarity of TWTR Stock Price
Adj Closing Price	Polarity of SNAP Stock Price
7-days Simple Moving Average	Polarity of GOOGL Stock Price
20-days Simple Moving Average	Polarity of MSFT Stock Price
7-days Exponential Moving Average	Polarity of AAPL Stock Price
20-days Exponential Moving Average	Price of DJIA
Closing Price predicted by ARIMA	Price of SPX
Polarity of AMAN Stock Price	Price of NDX

Stock market data is given in a Boolean format. 0 indicates that the price P_t of a competitor, at time t, increased in comparison to its price P_{t-1}, at $t-1$,

[4] https://textblob.readthedocs.io/en/dev.
[5] https://github.com/fnielsen/afinn.
[6] https://github.com/sfu-discourse-lab/SO-CAL.

and likewise 1. All the values are standardized by the formula: $z_i = \frac{x_i - \mu}{\sigma}$; where z_i is a standard score called also z-score, x_i is an observed value, μ is the mean value of the sample, and σ indicates the standard deviation of the sample.

Sentiment Feature. The extracted tweets are in raw form and need to be pre-processed before being used as input for the machine learning algorithms. In order to consider the Twitter dataset mentioning about Facebook as one feature in our model input, we perform the following steps to convert the tweets into the appropriate form:

- Lowercase conversion
- Removing emoticon
- Reducing special characters such as "?,.!"
- HTML handling: removing HTML tags such as "$< p >$" and "$< br >$"
- URL handling: replacing URL with "URL"
- @ handling: replacing @ with "USERNAME"
- $ handling: replacing $ with "ENTITY"
- Hashtag handling: replacing # with "HASHTAG"
- Number handling: replacing numbers like $100, 123, 0.98, 30/05/2017 with "money", "number", "ratio," and "date" respectively
- Laugh handling: replacing "hahahaha" with "laugh"
- Negation replacement: replacing negation with its antonym
- Repeated character handling: replacing repeated character such as sweeeeet with "sweet"
- Slang replacement: replacing slangs like "2day","aka" and "cuz" with "today", "also known as" and "because" respectively

For VADER and TextBlob, the pre-processed text is fed to obtain the sentiment score. However, in the case of SentiWordNet and Afinn, an additional word stemming and Part-of-Speech tagging steps are applied to obtain a sentiment score. For SO-CAL, the raw text data is handled by a python script and the sentiment score is computed by the Stanford CoreNLP[7]. Consequently, the obtained dataset consists of the date of tweets, five sentiment values, and a bot label. The mean value of sentiment scores is considered as a representative of the sentiment score in a day, which results in two datasets consisting of 80 days of sentiment scores for each sentiment analysis tool related to human and spambot accounts. The datasets sample, for both human and spambots, is shown in Tables 4 and 3 respectively.

The total number of days, where the mean sentiment score shows negative polarity, is computed and the ratio is obtained for each data. The result shows that spambots data has 30 days of negative polarity sentiment score out of the 80 days, which represents 37.5%. However, for human data, we found 8 days of negative polarity sentiment score out of the 80 days with a percentage of 10%. Thus, there is a tendency that spambot accounts post negative context more than genuine users.

[7] https://stanfordnlp.github.io/CoreNLP.

Table 3. Values of mean sentiment score for Human users

Date	SentiWordNet	VADER	TextBlob	Afinn	SO-CAL
2017-05-18	0.56	0.23	0.01	1.00	0.69
2017-05-19	0.67	–0.01	0.10	0.01	0.04
2017-05-20	0.61	0.20	0.16	1.00	1.08
2017-05-21	0.56	0.10	0.16	0.42	0.95
2017-05-22	0.52	0.07	0.09	0.14	0.40

Table 4. Values of mean sentiment score for Bot users

Date	SentiWordNet	VADER	TextBlob	Afinn	SO-CAL
2017-05-18	0.50	0.00	0.00	0.00	0.00
2017-05-19	0.57	0.08	0.09	0.45	0.43
2017-05-20	0.25	0.02	0.02	0.10	0.90
2017-05-21	0.55	0.07	0.23	0.30	0.71
2017-05-22	0.69	0.08	0.19	0.18	0.59

4.4 Model Generation

We selected the GAN model to predict the stock closing price of Facebook where both the generator and the discriminator are RNNs. Especially, LSTM is used due to its capability of handling sequential inputs. The general architecture of the used GAN model is depicted in Fig. 2.

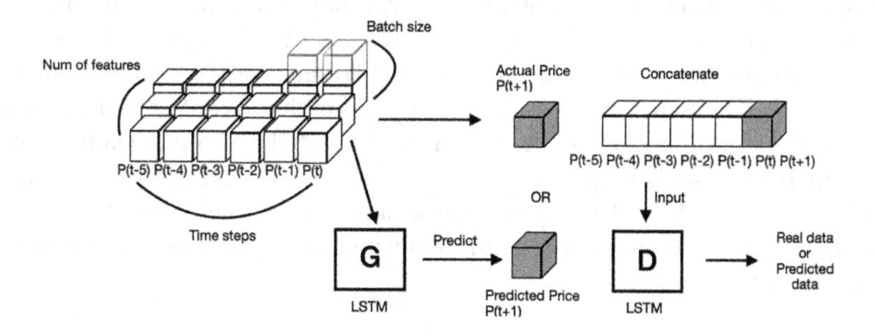

Fig. 2. The architecture of the GAN model

The generator, which is composed of an LSTM layer, takes an input with a 3-dimensional shape (batch size, time step, number of features). The time step indicates the number of steps being looked back. In this work, time step is equal to 5, which means that the input contains the value P from $t-5$ to t. Moreover, the number of features is the number of the collected data such as SMA, EMA, ARIMA, sentiment data, etc. The generator takes the selected features as input vectors, and based on a fully connected layer with a single perceptron, the closing price of Facebook at time $t + 1$ is predicted. Before feeding the input to the discriminator, the predicted closing price $P_{pred(t+1)}$, at $t + 1$, and the actual price $P_{actual(t+1)}$, at $t + 1$, are concatenated to the prices P, from $t - time\_steps$ to t. The discriminator, which also consists of an LSTM layer, takes the concatenated vector with a length of $timesteps + 1$ and predicts whether the input vector is real or generated by the generator.

5 Experimental Results

To investigate the performance of the GAN model, we test our approach with different experiments and compare the obtained results versus those of the state of the art models.

5.1 Experimental Setup

For our experiments, all the dataset, including textual and numerical data, is divided into two subsets. 80% of the dataset is used as the train set and 20% as the test set for evaluating the model. Our experiments were carried out under the configuration of macOS Catalina 10.15.4 (CPU: Intel(R) Xeon(R) CPU @2.30 GHz, RAM: 12 GB), in which Python (Version 3.6), Tensorflow (Version 2.2.0), and Keras (Version 2.3.1) have been installed.

5.2 Loss Assessment

For the training of the GAN model, the discriminator is trained with both spambots and human data. The assessed loss represents the average loss from the two datasets. On the other hand, the generator is trained indirectly by training the entire model. The generator loss is inferred from the loss of the discriminator based on the spambot dataset. A plot of the loss of the two models is shown in Fig. 3, where the x-axis indicates the number of epochs, and the y-axis indicates the loss. Thus, the loss of the generator is larger than the one of the discriminator. In addition, as more epochs are elapsing, the total loss becomes smaller and the model converges.

5.3 Evaluation Metrics

In order to assess the impact of spambot tweets on Facebook stock market closing price, we first build a GAN model and train it with the selected features described in Table 2. Consequently, the result of the prediction of the closing price sequence is compared to the actual price sequence to evaluate the model performance. By following that, we add an additional input feature, consisting in the twitter sentiment data, to the previous input features

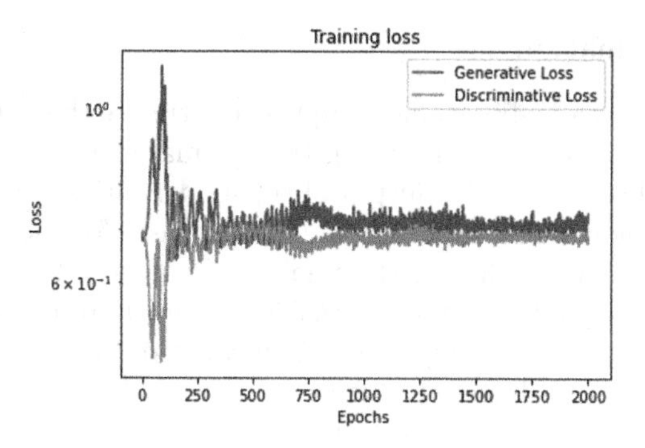

Fig. 3. The generator and discriminator loss

and carry out the same process to train and evaluate our model. These processes are repeated for bot and human Twitter sentiment data, to estimate whether the error increase when changing the input. For the calculation of an error between a predicted price sequence and an actual price sequence, we use three error metrics, i.e., Root Mean Squared Error (RMSE), Mean Absolute Error (MAE), and Mean Absolute Percentage Error (MAPE). Those evaluation metrics are defined respectively in Eqs. 2, 3, and 4, where N is the number of elements in the given input, y_i is the predicted value, and $\bar{y_i}$ is the actual value.

$$RMSE = \sqrt{\frac{1}{N}\sum_{i=1}^{N}(y_i - \bar{y_i})^2} \quad (2)$$

$$MAE = \frac{1}{N}\sum_{i=1}^{N}|y_i - \bar{y_i}| \quad (3)$$

$$MAPE = \frac{1}{N}\sum_{i=1}^{N}|10^2 \times \frac{y_i - \bar{y_i}}{y_i}| \quad (4)$$

5.4 Baseline Models

In the experiment, we adopt SVR and LSTM as the baselines.

- SVR is the same as SVM, which is one of the most popular models in the classification of financial stock. However, it is used for regression instead of classification. It uses the same terms and functionalities as SVM to predict continuous value.
- LSTM networks belong to the class of RNNs. The LSTM is composed of an input layer, one or more hidden layers, and an output layer. The number of neurons in the input layer (respectively the output layer) corresponds to the number of the feature space (respectively the output space). The hidden layers are constitute of the memory cells.

5.5 Model Evaluation

Before training all the combinations of inputs to estimate the impact of sentiment scores in tweets, we start by computing the optimal time steps where the error metric is the smallest. Since the output of the model varies in each new training, we run 10 times the training and the evaluation phases for each experiment, and we compute the median value as the final result. Figure 4 depicts the boxplot of the RMSE for each time step, which is obtained from the model trained with different time steps varying from 3 to 9. Indeed, both of the error and the variance increase as the time step increase.

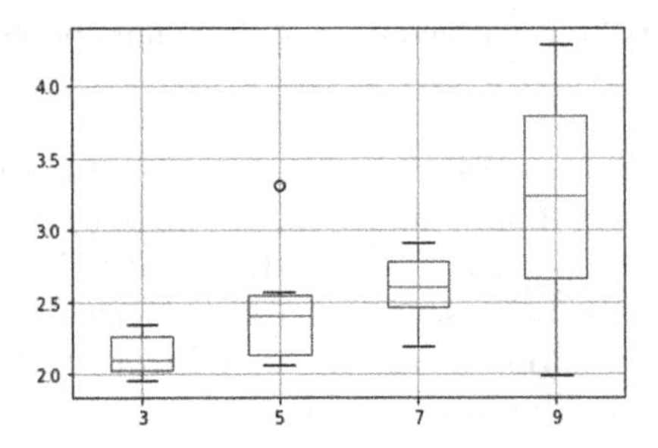

Fig. 4. Boxplot of RMSE value with time steps. X-axis indicates Time Steps and y-axis represents RMSE

Table 5. The median of the RMSE error for each time step

Time-Steps	3	5	7	9
RMSE	2.10	2.41	2.61	3.24

The error of the model without sentiment data is fixed as the base error to which other RMSE results are compared. Table 5 shows the median of RMSE for each time step. It indicates that the model trained with 3 time-steps has the smallest RMSE value. Hence, the RMSE value equal to 2.10, obtained with 3 time-steps, is chosen as a base error in our experiments. After obtaining the base error, we repeat training the model with all the combinations of the inputs to compute their related errors. The error results are depicted in Table 6. As underscored by Table 6, the input including bot tweets sentiment score captured the trend of the FaceBook's stock closing price, since it has smaller error than the input with human tweets. Moreover, by computing the average of the error, the tweets analyzed by the VADER sentiment analysis tool decrease the error the most. Since the error in Table 6 mostly decreases in comparison to the base error, it is beneficial to take the tweets sentiment score as one of the input features of the GAN model, in order to predict the stock price of Facebook.

Table 6. The GAN RMSE using five sentiment analysis tools

	SentiWordNet	VADER	TextBlob	Afinn	SO-CAL
Bot	1.98	**1.96**	2.04	2.61	2.03
Human	2.18	2.10	2.18	**1.98**	2.13
Average	2.08	**2.03**	2.11	2.29	2.08

We select the VADER sentiment tool for the remainder of the experiments since it achieved the best result as shown in Table 6. Indeed, VADER yields the lowest average RMSE loss, equal to 2.03, compared to the other sentiment analysis tools having an average RMSE between 2.08 and 2.29.

We compare our model with LSTM and SVR, in terms of RMSE, MAE, and MAPE metrics. For the training step, the LSTM model is trained with 3 time-steps, for each dataset. Whereas, SVR is trained with the same features, that have been of use for training the LSTM model, but without time steps. The comparison results, given in Table 7, show that the GAN model yields the lowest loss in terms of RMSE, MAE, and MAPE, for the bot and human datasets. For instance, in terms of RMSE, our model has an average loss of 1.88, whereas, the LSTM and The SVR generated a loss of 2.18 and 2.72 respectively. Besides, our model flags out a significant result in terms of MAPE. The latter, assessing how accurate a forecast system is, has a value equal to 0.92, outperforming those obtained by the LSTM and the SVR equal, respectively, to 1.07 and 1.34.

Table 7. The RMSE, MAE, and MAPE values computed by the GAN, LSTM and SVR models based on the VADER tool

Error metric	RMSE			MAE			MAPE		
	GAN	LSTM	SVR	GAN	LSTM	SVR	GAN	LSTM	SVR
Bot	**1.84**	2.30	2.92	**1.52**	1.84	2.42	**0.89**	1.07	1.42
Human	**1.92**	2.07	2.53	**1.61**	1.83	2.16	**0.95**	1.07	1.27
Average	**1.88**	2.18	2.72	**1.57**	1.83	2.29	**0.92**	1.07	1.34

Moreover, we compare the three models in terms of the closing price prediction quality. The plots of the predicted prices and the actual ones based on the three models, for both bot and human tweets, are shown respectively in Fig. 5a and Fig. 5b. The two plots show that the GAN prediction is the closest to the actual prices based on both spambot tweets, in Fig. 5a, and human tweets, in Fig. 5b. For instance, in Fig. 5a, specifically on day 76, the GAN model shows the closest predicted value to the actual price (equal to 172.9) with a value of 169.9 followed by the SVR and the LSTM with a value of 168.7.

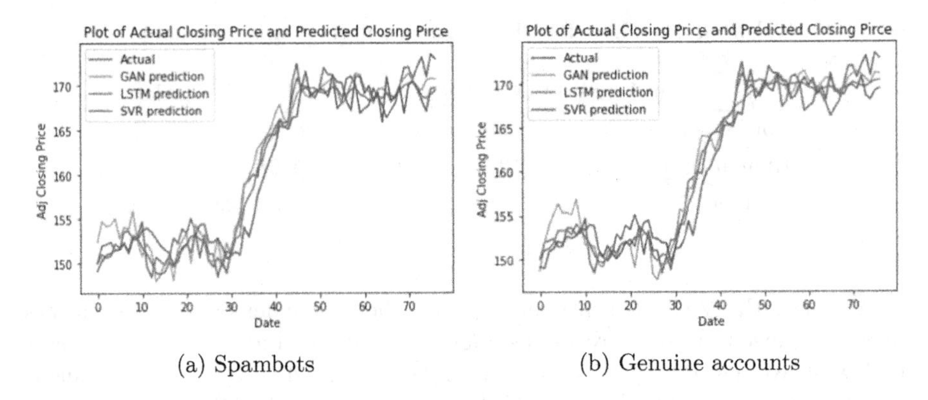

(a) Spambots (b) Genuine accounts

Fig. 5. Plot of predicted values derived from GAN, LSTM, and SVR: (5a) using spambot tweets and the actual closing price; and (5b) using human tweets and the actual closing price

6 Conclusion

In this paper, we built a GAN model to assess the impact of spambot tweets on financial stock market prices especially Facebook. The comparison of our model error, without sentiment data (called base error) to its error using different sentiment analysis tools, shows the impact of tweet sentiments to capture the trend of the FaceBook's stock closing price. Since the RMSE error obtained with the input including spambot tweets decreases more than the one including human tweets, it can be assumed that spambot tweets potentially grasp investors' attention and induce the decision to buy and sell. For future study, we plan to use additional stock price data, related to international companies, having a longer duration to investigate the error of our model. We also plan to integrate online news data into our model, including financial, political, and other online data, that can be inferred, for example, from Reuters[8] and Bloomberg[9], to study their impact on stock market prediction. Owe to the promising results we obtained, another possible direction is to study the capability of the GAN model to forecast multiple-step values.

Acknowledgements. The authors are supported by the Astra funding program Grant 2014–2020.4.01.16-032.

[8] https://www.reuters.com.
[9] https://www.bloomberg.com.

References

1. Ahirwar, K.: Generative Adversarial Networks Projects: Build Next-Generation Generative Models using TensorFlow and Keras. Birmingham: Packt Publishing Ltd, 1 edn. (2019)
2. Akita, R., Yoshihara, A., Matsubara, T., Uehara, K.: Deep learning for stock prediction using numerical and textual information. In: Proceedings of the IEEE/ACIS International Conference on Computer and Information Science. Okayama, Japan, pp. 1–6 (2016)
3. Bollen, J., Mao, H.: Twitter mood as a stock market predictor. Computer **44**(10), 91–94 (2011)
4. Cresci, S., Di Pietro, R., Petrocchi, M., Spognardi, A., Tesconi, M.: Fame for sale: efficient detection of fake twitter followers. Decis. Support Syst. **80**, 56–71 (2015)
5. Cresci, S., Di Pietro, R., Petrocchi, M., Spognardi, A., Tesconi, M.: Social fingerprinting: detection of spambot groups through DNA-inspired behavioral modeling. IEEE Trans. Dependable Secur. Comput. **15**(4), 561–576 (2018)
6. Cresci, S., Lillo, F., Regoli, D., Tardelli, S., Tesconi, M.: Cashtag piggybacking: uncovering spam and bot activity in stock microblogs on twitter. ACM Trans. Web **13**(2), 11:1–11:27 (2019)
7. Deng, S., Mitsubuchi, T., Shioda, K., Shimada, T., Sakurai, A.: Combining technical analysis with sentiment analysis for stock price prediction. In: Proceedings of the 9th International Conference on Dependable, Autonomic and Secure Computing. DASC 2011, IEEE Computer Society, USA, pp. 800–807 (2011)
8. Fernquist, J., Kaati, L., Schroeder, R.: Political bots and the swedish general election. In: IEEE International Conference on Intelligence and Security Informatics, pp. 124–129. Florida, USA, Miami (2018)
9. Goodfellow, I.J., et al.: Generative adversarial nets. In: Proceedings of the 27th International Conference on Neural Information Processing Systems. NIPS 2014, MIT Press, Cambridge, MA, USA, Vol. 2, pp. 2672–2680 (2014)
10. Hegazy, O., Soliman, O.S., Salam, A.M.: A machine learning model for stock market prediction. Int. J. Comput. Sci. Telecommun. **4**(12), 17–23 (2014)
11. Ibrahim, M., Abdillah, O., Wicaksono, A.F., Adriani, M.: Buzzer detection and sentiment analysis for predicting presidential election results in a twitter nation. In: Proceedings of the 2015 IEEE International Conference on Data Mining Workshop. Washington, DC, USA, pp. 1348–1353. IEEE (2015)
12. Khan, W., Ghazanfar, M.A., Azam, M.A., Karami, A., Alyoubi, K.H., Alfakeeh, A.S.: Stock market prediction using machine learning classifiers and social media, news. J. Ambient Intell. Humanized Comput. (2020)
13. Kogan, S., Moskowitz, T.J., Niessner, M.: Fake news: evidence from financial markets. SSRN (2019)
14. Koochali, A., Schichtel, P., Dengel, A., Ahmed, S.: Probabilistic forecasting of sensory data with generative adversarial networks - forgan. IEEE Access **7**, 63868–63880 (2019)
15. Li, X., Wu, P., Wang, W.: Incorporating stock prices and news sentiments for stock market prediction: a case of Hong kong. Inform. Process. Manag. p. 102212 (2020)
16. Liu, B.: Sentiment analysis and opinion mining. Synth. Lect. Human Lang. Technol. **5**(1), 1–167 (2012)
17. Moukalled, M., El-Hajj, W., Jaber, M.: Automated stock price prediction using machine learning. In: Proceedings of the Second Financial Narrative Processing Workshop. FNP 2019, Turku, Finland, pp. 16–24 (2019)

18. Nooralahzadeh, F., Arunachalam, V., Chiru, C.G.: 2012 presidential elections on twitter - an analysis of how the us and french election were reflected in tweets. In: Proceedings of the 19th International Conference on Control Systems and Computer Science. CSCS 2013, Bucharest, Romania, pp. 240–246 (2013)
19. Parsons, D.D.: The impact of fake news on company value: evidence from tesla and galena biopharma. Chancellor's Honors Program Projects (2020)
20. Sadia, K.H., Sharma, A., Paul, A., Padhi, S., Sanyal, S.: Stock market prediction using machine learning algorithms. Int. J. Eng. Adv. Technol. **8**(4), 25–31 (2019)

Integrating Adaptive Mechanisms into Mobile Applications Exploiting User Feedback

Quim Motger[1(✉)], Xavier Franch[1], and Jordi Marco[2]

[1] Department of Service and Information System Engineering (ESSI), Universitat Politècnica de Catalunya (UPC), Jordi Girona 1-3, 08030 Barcelona, Spain
{jmotger,franch}@essi.upc.edu

[2] Department of Computer Science (CS), Universitat Politècnica de Catalunya (UPC), Jordi Girona 1-3, 08030 Barcelona, Spain
jmarco@cs.upc.edu

Abstract. Mobile applications have become a commodity in multiple daily scenarios. Their increasing complexity has led mobile software ecosystems to become heterogeneous in terms of hardware specifications, features and context of use, among others. For their users, fully exploiting their potential has become challenging. While enacting software systems with adaptation mechanisms has proven to ease this burden from users, mobile devices present specific challenges related to privacy and security concerns. Nevertheless, rather than being a limitation, users can play a proactive role in the adaptation loop by providing valuable feedback for runtime adaptation. To this end, we propose the use of chatbots to interact with users through a human-like smart conversational process. We depict a work-in-progress proposal of an end-to-end framework to integrate semi-automatic adaptation mechanisms for mobile applications. These mechanisms include the integration of both implicit and explicit user feedback for autonomous user categorization and execution of enactment action plans. We illustrate the applicability of such techniques through a set of scenarios from the Mozilla mobile applications suite. We envisage that our proposal will improve user experience by bridging the gap between users' needs and the capabilities of their mobile devices through an intuitive and minimally invasive conversational mechanism.

Keywords: Mobile software ecosystems · Mobile applications · Adaptive software systems · Chatbots · Conversational agents · User feedback · User categorization

1 Introduction

The pervasiveness of smartphone devices and the use of mobile applications as fundamental tools around the globe is already a reality. By January 2020, around 5,190 million unique users were using a mobile phone [9], which implies

S. Cherfi et al. (Eds.): RCIS 2021, LNBIP 415, pp. 347–355, 2021.
https://doi.org/10.1007/978-3-030-75018-3_23

an increase of 2.4% compared to January 2019 reports. Despite being far from universal, and even though there are still significant usage gaps (e.g., rural-urban, gender or age), a wide range of services including instant messaging and social networking have become essential in a variety of personal and business cases [1].

This increasing trend has a direct impact not only in the number of users, but also in the complexity and heterogeneity of mobile software ecosystems. This complexity entails hardware specifications (e.g., manufacturers, sensors), software specifications (e.g., operating systems, mobile applications), features (e.g., web browsing, social networking) and context of use (e.g., personal vs. professional, private vs. public), among others. As users' goals and needs are unique, managing and fully exploiting the potential of the applications portfolio is a challenging task, which includes not only the ability of such ecosystems to unveil and adapt hidden features or settings from the user viewpoint (e.g., detecting and understanding hidden privacy settings [5]), but also their ability to adapt hardware and software components to match the users' needs.

A suitable method to overcome these challenges is the integration of adaptation mechanisms and decision-making features in software systems [18], a research area undergoing intense study in mobile-based systems [7]. However, smartphones present additional challenges related to the management of personal and sensitive data, as well as the additional knowledge that can be extracted from this data [15]. Therefore, they require from explicit user interaction for most changes in their mobile devices and applications.

Despite this limitation, the need for integrating the user in the adaptation loop can be conceived as an opportunity. In fact, effective evaluation of explicit user feedback is considered a key factor and a challenge in adaptive software systems [8]. Among explicit feedback collection techniques from users, the integration of virtual assistants, conversational agents or simply *chatbots* is beginning to grow exponentially. Nevertheless, chatbots are still an emerging technology, with a lack of scientific relevant presence in some research areas [2].

In this paper, we aim to depict a work-in-progress proposal of an end-to-end framework for **semi-automatic adaptation in the context of mobile software ecosystems**. We refer to semi-automatic adaptation as the set of mechanisms which combine (1) autonomous techniques for the collection of contextual and implicit feedback data, and (2) explicit feedback knowledge obtained through users interaction with a chatbot integrated in their smartphones.

2 Background

From the software engineering viewpoint, mobile-based systems or **mobile software ecosystems** as defined by Grua et al. [7] can induce adaptation mechanisms anywhere in the system. It is relevant to differentiate between adaptation at device level (e.g., mobile platform, device hardware) or at mobile application level (e.g., client app, back-end). With independence of where the adaptation takes place, one of the underlying goals of these approaches is to improve user satisfaction and the Quality of Service (QoS) delivered to these users [7].

If we focus on adaptation at the **mobile application** level, mechanisms and strategies to achieve these goals are diverse. Some examples include dynamic selection of user interfaces to improve usability dimensions at runtime [3], context-aware self-adaptation techniques for back-end infrastructures of mobile applications [14], and automatic reconfiguration of features to achieve customizable and adaptive personal goals [16]. On the other hand, the level of **automation** of these mechanisms is also manifold, whether adaptation is designed as a fully-automatic process transparent to users or as an assisted, semi-automatic process requiring explicit interaction between users and the application itself [4].

In practice, most of these adaptation strategies and mechanisms are transparent to the users. When measuring and evaluating adaptive mobile applications, evaluation focuses on QoS to enhance user experience [17]. Among these quality characteristics we highlight functional or **feature** suitability based on users needs, and non-functional or **quality** concerns including usability, reliability and performance efficiency as the most cited characteristics in mobile apps [10].

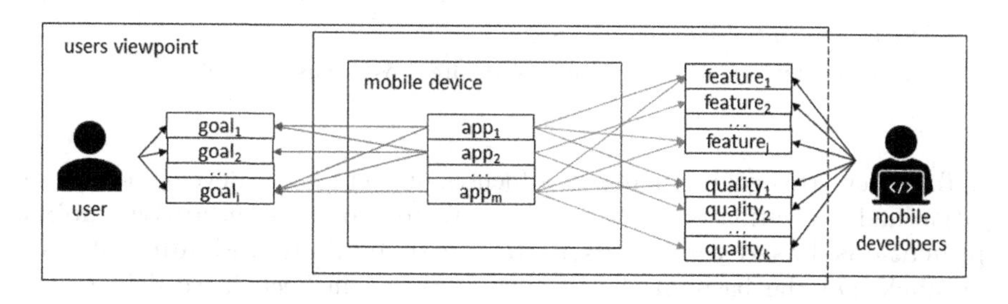

Fig. 1. Mobile software ecosystems from the user viewpoint

All things considered, from the **users' viewpoint**, mobile software ecosystems are conceived as support tools giving them access to a portfolio of **mobile applications** exposing a set of **features** and **qualities** to achieve their personal **goals**. In the context of enacting these ecosystems with adaptive tools, from the **mobile developer viewpoint**, the challenge is to identify, define, develop and integrate the underlying adaptation mechanisms these features and qualities from mobile applications require to help users achieve these goals.

To this end, context monitoring as well as implicit and explicit user feedback analysis are fundamental tools for runtime adaptation [13]. Regarding the latter, the use of **chatbots** to process user inquiries and feedback is recently growing at exponential levels, especially in specific domains like healthcare or business [2]. They offer not only the potential of collecting and processing natural language feedback at runtime from users to extend missing context information [11], but also to extend the user experience through a smart, human-like conversational interface they are actually familiarized with, which has been proved to be an effective strategy for increasing user engagement [6].

The potential and combination of the aforementioned strategies in the field of Human-Computer Interaction (HCI) is a subject of broad and current interest.

Some examples include implicit and explicit feedback collection in the HCI field for personalized mobile UI adaptation [19] and the integration of deep learning-based chatbots for user feedback collection [12]. However, these approaches cover these strategies partially, or they are focused on a limited object of adaptation.

3 The Framework

3.1 Research Method

Following the *Goal Question Metric* (GQM) approach, we state the research objective of this paper as follows:

Analyse	Semi-automatic adaptation mechanisms
for the purpose of	Enhancing user experience
with respect to	Features and qualities of mobile applications
from the point of view of	Users
in the context of	Mobile software ecosystems

To achieve this goal, our research focuses on the design, development, integration and evaluation of an **end-to-end framework for adaptive mobile applications based on the exploitation of explicit and implicit user feedback**. On the basis of the context described in Sect. 2, we define these adaptation mechanisms to be supported by our framework as follows:

1. Adapt features and qualities of mobile applications (including client apps, back-end and third-party services) at runtime.
2. Install and remove mobile applications to update users applications portfolio.
3. Update mobile applications to deliver customized solutions through user segmentation.

These mechanisms shall be enacted based on users needs and preferences, as well as additional contextual data. To this end, this framework is designed as the integration and combination of a sub-set of stand-alone software components, including: (1) the design and development of a conversational agent in users smartphones to collect and process users natural language feedback; (2) the integration of implicit feedback collection and context monitoring techniques based on users interaction with their smartphones and their applications; and (3) the combination of explicit and implicit feedback to learn and predict user categories and enactment plans for the adaptation of users applications portfolio.

3.2 Design Overview

We illustrate our framework proposal (Fig. 2) as the software components and data artefacts required to integrate the aforementioned adaptation mechanisms into an end-to-end cycle as a means of achieving the main goal of this research. The framework is depicted in the context of users and the applications portfolio designed and developed by mobile developers as depicted in Fig. 1.

User Mobile Device. The catalogue of applications installed in a user's device (→*AppsPortfolio*) acts as the bridge between that user's goals and the set of features and qualities exposed by those applications. To assist the adaptation mechanisms, we propose a cross-platform mobile application (→*ChatbotApp*) designed to (1) collect text/speech natural language data as the result of a smart conversational process (→*Request-Message*) through the integration of a chat application interface, and (2) collect contextual data based on the user interaction with the applications portfolio and the mobile device (→*Context-Data*).

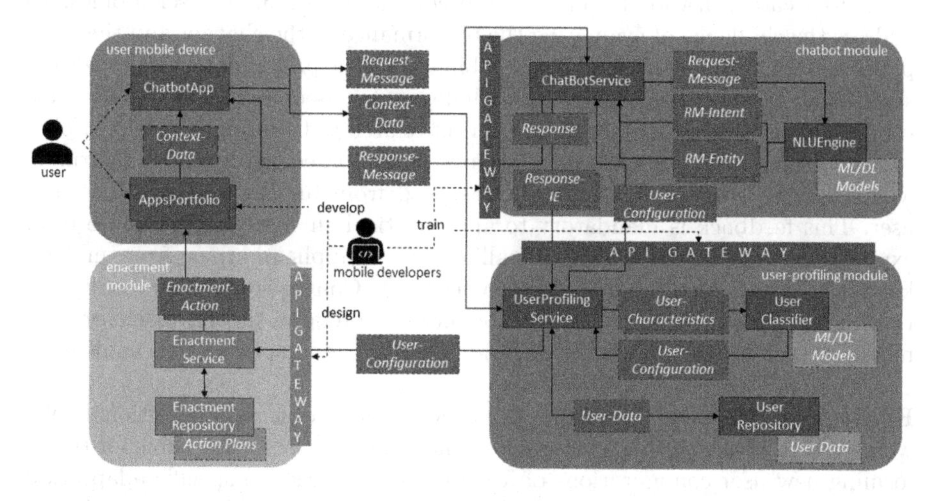

Fig. 2. The architecture of the proposed framework.

Chatbot Module. We define the chatbot module as a machine learning software system responsible for processing natural language information (→*Request-Message*) to extract interpretable knowledge from explicit user feedback. The technological core of this service (→*ChatBotService*) is the Natural Language Understanding (NLU) component (→*NLUEngine*), which is responsible for processing natural language data using previously-trained machine/deep learning models. The output of this NLU is two-fold: (1) the user intentions with respect to the applications portfolio to achieve their goals (→*RM-Intent*); and (2) the concepts or entities (i.e., applications, features and qualities) these intentions refer to, which require from these adaptations (→*RM-Entity*).

These intents and entities feed a response generation algorithm, which generates a response object (→*Response*) composed by (1) a natural language response message (→*Response-Message*) which is sent back to the user mobile device through the chat application interface, and (2) a set of intent-entity (IE) pairs which relate specific intents with the entities they refer to (→*Response-IE*).

User-Profiling Module. We define the user-profiling module as a machine learning software system responsible for integrating implicit (→*Context-Data*) and explicit (→*Response-IE*) user feedback to learn and predict user configuration models (→*User-Configuration*), which depict a set of parameterized features and qualities of the user applications portfolio. To compute this configuration, the user-profiling service (→*UserProfilingService*) integrates user feedback with additional data including historic interaction with the mobile applications portfolio and user profile information (→*User-Data*), which is persisted in the system (→*UserRepository*). User feedback and context data are combined to compute a set of structured, deterministic characteristics or metrics (→*User-Characteristics*). These characteristics are the input of a constantly-evolved user classifier (→*UserClassifier*) which uses machine/deep learning models to apply user categorization techniques to predict and learn about user profiles. To address the challenge of evaluating the performance of the chatbot and the user-profiling modules, we suggest the combination of a preliminary generalization stage using open-source, task-oriented dialogue data-sets and a fine-tuning stage using a supervised, domain-specific data-set related to the applications portfolio.

The user-profiling service must include a rule-based approach to determine whether newly computed configurations need from further feedback from the user. This feedback is mandatory to apply critical changes which require from explicit user confirmation (e.g. installing a new application) or from missing knowledge (e.g. uncertainties about a feature). Consequently, user configurations might be sent back to the chatbot service to require this feedback, or they might be sent to the enactment module to apply the adaptation mechanisms.

Enactment Module. We define the enactment module as a traditional software system implementing a service (→*EnactmentService*) responsible for transforming new user configurations of features and qualities to specific adaptation mechanisms or enactment actions (→*Enactment-Action*) to be executed in the user applications portfolio. These actions are eligible through a set of pre-defined adaptation or action plans stored in the system (→*EnactmentRepository*). The service inputs and processes the user configurations predicted by the user-profiling module and retrieves which action plans are required to achieve this new configuration. Each action plan is transformed into this set of enactment actions, which are sent to the user device, closing the end-to-end workflow of the framework.

4 Case-Study: The Mozilla Foundation

The Mozilla Foundation[1] is a community open source project founded in 1998. Its market-based work, the Mozilla Corporation, is responsible for developing a portfolio of open-source tools for web access and navigation (e.g. the Mozilla Firefox web browser) and a set of open-source mobile applications, including:

- **FirefoxDaylight**. Native Android application of the Firefox web browser.
- **FirefoxFocus**. Private browser for anonymous web navigation.
- **FirefoxNightly**. Developmental channel for users to test new features and provide feedback before publishing them to the stable releases.

Firefox implements an Enhanced Tracking Protection (ETP) feature[2] which allows enabling/disabling web trackers according to the user preferences. This feature allows 4 different configurations: *disabled*, *standard* (blocks all trackers except content tracking), *strict* (blocks all trackers) and *personalized* (customized manually by the user). By default, ETP is set to *standard*.

In this context, we depict three proof-of-concept scenarios to demonstrate how the adaptation mechanisms described in Sect. 3.1 can be integrated into the framework proposal depicted in Sect. 3.2. We identify two different users: Alice, a new user in the Mozilla context who has recently added FirefoxDaylight to her device; and Bob, a user with long experience with the Firefox suite.

Scenario A - Adaptation of Features And Qualities. The user-profiling module detects an uncertainty regarding Alice's security-related characteristics. The chatbot module sends a message to Alice's chatbot client app asking her about her security and personal data sharing concerns. Alice makes explicit her reluctance to share any personal data with unknown entities. The chatbot module processes this information and redirects the associated IEs to the user-profiling module, which updates Alice's persistent data, generating a new user configuration for Alice where the ETP feature in FirefoxDaylight is set to strict. Consequently, an enactment action is sent to Alice's device to apply this change.

Scenario B - Update of Users Applications Portfolio. The user-profiling module updates the classifier models and categorizes Alice under a profile of security-concerned users like Bob. Unlike Alice, Bob has additional applications from the Mozilla portfolio, including the FirefoxFocus anonymous browser. The chatbot module generates a message to inform Alice about this application which might be suitable for users like her. After responding with an explicit confirmation, a new adaptation mechanism is triggered to send a new enactment action to install this application in Alice's device, and her user profile information is updated according to this change in her applications portfolio.

Scenario C - Customization Through User Segmentation. Mozilla has published a new functionality F into the FirefoxNightly app to be evaluated by

[1] https://foundation.mozilla.org/en/who-we-are/.

[2] https://support.mozilla.org/en-US/kb/enhanced-tracking-protection-firefox-android.

users. After a few weeks of evaluation, the user-profiling module detects that users like Bob have successfully integrated F into their web navigation experience. On the other hand, users like Alice either have reported negative feedback about F or they have not used it at all. Consequently, Mozilla launches a segmented update of FirefoxDaylight including this new functionality, which will only be available for the sub-set of users categorized under Bob's profile.

These scenarios illustrate our framework as a holistic approach to adapt the Mozilla applications portfolio to their users by simplifying the interaction required from them. The approach benefits from implicit and explicit feedback to learn about users and adapt their applications towards a better user experience.

5 Future Work and Conclusions

Further research should be primarily devoted to the following tasks:

- Extend the scope of the depicted adaptation mechanisms that can be integrated into the proposed framework (e.g., software evolution).
- Review challenges from the chatbot domain, with emphasis on (1) analysing sociolinguistic features to increase user engagement and acceptance, and (2) comparing different strategies concerning the integration of a general-purpose NLU Engine with a fine-tuning process for task-specific purposes.
- Design and execute feature extraction techniques to identify relevant user characteristics for an accurate categorization in the context of this research.
- Design a domain-specific language to describe the mapping between user characteristics, user configurations, action plans and enactment actions.
- Research, discuss and elaborate on data collection and data management challenges for the development of the chatbot module and the user-profiling module, as well as for training, testing and evaluating the framework.

Our proposal aims at assisting users to achieve their goals through advanced feedback collection and analysis techniques. Among these, integrating a smart conversational process into the user's device and using machine/deep learning model for user categorization and segmentation are fundamental to guarantee the novelty of the solution. The scenarios of the Mozilla case-study give a glance at the potential application of our framework to real business cases. Ultimately, these preliminary results lay the groundwork for future research regarding state-of-the-art analysis and initial proof-of-concept development tasks towards a better user experience in mobile software ecosystems.

Acknowledgments. This work has been partially supported by AGAUR, code 2017-SGR-1694. The corresponding author gratefully acknowledges the Universitat Politècnica de Catalunya and Banco Santander for the financial support of his predoctoral grant FPI-UPC.

References

1. Bahia, K., Delaporte, A.: The state of mobile internet connectivity report 2020 - mobile for development (2020). https://www.gsma.com/r/somic/

2. Bernardini, A., Sônego, A., Pozzebon, E.: Chatbots: an analysis of the state of art of literature. In: Workshop on Advanced Virtual Environments and Education, Vol. 1, No. 1, pp. 1–6 (2018)
3. Braham, A., Buendía, F., Khemaja, M., Gargouri, F.: User interface design patterns and ontology models for adaptive mobile applications. Pers. Ubiquit. Comput. 1–17 (2021). https://doi.org/10.1007/s00779-020-01481-5
4. Brun, Y., et al.: Software Engineering for Self-Adaptive Systems. chap. Engineering Self-Adaptive Systems through Feedback Loops (2009)
5. Chen, Y., et al.: Demystifying hidden privacy settings in mobile apps. In: 2019 IEEE Symposium on Security and Privacy (SP) (2019)
6. Dev, J., Camp, L.J.: User engagement with chatbots: a discursive psychology approach. In: Proceedings of the 2nd Conference on Conversational User Interfaces. CUI 2020, New York, NY, USA (2020)
7. Grua, E.M., Malavolta, I., Lago, P.: Self-adaptation in mobile apps: a systematic literature study. In: 2019 IEEE/ACM 14th International Symposium on Software Engineering for Adaptive and Self-Managing Systems (SEAMS) (2019)
8. Jasberg, K., Sizov, S.: Human uncertainty in explicit user feedback and its impact on the comparative evaluations of accurate prediction and personalisation. Behav. Inf. Technol. (2020)
9. Kemp, S.: Digital 2020: global digital overview - global digital insights (2020). https://datareportal.com/reports/digital-2020-global-digital-overview
10. Maia, V., da Rocha, A., Gonçalves, T.: Identification of quality characteristics in mobile applications. In: CIbSE (2020)
11. Martens, D., Maalej, W.: Extracting and analyzing context information in user-support conversations on twitter. In: IEEE 27th International Requirements Engineering Conference (RE) (2019)
12. Nivethan, Sankar, S.: Sentiment analysis and deep learning based chatbot for user feedback. In: Data Engineering and Communications Technologies (2020)
13. Oriol, M., et al.: Fame: supporting continuous requirements elicitation by combining user feedback and monitoring. In: IEEE 26th International Requirements Engineering Conference (RE) (2018)
14. Orsini, G., Bade, D., Lamersdorf, W.: Cloudaware: a context-adaptive middleware for mobile edge and cloud computing applications. In: IEEE 1st International Workshops on Foundations and Applications of Self* Systems (FAS*W) (2016)
15. Picco, G.P., Julien, C., Murphy, A.L., Musolesi, M., Roman, G.C.: Software engineering for mobility: reflecting on the past, peering into the future. In: Future of Software Engineering Proceedings. New York, NY, USA (2014)
16. Qian, W., Peng, X., Wang, H., Mylopoulos, J., Zheng, J., Zhao, W.: Mobigoal: flexible achievement of personal goals for mobile users. IEEE Trans. Serv. Comput. **11**(2), 384–398 (2018)
17. Shafiuzzaman, M., Nahar, N., Rahman, M.R.: A proactive approach for context-aware self-adaptive mobile applications to ensure quality of service. In: 18th International Conference on Computer and Information Technology (2015)
18. Yang, Z., Li, Z., Jin, Z., Chen, Y.: A systematic literature review of requirements modeling and analysis for self-adaptive systems. In: Salinesi, C., van de Weerd, I. (eds.) REFSQ 2014. LNCS, vol. 8396, pp. 55–71. Springer, Cham (2014). https://doi.org/10.1007/978-3-319-05843-6_5
19. Yigitbas, E., Hottung, A., Rojas, S.M., Anjorin, A., Sauer, S., Engels, G.: Context- and data-driven satisfaction analysis of user interface adaptations based on instant user feedback. In: Proceedings of the ACM on Human-Computer Interaction, 3(EICS), pp. 1–20 (2019)

Conceptual Modeling Versus User Story Mapping: Which is the Best Approach to Agile Requirements Engineering?

Konstantinos Tsilionis[1(✉)], Joris Maene[1], Samedi Heng[2], Yves Wautelet[1], and Stephan Poelmans[1]

[1] KU Leuven, Leuven, Belgium
{konstantinos.tsilionis,yves.wautelet,stephan.poelmans}@kuleuven.be
[2] HEC Liège, Université de Liège, Liège, Belgium
samedi.heng@uliege.be

Abstract. User stories are primary requirements artifacts within agile methods. They are comprised of short sentences written in natural language expressing units of functionality for the to-be system. Despite their simple format, when modelers are faced with a set of user stories they might be having difficulty in sorting them, evaluating their redundancy, and assessing their relevancy in the effort to prioritize them. The present paper tests the ability of modelers to understand the requirements problem through a visual representation (named the Rationale Tree) which is a conceptual model and is built out of a user stories' set. The paper is built upon and extends previous work relating to the feasibility of generating such a representation out of a user stories' set by comparing the performance of the Rationale Tree with the User Story Mapping approach. This is achieved by performing a two-group quantitative comparative study. The identified comparative variables for each method were understandability, recognition of missing requirements/epics/themes, and adaptability. The Rational Tree was not easy to understand and did not perform as anticipated in assisting with the recognition of missing requirements/epics/themes. However, its employment allowed modelers to offer qualitative representations of a specific software problem. Overall, the present experiment evaluates whether a conceptual model could be a consistent solution towards the holistic comprehension of a software development problem within an agile setting, compared to more 'conventional' techniques used so far.

Keywords: User stories · User story · User Story Mapping · Rationale Tree · Agile requirements engineering

1 Introduction

User stories are artifacts often used in agile methods to describe requirements in a simple manner, demonstrating thusly the advantage of being easily understandable especially when read individually or in small sets. Nevertheless, user stories

S. Cherfi et al. (Eds.): RCIS 2021, LNBIP 415, pp. 356–373, 2021.
https://doi.org/10.1007/978-3-030-75018-3_24

can face various levels of quality and this is why Lucassen et al. [7,8] propose the Quality User Story (QUS) framework, i.e., a linguistic approach to evaluate and improve their quality individually and collectively. To unify their format, Wautelet et al. [20] collect and unify the templates mostly used by academics and agile practitioners. However, even when they are written with high quality, structured correctly and respecting defined semantics in their instances, understanding the *entire* software problem from a list of user stories remains challenging.

User Story Mapping (USM) [12] is used to address this challenge. This approach refers to a structuring method based on listing, under the scope of *Activities* (epic user stories), all of the related lower-level functions described in ordinary user stories. Meanwhile, conceptual modeling represents another approach to structuring desired system functionalities under certain criteria. Even though the latter is independent of a specific design method/technique, various notations/diagrams and/or their corresponding instantiations are often adopted in view of a modeling exercise aiming to represent and group certain functions/elements of the to-be system. In this regard, the Rationale Tree (RT) [21] offers, as a conceptual model, a visual representation of a user story structuring method, strongly inspired by i* [24]. The RT uses parts of the i* strategic rationale diagram constructs and visual notation to build various trees of relating user story elements in a single project (Fig. 1.a) with the purpose of identifying depending user stories, identifying Epic ones and group them around common Themes (Fig. 1.b).

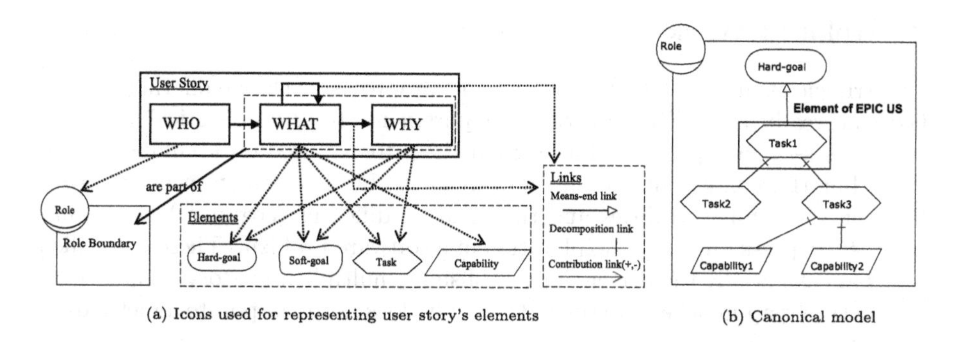

(a) Icons used for representing user story's elements (b) Canonical model

Fig. 1. Using Rationale Tree to structure user stories' sets.

Both of these techniques can be used for structuring sets of user stories but have different complexities in their application and different abilities to represent dependencies and decompositions. Intuitively, one could ask if the RT allows, as a conceptual model, for a better comprehension of the software problem or a simpler representation artifact derived from the implementation of the USM would already be sufficient. To provide more insights to this question we relay, in this paper, the results of a controlled experiment. Indeed, a first group of students has been required to employ the RT and build artifacts out of a given user stories' set; a second group has been asked to do the same with the USM approach. This study is based on the comparison of the results for these two groups. As so, the main contributions of this paper are based on:

- The evaluation of the applicability of the RT and USM by non-experienced modelers. The former has been evaluated preliminary in earlier studies. Nevertheless, the understandability/applicability of the latter has not been tested extensively, to the best of the authors' knowledge, despite its popularity in agile environments;
- The exploration of the applicability of conceptual modeling in agile requirements engineering. Indeed, we aim to evaluate whether the RT, based on a comprehensive feature decomposition, can perform efficiently compared to the USM technique which is, strictly speaking, not a conceptual model but a simple user story structuring approach. Such a comparison between two diverse techniques can impact the Computer-Aided Software Engineering (CASE) tools used to support requirements engineering in agile methods;
- An investigation into the pedagogical orientation of software engineering. Conceptual modeling has been traditionally associated with object-oriented development (i.e., taught through the use of Unified Modeling Language/UML [11]) and/or database modeling (i.e., the Entity-Relationship Model [1] etc.). However, we want to evaluate the impact of teaching/using conceptual models in the requirements engineering stage of agile developments. Thereby, the design of the present experiment aims to test the use of conceptual modeling out of its customary-taught modalities and study the possible pedagogical impact on students.

2 Related Work

Dimitrijević et al. [4] evaluate different software tools, each one offering diversified features in identifying functional requirements from user stories' sets. The study assesses the operational aspects of these tools based on a number of criteria, but the context of the entire exercise is the determination of a linkage between these functionalities and the array of different (cognitive) needs that modelers express during the exploration of a software problem. These diversified needs are essentially the drivers for establishing multiple user story management/structuring approaches. However, the study does not incorporate a method for evaluating the latter.

Tenso & Taveter [16] suggest the use of a simple goal-oriented approach to address the user stories' limitation in visualizing their proposed development trajectories. This approach negotiates the analysis of the sequence of activities and resource requirements within user stories and assigns them into functional/non-functional goals. However, it does not seem to proceed into a refined decomposition of these goals into simpler tasks that can be mapped directly to the user stories; nor does it analyze visually the inter-dependencies among the aforementioned elements to track redundant tasks and resource waste during the conceptualization of the requirements gathering process. Tenso et al. [15] interview experts so as to evaluate the previous method; its understandability is impacted without the use of implementation guidelines. Moreover, the authors seem to acknowledge that such an evaluation is limited without the use of a control group using another agile requirements method in comparison.

Dalpiaz et al. [2,3] perform an experiment to test the adequacy of two widely used natural language notations for expressing requirements (namely *use cases* and *user stories*) in delivering top-quality conceptual models. Their findings supported clearly the user stories' optimality, measured by the correctness and completeness of a manually derived UML class diagram by novice modelers. Nonetheless, Lucassen et al. [9] argue for a certain level of semantic ambiguity within the utilized words during the formation of user stories, ultimately jeopardizing the entire meaning of the story. To surpass this vulnerability, the authors suggest the utilization of an automated approach based on natural language processing, in order to produce representative (graphical) models from user story requirements.

Wautelet et al. [18] conduct an experiment to identify whether improving user story quality through the QUS framework [8] would lead to a better identification of different concepts of a user stories' set and a better development of the 'RT diagram'; this is the artifact produced when employing the RT method as described in [19,21]. Overall, the experiment was performed on novice modelers composed of two groups, one using a raw user stories set while the other using an abstract user stories set reshaped to be QUS-compliant. Overall, quality improvements in the formulation of user stories engaged the modelers' abilities to identify elements like tasks and capabilities.

Lastly, Tsilionis et al. [17] explore the performance of novice modelers when they apply the RT and USM in terms of providing artifacts that encapsulate efficiently the entire software problem as described in a specific case description. However, the study does not test the impact of understandability of these two approaches in correspondence to the modelers' performance; nor does it check the ease of use of these methods in the identification of missing requirements/epics/themes. These issues, including the search for which method can be considered more adaptable, are addressed in the present study.

3 Research Approach and Background

3.1 Research Goals

This paper aims to evaluate the RT as a user stories' structuring method. To this end, it was compared to one out of many industry-adopted approaches, namely USM. While the focus of the present experiment is the investigation of the context in which the RT is used, our current research focuses more on the comprehension of the RT as a conceptual modeling technique, rather than the case being fed to it. Therefore, the case studies and variables used in the experiment are sourced from [17,18] and they have been maintained to allow for their longitudinal comparison. As such, this research represents an extension of [17,18,22]; it attempts to evaluate and explain the problems faced in these earlier research iterations regarding the exploration and exploitation of the RT.

3.2 Sampling Method and Experimental Design

For the purposes of this controlled experiment, we chose students attending the Master program of Business Administration with a specialization track in

Business Information Management (BIM) from the 'Katholieke Universiteit Leuven (KULeuven)' (Brussels Campus) as our sample source to perform a quantitative comparative study [14]. The BIM specialization is addressed to students having a limited real-life working experience in software engineering. For this reason, it offers several courses aimed at developing multiple complementary views of software problems and their corresponding solutions. Even though the target population for the use of the RT is comprised of students, academics, and business users, the only group effectively performing the experiment was comprised of students. This can be considered as a limitation [5]. However, since no comprehensive sampling frame was available (especially for the academics and business users), we decided to use non-stochastic purposive sampling [14] in the form of typical cases [13] representing the students from the particular specialized curriculum. The participating BIM group counted originally 72 students; these were split up equally and randomly into two groups (i.e., 36 students per group). The first group was handed individual identical questionnaires dealing with the RT throughout the experiment; the questionnaires for the second group dealt with the USM.

The experiment was conducted as an extra activity during one teaching session of a compulsory spring-semester course included in the BIM curriculum and the time for completion was set to two hours. Overall, the experiment questionnaires consisted of three parts: **Part 1** was common for both groups and introduced a mix of open-ended and closed questions that explored the participants' prior software engineering knowledge and collected general background information (i.e., education level, occupation, etc.). Their domain knowledge was also assessed via a 'pre-test' evaluation asking participants to recognize the structure of a user story, recognize specific elements in an Activity diagram, and recognize the structure of a USM artifact. Due to size limitations, all the information collected in *Part 1* is presented in Appendix 1[1]. At the time of the experiment all students had already received courses in software design & modeling. Thereby, they had a theoretical understanding of user stories and several software modeling techniques (UML, Entity-Relationship Model, etc.). However, extra theoretical explanation was provided during the experiment (*Part 2*) when it comes to identifying missing requirements, epics, themes and the basics of the RT and USM approach.

Indeed, for **Part 2**, the questionnaires introduced a detailed theoretical explanation of the user story structuring approach assigned to each student group. Next, they presented a case description ('Company X' case, see Appendix 2.1) and a set of seven user stories derived from that case. Each student had to identify elements of the user stories' *WHO/WHAT/WHY*-dimension and correspond them to the modeling notations of his/her assigned approach. Next, each student had to design these modeling notations and their in-between links graphically on paper; in essence, the students had to draw a complete artifact based on information retrieved from the case description, the user stories and the theoretical instructions given in the beginning of *Part 2*. Basing themselves on

[1] All Appendices are available at: https://cutt.ly/ivvKHBT.

their previously drawn artifacts, the students had to recognize missing requirements/epics/themes; they also had to respond to six closed Likert-scale questions regarding the ease of use of each technique in identifying the previous elements. Appendix 3 provides a detailed description of the modeling exercise. *Part 2* concluded by asking the students to suggest improvements for the usability of the RT/USM.

For **Part 3**, the students had to check a separate attachment that was distributed with the original questionnaires. This attachment was introducing: i) a case description ('Film Finder' case, see Appendix 2.2), ii) a complete and complex USM model (artifact) modeling the 'Film finder' case description to be used by the USM group, and iii) a complete and complex RT diagram modeling the 'Film finder' case description to be used by the RT group. The first segment of the questionnaires asked the students to explain parts of these complex artifacts in order to test their understanding about the 'Film finder' case. The second segment tested the students' ability to adapt these artifacts by asking them to make changes and/or introduce new elements to them, on the premise of changing requirements.

3.3 Hypotheses

The hypotheses presented below are built upon existing literature that theorizes the advantages of the models proposed by Wautelet et al. [21] and Patton & Economy [12]. Conversely to the USM, the RT contains links and decompositions making it more difficult to be comprehended by novice modelers [22]. The latter incorporates also a broader choice of elements with semantics open to interpretation, adding thusly to its overall complexity [18]. Hence, we can formulate our first set of the null and alternative hypotheses:

- $H_0 1$: *The RT is as easy to understand as the USM.*
- $H_a 1$: *The RT is more difficult to understand than the USM.*

USM aims to create one-dimensional, purely hierarchical visual artifacts structuring the most basic user stories that satisfy intricate – to the software project – stakeholders [12]. Contrastingly, the RT is meant to relinquish artifacts with detailed feature decompositions assisting in the identification of missing requirements and higher-level epic user stories while grouping interrelated elements within sets of themes [21]. Therefore, the distinction between elements will probably be more difficult for the RT diagrams in the sense that a steeper learning curve may be required for a proper and qualitative representation of a software problem. This entails that more thought and especially **more time** should go into developing the RT diagram and the links among its elements. Nonetheless, the time given to complete the experiment was exactly the same for both groups (two hours). Hence, our next set of hypotheses:

- $H_0 2$: *The resulting RT diagrams and USM artifacts are equally good in providing qualitative representations.*

- ***H_a2***: *The resulting RT diagrams are worse than USM artifacts in providing qualitative representations.*

- ***$H_0$3***: *The resulting RT diagrams and USM artifacts are equally good in identifying missing requirements, epics and themes.*
- ***H_a3***: *The resulting RT diagrams are better than USM artifacts in identifying missing requirements, epics and themes.*

The complexity faced in recreating the RT diagram will eventually pay off due to its property of adaptability [21]. Once drawn, it is supposedly easier to adapt and better to maintain when requirements are changing due to its visual links. As such, we can formulate a fourth set of hypotheses:

- ***$H_0$4***: *The resulting RT diagrams and USM artifacts are equally good in being adaptable.*
- ***H_a4***: *The resulting RT diagrams are better than USM artifacts in being adaptable.*

3.4 Variables

This section identifies the variables testing the hypotheses. The answers and artifacts drawn by each student were nested together for i) the RT respondents, and ii) the USM respondents; this grouping between the two acted as our independent variable. The dependent variables evaluating the students' RT diagrams and USM artifacts are: i) Existing knowledge; ii) Pre-test evaluation; iii) Understandability; iv) Model (artifact) creation; v) Identification of missing requirements, epics and themes; vi) Adaptability. 'Existing knowledge' and 'Pre-test evaluation' acted as our control variables since most of the experiment participants had a harmonized theoretical knowledge of user stories but a rather limited knowledge in the debated user story structuring approaches.

4 Data Analysis and Validation of the Hypotheses

After processing the data received from the students, we analyzed the understandability of each method (validation of our first hypothesis). Following, we checked whether the employment of either of the two methods facilitated the students' dimension identification capabilities for the user stories' set for the 'Company X' case. Next, we evaluated their drawn RT diagrams and USM artifacts and compared the quality of their representations (validation of our second hypothesis). Our analysis concluded with a comparison between the answers of the two groups pertaining the identification of missing requirements/epics/themes (third hypothesis), and the adaptability of each method when requirements are changing (fourth hypothesis). These steps are detailed below.

4.1 $H_0$1: The RT is as Easy to Understand as the USM

The theoretical explanations for the RT and USM in the beginning of **Part 2** were purposed to educate the students about these techniques, optimize their comprehension of user stories/epics/themes, and describe the expectations of the upcoming modeling exercise. The theoretical explanations concluded by asking three Likert-scale questions to determine to what extent was: *Q1) the theory about the different elements and links – of each approach – understandable, Q2) the explanation of the upcoming modeling exercise understandable, and Q3) the expectation of the modeling exercise understandable.* The frequencies of the respondents' answers were mapped out based on the range of their understandability (i.e., the theory/explanation/expectation was 'Not at all', 'Slightly', 'Moderately', 'Very' or 'Extremely' understandable), where most of the students in both groups found the theory about different links and elements very understandable. Similarly, the modeling exercise explanation/expectation seemed also to be very understandable (see Appendix 4.1). However, when processing the answers to these three questions to recreate and compare the means of the students' responses by group and by question, we discovered that the understandability of the RT group seems to be lagging compared to the understandability of their counterparts in the USM group (Table 1). This discrepancy between the two groups takes its highest value when referring to Q1. The parametric independent-samples t-test represented in Table 2 measures whether the difference between the understandability means for the two groups relating to Q1, Q2, Q3 is significant. Due to the Central Limit Theorem (CLT), the variable used for recreating the means can be assumed normally distributed since our sample size per group is larger than 30. Equal variances were assumed after performing a Levene's test. The results show that the RT students had significant difficulty – compared to their counterparts – in understanding the theoretical concepts of the RT; the difference in the understandability between the two groups regarding the Q2 & Q3 was not significant. Hence, our *first null hypothesis can be rejected.* This difficulty in understanding the RT theory could be attributed to an insufficient theoretical explanation in the beginning of **Part 2** and not to the internal workings of the RT approach itself. However, this scenario does not seem to justify the answers provided by the RT group for questions Q2 & Q3. Additionally, the provided RT theoretical explanation seems to be the basis for the students' qualitative representations of the 'Company X' case as it will be shown during the validation of the second hypothesis.

Table 1. Understandability means by group and by question.

	USM mean	RT mean
Q1 Is the theory about the different elements and links understandable?	4.06	3.78
Q2 Is the modeling exercise explanation understandable?	3.69	3.49
Q3 Is the modeling exercise expectation understandable?	3.67	3.51

Table 2. Significance testing for the three questions: independent-samples T-test.

	t	df	Sig. (2-tailed)	Mean difference	Std. error difference	95% Confidence interval of the difference	
						Lower	Upper
Q1	2.061	70	.043	.273	.133	.009	.538
Q2	1.461	68	.148	.200	.137	−.073	.473
Q3	1.140	65.97	.258	.152	.134	−.114	.419

*The significance level is set at 5%.

4.2 $H_0$2: The Resulting RT Diagrams and USM Artifacts are Equally Good in Providing Qualitative Representations

We started exploring the students' model-creation capabilities by checking whether each group could identify correctly the elements from the *WHO/WHAT/WHY*-dimensions (roles, functionalities, etc.) within the set of seven user stories provided for the 'Company X' case. Next, we checked whether the students could correspond each of these elements to the modeling notations of their assigned approach (i.e., *Role/Task/Capability/Hard-Goal/Soft-Goal* for the RT, and *User/Activity/Task/Detail* for the USM approach). Eventually, we compared the students' artifacts resulting from the modeling exercise, between the two groups. These steps are described below.

User Stories' Dimension Identification for the RT Group: The *WHO*-dimension was identified correctly by 73% of the students assigned to the RT group. This was to be expected since the RT contains only one modeling construct (i.e., '*Role*') corresponding to this dimension. However, the group had difficulty in identifying elements within the *WHAT*-, and *WHY*-dimension in the provided user stories' set.

Table 3 validates our last statement. For instance, in the first row corresponding to the *WHAT*-dimension of the first user story, we notice a significant discrepancy in the percentage of the students' answers reporting a *Task* or a *Capability* element. In the second row for the *WHY*-dimension of the first user story, we also notice that the answers of the students are divided between the *Soft-Goal* and *Hard-Goal* element. These two examples encapsulate the students' challenge in distinguishing between the modeling constructs *Task*/*Capability* on the one hand, and *Soft-Goal*/*Hard-Goal* on the other. These results validate the ones found in the study of Wautelet et al. [22] stating the possibility of a limited semantic difference between such elements. Cells assigned with the number zero mean that no student reported that particular modeling element in his/her answer.

Table 3. *WHAT/WHY*-dimension analysis for the RT group.

US dimension	Task	Capability	Soft-goal	Hard-goal	Element not present
US2WHAT	45.9	**48.6**	5.4	0	0
US2WHY	2.7	5.4	**51.4**	40.5	0
US3WHAT	**94.6**	5.4	0	0	0
US3WHY	21.6	16.2	**56.8**	5.4	0
US4WHAT	29.7	**70.3**	0	0	0
US4WHY	0	0	0	0	100
US5WHAT	**59.5**	40.5	0	0	0
US5WHY	10.8	0	43.2	**45.9**	0
US6WHAT	16.2	**81.1**	2.7	0	0
US6WHY	0	0	13.5	**86.5**	0
US7WHAT	**62.2**	35.1	2.7	0	0
US7WHY	2.7	5.4	**54.1**	37.8	0

***Elements in bold font** indicate the most frequently identified elements within the group.

User Stories' Dimension Identification for the USM Group: The *WHO*-dimension was identified correctly by 62.9% of the USM group. This percentage is smaller compared to the one retrieved for the RT group. This discrepancy could be explained by the difference in the used terminology between the two approaches in terms of the identification of the *WHO*-dimension. RT contains the term *Role* (which is completely identifiable with the term provided in the theoretical explanation for the *WHO*-dimension of a user story) while the USM contains the term *User*. As for the *WHAT*-, and *WHY*-dimension, Table 4 reveals that the students tended to recognize the semantic difference between the *Activity* and *Task* element and assign them well to their proper dimensions. This is aided by the hierarchical structure of the USM where an *Activity* must be followed by a *Task* and finally a *Detail*. Nevertheless, the numbers reveal that the students experience ambiguity regarding the granularity-level associated with the elements belonging to the *WHAT*-dimension of the user stories. In particular, the students seem not to be able to differentiate well between the semantics of *Task/Detail* as the reported numbers depict in rows one, five, and seven.

Comparison of the Drawn RT Diagrams and USM Artifacts for the 'Company X' Case: This part describes the evaluation of the artifacts drawn by the students according to the tasks prescribed by the modeling exercise of **Part 2**. We evaluated the produced artifacts basing ourselves on methods elaborated in previous studies. For the drawn RT diagrams, we used the *Three Criteria* evaluation method namely completeness, conformity and accuracy [22], and the

Golden Standard method [18]. The latter was based on an 'ideal' artifact, created by the research team, whose every correct element and link was awarded with the maximum of points. The artifacts provided by the students approaching this 'ideal' solution the most gathered the most points. The artifacts drawn by the USM group were evaluated based on five identified criteria namely completeness, consistency, accuracy, correctness and accuracy. Appendix 4.2 provides a detailed description of each evaluation method.

Table 5 presents the descriptive elements related to the acquired points for each drawn artifact, based on their corresponded evaluation method. We observe that the means/medians of the gathered scores are similar for the two groups. Hence, despite the difficulty that RT students show in corresponding the *WHAT-/WHY*-dimension to the modeling constructs of the RT, they still manage to produce artifacts that gather similar points with the USM group (in terms of representing the requirements problem within the tasks of the modeling exercise). Thereby, our *second null hypothesis cannot be rejected.*

Table 4. *WHAT/WHY*-dimension analysis for the USM group.

US dimension	Activity	Task	Detail	Element not present
US2WHAT	5.7	**57.1**	37.1	0
US2WHY	**51.4**	11.4	34.3	2.9
US3WHAT	20	**77.1**	2.9	0
US3WHY	**71.4**	25.7	0	2.9
US4WHAT	0	37.1	**62.9**	0
US4WHY	2.9	2.9	0	**94.3**
US5WHAT	2.9	**74.3**	22.9	0
US5WHY	**62.9**	8.6	25.7	2.9
US6WHAT	8.6	**74.3**	17.1	0
US6WHY	**71.4**	5.7	20	0
US7WHAT	5.7	**74.3**	17.1	2.9
US7WHY	**51.4**	14.3	25.7	8.6

***Elements in bold font** indicate the most frequently identified element within the group.

4.3 $H_0 3$: The Resulting RT Diagrams and USM Artifacts are Equally Good in Identifying Missing Requirements, Epics and Themes

The last steps of the modeling exercise in **Part 2** were meant to test whether the employment of either of the RT/USM is significantly better in helping modelers to produce artifacts that facilitate with the identification of missing requirements,

Table 5. Drawn artifacts: descriptive statistics of acquired points per evaluation method.

	% of points on USM artifact	% of points on RT diagram based on Golden Standard evaluation	% of points on RT diagram based on Three Criteria evaluation
N	36	36	36
Mean	.5281	.5536	.5522
Median	.5690	.5806	.5965
Std. deviation	.13698	.20109	.17229
Minimum	.14	.03	.11
Maximum	.71	1.29	.83

epics and themes. Table 6 presents the means of the scores that the students' artifacts gathered, by group, when performing these 3 tasks. The numbers suggest that the USM group performed better in the identification of missing requirements. Conversely, the average of the achieved scores was higher for the RT group in respect to the identification of epics and themes. We wanted to test whether these performance variations, as measured by the differences in the score means for the two groups, are significant. Table 7 presents the confidence intervals corresponding to the differences in the score means for the two groups and reveals that while the USM group's performance is significantly better in identifying missing requirements, the difference in the performance between the two groups is not significant in terms of identifying epics and themes. This is a first –but not conclusive– indication that our *third null hypothesis cannot be rejected.*

Table 6. Descriptive statistics on the student-scores for the tasks of identifying Missing Requirements/Epics/Themes.

	Group	N	Mean	Std. deviation	Std. error mean
Score on the task of identifying Missing Requirements	USM group	36	1.2286	.68966	.11657
	RT group	36	.7794	.97849	.16781
Score on the task of identifying Epic US	USM group	36	.4071	.33258	.05622
	RT group	36	.4559	.33411	.05730
Score on the task of identifying Themes	USM group	36	1.7929	1.20276	.20330
	RT group	36	2.2574	1.33922	.22967

Table 7. Mean difference of the student-scores in identifying Missing Requirements/Epics/Themes: Confidence Intervals.

	Mean difference	Std. error difference	95% Confidence Interval of the difference	
			Lower	Upper
MR Score	.44916	.20332	.04333	.85499
Epic Score	−.4874	.08027	−.20897	.11149
Theme Score	−.46450	.30673	−1.07694	.14795

*The significance level is set at 5%.

To further support (or rebut) this indication, we checked the students' answers to six Likert-scale questions that were meant to establish the (possible) relationship between the *perceived* ease of use of each method in identifying missing requirements/epics/themes. These questions were: *Q1) How hard was it to find missing requirements in Part 2?, Q2) How hard was it to find epics in Part 2?, Q3) How hard was it to find themes in Part 2?, Q4) Did the RT/USM help you find missing requirements?, Q5) Did the RT/USM help you find epics?, Q6) Did the RT/USM help you find themes?.* We processed the answers to these questions to recreate and compare the means of the students' responses by group and by question. We used their descriptive elements in order to perform an independent-samples t-test to examine the significance in their perceived level of difficulty in identifying missing requirements/epics/themes between the two groups. Once again, the justification for using such a parametric test stems from the CLT; given the sample size of each group (larger than 30 participants) the variable used for recreating the means can be assumed normally distributed. A Levene's test was performed for each question ensuring the equality in the variances (see Appendix 4.3 for the detailed descriptive statistics for the comparison of the means, by group, for all six questions). Table 8 informs us that insofar the recognition of missing requirements/epics/themes, there are no significant differences between the perceived ease of use for either of the RT/USM. Thereby, our *third null hypothesis cannot be rejected.*

Table 8. Identification of Missing Requirements/Epics/Themes: T-test by question and by group.

	t	df	Sig. (2-tailed)	Mean difference	Std. error difference	95% Confidence interval of the difference	
						Lower	Upper
Q1	−1.818	68	.073	−.395	.218	−.829	.039
Q2	−.942	64.005	.350	−.225	.238	−.701	.251
Q3	−1.367	67.977	.176	−.371	.272	−.914	.171
Q4	−.077	66.522	.939	−.021	.273	−.565	.523
Q5	−1.185	65.185	.240	−.325	.274	−.873	.223
Q6	.573	67.192	.569	.152	.265	−.377	.681

*The significance level is set at 5%.

4.4 $H_0$4: The Resulting RT Diagrams and USM Artifacts are Equally Good in Being Adaptable

This section addresses the tasks that the students had to complete for **Part 3** of the experiment. Six questions were asked to determine the respondents' ability: i) to understand the structure of a complex model (artifact) provided for the 'Film Finder' case, and ii) to make adaptations to this model based on changing requirements. We followed the same process as the one used to test our third hypothesis. In particular, we collected and processed the participants' answers to all six questions to recreate the means of their responses by group and by question (see Appendix 4.4). Next, we used these descriptive elements in order to perform an independent-samples t-test to check whether the differences of the responses by group and by question were significant. Table 9 demonstrates that there were significant differences between the two groups concerning the time disposed to answer the first, second, and last question.

Table 9. Adaptability: independent-samples T-test by question and by group.

	t	df	Sig.	Mean	Std. error	95% Confidence	
						Lower	Upper
Q1	-2.763	69	.007	–.275	.099	–.538	–.011
Q2	-2.552	68	.013	–.286	.112	–.509	–.062
Q3	.802	67.452	.426	.19365	.24155	–.28842	.67572
Q4	–.457	68.854	.649	–.26984	.59069	–1.44827	.90859
Q5	–.196	68.996	.845	–.08532	.43450	–.95213	.78149
Q6	1.854	67.420	.068	.27500	.14835	.02759	.52241

*The significance level is set at 5%.

Q1 & Q2 demanded the (partly) explanation of the 'Film Finder' case with the aid of the provided models and they were answered better by the USM group. Of course, the 'Film Finder' case description addressed to this group was comprised of two pages, while the one for the RT group was over four pages. This was done in order to increase the visibility/readability between the links and elements of the provided RT diagram for this case. So, as the provided 'Film Finder' USM model (artifact) was more compact the students could have gotten more information in a shorter amount of time which inevitably leads to a faster, better understanding of the case. Q6 asked specific description of the models themselves and was answered better by the RT students. The remaining questions asking the respondents to adapt the models were slightly better for the RT group but the difference, compared to the USM group, was not significant. Therefore, our *fourth null hypothesis cannot be rejected.*

5 Discussion

Our analysis suggested that the RT seemed more difficult to understand compared to the USM. Although this created the expectation that the RT group would deliver artifacts which would not represent properly the software problem as described by the 'Company X' case (compared to the USM group), this was in fact not verified by our analysis. We will try to explain this contradiction by using the students' answers to an open question at the end of **Part 2** that gave them the opportunity to provide suggestions for improving further the RT and USM. Regarding the former, a recurring request from many students was the addition of extra elements complementing the existing set. For example, the students perceived that the addition of a decision point would facilitate its use. However, this would imply that the RT is process-oriented like a BPMN process diagram [10]. But its true purpose is to facilitate the decomposition of a feature and not to analyze a process. This observation suggests that participants 'anchored' on their previous trainings in UML and BPMN diagrams in order to conceive, comprehend and compare the RT. Since the latter is structurally different than the modeling elements the students were accustomed to, this can be the reason for their perceived difficulty in understanding the theory. However, the solved examples at the end of each step of the modeling exercise that were incorporated in **Part 2** guided the students during the conduct of their modeling exercise; at the end, the RT students provided qualitative artifacts (according to pre-set standards). Another recurring criticism referred to the difficulty in distinguishing between *Tasks/Capabilities* and *Hard-goals/Soft-goals*. This can be partially explained by the students' lack of experience with modeling frameworks such as i* [24] which incorporates such elements. Some participants even asked for stricter rules and guidelines to define the different RT elements and how to put them into practice each time. These 'criticisms' can reveal some of the bottlenecks that should be addressed when it comes to making non-experienced modelers exposed in the use of a conceptual model (i.e., the RT in our case). Vague semantics were also an issue for the use of USM, as the distinction between *Tasks/Details* was not clear for many participants.

6 Threats to Validity

Our presented results consider some threats to validity, according to Wohlin et al. [23].

Construct Validity. Our selected cases may affect the results. The 'Company X' case was considered complex and slightly unstructured and this factor in combination with the subjects' working inexperience with user stories can jeopardize the quality of their provided artifacts. However, the students did not have to extrapolate the user stories' set themselves for the build-up of their artifacts; the former was already provided in the questionnaire. This gave the students a well-established outset especially since the user stories' set was reviewed and optimized using the QUS framework.

Internal Validity. The questionnaire of the experiment was quite large amounting to fifteen pages for the RT group and fourteen pages for the USM group. A survey instrument of such size is prone to cause fatigue leading respondents ultimately to satisfice rather than optimize during their response effort. We tried to counter that effect by: i) applying correctional penalties for guessing; ii) boosting the students' motivation through an additional bonus grade (corresponding to their performance) to be applied on top of their final grade for the compulsory semester course in the session of which the current experiment was organized.

External Validity. The inclusion of students in the experiment may condition our results considering the participants' practical inexperience in software design & modeling. However, Kitchenham et al. [6] do not discourage the use of students as test subjects in software engineering experiments as long as the research questions match their level of experience. This has been the case in our experiment; the content of the questionnaires was the product of an iterative deliberation process among the members of the research team. In addition, the research questions and the ease of understanding of the theoretical explanations for the RT/USM were tested separately on three junior researchers (first-year PhD students). Their suggestions/proposed alterations were incorporated into the final version provided to the test subjects.

An additional concern is that the quality of the artifacts produced by the students (in the context of their modeling exercise) depends not only on their (in)experience but also on the cognitive complexity of each tested method. In principle, there seems to be some adversity between the two tested methods given that the USM represents essentially a structuring approach of user stories based on their level of granularity and that's relatively easier for the students to understand. Contrastingly, the subjects were not well versed in the i* framework whose elements/notations are used in the RT method. We acknowledge this confounding factor in the experimental design and this why we included a detailed theoretical explanation of each method – with one extra page for the RT – incorporating a complete set of solved examples at the beginning of each step of the modeling exercise in **Part 2**.

7 Conclusion

This paper analyzed the ability of novice modelers to understand a software problem by using a conceptual modeling approach (RT) and a structuring method (USM) for the formation of user stories. Our *first hypothesis* indicated that the RT seems not as easy to understand as USM. To reinforce the RT's applicability, more focus should be placed into making the semantics of its modeling elements self-evident along with a proper illustration of their in-between links. This hypothesis was tested on the basis of theoretical explanations provided within the questionnaires. Nevertheless, when the students receive practical, step-by-step guidance on how to apply the RT, they manage to use it to produce qualitative representations of the software problem (*second hypothesis*). This observation can influence the way conceptual modeling is taught within

IT curricula; first, our analysis highlights the possible transition from an ex-cathedra approach based on theory to a more empirical one where students practice modeling from the start. Second, the tutoring of conceptual modeling, to better understand the software problem, can be valuable in an agile setting as well; the RT itself – descending from an elaborate framework for socio-technical analyses (i*) – shows indeed promising results for agile requirements engineering. Contrastingly, our *third* and *fourth hypotheses* highlight a reoccurring discrepancy between the RT's intended purpose and actual performance. Theoretically, the RT's complexity is to be counterbalanced by delivering adaptable artifacts assisting modelers identify missing requirements/epics/themes more easily. However, our results showed neither a significant facilitation by the RT diagram in these tasks, nor by the USM (despite the latter's embedded simplicity). All in all, we believe that the teaching of the RT (i.e., a conceptual modeling-based approach for agile methods) next to the traditional USM method, furnishes an added value to IT students. It allows them to learn complementary ways of reasoning about a software problem, based on user stories, and they can experience on their own how it can be structured best. Learning the RT also reinforces their general skills on conceptual modeling and allows them to experience that the domain can be fruitfully used outside the scope of object-oriented modeling and database design.

References

1. Chen, P.P.S.: The entity-relationship model-toward a unified view of data. ACM Trans. Database Syst. **1**(1), 9–36 (1976)
2. Dalpiaz, F., Gieske, P., Sturm, A.: On deriving conceptual models from user requirements: an empirical study. Inf. Softw. Technol. **131**, 106484 (2020)
3. Dalpiaz, F., Sturm, A.: Conceptualizing requirements using user stories and use cases: a controlled experiment. In: Madhavji, N., Pasquale, L., Ferrari, A., Gnesi, S. (eds.) REFSQ 2020. LNCS, vol. 12045, pp. 221–238. Springer, Cham (2020). https://doi.org/10.1007/978-3-030-44429-7_16
4. Dimitrijević, S., Jovanović, J., Devedžić, V.: A comparative study of software tools for user story management. Inf. Softw. Technol. **57**, 352–368 (2015)
5. Falessi, D., et al.: Empirical software engineering experts on the use of students and professionals in experiments. Empirical Softw. Eng. **23**(1), 452–489 (2017). https://doi.org/10.1007/s10664-017-9523-3
6. Kitchenham, B.A., et al.: Preliminary guidelines for empirical research in software engineering. IEEE Trans. Softw. Eng. **28**(8), 721–734 (2002)
7. Lucassen, G., Dalpiaz, F., Van Der Werf, J.M.E., Brinkkemper, S.: Forging high-quality user stories: towards a discipline for agile requirements. In: RE2015, pp. 126–135. IEEE (2015)
8. Lucassen, G., Dalpiaz, F., van der Werf, J.M.E., Brinkkemper, S.: Improving agile requirements: the quality user story framework and tool. Req. Eng. **21**(3), 383–403 (2016)
9. Lucassen, G., Robeer, M., Dalpiaz, F., Van Der Werf, J.M.E., Brinkkemper, S.: Extracting conceptual models from user stories with visual narrator. Req. Eng. **22**(3), 339–358 (2017)

10. OMG: Business process model and notation specification version 2.0 (2011)
11. OMG: Unified modeling language. version 2.5. Tech. rep. (2015)
12. Patton, J., Economy, P.: User story mapping: discover the whole story, build the right product. O'Reilly Media, Inc. (2014)
13. Patton, M.Q.: Qualitative research & evaluation methods: integrating theory and practice. Sage publications (2014)
14. Saunders, M., Lewis, P., Thornhill, A.: Research methods for business students. Pearson education (2016)
15. Tenso, T., Norta, A., Vorontsova, I.: Evaluating a novel agile requirements engineering method: a case study. In: ENASE, pp. 156–163 (2016)
16. Tenso, T., Taveter, K.: Requirements engineering with agent-oriented models. In: ENASE, pp. 254–259 (2013)
17. Tsilionis, K., Maene, J., Heng, S., Wautelet, Y., Poelmans, S.: Evaluating the software problem representation on the basis of rationale trees and user story maps: premises of an experiment. In: Klotins, E., Wnuk, K. (eds.) ICSOB 2020. LNBIP, vol. 407, pp. 219–227. Springer, Cham (2021). https://doi.org/10.1007/978-3-030-67292-8_18
18. Wautelet, Y., Gielis, D., Poelmans, S., Heng, S.: Evaluating the impact of user stories quality on the ability to understand and structure requirements. In: Gordijn, J., Guédria, W., Proper, H.A. (eds.) PoEM 2019. LNBIP, vol. 369, pp. 3–19. Springer, Cham (2019). https://doi.org/10.1007/978-3-030-35151-9_1
19. Wautelet, Y., Heng, S., Kiv, S., Kolp, M.: User-story driven development of multi-agent systems: a process fragment for agile methods. Comput. Lang. Syst. Struct. **50**, 159–176 (2017)
20. Wautelet, Y., Heng, S., Kolp, M., Mirbel, I.: Unifying and extending user story models. In: Jarke, M., et al. (eds.) CAiSE 2014. LNCS, vol. 8484, pp. 211–225. Springer, Cham (2014). https://doi.org/10.1007/978-3-319-07881-6_15
21. Wautelet, Y., Heng, S., Kolp, M., Mirbel, I., Poelmans, S.: Building a rationale diagram for evaluating user story sets. In: RCIS 2016. pp. 1–12. IEEE (2016)
22. Wautelet, Y., Velghe, M., Heng, S., Poelmans, S., Kolp, M.: On modelers ability to build a visual diagram from a user story set: a goal-oriented approach. In: Proceedings of the 24th Intl. Working Conf. Req. Eng.: Foundation for Software Quality, pp. 209–226 (2018)
23. Wohlin, C., Runeson, P., Höst, M., Ohlsson, M.C., Regnell, B., Wesslén, A.: Experimentation in Software Engineering. Springer Science & Business Media (2012)
24. Yu, E., Giorgini, P., Maiden, N., Mylopoulos, J.: Social Modeling for Requirements Engineering. MIT Press (2011)

Design and Execution of ETL Process to Build Topic Dimension from User-Generated Content

Afef Walha[1,2](✉), Faiza Ghozzi[1,3], and Faiez Gargouri[1,3]

[1] Multimedia, InfoRmation systems and Advanced Computing (MIRACL) Laboratory, University of Sfax, Sfax, Tunisia

[2] Higher Institute of Information Science and Multimedia-Gabès, University of Gabès, Gabès, Tunisia

[3] Higher Institute of Information Science and Multimedia-Sfax, University of Sfax, Sfax, Tunisia

Abstract. Latest research studies on multi-dimensional design have combined business data with User-Generated Content (UGC). They have integrated new analytical aspects, such as user's behavior, sentiments, opinions or topics of interest, to ameliorate decisional analysis. In this paper, we deal with the complexity of designing topics dimension schema due to the dynamicity and heterogeneity of its hierarchies. Researchers addressed partially this issue by offering technical solutions to topics detection without focusing on the Extraction, Transformation and Loading (ETL) process allowing their integration in multi-dimensional schema. Our contribution consists in modeling ETL steps generating valid topic dimension hierarchies referring to UGC informal texts. In this research work, we propose a generic ETL4SocialTopic process model defining a set of operations executed following a specific order. The implementation of these steps offers a set of customized jobs simplifying the ETL designer's work by automating a large part of the process. Experimentation results show the consistency of ETL4SocialTopic to design valid topic dimension schemas in several contexts.

Keywords: User-generated content · Topic hierarchy design · Data warehouse · ETL process · Twitter · Social media

1 Introduction

User-generated content (UGC) is generally considered as extra element of online platforms such as social media websites (e.g. Twitter, Facebook). In this context, a novel area, called Social Business Intelligence (Social BI), has recently emerged. Authors, in [1], defined it as the discipline combining corporate data with UGC to make easier for decision makers to analyze and improve their business based on the observation of the user's trends and moods. In fact, UGC text may be extracted and extended in many ways; the most important of which is topic discovery since it plays a crucial role in contextual advertisement and offers a whole new set of analytical aspects to business analysts. Indeed, decision makers are interested in knowing how much people talk about a topic of interest.

S. Cherfi et al. (Eds.): RCIS 2021, LNBIP 415, pp. 374–389, 2021.
https://doi.org/10.1007/978-3-030-75018-3_25

In the existing Social Data Warehouse (SDW) design approaches dealing with the user's topic of interest integration [2–4], the topic was considered as a specific dimension in the multidimensional schema. In fact, topic hierarchies are not similar to standard hierarchies (of SDW dimensions) in terms of irregularity, dynamicity and semantic relationships between the various topic levels. Thus, in order to enable the aggregation of topics belonging to different levels, a topic hierarchy should be defined. Hence, building topic hierarchy is a challenging task in SDW multi-dimensional modeling. Consequently, the possibility of designing several structures of the topic hierarchy depending on the study context and the designer's preferences makes the modeling of ETL process to generate topic dimension more difficult. To solve this problem, we modeled and implemented an ETL process that aids the SDW designer build topic dimension schema by considering its hierarchies features.

This process, called ETL4SocialTopic, highlights the ETL steps followed to design the topic hierarchies. To this end, a generic ETL process model is introduced, in this study, to map UGCs into topic dimension schema. It was implemented and tested on real datasets collected from Twitter in different contexts including "mobile technology", "automobile" and "health".

This paper is organized as follows. Section 2 depicts topic integration in SDW design and shows the complexity of topic hierarchies design through an illustrative example. Then, the generic ETL process model of building of topic dimension from UGC is described in Sect. 3. This model presents the synchronization and execution order of ETL4SocialTopic steps. These steps gave birth to new ETL tool whose architecture is described in Sect. 4. In Sect. 5, ETL4SocialTopic workflows are executed on tweets data set, providing topic schemas interpreted by domain experts. In Sect. 6, experimental results are evaluated by applying Topic schema relevance metrics. The performance of the introduced process is discussed in Sect. 7. Finally, a conclusion and some future researches are provided in Sect. 8.

2 Research Context and Motivation: Topics Integration in Data Warehouse Modeling

In the last decade, SDW modeling has given more attention to UGC that became the focus of business owners. Besides, several recent studies have attempted to integrate user's topics of interests in social data warehouse design [2–8]. In [4], authors have applied data mining techniques to the UGC dataset by adding new measurements, straightforward mapping and knowledge discovery. This enrichment enables the modeling of the user's sentiment, UGC popularity as well as entity and topic detection. In this approach, data mining methods have been developed and trained on Twitter data sets in order to perform predictive analysis of *Tweets* and *Users* objects. Researchers, in [4] and [9], have focused on the relationships between these objects without paying attention to the inter-linking topics of interests.

Other researchers have considered that building topic hierarchy is a challenging task in SDW modeling. In [5], authors have introduced SDW model in which topic dimension has been designed as a set of relationships between topics using parent-child hierarchies. In fact, topic has been defined through two cases which can be either a basic strict hierarchy, defined with only one parent per node, or an extended non-strict hierarchy containing many-to-many relationships between its levels. Authors have distinguished topic hierarchies from traditional ones as a function of schemata and instances. As illustrated in Fig. 1, non-leaf topics can be related to a fact (social event). For example, clips may talk about *Smartphone* as well as of *Galaxy J7*. These topics show that grouping topics of interest at a given level may not provide a total partitioning of facts. Besides, the relationships between topics can have different semantics. For instance, the semantics in the relation "Galaxy J7 belongs to the company Samsung" and "Galaxy J7 has the operating system Android" are quite different. For traditional hierarchies design, these topics are designed relying on the semantics of aggregation levels (*Smartphone* is a member of the level "*Type*", while *Samsung* is a member of the level "*Company*"). Furthermore, in terms of instances, topic hierarchies are non-onto (they can have different instances length), non-covering (some nodes in the hierarchy skip one or more levels) and non-strict (many-to-many relationships may exist between topics).

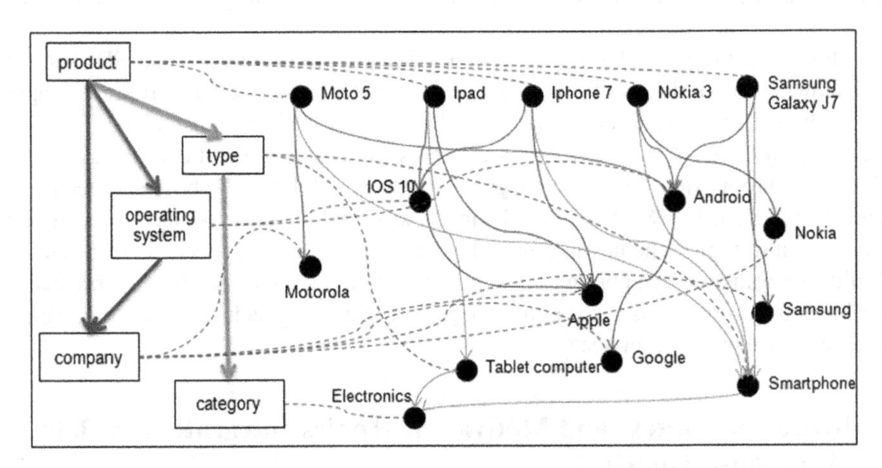

Fig. 1. An excerpt of the topic hierarchies for the «mobile technology» context.

Considering the topic as non-covering and non-strict hierarchy, authors, in [2], have studied topic hierarchy changes. Modeling topic hierarchies has been realized in ROLAP platforms combining classical dimension tables and recursive navigation tables. This work has been later extended, in [3], by a meta-model (called meta-stars) used to solve topic hierarchy issues by combining semantic and structural modeling aspects. Indeed, meta-stars model relies essentially on meta-modeling coupled with navigation and dimension tables to improve the flexibility and the expressiveness of modeling topic hierarchies. Its performance, compared with star schema, has been evaluated through OLAP queries. Although meta-stars are consistent to express queries, they are time-consuming.

Later, meta-stars approach (defined in [3]) has been utilized in [6] where the topic-based aggregation was realized through a set of classes defined in a domain ontology describing the subject of interest. Ontology concepts have been defined by domain experts as topics appearing during UGC analysis. These topics have been structured into hierarchies. For an effective modeling of topic hierarchy, authors have considered topic hierarchy features (heterogeneous, dynamic, non-onto, non-covering and non-strict). More recently, in [7], authors have integrated a contextual dimension (designed from social networks texts) into the SDW multi-dimensional model. This dimension consists of two components: the contexts, detected in the texts (*context* hierarchy), and the main topics treated in each context. Such dimension has been automatically created applying hierarchical clustering algorithms. Thus, it has allowed analyzing textual data similarly by contexts and topics. Consequently, business analysts can take decisions as they know the full extent of the information in a record. Despite this advantage, this research [7] represents the starting point of topics hierarchy modelling. Firstly, once the texts have been organized into contexts, texts entities could be extracted and incorporated, as a new dimension, into the SDW model. In [8], authors have considered topics of interests as a dimension (called *dim_topics*) of the SDW schema. They have applied classification techniques on UGC texts to discover data of *dim_topics*. Despites the good performance of this approach to classify UGC in terms of topics, we note that *dim_topics* store subjects of interests without defining the hierarchical relations between topics.

The existing approaches showed that designing topic hierarchy is a challenging task in multi-dimensional modelling. Their comparison demonstrates that topic design introduced in [3] presented the most advanced one dealing with topic hierarchy constraints. Nevertheless, the existing approaches did not focus on the process of building topic hierarchies. Moreover, the roll-up and semantic relationships between topics were manually generated. In SDW design, this process is known as ETL steps. As shown in [10], Data Warehouse projects use some vendor-provided ETL tools and software utilities (e.g. Ab Initio, Informatica, SQL Server Integration Service, Oracle Data Integrator, Talend Open Studio) in order to automate ETL process. These commercial tools provide advanced graphical user interfaces to ease ETL design. However, most of them apply the black-box optimization at the conceptual and the logical levels (e.g. re-ordering of the activities in ETL workflow).

In the literature, it was also proven that the manual definition of topic dimension and their hierarchies is a cumbersome task. Conversely, the fully automatic generation of a topic hierarchy expects a wide range of heterogeneous concepts to be manually restricted [3]. For this reason, our work introduces a semi-automatic process to generate topic hierarchies. We also model ETL process to map UGC data into the topic dimension schema following a specific workflow. This procedure was implemented on Talend Open Studio producing ETL4SocialTopic process whose components were executed by ETL designer to generate the topic dimension schema and its hierarchies.

3 ETL Process Conceptual Model for Topic Schema Building

Indeed, the ETL process controls the execution flows of extraction, transformation and loading steps. For a generic modeling of topic dimension building steps, an ETL process model involves the control flow of ETL operations performed to design topic hierarchies and the relations between topics. Considering an ETL process as a special type of business process, the existing studies [11–14] proved that BPMN standard is well-adapted to model ETL process ensuring an accurate design of its control aspects. As demonstrated in Fig. 2, the designed BPMN model specifies the execution order of ETL operations carried out to build topic dimension schema.

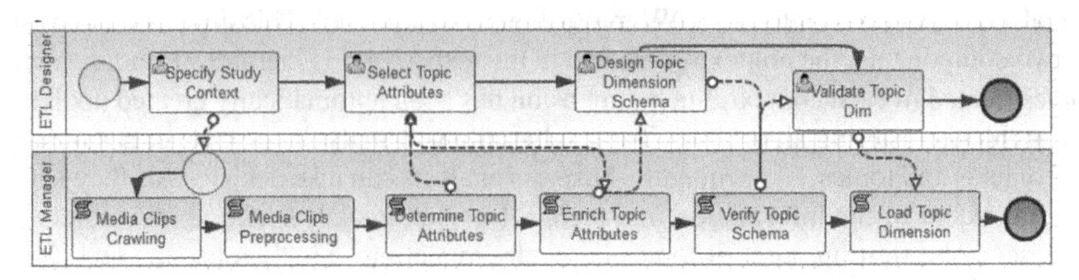

Fig. 2. A BPMN process model to «Build Topic Dimension».

In this research work, two actors (ETL designer and ETL manager) collaborate to build topic dimension. Indeed, the former is a person or group of individuals who intervenes in the integration of UGC data into the SDW, while the latter is an automatic system that helps designer during the building process. In the designed model, a BPMN «Collaboration» was used to model the interaction between two «Participants»: **ETL designer** and **ETL manager**. The interaction between these participants was realized through BPMN «Message Flows». Indeed, each of these participants had to perform a sequence of operations. Indeed, ETL designer operations were manually defined; whereas those established by ETL manager were automatically specified.

The execution order of operations, specific to the topic building, started by the «Media Clips Crawling» operation, in which UGC data available on social media were collected. Then, these data were pre-processed through the «Media clips Pre-processing» operation. This step relies on the study context introduced by the ETL designer through «Specify Study Context» operation. The next step consists in detecting, from the collected data, the possible topics related to the desired context. «Determine Topic Attributes» operation found these topics with reference to entities detection services that provided information about entity types such as *product*, *person*, *city*, *country* or *company*. The suggested entity types gave the ETL designer an idea about the candidate topic attributes. At this level, he/she could choose the desired ones from the collection of entity types.

Then, the ETL manager proposed other attributes related to the selected topic attributes. This operation, called «Enrich Topic Attribute», was established using external lexical resources (e.g. domain ontology, dictionary, etc.) providing topic attributes that were semantically related to the selected ones. At this point, the ETL designer classified the attributes into hierarchies through «Design Topic Dimension» operation. Then, the ETL manager verified the consistency of the introduced topic hierarchies through «Verify Topic Dimension» operation in which the semantic relationships between the different topic hierarchy levels were checked.

The ETL process model, shown in Fig. 1, serves as a pattern helping ETL designer build topic hierarchies and establish the relationships between them. This process, called ETL4SocialTopic, can be used to solve many problems related to the topic dynamic structure. It is generic because it may be customized according to the designer requirements and it is useful in various context and social media (such as Twitter and Facebook). To show the efficiency of this process, we implemented its operations and executed them following a specific order.

4 Implementation of ETL4SocialTopic

An ETL workflow can either be hand-coded or specified and executed via ETL tools. The latter were employed, in the experiments, mainly due to the graphical programming interfaces they provide as well as for their reporting, monitoring and recovery facilities. Among these tools, we can cite Talend Open Studio[1] (TOS) which is an open source offering a graphical user interface and allowing the integration of data and the creation of transformation jobs. The comparison of ETL tools (given in [14]) shows its ability to reduce the execution time. As TOS is a code generator, it makes possible to translate ETL tasks and jobs into Java code. For these reasons, we prototypically implemented ETL4SocialTopic workflows on TOS offering a set of new jobs to be executed to design Topic dimension schema. These jobs were implemented using the operations defined in Topic design conceptual model (see Fig. 2). Their execution, according to a specific order, allows the designer to build topic schema in a certain context and define the relationships between its hierarchical levels. ETL4SocialTopic jobs were performed on real UGC collection extracted from Twitter. The latter is considered as one of the main social media source frequently used to analyze sentiments [15]. Twitter was chosen because of on its data availability. Our process can be also applied on any type of social media (Facebook, Instagram, etc.).

The architecture of ETL4SocialTopic is presented in Fig. 3. It shows a sequence of Extraction, Transformation and Loading jobs realized according to a specific order (from 1 to 8). This architecture also presents the different APIs, programming languages and data employed to develop ETL4SocialTopic jobs.

In the first job called **Specify Study Context**, the designer determines his/her business requirements through a set of keywords expressing his/her desired analysis context. For example, the context "mobile technology" may be referred to using some terms such as "smartphone", "internet", "iPhone", etc. Based on these words, a query was formulated and sent to the Twitter Streaming API, giving low latency access to Twitter global stream of Tweet data. This query was executed by applying the methods defined in Twitter4J java library [16] to crawl tweets related to the desired context. In fact, a Tweet[2], known as status update, is a message that may include texts, links, photos, user mentions, hashtags, language, location or videos. The collected tweets data were, then, stored in «Tweets» XML files.

It is obvious that a tweet message is informal in comparison to the structured data. Its pre-processing is a crucial task. Thus, a tweet text was, subsequently, cleaned by the well-known pre-processing tasks including removing URL, consecutive characters, punctuations, numbers, stop words and HTML tags [17]. This cleaning was followed by a set of tasks including stemming and removing the user's mentions, emoticons, opinion words and modifiers which may be useless to topic detection. Afterwards, the pre-processed text was stored in «TweetsForTopicDetection.xml».

[1] https://www.talend.com/products/data-integration/.

[2] https://developer.twitter.com/en/products/tweets.

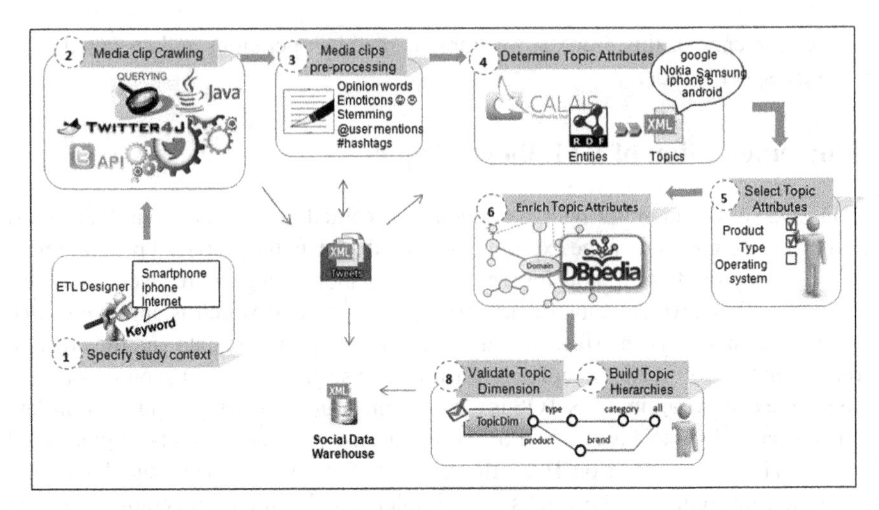

Fig. 3. Architecture of ETL4SocialTopic prototype for «Topic Dimension Building».

Topic dimension is the subject of interest of a specific Tweet event. In fact, **Determine Topic Attributes** job aims at detecting candidate attributes constituting Topic hierarchy. At this level, text mining APIs were utilized to semantically analyze a tweet text. Authors, in [4], showed the ability of Open Calais API to extract entities from tweet text and, thus, to return a list of entities (in RDF format) from pre-processed tweets. Indeed, an entity object is characterized by its name, its type and its relevance value. Figure 3 shows an excerpt of the detected entities specific to "mobile technology". For examples, the entity name *iPhone 5* corresponds to the type *product*, while *Nokia* is an entity of type *Company*. Subsequently, entities types were stored as topic attributes in «Topics.xml».

The possible topic attributes were presented to the ETL designer who selected the desired ones. Based on the chosen topics, Open Calais API was used to **enrich topic attributes** by other topics that were semantically related to the selected ones. At this level, the ETL designer built topic hierarchies. **Topic dimension** was validated by checking inter-topics relationships defined in a lexical resource (e.g. domain ontology, DBpedia, etc.).

In the ETL4SocialTopic software environment including programming languages, file formats, methods, tools and APIs may be substituted by another. Our choice of this environment is justified by its availability and its adaptability to our goals.

5 ETL4SocialTopic: Execution and Results Interpretation

To investigate ETL4SocialTopic performance, experimentations were carried out on Twitter real-world data of several contexts. In the next sub-section, the exhaustive execution of ETL4SocialTopic is performed on tweets of "mobile technology" context. Thereafter, topic schemas, obtained by applying the proposed process in other contexts, are presented and evaluated.

5.1 Execution Process for "Mobile Technology" Context

The process of designing topic dimension from tweets focusing on mobile technologies was performed as follows.

Media Clips Crawling. In this job, a set of keywords-based query was used to retrieve media clips in the scope of the subject "mobile technology trends". To respond to this query (specified by the designer), twitter crawling components collected *15,000 English tweets* published in *December 2020.* As demonstrated in Fig. 4, two filter components (*remove very short tweets* and *remove retweets)* were executed on the collected data to respectively discard retweets and very short tweets. Consequently, the number of tweets was reduced to *6741*. The obtained data were stored in «tweets», «tweets_hashtags» and «tweets_user_mentions» XML files.

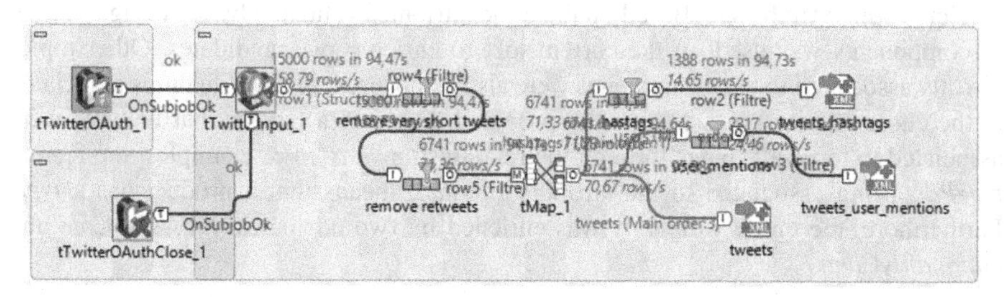

Fig. 4. Media Clips Crawling» Job.

Media Clips Preprocessing. The user-generated content, already stored in «tweets.xml», was cleaned through the pre-processing job which started by discarding useless information from tweet texts expressing the user's mentions and opinion symbols such as emoticons, opinion words and modifiers. Besides, a text cleaning component was executed on the tweet texts by using cleaning techniques given in [17] to remove diacritics (e.g., accent, unknown character), URLs, punctuations, stops words and stemming and obtain, therefore, pre-processed tweets.

Determine Topic Attributes. This job was performed to determine, from the pre-processed tweets, the attribute candidates that would be later used to design topic dimension. It analyzes each tweet, and returns a list of entities defined with their types. Figure 5(a) shows a fragment of the detected entity types. These types, stored in «topic_attributes.xml», correspond to the possible topic dimension attributes.

Select Topic Attributes. It is noted that some of the topic attributes, such as *musicGroup* and *TVShow*, did not belong to the subject area "mobile technology". For this reason, ETL designer should first restrict or enrich the list of the discovered topic attributes in order to keep only the interesting ones. Afterwards, he/she selected manually topic attributes. The entity types, surrounded by a red ellipse in Fig. 5(a), correspond to the desired topic attributes checked by the ETL designer.

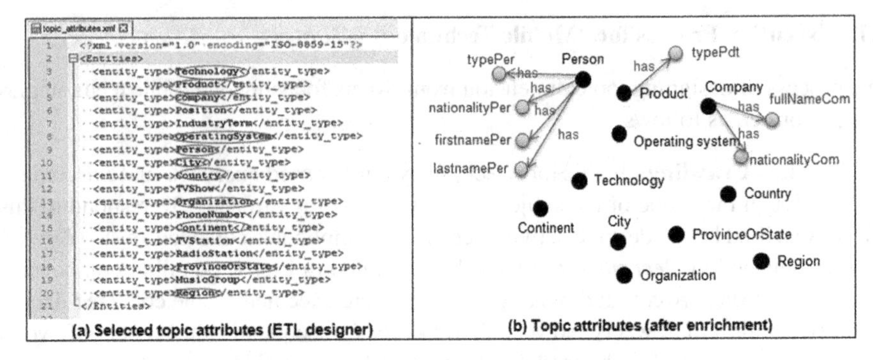

Fig. 5. Except of topic_attributes. (Color figure online)

Enrich Topic Attributes. Based on the topic attributes validated by the designer, a set of components was used, in the current job, to enrich topic candidates. Other topics directly associated to the desired ones were also discovered. A list of features associated to the chosen entity types was finally provided. Figure 5(a) shows that features were associated to topic attributes through the relationship "*has*". For examples, the feature *typePdt*, being associated to the attribute *Product*, means that a product has a *type*. Furthermore, the entity *Company* was enriched by two attributes: *fullNameCom* and *nationalityCom*.

Build Topic Hierarchies. At this level, candidate topic attributes were used to build topic schema modeled by the ETL designer. Figure 6(a) represents the designed topic schema. The relationships between topic attributes are represented by blue-dotted oriented arrows. For example, the relationship from *Product* to *Company* means that *Product* determines *Company*.

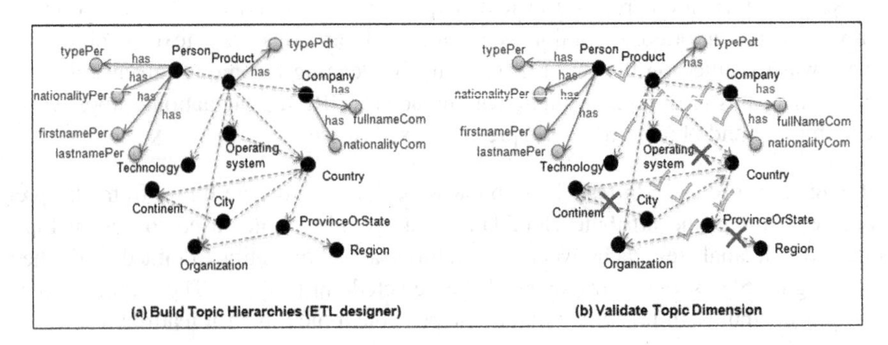

Fig. 6. Topic dimension schema. (Color figure online)

Validate Topic Dimension. For a consistent topic dimension schema, this job was developed to check inter-connected attributes considering its hierarchy features. The component corresponding to the current job consists in verifying the consistency of the existing semantic relationships of each couple of levels defined within the hierarchy. As given in [18], DBpedia is a rich knowledge source containing several topics of interest and the relationships between them. This lexical resource was employed by ***Validate Topic Dimension*** job to verify the inter-topics relationships between instances of its participant levels. The execution of this job provided a topic dimension schema (Fig. 6(b)) built with consistent hierarchies. Thus, some relationships (e.g. from *Product* to *Technology* and from *Product* to *Organization*) were allowed, while others were forbidden (e.g. from *Operating system* to *Country*). Moreover, transitive relations were omitted from inter-attributes semantic relationships. For example, the relation from *City* to *Continent* was omitted due to the existence of two relationships: (1) from *City* to *Country* and (2) from *Country* to *Continent.*

5.2 Interpretation of Topic Dimension Schemas

To validate ETL4SocialTopic, its workflow was also executed on other Twitter real-data covering different study contexts including "automobile" and "health" with several user's requirements. To check the relevance of the topic dimension schemas generated by the ETL4SocialTopic execution, we referred to the interpretations made by multidimensional design experts. We present, in Fig. 7, the experts interpretation do two schemas designed for **"mobile technology"** and **"automobile"** contexts.

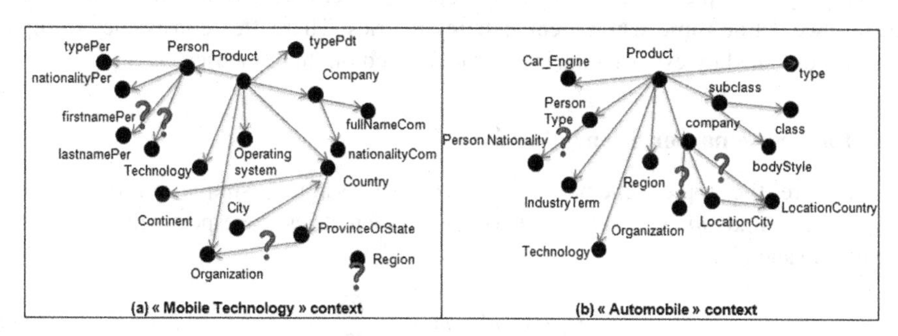

Fig. 7. Topic schemas for two contexts: (a) "Mobile technology" (b) "Automobile".

Interpretation of Schema Designed for "Mobile Technology" Context

Comparing the topic schema (illustrated by Fig. 7(a)) with the human-designed one (presented in Fig. 1), we observe a significant overlapping between the retrieved topics and those presented in the motivating example. Nevertheless, according to a domain expert, some of the detected relationships and topics (marked with "?" icon) were poorly-defined or had no semantic meaning. For examples, he/she deemed that the relation-ship from *ProvinceOrState* to *Organization* was inversely defined because the *Organization* determined *ProvinceOrState.* Besides, *firstnamePer* and *lastnamePer* were weak attributes. For this reason, it was not allowed to aggregate products per person names.

Moreover, the fact that *region* did not belong to any topic hierarchy, generated invalid multi-dimensional structure.

Interpretation of Schema Designed for "Automobile" Context
Figure 7(b) illustrates an example of the topic dimension schema generated by ETL4SocialTopic in the scope of "automobile" context. Its consistency was checked by another expert who deemed that term "Company" refers to any business organization so that no difference existed between *Organization* and *Company* instances in the context of "automobile". Thus, it was not possible to define a "parent-child" relationship from *Organization* to *Company.* Besides, the relation defined from *PersonType* to *PersonNationality* had no semantic relation. To this end, the latter should be attached directly to *Product* or omitted. In addition, *Engine* is a feature of cars that is a sub-class of product. For this reason, it should be directly related to *Sub-class* attribute.

6 Evaluation of ETL4SocialTopic Results

Based on the measures studied in [19] and [20], the **consistency**, describing the topic schema, can be defined as the extent to which the topic attributes and hierarchies are relevant. **Consistency** is a quality measure of the topic schema that may firstly be influenced by the compatibility of topic attributes to the context and to the user's requirements, and secondly by the topic relations satisfying topic hierarchy constraints. In the next subsection, we define **topic schema consistency** metrics. Thereafter, consistency of topic schemas obtained by experiments is evaluated based on these metrics.

6.1 Topic Schema Consistency Metrics

To measure the topic schema consistency, we assigned simple relevance: *topics_relevance* and *topics_relations_relevance.* These metrics are respectively formulated in Eqs. (1) and (2).

$$topics\_relevance = \frac{PT}{STA} \tag{1}$$

With

- *PT.* number of pertinent topics;
- *STA.* total number of the topic attributes in the designed topic schema;

$$topics\_relations\_relevance = \frac{PR}{STR} \tag{2}$$

With

- *PR.* number of correct topic relationships;
- *STR.* total number of inter-topics relationships in the designed topic schema;

6.2 Calculating Topic Schemas Consistency

The designers interpretation of topic schemas generated by the execution of ETL4SocialTopic for "mobile technology", "automobile" and "health" contexts are reported in Table 1. The latter illustrates *topics_relevance* and *topics_relations_relevance* scores computed for these topic schemas. In the ideal situation where schema topics are considered pertinent according to experts' evaluation, *topics_relevance* value is close to *(1)*. On the other hand, when inter-topics relationships of the resulted schema are totally accepted by human experts, *topics_relations_relevance* value should be close to *(1)*.

Table 1. Topic schemas relevance scores.

Study context	"Mobile technology"	"Automobile"	"Health"	Average
topics_relevance	0.95	1	0.91	**0.95**
topics_relations_relevance	0.76	0.78	0.77	**0.77**

Table 1 shows that ETL4SocialTopic execution process generated satisfactory results of topics. An average score of *topics_relevance* (equals to 0.95) was computed for three case studies. This value reveals how crucial the existence of ETL4SocialTopic jobs is for the successful execution of the ETL4SocialTopic process. A *topics_relevance* equal to 0.95 shows the consistency of **Determine Topic Attributes** job in generating relevant topics (very close to the designer expectations) from textual UGCs. Moreover, *topics_relations_relevance* score (with average 0.77) presents also the encouraging results of the valid topic hierarchies, which proves the performance of **Verify Topic Dimension** job. We also note that the relevance of the obtained topic hierarchies should be influenced by the choice of the lexical resource utilized to check inter-attributes relationships.

7 Discussion

The existing approaches (presented in Sect. 2) dealing with discovering topics of interest from textual UGC and their integration into the SDW proved that modeling topic hierarchies is complex due to their heterogeneity and dynamicity. In recent research works, topic dimension schemas have been used by to the SDW designer to extract manually related terms and topics from UGC data. Despite the good performance of some existing approaches in detecting data from social media texts and transforming them into topics in the SDW, these approaches did not focus on the complex ETL process to design topic schemas appropriate to the context. Our research addresses this issue at two levels: **conceptual modeling** and **implementation**.

As shown in Table 2, the above-studied approaches are compared with our proposal according to the following criteria:

Table 2. Comparison of ETL4SocialTopic with existing approaches.

Approaches	Flexibility			Consistency		ETL modeling	Process execution
	SMT	CC	DR	TRT	THT		
[4]	No	No	No	Topic dimension without hierarchy		No	Automatic
[5]	No	No	Yes	Standard	NS	No	Manual
[3, 6]	Yes	Yes	Yes	Semantic	NS	No	Manual
[7]	Yes	Yes	Yes	Standard	NS	No	Automatic
[8]	Yes	No	No	Topic dimension without hierarchy		No	Automatic
ETL4SocialTopic	Yes	Yes	Yes	Standard semantic	NS	Yes	Automatic

Flexibility. Flexibility can be defined as the ability of the ETL process to accommodate the previously-unknown, new or changing user's requirements [20]. Based on this definition, we propose three sub-criteria to measure the flexibility of the process introduced in this paper to design topic dimension schema.

- *Social Media Types (SMT).* specifies if the process supports several social media types (Twitter, Facebook, Youtube, etc.).
- *Context Changes (CC):* shows if the ETL process is suitable to any context.
- *Designer Requirements Customization (DRC):* reveals if ETL process tasks are customized to the designer's different requirements according to the context constraints.

Consistency. The correct instantiation of the Topic dimension schema is a major problem designing topic schema. Instantiation is generally validated depending on to what extend the topic hierarchy constraints is respected.

- *Topic Relation Type (TRT):* specifies if the topic hierarchies are designed by standard or semantic relationships between its levels.
- *Topic Hierarchy Type (THT):* demonstrates if topic dimension schema allows strict "S" or non-strict "NS" hierarchies.

ETL Design. Specifies if the approach does/doesn't propose an ETL conceptual model to design topic schema from UGC texts.

Process Execution. Refers to the degree of automation to which topics building steps are executed.

To the best of our knowledge, no work in the literature proposed ETL conceptual modeling of Topic dimension schema with respect to the crucial issues related to the nature of UGC data and the topic hierarchy constraints. ETL4SocialTopic is a starting point of designing complex ETL process applied to build topic dimension schema from user-generated texts. The major aim of our proposal consists in reducing the efforts made by the ETL designer through the process model (presented in Sect. 4). Indeed, the latter organizes ETL operations and controls their workflows in order to help designer automatically extract topics of interests from user-generated texts in the first step and, then, transform them in order to build topic dimension schema (designed with valid hierarchies). This flexible process, called ETL4SocialTopic, takes advantage of its independence of particular social media and specific study context. Besides, its generic operations may be customized to deal with the designer's specific constraints. For example, the designer chooses the necessary tasks for the execution of some operations (e.g. *Media clips pre-processing*), or the resources to be used in other operations (e.g. *Enrich Topic Attributes* or *Verify Topic Schema*).

It was expected that ETL4SocialTopic process would help ETL designer easily discover topics of interests appropriate to the study context and automatically execute topic hierarchies building steps according to a specific order. Furthermore, our process takes into account the main topic hierarchy constraints when designing their schemas and instances [5]. Firstly, complementary to the approaches that consider only strict topic hierarchies defined by one parent per node [4], ETL4SocialTopic also generates topic hierarchy schemas defined by many-to-many relations between its levels. On the other hand, different semantics relationships between topics were defined with reference to external resources.

The implementation of the whole process provided a palette of new jobs for each of its complex operations in order to be automatically executed according to a specific order. These jobs were trained on tweets data set in several contexts. According to expert-based evaluation, the generated topic dimension schemas were designed with consistent hierarchies. Experimentation results showed the good performance of the ETL4SocialTopic process in assisting the designer during the mapping of unstructured and informal texts into valid topic schemas. In terms of execution, this process achieved better degree of automation, in comparison to the existing approaches that manually defined topic hierarchies [3, 5, 6]. Indeed, most of its steps (Media Clips Crawling, Media Clips Preprocessing, Determine Topic Attributes, Enrich Topic Attributes and Validate Topic Dimension, etc.) were automatically realized.

8 Conclusion and Future Researches

This paper focused on ETL process modelling of UGC extraction, their transformation through the automatic detection of topic hierarchy attributes and their mapping into the SDW. The generic process model proposed in this paper may be exploited whatever the type of social media or the study context. Based on its defined ETL operations, ETL4SocialTopic was developed to automatically execute complex ETL workflows in order to generate valid topic dimension hierarchies. This process was tested on Twitter real data sets; each of which covers a specific study context. An expert-based evaluation of the topic schemas generated by ETL4SocialTopic showed its performance to remarkably facilitate the complex ETL workflow employed to crawl and pre-process Twitter data, to detect entities and to generate topic hierarchies schema defined by valid relationships.

This paper proposes a new ETL design solution that considers topic hierarchy constraints caused by integrating social media data into the data warehouse. Indeed,

ETL4SocialTopic helps designer build topic hierarchies defined by many-to-many relations between their levels. These topics were defined by different semantic relations.

This research is a starting point of topic integration into the ETL design process, opening up a broad range of future possibilities. Indeed, ETL4SocialTopic jobs provided consistent results of topic schemas. Otherwise, some of the developed jobs were specific to a particular development environment (twitter4J for Tweet crawling, open Calais API for entity detection API, DBpedia lexical resource for checking inter-topics semantic relations). In the near future, we intend to enrich ETL4SocialTopic palette by implementing jobs adequate to other social media and utilizing other resources to detect entities, enrich them and search inter-attributes relationships. Moreover, since the role of the recently-developed data warehousing is to support big data real-time or right-time capability, the introduced ETL will be extended to support the frequent social data changes.

References

1. Muntean, M., Cabău, L.G., Rinciog, V.: Social business intelligence: a new perspective for decision makers. Proc.-Soc. Behav. Sci. **124**, 562–567 (2014)
2. Gallinucci, E., Golfarelli, M., Rizzi, S.: Meta-stars: multidimensional modeling for social business intelligence. In: Proceedings of the Sixteenth International Workshop on Data Warehousing and OLAP, pp. 11–18 (2013)
3. Gallinucci, E., Golfarelli, M., Rizzi, S.: Advanced topic modeling for social business intelligence. Inf. Syst. **53**, 87–106 (2015)
4. Rehman, N.U., Weiler, A., Scholl, M.H.: OLAPing social media: the case of Twitter. In: 2013 IEEE/ACM International Conference on Advances in Social Networks Analysis and Mining (ASONAM), pp. 1139–1146. IEEE (2013)
5. Dayal, U., Gupta, C., Castellanos, M., Wang, S., Garcia-Solaco, M.: Of cubes, DAGs and hierarchical correlations: a novel conceptual model for analyzing social media data. In: Atzeni, P., Cheung, D., Ram, S. (eds.) ER 2012. LNCS, vol. 7532, pp. 30–49. Springer, Heidelberg (2012). https://doi.org/10.1007/978-3-642-34002-4_3
6. Francia, M., Gallinucci, E., Golfarelli, M., Rizzi, S.: Social business intelligence in action. In: Nurcan, S., Soffer, P., Bajec, M., Eder, J. (eds.) CAiSE 2016. LNCS, vol. 9694, pp. 33–48. Springer, Cham (2016). https://doi.org/10.1007/978-3-319-39696-5_3
7. Gutiérrez-Batista, K., et al.: Building a contextual dimension for OLAP using textual data from social networks. Expert Syst. Appl. **93**, 118–133 (2018)
8. Kurnia, P.F.: Business intelligence model to analyze social media information. Proc. Comput. Sci. **135**, 5–14 (2018)
9. Rehman, N.U., et al.: Building a data warehouse for twitter stream exploration. In: 2012 IEEE/ACM International Conference on Advances in Social Networks Analysis and Mining, pp. 1341–1348. IEEE (2012)
10. Mukherjee, R., Kar, P.: A comparative review of data warehousing ETL tools with new trends and industry insight. In: 2017 IEEE 7th International Advance Computing Conference (IACC), pp. 943–948. IEEE (2017)
11. El Akkaoui, Z., Mazón, J.-N., Vaisman, A., Zimányi, E.: BPMN-based conceptual modeling of ETL processes. In: Cuzzocrea, A., Dayal, U. (eds.) DaWaK 2012. LNCS, vol. 7448, pp. 1–14. Springer, Heidelberg (2012). https://doi.org/10.1007/978-3-642-32584-7_1
12. Oliveira, B., Belo, O.: BPMN patterns for ETL conceptual modelling and validation. In: Chen, L., Felfernig, A., Liu, J., Raś, Z.W. (eds.) ISMIS 2012. LNCS (LNAI), vol. 7661, pp. 445–454. Springer, Heidelberg (2012). https://doi.org/10.1007/978-3-642-34624-8_50

13. Walha, A., Ghozzi, F., Gargouri, F.: From user generated content to social data warehouse: processes, operations and data modelling. Int. J. Web Eng. Technol. **14**(3), 203–230 (2019)
14. Awiti, J., Vaisman, A.A., Zimányi, E.: Design and implementation of ETL processes using BPMN and relational algebra. Data Knowl. Eng. **129**, 101–837 (2020)
15. Nagamanjula, R., Pethalakshmi, A.: A novel framework based on bi-objective optimization and LAN 2 FIS for Twitter sentiment analysis. Soc. Netw. Anal. Min. **10**, 1–16 (2020)
16. Singh, S., Manjunanh, T.N., Aswini, N.: A study on Twitter 4j libraries for data acquisition from tweets. Int. J. Comput. Appl. **975**(2016), 8887 (2016)
17. Hemalatha, I., Saradhi Varma, G.P., Govardhan, A.: Preprocessing the informal text for efficient sentiment analysis. Int. J. Emerg. Trends Technol. Comput. Sci. (IJETTCS) **1**(2), 58–61 (2012)
18. Auer, S., Bizer, C., Kobilarov, G., Lehmann, J., Cyganiak, R., Ives, Z.: DBpedia: a nucleus for a web of open data. In: Aberer, K., et al. (eds.) ASWC/ISWC 2007. LNCS, vol. 4825, pp. 722–735. Springer, Heidelberg (2007). https://doi.org/10.1007/978-3-540-76298-0_52
19. El Akkaoui, Z., Vaisman, A.A., Zimányi, E.: A quality-based ETL design evaluation framework. In: ICEIS, no. 1 (2019)
20. Abran, A., et al.: Usability meanings and interpretations in ISO standards. Softw. Qual. J. **11**(4), 325–338 (2003)

Data Science and Decision Support

Predicting Process Activities and Timestamps with Entity-Embeddings Neural Networks

Benjamin Dalmas[1(✉)], Fabrice Baranski[2], and Daniel Cortinovis[2]

[1] Mines Saint-Etienne, Centre CIS, Saint-Etienne, France
benjamin.dalmas@emse.fr
[2] Logpickr, Cesson Sévigné, France
{fabrice.baranski,daniel.cortinovis}@logpickr.com

Abstract. Predictive process monitoring aims at predicting the evolution of running traces based on models extracted from historical event logs. Standard process prediction techniques are limited to the prediction of the next activity in a running trace. As a consequence, processes with complex topology (i.e. with several events having similar start/end time) are impossible to predict with these classical multinomial classification approaches. In this paper, the goal is to exploit an original features engineering technique which converts the historical event log of a process into different topological and temporal features, capturing the behavior and context of execution of previous events. These features are then used to train an Entity Embeddings Neural Network in order to learn a model able to predict, in a one-shot manner, both the remaining activities until the end in a running trace and the associated timestamp. Experiments show that this approach globally outperforms previous work for both types of predictions.

Keywords: Predictive process monitoring · Entity embedding · Neural network · Topological and temporal features

1 Introduction

Process mining is an important branch of data mining and business process management, and deals with the discovery, monitoring and improvement of business processes through the analysis of event logs [35]. Over the last decade, the process mining community has extensively developed algorithms, particularly in process discovery [5,20,37] and conformance checking [1,22]. More recently, Predictive Business Process Monitoring have seen an increase in research. This subfield of

This work was supported by Logpickr (https://www.logpickr.com) and carried out with *Process Explorer 360* technology. It has received funding from the European Union's Horizon 2020 research and innovation program under grant agreement No 869931 and is part of the Cogniplant project (https://www.cogniplant-h2020.eu/).

S. Cherfi et al. (Eds.): RCIS 2021, LNBIP 415, pp. 393–408, 2021.
https://doi.org/10.1007/978-3-030-75018-3_26

Process Mining is mainly concerned with predicting the evolution of running traces based on patterns extracted from a historical event log. The prediction of the next events in a process is of interest since it enables organizations to anticipate task scheduling, resource allocation or potential deviations from a recommended execution; and do what it takes to get back on the right track. In this context, several techniques have been investigated [12,17,29,36] for various tasks of business process predictions, e.g. the performance of the business operations, the time required to complete a particular task or the next activity to be executed. Benchmarks have shown that Machine Learning and Deep Learning techniques (e.g. predictive clustering tree inducer [3,26], Naive Bayes classifier [9], Long Short-Term Memory Neural Networks [8,13,31], Convolutional Neural Networks [23]) tend to outperform their competitor in this area, especially Long-Short Term Memory networks (LSTM) - a subtype of RNN - that are well suited to predict next events in traces since they are specifically designed to handle sequential inputs. Therefore, the underlying process generating a trace is modeled implicitly by the neural network itself.

However, existing techniques face two major limits. First, in their design, they are limited to the prediction of a single next event in a running trace. Although some techniques can be used in a Multi-step approach where each new prediction in a trace is used to feed the input for the following predictions, in this paper we are also interested in the prediction of all remaining activities in a trace in a single-shot manner. Then, this limit also implies the design of methods that output mutually exclusive predictions; i.e. only one activity is suggested. The underlying next-activity prediction refers to "the next activity to *start*". This is not a problem when the topology of the trace is relatively linear, but becomes problematic for more complex topologies. This research is supported by *Logpickr Process Explorer 360* tool, which has the particularity to detect and model an *enhanced* version of concurrent activities, whose behavior captures an activity starting *before* another ends, regardless of their respective starting timestamps (that could be different or similar). In the remaining of this paper, we will refer to these specific overlapping concurrent event executions as *concurrent events*, not to be mistaken with the traditional definition of *concurrent event* [4]. In this case, the underlying next-activity prediction refers to the next activity as a whole with a duration; rather than just an event represented by the starting timestamp. Therefore, there may be more than one next activity to predict at the same instance and the problem becomes a multi-output classification problem. To our knowledge, there are no study in the literature that investigates this complex problem.

To address the above-mentioned limits, the contribution of this paper is threefold. We propose a method able to predict (i) all remaining activities in a running trace alongside their respective duration, (ii) including enchanced concurrent events and (iii) in a single shot approach, i.e. with a model that predicts the entire forecast sequence at once, thus reducing passes through the network for the predictions, and avoiding prediction errors to accumulate such that accuracy performance is degraded as the trace time horizon increases. To do so, we explore an original features engineering technique which converts the historical event log of a process into different topological and temporal categorical variables, in the manner of time series approach. These variables allow us to consider concurrent events for processes with complex topologies. Then, we explore the use of Entity Embeddings Neural Networks (EENN), to efficiently deal with high cardinality categorical variables [14].

The remaining of this paper is organized as follows. Section 2 presents related work and Sect. 3 gives background concepts and definitions. In Sect. 4, our novel approach based on entity embedding and fully-connected neural networks for the next-activity and timestamps prediction is introduced. The application to remaining trace suffixes and durations is presented in Sect. 5. Finally, we conclude the paper and give further research perspectives in Sect. 6.

2 Related Work

Different research disciplines have developed methods to learn sequence-based models that can be used for the next-activity prediction problem. Tax et al. [29] propose a systematic review and relate three main families of approaches: grammar inference [11], process mining [35] and machine learning [2]. Although several models from these different fields, e.g. n-grams models, Probabilistic Finite Automaton or Markov models, have successfully been applied for sequence prediction, [6,7,18,19,34], recent benchmarks demonstrate that machine learning based techniques outperform their competitors in that area. In particular, the best performances are often achieved by Neural networks models [29,30]. To this end, the remaining of this section will focus on the recent applications of neural networks for the next-activity prediction problem.

The work in Evermann et al. [13] introduces a two hidden layer Long-Short Term Memory (LSTM) architecture for the next activity prediction of an ongoing trace, among other tasks. The technique includes a word embedding representation of categorical variables to train the network. Results showed that Neural Networks could achieve high accuracy and improve state-of-the-art techniques.

Previous results have been outperformed by a similar method investigated in Tax et al. [31], who predict next events also using LSTMs. Yet, in this work, categorical variables are transformed using a one-hot encoding procedure generating a vector where index i is set to 1 if it corresponds to the encoded activity. Although different architectures are benchmarked, the two hidden layer LSTM achieves the best results. The proposed techniques also allows to predict all remaining activities for a trace by recursively applying the next activity prediction until the end of the trace is reached. A different type of Neural network is used by Pasquadibisceglie et al. [23] for the next activity prediction task. In their recent work, the authors leverage a Convolutional Neural Network (CNN), while representing the spatial structure in a running case like a two-dimensional image. The experiments aim at fitting the prefix length to obtain the best accuracy results. The authors show an improvement over the previous LSTM-based architectures.

Another LSTM-based approach is later proposed in Camargo et al. [8]. Using an embedding technique to transform the resource and activity variables into continuous vectors, the authors consider three architecture variants to compare how sharing information between the layers can help differentiate execution patterns. Results show the technique obtains similar results to previous work for the next-activity task, but tends to outperform them in the prediction of the remaining activities in a trace. Lin et al. [21] propose *MM-Pred*, an RNN-based approach to predict the next event and the suffix of an ongoing case. In addition to the activity, this approach uses information related to other attributes of the events. The proposed architecture is composed of encoders, modulators and decoders to transform the events into hidden representations. This work is limited to the prediction of non-numerical attributes, therefore can not predict timestamps and durations.

Recently, the work proposed by Theis et al. [33] aims at predicting the next activity in a trace by leveraging performance metrics obtained with process model executions. The authors investigate a three-step technique in which first a process model is built with a process discovery algorithm. Then, the event log is replayed in this model to capture performance metrics, such as a decay function that enables the network to consider a time perspective during training. Finally, a vector is defined based on the metrics and fed into a neural network to predict the next activity. In addition to achieving state-of-the-art prediction accuracy, this method has the advantage to also provide comprehensible insights based on the process model generated in the first step.

Lastly, latest work include investigations of Generative Adversarial Networks [32], whose performances under specific conditions open new perspectives for the next activity prediction problem.

In these related work, we notice an over-representation of LSTM networks, that can be justified by its ability to capture the sequential behavior of process executions. In this paper, we propose a method to capture this behavior during the dataset generation, and feed the extracted information to a classical fully-connected neural networks instead.

3 Background and Definitions

In this section, we introduce concepts used in later sections of this paper. To remain consistent with existing work, the following definitions are based on [31].

3.1 Event Logs, Traces and Sequences

For a given set of activity A, A^* denotes the set of all sequences over A. $\sigma = \langle a_1, a_2, ..., a_n \rangle \; \forall a_i \in A$ is a trace of length n, $\sigma(i)$ representing the ith element of σ. $\langle\rangle$ is the empty trace and $\sigma_1.\sigma_2$ is the concatenation of traces σ_1 and σ_2. $hd^k(\sigma) = \langle a_1, a_2, ..., a_k \rangle$ is the prefix of length k $(0 < k < n)$ of sequence σ and $tl^k(\sigma) = \langle a_{k+1}, a_{k+2}, ..., a_n \rangle$ is its suffix. For example, for a sequence $\sigma_1 = \langle a, b, c, d, e \rangle$, $hd^2(\sigma_1) = \langle a, b \rangle$ and $tl^2(\sigma_1) = \langle c, d, e \rangle$. We extend hd^k and tl^k

to take into account concurrent events, noted $hd^k_{||}$ and $tl^k_{||}$. For example, for the trace $\sigma_i = \langle a, \{b, c, d\}, e, f, g \rangle$, $\{b, c, d\}$ is a parallel instance noted P with $P \subseteq A$ (Fig. 1). P is defined as the set of concurrent activities related to each other. Concurrent activities are activities that have the same start/end timestamps or overlapping activities executed in any order. For trace σ_i several prefixes and suffixes are possible according to the topology of P. In this extended definition, n represents the length of the trace in terms of number of *steps*, a parallel instance counting as one step. Figure 1 presents some illustrative examples of possible traces σ_i and the associated prefixes $hd^2_{||}(\sigma_i)$ and suffixes $tl^2_{||}(\sigma_i)$. For traces $\{\sigma_1, \sigma_2\}$ the topology of P is simple, so all prefixes and suffixes are the same for all activities of P. For traces $\{\sigma_3, \sigma_4\}$ the topology of P is slightly more complex and the prefixes and suffixes can change from the point of view of a specific activity of P.

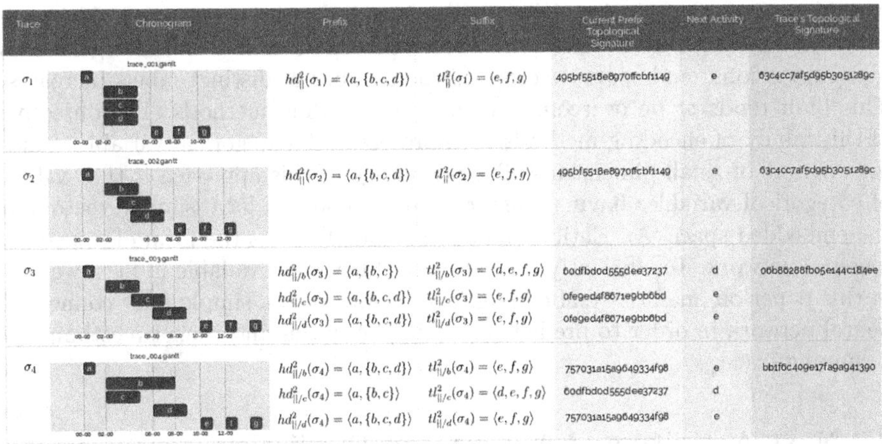

Trace	Chronogram	Prefix	Suffix	Current Prefix Topological Signature	Next Activity	Trace's Topological Signature
σ_1	trace_001gantt	$hd^2_{\|\|}(\sigma_1) = \langle a, \{b, c, d\} \rangle$	$tl^2_{\|\|}(\sigma_1) = \langle e, f, g \rangle$	495bf5518e8970ffcbf1149	e	63c4cc7af5d95b3051289c
σ_2	trace_002gantt	$hd^2_{\|\|}(\sigma_2) = \langle a, \{b, c, d\} \rangle$	$tl^2_{\|\|}(\sigma_2) = \langle e, f, g \rangle$	495bf5518e8970ffcbf1149	e	63c4cc7af5d95b3051289c
σ_3	trace_003gantt	$hd^2_{\|\|/b}(\sigma_3) = \langle a, \{b, c\} \rangle$	$tl^2_{\|\|/b}(\sigma_3) = \langle d, e, f, g \rangle$	60dfbd0d555dee37237	d	06b86288fb05e144c184ee
		$hd^2_{\|\|/c}(\sigma_3) = \langle a, \{b, c, d\} \rangle$	$tl^2_{\|\|/c}(\sigma_3) = \langle e, f, g \rangle$	0fe9ed4f8671e9bb6bd	e	
		$hd^2_{\|\|/d}(\sigma_3) = \langle a, \{b, c, d\} \rangle$	$tl^2_{\|\|/d}(\sigma_3) = \langle e, f, g \rangle$	0fe9ed4f8671e9bb6bd	e	
σ_4	trace_004gantt	$hd^2_{\|\|/b}(\sigma_4) = \langle a, \{b, c, d\} \rangle$	$tl^2_{\|\|/b}(\sigma_4) = \langle e, f, g \rangle$	757031a15a9649334f98	e	bb1f6c409e17fa9a941390
		$hd^2_{\|\|/c}(\sigma_4) = \langle a, \{b, c\} \rangle$	$tl^2_{\|\|/c}(\sigma_4) = \langle d, e, f, g \rangle$	60dfbd0d555dee37237	d	
		$hd^2_{\|\|/d}(\sigma_4) = \langle a, \{b, c, d\} \rangle$	$tl^2_{\|\|/d}(\sigma_4) = \langle e, f, g \rangle$	757031a15a9649334f98	e	

Fig. 1. Traces σ_i and the associated prefixes and suffixes according to the position in the parallel instance $P = \{b, c, d\}$, Current Prefix Topological Signature ($TS(hd^2_{||}(\sigma_i))$), Next Activity to predict, Trace's Topological Signature ($TS(\sigma_i)$).

Let $\mathcal{E}$ be the event universe, i.e., the set of all possible event identifiers, $\mathcal{E}^*$ the set of all sequences over $\mathcal{E}$ and $\mathcal{T}$ the time domain. We assume that events are defined by several attributes, however, the case id, timestamp, and activity label are mandatory for case identification, trace ordering and event labeling. We consider $\pi_A \in \mathcal{E} \rightarrow A$ and $\pi_\mathcal{T} \in \mathcal{E} \rightarrow \mathcal{T}$ functions that respectively assign to each event an activity from a finite set of process activities A and a timestamp. An event log is a set of traces, representing the executions of the underlying process. An event can only occur in one trace, however events from different traces can share the same activity.

We lift π_p functions to sequences over property p by sequentially applying π_p on each event of the trace; i.e., for a trace $\sigma{=}\langle e_1, e_2 \rangle$, with $\pi_A(e_1){=}a$ and $\pi_A(e_2){=}b$, $\pi_A(\sigma){=}\langle a, b \rangle$.

3.2 Neural Networks and Entity Embedding

A neural network is a model composed of neurons organized in layers, and connections between those layers. It commonly consists of one layer of input units, one layer of outputs units, and one or more hidden layers in-between. Each layer is fed with the outputs of the preceding layer, except the input layer which is fed by vectors sample from the dataset. The outputs of the output layer form the model predictions. The output of each neuron is a function over the weighted sum of its inputs. These weights are adjusted during the learning process, mainly with gradient-based optimizations, to approximate as accurately as possible the function that maps the inputs and the outputs.

A particularity of neural networks is that they handle only numerical features. As a consequence, categorical variables have to be encoded beforehand. *One-Hot Encoding* is one of the most used method: it represents each categorical variable with a binary vector whose length equals the number of distinct labels in that variable and marks the class label with a 1 and all other elements 0. Although easy to implement, the main downside of this method is it rapidly generates high-dimensional and sparse vectors as the number of distinct labels increases. This limit tends to be overcome by entity embedding methods. The objective of this family of encoding methods is to project each categorical variable values into vectors of small dimensions. The advantage of this approach is that values of categorical variables having similar output value will have similar vectors in the embedded space. An Entity Embedding usually takes the form of a layer in a neural network. To efficiently use categorical features available in logs, we rely in this paper on an entity embedding layer, coupled to a simple fully-connected neural network in order to predict remaining activities and their timestamps in a running trace.

4 Next Activity and Timestamp Prediction

In this section, we first present the approach developed to predict both the next activity in a trace and its related timestamp of execution. Then, we define the experimental setup and evaluate the approach.

4.1 Approach

This approach is based on two steps: (i) the extraction of vectors of topological ($\mathbf{V}_{topo}$) and temporal features ($\mathbf{V}_{temp}$) for each event (performed by *Logpickr Process Explorer 360*), and (ii) the training of an Entity Embeddings Neural Network (EENN) to predict the next activity and its timestamp. The objective is to learn an activity prediction function f_a^1 and a time prediction function f_t^1 such that $f_a^1(\mathbf{V}_{topo}^k, \mathbf{V}_{temp}^k) = hd_{||}^1(tl_{||}^k(\pi_A(\sigma)))$ and $f_t^1(\mathbf{V}_{topo}^k, \mathbf{V}_{temp}^k) = max(hd_{||}^1(tl_{||}^k(\pi_T(\sigma))))$.

For a trace σ, the topological features vector $\mathbf{V}_{topo}^k$ of event $\sigma(k)$ includes all information of the prefix $hd_{||}^k(\pi_A(\sigma))$ and all information of its topological representation (Fig. 1). This vector results from the core algorithm of *Logpickr Process Explorer 360* and aims at capturing the behaviors of the process execution preceding the current event. More precisely, as shown in Fig. 1, the prefix of each event is encoded into a unique signature called *Topological Signature* (TS). In Fig. 1, for the trace σ_3, at the end of the activity b, the topology of the prefix contains only information on activities a, b, and c where b and c are concurrent activities. The same logic can be applied to the trace σ_4, at the end of the activity c. From a topological point of view, these two prefixes are therefore identical which implies that $TS(hd^2_{||/b}(\sigma_3)) = TS(hd^2_{||/c}(\sigma_4))$. Conversely, the prefix topology of the trace σ_3, at the end of the activity c is slightly different from that of the trace σ_4, at the end of the activity b although the two prefixes contain information on the same activities, i.e., a, b, c and d where b, c and d are concurrent activities. From a topological point of view, these two prefixes are therefore different which implies that $TS(hd^2_{||/c}(\sigma_3)) \neq TS(hd^2_{||/b}(\sigma_4))$.

It is clear that the TS can represent categorical variables with high cardinality and allow the fully connected neural network to fully capture the dependencies among the elements inside the trace and their topology in the embedding space, which has a significant impact on the accuracy of the predictions.

Similarly, the temporal features vector $\mathbf{V}^k_{temp}$ includes all information related to the prefix $tl^m_{||}(hd^k_{||}(\pi_{\mathcal{T}}(\sigma)))$, with m a parameter defined to represent how far we look in the past to predict the next activity. The value of m is set to 3, resulting from a sensitivity analysis to obtain the best compromise between computation time and performance of the prediction models.

A first set of temporal features are the statistics (min(), max(), median(), mean()) of the duration of the m previous activities in the trace. A second set of temporal features are the statistics of the duration between the m previous activities. These temporal features only exist if events have both a start and end timestamps.

To take into account the hours and working days, we add the time and the weekday of (i) the start of the trace, (ii) the start of the current activity and (iii) the end of the current activity. Finally, to consider the effects of intra-month temporality and the effects of seasonality, we add the day of the month and the month for (i), (ii) and (iii) as well.

The temporal features allow the EENN to efficiently learn the dependencies between the duration of activity at different steps of the process and to discriminate the activities with close TS in the embedding space.

The first target is the next (concurrent events) activity encoded label(s) $\pi_A(\sigma(k+1)) = hd^1_{||}(tl^k_{||}(\pi_A(\sigma)))$.

A core feature of our approach is that it does not predict activity labels, but the Topological Signature of the suffix. This way, it is possible to predict one or several activities if a concurrent behavior is expected by the model.

The second target is the value of the next event duration or the maximal value of the next concurrent events duration $\pi_{\mathcal{T}}(\sigma(k+1)) = max(hd^1_{||}(tl^k_{||}(\pi_{\mathcal{T}}(\sigma))))$ having previously undergone a logarithmic transformation and a z-score normalization. A fully connected neural network architecture with embedding layers

Table 1. Entity Embeddings Neural Network parameters.

Parameter	Value
m	3
# layers	2
# neurons per layer	[emb dim, 500, 200, [output, 1]]
# dropout layer	3
Embedding dropout rate	0.2
Linear dropout rate	0.4
Batch normalization layers	3
Hidden layers activation functions	relu
Output layers activation functions	[softmax, -]
Loss function	[categorical crossentropy, MSE]

for categorical features is used in a multi-output learning setting. The schematic representation of the network architecture is presented in Fig. 2 and the details of layers parameters are illustrated in Table 1. The combination of parameter values presented is the one reaching the best empirical results.

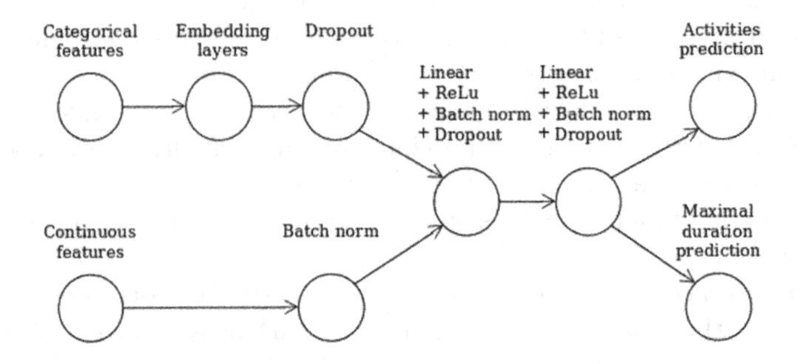

Fig. 2. Our Entity Embeddings Neural Network architecture.

An embedding layer is used to represent each categorical feature. Each embedding layer is followed by a dropout layer for regularization [28] as we found that it limits overfitting. For continuous features, a Batch normalization layer is used [15]. Two fully connected layers with fixed sizes of respectively 500 and 200 neurons, are used with Rectified Linear Unit (ReLU) activation functions. Batch normalization and dropout layers are applied between fully connected layers and between the second fully connected layer and the output layer. The output layer for the activities prediction uses a softmax activation function. During the training of the neural network, the optimization of the weighted sum of the categorical cross-entropy and Mean Square Error (MSE) loss functions is performed with Adaptive moment estimation (Adam) optimizer algorithm [16,27]. The presented approach is implemented in Python 3.8 64 bits version using the deep learning library Pytorch [24]. The training of the neural network was performed on a computer with an Intel i7-6700HQ CPU and 32 GB RAM.

4.2 Experimental Setup

We performed experiments to assess the effectiveness of our approach and in the aim to compare it to previous work [8,21,23,31,33]. However, we point out a lack of consensus in the configurations used in the literature to perform benchmark experiments. Several parameters impact the results of the different approaches, among which: (i) the split between the train and the test sets, (ii) the predictions of the first k events of a trace, (iii) the accuracy calculation, (iv) the introduction of artificial start/end events in the trace and even (v) the version of the dataset used. To allow a fair comparison, the different techniques should have the same configurations.

In this paper, we reproduced the configurations mentioned in [31] and [23]. Nonetheless, we will compare the results to others methods as well when the configuration is close but marked (*) to highlight the inconsistent configurations. Although some recent papers put forward good performances, a fair comparison can not be done regarding these aspects and were therefore not considered in the benchmark.

The chronologically ordered first 2/3 of the traces is used as training data and the remaining 1/3 of the traces is used as test data. To limit overfitting, a validation set of 20% of the training data is used in order to perform early stopping. The patience of the early stopping is set at five epochs. The quality of the next activity and timestamps predictions is evaluated at once for all traces of the test dataset. We use the Accuracy measure to evaluate the prediction quality of the activity label, and the Mean Absolute Error (MAE) for the timestamp predictions. Since the approach of [31] is not designed to predict events based on a 1-sized prefix, the following experiments start the predictions at the second event of each trace, as in [23,31]. Finally, to remain consistent with the later work, the classes to be predicted include only the log activities without any "end" activity (i.e. Scenario2 in [23]). The training phase is repeated five times with different random initialization of the network weights so that the performances can be measured as the average and the standard deviation of these tests.

4.3 Datasets

The performance of the next-activity and timestamp predictions is evaluated on four real-life benchmark datasets: **Helpdesk**[1], **Helpdesk final**[2] (similar to the previous dataset but with additional traces and attributes), **BPIC12 work complete**[3] and **Environmental Permit**[4].

[1] https://data.mendeley.com/datasets/39bp3vv62t/1.
[2] https://doi.org/10.4121/uuid:0c60edf1-6f83-4e75-9367-4c63b3e9d5bb.
[3] https://doi.org/10.4121/uuid:3926db30-f712-4394-aebc-75976070e91f.
[4] https://doi.org/10.4121/uuid:26aba40d-8b2d-435b-b5af-6d4bfbd7a270.

Table 2. Statistics of the evaluated datasets.

Dataset	# event instances	# concurrent event instances	# event classes	# traces	# attributes
Helpdesk	13710	0	9	3804	0
Helpdesk final	21348	260	14	4580	13
BPIC12 - *WC*	72413	0; 2070	6	9658	2
Environmental Permit	38944	18066; 38699	363	937	25

The statistics of these datasets in terms of number of event instances, concurrent event instances, event classes, traces, and attributes are presented in Table 2. The number of concurrent event instances can vary for BPIC12 - *work complete* and Environmental Permit, depending on whether competition between activities is taken into account or not. Most of the authors do not take into account the concurrence between activities. Indeed, they preprocess the dataset without taking into account the start or end date of the activities, which results, for certain dataset, by the sequentialization of the concurrent activities. As our approach can take into account concurrent activities, we take the part, here, to present the results with and without taking into account the concurrence.

4.4 Results

Table 3 summarizes the average accuracy and MAE for the next-activity and timestamp predictions. For the Helpdesk dataset, our approach outperforms [31] for the next-activity prediction, and reaches similar results in terms of timestamp predictions. Although we reach next-activity predictions similar to [23], our method has the additional ability to predict close-to-reality timestamps.

For the second version of the Helpdesk dataset, we tried to approximate the configuration used by [8] and [21], but an uncertainty related to the attributes used in the different implementations remains. The number of attributes used in [8] is not precised, therefore we mark this parameter as not communicated (N.C). Similarly, the work in [21] mentions the use of only 3 attributes (out the 11 available), but do not precise which ones. Still, our approach outperforms quite well, outperforming [8] with a 20% improvement in accuracy for the next-activity prediction when all the exploitable attributes are considered and a 1% improvement when only the 3 attributes used by [21] are considered. Compared to the best results achieved by [21], our approach yields a 3% increase in accuracy - from 0.916 to 0.944 - only when all the attributes are used. On the contrary, our results (0.798) are below those of [21] (0.916) when only 3 of them are considered. Yet, we wish to point out that among the 11 attributes, some are highly correlated with the remaining execution of the running trace (e.g. "*variant index*"), thus embedding in the prefix information about future events. This bias partly explains the good performance of our approach in this configuration,

Table 3. Next activity, remaining suffix and timestamp prediction results

				Next activity prediction		Suffix prediction	
Dataset	**Cce rate (%)****	**# attributes**	**Approach**	**Accuracy**	**MAE (days)**	**DLS**	**MAE (days)**
Helpdesk	0.0	0	Ours	0.7356 ± 0.0057	**3.74 ± 0.016**	**0.8893 ± 0.0013**	**3.91 ± 0.031**
			Pasquadibisceglie et al. [23]	**0.7393 ± 0.0038**	-	-	-
			Polato et al. [25]	-	-	0.2516	-
			Tax et al. [31]	0.7123	3.75	0.7669	6.04 ± 0.99
BPIC12 - *work complete*	0.028	2	Ours	**0.8802 ± 0.0013**	**0.0883 ± 0.00008**	**0.3717 ± 0.0057**	**7.25 ± 0.19**
	0.0		Ours	**0.8598 ± 0.0026**	1.61 ± 0.012	**0.3718 ± 0.0016**	**7.25 ± 0.08**
		0	Ours	**0.7916 ± 0.0026**	1.60 ± 0.012	**0.3718 ± 0.0016**	**7.25 ± 0.08**
			Pasquadibisceglie et al. [23]	0.7817 ± 0.0063	-	-	-
			Polato et al. [25]	-	-	0.0458	-
			Tax et al. [31]	0.76	1.56	0.3533	9.09 ± 2.98
Environmental permit	0.9937	2	Ours	-	-	**0.4108 ± 0.0044**	**32.78 ± 3.09**
	0.0		Ours	-	-	**0.2741 ± 0.0023**	**33.58 ± 1.32**
		0	Ours	-	-	**0.2743 ± 0.0035**	**38.31 ± 4.49**
			Tax et al. [31]	-	-	0.1522	41.8 ± 8.35
			Polato et al. [25]	-	-	0.0260	-
Helpdesk final	0.012	11	Ours	0.9442 ± 0.0035	7.61 ± 0.868	-	-
		3	Ours	0.7986 ± 0.0014	8.97 ± 0.629	0.904 ± 0.001	7.44 ± 0.371
			Lin et al. [21] (*)	0.916	-	0.874	-
		N.C	Camargo et al. [8] (*)	0.789	-	0.917	7.36 ± 1.194

(*) Inconsistent configurations with our approach - (**) Concurrence rate.

and might be the case for other implementations using these attributes as well. In terms of MAE for the timestamp prediction, the results are not as good as the initial version of the Helpdesk dataset, reaching an error of 8.97 days.

For the BPIC12 - *work complete*, on the same configuration of [31] and [23], our approach reaches 79% in accuracy, outperforming the work of [31] by 3% points. However, the timestamps predictions are similar - although slightly lower - to [31], with only a 0.04 days difference in MAE. Again, the quality in the next-activity prediction are close - but this time better - to [23]. Also in this case, our method has the advantage of predicting both the next-activity and timestamps, of good quality.

Better results are obtained when taking into account additional attributes and/or concurrent events in the BPIC12 - *work complete* log. When only the additional attributes are considered, the MAE is not impacted, while the next-activity predictions are improved in terms of accuracy, with a 7% points increase (86%) compared to [23]. Our approach performs best when both the attributes and concurrent events are taken into account, reaching an accuracy of 88% and a MAE of 0.09 days. We outperform the results in [23] by 9.35% points in accuracy and by 1.47 days in MAE.

5 Suffix and Remaining Trace Time Prediction

In the following, we define the experimental setup and evaluate the approach.

5.1 Approach

Our approach is designed in such a way that it does not iteratively predict the next activity and its timestamp, each prediction feeding the next, until the end of the case is predicted. Instead, the suffix prediction is based on the assumption that a topological signature, $TS(\sigma_i)$, can be assigned to each trace $\sigma_i \in L$ (Fig. 1). Following this intuition, the topological signature of the trace, $TS(\sigma_i)$, and the remaining trace time can be predicted from each event of the trace, in a one-shot manner. From this trace topological signature is then extracted the desired prefix with regard to k the current event in the trace. This approach allows the use of the EENN architecture as presented in Sect. 4 outputing an encoded vector of the trace's activities, as well as their potential concurrency behavior. This way, it is possible to predict, in a one-shot manner, the suffix and the remaining time.

The first target is the topological signature of the trace, $TS(\sigma_i)$, and the second target is the value of the remaining trace time, $\pi_{\mathcal{T}}(tl^k_{||}(\sigma_i))$ having previously undergone a logarithmic transformation and a z-score normalization. The parameters of the EENN layers are the same as those presented in Table 1.

5.2 Experimental Setup

The experimental setup used is strictly the same as that described in Sect. 4. To be consistent with [23,31], the suffix prediction is evaluated with the Damerau-Levenstein Similarity (DLS), that equals the Damerau-Levenstein distance (DLD) subtracted to one [10]. The DLD is a metric that outputs the minimum number of operations to transform one sequence into another. The DLS is then normalized by the maximum of the length of the ground truth suffix and the length of the predicted suffix. The remaining trace time is evaluated using the MAE metric. The approach is evaluated using the four datasets introduced in Sect. 4.3.

5.3 Results

Table 3 summarizes the average DLS and MAE for the suffix and timestamp predictions. Globally and similarly to the next-activity and timestamp prediction, our approach performs better than the other techniques, regardless of the dataset. For the traditional Helpdesk dataset, our approach largely outperforms [31] for both the suffix and the remaining trace time prediction, respectively improving the DLS by 16% (0.12 point) and reducing the MAE by 35% (2.13 days).

On the enhanced version of the Helpdesk dataset, our approach outperforms [21], but could not reach better results that those of [8]. However, we remind the differences in the attributes considered, since highly correlated resources could have been used in their implementation. While the prediction of the suffix is improved compared to the other version of the Helpdesk dataset, the remaining time prediction is negatively impacted by the additional traces present in the log, with a mean error reaching 7.44 days. However, it is to be noticed that the remaining time prediction errors are similar to those obtained with the next event timestamp predictions, which shows robustness in predictions regardless of the projection in time.

For the BPIC12 - *work complete* on the same configuration, our approach performs only slightly better than [31] for the suffix prediction, reaching a DLS of 0.37, therefore improving by 5% previous results. However, our approach takes the lead in the remaining time prediction, reducing by 20% the error in days, reaching a MAE of 7.25.

Contrary to what was stated in the previous section, our approach does not reach better results when taking into account additional attribute and/or concurrent events in the BPIC12 - *work complete* log, giving similar score both in terms of DLS and MAE. In this case, the consideration of additional attributes does not provide relevant information helping the prediction. Alternatively, it also mean that our approach handles the task of predicting concurrent events as efficiently as sequential events.

Our approach particularly distinguishes itself of the Environmental permit log. It is to be noticed that we did not compare the next-activity prediction results on this dataset since no previous work benchmarked this dataset on this problem, but on the suffix prediction only. On the basic configuration and compared to [31], the DLS for the suffix prediction is exceptionally increased by 80%, from 0.15 to 0.27. The MAE for the remaining time prediction is reduced by 8% in this case. This time, we notice even better results when considering new attributes and concurrent events in the log, reaching 0.41 in DLS (a 50% improvement) and 32.78 in MAE (14% reduction). This reveals the robustness of the approach.

5.4 Discussion

The experiments performed in the previous section highlight the applicability and performance of the method proposed in this paper. In particular, three aspects are to be pointed out. Firstly, the method aims at considering enhanced versions of concurrent activities in traces. As presented in Table 3, it is highly capable of handling the presence of such events in the prediction of the next event and the suffix of the traces. In addition, we also notice that the method often output results at least as good as the existing methods when no concurrent event is present in the log. It shows that the method is not just robust in particular situations, but can also be used in a wider range of process topologies.

Then, the one-shot prediction of the remaining events of a running case is the second contribution to highlight. At the best of our knowledge, existing methods could only approximate the suffix of a running case by predicting the next events in an iterative manner, until the end of the trace is predicted. The method proposed in this paper outputs the whole suffix in a single-shot manner. In addition to perform better than the existing methods, this approach also allows for a speed up in the computation time as only one pass in the predictive model is required to get the suffix.

Finally, a third major aspect to point out in the fact that the proposed method implements a basic fully connected neural network. Most existing techniques investigated other network architectures, such as LSTMs, CNNs or GANs. Justified by their ability to capture time and/or topology based relations in the log, the use of these architectures is complex and requires lots of hyperparameter tuning. The results obtained in this paper by a more traditional EENN architecture shows that it is possible to capture the underlying time and topology relations by transforming the dataset instead, therefore transferring the complexity of the predictive models into the pre-processing phase.

6 Conclusion and Future Work

This paper addresses the problem of predicting the next activity/suffix and the related timestamps of a running case. The main contributions are the proposition of a method able to include enhanced concurrent events as designed by *Logpickr Process Explorer 360* and in a one-shot prediction of the remaining activities. To the best of our knowledge, no other existing method is able to do so. Moreover, the gain in performance of the approach presented in this paper, compared to the existing methods, is significantly increased as the level of enhanced concurrent events increases. The approach explores topological and temporal categorical variables processed in an Entity Embeddings Neural Networks (EENN). The achieved performance also questions the relative superiority of LSTM networks to address the next-activity prediction problem. Relevant information can be obtained through the temporal and behavioral context of the log, and processed using simpler neural architectures. However, several aspects limit the efficiency of our approach. First, we noticed a relatively important number of unique suffixes. This characteristic makes the prediction task hard. A workaround would be to consider a generative approach; e.g. using Generative Adversarial Networks, to learn the distribution of activities in such suffixes and increase the sample size. Although the recent research in that area didn't meet the benchmark requirement, the approach is worth exploring to hybrid our EENN with, as it seems to solve this first limit. A second limit lies in the use of the DLS that computes the similarity between two sequences. The consideration of concurrent events makes the sequence formalism - and by extension the DLS - unsuitable to evaluate the quality of the predictions. Finally, in terms of timestamps and duration predictions, our approach is limited to the prediction of the min/max/mean value in case of concurrent events, and would require the execution of two decoupled models to correctly predict the duration of concurrent events. These limits are baseline research directions to explore in future work.

References

1. Adriansyah, A., van Dongen, B.F., van der Aalst, W.M.: Conformance checking using cost-based fitness analysis. In: 2011 IEEE 15th International Enterprise Distributed Object Computing Conference, pp. 55–64. IEEE (2011)
2. Alpaydin, E.: Introduction to Machine Learning. MIT Press, Cambridge (2020)
3. Appice, A., et al.: Business event forecasting. In: 10th International Forum on Knowledge Asset Dynamics, pp. 1442–1453 (2015)

4. Armas-Cervantes, A., Dumas, M., Rosa, M.L., Maaradji, A.: Local concurrency detection in business process event logs. ACM Trans. Internet Technol. **19**, 1–23 (2019)
5. Augusto, A., Conforti, R., Dumas, M., La Rosa, M.: Split miner: discovering accurate and simple business process models from event logs. In: 2017 IEEE International Conference on Data Mining, pp. 1–10. IEEE (2017)
6. Becker, J., Breuker, D., Delfmann, P., Matzner, M.: Designing and implementing a framework for event-based predictive modelling of business processes. In: Enterprise Modelling and Information Systems Architectures (2014)
7. Breuker, D., Matzner, M., Delfmann, P., Becker, J.: Comprehensible predictive models for business processes. MIS Q. **40**(4), 1009–1034 (2016)
8. Camargo, M., Dumas, M., González-Rojas, O.: Learning accurate LSTM models of business processes. In: Hildebrandt, T., van Dongen, B.F., Röglinger, M., Mendling, J. (eds.) BPM 2019. LNCS, vol. 11675, pp. 286–302. Springer, Cham (2019). https://doi.org/10.1007/978-3-030-26619-6_19
9. Ceci, M., Spagnoletta, M., Lanotte, P.F., Malerba, D.: Distributed learning of process models for next activity prediction. In: Proceedings of the 22nd International Database Engineering & Applications Symposium, pp. 278–282 (2018)
10. Damerau, F.J.: A technique for computer detection and correction of spelling errors. Commun. ACM **7**, 171–176 (1964)
11. De la Higuera, C.: Grammatical Inference: Learning Automata and Grammars. Cambridge University Press, Cambridge (2010)
12. Di Francescomarino, C., Ghidini, C., Maggi, F.M., Milani, F.: Predictive process monitoring methods: which one suits me best? In: Weske, M., Montali, M., Weber, I., vom Brocke, J. (eds.) BPM 2018. LNCS, vol. 11080, pp. 462–479. Springer, Cham (2018). https://doi.org/10.1007/978-3-319-98648-7_27
13. Evermann, J., Rehse, J.-R., Fettke, P.: Predicting process behaviour using deep learning. Decis. Support Syst. **100**, 129–140 (2017)
14. Guo, C., Berkhahn, F.: Entity embeddings of categorical variables. arXiv preprint arXiv:1604.06737 (2016)
15. Ioffe, S., Szegedy, C.: Batch normalization: accelerating deep network training by reducing internal covariate shift. In: Bach, F., Blei, D. (eds.) Proceedings of the 32nd International Conference on Machine Learning. Proceedings of Machine Learning Research, Lille, France, 07–09 July 2015, vol. 37, pp. 448–456. PMLR (2015)
16. Kingma, D.P., Ba, J.: A method for stochastic optimization (2014)
17. Koshy, C.: A literature review on predictive monitoring of business processes. Master's thesis, University of Tartu, Estonia (2017)
18. Lakshmanan, G.T., Shamsi, D., Doganata, Y.N., Unuvar, M., Khalaf, R.: A Markov prediction model for data-driven semi-structured business processes. Knowl. Inf. Syst. **42**(1), 97–126 (2013). https://doi.org/10.1007/s10115-013-0697-8
19. Le, M., Gabrys, B., Nauck, D.: A hybrid model for business process event prediction. In: Bramer, M., Petridis, M. (eds.) SGAI 2012, pp. 179–192. Springer, London (2012). https://doi.org/10.1007/978-1-4471-4739-8_13
20. Leemans, S.J.J., Fahland, D., van der Aalst, W.M.P.: Discovering block-structured process models from event logs - a constructive approach. In: Colom, J.-M., Desel, J. (eds.) PETRI NETS 2013. LNCS, vol. 7927, pp. 311–329. Springer, Heidelberg (2013). https://doi.org/10.1007/978-3-642-38697-8_17
21. Lin, L., Wen, L., Wang, J.: MM-Pred: a deep predictive model for multi-attribute event sequence. In: Proceedings of the 2019 SIAM International Conference on Data Mining, pp. 118–126. SIAM (2019)

22. Munoz-Gama, J., et al.: Conformance Checking and Diagnosis in Process Mining. Springer, Cham (2016)
23. Pasquadibisceglie, V., Appice, A., Castellano, G., Malerba, D.: Using convolutional neural networks for predictive process analytics. In: 2019 International Conference on Process Mining (ICPM), pp. 129–136. IEEE (2019)
24. Paszke, A., et al. (eds.) Advances in Neural Information Processing Systems 32, pp. 8024–8035. Curran Associates Inc. (2019)
25. Polato, M., Sperduti, A., Burattin, A., de Leoni, M.:Time and activity sequence prediction of business process instances. CoRR,abs/1602.07566 (2016)
26. Pravilovic, S., Appice, A., Malerba, D.: Process mining to forecast the future of running cases. In: Appice, A., Ceci, M., Loglisci, C., Manco, G., Masciari, E., Ras, Z.W. (eds.) NFMCP 2013. LNCS (LNAI), vol. 8399, pp. 67–81. Springer, Cham (2014). https://doi.org/10.1007/978-3-319-08407-7_5
27. Ruder, S.: An overview of gradient descent optimization algorithms. arxiv:1609.04747 (2016)
28. Srivastava, N., Hinton, G., Krizhevsky, A., Sutskever, I., Salakhutdinov, R.: Dropout: a simple way to prevent neural networks from overfitting. J. Mach. Learn. Res. **15**(56), 1929–1958 (2014)
29. Tax, N., Teinemaa, I., van Zelst, S.J.: An interdisciplinary comparison of sequence modeling methods for next-element prediction. arXiv preprint arXiv:1811.00062 (2018)
30. Tax, N., van Zelst, S.J., Teinemaa, I.: An experimental evaluation of the generalizing capabilities of process discovery techniques and black-box sequence models. In: Gulden, J., Reinhartz-Berger, I., Schmidt, R., Guerreiro, S., Guédria, W., Bera, P. (eds.) BPMDS/EMMSAD -2018. LNBIP, vol. 318, pp. 165–180. Springer, Cham (2018). https://doi.org/10.1007/978-3-319-91704-7_11
31. Tax, N., Verenich, I., La Rosa, M., Dumas, M.: Predictive business process monitoring with LSTM neural networks. In: Dubois, E., Pohl, K. (eds.) CAiSE 2017. LNCS, vol. 10253, pp. 477–492. Springer, Cham (2017). https://doi.org/10.1007/978-3-319-59536-8_30
32. Taymouri, F., La Rosa, M., Erfani, S., Bozorgi, Z.D., Verenich, I.: Predictive business process monitoring via generative adversarial nets: the case of next event prediction. arXiv preprint arXiv:2003.11268 (2020)
33. Theis, J., Darabi, H.: Decay replay mining to predict next process events. IEEE Access **7**, 119787–119803 (2019)
34. Unuvar, M., Lakshmanan, G.T., Doganata, Y.N.: Leveraging path information to generate predictions for parallel business processes. Knowl. Inf. Syst. **47**(2), 433–461 (2015). https://doi.org/10.1007/s10115-015-0842-7
35. Van Der Aalst, W.: Data science in action. In: Van Der Aalst, W. (ed.) Process Mining, pp. 3–23. Springer, Heidelberg (2016). https://doi.org/10.1007/978-3-662-49851-4_1
36. Verenich, I., Dumas, M., Rosa, M.L., Maggi, F.M., Teinemaa, I.: Survey and cross-benchmark comparison of remaining time prediction methods in business process monitoring. ACM Trans. Intell. Syst. Technol. **10**(4), 1–34 (2019)
37. Weijters, A.J.M.M., Ribeiro, J.T.S.: Flexible heuristics miner (FHM). In: 2011 IEEE Symposium on Computational Intelligence and Data Mining (CIDM), pp. 310–317. IEEE (2011)

Data-Driven Causalities for Strategy Maps

Lhorie Pirnay(✉) and Corentin Burnay

Namur Digital Institute, Université de Namur, Namur, Belgium
{lhorie.pirnay,corentin.burnay}@unamur.be

Abstract. The Strategy Map is a strategic tool that allows companies to formulate, control and communicate their strategy and positively impact their performance. Created in 2000, the methodologies applied to develop Strategy Maps have evolved over the past two decades but always rely solely on human input. In practice, Strategy Map causalities - the core elements of this tool - are identified by managers' opinion and judgment which may result with a lack of accuracy, completeness and longitudinal perspective. Even though authors in the literature have highlighted these issues in the past, few recommendations have been made as to how to address them. In this paper, we present a preliminary work on the use of business operational data and data mining techniques to systematize the detection of causalities in Strategy Maps. We describe a framework we plan to develop using time series techniques and Granger causality tests in order to increase the efficiency of such strategic tool. We demonstrate the feasibility and relevance of this methodology using data from *skeyes*, the Belgian air traffic control company.

Keywords: Strategy Map · Causalities · Data mining · Performance measurement models · Strategic management · Strategic decision-making

1 Introduction

Introduced in 2000, Strategy Map (SM) is a performance management tool widely adopted by companies. After creating the Balanced Scorecard (BSC) in 1992, Kaplan and Norton developed the SM to add causal relationships between the indicators of the BSC. A SM gathers key indicators of a company into four perspectives: Financial, Customer, Internal Business Processes and Learning and Growth. It connects the indicators into a causal map and creates a visual representation that helps understanding the side effects of some change in an indicator. This concept of causality, which will be discussed deeper in Sect. 2, distinguishes a SM from a simple performance measurement scorecard [1]. Its usefulness for companies has been demonstrated in the literature [2].

SMs (and BSCs) have been used by companies in order to formulate, control [3] and communicate [4,5] their strategy. Moreover, managers can use them as

S. Cherfi et al. (Eds.): RCIS 2021, LNBIP 415, pp. 409–417, 2021.
https://doi.org/10.1007/978-3-030-75018-3_27

tools with the purpose of decision-making and decision-rationalizing [6]. The SMs have a decision-facilitating impact for the managers to judge the relevance of external information as well as to evaluate if a strategy is appropriate [7]. SMs are thus considered as Decision Support Systems (DSS) in the sense that they can explore "what if" scenarios thanks to inherent causalities to help managers in a decision-making intention. Indeed, DSS can have a role in the support of strategic decision making in a company [8].

Human input intervenes in the development of the SM through manager's experience and intuition. They are *experts* of the company and their knowledge is considered sufficient to evaluate whether an indicator should be included in the SM and if a causal link exists. However, experts' opinion raises critical issues, that will be further developed in Sect. 3, that could be detrimental to the tool and consequently to the company. In the literature, there is no framework that uses business data to counter the subjectivity induced by human input in the context of SM. Yet, it has been recognized that firms which base their decision on data perform better [9]. As a consequence, we suggest in Sect. 4 to use data and apply data mining techniques in the creation process of the SM. A data-driven procedure with the purpose of decision-making integrates a Business Intelligence [10] dimension in the SM. Therefore, we position this paper as a decision information systems, data mining and business analytics paper.

2 Causalities in Strategy Maps

In the SM literature, authors have investigated several aspects of the practical development of such models in companies which we can divide in three stages:

1. The selection of the indicators to put in the four perspectives
2. The identification of causalities between chosen indicators
3. The validation of these identified causalities

We insist on the distinction between causality identification and causality validation considering that among the companies which create their SM, only a small number pursuit to validate it [2]. According to Kaplan and Norton, the possible causal links between the indicators can be made within the same perspective or toward an upward perspective. A generic SM is illustrated in Fig. 1, the arrows between the indicators representing the causalities.

While indicators selection has not been discussed much in the literature, causality identification and validation are the steps that have been the most investigated and criticized, and important issues have been highlighted among the years. First, Norreklit argues that some causalities assumed by Kaplan and Norton are not valid in real cases [11]. Bukh and Malmi advocate that Kaplan and Norton's intention was not to create a generic model - which, if applicable to all companies as such, would lose its strategic benefit for competition - but wanted a model based on assumed relationships between a selection of indicators in a certain company at a certain point in time [12]. None of the causalities are pre-established but rather assumed by the managers and revised if proved

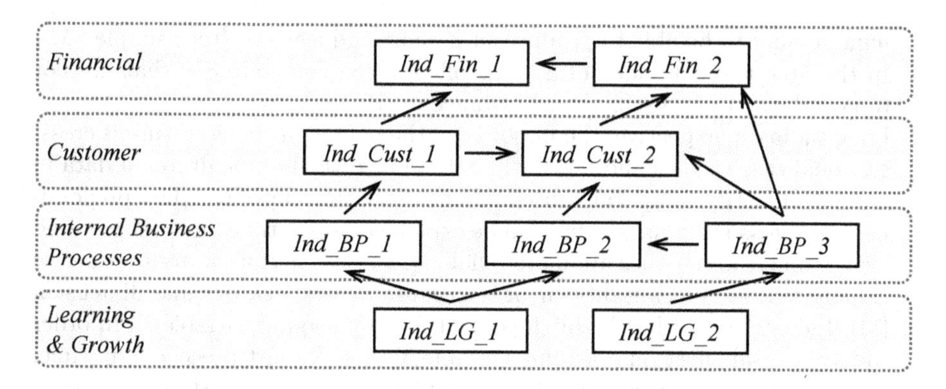

Fig. 1. Representation of a simple generic Strategy Map.

wrong later. The authors also admit that, ideally, the relationships should be validated with data if available. Second, Norreklit also question the relationships between the four perspectives stating that there exist interdependence instead of causality [11]. Once again, Bukh and Malmi replied that these relationships could be indeed interdependent in practice but that the backward link only reflects feasibility and should not be taken into account in the SM [12].

3 Challenges

Collecting experts' opinion can be a long and costly process. It requires time for the firms' experts to elicit their tacit knowledge [13] and mapping true causality relationships is costly and require a significant amount of resources [5]. Moreover, human participation in the development of SMs can be criticized on several aspects that can directly affect the SM itself in terms of: accuracy, completeness and longitudinal perspective. In the literature, the previous issues were highlighted but not necessarily linked with the human input used to produce the maps.

- Accuracy: human opinion is prone to biases, lobbying or irrationality. Causal relationships assessment is subject to human cognitive limitations [5]. The literature on human judgment in decision-making is vast and highlights accuracy issues. During decision-making based on beliefs and under uncertainty, people tend to use heuristics to simplify the task of assessing the probability of an event occurrence and being able to produce a judgment. These heuristics can lead to systematic errors and biases [14];
- Completeness: an efficient SM must be complete enough in order to be useful for decision makers. During the development process of a SM, the experts of the company have to evaluate all the possible causal links and state if they exist or not. If we consider a SM with 20 indicators distributed as 5 per perspectives, a total of 230 links have to be evaluated by the experts according to Kaplan and Norton's rule. Rapidly, it becomes too long and complex for a

human mind to be able to produce such effort and leads to (too) simple SMs. In the literature, the idea of a trade off between complete SM that are not too overloaded are discussed for instance in [15] and [16];

- Longitudinal perspective: the majority of the papers in the literature is cross-sectional case studies and few authors have investigated longitudinal data in order to identify temporal cause-and-effect relationships [17]. The predominance of cross-sectional studies can be explained by the time and cost required even if longitudinal ones are more reliable [18]. BSC detractor argues that we cannot talk about causality in SMs because of the lack of time dimension [11]. Indeed, the author highlighted that for any lagging variable X, in order to have causal effect on a leading variable Y then X must precede Y in time. However, the time dimension is not part of Kaplan and Norton's scorecard thus the author states that relationships cannot be causal.

In the literature related to SM development, we observe the prevalence of human input for each stage of the development process. Although human input questions the accuracy of BSCs and SMs, managers still play a role of organizational guide [5]. Many authors working on BSCs and SMs acknowledge the subjectivity issue of human data and use different techniques or triangulates multiple methods to try to counter subjectivity (see for instance [3,19–21]). While most papers focus on managerial contribution, it is hard to justify the use and implementation of complex methods for practitioners in order to create their SMs. Moreover, data is now at the core of essential business processes. The paradigm has shifted from simple decision-making to data-driven decision-making in many companies. In 2015, a study revealed that 81% of the companies agreed that data should be put at the heart of all decision-making [22]. Firms have evolved in their relationship with data through time from descriptive to predictive and prescriptive analyses. The rise of Artificial Intelligence and Experts Systems make Decision-Making prone to be increasingly based on data. As a consequence, we view the lack of use of data in the development of SM as a significant and relevant gap in the literature.

4 Proposed Solution and Case Study

Following the recommendations of [12], the work of [3] and the econometric literature, the solution we propose is decomposed in the following steps:

1. Exploratory protocol for causality identification between indicators: we investigate the relationships between indicators with the use of plots, correlation coefficients and regression techniques;
2. Time series graphical representations for managers and decision-makers;
3. We incorporate the time dimension into the SM through time series models. We ensure stationarity through Augmented Dickey-Fuller Test and lags selection with Akaike information criterion. Time dimension is a way to be able to validate causality between two indicators which is not possible with cross-sectional data;

4. Application of a vector auto-regressive (VAR) model [23] for causality validation. We use a VAR model to capture the linear interdependencies among multiple time series. We couple this VAR model with a Granger Causality test [24] which determines whether one time series is useful in forecasting another and is commonly used in scientific papers dealing with causality;
5. Automatic feeding of the SM based on VAR model results.

To illustrate what the application of our protocol would look like, we report preliminary tests on the steps of our proposed solutions that require the most attention. To do this, we use operational data provided by *skeyes*. Skeyes is the Belgian air traffic control company, it employs 891 persons and is in charge of the five airports located in Belgium and two radar stations. In 2019, it controlled more than one million flights and had a turnover of 245.2 million euros. We selected four key indicators of skeyes to include in their SM, the distribution of those indicators within the four perspectives of the SM has been carried out by skeyes' performance manager:

1. The *Vertical Traffic Complexity* (VTC) indicator represent the number of aircrafts present vertically within the air zone at different altitudes. This indicator belongs to the Learning and Growth perspective of the SM.
2. The *ATCO Hours On Duty* (AHD) indicator measures the total working time of the Air Traffic Control Officers. This indicator belongs to the Internal Business Processes perspective of the SM.
3. The *CDO Fuel Flag* (CFF) indicator is the number of aircrafts that did not respect the fuel regulations for their descent. This indicator belongs to the Customer perspective of the SM.
4. The *Service Units* (SU) indicator represents the multiplication of aircraft weight factor by distance factor and is an approximation of skeyes' invoice amount. This indicator belongs to the Financial perspective of the SM.

According to Kaplan and Norton's recommendations, potential relationships between indicators of the SM can only happen within the same perspective or towards an upper one. In our case, there could thus only exist 6 potential causal links between our selected indicators: from VTC to AHD, from VTC to CFF, from VTC to SU, from AHD to CFF, from AHD to SU and, lastly, from CFF to SU. Those potential relationships are represented in Fig. 2 and 3. In Fig. 2, we observe positive linear relationships between (i) VTC and CFF, (ii) VTC and SU and (iii) CFF and SU. However, there is no apparent relationship for the three other combination.

We then confirm the graphical relationship identification using Pearson correlation and Ordinary Least Squares (OLS) regression analysis. The relationships are indeed strong (corr > 0.7) and significant (p-values < 0.05) for the three observed relationships but weak (corr < 0.25) and unsignificant (p-values > 0.05) for the three others as shown in Table 1. In skeyes' SM, we can already remove the 3 potential links where no relationships were identified (Fig. 3). The existing relationships are not yet defined as causal and need further investigation in order to keep them in skeyes' SM.

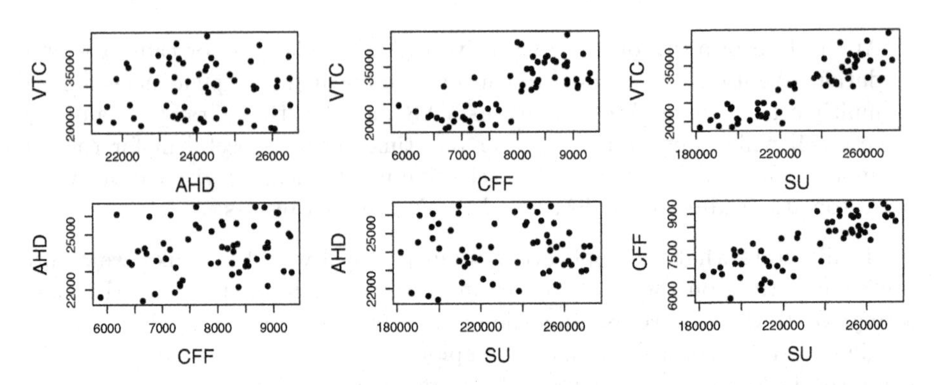

Fig. 2. Possible relationships between the 4 indicators (monthly data from 2015–2019).

Table 1. Pearson correlations and OLS results for the 6 potential relationships.

	DV: AHD IV: VTC	DV: CFF IV: VTC	DV: SU IV: VTC	DV: CFF IV: AHD	DV: SU IV: AHD	DV: SU IV: CFF
Pearson coefficient	0.0167	0.7316	0.8930	0.2361	-0.0277	0.8265
OLS coefficient	3.262e-03	9.725e-02	3.423e+00	1.609e-01	-5.454e-01	23.832
OLS p-val.	0.899	3.14e-11***	<2e-16***	0.0693	0.833222	4.2e-16***
Causality identification	no	yes	yes	no	no	yes

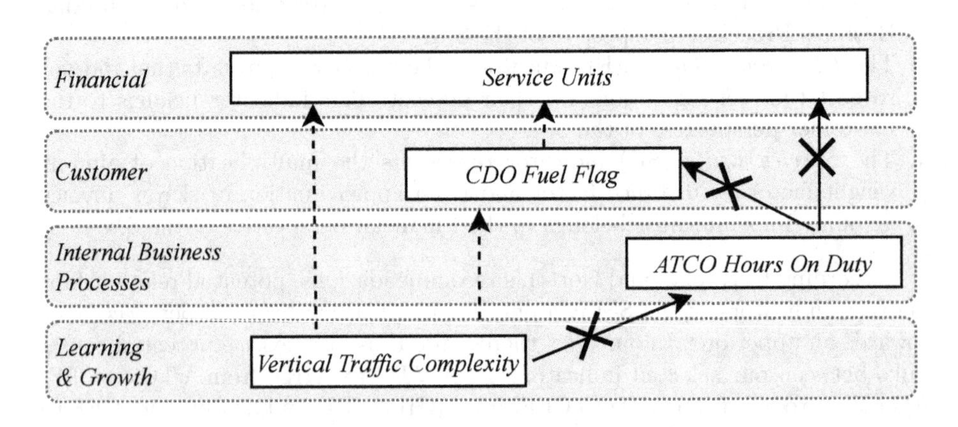

Fig. 3. SM after causality identification step.

To establish if the three identified relationships are indeed causal, we transform our data into time series and use Granger causality tests. We ensure the stationarity of our time series with Augmented Dickey-Fuller Test and select the optimal lag numbers recommended with the Akaike information criterion for each pair of indicators. Finally, the Granger test is performed based on the respective VAR model. The results summarized in Table 2 show that there is a Granger causality from VTC to CFF and from VTC to SU (null-hypothesis is the non-Granger causality). However, the indicator CFF does not Granger cause

Table 2. Granger results for causality validation.

	Dependent Variable: CFF Independent Variable: VTC	Dependent Variable: SU Independent Variable: CFF	Dependent Variable: SU Independent Variable: VTC
Optimal lag number	VAR(5) model	VAR(9) model	VAR(10) model
Granger test p-val.	0.01445***	0.8508	0.0004497***
Causality validation	yes	no	yes

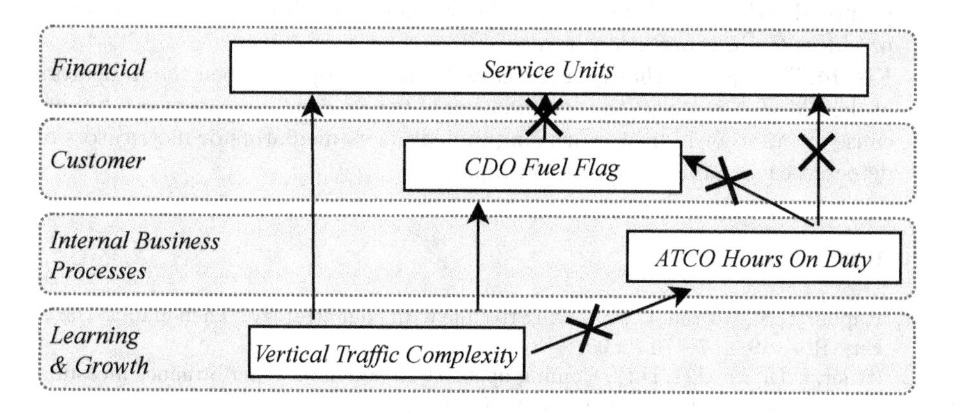

Fig. 4. Final SM resulting from causality validation.

SU, thus, although a relationship was previously identified the link was removed from the final SM because it is not causal in the sense of Granger (Fig. 4). In terms of interpretation for skeyes, this analysis and the final produced SM shows that they must be very attentive to the Vertical Traffic Complexity. Indeed, this indicator has a causal impact on the Service Units and on the CDO Fuel Flag.

5 Conclusion

In this paper, we presented our vision of a methodology to develop SM based on operational data and data mining. This methodology would allow to counter issues related to the human input involved in this process. The preliminary results show that we can identify and validate causality in the sense of Granger between indicators selected for the SM. Although the results look relatively obvious with the four selected indicators for this paper, the issue becomes quite complicated when a company faces more than 200 indicators. In this case, our proposed framework is much more valuable. Thanks to the previous sections, we can formulate further research directions (FRD) related to SMs development:

- **FRD1.** The automation of the creation of the SM: the managers of any company could add all the indicators in the model as input and obtain a SM as output. The model can test all the possible causal relationships of the map, even un-suggested causal links by the experts.

- **FRD2.** The optimization of the SM: the total number of causal links could be optimized with a strength threshold under which the causalities are not represented in the visual SM. Similarly we could use the model to eliminate the redundancy between indicators that would be too correlated.
- **FRD3.** The illustration of strength and direction of causal links between indicators: since the causal effects are detected by quantitative model and do not emerge anymore from intuition of the experts of the company. The proposed SM should thus include the strength and directions of the links it produces for interpretation purpose.
- **FRD4.** To explore other types of causal relationships between the indicators of the SM. For instance, the combination of two or more indicators as a unique cause for another indicator or using indicators as mediators or moderators of detected cause and effect relationships.

References

1. Kaplan, R.S., Norton, D.P.: Having trouble with your strategy? Then map it. Harv. Bus. Rev. **49**, 167–176 (2000)
2. Ittner, C.D., Larcker, D.F.: Coming up short on non nancial performance measurement. Harv. Bus. Rev. **81**(11), 88–95 (2003)
3. Malina, M.A., Nørreklit, H.S., Selto, F.H.: Relations among measures, climate of control, and performance measurement models. Contemp. Account. Res. **24**(3), 935–982 (2007)
4. Ritter, M.: The use of balanced scorecards in the strategic management of corporate communication. Corp. Commun. Int. J. **8**(1), 44–59 (2003)
5. Kasperskaya, Y., Tayles, M.: The role of causal links in performance measurement models. Manag. Audit. J. **28**(5), 426–443 (2013)
6. Wiersma, E.: For which purposes do managers use balanced scorecards?: an empirical study. Manag. Account. Res. **20**(4), 239–251 (2009)
7. Cheng, M.M., Humphreys, K.A.: The differential improvement effects of the strategy map and scorecard perspectives on managers' strategic judgments. Account. Rev. **87**(3), 899–924 (2012)
8. Power, D.J.: Decision support systems: concepts and resources for managers. Greenwood Publishing Group (2002)
9. Brynjolfsson, E., Hitt, L.M., Kim, H.H.: Strength in numbers: how does data-driven decisionmaking affect firm performance? Available at SSRN 1819486 (2011)
10. Negash, S., Gray, P.: Business intelligence. In: Burstein, F., Holsapple, C.W. (eds.) Handbook on Decision Support Systems 2, pp. 175–193. Springer, Heidelberg (2008). https://doi.org/10.1007/978-3-540-48716-6_9
11. Nørreklit, H.: The balance on the balanced scorecard a critical analysis of some of its assumptions. Manag. Account. Res. **11**(1), 65–88 (2000)
12. Bukh, P.N., Malmi, T.: Re-examining the cause-and-effect principle of the balanced scorecard. In: Accounting in Scandinavia-The Northern Lights, pp. 87–113 (2005)
13. Abernethy, M.A., Horne, M., Lillis, A.M., Malina, M.A., Selto, F.H.: Building performance models from expert knowledge. Available at SSRN 403220 (2003)
14. Tversky, A., Kahneman, D.: Judgment under uncertainty: heuristics and biases. Science **185**(4157), 1124–1131 (1974)

15. Quezada, L.E., López-Ospina, H.A.: A method for designing a strategy map using AHP and linear programming. Int. J. Prod. Econ. **158**, 244–255 (2014)
16. López-Ospina, H., Quezada, L.E., Barros-Castro, R.A., Gonzalez, M.A., Palominos, P.I.: A method for designing strategy maps using DEMATEL and linear programming. Manag. Decis. **55**(8), 1802–1823 (2017)
17. Slapničar, S., Buhovac, A.R.: Identifying temporal relationships within multidimensional performance measurement. J. Bus. Econ. Manag. **15**(5), 978–993 (2014)
18. Van der Stede, W.A., Young, S.M., Chen, C.X.: Assessing the quality of evidence in empirical management accounting research: the case of survey studies. Acc. Organ. Soc. **30**(7–8), 655–684 (2005)
19. Malina, M.A., Selto, F.H.: Communicating and controlling strategy: an empirical study of the effectiveness of the balanced scorecard. J. Manag. Account. Res. **13**(1), 47–90 (2001)
20. Abernethy, M.A., Horne, M., Lillis, A.M., Malina, M.A., Selto, F.H.: A multi-method approach to building causal performance maps from expert knowledge. Manag. Account. Res. **16**(2), 135–155 (2005)
21. Acuña-Carvajal, F., Pinto-Tarazona, L., López-Ospina, H., Barros-Castro, R., Quezada, L., Palacio, K.: An integrated method to plan, structure and validate a business strategy using fuzzy dematel and the balanced scorecard. Expert Syst. Appl. **122**, 351–368 (2019)
22. EY. Becoming an analytics driven organization to create value, report (2015)
23. Zivot, E., Wang, J.: Vector autoregressive models for multivariate time series. In: Modeling Financial Time Series with S-Plus, pp. 385–429 (2006)
24. Granger, C.W.: Investigating causal relations by econometric models and crossspectral methods. Econometrica J. Econometric Soc. **37**, 424–438 (1969)

A Novel Personalized Preference-based Approach for Job/Candidate Recommendation

Olfa Slama(✉) and Patrice Darmon

Umanis - Research & Innovation, Levallois Perret, France
{oslama,pdarmon}@umanis.com
https://umanis.com/fr

Abstract. Although *fuzzy-based recommendation systems* are widely used in several services, scanty efforts have been carried out to investigate the efficiency of such approaches in job recommendation applications. In fact, most of the existing *fuzzy-based job recommendation systems* are only considering two crisp criteria: *Curriculum Vitae (CV) content* and *job description*. Other factors like *personalized users needs* and the fuzzy nature of their *explicit* and *implicit preferences* are totally ignored. To fill this gap, this paper introduces a new *fuzzy personalized job recommendation approach* aiming at providing a more accurate and selective job/candidate matching. To this end, our contribution considers a *Fuzzy NoSQL Preference Model* to define the candidates profiles. Based on this modeling, an efficient *Fuzzy Matching/Scoring algorithm* is then applied to select the top-k personalized results. The proposed framework has been added as an extension to TeamBuilder software. Through extensive experimentations using real data sets, achieved results corroborate the efficiency of our approach in providing accurate and personalized results.

Keywords: Fuzzy logic · User preferences · Personalization · Recommender systems · MongoDB database

1 Introduction

Recommender Systems [3,9,17] have proven their efficiency in addressing the problem of information overload in many domains like news, entertainment, e-learning, social networking, search engines, etc. In addition, with the integration of user preferences, recommendation techniques offer the best promises of being more precise and flexible. Indeed, user preferences and profiling play a key role to guide users choosing easily and fastly the best information, product or services they are searching for, among the enormous volume of data available to them. *Users needs and preferences* are known to be *subjective* and *imprecise* by nature. In fact, this lack of precision is mainly due to the fact that item features can have a very large interval of extent (i.e., low to high) leading to several possible values.

S. Cherfi et al. (Eds.): RCIS 2021, LNBIP 415, pp. 418–434, 2021.
https://doi.org/10.1007/978-3-030-75018-3_28

As an example, the job feature called `duration` may have multiple possible values such as `very short`, `short`, `long`, etc.

To mitigate the impact of user preferences impreciseness, fuzzy logic [23,24] has been extensively used by researchers to provide more precise services in recommendation systems. This is done through selectively promoting suitable items to end-users based on their preferences analysis.

While *fuzzy-based recommendation systems* represent nowadays a key pillar for developing several domains such as tourism [13,14], healthcare [12,20], movie [5,22,26], E-commerce [11,15], E-government [7,19], the fuzzy job recommendation domain is less explored.

In fact, the scanty efforts on *fuzzy job recommendation systems* [4,6] are mostly focusing on content analysis of candidates resumes and job descriptions. Nevertheless, these contributions neglect the importance of dealing with the personalized candidates needs and the fuzzy nature of their explicit and implicit preferences.

Example 1 (Motivating example). Consider two users, *Jhon* and *Anna*, have almost the same proficiencies in their CVs and both of them are looking for a new job that best captures their interests. *Anna* (married) wants to work on `Data Science` and `long-term` missions, while *Jhon* (single) prefers `development` missions on `Python` and accepts `short-term` missions as long as they are located in `Paris` region. Each job seeker preferences can be stored in their respective *user profile*. Then, the system could automatically make use of them when looking for candidates for a new job offer. In this way, the system could give personalized recommendation by returning more appropriate jobs that are ranked according to the interest of each job seeker. *Anna* would be more satisfied with the results of `Data science` jobs with a long `duration` which is not the case for *Jhon*.

Therefore, through this example, we can clearly see that there is a crucial need to provide a job recommendation system that efficiently match potential candidates to the concerned job positions. The advantage of such a system is that apart of centralizing information, it can save valuable time and efforts of the job seekers/providers. This is done by making job providers reach more easily potential candidates on the one hand and on the other hand helping job seekers to find right career opportunities. Moreover, such a system may avoid a higher number of dissatisfied job seekers and potentially longer unemployment durations.

To help achieve these goals, we rely on the work of [10], where they developed a software called *TeamBuilder* to help job providers and recruiters reach out to potential candidates or employees during recruitment process. Nevertheless, this software is based only on the skills provided in the CV and then candidates preferences about the desired jobs are completely neglected. In this kind of situations, the skills provided in the CV indicate simply the mastered skills of the candidates and they could not perfectly reflect their needs and intentions for the job. This situation makes it more difficult for recruiters to find easily and quickly the best candidates that fit the job in consideration among the vast quantity of information available to them.

Based on these findings, this paper fills the gap by extending TeamBuilder software [10] to incorporate *multi-criteria crisp and fuzzy user preferences* stored in their submitted profiles. Indeed, job seekers preferences can be *imprecise* or *vague* and include *negative* and *positive* scores. Thus, these preferences should be carefully analysed using fuzzy logic for optimal filtration. Moreover, we have proposed a new *personalized fuzzy matching and scoring function* that aims to select the most relevant and appropriate jobs or candidates.

The main goal of our contribution resides in developing a *fuzzy preference-based recommender approach* for personalized job and candidate recommendations. This approach aims at returning items that faithfully reflect users needs and intentions and then improve the quality of theses recommendations. To the best of our knowledge, our proposal is the first attempt to address the issue of fuzzy personalization for job and candidate recommendation in the NoSQL context.

The rest of this paper is organized as follows. Section 2 presents some necessary background notions. In Sect. 3, we first introduce our proposed profile model used to define the *fuzzy user preferences*. Then, we describe our personalized scoring function proposal which is based on the *Fuzzy Matching/Scoring algorithm*, and aims to select the top-k results. Details about our implementation and conducted experiments are highlighted in Sect. 4 along with the obtained results. Related work is reported in Sect. 5. Finally, Sect. 6 concludes the paper and outlines some future work.

2 Background Notions

In this section, we recall important notions about the NoSQL Database Management System through introducing MongoDB and then we give an overview of the Fuzzy Logic theory.

2.1 NoSQL Database Management System: MongoDB

Not **O**nly **S**tructured **Q**uery **L**anguage (**NoSQL**) is a class of database management system that outperforms the **R**elational **D**atabase **M**anagement **S**ystems (**RDBMS**) [16], since it is able to offer new capabilities such as *horizontal scalability*, *high-availability* and *flexibility* to handle *semi structured data.*

NoSQL DBs are usually designed using one of the following type of databases: *Document-based* (`MongoDB, Apache CouchDB`), *Column-based* (`Casandra, HBase`), *Key-Value pair* (`Redis, DynamoDB`), and *Graph-based* (`Neo4J, OrientDB`).

In this paper, we consider the NoSQL open source DBMS MongoDB [2], released in 2009, that uses a *document-oriented data model.* MongoDB documents are stored internally using a binary encoding of JSON called BSON [1]. They are grouped together in the form of *collections*, where a *collection* is the equivalent of an RDBMS table and exists within a single database. Under this design, a document corresponds to records in Relational DB context. To well illustrate MongoDB collection structure, we give hereinafter a brief example.

Example 2. Let us consider two MongoDB collections: *Persons* and *Jobs* denoted respectively by $C_{Persons}$ and C_{Jobs}.

The collection $C_{Persons}$ contains information extracted from the users and then stored in a document. This latter can be represented as follows:

U_{User} : {`name, mastered skills, diploma, disponibility, name manager`}.

Given four job seekers named `John`, `Sophia`, `Julia` and `Paul` have the following profiles:

- U_{John} : {`John, [Data Science, Machine Learning, Python, Java, JEE], PhD, yes, James`},
- U_{Sophia} : {`Sophia, [Data Science, Machine Learning, Python, NoSQL], PhD, yes, David`},
- U_{Julia} : {`Julia, [Data Science, Machine Learning, Python, R/MATLAB], PhD, yes, Peter`},
- U_{Paul} : {`Paul, [Java, JavaScript, PHPL, SQL], Engineer, yes, Sarrah`}.

The second collection C_{Jobs} contains descriptions about the active jobs that have been recently posted by the recruiter and they have the following document structure:

Job_j : {`required education, required skills, duration, location`}.

We consider two jobs with the following descriptions:

- Job_{DS} : {`PhD, [Data Science, Machine Learning, Python], 4, Paris`},
- Job_{Dev} : {`Engineer, [Python, Java, JEE, MysQL, NoSQL], 24, Paris`}.

Moreover, one key feature of MongoDB DBs is that they are flexible in nature since documents have dynamic schema. Under this scheme, documents in the same collection can have completely different fields and common fields may hold different types of data. Although MongoDB is non-relational, it implements many features of relational DB, such as *sorting* and *range queries*. Operators like *create*, *insert*, *update* and *remove* as well as *manual indexing* are also supported.

2.2 Fuzzy Logic Theory

Zadeh work in [24] is considered a key milestone towards the definition of the fuzzy set theory. In fact, while the results of classical set theory are binary ("true or false" or "1 or 0"), Zadeh introduced for the first time the concept of *gradual membership* to model classes whose borders are not clear-cut. Within his approach, a fuzzy set, as presented in Definition 1, is associated with a membership function in the range of $[0, 1]$, which means that graduations are allowed and an element may belongs more or less to a fuzzy set.

Definition 1. *Let* $U = \{x_1, x_2, ..., x_n\}$ *be a classical set of objects called the Universe of discourse. A fuzzy set* A *in* U $(A \subset U)$ *is defined as a set of ordered pairs:*

$$A = \{(x_i, \mu_A(x_i))\} \text{ with } x_i \in U, \mu_A : U \to [0, 1],$$

where $\mu_A(x) \in [0,1]$ *is the degree of membership of* x *in* A *that quantifies the membership grade of* x *in* A. *The closer the value of* $\mu_A(x)$ *to 1, the more* x *belongs to* A. $\mu_A(x) = 0$ *means that* x *does not belong to* A *at all*, $0 < \mu_A(x) < 1$ *if* x *belongs partially to* A *and* $\mu_A(x) = 1$ *means that* x *belongs entirely to* A.

In [25], Zadeh introduces an essential concept in the fuzzy logic theory called a *linguistic variable.* It is a variable whose values are words or terms from a natural or artificial language instead of numerical values. Each linguistic variable is characterised by its name, *job duration* for instance and a set of linguistic values or terms, such as "short-term", "mid-term," and "long-term". The relation between numerical and linguistic values can be defined by trapezoidal membership functions of fuzzy sets. The numerical values of a linguistic variable can belong to one or more fuzzy sets with different degrees of membership between 0 and 1.

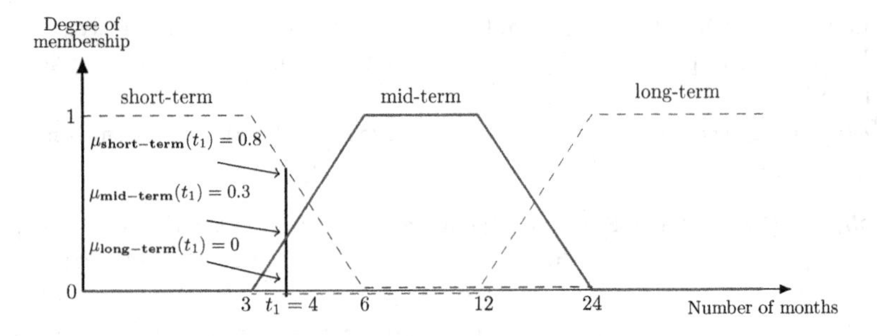

Fig. 1. Trapezoidal membership functions of *job duration* variable

Example 3. Figure 1 illustrates an example of the linguistic variable "job duration", with three possible linguistic values "short-term", "mid-term," and "long-term" as functions of the *job duration.* These linguistic values can be precisely defined in the system, where for instance "short-term" refers to a job duration between 3 and 6 months. Each numerical value of the job duration is assigned to at least one fuzzy set. The trapezoidal membership function of each set determines the degree to which a certain duration belongs to the set. For the linguistic variable "job duration", we define the following three membership functions: $\mu_{short-term}(t)$, $\mu_{mid-term}(t)$, and $\mu_{long-term}(t)$. As highlighted in Fig. 1, with duration t_1, a job may belong to three fuzzy sets with different degrees of membership. Thus, duration $t_1 = 4$ is considered to be *short-term* to a degree of 0.8, *mid-term* to a degree of 0.3 and *long-term* to a degree of 0, with $\mu_{short-term}(4) = 0.8$, $\mu_{mid-term}(4) = 0.3$ and $\mu_{long-term}(4) = 0$ respectively.

3 Contribution: Personalized Preference-Based Recommender Approach

In this section, we introduce a new *personalized preference-based recommender approach driven by fuzzy logic technique.* The proposed approach is able to provide personalized recommendations following two objectives: 1) *job recommendation* in which relevant job with higher matching degree with the job seeker's profile is recommended to him/her, and 2) *job-seeker recommendation* in which the job seeker that his/her profile get the higher matching degree with the specified job is recommended to the recruiter, which is the focus of this paper. These two types of recommendations are almost similarly designed and both of them are based on ranking items. These latter are either the *top-k candidates* that best fit the concerned job or the *top-k jobs* that best fit the candidates preferences.

The key idea behind our proposal is to efficiently exploit the candidates preferences recorded in their profiles. This information can essentially be collected during user interactions with the system and can be either *implicit* or *explicit. Explicit preferences* are about the job attributes, such as *desired job type*, *required experience* or *desired location.* On the other side, *implicit preference* are inferred by observing the user's actions or rating past experiences.

In this paper, our *fuzzy user profile model* covers both kinds of preferences aiming at providing more accurate and personalized recommendations. Without loss of generality, we suppose that *explicit preferences* are defined in the profile by the users and *implicit preferences* can be learned from them using machine learning mechanism. However, the way those *implicit preferences* are constructed is out of the scope of this paper.

The management of personalized recommendations require two-step process:

1. Generation a *fuzzy user profile model* by collecting candidates information and their multi-criteria preferences about the target job.
2. Development of a *Fuzzy Matching/Scoring algorithm* that:
   - filters out candidates whose profiles do not match the selected job,
   - generates the personalized recommendation list,
   - ranks the candidates in the recommendation list using a scoring function and returns the top-k recommendations.

3.1 Fuzzy User Preferences Profile Model in MongoDB

A key feature of our approach is its ability to store relevant information about users that will be used to infer their preferences and needs. Such information are stored in an individual user profile that should be dynamic in order to track the user's preferences change over time as they progress in their careers. *As an example, a person looking for a job at X location might not be interested in this location a few years later. Similarly, a job that is relevant for a person now might not be the case in the future because of a possible upskilling.*

As such, a user's profile consists of a list of attribute values about each company's employee. The attributes can concern, for example, *skills, email, disponibility, name of the manager, diploma* and *CV.*

User preferences are obtained when the employee logs into the system and provides them when requested. These preferences are *quantitative* and may concern several job attributes such as *desired skills*, *job duration* or *location*, *domain of interest*, *salary*, *future prospects*, etc.

In this work, and for simplicity sake, we only consider a set of attributes A = {`skills, duration, location`} and we assume that attributes like *skills*, *duration* or *location* are the most used when a candidate is looking for a job. In this case, each attribute can take different k preferences values.

In order to create our *fuzzy user preference profile model*, we add for each user its preferences about the job attributes along with their respective weights. This can be represented as follows:

$$Prefs_{User} : \{pref_{skills}, pref_{duration}, pref_{location}, W_{skills}, W_{duration}, W_{location}\}.$$

In the following, we details the definition of each attribute preferences:

- The preferences about the *skills* attribute, denoted by $pref_{skills}$, can be represented by a set of linguistic descriptors such as "`not interested, little interested, moderately interested, strongly interested`". For each attribute value $skill_k$ from *skills* where $k \in [0, m]$, we define the score $AScore_{skill_k} \in [-1, 1]$. This score corresponds to a real number in the range $[-1, 1]$ and indicates its *degree of interest* related to the $skill_k$. It can be of many types:
  - *positive* score $\in]0, 1]$ expresses a high interest (expressing liking, "`I am strongly interested on DevOps missions`"), with degree 1 indicates extreme interest. Thus, the more the score is, the higher the interest is.
  - *negative* score (expressing dislike, "`I am not interested in C++ missions`"), with degree -1 for "most-unpleasant" values.
  - *zero-valued score* models "indifference/don't care" situation with a degree equal to 0. In this case, this score indicates that we express neither a positive nor a negative preference over an attribute. For example, we can say that "`we are interested in Data Science missions, we don't like C++ missions, and we are indifferent to Python missions`".
    Thus, combination of *positive preferences* should give us a *higher score*, while combination of *negative ones* should give us a *lower score*. Moreover, an indifferent element should also behave like the unit element in a usual don't care operator. That is, when combined with any preference (either positive or negative), it should disappear. For example, if `we like data science missions` and `we are indifferent to Python ones`, `a mission with data science and Python` would have overall a positive score.
- The user preferences about the *job duration*, denoted by $pref_{duration}$, are associated with the following score $AScore_{duration_k} \in [0, 1]$, where $duration_k$ represents the kth preference about duration with $k \in [0, m]$.
  Job duration preferences can be modeled by *crisp* or *fuzzy* preferences. *Crisp* preferences are about the number of days, months or years of the desired job.

To do so, we use relational operators like "$<, >, !=, =$" to define an expression like "$duration_k > 2$ `months`", and then, we obtain a *Boolean score* (0 or 1). However, fuzzy preferences are modeled by *linguistic values* like *short-term*, *mid-term* or *long-term* job duration that can be predefined in the system. As illustrated in Fig. 1, the linguistic value "long-term" refers to job duration between 12 and 24 months for instance and their satisfaction is a question of *satisfaction degree* rather than an "all or nothing" notion.

- The same principle is applied to *job location preferences*, denoted by $pref_{location}$, where the satisfaction score for the kth preference about location is represented by $AScore_{location_k} \in [0, 1]$.
  Fuzzy preferences are also modeled by *linguistic values* like *near*, *moderately-near/far* or *far* job location. However, *crisp preferences* about job location may concern the *department/city/country name* or simply the *ZIP Code* of the desired job. This can be calculated using the geographic coordinates of the job and the user locations.
- The attribute *weight*, denoted by $W_{A_i}(u) \in [1, 10]$, refers to the importance degree of the respective job attribute A_i where $i \in [1, n]$ and aims to emphasize its priority regarding other attributes. For example, a user may assign a value 5 to the job duration ($W_{duration}(u) = 5$) and a value 2 to the job location ($W_{location}(u) = 2$), that's to say that a user is interested in the job *duration* more than its *location*. Intuitively, the more the attribute is preferred the higher the degree is.

All the above information form the *fuzzy user preferences profile model* which can be illustrated in Example 4.

Example 4. Let us consider the collection $C_{Persons}$ that contains `John, Sophia, Julia and Paul`'s profiles respectively denoted by $\boldsymbol{U_{John}}$, $\boldsymbol{U_{Sophia}}$, $\boldsymbol{U_{Julia}}$ and $\boldsymbol{U_{Paul}}$, as illustrated in Example 2. In order to represent their preferences about the ideal job, in each user's profile we add preferences about the skills, duration and location along with its weights. The preferences of each candidate are described in the following:

- $\boldsymbol{Prefs_{John}}$: {`[Data Science(1), Machine Learning(1), Python(0.8), Java(0.5), JEE(0)], short-term, Paris, 5, 3, 2`},
- $\boldsymbol{Prefs_{Sophia}}$: {`[Data Science(0.8), Machine Learning(0.8), Python(0.4), NoSQL(0)], short-term, Paris, 4, 2, 3`},
- $\boldsymbol{Prefs_{Julia}}$: {`[Data Science(0.5), Machine Learning(0.5), Python(-1), R/MATLAB(1)], Mid-term, Paris, 5, 1, 3`},
- $\boldsymbol{Prefs_{Paul}}$: {`[Java(0.8), JavaScript(0.8), PHP(0.5), SQL(0)], long-term, Lyon, 2, 5, 7`}.

For example, all of `John`'s preferences for his ideal job are stored in his profile $\boldsymbol{U_{John}}$ as $\boldsymbol{Pref_{John}}$. `John`, as a PhD, is strongly interested in `Data science and Machine Learning missions` ($pref_{skill_{DataScience}}$ with degree 1 and $pref_{skill_{MachineLearning}}$ with degree 1). He is interested in `Python` ($pref_{skill_{Python}}$ with degree 0.8), moderately interested in `Java` ($pref_{skill_{Java}}$ with degree 0.5) and he doesn't care if it is a JEE mission or not ($pref_{skill_{JEE}}$ with degree 0). He also prefers mission located in Paris ($pref_{location}$ = Paris) with short-term duration ($pref_{duration}$ = short-term). Moreover, John considers the *skills* attribute of the mission is more important than its *duration* and *location* (resp., W_{skills}(John) = 5, $W_{duration}$(John) = 3 and $W_{location}$(John) = 2).

3.2 Fuzzy Matching/Scoring Function

An efficient exploitation of the *fuzzy user preferences profile model*, already described in Subsect. 3.1, is mandatory to propose the best recommendations to the user. To meet this requirement, we developed a new **F**uzzy **M**atching/**S**coring **A**lgorithm (denoted by **FMSA**) that is illustrated below in Algorithm 1. A unique feature of our proposal resides in its capability to handle *fuzzy profiles models* containing fuzzy job preferences and then its ability to match a job description with the best user profiles. The output of our algorithm corresponds to the top-k list of candidates matching the job description. **FMSA** is based on the following key steps:

Algorithm 1: FMSA algorithm

Input: $C_{Persons}$, C_{Jobs}
Output: List of the best Candidates ranked by *PScore*
1 Generate all Candidate Preferences in $C_{Persons}$
2 $j \rightarrow$ Extract Job Attributes from C_{Jobs}
3 $u \rightarrow$ Select and Extract the k Best Candidate Preferences from $C_{Persons}$ that are relevant to j
4 Compute $PScore(u, j)$ (using Equation 1)
5 Apply the α-cut function
6 **return** top-k list of ranked Candidates with their Satisfaction Score

- *User Profiles Generation (line 1 of Algorithm 1):* In this step, the user logs into the system and defines his/her crisp or fuzzy preferences about the desired job attributes (such as the *job location, duration, desired skills* and the *weights* of each job attribute). These preferences are then stored in his/her profile in the collection $C_{Persons}$, as it is presented in Subsect. 3.1.
- *Attribute Job Selection (line 2 of Algorithm 1):* For each new job j selected by the recruiter, **FMSA** identifies and extracts all the required information (namely *skills, job location* and *duration*) and stores it in the collection C_{Jobs}.
- *User Preference Selection and Integration (line 3 of Algorithm 1):* In this phase, our technique identifies and extracts the k (i.e., best) selected preferences recorded in each user profile that are relevant to the selected job j. The idea behind this approach is to find the best matching between the selected attribute job j and the job preferences retrieved from the user profile u. For each job attribute A_i, we retrieve the related user preferences that match this attribute and should be taken into consideration for the calculation of

this *attribute score* $\tilde{A}Score_{A_i}(u,j)$. This latter is expressed as the *sum* of the scores related to different user preferences for the same attribute A_i.

- *Personalized Scoring Computing (lines 4 and 5 of Algorithm 1):* In order to produce a personalized result for each item returned in the result set, we calculate the *Personalized Score.* It is calculated by the *Personalized Scoring function*, denoted by $PScore(u,j)$, which is the *sum* of the scores of all fuzzy user preferences for each attribute job ($\tilde{A}Score_{A_i}(u,j)$) multiplied by its weight. The *PScore* is depicted in Eq. 1.

$$PScore(u,j) = \sum_{i=1}^{n} \tilde{A}Score_{A_i}(u,j) * W_{A_i}(u) \tag{1}$$

  Where $\tilde{A}Score_{A_i}(u,j) = \sum_{k=1}^{m} AScore_{a_{i_k}}(u,j)$, with the obvious meaning for user (u) and job (j) and assuming that each user profile has n attributes $\{A_1, A_2, ..., A_n\}$. Each attribute A_i takes i_k preferences values from the set $\{a_{i_1}, a_{i_2}, ..., a_{i_k}\}$.
  Finally, results are sorted in a decreasing order based on the *PScore*, where the items with the highest score appear at the top of the list. It is likely that users will receive several candidates in their recommendation list. So, an α-cut is required in order to limit the number of the returned results. It is worth noting that, contrary to our previous work [18], where we automatically exclude users having at least one preference with a negative score, our proposed **FMSA** technique considers that such preferences could be useful to offer more flexibility. In fact, negative preferences doesn't mean an automatic rejection of the candidate as long as *PScore* is positive.

Example 5. illustrates how the *PScore* is calculated for a specific job. Let us consider the job (denoted by Job_{DS}) from Example 2, for which we are looking for a candidate. `John`, `Sophia`, `Julia` and `Paul` are four candidates whose job preferences are already described in their respective profile in Example 4. To interpret this request, for each job attribute A_i in $A_{Job_{DS}}$ = {`skills :[Data Science, Machine Learning, Python]`, `duration: 4`, `location: Paris`}, we retrieve all the preferences needed from the user profiles that match A_i. These selected preferences should then be taken into account when calculating the *PScore* of each user. In fact, we first collect the scores of each user skills that match those of Job_{DS}. Then, we calculate the membership degree of the linguistic value related to the job duration ($\mu_{short-term}(4) = 0.8$, $\mu_{mid-term}(4) = 0.3$ and $\mu_{long-term}(4) = 0$ as illustrated in Fig. 1). Finally, we assign a score of 1 for `Paris` location and 0 for other cases since location is a non-fuzzy preference. These latter can be expressed as:

$\boldsymbol{Pscore}(U_{Jhon}, Job_{DS})= (\boldsymbol{AScore}_{skill_{DataScience}}(\text{Jhon})$
$+ \boldsymbol{AScore}_{skill_{MachineLearning}}(\text{Jhon})$
$+ \boldsymbol{AScore}_{skill_{Python}}(\text{Jhon})) \times \boldsymbol{W}_{skills}(\text{Jhon}) + \boldsymbol{AScore}_{duration}(\text{Jhon}, Job_{DS}) \times \boldsymbol{W}_{duration}(\text{Jhon})$
$+ \boldsymbol{AScore}_{location}(\text{Jhon}, Job_{DS}) \times \boldsymbol{W}_{location}(\text{Jhon}) = (1 + 1 + 0.8) \times 5 + 0.8 \times 3 + 1 \times 2 = 18.4,$

$$\boldsymbol{Pscore}(U_{Sophia}, Job_{DS}) = (\boldsymbol{AScore}_{skill_{DataScience}}(\text{Sophia}) + \boldsymbol{AScore}_{skill_{MachineLearning}}(\text{Sophia}) + \boldsymbol{AScore}_{skill_{Python}}(\text{Sophia})) \times \boldsymbol{W}_{skills}(\text{Sophia}) + \boldsymbol{AScore}_{duration}(\text{Sophia}, Job_{DS}) \times \boldsymbol{W}_{duration}(\text{Sophia}) + \boldsymbol{AScore}_{location}(\text{Sophia}, Job_{DS}) \times \boldsymbol{W}_{location}(\text{Sophia}) = (0.8 + 0.8 + 0.4) \times 4 + 0.8 \times 2 + 1 \times 3 = 12.4,$$

$$\boldsymbol{Pscore}(U_{Julia}, Job_{DS}) = (\boldsymbol{AScore}_{skill_{DataScience}}(Julia) + \boldsymbol{AScore}_{skill_{MachineLearning}}(Julia) + \boldsymbol{AScore}_{skill_{Python}}(Julia)) \times \boldsymbol{W}_{skills}(Julia) + \boldsymbol{AScore}_{duration}(Julia, Job_{DS}) \times \boldsymbol{W}_{duration}(Julia) + \boldsymbol{AScore}_{location}(Julia, Job_{DS}) * \boldsymbol{W}_{location}(Julia) = (0.5 + 0.5 + (-1)) \times 5 + 0.3 \times 1 + 1 \times 3 = 3.3,$$

$\boldsymbol{Pscore}(U_{Paul}, Job_{DS}) = 0$, since `Paul` is not skilled in `Data Science, nor in Machine Learning` and `Python` and has therefore $\boldsymbol{AScore}_{skills}(Paul) = 0$.

Moreover, his $\boldsymbol{AScore}_{location}(Paul, Job_{DS}) = 0$ because he is looking for a job in `Lyon` instead of `Paris` and he prefers a `long-term` job with $\mu_{long-term}(4) = 0$ as shown in Fig. 1. Thus, his $\boldsymbol{AScore}_{duration}(Paul, Job_{DS}) = 0$

After carrying out the above calculation, the satisfaction scores of `Jhon`, `Sophia` and `Julia` related to the job Job_{DS} are respectively 18.4, 12.4, and 3.3. The higher the score is the better the candidate is matching the indicated job. `Paul` will be automatically removed from the final result set since his *Pscore* is null.

4 Results

4.1 Proposal Implementation Overview

We have implemented our new flexible and personalized preference-based recommender approach using the TeamBuilder Software [10]. TeamBuilder is based on a containerized Big Data architecture using micro services. It allows to make a multi-criteria matching between the *skills of the job offer* (inserted by the recruiter) and the *skills of the existing CVs* (previously stored and scored in a MongoDB collection). The returned CVs are, then, ranked from most to least relevant ones. Our implementation follows the same methodology implementation of TeamBuilder and we used some of its functionalities to build our new approach, like *CV annotation functionality* provided by the Natural Language Processing service.

As TeamBuilder software doesn't handle job user preferences, our implementation extends TeamBuilder to make it more expressive and flexible. This contribution is carried out by integrating a fuzzy NoSQL user profile model that stores *multi-criteria crisp and fuzzy job preferences* and calculating the personalized scores to rank final results using our **FMSA** technique. Unlike the old version of TeamBuilder, this new version of the prototype is bidirectional and works both for *job* and *job seeker recommendation.* Hence, we have implemented two interfaces for these two different scenarios that interact with the two MongoDB collections $C_{Persons}$ and C_{Jobs}. Figure 2 illustrates both job seeker and recruiter implementation architecture.

1. *Job seeker interface design:* Through this interface an employee is capable to create his/her own profile by uploading personal information, updating CV or expressing preferences about his/her preferred jobs.The user profile is then stored in the collection persons $C_{Persons}$, letting the applicant to reuse it for other job position. We first perform a *preference selection* to select the top-k user preferences attributes with information needed to calculate each job attribute score ($\tilde{A}Score_{A_i}$). Then, we apply our **FMSA** algorithm which aims to recommend available top-k jobs to the concerned employee.
2. *Recruiter interface design:* This interface allows to automatically store each new job description in the collection jobs C_{Jobs} as soon as it is entered into the system. For each new selected job by the recruiter, its crisp attributes are retrieved and will be used for matching the employee preferences and calculating the final score $Pscore$. Then, we apply our **FMSA** algorithm that aims to recommend the appropriate available top-k employees matching the selected job description. Finally, these results are sent to the human resource department for more processing.

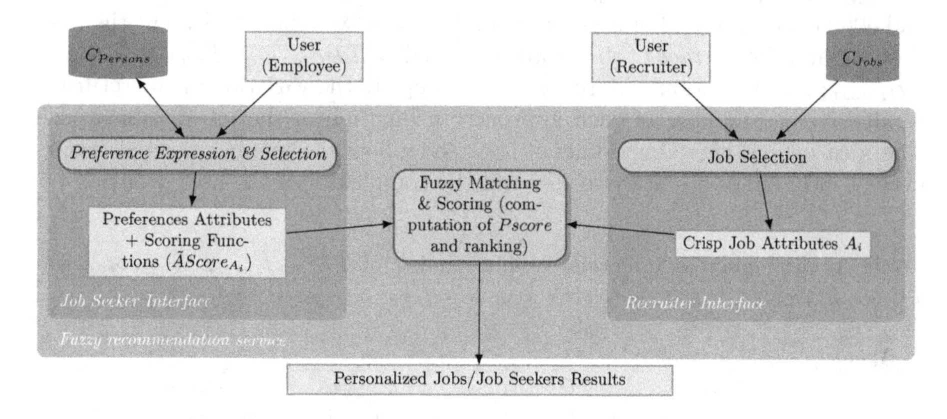

Fig. 2. Fuzzy recommendation service architecture

4.2 Performance Evaluation

In order to evaluate the performances of our proposed approach, we ran several preliminary experiments with real data sets coming from Umanis company. The tested data contains information about over 3587 employees of the company as well as their CVs and crisp or fuzzy job preferences stored in a MongoDB collection. Each employee has over 100 attributes retrieved from Umanis's CV library and the human ressource database.

To prepare the setting up for our experiments, we created for each candidate in the collection a number of default user profiles based on the (a) duration, (b) location and (c) job skills preferences. Note that, these preferences are around min 5 preferences by user and can be fuzzy or crisp ones with positive or negatives scores. Afterwards, we considered a new MongoDB collection jobs that contains *cisp job attributes*, such as *location* (ZIP Code/City), *duration* (number of months) and *required skills* with different number of document ($k = 20, 1000, 3000, 5000$).

As aforementioned, our approach extends TeamBuilder [10] by introducing *fuzzy candiates preferences profiles*. In order to demonstrate the benefits of adding these fuzzy job preferences, we conducted two set of experiments.

In the first experimentation, a *crisp preferences-based approach* was considered, denoted by $TB_{CrispPref}$, in which we use only non-fuzzy job seeker preferences in the collection. In the second experiment, we use a *fuzzy preferences-based approach*, denoted by $TB_{FuzzyPref}$, for which the collection can contains both crisp and fuzzy preferences. For each approach ($TB_{CrispPref}$ or $TB_{FuzzyPref}$), we run the **FMSA** algorithm. In these experiments, we aim to compare the results set of both $TB_{CrispPref}$ and $TB_{FuzzyPref}$ techniques to the ones of the classical approach [10], denoted as $TB_{Classical}$. This latter does not support *fuzzy job preferences* and does not need the use of **FMSA** algorithm.

For these experiments, we used four different sizes of job databases ($\boldsymbol{DB_{20}}$, $\boldsymbol{DB_{1000}}$, $\boldsymbol{DB_{3000}}$, and $\boldsymbol{DB_{5000}}$ with a number of jobs equal to 20, 1000, 3000 and 5000 respectively). For each different database, we report in Table 1 the *min*, the *max* and the *average* of the results returned by $TB_{Classical}$, $TB_{CrispPref}$ and $TB_{FuzzyPref}$ evaluations. Moreover, Fig. 3 depicts the variation of the returned results average number of each approach in function of the job database size. The idea behind these experiments is to show how the number of final results evolves in function of database size and the complexity of the user profile.

Table 1. *min*, *max* and *average* results number of $TB_{Classical}$, $TB_{CrispPref}$ and $TB_{FuzzyPref}$

Approach	Databases											
	DB_{20}			DB_{1000}			DB_{3000}			DB_{5000}		
	Min	Max	Avg	Min	Max	Avg	Min	Max	Avg	Min	Max	Avg
$TB_{Classical}$	0	41	14	0	1033	54	0	1045	55	0	1140	60
$TB_{CrispPref}$	0	30	9	0	650	30	0	800	32	0	870	39
$TB_{FuzzyPref}$	0	20	6	0	444	24	0	650	27	0	772	32

A clear observation is that for the three approaches the number of returned results is proportional to the job size. This is primarily due to the fact that, when we increase the number of jobs, candidates will be more able to satisfy the job requirements, and then, we have more returned results.

As it can be observed from Fig. 3, $TB_{FuzzyPref}$ approach outperforms the $TB_{Classical}$ one in terms of average results number. In fact, this latter of $TB_{FuzzyPref}$ is almost 50% less on average than $TB_{Classical}$. This can be explained by the fact that $TB_{FuzzyPref}$ recommends better results than the classical one by returning more personalized and less number of results. Indeed,

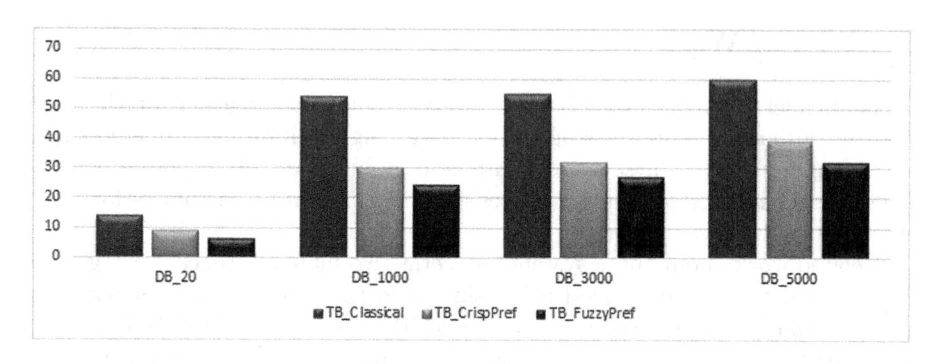

Fig. 3. $TB_{Classical}$, $TB_{CrispPref}$ and $TB_{FuzzyPref}$ experimental results

a personalized profile contains more preferences than a simple (non-personalized) one. Those preferences play the role of a filter that reduces the number of matching items. Thus, $TB_{FuzzyPref}$ approach can be seen as a refinement of the $TB_{Classical}$ approach. This is a very important feature since it makes it easier to the user to pickup the items that is searching for among huge result sets.

A similar behavior is also observed for the $TB_{CrispPref}$ approach since the average of returned results for each database is inferior to the one returned by $TB_{Classical}$. In addition, we can notice that, $TB_{FuzzyPref}$ performs better than $TB_{CrispPref}$ by reducing the number of returned results. This can be naturally explained by the more we introduce *fuzzy conditions* in the profile, the less items in the database will be satisfied. This is as well explained by the impact of our used *personalized scoring function*. In fact, the negative score in the profile indicating a dislike preferences will help to discard some unwanted responses (i.e., with negative scores) form the final result. As a conclusion, our technique performs better than the *classical* and the *crisp preferences* methods as well.

Interestingly, during these experiments, we noticed also that the processing time of the overall process is proportional to the database size and the fuzzy conditions numbers. Even though our proposal $TB_{FuzzyPref}$ shows a little increase in the processing time compared to $TB_{Classical}$, this raise is clearly very scanty and is expressed in term of milliseconds. Nevertheless, the gain achieved by our proposal in term of returned personalized results is very striking compared to other approaches.

Based on all the aforementioned findings and results, we can clearly observe that the experimental results are very encouraging and show the efficiency of our $TB_{FuzzyPref}$ approach by integrating fuzzy user preferences profiles into MongoDB databases. Indeed, our current approach outperforms the work of [10], in the way that it returns *smaller* and *more user-centered result set* and also entails a *very small increase of the overall processing time.*

5 Related Work

Recommender Systems [3,9,17] have received a lot of attention for the past years in various domains and applications (e.g., digital libraries, online booking, search engines, etc.). These systems are able to automatically generate personalized suggestions of products, services and information to customers for their individual or business purposes.

Related work about these systems concerns two main approaches categories: i) those that try to recommend items similar to the ones a particular user has already liked (*content-based approach*), and ii) those that try to identify users whose preferences are similar to those of the particular user and recommend items they have liked (*collaborative approach*). Moreover, these two approaches may be combined to form an *hybrid approach* trying to benefit from their advantages and reduce simultaneously each approach's drawbacks.

The literature review reveals that many soft computing techniques, such as neural networks, Markov models, fuzzy logic, genetic algorithms and Bayesian approaches, [8,21] are utilized in recommender systems to manage user preferences and interests.

In this paper, we leverage fuzzy logic technique [24] to deal with imprecision in the user preferences. This choice is based on the fact that fuzzy logic is more faithful to human reasoning and covers all intermediate values of acceptance and rejection. The introduction of fuzzy logic in the recommender system dates back to 2003 by Yager [23]. Afterwards, many researchers adopt this technique and propose new personalized approaches in order to handle *imprecise data* and *gradual user preferences* and then, to be able to provide more accurate and effective recommendations.

Although, fuzzy-based recommendation systems have witnessed a growing interest in several services, to name few, tourism [13,14], healthcare [12,20], movie [5,22,26], E-commerce [11,15], applications about *fuzzy job recommendation* are still less explored. To the best of our knowledge, most of the existing fuzzy job recommendation systems [4,6] are very limited since they are mostly focused on content analysis of the similarity between the candidates resumes and the job descriptions. Other factors like personalized user's needs and the fuzzy nature of their *explicit* and *implicit* preferences are totally ignored, which is the core goal of this work. Moreover, as far as we know, none of the existing fuzzy job approaches in the literature have dealt with the fuzzy MongoDB Data setting.

In our previous work [18], we have recently investigated the same issue of fuzzy personalization in the semantic web context dealing with fuzzy SPARQL queries and fuzzy RDF databases. The fuzzy user profiling is also addressed but in a querying point of view, where the SPARQL query is enhanced with the relevant user preferences recorded in his/her profile. However, in this paper, we are focusing on NoSQL data rather than on the querying step which is more adaptable and easy to use for a non-expert user.

In order to deal with fuzzy preferences in a MongoDB context, we propose in this paper a fuzzy extension of the approach introduced in [10] where they propose a *non-fuzzy based recommender system*, that is only based on a matching between the *skills of the job offer* and the *mastered skills in the CV*. To do so, we propose to build a *new personalized job recommendation approach* based on fuzzy logic which aims to take into consideration different type of implicit and explicit candidates preferences. In addition, we defined an *unified NoSQL preference model* that stores *multi-criteria crisp or fuzzy preferences* in candidates profiles including *negative* and *positive* scores, which has not been addressed before.

6 Conclusion

In this paper, we were interested in job/candidate recommendation systems and proposed a novel fuzzy preference-based technique to provide a more selective and personalized job/candidate matching. To do so, we first introduced the *fuzzy NoSQL preference profile model* for defining the candidates job preferences. Then, we proposed an efficient *Fuzzy Matching/Scoring algorithm* for the selection of the top-k personalized results and the final results rank. Our proposed approach was also integrated to TeamBuilder software for experimental validation with real data sets. Reported results corroborate the efficiency and practicability of our proposed personalized technique. As a future work, we plan to integrate more complex user preferences into the developed system, such as conditional preferences (as in "`If A happens, then I prefer B to C`") and contextual preferences like the current *spatial* and *temporal* position of the user.

References

1. Binary JSON (2009). http://bsonspec.org/
2. MongoDB (2009). https://www.mongodb.com/
3. Adomavicius, G., Tuzhilin, A.: Toward the next generation of recommender systems: a survey of the state-of-the-art and possible extensions. IEEE Trans. Knowl. Data Eng. **17**(6), 734–749 (2005)
4. Alksasbeh, M., Abukhalil, T., Alqaralleh, B.A., Al-Kaseasbeh, M.: Smart job searching system based on information retrieval techniques and similarity of fuzzy parameterized sets. Int. J. Electr. Comput. Eng. **11**(1), 636 (2021)
5. Anand, D., Mampilli, B.S.: Folksonomy-based fuzzy user profiling for improved recommendations. Expert Syst. Appl. **41**(5), 2424–2436 (2014)
6. Chen, P.C., et al.: A fuzzy multiple criteria decision making model in employee recruitment. Int. J. Comput. Sci. Netw. Secur. **9**(7), 113–117 (2009)
7. Cornelis, C., Lu, J., Guo, X., Zhang, G.: One-and-only item recommendation with fuzzy logic techniques. Inf. Sci. **177**(22), 4906–4921 (2007)
8. Kaur, R., Bhola, A., Singh, S.: A novel fuzzy logic based reverse engineering of gene regulatory network. Future Comput. Inform. J. **2**(2), 79–86 (2017)
9. Lu, J., Wu, D., Mao, M., Wang, W., Zhang, G.: Recommender system application developments: a survey. Decis. Support Syst. **74**, 12–32 (2015)
10. Manad, O., Bentounsi, M., Darmon, P.: Enhancing talent search by integrating and querying Big HR Data. In: Proceedings of the International Conference on Big Data (Big Data 2018), pp. 4095–4100 (2018)

11. Mao, M., Lu, J., Zhang, G., Zhang, J.: A fuzzy content matching-based e-Commerce recommendation approach. In: Proceedings of the International Conference on Fuzzy Systems (FUZZ-IEEE 2015), pp. 1–8 (2015)
12. Mulla, N., Kurhade, S., Naik, M., Bakereywala, N.: An intelligent application for healthcare recommendation using fuzzy logic. In: Proceedings of the International Conference on Electronics, Communication and Aerospace Technology (ICECA 2019), pp. 466–472 (2019)
13. Nilashi, M., bin Ibrahim, O., Ithnin, N., Sarmin, N.H.: A multi-criteria collaborative filtering recommender system for the tourism domain using Expectation Maximization (EM) and PCA-ANFIS. Electron. Commerce Rese. Appl. **14**(6), 542–562 (2015)
14. Nilashi, M., Yadegaridehkordi, E., Ibrahim, O., Samad, S., Ahani, A., Sanzogni, L.: Analysis of travellers' online reviews in social networking sites using fuzzy logic approach. Int. J. Fuzzy Syst. **21**(5), 1367–1378 (2019)
15. Ojokoh, B., Omisore, M., Samuel, O., Ogunniyi, T.: A fuzzy logic based personalized recommender system. Int. J. Comput. Sci. Inf. Technol. Secur. **2**(5), 1008–1015 (2012)
16. Parmar, R.R., Roy, S.: MongoDB as an efficient graph database: an application of document oriented NOSQL database. In: Data Intensive Computing Applications for Big Data, vol. 29, p. 331 (2018)
17. Resnick, P., Varian, H.R.: Recommender systems. Commun. ACM **40**(3), 56–58 (1997). https://doi.org/10.1145/245108.245121
18. Slama, O.: Personalized queries under a generalized user profile model based on fuzzy SPARQL preferences. In: Proceedings of the International Conference on Fuzzy Systems (FUZZ-IEEE 2019), pp. 1–6 (2019)
19. Terán, L.: A fuzzy-based advisor for elections and the creation of political communities. In: Proceedings of the International Conference on Information Society (i-Society 2011), pp. 180–185 (2011)
20. Thong, N.T., Son, L.H.: HIFCF: an effective hybrid model between picture fuzzy clustering and intuitionistic fuzzy recommender systems for medical diagnosis. Expert Syst. Appl. **42**(7), 3682–3701 (2015)
21. Vonglao, P.: Application of fuzzy logic to improve the Likert scale to measure latent variables. Kasetsart J. Soc. Sci. **38**(3), 337–344 (2017)
22. Wu, Y., ZHao, Y., Wei, S.: Collaborative filtering recommendation algorithm based on interval-valued fuzzy numbers. Appl. Intell. **45**(12), 1–13 (2020)
23. Yager, R.R.: Fuzzy logic methods in recommender systems. Fuzzy Sets Syst. **136**(2), 133–149 (2003)
24. Zadeh, L.A.: Fuzzy sets. Inf. Control **8**(3), 338–353 (1965)
25. Zadeh, L.A.: The concept of a linguistic variable and its application to approximate reasoning–i. J. Inform. Sci. **8**(3), 199–249 (1975)
26. Zenebe, A., Zhou, L., Norcio, A.F.: User preferences discovery using fuzzy models. Fuzzy Sets Syst. **161**(23), 3044–3063 (2010)

A Scalable Knowledge Graph Embedding Model for Next Point-of-Interest Recommendation in Tallinn City

Chahinez Ounoughi[1,2](✉), Amira Mouakher[3], Muhammad Ibraheem Sherzad[1], and Sadok Ben Yahia[1]

[1] Department of Software Science, Tallinn University of Technology, Tallinn, Estonia
chahinez.ounoughi@taltech.ee
[2] Université de Tunis El Manar, Faculté des Sciences de Tunis, LR11ES14, 2092 Tunis, Tunisia
[3] IT Institute, Corvinus University of Budapest, 1093 Budapest, Hungary

Abstract. With the rapid growth of location-based social networks (LBSNs), the task of next Point Of Interest (POI) recommendation has become a trending research topic as it provides key information for users to explore unknown places. However, most of the state-of-the-art next POI recommendation systems came short to consider the multiple heterogeneous factors of both POIs and users to recommend the next targeted location. Furthermore, the cold-start problem is one of the most thriving challenges in traditional recommender systems. In this paper, we introduce a new Scalable Knowledge Graph Embedding Model for the next POI recommendation problem called SKGEM. The main originality of the latter is that it relies on a neural network-based embedding method (*node2vec*) that aims to automatically learn low-dimensional node representations to formulate and incorporate all heterogeneous factors into one contextual directed graph. Moreover, it provides various POIs recommendation groups for cold-start users, e.g., nearby, by time, by tag, etc. Experiments, carried out on a location-based social network (Flickr) dataset collected in the city of Tallinn (Estonia), demonstrate that our approach achieves better results and sharply outperforms the baseline methods. Source code is publicly available at: https://github.com/Ounoughi-Chahinez/SKGEM

Keywords: Node embedding learning · Knowledge graph · Point-of-interest · Recommender system · Location-based social networks

1 Introduction

Recently, the maturation of location-based services has extremely affected social networking services, in which users can easily share their geographical locations and experiences (e.g. photos, tags, and comments) with their friends by checking-in points-of-interest (POIs) via online platforms. The latter are referred to as

S. Cherfi et al. (Eds.): RCIS 2021, LNBIP 415, pp. 435–451, 2021.
https://doi.org/10.1007/978-3-030-75018-3_29

location-based social networks (LBSNs), such as Foursquare, Gowalla, Facebook, and Flickr, etc. Such shared check-in information generates a large amount of historical data about the users' behaviors especially with the spread of smartphones among large popularity of youngs.

The next POI recommendation issue has been derived as a new fresh research focus of recommendation systems. This is very challenging for mobile-based applications to better understand user preferences and help them discover interesting places by providing personalized recommendations, where a user ought to visit next destination based on temporal and spatial information. Furthermore, one of the major issues in recommender systems is the user cold-start problem. To deal with these challenging tasks, several approaches have been proposed to extract users' movement patterns based on their historical behaviors and to provide personalized POI recommendations according to their latest check-ins [1]. A few researches have addressed these issues using traditional recommendation methods such as Matrix Factorization (MF). These latter obtain the user-location frequency matrix, which shows the number of occurrence of check-ins of users to POIs [2]. However, it is difficult for these MF-based approaches to provide satisfying recommendation results due to the data sparsity problem (absence of check-in data). To overcome this issue, some recent approaches, e.g., [3–5], to cite but a few, tried to take better advantage from spatial and temporal information to better train the recommendation models with deep recurrent neural networks (RNNs) [6] and rely on embedding learning-based techniques [7], that show promising performances for next POI recommendation. Notwithstanding, existing next POI recommender systems often focus on time and location dimensions and failed to incorporate the multiple heterogeneous factors of both POIs and users to recommend the user's next should visit locations. At the same time, they were unable to tackle the user cold-start challenge by providing satisfying recommendations for new users.

To this end, in this paper, we introduce a new approach called SKGEM for the next Point of Interest recommendation. Adopting the node2vec embedding technique is particularly useful to unify the representation of all the heterogeneous factors using one contextual directed graph to recommend the next *top-k* POIs. To overcome the cold-start problem, we also provide relevant *personalized groups/lists* recommendations according to temporal, spatial, and users' preferences (tags, categories, etc.) in a real-time manner. To sum up, our contribution steps are listed as follows:

1. Analyze the provided data by the LBSN to create our knowledge graph through a contextual directed graph. Through this knowledge graph, we gather different relationships between different types of nodes, e.g., poi-poi, poi-user, poi-category, poi-time, poi-region, poi-tag, poi-view, to name but a few.
2. Consider each node as a unique word in the directed graph to extract the model's vocabulary.

3. Use the biased random walks mechanism to walk across the directed graph and generate the sentences. Then, we have to train a node2vec model to create the embedded vectors of nodes for each POI.
4. Finally, the resulting model can be used to provide the recommendations of the top-k next-POI that should be visited given a user, as well as providing personalized groups/lists next-POI recommendations for new users of the system.
5. To evaluate our proposed approach, we carried out extensive experiments on an LBSN dataset collected in the city of Tallinn (Estonia). The harvested output, for the considered evaluation criteria, shows that we sharply outperform that obtained by the pioneering ones of the literature.

The remainder of this paper is organized as follows: Sect. 2 scrutinizes a literature review about POI recommendation. Then, Sect. 3 describes the next POI recommendation problem and proposes the SKGEM approach. Section 4 shows the experimental results of our proposed model versus its competitors. Finally, Sect. 5 concludes the paper and presents some future work.

2 Related Work

The task of the next POI recommendation has been studied extensively in recent years. In this section, we review some of the most relevant approaches that addressed such a task. A thorough study of the pioneering approaches of the literature drives us to split them through four main streams: (*i*) Matrix factorization-based approaches; (*ii*) Recurrent Neural Network-based approaches; (*iii*) Attention mechanism-based approaches; and (*iv*) Graph-based approaches. These latter main streams are sketched in the following.

2.1 Matrix Factorization-Based Approaches

Early studies on the next POI recommendation were based on Collaborative Filtering (CF), especially Matrix Factorization (MF) based techniques to capture users' preferences and mobility patterns to recommend POIs. Worth mentioning Rahmani et al. that proposed the following models: the first one is called LGLMF [8], which is a fusion of an effective local geographical model into a logistic Matrix Factorization. In this approach, the local geographical model generates the user's main region of activity and the relevance of each location within that region. By emerging the results to the logistic Matrix Factorization, the accuracy of POI recommendation is highly improved. The second model is called STACP [9], and is a spatio-temporal activity center POI approach aiming to model users' mobility patterns based on check-ins happening around several centers. The influence of their current temporal and geographical state is incorporated into a matrix factorization model for more accurate recommendations. Most of MF-based approaches do not deal with both data sparsity and cold-start problems.

2.2 Recurrent Neural Network-Based Approaches

Recent studies on next POI recommendation mainly focus on predicting users' targeted locations using RNNs-based models to extract the spatial correlation and their temporal dependencies patterns from the sequential historical user's trajectories. Worth mentioning, Kong et al. [6] have paid heed to the benefit of using the recurrent architecture Long Short Tern Memory (LSTM) with the encoder-decoder mechanism for real-time recommendations, to accurately combine spatial-temporal influence and mitigate the problem of data sparsity. Zhao et al. added four more gates to the basic LSTM architecture [10]. Two of them were dedicated to time dependencies and the remaining ones to spatial correlations in order to capture the influence of the latest visited POI on the next one. In a similar study, Wu et al. [7] introduced a combination of long and short-term modules that use the embedding technique and an LSTM-based architecture for the next POI recommendation. Subsequently, a deep architecture was presented by Zhou et al. [11] to integrate the topic model and memory network, capitalizing on the strengths of local neighborhood-based features to exploit user-specific spatial preference and POI-specific spatial influence to enhance the recommendations. Later, Sun et al. [12] developed a context-aware non-local network for long-term preference modeling and a geo-dilated RNN for short-term preference learning to explore the temporal and spatial correlations between historical and current trajectories. Chang et al. [13] proposed a content-aware model with two different layers: a context and a content layers. The former is used to capture the geographical influence from the check-in sequence of a user, while the content layer is used to extract the characteristics of POIs for better-personalized recommendations. RNN-based approaches prove their efficiency to capture the spatio-temporal relationships between successive check-ins, but these approaches are computationally very intensive and suffer with cold-start problem as long as it needs previous data to learn from.

2.3 Attention-Based Approaches

Other researches attempted to leverage from the contextual temporal and spatial users' and POIs' information provided by the LBSNs to build a spatio-temporal context, and social-aware models for better recommendations. Huang et al. in [1] presented a deep attentive network for social-aware next POI recommendation that makes use of the self-attention mechanism instead of the architecture of RNNs to model both sequential and social influences. Ma et al. [14] proposed a novel autoencoder-based model to learn the non-linear user-POI relations, that use a self-attentive encoder (SAE) and a neighbor-aware decoder (NAD) to make users' reachable to similar and nearby neighbors of checked-in POIs. Zhang et al. [5] introduced a simple effective neural network framework that incorporates different factors in a unified manner to recommend users' next move. The success of using the attention mechanism has motivated Liu et al. [15] to establish a geographical and temporal attention network. That synchronously learn to dynamically change user preferences by selecting relevant activities from check-in histories and then make the POI recommendation using a conditional probability distribution function. Guo et al. [16] introduced a recommender model that incorporates the embeddings of spatial patterns of user's relative positions of POIs and check-ins time into the self-attentive network to create an accurate POIs relation-aware self-attention module for next-POI recommendation. Huang et al. in [17] introduced an RNN-attention-based approach, which recommends personalized next POI according to user preferences. The latter used an LSTM architecture to extract spatial information and their temporal dependencies from users' historical check-ins and uses an attention mechanism to focus more on relevant features in the user's sequential trajectories. the benifit of the attention mechanism is that it assigns greater weight to relevant factors, but in fact it does ignores the exceptions/special cases.

2.4 Graph-Based Approaches

A few previous works of next POI recommendation have used the structure of *graph* to project the user's behavior or its sequential check-in patterns of their visited POIs. Xie et al. proposed in [4] for the first time, a unified solution for several challenges of POI recommendations (data sparsity, cold-start, context awareness, and the dynamic user preferences) using the embedding of bipartite graphs to represent the relationships in between temporal and spatial factors of the system to provide accurate recommendations in a real-time manner. Li et al. [18] introduced a solution to construct a multi-modal check-in heterogeneous graph that employs an attentional RNN-based for successive POI recommendation. *RELINE* [19] is another graph embedding approach, which is worth citing. It consists of a first-order proximity approach that embeds the local pairwise closeness of nodes and a second-order proximity approach that embeds the knowledge of nodes that belongs to the same neighborhood in the network structure. Knowledge graphs have been used in various recommendation systems to enhance the graphs with heterogeneous features for better recommendation, since their proposition by Google in 2012. Worthy to mention, tweet and followers personalized recommendation [20], differentiated fashion recommendation [21], points of interest recommendation [22,23], etc. Furthermore, these existing approaches often focus on time and location dimensions and ignore other crucial context dimensions.

By and large, a wealthy number of next-POI recommendation approaches have been proposed so far. The incorporation of the neural network-based embedding techniques has shown undoubtedly evidence for their better representation of "hidden" POIs relationships and users' behavior patterns. In addition, the interpretation of the users' check-ins network as a multi-factors graph has provided more accurate recommendations for the next-POIs. To this end, we rely on both notions to introduce a new next-POI recommendation approach. A neural network-based embedding method (node2vec) is exploited to learn the user and POI representations. The latter relies on the unified representation of the knowledge graph's heterogeneous relationships to create the nodes embedding. Further insights about the approach details are given in the remainder.

3 The Proposed Approach

In this section, we present the SKGEM approach that stands within the graph-based approaches stream. The latter aims to learn implicit users' preferences according to their check-in history using a neural network-based embedding method (node2vec). At first, we sketch necessary notations and formalize our POI recommendation problem.

3.1 Formalization of the Problem

At first, we introduce the key notions used through the reminder to define the POI recommendation problem.

Definition 1 (Location Based Social Network). *The LSBN is a social network graph $G = (V, E)$, where V is a set of users, and E denotes their relationships. Using this kind of platform, users can share their daily life experiments in different locations.*

Definition 2 (Point of Interest). *A POI represents a spatial component associated with a geographical location (e.g. theatre, fitness center, museum, etc.). In general, a POI has two attributes: an identifier, and a content. We use p to represent a POI identifier. W_p stands for a set of textual semantic words (e.g. category/type, tag words, etc.) describing p.*

Definition 3 (Check-in activity). *Let U denotes a set of users, a check-in c is a behavior performed by a user u in a location (i.e. POI) p, at a specific time t. The latter is denoted by the triple $(u,\ p,\ t) \in U \times P \times T$.*

Definition 4 (Check-ins sequence). *A check-ins sequence (tour) is a time-ordered consecutive check-ins sequence visited by a user u which is denoted by: $s_u = \{(p_1, t_1), (p_2, t_2), \ldots, (p_n, t_n)\}$, where n is the sequence length.*

Definition 5 (Knowledge Graph). *A knowledge graph $G = (V, E)$ is a directed graph, where V denotes the set of nodes/entities, and E is the set of edges or triple facts of the form subject-property-object. Each edge is denoted as $\langle h, r, t \rangle$ to indicate a relationship of $r \in R$ from a head entity $h \in V$ to a tail entity $t \in V$.*

In a typical LBSN, the main goal of the POI recommendation problem, is to offer, for a target user u, the most likely list of non-visited POIs $\in P$ to visit at the (future) time according to its historical tours s_u. For new users, most of the recommender systems are likely to fail to gather enough knowledge, resulting in ignoring them during recommendations.This scenario is popularly known as the cold-start user problem. In our approach, we overcome this problem. Indeed, for a given new user u defined with its current location l at time t, our goal is to recommend groups/lists of POIs that u may be interested in according to a hyper-locality information, e.g., in the nearby l and/or at time t or other implicit preferences.

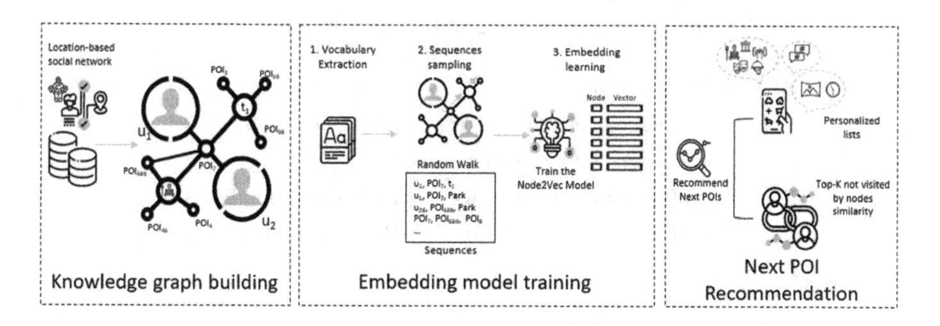

Fig. 1. The SKGEM recommender overall architecture.

3.2 The SKGEM for Next POI recommendation

In the following, we introduce the SKGEM recommender that aims to improve user satisfaction and experience by providing personalized suggestions of targeted locations they might like. The latter deals with the multiple heterogeneous factors of both POIs and users. It relies on a feature learning approach (node2vec) to predict missing relations in a knowledge graph previously designed. Furthermore, it can make effective recommendations to new users by extracting high-level representations, and thus solves the user cold start problem. The global architecture of the SKGEM recommender, depicted by Fig. 1, shows three main steps: *(i)* The knowledge graph building; *(ii)* The knowledge graph embedding model training; and *(iii)* The next POI recommendation. The former identifies the directed graph's *nodes*, and their in-between relationships. Then, in the following step, after mapping the entities and relations into a vector space, the embedding vector of each node is generated. Finally, for the next POI recommendation step, the model offers two different options: the first one is to recommend the user's next POIs according to its previous visits. Otherwise, if the user is utterly new to the system, then the model recommends personalized groups/lists according to the user's location or any other specific preferences.

Step 1 (A Knowledge Graph Building): As a rule of thumb, user tours data S are defined as a sequence of consecutive historical visited check-in. A given user u ($u \in U$), has already visited the POI p ($p \in P$) with the corresponding timestamp t ($t \in T$). Each POI is described by a set of textual words w ($w \in W$). Based on these information, we design, during this step, a *knowledge graph*. The latter is a graph-structured knowledge base that stores factual information in the form of relationships between entities [24]. Roughly speaking, our knowledge graph can be seen as a layered graph, where each layer stands for one type of relationship. In our context, the designed knowledge graph is defined as follows: Let $G = (V, E)$ be a directed graph, where $V = (U \cup P \cup T \cup W)$ denotes the set of nodes, and $E = (E_{up} \cup E_{pp} \cup E_{pt} \cup E_{pw})$ represents their in-between relationships. Table 1 describes the different interpretation of each type of edge used in the directed graph.

Table 1. The knowledge graph's edges interpretation.

Edge	Interpretation
E_{up}	Set of edges between the users and their visited POIs
E_{pp}	Set of edges between successive POIs
E_{pt}	Set of edges between POIs and their corresponding time
E_{pw}	Set of edges between POIs and their associated words

Once the knowledge graph has been designed, we adopt the node embedding to infer new knowledge (similar contexts, similar users, etc.) and finding the hidden connections. The main advantage of using embedding models is representing entities and relations by a low-dimensional embedding vector space while preserving the structure of the graph.

By contrast to the existing KG embedding models which ignore contextual information, in our approach, we incorporate the context dimensions into the KG. This aims to automatically learn entity/node (i.e. user, POI) by exploiting their corresponding contexts.

Step 2 (The Embedding Model Training): The success of the modern embedding techniques is owed to their ability to unify the heterogeneous factors in order to extract high-level representations. In the following, we first introduce the general definition of the adopted node2vec embedding algorithm for nodes representation as a straightforward way to improve the robustness of the next-POI recommendations.

The node2vec Embedding Method: is an efficient scalable model for feature learning in networks proposed by [25]. The latter learns nodes representations in a graph through the application of the word2vec model on sequences of nodes sampled through random walks. Indeed, the main principle of the word2vec model is to group words with similar contexts in near neighborhoods. The innovation brought by the node2vec method is the definition of a random walk exploration process for the sequences of nodes, which are interpreted as if they were words appearing together in a sentence [26]. Therefore, the main idea is to embed the nodes of the previously designed knowledge graph into vectors in a way that the distance (or similarity) between vectors would faithfully assess the distance (or similarity) between nodes. Roughly speaking, the node2vec model scans over the nodes of a given graph, and for each node, it aims to embed it such that the node's features can predict nearby nodes (i.e., nodes inside some context window). The node feature representations are learned by optimizing the likelihood objective function using *SGD*[1] with a negative sampling [27]. In order to train the nod2vec model, we proceed as follows:

1. Extracting all the vocabulary (words) from the created knowledge graph nodes (e.g. Users ids, POIs ids, categories, tags, etc.).

[1] SGD: Stochastic gradient descent optimizer.

2. Sequences sampling using the random walks mechanism. Some examples of the generated sequences are given as follows: *"User_1 went to POI_65 that is a restaurant"*, *"User_1 went to POI_65 described by Delicious_Food"*.
3. Training of the node2vec model to create the nodes embedded vectors by specifying a set of parameters: the embedded nodes vectors dimension, the number of walks for each node, the length of each walk, and the context size or window to generate the dimensions' weights.

Step 3 (The Next POI Recommendation): In this step, the output of the node2vec can be interpreted as a set of embedded vectors that will be used for the next-POI recommendation. Given that these nodes embedding vectors are simply vectors of numbers, the recommendation is performed by computing the similarity in-between vectors using the *cosine similarity* [26]. In general, the latter is one of the most widely used measures that presents geometrically the angle between vectors. At this level, we distinguish two different scenarios for a target user u to recommend the top-k likely next-POIs that might be visited:

- Existing user u: recommend for u the most likely *top-k* list of unvisited POIs to visit in future time according to its historical tours S_u.
- New user u: recommend for u the most likely groups/lists of POIs that u could be interested in according to nearby its location and/or at a specific time and/or other specific preferences (category, tag, etc.).

The different steps of the SKGEM training algorithm are summarized in Algorithm 1. First, we initialize our directed graph and then start adding the nodes and their relationships i.e. edges using the provided users' dataset U. Each user shares a set of tours of its check-ins besides its experiment description content (lines 1–13). After the knowledge graph creation, we proceed to define the models training hyper-parameters (line 14) and then launch the *node2vec* training process in order to create the nodes embedding vectors (line 15). To make the recommendations, first, we need to define the identity of the user. If we deal with an existing user in the system, its next POIs recommendation would be according to the similarity of its POIs embedding vectors with non-visited ones (line 18). Otherwise, if the user is new to the system, then we use the model to recommend groups/lists of POIs according to the input personal preferences and/or POIs that are geographically nearby (wrt a threshold th) or being the most likely visited at its current picked time (lines 19–26).

4 Experiments

In this section, we describe the experimental setup, providing information about the dataset used in the experiments and how we have configured and evaluated the recommendation performance of our proposed approach. We compared the obtained results with other related state-of-the-art existing methods. The details of the experiments are discussed in the following. Our experiments are based on

Algorithm 1. The SKGEM for next POI recommendation

Require: Users tours dataset U, and POIs descriptions dataset P;
where a user u has the list of tours $\{S_1, S_2, \ldots, S_m\}$ and each tour S_i is represented as a sequence of check-in activities $S_i = \{(p_1, t_1), (p_2, t_2), \ldots, (p_k, t_d)\}$.
Each $p \in P$ is described by a set of words w_p.
Ensure: The recommendation of top-k Next-POIs.

1: G = DirectedGraph()
2: **for** $u \in U$ **do**
3:   **for** $s \in S_u$ **do**
4:     **for** p, t in s **do**
5:       G.addEdge(u, p)
6:       G.addEdge(p, t)
7:       **for** w in $P[p]$ **do**
8:         G.addEdge(p, w)
9:       **end for**
10:       G.addEdge($p_{previous}$,p) // *Two successive visited POIs.*
11:     **end for**
12:   **end for**
13: **end for**
14: Initialize the parameters: $VecD$, $NWalks$, $WalkL$, $ContextS$.
15: model = node2vec.train(G,$VecD$, $NWalks$, $WalkL$, $ContextS$)
16: *//Make top-k POI recommendations for a target user u:*
17: **if** $u \in U$ **then**
18:   predictions[u] = model.predict_output(S_u, K)
19: **else**
20:   *//Make recommendations according to the location/time/other preferences of u:*
21:   predictions_time[u] = model.predict_output(t, K)
22:   predictions_nearby[u] = Get_nearby(l,L,th) // *L: Pois coords, th: threshold.*
23:   predictions_category[u] = model.predict_output(w, K) // *w: category.*
24:   ...
25:   prediction[u] = predictions_time[u] $\cap$ predictions_nearby[u] $\cap$ predictions_category[u] $\cap$ ...
26: **end if**
27: **return** predictions[u],

a Flickr dataset collected in the city of Tallinn (Estonia) from the 1st of January 2003 to the 25th of September 2017. The dataset provides user tours (check-ins sequences) in different POIs. A single check-in from the dataset is defined as follows: "user_ID", "POI_ID", and the "timestamp". Each POI is geocoded by its "GPS coordinates" (Latitude, longitude) and respectively described by its: "view", "category", a set of "images IDs", a set of "tags", and its containing "region". The "region" contains an IDs' list of closer "regions". The figure below depicts the generated knowledge graph and the relationships between the different types of nodes according to the SKGEM recommender. Table 2 gives an overview of the characteristics of this dataset.

Table 2. The generated knowledge graph from Tallinn dataset.

Features	Tallinn (Estonia)
Number of Users	1,911
Number of POI	1054
Number of Check-ins	12,413
Type of nodes	8
Total graph nodes	144,594
Total graph edges	894,847
Data sparsity	99.38%

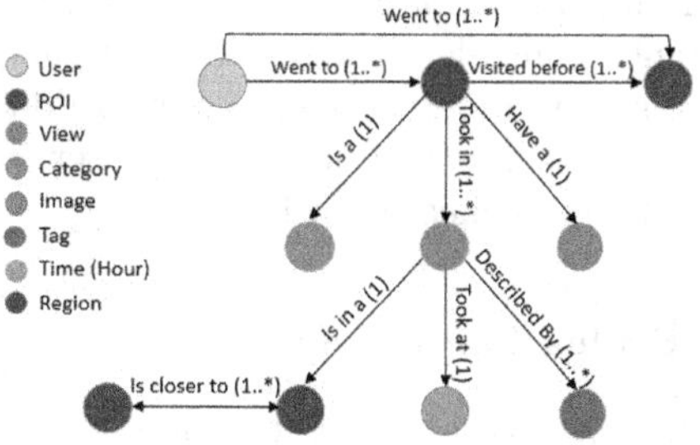

4.1 Experimental Setups

To evaluate the performances of our proposed model, we perform two different experiments. On a first time, we make a non cold-start evaluation, where 80% of the tour data for each user is selected to create the knowledge graph and train the node2vec model, while the remaining 20% are used as a test set for the evaluation. We also conduct experiments with cold-start settings to test the efficiency of our approach. In this case, 80% of the users are used to create the knowledge graph and train the model and the remaining 20% are considered as utterly new users to the system. Thus, we perform the recommendations according to some selected categories and hours of the day for each new user in the test data. The next step, after designing the knowledge graph from the dataset, is to fine-tune and initialize the model's parameters to ensure better embedding representations. It is important to mention that we fit the node's vectors embedding into R^{80} dimension, the number of walks is set to 300 per each node, and both walk length and context window size are set to 4. Our experiments are carried out under the configuration of a Linux server (Intel(R) Xeon(R) CPU $E5-2690v3$ @ 2.60 GHz × 48) with a 3.7 Python version.

4.2 Baseline Methods

To accurately evaluate our proposed approach, we led a comparison with the freshest next-POIs recommendation baselines.

- STACP[2] [9]: is a spatio-temporal algorithm that extracts the users' mobility patterns according to the historical check-ins center of activity depending on their current temporal state.
- LGLMF[3] [8]: uses a logistic Matrix Factorization to formulate the generated users' main regions of activities by a local geographical model to recommend the similar checked-in POIs in the zone of each user's activity.

[2] https://github.com/rahmanidashti/STACP.
[3] https://github.com/rahmanidashti/LGLMF.

- SAE-NAD[4] [14]: is a two phases model that uses an auto-encoder to learn the non-linear relationship between users and POIs. The first phase applies a self-attentive encoder (SAE) to extract the personalized preferences of each user. The second one is a neighbor-aware decoder (NAD) to incorporate the geographical context information of users to recommend the similar and nearby neighbors of checked-in POIs.

4.3 Evaluation Metrics

A next-POI recommender typically produces an ordered list of recommendations for each user in the test set. The recommendations performance of our model and the baselines' models are evaluated using six relevant metrics *Precision@K*, *Recall@K*, *Novelty@K*, *Serendipity@K*, *nDPM@K*, and *Kendal tau correlation@K*.

- The *Precision@K* yields insight into how relevant the list of recommended POIs are.
- The *Recall@K* gives insight into how well the recommendation model is able to recall all the POIs the user has visited in the test set.
- The *Novelty@K* is used to analyze if the model is able to recommend POIs that have a low probability of being already known by a user. This metric does not consider the correctness of the recommended POIs, but only their novelty [28].
- The *Serendipity@K* defines the capability of the recommender to identify both attractive and unexpected POIs. The Serendipity resulting value would be in the interval $[0, 1]$, lower than or equal to precision. The difference between precision and serendipity represents the percentage of obvious items that are correctly suggested.
- The value of *nDPM* is used to measure the similarity of the orderings of the recommended POIs compared to the actual order of visited POIs, it is computed according to all the possible pairs of POIs available in the KG, it will result close to 1 when the sequences generated by the recommender are contradictory, to 0 when they have the same ranking, and to 0.5 when the ordering is irrelevant because they contain different items.
- The *Kendall tau Correlation@K* is used to measure the similarity of the orderings of the recommended POIs compared to the actual order of visited POIs. The computation of the Kendall tau correlation value is based on the order of the different pairs of the recommended POIs, the closer the coefficient is to 1 the perfect the order between the two sets is.

4.4 Results and Discussion

Table 3, Table 4, and Table 5 show the recommendations performances of the SKGEM system versus those of its competitors using all the above mentioned

[4] https://github.com/allenjack/SAE-NAD.

evaluation metrics with $K = \{5, 10, 15, 20\}$. Table 3 shows that our approach gives the most efficient recommendations for both precision and recall metrics. A good look at our results underscores that our model sharply outperforms the other baseline methods in terms of recommending serendipitous Next-POIs with an acceptable rate of novelty (Table 4). As reported in (Table 5), SKGEM gives the best order of the recommended next PIOs according to Kendall correlation. The STACP approach is the worst performer regarding almost all metrics. In fact, the latter doesn't take into account any contextual information about users or POIs. Whereas, according to Table 5, it shows a good performance when considering the order of recommendations according to the global dataset's tours using the nDPM metric. Therefore, we can come to the conclusion that unifying the representations of all the system's components, through this knowledge graph, and its contextual information have lead us to sharply enhance the quality of the recommendations. Table 6 displays the achieved next POI recommendation performances for the users, within the cold-start settings, using three options of lists/groups, to wit: category, hour of the day, and the combination of both. It is clear that recommending POIs based on the category lists performances are more relevant than that based on the hour of the day's lists or their intersection on the considered dataset.

Table 3. Non cold-start performance evaluation (Precision and Recall).

Metrics	Precision				Recall			
Method	@5	@10	@15	@20	@5	@10	@15	@20
STACP	0.0178	0.0124	0.0091	0.0097	0.0160	0.0216	0.0236	0.0306
LGLMF	0.0557	0.0436	0.0387	0.0343	0.0593	0.0904	0.1169	0.1341
SAE-NAD	0.0512	0.0375	0.0300	0.0256	0.1872	0.2619	0.3089	0.3491
SKGEM	**0.1765**	**0.1071**	**0.0795**	**0.0611**	**0.3578**	**0.4113**	**0.4403**	**0.4479**

Table 4. Non cold-start performance evaluation (Novelty and Serendipity).

Metrics	Novelty				Serendipity			
Method	@5	@10	@15	@20	@5	@10	@15	@20
STACP	−4.9561	−6.7905	−7.4941	−7.9233	0.0178	0.0124	0.009	0.0097
LGLMF	**−7.2704**	**−7.6843**	**−7.9648**	**−8.1714**	0.0268	0.0133	0.01042	0.0091
SAE-NAD	−4.1262	−4.7285	−5.0310	−5.3108	0.0512	0.0375	0.0300	0.0256
SKGEM	−4.7787	−5.5072	−5.9181	−6.0115	**0.1765**	**0.1071**	**0.0795**	**0.0611**

Table 5. Non cold-start performance evaluation (nDPM and Kendall tau correlation).

Metrics	nDPM				Kendall tau correlation			
Method	@5	@10	@15	@20	@5	@10	@15	@20
STACP	**0.000**	**4.65-05**	**0.0002**	**0.0007**	−0.0572	−0.0530	−0.0502	−0.0461
LGLMF	0.0024	0.0084	0.0152	0.0195	0.0022	0.0050	0.0082	0.0077
SAE-NAD	0.0043	0.0113	0.0180	0.0230	−0.0017	−0.0035	−0.0037	−0.0037
SKGEM	0.0320	0.0522	0.1255	0.1791	**0.0549**	**0.0496**	**0.0500**	**0.0507**

Table 6. Cold-start performance evaluation.

Metrics	Precision				Recall			
Search by	@5	@10	@15	@20	@5	@10	@15	@20
Category (C)	**0.0783**	**0.0577**	**0.0480**	**0.0446**	**0.0801**	**0.1096**	**0.1270**	**0.1804**
Hour of the day (HOD)	0.0010	0.0010	0.0008	0.0007	0.0027	0.0033	0.0042	0.0045
C and HOD	0.0020	0.0018	0.0015	0.0015	0.0043	0.0055	0.0059	0.0067

Impact of Embedding Vector Dimension. Table 7 shows the performance of the SKGEM approach based on different dimensions of the embedding vector of each node in the graph using both metrics. From the results, the best performance' vector dimension value is obtained by 80. The experiments underscore the importance of fine-tuning of the vector's dimension value according to the available contextual information of the considered LBSN dataset.

Table 7. Impact of the variation of embedding vector dimension.

Metrics	Precision				Recall			
Variants-VecDim	@5	@10	@15	@20	@5	@10	@15	@20
SKGEM-20	0.1330	0.0801	0.0554	0.0416	0.2824	0.3250	0.3313	0.3314
SKGEM-40	0.1710	0.1077	0.0783	0.0594	0.3439	0.4089	0.4323	0.4355
SKGEM-60	0.1684	0.1041	0.0760	0.0583	0.3443	0.4020	0.4249	0.4305
SKGEM-80	**0.1765**	**0.1071**	**0.0795**	**0.0611**	**0.3578**	**0.4113**	**0.4403**	**0.4479**
SKGEM-100	0.1716	0.1047	0.0773	0.0595	0.3526	0.4079	0.4349	0.4409

Impact of Context and Walk Length. In the aspect of the evaluation, we compare the performances of the proposed model using different contexts and walk lengths. We always consider its values equally in each experiment task $\{4, 8, 12, 16\}$ to preserve the context of the sentence. Table 8 shows the degree of stability from the achieved results using each of the above-mentioned values for the considered dataset. This highlights that the context size and the walk length don't significantly affect the performance of the model's next POIs recommendations.

Table 8. Impact of context size and walk length.

Metrics	Precision				Recall			
Variants-Walk	@5	@10	@15	@20	@5	@10	@15	@20
SKGEM-4	**0.1765**	**0.1071**	**0.0795**	**0.0611**	**0.3578**	**0.4113**	**0.4403**	**0.4479**
SKGEM-8	0.1731	0.1059	0.0778	0.0595	0.3527	0.4061	0.4314	0.4353
SKGEM-12	0.1732	0.1037	0.0758	0.0582	0.3542	0.4036	0.4283	0.4357
SKGEM-16	0.1710	0.1037	0.0754	0.0572	0.3591	0.4030	0.4252	0.4283

5 Conclusion and Future Work

In this paper, we introduced the SKGEM for next POI recommendation, that unifies the representation of the heterogeneity of different factors, through a knowledge graph. We carried out experiments on a real-world dataset, which provided backing up evidences that our approach achieved better results and sharply outperforms the most recent and pioneering baseline methods. The node2vec generates vector representations of the users and of the POIs, and of other features without taking into consideration the type of the relationships in-between. Thus, in future work, we would incorporate into the model a hybrid vector representations of nodes and relationships using an extensive datasets with more contextual information to further investigate its effectiveness and performance.

References

1. Huang, L., Ma, Y., Liu, Y., He, K.: DAN-SNR: a deep attentive network for social-aware next point-of-interest recommendation, CoRR, vol. abs/2004.12161 (2020)
2. Li, X., Cong, G., Li, X., Pham, T.N., Krishnaswamy, S.: Rank-geofm: a ranking based geographical factorization method for point of interest recommendation. In: Proceedings of the 38th International ACM SIGIR 2015, New York, NY, USA, pp. 433–442 (2015)
3. Doan, K.D., Yang, G., Reddy, C.K.: An attentive spatio-temporal neural model for successive point of interest recommendation. In: Yang, Q., Zhou, Z.-H., Gong, Z., Zhang, M.-L., Huang, S.-J. (eds.) PAKDD 2019. LNCS (LNAI), vol. 11441, pp. 346–358. Springer, Cham (2019). https://doi.org/10.1007/978-3-030-16142-2_27
4. Xie, M., Yin, H., Wang, H., Xu, F., Chen, W., Wang, S.: Learning graph-based poi embedding for location-based recommendation. In: Proceedings of the 25th ACM CIKM 2016, New York, NY, USA, pp. 15–24 (2016)
5. Zhang, Z., Li, C., Wu, Z., Sun, A., Ye, D., Luo, X.: NEXT: a neural network framework for next POI recommendation. Front. Comput. Sci. **14**(2), 314–333 (2019). https://doi.org/10.1007/s11704-018-8011-2
6. Kong, D., Wu, F.: HST-LSTM: a hierarchical spatial-temporal long-short term memory network for location prediction. In: Proceedings of the 27th IJCAI 2018, pp. 2341–2347 (2018)
7. Wu, Y., Li, K., Zhao, G., Qian, X.: Long- and short-term preference learning for next poi recommendation. In: Proceedings of the 28th ACM CIKM 2019, New York, NY, USA, pp. 2301–2304 (2019)

8. Rahmani, H.A., Aliannejadi, M., Ahmadian, S., Baratchi, M., Afsharchi, M., Crestani, F.: LGLMF: local geographical based logistic matrix factorization model for POI recommendation. In: Information Retrieval Technology, pp. 66–78 (2020)
9. Rahmani, H.A., Aliannejadi, M., Baratchi, M., Crestani, F.: Joint geographical and temporal modeling based on matrix factorization for point-of-interest recommendation. In: Jose, J.M., et al. (eds.) ECIR 2020. LNCS, vol. 12035, pp. 205–219. Springer, Cham (2020). https://doi.org/10.1007/978-3-030-45439-5_14
10. Zhao, P., et al.: Where to go next: a spatio-temporal gated network for next POI recommendation. In: Proceedings of the AAAI 2019 Conference, vol. 33, pp. 5877–5884 (2019)
11. Zhou, X., Mascolo, C., Zhao, Z.: Topic-enhanced memory networks for personalised point-of-interest recommendation. In: Proceedings of the ACM SIGKDD 2019, pp. 3018–3028 (2019)
12. Sun, K., Qian, T., Chen, T., Liang, Y., Hung, N., Yin, H.: Where to go next: modeling long- and short-term user preferences for point-of-interest recommendation. In: Proceedings of the AAAI Conference, vol. 34, pp. 214–221 (2020)
13. Chang, B., Park, Y., Park, D., Kim, S., Kang, J.: Content-aware hierarchical point-of-interest embedding model for successive poi recommendation. In: Proceedings of the 27th IJCAI 2018, Stockholm, Sweden, pp. 3301–3307 (2018)
14. Ma, C., Zhang, Y., Wang, Q., Liu, X.: Point-of-interest recommendation: Exploiting self-attentive autoencoders with neighbor-aware influence. In: Proceedings of the 27th ACM CIKM 2018, Torino, Italy, pp. 697–706. ACM (2018)
15. Liu, T., Liao, J., Wu, Z., Wang, Y., Wang, J.: Exploiting geographical-temporal awareness attention for next point-of-interest recommendation. Neurocomputing **400**, 227–237 (2020)
16. Guo, Q., Qi, J.: SANST: A Self-Attentive Network for Next Point-of-Interest Recommendation. CoRR, vol. abs/2001.10379 (2020)
17. Huang, L., Ma, Y., Wang, S., Liu, Y.: An attention-based spatiotemporal LSTM network for next POI recommendation. IEEE Trans. Serv. Comput. **12**, 1 (2019)
18. Li, L., Liu, Y., Wu, J., He, L., Ren, G.: Multi-modal representation learning for successive poi recommendation. In: Proceedings of PMLR 2019, Nagoya, Japan, 17–19 November 2019, pp. 441–456 (2019)
19. Christoforidis, G., Kefalas, P., Papadopoulos, A.N., Manolopoulos, Y.: RELINE: point-of-interest recommendations using multiple network embeddings. Knowl. Inf. Syst. (2), 1–27 (2021). https://doi.org/10.1007/s10115-020-01541-5
20. Pla Karidi, D., Stavrakas, Y., Vassiliou, Y.: Tweet and followee personalized recommendations based on knowledge graphs. J. Ambient. Intell. Humaniz. Comput. **9**(6), 2035–2049 (2017). https://doi.org/10.1007/s12652-017-0491-7
21. Yan, C., Chen, Y., Zhou, L.: Differentiated fashion recommendation using knowledge graph and data augmentation. IEEE Access **7**, 102239–102248 (2019)
22. Christoforidis, G., Kefalas, P., Papadopoulos, A., Manolopoulos, Y.: Recommendation of points-of-interest using graph embeddings. In: IEEE 5th DSAA 2018, pp. 31–40 (2018)
23. Hu, S., Tu, Z., Wang, Z., Xu, X.: A poi-sensitive knowledge graph based service recommendation method. In: IEEE SCC 2019, pp. 197–201 (2019)
24. Nickel, M., Murphy, K., Tresp, V., Gabrilovich, E.: A review of relational machine learning for knowledge graphs. Proc. IEEE **104**, 11–33 (2016)
25. Grover, A., Leskovec, J.: Node2vec: scalable feature learning for networks. In: Proceedings of the 22nd ACM SIGKDD, KDD 2016, New York, NY, USA, pp. 855–864 (2016)

26. Grohe, M.: Word2vec, node2vec, graph2vec, x2vec: towards a theory of vector embeddings of structured data. In: Proceedings of the 39th ACM SIGMOD-SIGACT-SIGAI, PODS 2020, pp. 1–16, New York, NY, USA (2020)
27. Mikolov, T., Sutskever, I., Chen, K., Corrado, G.S., Dean, J.: Distributed representations of words and phrases and their compositionality. In: Proceedings of the 26th NIPS 2013, Red Hook, NY, USA, pp. 3111–3119 (2013)
28. Palumbo, E., Monti, D., Rizzo, G., Troncy, R., Baralis, E.: entity2rec: property-specific knowledge graph embeddings for item recommendation. Expert Syst. Appl. **151**, 113235 (2020)

Spatial and Temporal Cross-Validation Approach for Misbehavior Detection in C-ITS

Mohammed Lamine Bouchouia[1(✉)], Jean-Philippe Monteuuis[2], Ons Jelassi[1], Houda Labiod[1], Wafa Ben Jaballah[3], and Jonathan Petit[2]

[1] Télécom Paris, Institut Polytechnique de Paris, Paris, France
{mohammed.bouchouia,ons.jelassi,houda.labiod}@telecom-paris.fr
[2] Qualcomm Technologies Inc, San Diego, USA
{jmonteuu,petit}@qti.qualcomm.com
[3] Thales Group, Courbevoie, France
wafa.benjaballah@thalesgroup.com

Abstract. This paper proposes a novel approach to apply machine learning techniques to data collected from emerging cooperative intelligent transportation systems (C-ITS) using Vehicle-to-Vehicle (V2V) broadcast communications. Our approach considers temporal and spatial aspects of collected data to avoid correlation between the training set and the validation set. Connected vehicles broadcast messages containing safety-critical information at high frequency. Thus, detecting faulty messages induced by attacks is crucial for road-users safety. High frequency broadcast makes the temporal aspect decisive in building the cross-validation sets at the data preparation level of the data mining cycle. Therefore, we conduct a statistical study considering various fake position attacks. We statistically examine the difficulty of detecting the faulty messages, and generate useful features of the raw data. Then, we apply machine learning methods for misbehavior detection, and discuss the obtained results. We apply our data splitting approach to message-based and communication-based data modeling and compare our approach to traditional splitting approaches. Our study shows that traditional splitting approaches performance is biased as it causes data leakage, and we observe a 10% drop in performance in the testing phase compared to our approach. This result implies that traditional approaches cannot be trusted to give equivalent performance once deployed and thus are not compatible with V2V broadcast communications.

Keywords: Misbehavior detection · V2X · Machine learning · Cross-validation sets · Time series

1 Introduction

V2V communication is a technology in C-ITS systems that aims to improve traffic safety and efficiency through exchanged information between vehicles.

S. Cherfi et al. (Eds.): RCIS 2021, LNBIP 415, pp. 452–468, 2021.
https://doi.org/10.1007/978-3-030-75018-3_30

This communication relies on Basic Safety Messages (BSMs) that are defined in the SAE J2735 standard [19] and Cooperative Awareness Message (CAM) in the ETSI standard [6]. A CAM contains vehicle state such as its location and speed. A vehicle emits its CAM to all surrounding vehicles following dissemination requirements. For instance, the time interval between two emitted CAMs shall not be inferior to 100 ms nor superior to 1 s [6]. Such requirement improves the vehicle decision and driver's safety.

However, this scenario could be exploited by malicious attackers that may broadcast CAMs containing false information such as a fake vehicle location to provoke traffic jams or even fatalities [13]. Therefore, there is an urgent need to guarantee the correctness of the data. This can be achieved through misbehavior detection (MBD) [8,14,21]. Machine Learning (ML) methods could be used since they proved to be reliable in the security context and in particular for anomaly detection [3]. The application of these methods relies on two critical tasks, data preprocessing and training. During the training task, the data is split in two sets named "train" and "test". In an attempt to represent real-life scenarios, the training step must not use data from the test set.

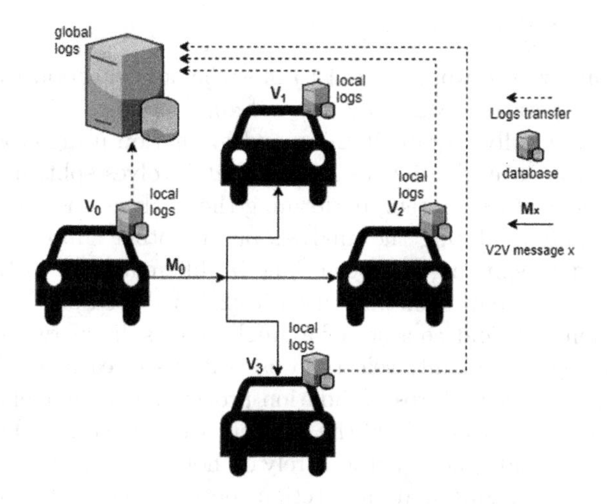

Fig. 1. Broadcast scenario

In the context of V2V communication, in order to create the training dataset for the machine learning model, the broadcast data is collected from different vehicles. Figure 1 depicts an example where each vehicle broadcasts CAM messages to the surrounding vehicles, then receives, processes and logs these CAM messages in local data storage. Afterwards, at the global level, servers will be able to store and process local logs received from vehicles.

In particular, Fig. 1 shows a scenario where vehicle V_0 broadcasts a message M_0 to its neighbors (V_1, V_2, V_3). These vehicles receive this message and store it. Afterwards, the messages are collected in a global storage which contains 3 different copies of the original message at different timestamps related to the reception times.

This specificity makes data preprocessing critical, as it makes classical data split inconsistent with test set assumptions as they cause data leakage. In this paper, our contributions are threefold. First, we address the problem of data splitting in the training step for data issued from V2V communications and carry out a statistical analysis on VeReMi dataset as a baseline for MBD. Second, we propose a novel cross-validation approach based on temporal and spatial aspects in the context of C-ITS broadcast data. Finally, we provide an empirical evaluation of different supervised ML methods for MBD in C-ITS to validate our approach.

Our paper is structured as follows. First, we present the related work in Sect. 2. Then, we present a statistical analysis of a commonly-used dataset called VeReMi in Sect. 3. Afterwards, we describe the cross-validation issue for broadcast data and the proposed approach in Sect. 4. We compare our proposed approach with the traditional splitting one using a variety of ML methods in Sect. 5. Section 6 concludes the paper.

2 Related Work

This section surveys the work related to misbehavior detection (MBD) with a focus on data preparation, ML datasets, and applications.

ML solutions usually require training and evaluation using cross-validation. Cross-validation is an evaluation technique that involves splitting a sample of data into complementary subsets, performing the analysis on one subset (called the train set), and validating the analysis on the other subset (called validation set). This data splitting has been done in different ways in the literature. The basic method for data splitting (used in [22]) is based on the Hold-out (or simple validation) [5], and consists of a single data split in two sets (training and validation) with randomly selected observations in each set. For instance, in [1], the authors surveyed cross-validation procedures for model selection and train-test splitting. They described the different variants such as Leave-one-out, Leave-p-out and V-fold. These methods rely on how train and test sets are built, mainly varying proportions, and intersections between sets and randomly selecting elements of each one. These methods, when applied to data from broadcast messages, fail to guarantee the assumption of unseen data in the test set and thus create a data leakage. Therefore, training and validation sets must be created such that the dependence between observations is considered.

Similarly, authors in [18] proposed a "Blocking cross validation" where they considered data with temporal, spatial relationships, group dependencies, and hierarchical structures. In case of highly homogeneous data where the homogeneous examples cannot be removed, the algorithm splits those examples between train and validation sets, which also causes a data leakage (Sect. 4.1). With this respect, in our paper, we propose a different approach for obtaining train, validation, and test sets in the case of broadcast data messages. Specifically, we further apply our methodology to MBD in V2V communications.

There are two different MBD approaches commonly used in the literature: communication MBD [21,22] and message MBD [10,14]. Communication MBD aims to classify the whole communication as anomalous or not. Different statistics and measurements are computed on the whole communication, such as the rate of messages and the average plausibility of all reported locations [22]. These measures create a new dataset on which ML methods are applied. The second approach is message MBD, where the ML method uses the original features of the message and additional features extracted to improve the performance to learn the underlying behavior and make decisions.

Several work applied ML for MBD. For instance, authors in [22] proposed to use plausibility checks as input features for ML methods. Their work is a baseline ML application for MBD tested with K-Nearest Neighbors (K-NN) and Support Vector Machine (SVM). Overall, both methods have similar performances but detect poorly attacks that mimic the movement of a real vehicle. Thus, the authors extended their work by verifying the plausibility of the communication content at the signal level. To this end, their work added the receive signal strength indicator (RSSI) as a new input feature. Moreover, the authors proposed three novel physical-layer plausibility checks [21], where their study outperformed their previous work in detecting attacks.

As one can see, previous work investigated ML use for MBD, but did not perform a statistical analysis to assess the quality of the dataset. For instance, the broadcasting nature of the communication creates redundant entries in the dataset that impacts the performance of the ML models. Hence, in this paper, we carry out a statistical analysis of the considered dataset. Then, we propose a new data splitting approach that considers the broadcast nature. Lastly, we compare it to traditional data splitting.

3 VeReMi Dataset: Statistical Analysis and Feature Engineering

In this section, we provide an analysis of the *Vehicular Reference Misbehavior (VeReMi) dataset* [10]. In particular, we focus on the position feature of the CAM messages and show how feature engineering improves MBD performances.

3.1 VeReMi Dataset

We use the last version of VeReMi simulated dataset [21] which presents the same characteristics as a real dataset. This dataset has proven reliable and is used by several researchers [9,11,14,20,22]. This dataset is generated based on 225 simulations with five different attacks presented in the next section. Each simulation uses three different attacker densities. Each parameter set is repeated 5 times with different random seeds. Each simulation was made in the area of Luxembourg and lasts for 100 s, with a communication bit rate of 6 Mbps. Our work uses the sub-dataset with the following parameters: attack probability of 0.3, simulations start at 7 am (which corresponds to the highest density).

3.2 Attacks

The VeReMi dataset includes five types of attacks. Each attack has a label and a set of generation parameters. These attacks tamper with the location of the transmitting vehicle in different ways. First, an attacker can transmit a fixed location (Constant). Second, an attacker could transmit a fixed offset of its real location(Constant Offset). An attacker sends a uniformly random position (Random). An attacker sends a random location in an area around the vehicle (Random offset). Lastly, an attacker that behaves normally and then transmits the same location repeatedly (Eventual Stop).

3.3 Descriptive Statistical Analysis

We compute several statistics and analyze each feature of our dataset[1]. Table 1 summarizes the features statistics.

Table 1. Summary statistics

Reception time		Mean	Std	Min	Q1	Median	Q3	Max
		21798,3	105,2	21600,0	21704,3	21817,4	21885,8	21959,9
Receiver	X position	4294,37	1018,19	2325,41	3597,82	3673,08	5023,85	6324,99
	Y position	5510,63	258,74	5180,04	5255,00	5470,59	5738,24	6079,99
Transmission time		21798,3	105,2	21600	21704,3	21817,4	21885,8	21959,9
Transmit	X position	5020,44	3288,29	0,41	3602,46	3858,48	5560	27278,9
	Y position	5939,26	2325,82	7,79	5254,50	5538,36	5819,28	22998,1
	X velocity	0,04	8,63	−40,38	−3,95	0	3,83	41,12
	Y velocity	1,51	20,67	−44,25	−4,36	0	11,93	48,90
RSSI		2,5E-07	2,9E-06	1,2E-09	3,3E-09	8,4E-09	3,1E-08	2,3E-03

From Table 1, we observe that the standard deviation of the receiver and the transmitter position distributions differ largely (10 times bigger in Y position). However, both features are emitted from vehicles interacting in the same context, i.e., vehicles are located in the same geographic area and hence they should have similar coordinates. Thus, we assume the presence of some anomalies in either or both position features.

We plot the histogram of some features in Fig. 2 to study their distributions. Our observations are as follows:

- The distributions of the receiver X and Y positions compared to the transmitter ones are very different. This confirms our initial intuition. We can see that transmitter X and Y position values are spread in a wider set of values $[0, 28000]$ while most of these values are in the same interval as the receivers

[1] Details about the dataset can be found here: https://anonymous.4open.science/r/5de28865-7f74-4360-b3fa-daa68c97bd83/.

ones [2000, 7000] (Fig. 2). We can assume that only a portion of values are anomalous.

- We observe that the transmitter X and Y velocity distributions are symmetric w.r.t 0 for both sets of values, which we assume correct since most roads have two ways. We also observe a high number of null velocities, which might be the result of traffic light or stop signs.

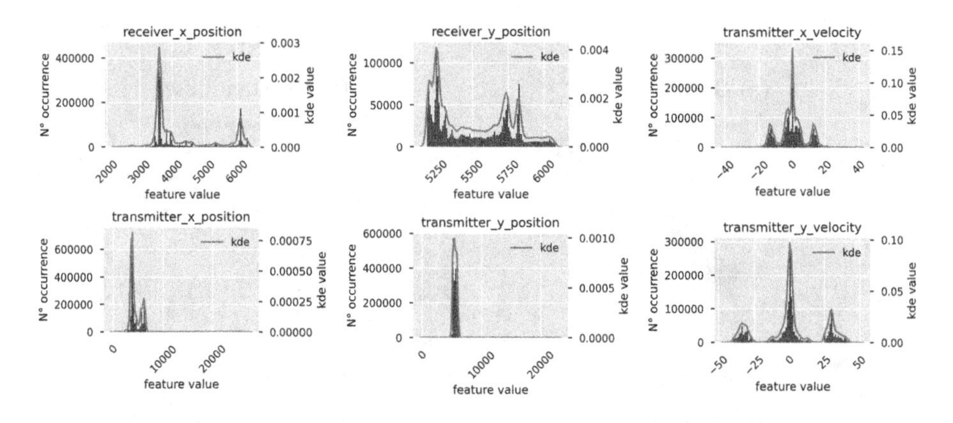

Fig. 2. VeReMi's features distribution analysis

Now that we established that there are anomalies in the transmitted positions, we plot transmitter and receiver position values against each other for each attack and for genuine data. In Fig. 3, we show a density plot of these values and we make the following observations:

- As expected, plotting position values for genuine data form a linear scatter plot following the diagonal line $y = x$. Note that the width of this line reflects the transmission range of the vehicles.
- For the attack "constant offset", the figure shows a translated version of the genuine one that is caused by the constant change applied by the attacker.
- For the attack "random offset", we observe an almost identical plot as we did for genuine data. The difference lays in the left and right extremities of the observed data. We identify in these extremities a sparse structure formed along the maximum transmission range. This is due to the fact that some attacker vehicles positioned at the edge of the transmission area of a benign can transmit a position that is outside that area.
- For the attacks "constant", "random" and "eventual stop", the difference in the data is clearly shown. Only a small portion of the transmitter values intersects with those of the receiver.

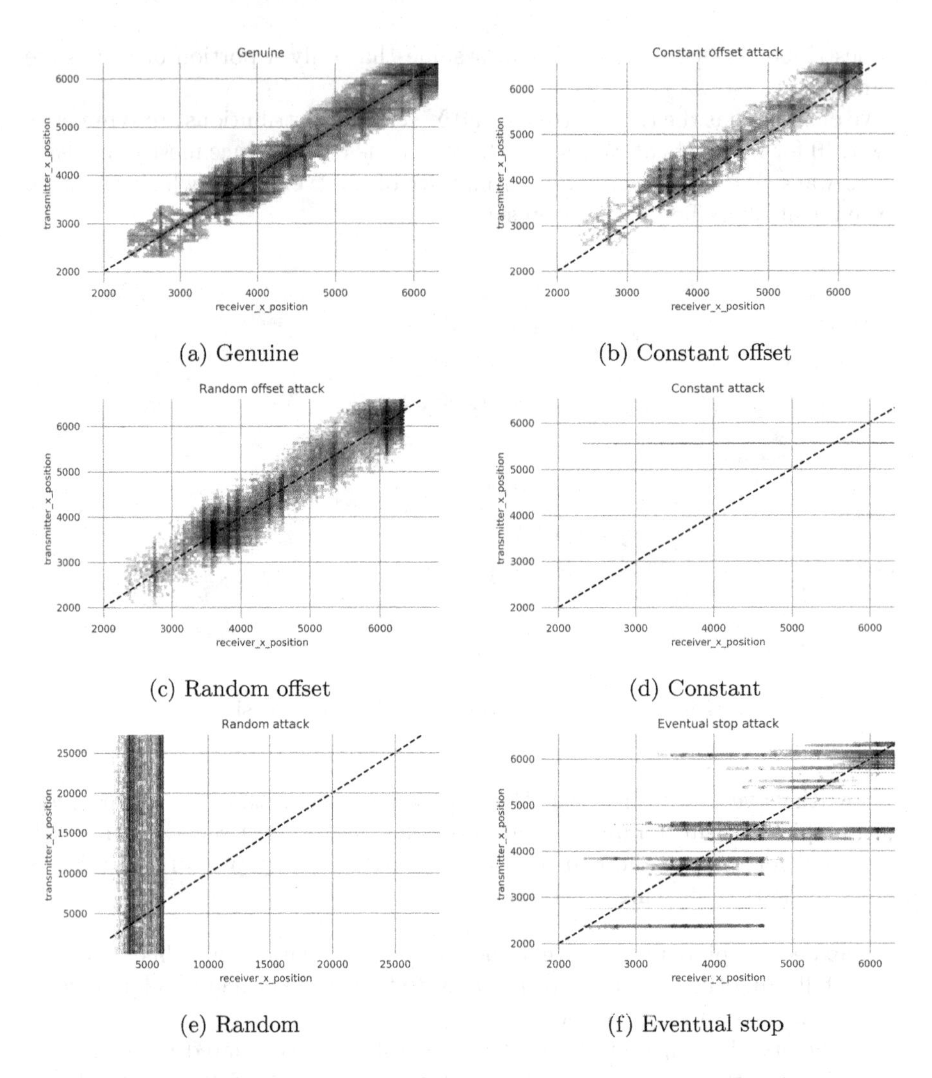

(a) Genuine (b) Constant offset

(c) Random offset (d) Constant

(e) Random (f) Eventual stop

Fig. 3. Comparison of X position of receiver and transmitter values

These computed statistics do not capture the broadcast aspect of the data. Hence, we compute the number of copies of each unique message, i.e. the same message being received by multiple receivers. In the following sections, we refer to the original CAM message as the unique message. Figure 4 shows a histogram of the number of copies created from each unique message and the density estimation per number of copies in the data. We observe that the area under the curve for messages with a number of copies higher than 10 dominates the density estimation, meaning that most of the dataset contains redundant messages (more than 50%). Such characteristic of the data must be handled when modeling a machine learning solution.

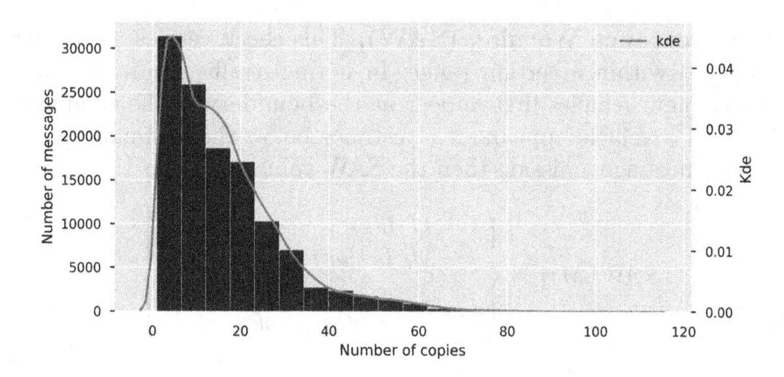

Fig. 4. Number of CAM copies for each unique message

From the aforementioned analysis, we conclude that the transmitted position values include outliers in an anomalous way compared to receivers positions and is proof of tampering. The data allowed us to assume that the transmitted time is coherent. Thus, we use the positions to compute the transmitter speed rather than relying on the transmitted velocities. Comparing the values gives an interesting metric to use for detection.

Moreover, the dataset needs preprocessing such as removing constant and id features detected in the analysis because these features do not correlate with the target task and only induce additional computation costs. A last point is that Fig. 4 presents a high redundancy of data that needs to be processed accordingly (see Sect. 4). In the next section, we create new features to improve the misbehavior detection.

3.4 Feature Engineering

Based on our statistical analysis, we rely on the following checks output as dataset features. Note that ($T_{X,Y}$, $T_{t,X,Y}$,$T_{t,v}$) represents the position vector, the position at time t and the speed at time t for the transmitter vehicle (receiver vehicle respectively).

Acceptance Range Threshold (ART). This check verifies if the distance between the CAM emitter and receiver is above the maximum theoretical communication range.

$$ART(M) = \begin{Bmatrix} 1 \; if \; d(T_{X,Y}, R_{X,Y}) > \Delta_r \\ 0 \qquad otherwise \end{Bmatrix} \tag{1}$$

where $d(x, y)$ is the Euclidean distance and Δ_r denotes the theoretical value of the communication range.

Sudden Appearance Warning (SAW). This check verifies if a vehicle suddenly appeared within a certain range. In normal traffic conditions, it can be assumed that new vehicles first appear at the boundary of the communication range. Thus, if a vehicle appears at a distance below the communication range without prior message emission then the SAW value equals to 1.

$$SAW(M_0) = \begin{Bmatrix} 1 & if\ d(T_{X,Y}, R_{X,Y}) < \rho \\ & \cap\ M_0\ is\ the\ first\ message \\ & \\ 0 & otherwise \end{Bmatrix} \tag{2}$$

where ρ is the threshold value for first appearance.

Simple Speed Check (SSC). This check verifies if the difference between the transmitter speed and the estimated speed from the position and time differences Δ_t between two consecutive messages is less than a threshold value Δ_v.

$$SSC(M_t) = \begin{Bmatrix} 1\ if\ \frac{d(T_{t,X,Y}, T_{t-1,X,Y})}{\Delta_t} - T_{t,v} > \Delta_v \\ \\ 0 \qquad\qquad otherwise \end{Bmatrix} \tag{3}$$

where Δ_v is the threshold for the speed difference. M_t is the message at time t.

We notice that all the extracted features are related to the position, speed, and displacement. Indeed, based on our statistical analysis, the position represents the main anomalous feature.

4 Broadcast Data Splitting Approach for MBD Using ML Methods

In this section, we explain the issues related to broadcast dataset splitting and propose a spatial and temporal approach to efficiently split data and apply ML.

4.1 Motivation: Broadcast Data Splitting Issues

Figure 5 shows the issues that arise from using a classical random split (hold-out) on the full dataset with a 10% validation proportion. Results show that copies of a unique message are present multiple times in both validation and train sets (refer to black and white dots in Fig. 5) where each colored column represents a unique message and a black dot means that a copy of the message is present in the train set (a white dot for the test set). Note that the expected result should have only white (resp. black) colored dots for each unique message. This means that the observations are repeated in both sets which leads to a biased performance as shown in Sect. 5. The same behavior happens when performing *communication MBD*. In particular, train and validation sets contain some portions of the same messages on which the measures are computed and leads to biased performances.

Relying on the broadcast nature of the communication, we claim that in both communication and message MBD approaches, the commonly used cross-validation with random splits is incoherent with this type of dataset and over-estimates the model's performance. The same occurs for time-series splits with moving windows because of possible delays between the reception times of different copies as we explain in the next section.

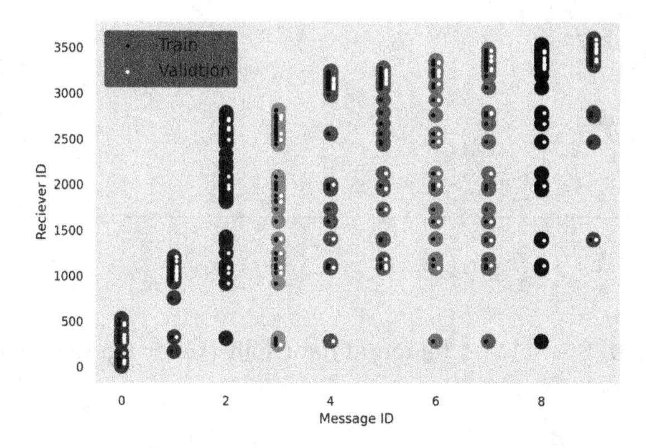

Fig. 5. Sample of messages with random split. Each unique message have a unique color. Black (white) dots refer to the existence of a copy of the unique message in the train (validation) set. (Color figure online)

4.2 Proposed Data Split Approach

To reduce the problem of data leakage when using a random split, we take into account the split with consideration of time used for time series data. The temporal split helps reducing the data leakage, yet, it does not solve the problem entirely, i.e., a portion of messages still ends up in both train and validation sets because of possible delays.

To explain this behavior, let us consider a message M sent from a vehicle to other 20 vehicles within the range of 500 m. All messages M_0 till M_{19} have different receiving times due to the surrounding context and the recording time. T_{early}, T_{late} represent respectively the earliest and latest recorded messages. Any time split T_{split} between T_{early} and T_{late} puts copies of the message M in both train and validation sets violating the assumption of unseen data.

Figure 6 presents a scenario where this issue is observable. The x-axis on Fig. 6 represents the time, and the y-axis represents the vehicle's position. The scenario consists of four different messages represented by black dots from which two copies are created each time (blue boxes). To perform a temporal split, we must choose a discrete time to split the data. If T_1 is chosen for the temporal split, then the broadcast copies of the message M_1 have reception times earlier and later than T_1 as shown in Fig. 6, which means that the temporal split on T_1 would put the message M_1 in both train and validation sets which leads to a data leakage.

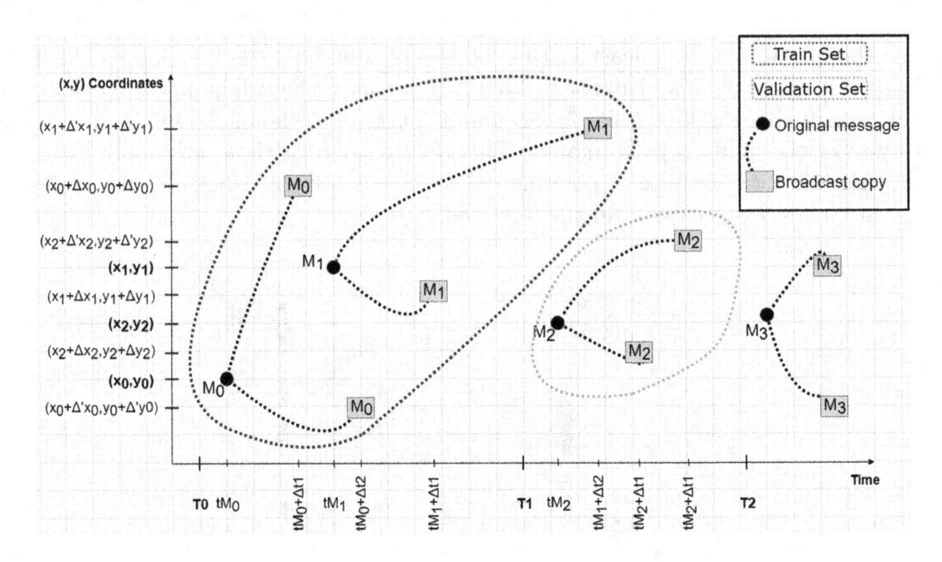

Fig. 6. Spatial and temporal data split (Color figure online)

To solve this problem, we propose a novel data split (Algorithm 1) that keeps the assumption of an unseen validation/test set valid.

Algorithm 1. Proposed split approach

Require: $M\{msg_{id}, time, sender_{id}, ...\}, train\_prop$

1: **procedure**
2: **sort**$(M, time)$
3: $T_{split} = M.time[train\_prop * sizeof(M)]$
4: $T_{set} = M[M.time \leq T_{split}]$
5: $V_{set} = M[M.time > T_{split}]$
6: $intersect_{id} =$ **intersect**$(T_{set}.msg_{id}, V_{set}.msg_{id})$
7: $intersect = V_{set}.$**pop**$(V_{set}.msg_{id} \in intersect_{id})$
8: $T_{set}.$**add**$(intersect)$
9: **return** T_{set}, V_{set}
10: **end procedure**

The algorithm first sorts the data w.r.t time to ensure temporal flow of the data (Algorithm 1, line 2). The algorithm then splits the data with respect to a given *time_split* (Algorithm 1, lines 3–5). Then, we check for spatial dependencies between the train and validation sets (Algorithm 1, line 6) by computing the possible intersections between copies of the same message in the train and validation sets. The Algorithm then ensures the respect of these spatial dependencies (Algorithm 1, lines 7–8) and outputs the resulting train and validation sets.

5 Evaluation

To prove the benefit of the proposed data splitting, we run multiple ML methods on our dataset while varying the data split approaches. We present and analyze the results of each method with each setup. For both split methods, we fit our models with the same standard scikit-learn parameters from [15]. We tested the following ML methods: AdaBoost [7], Decision Tree [16], Naive Bayes (NB) [17], Nearest Neighbors [4], Neural Net[2], and Random Forest (RF) [12][2].

To evaluate both data splits, we first split the data into train and test sets considering the temporal and broadcast aspects of the data. Then, the train set is split into training and validation sets using both random and our splitting approach separately for performance comparison. Also, we evaluate the MBD performance with and without using the previously extracted features. Overall, we consider 5 attacks, 6 ML methods, 2 splitting methods, 2 sets (validation and test) with (or without) engineered features.

5.1 Metrics

In MBD, there are less bogus than normal messages resulting in an imbalanced classes problem. Therefore, we use the harmonic mean of precision and recall, named $F_1 - score$.

$$F_1 - score = 2. \frac{precision \, . \, recall}{precision + recall} \tag{4}$$

Thus, a high $F_1 - score$ value means that the model classifies both the positive (attack) and negative (benign) classes successfully.

5.2 Results and Discussion

Results show that a random splitting approach gives biased performances, i.e., the model does not generalize the learned behavior during the learning phase and gets a significantly lower (10%) performance during the testing phase. To observe this, we plot the best performances obtained among all methods for each attack in the learning phase in Fig. 7a. This shows the obtained $F_1 - score$ at the learning phase (validation) and testing phase (test). We notice that the learning phase's performance fits perfectly for each attack with a minimum of 0.99 $F_1 - score$. We expect the model to have a similarly good performance in the testing phase.

However, the model tested on unseen data, i.e., the test set, has obtained worse performance in the testing phase than what was expected ($F_1 - score$ drops to 0.88 in case of eventual stop attack which makes a performance 10% worse). This questions the high performance observed in the learning phase, and can be explained by the data leakage caused by the random splitting. Therefore, our

[2] The sources and dataset for our work are provided here https://anonymous.4open.science/r/bf9bb344-bd86-4cec-9015-7f561b0c77e2/.

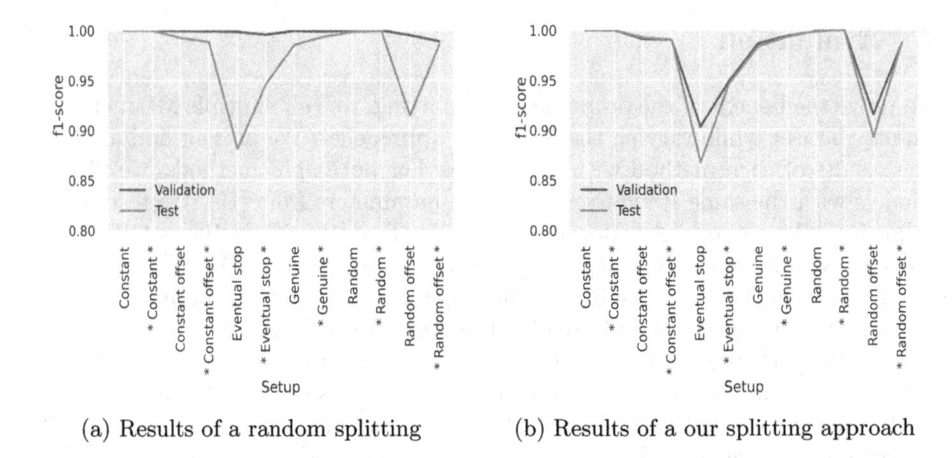

(a) Results of a random splitting (b) Results of a our splitting approach

Fig. 7. Splitting methods comparison on models generalization

proposed splitting fixes this problem and our learned model generalizes better. Thus, the model should perform in the testing phase as well as in the learning phase.

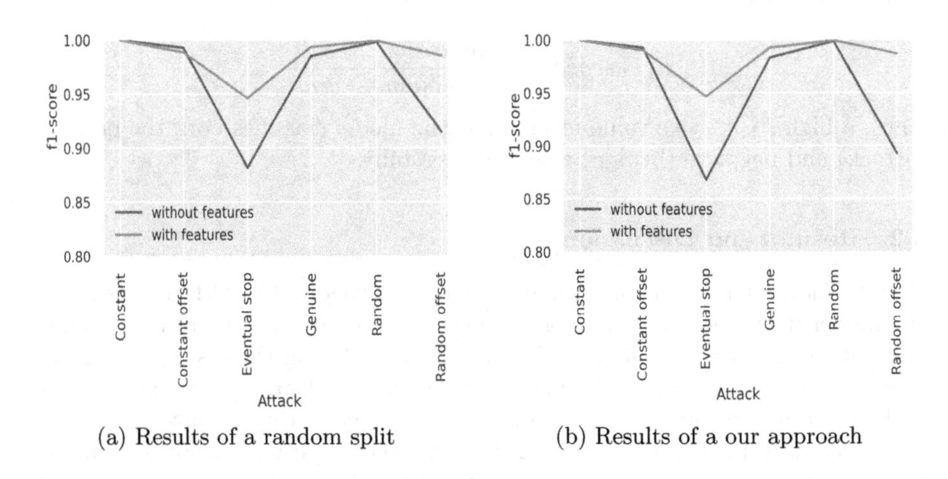

(a) Results of a random split (b) Results of a our approach

Fig. 8. Features influence on models performance

Compared to the random splitting (Fig. 7b), the performance in the learning phase for our splitting is not a perfect fit for the data ($F-1score$ varies between 0.9 and 1 depending on the attack). Compared to the performance on the testing phase, we notice that both performances are similar (3% lower performance in the worst case).

The result confirms that random splitting is not a good approach when modeling broadcast data as it induces data leakage in the learning phase.

Our approach fits better in the broadcast scenario and mitigates the data leakage by ensuring the respect of spatial and temporal dependencies of the broadcast.

Furthermore, to assess the impact of the extracted features on the models, we plot the performance of each model with and without the extracted features. Figure 8 shows the obtained $F1 - score$ for all attacks and splitting methods. Figure 8 shows improved results for each attack on the testing phase. We notice an improvement between 0.07 and 0.1 in the case of eventual stop attack.

Thus, the extracted features (ART, SAW, SSC) improved the detection of attacks, especially the ones that were more difficult to detect.

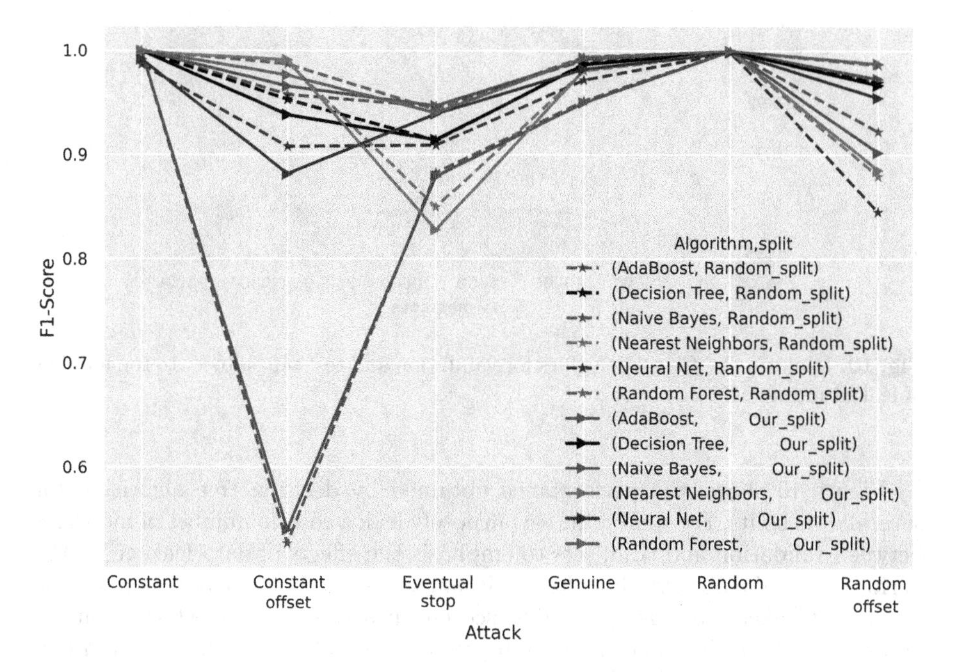

Fig. 9. $F_1 - score$ using different splitting and ML methods

In Fig. 9, we plot the performance of each method, where the $F_1 - score$ is computed on the test set for each data splitting approach. As seen, the performance using a random splitting is slightly better than the performance obtained using our approach for some pairs of methods and attacks, particularly for NB and RF methods and the Random attack. For RF, the difference in $F_1 - measure$ is very small (less than 0.02), meaning that the two approaches are relatively equivalent. The same observation can be made on the random attack with the NB method.

On the other hand, the performance using our approach is better using neural networks with random offset attacks; in fact, we can see a 0.1 increase in performance for this setup (0.954 for our approach and 0.845 for a random splitting). We observe that the NB method has the worst performance in most cases (for each attack). The methods RF and AdaBoost have the best overall performance with RF performing slightly better (about 0.01 increase in $F1-score$). This suggests that boosting-based methods perform better in the task of MBD, because those methods fit many small classifiers that can model the specificity of each attack.

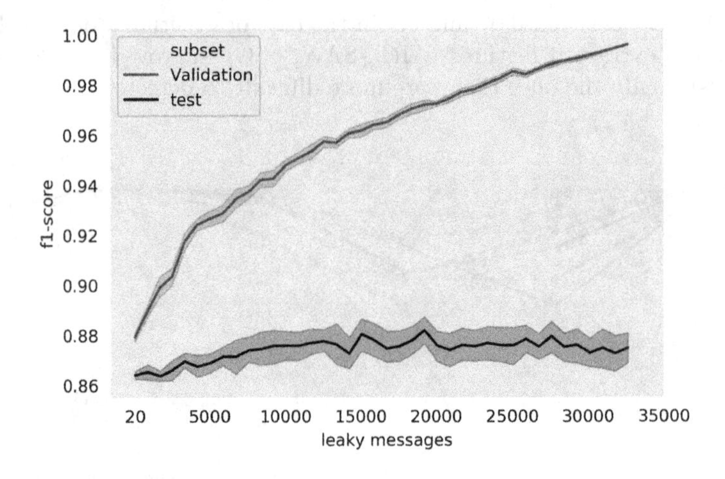

Fig. 10. Evolution of $f_1-score$ values for validation and test sets subject to the number of leaked messages

Figure 10 shows the performance obtained by decision tree algorithm for several data splits. For each split, we purposely leak a certain number of messages between validation and train sets to emphasis the effects of data leakage on the performance. We observe that the validation score gets better as we increase the number of leaked messages (from 0.88 score to nearly 1.0). The test score on the other hand stays the same (roughly between 0.86 and 0.88). The observed gap in the score at highest number of leaks leads to an overestimation of the model and an incoherent performance in the real world.

Overall, random splitting datasets of a broadcast time series overestimates the learning performance and lowers the performance on the test set. However, the use of engineered features improves the performance.

6 Conclusion

In this paper, we introduced a novel approach for data splitting of datasets originating from broadcast V2V messages. Our approach solves the biased learning performance obtained when using random splitting on this type of data. We also provided an empirical evaluation of different supervised ML methods for misbehavior detection in C-ITS with our proposed splitting approach. Our spatial and temporal approach uses the position and the time of occurrence of CAMs for cross-validation and is adapted to the use of unsupervised ML techniques for misbehavior detection. As future work, we will consider a more complex dataset (longer time period and smarter attacks) to get realistic performance of misbehavior detection system when deployed (compared to random splitting previously used by the community). Another step forward is to optimize the hyper-parameters for each algorithm when using our approach. We also want to consider more features as these are crucial to improve the performance of all ML-based misbehavior detection systems. Another possible research track would be to analyze process models discovered through the application of process mining, which might help linking related messages in this case and eventually reduce data leakage.

Acknowledgment. This work is supported by the research chair Connected Cars and Cyber Security (C3S) founded by Renault, Télécom Paris, Fondation Mines-Télécom, Thales, Nokia, Valeo, and Wavestone.

References

1. Arlot, S., Celisse, A., et al.: A survey of cross-validation procedures for model selection. Stat. Surv. **4**, 40–79 (2010)
2. Beale, M.H., Hagan, M.T., Demuth, H.B.: Neural network toolbox user's guide. The Mathworks Inc (1992)
3. Buczak, A.L., Guven, E.: A survey of data mining and machine learning methods for cyber security intrusion detection. IEEE Commun. Surv. Tutor. **18**, 1153–1176 (2015)
4. Cover, T., Hart, P.: Nearest neighbor pattern classification. IEEE Trans. Inf. Theory **13**, 21–27 (1967)
5. Devroye, L., Wagner, T.: Distribution-free performance bounds for potential function rules. IEEE Trans. Inf. Theory **25**, 601–604 (1979)
6. ETSI EN 302 637-2 v1. 3.1-intelligent transport systems (ITS); vehicular communications; basic set of applications; part 2: Specification of cooperative awareness basic service. ETSI (2014)
7. Freund, Y., Schapire, R.E.: A desicion-theoretic generalization of on-line learning and an application to boosting. In: Vitányi, P. (ed.) EuroCOLT 1995. LNCS, vol. 904, pp. 23–37. Springer, Heidelberg (1995). https://doi.org/10.1007/3-540-59119-2_166
8. Ghaleb, F.A., Zainal, A., Rassam, M.A., Mohammed, F.: An effective misbehavior detection model using artificial neural network for vehicular ad hoc network applications. In: 2017 IEEE Conference on Application, Information and Network Security (AINS), pp. 13–18. IEEE (2017)
9. Gyawali, S., Qian, Y.: Misbehavior detection using machine learning in vehicular communication networks. In: ICC 2019-2019 IEEE International Conference on Communications (ICC), pp. 1–6. IEEE (2019)
10. van der Heijden, R.W., Lukaseder, T., Kargl, F.: VeReMi: a dataset for comparable evaluation of misbehavior detection in VANETs. In: Beyah, R., Chang, B., Li, Y., Zhu, S. (eds.) SecureComm 2018. LNICST, vol. 254, pp. 318–337. Springer, Cham (2018). https://doi.org/10.1007/978-3-030-01701-9_18

11. Kamel, J., Ansari, M.R., Petit, J., Kaiser, A., Jemaa, I.B., Urien, P.: Simulation framework for misbehavior detection in vehicular networks. IEEE Trans. Veh. Technol. **69**(6), 6631–6643 (2020)
12. Louppe, G.: Understanding random forests: From theory to practice. preprint arXiv:1407.7502 (2014)
13. Monteuuis, J.P., Petit, J., Zhang, J., Labiod, H., Mafrica, S., Servel, A.: Attacker model for connected and automated vehicles. In: ACM Computer Science in Car Symposium (2018)
14. Monteuuis, J.P., Petit, J., Zhang, J., Labiod, H., Mafrica, S., Servel, A.: "My autonomous car is an elephant": a machine learning based detector for implausible dimension. In: 2018 Third International Conference on Security of Smart Cities, Industrial Control System and Communications (SSIC), pp. 1–8. IEEE (2018)
15. Pedregosa, F., et al.: Scikit-learn: machine learning in python. J. Mach. Learn. Res. **12**, 2825–2830 (2011)
16. Quinlan, J.R.: Induction of decision trees. Mach. Learn. **1**, 81–106 (1986)
17. Rish, I., et al.: An empirical study of the Naive Bayes classifier. In: IJCAI 2001 Workshop on Empirical Methods in Artificial Intelligence, p. 41 (2001)
18. Roberts, D.R., et al.: Cross-validation strategies for data with temporal, spatial, hierarchical, or phylogenetic structure. Ecography **40**, 913–929 (2017)
19. SAE: DSRC implementation guide (2010)
20. Singh, P.K., Gupta, S., Vashistha, R., Nandi, S.K., Nandi, S.: Machine learning based approach to detect position falsification attack in VANETs. In: Nandi, S., Jinwala, D., Singh, V., Laxmi, V., Gaur, M.S., Faruki, P. (eds.) ISEA-ISAP 2019. CCIS, vol. 939, pp. 166–178. Springer, Singapore (2019). https://doi.org/10.1007/978-981-13-7561-3_13
21. So, S., Petit, J., Starobinski, D.: Physical layer plausibility checks for misbehavior detection in v2x networks. In: Proceedings of the 12th Conference on Security and Privacy in Wireless and Mobile Networks, pp. 84–93 (2019)
22. So, S., Sharma, P., Petit, J.: Integrating plausibility checks and machine learning for misbehavior detection in VANET. In: 2018 17th IEEE International Conference on Machine Learning and Applications (ICMLA), pp. 564–571. IEEE (2018)

Information Systems and Their Engineering

Towards an Efficient Approach to Manage Graph Data Evolution: Conceptual Modelling and Experimental Assessments

Landy Andriamampianina[1,2(✉)], Franck Ravat[1], Jiefu Song[1,2], and Nathalie Vallès-Parlangeau[1]

[1] IRIT-CNRS (UMR 5505) - Université Toulouse 1 Capitole (UT1), 2 Rue du Doyen Gabriel Marty, 31042 Toulouse Cedex 09, France
{landy.andriamampianina,franck.ravat,jiefu.song, nathalie.valles-parlangeau}@irit.fr

[2] Activus Group, 1 Chemin du Pigeonnier de la Cépière, 31100 Toulouse, France
{landy.andriamampianina,jiefu.song}@activus-group.fr

Abstract. This paper describes a new temporal graph modelling solution to organize and memorize changes in a business application. To do so, we enrich the basic graph by adding the concepts of *states* and *instances*. Our model has first the advantage of representing a complete temporal evolution of the graph, at the level of: (i) the graph structure, (ii) the attribute set of entities/relationships and (iii) the attributes' value of entities/relationships. Then, it has the advantage of memorizing in an optimal manner evolution traces of the graph and retrieving easily temporal information about a graph component. To validate the feasibility of our proposal, we implement our proposal in Neo4j, a data store based on property graph model. We then compare its performance in terms of storage and querying time to the classical modelling approach of temporal graph. Our results show that our model outperforms the classical approach by reducing disk usage by 12 times and saving up to 99% queries' runtime.

Keywords: Temporal graph · Graph snapshots · Temporal evolution · Graph data stores

1 Introduction

In the real world, entities (i.e. objects, concepts, things with an independent existence) and the relationships between them change over time so information about them also changes. They can evolve over time in terms of (i) their topology (how entities are linked, when entities/relationships are present or absent), (ii) their inherent features (the attributes set that describes an entity or a relationship) and (iii) their status (the values of the set of descriptive attributes at a particular time). Finding and analyzing these evolutions enable to get a deeper understanding of an application notably to exploit temporal correlations and

S. Cherfi et al. (Eds.): RCIS 2021, LNBIP 415, pp. 471–488, 2021.
https://doi.org/10.1007/978-3-030-75018-3_31

causality [3,9], to make simulations [8] or to make predictions [16]. It is therefore necessary to be able to manage the temporal evolution of data to exploit them. The management of evolving data implies the following challenges: (i) the formalization of a conceptual model to capture the three aspects of evolution of an application that we mentioned before, (ii) the implementation of the conceptual model into a data store and (iii) the efficient querying of the temporal aspects of an application.

Regarding the first challenge, a growing part of the literature proposes conceptual models, called *temporal graphs*, based on graphs because of their flexible nature. It incorporates time dimension in graphs and captures the temporal evolution of graph data. The basic representation of temporal graphs is the *sequence of graph snapshots*[1]. However, existing snapshots-based solutions focus on specific evolution aspects according to an application's needs. Particularly, they do not capture the addition or deletion of entities and relationships' attributes over time. Regarding the second challenge, to our knowledge, no works formalize translation rules of a conceptual model of temporal graphs into a data store [2,24,27]. Regarding the third challenge, to exploit temporal graphs efficiently, some works propose optimization methods to reduce data redundancy generated by snapshots but they are not effective enough [14,26,28]. Other works focus on the performance of graph data stores supporting temporal graphs [5,10,19,25].

In response to the previous issues, our contribution is three-fold: (i) a generic conceptual model to capture a complete temporal evolution of graph data, (ii) that is directly convertible into a graph data store through formalized translation rules (iii) and that supports efficiently the querying of multiple evolution aspects of a graph. In this paper, first, we discuss the challenges posed by existing works on the management of graph data evolving over time (Sect. 2). Second, we propose novel concepts of the temporal graph to overcome the limits of existing concepts (Sect. 3). Finally, we implement our model in a graph data store, namely Neo4j, and compare its performance to the classical snapshot-based implementation and an optimized snapshot-based implementation (Sect. 4).

2 Related Works

In this section, we analyze existing approaches to manage the evolution of graph data at three levels: conceptual, logical, and physical levels. Then, we present our contributions in relation to existing works.

At the conceptual level, the classical approach to model graph data evolving over time is the sequence of snapshots [14]. It generally consists in sampling graph data periodically to obtain snapshots at a fixed time interval (e.g. per hour, day, month or year) [18]. The advantages of this modelling approach are that it is simple and that it represents accurately the state of the graph at a specific time instance [18]. Nevertheless, existing works based on this approach are

[1] Denoted $G_1, G_2, ..., G_T$ where G_i is an image of the entire graph at the time instance i and $[1; T]$ is the timeline of the application.

limited in taking into account evolution. The evolution of the graph topology[2], i.e. the addition and deletion of edges only [2,27] or both nodes and edges [24] over time, is the most studied evolution type. To meet more complex needs, some models include attributes of nodes [6,7] or both edges and nodes' attributes [11] to capture the temporal evolution in their values. In the previous cited works, they generally consider the attribute set of nodes or edges as fixed while it can evolve over time in real-world applications. Indeed, some applications require to model evolution that happened at all levels in a graph [4]. To the best of our knowledge, there is no modelling solutions of temporal graphs including all evolution types in order to be used in any desired application. Last but not least, some works propose a modelling approach of evolving graphs completely in break with snapshots [15,17]. They attach a valid time interval to each graph component (i.e. node or edge) to track the graph evolution. However, as snapshots, they focus on specific evolution types.

At the logical level, property-graph and RDF data models are commonly used in the graph domain. Traditionally, the transformation between the conceptual level and the logical level is done in an automatic way such as in the relational databases domain. However, to our knowledge, this automation is not studied in the domain of graphs. The works that propose a conceptual model completely ignore the formalization of translation rules from the conceptual model to the logical model [2,24,27]. No standard is defined at the present time to guarantee a compliant implementation of a conceptual model of temporal graphs at the logical level.

At the physical level, existing works try to maximize the implementation and query efficiency of temporal graphs. We distinguish two research axis in existing works: data redundancy reduction and performance improvement. Regarding data redundancy reduction, snapshots inevitably introduce data redundancy since consecutive snapshots share in common nodes and edges that do not change over time [14]. There exist optimization techniques to partially reduce data redundancy. For instance, [26] proposes a strategy to determine which snapshots should be materialized based on the distribution of historical queries. [11] introduces an in-memory data structure and a hierarchical index structure to retrieve efficiently snapshots of an evolving graph. [22] proposes a framework to construct a small number of representative graphs based on similarity. These techniques are unfortunately not effective enough.

Regarding the performance improvement, some works focus on the performance of graph data stores supporting evolving graphs via experimental assessments. Some experiments are based on property-graph based NoSQL databases. For instance, [5] uses Neo4j to store time-varying networks and to retrieve specific snapshots. The authors in [10] have developed a graph database management system based on Neo4j to support graphs changing in the value of nodes and edges' properties but with a static structure. Other experiments rely on

[2] Graph topology is the way in which nodes and edges are arranged within a graph.

RDF triple stores, such as Virtuoso[3] or TDB-Jena[4], to store the evolution of Linked Open Data (LOD) in the Semantic Web area [19,25]. It is already known that property-graph based NoSQL databases are more efficient than RDF triple stores when querying RDF data [20]. It is necessary to see if property-graph based databases are as efficient in the context of temporal graphs.

Contributions. We propose a complete solution to manage the evolution of graph data. From a conceptual point of view, we propose a graph-based modelling that does better than snapshots by capturing temporal evolution at all levels - the graph topology, the attributes' set and the value of attributes - in order to be implemented in any desired application (Sect. 3). From a logical point of view, we propose translation rules between our conceptual model and a graph data store to automate the implementation of our model (Sect. 4). We have decided to focus on a property-graph data store as it provides a more efficient environment for analytical queries than RDF triple stores. From a physical point of view, to highlight the advantage of using our model instead of snapshots, we present a comparative study of the implementation of both models using Neo4j as a property-graph data store. On the one hand, we compare the creation time and space requirements to evaluate the proportion of data redundancy in both models. On the other hand, we compare the querying performance of these implementations based on benchmark queries highlighting the temporal evolution concepts proposed by our model and using the native query language of Neo4j (Sect. 4).

3 Proposition

In this section, we present our modelling solution of a temporal graph. We keep the concepts of entities and relationships as in basic graphs. We incorporate the notion of time to represent the evolution of entities and their relationships. We model time as linear and discretized according to a time unit. A time unit is a partition of the timeline into a set of disjoint contiguous time intervals.

Definition 1. *A time interval defines a set of instants between two instant limits. We denote it* $T = [t_{begin}, t_{end}]$. *An instant defines a point on a timeline, that is* $T = [t_{begin}, t_{end}]$ *where* $t_{begin} = t_{end}$.

In order to respond to the current needs for capturing multiple evolution types of an application (change in the topology of entities/relationships, in the attributes set of entities/relationships or in the attribute values of entities/relationships), we cannot rely on the current works in the literature. To overcome this limitation, we propose a new model capable of capturing three types of temporal evolution of entities and relationships in an unique representation. In our model, an entity or relationship that evolves over time is modelled

[3] https://virtuoso.openlinksw.com/.
[4] https://jena.apache.org/documentation/tdb/.

through three levels of abstraction: (i) the topology level to capture its presence and absence over time (ii) the state level to capture the evolution in its attributes set and (iii) the instance level to capture the evolution in the value of its attributes.

Instead of attaching time to an entire graph as in snapshots, we attach a valid time interval to each abstraction level of entities/relationships. This valid time interval expresses the validity and existence of the information associated to each abstraction level of entities/relationships inside a certain time interval. This time management method allows to keep the strict and necessary data and then avoid data redundancy.

Definition 2. *A temporal entity, called* $e_i \in E$*, is defined by* $\langle T^{e_i}, id^{e_i}, S^{e_i} \rangle$ *where* T^{e_i} *is the valid time interval of* e_i*,* id^{e_i} *is the identifier of* e_i *and* $S^{e_i} = \{s_1^{e_i}, ..., s_m^{e_i}\}$ *is the non-empty set of states of* e_i*. Each state* $s_j^{e_i} \in S^{e_i}$ *is defined by* $\langle T^{s_j}, A^{s_j}, I^{s_j} \rangle$ *where:*

- T^{s_j} *is the valid time interval of* $s_j^{e_i}$*.*
- $A^{s_j} = \{a_1^{e_i}; ...; a_n^{e_i}\}$ *is the non-empty set of attributes of* $s_j^{e_i}$ *during* T^{s_j}*. It is called the schema of* e_i *during* T^{s_j}*.*
- $I^{s_j} = \{i_1^{s_j}; ...; i_p^{s_j}\}$ *is the non-empty set of instances of* $s_j^{e_i}$ *during* T^{s_j}*. Each instance* $i_k^{s_j} \in I^{s_j}$ *is defined by* $\langle T^{i_k}, V^{i_k} \rangle$ *where:*
  - T^{i_k} *is the valid time interval of* $i_k^{s_j}$*.*
  - $V^{i_k} = \{v(a_1^{e_i}); ...; v(a_n^{e_i})\}$ *is a non-empty set of attributes' values. Each* $v(a_q^{e_i}) \in V^{i_k}$ *is the value of each attribute* $a_q^{e_i} \in A^{s_j}$ *during* T^{i_k}*.*

The highest abstraction level of a temporal entity e_i is the topology level. At this level, a temporal entity evolves only according to its presence or absence in the application reflected by the change of its valid time T^{e_i} over time.

The middle abstraction level of a temporal entity e_i is the state level under which its schema, denoted A^{s_j}, can evolve. At this level, two states of the same entity have different schemas. When a new attribute is added or removed from an entity, a new state is created instead of overwriting the old state version.

The lowest abstraction level of a temporal entity e_i is the instance level. It captures the evolution in the value V^{i_k} of its attributes A^{s_j}. At this level, between two instances of the same entity, the schema is the same but the values of its attributes are different. When the values of an entity's attributes change, a new instance is created instead of overwriting the old instance version.

The changes at the topology and state levels impact the instance level. At the topology level, when an entity is present/absent at a particular time, this translates by the presence/absence of its states and the instances that composed them at this particular time. At the state level, when there is a change in the schema of an entity, a new state is created. Moreover, at least one instance of this state is created. At each change on an abstraction level, this ends the valid time of the last instance at the time of the change and starts the valid time of the new created instance at the time of the change. So the valid times of the abstraction levels higher than the instance level are deduced by calculation as described in following definition.

Definition 3. *The valid time interval of each instance of a temporal entity* $i_k^{s_j} \in I^{s_j}$ *is defined by* $T^{i_k} = [t_{begin}, t_{end}]$ *where* $t_{begin} \neq \emptyset$ *and* $t_{end} \neq \emptyset$*. There is only one case where an instance has not yet got a pre-defined ending time: if some instances under the current state* $s_m^{e_i}$ *are current in the application.*

The valid time interval of each state of a temporal entity $s_j^{e_i} \in S^{e_i}$ *is obtained by calculation:*

$$T^{s_j} = \cup_{k=1}^{k=p} T^{i_k} \text{ where } i_k \in I^{s_j} \tag{1}$$

The valid time interval of each temporal entity $e_i \in E$ *is obtained by calculation :*

$$T^{e_i} = \cup_{j=1}^{j=m} T^{s_j} \text{ where } s_j \in S^{e_i} \tag{2}$$

The temporal evolution of relationships includes the evolution in the graph topology, in their attribute set and in the value of their attributes. We use the same evolution mechanisms as in temporal entities for relationships. In fact, a temporal relationship is also modelled through the concepts of states and instances.

Definition 4. *A temporal relationship, called* r_i*, is defined by* $\langle T^{r_i}, S^{r_i} \rangle$ *where* T^{r_i} *is the valid time interval of* r_i *and* $S^{r_i} = \{s_1^{r_i}, ..., s_u^{r_i}\}$ *is the non-empty set of states of* r_i*. A state* $s_b^{r_i} \in S^{r_i}$ *is defined by* $\langle T^{s_b}, A^{s_b}, I^{s_b} \rangle$ *where:*

- T^{s_b} *is the valid time interval of* $s_b^{r_i}$*.*
- $A^{s_b} = \{a_1^{r_i}; ...; a_w^{r_i}\}$ *is the non-empty set of attributes of* $s_b^{r_i}$ *during* T^{s_b}*. It is called the schema of* r_i *during* T^{s_b}*.*
- $I^{s_b} = \{i_1^{s_b}; ...; i_x^{s_b}\}$ *is the non-empty set of instances of* $s_b^{r_i}$ *during* T^{s_b}*. Each instance* $i_c^{s_b} \in I^{s_b}$ *is defined by* $\langle T^{i_c}, V^{i_c} \rangle$ *where:*
  - T^{i_c} *is the valid time interval of* $i_c^{s_b}$*.*
  - $V^{i_c} = \{v(a_1^{r_i}); ...; v(a_w^{r_i})\}$ *is a non-empty set of attributes' values. Each* $v(a_d^{r_i}) \in V^{i_c}$ *is the value of each attribute* $a_d^{r_i} \in A^{s_b}$ *during* T^{i_c}*.*

Definition 5. *A temporal relationship is defined based on the same concepts as a temporal entity. The valid time of each state* $s_b^{r_i} \in S^{r_i}$*, denoted* T^{s_b}*, is obtained by calculation as in Definition 3. The valid time of each temporal relationship* $r_i \in R$*, denoted* T^{r_i}*, is obtained by calculation as in Definition 3. The particularity of a temporal relationship is that it does not have an independent existence contrary to temporal entities. This implies in our modelling that:*

- *An instance* $i_c^{s_b} \in I^{s_b}$ *is a relationship between a couple of instances* (i_h, i_l) *belonging respectively to entities* e_i *and* e_j*.*
- *The valid time of each instance* $i_c^{s_b} \in I^{s_b}$ *is defined by* $T^{i_c} = [t_{begin}, t_{end}]$ *where* $t_{begin} \neq \emptyset$ *and* $t_{end} \neq \emptyset$*. There is only one case where it has not yet got a pre-defined ending time: if some instances under the current state* $s_u^{r_i}$ *are current in the application and both connected entities' instances* i_h *and* i_l *do not have yet a pre-defined ending time.*
- $T^{i_c} d (T^{i_h} \cap T^{i_l})$[5] *where* T^{i_h} *is the valid time of an instance* i_h *of* e_i *and* T^{i_l} *is the valid time of an instance* i_l *of* e_j*.* $(T^{i_h} \cap T^{i_l}) \neq \emptyset$ *because* $(T^{i_h} \circ T^{i_l})$[6]*.*

[5] d is an ALLEN temporal operator to express that a time interval X occurs "during" a time interval Y, i.e. XdY [1].

[6] $\circ$ is an ALLEN temporal operator to express that a time interval X "overlaps" a time interval Y, i.e. $X \circ Y$ [1].

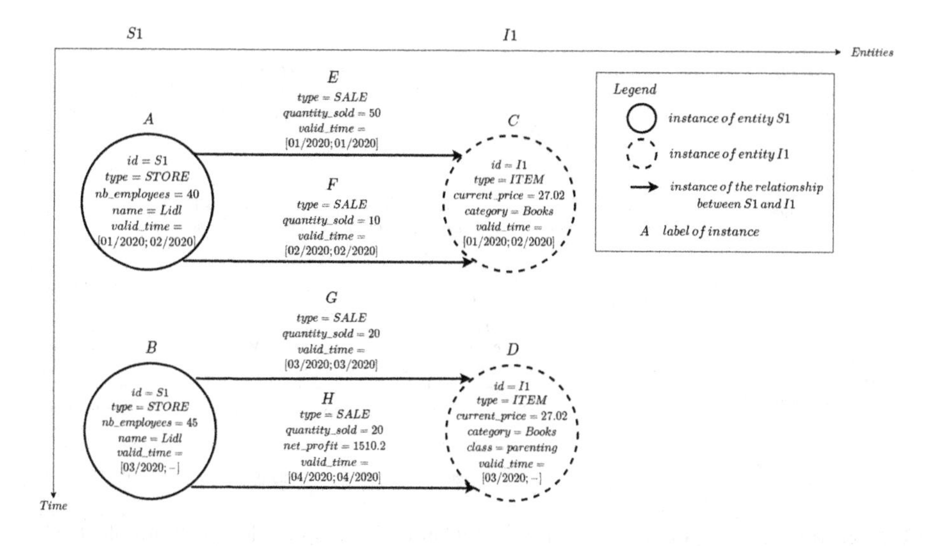

Fig. 1. Management of the temporal evolution of the application in Example 1 with our modelling solution.

Example 1. We propose in this example an application to show the implementation of our modelling concepts. We consider two entities: a store and an item. At the creation of the application at the month 01/2020, the store and the item are characterized by the following set of attributes: an identifier (denoted *id*) and a type (denoted *type*). In addition, the store is described by the number of its employees (denoted *nb_employees*) and a name (denoted *name*). The item is also described by a price (denoted *current_price*) and the category to which it belongs (denoted *category*). These two entities are linked by the sale of the item by the store. This sale is characterized by a type (denoted *type*) and the quantity sold of the item by the store (denoted *quantity_sold*). The store is identified by "$S1$" and named "Lidl". Its type is "Store". It has 40 employees. The item is identified by "$I1$". Its type is "Item". It has a price of 27.02$. Its category is "Books". The type of the sale between of $I1$ by $S1$ is "Sale". The quantity sold of the latter is 50.

Since the application creation, both entities have not evolved until 02/2020. However, the quantity sold of $I1$ by $S1$ has decreased by 40 at the month 02/2020. At the month 03/2020, several evolutions took place. The store $S1$ has recruited 5 employees. The item $I1$ is described by a new attribute called *class*. The item $I1$ has been affected to the class "parenting". The quantity sold of $I1$ by $S1$ has increased by 10. Since the month 03/2020, both entities have not evolved anymore. At the month 04/2020, the sale of $I1$ by $S1$ is described by the new attribute *net_profit*. It is the net profit made by $S1$ on $I1$. Its value is 1510.2$. Finally, there is no sale of $I1$ by $S1$ since the month 05/2020.

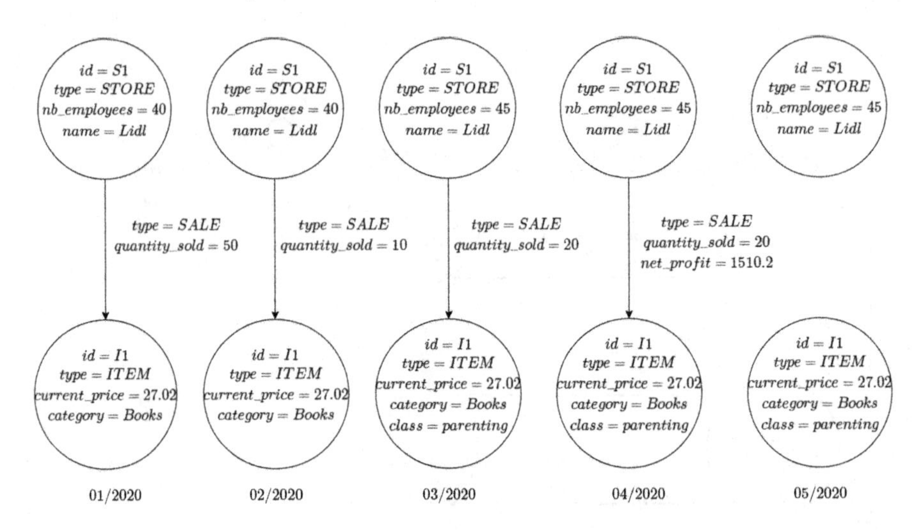

Fig. 2. Management of the temporal evolution of the application in Example 1 with the snapshots-based solution.

To answer the need of capturing these evolutions, we show in Fig. 1 the implementation of our modelling concepts to manage the temporal evolution of the application. The sale of $I1$ by $S1$ corresponds to a relationship between the two entities. An instance is illustrated graphically by a node for entities and by an edge for relationships in Fig. 1. Similarly, a state is illustrated graphically by a set of nodes for entities and a set of edges for relationships in Fig. 1.

Both entities have not changed from 01/2020 to 02/2020 neither in terms of their presence/absence nor their schema nor their attributes' value. At the level of our model, this is translated by one state of $S1$ with the schema $\{id, type, nb\_employees, name\}$. One instance of this state is created to initialize the value of $S1$'s attributes. The latter is illustrated by the node A in Fig. 1. Moreover, one state of $I1$ is created with the schema $\{id, type, current\_price, category\}$. One instance of this state is created to initialize the value of $I1$'s attributes. It is illustrated by the node C in Fig. 1. Instances A and C have a valid time starting from 01/2020 and ending at 02/2020 during which they did not change.

The first sale of $I1$ by $S1$ generates at the level of our model one state of the relationship between both entities with the schema $\{type, quantity\_sold\}$. One instance of this state, illustrated by the edge E in Fig. 1, is created to initialize the value of the sale's attributes. At the month 02/2020, the value of the attribute *quantity_sold* of the sale of $I1$ by $S1$ has decreased under the same schema of the instance E. This generates in our model a new instance, labelled F in Fig. 1, with the updated value of *quantity_sold* under the same state in which the instance E belongs. The valid time of F begins at the time of the change it captures i.e. 02/2020.

At the month 03/2020, $S1$ experienced an increase in the value of the attribute *nb_employees* under the same schema of its instance A. This creates at the level of our model a new instance of $S1$, labelled B in Fig. 1, with the updated value of *nb_employees* under the state in which the instance A belongs. As $S1$ does not change anymore since 03/2020, the valid time of instance B is starting from 03/2020 but its ending date is not specified. It is worthy to notice that $S1$ has never experienced a change in its schema. It has only one state with the schema $\{id, type, nb\_employees, name\}$ and which gathers the instances A and B.

Moreover, at the month 03/2020, the attribute *class* has been added to the schema of $I1$. From our modelling point of view, this generates a new state with the new schema $\{id, type, current\_price, category, class\}$. A new instance of this state is created to specify the value of $I1$'s attributes. It is illustrated by the node D in Fig. 1. As $I1$ does not change anymore since 03/2020, the valid time of instance D is starting from 03/2020 but its ending date is not specified. To sum up, $I1$ has two states: one with the schema $\{id, type, current\_price, category\}$ and composed of the instance C and another one with the schema $\{id, type, current\_price, category, class\}$ and composed of the instance D.

Last but not least, also at the month 03/2020, the value of the attribute *quantity_sold* describing the sale of $I1$ by $S1$ has increased under the same schema of instances E and F. This is translated in our model by the creation of a new instance G in Fig. 1 with the updated value of *quantity_sold*. This instance belongs to the state composed of instances E and F. The valid time of G starts at the time of the change it captures i.e. 03/2020. At 04/2020, the attribute *net_profit* has been added to the schema of the relationship. From our modelling point of view, this generates a new state of the relationship with the new schema $\{type, quantity\_sold, net\_profit\}$. A new instance of this state is created to specify the value of the relationship's attributes. It is illustrated by the edge H in Fig. 1. To sum up, the relationship between $I1$ and $S1$ has two states: one with the schema $\{type, quantity\_sold\}$ and composed of three instances (E, F and G) and another one with the schema $\{type, quantity\_sold, net\_profit\}$ and composed of one instance (H). Finally, there is no sale of $I1$ by $S1$ since the month 05/2020. This corresponds in our model to the absence of relationship between $I1$ and $S1$ at the month 05/2020. Consequently, no instance or state of this relationship with a valid time including the month 05/2020 is created.

In a nutshell, our model translates the different evolutions of the application into 1 graph with 4 nodes and 4 edges. We present in Fig. 2 the representation of the same application if we would have adopt the snapshot-based approach to manage the temporal evolution. We would have 5 graph snapshots with 10 nodes and 4 edges.

As a result of the previous definitions, our *temporal graph* is defined as follows:

Definition 6. *A Temporal Graph, called G, is defined by $\langle L, E, R\rangle$ where:*
- *L is the timeline of the temporal graph,*
- *$E = \{e_1, ..., e_g\}$ is a non-empty set of temporal entities,*
- *$R = \{r_1, ..., r_h\}$ is a non-empty set of temporal relationships.*

Definition 7. *The timeline L of a temporal graph G only depends on the valid times of temporal entities as they have an independent existence. L is obtained by calculation:*

$$L = \cup_{i=1}^{i=g} T^{e_i} \text{ where } e_i \in E \quad (3)$$

4 Experimental Evaluation

In this section, we present an experimental comparison of three approaches for modelling an evolving graph: the classical sequence of snapshots, an optimized sequence of snapshots and our temporal graph. As we have discussed in Sect. 2, the classical snapshots consists in sampling of graph data at a regular time period (here we chose a month). Our optimized snapshots approach consists in creating snapshots only if they differ. In other terms, we create a snapshot only if it includes a change compared to a previous snapshot.

This experiment has two goals: (i) to study the feasibility of our model, i.e. illustrate if our modelling is easily implementable (stored and queried) in a graph-oriented data store and (ii) to study the efficiency of our model by comparing its storage and query performance to the classical sequence of snapshots and the optimized sequence of snapshots.

In Sect. 4.1, we present the technical environment of our experiment. Then, in Sect. 4.2, we present the datasets we used for the three implementations. We stored these datasets in Neo4j based on defined translation rules of our model presented in Sect. 4.3. Finally, we query the three approaches according to different querying criteria and compare their runtime in Sect. 4.4. We present the details of our experiment at the following web page https://gitlab.com/2573869/temporal_graph_modelling.

4.1 Technical Environment

The hardware configuration is as follows: PowerEdge R630, 16 CPUs x Intel(R) Xeon(R) CPU E5-2630 v3 @ 2.40 Ghz, 63.91 GB. One virtual machine is installed on this hardware. This virtual machine has 6 GB in terms of RAM and 100 GB in terms of disk size. We installed on this virtual machine Neo4j (community version 4.1.3) as a data store for our datasets.

4.2 Datasets

To run our experimental comparison, we needed a dataset that reflect realistic applications with temporal evolutions. We therefore used a dataset from a reference benchmark namely TPC-DS[7]. Temporal evolutions exist in this benchmark

[7] http://www.tpc.org/tpc_documents_current_versions/pdf/tpc-ds_v2.13.0.pdf.

Table 1. Characteristics of datasets.

Implementations	# Nodes	# Edges	# Snapshots
Temporal graph	112.897	1.693.623	N/A
Classical snapshots	7.405.461	4.207.657	60
Optimized snapshots	5.347.477	4.044.481	53

and allow us to find all the three types of evolution mentioned in Sect. 3. We transformed the dataset provided by TPC-DS into three datasets having the temporal graph, the classical snapshots and the optimized snapshots representations. All transformation details of the TPC-DS dataset into the three representations are available on the website https://gitlab.com/2573869/temporal_graph_modelling. In Table 1, we found as a result of the transformation steps, the number of nodes, edges and snapshots of the dataset used for each implementation.

4.3 Translation of Temporal Graph into Neo4j

To evaluate the feasibility of our modelling solution, we searched for translation rules to map our conceptual model of temporal graph into the graph data model supported by Neo4j, the property graph model [23]. In Table 2, we define the translation rules between our model and the property graph. The concepts of our temporal graph are directly translatable into the property graph of Neo4j. An instance of an entity or relationship in our model can be represented respectively by a node and an edge in Neo4j. The value of the attributes set and valid times of instances correspond to the key-value properties in Neo4j. An entity, relationship or state is composed of instances. Then, they are represented by a set of nodes or edges in Neo4j. Schemas and valid times of a state, an entity or relationship can be retrieved by query in Neo4j.

For each implementation, we stored the relative dataset in a database instance of Neo4j. Table 3 shows the size (in GB) and the creation time (in seconds) of each database instance in Neo4j. The two snapshots approaches use a different time management method than our model which leads to larger sizes of their database instances. Our model reduces respectively 12 times and 9 times the size of database instance storing classical snapshots and optimized snapshots. To load the datasets into Neo4j, we designed a program based on the CSV importing system of Neo4j. Again, the datasets based on snapshots approaches require more time to be imported since they contain more nodes and edges than our model (Table 1).

4.4 Query Performance

To evaluate the efficiency of our model, we compare its querying performance with the classical snapshots and the optimized snapshots based implementations.

Table 2. Translation rules of our model into Neo4j. **start_valid_time* and *end_valid_time*.

Our model's concepts	Neo4j's concepts
An instance of an entity state $i_k^{s_j}$	A node
An instance of a relationship state $i_c^{s_b}$	An edge
Valid time of an entity instance T^{i_k}	Two properties*
Valid time of a relationship instance T^{i_c}	Two properties*
A state of an entity $s_j^{e_i}$	A set of nodes (with different valid times)
A state of a relationship $s_b^{r_i}$	A set of edges (with different valid times)
Valid time of an entity state T^{s_j}	By query
Valid time of a relationship state T^{s_b}	By query
A schema of an entity state A^{s_j}	By query
A schema of a relationship state A^{s_b}	By query
An entity e_i	A set of nodes (with different valid times)
A relationship r_i	A set of edges (with different valid times)
An attribute of an entity $a_q^{e_i}$	A property
An attribute of a relationship $a_d^{r_i}$	A property
A temporal entity's identifier id^{e_i}	A property
Valid time of an entity T^{e_i}	By query
Valid time of a relationship T^{r_i}	By query

Table 3. Size and creation time of graph database instances.

Implementations	Size (in GB)	Creation time (in sec)
Temporal graph	0,3	15,795
Classical snapshots	3,7	56,529
Optimized snapshots	2,8	45,827

To do so, we created benchmark queries that cover a large range of scenarios to get insights about the temporal aspects of a graph (Table 4). We classified them into the following criteria: the entity scope, the time scope, the temporal evolution type and the operations type [12,13]. Then, we translated these benchmark queries in the native query language of Neo4j: Cypher. Finally, we recorded for each benchmark query its execution time which is the elapsed time in seconds for processing the query (Fig. 3). We run each query ten times and take the mean time of all runs as final execution time. To avoid any bias in the disk management and querying performance, we do not use any customized optimization techniques but rely on default tuning of Neo4j.

Observations. In Fig. 3, we observe that queries Q1–Q6 are instantaneous (close to 0) for all three implementations. Q17–Q21 and Q27 record execution spikes for the two snapshots implementations. Moreover, we notice that the runtimes of Q28 explode for the snapshots and the temporal graph implementations.

Table 4. Benchmark queries. *SE = Single Entity, SU = Subgraph, EN = Entire Graph, S = Schema, I = Instance, T = Topology, SP = Single Point, MP = Multiple Points, SI = Single Interval, MI = Multiple Intervals, C = Comparison, A = Aggregation.*

		Graph component	Evolution type	Time scope	Operation type
Q1	The descriptive attributes of a store at the month X	SE	S	SP	
Q2	The descriptive attributes of a store at the months X and Y	SE	S	MP	
Q3	The changes that occurred on the descriptive attributes of a store between the months X and Y	SE	S	MP	C
Q4	The descriptive attributes of a store from the month X to the month Y	SE	S	SI	
Q5	The descriptive attributes of a store every year of a period	SE	S	MI	
Q6	The changes that occurred on descriptive attributes of a store from the month X to the month Y	SE	S	SI	C
Q7	The price of an item at the month X	SE	I	SP	
Q8	The price of an item at the months X and Y	SE	I	MP	
Q9	Measure the change in the price of an item between the months X and Y	SE	I	MP	C
Q10	The price(s) of an item from the month X to the month Y	SE	I	SI	
Q11	Measure the average price of an item every year of a period	SE	I	MI	A
Q12	The customers that shopped in a store at the month X	SU	T	SP	
Q13	The customers that shopped in a store at the months X and Y	SU	T	MP	
Q14	Count the number of customers that shopped in a store at the month X	SU	T	SP	A
Q15	Count the number of customers that shopped in a store at the months X and Y	SU	T	MP	A
Q16	The customers that shopped in a store from the month X to the month Y	SU	T	SI	
Q17	The customers that shopped in a store every year of a period	SU	T	MI	
Q18	Count the number of customers in a store every year of a period	SU	T	MI	A
Q19	The household attributes of a customer at the month X	SU	S	SP	
Q20	The household attributes of a customer at the months X and Y	SU	S	MP	
Q21	The changes that occurred on the household characteristics of a customer between the months X and Y	SU	S	MP	C
Q22	The household attributes of a customer from the month X to the month Y	SU	S	SI	
Q23	The changes that occurred on the household characteristics of a customer from the month X to the month Y	SU	S	SI	C
Q24	The sold quantity of an item by a store at the month X	SU	I	SP	
Q25	The sold quantity of an item by a store at the months X and Y	SU	I	MP	
Q26	The sold quantity of an item by a store from the month X to the month Y	SU	I	SI	
Q27	Measure the average sold quantity of an item by a store every year of a period	SU	I	MI	A
Q28	The historical state of the store sales at the month X	EG		SP	

The rest of benchmark queries (Q7–Q16 and Q22–Q26) does not exceed 6 s for the three approaches. Overall, the execution query times of the temporal graph are more stable than both snapshot-based approaches.

Discussion. The gap between the temporal graph and the two snapshots based implementations is partly due to difference in the volume of data involved in queries. As we can see in Table 1, the classical snapshots based implementation results in 66 times more nodes and 2 times more edges than the temporal graph. The optimized snapshots based implementation enables to reduce significantly the number of nodes but still it counts 47 times more nodes than the temporal graph. Inevitably, both snapshots approaches use more disk space and require more time to process during querying.

Queries' runtime are also impacted by their types. First, we analyze the querying performance of the temporal graph according to the entity scope, that is requesting information about the history of the graph at the level of a single entity (Q1–Q11) or a set of entities (subgraph) (Q12–Q27) or the entire graph (Q28). Most queries on a single entity are instantaneous as they involve the least data for the three approaches. The temporal graph approach outperforms the classical and the optimized snapshots approaches on querying a subgraph by respectively reducing their runtimes by 58%–99% and 74%–99%. The same trend is observed on querying the entire graph. The temporal graph saves 35% of the classical snapshots' runtime. Neo4j was not able to process Q28 for the optimized snapshots approach due to main memory limitations.

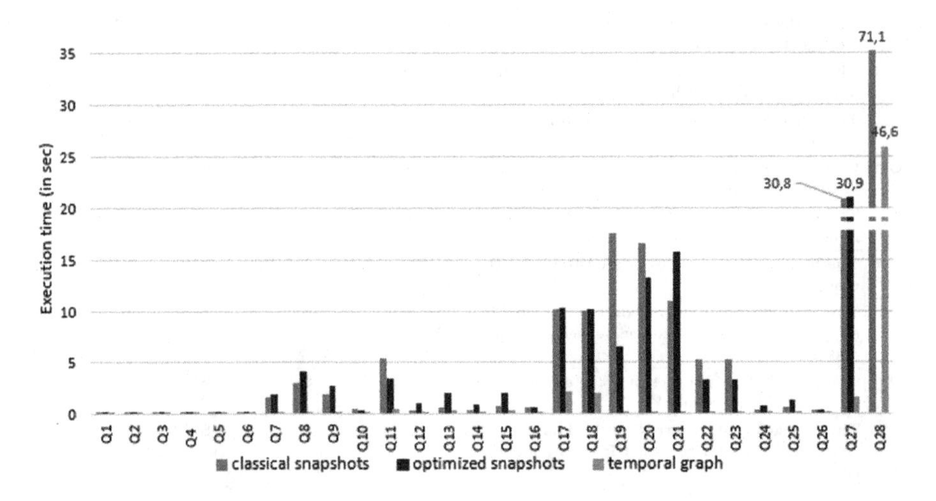

Fig. 3. Execution times of 28 benchmark queries.

Second, we analyze the impact of evolution type over queries' runtime: the evolution of schemas (Q1—Q6 and Q19–Q23), instances (Q7–Q11 and Q24–Q27) or topology (Q12 to Q18). The retrieval tasks relative to this scope enable to evaluate the cost of retrieving a specific information about graph changes. Excluding instantaneous queries, the gap between the two snapshots and the temporal graph implementations is the largest when querying schema. Indeed, queries on schema involve one specific operator[8]. Particularly, the temporal graph decreases the runtimes of Q19–Q23 in both classical and optimized snapshots by 98%–99%.

Third, we focus on the impact of time scope over queries' runtime to evaluate the cost of time travelling in the graph: querying a single time point (Q1, Q7, Q12, Q14, Q19, Q24 and Q28), a single interval (Q4, Q6, Q10, Q16, Q22, Q23 and Q26), multiple time points (Q2, Q3, Q8, Q9, Q13, Q15, Q20, Q21 and Q25) or multiple time intervals (Q5, Q11, Q17, Q18 and Q27). On the one hand, we observe that for queries with a complex time view (i.e. concerning multiple time points or multiple time intervals) the execution time explodes for both snapshots approaches while our model is still effective. Particularly, queries Q17–Q18 and Q27, involving multiple time intervals, reach respectively 10s and 31s for the two snapshots approaches. Our temporal graph allows to reduce those runtimes by 79%–95%. Moreover, queries Q20–Q21, involving multiple time points, exceed 10s for the two snapshots approaches. Our temporal graph enables to save 99% of both snapshots approaches on those queries. On the other hand, surprisingly, we notice that some queries' runtimes with the optimized snapshots such as Q7, Q8, Q9 or Q21 are higher than the classical snapshots even if they involve less data. Indeed, the translation of these queries into Cypher differs between the three implementations. As the time management method differs in the three models, the predicate on valid times differs even if they answer to the same business insights. Particularly, the translation of queries on a single time and multiple time points in Cypher for the optimized snapshots is more complex. These queries imply a sub-query to search for the snapshot that is the closest to the requested time instance.

Last but not least, we focus on the impact of operation types over queries' runtime: (i) comparison queries aiming at evaluating how does a graph component change over time with respect to a temporal evolution type (Q3, Q6, Q9, Q21 and Q23), (ii) aggregation queries aiming at evaluating an aggregate function (Q11, Q14, Q15, Q18 and Q27). Excluding instantaneous queries, both snapshots approaches perform the worst runtimes on aggregation and comparison queries. The temporal graph based implementation allows to save 61%–99% of classical snapshots' runtimes and 80%–99% of optimized snapshots' runtimes.

Implications. The choice of a data model to manage evolving graph data impacts significantly the storage and querying efficiency. Our model has a double advantage. First, it allows to get rid of data redundancy. So it saves a significant amount of space on the disk compared to snapshots. Second, it supports efficiently a wide range of queries while keeping the query runtime low and stable. In particular, querying an entire graph snapshot (Q28), which is the basic task

[8] The operator *keys* allows to extract the schema of a node or an edge. https://neo4j.com/docs/cypher-manual/current/functions/list/.

in the literature, is costly in snapshots approaches. The implementation with our model allows to save 35% of runtime compared to the classical snapshots implementation.

5 Conclusion and Future Works

This paper has presented a complete solution to manage graph data evolution. The power of our solution lies on the proposition of a conceptual modelling and experimental assessments to illustrate its feasibility and efficiency.

Our conceptual modelling proposes concepts allowing representing the evolution of a graph at different levels: the graph topology, the attributes' set and the attributes' value of entities and relationships. Thus, it is generic enough to be compatible with any desired applications. Moreover, it does not introduce data redundancy thanks to a different time method from snapshot-based approaches. Time is attached to each individual graph component while it is attached to the entire graph in snapshots.

To validate the feasibility of our model, we implemented it in Neo4j based on a dataset containing temporal evolution. We showed that our model is directly convertible to the data model of Neo4j based on a set of translation rules we formalized. Then, we implemented several queries. We were able to query the evolution types proposed by our model using the native querying language of Neo4j.

To highlight the efficiency of our model, we made a comparative study of its implementation with the traditional sequence of snapshots and an optimized version of snapshots based on the same dataset. We observed that our model performs better than the sequence of snapshots by reducing 12 times disk usage and by saving up to 99% on queries' execution time. In comparison to the optimized sequence of snapshots, our model reduces 9 times disk usage and saves until 99% on queries' runtime. In a nusthell, our model is an efficient solution for storing and querying a dataset with temporal evolution.

In our future works, we will extend our experiments to other types of data stores such as relational data stores since they can outperform both NoSQL graph stores and RDF triples stores [21]. This will require to extend the translation rules between the conceptual and logical level to be applicable to relational data stores. Then, we will compare the performance of these data stores in terms of storage and querying with different query languages than Cypher.

References

1. Allen, J.F.: Maintaining knowledge about temporal intervals. Commun. ACM **26**(11), 832–843 (1983). https://doi.org/10.1145/182.358434
2. Aslay, C., Nasir, M.A.U., De Francisci Morales, G., Gionis, A.: Mining frequent patterns in evolving graphs. In: Proceedings of the 27th ACM International Conference on Information and Knowledge Management, pp. 923–932. ACM, October 2018

3. Beheshti, S.M.R., Motahari-Nezhad, H.R., Benatallah, B.: Temporal Provenance Model (TPM): Model and Query Language. arXiv:1211.5009 [cs] abs/1211.5009, November 2012
4. Brunsmann, J.: Semantic exploration of archived product lifecycle metadata under schema and instance evolution. In: SDA, pp. 37–47. Citeseer (2011)
5. Cattuto, C., Quaggiotto, M., Panisson, A., Averbuch, A.: Time-varying social networks in a graph database: a Neo4j use case. In: First International Workshop on Graph Data Management Experiences and Systems, GRADES 2013, pp. 1–6. Association for Computing Machinery (2013). https://doi.org/10.1145/2484425.2484442
6. Desmier, E., Plantevit, M., Robardet, C., Boulicaut, J.-F.: Cohesive co-evolution patterns in dynamic attributed graphs. In: Ganascia, J.-G., Lenca, P., Petit, J.-M. (eds.) DS 2012. LNCS (LNAI), vol. 7569, pp. 110–124. Springer, Heidelberg (2012). https://doi.org/10.1007/978-3-642-33492-4_11
7. Fournier-Viger, P., He, G., Lin, J.C.-W., Gomes, H.M.: Mining attribute evolution rules in dynamic attributed graphs. In: Song, M., Song, I.-Y., Kotsis, G., Tjoa, A.M., Khalil, I. (eds.) DaWaK 2020. LNCS, vol. 12393, pp. 167–182. Springer, Cham (2020). https://doi.org/10.1007/978-3-030-59065-9_14
8. Hartmann, T., Fouquet, F., Moawad, A., Rouvoy, R., Le Traon, Y.: GreyCat: efficient what-if analytics for data in motion at scale. Inf. Syst. **83**, 101–117 (2019). https://doi.org/10.1016/j.is.2019.03.004
9. Holme, P., Saramäki, J.: Temporal networks. Phys. Rep. **519**(3), 97–125 (2012)
10. Huang, H., Song, J., Lin, X., Ma, S., Huai, J.: TGraph: a temporal graph data management system. In: Proceedings of the 25th ACM International on Conference on Information and Knowledge Management, pp. 2469–2472. ACM (2016)
11. Khurana, U., Deshpande, A.: Efficient snapshot retrieval over historical graph data. In: 2013 IEEE 29th International Conference on Data Engineering (ICDE), pp. 997–1008. IEEE, April 2013. https://doi.org/10.1109/ICDE.2013.6544892
12. Khurana, U., Deshpande, A.: Storing and Analyzing Historical Graph Data at Scale. arXiv:1509.08960 [cs], September 2015
13. Koloniari, G., Souravlias, D., Pitoura, E.: On Graph Deltas for Historical Queries. arXiv:1302.5549 [cs] (2013)
14. Kosmatopoulos, A., Giannakopoulou, K., Papadopoulos, A.N., Tsichlas, K.: An overview of methods for handling evolving graph sequences. In: Karydis, I., Sioutas, S., Triantafillou, P., Tsoumakos, D. (eds.) ALGOCLOUD 2015. LNCS, vol. 9511, pp. 181–192. Springer, Cham (2016). https://doi.org/10.1007/978-3-319-29919-8_14
15. Kosmatopoulos, A., Gounaris, A., Tsichlas, K.: Hinode: implementing a vertex-centric modelling approach to maintaining historical graph data. Computing **101**(12), 1885–1908 (2019). https://doi.org/10.1007/s00607-019-00715-6
16. Li, J., et al.: Predicting path failure in time-evolving graphs. In: Proceedings of the 25th ACM SIGKDD International Conference on Knowledge Discovery and Data Mining, KDD 2019, pp. 1279–1289. Association for Computing Machinery (2019)
17. Maduako, I., Wachowicz, M., Hanson, T.: STVG: an evolutionary graph framework for analyzing fast-evolving networks. J. Big Data **6**(1), 55 (2019). https://doi.org/10.1186/s40537-019-0218-z
18. Moffitt, V.Z., Stoyanovich, J.: Towards sequenced semantics for evolving graphs (2017). https://doi.org/10.5441/002/EDBT.2017.41
19. Pernelle, N., Saïs, F., Mercier, D., Thuraisamy, S.: RDF data evolution: automatic detection and semantic representation of changes. In: SEMANTiCS (2016)

20. Ravat, F., Song, J., Teste, O., Trojahn, C.: Improving the performance of querying multidimensional RDF data using aggregates. In: Proceedings of the 34th ACM/SIGAPP Symposium on Applied Computing, SAC 2019, pp. 2275–2284. Association for Computing Machinery (2019)
21. Ravat, F., Song, J., Teste, O., Trojahn, C.: Efficient querying of multidimensional RDF data with aggregates: comparing NoSQL, RDF and relational data stores. Int. J. Inf. Manag. **54**, 102089 (2020)
22. Ren, C., Lo, E., Kao, B., Zhu, X., Cheng, R.: On querying historical evolving graph sequences. Proc. VLDB Endow. **4**(11), 726–737 (2011)
23. Rodriguez, M.A., Neubauer, P.: Constructions from Dots and Lines. arXiv:1006.2361 [cs] (2010)
24. Rossi, R.A., Gallagher, B., Neville, J., Henderson, K.: Modeling dynamic behavior in large evolving graphs. In: Proceedings of the Sixth ACM International Conference on Web Search and Data Mining - WSDM 2013, pp. 667–676. ACM Press (2013)
25. Roussakis, Y., Chrysakis, I., Stefanidis, K., Flouris, G., Stavrakas, Y.: A flexible framework for understanding the dynamics of evolving RDF datasets. In: Arenas, M., et al. (eds.) ISWC 2015. LNCS, vol. 9366, pp. 495–512. Springer, Cham (2015). https://doi.org/10.1007/978-3-319-25007-6_29
26. Xiangyu, L., Yingxiao, L., Xiaolin, G., Zhenhua, Y.: An efficient snapshot strategy for dynamic graph storage systems to support historical queries. IEEE Access **8**, 90838–90846 (2020). https://doi.org/10.1109/ACCESS.2020.2994242
27. Yang, Y., Yu, J.X., Gao, H., Pei, J., Li, J.: Mining most frequently changing component in evolving graphs. World Wide Web **17**(3), 351–376 (2014)
28. Zaki, A., Attia, M., Hegazy, D., Amin, S.: Comprehensive survey on dynamic graph models. Int. J. Adv. Comput. Sci. Appl. **7**(2), 573–582 (2016). https://doi.org/10.14569/IJACSA.2016.070273

DISDi: Discontinuous Intervals in Subgroup Discovery

Reynald Eugenie(✉) and Erick Stattner

LAMIA Laboratory Université des Antilles, Pointe-à-Pitre, France
{reynald.eugenie,erick.stattner}@univ-antilles.fr

Abstract. The subgroup discovery problem aims to identify, from data, a subset of objects which exhibit interesting characteristics according to a quality measure defined on a target attribute. Main approaches in this area make the implicit assumption that optimal subgroups emerge from continuous intervals. In this paper, we propose a new approach, called DISDi, for extracting subgroups in numerical data whose originality consists of searching for subgroups on discontinuous attribute intervals. The intuition behind this approach is that disjoint intervals allow refining the definition of subgroups and therefore the quality of the subgroups identified. Thus unlike the main algorithms in the field, the novelty of our proposal lies in the way it breaks down the intervals of the attributes during the subgroup research process. The algorithm also limits the exploration of the search space by exploiting the closure property and combining some branches. The efficiency of the proposal is demonstrated by comparing the results with two algorithms that are references in the field of several benchmark datasets.

Keywords: Data science · Subgroup discovery · Knowledge extraction · Algorithm

1 Introduction

Over the last few decades, the field of data science has undergone strong development. Several factors may explain this interest: (i) The improvement of storage and calculation capacities, (ii) the explosion and heterogeneity of data available today and (iii) the heterogeneity of problems that can be addressed through data analysis approaches.

One of the most widely explored branches of data science is the search for applicable descriptive analysis methods. One of the recent approaches concerns the problem of "*subgroup discovery*" that aims to identify, from data, a subset of objects which exhibit interesting characteristics according to a quality measure defined on a target attribute. Main approaches in this area make the implicit assumption that optimal subgroups emerge from continuous intervals and attempt to identify subgroups defined with continuous attribute intervals.

In this paper, we focus on the subgroup discovery problem and we propose a new approach implemented in an algorithm called DISDi, which the originality

S. Cherfi et al. (Eds.): RCIS 2021, LNBIP 415, pp. 489–505, 2021.
https://doi.org/10.1007/978-3-030-75018-3_32

consists of searching for subgroups defined on discontinuous attribute intervals. Indeed the main approaches in the field identify subgroups only over continuous intervals that results in the identification of groups defined over wider intervals thus containing some irrelevant objects that degrade the quality function. The intuition behind the approach we propose is that disjoint intervals allow refining the definition of subgroups and therefore the quality of the subgroups identified. This approach could help to better exploit the knowledge lying in Information System when the quality can be altered by external factors which also depends on the attributes, such as pest proliferation for the agricultural sector.

For this purpose, the algorithm DISDi breaks down the intervals of the attributes during the subgroup research process to identify best attribute intervals maximizing the quality function. The algorithm also optimizes the extraction process by limiting the exploration of the search space by exploiting the closer upper-bound property and combining elements on the branches of the underlying DISDi. Finally, the approach works directly on the numerical attributes and does not require a prior discretization of attributes. The efficiency of the proposal is demonstrated by comparing the results, on several benchmark datasets, with two algorithms that are references in the field.

The paper is organized as follows. Section 2 presents the main related works. Section 3 formally defines the concept of subgroups and describes our proposal. Section 4 is devoted to the experimental results. Section 5 concludes and presents our future directions.

2 Related Works

Mining hidden information in data has become a key area to explore in many sectors. One of the recent Knowledge Extraction approaches, for descriptive purposes, is the *subgroup discovery*. The aim of subgroup discovery is to find a subset of transaction in a dataset that share similarity while maximizing a "quality" level define through a quality function. The quality function is usually defined on one or many attributes of the datasets, which are called *target variables*.

In [3], Aumann et al. presented the first version of a quality function based on association rules that linked a subset with the left hand and a particular behaviour observed in the set in the right hand. Later, many other quality measures have been proposed, such as the ones described in [11], used in order to improve the quality of the subgroups extracted. More generally, Alzmueller et al. [1] categorized them in two types: the data-driven measures, called *objective* aspect and user-driven type, the *subjective* aspect. This paper presents an overview of the main quality functions with examples of significant quality function for each type of target variable. The quality function depicted in their section Numeric Target Quality Function (see (1)) being the more significant methods will be used as the quality function in this paper.

$$q_\alpha(P) = n^\alpha(m_P - m_0) \tag{1}$$

In this equation, q_α is the quality function, P is the subgroup, n is the number of elements in the subgroup, $\alpha \in [0;1]$ is a parameter to adjust the weight of

n in the final result, and finally m_P and m_0 are respectively the means of the target value calculated on the subgroup and the whole dataset.

Regarding the subgroup discovery methods, Herrera et al. [11] introduce a classification according to three main families.

(i) **Extensions of classification algorithms.** This family of approach is based on algorithms that were devoted to find rules separating classes. They were modified to fit the task of subgroup discovery. Many of the first approaches in the field are in this category. We can cite EXPLORA [13] and MIDOS [18], which are considered as pioneers in the domain. They share their main idea which is based on the exhaustive exploitation of decision trees, but differ in the pruning method as EXPLORA use a unique table shaped dataset and doesn't prune during its search while MIDOS uses safe pruning and optimistic estimation on a multi-relational database. Some other approaches, that use the beam search strategy [17], have also been proposed, like SubgroupMiner [14] designed to extract spacial and temporal mining tools, the SD algorithm [8], which allow the user to define the *true positive* and *false positive* to guide the subgroup search, or SN2-SD [15] which is base on the CN2 algorithm [6] for instance.

(ii) **Evolutionary algorithms for extracting subgroups.** This family of approach falls into the bio-inspired methods. The main idea of these kinds of approaches is to use the share an ability in extracting fuzzy rules based description language. They are usually derived from genetic algorithms, considering each subgroup as an individual and use the quality function to determine which of them will survive through the next generation. We can especially cite MES-DIF [4], a multi-objective genetic algorithm which uses the principle of elitism in rule selection, SDIGA [7] which use linguistic rules as description languages and NMEEF-SD [5], which also use elitism but also favours simplicity and qualitative rules.

(iii) **Extensions of association algorithms.** While the previous categories are more focused towards nominal or categorical variables as target values, this family of approach cover methods that focus on the use of other types of variable. Some papers use categorical target value [2], but also binary variable [10] and numerical variables [2,16]. In this last category, the SD-MAP [2] proposed by Atzmueller et al. showed excellent results and was a reference to the domain for years. More recently, Millot et al. proposed OSMIND [16] which is considered today as the benchmark of the domain. Although it doesn't need a prior discretization of the data, their method is able to extract optimal subgroups through a fast but exhaustive search, surpassing the results of SD-MAP.

If these approaches are all able to extract subgroups, they make the implicit assumption that subgroups are only identified over continuous attribute intervals. Indeed, they consider continuous intervals, while in fact meaningful information can be found by taking discontinuous algorithms into account. In this paper, we propose the DISDi algorithm, which falls in the third family of algorithms and that aims to identify subgroups possibly define on discontinuous attribute intervals.

3 DISDi Algorithm

3.1 Preliminaries

Let D be a dataset constituted with a set of attributes A and a set of transactions T such as: $\forall t \in T, \forall a \in A, \exists v$ such that $t[a] = v$. The search for subgroup discovery aims to find interesting patterns which describe a particular set of objects according to a quality function q_α (see Eq. 1).

In [2], Atzmueller et al. pinpoints 4 properties needed in order to conduct a Subgroup Discovery: (1) A quality function q_α that evaluate the quality of the subgroup, (2) a target variable a_{target} (or a group of target variables), used in the quality function, (3) a subgroup description language in which the format of the subgroup description is defined and (4) a search strategy, essentially the concept of the algorithm used for the extraction.

Obviously, the target variable depends on the dataset; nevertheless in this study we always work with non-discretized numerical variable as targets. As for the description language, we define a subgroup g as a set of objects called "selectors", s_i composed of a left part and a right part. The left part is an attribute a_i in A, while the right part is an interval or a set of intervals leading to a restriction on the value upon the a_i attribute.

For the quality function, we consider the function which is commonly used for the numeric target quality function [1] described previously in the Eq. 1.

At last, the search strategy used the principle of a FP-Tree which specificity will be explained further.

More formally, for each attribute a_i in A, the values Min_i and Max_i are defined respectively as the minimal and maximal value of the dataset on the attribute a_i.

Definition 1: Selector. A selector s_j is defined as a couple of objects (l_j,r_j) with $l_j = a_i \in A$ and r_j such as

$$r_j = \bigcup_{1 \to nb_I}^{k} [min_k; max_k] \tag{2}$$

where $min_1 \geq Min_i$, $max_{nb_I} \leq Max_i$ and $max_k < min_{k+1}$

We can then define the two functions lh the function which return the left part of a given selector and rh which return its right part, namely $lh : s_j \to l_j$ and $rh : s_j \to r_j$. We note S the set of all possible selectors.

Definition 2: Extent of a selector. For every selector s_j, we can define its extent $ext(s_j)$ as the transactions of T for which the value of the attribute $lh(s_j)$ is in the range of $rh(s_i)$.

$$ext(s_j) = \{t \in T \text{ such as } t\left[lh\left(s_j\right)\right] \in rh\left(s_j\right)\} \tag{3}$$

Definition 3: Extent of a subgroup. The extent $ext(g)$ of a subgroup g composed by the selectors $s_1, s_2, ..., s_l$ is the intersection of the extent of its selectors.

$$ext(g) = \bigcap_{1 \to l}^{k} ext(s_k) \tag{4}$$

Property 1: Closer Upper-Bound. For a subgroup g, a closer upper-bound $ub(g)$ can be identified as the highest value theoretically reachable with the combination of the transactions in $ext(g)$. This bound can be found by the formula:

$$ub(g) = max\left(q_\alpha(Top_1), q_\alpha(Top_2), ..., q_\alpha(Top_{\|ext(g)\|}),\right) \tag{5}$$

with Top_n the set of the n transactions of $ext(g)$ with the highest target value.

Proof. Let consider a set of transactions g_{small} with nb_{small} elements and sum_{small} the sum of the targets value of its transactions. For two transactions t_1 and t_2 with val_1 and val_2 as their value on the target variable, with $val_1 \geq val_2$ we can calculate the score of the new sets created by adding t_1 and t_2 to g_{small}, respectively g_1 and g_2:

$$val_1 \geq val_2 \Rightarrow sum_{small} + val_1 \geq sum_{small} + val_2$$

$$\Rightarrow mean_1 = \tfrac{sum_{small}+val_1}{nb_{small}+1} \geq \tfrac{sum_{small}+val_2}{nb_{small}+1} = mean_2$$

$$\Rightarrow q_\alpha(g_1) = n^\alpha\left(mean_1 - m_0\right) \geq n^\alpha\left(mean_2 - m_0\right) = q_\alpha(g_2)$$

In this way, using any subgroup g allows to create the best subsets of elements maximizing the quality function in the Eq. 1 for each possible size. Thus, the highest value determines the best score that any subset of g can achieve.

3.2 Algorithm

The DISDi algorithm aims to identify the ranges of value for each attributes which can define meaningful subgroups. However, unlike the existing main approaches this method can extract subgroups with discontinuous intervals for the attributes through unions of disjoint intervals.

The main idea behind the approach is that the subgroups defined on discontinuous intervals better describe the complexity of the phenomena studied.

As it can be seen in Fig. 1, DISDi performs the search for subgroups in 3 main steps:

1. **Extraction of the raw selectors**, the first intervals which will serve as a basis for the composition of the subgroups (detailed in Algorithm 2).
2. **Construction of the FP-Tree** by using the extracted raw selectors (see Algorithm 3).
3. **Combination of the nodes of the FP-Tree** to create the subgroups. Their score will be determined at this point, and the bests will be conserved (as shown is Algorithm 4).

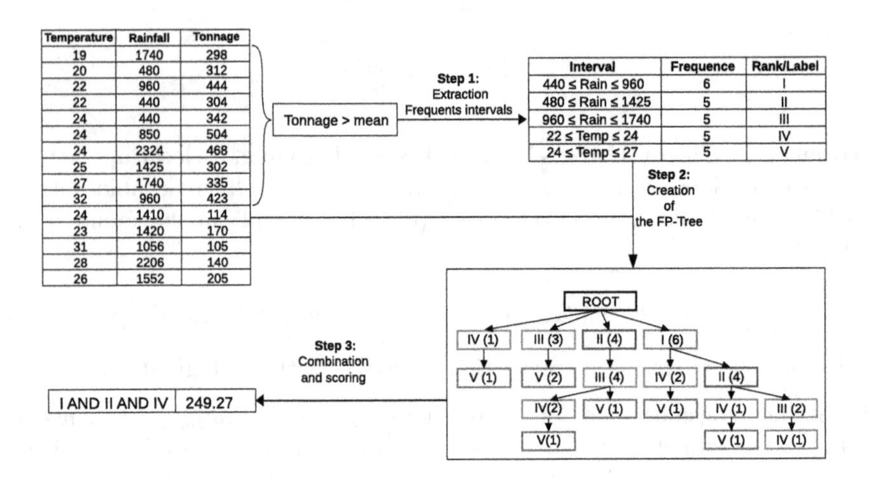

Fig. 1. Main steps of DISDi Algorithm

Furthermore, the algorithm presents two other notable features. The first one concerns the selectors extracted, as they can now be unions of intervals. As such, a corresponding extraction methods was implemented, using the closer upper-bound properties on the subgroup in the FP-Tree (see Property 1). The other feature is caused by the structure of conventional FP-Trees. Usually, in the process of creating an FP-Tree, the selectors using the same attributes are disjoints. As such, on one branch we should have a maximum of only $\|A\|$ elements, which is the number of attributes. However, in the case of DISDi we can have many selectors of the same attribute on the same branch, as it can be seen in Fig. 1.

The result of the process is a set of subgroups that maximize the quality function, with either an interval or the union of two discontinuous intervals. The interest in this discontinuity lies in the fact that inside a promising subgroup, they can be sub-part because of which the quality function drop significantly.

An example can be taken on the banana crop: In [9], Ganry states that the growth temperature of the banana crop is defined between 9 degree Celsius and 40 degree Celsius, and that the optimal temperature should be around 28 degree Celsius. As an example, let's consider a range of five degrees around this optimal value as the optimal interval. The interval $[23; 33]$ will be considered as the interval of temperature for a good harvest. However in some region a fungus named black sigatoka parasite the leaves of the banana tree. From the infection results harmful effect on the growth of the crops and on the overall productivity. In [12], Jacome et al. define the optimal temperature of this fungus is in the range of $[25; 28]$ degree. The existence of this parasite drops the value of the $[23; 33]$ interval. With our methods, we should be able to remove $[25; 28]$, and extract the optimal $[23; 25] \cup [28; 33]$ intervals.

The tasks of the DISDi algorithm can be divided in three main steps as shown on Algorithm 1: (i) The creation of the firsts basic selectors that will be used to create the complete and final selectors, which we call raw selectors (line 4), (ii) the creation of the FP-Tree using those raw selectors (line 6) and finally (iii) the combination and scoring of the branches of the tree from which result the final subgroups (lines 7 and 8).

Algorithm 1. DISDi

Require: A : list of attributes, a_{target} : target variable, T : list of transactions , β : support threshold
Ensure: *listSubGroup* : list of the subgroup sorted by their quality
1: S_{raw} : set of selectors
2: $Tree$: FP-Tree
3: *listSubGroup*: list of the identified subgroup
4: $S_{raw} = MAKE\_RAW\_SELECTORS(A, a_{target}, T)$
5: $sort(S_{raw})$
6: $Tree = MAKE\_TREE(T, S_{raw})$
7: $listSubGroup = BRANCH\_COMBINER(FPTree)$
8: $getBestScore(listSubGroup)$

The objective of the first step is to extract raw selectors which will be used in the FP-Tree (see Algorithm 2).

In order to extract the raw selectors S_{raw}, DISDi bases its treatment on $pos(T)$, the subset of transactions with a higher value on their target variable than the mean of the population. Then DISDi starts with the complete interval of each attribute a_i and erodes them into smaller sets in the method *createSubIntervalWithErosion* (line 5).

Each set extracted have to verify the following rules:

1. The subset can be defined by either a continuous interval or the union of two intervals $[a; b] \cup [c; d]$ such as $[a; b] \cap [c; d] = \emptyset$.
2. The number of transactions of $[a; b]$ has to be higher than a fifth of the number of elements in $[c; d]$ and conversely, in order to mitigate the union between a meaningful interval and an irrelevant one.
3. The number of transactions of the subset have to be higher than a given support threshold β.

At the end of this first step, the algorithm creates for each attribute a_i a set S_i of selectors $s_{i,j}$ which are merged in S_{raw}.

For instance, in Fig. 1, the considered target variable is Tonnage, which has an average value of 298. Thus, all of the transaction with a higher value on the Tonnage attribute were taken and considered as the basis for the extraction of the raw selectors. The range of the temperature of the interesting subpart is from 19 to 32. By removing an existing value between these limits, we can obtain two kinds of selectors, with continuous intervals (for example [20; 32]) or discontinuous intervals (for example $[19; 20] \cup [24; 32]$).

Algorithm 2. MAKE_RAW_SELECTORS

Require: A : list of attributes, a_{target} : target variable, T : list of transactions , β : support threshold
Ensure: S_{raw} : List of the selectors s for which $ext(s) \cap pos(T) > \beta$
1: $S = \{\}$
2: **for** i **from** 0 **to** $|A|$ **do**
3: $interval = \{Min_i; Max_i\}$
4: $S_i = createSubIntervalWithErosion(a_i, a_{target}, pos(T), interval, \beta)$
5: $add(S_i, S_{raw})$
6: **end for**
7: **return** S_{raw}

In both cases, the intervals are eroded. The erosion consists of the suppression of the boundaries of the intervals, leading to two potential subgroups when applied on a continuous interval and up to four when applied to a discontinuous interval:

$$erode([20;32]) : \{[22;32], [20;27]\}$$

$$erode([19;20] \cup [24;32]) : \{ [20;20] \cup [24;32],\ [19;19] \cup [24;32],\ [19;20] \cup [25;32],\ [19;20] \cup [24;27]\}$$

In this example, DISDi goes on with the continuous interval for the sake of understanding. Then, the intervals are eroded until they reach the threshold β, which is fixed at 33% of the size of the dataset in this case.

As a result, the final selectors extracted are the **I**, **II**, and **III** for the Rainfall attribute and the **IV** and **V** for the Temperature attribute.

In the second part, DISDi uses the selectors extracted in step 1 in order to build the FP-Tree. This step is detailed in Algorithm 3. Each node of the tree represents an object constituted by a selector, the list of the transaction IDs which had reached the node and the sum of the value of their target variable. In order to obtain the final tree, the algorithm classifies all of the selectors by their frequencies.

For each transaction of the database, the FP-Tree is modified as follows: The process starts at the root and check if the transaction t is included in the first selector s_1. While it's not included, DISDi recursively move to the next selector s_{i+1}. When t matches s_i, if the current node has a child which corresponds to the selector, the values of this child are increased accordingly. Otherwise, the algorithm creates the corresponding child node. Then, the child becomes the current node, and DISDi continue to browse the selectors until the last one.

Following the previous example of Fig. 1, the 5 raw selectors were extracted. Thus, starting from the root, the tree is created using the transactions.

The first transaction only matches the selector **III**, thus at this point of the process a node $node_{III}$ is created with the label of the selector and the information of the transaction. Then the node is added as the descendant of the root. Likely, the second transaction matches the selectors **I** and **II**. Thus, a node $node_I$ is created below the root with the higher selector **I**, and $node_{I,II}$ its

Algorithm 3. MAKE_TREE

Require: T : list of transactions, S_{raw} : list of selectors
Ensure: $FPTree$: the FP-Tree of the dataset

```
 1: FPTree = newRootTree()
 2: for all t ∈ T do
 3:    actNode = root(FPTree)
 4:    for all s ∈ S_raw do
 5:       if valid(t, s) then
 6:          if s ∈ children(actNode) then
 7:             actNode = child(actNode, s)
 8:             addToNode(t, actNode)
 9:          else
10:             childNode = newNode(t, s, actNode)
11:             actNode = childNode
12:          end if
13:       end if
14:    end for
15: end for
16: return FPTree
```

descendant with the second selector **II**. For both of them, the information of the second transaction is stocked.

In the case of the third transaction which matches the selectors **I**, **II**, **III** and **IV**, the nodes corresponding to the first and second selector already exist, so the information of the current transaction is added on $node_I$ and $node_{I,II}$, then new nodes are created with the selector **III**, and finally **IV**.

At last, the complete FP-Tree is obtained when all of the transactions went through this process.

In the last part of our method, DISDi has to aggregate the information of the generated FP-Tree in order to extract the subgroups with the highest score. In Algorithm 4, for each selector the algorithm aggregates the information of the branches to generate the other more frequent selectors who could be associated with. Then, subgroups are extracted by combination. In order to decrease the number of combinations that need to be tested, the first step of this task is to separately generate the intervals for each attribute, in order to mitigate the redundancy of combinations with the same result. Then we use the closer upper-bound property in order to prune the subgroups which has no chance of giving a higher score than the current-best subgroups.

In the case of the Fig. 1, the combination starts with the selector **V**. The subgroup composed of this selector only contains 7 transactions with an average of 324.28 on the target value. Using the Eq. 1, the score of 70.25 is calculated, and with the Property 1 its closer upper-bound of 266.25 is obtained. Then, the best score registered is 70.25, and as the upper-bound is higher, the process can resume with combinations of **V**, starting with **{IV,V}**.

This subgroup is composed of 4 transactions with an average value of 357. As previously done, the score 118.53 and the closer upper-bound 266.25

Algorithm 4. BRANCH_COMBINER

Require: $FPTree$: the generated FP-Tree, $listSelector$: list of the selectors
Ensure: $listSubGroup$: List of the candidate subgroups with their quality

```
1: listSubGroup = {}
2: topSubGroup = {}
3: for all interval_i ∈ listSelector do
4:    combiSelec = allBranchesWith(interval_i)
5:    for all a_i ∈ A do
6:       S_i = listCombi(a_i, combiSelec)
7:    end for
8:    for all i : 1 → ||A|| do
9:       for all s ∈ S_i do
10:         newCandidate = {}
11:         for all g ∈ listSubgroup do
12:            ng = combi(s, g)
13:            updateIfHigher(ng, topSubGroup)
14:            if up(ng) > q_α(topSubGroup) then
15:               add(ng, newCandidate)
16:            end if
17:         end for
18:         addAll(newCandidate, listSubgroup)
19:      end for
20:   end for
21: end for
22: return listSubGroup
```

are calculated. As the quality of the current subgroup outperform the quality of the previous one, the best subgroup is updated. However, the upper-bound is still higher than the best score, thus the combination continues.

At some point, the case of the subgroup **{III,V}** will be treated. Its also have 4 transactions, but the average on the target value is only 239, leading to a score of -356.46. Even its closer upper-bound proves to be 29.36, and this value is far from the 118.53, the score of the best current subgroup. Thus, DISDi will not extract the subgroups resulting from a combination of **{III,V}**.

An implementation in java of DISDi algorithm has been implemented in *Java* and it is available on GitHub[1].

4 Experimental Results

This section describes the performances of our algorithm through comparison with SD-MAP and OSMIND, that are reference algorithms in the field. They are two different algorithms since SD-MAP is based on an exhaustive search method which uses a FP-Tree, while OSMIND relies on the properties of the subgroup discovery in order to prune the search space considerably.

[1] https://github.com/rey-sama/DISDi.git.

First, the datasets used in the experiments are detailed, then we focus on the subgroup which presents the best score for each algorithm and raw dataset. Afterward, the impact of the size of the dataset on the quality is shown by altering it. At last, the structure of subgroups is studied to show the difference provided by DISDi compared to the others.

4.1 Test Environment

The 4 datasets which were used come from the Bilkent repository[2]. They are traditionally used as a benchmark for evaluated performances of subgroup discovery algorithms. (1) Airport (AP), which contains air hubs in the United States as defined by the Federal Aviation Administration. (2) Bolt (BL), which gathers data from an experiment on the effects of machine adjustments on the time to count bolt. (3) Body data (Body) which represents data on body Temperature and Heart Rate. (4) Pollution (Pol) which are data on pollution of cities. The number of attributes as well as the number of transactions varies from a dataset to another, as shown in Table 1.

Table 1. Description of the datasets

	Airport	Bolt	Body	Pollution
Nb. attributes	5	7	2	15
Nb. transactions	135	40	130	60

For each dataset, all attributes are numeric attributes and they have not been discretized beforehand. Such a comparison is interesting as the discretization may not be an intuitive operation for a complex dataset, due to the multiple existing ways. Thus observing these results under those circumstances may reveal the actual capacity of the subgroup discovery algorithm in front of this configuration. In our experiments, we always use the lowest β threshold with DISDi that gives the best results.

4.2 Best Quality on Raw Dataset

In a first step, we have studied the performances of the algorithm by comparing the best subgroups. The best score overall was used to normalize the value. The results can be seen in Fig. 2.

[2] http://pcaltay.cs.bilkent.edu.tr/DataSets/.

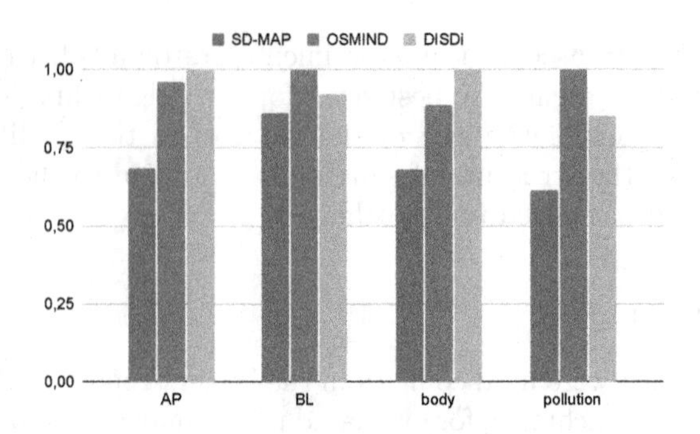

Fig. 2. Comparison of the quality value of the best subgroup identified

The first observation which can be made is that for all of the tested datasets, DISDi performs better than SD-MAP. On average, the gain brought by DISDi is 29.14%. Thus a great margin can be observed on every studied dataset, except in the case of the BL dataset where the scores obtained by the 3 algorithms are pretty close.

In the case of BL, this result suggests that the interval splitting performed by DISDi does not improve the quality on the BL dataset. We can also note that it is the unique dataset for which DISDi returned a non-split subgroup definition as detailed later in Table 2.

Regarding the comparison with OSMIND, we can observe that the scores are quite close for every datasets. In two of them (AP and body), DISDi extracts subgroups with a better quality. These results thus show the interest of the approach and the discontinuous subgroup search process it introduces.

More globally, for the datasets for which the splitting was done, the average gain provided by the approach proposed is 0.65% compared to OSMIND and 44.26% compared to SD-MAP.

4.3 Best Quality on Resized Dataset

In the second part, we focus on the evolution of the gain provided by our approach according to different dataset sizes. The gain is calculated as the difference between our algorithm and the others, divided by their own score as depicted in the equation below.

$$GAIN_{DISDi} = \frac{Score_{DISDi} - Score_{their}}{Score_{their}}$$

We decided to take into account 4 thresholds for the size of the datasets: 10, 20, 50 and 100 when the dataset was large enough.

Figure 3 shows the evolution of the gain on the quality score of the best subgroups for (a) Airport, (b) Bolt, (c) Body and (d) Pollution with different dataset sizes.

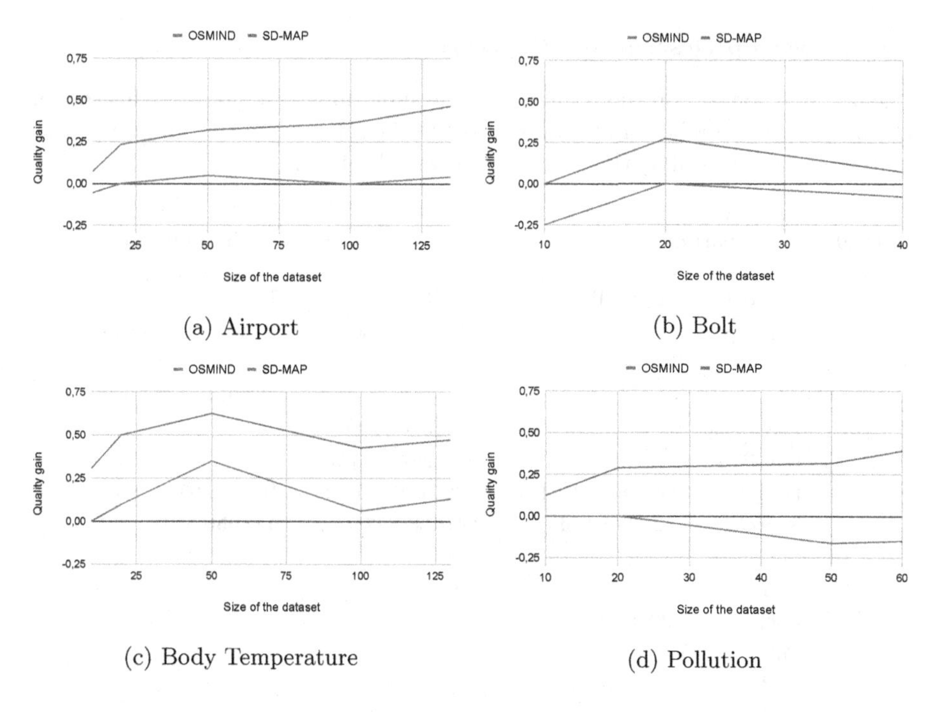

(a) Airport

(b) Bolt

(c) Body Temperature

(d) Pollution

Fig. 3. Evolution of quality of the best subgroup according to the dataset size

First of all, we can observe that DISDi always performs better than SD-Map since the gain on the score is higher. In most of the cases, the gain exceeds 25% compared to SD-Map. This demonstrates that the approach we propose is able to maintain good performances even when the number of transactions changes.

On the other hand, the results are less homogeneous with OSMIND.

For most of the other datasets, the results are quite positive. For instance, on the Bolt dataset (see Fig. 3b), we observe that at first DISDi starts with a great disadvantage (−25%) but then reduce the gap to less than 8% with more data.

The Airport dataset (see Fig. 3a) is interesting, because we can see that OSMIND and DISDi are very close. In some configurations, the gain is even positive, that reflects the advantage provided by DISDi compared OSMIND on this dataset.

The best results are shown in the Body dataset where the average gain of 12.5%. The gain for this dataset is less subtle than the others, with a maximum gain reaching almost 25% on the dataset with the higher number of transactions.

Nevertheless, in the case of the pollution dataset (see Fig. 3d), at first DISDi seems to match the result of OSMIND with a neutral gain when the number of transactions is low, but the advantage seems to be in favour of OSMIND when the number of transaction increase, with a final gain of approximately 15%. However, the subgroup found in DISDi, even in this situation are still pertinent considering their structure.

4.4 Subgroup Description Structure

The last part focuses on the structure of the subgroups extracted. In this section we compare the number of attributes used in the selectors of the subgroups that were identified as well as the score which was obtained.

Table 2. Comparison of the attributes involved in the best subgroups identified

	Attributes	SD-MAP	OSMIND	DISDi
AP	Sch_Depart		[35891;322430]	[154067.0;322430.0] ∪ [35891.0;80651.0]
	Perf_Depart		[35273;332338]	
	Enp_Pass		[1362282;25636383]	
	Freight	[300463.8;300463.8]	[142660.95;352823.5]	[127815.09;352823.5]
	Score	**128949.184**	**181638.8478**	**188956.3515**
BL	Col0		[6;39]	
	Col1	[6;6]	[6;6]	
	Col2	[30;30]		
	Col3			
	Col4			
	Col5			
	Col6		[28.89;134.01]	[39.74;134.01]
	Score	**117.9793522**	**137.1097193**	**126.4146843**
Body	body_temp	[98.6;98.6]	[98.3;98.6]	[98.3;98.6]∪[98.8;99.1]
	gender	[2;2]	[2;2]	
	Score	**17.476**	**22.77044306**	**25.70255285**
POL	prec		[30.0;54.0]	[37.0;54.0]
	jant		[23.0;54.0]	[23.0;26.0]∪[33.0;54.0]
	jult		[70.0;82.0]	
	ovr65		[7.3;11.1]	[6.5;9.3]
	popn		[3.03;3.49]	
	educ		[9.6;11.3]	
	hous		[66.8;87.5]	
	dens		[2302.0;7462.0]	
	nonw		[3.5;38.5]	
	wwdrk		[41.3;50.7]	
	poor	[24.2;24.2]	[10.7;26.4]	
	hc		[8.0;88.0]	
	nox		[8.0;63.0]	
	so			
	humid		[53.0,62.0]	
	Score	**176.8148791**	**289.2901592**	**246.0609474**

Table 2 details the subgroups extracted on each dataset by the three algorithms. This study highlights very interesting results. Each group of line concern a dataset, with each individual line representing either an attribute of the dataset or the score. Then, each column defined an algorithm and the inner cells the restriction of the interval found by the algorithm for its best subgroup.

Indeed, while the Subsect. 4.2 pinpointed a constant better quality score of DISDi than SD-MAP, we can see in Table 2 that for every dataset, the number of attributes used by our algorithm is at most half of the number used by OSMIND and SD-MAP, except for the pollution dataset with the latter.

For the dataset Pollution, DISDi used a fifth of the attributes while OSMIND used almost all of them. Nevertheless, its only result in a drop of less than 15% of the overall quality. A similar observation can be made in the case of the Bolt dataset. Moreover, it is the only dataset for which DISDi didn't use any dissociate intervals, leaving another room for improvement.

However, the strong point of our approach can be seen in the datasets Aiport and Body, where even with the use of fewer attributes, we were able to find subgroups with better score than OSMIND, especially in the case of the Body dataset.

5 Conclusion

In this paper, we have addressed the problem of subgroups discovery in numerical data and we have presented DISDi, a new algorithm able to extract unusual subgroups composed of discontinued intervals.

Unlike the main approaches in the field that only extract subgroups defined on continuous attribute intervals, the method we have proposed uses successive erosion of intervals to generate the first raw selectors. These selectors are then used in a fitted FP-Tree, allowing the existence of branches with multiple selectors on the same attributes. To minimize the complexity of such tree, some optimizations have been added at the creation to subgroups, by merging the information of the branches which share the same raw selector, then precombine the nodes with similar attributes. Furthermore, the search space was also reduced by exploiting the closer upper-bound property.

We have conducted experiments to compare DISDi to the two reference algorithms in the field. The results have highlighted interesting features since we have shown that in several cases the performances were better for DISDi with more simply defined subgroups. Thus these results have demonstrated the interest of our approach that lies in the search for discontinuous intervals in subgroup discovery.

As a short-term perspective, we plan to address the scaling up of the approach and particularly the subgroup discovery on large datasets. For this purpose, the first tracks would be a better exploitation of the properties linked to the subgroup and also overcome the constrains linked to the use of FP-Trees. Finally, in the medium term, it would be interesting to study the portability of the algorithm on big data frameworks such as Hadoop or Spark.

References

1. Atzmueller, M.: Subgroup discovery. Wiley Interdiscip. Rev. Data Min. Knowl. Discov. **5**(1), 35–49 (2015)
2. Atzmueller, M., Puppe, F.: SD-Map – a fast algorithm for exhaustive subgroup discovery. In: Fürnkranz, J., Scheffer, T., Spiliopoulou, M. (eds.) PKDD 2006. LNCS (LNAI), vol. 4213, pp. 6–17. Springer, Heidelberg (2006). https://doi.org/10.1007/11871637_6
3. Aumann, Y., Lindell, Y.: A statistical theory for quantitative association rules. J. Intell. Inf. Syst. **20**(3), 255–283 (2003)
4. Berlanga, F., del Jesus, M.J., González, P., Herrera, F., Mesonero, M.: Multiobjective evolutionary induction of subgroup discovery fuzzy rules: a case study in marketing. In: Perner, P. (ed.) ICDM 2006. LNCS (LNAI), vol. 4065, pp. 337–349. Springer, Heidelberg (2006). https://doi.org/10.1007/11790853_27
5. Carmona, C.J., González, P., del Jesus, M.J., Herrera, F.: NMEEF-SD: non-dominated multiobjective evolutionary algorithm for extracting fuzzy rules in subgroup discovery. IEEE Trans. Fuzzy Syst. **18**(5), 958–970 (2010)
6. Clark, P., Niblett, T.: The CN2 induction algorithm. Mach. Learn. **3**(4), 261–283 (1989)
7. Del Jesus, M.J., González, P., Herrera, F., Mesonero, M.: Evolutionary fuzzy rule induction process for subgroup discovery: a case study in marketing. IEEE Trans. Fuzzy Syst. **15**(4), 578–592 (2007)
8. Gamberger, D., Lavrac, N.: Expert-guided subgroup discovery: methodology and application. J. Artif. Intell. Res. **17**, 501–527 (2002)
9. Ganry, J.: Étude du développement du système foliaire du bananier en fonction de la température (1973)
10. Grosskreutz, H., Rüping, S., Shaabani, N., Wrobel, S.: Optimistic estimate pruning strategies for fast exhaustive subgroup discovery. Technical report, Fraunhofer Institute IAIS (2008)
11. Herrera, F., Carmona, C.J., González, P., Del Jesus, M.J.: An overview on subgroup discovery: foundations and applications. Knowl. Inf. Syst. **29**(3), 495–525 (2011)
12. Jacome, L.H., Schuh, W., et al.: Effects of leaf wetness duration and temperature on development of black sigatoka disease on banana infected by mycosphaerella fijiensis var. difformis. Phytopathology **82**(5), 515–520 (1992)
13. Klösgen, W.: Explora: a multipattern and multistrategy discovery assistant. In: Advances in Knowledge Discovery and Data Mining, pp. 249–271 (1996)
14. Klösgen, W., May, M.: Census data mining-an application. In: Proceedings of the 6th European Conference on Principles of Data Mining and Knowledge Discovery, pp. 65–79 (2002)
15. Lavrač, N., Kavšek, B., Flach, P., Todorovski, L.: Subgroup discovery with CN2-SD. J. Mach. Learn. Res. **5**(Feb), 153–188 (2004)
16. Millot, A., Cazabet, R., Boulicaut, J.-F.: Optimal subgroup discovery in purely numerical data. In: Lauw, H.W., Wong, R.C.-W., Ntoulas, A., Lim, E.-P., Ng, S.-K., Pan, S.J. (eds.) PAKDD 2020. LNCS (LNAI), vol. 12085, pp. 112–124. Springer, Cham (2020). https://doi.org/10.1007/978-3-030-47436-2_9

17. Ney, H., Haeb-Umbach, R., Tran, B.H., Oerder, M.: Improvements in beam search for 10000-word continuous speech recognition. In: IEEE International Conference on Acoustics, Speech, and Signal Processing, vol. 1, pp. 9–12. IEEE Computer Society (1992)
18. Wrobel, S.: An algorithm for multi-relational discovery of subgroups. In: Komorowski, J., Zytkow, J. (eds.) PKDD 1997. LNCS, vol. 1263, pp. 78–87. Springer, Heidelberg (1997). https://doi.org/10.1007/3-540-63223-9_108

Building Correct Taxonomies with a Well-Founded Graph Grammar

Jeferson O. Batista[1], João Paulo A. Almeida[1(✉)], Eduardo Zambon[1], and Giancarlo Guizzardi[1,2]

[1] Federal University of Espírito Santo, Vitória, Brazil
jeferson.batista@aluno.ufes.br, jpalmeida@ieee.org, zambon@inf.ufes.br

[2] Free University of Bozen-Bolzano, Bolzano, Italy
gguizzardi@unibz.it

Abstract. Taxonomies play a central role in conceptual domain modeling having a direct impact in areas such as knowledge representation, ontology engineering, software engineering, as well as in knowledge organization in information sciences. Despite their key role, there is in the literature little guidance on how to build high-quality taxonomies, with notable exceptions such as the OntoClean methodology, and the ontology-driven conceptual modeling language OntoUML. These techniques take into account the ontological meta-properties of types to establish well-founded rules for forming taxonomic structures. In this paper, we show how to leverage on the formal rules underlying these techniques to build taxonomies which are *correct by construction*. We define a set of correctness-preserving operations to systematically introduce types and subtyping relations into taxonomic structures. To validate our proposal, we formalize these operations as a graph grammar. Moreover, to demonstrate our claim of correctness by construction, we use automatic verification techniques over the grammar language to show that: (i) all taxonomies produced by the grammar rules are correct; and (ii) the rules can generate all correct taxonomies.

Keywords: Conceptual modeling · Taxonomies · Graph grammar

1 Introduction

Taxonomies are structures connecting types via *subtyping* (i.e., type specialization) relations. They are fundamental for conceptual domain modeling and have a central organizing role in areas such as knowledge representation, ontology engineering, object-oriented modeling, as well as in knowledge organization in information sciences (e.g., in the construction of vocabularies and other lexical resources). Despite their key role in all these areas, there is in the literature little guidance on how to build high-quality taxonomies.

A notable exception is OntoClean [4]. OntoClean was a pioneering methodology that provided a number of guidelines for diagnosing and repairing taxonomic relations that were inconsistent from an ontological point of view.

S. Cherfi et al. (Eds.): RCIS 2021, LNBIP 415, pp. 506–522, 2021.
https://doi.org/10.1007/978-3-030-75018-3_33

These guidelines were grounded on a number of *formal meta-properties*, i.e., properties characterizing types. Derived from these meta-properties, the methodology would offer a number of formal rules governing how types characterized by different meta-properties could be associated to each other in well-formed taxonomies.

OntoClean has been sucessfully employed to evaluate and suggest repairs to several important resources (e.g., WordNet [13]). However, being a methodology, it does not offer a representation mechanism for building taxonomies according to its prescribed rules. Also with the intention of addressing that problem, in [8], the authors (including one of OntoClean's original authors) proposed a UML profile with modeling distinctions based on an extension of OntoClean's meta-properties and rules. That profile would later become the basis of the OntoUML modeling language [5], incorporating syntactic rules to prevent the construction of incorrect taxonomies in conceptual models. In [6], the language has its full formal semantics defined in terms of a (proved-consistent) ontological theory, and its abstract syntax defined in terms of a metamodel. In particular, the latter is an extension of the UML 2.0 metamodel, redesigned to reflect the ontological distinctions and axiomatization put forth by that theory. These distinctions and constraints, in turn, have influenced other prominent modeling languages, e.g., ORM [9].

As argued in [15], instead of leveraging on this axiomatization by proposing methodological rules (as in OntoClean) or semantically-motivated syntactical constraints (as in the OntoUML metamodel), a representation system based on this ontological theory could employ a more productive strategy. It could leverage on that fact that the theory's formal constraints impose a correspondence between each particular type of type (characterized by those ontological meta-properties) and certain modeling *structures* (or modeling *patterns*). In other words, a representation system grounded on this ontological theory is a *pattern language*, i.e., a system whose basic building blocks are not low-granularity primitives such as types and relations but higher-granularity patterns formed by types and relations. A MOF-based metamodel (such as UML's) simply isn't capable of naturally capturing this fundamental aspect of such a representation system.

In [17], some of us have proposed a first attempt to formalize a representation system based on that ontological theory as a true Pattern Grammar, i.e., as a Graph Grammar with transformation rules capturing these patterns and their possible relations. Hence, this paper can be seen as an extension of that work. On one hand, it is focused on types and taxonomic relations. On the other hand, it extends that original work in providing a complete set of graph transformation rules. Moreover, we use automatic verification techniques over the grammar state space (language) to show the correctness of the taxonomies produced by the grammar and the capability of the grammar to generate all correct taxonomies.

This work contributes to the foundations of rigorous conceptual modeling by identifying the set of rules that should be considered as primitives in the design of correct taxonomies. Moreover, it does that in a metamodel-independent way, so the results presented here can be incorporated into different modeling languages (again, e.g., ORM) as well as different tools used by different communities (e.g., as a modeling plugin to Semantic Web tools such as Protégé[1]).

The remainder of this paper is structured as follows. In Sect. 2, we review the ontological foundations used in this work. In particular, we present a number of ontological meta-properties, a typology of types derived from them, and the formal constraints governing the subtyping relations between these types. In Sect. 3, we present the graph transformation grammar with operations that take into account the distinctions and constraints discussed in Sect. 2. In Sect. 4, we discuss the formal verification of the grammar. Finally, Sect. 5 presents some concluding remarks.

2 Ontological Foundations

In this section, we present some ontological distinctions that are the basis for the remainder of this paper. These notions and the constraints governing their definitions and relations correspond to a fragment of the foundational ontology underlying OntoUML, and which incorporates and extends the theory of types underling OntoClean [5,7]. For an in depth discussion, philosophical justification, empirical support, and full formal characterization of these notions, one should refer to [5,6].

Types represent properties that are shared by a set of possible instances. The set of properties shared by those instances is termed the *intension* of type; the set of instances that share those properties (i.e., the instances of that type) is termed the *extension* of that type. Types can change their extension across different circumstances, either because things come in and out of existence, or because things can acquire and lose some of those properties captured in the intension of that type.

Taxonomic structures capture *subtyping* relations among types, both from *intensional* and *extensional* points of view. In other words, subtyping is thus a relation between types that govern the relation between the possible instances of those types. So, if type B is a subtype of A then we have that: (i) it is necessarily the case that all instances of B are instances of A, i.e., in all possible circumstances, the extension of B subsets the extension of A; and (ii) all properties captured by the *intension* of A are included in the *intension* of type B, *i.e.*, B's are A's and, therefore, B's have all properties that are properties defined for type A.

Suppose all instances that exist in a domain of interest are *endurants*[6]. Endurants roughly correspond to what we call *objects* in ordinary language, i.e., things that (in contrast to occurrences, events) endure in time changing their properties while maintaining their identity. Examples include you, each author of this paper, Mick Jagger, the Moon, the Federal University of Espírito Santo.

Every endurant in our domain belongs to one **Kind**. In other words, central to any domain of interest we will have a number of object kinds, i.e., the genuine fundamental

[1] https://protege.stanford.edu/.

types of objects that exist in that domain. The term "kind" is meant here in a strong technical sense, i.e., by a kind, we mean a type capturing *essential* properties of the things it classifies. In other words, the objects classified by that kind could not possibly exist without being of that specific kind [6].

Kinds tessellate the possible space of objects in that domain, i.e., all objects belong to exactly one kind and do so necessarily. Typical examples of kinds include Person, Organization, and Car. We can, however, have other static subdivisions (or subtypes) of a kind. These are naturally termed **Subkinds**. As an example, the kind 'Person' can be specialized in the (biological) subkinds 'Man' and 'Woman'.

Endurant kinds and subkinds represent essential properties of objects. They are examples of **Rigid Types** [6]). Rigid types are those types that classify their instances necessarily, i.e., their instances must instantiate them in every possible circumstance in which they exist. We have, however, types that represent *contingent* or *accidental* properties of endurants termed **Anti-Rigid Types** [6]). For example, in the way that 'being a living person' captures a cluster of contingent properties of a person, that 'being a puppy' captures a cluster of contingent properties of a dog, or that 'being a husband' captures a cluster of contingent properties of a man participating in a marriage.

Kinds, subkinds, and the anti-rigid types specializing them are categories of endurant **Sortals**. In the philosophical literature, a sortal is a type that provides a uniform principle of identity, persistence, and individuation for its instances [6]. To put it simply, a sortal is either a kind (e.g., 'Person') or a specialization of a kind (e.g., 'Student', 'Teenager', 'Woman'), i.e., it is either a type representing the essence of what things are or a sub-classification applied to the entities that "have that same type of essence", be it rigid, i.e., a **Subkind**, or anti-rigid, i.e., an **Anti-Rigid Sortal**.

In general, types that represent properties shared by entities of *multiple kinds* are termed **Non-Sortals**, i.e., non-sortals are types whose extension possibly intersect with the extension of more than one kind. Non-sortals too can also be further classified depending on whether the properties captured in their intension are essential (i.e., rigid) properties or not.

Now, before we proceed, we should notice that the logical negation of rigidity is not anti-rigidity but *non-rigidity*. If being rigid for a type A means that all instances of A are necessarily instances of A, the negation of that (i.e., non-rigidity) is that there is at least one instance of A that can cease to be an instance of A; anti-rigidity is much stronger than that, it means that all instances of A can cease to be instances of A, i.e., A's intension describes properties that are contingent for all its instances. Finally, we call a type A *semi-rigid* iff it is non-rigid but not anti-rigid, i.e., if it describes properties that are essential to some of its instances but contingent to some other instances. Because non-sortal types are dispersive [11], i.e., they represent properties that behave in very different ways with respect to instances of different kinds, among non-sortal types, we have: those that describe properties that apply *necessarily to the instances of all kinds* it classifies (i.e., Rigid Non-Sortals, which are termed **Categories**); those

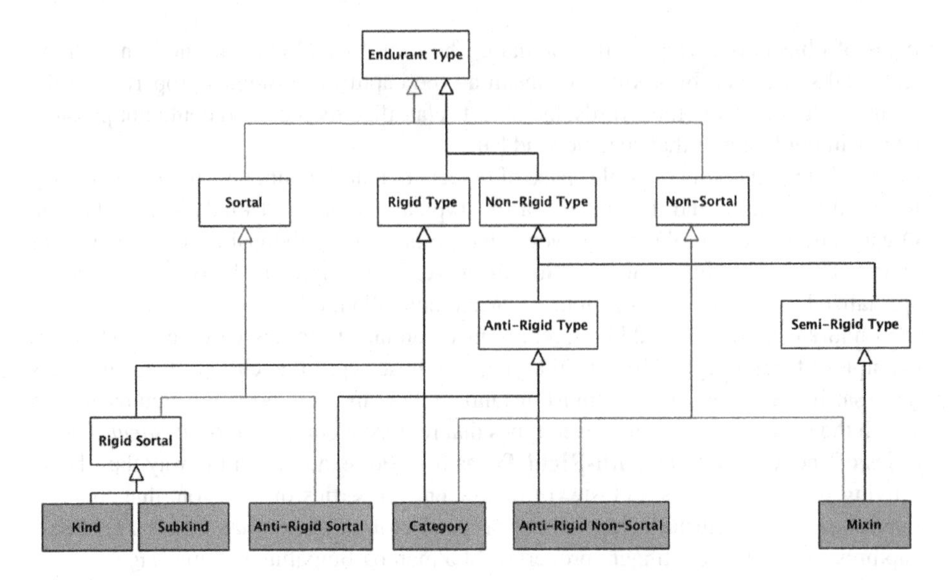

Fig. 1. A taxonomy for Endurant Types. (Color figure online)

that describe properties that apply *contingently to the instances of all kinds* it classifies (**Anti-Rigid Non-Sortals**); those that describe properties that apply *necessarily to the instances of some of the kinds it classifies* but that also apply *contingently to the instances of some other kinds it classifies* (i.e., Semi-Rigid Non-Sortals, termed **Mixins**). An example of a category is 'Physical Object' representing properties of all kinds of entities that have masses and spatial extensions (e.g., people, cars, watches, building); an example of a anti-rigid non-sortal is 'Customer' representing contingent properties for all its instances (i.e., no customer is necessarily a customer), which can be of the kinds 'Person' and 'Organization'; an example of a mixin is the 'Insurable Item', which describe properties that are essential to entities of given kinds (e.g., suppose that cars are necessarily insured) but which are contingent to things of other kinds (e.g., houses can be insured but they are not necessarily insured).

Figure 1 represents this typology of endurant types generated by the possible values of these two properties. As always, UML arrows connect subtypes to their supertypes (the arrowhead pointing to the supertype). Two subtyping relations joined in their arrowheads form a *generalization set*, which here we assume to tessellate the extension of the supertype (pointed to by the joint arrowhead), i.e., these are disjoint and complete generalization sets. The red subtyping relations and generalization sets here represent an inheritance line created by the *sortality* meta-property, i.e., all endurant types are either sortals (i.e., either kinds or specializations thereof) or non-sortals (crossing the boundaries of multiple kinds) but not both. Finally, the blue subtyping relations and generalization sets here represent an inheritance line created by the *rigidity* meta-property, i.e., all endurant types are either rigid (i.e., essentially classifying all their instances), anti-rigid (i.e., contingently classifying all their instances), or semi-rigid (essentially classifying some of their instances, and contingently classifying others). As a result of the combination of these two meta-properties, we have the following six (exhausting and mutually disjoint) types of types (i.e., meta-types): **Kinds**, **Subkinds**, **Anti-Rigid Sortals**, **Categories**, **Anti-Rigid Non-Sortals**, and **Mixins** (in grey in Fig. 1).

The ontological meta-properties that characterized these different types of types also impose constraints on how they can be combined to form taxonomic structures [6]. As we have already seen, since kinds tessellate our domain and, because all sortals are either kinds or specializations thereof, we have both that: no kinds can specialize another kind; every sortal that is not a kind specializes a unique kind. In other words, every sortal hierarchy has a unique kind at the top. Moreover, from these, we have that any type that is a supertype of a kind must be a non-sortal. But also that, given that every specialization of a kind is a sortal, non-sortals cannot specialize sortals. Finally, given the formal definitions of rigidity (including anti-rigidity), it just follows logically that anti-rigid types (sortals or not) cannot be supertypes of semi-rigid and rigid types (sortals or not) (see proof in [6]). For example, if we determine that 'Customer' applies contingently to persons in the scope of business relationships, then a taxonomy in which a rigid type 'Person' specializes an anti-rigid type 'Customer' is logically incorrect. Intuitively, a person will be at the same time required through the specialization to be statically classified as a 'Customer' while at the same time, being defined dynamically classified as a 'Customer', in virtue of the definition of that type. So, either: (i) the definition of 'Customer' should be revised to capture only essential properties, becoming a rigid type and thus solving the incorrect specialization problem; or (ii) 'Customer' should be an anti-rigid specialization of the rigid type 'Person', inverting the direction of the original (but incorrect) taxonomic relation.

3 Graph Transformation Rules to Build Taxonomies

Graph transformation (or *graph rewriting*) [10] has been advocated as a flexible formalism, suitable for modeling systems with dynamic configurations or states. This flexibility is achieved by the fact that the underlying data structure, that of graphs, is capable of capturing a broad variation of systems. Some areas where graph transformation is being applied include visual modeling of systems, the formal specification of model transformations, and the definition of graph languages, to name a few [3, 16].

The core concept of graph transformation is the rule-based modification of graphs, where each application of a rule leads to a graph transformation step. A transformation rule specifies both the necessary preconditions for its application and the rule effect (modifications) on a *host graph*. The modified graph produced by a rule application is the result of the transformation.

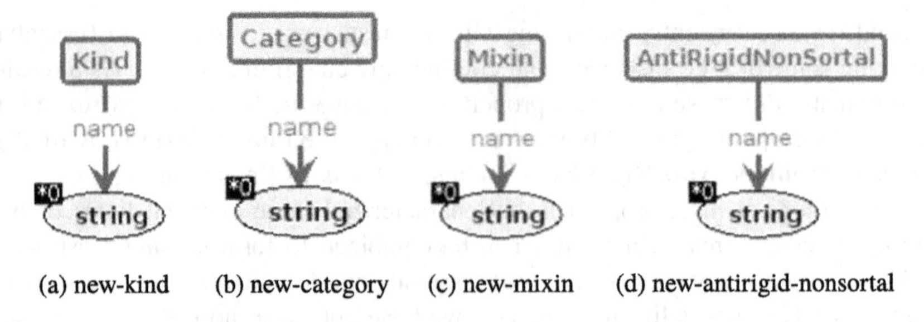

(a) new-kind (b) new-category (c) new-mixin (d) new-antirigid-nonsortal

Fig. 2. Transformation rules to introduce an independent type. (Color figure online)

In this work, we use graph transformations to formally model the operations for the construction of a taxonomy. A set of graph transformation rules can be seen as a declarative specification of how the construction can evolve from an initial state, represented by an initial (empty) host graph. This combination of a rule set plus an initial graph is called a *graph grammar*, and the (possibly infinite) set of graphs reachable from the initial graph constitute the *grammar language*.

Our main contribution in this paper is to formally define a graph grammar that, starting from an empty taxonomy, allow us to build any (and only) correct taxonomies. To put this more precisely: in the area of formal verification, statements about a system are usually split between *correctness* and *completeness* properties. The correctness of a modeled system ensures that only desirable models are possible. In our setting, this means that only correct taxonomies can be part of the grammar language. On the other hand, *completeness* ensures that if a desirable system configuration can exist "in the real world", then a corresponding model is reachable in the formalization. In our setting, this means that any correct taxonomy can be created using the proposed graph grammar.

The grammar described in this section was created with GROOVE [3], a graph transformation tool suitable for the (partial) enumeration of a grammar language, which the tool calls the *state space exploration* of the graph grammar.

3.1 Introducing New Types

We start by defining transformation rules to introduce a new type in the taxonomy. Types for four of the leaf ontological metatypes given in Fig. 1 can be introduced in the taxonomy without being related with a previously introduced type: these include all **Kinds** and all the non-sortals: **Categories**, **Mixins** and **Anti-Rigid Non-Sortals**.

Figure 2 shows the four rules that introduce independent types, using the GROOVE visual notation for presenting rules. Each rule is formed only by a green box representing the type that will be *created* during rule application. A type has an ontological metatype (the label inside the box) and a name attribute. The "string" ellipses in Fig. 2 are the tool notation to indicate that the name must be provided (perhaps by the tool user) upon the type creation. No rule in Fig. 2 have preconditions. Therefore, types for these four ontological metatypes can be introduced without requiring the existence of other types or relations in the taxonomy.

3.2 Introducing Dependent Types

In contrast to non-sortals and kinds, **Subkinds** and **Anti-Rigid Sortals** have preconditions upon their introduction.

In the case of **Subkinds**, their introduction requires the existence of a previous sortal, from which the subkind will inherit a principle of identity. In addition, this sortal must be rigid, to respect the ontological principle that a rigid type cannot specialize an anti-rigid one. These preconditions for the introduction of a new **Subkind** are captured in the rule shown in Fig. 3. The *existing* **Rigid Sortal** is shown as a black box in the figure. The green "subClassOf" arrow states that a new direct subtyping relation will be introduced in the model.

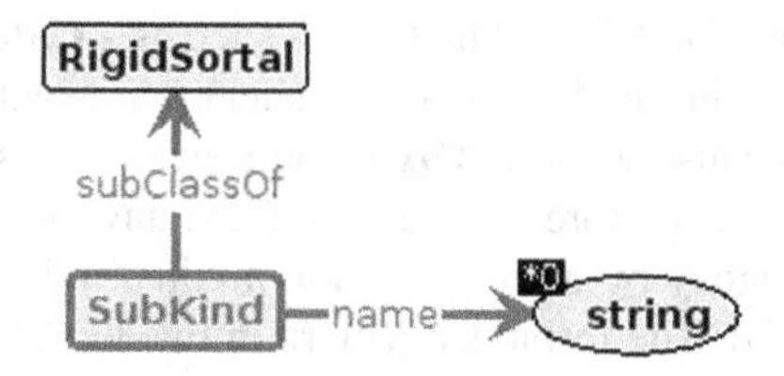

Fig. 3. Transformation rule to introduce a **Subkind** type. (Color figure online)

In the case of an **Anti-Rigid Sortal** type, the only precondition is the existence of a previous sortal, from which the newly introduced Anti-Rigid Sortal will inherit a principle of identity. This rule is shown in Fig. 4. Differently from a Subkind, an Anti-Rigid Sortal can specialize any Sortal (and not only Rigid ones).

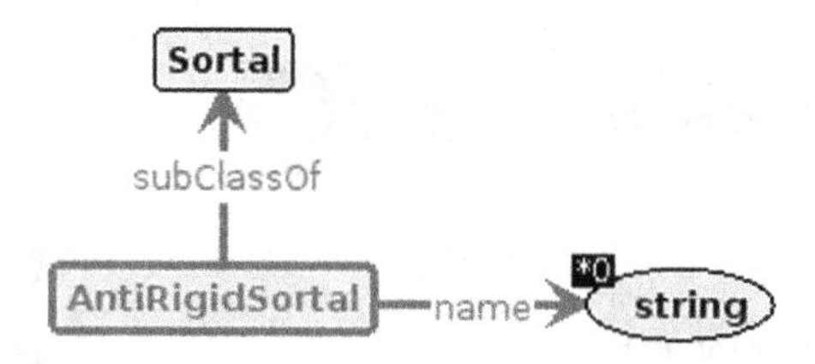

Fig. 4. Transformation rule to introduce an **Anti-Rigid Sortal** type. (Color figure online)

3.3 Introducing Specializations for Existing Non-sortal Types

Having defined rules for the introduction of types, we proceed with rules to insert subtyping relations between two types already present in the model. We start with **Category** and **Mixin** specializations, as both of these ontological metatypes have metaproperties that allow their types to be specialized in any **Endurant Type**, without breaking formal ontology principles.

Figure 5(a) shows a rule that creates a subtyping relation between an existing **Category** supertype and an existing **Mixin** subtype. The red arrow in the figure prevents the introduction of a circularity in the relations. Red elements in GROOVE rules indicate *forbidden* patterns, *i.e.*, elements that, if present, prevent the rule application. The label "subClassOf+" indicates direct or indirect subtyping. Circularity of specializations may be tolerated in taxonomies structured with improper specialization relations, such as `rdfs:subClassOf` in the Semantic Web. A consequence of circular specializations in that case is that mutually specializing classes become equivalent, and hence, should have the same ontological nature. Because of this, we rule out cases of circularity involving types of different metatypes such as a **Category** and a **Mixin**.

The forbidden pattern in Fig. 5(a) is not sufficient to prevent any circular subtyping relation. This occurs because while a **Mixin** can specialize a **Category**, the opposite relation is also possible. Therefore, in order to avoid any circularity, we separate the specialization of a **Category** by mixins and non-mixins Endurant Types. This second case is shown in Fig. 5(b). The forbidden pattern in this figure prevents cycles of subtyping relations involving Categories, Mixins and other Endurant Types. The red label "!Mixin" in Fig. 5(b) indicates that the existing **Endurant Type** cannot be a **Mixin**.

Analogously, we created two additional transformation rules to define how the specialization of a **Mixin** type can be made. These rules are not shown here due to their similarities to the ones in Fig. 5. Finally, the rule depicted in Fig. 6 allows the specialization of an **Anti-Rigid Non-Sortal** by another **Anti-Rigid Type**.

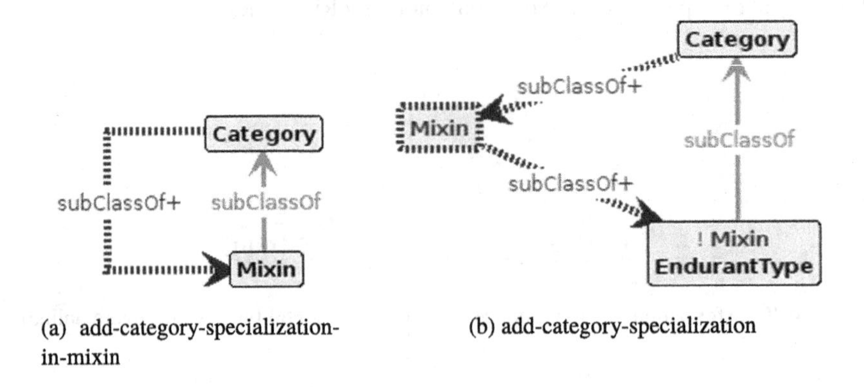

(a) add-category-specialization-in-mixin

(b) add-category-specialization

Fig. 5. Transformation rules to specialize a **Category**. (Color figure online)

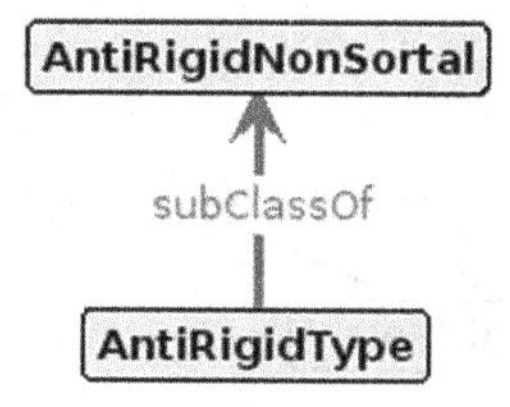

Fig. 6. Transformation rule to specialize an **Anti-Rigid Non-Sortal** type. (Color figure online)

3.4 Introducing Generalizations for Existing Sortal Types

Kind types appear on the top of **Sortal** types hierarchies because kinds provide a principle of identity for all their instances. By definition, kinds cannot specialize other kinds. Therefore, they can only specialize **Non-Sortal** types, more specifically **Categories** and **Mixins**. These specializations can already be constructed with the rules presented in Sect. 3.3.

Subkind types, on the other hand, carry a principle of identity from their supertypes and, ultimately, from exactly one **Kind** type. The rule shown in Fig. 7 properly captures this restriction. If there are distinct (as defined by the *not equal* red dashed edge) **Sub-Kind** and **Rigid Sortal** types that carry a principle of identity from the same **Kind**, then a direct subtyping relation can be created between the two. The black edges with labels "subClassOf*" and "subClassOf+" indicate that, for the rule to be applied, a specialization relation from the new super-type and from the **Subkind** to the same **Kind** must already be present, or at least that the new (direct) super-type of the **Subkind** is its own **Kind**. Subkinds can also specialize any rigid or semi-rigid non-sortal, but these cases are already covered by the rules presented in Sect. 3.3. A similar construction for **Anti-Rigid Sortal** types can be seen in Fig. 8.

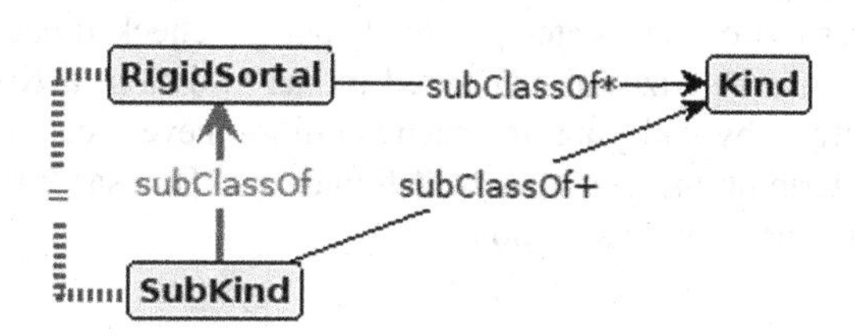

Fig. 7. Transformation rule to generalize a **Sub-Kind** type. (Color figure online)

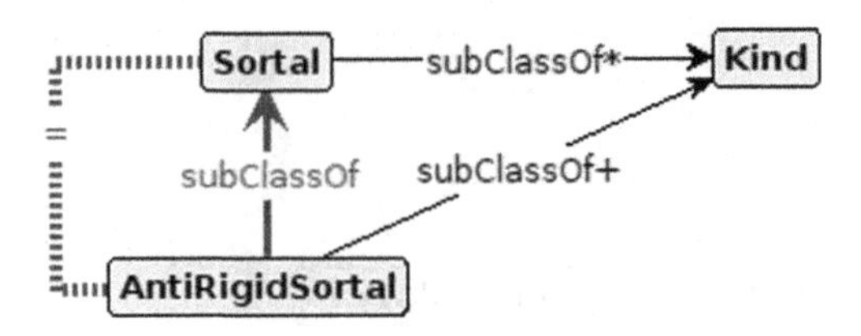

Fig. 8. Transformation rule to generalize an **Anti-Rigid Sortal** type. (Color figure online)

4 Formal Verification

We use the GROOVE graph transformation tool to carry out a formal verification of the graph grammar presented in Sect. 3. To do so, we employ verification conditions in GROOVE, which formally define the ontological restrictions described in Sect. 2, and allow us to perform an analysis over any given taxonomy (graph state model). We then use the state space exploration functionality of the tool to check that all states (taxonomies) satisfy the restrictions.

As stated in Sect. 3, our objective with the verification is two-fold: to demonstrate the *correctness* and *completeness* of the proposed graph grammar. Correctness ensures that the grammar rules only produce correct taxonomies, *i.e.*, those that do not invalidate well-formedness constraints. Completeness ensures that any and all correct taxonomies can be produced by a sequence of rule applications.

A *graph condition* in GROOVE is represented diagrammatically in the same way as transformation rules, albeit without creator (green) elements. A graph condition is satisfied by a taxonomy model if all reader (black) elements of the condition are present in the model, and all forbidden (red) elements are absent.

Figure 9 shows our first graph condition, capturing the restriction that **Kinds** must appear at the top of sortal hierarchies, hence not specializing another **Sortal**. It is important to note that restrictions are stated *positively* but are checked *negatively*. Thus, the condition in Fig. 9 characterizes an undesired model violation (a **Kind** specializing a **Sortal**), and therefore, by verifying that such condition never occurs in any taxonomy model, we can determine the grammar well-foundness. This same rationale holds for all other conditions shown in this section.

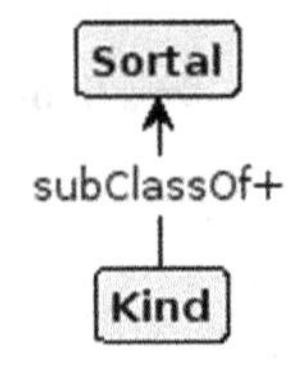

Fig. 9. Restrictive condition of a **Kind** specializing another **Sortal**.

Figure 10 formalizes a second restrictive condition, stating that a **Sortal** cannot inherit its principle of identity from more than one **Kind**. A third condition, shown in Fig. 11, captures the situation in which the *rigidity* meta-property is contradicted, that is, when a rigid or semi-rigid type specializes an anti-rigid one. Similarly, the fourth restrictive condition, depicted in Fig. 12, represents the situation in which the *sortality* meta-property is contradicted, that is, when a **Non-Sortal** type specializes a **Sortal** one.

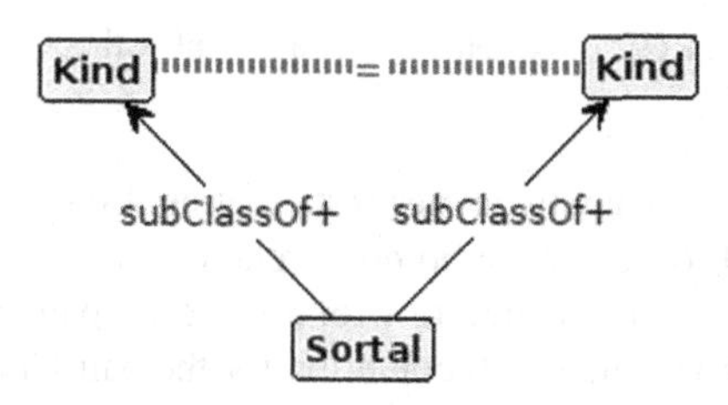

Fig. 10. Restrictive condition of a **Sortal** with more than one **Kind**.

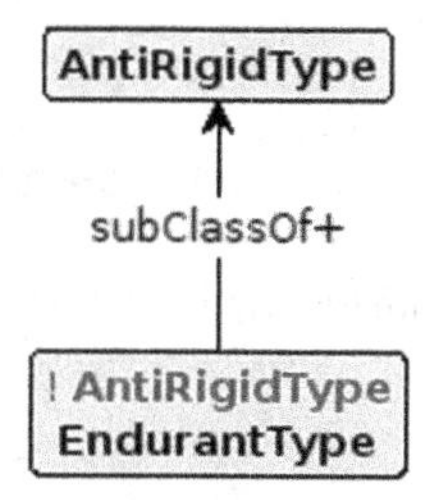

Fig. 11. Restrictive condition of a rigid or semi-rigid type specializing an anti-rigid one.

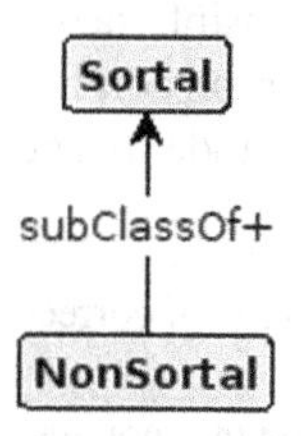

Fig. 12. Restrictive condition of a **Non-Sortal** type specializing a **Sortal** one.

To specify a fifth restrictive condition, we consider that all **Sortals** ultimately should specialize (or be) a **Kind**, from which they inherit a principle of identity. The violating situation, in which a **Sortal** does not specializes a **Kind**, is shown in Fig. 13.

Fig. 13. Restrictive condition of a **Sortal** without a **Kind**.

A final restriction is that any two types instantiating different ontological metatypes cannot have a mutual (circular) subtyping relation between them. We represent such restriction with 15 graph conditions, one for each pair of different ontological metatypes. Figure 14 shows the graph condition for the pair **Category** and **Mixin**. The remaining 14 conditions all have the same structure, and thus are not shown.

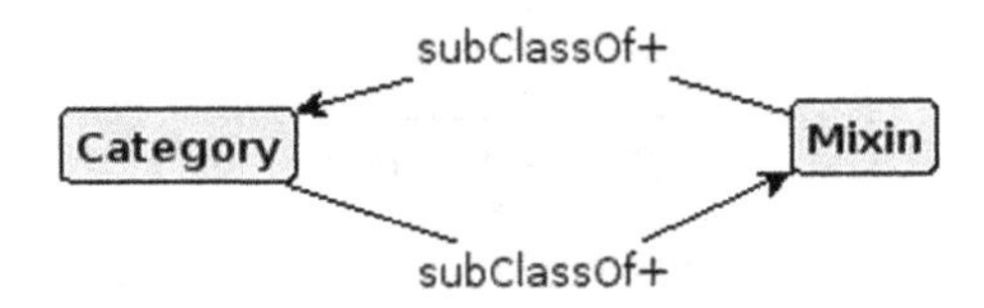

Fig. 14. An example of a condition with two equivalent types of different ontological metatypes.

4.1 Verifying Correctness

The first step in verifying the correctness of the graph grammar proposed is to enumerate its language, i.e., construct all possible taxonomies reachable by any sequence of rule applications. Subsequently, the graph conditions just presented are checked against these constructed taxonomies. If any model triggers one or more graph conditions, then

Table 1. Results of correctness analysis.

# types (N)	Produced taxonomies	Incorrect taxonomies
1	4	0
2	24	0
3	223	0
4	3,865	0
5	146,882	0
6	?	?

we know the model violates some ontological restrictions, and therefore it is incorrect. Consequently, the goal of the correctness analysis is to verify that no taxonomy in the language is incorrect. To perform the grammar state space exploration we use the GROOVE Generator, a command-line tool designed for this task. Details of GROOVE usage can be found at the tool manual[2], and additional case studies that illustrate the tool functionalities are presented in [3].

A major caveat in the first step above is that the grammar language is *infinite*, thus preventing a complete enumeration in a finite amount of time. To cope with this situation, we need to perform a *bounded* exploration with the GROOVE tool. In this setting, our bound N is the maximum number of types present in a taxonomy. When performing the exploration, the tool managed to generate a total of 150,998 taxonomies up to a bound $N = 5$, with a breakdown of this total per bound value shown in Table 1. The table also shows that our correctness goal was validated (at least up to $N = 5$), with no taxonomies being flagged as incorrect by the graph conditions.

Given the inherently exponential growth of the number of possible taxonomies with respect to bound N, it was not possible to continue the exploration for $N = 6$ and beyond due to memory limitations (the execution was halted after several million models partially produced.) This *state space explosion* is a common problem for all explicit state model checkers, such as GROOVE [3].

To support that the correctness results in Table 1 are significant, we rely on the *small scope hypothesis*, which basically claims most design errors can be found in small counterexamples [2]. Experimental results suggest that exhaustive testing within a small finite domain does indeed catch all type system errors in practice [14], and many case studies using the tool Alloy have confirmed the hypothesis by performing an analysis in a variety of scopes and showing, retrospectively, that a small scope would have sufficed to find all the bugs discovered [12].

Table 2. Results of completeness analysis.

# types (N)	All taxonomies	Incorrect taxonomies	Correct taxonomies
1	6	2	4
2	78	54	24
3	2,456	2,233	223
4	228,588	224,723	3,865
5	?	?	?

[2] Available at https://sourceforge.net/projects/groove/.

4.2 Verifying Completeness

The verification described in the previous section assures that all taxonomies produced are correct, but does nothing to persuade us that any and all possible correct taxonomies can be produced. To provide this kind of assurance is the goal of the completeness verification described below.

To perform the completeness analysis we need to consider not only correct taxonomies but also the incorrect ones. To this end, we developed another, completely permissible, graph grammar that allows the creation of both correct and incorrect models. The grammar is quite simple, with six rules for the unrestricted creation of the leaf types of types in Fig. 1, and one rule allowing the introduction of a subtyping relation between any two endurant types.

The results of the exploration with this new permissible grammar are presented in Table 2. As expected, the rate of growth in this scenario is even steeper, given that more models can be produced. The tool was able to perform a bounded exploration up to $N = 4$, with larger bounds exceeding the available memory. The second column of Table 2 lists all taxonomies created with the new grammar, both correct and incorrect. We again use the graph conditions to flag violations of ontology restrictions in the models. If a taxonomy triggers *any* of the graph conditions, then it is considered incorrect. Conversely, if *no* graph condition is triggered by a model, then it certainly describes a correct taxonomy. The last two columns in the table summarize this classification.

The completeness goal can be verified by a comparison between the **Correct taxonomies** column of Table 2 and the **Produced taxonomies** column of Table 1. It can be seen immediately that all values up to $N = 4$ match. Given that the permissible grammar produces all possible models (correct and incorrect), this allows us to conclude that the taxonomy grammar of Sect. 3 produces *all* correct taxonomies, and *only* the correct ones. To strengthen this validation claim we once again rely on the small scope hypothesis: although the completeness result is not formally proven for models of arbitrary size, the bounded values shown provide strong evidence that such result holds. Also, the bound limit could be pushed (at least a bit) further with additional computational resources and time.

5 Final Considerations

In this paper, we propose a systematic approach for building ontologically well-founded and logically consistent taxonomic structures. We do that by leveraging on a *typology of endurant types*. This typology, in turn, is derived from an ontological theory that is part of the Unified Foundational Ontology (UFO) [7], and which underlies the Ontology-Driven Conceptual Modeling language OntoUML [6].

The original theory puts forth a number of ontological distinctions based on formal meta-properties. As a result of the logical characterization of these meta-properties, we have that certain structures (patterns) are imposed on the language primitives representing these distinctions [15]. We have identified a set of primitive operations on taxonomic structures that, not only guarantees the correctness of the generated taxonomies, but also is capable of driving the construction of any correct taxonomy. This forms the basis for the systematic design of such structures at a higher level of abstraction.

Given the limitations of metamodels as a mechanism for representing a language's abstract syntax, these structures were not treated as first-class citizens before and have remained hidden in the abstract syntax of the original OntoUML proposal [5]. This paper addresses this exact problem. By leveraging on that theory, and propose a *pattern grammar* (graph transformation grammar) that embeds these distinctions and that guarantees *by design* the construction of taxonomic structures that abide by the formal constraints governing their relations. The work proposed here advances the work initiated in [17]. For example, by employing the state exploration mechanism supported by GROOVE, we managed to detect important omissions in the rule set proposed in that original work.

Another important aspect is that our proposal captures the representation consequences of that ontology theory in a way that is metamodel-independent. For this reason, these results can be carried out to other languages and platforms. In particular, we are currently developing a plugin for Protégé that, among other things, implements the primitive operations proposed in this paper. This plugin is intended to be used in tandem with the gUFO ontology (a lightweight implementation of UFO) [1]. In that implementation, these operations take the form of ontology patterns to be applied, to support its users in modeling consistent Semantic Web ontologies.

Acknowledgments. This research is partly funded by Brazilian funding agencies CNPq (grants numbers 312123/2017-5 and 407235/2017-5) and CAPES (Finance Code 001 and grant number 23038.028816/2016-41).

References

1. Almeida, J.P.A., Guizzardi, G., Falbo, R.A., Sales, T.P.: gUFO: a lightweight implementation of the Unified Foundational Ontology (UFO) (2019)
2. Gammaitoni, L., Kelsen, P., Ma, Q.: Agile validation of model transformations using compound f-alloy specifications. Sci. Comput. Program. **162**, 55–75 (2018)
3. Ghamarian, A.H., de Mol, M., Rensink, A., Zambon, E., Zimakova, M.: Modelling and analysis using GROOVE. Int. J. Softw. Tools Technol. Transfer **14**(1), 15–40 (2012)
4. Guarino, N., Welty, C.A.: An overview of OntoClean. In: Staab, S., Studer, R. (eds.) Handbook on Ontologies, pp. 151–171. Springer, Heidelberg (2004). https://doi.org/10.1007/978-3-540-24750-0_8
5. Guizzardi, G.: Ontological foundations for structural conceptual models. No. 15 in Telematica Institute Fundamental Research Series, University of Twente (2005)
6. Guizzardi, G., Fonseca, C.M., Benevides, A.B., Almeida, J.P.A., Porello, D., Sales, T.P.: Endurant types in ontology-driven conceptual modeling: towards OntoUML 2.0. In: Trujillo, J.C., et al. (eds.) ER 2018. LNCS, vol. 11157, pp. 136–150. Springer, Cham (2018). https://doi.org/10.1007/978-3-030-00847-5_12
7. Guizzardi, G., Wagner, G., Almeida, J.P.A., Guizzardi, R.S.: Towards ontological foundations for conceptual modeling: the unified foundational ontology (UFO) story. Appl. Ontol. **10**(3–4), 259–271 (2015)

8. Guizzardi, G., Wagner, G., Guarino, N., van Sinderen, M.: An ontologically well-founded profile for UML conceptual models. In: Persson, A., Stirna, J. (eds.) CAiSE 2004. LNCS, vol. 3084, pp. 112–126. Springer, Heidelberg (2004). https://doi.org/10.1007/978-3-540-25975-6_10
9. Halpin, T., Morgan, T.: Information Modeling and Relational Databases. Morgan Kaufmann, Burlington (2010)
10. Heckel, R.: Graph transformation in a nutshell. Electron. Notes Theor. Comput. Sci. **148**(1), 187–198 (2006)
11. Hirsch, E.: The Concept of Identity. Oxford University Press, Oxford (1992)
12. Jackson, D.: Alloy: a language and tool for exploring software designs. Commun. ACM **62**(9), 66–76 (2019)
13. Oltramari, A., Gangemi, A., Guarino, N., Masolo, C.: Restructuring WordNet's top-level: The OntoClean approach. LREC2002, Las Palmas, Spain 49 (2002)
14. Roberson, M., Harries, M., Darga, P.T., Boyapati, C.: Efficient software model checking of soundness of type systems. ACM SIGPLAN Notices **43**(10), 493–504 (2008)
15. Ruy, F.B., Guizzardi, G., Falbo, R.A., Reginato, C.C., Santos, V.A.: From reference ontologies to ontology patterns and back. Data Knowl. Eng. **109**, 41–69 (2017)
16. Zambon, E.: Abstract Graph Transformation - Theory and Practice. Centre for Telematics and Information Technology, University of Twente (2013)
17. Zambon, E., Guizzardi, G.: Formal definition of a general ontology pattern language using a graph grammar. In: 2017 Federated Conference on Computer Science and Information Systems (FedCSIS), pp. 1–10. IEEE (2017)

Microservice Maturity of Organizations

Towards an Assessment Framework

Jean-Philippe Gouigoux[1(✉)], Dalila Tamzalit[2(✉)], and Joost Noppen[3(✉)]

[1] Group CTO SALVIA Développement, Bât. 270, 45, Avenue Victor Hugo, 93300 Aubervilliers, France
jp.gouigoux@salviadeveloppement.com

[2] Université de Nantes, CNRS, LS2N, 44000 Nantes, France
Dalila.Tamzalit@univ-nantes.fr

[3] BT Applied Research Adastral Park Barrack Square, Martlesham, Ipswich IP5 3RE, UK
johannes.noppen@bt.com

Abstract. This early work aims to allow organizations to diagnose their capacity to properly adopt microservices through initial milestones of a Microservice Maturity Model (*MiMMo*). The objective is to prepare the way towards a general framework to help companies and industries to determine their microservices maturity. Organizations lean more and more on distributed web applications and Line of Business software. This is particularly relevant during the current Covid-19 crisis, where companies are even more challenged to offer their services online, targeting a very high level of responsiveness in the face of rapidly increasing and diverse demands. For this, microservices remain the most suitable delivery application architectural style. They allow agility not only on the technical application, as often considered, but on the enterprise architecture as a whole, influencing the actual financial business of the company. However, microservices adoption is highly risk-prone and complex. Before they establish an appropriate migration plan, first and foremost, companies must assess their degree of readiness to adopt microservices. For this, *MiMMo*, a Microservices Maturity Model framework assessment, is proposed to help companies assess their readiness for the microservice architectural style, based on their actual situation. *MiMMo* results from observations of and experience with about thirty organizations writing software. It conceptualizes and generalizes the progression paths they have followed to adopt microservices appropriately. Using the model, an organization can evaluate itself in two dimensions and five maturity levels and thus: (i) benchmark itself on its current use of microservices; (ii) project the next steps it needs to achieve a higher maturity level and (iii) analyze how it has evolved and maintain a global coherence between technical and business stakes.

Keywords: Microservices · Maturity model · Assessment · Information systems

1 Introduction and Problem Statement

With an increasingly connected world and the expectation of services being available online, organizations are increasingly faced with the challenge of delivering or use their

S. Cherfi et al. (Eds.): RCIS 2021, LNBIP 415, pp. 523–540, 2021.
https://doi.org/10.1007/978-3-030-75018-3_34

software in a shape that can handle demand at scale and ready for the Cloud. This is much more relevant during the current crisis, where companies are even more challenged to offer their services online, targeting a very high level of responsiveness in the face of rapidly increasing and diverse demands.

In recent years, service-oriented architectures [7–9] have emerged as the most popular paradigm in this space, with in particular the concept of microservices [4], hyper-scalable small algorithms of a transactional nature, becoming one of the core building blocks to achieving these goals [10, 11]. The fine-grained nature of these microservices combined with their horizontal scaling properties allows companies to easily pivot their services while at the same time supporting large workloads inherent to modern online systems [4]. Microservices are a good targeted architecture for the modernization of software systems [12, 13]. However, for all the benefits microservice-based architecture offer, the journey for a company to migrate to this architectural style can be challenging and perilous. In fact, legacy processes and lack of knowledge are the main hurdles that companies face for adopting microservices [1–3]. In addition, several authors consider that microservices are not viable for every software system, as there are numerous trade-offs to consider [5, 6] and reasons to adopt microservices and how may vary considerably between different organizations.

In an ideal situation, an organization that delivers its software through this paradigm is fully aligned in both its technical and business parts. For example, from a technical point of view the organization has a comprehensive understanding of the size of its user base and the performance implications this has. The organization also understands which parts of the software architecture are most affected by this scale (e.g., a payment component in a webshop) and has isolated this to become one of the aforementioned microservices to support the scaling demand. In addition, the organization also has aligned its organizational structure to support this mode of development through hiring the right talent, empowering teams for rapid feature deployment and technology use, service-oriented earnings models, and having a fundamental understanding of the up- and downsides of the service-oriented paradigm across the organization. In this situation an organization is best placed to take full advantage of the benefits offered by a microservices architecture from both an economic and technical perspective while at the same time minimizing constraints and managing risks inherent to the approach. The organization in such situation can therefore be described as a *Mature Microservice Organization.*

However, the large majority of companies do not find themselves in the position described above. Many larger organizations are still in the early stages of the migration towards being primarily a software company and ensuring their software is of high quality and delivered at speed. Adopting microservices is much more than simply leveraging APIs as microservices, as, regrettably, many enterprises are understanding. Technical challenges in such migration paths typically include migrating legacy systems to scalable cloud architectures, defining and implementing software delivery pipelines, reimplementing software that in its original form does not support cloud-based deployment, etc. In addition, from an organizational perspective, the organization typically has to redefine its software development methods, upskill its staff and redefine how it makes money from the services it offers. For example, the company might have to shift from selling software wholesale to offering the functionality up as a service with a pay-as-you-go model for monetization. An organization who finds itself on this migration trajectory is less able to take maximum advantage of microservice-based software development and can therefore be classified as *Immature Microservice Organization.*

Naturally every organization will have completed a distinct set of challenges in this migration process, some focusing more on addressing legacy software and technical challenges first, while others emphasize change management of the business processes first. And while those steps do not necessarily make an organization mature, they can already enable the organization to gain initial benefits of microservice-based development. As such it can be argued that microservice maturity of an organization needs to be considered from several dimensions' points of view, like the usual business and technical dimensions.

The paper is organized as follow: this first section introduces the context and the problem statement. Section 2 presents *MiMMo*, the proposed Microservice Maturity Model. Section 3 illustrate the results of using the *MiMMo* through two organizations. Section 4 is dedicated to related works and Sect. 5 discuss the work and open some future research tracks to conclude.

2 MiMMo: Towards a Microservice Maturity Assessment Framework

MiMMo proposes the initial milestones towards a general framework to help companies and industries determine their microservices maturity, one of the main challenges for organizations. It helps to determine at what stage of maturity they are before considering to build an appropriate strategy to adopt properly microservices with a substantial Return Over Investment.

2.1 General Presentation

MiMMo proposes to consider two main dimensions of importance for companies: the *organizational dimension*, that supports the business strategy, and the *technical dimension*. In order to assess the degree of maturity, each dimension is declined in different levels of maturity. The maturity assessment obtained will represent a good starting point for organizations to evaluate the necessary effort to adopt microservices and if it is worth doing it. The strategy of adoption microservices can be thus built appropriately to the context of each organization.

The proposed MiMMo framework has been derived from authors' experience, mainly based on 6-years field observations of about thirty organizations, each having between 40 and 8000 users (Table 1[1]). By working with and advising these organizations, one of the industrial authors has observed the journeys of these organizations on their trajectory towards using microservices. By comparing journeys, identifying recurring patterns and successful actions taken, the authors have compiled their observations into a generalized framework that can be used by organizations to assess their microservices maturity and

[1] Names of companies are not given for aims of confidentiality but their type is specified.

readiness to take this paradigm to the next level. This maturity assessment framework therefore is a heuristic advice mechanism that captures observed industry best practices. This paper presents the first steps.

Table 1. 29 Organizations observed during 6 years.

20 Observed organizations (2014-2018)					9 Observed organizations (2018-2019)				
Index	Type	Year	#Users	Domain	Index	Type	Year	#Users	Domain
1	Regional Council	2014	450	Complete map	21	Agriculture	2018	1200	Complete map
2	Departmental Council	2014	200	Persons + Finance	22	Pollutants management	2018	900	Complete map
3	Regional Council	2014	300	IAM + Persons	23	Lawyers	2018	200	IAM + Persons
4	Regional Council	2014	500	Persons	24	News industry	2018	1500	Geographical
5	Regional Council	2014	450	Persons + Finance	25	Agriculture	2019	4300	Persons
6	Regional Council	2014	300	Persons	26	Food transformation	2019	1000	Data ontology
7	Software Editor	2014	130	Business Intelligence	27	Software Editor	2019	800	Persons
8	Equipment Industry	2014	8000	Complete map	28	Software Editor	2019	40	Persons + IAM
9	Regional Council	2015	400	Persons	29	Government agency	2019	80	Data ontology
10	Regional Council	2015	650	Persons + EDM + IAM					
11	Regional Council	2015	200	Complete map					
12	Chamber of Commerce	2015	300	Professionnal trainin					
13	Departmental Council	2016	80	Complete map					
14	Regional Council	2016	800	IAM					
15	Regional Council	2016	300	Complete map					
16	Equipment Industry	2016	1200	IAM					
17	Software Editor	2016	170	Planning + Persons					
18	City	2017	120	Persons					
19	Chemical Industry	2017	200	Finance + BI					
20	Regional Council	2018	650	IAM + Persons					

2.2 Followed Methodology

The derivation of the Microservice Maturity Model (MiMMo) came in two main stages: *observations* and *elaboration*:

2.2.1 Observations

This observations stage lasted from 2014 to 2019. It represents the period where one of the authors was working with and advising around thirty organizations. These studied organizations include public agencies, like ministries, regional and departmental councils mainly in France, as well as some large cities and some mid-sized private enterprises.

Phase 1 – Implicit Observations (2014–2018): from 2014 to 2016, only public organizations have been addressed with projects of Information System alignment around a modular software suite. The evolution in time of maturity did not clearly appear as closely related with the technical aspect of Service Oriented Architecture, since the domains were so close (almost the same) and the organizations have the same public status. It was only logical that they behave and evolve the same way. In 2017, the approach of what started to get called a microservice architecture became a significant advantage for the organizations addressed and the board of the company decided to create a dedicated Business Unit to approach other categories of customers. New categories of companies started to be advised in 2018. The 20 companies concerned by this first phase are presented in Table 1 – Left side.

Phase 2 – ***Explicit Observations (2018–2019)***: the same step in evolution of the architecture appeared among the different customers. And although the method to help them changed radically from one to the other (in terms of length and mission content, but also in actors), the experience of the first phase helped to clearly identify a pattern of evolution. All companies that were accompanied, were they small (40 users) or big (8000 users), were they using one technology or another, were they operating on one business domain or some that were completely different, went through steps in their Information System evolution towards Service Orientation that were basically similar to each other, and also to the steps observed in the first phase. The 9 companies concerned by this second phase are presented in Table 1 – Right side.

2.2.2 Elaboration

Afterwards, in 2019, the same experience was shared between the authors, coming from different backgrounds, and since the evolution of maturity towards microservices architecture seemed to have common features whatever the context, the idea of an assessment model was devised among the authors. In 2020, based on their respective expertise, the authors analyzed notes, observations, and extrapolated and generalized observed best practices of successful transformational journeys. As a general methodology for derivation of MiMMo, a comparative analysis was performed of the experiences and best practices observed in the organizations by the authors. In particular shared successful behavior was identified, such as the application of enabling technologies and the restructuring of the organization with respect to new challenges in licensing. The identified patterns in turn were ordered chronologically based on observed change management to understand their logical progression. Finally, 5 stages were identified based on observable evolution steps inside organizations. The key thoughts are formalized within the MiMMo framework in terms of levels and dimension of maturity, detailed in Sect. 3.

As this was a retrospective rather than an in-situ exercise, and therefore no systematic data collection and analysis could be performed, MiMMo was decided to be a heuristic assessment framework representative of observed industry experience, as a first step for a further research objective to form the foundation for a formalized maturity model.

3 Levels and Dimensions of the MiMMo Framework

The proposed Microservice Maturity Model (MiMMo) aims to capture the maturity of organizations for software delivery using microservices by identifying five distinct *levels of maturity* applied on *two dimensions.*

3.1 Maturity Levels

The authors identified 5 levels per dimension, totally based on observations from the field starting at level 1 (least mature) and up to level 5 (most mature). Each of these levels consists of a set of attributes and behaviors that can be observed in an organization that puts them at this level of maturity:

- **Level 1: Theory Understood but not Applied:** at this stage, the organization has received training and/or has gained a basic understanding of the microservices approach, but no effort has been taken in applying it. No projects have been defined to serve as a first application and no business plans have been put in place for the new methods of software delivery. The knowledge of microservices at this point is purely theoretical.
- **Level 2: Unskilled Application of Principles:** This second level starts when the first initiatives are taken to apply the new knowledge on microservices. Application projects start and the first microservices are created without a complete grasp of the implication of granularity nor the organizational implications. Generally, the first technical realizations are being delivered but the organization is not in a position to take advantage of the opportunities offered from a technical and business perspective.
- **Level 3: Microservices by the Book:** This is the level that should in theory be used as soon as the project starts and the team leaves level 1, but both the technical application and embedding in the organization and business model of microservices requires understanding them in the specific context of the organization. After acquiring this additional contextual knowledge at level 3 the organization is now capable of applying microservices by the book. Technically the software produced is sound and the organization has realigned its business model to take advantage of the new mode of software development and productization. At this level the organization can also be observed correcting some of the mistakes made at level 2, such as re-architecting software systems and redefining business roles.
- **Level 4: Expertise:** This level 4 corresponds to a level of maturity where the external principles recommendations have been digested by the team and are routinely used. Best practices are shared and teams not only follow them but understand what they stand for and what will be the risk of not following them. In some cases, adaptations are made to the best practices, but this is done with full consciousness of its impact to the software and the organization itself.
- **Level 5: Application Beyond Best Practice:** The highest level of maturity is considered reached when the principles of level 4 are constantly applied (not only a few best practices, but a major part of the state of the art on the domain) and the organization starts new best practices or advanced experimentation on its own. Generally, this level will be achieved on a few domains only where the organization has gained complete expertise and can now explore disruptive approaches to push the microservices benefits further.

3.2 Maturity Dimensions

The levels of maturity defined in the previous section can serve as a framework for organizations to assess how far along they are in the journey towards a full microservice-oriented organization. By determining their own behavior against the core elements described above, these organizations can determine their next steps to further their maturity. However, maturity with respect to microservices covers many different aspects of an organization. In addition to purely the technical challenges there are also organizational challenges, such as management buy-in and licensing models, and sustainability considerations, such as environmental and social sustainability concerns and implications for employees. To accommodate these specialized dimensions of maturity in this section, authors explore the most prominent maturity dimensions, i.e., technical and organizational maturity, and illustrate how the aforementioned maturity levels translate to these specific domains.

3.3 Technical Maturity Dimension

Most of the microservices adoption stories start from a grassroot experimentation from the developers and technical experts and, though many managers now know that the technical bits are not worth much when they are not accompanied with the right governance, there is an old craftsmanship reflex in IT that focuses attention for the information system on its technical implementation, since this is the easier part to observe changes on.

The global overview of the maturity-level applied on the technical dimension is given in Fig. 1. While Table 2 gives examples and is an illustration of the maturity levels in the technical dimensions. It lists typical behaviors and practices observed depending on the level of maturity of the company on its technical path to microservices use. The correspondence between Fig. 1. and the correspondence matrix Table 2 is made with corresponding letters (A), (B)…. When there is no letter, that means that the observation is generic.

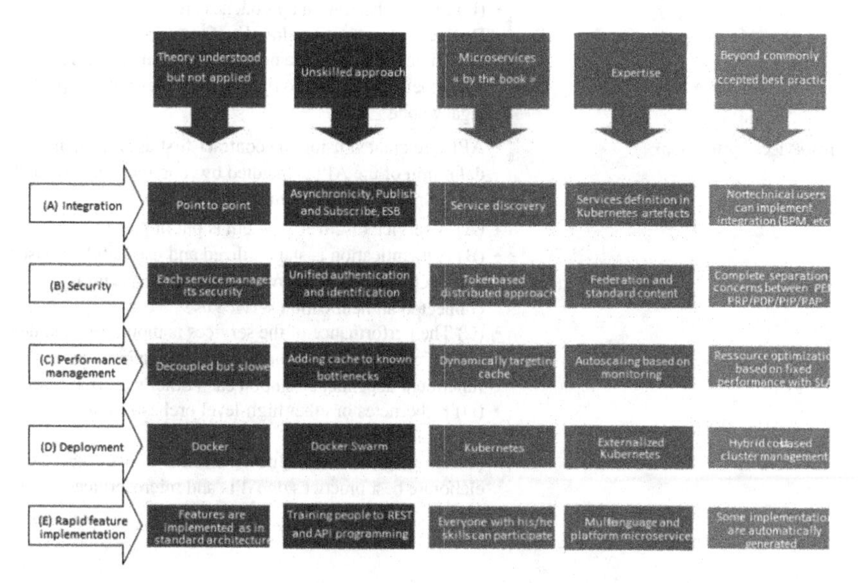

Fig. 1. Maturity-level correspondence matrix for the technical dimension.

Table 2. Maturity-level correspondence matrix illustration for the technical dimension.

Maturity levels	Technical observations
Theory understood but not applied	• A few APIs have been coded but do not respect the REST best practices (there is a dedicated maturity model for RESTful APIs, developed by Leonard Richardson) • (A) Integration between them or between them and the legacy systems is pure point to point, without any interfaces • (B) The services deal with security in exactly the same way as the legacy system, without any contextual adaptation • (C) First step of decoupling appears in the system, but this is mainly done at the cost of performance, since separation of responsibility is not compensated by adequate actions and the result is thus slower than the old monolith • (D) These first tests are deployed with dedicated tools, or with Docker used in its simplest way, managing containers one by one • (E) The features are developed using the same tools as for the legacy systems
Unskilled approach	• Actual REST API are created and an external contract is created • (A) A middleware is used to handle integration and calls between APIs, sometimes using publish and subscribe and sometimes direct calls • (B) A unified authentication method is dedicated to microservices • (C) Cache is added to restore performance of the whole, by choosing bottlenecks to correct • (D) First orchestration approaches are attempted with Docker Swarm or other low-level techniques • (E) Though the tools are not adapted to microservices, developers are trained to their specificities with respect to legacy code
Microservices by the book	• APIs are created using the contract-first approach, and the definition of the API is handled by functional experts and not technical people anymore • (A) A service discovery system is put in place • (B) Authentication is standardized and uses a token-based approach to avoid performance impact of a central connected authentication service use • (C) The performance of the services is monitored and dealt dynamically on each of them, while taking into account their functional dependencies upon each other's service level • (D) Kubernetes or other high-level orchestration systems are put in place • (E) Training has been achieved and developers start elaborate best practices on APIs and microservices

(continued)

Table 2. *(continued)*

Maturity levels	Technical observations
Expertise	• (A) All services are contracted and exposed in a central directory based on the orchestration system • (B) Federated security and external identity providers are routinely used for the microservices security • (C) Performance is measured and adjusted continuously, depending on Service Level Agreement, current load and financial cost of the resources • (D) The orchestrator is externalized or even hybrid, managing several cloud systems • (E) Services are developed in the best platform for each usage, using the promise of the best tool for each service
Beyond commonly accepted best practices	• The whole company functions (not only the applications) is exposed in an API platform • (A) Non-technical users are enabled to create value-added integration by plugging APIs together using dedicated middleware or low code platforms • (B) Authentication, identification, authorization are completely isolated responsibilities • (C) Resource use is balanced with performance for optimal usage depending on the business constraints solely • (D) A multiple cloud system is used and the location of containers is fully hybrid, depending on cost and proximity to the source or the consumer of the service • (E) Implementation of some low-level services are generated without any developer intervention

Even if some manifestation from one level can be observed at the same time as some from another level, it is rare that a company has a high level of maturity on one axis and a low one on another. In the end, the global technical maturity of the observed entity is an average of the possible behaviors listed below.

3.4 Organizational Maturity Dimension

As said previously, when considering microservice maturity it can be tempting to focus primarily on technical aspects, such as understanding of engineering principles and deployment. However, a second major component in the successful application of microservices is to have an organizational structure that is able to maximize the business potential of the benefits microservices have to offer. This not only includes providing development teams with access to relevant knowledge and technology, but also realignment of for example how software products are sold and which unique selling points these software products will have. The shift to microservices can lead to a realignment in target markets and even bring the company in competition with organizations it did not have to consider before. The global overview of the maturity-level applied on the organizational dimension is given in Fig. 2 is illustrated with Table 3.

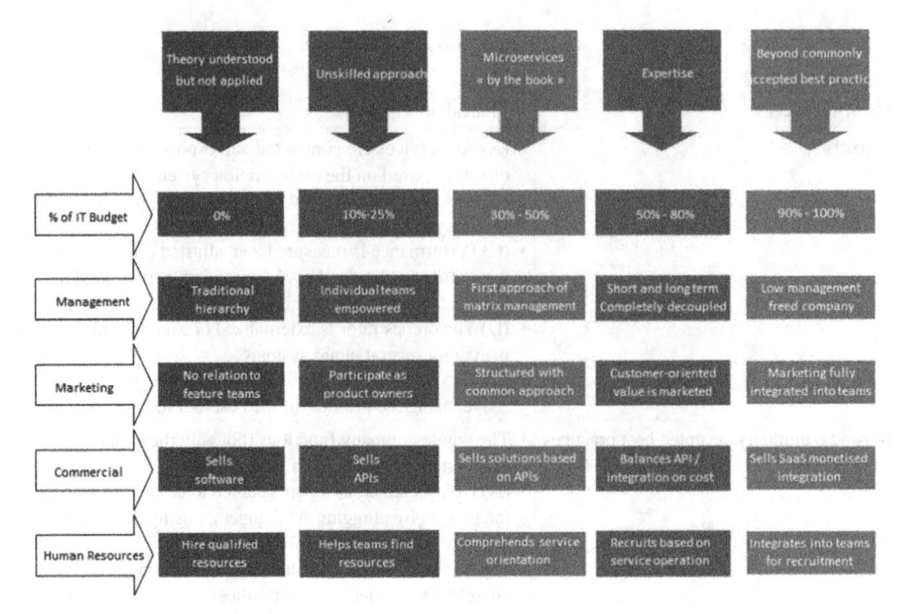

Fig. 2. Maturity-level correspondence matrix for the organizational dimension.

It is thus an illustration of the maturity levels for the organizational dimensions. It identifies behavior and attributes that can be observed in an organization at the corresponding level of maturity and will help the organization identify which steps need to be taken to drive the maturation process forward from an organizational perspective.

As a result, the proposed model not only highlights the current maturity level but also a path to new attributes and behaviors that will make the organization as a whole better suited to microservice-based software delivery. It is good to note that these attributes and observations do not always apply uniformly and are not considered to be complete. However, they do highlight elements that have been observed in practice within companies with various levels of organizational maturity.

4 Illustration on Two Organizations

Out of 29 customers of one of the authors, two organizations illustrating very different trajectories in the maturity model have been chosen. The first one (for confidentiality reasons, let's call it *company A*) is a mid-sized established vertical software editor, with a strong technical culture. It is locally recognized as a pioneer in Service Oriented Architecture. The change to microservices was grassroot: the architects and technical leaders started the implementation as a full-blown replacement of the old monolithic architecture, while the financial and operational impacts were largely ignored. The maturity level on most of the technical axes is high and has reached target in most of them, while only some of the organizational axes have moved and some of them remain extremely low (Table 4) and radar diagram (Fig. 3). The use of the maturity model has helped in raising managers attention and internal as well as external training has been focused

Table 3. Maturity-level correspondence matrix illustration for the organizational dimension.

Maturity levels	Organizational observations
Theory understood but not applied	• The concept of microservices is understood uniformly across the organization • Benefits and downsides can be discussed from a technical and business perspective without entrenched positions • Implications for products offered and target market understood • Implications for employees understood in terms of training and role definitions • No decisions have been made and actions taken to initiate the creation and use of microservices in the organization
Unskilled approach	• The organization has invested into creating their first microservices • A small number of teams have gone through training and have been provided with tools and infrastructure • Microservice versions of a small number of products are developed in parallel with existing software • Market research is being done to determine how to monetize the new software products • Information streams from technical teams to management to inform of product attributes, which needs to be translated to organizational change • Initial disillusionment due to lack of expertise and early mistakes • Recruitment of talent difficult due to a lack of understanding of what skillset is required
Microservices by the book	• Having learned from the previous stage, technical and organizational blockers have been removed • Relevant contracts for supporting developments have been agreed (e.g., cloud providers) • Information stream between technical teams and management, with business requirements influencing development and technical knowledge influencing planning and feature strategy • Talent recruitment is easier as a better appreciation of job expectations is put in place • Software licensing has shifted towards selling software as a service rather than a product • Management has redefined its business model and future planning to center around microservices

(*continued*)

Table 3. (*continued*)

Maturity levels	Organizational observations
Expertise	• Substantial earnings and revenue of the organization is generated by microservice-based software • Organization is comfortable expanding feature sets and moving into new markets, trusting their software to cope • Development teams have been empowered to develop and restructure software systems based on technical considerations • The organization explores and experiments with product and product features in rapid fashion, with minimal impact on workload and management • New markets are now fully available to the organization and competition with technically capable competitors is possible on a consistent basis
Application beyond best practice	• The majority of software products offered by the company are now centered around microservice architectures • Understanding of microservice benefits and limitations from a technical perspective and business implications permeate the entire organization • Measures have been put in place to isolate the organization from vendor lock-in challenges • Tooling support is explored and encouraged to ease development beyond core software teams and upskill relevant parts of the organization • Active participation in microservices community is encouraged with employees being allowed to make in-house tools publicly available and attend and present at tech conferences • Experimentation and sandboxing are supported and expected to be regular practice to ensure staying ahead of the curve • Active knowledge sharing across the organization with a common sense of pride with respect to the level that has been reached • Organizational image has changed towards being a high-tech company with customer trust in software offerings • Able to compete with the best in the business and a business model that aims to achieve this • Old software products (almost) completely phased out and maintenance no longer invested in

on functional- and commercial-oriented workforce. A remaining lack in integration and earning model still hurts financial return on the technical investment. Company A has been chosen because it represents, at its paramount level, the maturity path of a fair share

Table 4. Microservice maturity assessment of company A.

		Company A		
		Objective	*Achieved*	*Last eval*
Technical	Integration	5	2	2
	Security	4	3	3
	Performance	4	2	1
	Deployment	3	3	1
	Rapid features	3	2	2
Organizational	Earning model	3	1	0
	Commercialization	3	1	0
	HR and support	2	2	1
	Knowledge management	4	2	1
	Business strategy	4	0	0

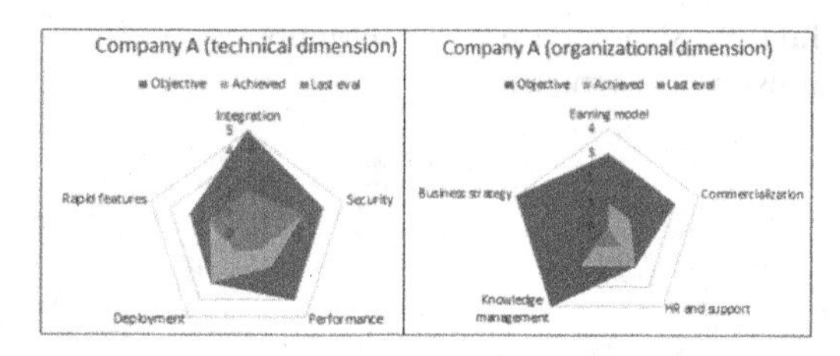

Fig. 3. Maturity radar diagram of company A.

of companies that have been observed by the authors. The corresponding maturity radar diagrams are established in Fig. 3.

The second one (for confidentiality reasons, let's call it *company B*) is a slightly larger but still middle-sized company that operates in retail services, also on a national scale. Though it does not belong to the software market, it could almost be considered as digital native, since most of its organization has been thought from the beginning around its information system. Company B has progressively come to a microservices approach, due to the same problems as company A, namely the increasingly problematic rate of evolution due to its monolithic information system. The main difference between the two companies, which are by other means quite comparable, is that company B has a financial approach to its software systems, and has prolonged the use of the legacy system until the risks indicators made it needed to think of a replacement. This replacement activity has been carefully thought of, based on a benchmark using the proposed maturity model in its technical dimension and evolution plan where costs, benefits and risks are modeled and adjusted along a three-year planning.

Though the objectives are high, the rate of evolution is more than satisfying. The drive on this plan, backed up by the managers, direction and even financial stakeholders is identified as the main reason for the high rate of transformation. Company B's maturity is stated through its assessment (Table 5).

Company B's maturity radar diagrams are represented above (Fig. 4). It should be noted that these diagrams cannot be used to compare the rate of maturity change, but only the state of maturity itself, since the time between the last evaluation against the maturity model and the current evaluation that represents the achieved maturity is not the same for the two companies (more than two years for company A and less than a year for company B, which has started its microservices journey several years later but evolves much faster, certainly due to the fact that much more return of experience is now available).

Table 5. Microservice maturity assessment of company B

		Company B		
		Objective	*Achieved*	*Last eval*
Technical	Integration	3	2	1
	Security	2	2	1
	Performance	2	1	0
	Deployment	4	1	0
	Rapid features	2	2	1
Organizational	Earning model	3	2	2
	Commercialization	3	3	2
	HR and support	4	3	2
	Knowledge management	4	4	2
	Business strategy	4	4	4

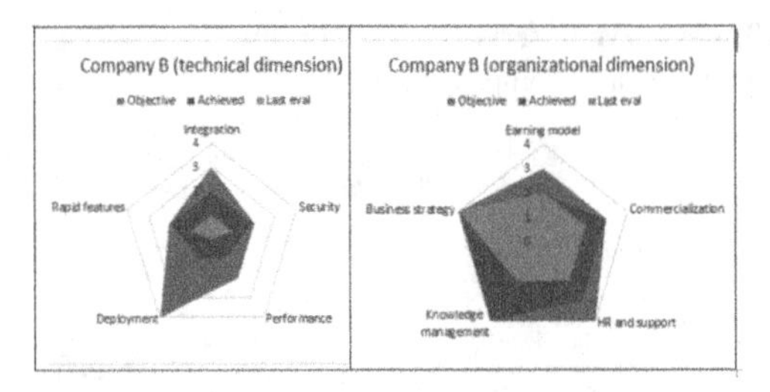

Fig. 4. Maturity radar diagram of company B

5 Related Work

Maturity is a measurement of the ability of an organization for continuous improvement in a particular discipline [18]. Even if there is no consensus nor theoretical foundations on how to build them [19], there are multiple approaches for both researchers and practitioners to develop maturity models and a wide range of maturity assessment models have been developed as well by practitioners and academics over the past years. Almost each field (Analytics, Change Management, Continuous Delivery, Enterprise Architecture, Information Technology, Business Process Management…) has its proper maturity models. There are also universal maturity models like the most know of maturity models, Capability Maturity Model Integration (CMMI) [20, 23, 24]. The main idea of a maturity model is to briefly describe the typical behavior (activities) exhibited by an organization at a number of levels of maturity [21]. For each activity, it provides a description of the activity as it might be performed at each defined maturity level. Maturity models are designed to assess the maturity of a selected domain [22] and provides guidelines how to reach the next, higher maturity level [21]. All maturity models serve as informed approach for continuous improvement [20, 21] or as means of self or third-party assessment [21, 25]. MiMMo falls under the second category. It has been proposed to assess the current state and the desired future state of maturity of organizations regarding microservices. This paper proposes the initial milestones towards a general framework, with the objective to serve as a foundation for future research into a fully formalized maturity model, by involving as well academics and practitioners.

Even if there are reference architectures available in the service-oriented field, like the Open Group SOA Reference Architecture[2], there is no standard or reference architecture for micro-services. There are some beginning works, like the microservices capability model and a maturity model proposed in the book [26]. As for MiMMo, it is based on experience in industry. The capability model is divided in four areas: Core Capabilities (for components of a MS), Supporting Capabilities (not directly linked to MSs but to necessary for their development), Process & Governance Capabilities (tools and guidelines about MSs implementations) and Infrastructure Capabilities (for deployment and management of MSs). A maturity model presents 4 levels of maturity on 5 layers (application, database, infrastructure, monitoring and processes). It is interesting on the technical side but no organizational dimension is considered. In addition, no opening is considered to embody other dimensions.

[2] http://www.opengroup.org/soa/source-book/soa_refarch/index.htm .

From the academic view, regarding the microservice domain, several research works start to give some good pointers to the use of microservices and research trends. Among the most cited papers, Pahl et al. [15] proposed a mapping study and a characterization method but from the perspective of continuous development context, cloud and container technology but there is no organizational consideration. Jaramillo et al. [16] address leveraging microservices architecture via Docker technology. The book of Nadareishvili et al [17] addresses principles and practices of microservice architecture. These works are just an excerpt of numerous research contributions on the topic. However, the authors found only one contribution dedicated to the assessment of Microservices Maturity Models. Behara et al. [14] propose a Microservices Maturity Model. The paper outlines the problem of considering microservices by companies only from the technical dimension. They consider different assessment parameters (architecture, functional decomposition, codebase, data...) and, as for our MiMMo framework, different levels of maturity. They propose an assessment methodology but it is completely tied to the parameters they considered, making this methodology not applicable for any specific situation. According to the lack of research works on the topic and the important need of companies to assess their microservices maturity before considering their adoption and how, the authors considers that this field is in emergence. They thus proposed the first steps of MiMMo, that can continue to mature by leaning of all existing initiatives.

6 Discussions and Conclusion

6.1 Discussion

The MiMMo proposed in this paper aims to provide a framework and guidance for organizations who are keen to embark on and improve their use of microservices as the foundation for their software development. As MiMMo is a generalization of observed best-practice in industry across a large number of organizations, it will have general applicability. However, there are a number of challenges and discussion points that need to be considered.

Generalizability Across Domains and Organizations: While MiMMo is grounded in real-world observations of best practice in industry, it can be argued that further work is needed to establish its applicability across a wider range of domains. Depending on the starting point and knowledge inherent to the organization as well as the core business domain, refinement or adjustment of the model is required for aspects it currently does not consider. For example, it is highly likely that the organizations studied have gone through knowledge acquisition, training and experimentation even before making organizational changes. The current study does not consider such influences, making it a heuristic advice framework at this point rather than a full-fledged model. To ascertain completeness and to identify such refinement a more in-depth analysis and systematic evaluation of MiMMo is required. Another research track is to lean and to sustain the building of the model with the theory of design science.

Longevity and Technology Progress: A second consideration is the applicability of MiMMo in the long-term. Microservices are currently gaining in popularity, but their technology and management is rapidly changing and improving. In particular, the creation and management of microservices and serverless functions has been considerably streamlined over the last few years, which in turn will lower the bar for adoption of the technology. However, designing and architecting a software system and company infrastructure that is capable of taking advantage of this capability will remain as hard as before. It is likely that MiMMo will require continual updating with current best practices and deeper understanding of technical and business challenges to remain relevant. Further analysis of this is needed over a longer period of time to ensure the framework is up to date and has extension mechanisms that can cover these evolutions.

6.2 Conclusions

The main hurdles companies face for adopting microservices is lack of knowledge of how to adopt, in an appropriate way and according to their context, the microservice architectural style [1–3]. In this paper the authors proposed a Microservice Maturity Model (MiMMo) to help organizations to assess their degree of maturity in order to adopt the microservice architectural style by leaning before all on their situation, weakness and strengths. The proposed MiMMo represents the first milestones of an assessment framework upon which an organization can: (i) benchmark itself on its current use of microservices; (ii) project the next steps it needs to make in order to achieve a higher microservices maturity level and (iii) analyze how it has evolved and which area needs improvement to maintain global coherence between technical and business stakes.

The proposed MiMMo has been defined on the two most important dimensions of an organization: the technical and the organizational dimensions. Each of them has been declined in 5 levels of maturity in a correspondence matrix (Fig. 1 and Fig. 2). Each of this matrix has been illustrated on encountered situations (Table 2 and Table 3). However, depending on the type of organization (for-profit, foundation, open-source, etc.) as well as the domain in which they are active, not only the technical and organizational dimensions can be refined, but likely additional dimensions can be identified and detailed as well the levels of maturity.

This paper presents the first steps, with the objective to serve as a foundation for future research into a fully formalized maturity model, by involving as well academics and organizations. For this, MiMMo is intended to be extensible by design, with the levels of maturity as a general categorization that is relevant and relatable across all dimensions. Adding a new dimension needs to establish the maturity-level correspondence matrix of the new dimension (for instance *Sustainability* dimension) by making the projection of the MiMMo level on the considered dimension, like in Fig. 1 and Fig. 2 for the Technical and Organizational dimensions. This creates the flexibility to define new and refined dimensions for specific domains and types of organizations in parallel to the dimensions already addressed in this article.

The overall maturity of an organization can then be interpreted as a combination of the score in each individual dimension, which can be represented for example as a score card or a spider chat. The authors did not propose a detailed methodology on how to assess the maturity of an organization with MiMMo. Proposing a methodology is not viable since there are so many numerous trade-offs to consider. Reasons to adopt microservices and how may vary considerably between different organizations [5, 6]. It completely depends on the organizations, their context and the adopted business strategy. The authors' position is to propose the MiMMo and explain its use through the case of two organizations and then let each organization find its proper barycenter of maturity. This is completely tied to the business strategy. Moreover, MiMMo is proposed based on authors experience. It needs to be improved in the future with interviews of industry experts to help practitioners develop their assessment capabilities, tied with the objective to facilitate academic contributions, ideally around a formal framework.

References

1. Beyond agile: is it time to adopt microservices (2017). https://info.leanix.net/hubfs/leanIX_Microservices-Study.pdf
2. Balalaie, A., Heydarnoori, A., Jamshidi, P.: Microservices architecture enables devops: migration to a cloud-native architecture. IEEE Softw. **33**(3), 42–52 (2016)
3. Knoche, H., Hasselbring, W.: Drivers and barriers for microservice adoption-a survey among professionals in Germany. Enterp. Model. Inf. Syst. Arch. (EMISAJ)-Int. J. Concept. Model. **14**(1), 1–35 (2019)
4. Lewis, J., Fowler, M.: Microservices (2014). http://martinfowler.com/articles/microservices.html
5. Killalea, T.: The hidden dividends of microservices. Commun. ACM **59**(8), 42–45 (2016)
6. Singleton, A.: The economics of microservices. IEEE Cloud Comput. **3**(5), 16–20 (2016)
7. Erl, T.: Service-Oriented Architecture. Pearson Education Incorporated, Upper Saddle River (1900)
8. Krafzig, D., Banke, K., Slama, D.: Enterprise SOA: Service-Oriented Architecture Best Practices. Prentice Hall Professional, Hoboken (2005)
9. MacKenzie, C.M., Laskey, K., McCabe, F., Brown, P.F., Metz, R., Hamilton, B.A.: Reference model for service oriented architecture 1.0. OASIS Standard, 12(S 18) (2006)
10. Hasselbring, W.: Microservices for scalability: keynote talk abstract. In: Proceedings of the 7th ACM/SPEC on International Conference on Performance Engineering, pp. 133–134 (2016)
11. Hasselbring, W., Steinacker, G.: Microservice architectures for scalability, agility and reliability in e-commerce. In: 2017 IEEE International Conference on Software Architecture Workshops (ICSAW), pp. 243–246. IEEE (2017)
12. Newman, S.: Building Microservices: Designing Fine-Grained Systems. O'Reilly, Sebastopol (2015)
13. Wolff, E.: Microservices: Flexible Software Architecture. Addison-Wesley Professional, Boston (2016)
14. Behara, G.K., Khandrika, T.: Microservices maturity model. Int. J. Eng. Comput. Science **6**(11), 22861–22864 (2017)
15. Pahl, C., Jamshidi, P.: Microservices: a systematic mapping study. In: CLOSER, pp. 137–146 (2016)
16. Jaramillo, D., Nguyen, D.V., Smart, R.: Leveraging microservices architecture by using Docker technology. In: SoutheastCon 2016, pp. 1–5. IEEE (2016)
17. Nadareishvili, I., Mitra, R., McLarty, M., Amundsen, M.: Microservice Architecture: Aligning Principles, Practices, and Culture. O'Reilly Media, Inc., Sebastopol (2016)
18. Aceituno, V.: Open information security maturity model. Accessed 18 Mar 2021
19. Mettler, T.: Maturity assessment models: a design science research approach. Int. J. Soc. Syst. Sci. **3**(1–2), 81–98 (2011)

20. SEI - CMMI Product Team: CMMI for Development, version 1.2. Software Engineering Institute, Carnegie Mellon University, Pittsburgh, Pennsylvania (2006)
21. Fraser, P., Moultrie, J., Gregory, M.: The use of maturity models/grids as a tool in assessing product development capability. In: IEEE International Engineering Management Conference, vol. 1, pp. 244–249. IEEE (2002)
22. De Bruin, T., Rosemann, M., Freeze, R., Kaulkarni, U.: Understanding the main phases of developing a maturity assessment model. In: Australasian Conference on Information Systems (ACIS), pp. 8–19. Australasian Chapter of the Association for Information Systems (2005)
23. Paulk, M.C., Curtis, B., Chrissis, M.B., Weber, C.V.: Capability maturity model, version 1.1. IEEE Softw. **10**(4), 18–27 (1993)
24. Ahern, D.M., Clouse, A., Turner, R.: CMMI Distilled: A Practical Introduction to Integrated Process Improvement. Addison-Wesley Professional, Boston (2004)
25. Hakes, C.: The Corporate Self Assessment Handbook: For Measuring Business Excellence. Chapman & Hall, London (1995)
26. Rajesh, R.V.: Spring 5.0 Microservices. Packt Publishing Ltd., Birmingham (2017)

Dealing with Uncertain and Imprecise Time Intervals in OWL2: A Possibility Theory-Based Approach

Nassira Achich[1,2](✉), Fatma Ghorbel[1,2], Fayçal Hamdi[2], Elisabeth Metais[2], and Faiez Gargouri[1]

[1] MIRACL Laboratory, University of Sfax, Sfax, Tunisia
nassira.achich.auditeur@lecnam.net, fatmaghorbel6@gmail.com, faiez.gargouri@isims.usf.tn
[2] CEDRIC Laboratory, Conservatoire National des Arts et Métiers (CNAM), Paris, France
{faycal.hamdi,elisabeth.metais}@cnam.fr

Abstract. Dealing with temporal data imperfections in Semantic Web is still under focus. In this paper, we propose an approach based on the possibility theory to represent and reason about time intervals that are simultaneously uncertain and imprecise in OWL2. We start by calculating the possibility and necessity degrees related to the imprecision and uncertainty of the handled temporal data. Then, we propose an ontology-based representation for the handled data associated with the obtained measures and associative qualitative relations. For the reasoning, we extend Allen's interval algebra to treat both imprecision and uncertainty. All the proposed relations preserve the desirable properties of the original algebra and can be used for temporal reasoning by means of a transitivity table. We create a possibilistic temporal ontology based on the proposed semantic representation and the extension of Allen's relations. Inferences are based on a set of SWRL rules. Finally, we implement a prototype based on this ontology and we conduct a case study applied to temporal data entered by Alzheimer's patients in the context of a memory prosthesis.

Keywords: Uncertain and imprecise temporal data · Temporal representation · Temporal reasoning · Possibility theory · Allen's interval algebra · Possibilistic temporal ontology

1 Introduction

Human-made data in the semantic web field are mostly prone to different types of imperfection including imprecision, incompleteness and uncertainty. Temporal data is no exception [1]. Besides, data may suffer from multiple imperfections at the same time. For instance, information like "*I think I was living in Paris between the 60's and the 70's*" encompasses two kinds of imperfections that are

S. Cherfi et al. (Eds.): RCIS 2021, LNBIP 415, pp. 541–557, 2021.
https://doi.org/10.1007/978-3-030-75018-3_35

uncertainty expressed by "*I think*" and imprecision expressed by "*between the 60's and the 70's*". Representing and reasoning about this kind of data is what we specifically addressed in this work.

In the semantic web field, several approaches have been proposed to deal with perfect time intervals. In our previous works, we proposed approaches to deal with imperfect temporal data in OWL2, specifically imprecise temporal data [2,4] or uncertain temporal data [3]. However, dealing with simultaneously uncertain and imprecise temporal data is another matter that needs to be solved. To our knowledge, there is no approach that has addressed this problem in the context of Semantic Web. Our previous proposed approaches are based on theories that are devoted to deal with only imprecision (using fuzzy theory) or uncertainty (using probability theory). Temporal data, we are processing in this work, are simultaneously uncertain and imprecise. Possibility theory provides models that can handle, at the same time, different types of information and different forms of imperfection [35]. Adapting this theory to the context of the semantic web leverages the use of semantic technologies on data that could not fully exploit due to their imprecision and uncertainty or any other imperfection.

Thus, to represent and reason, in OWL2, about time intervals that are both uncertain and imprecise at the same time, we propose an approach based on the possibility theory. Indeed, according to [33], this theory is devoted to deal with both imprecise and uncertain information. Our approach consists of: *(1)* Proposing a set of rules that calculate possibility and necessity degrees related to the imprecision and the uncertainty of the time interval. *(2)* Proposing a semantic representation for the handled temporal data based on the obtained possibility and necessity measures, and the associated qualitative relations. *(3)* Reasoning about uncertain and imprecise time intervals by extending the Allen's interval algebra [5] (that handle only qualitative relations between perfect time intervals) with qualitative temporal relations between uncertain and imprecise time intervals. This extension preserves important properties of the original algebra. All relations can be used for temporal reasoning by means of a transitivity table. *(4)* Proposing an OWL 2 possibilistic temporal ontology called "*PossibilisticTemporalOnto*". This ontology is implemented based on the proposed semantic representation and Allen's extension. Inferences are carried out using SWRL rules.

The structure of this paper is as follows: Sect. 2 presents some related work in the fields of temporal data representation and reasoning in the Semantic Web. Section 3 introduces our approach to deal with uncertain and imprecise temporal data in OWL 2 using possibility theory. Section 4 presents our proposing possibilistic temporal ontology. Section 5 presents a case study that we conduct in the context of Captain Memo [31] the memory prosthesis dedicated to Alzheimer's patients based on PersonLink [32] ontology. Section 6 presents the principal conclusions of the presented work and some future works.

2 Related Work

In the literature, a variety of approaches have been proposed to represent and reason about temporal information in Semantic Web. In this section, we review the main ones.

2.1 Temporal Data Representation in Semantic Web

Several ontology-based approaches have been proposed to represent temporal data. Some of these approaches extend OWL or RDF Syntax such as Temporal Description Logics [6], Concrete Domains [7] and Temporal RDF [10], and others rely on the existing OWL or RDF constructs without extending their syntax such as Versioning [12], Reification [13], N-ary Relations [14], 4D-fluents approach [15] and Named Graphs [17].

Temporal Description Logics extend the standard description logics with new temporal semantics such as "until". This approach does not suffer from data redundancy and retain decidability [3]. However, it is an avoidable solution because it extends OWL or RDF, which is a tedious task. Concrete Domains requires introducing additional data types and operators to OWL. Several implementations, such as OWL-MeT [8] and TL-OWL [9] have been proposed based on this approach. Temporal RDF uses only RDF triples and does not have all the expressiveness of OWL language. In addition, it cannot express qualitative relations. In [11], the authors present a comprehensive framework to incorporate temporal reasoning into RDF. Versioning handles changes in ontology by creating and managing different variants of it. However, all the versions are independent from each other which require exhaustive searches in the different versions. Reification is a technique for representing N-ary relations when only binary relations are allowed. Whenever a temporal relation has to be represented, a new object is created. This approach suffers from data redundancy. N-ary Relations proposes to represent an N-ary relation as two properties each related to a new object. It maintains property semantics. However, it also suffers from data redundancy. The 4D-fluents approach represents time intervals and their evolution in OWL. It minimizes the problem of data redundancy, as the changes occur only in the temporal parts and keeps the static part unchanged. Concepts varying in time are represented as 4-dimensional objects with the 4th dimension being the temporal data. Many approaches adopt the 4D-fluents approach such as [16]. The Named Graphs approach represents each time interval by exactly one named graph, where all triples belonging share the same validity period. Reasoning and querying are supported in [6,18–20] and [21].

All these approaches have been proposed to represent only perfect temporal data in Semantic Web and neglect imperfect ones.

2.2 Temporal Data Reasoning in Semantic Web

Most of the proposed approaches extend Allen's Interval Algebra. Allen has proposed 13 perfect qualitative relations between two precise time intervals.

A number of approaches extend Allen's interval algebra to propose temporal relations between precise time intervals. In [22], the authors represent a precise time interval as a pair of possibility distributions that define the possible values of the bounds of the interval. This approach proposes some imprecise relations such as "Long Before". In [23], the authors propose a fuzzy extension of Allen's interval algebra. Imprecise temporal relations are not studied.

Several approaches extend Allen's interval algebra to propose temporal relations between imprecise time intervals. In [24], the authors represent these intervals as fuzzy sets. They introduce a set of auxiliary operators on time intervals and define fuzzy counterparts of these operators. However, many of the properties of the original Allen's interval algebra are lost. Thus, the compositions of the resulting relations cannot be studied by the authors. In [25], the authors propose a generalization of Allen's interval algebra. In this approach, Allen's temporal relations, as well as some imprecise relations, are handled. This approach preserves a good number of the properties of the Allen's algebra and the resulting relations could be used for fuzzy temporal reasoning by means of a transitivity table. However, not all the imprecise temporal relations are studied by the authors. In [26], the authors propose an approach that allows uncertain temporal inference. They extend Allen's algebra to handle imprecise time intervals by representing them as trapeziums with distinct beginning, middle and end. They developed an uncertain version of the transitivity table. In [27], the authors generalize Allen's relations to make them applicable to imprecise time intervals in conjunctive and disjunctive ways. The compositions of the resulting relations are not studied by the authors. Imprecise temporal interval relations are not proposed by this approach. In [28], the authors propose a Fuzzy-based approach to reason about imprecise temporal relations by extending Allen's Algebra. In our previous work [3], we propose an approach to reason about certain and uncertain temporal relations by extending the Allen's Interval relations. Certainty degrees were calculated using Bayesian Network.

Most of the proposed approaches that represent and reason about imperfect temporal data, mainly deal with imprecise temporal data or uncertain temporal data and use fuzzy and probability theories. However, to the best of our knowledge there is no approach to deal with temporal data that are both uncertain and imprecise at the same time, in an ontology. We believe that possibility theory can deal with temporal data subject to this kind of imperfection, in OWL2.

3 Our Approach to Deal with Jointly Uncertain and Imprecise Temporal Data in OWL 2

The approach that we propose in this paper deals with jointly uncertain and imprecise time intervals using possibility theory. This theory characterizes events by two measures which are possibility Π and necessity (or certainty)N.

Possibility theory is based on possibility distributions. A possibility distribution, denoted by $\pi_x(u)$, is an application from the universe of discourse to the scale [0, 1] translating a partial knowledge about the universe [33].

According to [29], the possibility measure of an event A, denoted by Π, is deduced from the possibility distribution $\pi_x(u)$ by:

$$\Pi(A) = sup_{u \in A}\ \pi_x(u) \tag{1}$$

$$N(A) = 1 - \Pi(\overline{\mathrm{A}}) \tag{2}$$

Our purpose is to:

- Estimate possibility and necessity degrees related to the imprecision. Thus, we calculate the possibility and necessity degrees of different possible intervals ($I_{i=1..n}$), that can represent the time interval I. I_i are defined by a domain expert. We rely on the equations defined by [29]. As a result, we obtain a set of measures for each interval I_i and then a decision maker can evaluate these measures and select the most possible interval (which has the greatest possibility degree).
- Estimate the possibility and necessity degrees related to the uncertainty. Indeed, according to [29], "A probable (or uncertain) event must be possible". According to [34], a possibility degree is the upper bound of a probability degree and the necessity degree is its lower bound since an uncertain event must be probable and the probable one must be possible (i.e., N(A) $\leq$ P(A) $\leq$ Π(A)). Indeed, necessity N represents the certainty degree of information. According to [35], If "N = 1", then the information is certain (absolute certainty). In our case, the temporal information is uncertain, thus N must be strictly less than 1 (N < 1).

3.1 Possibility and Necessity Measures

Let $[L, U]$ be a temporal interval representing the extreme bounds of the jointly uncertain and imprecise temporal information, where "L" is the extreme lower bound and "U" is the extreme upper bound of the interval. For example, if we have the information *"I think I was living in Paris between the 60's and the 70's"*, $[L, U] = [60's, 70's]$, precisely $[1960, 1979]$. Let $I_i = [I_i^-, I_i^+]$ representing the different possible intervals that can represent this information, defined by a domain expert, where: $I_i = \{I_1, I_2, \ldots, I_n\}$ and L $\leq I_i \leq$ U.

Let $I_i = [I_i^-, I_i^+]$ be each possible time interval represented by its imprecise lower and upper bounds; where $I_i^- = [I_i^{-(1)}, I_i^{-(N)}]$ and $I_i^+ = [I_i^{+(1)}, I_i^{+(N)}]$.

To calculate possibility and necessity measures, we propose five rules. The first four rules concern the imprecision of the time intervals. The fifth rule concerns the uncertainty of the whole given information.

Rule 1. Let "R_1" be a rule specified by means of the binary relation "$\geq$" and a fixed extreme lower bound of the temporal information "L". This rule means that the starting lower bound "$I^{-(1)}$" has to be greater or equal to "L":

$$R_1(\geq, I_i^{-(1)}, L) : I_i^{-(1)} \geq L \tag{3}$$

Possibility and necessity degrees related to each I_i and satisfying R_1, can be expressed, respectively, as "$\Pi_{(R_1(I_i))}(True)$" and "1 - $\Pi_{(R_1(I_i))}(False)$" and can be calculated as follows:

$$\Pi_{(R_1(I_i))}(True) = sup_{I_i^{-(1)} \leq w} \ \pi_L(w) \tag{4}$$

$$1 - \Pi_{(R_1(I_i))}(False) = inf_{I_i^{-(1)} > w} \ 1 - \ \pi_L(w) \tag{5}$$

To simplify the notation, we denote "$\Pi_{(R_1(I_i))}(True)$" as "P($R_1(I_i)$)" and "1 - $\Pi_{(R_1(I_i))}(False)$" as "N($R_1(I_i)$)":

$$P(R_1(I_i)) = sup_{I_i^{-(1)} \leq w} \ \pi_L(w) \tag{6}$$

$$N(R_1(I_i)) = inf_{I_i^{-(1)} > w} \ 1 - \ \pi_L(w) \tag{7}$$

Rule 2. Let "R_2" be a rule, specified by means of the binary relation "$\leq$" and a fixed extreme upper bound of the information "U". This rule means that the ending upper bound "$I_i^{+(N)}$" has to be lower or equal to "U":

$$R_2(\leq, I_i^{+(N)}, U) : I_i^{+(N)} \leq U \tag{8}$$

The possibility degree $P(R_2(I_i))$ and necessity degree $N(R_2(I_i))$ of I_i satisfying "R_2" can be calculated as follows:

$$P(R_2(I_i)) = sup_{I_i^{+(N)} \geq w} \ \pi_U(w) \tag{9}$$

$$N(R_2(I_i)) = inf_{I_i^{+(N)} < w} \ 1 - \ \pi_U(w) \tag{10}$$

Rule 3. Let "R_3" be a rule, specified by means of the binary relations "$\leq$". This rule means that the starting upper bound "$I_i^{+(1)}$" has to be greater or equal to the ending lower bound "$I_i^{-(N)}$":

$$R_3(\leq, I_i^{-(N)}, I_i^{+(1)}) : I_i^{-(N)} \leq I_i^{+(1)} \tag{11}$$

The possibility degree $P(R_3(I_i))$ and necessity degree $N(R_3(I_i))$ of I_i satisfying "R_3" can be calculated as follows:

$$P(R_3(I_i)) = sup_{I_i^{-(N)} \leq w \leq I_i^{+(1)}} \ \pi_Z(w) \tag{12}$$

$$N(R_3(I_i)) = inf_{I_i^{-(N)} > w > I_i^{+(1)}} \ 1 - \ \pi_Z(w) \tag{13}$$

Rule 4. To calculate the possibility and necessity degrees of I_i by means of the previous Rules, we propose a fourth one "R_4" that combines the first three ones. This means that this rule presents the conjunction of the three rules:

$$(R_4 = R_1 \wedge R_2 \wedge R_3) \tag{14}$$

The conjunction provides a more precise result than if each source is considered separately [34]. The possibility and necessity degrees in this case can be calculated using "min" operation [33]:

$$P(R_4(I_i)) = min(P(R_1(I_i)), P(R_2(I_i)), P(R_3(I_i))) \quad (15)$$

$$N(R_4(I_i)) = min(N(R_1(I_i)), N(R_2(I_i)), N(R_3(I_i))) \quad (16)$$

Rule 5. The uncertainty of the whole information means that all possible intervals I_i representing the imprecise time interval are uncertain. Thus, we propose a fifth rule "R_5" to estimate possibility and necessity degrees related to the uncertainty of the whole temporal information. P and N are deduced from the obtained results of "R_4" related to the imprecision. We rely on the equations proposed by [30]. In our case:

$$P(R_5(I_i)) = P(R_4(I_1)) \cup ... \cup P(R_4(I_n)) \quad (17)$$

$$N(R_5(I_i)) = N(R_4(I_1)) \cap \ldots \cap N(R_4(I_n)) \quad (18)$$

This means that:

$$P(R_5(I_i)) = max(P(R_4(I_1)), ..., P(R_4(I_n))) \quad (19)$$

$$N(R_5(I_i)) = min(N(R_4(I_1)), ..., N(R_4(I_n))) \quad (20)$$

3.2 Representation of Jointly Uncertain and Imprecise Time Interval in OWL 2

To represent an uncertain and imprecise time interval, we define a set of ontological components, as depicted by Fig. 1. To represent information, we define two instances "ClassInst1" and "ClassInst2" related through an object property "Relation". To represent the temporal part, we introduce a class named "TimeFrame" related to both "ClassInst1" and "ClassInst2" through an object property named "HasTimeFrame".

Let $I = [I^-, I^+]$ be a simultaneously uncertain and imprecise time interval; where $I^- = \{I^{-(1)}...I^{-(N)}\}$ and $I^+ = \{I^{+(1)} \ldots I^{+(N)}\}$ associated with possibility and necessity degrees related to imprecision and possibility and necessity degrees related to uncertainty. We introduce a class "Uncert_Imp_Time_Interval" to represent I. It is a subclass of the class "TimeFrame". We introduce two classes "Lower_Bound" and "Upper_Bound" to represent both bounds I^- and I^+ of I. We define two object properties "Has_Lower_Bound" and "Has_Upper_Bound" to relate, respectively, "Uncert_Imp_Time_Interval" and "Lower_Bound" and "Upper_Bound" classes. We add four crisp datatype properties "Starts_At", "Starts_To", "Ends_At" and "Ends_To", where "Starts_At" has the range $I^{-(1)}$, "Starts_To" has the range $I^{-(N)}$, "Ends_At" has the range $I^{+(1)}$ and "Ends_To" has the range $I^{+(N)}$. We introduce two datatype properties "Pos_Imp_Degree" and "Nec_Imp_Degree" related to "Uncert_Imp_Time_Interval" to represent respectively possibility and necessity degree associated to I (i.e., most possible interval I_i, which has the greatest possibility degree). "Pos_Imp_Degree" has the range "P_{Im}" and "Nec_Imp_Degree" has the range "N_{Im}". We define two datatype properties "Poss_Uncert_Degree" and "Nec_Uncert_Degree" to represent both possibility and necessity degrees related to uncertainty. It relates "Uncert_Imp_Time_Interval" with, respectively, "P_{Un}" and "N_{Un}" associated to I.

To represent the qualitative relations between two uncertain and imprecise time intervals, we introduce the object property "Relation_Intervals". It relates two instances of the class "Uncert_Imp_Time_Interval".

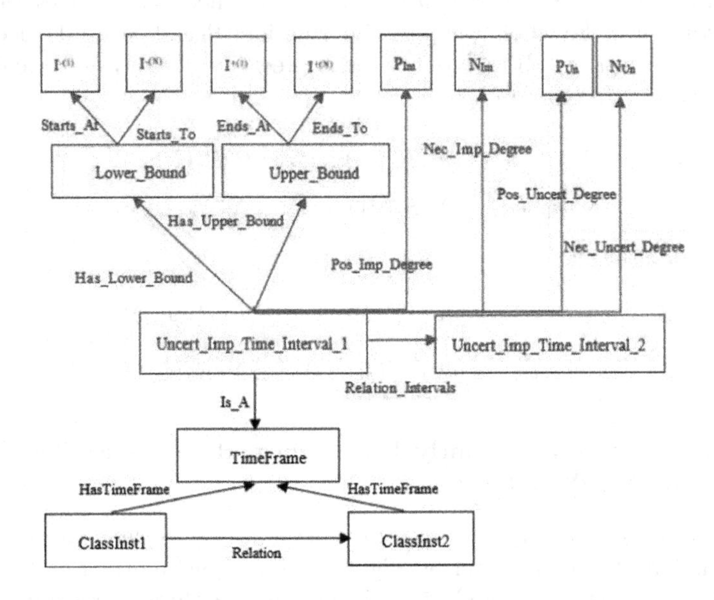

Fig. 1. Our semantic representation of simultaneously uncertain and imprecise time intervals

3.3 Reasoning About Jointly Uncertain and Imprecise Time Interval in OWL 2

We redefine Allen's relation to reason about jointly uncertain and imprecise time intervals based on the defined rules and the corresponding boolean function. For instance, let $I = [I^-, I^+]$ and $J = [J^-, J^+]$ two imprecise time intervals, where $I^- = [I^{-(1)}, I^{-(N)}]$, $I^+ = [I^{+(1)}, I^{+(N)}]$, $J^- = [J^{-(1)}, J^{-(E)}]$ and $J^+ = [J^{+(1)}, J^{+(E)}]$. We redefine I before J as follows:

$$I\ before\ J \rightarrow R(<, I^{+(N)}, J^{-(1)}) \tag{21}$$

This means that "I before J" holds if the following rule "R (<, $I^{+(N)}$, $J^{-(1)}$)" is satisfied. It means that the boolean relation "<" must hold between the ending

Table 1. Temporal relations between simultaneously uncertain and imprecise time intervals I and J

Relation	Inverse	Definition
I Before J	J After I	R ($<$, $I^{+(N)}$, $J^{-(1)}$)
I Meets J	J MetBy I	R ($=$, $I^{+(1)}$, $J^{-(1)}$) $\wedge$ R ($=$, $I^{+(N)}$, $J^{-(N)}$)
I Overlaps J	J OverlappedBy I	R($<$, $I^{-(N)}$,$J^{-(1)}$) $\wedge$ R ($<$,$J^{-(N)}$, $I^{+(1)}$) $\wedge$ R ($<$, $I^{+(N)}$, $J^{+(1)}$)
I Starts J	J StartedBy I	R ($=$, $I^{-(1)}$,$J^{-(1)}$) $\wedge$ R ($=$, $I^{-}(N)$,$J^{-(N)}$) $\wedge$ R ($<$,$I^{+(N)}$,$J^{+(1)}$)
I During J	J Contains J	R ($<$, $J^{-(N)}$,$I^{-(1)}$) $\wedge$ R ($<$, $I^{+(N)}$,$J^{+(1)}$)
I Ends J	J EndedBy I	R ($<$, $J^{-(N)}$,$I^{-(1)}$) $\wedge$ R ($=$,$I^{+(1)}$,$J^{+(1)}$) $\wedge$ R ($=$, $I^{+(N)}$,$J^{+(N)}$)
I Equals J	J Equals I	R ($=$, $I^{-(1)}$,$J^{-(1)}$) $\wedge$ R ($=$, $I^{-(N)}$,$J^{-(N)}$) $\wedge$ R ($=$, $I^{+(1)}$,$J^{+(1)}$) $\wedge$ R ($=$, $I^{+(N)}$,$J^{+(N)}$)

of the lower bound $I^{+(N)}$ of I and the initial upper bound $J^{-(1)}$ of J. Likewise we redefine the other Allen's relations as shown in Table 1.

Properties. Our temporal relations preserve many properties of the Allen's algebra. We obtain generalizations of the reflexivity/irreflexivity, symmetry/asymmetry and transitivity properties. Let $I = [I^-, I^+]$, $J = [J^-, J^+]$ and $K = [K^-, K^+]$ be simultaneously uncertain and imprecise time intervals.

- ***Reflexivity/irreflexivity***: The temporal relations {Before, After, Meets, Met-by, Overlaps, Overlapped-by, Starts, Started-by, During, Contains, Ends and Ended-by} are irreflexive, i.e., let "TR" be one of the aforementioned relations. It holds that: $TR(I,I) = 0$. For instance, $Before(I,I) = R(<, I^{+(N)}, I^{-(1)}) = 0$ as $I^{+(N)} > I^{-(1)}$. Furthermore, the relation Equals is reflexive. It holds that : $Equals(I,I) = R(=, I^{-(1)}, I^{-(1)}) \wedge R(=, I^{-(N)}, I^{-(N)}) \wedge R(=, I^{+(1)}, I^{+(1)}) \wedge R(=, I^{+(N)}, I^{+(N)}) = 1$.
- ***Symmetry/asymmetry***: The temporal relations {Before, After, Meets, Met-by, Overlaps, Overlapped-by, Starts, Started-by, During, Contains, Ends and Ended-by} are asymmetric, i.e., let "TR" be one of the aforementioned relations. It holds that : TR (I, J) and TR(J, I) $\Rightarrow$ I = J. For instance, it can be deduced from "Before(I, J)" and "Before (J, A)" that "I = J" holds. Indeed, by "Before (I, J)", "R ($<$, $I^{+(N)}$, $J^{-(1)}$)" is deduced, and by "Before (J, I)", "R ($<$, $J^{+(N)}$, $I^{-(1)}$)" is deduced. From "($I^{+(N)} < J^{-(1)}$)" and "($J^{+(N)} < I^{-(1)}$)", it is concluded that I = J. Furthermore, the relation Equals is symmetric. It holds that : Equals (I, J) = Equals (J, I).

- ***Transitivity***: The temporal relations {Before, After, Overlaps, Overlapped-by, Starts, Started-by, During, Contains and Equals} are transitive, i.e., let "TR" be one of the aforementioned relations. It holds that TR (I, J) and TR (J, K) ⇒ TR (I, K). For instance, it can be deduced from "Before (I, J)" and "Before(J, K)" that "Before(I, K)" holds. Indeed by "Before(I, J)", "R (<, $I^{+(N)}$, $J^{-(1)}$)" is deduced, and by "Before(J, K)", "R (<, $J^{+(N)}$, $K^{-(1)}$)"is deduced, consequently "R (<, $I^{+(N)}$, $K^{-(1)}$)" holds. This means that "Before(I, K)" holds.

Transitivity Table. Allen's interval algebra lets us reason from TR1 (I, J) and TR2 (J, K) to TR3 (I, K), where $I = [I^-, I^+]$, $J = [J^-, J^+]$ and $K = [K^-, K^+]$ are crisp time intervals and TR1, TR2 and TR3 are Allen's interval relations. For instance, using Allen's original definitions, we can deduce from During (I, J) and Meet (J, K) that Before (I, K) holds. Indeed by During (I, J), we have $(I^- > J^-)$ and $(I^+ < J^+)$, and by Meet (J, K), we have $J^+ = K^-$. From $(I^+ < J^+)$ and $(J^+ = K^-)$, we conclude Before (I, K).

We generalize such deductions using the three jointly uncertain and imprecise time intervals $I = [I^-, I^+]$, $J = [J^-, J^+]$ and $K = [K^-, K^+]$. Based on Table 1, we can deduce from During (I, J) and Meet (J, K) that Before (I, K) holds. Indeed by During (I, J), we have $R(<, J^{-(N)}, I^{-(1)}) \wedge R(<, I^{+(N)}, J^{+(1)})$, and by Meet (J, K), we have $R(=, J^{+(1)}, K^{-(1)}) \wedge R(=, J^{+(N)}, K^{-(N)})$. From $R(<, I^{+(N)}, J^{+(1)})$ and $R(=, J^{+(1)}, K^{-(1)})$, we conclude Before (I, K). Our transitivity table coincides with Allen's one.

4 Possibilistic Temporal Ontology to Deal with Jointly Uncertain and Imprecise Temporal Data

We propose our possibilistic temporal ontology called *"PossibilisticTemporalOnto"*[1] that implements our proposed semantic representation which is instantiated based on our extension of Allen's relations. Our possibilistic temporal ontology is a classical-based ontology containing new components representing possibility and necessity measures of a jointly uncertain and imprecise time interval. We use the ontology editor Protégé and the Pellet reasoner. Our ontology contains 5 classes, 17 object properties and 8 data properties. We infer via a set of SWRL rules our extension of Allen's algebra. For example:

$$\begin{gathered}
Uncert_Imp_Time_Interval(?I) \wedge Has_Upper_Bound(?I, ?I^-) \wedge \\
Starts_At(?I^-, ?I^{-(1)}) \wedge Starts_To(?I^-, ?I^{-(N)}) \wedge \\
Has_Lower_Bound(?I, ?I^+) \wedge Ends_At(?I^+, ?I^{+(1)}) \wedge Ends_To(?I^+, ?I^{+(N)}) \wedge \\
Pos_Im_Degree(?I, P_{Im}) \wedge Nec_Imp_Degree(?I, N_{Im}) \wedge \\
Pos_Uncert_Degree(?I, P_{Un}) \wedge Nec_Uncert_Degree(?I, N_{Un}) \wedge \\
Uncert_Imp_Time_Interval(?J) \wedge Has_Upper_Bound(?J, ?J^-) \wedge \\
Starts_At(?J^-, ?J^{-(1)}) \wedge Starts_To(?J^-, ?J^{-(E)}) \wedge
\end{gathered}$$

[1] https://cedric.cnam.fr/isid/ontologies/PossibilisticTemporalOnto.owl.

$$Has\_Lower\_Bound(?J, ?J^{+}) \wedge Ends\_At(?J^{+}, ?J^{+(1)}) \wedge Ends\_To(?J^{+}, ?J^{+(E)}) \wedge Pos\_Imp\_Degree(?J, P_{Im}) \wedge Nec\_Imp\_Degree(?J, N_{Im}) \wedge Pos\_Uncert\_Degree(?J, P_{Un}) \wedge Nec\_Uncert\_Degree(?J, N_{Un}) \wedge swrlb : equal(?I^{-(1)}; ?J^{-(1)})) \wedge swrlb : equal(?I^{-(N)}; ?J^{-(E)})) \wedge swrlb : equal(?I^{+(1)}; ?J^{+(1)})) \wedge swrlb : equal(?I^{+(N)}; ?J^{+(E)})) \Rightarrow Equals(?I, ?J)$$

5 Experimentation

We experiment our approach by implementing a prototype based on the proposed ontology. We conduct a case study in the context of Captain Memo prothesis.

5.1 Our Ontology-Based Prototype

Our ontology-based prototype, depicted by Fig. 2, offers user interfaces to explore our approach. It is implemented in JAVA. It allows users to enter and save all the possible time intervals and to calculate possibility and necessity degrees related to imprecision and uncertainty to make decisions based on the obtained measures. Qualitative temporal interval relations are executed based on the proposed SWRL rules.

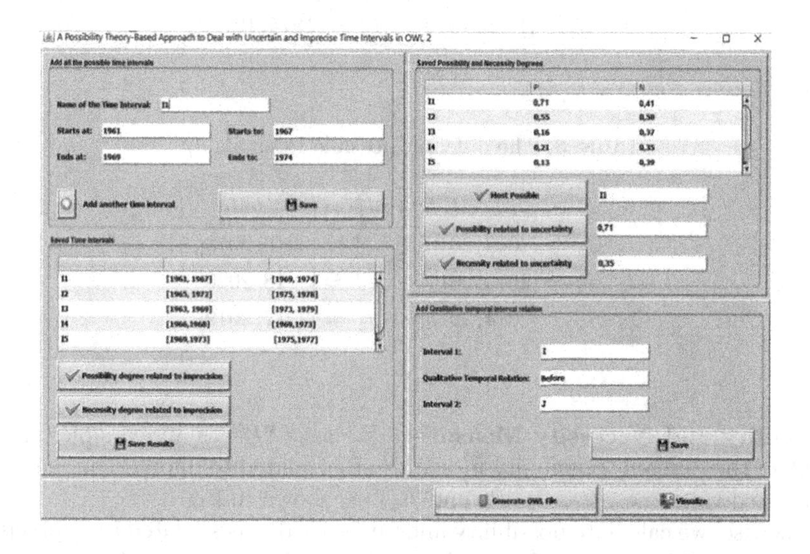

Fig. 2. Our ontology-based implemented prototype

5.2 Case Study : Application to Alzheimer's Patients

We apply our work to Captain Memo, which is a memory prosthesis dedicated to Alzheimer's patients, to handle temporal data that are, simultaneously, uncertain and imprecise, in the context of the PersonLink ontology.

For instance, if we have the information *"I think Françoise was living in France between the 60's and the 70's. Then, she moved to Germany maybe since about 5 years before leaving to Canada"*. Let $[L_1, U_1] = [60's, 70's]$ which means that: $[L_1, U_1] = [1960, 1979]$. Let $I_i = [I_i^-, I_i^+]$ be the different possible time intervals in $[L_1, U_1]$, representing the duration of Françoise's life in France, where $I_i^- = [I_i^{-(1)}, I_i^{-(N)}]$ and $I_i^+ = [I_i^{+(1)}, I_i^{+(N)}]$ represented by Table 2. Let $[L_2, U_2] = [2013, 2020]$. Let $J_j = [J_j^-, J_j^+]$ be the different possible intervals "J" in $[L_2, U_2]$, representing Françoise's move to Germany, where $J_j^- = [J_j^{-(1)}, J_j^{-(E)}]$ and $J_j^+ = [J_j^{+(1)}, J_j^{+(E)}]$ represented by Table 3. All possible time intervals are given by a domain expert.

Table 2. The different possible Intervals I_i

I_i	$I_i^- = [I_i^{-(1)}, I_i^{-(N)}]$	$I_i^+ = [I_i^{+(1)}, I_i^{+(N)}]$
I_1	$I_1^- = [1961, 1967]$	$I_1^+ = [1969, 1974]$
I_2	$I_2^- = [1965, 1972]$	$I_2^+ = [1975, 1978]$
I_3	$I_3^- = [1963, 1969]$	$I_3^+ = [1973, 1979]$
I_4	$I_4^- = [1966, 1968]$	$I_4^+ = [1969, 1973]$
I_5	$I_5^- = [1969, 1973]$	$I_5^+ = [1975, 1977]$

Table 3. The different possible Intervals J_j

J_j	$J_j^- = [J_j^{-(1)}, J_j^{-(E)}]$	$J_j^+ = [J_j^{+(1)}, J_j^{+(E)}]$
J_1	$J_1^- = [2013, 2016]$	$J_1^+ = [2016, 2018]$
J_2	$J_2^- = [2015, 2017]$	$J_2^+ = [2018, 2020]$
J_3	$J_3^- = [2014, 2015]$	$J_3^+ = [2017, 2019]$

Possibility and Necessity Measures. We take "I_1" as an example, and we calculate the different possibility measures of I_1 related to imprecision, based on the defined rules (i.e., R_1, R_2, R_3 and R_4), as shown in Fig. 3.

Likewise, we calculate possibility and necessity degrees related to imprecision of all the possible intervals I_i (i.e., I_2, I_3, I_4 and I_5) as well as all the intervals J_j (i.e., J_1, J_2, J_3). Then, we calculate, from the obtained measures, the possibility and necessity degrees related to the uncertainty based on the introduced equations in Rule 5 (R_5). Tables 4 and 5 present the results.

I_1 has the greatest possibility degree ($P(R_4(I_2)) = 0,71$). This means that I_1 represents the most possible in the set of intervals I_i that fits to be the imprecise interval I.

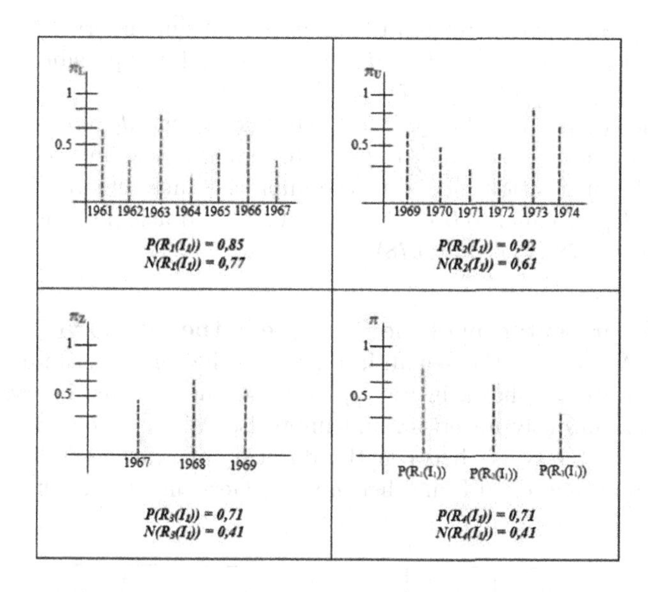

Fig. 3. Possibility and necessity measures of I_1 based on the defined rules

Table 4. Possibility and necessity measures of the jointly uncertain and imprecise time interval I

	P(R_i)				N(R_i)			
I_i	R_1	R_2	R_3	R_4	R_1	R_2	R_3	R_4
I_1	0,85	0,92	0,71	0,71	0,77	0,61	0,41	0,41
I_2	0,92	0,62	0,55	0,55	0,58	0,66	0,76	0,58
I_3	0,16	0,27	0,26	0,16	0,42	0,37	0,44	0,37
I_4	0,5	0,41	0,21	0,21	0,51	0,35	0,38	0,35
I_5	0,13	0,3	0,4	0,13	0,38	0,4	0,6	0,38
P(R_5) = 0,71					N(R_5) = 0,35			

Table 5. Possibility and necessity measures of the jointly uncertain and imprecise time interval J

	P(R_i)				N(R_i)			
J_j	R_1	R_2	R_3	R_4	R_1	R_2	R_3	R_4
J_1	0,66	0,85	0,79	0,66	0,58	0,29	0,25	0,25
J_2	0,62	0,95	0,73	0,62	0,59	0,26	0,59	0,26
J_3	0,91	0,78	0,96	0,78	0,32	0,29	0,15	0,15
P(R_5) = 0,78					N(R_5) = 0,15			

The whole information related to the imprecise time interval I is uncertain at least to a degree equal to 0.35 (N(R_5) = 0,35) and it is possible at most to a degree equal to 0,71 (P(R_5) = 0,71).

J_3 has the greatest possibility degree. This means that J_3 represents the most possible in the set of intervals J_j that fits to represent the imprecise interval J.

The whole information related to the imprecise time interval J is uncertain at least to a degree equal to 0.15 (N(R_5) = 0,15) and it is possible at most to a degree equal to 0,78 (P(R_5) = 0,78).

Semantic Representation of the Example in the Context of PersonLink Ontology. We present the semantic representation of the example using the obtained measures as shown in Fig. 4. We represent the time intervals I and J that are simultaneously uncertain and imprecise. We represent the qualitative relation "Before_Intervals" between the duration of Françoise's life in France, represented by the interval I, and her move to Germany, represented by J.

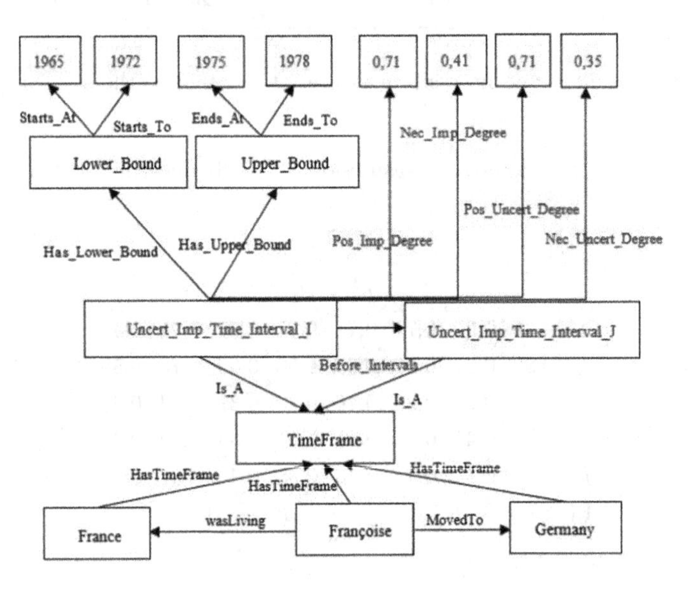

Fig. 4. Semantic representation of the example in the context of PersonLink ontology

6 Conclusion and Future Directions

This paper presents a novel approach to deal with simultaneously uncertain and imprecise time intervals in OWL 2. It is based on the possibility theory. Our first contribution consists of calculating the possibility and necessity degrees based on a set of rules that we defined. Our second contribution is about proposing a semantic representation for the handled temporal data based on the obtained measures. Our third contribution consists of extending Allen's interval algebra to reason about the handled data. We propose 13 temporal relations between simultaneously uncertain and imprecise time intervals. Our extension is favored by keeping reflexivity/irreflexivity, symmetry/asymmetry and transitivity. Our fourth contribution focuses on proposing a possibilistic temporal ontology that implements our proposed semantic representation and Allen's extension. Finally, we implement a prototype based on our ontology.

Compared to approaches based on fuzzy and uncertainty theory which gives each of all possible intervals the same degree of certainty, our approach associates to each possible interval a degree of certainty that differs from the others. This helps decision makers to have more accuracy of the needed information.

In the future, we plan to compare the current approach to other previous fuzzy and probability theories-based approaches. Besides, we plan to extend our approach to deal, in addition to time intervals, with simultaneously uncertain and imprecise time points.

References

1. Achich, N., Ghorbel, F., Hamdi, F., Metais, E., Gargouri, F.: A typology of temporal data imperfection. In KEOD, pp. 305–311 (2019)
2. Achich, N., Ghorbel, F., Hamdi, F., Metais, E., Gargouri, F.: Representing and reasoning about precise and imprecise time points and intervals in semantic web: dealing with dates and time clocks. In: International Conference on Database and Expert Systems Applications, pp. 198–208. Springer, Cham (2019)
3. Achich, N., Ghorbel, F., Hamdi, F., Métais, E., Gargouri, F.: Approach to reasoning about uncertain temporal data in OWL 2. Procedia Comput. Sci. **176**, 1141–1150 (2020)
4. Ghorbel, F., Hamdi, F., Métais, E., Ellouze, N., Gargouri, F.: Ontology-based representation and reasoning about precise and imprecise temporal data: a fuzzy-based view. Data Knowl. Eng. **124** (2019)
5. Allen, J.F.: Maintaining knowledge about temporal intervals. In: Communications of the ACM, pp. 832–843 (1983)
6. Artale, A., Franconi, E.: A survey of temporal extensions of description logics. In: Annals of Mathematics and Artificial Intelligence, pp. 171–210 (2000)
7. Lutz, C.: Description Logics with Concrete Domains. Advances in M.L., pp. 265–296 (2003)
8. Ermolayev, V., et al.: An agent-oriented model of a dynamic engineering design process. Agent-Oriented Information Systems III, pp. 168–183. LNCS 3529 (2006)
9. Kim, S.-K., Song, M.-Y., Kim, C., Yea, S.-J., Jang, H., Lee, K.-C.: Temporal ontology language for representing and reasoning interval-based temporal knowledge. In: 3rd Asian Semantic Web Conference on the Semantic Web, pp. 31–45, 5367 (2008)
10. Gutierrez, C. H.: Temporal RDF. Conference (ESWC'05), pp. 93–107. Springer (2005)
11. Hurtado, C., & Vaisman, A.: Reasoning with temporal constraints in RDF. In International Workshop on Principles and Practice of Semantic Web Reasoning, pp. 164–178. Springer, Heidelberg (200)
12. Klein, M.C., Fensel, D.: Ontology versioning on the Semantic Web. In: SWWS, pp. 75–91 (2001)

13. Buneman, P., Kostylev, E.: Annotation algebras for RDFS. CEUR Workshop Proceedings (2010)
14. Noy, N.R.: Defining N-Ary Relations on the Semantic-Web. W3C Working Group (2006)
15. Welty, C., Fikes, R.: A reusable ontology for fluents in OWL. In: FOIS, pp. 226–336 (2006)
16. Batsakis, S., Petrakis, E.G., Tachmazidis, I., Antoniou, G.: Temporal representation and reasoning in OWL 2. Semantic Web **8**(6), 981–1000 (2017)
17. Tappolet, J. & Bernstein, A.: Applied Temporal RDF: Efficient Temporal Querying of RDF Data with SPARQL. European Semantic Web Conference (pp. 308–322). Springer. (2009)
18. O'Connor, M.J.: A method for representing and querying temporal information in OWL. Biomed. Eng. Syst. Technol. pp. 97–110 (2011)
19. Harbelot, B.A.: Continuum: a spatiotemporal data model to represent and qualify filiation relationships. In: ACM SIGSPATIAL International Workshop, pp. 76–85 (2013)
20. Batsakis, S., Petrakis, E.G.: SOWL: a framework for handling spatio-temporal information in OWL 2.0. In: International Workshop on Rules and Rule Markup Languages for the Semantic Web, pp. 242–249. Springer, Heidelberg (2011)
21. Herradi, N.: A semantic representation of time intervals in OWL2. In: KEOD, pp. 1–8 (2017)
22. Dubois, D., Prade, H.: Processing fuzzy temporal knowledge. In: IEEE Transactions on Systems, Man, and Cybernetics, pp. 729–744 (1989)
23. Badaloni, S., Giacomin, M.: The algebra IAfuz: a framework for qualitative fuzzy temporal. J. Artif. Intell. **170**(10), 872–902 (2006)
24. Nagypal, G., Motik, B.: A fuzzy model for representing uncertain, subjective, and vague temporal knowledge in ontologies. In: OTM Confederated International Conferences on the Move to Meaningful Internet Systems, pp. 906–923. Springer, Heidelberg (2003)
25. Schockaert, S., De Cock, M., Kerre, E. E.: Fuzzifying Allen's temporal interval relations. In: IEEE Transactions on Fuzzy Systems, pp. 517–533 (2008)
26. Sadeghi, K.M.: Uncertain interval algebra via fuzzy/probabilistic modeling. In: IEEE International Conference on Fuzzy Systems, pp. 591–598 (2014)
27. Gammoudi, A., Hadjali, A., Yaghlane, B.B.: Fuzz-TIME: an intelligent system for managing fuzzy temporal information. Int. J. Intell. Comput. Cybernetics (2017)
28. Ghorbel, F., Hamdi, F., Métais, E.: Ontology-based representation and reasoning about precise and imprecise time intervals. In: 2019 IEEE International Conference on Fuzzy Systems (FUZZ-IEEE), pp. 1–8. IEEE (2019)
29. Zadeh, L.A.: Fuzzy sets as a basis for a theory of possibility. Fuzzy sets and syst. **1**(1), 3–28 (1978)
30. Dubois, D., Prade, H.: Théorie des possibilités. REE **8**, 42 (2006)
31. Métais, E., Ghorbel, F., Herradi, N., Hamdi, F., Lammari, N., Nakache, D., Soukane, A.: Memory prosthesis. Non-pharmacological Therapies in Dementia, **3**(2), 177 (2012)
32. Herradi, N., Hamdi, F., Metais, E., Ghorbel, F., Soukane, A.: PersonLink: an ontology representing family relationships for the CAPTAIN MEMO memory prosthesis. In: International Conference on Conceptual Modeling, pp. 3–13 (2015)
33. Dubois, D., Prade, H.: Possibility theory: qualitative and quantitative aspects. In Quantified Representation of Uncertainty and Imprecision, pp. 169–226. Springer, Dordrecht (1998)

34. Dubois, D., Prade, H.: Teoria Vozmojnostei (Traduction Russe de "Théorie des Possibilités", Masson, Paris, 1985/1987). Radio i Sviaz, Moscou (1990)
35. Ammar, S.: Analyse et traitement possibiliste de signaux ultrasonores en vue d'assistance des non voyants (Doctoral dissertation, Ecole Nationale d'Ingénieurs de Sfax (ENIS)) (2014)

[illegible] "Théorie des Probabilités" [illegible] Moscow (1960)
[illegible] C. R. Acad. Sci. Paris [illegible] (1914)

Poster and Demo

KEOPS: Knowledge ExtractOr Pipeline System

Pierre Martin[1,2](✉), Thierry Helmer[3], Julien Rabatel[3], and Mathieu Roche[4,5]

[1] CIRAD, UPR AIDA, 34398 Montpellier, France
pierre.martin@cirad.fr
[2] AIDA, Univ Montpellier, CIRAD, Montpellier, France
[3] CIRAD,DSI, 34398 Montpellier, France
thierry.helmer@cirad.fr
[4] CIRAD,UMR TETIS, 34398 Montpellier, France
mathieu.roche@cirad.fr
[5] TETIS, Univ Montpellier, AgroParisTech, CIRAD, CNRS, INRAE, Montpellier, France

Abstract. The KEOPS platform applies text mining approaches (e.g. classification, terminology and named entity extraction) to generate knowledge about each text and group of texts extracted from documents, web pages, or databases. KEOPS is currently implemented on real data of a project dedicated to Food security, for which preliminary results are presented.

Keywords: Knowledge management system · Text mining

1 Introduction

Many tools and platforms are available for exploring textual data and highlighting new knowledge. TyDI (Terminology Design Interface) [5] is a collaborative platform for manual validation and structuring of terms from existing terminologies or terms extracted automatically using dedicated tools [1]. Other tools like NooJ [8] use linguistic approaches to build and manage dictionaries and grammars. NooJ integrates several NLP (Natural Language Processing) methods like named entity recognition approaches. Other platforms integrate text mining components like CorTexT [2]. CorTexT allows the extraction of named entities and advanced text mining approaches (e.g. topic modeling, word embedding, etc.) are integrated in this platform. Finally some platforms such as UNITEX rely on dictionaries and grammars [6].

KEOPS (Knowledge ExtractOr Pipeline System) is a platform that contains various indexing and classification methods to be applied to the texts that come from databases, documents, or web pages. As output, KEOPS combines classification and indexing results to generate knowledge about each text and group

Supported by Leap4FNSSA H2020 project, SFS-33-2018, grant agreement 817663.

S. Cherfi et al. (Eds.): RCIS 2021, LNBIP 415, pp. 561–567, 2021.
https://doi.org/10.1007/978-3-030-75018-3_36

of texts. KEOPS is currently implemented in different projects dedicated to agriculture domain, e.g. LEAP4FNSSA[1].

This paper introduces the four-step process of the KEOPS platform in Sect. 2 and presents first results of KEOPS applied to LEAP4FNSSA documents in Sect. 3. Section 4 concludes this paper.

2 The KEOPS Platform

The KEOPS platform is made up of autonomous modules linked together to perform the comprehensive processing of the text, extract knowledge, and make it visible to users. KEOPS process is based on 4 main phases presented in Fig. 1 and summarized in the following subsections.

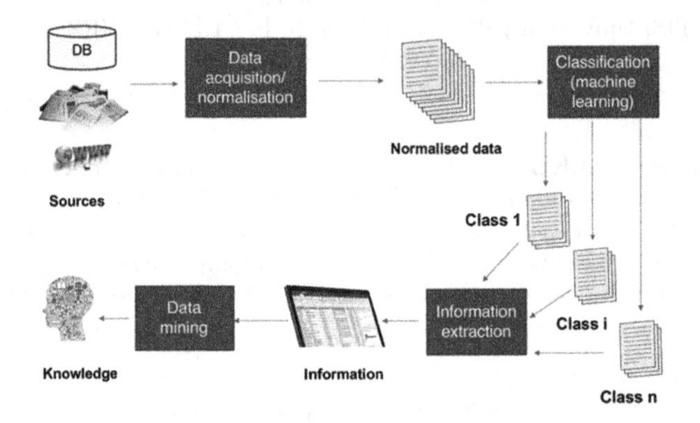

Fig. 1. The KEOPS process.

2.1 Step 1: Data Acquisition

The textual data is collected using three successive tasks. The first one consists in importing a document or a set of documents (i.e. txt, doc, html, pdf). In the case of a website address, the website is copied up to the crawling depth indicated by the user. The second task transforms the imported documents into normalized plain text (deleting images, menus, etc.). The third one identifies the language used in each text.

2.2 Step 2: Document Classification

This step aims to classify the documents according to classes predefined by the user (e.g. Food production, Processing, Distribution, and Consumption). The adopted process is based on a supervised learning method (machine learning - See Sect. 3.1). To proceed, some documents are associated with the predefined

[1] https://www.leap4fnssa.eu/.

classes and a model is learned from this training data. For each new text, the learned model predicts the class to be assigned. This classification is based on the premise that "if documents have a common vocabulary then they can be grouped into common classes (themes)". It should be noted that the texts are first represented in vector form (i.e. bag-of-word representation).

2.3 Step 3: Indexing and Information Extraction

This step aims to extract information from documents through the semantic features and to position a tag next to each occurrence of indexed terms (e.g. keywords, named entities, etc.) in the document (see Fig. 3) according to the following methods and resources:

- Terms of the thesaurus Agrovoc[2] dedicated to agriculture;
- Keywords provided by the users (identified during specific workshops [7]);
- Expert keywords provided by reference databases;
- A terminology (thematic entities) acquired automatically (using BioTex[3]);
- A set of named entities (people, places, organizations, etc.) extracted by SpaCy[4].

Note that the spatial information identified using SpaCy is managed through Gazetteers (e.g. Geonames).

The extracted information, used by step 4, can also be useful for the document indexing task as follows:

- Examples of generic information: location, organization, etc.
- Examples of information related to a Food security domain: water management, food security, crops, etc.

2.4 Step 4: Extraction and Visualization of Knowledge

Using the information obtained in the previous steps (i.e. types of documents in step 1, classes in step 2, and indexed terms in step 3), some results based on data-mining and visualisation algorithms are proposed. The extracted knowledge is then aggregated and presented as maps, graphs, curves, and Venn diagrams in order to enable their validation by experts. An example of output is presented in Fig. 2.

[2] http://www.fao.org/agrovoc/.
[3] http://tubo.lirmm.fr/biotex.
[4] https://spacy.io/.

Fig. 2. Example of Venn diagram result from a subset of projects explored by KEOPS. This representation compares spatial meta-data related to the projects (called P16) and locations extracted with SpaCy in the description of the projects (P17). For instance, this visualisation highlights specific locations (e.g. Nairobi, Australia) cited in the contents of the documents but not as meta-data.

Fig. 3. KEOPS screenshot: example of tags on a LEAP4FNSSA project document. An orange, black, or blue label corresponds respectively to an Agrovoc concept, a user term, or a term extracted using BioTex or Spacy.

3 Case Study

Applied to the LEAP4FNSSA project, the objective of KEOPS is to enable the analysis of the corpus of the projects described in the FNSSA database[5],

[5] https://library.wur.nl/WebQuery/leap4fnssa-projects/.

using associated documents (e.g. report, publication, etc.). The current corpus includes 208 project descriptions, 1227 documents, and 156 website references. The analysis output, based on the documents, can be provided at the project level.

3.1 Classification

In this case study, two classification levels of the documents are considered, i.e. document type and thematic. Classes are identified through an iterative evaluation process taking into account the corpus content.

For the document type level, 8 classes were initially identified during a workshop [7], i.e. Case studies, Facts sheet, Policy brief, Presentation/news/poster, Project report, Publication, Thesis, and Workshop report. Their evaluation on 386 documents, obtained using the multi-layer perceptron classifier[6], provided a best score of 51.75% (average accuracy in a 5-fold cross validation protocol). Merging some of them to get 3 classes (i.e. Information document, Report, Publication) then provided a best score of average accuracy of 82.29% using the Random Forest Classifier (with 50 trees with maximal depth 15). The average precision, recall, and f1-score for this model respectively were 0.80, 0.79, and 0.80.

For the thematic level, 4 classes describing agri-food system were initially suggested, i.e. Food production, Processing, Distribution, and Consumption. An initial evaluation of these classes on 15 documents during a workshop, conducted by 10 experts, showed the need to group 3 classes (i.e. Processing, Distribution, and Consumption), and to add an additional one, i.e. Health. This new set of classes is under testing.

3.2 Indexing

Terminology of KEOPS for indexing is extracted using generic parameters of the BioTex tool [4]. BioTex uses both statistical and linguistic information to extract terminology from free texts. Candidate terms are first selected if they follow defined syntactic patterns (e.g. adjective-noun, noun-noun, noun-preposition-noun, etc.). After such linguistic filtering, a statistical criterion is applied. This measures the association between the words composing a term by using a measure called C-value [3] and by integrating a weighting (i.e. TF-IDF - Term Frequency - Inverse Document Frequency). The goal of C-value is to improve the extraction of multi-word terms while the TF-IDF weighting highlights the discriminating aspect of the candidate term. In our experiments with the LEAP4FNSSA corpus, a terminology is extracted by applying 5 strategies:

- **M1**: Frequent Agrovoc keywords;
- **M2**: Words and multi-word terms extracted with discriminative criteria (i.e. F-TFIDF-C) of BioTex;

[6] The multi-layer perceptron uses the default configuration available in the scikit-learn library.

- **M3**: Multi-word terms extracted with discriminative criteria (i.e. F-TFIDF-C) of BioTex;
- **M4**: Words and multi-word terms extracted with C-Value;
- **M5**: Multi-word terms extracted with C-Value.

In this context, 10 participants of the project analyzed the first terms according to these strategies. The results (see Table 1) highlight that multi-word terms extracted with discriminative measures (i.e. M3) are more relevant for indexing tasks.

Table 1. Quality of terms evaluated by 10 participants of the LEAP4FNSSA project.

	Very relevant	Relev. but too general	Not really relevant	Irrelevant	I don't know
M1	21 (19.0%)	53 (48.1%)	21 (19.0%)	12 (10.9%)	3 (2.7%)
M2	34 (33.0%)	42 (40.7%)	15 (14.5%)	12 (11.6%)	0 (0.0%)
M3	73 (73.0%)	17 (17.0%)	3 (3.0%)	3 (3.0%)	4 (4.0%)
M4	24 (22.6%)	56 (52.8%)	11 (10.3%)	15 (14.1%)	0 (0.0%)
M5	64 (64.0%)	19 (19.0%)	7 (7.0%)	8 (8.0%)	2 (2.0%)

4 Conclusion and Future Work

The classification and indexing steps of the KEOPS process have been implemented and evaluated on real data from the LEAP4FNSSA project. KEOPS is continuously developed in order to meet users' objectives. Within the framework of other European projects, multi-language processing is being integrated.

Acknowledgement. We thank the WP3 members of the LEAP4FNSSA project for their contribution to the indexing and classification tasks. We thank Xavier Rouviere for his contribution to the development of the user interface.

References

1. Aubin, S., Hamon, T.: Improving term extraction with terminological resources. In: Salakoski, T., Ginter, F., Pyysalo, S., Pahikkala, T. (eds.) FinTAL 2006. LNCS (LNAI), vol. 4139, pp. 380–387. Springer, Heidelberg (2006). https://doi.org/10.1007/11816508_39
2. Barbier, M., Cointet, J.P.: Reconstruction of socio-semantic dynamics in sciences-society networks: Methodology and epistemology of large textual corpora analysis. Science and Democracy Network, Annual Meeting (2012)
3. Frantzi, K., Ananiadou, S., Mima, H.: Automatic recognition of multi-word terms: the c-value/nc-value method. Int. J. Digital Libraries **3**(2), 115–130 (2000)

4. Lossio-Ventura, J., Jonquet, C., Roche, M., Teisseire, M.: Biomedical term extraction: overview and a new methodology. Inf. Retr. J. **19**(1–2), 59–99 (2016)
5. Nedellec, C., Golik, W., Aubin, S., Bossy, R.: Building large lexicalized ontologies from text: a use case in automatic indexing of biotechnology patents. In: Proceedings of EKAW, pp. 514–523 (2010)
6. Paumier, S.: Unitex - Manuel d'utilisation, November 2011. https://hal.archives-ouvertes.fr/hal-00639621, working paper or preprint
7. Roche, M., et al.: LEAP4FNSSA (WP3 - KMS): Terminology for KEOPS - Dataverse (2020). http://doi.org/10.18167/DVN1/GQ8DPL
8. Silberztein, M.: La formalisation des langues : l'approche de NooJ. ISTE, London (2015)

Socneto: A Scent of Current Network Overview
(Demonstration Paper)

Jaroslav Knotek, Lukáš Kolek, Petra Vysušilová, Julius Flimmel, and Irena Holubová(✉)

Faculty of Mathematics and Physics, Charles University, Prague, Czech Republic
holubova@ksi.mff.cuni.cz

Abstract. For more than a decade already, there has been an enormous growth of social networks and their audiences. As people post about their life and experiences, comment on other people's posts, and discuss all sorts of topics, they generate a tremendous amount of data that are stored in these networks. It is virtually impossible for a user to get a concise overview about any given topic.

Socneto is an extensible framework allowing users to analyse data related to a chosen topic from selected social networks. A typical use case is studying sentiment about a public topic (e.g., traffic, medicine etc.) after an important press conference, tracking opinion evolution about a new product on the market, or comparing stock market values and general public sentiment peaks of a company. An emphasis on modularity and extensibility of *Socneto* enables one to add/replace parts of the analytics pipeline in order to utilise it for a specific use case or to study and compare various analytical approaches.

Keywords: Social networks · Sentiment analysis · Topic modelling

1 Introduction

Social networks, such as *Twitter*[1] and *Reddit*[2], allow users to easily subscribe to a content producer or to a group interested in some topic. This personalisation may, however, result in a user enclosed in a bubble without being confronted with opposite viewpoints and opinions. It is then easy for the content producers (*influencers*) to influence their subscribers in any way.

Another problem social networks posses is the large amount of data that is impossible to read to form one's opinion. Social networks do not typically offer a tool helping the user to understand the vast amount of data with comprehensive statistics of related topics, sentiment information etc.

[1] https://twitter.com/
[2] https://www.reddit.com/

Supported by the SVV project no. 260588.

S. Cherfi et al. (Eds.): RCIS 2021, LNBIP 415, pp. 568–574, 2021.
https://doi.org/10.1007/978-3-030-75018-3_37

And, last but not least, although social networks have their data publicly accessible (at least in theory), it is not easy to access it, even for, e.g., research purposes. Access to the data is typically limited (see, e.g., [7]) either by the number of posts that can be downloaded per a given time period, or by the age of posts that can be downloaded which disallows an access to historical data.

Naturally, there exist various tools (see Sect. 2) that focus on downloading and/or analysing data from social networks. There are full-fledged services whose level of customisation is limited. Or, there are open-source customisable tools that focus either on data acquisition or data analysis, but they do not combine advantages of both sufficiently. Often they also lack user-friendly outputs.

In this demonstration we introduce *Socneto*[3], an open-source extensible framework that enables one to solve the above described issues comfortably. In a typical use case the user specifies a topic of interest and selects type(s) of required analyses and social networks to be used as data sources. *Socneto* then starts collecting respective data, forwards them to analysers, and stores the results. The user can then study the results either in a tabular version or visualised using various customised charts. The modularity of *Socneto* enables easy extensions and modifications suitable for many use cases of both researchers and practitioners. The users can add/replace parts of the analytics pipeline in order to utilise it for specific requirements or to study and compare different approaches to a particular analytical step.

The main contributions of *Socneto* are as follows:

- *API Limits of Social Networks*: *Socneto* overcomes the API limits by downloading the data continuously and exploiting the given limits to their maximum. Hence, both higher amounts of historical data can be gathered. In addition, when a user submits a job, the results can be seen immediately – *Socneto* is designed to calculate the analyses on the fly.
- *User-friendly Data Insight*: The current release of *Socneto* supports two types of data analyses: (1) *Topic modelling* enables one to identify popular and related topics people talk about. (2) *Sentiment analysis* provides a view of people's opinion on these topics. The results can be visualised using various types of charts. The user can see the number of posts related to a given topic on the timeline, sentiment development in time, top related topics etc.
- *Customisation*: When the user submits a job, (s)he can select data acquirers and data analysers as well as customise result visualisations. As *Socneto* was designed as an extensible framework, users can also add a support for social network data acquisition and data analysis out of the box. The current release supports social networks *Twitter* and *Reddit*. For topic modeling the *Latent Dirichlet Allocation* (LDA) [2] is used. Sentiment analysis is based on the *Bidirectional Encoder Representations from Transformer* (BERT) [3].

Paper Outline: In Sect. 2 we overview related work. In Sect. 3 we introduce the architecture of *Socneto* and its visualisation capabilities. In Sect. 4 we outline the demonstration. In Sect. 5 we conclude.

[3] https://www.ksi.mff.cuni.cz/sw/socneto/

2 Related Work

Naturally there exists a number of related tools. On the one hand, there exists a set of single-purpose (mostly open-source) scripts and simple tools that enable one to process a given set of social network data using a single (or a limited set of) analytical approaches. For example *Analyze Tweets* [1] applies LDA to a given set of Twitter tweets and outputs a JSON document with results.

On the other hand, there is a group of robust (typically commercial) applications. They can be classified according to their core targets: (1) social network data management and access and (2) web monitoring and analysis. Due to space limitations we mention only the most popular representatives.

A tool focusing primarily on presentation and brand management is *Zoomsphere* [8] whose goal is to help companies or influencers to thrive on the supported social networks offering an extensive analysis of a current brand status focused on measuring the impact of created posts. On the other hand, *Socialbakers* [6] offers a solution to the majority of problems stemming from managing social networks. Customers' needs are monitored at various levels ranging from conversational level (hot topic classification) to high-level brand sentiment.

Media monitoring tools are represented, e.g., by *Monitora* [5] that not only scrapes, but also analyses and aggregates the scraped data. While the former tool is used by users for data gathering, the latter one is a paid service that is claimed to employ a team of specialists to collect and interpret the results. This service is used by customers wishing to be informed on a public opinion.

An example of a special-purpose service keeping a track of web content is a recently shutdown service *Google Flu Trends* [4]. It monitored Google Search activity related to searches of influenza to predict the start of a "flu season" in more than 25 countries.

Socneto does not (and cannot) compete with the robust commercial tools. Also because its aims are different. We wanted to create a tool that is:

- *user-friendly*, mainly in deploying, data gathering, and analysis of results,
- *widely applicable* in both research and applied use cases, i.e., not limited to a particular topic or problem domain, and
- *extensible* thanks to openness of code and modular design.

The first release of *Socneto* can be viewed as a proof of the concept that can be easily extended to functionalities of other tools, such as broad scope of sources in *Monitora*, topics related to one user (profile) like in *Zoomsphere* and *Socialbakers*, or even prediction of future trends similarly to *Google Flu Trends*.

3 Architecture

Socneto is a distributed application whose components are loosely coupled. The application is divided into services by their functionality. Everything is connected via *Kafka messaging*[4] or internal REST API. As depicted in Fig. 1, *Socneto* is divided into the following logical parts[5]:

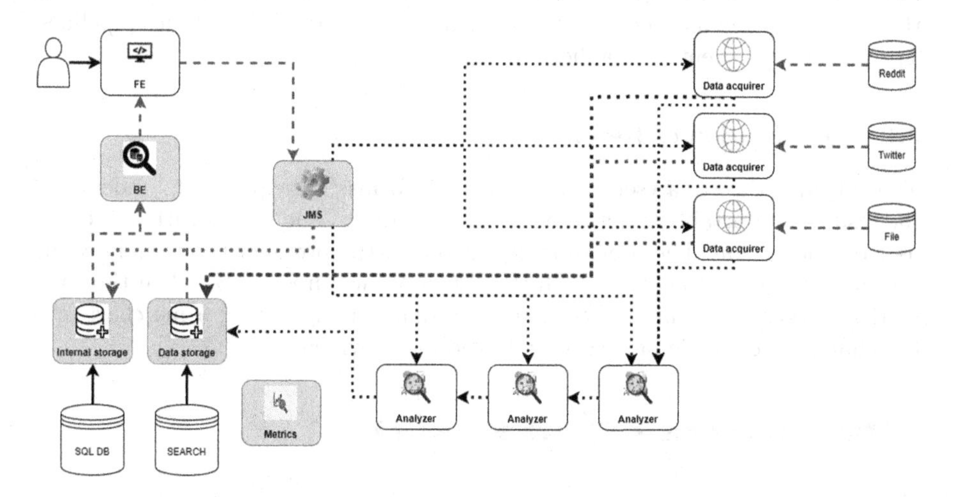

Fig. 1. The components of *Socneto* and their mutual communication. Black lines represent communication via Kafka, red lines via the REST API. (Color figure online)

- *Frontend* (FE): A web-based application with GUI.
- *Backend* (BE): A middle component between frontend and the rest of the platform which provides means to retrieve different data from the platform, creates new jobs, and authenticates users.
- *Job Management Service* (JMS) keeps a track of all registered components, accepts submitted jobs, and distributes jobs among all components (mainly acquirers and analysers) involved.
- *Data Acquirers* (currently for *Reddit*, *Twitter*, or files) download data from a social network (or any source) tackling the respective limits (if any).
- *Data Analysers* (currently topic modelling using LDA and sentiment analysis based on BERT) consume posts and produce results of per-post analyses.
- *Messaging*: Acquired posts are asynchronously sent to analysers and storage. Analysers subscribe to assigned queues and send results to storage.
- *Internal/Data Storages* provide an abstraction of physical databases (*PostgreSQL*[6] and *Elasticsearch*[7]) and store posts, internal data, and results.
- *Monitoring*: *ELK Stack*[8] is used for platform monitoring. Every component can log its events using HTTP or *Kafka* messaging into *Logstash*[9].

[4] https://kafka.apache.org/
[5] Technical details can be found in the documentation at the web page of *Socneto*.
[6] https://www.postgresql.org/
[7] https://www.elastic.co/
[8] https://www.elastic.co/what-is/elk-stack
[9] https://www.elastic.co/logstash

The main aim of the chosen architecture is to ensure an easy adding or replacement of components for both data acquisition and data analysis. In the former case it enables both scalability and extensibility to new data sources. In the latter case the modules can be chained to form complex analytics pipelines. The only requirement is to adhere to the internal API.

3.1 Visualisation of Results

The output of data analysers can have various forms. To help users to understand the results comfortably, *Socneto* offers tables, graphs, and charts with additional user customisation. The user running the out-of-the-box sentiment analysis can first bind the data to a table with the list of all acquired posts. Then the summaries of the sentiment analysis can be visualised, e.g., using a pie chart or a bar chart. An example of such visualisation is provided in Fig. 2.

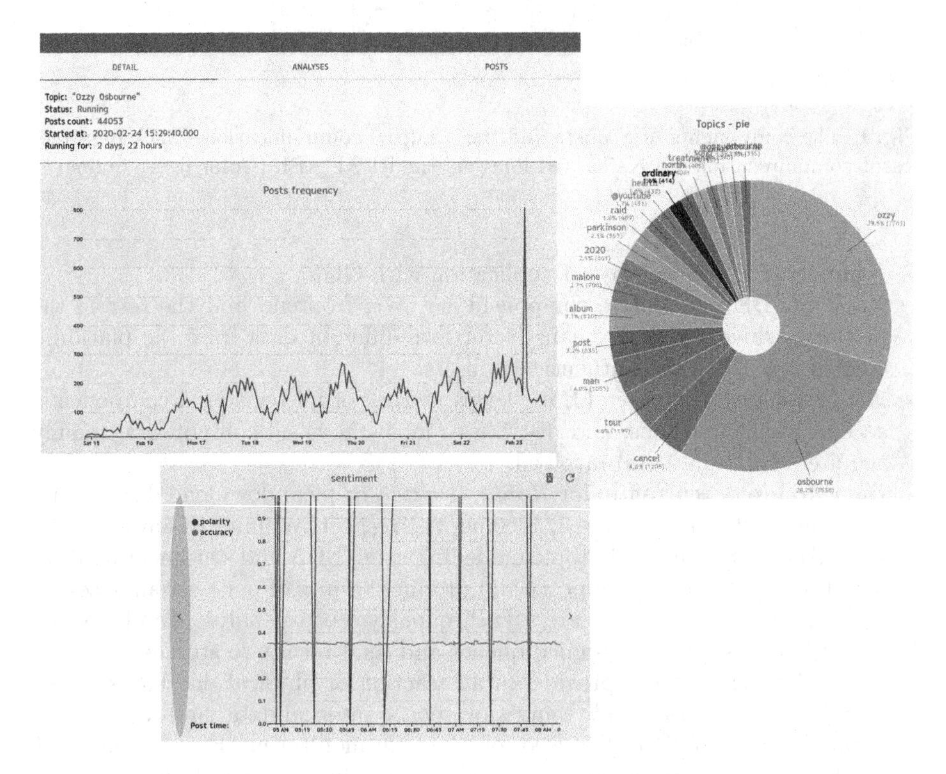

Fig. 2. Examples of visualisations in *Socneto*: a line chart of posts frequency in time, a pie chart of topics frequency, and a line chart of sentiment in time.

4 Demonstration Outline

The demonstration will show a real-world use case where *Socneto* was successfully applied. We will go through the whole process of creating and running own job, as well as showing results of the use case that run for a longer time period. We will also show where and how *Socneto*, being a modular framework, can be easily extended with a new functionality, such as data acquirers, analysers etc.

Médecins Sans Frontières (MSF) Socneto was used for analysis of topics related to measles and snakebites on Twitter. In particular, topic "snakebite" was chosen to see whether it is possible to monitor Twitter to find people that were recently bitten. Topic "measles" was supposed to reveal relations to other topics. The analysis consisted of running two separate jobs for each topic and gathering data for a period of 40 days.

According to the IT representative of the MSF Czech Republic[10], the results confirmed their hypothesis of misleading nature of tweets. Although the query was given in three languages (English, French, and Arabic), the results were mostly in English (as can be seen in Table 1). The finding indicates that Twitter is used mainly as a tool for reporting the news to the world and not for communication among locals. Another analysis led by the MSF themselves showed that Facebook is the primary platform for the latter purpose.

Additionally, the analysis of "measles" helped to identify influential figures with anti-vaccine attitude. Such findings can be used to properly understand the motivation behind defensive attitude towards the prevention of disease outbreaks. On the other hand, the analysis of "snakebites" related tweets did not yield any significant results due to the global nature of the tweeting as described above. It is important to mention that the MSF have their internal analytical department and *Socneto* analysis was complementary to theirs.

Table 1. The distribution of usage of languages for query "measles". Total number of records was 54,211.

Language	# of posts
English	46,998
French	1,855
Arabic	1,211

5 Conclusion

Socneto was designed as an extensible platform for downloading and analysing data primarily from social networks. It enables practitioners to easily study

[10] https://www.lekari-bez-hranic.cz/

particular topics and their sentiment evolving in time. It also helps researchers to gain real-world data and to test and compare various analytical approaches.

As a future work we plan to extend data acquirers to utilise more data offered by social networks (e.g., geo codes, post statistics, or comments). Another direction can be interlinking with other publicly available data.

References

1. Algorithmia: Analyze Tweets (2021). https://algorithmia.com/algorithms/nlp/AnalyzeTweets
2. Blei, D.M., Ng, A.Y., Jordan, M.I.: Latent dirichlet allocation. J. Mach. Learn. Res. **3**, 993–1022 (2003)
3. Devlin, J., Chang, M., Lee, K., Toutanova, K.: BERT: pre-training of deep bidirectional transformers for language understanding. In: NAACL-HLT 2019, pp. 4171–4186. Association for Computational Linguistics (2019)
4. Ginsberg, J., Mohebbi, M.H., Patel, R.S., Brammer, L., Smolinski, M.S., Brilliant, L.: Detecting influenza epidemics using search engine query data. Nature **457**, 1012–1014 (2009)
5. Monitora: Media Intelligence (2020) https://monitoramedia.com/
6. Socialbakers: Unified Social Media Marketing Platform (2020). https://www.socialbakers.com/
7. Twitter: Rate Limits: Standard v1.1 (2020). https://developer.twitter.com/en/docs/twitter-api/v1/rate-limits
8. Zoomsphere: Social Media Analytics (2020), https://www.zoomsphere.com/social-media-analytics

STOCK: A User-Friendly Stock Prediction and Sentiment Analysis System
(Demonstration Paper)

Ilda Balliu, Harun Ćerim, Mahran Emeiri, Kaan Yöş, and Irena Holubová(✉)

Faculty of Mathematics and Physics, Charles University, Prague, Czech Republic
holubova@ksi.mff.cuni.cz

Abstract. Determining a future value of a company in order to find a good target for investing is a critical and complex task for stock marketers. And it is even more complicated for non-experts.

STOCK is a modular, scalable, and extensible framework that enables users to gain insight in the stock market by user-friendly combination of three sources of information: (1) An easy access to the companies' current position and evolution of prices. (2) Prediction models and their customisation according to users' needs and interests, regardless of their knowledge in the field. (3) Results of sentiment analysis of related news that may influence the respective changes in prices.

Keywords: Stock price prediction · Sentiment analysis · Big Data

1 Introduction

Stock markets have always been an interesting area for both practitioners and researchers. The evolution of prices of companies reacts on various events occurring almost anywhere and anytime. It is not only the demand/supply influence, but also various changes in politics or climate, occurrence of new products/technologies, or even just a single Twitter post of a strong influencer.

All these aspects are difficult to grasp even for an expert. Even for him/her the determining a future value of a company in order to find a good target for investing is a critical and complex task. But, there are also common users, who want to explore this area at a non-professional level. Or, there are researchers who want to study this specific challenging world and experiment with novel approaches for stock price prediction.

Naturally there exist tools which help in this process. However, they are usually complex and thus expensive, whereas their functionality is fixed and cannot be easily modified and extended according to users' needs or in order to incorporate a new custom approach.

Supported by the SVV project no. 260588.

S. Cherfi et al. (Eds.): RCIS 2021, LNBIP 415, pp. 575–580, 2021.
https://doi.org/10.1007/978-3-030-75018-3_38

In this demonstration we introduce STOCK[1], a modular, scalable, and extensible framework, where users can gain more insight in the stock market by user-friendly combination of three sources of information:

1. An easy access to the companies' current position and historical evolution of prices.
2. Prediction models and their customisation according to users' needs and interests, regardless of their knowledge in the field.
3. Results of sentiment analysis of related news that may influence the respective changes.

STOCK was designed to be used by three types of target users with distinct needs and expectations:

- *Inexperienced users*, which include users that do not have any knowledge of the stock market or machine learning (ML), but they still want to get some information with easy indicators on how recent events affect the prices.
- *Casual/standard users*, which include users that have a limited knowledge of the stock market and ML, but not enough technical skills to be able to build prediction models themselves.
- *Experienced users,* which include users that have more advanced knowledge of the stock market and ML models building and customisation, but they lack the ability to build them without technical skills, and/or need different types of information and analytical visualisations at one place.

The ML part of *STOCK* focuses on creating user-customised prediction models and predicting future stock prices. It involves two types of stock prediction. The *default stock prediction* predicts stock prices using a Recurrent Neural Network with custom parameters assigned by the development team. This model is responsible to show forecast stock prices when the user visits the company dedicated page without any further requirements on parameters etc. The second type, called *custom stock prediction*, gives the user the power of creating prediction models by selecting from a wide (and extensible) set of verified prediction approaches and configuring their own parameters.

The sentiment analysis part searchers for articles where the particular company is mentioned and evaluates their sentiment. This saves time of the user who does not need to search for such articles and read them in detail (though their full text is available in *STOCK* too).

Combining these information (connected via time) with the history of prices of a company and its description provides a more comprehensive information about promising investment targets.

And, last but not least, the modularity of *STOCK* enables easy extensions and modifications suitable for many use cases of both researchers and practitioners. More types of prediction models and sentiment analysis approaches can

[1] https://github.com/Rinqt/stock

be added and compared, whereas the data are provided at one place and there is the support for visualisation and comparison of the results.

Paper Outline: In Sect. 2 we overview related work. In Sect. 3 we introduce the architecture of *STOCK*. In Sect. 4 we outline the demonstration. In Sect. 5 we conclude.

2 Related Work

As we have mentioned, there exist several tools with similar aims. We will briefly describe and compare with *STOCK* three of the most popular, the most similar, and in terms of functionalities probably also the richest ones.

MarketWatch [3] is an American financial information website that provides business news, analysis, and stock market data. It provides a large amount of information from real time stock prices information to articles and watchlists, but they only focus on providing information and do not make any predictions on the data they provide.

Wallet Investor [1] is a tool that offers cryptocurrency, stocks, forex, fund, and commodity price predictions using ML. Cryptocurrency and other forecasts are based on changes in the exchange rates, trade volumes, volatilities of the past period, and other important economic aspects. The accuracy of the prediction depends on the quantity and the quality of the data, so it is also difficult to anticipate anything in the case of newer cryptocurrencies. However, there is no information on what ML models and their parameters they use to build the predictions.

Wallmine [6] is a tool for financial data visualisation and analysis. It provides various tools for displaying financial information, more precisely stocks, forex, and cryptocurrencies that can help financial experts in making smarter financial decisions. Moreover, they offer information for most of the stock markets similarly to *Wallet Investor* and *Market Watch*. However, the tool lacks ML capabilities and does not focus on stock price predictions.

By analyzing the three (and several other similar) tools, we can conclude that their services cover different parts of *STOCK*, but none of them provides them all. *STOCK* involves several ML models for the user to use, customize, and compare. Another strong difference is that *STOCK* is a modular framework that can be modified and serve multiple, research and practical, purposes.

3 Architecture

The architecture of *STOCK* is depicted in Fig. 1. The key modules are as follows:

- *Client Module* (frontend) is a web application for interaction with *STOCK*.
- *Authentication Server Module* is responsible for authentication and authorization of users.
- *Database Module* stores users' data, financial articles, stock prices, companies' information, and results of ML models.

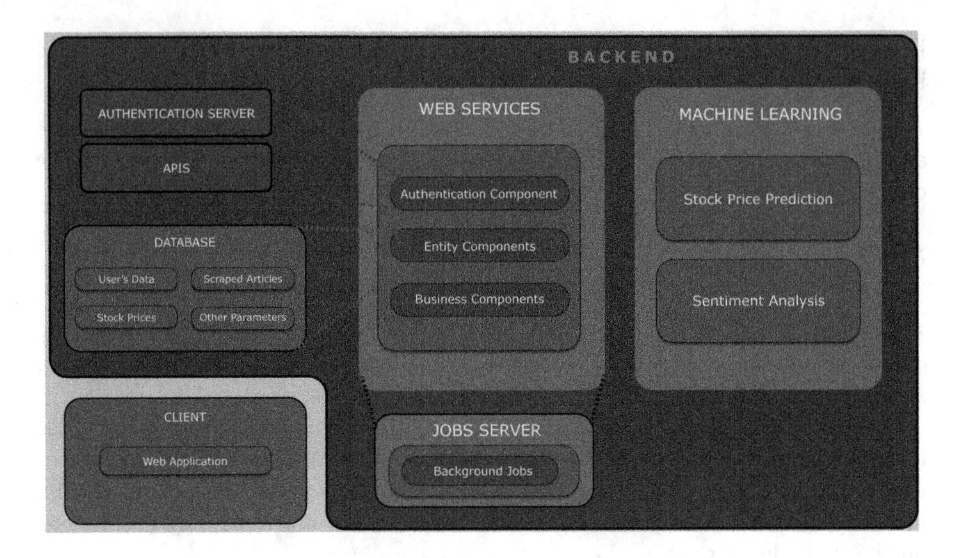

Fig. 1. Architecture of *STOCK*

- *Machine Learning Module*, the core part of *STOCK*, is responsible for:
  - Creating default/custom prediction models; namely in the current release of *STOCK* these are:
    - Regression algorithms [4] (in particular Decision tree, Random forest, Standard regression, Bayesian Ridge regression, Elastic regression, Lasso regression, Lasso Lars regression, and Ridge regression), and
    - Neural network algorithms (in particular Recurrent Neural Network with long-short term memory [5]).
  - Sentiment analysis functionality based on *Vader* [2] using *VaderSharp*[2].
- *Web Services Module* is a middleware responsible for dataflow and business logic between other modules.

When the user creates a custom model with tuned parameters, the request goes to backend. Backend validates the requests and stores the parameters in the database. After that, the backend schedules a job to build the model and sends the parameters to the machine learning module which creates the model and sends back the results to the backend. After the results are stored in the database, they can be retrieved by the frontend upon request.

4 Demonstration Outline

In the demonstration we will show how the tool can be used by the three types of target users. We will go through the whole process of creating and running own predictions, both default and custom, as well as showing and comparing the

[2] https://github.com/codingupastorm/vadersharp

results. As we can see in Fig. 2, we will depict all the possible results we can get using *STOCK* via user-friendly intuitive graphs and charts. We will also show where and how *STOCK*, being a modular framework, can be easily extended with new functionality.

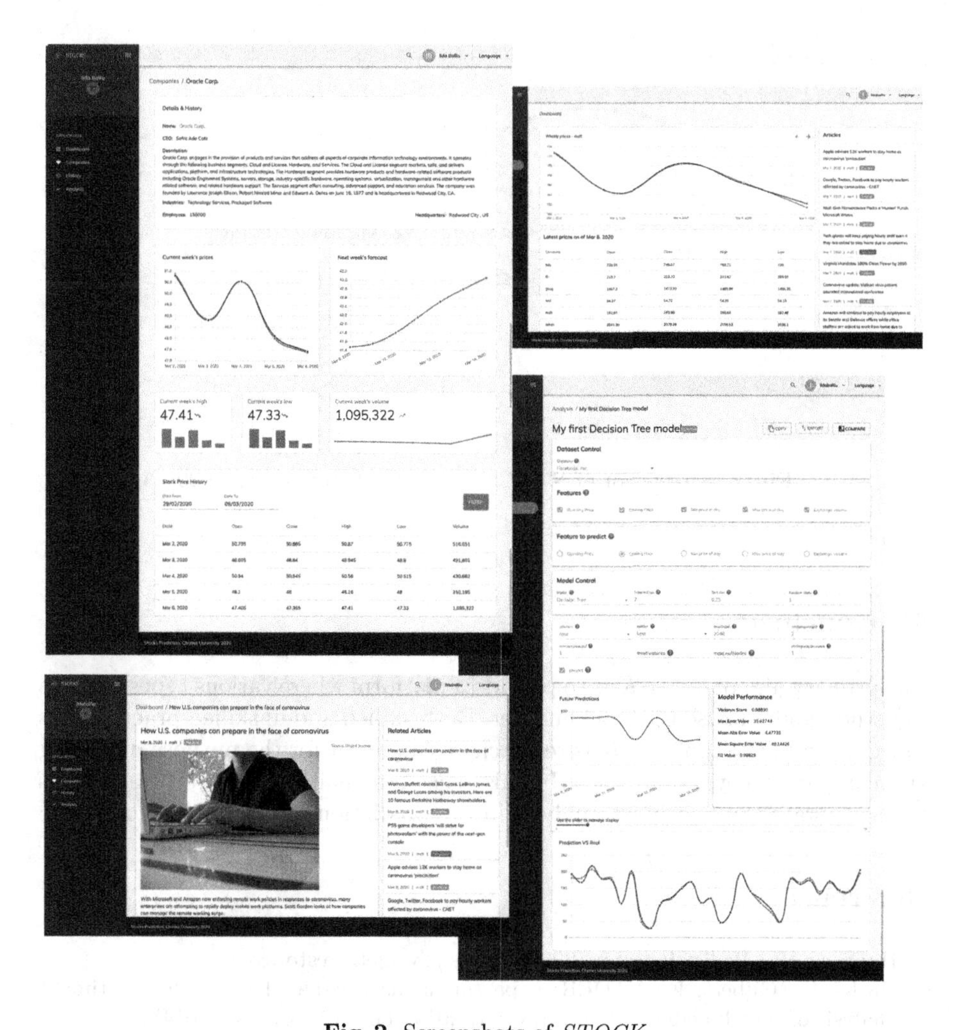

Fig. 2. Screenshots of *STOCK*

For the purpose of the demonstration we will use the context of COVID-19. In particular, we will show results of two situations: (1) the latest results from the time period before the conference (whose predictive value is hard to predict at the moment) and (2) the results of historical analyses from spring 2020. Especially at the beginning of the first wave we found *STOCK* particularly useful in the context of the latest events of a new, unprecedented situation. Almost every day there was an impact on the prices of stock market companies. For example,

Apple, Facebook, Amazon, Microsoft, and Google lost more than $238 billion as reported on February 24, 2020. Articles related to this were also retrieved and sentiment analysed in *STOCK* giving indicators if they were positive, negative, or neutral and then reflected in the charts of current week's prices (see Fig. 3).

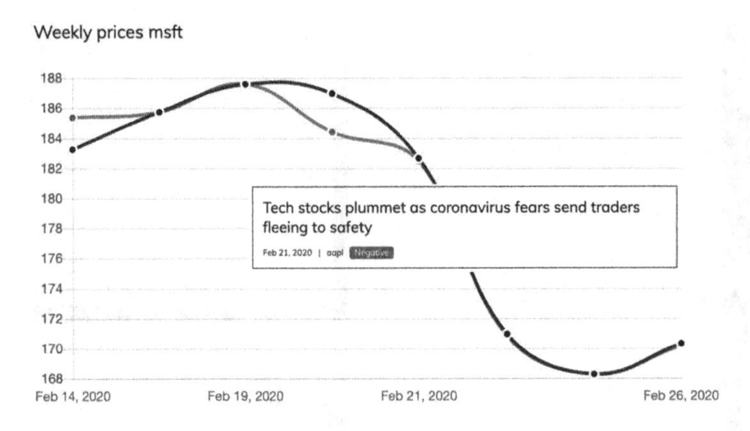

Fig. 3. Screenshot of *STOCK* – drop on February 24, 2020

5 Conclusion

The primary aim of *STOCK* is to provide a platform where various types of users can study and analyse the stock market. Both skilled and unskilled practitioners can work with the tool, whereas researchers can use it for the purpose of testing and comparing new approaches. In this sense our main planned future work is to incorporate the sentiment analysis in the prediction of the stock prices.

References

1. Hungary, W.: Wallet Investor (2020). https://walletinvestor.com/
2. Hutto, C., Gilbert, E.: VADER: a parsimonious rule-based model for sentiment analysis of social media text. In: ICWSM 2014. The AAAI Press (2014)
3. MarketWatch, I.: MarketWatch (2020). https://www.marketwatch.com/
4. Ryan, T.P.: Modern Regression Methods. Wiley (2008)
5. Sherstinsky, A.: Fundamentals of Recurrent Neural Network (RNN) and Long Short-Term Memory (LSTM) Network. Physica D: Nonlinear Phenomena **404** (2020)
6. Wallmine.com: Wallmine (2020). https://wallmine.com/

Interoperability in the Footwear Manufacturing Networks and Enablers for Digital Transformation

Claudia-Melania Chituc(✉)

DIPF | Leibniz Institute für Bildungsforschung und Bildungsinformation, Frankfurt, Germany
Chituc@dipf.de

Abstract. The digital transformation of the manufacturing industry is accelerated by the advancements of the digital technologies (e.g., Internet of Things, big data analytics), enabling the emergence of new business models and digital networks. The footwear manufacturing networks face numerous interoperability challenges due to the high heterogeneity of the enterprises, software systems and resources they comprise. The aim of this article is to analyze interoperability approaches in the footwear manufacturing networks up-stream segment and discuss enablers and challenges that need to be tackled towards ensuring digital transformation in this rather traditional manufacturing sector. The enablers are grouped in five categories in a digital radar: digital data and insights, automation, digital access, customer-centric manufacturing, and networking.

Keywords: Interoperability · Digital transformation · Footwear industry

1 Introduction

The digital tools and technologies (e.g., big data analytics, cloud computing, machine learning, Internet of Things (IoT), sensing technologies, 3D printing, actuation technologies, social media) accelerate the digital transformation of the manufacturing industry [1], and enable new and improved product features [2]. Industry 4.0 merges embedded production system technologies with intelligent production processes, transforming the manufacturing industry value chains and business models [3]. As a consequence, digital production networks [4] or digital manufacturing networks (DMNs) are emerging [5], which comprise enterprises that join their resources towards attaining a specific goal in the context of Industry 4.0, and act without human interference, being able to autonomously control their operations in view of environment changes and strategic goals [6].

The DMNs generate, exchange, store and share data, and perform complex data analytics in order to realize the goal(s) set (e.g., manufacture a car or a shoe, or deliver a digital service), obtain increased revenue, increase the operational efficiency (e.g., of the DMN, and of each enterprise in the DMN), and deliver improved customer experience. The digital technologies have the potential to rejuvenate the footwear industry that has

S. Cherfi et al. (Eds.): RCIS 2021, LNBIP 415, pp. 581–587, 2021.
https://doi.org/10.1007/978-3-030-75018-3_39

a rather rigid production chain and steady typology, influenced by seasonal demand, with quite stable and immutable business relationships, which limit their capacity offer and ability to exploit new business opportunities [7]. This industry is characterized by a dynamic season-driven product demand, with short design and production cycles. Although different models are manufactured, their volume is very small, which determines traditional shoe producers to focus on high-fashion shoes made available in rather small quantities, in a make-to-order approach [7]. The operations executed towards the final product are diverse (e.g., cutting, stitching, assembly, finishing) and are often executed by different outsourced companies [8], e.g., due to the high specialization needed for each shoe [9]. The most relevant companies operating in the footwear manufacturing up-stream segment are [7]: the shoe maker or shoe producer which produces the final product, sub-contracted companies (which are companies subcontracted by the shoe maker to manufacture parts of the shoe or the entire shoe), and supply companies which supply raw materials (e.g., leather, textile) and/ or shoe components (e.g., heels, soles, uppers, metallic accessories).

The digital collaboration in the footwear industry is rather challenging due to the numerous business and technology needs and specificities [10]. Interoperability must be ensured to support the exchange of data, execution of inter-organizational activities, and (remote) management and monitoring of manufacturing equipment, and inter-connected software systems and "things". Interoperability, in a broad sense, refers to capability of two or more systems or components to exchange information and use it [11]. The lack of interoperability disrupts the execution of the collaborative manufacturing activities [12]. Although some initiatives exist, attaining interoperability in the footwear sector, and, in general, in the fashion industry is challenging [10, 13]. An up-to-date analysis of interoperability initiatives in the footwear industry up-stream segment is not available, although highly relevant. This article addresses this gap.

The aim of this article is to present an up-to-date analysis of prominent interoperability initiatives in the footwear manufacturing industry up-stream segment, and discuss enablers for digital transformation depicted in a digital radar, and challenges to be further addressed. As numerous interoperability initiatives are quickly emerging and changing, it is not easy to understand them. This work offers a unique niche for researchers, practitioners, and software engineers to make significant contributions.

This article is organized as follows. Related work and relevant initiatives are analyzed next. Enablers and challenges are discussed in Sect. 3. The article concludes with a section addressing the need for further work.

2 Research Approach, Discussion of Related Work and Prominent Initiatives

Aiming at identifying and analyzing prominent interoperability initiatives in the footwear manufacturing industry, a literature review was conducted following PRISMA guidelines [14]. The digital libraries of IEEE, ACM, Elsevier and Springer were searched as they represent the most important databases in the area of interoperability and footwear manufacturing. Queries on Google Scholar were also performed. Keywords identified include: "interoperability", "footwear manufacturing", "footwear industry", "interoperability framework", "digital manufacturing", "IoT", "Industry 4.0". Queries executed included the Boolean operators OR, AND, NOT, e.g., (("interoperability" AND "footwear manufacturing") OR ("interoperability framework" AND "footwear manufacturing")). As the list of articles retrieved was vast, inclusion/exclusion criteria were defined, e.g., by reading the title and abstract, the clearly out-of-scope articles were excluded. Articles in a language other than English were also excluded. The relevant articles were read in full and an analysis of related work was made. The websites and technical reports of R&D projects were also analyzed.

Relevant interoperability initiatives in the footwear industry can be grouped into: R&D projects, architectures and frameworks, interoperability standards. R&D projects executed during the past 20 years focusing on ensuring interoperability in this sector include: the European Footwear Network for Electronic Trading (EFNET, cordis.europa.eu/project/id/FP4_28442) aiming at building a communication infrastructure for information distribution in the footwear supply chain, SHOENET (cordis.europa.eu/project/id/IST-2001-35393) aiming to adopt solutions through the implementation of information systems and novel tools to develop the innovative capacity of the SMEs in this sector, MODA-ML initiative (www.moda-ml.org), Cec-made-shoe (www.cec-made-shoe.com) aimed at attaining seamless interoperability, eBIZ of the eBIZ-TFC project (www.ebiz-tfc.eu) – an initiative for e-business harmonization in the European textile clothing and footwear industry promoted by EURATEX, CEC and ENEA. Except for EFNET, software implementations exist that follow the specifications of these initiatives.

All the above-mentioned initiatives contain a messaging interoperability layer that supports the exchange of e-documents. However, providing a messaging layer is not sufficient to attain broad scale interoperability in DMNs because other interoperability aspects need to be tackled as well, e.g., the execution of inter-organizational business processes, choreography of the e-documents exchanged, semantic interoperability to ensure the information exchanged is interpreted in the same way by all the enterprises.

By providing a common set of e-documents, the Shoenet initiative tackles semantic interoperability. However, it does not tackle the choreography of the e-documents exchanged or orchestration of business processes. The Cec-made-shoe initiative builds on the results of previous initiatives and addresses this gap. However, the Cec-made-shoe operational ICT messaging infrastructure is proprietary and non-compliant with the ebXML messaging specifications, and this obstructs interoperability [7].

The eBIZ Reference Architecture 4.0 [15] tackles technical, semantic, and business interoperability. However, few pilots exist in the footwear industry to illustrate the digital transformation. A pilot developed for an e-business solution for SMEs in the clothing sector using eBIZ profile of the UBL, enhanced with ebXML messaging, GLN, GTIN, GS1 identification standards is advanced in [16]. Main obstacles in implementing eBIZ 4.0 (e.g., high effort, lack of knowledge) are discussed in [17].

The Shoe Process INTeroperability Standard (SPRINTS) – an XML-based language to define a data exchange protocol among systems and machines in the footwear production field is introduced in [18]. However, the focus is on CAD communication.

Case studies conducted at national or regional level reflect the relationships among the numerous stakeholders in the footwear manufacturing sector and the need to ensure interoperability, e.g., [8] in Brazil, [10] in Northern Portugal. A framework for ensuring interoperability in a collaborative networked environment and an implementation example are presented in [19] and [20]; it relies on the concept of business enabler system that supplies different services (e.g., messaging, performance assessment) as SaaS. However, this initiative did not receive wide acceptance.

The use of the following standards for exchanging data or e-documents in the apparel, footwear, and fashion sector is reported in [21]: GS1 EANCOM (www.gs1.org/standards/eancom - a sub-set of the UN/EDIFACT standard) and GS1 XML, Universal Business Language (UBL, ubm.xml.org), PRANKE (pranke.com), eBIZ, Ryutsu Business Message Standards (the Japanese equivalent of a supply and demand chain, www.gs1jp.org/2018/service-and-solution/2_4.html).

Digital technologies are used in recent years in selecting specific footwear, e.g., the use of artificial neural networks in choosing shoe lasts for persons with mild diabetes is illustrated in [22]. Technology enablers in traditional manufacturing sectors are analyzed in [23]. The authors conclude that traditional sectors have limited capacity to invest in digital production technologies and cannot take full advantage of Industry 4.0.

The analysis of related work and main initiatives illustrated the importance to ensure interoperability in the footwear manufacturing industry and allowed identifying enablers and challenges for digital transformation, which are referred next.

3 Enablers and Challenges

Towards attaining seamless interoperability in the footwear manufacturing up-stream segment, digital transformation is required. However, the digitalization of this traditional sector is complex and expensive for the footwear enterprises [23].

Several challenges need to be addressed, not tackled by current initiatives:

- *Analytics in IoT Manufacturing* [24], including *Scalability* and *Data cleaning*. The digital transformation determines an increase in the volume of data that needs to be stored and managed. New applications need to be developed to support large scale data management and analytics [24]. Data in manufacturing activities may be inaccurate or noisy, e.g., due to defected sensors. It is rather challenging to clean huge volumes of data to perform accurate analytics.
- *Impact of digital transformation.* New models need to be developed and implemented to assess the economic impact of digital transformation in the footwear manufacturing sector, giving advantages over the competition in changing markets [23].
- *Social manufacturing* is a new paradigm to improve customization accuracy and efficiency by using big data and crowdsourcing [25]. Recent developments in 3D printing and 3D manufacturing support shoe customization; however, they need to be complemented with biomedical information necessary for personalization (e.g., internal tension) [23], behavior analysis and dynamic netizens [25], which is challenging. Despite certain advances (e.g., in the design of orthopedic footwear), it is not yet possible to automatically construct a shoe from a digitalized foot model, and enterprises still focus on low-level personalization [23].

Towards attain digital transformation in the footwear manufacturing sector, five categories of enablers are identified by analyzing related work and relevant initiatives, illustrated in Fig. 1. The digital radar in [26] and [27] is extended here with the *customer-centric manufacturing* enabler, which reflects the current trend for footwear personalized customization in the context of IoT and Industry 4.0 in this industry [23, 25]. Supporting applications and technologies are also referred. Adequate personalization assessment metrics need to be developed (e.g., to assess the customer comfort, readiness to change as for shoes or shoe models and volume variations).

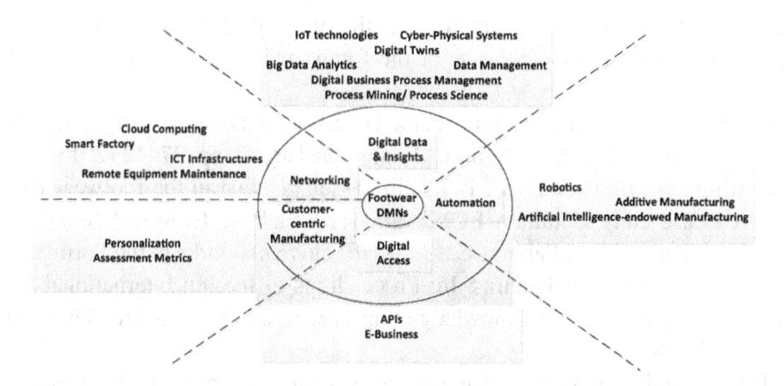

Fig. 1. Digital radar for the footwear DMNs (Source: adapted after [26, 27])

4 Conclusions and Future Work

The digital technologies have the potential to rejuvenate the traditional footwear manufacturing industry. The current trend for high customization in the context of IoT and Industry 4.0 in the footwear industry [22, 23] require highly dynamic forms of collaboration, such as the DMNs. Interoperability must be ensured to support the exchange of data and execution of inter-organizational business processes. The most relevant interoperability initiatives in the footwear industry sector up-stream segment include: R&D projects, interoperability frameworks and architectures, standards. Five enablers for digital transformation (Fig. 1) are identified: digital data & insights, automation, digital access, customer-centric manufacturing, networking.

Future research work will focus on assessing the impact of interoperability and digital transformation in the footwear industry. For example it would be useful to analyze the gains (of an individual organization and of a DMN), costs and risks associated with the digital transformation in this sector and compare the results with other industries.

References

1. Borangiu, T., Trentesaux, D., Thomas, A., Laitao, P., Barata, J.: Digital transformation of manufacturing through cloud services and resource virtualization. Comput. Ind. **108**, 150–162 (2019)

2. Ross, J.W., Beath, C.M., Mocker, M.: Designing for Digital: How to Architect Your Business for Sustained Success. MIT Press, Cambridge (2019)
3. Zhong, R.Y., Xu, X., Klotz, E., Newman, S.T.: Intelligent manufacturing in the context of Industry 4.0: a review. Engineering **3**(5), 616–630 (2017)
4. Pereira, A.C., Romero, F.: A review of the meanings and implications of the Industry 4.0 concept. Procedia Manuf. **13**, 1206–1214 (2017)
5. Dakhnovich, A.D., et al.: Applying routing to guarantee secure collaboration of segments in digital manufacturing networks. Autom. Control Comput. Sci. **52**(8), 1127–1133 (2018)
6. Erol, S., et al.: Tangible Industry 4.0: a scenario-based approach to learning for the future of production. Procedia CIRP **54**, 13–18 (2016)
7. Chituc, C.-M., Toscano, C., et al.: Interoperability in collaborative networks: independent and industry-specific initiatives – the case of the footwear industry. Comput. Ind. **59**, 741–757 (2008)
8. Fani, V., et al.: Supply chain structures in the Brazilian footwear industry: outcomes of a case study research. In: XX Summer School "Francesco Turco", pp. 37–42 (2015)
9. Fani, V., Bindi, B., Bandinelli, R.: Balancing assembly line in the footwear industry using simulation: a case study. Commun. ECMS **34**(1) (2020). Proc. ECMS M. Steglich et al. (Eds.)
10. Ribeiro, S.V., Santos, V.R., Pereira, C.S.: Collaborative networks in the Portuguese footwear sector and the cluster of Felgueiras. In: Proceedings of the 9th International Joint Conference on Knowledge Discovery, Knowledge Engineering and Knowledge Management (KMIS 2017), pp. 197–204 (2017)
11. IEEE: IEEE Standard Computer Dictionary: A Compilation of IEEE Standard Computer Glossaries. Institute of Electrical and Electronics Engineers, NY (1990)
12. Jardim-Goncalves, R., Grilo, A., Popplewell, K.: Novel strategies for global manufacturing systems interoperability. J. Intell. Manuf. **27**, 1–9 (2016)
13. Bindi, B., Fani, V., Bandinelli, R., Brutti, A., Ciaccio, G., De Sabbata, P.: eBusiness standards and IoT technologies adoption in the fashion industry: preliminary results of an empirical research. In: Rinaldi, R.., Bandinelli, R.. (eds.) IT4Fashion 2017. LNEE, vol. 525, pp. 139–150. Springer, Cham (2019). https://doi.org/10.1007/978-3-319-98038-6_11
14. Moher, D., et al.: Preferred reporting items for systematic review and meta-analyses: the PRISMA statement. PLoS Med. **6**(7), e1000097 (2009)
15. CEN: Reference architecture for eBusiness harmonisation in textile/clothing and footwear sectors, CWA 16667, July 2013
16. Ponis, S.T., et al.: Supply chain interoperability for enhancing e-business adoption by SMEs: a case study from the European clothing sector. Int. J. Bus. Inf. Syst. **10**(4), 417–435 (2012)
17. Bindi, B., et al.: Barriers and drivers of eBIZ adoption in the fashion supply chain: preliminary results. In: 2018 5th International Conference on Industrial Engineering and Applications (ICIEA), pp. 555–559 (2018)
18. Danese, G., et al.: A novel standard for footwear industrial machineries. IEEE Trans. Ind. Inf. **7**(4), 713–722 (2011)
19. Chituc, C..-M.., Toscano, C.., Azevedo, A.: Towards seamless interoperability in collaborative networks. In: Camarinha-Matos, L..M.., Afsarmanesh, H.., Novais, P.., Analide, C.. (eds.) PRO-VE 2007. ITIFIP, vol. 243, pp. 445–452. Springer, Boston (2007). https://doi.org/10.1007/978-0-387-73798-0_47
20. Chituc, C.-M., Azevedo, A., Toscano, C.: A framework proposal for seamless interoperability in a collaborative networked environment. Comput. Ind. **60**, 317–338 (2009)
21. GS1: Implementation of GS1 EDI standards in 2018, Detailed Report, 24 April 2019. www.gs1.org/sites/default/files/docs/EDI/edi_implementation_2018_public.pdf
22. Wang, C..-C., et al.: Artificial neural networks in the selection of shoe lasts for people with mild diabetes. Med. Eng. Phys. **64**, 37–45 (2019)

23. Jimeno-Morenilla, A., et al.: Technology enablers for the implementation of Industry 4.0 to traditional manufacturing sectors: a review. Comput. Ind. **125**, 103390 (2021)
24. Dai, H.-N., et al.: Big data analytics for manufacturing internet of things: opportunities, challenges and enabling technologies. Enterp. Inf. Syst. **14**(9–10), 1279–1303 (2020)
25. Shang, X., et al.: Moving from mass customization to social manufacturing: a footwear industry case study. Int. J. Comput. Integr. Manuf. **32**(2), 194–2015 (2019)
26. Boueé, C., Schaible, S.: Die Digitale Transformation der Industrie (2015)
27. Schallmo, D., et al.: Digital transformation of business models - best practice, enablers, and roadmap. Int. J. Innov. Manage. **21**(8), 1740014 (2017)

SIMPT: Process Improvement Using Interactive Simulation of Time-Aware Process Trees

Mahsa Pourbafrani[1(✉)], Shuai Jiao[2], and Wil M. P. van der Aalst[1]

[1] Chair of Process and Data Science, RWTH Aachen University, Aachen, Germany
{mahsa.bafrani,wvdaalst}@pads.rwth-aachen.de
[2] RWTH Aachen University, Aachen, Germany
shuai.jiao@rwth-aachen.de

Abstract. Process mining techniques including process discovery, conformance checking, and process enhancement provide extensive knowledge about processes. Discovering running processes and deviations as well as detecting performance problems and bottlenecks are well-supported by process mining tools. However, all the provided techniques represent the past/current state of the process. The improvement in a process requires insights into the future states of the process w.r.t. the possible actions/changes. In this paper, we present a new tool that enables process owners to extract all the process aspects from their historical event data automatically, change these aspects, and re-run the process automatically using an interface. The combination of process mining and simulation techniques provides new evidence-driven ways to explore "what-if" questions. Therefore, assessing the effects of changes in process improvement is also possible. Our Python-based web-application provides a complete interactive platform to improve the flow of activities, i.e., process tree, along with possible changes in all the derived activity, resource, and process parameters. These parameters are derived directly from an event log without user-background knowledge.

Keywords: Process mining · Process tree · Interactive process improvement · Simulation · Event log · Automatic simulation model generation

1 Introduction

The real value of providing insights by process mining emerges when these insights can be put into action [1]. Actions include the improvement of discovered running processes, performance problems, deviations, and bottlenecks.

Funded by the Deutsche Forschungsgemeinschaft (DFG, German Research Foundation) under Germany's Excellence Strategy – EXC 2023 Internet of Production- Project ID: 390621612. We also thank the Alexander von Humboldt (AvH) Stiftung for supporting our research.

S. Cherfi et al. (Eds.): RCIS 2021, LNBIP 415, pp. 588–594, 2021.
https://doi.org/10.1007/978-3-030-75018-3_40

Process owners should be able to take some actions based on this information with a certain level of confidence. To do so, they need to improve/change their processes interactively. Therefore, simulation and prediction techniques are taken into account to foresee the process after changes and improvement. Simulation techniques are capable of replaying processes with different scenarios.

Process mining also enables designing data-driven simulation models of processes [2]. However, in the current tools for simulation in process mining either interaction with the user and user knowledge is a prerequisite of designing a simulation model or the tools are highly dependent on the interaction of multiple simulation tools. In [5], an external tool, i.e., ADONIS for simulating the discovered model and parameters are used. The combination of BPMN and process mining is presented in [4] in which BIMP is used as a simulation engine. However, the possibility of interaction for changing the process model is not available for the user. Also, the authors in [14] propose a Java-based discrete event simulation of processes using BPMN models and user interaction where the user plays a fundamental role in designing the models. Generating a CPN model based on CPN tools [18] is presented in [17]. The user needs to deal with the complexity of CPN tools and *SML*. In [7], the focus is also to generate CPN models and measuring performance measurements using the *Protos* models which can be used easier but more restricted than CPN tools. [16] performs simulation on top of discovered Petri nets and measure the performing metrics and not re-generating the complete behavior of a process. The *Monte Carlo* simulation technique, as well as generating sequences of activities based on process trees, are also proposed in Python [3]. However, the simulation results are not in the form of an event log, and they lack the time perspective. Also, the tool in [10] as a python library simulates the Petri nets of processes based on their event logs. In [13], aggregated simulations which are useful for what-if analyses in high-level decision-making scenarios are introduced. The *PMSD* tool represents the aggregated approach and generates a simulation model at a higher level of detail [8] based on the approach in [11]. Different process variables are introduced in [9] that makes the different levels of process simulations possible, e.g., simulating the daily behavior of a process instead of simulating every event in the process.

The interactive improvement/changes of processes is not a straightforward task when it comes to changing the process models and parameters by the user. Therefore, we use the discovered process tree and provide an interface for the user to discover and design a new process model including all the performance and environmental attributes, e.g., changing business hours, or resource capacity. All of these changes are supported by the information derived from event logs of processes using process mining techniques as shown in Fig. 1. In this paper, we present our tool which is designed to support process improvement using simulation and process mining. Our tool is implemented as an integrated Python web-application using *Django* framework, where all the modules are also accessible outside the user interface for the users to re-use or add their desired modification to the code. Moreover, to the best of our knowledge, it is the first tool that runs the possible changes in the process tree while considering perfor-

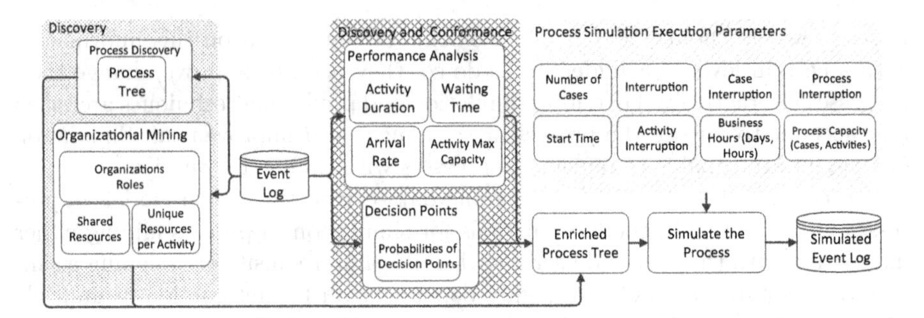

Fig. 1. The general framework of our tool for generating a process tree using process mining techniques and enriching the process tree with the possible information from an event log. The resulting process model can be executed to re-run the process with the user-provided configuration.

Table 1. The general parameters in the tool are listed. Most can be derived using process mining. Also, the required execution parameters. All the parameters discovered using process mining from event logs by default and are filled in the tool with the real values automatically. The execution values guaranteed the default values in case that users do not change/provide the parameters. Note that the handover matrix is used for logging resources.

	Process Mining											Simulation Execution Parameters	
	Process Model (Tree)	Arrival Rate	Activity Duration, Deviation	Activities Capacity	Unique Resources (Shared Resources)	Social Network (Handover Matrix)	Waiting Time	Business Hours	Activity-flow Probability	Process Capacity (cases)	Interruption (Process, Cases, Activities)	Start Time of Simulation	Number of Cases
Automatically Discovered	+	+	+	+	+	+	+	+	+	+	+	-	-
Changeable by User	+	+	+	+	+	-	+	+	+	+	+	+	+

mance aspects such as resource, activity, and process capacity, accurate time, as well as business hours. These capabilities are directly used to address interactive process discovery as well as process improvement.

2 SIMPT

As shown in Fig. 1, our tool automatically extracts all the existing aspects of a process based on general event log attributes. These quantitative aspects are used for running the process tree w.r.t. different scenarios. The main aspect is the discovered process tree which is used for interaction with users since it is limited to 4 operations. The user-interaction using process trees is easier compared to the complexity of Petri nets. The sequence, parallel, loop, and XOR operators are easy to be represented and understandable by the user for further

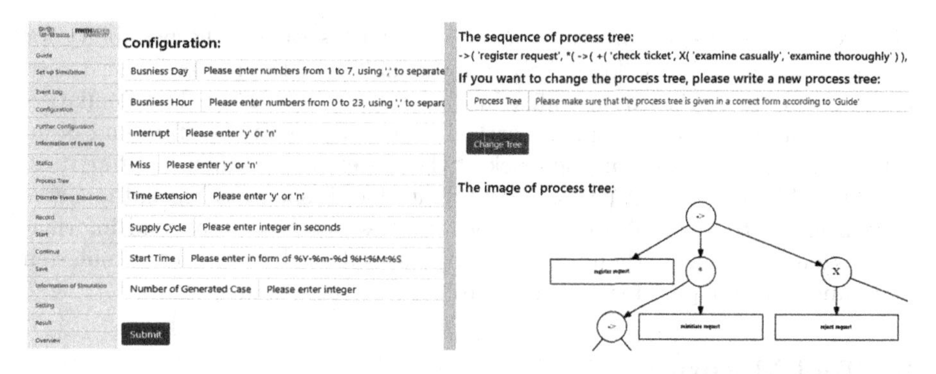

Fig. 2. A part of the tool parameters configuration to apply the changes to the basic performance elements as well as the process tree structure tab for the possible changes.

changes. The process structure and the flow of activities are represented using these operators. We extend the implementations of the process tree method in [3] to generate a comprehensive tree including the probability of choices (XOR) and loop restrictions, e.g., the maximum length of traces and execution of loops. For instance, measuring the performance KPIs of a process in case that activity a and b are parallel instead of being sequential is possible. Not only the possible traces are generated but also generating the complete event log gives all the performance aspects of the new process, e.g., the length of the queues, the service time of cases, and other possible aspects from an event log. The provided insights also include the possibility of checking the newly generated behaviors by the new process structure (process tree) and configuration for conformance checking too. Table 1 shows the general overview of the parameters and the possibility for the user to interact with the process and reproduce the new process behavior (event log) w.r.t. the changes in that parameters. Here, we explain some of the main modules. All the details along with the tool source code and a representing video are presented extensively.[1]

The tool has three main modules. The first module runs the discovery, extracts the current parameters in the event logs, and presents the model and the parameters to the user to decide on the possible changes, e.g., process tree, deviations, or waiting time. For the performance analysis, both event logs with start and complete timestamps and only one timestamp can be considered. The activities' durations are also taken from their real averages and deviations. The second module is configuring the new process parameters for simulating and running the simulation for the given parameters, e.g., the number of cases to be generated or the start time of the simulation. Furthermore, the interruption concept for process, activities, and traces is introduced. The user can define whether in specific circumstances, e.g., when a running case or activities is passing the business hours, the interruption can happen and it is logged for the user. The last module is running and simulating the defined and configure process tree

[1] https://github.com/mbafrani/SIMPT-SimulatingProcessTrees.git.

in which the results are presented as an overview as well as the possibility for downloading as an event log. The handover matrix of the process is also used to log the resources based on reality in the generated event log. The simulation is generating new events, e.g., the arrival of a new case or the start/end of an activity for a case, based on the clock of the system and configured properties, e.g., available resources. A part of the tool interface is shown in Fig. 2, the *Guide* section in the tool provides features, possibilities, required steps, and information, extensively. The python library *simpy*[2] is used for discrete event simulation and handles the required system clock to generate new events.

3 Tool Maturity

The tool has been used in different projects to design/improve a process model interactively in different situations and generate different event logs. In the IoP project[3], the tool is used to simulate multiple production lines to estimate the effect of the capacity of activities on the production process, e.g., average production speed. Moreover, [12] exploits the tool for car company production analyses, different arrival rates and activities' duration for the same process has been selected and the tool event logs are generated. Also, we use the tool as the base of the interactive design of the job-shop floor. The possible flow of jobs in the job-shop floor, i.e., the flow of activities, is presented as a process tree. These trees omit forbidden actions in the production line using the knowledge of the production manager and simulate the production line with the desired setting.

Figure 3 presents a sample scenario of changing the process structure and measuring the differences after the changes. Note that the inserted behaviors are generated based on the choices and loops in the rest of the process. As mentioned, having both simulated and original behavior of the process (with or without modifications) creates the possibility of the comparison between two processes which is available using the existing process mining tools and techniques. To demonstrate the tool functionality and validity of the re-generated event log, we used the BPI Challenge 2012 event log. We assessed the similarity of the original event log with the re-generated one using *Earth-Mover Distance* (EMD) technique as presented in [6] using the Python implementation in [15]. EMD calculates the shortest distance

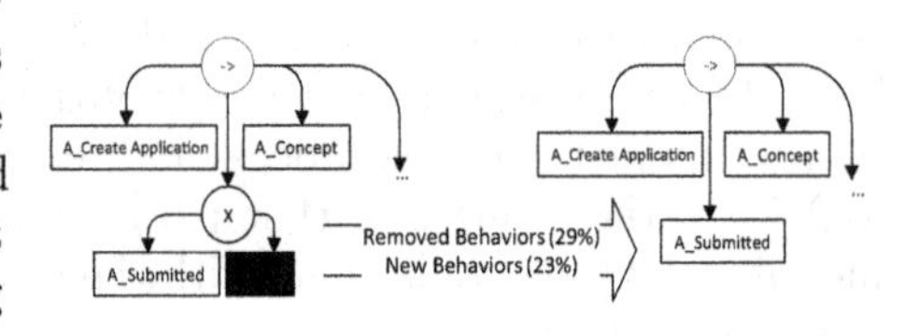

Fig. 3. A sample scenario for the process model of the BPI Challenge 2017 event log (application requests) in the tool. Activity *A-Create Application* can be skipped in the discovered process tree (left). By changing the choice to a sequence (right), i.e., this activity is required for all the cases, the removed and new inserted behaviors in the process can be measured.

[2] simpy.readthedocs.io.

[3] www.iop.rwth-aachen.de.

between the two event logs w.r.t. the minimum movement over the minimum distance between traces. The process is re-run without any changes in performance parameters to check the process behavior w.r.t. the flow of activities. The value of 0.34 as the EMD measure indicates the similarity of the two event logs. Note that the choices in the process model are the reason to have more behavior than the real event log which is expected w.r.t. *precision metrics* of discovery algorithm. Given the closeness of the simulation results and the original event log, the next changes can be applied to the process tree and other aspects of the process with enough confidence to reproduce the new event log including the effects of changes.

4 Conclusion

Given the fact that process improvement is the next step in the process mining path, simulation techniques will become more important. The combination of process mining and simulation techniques makes it possible to improve and redesign the processes w.r.t. the discovered possible change points in processes. Our tool is designed and implemented with the purpose of making process improvement using process mining and simulating the processes with the user's changes possible. The process tree notation along with all the performance and execution aspects of the process make the generated new behavior of the process w.r.t. user possible improvement reliable. Based on the provided reliable platform, the possibility of recommending the best process model interactively with the user considering both performance and activity flow is the next step.

References

1. van der Aalst, W.M.P.: Process Mining - Data Science in Action, 2nd edn. Springer, Heidelberg (2016). https://doi.org/10.1007/978-3-662-49851-4
2. van der Aalst, W.M.P.: Process mining and simulation: a match made in heaven! In: Computer Simulation Conference, pp. 1–12. ACM Press (2018)
3. Berti, A., van Zelst, S.J., van der Aalst, W.M.P.: Process mining for python (PM4PY): bridging the gap between process- and data science. CoRR abs/1905.06169 (2019)
4. Camargo, M., Dumas, M., Rojas, O.G.: SIMOD: a tool for automated discovery of business process simulation models. In: Demonstration Track at BPM (2019)
5. Gawin, B., Marcinkowski, B.: How close to reality is the as-is business process simulation model? Organizacija **48**(3), 155–175 (2015)
6. Leemans, S.J.J., Syring, A.F., van der Aalst, W.M.P.: Earth movers' stochastic conformance checking. BPM Forum **2019**, 127–143 (2019)
7. Netjes, M., Reijers, H., Aalst, W.M.P.: The PrICE tool kit: tool support for process improvement. In: CEUR Workshop Proceedings, vol. 615, January 2010
8. Pourbafrani, M., van der Aalst, W.M.P.: PMSD: data-driven simulation using system dynamics and process mining. In: Proceedings of the Best Dissertation Award, Doctoral Consortium, and Demonstration(BPM 2020), vol. 2673, pp. 77–81 (2020). http://ceur-ws.org/Vol-2673/paperDR03.pdf

9. Pourbafrani, M., van der Aalst, W.M.P.: Extracting process features from event logs to learn coarse-grained simulation models. In: Advanced Information Systems Engineering. Springer, Cham (2021)
10. Pourbafrani, M., Vasudevan, S., Zafar, F., Xingran, Y., Singh, R., van der Aalst, W.M.P.: A python extension to simulate petri nets in process mining. CoRR abs/2102.08774 (2021)
11. Pourbafrani, M., van Zelst, S.J., van der Aalst, W.M.P.: Scenario-based prediction of business processes using system dynamics. In: On the Move to Meaningful Internet Systems: COOPIS 2019 Conferences, pp. 422–439 (2019). https://doi.org/10.1007/978-3-030-33246-4_27
12. Pourbafrani, M., van Zelst, S.J., van der Aalst, W.M.P.: Semi-automated time-granularity detection for data-driven simulation using process mining and system dynamics. In: Dobbie, G., Frank, U., Kappel, G., Liddle, S.W., Mayr, H.C. (eds.) ER 2020. LNCS, vol. 12400, pp. 77–91. Springer, Cham (2020). https://doi.org/10.1007/978-3-030-62522-1_6
13. Pourbafrani, M., van Zelst, S.J., van der Aalst, W.M.P.: Supporting automatic system dynamics model generation for simulation in the context of process mining. In: Abramowicz, W., Klein, G. (eds.) BIS 2020. LNBIP, vol. 389, pp. 249–263. Springer, Cham (2020). https://doi.org/10.1007/978-3-030-53337-3_19
14. Pufahl, L., Wong, T., Weske, M.: Design of an extensible BPMN process simulator. In: Proceedings of Demonstration Track at BPM 2017, pp. 782–795
15. Rafiei, M., van der Aalst, W.M.P.: Towards quantifying privacy in process mining. In: International Conference on Process Mining - ICPM (2020), International Workshops, pp. 385–397 (2020)
16. Rogge-Solti, A., Weske, M.: Prediction of business process durations using non-Markovian stochastic Petri nets. Inf. Syst. **54**, 1–14 (2015)
17. Rozinat, A., Mans, R.S., Song, M., van der Aalst, W.M.P.: Discovering simulation models. Inf. Syst. **34**(3), 305–327 (2009)
18. Westergaard, M.: CPN Tools 4: multi-formalism and extensibility. In: 34th International Conference, Petri net 2013. Proceedings, pp. 400–409 (2013)

Digitalization in Sports to Connect Child's Sport Clubs, Parents and Kids: Simple Solution for Tackling Social and Psychological Issues

Irina Marcenko and Anastasija Nikiforova(✉)

Faculty of Computing, University of Latvia, Riga, Latvia
anastasija.nikiforova@lu.lv

Abstract. Today, the topic of child's sporting has become a crucial, not only because, in the 21st century, computer games and social networks are the most common way of spending a child leisure time (shift from sports to eSports took place), but also because in 2020, Covid-19 and the associated restrictions give parents even more stress on visits to sports clubs. In addition, sports may lead to unpleasant situations when a child is not successful enough in the particular discipline and is publicly criticized, thereby undermining his willingness to sport. We suppose that the trends of digitalization and some aspects of Industry 4.0, would be able to solve these issues at least partly, without requiring a lot of resources from child's sports clubs. This paper is devoted to a simple technological solution that would improve the sports club business by facilitating the exchange of information between a child, parents and sports clubs.

Keywords: Industry 4.0 · Sport 4.0 · Business · Child's sporting · Sports club

1 Introduction

Nowadays, more and more kids experience the shift from sports to eSports. However, the lack of real sports may increase stress, may be a reason for mood swings, reduced performance, fatigue, less developed eye tracking, coordination and increase the risks of diseases [1, 2]. According to a BBC survey, one of three children is not sportive and active enough [3]. Therefore the movement for healthy children is becoming active [4] and we should support this initiative facilitating their involvement in sports.

In many cases sports, which aim to make kids healthier, more sportive, developing skills, including team properties, managing emotional control, social functioning etc. [1], have the opposite results. It may negatively impact kids' psychology and emotional side by raising fear, anxiety, negativity, doubt. This is also the case when a kid is criticized publicly because although a coach might be doing it to make him better, this might bring only the stress. With these effects kids may refuse sporting that is the case for 30–70% of sporting as sport is no longer fun but rather stress [6].

Another point that came into force in 2020 is the Covid-19 pandemic. Parents are less sure that their kids are safe because not always kids are registered during the sport

S. Cherfi et al. (Eds.): RCIS 2021, LNBIP 415, pp. 595–601, 2021.
https://doi.org/10.1007/978-3-030-75018-3_41

activities. It means that it is almost impossible to indicate all the contact persons. This limits the number of kids attending the sports clubs significantly, even when there are no strict restrictions in the country and parents along with their kids would likely attend them. It also makes it harder to find out the achievements of their kids since the only way to find it out is to make a visit to a coach training their child.

Although child's sports clubs are not of high business value as adult sports where Sport 4.0 trends take place more frequently, the establishment of the communication and information exchange channel between involved parties is rarely ensured. As a result, a lack of information of different types, that could have a number of negative effects, may take place. Therefore, the aim of this paper is to propose a system that creates a channel between child's sports club, child and parents and resolves social and psychological issues that disrupt a child's motivation for sport. The paper is of practical nature proposing a real developed solution. It is planned that the system could be extended in the near future covering the majority of sport clubs in Latvia.

The following research question (RQ) was therefore raised: *Can social and psychological issues be resolved through a technological solution?* To answer this question, a list of sub-questions was established: *(RQ1) What are the main motivators for sport and the main barriers leading to the dropout of children? (RQ2) How to protect kids in the way of their emotional health, while trying to improve their performance? (RQ3) How to establish an interaction channel for children's sports clubs and parents?*

The paper is structured as follows: Sect. 2 forms a theoretical background, addressing the main motivators for the sporting of children and the barriers for their dropout, Sect. 3 presents a solution, Sect. 4 provides an analysis of the proposed solution, Sect. 5 provides research findings, as well as conclusions in Sect. 6.

2 Theoretical Background

Given the potential positive effects of sports on the physical and mental health of kids [3], its promotion is considered an important strategy [7]. Therefore, a number of studies have been conducted in recent years, focusing on identifying key motivators for child sporting. We will focus mainly on [1], where findings of 43 studies are compiled and [6], where an in-depth analysis of the factors identified from all stakeholder groups is conducted. Most of the studies reveal that "*fun*" is the most common intrinsic motivator for sport participation among children, followed by the challenge and excitement of competing, and opportunities to test or improve existing skills or learn new skills. The comments collected on the term of "*fun*" show that kids understand by it, *a lack of playing time or opportunities, frustration or dissatisfaction with the coach*, and sometimes *too much workout time* [1]. Many children also feel *a lack of competence*. These factors have a significant impact on the dropout of children.

In [6] comprehensive analysis and conceptualization of the determinants of "*fun*" has been presented. The analysis resulted in 81 fun-determining factors, which were classified into 11 dimensions. Identified clusters were then analyzed, concluding that the most significant aspect is "*positive team dynamics*", followed by "*trying hard*", "*positive coaching*", "*learning and improving*", "*game time support*", "*games*", "*practices*". However, *achievement status* (extrinsic factor) is generally less important, and can even be seen as a barrier, while being important for most parents.

Moreover, [1, 8–10] shows that one of the most challenging barriers affecting children's motivation is the pressure of parents, coaches or friends. Although parents have great potential to have a positive impact on children's sporting experience, they can also have a negative impact. Parents' post-sporting behaviors tend to draw kids negative conclusions about the results of sporting activities. Therefore, many psychologists ask parents to opt out of visiting children's lessons and participating in exchanges of views with kids and coaches [5]. However, parents have to be able to know about the success of their child – *but how to combine these two aspects*? Although this barrier cannot be disrupted without understanding of this fact, it may be reduced at least partly. To satisfy both needs, we (including the children's club) offer to distinguish the "achievement status", which is important mainly for parents, from sports activities within the club, remaining it in the background – make it known in the app. This would allow both to gain information and reflect on what to say to their child, thereby supporting and motivating for future success.

In [7, 10, 11] along with the factors above, the importance of motivators have been stressed. *Robinson et al.* [7] distinguish (1) *autonomous motivation*, which includes regulating behavior with psychological freedom experiences and reflective self-endorsement, (2) *controlled motivation*, which refers to the pressured involvement in action. In addition, motivation is closely linked to *perceived competence*. The authors also emphasize that there is a positive relationship between perceived motor competence and motivation for sports, i.e. children who feel more competent will have more independent motivation for sports. While autonomous motivation is closely associated with a child, controlled motivation involves parents and coaches. Autonomous motivation is the preferred option that can be achieved by reducing stress and pressure and by developing perceived motor competence. Here, the proposed system could be the solution.

3 Social and Psychological Issues to Be Resolved

In view of the issues addressed in the literature, we have selected aspects which could be resolved by a technological solution. This list is based on [6], where 7 out of 11 clusters are considered important, i.e. 56 out of 81 determinants. Not all of them are of the same weight, therefore, we exclude those that have been assessed with less than 4 points. As a result, 33 determinants were further considered. 25 of them were found as those which can be covered at least partly by a very simple technological solution:

- **positive team dynamics** - (1) *playing well together as a team,* (2) *being supported by teammates,* (3) *supporting teammates,* (4) *when players show good sportsmanship,* (5) *getting help from teammates*;
- **trying hard** - (6) *setting and achieving goals*;
- **positive coaching** - (7) *when a coach treats players with respect,* (8) *when a coach encourages the team,* (9) *having a coach who is a positive role model,* (10) *getting clear,* (11) *consistent communication from coaches,* (12) *a coach who knows a lot about the sport,* (13) *a coach who allows mistakes,* (14) *while staying positive,* (15) *a coach who listens to players and takes their opinions into consideration,* (16) *a coach who you can talk to easily,* (17) *a nice friendly coach*;

- **learning and improving** - (18) *being challenged to improve and get better at your sport*, (19) *learning from mistakes*, (20) *ball touches*, (21) *improving athletic skills to play at the next level*, (22) *learning new skills*;
- **game time support** - (23) *when parents show good sportsmanship*;
- **games** – (24) *getting playing time*;
- **practices** - (25) *having well-organized practices.*

The list was then supplemented with additional aspects to be addressed by the solution. They are "*feeling*" a lack of competence, i.e. "*not being good enough*" and "*lack of skill improvement*", "*optimally challenging tasks*". We argue that a technological solution with some aspects of Industry 4.0, even very simple, is capable of at least partly resolving these key challenges. Just as in the digital economy, we propose changing the assets by shifting focus from seeking new categories of consumer to identifying individual characteristics and meeting his needs.

4 The Proposed Solution

The system is designed to improve the exchange of information between a sports club, children and child's parents. It allows kids and their parents to apply for sports lessons from the available, and to see all the additional information they need about it, i.e. activities, schedules etc. After the end of the lesson, the trainer and the club administrator have the option to enter a reference to the results achieved, which will provide an opportunity to observe the child's progress over a longer period of time.

Child's sports clubs deal with continuous interaction of groups of stakeholders, more precisely, children who do sports, coaches who train children and parents. This means that compared to sports clubs for adults, another group (parents) is involved, which communicates with both groups, i.e. children and trainers, and complements the club's ecosystem. As a result, because of the higher number of communication channels, which cannot always be realized offline, together with the fact that children are more emotionally affected than adults, the topic of child sports clubs is becoming more complicated and sophisticated.

The system, therefore, has 6 user groups and the functionalities of these actors are categorized by 5 modules - "Authentication", "User", "Club", "Coach" and "Parent". The functionality of the system consisting of 26 functions is shown in Fig. 1.

The system was developed in C#, using the ASP.net framework, which uses the IIS Express 10.0 and ASP.net framework 4.8. These technologies made it easy to achieve the aims pursued, and we argue that they would support the development of this product, even for a programmer with relatively low experience and skills.

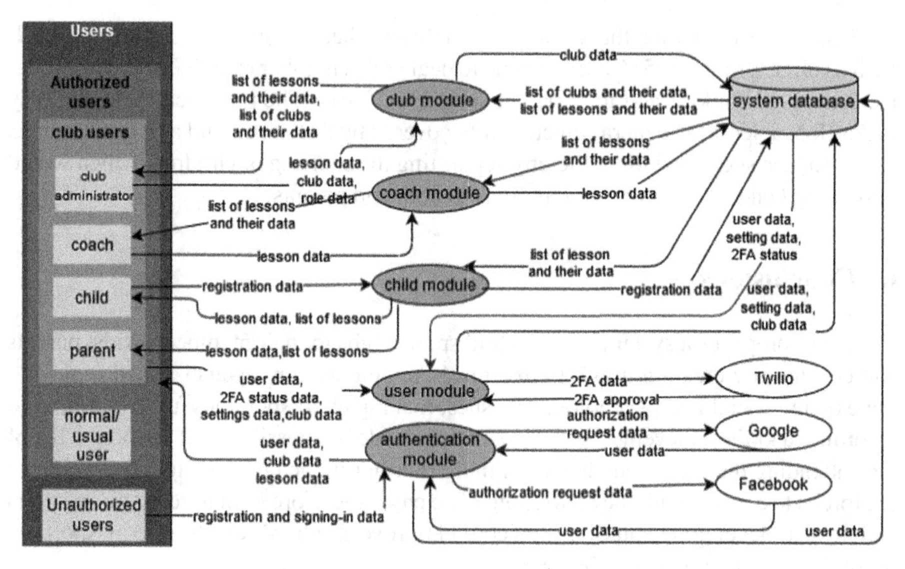

Fig. 1. Data flow chart: 1st level.

5 Research Findings

Now, when the key technical aspects have been addressed, let us come back to the social factors we are dealing with and to the issues we are trying to resolve. This will be done by mapping the aspects proposed between the issues found in Sect. 3 to the technical aspects of our solution (Table 1).

Table 1. Aspects addressed by the solution.

Aspect	Way of addressing
Positive team dynamics	Coach fix in the description of the lesson (after the lesson) for parents and child
Positive coaching	Communication channel (parents → coach) Helping selection of other coach OR club
Learning and improving	Coach fix in the description of the lesson (after the lesson) for parents and child
Game time support	Description of the lesson AND achievements over the time
Games	Description of the lesson. Helping selection of other coach OR club
Practices	Description of the lesson (prior) AND Description of the lesson (after the lesson); Description of other lessons (facilitating selection of other lessons OR club)
Tasks that are optimally challenging	Description of the lesson (prior) AND Description of the lesson (after the lesson); Description of other lessons
"Feeling" a lack of competence	Coach fix in the description of the lesson (after the lesson) for child

This allows us stating, that even very simple and cheap solution (according to PERT, such a solution requires 516 h) is capable to deal with a number of social and psychological issues, which kids and their parents may experience. The proposed system is easy to develop, at least the general functionality covered by this paper, and as a result, others can introduce such a solution, thereby supporting the sporting of children, which would only bring benefits and positive emotions to both and parents.

6 Conclusions

The paper proposes a system linking child sports clubs to their members - kids, parents and coaches, by creating a multi-directional communication channel aimed at resolving existing social and psychological issues, making child sports joyful. In addition to recording a kid's achievements, this solution provide the possibility of keeping a list of kids attending the class, which is even more relevant in the current situation, when we are forced to comply with the restrictions. The paper therefore is an urge for every sports club to start developing solutions that could improve children's experience by sporting, becoming healthier and socially active.

The digital world and the era of digitalization shift the focus from the search for consumer categories towards the identification of the characteristics of the individual. This also means that if sports clubs have sponsorship there will be a number of options available, taking into account all those offered by Sport 4.0 related to sensors, artificial intelligence and the new possibilities that open up for coaching methods etc. However, at that point, at least in Latvia, children's sports clubs have to deal with the funds they receive from parents. The proposed system is therefore simple enough to make it possible to develop and involve it in all clubs and to start a way for a brighter future for children by means of elimination of social and psychological barriers and facilitating motivation for sports.

Acknowledgements. This work has been supported by University of Latvia.

References

1. Crane, J., Temple, V.: A systematic review of dropout from organized sport among children and youth. Eur. Phys. Educ. Rev. **21**(1), 114–131 (2015)
2. Taliaferro, L.A., Rienzo, B.A., Donovan, K.A.: Relationships between youth sport participation and selected health risk behaviors from 1999 to 2007. J. Sch. Health **80**, 399–410 (2010)
3. BBC News: One in three children 'not active enough', finds sport survey (2018). https://www.bbc.com/news/health-46456104. Accessed 1 Feb 2021
4. Hardy, K., Hooker, L., Ridgway, L., Edvardsson, K.: Australian parents' experiences when discussing their child's overweight and obesity with the maternal and child health nurse: a qualitative study. J. Clin. Nurs. **28**(19–20), 3610–3617 (2019)
5. Taylor, J.: Sports parents, we have a problem, psychology today (2018). https://www.psychologytoday.com/us/blog/the-power-prime/201812/sports-parents-we-have-problem. Accessed 1 Feb 2021

6. Visek, A.J., Achrati, S.M., Mannix, H.M., McDonnell, K., Harris, B.S., DiPietro, L.: The fun integration theory: toward sustaining children and adolescents sport participation. J. Phys. Act. Health **12**(3), 424–433 (2015)
7. Robinson, L.E., et al.: Motor competence and its effect on positive developmental trajectories of health. Sports Med. **45**(9), 1273–1284 (2015). https://doi.org/10.1007/s40279-015-0351-6
8. Elliott, S.K., Drummond, M.J.: Parents in youth sport: what happens after the game? Sport Educ. Soc. **22**(3), 391–406 (2017)
9. The Australian Parenting Website: Sport: encouraging children to have a positive attitude (2020). https://raisingchildren.net.au/school-age/play-media-technology/active-play/sport-positive-attitude. Accessed 1 Feb 2021
10. Pannekoek, L., Piek, J., Hagger, M.: Motivation for physical activity in children: a moving matter in need for study. Hum. Mov. Sci. **32**(5), 1097–1115 (2013)
11. Teixeira, P.J., Carraça, E.V., Markland, D., Silva, M.N., Ryan, R.M.: Exercise, physical activity, and self-determination theory: a systematic review. Int. J. Behav. Nutr. Phys. Act. **9**(1), 1–30 (2012)

Open Government Data for Non-expert Citizens: Understanding Content and Visualizations' Expectations

Abiola Paterne Chokki(✉), Anthony Simonofski, Benoît Frénay, and Benoît Vanderose

University of Namur, Namur, Belgium
{abiola-paterne.chokki,anthony.simonofski}@unamur.be

Abstract. Open government data (OGD) refers to data made available online by governments for anyone to freely reuse. Non-expert users, however, lack the necessary technical skills and therefore face challenges when trying to exploit it. Amongst these challenges, finding useful datasets for citizens is very difficult as their expectations are not always identified. Furthermore, findings the appropriate visualization that is more understandable by citizens is also a barrier. The goal of this paper is to decrease those two entry barriers by better understanding the expectations of non-expert citizens. In order to reach that goal, we first seek to understand their content expectations through the usage statistics analysis of the OGD portal of Namur and through a complementary online survey of 43 participants. Second, we conduct interviews with 10 citizens to obtain their opinion on the appropriate and well-designed visualizations of the content they seek. The findings of this multi-method approach allow us to issue 5 recommendations for OGD portal publishers and developers to foster non-expert use of OGD.

Keywords: Open Government Data · Visualization · Content · Non-expert

1 Introduction

Open government data (OGD) refers to data made available online by governments for anyone to freely reuse. OGD initiatives increase government transparency and accountability, but also involve many challenges such as its potential reuse by non-experts [1,2]. These challenges have been minimized by developers who have implemented many services or applications for citizens using open data. However, this approach has two issues. First, the developers and OGD publishers are not aware of the datasets that are likely to be of interest to citizens [3]. Therefore, our first research question **(RQ1)** is as follows: "What data are non-experts interested in?". Second, the OGD publishers and especially the developers are not aware of the needs of citizens in terms of appropriate visualization design to represent data in an understandable manner [4]. Our second

S. Cherfi et al. (Eds.): RCIS 2021, LNBIP 415, pp. 602–608, 2021.
https://doi.org/10.1007/978-3-030-75018-3_42

research question **(RQ2)** is therefore formulated as follows: "How to optimally visualize OGD to non-experts?".

The goal of this paper is to better understand citizens' expectations, the useful datasets and the adequate visualizations they expect on OGD portals. The study seeks to identify the datasets needed by non-experts by analyzing the dataset usage statistics on the open data portal of Namur, but also by doing an online survey with 43 participants to find out the real expectations of non-experts in order to provide recommendations to developers about the interested datasets to used in applications and to OGD publishers about the datasets to publish on portals. To find answers to RQ2, we conduct interviews with 10 citizens to get their opinion on the appropriate and well-designed type of visualization for OGD. The data recommendation tool NeDVis[1] under development in our laboratory is used to support the interviews.

2 Methodology

2.1 Usage Statistics and Survey (RQ1)

In order to address RQ1, we combined three resources. First, we used the OGD portal of the city of Namur (Belgium)[2] as use case to study the actual consultation statistics of the datasets on the portal. We chose this portal as it is the most advanced portal in Wallonia (Belgium) and access with key stakeholders of this portal was possible. This information was collected through a file sent by the OGD manager of the city to the researchers. Second, the list of High-Value Datasets[3] (HVDs) representing datasets with significant benefits to society, from the data portal of the Dutch government, was used to initiate the survey. The list was also used to verify if it matches with the real expectations of non-expert users. Third, to complement the findings from these statistics, we issued a survey[4] to the citizens of Namur asking them what datasets they expect to find on portals.

The survey was implemented using Google forms and pretested by two users to ensure all kinds of errors that are associated with survey research are reduced [5]. The survey was later shared on Facebook groups and was filled in by 43 non-experts. This low participation rate can be explained by three reasons: (i) we focused here on participants interested on OGD which represent a very specific sub-set of the population, (ii) we only used online channels due to the COVID situation and (iii) the survey was conducted as a complement to the usage statistics.

2.2 Interviews (RQ2)

We conducted interviews with 10 non-expert citizens of Namur, interested to know more about OGD, to answer RQ2. These 10 citizens were recruited on

[1] https://rb.gy/7sgpqo.
[2] https://data.namur.be/pages/accueil/.
[3] https://data.overheid.nl/community/maatschappij/high-value/gemeenten.
[4] https://rb.gy/2wjtgd.

voluntary basis based on their previous answers in the survey described in Sect. 2.1. The reasons for low participation are the same as above, with the exception of the third. NeDVis was used to facilitate the data collection for the interviews. This tool was selected because it allows to easily take into account the user feedback compared to the existent solutions.

Datasets and Predefined Tasks. We selected three datasets from the open data portal of Namur for the interviews. These datasets were chosen because they are easy to understand by participants and also are among the most visited datasets according to the usage statistics file collected from the OGD manager of Namur. For each dataset, we have defined 2 tasks that the participants need to do in order to record their feedback. The predefined tasks were also well selected in order to cover different use cases of data visualization. All the datasets and predefined tasks were later integrated in NeDVis in order to facilitate the interview process and especially to not lose time during the interview. Table 1 summarizes the information about the datasets (name, link for more details and predefined tasks).

Table 1. List of datasets and predefined tasks for interviews.

Datasets	Predefined tasks
COVID-19 Pandemic - Province of Namur - New contaminations by commune Link: https://rb.gy/4r0ht7	(T1) Total new cases over date (T2) Total new cases per municipality
Namur - Mobility - Parking Link: https://rb.gy/b840w5	(T3) Total places per parking type (T4) Total places per parking type and per Municipality
Namur - Ordinary budget by function Link: https://rb.gy/1q79nd	(T5) Total revenues and total expenses across function (T6) Total revenues and total expenses across Function over year

Data Collection. In order to reduce the duration of the interview, we launched NeDVis on our computer and asked participants to evaluate the generated visualizations. For each predefined task, NeDVis generated at least 2 different visualizations. Participants were then asked to give a score between 1 (very inappropriate) to 10 (very appropriate) to each generated visualization. In addition, participants were asked to verbalize their thoughts during the study about why they gave a certain score for a specific visualization and also how they would like the system to represent the visualization to facilitate understanding. These thoughts were recorded so that nothing was missed from their feedback. Each subject spent approximately 30 min to note in total 22 visualizations for all the predefined tasks.

Data Analysis. After collecting user feedback, the final score of each proposed visualization type for each predefined task was calculated using the average of user ratings. The different scores were then used to find the best visualization type (visualization with the highest score) for each predefined task.

3 Results

3.1 Content Expectations: Usage Statistics and Survey Results

The file collected from the OGD manager of Namur portal concerns the consultation of the portal's data from January to December 2020. This file contains 902 573 rows and 34 columns such as timestamp, user_ip_addr, dataset_id, exec_time and so on. Based on this file, we determine how many times each dataset was visited between January and December 2020. Table 2 shows the top 10 datasets consulted on the OGD portal of Namur.

Table 2. Top 10 datasets visited between January and December 2020 on the OGD portal of Namur.

No	Dataset	Dataset Category in Survey	Number of records	% records
D1	Number of confirmed COVID-19 cases by municipality	COVID	298498	33.1
D2	Number of new confirmed COVID-19 cases per municipality per day	COVID	57130	18.4
D3	Number of new hospitalizations of COVID-19 per province per day	COVID	51232	6.33
D4	List of deceased related to cemetery locations	Non present	24260	5.68
D5	Administrative boundaries - Municipalities of the Province of Namur	Non present	20108	2.69
D6	Polygons of 26 localities of the commune of Namur	Non Present	17776	2.23
D7	Boundaries of districts of Namur	Non present	16345	1.97
D8	Location of Public Cemeteries	Non present	14588	1.81
D9	Photos and geolocalized old postcards	Non present	10497	1.62
D10	List of the deceased linked to the cemetery sites in the commune of Namur	Non present	8756	1.16

Referring to Table 2, the order of the datasets from most to least visited, is as follows: COVID datasets, datasets on cemeteries, data on communities, localities, addresses, and buildings, mobility data and population data. Another observation is that some expected datasets, such as budget data to achieve transparency, were less visited but were among the 100 most visited datasets. Also, many datasets in the list of HVDs are not found in the list of datasets visited on the Namur portal.

Regarding the survey, a total of 43 users completed it. 63% of users had heard about open data, 53% had used an open data portal and 70% had general computer knowledge. First, we asked participants to quantify the importance of the predefined datasets (coming from the list of HVDs) using a scale from "Not important at all" to "Very Important" . The importance was calculated as the median response of the 43 respondents. The survey results show that most of the datasets are important (median = 3) for citizens except the datasets about street lighting, places to walk dogs, information on trees and spreading routes, which have a median less than 3 (not important). Second, we asked the following question to participants: "What data (other than those listed) would you like to see on an Open Data site?". 13 participants answered it. The list of suggested data included: nurseries libraries, road work schedule, local business statistics, position of the refugee centers and their age pyramid, collection and use of tax and information on essential shops.

Based on these findings, we suggest publishers to highlight on the portal (respectively developers to offer services based on) the high-value datasets, COVID-Related Data (or, more generally, data relevant to analyze a current crisis and/or societal debate in an objective manner), administrative boundaries and population data, a list of buildings, mobility data and old photos from the city. On the other hand, publishers should also provide, in addition to the current data, datasets about nurseries libraries, road work schedule, local business statistics, position of the refugee centers and their age pyramid, collection and use of tax and information on essential shops. They should also have a feedback feature which can help collect user expectations in terms of the datasets to be published on the portal.

3.2 Visualization Expectations: Results from Interviews

In total, 10 users participated to the interviews. All participants had average to low computer skills and had not previously analyzed the studied datasets. Table 3 presents the adequate visualization type for each predefined task based on the user feedback. Note that the best visualization type is determined by taking the visualization type that has the highest final score calculated using the average of user ratings.

Referring to Table 3, we can note that the best visualization type for visualizing geographic data is the bubble map, for comparing categorical data is the bar graph, and for seeing the evolution over time is the line graph. In addition, we find that the design of the visualization types is very important for non-experts to help them understand them easily. Thus, based on user feedback on

Table 3. Best visualization type for each predefined task.

Datasets	Tasks Predefined	Best Visualization Type
COVID-19 Pandemic - Province of Namur - New contaminations by commune	(T1) Total new cases over date	Line chart
	(T2) Total new cases per municipality	Bubble map
Namur - Mobility - Parking	(T3) Total places per parking type	Bar chart with horizontal orientation & Doughnut & Pie chart
	(T4) Total places per parking type and per municipality	Grouped bar chart with horizontal orientation
Namur - Ordinary budget by function	(T5) Total revenues and total expenses across function	Grouped bar chart with vertical orientation
	(T6) Total revenues and total expenses across function over year	Multiple line charts

suggested visualizations, we propose that programmers and publishers take the following actions to incorporate these user expectations. First, they should have a visualization review feature that allows users to provide suggestions on how to improve visualizations. Second, they should allow users to access the low-level visual encodings such as graph orientation, axis labels, order of data in graph and color, in order to change them if necessary. Third, they should provide search functionality for each visualisation to allow only the desired data to be displayed rather than all data.

4 Conclusion and Further Research

The aim of this paper was to understand the content (RQ1) and visualization expectations (RQ2) of non-experts towards OGD. To achieve that goal, we used a multi-method approach including an analysis of the usage statistics of the OGD portal of Namur, a complementary online survey of 43 participants to find out the needs of the end-users in terms of datasets and interviews with 10 participants to get their opinion on the correct and well-designed visualizations of datasets. Using this multi-method approach, we identify end-users' expectations for content and visualizations, and then provide useful recommendations to programmers and publishers. This study differs from existing literature in two aspects. First, to our knowledge, this study is the first attempt to use the usage statistics of portal combined with a survey to understand content expectations.

Second, in previous researches, only few visualization types were used [6] and general interactivity (not based on tasks and feedback from citizens as done here) were suggested [7]. For future work, we first plan to increase the number of participants and cover more visualization types in order to have statistical significance. Second, we plan to improve NeDVis tool by integrating recommendations gathered from the interviews: (A) which type of visualization is appropriate for a specific task? (from scores), and (B) how to represent the visualization to make it easier to understand? (from verbal thoughts). The integration of (A) will be handled by recording the score and related features (e.g., visualization type, number of numerical attributes) of each rated visualization in the system, which will help improving the recommendation module of NeDVis. For (B), we will need to modify the representation of some visualization types and also allow users to make changes to low-level visual encodings when selecting an attribute to visualize.

References

1. Zuiderwijk, A., Janssen, M., Choenni, S., Meijer, R., Alibaks, R.S.: Socio-technical impediments of open data. Electron. J. Electron. Gov. **10**, 156–172 (2012)
2. Tammisto, Y., Lindman, J.: Definition of open data services in software business. In: Cusumano, M.A., Iyer, B., Venkatraman, N. (eds.) ICSOB 2012. LNBIP, vol. 114, pp. 297–303. Springer, Heidelberg (2012). https://doi.org/10.1007/978-3-642-30746-1_28
3. Crusoe, J., Simonofski, A., Clarinval, A., Gebka, E.: The impact of impediments on open government data use: insights from users. In: 13th International Conference on RCIS, pp. 1–12 (2019)
4. Barcellos, R., Viterbo, J., Miranda, L., Bernardini, F., Maciel, C., Trevisan, D.: Transparency in practice: using visualization to enhance the interpretability of open data. In: 18th Annual International Conference on Digital Government Research, pp. 139–148 (2017)
5. Grimm, P.: Pretesting a questionnaire. Wiley Int. Encycl. Mark. (2010)
6. Ornig, E., Faichney, J., Stantic, B.: Empirical evaluation of data visualizations by non-expert users **10**, 355–371 (2017)
7. Khan, M., Shah Khan, S.: Data and information visualization methods, and interactive mechanisms: a survey. Int. J. Comput. Appl. **34**, 1–14 (2011)

Domain Analysis and Geographic Context of Historical Soundscapes: The Case of Évora

Mariana Bonito, João Araujo(✉), and Armanda Rodrigues

NOVA LINCS, Universidade NOVA de Lisboa, Lisbon, Portugal
m.bonito@campus.fct.unl.pt, {joao.araujo,a.rodrigues}@fct.unl.pt

Abstract. Soundscape is the technical term used to describe the sound in our surroundings. Experiencing Historical Soundscapes allows for a better understanding of life in the past and provides clues on the evolution of a community. Interactive and multimedia-based Historical Soundscape environments with geolocation is a relatively unexplored area but, recently, this topic has started to call the attention of researchers due to its relevance in culture and history. This work is part of the PASEV project, which is developing several types of digital tools, designed to interactively share the Historical Soundscapes of the Portuguese City of Evora. This paper presents an initial domain requirements analysis for the interactive and multimedia-based Historical Soundscapes domain, which involves handling geolocations. Thus, projects in this domain, such as PASEV, can be part, and take advantage of the benefits of this work, which is the reuse of Soundscape domain requirements, reducing the time needed to develop applications in such domain.

Keywords: Domain Analysis · Historical Soundscapes · Feature Models

1 Introduction

The concept of Soundscape describes the sound in our surroundings. This "environment" can be created in many ways through music, historical recordings, and can even be the product of reminiscing and imagining the sound [3]. As Emily Thompson states, "Soundscape is simultaneously a physical environment and a way of perceiving that environment" [9]. Hence, experiencing Historical Soundscapes allows for a better understanding of life in the past and acts as an indicator of the evolution of a community [3]. This work is part of the PASEV [6] project which is developing a set of digital tools designed to interactively share and disseminate the Historical Soundscapes of Évora (Portugal) with the user.

In this paper, an initial domain requirements analysis for the *interactive and multimedia-based Historical Soundscapes* domain, involving handling geolocations, is presented. The purpose of domain analysis is to establish guidelines that allow for the reuse of common components amongst projects in the same

S. Cherfi et al. (Eds.): RCIS 2021, LNBIP 415, pp. 609–615, 2021.
https://doi.org/10.1007/978-3-030-75018-3_43

domain, reducing the time to develop and costs; this technique has been largely adopted in software product lines [10]. There are some suggested methods on how to perform domain analysis [1,2,4]. However, as it is difficult to obtain a *one-size-fits-all* approach, we will select artifacts from different methods to propose a modified approach. The proposed Soundscape Domain Model is sufficiently flexible to incorporate updates, whenever there is a change or new domain software becomes available. Besides, this project also contributes with an extension of the open-source FeatureIDE plug-in for Eclipse IDE[1], used to build feature models, here used for domain analysis.

2 Background

Historical Soundscapes. The term Soundscape was originally presented by R. Murray Schafer at Simon Fraser University with a purpose of "raising public awareness of sound" [11]. One of the best ways to understand the concept is by picturing it as "an auditory or aural landscape" [9]. In addition, a reoccurring key concept found in literature is *the importance of how the sound is perceived. Historical Soundscape* is thus, the acoustic environment of the past, which might also require a context to be provided, as the perception of the sounds will likely differ over time. Lee et al. define Historical Soundscapes as being a way to describe the past through sound [5]. They also assert that *Historical Soundscapes* are important as they "can inform our understanding of the past by opening new spaces for examining, communicating, and understanding the past using sound" [5]. Given the importance of Soundscapes, and more specifically, Historical Soundscapes, there have been several attempts, by different international organisations, such as the "Early Modern Soundscapes" or the "Simon Fraser University", to explore and offer, to the public, information and access to Soundscapes of the past [11,12]. The topic is also currently under study by European research groups. A specific example is the Spanish platform developed to associate multimedia to geographically referenced events, to create an immersive Soundscape experience for the user in Spanish cities [8]. A similar effort is currently under way for the city of Évora, in Portugal, where different geo-referenced digital tools are being developed with a similar objective (PASEV project) [6].

Domain Analysis and Approaches. A Domain Model is intended to represent commonalities and variabilities of a domain. One of the popular ways to represent an application domain is through a Feature Model, used in the Feature Oriented Domain Analysis (FODA) method, which focuses on domain features. According to Kang et al. [4], a feature is a property that can be shared with a family of systems. The domain analysis in FODA is divided into context analysis, domain modeling, and architectural modeling. In the Domain Analysis and Reuse Environment (DARE) approach [2], the Domain Model output is referred

[1] The original plugin is available at https://featureide.github.io/.

to as the domain book. Its content is structured into domain sources, vocabulary analysis and architectural analysis. The Product-Line Software Engineering-Customizable Domain Analysis (PuLSE-CDA) method [1] begins by analyzing the topics covered by the domain (scope definition). Then, raw/unstructured domain knowledge is gathered and linked to its source. When using PuLSE-CDA, the Domain Model is never expected to be stable allowing constant re-analysis of the requirements and domain knowledge. The link facilitates the update on the model domain knowledge. The third and final step delivers the domain model and a domain decision model. These three approaches are combined to form our combined method, described next.

3 A Domain Analysis for Historical Soundscapes

This section describes our approach for the domain analysis. PuLSE-CDA inspired the idea of linking sources to requirements, as this will allow for an efficient evolution of the Domain Model. The book metaphor and the completion criteria (when the whole outline has been filled) is based on the DARE approach. From the FODA method, we adopt the Feature Model, which plays a major role. However, we need a conceptual model, in our case expressed using a class diagram. The need for a class diagram comes from the need for a representation of the entities and their relationships, required by the domain as well as the relevant attributes, leading to a simpler future software implementation. The domain analysis method used consists of creating a proposal of a domain book of sorts, where the focus is solely on the domain requirements (see Table 1).

Table 1. Domain model outline for this project

Domain scope	Detailed limits of domain scope and target users for systems in the domain
Definitions	Dictionary of technical terms and concepts the reader may not be familiar with
Software analysis commonalities	Structured list of assumptions that are true for all systems in the domain
Software analysis variabilities	Structured list of assumptions on how systems in the domain differ
Domain requirements	Structured list of mandatory and optional, functional and non-functional requirements for all systems in the domain This will include a link to the requirement source
Domain modeling	Class diagram and Feature diagram
Issues	A record of important domain model decisions and Alternatives

A plug-in extension for the creation of feature models was developed, in our case, FeatureIDE. Features in the feature model may include online links

(URLs) to examples. Feature diagrams allow the expression of information about a specific feature. In particular, the FeatureIDE plug-in includes a description of each feature. However, as features are user-visible characteristics, each feature can have a different level of abstraction. For example, a color can be a feature, but a Log-in page can also be a feature in the same Feature Model. Developers may require a detailed explanation of what the feature is meant to do, specially in this domain where multimedia plays a key role. Hence, allowing features to include links to actual examples, by associating them with multimedia resources, provides the developers with an improved understanding of what is intended with the feature. The solution allows the user to associate several URLs per feature.

4 Towards a Domain Model for Historical Soundscapes

In a Domain Model, we cannot guarantee identification of all requirements. Hence, there is a need to scope the domain and properly define its limits. An important factor was the target users. Thus, the contents must be accessible not only for developers, but also for readers without experience in Domain Modeling. This led to the choice of representing the domain requirements and their sources in different forms, such as table templates and models. Thus, our Domain Model is described through a conceptual model, and two Feature Models; a brief explanation of their interpretation is available in the appendix of the full domain analysis document[2]. The document also includes the description of the terms and concepts relevant to the Soundscape domain under analysis.

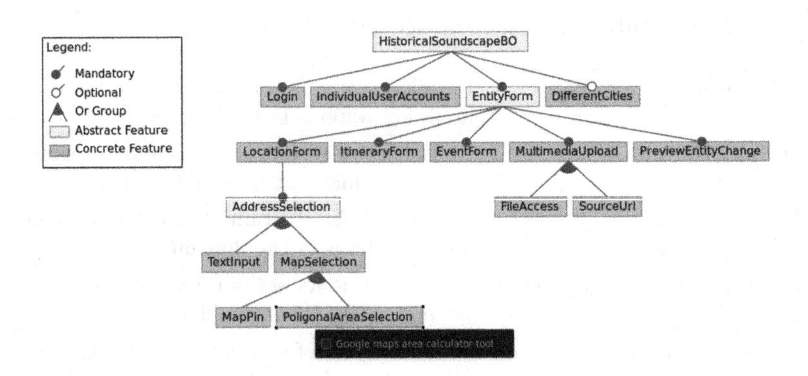

Fig. 1. Back-office feature model of the domain model

The Soundscape Domain Model is a result of the analysis of both the PASEV and the Spanish Historical Soundscapes platforms. It covers the mandatory

[2] The Domain Model is available at: https://github.com/marianaBonito/APDC-Investigation-HistoricalSoundscapesCaseOfEvora-DomainAnalysis/blob/master/Domain_Analisis-Historical_Soundscapes.pdf.

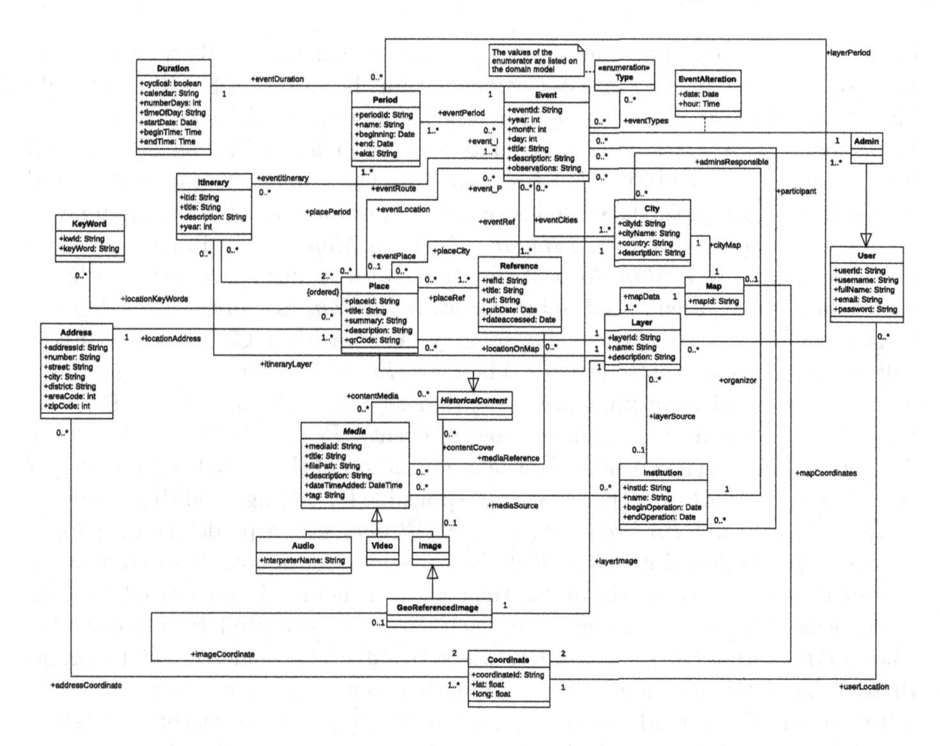

Fig. 2. Class diagram of the domain model

and optional requirements for systems in the domain. Figure 1 shows the Feature Model developed for the back-office module of a software platform for the domain. The Feature Models were developed using the FeatureIDE plug-in extension, developed in the context of this work. The diagram shows an example of a feature linked online reference to demonstrate one of the visualization options[3].

The conceptual model was the least consensual part, as there are many ways to structure the domain's entities and their relationships. All decisions for this diagram and any other conflicting observations that were encountered during the domain analysis, are justified in the full Domain Model. An understanding of the conceptual model can be obtained from the analysis of the class diagram in Fig. 2, which presents the domain entities as Classes and their relationships.

Since the known platforms developed for the domain focus on Historical Soundscapes, everything on the class diagram must be associated to some *Period* in time. This *Period* is represented by an entity with its corresponding attributes. When using a platform in the domain the *User* will be interested in viewing all sorts of historical information associated to a specific location, so the purpose of an immersive experience can be achieved. This is represented with the *Place*

[3] Plug-in extension along with further detail is available at https://github.com/marianaBonito/APDC-Investigation-HistoricalSoundscapesCaseOfEvora-DomainAnalysis/blob/master/FeatureIDE_Plugin_Extension_Manual.pdf.

entity and its corresponding attributes. A *Place* may have *Key Words* associated to it, to facilitate filtering or associations within the software. It will necessarily include an *Address* and *Coordinates* associated to said *Address* to represent its geolocation. A *Place* will be associated to one or more *Map Layers* and will have *Media* associated to it. *Map Layers* are used to display geographic data and represent location pins, show the historical cartography over the basemap layer, and even display routes of an *Itinerary*. Hence, a *Map Layer* will logically need to be associated to a *Map*. Also, if the *Map Layer* is historical cartography or something similar, it will need to include an *Institution* as source. Each *Map* will be associated to a City. Various *Events* may take place in a City, but each *Event* will be linked to at least one *City*. The class *Event* is central to the platform, as most historical recordings are generated as part of events. Each *Event* is related to other concepts, such as *Type* (of event), *Period*, *Reference*, *Duration*, *Institution* (the one responsible for the organisation of the event), *Administrator* (member of the platforms organization responsible for adding or editing the event in the system), and *Itinerary* or *Place*. An *Itinerary* is a predetermined route between specific locations, represented as a set of contiguous lines connecting the event's locations on the map. Hence, the itinerary is associated to 2 or more places. Also, at a given time, each *User* is associated to a geographic *Coordinate*, and a *Place* has a QR-Code attribute. The reader might recognise these as being two common ways of presenting location content to the user. The software can either read the user's current location from a sensor on his/her mobile device and start displaying the location multimedia automatically, or the software can request the user to use his/her device to read the QR-code present at each location and display the information linked to it. As this model represents different approaches allowed for all tools currently in the domain, we opted not to restrict to one approach. In Fig. 2, the entity *Type* is an enumerator, including Civic and Military Demonstrations, and Religious Manifestations.

5 Conclusion

Historical Soundscapes are of great importance. Hence, new projects are emerging within the proposed domain. This document presented the context for an initial domain requirements analysis, the approach taken to develop it and, briefly, described its results. It also presented an extension of the FeatureIDE plug-in, which is a tool used for creating Feature Models in the context of this domain. As future work, we will continue to improve the Domain Model and will perform a full survey with domain experts, to evaluate the produced domain artifacts.

Acknowledgment. We thank NOVA LINCS UID/CEC/04516/2019 and PASEV project PTDC/ART-PER/28584/2017.

References

1. Bayer, J., Muthig, D., Widen, T.: Customizable domain analysis. In: Czarnecki, K., Eisenecker, U.W. (eds.) GCSE 1999. LNCS, vol. 1799, pp. 178–194. Springer, Heidelberg (2000). https://doi.org/10.1007/3-540-40048-6_14

2. Frakes, W., Prieto-Diaz, R., Fox, C.: DARE: domain analysis and reuse environment. Ann. Softw. Eng. **5**, 125–141 (1998)
3. Guzi, M.: The Sound of Life: What Is a Soundscape? 4 May 2017. https://folklife.si.edu/talkstory/the-sound-of-life-what-is-a-Soundscape. Accessed Mar 2020
4. Kang, K.C., Cohen, S.G., Hess, J.A., Novak, W.E., Peterson, A.S.: Feature-oriented domain analysis feasibility study, pp. 1–147. CMU/SEI-90-TR-21 (1990)
5. Lee, J., Hicks, D., Henriksen, D., Mishra, P.: The Deep-Play Research Group: Historical Soundscapes for Creative Synthesis (2015)
6. PASEV project (2019). https://pasev.hcommons.org/
7. Rabiser, R., Schmid, K., Eichelberger, H., Vierhauser, M., Guinea, S., Grünbacher, P.: A domain analysis of resource and requirements monitoring: towards a comprehensive model of the software monitoring domain. Elsevier, IST (2019)
8. Ruiz Jiménez, J., Lizarán Rus, I.J.: Paisajes sonoros históricos (c.1200-c.1800) (2015). http://www.historicalSoundscapes.com/
9. Sterne, J.: Soundscape, Landscape, Escape. De Gruyter (2013). https://www.degruyter.com/
10. Thurimella, A.K., Padmaja, T.M.: Economics-driven software architecture. (Ivan, M., Bahsoon, R., Kazman, R., Zhang, Y. eds.) (2014)
11. Truax, B., Westerkamp, H., Woog, A. P., Kallmann, H., Mcintosh, A.: World Soundscape Project 7 February 206AD. https://thecanadianencyclopedia.ca/en/article/world-Soundscape-project. Accessed 2 Mar 2020
12. Willie, R., Murphy, E.: Soundscapes in the early modern world (2020). https://emSoundscapes.co.uk/. Accessed 2 Mar 2020

Towards a Unified Framework for Computational Trust and Reputation Models for e-Commerce Applications

Chayma Sellami[1,2](✉), Mickaël Baron[1](✉), Mounir Bechchi[2](✉), Allel Hadjali[1](✉), Stephane Jean[1](✉), and Dominique Chabot[2](✉)

[1] LIAS - ISAE-ENSMA/University of Poitiers, Chasseneuil, France
{chayma.sellami,baron,allel.hadjali,stephane.jean}@ensma.fr
[2] O°Code, 322 Bis Route du Puy Charpentreau, 85000 La Roche-sur-Yon, France
{mounir,dominique}@o-code.co

Abstract. Evaluating the quality of resources and the reliability of entities in a system is one of the current needs of modern computer systems. This assessment is the result of two concepts that dominate our real life as well as computer systems, which are Trust and Reputation. To measure them, a variety of computational models have been developed to help users make decisions, and to improve interactions with the system and between users. Due to the wide variety of definitions for reputation and trust topics, this paper attempts to unify these definitions by proposing a unique formalization in terms of graphical and textual notations. It introduces also a deep analysis to understand the behavior and the intuition behind each computational model.

Keywords: Trust · Reputation · Computational model · Graphical/textual representation

1 Introduction

The concepts of trust and reputation are of paramount importance in human societies. Several disciplines resort to their use in different ways according to their own visions and perspectives. In this paper, we highlight the use of these concepts in an area that is becoming omnipresent in our lives, which is computer system. Within the past few decades, an impressive sum of inquires has been conducted on the subjects of computational trust and reputation models. One of the beginning focuses for considering computers and trust within the same setting was Marsh in [10]. Numerous commonsense approaches on high-profile applications are still right now widespread. For example, the reputation frameworks on websites like eBay, Amazon, or person rating websites such as Tripadvisor and Goodreads. To meet the challenges posed in this field, researchers began to develop theoretical and practical models to better understand the field and to improve existing solutions. Given that this is a trendy research area, several

S. Cherfi et al. (Eds.): RCIS 2021, LNBIP 415, pp. 616–622, 2021.
https://doi.org/10.1007/978-3-030-75018-3_44

researchers are still developing other solutions [1,2,6]. However, we notice that there are several definitions related to trust and reputation, which lead to an ambiguity in the understanding of these concepts. Our first contribution proposes a unification of the definitions related to trust and reputation. It suggests a unique formalization with graphical and textual representations of these two concepts. We also found that it is not easy to understand the semantics and intuition behind the computations performed by the various computational models. Our second contribution attempts to make more transparent the "black-box" of the behavior of each of these models.

The rest of the paper is made up as follows; Sect. 2 presents definitions and properties related to trust and reputation. This section also introduces our first contribution, which is the graphical and textual formalization of trust and reputation principles. Section 3 describes the different types of trust and reputation computational models as well as our second contribution in section regarding the behavior of computational models. Some related works are discussed in Sect. 4. Finally, the points to remember and perspectives are presented in Sect. 5.

2 Definitions and Properties

In this section, we revisit the definitions and the behaviors of trust and reputation and other related concepts. For each notion, both graphical notation and mathematical formalization are introduced.

2.1 Trust

- **Definition:** Trust is a concept that we apply daily. Unfortunately, trust suffers from the problem of definition, in the absence of a precise definition commonly used in the literature. According to [8], it is possible to segment the social perspectives of trust into three segments categories: (i) that of personality, (ii) that of sociologists, and (iii) that of psychosociologists. It can generally be said that trust is a relationship between a trustor and a trustee. The trust relationship can thus be modeled as in Fig. 1, where the user U_1 (Trustor) trusts another user U_2 (Trustee) with a value X:

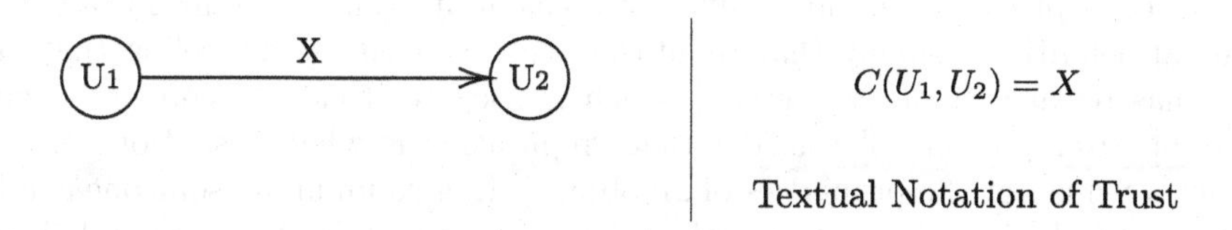

Fig. 1. Graphical notation of trust

The function $C(U_1, U_2)$ has two arguments the trustor "U_1" and the trustee "U_2", the result of this function is X "the value of the trust".

- **Context:** According to [11], when defining trust, the context is an important factor. It indicates the situation in which the relationship is established. The graphical notation of the context can be shown in Fig. 2. U_1's trust in U_2 in a context c is X, we note:

$$C_c(U_1, U_2) = X \tag{1}$$

- **Transitivity:** A graphical notation of transitivity is given in Fig. 3. If U_1 trusts U_2 and U_2 trusts U_3, then U_1 trusts U_3, we note:

$$C(U_1, U_2) = x \wedge C(U_2, U_3) = y \Rightarrow \exists f / f(x, y) = z. \tag{2}$$

  As Josang and Pope prove in [4], transitivity is possible only in some cases. However, in the case of transitivity, as the number of referrals increases, the level of trust is likely to decrease. For example, if Bob asks Alice for a dentist referral. Alice responds, my sister was telling me about a dentist that her friend had referred to her from a trusted friend. The level of trust Bob will have in this referral is less than if it were a dentist that Alice had seen directly.

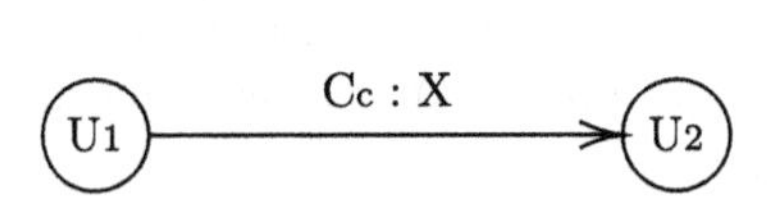

Fig. 2. Graphic notation of the context

Fig. 3. Transitivity of trust

- **Transaction** In our proposal, a transaction is an action of a user on the network within a specific context that plays a role in the computation of trust and reputation. For example, in the context of online sales sites, placing an order, giving an opinion on an item or on the seller, are considered transactions.

2.2 Reputation

The second key concept considered in this paper is reputation. Several definitions of this concept can be found in different areas of literature. The first is a rather general definition, namely that reputation can be seen as the feeling that one user has towards another user [7], which is used to decide to cooperate with him [6]. Jøsang et al. [3] consider that "reputation is what is said or believed about a person or the properties of an object". In a community, someone can be trusted if (s)he has a good reputation. According to Abdul-Rahman and Hailes [1], reputation is an estimate of an entity's behavior in the community, based on its past behaviors. Reputation is in fact an intangible asset (an opinion, a feeling) over which an individual does not have total control since it emanates from the community. Thus, by instantiation in the field of computer science, reputation is the opinion of a system towards a user. The concept of reputation can thus be represented as in Fig. 4, where the system assigns a reputation rating to a user, based on community opinions and behavior in the system. The reputation of U_1 in the system S is X, we note:

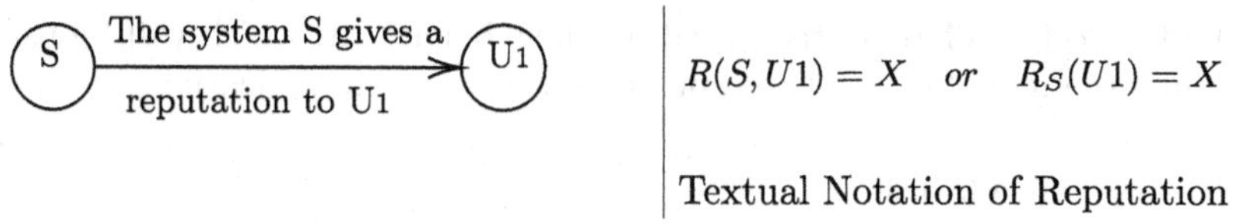

Fig. 4. Graphical notation of reputation

But above all, to talk about a computational model, we must define the measurements taken into account in this process.

2.3 Measurement

In order to quantify trust and reputation, an appropriate measure is needed. Four types of values of such measure are generally used:

- **Unique value:** It is the measure used to ensure the quality of products in a production line. For example, if an item does not conform with manufacturing requirements, it is withdrawn from the chain and nothing is reported otherwise.
- **Binary values:** binary values are used to distinguish between a trusted and untrusted entity. For example, if we trust a user, we assign him a rating of 1, and 0 otherwise.
- **Multiple values:** allow to take into account the history of cooperation between two entities. For example, possible values are "very low, low, medium, high and very high" levels of trust.
- **Continuous values:** Continuous values give a wider range of possible values of the trust level. Typically, this value varies along the range [0,1]; it measures trust in the form of probability.

To measure the degree of trust and reputation in the form of any value, computer systems have relied on models using different processes depending on the need, as can be seen in the rest of this paper.

It is important to understand the functioning and mathematical process of each model. This will facilitate their classification according to their behavior.

3 Computational Models Choice

Systems based on trust and reputation must, as noted below, have a computing model. Indeed, the computation process must make it possible to take a decision. For example, a high degree of trust in an entity makes it possible to judge that entity to be reliable and to take the decision to trust it. The same applies to reputation. Different models have been proposed to represent and compute trust and reputation in systems. These models can be classified into: Bayesian models, Belief-based models, Discrete value models and Flow models. In this section, for each computational model, we specify its semantics and intuition. This will allow the models to be differentiated based on their behaviour, which will be used to determine the model to use based on the needs of each application.

3.1 Bayesian Model

Bayesian models use probability distribution functions to estimate trust and reputation values. The distribution function of a real random variable X is the function F_X which, at any real x, associates the probability of obtaining a value such as:

$$F_X(x) = \mathbb{P}(X \leq x). \tag{3}$$

The F_X function depends on the law used by the computational model. In probability theory, the machine procedure must be replicated many times in order to make a final decision. This approach induces a slow shift in the expected values. Therefore, to gain good trust and reputation rates, it is important to make many transactions. This strategy is beneficial in the sense that it allows a consumer who made a bad transaction the ability to regain his credibility. But eventually, it will punish him. The downside is that the model can not detect it explicitly in the event of malicious use of the device.

3.2 Belief-Based Model

Like Bayesian models, belief theory is related to probability theory, the difference being that the sum of the probabilities on all possible outcomes is not necessarily equal to 1, and the remaining probability is interpreted as uncertainty. This model category behaves in much the same way as the Bayesian model.

3.3 Discrete Value Model

The trust value of a newcomer is equal to zero. Since this model does not use a specific probability function, the choice of the appropriate function depends on system's needs.

3.4 Flow Model

Flow models compute trust or reputation values by transitive iterations through looped chains. This model does not impact the initial value for newcomers, as in Google's PageRank system. To build a strong reputation, one has to start detecting incoming trust flows. The benefit here is that the methods for estimating data flows rapidly update the estimated values each time a new flow is detected. In the case of cheating, the machine explicitly detects a series of malicious acts. The limitation of this technique is that a neutral value of trust or reputation is equal to zero, which can be considered penalizing.

3.5 Summary

In today's IT systems, trust and reputation are two principles that have become very important. Since there are many works that have discussed these concepts in the literature, it leads to a variety of descriptions. On the one hand, for these definitions, we have suggested a global graphical and textual formalization. On the other hand, to the best of our knowledge, there is little work that clarifies what sort of trust and reputation modeling they use. This makes their use in applications a bit complicated. That is why it will be easier to select which model to adapt, if we set the system specifications from the beginning.

4 Related Works

In recent years, computational trust and reputation models have become quite important methods to improve interaction between users and with the system. And since their appearance, several research works have been published to solve the problems linked to these concepts. Other types of work were carried out which gave an additional aspect to this research, an aspect of analysis and comparison of reputation and trust models. Among these works we can cite a work published in [9] whose aim is to present the most popular and widely used computer models of trust and reputation. Then in 2017, a survey was carried out to classify and compare the main findings that have helped to address trust and reputation issues in the context of web services [12]. And finally in 2018, Braga, Diego De Siqueira, et al. conducted a survey which provided additional structure to the research being done on the topics of trust and reputation [5]. A new integrated system for analyzing reputation and trust models has been proposed. There are therefore several works and classifications, but they do not help to clarify which model to take and why to take it. Moreover, the comparison made in these papers is static; in common community application scenarios, it does not help to explain the dynamic models' behavior. Furthermore, they do not provide formalized and graphically illustrated definitions of the concepts used in these models.

5 Conclusion and Perspectives

In this paper, we have tackled the problem of computational models of trust and reputation. Due to the numerous studies made in the literature about these two concepts, we have tried to unify these notions. In particular, we have revised their definitions and restate their basic properties. The analysis done show that our requirements proposal helps to differentiate the various models and select the most suitable ones according to the users needs. This paper constitutes our first step towards a new general model of trust/reputation that can fit each application's context. As an immediate future work, we plan to identify a set of requirements that make the model choice more practical and intelligent, in the sense that it meets the desired needs.

References

1. Abdul-rahman, A., Hailes, S.: Supporting trust in virtual communities. In: Proceedings of 33rd Hawaii International Conference on System Sciences, vol. 0, no. c, pp. 1–9. IEEE Computer Society (2000)
2. Jøsang, A., Ismail, R.: The beta reputation system. In: 15th Bled Electronic Commerce Conference, pp. 2502–2511 (2002)
3. Jøsang, A., Ismail, R., Boyd, C.: A survey of trust and reputation systems for online service provision. Decis. Support Syst. **43**(2), 618–644 (2007)
4. Jøsang, A., Pope, S.: Semantic constraints for trust transitivity. In: Conferences in Research and Practice in Information Technology Series, vol. 43, pp. 59–68 (2005)
5. Braga, D.D.S., Niemann, M., Hellingrath, B., Neto, F.B.D.L.: Survey on computational trust and reputation models. ACM Comput. Surv. (CSUR) **51**(5), 1–40 (2018)
6. Pinyol, I., Sabater-Mir, J.: Computational trust and reputation models for open multi-agent systems: a review. Artific. Intell. Rev. **40**(1), 1–25 (2013)
7. Kravari, K., Bassiliades, N.: DISARM: a social distributed agent reputation model based on defeasible logic. J. Syst. Softw. **117**, 130–152 (2016)
8. Lewicki, R.J., Bunker, B.B.: Developing and maintaining trust in work relationships. Trust Organ. Front. Theory Res. **114**, 139 (1996)
9. Medić, A.: Survey of computer trust and reputation models-the literature overview. Int. J. Inf. Commun. Technol. Res. **2**(3) (2012)
10. Marsh, S.P.: Formalising Trust as a Computational Concept. Ph.D. thesis. University of Stirling (1994)
11. Vu, V.-H.: Infrastructure de gestion de la confiance sur internet. Ph.D. thesis, Ecole Nationale Supérieure des Mines de Saint-Etienne, France (2010)
12. Wahab, O.A., Bentahar, J., Otrok, H., Mourad, A.: A survey on trust and reputation models for Web services: single, composite, and communities. Decis. Support Syst. **74**, 121–134 (2015)

Improving Web API Usage Logging

Rediana Koçi(✉), Xavier Franch, Petar Jovanovic, and Alberto Abelló

Universitat Politècnica de Catalunya, BarcelonaTech, Barcelona, Spain
{koci,franch,petar,aabello}@essi.upc.edu

Abstract. A Web API (WAPI) is a type of API whose interaction with its consumers is done through the Internet. While being accessed through the Internet can be challenging, mostly when WAPIs evolve, it gives providers the possibility to monitor their usage. Currently, WAPI usage is mostly logged for traffic monitoring and troubleshooting. Even though they contain invaluable information regarding consumers' behavior, they are not sufficiently used by providers. In this paper, we first consider two phases of the application development lifecycle, and based on them we distinguish two different types of usage logs, namely development logs and production logs. For each of them we show the potential analyses (e.g., WAPI usability evaluation) that can be performed, as well as the main impediments, that may be caused by the unsuitable log format. We then conduct a case study using logs of the same WAPI from different deployments and different formats, to demonstrate the occurrence of these impediments and at the same time the importance of a proper log format. Next, based on the case study results, we present the main quality issues of WAPI logs and explain their impact on data analyses. For each of them, we give some practical suggestions on how to deal with them, as well as mitigating their root cause.

Keywords: Web API · Usage logs · Log format · Pre-processing

1 Introduction

An increasing number of organizations and institutions are exposing their data and services by means of Application Programming Interfaces (APIs). Different from statically linked APIs, which are accessed locally by consumers, web APIs (WAPIs) are exposed, thus accessed, through the network, using standard web protocols [3]. As the interaction between WAPIs and their consumers is done typically through the Internet, both parts end up loosely connected.

This loosely coupled connection becomes eventually challenging, mostly during WAPI evolution, when as a boomerang effect, consumers end up strongly tight to WAPIs [1]. If providers release a new version and decide to discontinue the former ones, consumers are obliged to upgrade their applications to the new version and adapt them to the changes. Consequently, WAPIs end up driving the evolution of their consumers' application [6,7]. Knowing the considerable impact

S. Cherfi et al. (Eds.): RCIS 2021, LNBIP 415, pp. 623–629, 2021.
https://doi.org/10.1007/978-3-030-75018-3_45

WAPIs have on their consumers, providers would benefit from their feedback to understand their needs and problems when using the WAPI [4].

Currently, API providers face a lot of difficulties in collecting and analyzing consumers' feedback from several sources, e.g., bug reports, issue tracking systems, online forums [5]. Furthermore, feedback collection and analysis turns out to be expensive in terms of time, thus difficult to scale. Actually, in the WAPI case, this feedback can be gathered in a more centralized way. While being accessed through the network poses some challenges for consumers, it enables providers to monitor the usage of their WAPIs, by logging every request that consumers make to them (see Fig. 1). WAPI logs, besides coming from a trustworthy source of information, can be gathered in a straightforward, inexpensive way, and completely transparent to the WAPI consumers.

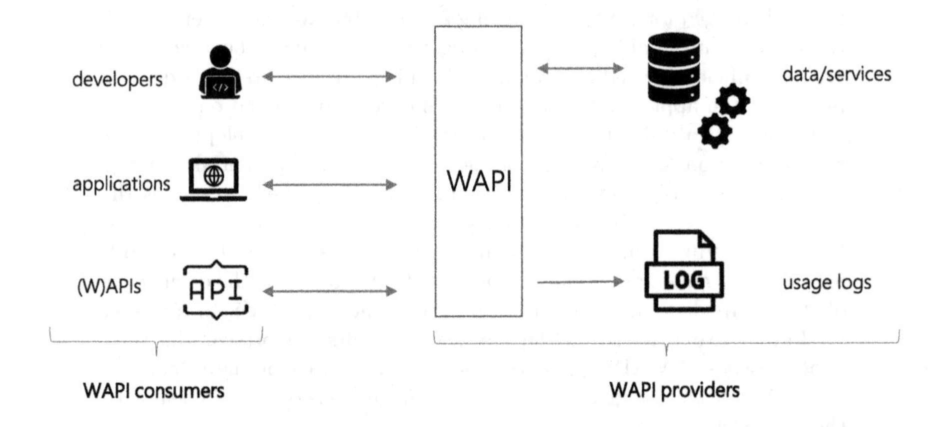

Fig. 1. The interaction between consumers, providers and WAPIs

This paper is building upon our previous work [2], where we measured the usability of WAPIs by analyzing their usage logs generated during the development phase of consumers' applications. Based on the challenges faced while working with WAPI usage logs, and the surprising lack of attention this topic (i.e., WAPI usage logs analysis) had gained, we saw convenient to summarize our experience and research in the field, into a set of practical suggestions to enhance the logging of WAPI usage for more specialised analyses. The extended version of this work is available in [11].

2 The Potential of WAPI Usage Logs

Providers typically log their WAPIs' usage by recording all requests done against the WAPIs. As applications are their actual consumers, we should consider the different ways they consume WAPIs over their own lifecycle. Basically, applications interact with the WAPIs during design time and runtime, over both of which they manifest different aspects of their behavior. Following on from this, we distinguish two types of logs: (i) development logs, and (ii) production logs.

Development logs are generated at design time, while developers build and test their applications. Thus, these logs show their attempts in using the WAPI, the endpoints they struggle more with, specific mistakes they do while using and learning the WAPI, etc. [2,10]. By analyzing these logs, providers may evaluate the usability of their WAPI from the consumers' perspective. On the other hand, production logs are generated during applications runtime, while application are being used by end users. WAPI requests are predetermined by the implemented functionalities of the applications, containing real and solid WAPI usage scenarios and the right order in which developers make the requests to WAPI. By analyzing these logs, providers may identify consumers' needs for new features, and implement the corresponding endpoints.

Even though both types of logs provide useful information about WAPI consumption and perception from consumers, preparing and analyzing them is arduous. First, it is not always trivial distinguishing these logs from each other, as they often are stored together in the same files. Secondly, consumers' applications design and the way users interact with them will be manifested in the production logs, obfuscating the inference of the real WAPI usage patterns. Finally, as providers store these logs typically for traffic monitoring, they do not consider the requirements that specific analyses may have. Thus, unawarely, they may neglect the importance of the log format, and even leave out crucial information for consumers' identification, adversely affecting not only the analysis results, but also the logs pre-processing.

3 How Does the Logs Format Affect the Pre-processing?

The pre-processing phase typically consists of four main steps: (i) data fusion, (ii) data cleaning, (iii) data structuring, and (iv) data generalization [2,8]. In this section we will cover two challenges from WAPI logs pre-processing, namely field extraction from data cleaning phase, and session identification from data structuring, as the two challenges of pre-processing that are directly affected by the log format and the way the usage is being logged (Fig. 2).

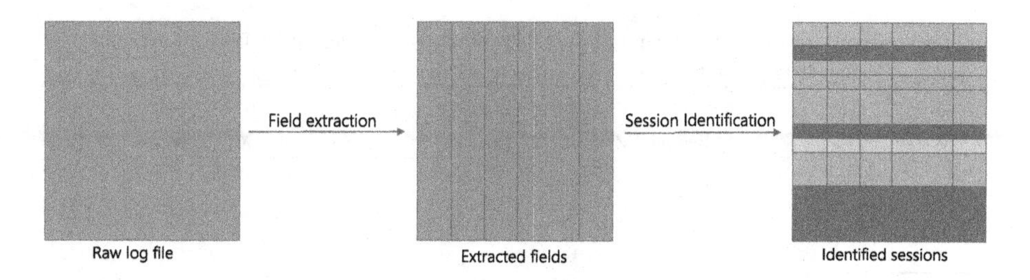

Fig. 2. Field extraction and session identification

Field Extraction. Usage logs are stored in text files, where each log entry (line) contains several fields. Field extraction consists exactly in the separation of the log entries into fields. It is typically performed before data cleaning, so that log entries can be filtered based on the value of their specific fields (e.g., request method, request body). There are several ways to parse log files information, including regular expressions, predefined parsers, custom grok parsers (pattern matching syntax used by ElasticSearch). Providers should decide on a log format that can be easily parsed, in order to enable a simple querying of fields value.

Session Identification. This challenge (often called *sessioning*), refers to grouping together into the same session, all the log entries (i.e., requests) coming from each user during the time frame of a visit. Most of the WAPIs are stateless, meaning that the server does not store the state, thus no sessions are generated. Session identifiers must be inferred from other available information in the logs, applying sessioning heuristics (i.e., methods for constructing sessions based on assumptions about users' behavior or the site/application characteristics). Two of the most applied methods are (i) time-based heuristics, which construct the sessions based on the duration of a user's visit on one page (i.e., page-stay heuristic) or the entire visit to the application, and (ii) navigation-based heuristics, which construct the sessions based on the assumption on how the applications' pages are linked [9]. As both of them are built under the hypothesis of an already launched application, they apply only to the production logs.

4 Case Study

We perform field extraction and session identification to demonstrate the importance of specific fields of the log format, and the impact their lack may cause to both of these challenges. We conduct a case study using production logs from two instances of the District Health Information Software 2 (DHIS2) WAPI[1], namely World Health Organization (WHO) Integrated Data Platform[2] (WIDP), and Médecins Sans Fontières (MSF). Being deployed and used independently, the logs coming from them have different formats (Table 1).

Table 1. Log formats of the two DHIS2's deployments under study

Deployment	Client IP address	Timestamp granularity	Duration	Request	Status code	Object size	Referer	User agent
MSF	✗	Second	✓	✓	✓	✓	✓	✓
WIDP	✓	Millisecond	✓	✓	✓	✓	✗	✓

[1] https://www.dhis2.org/about.
[2] http://mss4ntd.essi.upc.edu/wiki/index.php?title=WHO_Integrated_Data_Platform_(WIDP).

1. **Field extraction.** We perform field extraction by using regular expressions in JAVA. Request body, referer and user-agent, are the parts that generate more errors while parsing, as they may include spaces and special characters, sometimes used to separate the fields. We have to perform some extra manual work to handle the errors, like splitting these fields into several parts, and then joining them, without cluttering parts of different fields.
2. **Session identification.** We apply the page-stay heuristic and the navigation one combined with time constraint, using timeout thresholds 5 and 15 min for both of the methods. We perform the experiments on log data from MSF, since the log format contains information about the referer (Table 1), required in navigation-based method. The results of the analysis are shown in Table 2.

Table 2. Statistics for the defined sessions

Heuristic	No. of sessions	Avg. duration	Avg. size
Time 5 min	15,804	110 s	63
Time 15 min	15,937	127 s	63
Time 5 min, navigation	8,233	266 s	122
Time 15 min, navigation	6,586	413 s	152

As seen from Table 2, the metrics from the navigation method (two last rows) are significantly different from the ones when only the time heuristic was used (two first rows). After using the referer information, for the same logs we have less number of sessions, but larger ones in terms of number of requests and session total duration. This means that, when using only the time heuristic, we are over-splitting the sessions, thus potentially loosing sequences of requests. Besides this, the new sessions created, likely contain mixed requests from different users and different applications, thus possibly creating fake sequences of requests.

Assessment. The performance of the heuristics could be evaluated by comparing the constructed sessions with the real ones. As in WAPI usage logs we cannot have the real sessions, we compare the reconstructed sessions of logs from MSF and WIDP (using client IP and timeout 15 min), in the context of four specific applications. For each application, we extract the distinct requests assigned on both instances (Table 3). We saw that when using only the time heuristic in MSF, even though the sessions are in average shorter in terms of number of requests (Table 2), too many distinct and different requests are assigned to each application. The same happen with WIDP, whose logs do not have information about the referer. For each application we explore in detail the distinct requests assigned to them, for all the sessions. We saw that there were WAPI requests, that even though not related to the applications, were assigned to them because of the missing information in the logs.

Table 3. WAPI requests assigned to four applications installed in MSF and WIDP

Application	MSF (time)	MSF (time, navigation)	WIPD (time)
dhis-web-event-capture	106	28	177
dhis-web-event-reports	139	25	118
dhis-web-tracker-capture	202	48	124
HMIS-Dictionary	136	31	57

5 Common WAPI Logs Issues

In this section, deriving from the case study, we introduce the main WAPI usage logs quality issues, that are responsible for the problems surged during field extraction and session identification.

1. **Field extraction**
   - Fields' separators part of the fields' body. When the fields themselves contain in their body the characters used as separators (e.g., comma, semi-colon, space), field extraction becomes difficult to automate. To overcome this challenge, it is recommended to double-quote the fields that might have special characters.
2. **Session identification**
   - Insufficient fields. As WAPI logs are usually not stored to analyze consumers' behavior, they often suffer from missing crucial fields for the application of several analysis. To strike a balance between not leaving out important fields, and not logging too many ones, providers should decide beforehand on the analyses they will perform on the usage data.
   - Missing applications' identifiers. Applications' identifiers are unique identifiers that providers generate for their consumers, to track their usage. The lack of these identifiers may affect the evaluation and the prioritization of the found usage patterns. Additionally, to differentiate between development and production logs, providers should generate different identifiers for each of the phases.
   - Hidden client IP address. If the consumers are using proxy servers, the IP address that appears in the logs will not be of the original user, resulting in different users under the same IP address. Thus, providers should not rely on this field for users and sessions' identification. Instead they should include other fields (e.g., referer, user agent), that will help them in better structuring the logs.
   - Timestamp granularity. The WAPI requests are partially ordered in the usage file: a log entry printed after another one, may have been submitted earlier. If the timestamps are not logged precisely enough, the log entries may appear with the same timestamp. To be able to order them in an exact chronological way, providers should log the timestamp with high precision (e.g., milliseconds).

We have summarized in Table 4, the mitigation suggestions, based on the main problem they aim to solve.

Table 4. Issues' mitigation for a better WAPI usage logging

WAPI usage log issue	Mitigation
Field extraction	Use a machine parse-able format for logs
Session Identification	Provide application identifiers
	Provide different application identifiers for development phase
	Log the referer, user agent
	Log the timestamp in high precision

6 Conclusion and Future Work

Our results indicate that WAPI logs contain invaluable information about consumers' behavior, which comes at the cost of the logs tedious pre-processing. WAPI logs suffer from several issues, that should be properly mitigated, to be further analyzed. While some of these issues are related to the nature of the communication between WAPI and its consumers, others may occur because of improper logging. Furthermore, there are many demanding analyses, whose requirements should drive providers in the way they log the usage of their WAPIs.

As a future work, we plan to perform the proposed analyses on the WAPI usage logs, applying first the suggestions in mitigating the existing quality issues.

References

1. Espinha, T., et al.: Web API growing pains: loosely coupled yet strongly tied. J. Syst. Softw. **100** (2015)
2. Koçi, R., et al.: A data-driven approach to measure the usability of web APIs. In: Euromicro, SEAA. IEEE (2020)
3. Tan, W., et al.: From the service-oriented architecture to the web API economy. IEEE Internet Comput. **20**(4) (2016)
4. Murphy, L., et al.: API designers in the field: Design practices and challenges for creating usable APIs. In: VL/HCC. IEEE (2018)
5. Zhang, T., et al.: Enabling data-driven API design with community usage data: a need-finding study. In: CHI (2020)
6. Espinha, T., et al.: Web API growing pains: stories from client developers and their code. In: CSMR-WCRE. IEEE (2014)
7. Eilertsen, A.M., Bagge, A.H.: Exploring API: client co-evolution. In: WAPI (2018)
8. Tanasa, D., Trousse, P.: Advanced data preprocessing for intersites web usage mining. IEEE Intell. Syst. **19**(2) (2004)
9. Berendt, B., et al.: Measuring the accuracy of sessionizers for web usage analysis. In: Workshop on Web Mining at SDM (2001)
10. Macvean, A., et al.: API usability at scale. In: PPIG (2016)
11. Koçi, R., et al.: Improving Web API Usage Logging. arXiv:2103.10811 [cs.SE] (2021)

Towards a Hybrid Process Modeling Language

Nicolai Schützenmeier[1(✉)], Stefan Jablonski[1], and Stefan Schönig[2]

[1] Institute for Computer Science, University of Bayreuth, Bayreuth, Germany
{nicolai.schuetzenmeier,stefan.jablonski}@uni-bayreuth.de
[2] University of Regensburg, Regensburg, Germany
stefan.schoenig@ur.de

Abstract. Nowadays, business process management is getting more and more important. A wide variety of process modeling languages is available. Hence one of the most complicated tasks of entrepreneurs is to choose the modeling language which suits their respective problems and purposes best. Each of the modeling languages has its own advantages and disadvantages depending on the properties of the process to be modeled. None of the existing approaches satisfies requirements for a "good" modeling language completely. Thus, we formulate our goal to develop a new concept for a hybrid modeling language based on BPMN.

Keywords: Business process modeling · Hybrid process modeling

1 Introduction

Business processes are usually classified as imperative (procedural) and declarative. Procedural modeling language are typically applied when routine processes have to be modelled. Declarative modeling languages are well suited to represent so-called flexible processes [1]. Since in real life many processes consist of both, routine and flexible parts, the question arises, what type of modelling language to apply for such applications. This paper contributes a novel method for this general process modeling problem.

We present some scenarios where the advantages, but also the disadvantage of common process modeling languages become apparent. As a representative of a procedural language we choose BPMN [2]. As representative for a declarative process modeling language, MP-Declare [3] is chosen.

Let us first have a look at a simple but relevant example: suppose there are only the three different activities A, B and C which have to be executed in a sequence where activity A must occur twice and the activities B and C each once. That means that there are twelve different possibilities: $AABC$, $AACB$, $ABAC$, $ACAB$, $ABCA$, $ACBA$, $CAAB$, $BAAC$, $BACA$, $CABA$, $BCAA$ and $CBAA$. Due to technical restriction, overlapping is not allowed, i.e. strict sequential execution is enforced. To model this situation in BPMN, it is necessary to model each of these twelve possibilities separately (see Fig. 1). It is easy to recognize

S. Cherfi et al. (Eds.): RCIS 2021, LNBIP 415, pp. 630–636, 2021.
https://doi.org/10.1007/978-3-030-75018-3_46

that this process model is almost not readable and interpretable. However, this sequence can be modeled easily when the declarative language Declare is used. Only three templates are needed: exactly$(A, 2)$, exactly$(B, 1)$ and exactly$(C, 1)$. The use of these templates means that the two activities B and C have to occur in the process execution, but they may occur only once whereas activity A must occur exactly twice. Adding more activities to this example would extend the BPMN model enormously. Remember that for n different activities there are $\frac{n!}{2} = \frac{n \cdot (n-1) \cdot \dots \cdot 2 \cdot 1}{2}$ different orders.

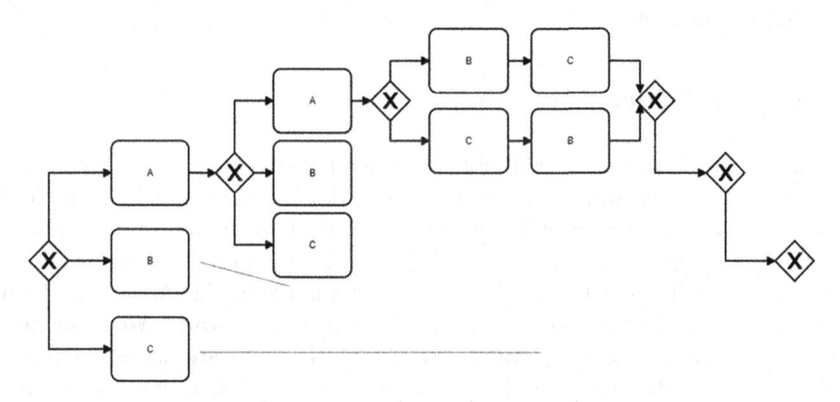

Fig. 1. Cutout of the twelve paths of the example process

To show an advantage of BPMN over MP-Declare, we modify our example. Suppose that there is now only one valid sequence of the three activities A, B and C where each activity has to occur exactly once, e.g. ABC. We can model this scenario without any problems using only one of the six paths in the first example. This is shown in Fig. 2. To model this situation in Declare, the three exactly templates and additional templates which guarantee the required order are necessary. So we need two additional constraints: chainResponse(A, B) and chainResponse(B, C). The chainResponse (A, B) template means that after executing activity A, activity B has to be executed immediately afterwards. The complete model is shown in Fig. 2 which, however, is not very illustrative. Readability and comprehensibility are hampered. Besides, if new activities have to be added, the model will become more and more unreadable. Hence, a model of a sequence of n activities would consist of n existence and $n-1$ chainResponse templates.

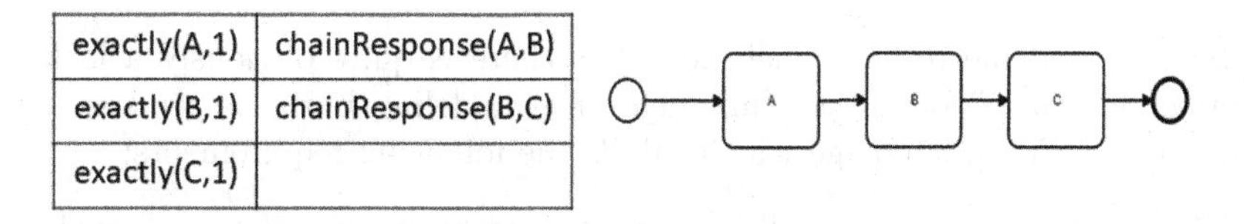

exactly(A,1)	chainResponse(A,B)
exactly(B,1)	chainResponse(B,C)
exactly(C,1)	

Fig. 2. Sequence of three activities in given order modeled in Declare and BPMN

To give a third example let us consider a process with six activities A, B, C, D, E and F. The three activities A, B and C must be executed in an arbitrary sequence where activity A must be executed twice and B and C only once, as can be seen in the first example. D, E and F have to be executed exactly once after the first sequence and in the order DEF. This is a typical situation where both kinds of application requirements show up in the same scenario. In this example we can see both the advantages and the disadvantages of Declare and BPMN. Consequently, the two models may get quite confusing because of their inconvenients. Our goal is to create a language which combines the advantages of both languages.

2 Related Work

Due to space restrictions we will not introduce BPMN and MP-Declare, respectively. However, their pros and cons with regard to specific modelling challenges are already discussed in Sect. 1. Here we just want to discuss current research that tries to make use of the two paradigms in so-called Hybrid Process Models. In general, two different types of hybrid process modeling languages can be distinguished: *separate* notations and *mixed* notations. *Separate Notation* means that the declarative and imperative modeling elements are strictly separated in the model which leads to a clear and easy comprehensibility of the resulting models and to clearly defined semantics. For example, the authors in [4] combine Petri Nets and Declare templates.

A major disadvantage of the paradigm of separate notation is the fact that the different methods can only be applied to subprocesses. These efforts have certain weaknesses that disqualify them from being adopted: there is no tool support, i.e. there is no execution engine available, and a lack of multi-perspectivity. Both drawbacks rule out this approach. The second paradigm of hybrid process modeling is the so-called *Mixed Notation*. Here, the declarative and the imperative elements are completely mixed in the model. In [5], the authors also combine Petri Nets and Declare templates.

The advantage over the separate notation is the fact that two activities can be combined. Hence almost every situation referring to the control-flow perspective can be modeled. But unfortunately the efforts using mixed notations also have their weak points: the semantics are often not defined clearly. Apart from that there is a lack of multi-perspectivity. Finally, we have no tool support.

3 Concept

In Sect. 2 we come to the conclusion that there is quite obviously a lack of a "perfect language" or "hyper language" for modeling business processes. Our aim is to develop a language which fulfills the following requirements:

1. The language must cover all important aspects of a process, e.g. all the different perspectives.
2. The language should fulfill the requirements of a model [6].

3. The language should be "clear" and "easy to understand". This means that the result should be easily readable and understandable.
4. As the model is a means of communication, we claim that a graphical language should be preferred to a textual language (see also [7]).

In this part of the paper we will demonstrate how a language that meets all the requirements posted above can be conceived. As "basic language" for our "hyper language", we opt for BPMN because it is a graphical, well documented and widespread modeling language.

One big disadvantage of BPMN is that process models become large and unreadable when flexibility has to be incorporated into processes. For scenarios like that we propose the following method:

1. Define the original BPMN model that represents the underlying process structure.
2. Analyse the major elements and principles that need to be identified in order to specify a process model like this one.
3. Create a suitable symbol that "communicates" the basic behavior of the process model.
4. Implement the semantics of the process model in the sense of a "macro" and connect it with the process symbol.
5. Offer the macro - including its implementation - in a process modeling workbench.

We apply the above defined method to our first example introduced in Sect. 1. A cutout of step 1 can be seen in Fig. 1. In step 2 we analyse that the model mainly consists of different sequences of a set of given activities. Besides, we have to specify how often an activity must be executed. Also this information must be depicted by the newly introduced modeling construct. One way of representing such a scenario is to present this set of activities within a big arrow (cf. Fig. 3 (a)) (step 3). The number of executions for each activity is represented as a superscript for such an activity. Connecting the original process model as implementation of this new modeling construct to this arrow makes the model clearer and "smaller" (see Fig. 3 (a)). Remember that the big arrow only symbolizes the semantics of the example process. The resulting process structure must be implemented and connected to this symbol, i.e. modeling construct. Start and end state are kept out. The new comprehensive modeling construct is finally provided in a modeling workbench based on the Camunda Modeler[1].

Comparing the non-readable process model in Fig. 1 with the process models of Fig. 3(a) demonstrates that the compact new modeling constructs alleviate the representation and comprehension of a process model. It is obvious that the semantics of this new modeling construct must be clearly communicated to process modellers to correctly apply it. We can see that the twelve different paths have disappeared and only one big arrow is left. The "2" in the upper right corner of activity A represents the fact that this activity has to occur twice in the execution of the sequence.

[1] www.camunda.com.

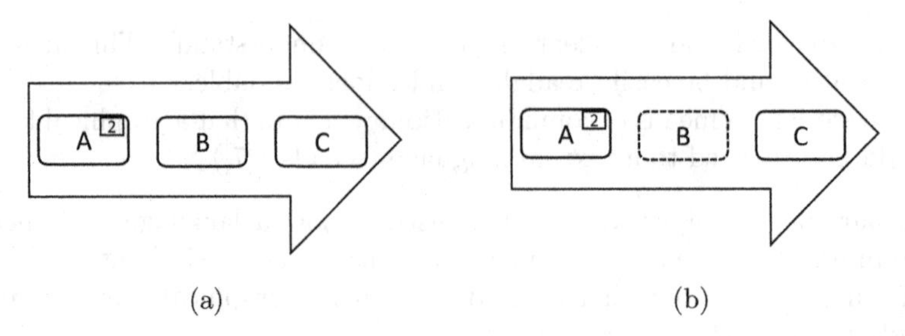

Fig. 3. Sequence of three activities in any order (a) and optional occuring of B (b)

Of course we can extend this procedure to random sequences with n activities. Instead of $\frac{n!}{2}$ different paths, only one single arrow with n activities remains. The semantics stays the same. Hence we can define a map which maps a complicated sequence to an arrow containing the activities occurring in the sequence including their number of occurences.

We can make this example more complicated. Assume that activity B is optional. That means that B can be executed but does not have to. In standard BPMN the process model would increase. Using dashed lines, we can implement this fact easily (see Fig. 3 (b)).

To complicate matters further, let us assume that there are several optional activities and more activities in general. The resulting BPMN model would increase then.

The arrow construct can be extended. Suppose we have got four activities A, B, C and D which can be executed in any order and with just one limitation: A and B must be executed directly one after another (but the order is irrelevant). So we would have e.g. $ABCD, BACD, ABDC$ as possibilities. In BPMN this would mean that we have to model each of these possibilities with a single path. With our new construction, this can be done very easily by using the arrow "recursively" (see Fig. 4 line 4). Figure 4 shows the basic building blocks and their corresponding BPMN diagrams. The resulting models are definitely better readable than the original ones.

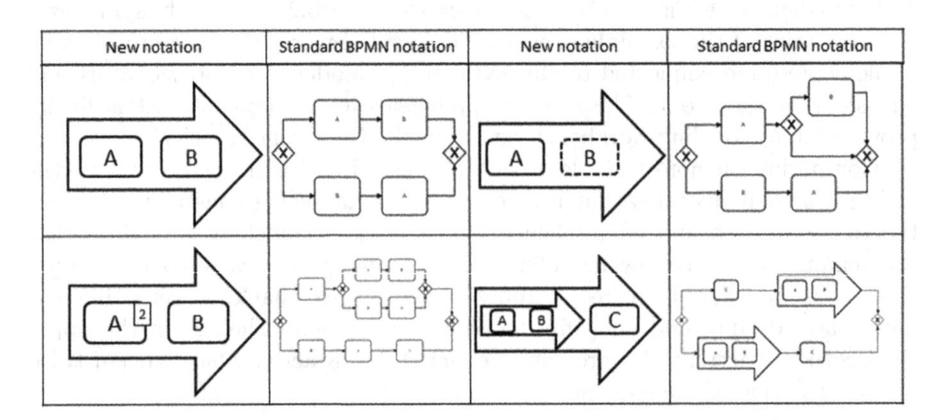

Fig. 4. Basic building blocks and their corresponding BPMN diagrams

4 Conclusion and Future Work

In this paper we gave a survey of existing business process modeling languages. The first part was concerned with the explanation of the two paradigms of modeling: the imperative and the declarative process modeling. We gave the most commonly used representatives of each paradigm and discussed their advantages and disadvantages regarding some example processes. We came to the conclusion that neither an existing imperative modeling language nor a declarative modeling language is sufficient to fulfill all our requirements of a language which is supposed to be "clear" and "easy to understand".

The existing hybrid approaches, which combine the imperative and the declarative paradigms, cannot really meet our expectations. Their semantics is either hardly or not at all understandable (this aspect mainly refers to the so-called "separate notation") or the process has to be divided into subprocesses (this refers to the so-called "mixed notation"). The disadvantages of both approaches are rather serious, and that is the reason why they cannot be applied in reality.

In addition to these arguments, all the different modeling languages cannot express the different process perspectives which we formulated in Sect. 1.

Considering the disadvantages of all these business modeling languages, we fixed our goal to create a new modeling language. For many reasons we decided to choose BPMN as basic language and to expand it by useful and necessary elements and macros.

Of course there are still a lot of problems which will have to be solved in the future. We first want to calculate and compare the Expresivenesse of BPMN and MP-Declare. We need this calculation to have a theoretical reason to choose either the one or the other as basic language for our new hybrid modeling language. It seems that for the time being BPMN might be the best choice.

Afterwards, we will look for "useful" and "necessary" extensions of the chosen language regarding the different perspectives of a process and then define them. These extensions will have to be described in detail and then be added to the existing syntax of the language. Furthermore, we will have to find graphical elements which represent the extension in an "easy" and "clear" way.

After documenting the new hybrid language formally, we will also try to build a modeler including an execution engine.

References

1. van der Aalst, W.: Process Mining: Discovery, Conformance and Enhancement of Business Processes. Springer, Heidelberg (2011). https://doi.org/10.1007/978-3-642-19345-3
2. OMG: Business Process Model and Notation (BPMN), Version 2.0, January 2011
3. Burattin, A., Maggi, F.M., Sperduti, A.: Conformance checking based on multi-perspective declarative process models. Expert Syst. Appl. **65**, 194–211 (2016)
4. Slaats, T., Schunselaar, D.M.M., Maggi, F.M., Reijers, H.A.: The semantics of hybrid process models. In: Debruyne, C., et al. (eds.) OTM 2016. LNCS, vol. 10033, pp. 531–551. Springer, Cham (2016). https://doi.org/10.1007/978-3-319-48472-3_32

5. Smedt, J.D., Weerdt, J.D., Vanthienen, J., Poels, G.: Mixed-paradigm process modeling with intertwined state spaces. Bus. Inf. Syst. Eng. **58**(1), 19–29 (2016)
6. Stachowiak, H.: Allgemeine Modelltheorie. Springer, New York (1973)
7. Chen, J.-W., Zhang, J.: Comparing text-based and graphic user interfaces for novice and expert users. In: AMIA ... Annual Symposium Proceedings/AMIA Symposium. AMIA Symposium, vol. 11, pp. 125–129, February 2007

A Metadata-Based Event Detection Method Using Temporal Herding Factor and Social Synchrony on Twitter Data

Nirmal Kumar Sivaraman(✉), Vibhor Agarwal, Yash Vekaria, and Sakthi Balan Muthiah

The LNM Institute of Information Technology, Jaipur, India
{nirmal.sivaraman,vibhor.agarwal.y16,yash.vekaria.y16, sakthi.balan}@lnmiit.ac.in

Abstract. Detecting events from social media data is an important problem. In this paper, we propose a novel method to detect events by detecting traces of herding in the Twitter data. We analyze only the metadata for this and not the content of the tweets. We evaluate our method on a dataset of 3.3 million tweets that was collected by us. We then compared the results obtained from our method with a state of the art method called Twitinfo on the above mentioned 3.3 million dataset. Our method showed better results. To check the generality of our method, we tested it on a publicly available dataset of 1.28 million tweets and the results convey that our method can be generalised.

Keywords: Event detection · Temporal Herding Factor · Social network analysis

1 Introduction

In this work, we study the Twitter activities of the users and examine if we can find a definite behavioral trait for tweets concerning events without looking at the content of the tweets. The working definition of an *event* is as follows – something that happens and captures the attention of many people. In case of online social media like Twitter, *measuring the attention* is equivalent to measuring whether they are putting any tweet about what has happened.

We propose a novel method for event detection using a novel measure called *Temporal Herding Factor (THF)*. Any event that has a substantial impact on the society will be a talking point in the social media for at least a few days. In this work, we use one day as the granularity of time. Our approach to event detection is a term interestingness approach [5], where we consider hashtags as the terms at a granularity of time of one day. We use the idea of social synchrony [9] to detect events using THF to quantify the traces of herding in the Twitter data. When there is herding, we consider that there is a corresponding event. Importantly, we use only metadata to detect events. For evaluation of our work, we collected a

S. Cherfi et al. (Eds.): RCIS 2021, LNBIP 415, pp. 637–643, 2021.
https://doi.org/10.1007/978-3-030-75018-3_47

dataset that contains 3.3 million tweets geotagged for India. We call this dataset as 3.3M dataset[1]. We got precision, recall and $F1$ score of 0.76, 0.89 and 0.82 respectively. To check the generality of our method, we considered the generic dataset that has no geotags and is from a different time period. We call this dataset as generic dataset. We tested this dataset using the same thresholds that were calculated for the 3.3M dataset. We got a precision, recall and $F1$ score of 0.70, 0.97 and 0.81 respectively. The dataset that is available publicly contains 1.28 million tweets. Also we compared our results with a state of the art method called Twitinfo that is closest to our approach. We observed that our method has more F1 score.

2 Related Works

There are a lot of works on event detection in the literature. According to [5], the event detection methods can be broadly classified into four,

- Term-interestingness-based approaches,
- Topic-modeling-based approaches,
- Incremental-clustering-based approaches, and
- Miscellaneous approaches.

Term-interestingness-based approaches rely on tracking the terms that are likely to be related to an event [7]. Twitinfo method [7] has the best F1 score among the term interestingness approaches [5]. Topic-modeling-based approaches depend on the probabilistic topic models to detect real-world events by identifying latent topics from the Twitter data stream [3]. Incremental-clustering-based approaches follow an incremental clustering strategy to avoid having a fixed number of clusters [4]. Miscellaneous approaches are the ones that adopt hybrid techniques, which do not directly fall under the three categories [1].

3 A Model to Detect Online Events

We detect events by using the ideas of herding that is calculated as THF and social synchrony. In this section, we discuss Herding, our formulation of THF, social synchrony and our methodology.

3.1 Social Synchrony

According to [9], surge and social synchrony are defined as follows:

Surge: *A social phenomenon where many agents perform some action at the same time and the number of such agents first increases and then decreases.*

Social Synchrony: *A surge where the agents perform the same action.*

The problem of detecting the presence of events may be described as detecting social synchronies in Twitter with the following criteria:

[1] Dataset is available at https://tinyurl.com/244t7t46.

- The criteria for agents to be considered for observation – all the users tweeting with the same hashtag
- Find the surge in the number of agents by using the Algorithm given in [9].
- The criteria to measure the *sameness* of the agents' actions – tweeting with the same hashtag and the parameter that we introduce in this paper called *Temporal Herding Factor* of the surge being above a threshold value. This is discussed in detail in Sect. 3.2.

3.2 Temporal Herding Factor (THF)

At a behavioural level, the most popular form of herding behaviour is the tendency to imitate results [2]. Retweets can be taken as markers of *the tendency to imitate results* in case of Twitter [6]. To detect herding behavior in the Twitter users we observe their tweeting activity. At each time slice, we consider the new users with respect to the previous time slice and find out the fraction of them who retweets. We call this parameter *Temporal Herding Factor (THF)*.

We consider all the hashtags that are present in the dataset. We first take the list of all the hashtags and consider the set of hashtags as $H = \{h_1, h_2, h_3, ..., h_n\}$. The set of users who tweet regarding a topic h_j are represented as:

$$U^{h_j} = \{u_{j1}, u_{j2}, u_{j3}, ..., u_{jm}\}$$

A surge is the distribution of tweets regarding a hashtag where the number of tweets increases first and then decreases. Let a surge with respect to hashtag h is represented as S_h. S_h is divided into N time slices of equal-length and t_i denote the ith time slice of the surge where $i \in \{1, 2, ..., N\}$.

Let $U_T^h(t_i)$ denote the set of all the unique users who posted *tweet(s)* that are not *retweets* related to the hashtag h in the time slice t_i, $U_{RT}^h(t_i)$ denotes the set of all the unique users who retweeted related to the hashtag h in the time slice t_i and $U_{all}^h(t_i)$ denotes the set of all the unique users involved in the tweeting or retweeting activity related to the hashtag h in the time slice t_i.

$$U_{all}^h(t_i) = U_T^h(t_i) \cup U_{RT}^h(t_i)$$

THF at the ith time slice (t_i) of S_h is defined as follows:

$$THF(t_i) = \begin{cases} \frac{|U_{RT}^h(t_i)|}{|U_{all}^h(t_i)|} & : \text{if } t_i = t_1 \\ 0 & : \text{if } |U_{all}^h(t_i) - U_{all}^h(t_{i-1})| = 0 \\ \frac{|U_{RT}^h(t_i) - U_{all}^h(t_{i-1})|}{|U_{all}^h(t_i) - U_{all}^h(t_{i-1})|} & : \text{otherwise} \end{cases}$$

Here, $|U_{RT}^h(t_i) - U_{all}^h(t_{i-1})|$ represents the number of all the unique users who have retweeted with the hashtag h in the time slice t_i but have not tweeted or retweeted in t_{i-1}. When the combined set of all the unique users tweeting or retweeting with the hashtag h are same for two consecutive time slices t_i and t_{i-1} (i.e., $|U_{all}^h(t_i) - U_{all}^h(t_{i-1})| = 0$), then $THF(t_i)$ is considered as 0. The above formula is used for computing *THF* values for every time slice $t_i \in \{t_2, t_3, ..., t_N\}$.

At time slice $t_i = t_1$, we are assuming that all the users are new users (i.e. they are involved in the surge for the first time) and hence,

$$THF(t_1) = \frac{|U^h_{RT}(t_1)|}{|U^h_{all}(t_1)|}$$

Now that we have the values $THF(t_i)$ at every time slice t_i, we aggregate them by taking average.

$$THF_{avg} = \frac{1}{N}\sum\nolimits_{i=1}^{N} THF(t_i)$$

We hypothesize that the value of THF_{avg} is higher for the tweets regarding an event as compared to the tweets regarding random topics. Our method is outlined in Fig. 1.

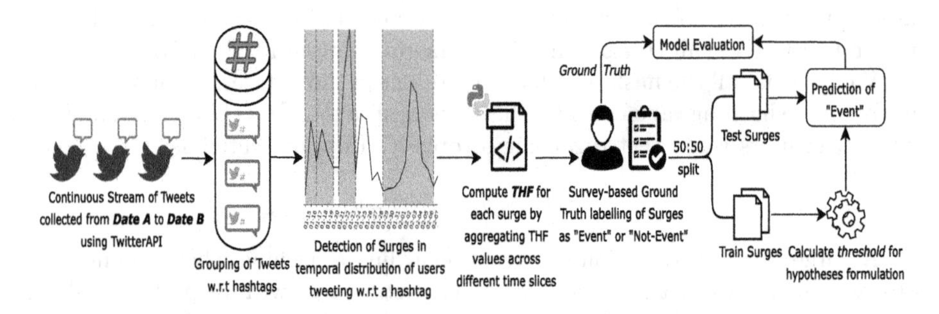

Fig. 1. Methodology for Event Detection using THF.

4 Evaluation

In this section, we evaluate our event detection model described in the previous section. The 3.3 M dataset that is used for evaluation was downloaded using the Twitter API. This dataset contains 3, 360, 608 tweets from 15th *Jan* 2018 to 4th *Mar* 2018.

We took 28, 415 tweets randomly out of all the tweets scraped for each day. This was done so that the dataset can be uniformly distributed over all the days. The number 28415 was chosen because this was the smallest number of tweets that were captured on a single day during this time period. After this sampling, we had 1363920 tweets posted by 280286 unique users. We detected 244 surges in our dataset. Out of these 244 surges, we dropped 41 surges since they had less than 50 tweets. We computed the THF values for each one of the 203 surges.

Labelling: We conducted a comprehensive survey on the tweets in each of the Candidate surges and labelled them as events or non-events. We randomly picked 50 tweets from each surge. Each of these surges are then annotated by 3 people. The survey was conducted amongst 27 volunteers of age group 17–23 years, who were familiar with Twitter. The questions that were asked in the survey form are:

- How many tweets are talking about an event? (this is to find out all the tweets regarding events)
- How many tweets are there in the largest set of tweets that are talking about the same event? (this is to find the largest cluster among the tweets that are talking about an event)

If the answer to the second question is more than 17 (33% of 50 tweets), we label them as events. The Fleiss' Kappa coefficient is 0.73.

We labelled surges as events and non-events. Here, *Events* imply that the corresponding surge has at least one event. The THF_{avg} value was computed for all the surges in each method. We considered manual classification labelling as the ground truth. We then divided our dataset randomly into two equal parts – one for training and the other for testing. We randomly selected 50% of our data for the training set. We calculated the Mean and Standard Deviation of the THF_{avg} values corresponding to the surges in the training set that are labeled as events. We then selected threshold T as discussed further in order to define a range as our hypothesis for predicting whether a surge corresponds to an event or not. The hypothesis is as follows:

Hypothesis: If $Mean_E - (T \times SD_E) < THF_{avg} < Mean_E + (T \times SD_E)$, then there is at least one event in the corresponding surge.

In the above, $Mean_E$ and SD_E represent the mean and standard deviation of the THF_{avg} values respectively, corresponding to the surges in the training set that are labelled as events. T is the number of standard deviations we consider to detect the outliers.

Choosing Best T by Multiple Runs: In the hypothesis given above, choosing the right value of T is a crucial part. In order to select the value of T that gives the most accurate results, we evaluated our method on different values of T. Further, we carried out 10 random runs of training-testing on our dataset for each value of T. The average precision, average recall and F1 score are 0.76, 0.89 and 0.82 respectively.

4.1 Comparing with the Event Detection Method Twitinfo

In this section, we report the results of the comparison between our model and the Twitinfo model; both implemented on the 3.3M dataset. We compare our results with Twitinfo model because that is the closest to our approach.

Detecting events using Twitinfo on Our Dataset: Using the same values of T and α as Twitinfo uses, would not be an optimal decision since the granularity at which they analyze the tweets is at minute-level whereas we deal with the day-level analysis in the THF_{avg} model. As a result, we test the Twitinfo algorithm on our dataset using different values of T and α.

We applied the Twitinfo method on our dataset for differnt values of T and α. The best results are obtained for $T = 3.0$ and $\alpha = 0.225$. However, Recall in detecting Events is relatively poor in this case. The Precision, Recall and F1-score of Twitinfo method are 0.81, 0.53 and 0.64 respectively, whereas, The Precision, Recall and F1-score of our method are 0.76, 0.89 and 0.82 respectively.

5 Generality of the Hypothesis

To test the generality of our hypothesis, we verify the hypothesis on a generic dataset that contains 1280000 tweets from 14th *Dec* 2011 to 11th *Jan* 2012. This dataset is not restricted to any particular region and is from a different time period. We downloaded the Twitter firehose dataset that was used in [8]. This dataset is also listed in the *ICWSM* website[2] and is publicly available.

There are 77 hashtags and 547 surges in the dataset. Out of them, majority of the tweets in 423 surges are non-English. There were 14 surges that were too small – having less than 50 tweets. We discarded all such surges. Hence, we were left with 110 surges.

To test the hypothesis, we manually labeled the surges that represent events as described in previous sections. We then tested the same hypothesis that we formulated from the 33m dataset, on these surges. The precision, recall and F1 score of the method on Generic Dataset are 0.70, 0.97 and 0.81 respectively for $T = 1$.

6 Conclusion

In this paper, we proposed a method to detect events from Twitter data, based on our hypothesis that herding occurs in surges during events. Results obtained from our method show that it performs better than the state of the art method Twitinfo. Moreover, we tested our method on an openly available dataset (Generic dataset). We used the same boundary values that we calculated from 3.3M dataset and showed that our algorithm works with F1-score of 0.81 even with the Generic dataset. This indicates that herding is a distinguishing factor when it comes to the activities of the users during events versus the activities when there is no evet.

References

1. Adedoyin-Olowe, M., Gaber, M.M., Dancausa, C.M., Stahl, F., Gomes, J.B.: A rule dynamics approach to event detection in Twitter with its application to sports and politics. Expert Syst. Appl. **55**, 351–360 (2016)
2. Banerjee, A.V.: A simple model of herd behavior. Q. J. Econ. **107**(3), 797–817 (1992)
3. Cai, H., Yang, Y., Li, X., Huang, Z.: What are popular: exploring Twitter features for event detection, tracking and visualization. In: Proceedings of the 23rd ACM International Conference on Multimedia, pp. 89–98. ACM (2015)
4. Hasan, M., Orgun, M.A., Schwitter, R.: TwitterNews+: a framework for real time event detection from the Twitter data stream. In: Spiro, E., Ahn, Y.-Y. (eds.) SocInfo 2016. LNCS, vol. 10046, pp. 224–239. Springer, Cham (2016). https://doi.org/10.1007/978-3-319-47880-7_14

[2] https://www.icwsm.org/2018/datasets/.

5. Hasan, M., Orgun, M.A., Schwitter, R.: A survey on real-time event detection from the Twitter data stream. J. Inf. Sci. (2017)
6. Li, H., Sakamoto, Y.: Re-tweet count matters: social influences on sharing of disaster-related tweets. J. Homel. Secur. Emerg. Manage. **12**(3), 737–761 (2015)
7. Marcus, A., Bernstein, M.S., Badar, O., Karger, D.R., Madden, S., Miller, R.C.: Twitinfo: aggregating and visualizing microblogs for event exploration. In: Proceedings of the SIGCHI Conference on Human Factors in Computing Systems, pp. 227–236. ACM (2011)
8. Morstatter, F., Pfeffer, J., Liu, H., Carley, K.M.: Is the sample good enough? comparing data from Twitter's streaming API with Twitter's firehose. In: ICWSM (2013)
9. Sivaraman, N.K., Muthiah, S.B., Agarwal, P., Todwal, L.: Social synchrony in online social networks and its application in event detection from twitter data. In: Proceedings of the 2020 IEEE/WIC/ACM International Joint Conference on Web Intelligence and Intelligent Agent Technology (WI-IAT 2020) (2020)

Data and Conceptual Model Synchronization in Data-Intensive Domains: The Human Genome Case

Floris Emanuel[1,2(✉)], Verónica Burriel[2], and Oscar Pastor[1]

[1] Centro de Investigación en Métodos de Producción de Software, Universitat Politècnica de València, Valencia, Spain
florisldn@gmail.com, opastor@pros.upv.es

[2] Department of Information and Computing Sciences, Utrecht University, Utrecht, The Netherlands
v.burriel@uu.nl

Abstract. Context and Motivation: With the increasing quantity and versatility of data in data-intensive domains, designing information systems, to effectively process the relevant information is becoming increasingly challenging. Conceptual modeling could tackle such challenges in numerous manners as a preliminary phase in the software development process. But assessing data and model synchronization becomes an issue in domains where data are heterogeneous, have a diverse provenance and are subject to continuous change. **Question/problem:** The problem is how to determine and demonstrate the ability of a conceptual schema to represent the concepts and the data in the particular data-intensive domain. **Principal Ideas/Results:** A validation approach has been designed for the Conceptual Schema of the Human Genome by investigating the particular issues in the genetic domain and systematically connecting constituents of this conceptual schema with potential instances in samples of genome-related data. As a result, this approach provided us accurate insight in terms of attribute resemblance, completeness, structure and shortcomings. **Contribution:** This work demonstrates how the strategy of conceptualizing a data-intensive domain and then validating that concept by reconnecting this with the attributes of the real world data domain, can be generalized. Conceptual modeling has a limited resistance to the evolution of data, which is the next problem to face.

Keywords: Information systems · Genome · Conceptual modeling · Validation

1 Introduction

Software systems are becoming more complex due to the evolution of related techniques, as a result of the high expectations from our advancing society.

S. Cherfi et al. (Eds.): RCIS 2021, LNBIP 415, pp. 644–650, 2021.
https://doi.org/10.1007/978-3-030-75018-3_48

To align with this trend, software and data models must be integrated with models of the application domain, which would be technical, organizational, people centered or a mixture thereof [8]. In this work, we are especially interested in data-intensive domains (DIDs), domains where the data perspective is the most relevant one, and where applications must deal with large quantities of (more or less) structured data, suing basic operations to extract valuable information. Hence, both the domain and related data should be understood.

Conceptual modeling (CM) could be applied to provide a solution to the problem context by eliciting and describing the general knowledge a particular information system needs to know [7], which tackles the complexity of managing the data of a particular domain. CM can also synergize work between experts of different domains (multiple stakeholders) and capture and structure existing knowledge [6]. Specifically testing (validate) the general (conceptualized) rules that have been created from a collection of specific observations in the problem domain (context) could tackle big data management as an overall approach. In this paper, we demonstrate this idea by introducing a validation approach to the established Conceptual Schema of the Human Genome (CSHG[1]), which has been developed at PROS Research Center, Valencia.

Understanding the Human Genome is probably the biggest challenge of this century. Its main direct implication is already affecting the development of 'precision medicine' (PM), an emerging approach for disease treatment and prevention that takes into account individual variability in genes, environment and lifestyle [3]. PM is a practise of the interdisciplinary field of biomedical informatics. Complex genome data has exploded since the first complete read in 2003 [2,4]. The CSHG tackles the lack of the formalization of the genome concept by capturing existing knowledge by providing structure, allowing integration from numerous data sources and provides structure for the design of a data management tool. The problem is to validate the adequacy and correctness of the CSHG by assessing how the data available in existing genome data sources comply with the structure of the model, in order to demonstrate its significance. Without validation, its adequacy can only be assumed.

According to Design Science Methodology by Roël Wieringa [11], this issue can be classified a knowledge question with an underlying design problem. Because in this case we are validating the CSHG, our validation approach is the artefact that has been designed. Therefore, the question is to what extend our validation approach is able to manage the model synchronization in this context. In the next section we introduce the design of the validation approach, in the Treatment Validation section its performance is discussed. In the Conclusion and Future work we generalize this particular results to discuss the overall approach to tackle big data management, which is the overarching problem context.

[1] https://www.dropbox.com/s/y06ov4kl6dmdgqg/CSHG.pdf?dl=0.

2 Validation Artefact Design

To design this artefact to get a useful insight into the state of the CSHG, we initially analyzed the problem domain concerning the complexity of genome-related data and its related issues. Subsequently, we investigated the issues specific to corresponding the CSHG to genome-related data, rather than investigating methods to validate conceptual models in general, because our research purpose is to connect the data-world to the modeling-world. For the matching procedure itself, general approaches were investigated from information systems related literature. In Fig. 1, the validation artefact is depicted as a process deliverable diagram (PDD) to concisely depict was has been designed in this work. The PDD has been created on the basis of the guidelines by I. Weerd and S. Brinkkemper [10].

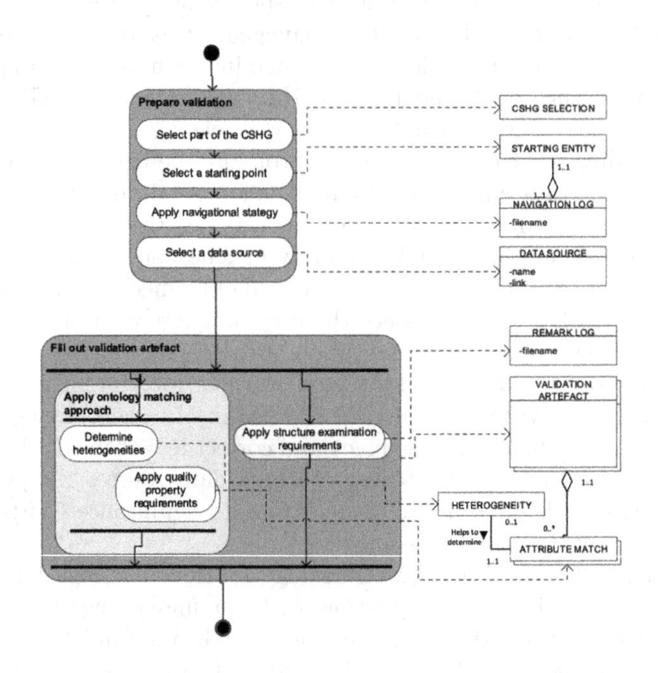

Fig. 1. A process-deliverable diagram (PDD) of the designed validation artefact.

The artefact contains two main activities, namely *preparing the validation* and *carrying out the validation.*

Prepare Validation. The preparation entails the process before establishing connections between the CSHG and the real-world data that it should represent. First, a preferred sample of the CSHG is selected. Subsequently, an entity, preferably central or less complex is chosen as a starting point. An entity could be a 'variation' in the DNA. An example attribute could be whether this is 'benign'. Both the model and the related databases start by describing more central themes of the genome, gradually moving to more specific topics. Therefore, we adopt an 'inside out' strategy as a principle, combined by following the paths of the cross references between repositories, and create a *log* to keep track of the movements.

Fill Out Validation Artefact. To report findings, we created a table component to be filled out for every entity, and every repository. We store all validated entities vertically and all different sources for that same component horizontally in a spreadsheet for a structured execution. For every attribute it is determined whether it corresponds to parts of the required information from a given data record.

In order to avoid the need to justify each correspondence that is made, 'minimum requirements' are applied during each correspondence attempt. Justifying the abstract properties of a valid correspondence can effectively contribute to the repeatability and validity of this work. The heterogeneity amongst sources means that we will often deal with different ontologies. Therefore, we adopted an ontology matching approach by Euzenat and Svaiko [1]. This is an abstract lifecycle that guides the ontology matching workflow from analysis of the problem domain to the creation of a fitting matching approach, on the basis of an assembly of existing techniques. They state 'no one size fits all and every case is unique'. Therefore, we adopted this approach, and used only what is relevant in our case. Along these properties, we use only two requirements for now, which is that the *data type* of a required attribute and its potential instance should always be the same. Secondly, An attribute of the CSHG and a potential instance in an external data source should always be *conceptually* the same, regardless of *terminological heterogeneity* (different definition). We think identifying and acknowledging such heterogeneities is critical to making the correspondences because ignoring them results in numerous unwanted and avoidable false positives and false negatives.

As we closely analyze the CSHG, and the data, we list discrepancies concerning how the attributes are grouped together in a *remark log*. Subsequently, we assess these with literature.

3 Validating the 'Validation Artefact'

The validation artefact is applied to the CSHG context on the basis of genome related data sources. The results are divided into relevant general perspectives.

3.1 Results

Regarding the CSHG, our goal was to determine and demonstrate its essential ability to support the management of genomic data. Table 1 summarizes the 62 attributes of the CSHG that were validated at the hand of multiple different data

Table 1. Summary statistics of the validation component sheet (A view only copy of the correspondence recording data can be found here: https://www.dropbox.com/s/gu4893inqky0pds/View_CSHG_Validation_Record.xlsx?dl=0)

Description	Result
Total correspondence attempts	118
Number of attributes validated	62
Average number of sources per attribute	2
Ratio of present correspondences/total	78.8%
Ratio of non-present correspondences	18.6%
Ratio of undefinable correspondences	2.5%

sources per attribute, resulting in 118 correspondence attempts. Hence, regarding the correspondence between the CSHG and real-world genome related data, no perfect compliance was observed. The resemblance was however a promising 80%, taking into account *overfitting*, *derivable values* and *intended heterogeneities* in the conceptual schema (making 100% impossible). There were also no colliding flows of information under the current structure, solely discrepancies. However, discussion is always possible. Such as that there is additional information thinkable, and there were also underrepresented parts, meaning we found no real-world representation of these attributes in the data sources used. This way we demonstrate proficiency of the CHSG while remaining critical. These useful results demonstrate the success of the validation approach. This was also confirmed after presenting the results to the model authors and information systems experts from our academic network. The model authors were not actively involved in the project but were of help in understanding the problem domain, validate the results and to improve the method from a scientific point of view.

3.2 Discussion

We could generalize the essence of these two approaches and see them as subsequent or perhaps simultaneous phases. In phase one, a solution (the CSHG) is proposed by conceptualizing the problem domain, in order to provide structure for a complex concept that encompasses all kinds of related data. In subsequent phase, this is tested by using this data to examine its fit to the solution. While the artefact was initially tuned to the problems within this domain and scope, we hypothesize that this generic strategy could be useful to problem contexts of a similar nature.

This could be a problem domain where big data driven decision support is required. In such a complex DID, the related available data has properties like 'messy', 'heterogeneous', 'vast', 'growing number of stakeholders and parameters'. An example of this could be the housing market, a highly dynamic environment with all kinds of constant changes. What makes this environment complex are the varying regulatory influences which cannot be withstood by conventional house pricing models. Also, the definition of regulation is lacking due to the complexity and potential interaction of different regulatory aspects [9]. Furthermore, there are numerous heterogeneous data sources for housing data and for all kinds of environmental factors that influence the market.

4 Conclusion and Future Work

In this work, we proposed and tested a solution that should tackle the problems related to validating a conceptual schema on the basis of its real-world data that it should represent, in an exploratory manner. Some problems were specific to the domain of the management of genome related data, for which our solution has been created. In a DID where complex data is constantly evolving and valuable information is spread across heterogeneous data sources in a vast lake of data, conceptual modeling has not only been a potential solution to the data-related challenges. It also tackled the issue of the constant evolution of genome fundamental knowledge, which formed an extra challenge to IS design.

We demonstrated that this validation artefact is effective, and that the CSHG can improve through the application of this validation method; we propose it can be generalized and applied to other environments with similar properties, or used for subsequent work either in- or outside the genome domain. As the domain rapidly evolves, its related data does so as well. Where CM is a first step [5], future work should focus on how an information system could deal with data evolution.

References

1. Euzenat, J., Shvaiko, P., et al.: Ontology Matching, vol. 18. Springer, Heidelberg (2007). https://doi.org/10.1007/978-3-540-49612-0
2. Collins, F.S., Morgan, M., Patrinos, A.: The Human Genome Project: lessons from large-scale biology. Science **300**(5617), 286–290 (2003)
3. Larry Jameson, J., Longo, D.L.: Precision medicine-personalized, problematic, and promising. Obstetr. Gynecol. Survey **70**(10), 612–614 (2015)
4. Mukherjee, S., et al.: Genomes OnLine Database (GOLD) v. 6: data updates and feature enhancements. Nucleic Acids Res. D446–D456 (2016)
5. Pastor, O., Levin, A.M., Casamayor, JC., Celma, M., Eraso, L.E., Villanueva, M.J., Perez-Alonso, M.: Enforcing conceptual modeling to improve the understanding of human genome. In: 2010 Fourth International Conference on Research Challenges in Information Science (RCIS) (2010), pp. 85–92. IEEE (2010)
6. Pastor, O., et al.: Conceptual modeling of human genome: integration challenges. In: Düsterhöft, A., Klettke, M., Schewe, K.-D. (eds.) Conceptual Modelling and Its Theoretical Foundations. LNCS, vol. 7260, pp. 231–250. Springer, Heidelberg (2012). https://doi.org/10.1007/978-3-642-28279-9_17
7. Fabián Reyes Román, J.: Diseño y Desarrollo de un Sistema de Información Genómica Basado en un Modelo Conceptual Holıstico del Genoma Humano. PhD thesis (2018)

8. Sølvberg, A.: On models of concepts and data. In: Düsterhöft, A., Klettke, M., Schewe, K.-D. (eds.) Conceptual Modelling and Its Theoretical Foundations. LNCS, vol. 7260, pp. 190–196. Springer, Heidelberg (2012). https://doi.org/10.1007/978-3-642-28279-9_14
9. Tu, Q., de Haan, J., Boelhouwer, P.: The mismatch between conventional house price modeling and regulated markets: insights from The Netherlands. J. Housing Built Environ. **32**(3), 599–619 (2017)
10. van de Weerd, I., Brinkkemper, S.: Meta-modeling for situational analysis and design methods. In: Handbook of Research on Modern Systems Analysis and Design Technologies and Applications, pp. 35–54. IGI Global (2009)
11. Wieringa, R.J.: Design Science Methodology for Information Systems and Software Engineering. Springer, Heidelberg (2014). https://doi.org/10.1007/978-3-662-43839-8

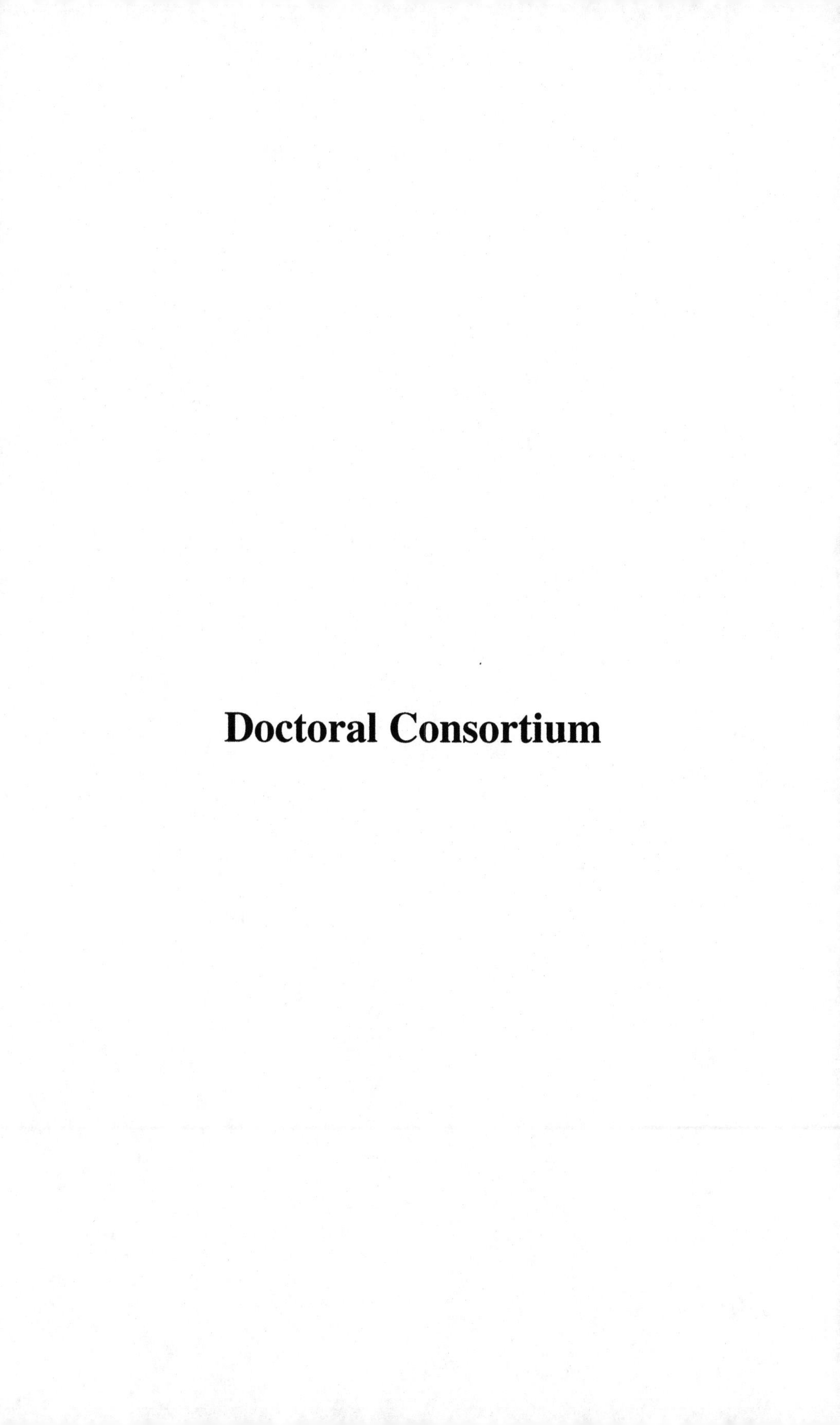

Doctoral Consortium

Simplified Timed Attack Trees

Aliyu Tanko Ali(✉)

Department of Applied Informatics, Comenius University, Bratislava, Slovakia
tanko2@uniba.sk

Abstract. This paper considers attack trees, a graphical security model that can be used to visualised varying ways an asset may be compromised. We proposed an extension of this model, termed *Simplified Timed Attack Trees* (STAT). The primary aim here is to use STAT for the analysis of CPS assets. STAT extend attack trees gate refinements with time parameters. In order to reach a parent node, an attacker has to achieve the child nodes within a specified time interval. This adds a level of security to the gates refinement. We propose how to translate STAT to a parallel composition of timed automata (TA). We reduce the root reachability of STAT to place reachability in the TA. This reachability can be checked; using a formal verification tool UPPAAL.

Keywords: Attack trees · Simplified timed attack trees · Cyber-physical systems · Threat modelling · Security · Timed automata · Reachability

1 Introduction

Cyber-physical systems (CPS) [1] has become the key link between information systems (IT) and the devices that control industrial production and maintain critical infrastructure (CI). A CPS system exists in different forms, ranging from SCADA systems, autonomous vehicles to smart-doors. Unlike the IT systems, CPS does not adhere to the CIA triad [2] for information security model (followed by IT systems). Most of its operations rely on interacting with objects from the physical environment (that are observable), therefore breaking the strict needs of 'C' confidentiality. Such interaction enables the asset to detect/perceive its surrounding in real-time. For instance, an autonomous vehicle perceives its surroundings (i.e. cars, infrastructures, on-road signs) to perform different activities ranging from avoiding collision, identifying danger and, energy synchronisation. This openness (i.e. easy to view, influence the surrounding objects) between an asset (i.e. vehicle) and the set of objects from the physical environment (i.e. on-road sign) make it easy for a potential attacker to observe (from the physical environment) and; potentially perform some actions (i.e. add, block, blur) that can

This work was supported by the Slovak Research and Development Agency under the Contract no. APVV-19-0220 (ORBIS) and by the Slovak VEGA agency under Contract no. 1/0778/18 (KATO).

S. Cherfi et al. (Eds.): RCIS 2021, LNBIP 415, pp. 653–660, 2021.
https://doi.org/10.1007/978-3-030-75018-3_49

- misleads an asset into issuing false control operations, which can result in, other consequences or,
- hides the malicious consequences to delaying remedy procedures.

Performing such actions can result in dangerous attacks such as DoS, message falsification attack and message spoofing attack. Over the years, different methods and approaches have been proposed to evaluate and identify these kinds of threats in different assets.

One such approach is the attack trees formalism [3]. An attack tree provides a visual representation (static view) of; how an asset may be at risk in a tree format, usually from an external malicious person known as an attacker (i.e. varying ways an attacker may compromise an assets). The root node of the tree represents the attackers' target, this is broken down into smaller units (subgoals); for easy identification of how it can be reached. This process is repeated until a set of leaf nodes is reached. The leaf nodes represents atomic actions that an attacker needs to carry out to initiate an attack. The attackers' actions can be studied and evaluated; when enriched with attributes such as the cost of an attack or time required to execute an attack [4]. Several extensions of attack trees were introduced to analyse different attack scenarios. Some of which includes attack-defence trees, attack countermeasure, sequential and parallel attack tree, attack protection trees [6–10].

Main Challenges: An attack tree is a tree-based formalism inspired by *fault trees* [13] while systems such as CPS are hybrid [5] that are equipped with communications and do necessarily includes timing-sensitive (safety-critical) between different objects that can sometimes run concurrently. These pose a great challenge when applying attack trees for threat modelling because the *threat environment* (in CPS) changes due to agents behaviour (e.g. increase in attacker's knowledge) as some parts of the system can be physically observed. Also, the *vulnerability landscape* of these systems is ever-changing due to infrastructure updates (e.g. interaction with other components). As a result, if such a system is to be modelled; using attack trees, the estimated annotations of the tree (e.g. nodes) needs to be updated regularly to reflect both behaviours. Furthermore, an attack tree formalism is limited to identify varying ways an asset can be compromised (static view of the asset) which does not take into considerations other systems/object that interacts with the asset over time.

Research Questions and Goal: CPS systems are available in all forms and present in many elements of our daily lives. Their security threats are ever increasing due to their popularity and adaptation in different sectors. Furthermore, their vulnerability landscape is ever-changing. Attack trees are static model, while CPS are dynamic and interact with external objects over time. So, the intriguing question is, can a static model be effective in identifying and analysing potential threat in a system that dynamic and runs concurrency?.

Our main objectives are to study the security threats in CPS systems and propose how to model and analyse these threats using an attack trees formalism. Our goals at the end are to,

- propose an extension of attack trees formalism that; can be used to identify, describe, and analyse potential ways a CPS asset may be compromised,
- propose protection mechanism to repel identified attack paths,
- to identify varying ways the asset may be compromised over time as it interacts with a set of objects from the physical environment.

In this paper, we present part of our result, a proposed extension of attack trees termed *Simplified Timed Attack Trees.* STAT adds a time constraint at the gates refinement of attack trees formalism. This added constraint is to serve; as a security mechanism at (parent) nodes, allow attack actions to succeed on these (parent) nodes only; if it is carried out within a given time interval. In this work, we informally describe and evaluate this idea, and also use a formal verification tool UPPAAL to analyse some examples. We plan to provide a formal definition as well as prove some security properties in the future work.

Research Methodology and Open Science Principles: Throughout this paper, we will adopt the use of working examples and case study to demonstrate and model the proof of concept. Most notably, we will use an autonomous vehicle (a CPS example) in these working examples. We plan to translate the model (STAT) into timed automata (TA) and use an open-source formal verification tool, UPPAAL [12] for analysis. All working projects, definitions, including translation to TA and verification with UPPAAL, will be made available to open-science community.

The paper is organised as follows. In Sect. 2, we describe and recall attack trees formalism. In Sect. 3, we present simplified timed attack trees. In Sect. 4, we translate STAT into TA and, in Sect. 5, contribution and future work.

2 Attack Trees

Attack Tree (AT) is a methodological way of describing varying ways an asset may be compromise. The root node of the tree represents the attack target. It is further breakdown into smaller units that are easier to solve called sub-goals (parent node). A sub-goal is associated with a gate refinement which indicates the fashion/order of how it can; be reached. In the case of a large/complicated system, a sub-goal can be divide into (sub)-sub-goals other-wise, a set of leaf nodes marked at the end of the tree. The leave nodes represent atomic nodes or vulnerability, indicating an attack step. The set of gates refinement we consider for this paper is the AND and OR gates. For a (parent) node with AND gate refinement, it is said to have a set of (child) nodes that are linked (to the parent node) by a set of edges and these (child) nodes most be compromised first before the parent node is satisfied. While in the case of a (parent) node with OR refinement, a single node from the set of child nodes when compromised is enough for the (parent) node with gate refinement to be satisfied.

Example 1. As an example, consider Fig. 1 (A). The figure shows a simple attack tree of how to steal a car. The root node **steal car** consists of two sub-goals,

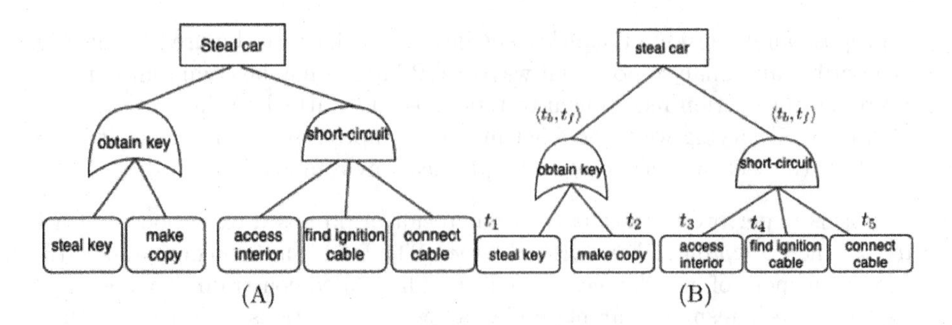

Fig. 1. Steal a car attack tree

obtain key and **short-circuit** which by compromising either, an attacker can reach the desired goal. Sub-goal obtain key is of OR refinement therefore, either of the leaf nodes **steal key** or **make copy** when compromised is enough for the parent node **obtain key** to be satisfied. While the sub-goal **short-circuit** is of AND refinement and all the leaf nodes **access interior, find ignition cable, connect cable** has to be compromised to satisfied the sub-goal **short-circuit**.

Definition 1. *An attack tree is a tuples $\mathcal{T}_r = (\mathcal{Q}, q_0, \mathcal{E}, \mathcal{G})$ where, $\mathcal{Q}$ is finite set of nodes in the tree, $q_0 \in \mathcal{Q}$ is special kind of node that represent the attack target and every node in the tree is reachable from q_0, the set $\{q^{'} | (q^{'}, q) \in \mathcal{E}\}$ is well-ordered nodes linked by a set of edges $\mathcal{E}$, finally $\mathcal{G}$ represent the gate refinement associated with each parent node.*

Extending Attack Trees: Several attack tree extensions have been proposed, amongst which are attack-defence trees (ADT) [14], attack response tree (ART) and attack countermeasures tree (ACT) [7]. ADT introduced defenders' actions and model their interplay as a form of game theory, portraying the attacker-defender repelling each other's move. ACT introduced a countermeasure to mitigate attackers actions. The countermeasure node is attached to block any attack path identified. Attack response tree (ART) formalism extends the attacker-defender game to find an optimal policy to stop the attacker's action. Others include [6–10]. Using attack trees, assets such as SCADA [16] and some attack scenarios in a CPS asset [15] has been assessed. To the best of our knowledge, non of the work from the mentioned attack trees extensions or other papers we came across; come closest to our work.

In our previous work (submitted for publication), we introduced *Timed Attack Trees* (TAT), an extension of attack trees to model assets whose vulnerability landscape changes due to interaction with a set of objects from the physical environment. In this paper, we study the security aspect of timed attack trees, most notably the gates refinement. We introduce a time parameter for each parent node such that to achieve the gate associated with the node, the attackers' action has to be done within a time interval. The main difference between *Timed Attack Trees* and *Simplified Timed Attack Trees* (STAT) is that in TAT, we consider the evolution of the tree at a different analysis time point (as defined in timed attack trees), while in STAT, we focus on how an attacker can achieve the child nodes within some time interval.

3 Simplified Timed Attack Trees

Informally, our idea is to add time parameters to the gates refinement, restricting the fashion at which an attacker can achieve a (parent) node. This time parameters that are added to the set of gates are; attack *begin time* t_b and attack *finish time* t_f, denoted as $\mathcal{G}\langle t_b, t_f\rangle$. With this, in addition to the fashion ('all' for AND and 'any' for OR) at which a parent node can be reached, the attacker has to compromise the (child) nodes; within a time interval (begin and finish) otherwise, the attack fails. For example, let us assume that, the node has an attack time t_i that is needed for an attacker to perform some attack action (i.e. in Fig. 1 attack time for *short-circuit* is 4 min). For this, $t_b > 1$ and $t_f \leq t_i$, the attacker is must complete the attack within this time interval for the (parent) node to be reached. Since each child node has different difficulties when trying to achieve by an attacker, in our idea, we do not consider attack time for each child node. Hence, we focus on reaching the parent node. In the case of a node with AND gate refinement, then all the child nodes have to be achieved by t_i while in the case of OR gate refinement, a single child not is enough to reach the parent node.

This new time parameter provides an added restriction on the set of gates refinement and can be used to analyse the interval between different actions carried out by the attacker. For the purpose of illustration, consider Fig. 1 (B) as explained with the following examples.

Example 2. Let us assume that the car in the attack tree presented in Fig. 1 can synchronise a set of external devices (i.e. remote starter, mobile phone) that; can be used from a remote distance (i.e. open doors or start engine). Assuming the nodes that represent; these external devices are extended from a sub-goal *external devices* with OR gate refinement and linked to the root node. A (child) node (from external devices) is *remote starter*, and it is of AND refinement that has a set of leaf nodes *stand within proximity, avoid sighted, press remote, physically open door.* Now, let us assume that, an attack tree for example that represent this tree is depicted. We assume that 50 s of time is given to achieve the sub-goal. That is, for each sub-goal, the $t_b \geq 1$ and $t_f \leq 50$.

Example 3. In order to compromise a sub-goal, if the sub-goal is of OR gate, then $\exists t_i \in \langle 1, 50\rangle$ and if the sub-goal is of AND gate, then $\forall t_1, ..., t_n \in \langle 1, 50\rangle$.

4 From STAT to Timed Automata

In this section, we translate simplified timed attack trees into a version of timed automata, called *weighted timed automata* (WTA) [11]. There exists an open-source formal verification tool, UPPAAL that, accepts WTA as its formal language.

A Weighted timed automata, otherwise known as price timed automata (PTA), is an extended version of timed automata (TA) with weight/cost information added on both locations and edges. To arrive at a state, the weight value defined in that state has to be satisfied. Also, make a transition via an edge, the weight value at that edge has to be satisfied. To be at the final/desired location, a global weight/cost, which is the accumulated weight/cost along the run, is calculated. With the accumulative weight/cost value, it is easy to calculate the distance or cost of travelling from point A to point B in different case studies.

The trace in a weighted timed automata is a sequence of states, with the transitions across the states given as $\pi = l_0 \overset{a_0}{\underset{c_0}{\longrightarrow}}{}^{w_0}\ l_1 \overset{a_1}{\underset{c_1}{\longrightarrow}}{}^{w_1}\ l_2 ...$ such that

- there is always an initial location l_0 with an initial clock valuation $c_0 = 0$,
- for every $i \in \{1, .., k\}$, there is some transition $\rightarrow = (l_i, a_i, g, c_i, l_{i+1}) \in$ E,
- a transition is only enable if for every clock valuation v, there exists a guard g such that v satisfies g,
- for every successful transition, a new clock valuation C_{i+1} is obtained by increasing every clock variable in C_i by a transition i and resetting all previous clocks 0.

For each leaf node in STAT, we have a weighted timed automaton that represents a linear path; from the leaf to the root node. Altogether, there are as many WTAs as the leaf nodes in the simplified timed attack tree. The initial location of the first automaton has an initial weight value of $n = 0$. The succeeding automaton has an initial location weight value of; the previous automaton final location weight value +1. To translate the gates refinement, we give each final location a weight value that must be satisfied. If the automaton corresponds to a path with an OR gate refinement, it requires the first automaton; to reach the final location for the OR gate refinement to be satisfied. Whereas if the path is that of AND gate refinement (i.e. two leaf nodes), all the automata have to reach the final location for the AND gate refinement to be satisfied. The idea here is that; when the (first) automaton with final location $n = 1$ is satisfied, the OR gate refinement in the attack tree requires the execution of attack action on one; out of many leaf nodes. And this first automata satisfied that. In the case of an AND gate refinement, the run continues until the last automaton reached the final location. In general, a simplified timed attack tree is translated into a parallel composition of timed automata $A_1, ..., A_z$ that represents the linear path from the leaves; to the root node. As a working example of our concept, we continue with Example 2. This time, we model a scenario and analyse using; UPPAAL. We assume that an attacker tries to use external devices to access the vehicle.

In Fig. 2, We show a UPPAAL model of 3 pieces of automata, the attackers' model, the vehicles' model and the STAT model. The figure model a scenario of an intruder who tries to steal a car. In this scenario, the attacker attempt to have access by opening it with an external device. This happens only when the attacker is within proximity *near!* and *press!*. The vehicle is locked initially, and when the attacker performed the action *press!*, the action's model receives *press?*

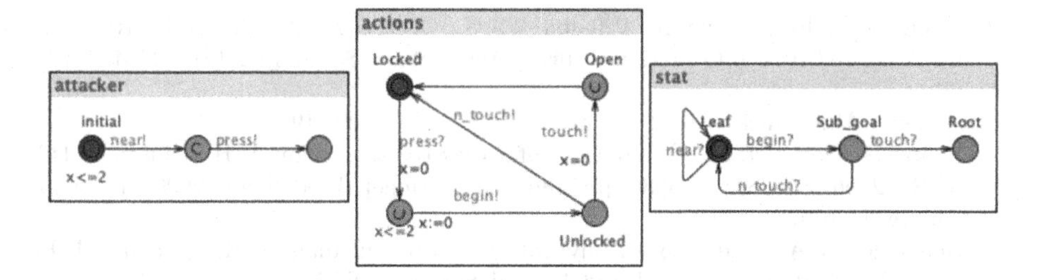

Fig. 2. UPPAAL model of STAT.

and, from then the attacker has to; mechanically open the door *touch!* otherwise, it went back to a locked state within some mins. In the STAT model, the initial location is the *Leaf* and, it receives the action message when the attacker is within proximity *near?*. It remains in that location until the *begin?* message is received. When the *begin?* is receives, the leaf node has been reached, from the location *Sub_goal*, if the vehicle is not physically touched *n_touch?*, the process fails as the vehicle; is back to a locked state.

We plan to formally define and extend this idea of simplified timed attack trees and further investigate how an attacker can learn from observing from the physical environment, sets of external objects a CPS can detect/perceive and possibly deduce the response of the system. This observation ability is difficult to analyse with attack trees. In the next phase of our work, we plan to study and work with the notion of *opacity*. This is an information flow property; that verifies whether an external observer (intruder) can deduce a secret of a system by observing its behaviour.

5 Conclusion

In this paper, we have presented simplified timed attack trees as a new extension of attack trees. We also proposed how to translate simplified timed attack trees into weighted timed automata. Modern systems constitute many components, the means that to analyse an asset as such, STAT can have many nodes and time restriction. We propose how to model STAT using a formal verification tool UPPAAL and presented a working example.

We hope that; our work will encourage research and experimentation that uses attack trees and related extensions for threats analysis. These will give the security managers and relevant stakeholders a clear picture of all possible threats and make it easy to apply solutions towards protecting the asset.

References

1. Baheti, R., Gill, H.: Cyber-physical systems. Impact Control Technol. **1**(12), 161–166 (2011)

2. de Oliveira Albuquerque, R., Villalba, L.J.G., Orozco, A.L.S., Buiati, F., Kim, T.-H.: A layered trust information security architecture. Sensors **14**(12), 22754–22772 (2014)
3. Schneier, B.: Attack trees. Dr. Dobb's J. **24**(12), 21–29 (1999)
4. Mauw, S., Oostdijk, M.: Foundations of attack trees. In: Won, D.H., Kim, S. (eds.) ICISC 2005. LNCS, vol. 3935, pp. 186–198. Springer, Heidelberg (2006). https://doi.org/10.1007/11734727_17
5. Henzinger, T.A.: The theory of hybrid automata. In: Inan, M.K., Kurshan, R.P. (eds.) Verification of Digital and Hybrid Systems. NATO ASI Series (Series F: Computer and Systems Sciences), vol. 170. Springer, Heidelberg (2000). https://doi.org/10.1007/978-3-642-59615-5_13
6. Ali, A.T., Gruska, D.P.: Attack protection tree. In: Proceedings of the 28th International Workshop on Concurrency, Specification and Programming, vol. 1, no. 12, pp. 161–166 (2019)
7. Roy, A., Kim, D.S., Trivedi, K.S.: Attack countermeasure trees (act): towards unifying the constructs of attack and defense trees. Secur. Commun. Netw. **5**(8), 929–943 (2012)
8. Siddiqi, M.A., Seepers, R.M., Hamad, M., Prevelakis, V., Strydis, C.: Attack-tree-based threat modeling of medical implants. In: PROOFS@ CHES, pp. 32–49 (2018)
9. Jhawar, R., Kordy, B., Mauw, S., Radomirović, S., Trujillo-Rasua, R.: Attack trees with sequential conjunction. In: Federrath, H., Gollmann, D. (eds.) SEC 2015. IAICT, vol. 455, pp. 339–353. Springer, Cham (2015). https://doi.org/10.1007/978-3-319-18467-8_23
10. Ten, C.-W., Liu, C.-C., Manimaran, G.: Vulnerability assessment of cybersecurity for SCADA systems using attack trees. In: 2007 IEEE Power Engineering Society General Meeting, pp. 1–8. IEEE (2007)
11. Bulychev, P., et al.: UPPAAL-SMC: statistical model checking for priced timed automata. arXiv preprint arXiv, pp. 1207–1272. Elsevier (2012)
12. Bengtsson, J., Larsen, K., Larsson, F., Pettersson, P., Yi, W.: UPPAAL—a tool suite for automatic verification of real-time systems. In: Alur, R., Henzinger, T.A., Sontag, E.D. (eds.) HS 1995. LNCS, vol. 1066, pp. 232–243. Springer, Heidelberg (1996). https://doi.org/10.1007/BFb0020949
13. Brooke, P.J., Paige, R.F.: Fault trees for security system design and analysis. Comput. Secur. **22**, 256–264 (2003)
14. Fraile, M., Ford, M., Gadyatskaya, O., Kumar, R., Stoelinga, M., Trujillo-Rasua, R.: Using attack-defense trees to analyze threats and countermeasures in an ATM: a case study. In: Horkoff, J., Jeusfeld, M.A., Persson, A. (eds.) PoEM 2016. LNBIP, vol. 267, pp. 326–334. Springer, Cham (2016). https://doi.org/10.1007/978-3-319-48393-1_24
15. Depamelaere, W., Lemaire, L., Vossaert, J., Naessens, V.: CPS security assessment using automatically generated attack trees. In: Proceedings of the 5th International Symposium for ICS & SCADA Cyber Security Research 2018. British Computer Society (BCS) (2018)
16. Sabaliauskaite, G., Mathur, A.P.: Aligning cyber-physical system safety and security. In: Cardin, M.-A., Krob, D., Lui, P.C., Tan, Y.H., Wood, K. (eds.) Complex Systems Design & Management Asia, pp. 41–53. Springer, Cham (2015). https://doi.org/10.1007/978-3-319-12544-2_4

A Model-Driven Engineering Approach to Complex Performance Indicators: Towards Self-Service Performance Management (SS-PM)

Benito Giunta(✉)

NaDI, Namur Digital Institute, PReCISE Research Center,
Université de Namur, Namur, Belgium
benito.giunta@unamur.be

Abstract. Every modern organization nowadays produces data and consumes information through Decision-Support Systems (DSS) which produce more and more Complex Performance Indicators (CPI). This allows business monitoring, decision-making support and tracking of decisions effects. With the increasing complexity, DSS suffer from two main limitations that inhibit their use. First, DSS tend to be opaque to Business Managers who cannot observe how the data is treated to produce indicators. Second, DSS are owned by the technicians, resulting in an IT-bottleneck and a business-exclusion. From a Business Management perspective, the consequences are damaging. DSS result in sunk costs of development, fail to receive full confidence from Business Managers and to fit dynamic business environments. In this research, preliminary insights are proposed to build a solution that tackles the previous limitations. The literature review, the research contributions and methodology are presented to conclude with the work plan of the PhD.

Keywords: Decision Support System · Model-Driven Engineering · Performance Management · Complex Performance Indicators

1 Context and Motivation

It is now broadly accepted that organizations produce data and consume information as a way to produce knowledge, and ultimately wisdom [3]. This principle has been addressed in various ways in Computer Science and Management Science. Technological architectures like Business Intelligence, Big Data and more generally Decision Support Systems (DSS) [29] deal with the technical issues related to the processing of heterogeneous data sources as a way to produce information. DSS produce a series of measures necessary to inform Business Managers about the situation of their company, the past/future decisions and their effects. The measures are also referred to as Indicators, or more specifically Key Performance Indicators (KPI) [24].

S. Cherfi et al. (Eds.): RCIS 2021, LNBIP 415, pp. 661–669, 2021.
https://doi.org/10.1007/978-3-030-75018-3_50

While DSS are extremely rich and powerful they still suffer from low success rates [4]. Money is often invested in systems which are not used at full potential or even not adopted. This, in turn, tends to limit the return on investment for organizations and the benefits for corporate decision-making. While investigating the possible explanations for these failures, two main problems can be identified. First, DSS tend to be *opaque to the business* [7], meaning that Business Managers cannot observe how the data is manipulated, transformed and aggregated to produce information. Second, the design of DSS is *owned by the technicians* (computer scientists, developers, "IT departments", etc.) and tends to exclude the business. Every change request on the DSS necessarily implies the involvement of IT people. The business has then little control over what the DSS really does. With IT-ownership and KPIs that change often and rapidly, the risk of bottlenecks increases dramatically and DSS fail to fit highly dynamic environments.

Former limitations are true in general but become even more salient when the DSS produce Composite (or Complex, used as synonym) Performance Indicators (CPI). A CPI is the assembling of individual indicators following an underpinning model for the measurement of multidimensional aspects [22]. For instance, a corporate sustainability CPI measures multidimensional aspects and needs to assemble various individual indicators to be computed. They are not to be confused with KPIs, which typically result from the aggregation of one data along with one or several business dimensions. For instance, a sales growth KPI results from the aggregation of one data, namely the sales. The use of CPIs has become ubiquitous in many recent performance areas, including environment [31], sustainability [10] or finance [14]. This adds to more traditional measurements challenges like customer satisfaction [30], supply chain monitoring [23] or management by objectives [25]. Regardless of the field, CPIs are complex from both a methodological point of view (i.e., how to analyze, to model and to document them?) and a technical one (i.e., how to implement, to process and to update them?). The combination of CPIs complexity with the existence of limitations when DSS produce CPIs makes the design of successful DSS and the computation of CPIs particularly challenging.

2 Research Challenges and Questions

The main conclusions from the context of interest can be summarized under the form of a set of assumptions that are investigated in this PhD research:

- Current approaches to DSS and CPIs design tend to hide the technicality of data processing, resulting in a rather oblivious set of information with definitions that are not always clearly exposed and in IT-bottlenecks appearing when CPIs need to be changed;
- Business Managers do not want to be exposed to the full complexity implemented in a Decision Support System in order to produce a CPI, but would gain in confidence if exposed to the main actions/operations performed to produce that very CPI;

- The more an indicator is complex and intricate, the more trust is required for a manager to use it, but the less trust there will actually be due to the various operations and manipulations that have to be performed to compute the indicator (trade-off);
- Considering the three previous assumptions, a solution can be found, that would empower business decision-makers with the capability of designing CPIs in a DSS without making any technical decision, which would reduce the workload of IT departments, increase the level of trust in CPIs, and eventually increase the chance of success of the underlying DSS.

From these conclusions, three research questions can be drawn to address the limitations presented earlier:

- **RQ1:** What are the limitations of existing DSS frameworks when it comes to the operationalization of CPIs?
- **RQ2:** How to address limitations of DSS and CPIs while balancing the trade-off between complexity and trust in a CPI?
- **RQ3:** How can we make DSS implementation more "business-friendly" by allowing decision-makers to design parts of a DSS back-end by themselves?

3 Related Work

KPIs, and more generally indicators, are traditionally handled by DSS. These systems are predominant in several fields, through various architectures and technologies. DSS are recognized as the main asset to monitoring and improving businesses through indicators [16]. However, no proposition seems to present DSS design that overcomes the limitations presented before.

The essential problem in this PhD is a *Performance Management* (PM) one, referring to practices and models used in an organization to track and improve its overall performance. The field is mainstream and mature. Some of its fundamental contributions are reviewed to better position this research. The Balanced Scorecard (BSC), a well-known PM model, identifies four business dimensions for monitoring a company [18]. The perspectives highlighted by the BSC, together with the Strategy Map, provide a framework along which CPIs of an organization can be studied. This PhD is also influenced by other historical models, such as the GRAI Grid [9] or the ARIS framework [8], which both provide mechanisms to model business dimensions from a PM perspective. All these works will confer valuable inputs as a way to produce enhanced notation for CPIs. In [6], authors extend the framework of Semantics of Business Vocabulary and Business Rules (SBVR) from Object Management Group to model KPI in a language readable by non-experts (using SBVR) along with a machine-readable outcome (using MathML tool). The proposed framework offers KPI vocabulary focused on definition, but not a CPIs model focused on operationalization (how indicators are computed from raw data). The paper opens the door for future *Model-Driven Engineering* (MDE) approaches but leaves the problem unexplored.

Directly following from PM is the issue of defining relevant measurements for organizations. PM provides the framework but does not focus on the operationalization of measures, central in this research project. In general, there are few scientific works on how to implement CPIs. In [22], the Statistics Directorate and the Directorate for Science, Technology, and Industry (OECD) and the Econometrics and Applied Statistics Unit of the Joint Research Centre (JRC) present a methodology to handle the creation of CPIs. Ten important steps are documented and will be followed in this PhD. Beside methodological aspects, some references present mathematical and/or statistical methods for the creation of CPIs. A review of all the pros and cons of these methods is proposed in [22]. It is worth noticing that other approaches like Multi-criteria Decision Making Models have been considered to assemble various measures into richer CPIs [19,26]. These techniques provide valuable insights for this project but stick to some general guidelines as to how CPIs are to be produced, maintained and updated. Moreover, no tool seems to implement these methodologies while overcoming previous limitations of DSS.

The question of designing systems aligned with expectations of future users has been widely covered by the *Requirements Engineering* (RE) research community. RE refers to the practices of identifying, modelling, analyzing and validating requirements of stakeholders for a future system. Various models have been proposed in RE to support the design of DSS. In [11], a goal-oriented approach is introduced which allows relating DSS measures and dimensions to strategic business intentions. Similarly, models like [12] focus on the modelling and the representation of data warehouses. In [15], the BIM model is introduced, where traditional requirements languages are combined with decision-making concepts such as indicators to help produce DSS better aligned with an organization's strategy. Other examples include [28], where an alternative notation for DSS concepts (e.g.: indicators, reports, ...) is introduced in UML activity diagrams to facilitate the identification of relevant indicators in a process-oriented approach or [2] where authors develop a method to reason on indicators as a way to design enhanced DSS. RE does not propose any modelling notation for the operationalization of indicators.

An MDE approach refers to the practices of defining a meta-model and models transformations for the development of several pieces of software [27]. It is now a well-accepted and established approach. Besides, MDE has already been applied to DSS several times, which suggests the method is well suited for the current research objectives. For instance, [1] introduces Mozart, a tool to mine KPIs and their correlations from historical data as a way to implement monitoring applications. In a similar mood, [20] addresses the problem of misalignment between DSS and the business context. Authors automate the design of KPIs in traditional BI vendors using an MDE approach. Overall, the use of MDE in DSS is still largely unexplored, and research avenues on the topic are still numerous.

4 Research Methodology

The current project is the strengthening of the research proposal in [5]. This PhD follows a Design Science (DS) approach, a scientific problem-solving methodology that mainly focuses on research contributions and well-suited to an information system context [13]. DS essentially aims to theorize and to build new artifacts in order to understand and to improve Information Systems, and especially DSS [13]. It ensures the rigour and the relevance of the research through seven guidelines [13]. Two of them – the *research contributions* and the *design evaluation* – are discussed in more details in Sect. 5.

5 Proposed Solutions

Starting from assumptions identified in previous sections, this project would balance between methodological contributions (how to design CPIs in a more transparent way by embedding the business?) and more technical ones (how to transform a business-readable specification of CPIs into a workable piece of software to actually compute the CPIs?). The objective is to design a robust Model-Driven Engineering approach to empower Business Managers in the production of CPIs in a self-service mood. The practical implications and mechanisms are further detailed in Sect. 5.1. The PhD would also focus on the transparency issue in a way that every decision-maker in the organization, and not only the author of the CPI, can understand how a CPI has been produced and what it actually measures.

5.1 Research Contributions

As mentioned earlier, the research project will adopt a Design Science approach to produce its three contributions.

The First Main Contribution is the Proposition of a New Modelling Framework for the Documentation of CPIs. As discussed in Sect. 3, ways to approach the design of KPIs are varied. However, only some of them apply to CPIs, and very few of them provide modelling support to actually formalize the CPIs and the way they are produced (which transformations? On which data? Which weights and decision rules? Why? When?) in a manner that is interpretable by business people. Following a rigorous approach for the creation of new languages [17], a new modelling notation for the operationalization of CPIs would be proposed. This clearer and systematical documentation would ease the implementation of CPIs and would result in a better understanding and stronger confidence in the indicators.

The Second Contribution is the Proposition of the MDE Framework for the Computation of CPIs. As already discussed, DSS heavily rely on the expertise of programmers in charge of developing and maintaining the solution. Every change regarding an indicator (definition, source, etc.) results in new developments by technicians. In turn, it suggests costs of development and most importantly time with a risk of bottlenecks. The proposition here is to design and to implement a processor for CPIs, whose code and internal functioning would depend on a business model produced by Business Managers. The new artifact would be composed of two parts; a business interface and an MDE system. Through the interface, the Business Managers would themselves design a model under the form of simple and explicit visual artifacts to directly define and adapt their CPIs without interference with technicians. This interface will be implemented in a way that a non IT expert would perfectly understand, using user-centric design [21]. The second part, that is the MDE mechanism, would translate the business model provided by managers into a program that effectively implements the CPIs. To summarize, Business Managers define in their language the CPIs and the system builds them. This approach would enable to reduce the cost of implementing changes in indicators, to track more CPIs and to make the system and the business more responsive to dynamic environments.

The Third Contribution is the Proposition of a New Indicator Processing Visualisation Technique. Contributions 1 and 2 do only solve a part of the problem of trust in CPIs. Throughout the organization, Business Managers who use the CPIs must have somehow access to the mathematical/logical process applied in order to produce the indicator, even if they were not the author of that CPI. The MDE system of contribution 2 should help increase the trust that the specifier of the indicator has in the CPI, but it would not improve the trust of all other consumers of that indicator. To solve this "CPI distribution and communication" issue, this project also attempts to implement a visualization tool for Business Managers, building on the same MDE approach of contribution 2. That visualization tool would not focus on the indicator. Indeed, there are already several contributions on the representation of data, and it is not the ambition of this project to propose new ways of representing a measure. The focus would be on the manipulations applied to raw data that have been used to produce the indicator (intermediary steps and values, underlying variables, etc.). Concretely, anyone confronted with a CPI would have access to an interface that presents how the CPI was built. Even if a decision-maker did not create the CPI, that decision-maker would be able to understand, first, how it has been designed, and, second, to which extent the underlying variables contribute to the final CPI value. Moreover, if a CPI is subject to various changes, business people would have the ability to track the changes history a posteriori.

5.2 Research Validation

According to DS, the effectiveness of the three contributions in addressing the initial problem must be rigorously demonstrated through a precise evaluation methodology to assess the feasibility and the value of this research [13]. The outcome of this project will be evaluated through real-world cases possible thanks to existing relationships of the research team; notably with *Civadis* and *Skeyes.*

Civadis is a company that provides IT solutions for the local government of municipalities in Wallonia and Brussels (in Belgium). A collaboration for the current project would be an extremely valuable case-study and would offer a platform to interactions with Belgian municipalities. Moreover, a relationship through a research convention is shared with *Skeyes*, the Belgian air traffic control agency. Therefore, the team has access to experts and to virtually all relevant data.

As the project is not tied to a particular company and the topic is relevant for virtually any organization, other real-world cases can be found.

5.3 Work Plan

This PhD research will be conducted for four to five years. It will be articulated in four iterative phases. Figure 1 depicts these phases and their underlying tasks. We are currently heading Phase 1.

Phase 1 will focus on CPI conceptualization (what is it? How does it differ from regular KPIs? What are the characteristics that discriminate complex and non-complex indicators? Etc). Then, frameworks for modelling indicators will be investigated to determine their advantages and limitations. This will allow to better position this project in the literature. Phase 1 addresses RQ1.

Phase 2 will concentrate on contribution 1. The objective is to produce a CPI modelling notation readable by Business Managers. To do so, a framework identified during the previous phase will be selected. Based on its limitations, candidate solutions will be designed. The new notation will require insights from modelling theories and the involvement of Business Managers. Since the targeted users of the notation are Business Managers, a lot of efforts will be dedicated to involve them and to the empirical evaluation of the notation. Successful achievement of Phase 2 will rely on this evaluation. Phase 2 will contribute to RQ2.

Phase 3 will consolidate contribution 1 and 2. The concepts (objects, relationships, constraints) needed will be finalised. Then, a focus will be given to meta-modelling and model transformations to produce the MDE system. It will then be tested and validated with practitioners. This phase addresses RQ3.

Phase 4 will focus on contribution 3. A literature review will be conducted regarding how to measure the contribution of a variable. Then, a *CPI processing visualisation* will be defined, implemented, evaluated and integrated. RQ2 will be addressed during this phase.

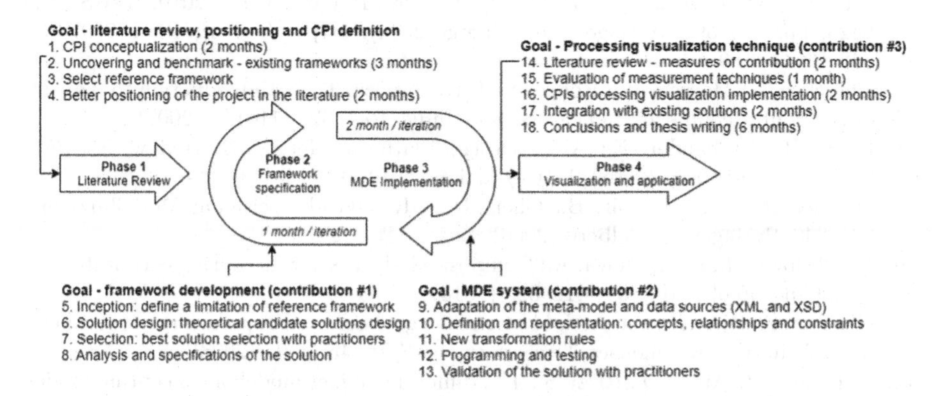

Fig. 1. The four phases of the work plan

6 Discussion

In this paper, we propose a complete approach to tackle the limitations of current DSS regarding CPIs; the issues of *opaqueness* and *IT-ownership*. The three contributions try to involve Business Managers in CPI design and computation to increase transparency and trust facing the complexity of CPIs. Business Managers will be part of the CPI creation process and will gain a more transparent lens on what the CPIs effectively capture. This transparency will increase the trust in the CPIs. The decisions taken based on the CPIs will gain in quality since Business Managers will better grasp them. The MDE system will allow to reduce IT workload and the cost of producing and maintaining CPIs. All in all, success rates of CPI and ultimately of DSS are expected to increase. The system will be more responsive to fit dynamic environments and will provide better quality decision-support.

References

1. Abe, M., Jeng, J., Li, Y.: A tool framework for kpi application development. In: IEEE International Conference on e-Business Engineering (ICEBE 2007), pp. 22–29 (2007)
2. Barone, D., Jiang, L., Amyot, D., Mylopoulos, J.: Composite indicators for business intelligence. In: Jeusfeld, M., Delcambre, L., Ling, T.-W. (eds.) ER 2011. LNCS, vol. 6998, pp. 448–458. Springer, Heidelberg (2011). https://doi.org/10.1007/978-3-642-24606-7_35
3. Bellinger, G., Castro, D.: Data, information, knowledge, and wisdom (2004)
4. Bitterer, A., Schlegel K., Laney, D.: Predicts 2012: business intelligence still subject to nontechnical challenges. Retrieved from Gartner Database (2012)
5. Burnay, C.: A model driven engineering approach to key performance indicators: towards self-service performance management (SS-PM project). In: 14th International Conference on Research Challenges in Information Science, RCIS (September 2020)
6. Caputo, E., Corallo, A., Damiani, E., Passiante, G.: KPI modeling in MDA perspective. In: Meersman, R., Dillon, T., Herrero, P. (eds.) OTM 2010. LNCS, vol. 6428, pp. 384–393. Springer, Heidelberg (2010). https://doi.org/10.1007/978-3-642-16961-8_59
7. Cherchye, L., Moesen, W., Rogge, N., Puyenbroeck, T.: An introduction to 'benefit of the doubt' composite indicators. Soc. Indic. Res. **82**, 111–145 (2007)
8. Davis, R., Brabander, E.: ARIS Design Platform: Getting Started with BPM. Springer, Heidelberg (2008). https://doi.org/10.1007/978-1-84628-613-1
9. Doumeingts, G., Vallespir, B., Chen, D.: GRAI Grid Decisional Modelling, pp. 321–346. Springer, Heidelberg (2006)
10. Dočekalová, M., Kocmanová, A.: Composite indicator for measuring corporate sustainability. Ecol. Indic. **61**, 612–623 (2015)
11. Giorgini, P., Rizzi, S., Garzetti, M.: Grand: a goal-oriented approach to requirement analysis in data warehouses. Decis. Support Syst. **45**, 4–21 (2008)
12. Golfarelli, M., Maio, D., Rizzi, S.: The dimensional fact model: a conceptual model for data warehouses. Int. J. Coop. Inf. Syst. **7**, 215–247 (1998)

13. Hevner, A., March, S., Park, J., Ram, S.: Design science in information systems research (2013)
14. Hoffmann, P., Kremer, M., Zaharia, S.: Financial integration in Europe through the lens of composite indicators. Econ. Lett. **194**, 109344 (2020)
15. Horkoff, J., et al.: Strategic business modeling: representation and reasoning. Softw. Syst. Model. **13**, 1–27 (2014)
16. Issar, G., Navon, L.R.: Decision support systems (DSS). Operational Excellence. MP, pp. 17–20. Springer, Cham (2016). https://doi.org/10.1007/978-3-319-20699-8_4
17. Jureta, I.: The Design of Requirements Modelling Languages. Springer, Cham (2015). https://doi.org/10.1007/978-3-319-18821-8
18. Kaplan, R., Norton, D.: Linking the balanced scorecard to strategy. Calif. Manag. Rev. **39**, 53–79 (1996)
19. Karagiannis, G.: On aggregate composite indicators. J. Oper. Res. Soc. **68**, 741–746 (2016)
20. Letrache, K., El Beggar, O., Ramdani, M.: Modeling and creating KPIs in MDA approach. In: 2016 4th IEEE International Colloquium on Information Science and Technology (CiSt), pp. 222–227 (October 2016)
21. Marcus, A.: HCI and User-Experience Design. HIS. Springer, London (2015). https://doi.org/10.1007/978-1-4471-6744-0
22. Nardo, M., Saisana, M., Saltelli, A., Tarantola, S., Hoffman, A., Giovannini, E.: Handbook on Constructing Composite Indicators and User Guide, vol. 2005 (2008)
23. Oliveira, R., et al.: A composite indicator for supply chain performance measurement: a case study in a manufacturing company, pp. 1611–1615 (December 2019)
24. Parmenter, D.: Key Performance Indicators: Developing, Implementing, and Using Winning KPIs. Wiley, New Jersey (2010)
25. Prendergast, C.: The provision of incentives in firms. J. Econ. Lit. **37**, 7–63 (1999)
26. Samira, E.G., Núñez, T., Ruiz, F.: Building composite indicators using multicriteria methods: a review. J. Bus. Econ. **89**, 1–24 (2019)
27. Schmidt, D.: Model-driven engineering. IEEE Comput. **39**, 41–47 (2006)
28. Stefanov, V., List, B., Korherr, B.: Extending UML 2 activity diagrams with business intelligence objects. In: Tjoa, A.M., Trujillo, J. (eds.) DaWaK 2005. LNCS, vol. 3589, pp. 53–63. Springer, Heidelberg (2005). https://doi.org/10.1007/11546849_6
29. Vera-Baquero, A., Colomo-Palacios, R., Molloy, O.: Towards a process to guide big data based decision support systems for business processes. In: International Conference on ENTERprise Information Systems, CENTERIS, vol. 16 (October 2014)
30. Zani, S., Milioli, M.A., Morlini, I.: Fuzzy composite indicators: an application for measuring customer satisfaction. In: Torelli, N., Pesarin, F., Bar-Hen, A. (eds.) Advances in Theoretical and Applied Statistics. Studies in Theoretical and Applied Statistics. Springer, Heidelberg (2013). https://doi.org/10.1007/978-3-642-35588-2_23
31. Zhang, L., Zhou, P., Qiu, Y., Su, Q., Tang, Y.: Reassessing the climate change cooperation performance via a non-compensatory composite indicator approach. J. Clean. Prod. **252**, 119387 (2019)

Robust and Strongly Consistent Distributed Storage Systems

Andria Trigeorgi(✉)

University of Cyprus, Nicosia, Cyprus
atrige01@cs.ucy.ac.cy

Abstract. The design of Distributed Storage Systems involves many challenges due to the fact that the users and storage nodes are physically dispersed. In this doctoral consortium paper, we present a framework for boosting the concurrent access to *large* shared data objects (such as files), while maintaining strong consistency guarantees. In the heart of the framework lies a fragmentation strategy, which enables different updates to occur on different fragments of the object concurrently, while ensuring that all modifications are valid.

Keywords: Distributed storage · Large objects · Concurrency · Linearizability (strong consistency)

1 Problem and Motivation

Nowadays, data are rapidly generated through applications, social media, browsers and so on. The challenge for many organizations and companies is to design an efficient storage system to cope with this data explosion. A Distributed Storage System (DSS) [17] provides data survivability and system availability. Data replication on multiple storage locations is a well known technique to cope with these issues. A main challenge due to replication, caused when the shared data are accessed concurrently, is data inconsistency.

Numerous platforms prefer high availability over consistency, due to the belief that strong consistency will burden the performance of their systems. As a result, they devise strategies to address the issue of consistency, but they rely on system coordinators to provide weaker consistency guarantees. However, modern storage systems attempt to find the balance between the consistency of the data and the availability of the system. In this work we aim to explore the development of a Robust and Strongly Consistent DSS while providing highly concurrent access to its users.

Our design is based on fundamental research in the area of distributed shared memory emulation [1,2]. These emulations provide a strong consistency guarantee, called *linearizability* (atomicity) [15], which is especially suitable for concurrent systems. Currently, such emulations, are either limited to small-size objects,

The work is supported in part by the Cyprus Research and Innovation Foundation under the grant agreement POST-DOC/0916/0090 (COLLABORATE).

S. Cherfi et al. (Eds.): RCIS 2021, LNBIP 415, pp. 670–679, 2021.
https://doi.org/10.1007/978-3-030-75018-3_51

or if two writes occur concurrently on different parts of the object, only one of them prevails. To address these limitations, we introduce a framework based on data fragmentation strategies that boost concurrency, while maintaining strong consistency guarantees, and minimize the operation latencies.

2 Existing Knowledge

In this section, we briefly review existing distributed shared memory emulations, proposed distributed file systems and discuss their strengths and limitations. Table 1 presents a comparison of the main characteristics of the distributed algorithms and storage systems that we will discuss in this document.

Attiya *et al.* [2] presents the first fault-tolerant emulation of atomic shared memory, later known as *ABD*, in an asynchronous message passing system. It implements Single-Writer Multi-Reader (SWMR) registers in an asynchronous network, provided that at least a majority of the servers do not crash. The writer completes write operations in a single round by incrementing its local timestamp and propagating the value with its new timestamp to the servers, waiting acknowledgments from a majority of them. The read operation completes in two rounds: (i) it discovers the maximum timestamp-value pair that is known to a majority of the servers, (ii) it propagates the pair to the servers, in order to ensure that a majority of them have the latest value, hence preserving atomicity. This has led to the common belief that "atomic reads must write". This belief was refuted by Dutta *et al.* [5] who showed that it is possible, under certain constraints, to complete reads in one round-trip. Several works followed, presenting different ways to achieve one-round reads (e.g., [11,12,14]). The ABD algorithm was extended by Lynch and Shvartsman [16], who present an emulation of Multi-Writer and Multi-Reader (MWMR) atomic registers.

The above works on shared memory emulations were focused on small-size objects. Fan and Lynch [7] proposed an extension, called *LDR*, that can cope with large-size objects (e.g. files). The key idea was to maintain copies of the data objects separately from their metadata; maintaining two different types of servers, replicas (that store the files) and directories (that handle metadata and essentially run a version of ABD). However, the whole object is still transmitted in every message exchanged between the clients and the replica servers. Furthermore, if two writes update different parts of the object concurrently, only one of the two prevails.

From the dozens of distributed file systems that exist in the market today, we focus on the ones that are more relevant to our work. The Google File System (GFS) [13] and the Hadoop Distributed File System (HDFS) [22] were built to handle large volume of data. These file systems store metadata in a single node and data in cluster nodes separately. Both GFS and HDFS use data stripping and replicate each chunk/block for fault tolerance. HDFS provides concurrency by restricting the file access to one writer at a time. Also, it allows users to perform only append operations at the end of the file. However, GFS supports record append at the offset of its own choosing. This operation allows multiple clients to append data to the same file concurrently without extra locking. These systems are designed for data-intensive computing and not for normal end-users [6].

Dropbox [19] is possibly the most popular commercial DSS with big appeal to end-users. It provides eventual consistency (which is weaker than linearizability), synchronising a working object for one user at a time. Thus, in order to access the object from another machine, a user must have the up-to-date copy; this eliminates the complexity of synchronization and multiple versions of objects.

Blobseer [4] is a large-scale DSS that stores data as a long sequence of bytes called BLOB (Binary Large Object). This system uses data stripping and versioning that allow writers to continue editing in a new version without blocking other clients that use the current version. A version manager, the key component of the system, deals with the serialization of the concurrent write requests and assigns a new version number for each write operation. Unlike GFS and HDFS, Blobseer does not centralize metadata on a single machine, but it uses a centralized version manager. Thus linearizability is easy to achieve.

Our work aims in complementing the above systems by designing a highly fault-tolerant distributed storage system that provides concurrent access to its clients without sacrificing strong concurrency nor using centralized components.

Table 1. Comparative table of distributed algorithms and storage systems.

Algorithm/System	Data scalability	Data access Concurrency	Consistency guarantees	Versioning	Data Stripping
MWMR ABD [16]	NO	YES	Strong	NO	NO
LDR [7]	YES	YES	Strong	NO	NO
CoABD [8]	NO	YES	Strong	YES	NO
GFS [13]	YES	Concurrent appends	Relaxed	YES	YES
HDFS [22]	YES	Files restrict one writer at a time	Strong (centralized)	NO	YES
Dropbox [19]	YES	Creates conflicting copies	Eventual	YES	YES
Blobseer [4]	YES	YES	Strong (centralized)	YES	YES
CoBFS [our work]	YES	YES	Strong	YES	YES

3 Research Plan and Stage of Research

For the purpose of accomplishing a prototype of a Robust Distributed Storage System, with strong consistency guarantees, my research will include the following stages (quoting the estimated time for each one):

1. From existing emulations of distributed shared memory [2,7,8,10], we want to implement an optimized version of the most efficient one, in order to establish *linearizable consistency* to a unit of storage, we call a *block* (3 months).
2. Survey Data Fragmentation Strategies, focusing on block strategies. This would lead to our own fragmentation strategy, aiming to reduce the communication cost of write/read operations by splitting data into smaller atomic data objects (blocks), while enabling concurrent access to these blocks (4 months).
3. Integrate the different algorithmic modules and strategies, envisioned via a system architecture (see next section). This would entail our design and implementation framework. Based on that, we aim to introduce new consistency guarantees, that characterize the consistency of the whole object, which is composed by smaller atomic objects (blocks) (3 months).
4. Implement an erasure-coding (EC) storage (such as *ARES* [3]) which divides the object into encoded fragments and deliver each fragment to one server. The object can be recovered from a subset of the fragments. However, operations are still applied on the entire object. Thus, we can evaluate the performance of the system by combining our fragmentation approach with EC (2 months).
5. Implement a Reconfiguration service in order to mask host failures or switching between storage algorithms without service interruptions. It is expected that an existing reconfigurable algorithm (such as *ARES* [3]) may be extended to address this objective (2 months).
6. A failure prediction service can be used to estimate the risk of a device failing in order to trigger the reconfiguration service. It could be based on a monitoring service that would collect S.M.A.R.T. (Self-Monitoring, Analysis and Reporting Technology) metrics of the servers, indicating a possible drive failure. Machine Learning would be used to identify correlations on the metrics so to predict drive failures. We will integrate the failure prediction service with reconfiguration. Also, we need to specify the aggressiveness of reconfiguration: reconfiguring in every failure notification may result in many frequent reconfigurations, whereas waiting too long may disable the service due to many failures (5 months).
7. Design easy-to-use user interfaces to facilitate the use of our storage system by users that are not necessarily highly technology-trained (5 months).
8. Deploy and evaluate the system in network testbeds. An emulation testbed such as Emulab [20] will be used for developing and debugging the components of our system. However, an overlay planetary-scale testbet such as PlanetLab [23] will help us examine the performance of our system in highly-adverse, uncontrolled, real-time environments (7 months).
9. Deploy the prototype on small devices with limited computing capabilities (e.g. Raspberry Pie). During these experiments we will have the opportunity to test the durability of our storage in high concurrency conditions. Also, it will help us examine the performance of the reconfiguration operations by physically replacing the serves (5 months).

10. Further enhance our prototype implementation with more functionality and features, having the ultimate goal of developing a fully-functioning and scalable DSS, that provides high concurrency and strong consistency (5 months).

Stage of Research. I have been doing this research for the past fourteen months. During this period, items (1) to (3) and part of item (8) have been completed. We are currently working on items (4) and (5). As a proof of concept implementation, we developed a prototype implementation realizing the proposed framework [9]. Furthermore, we conducted a preliminary evaluation on Emulab [20], using Ansible Playbooks [18] for the remote execution of tasks. The evaluation shows the promise of our design; we overview the results obtained so far in the next two sections.

4 Development and Prototype Implementation

Our prototype DSS is a Distributed File System, called CoBFS, which utilizes coverable linearizable fragmented objects. The object (file), is composed of blocks, and *fragmented linearizability* [9] guarantees that all concurrent updates on different blocks are valid, and only concurrent updates on the same blocks are conflicting with each other. *Coverability* [8] extends linearizability with the additional guarantee that an update succeeds when the writer has the latest version of the object before updating it. Otherwise, an update becomes a read and returns the latest version with its associated value. The coverable version of MWMR ABD (CoABD) [8] is used as the distributed shared memory service in our system in order to ensure consistency. It allows multiple concurrent updates (writes) and reads, in an asynchronous, message-passing, crash-prone environment. We now proceed to more implementation details.

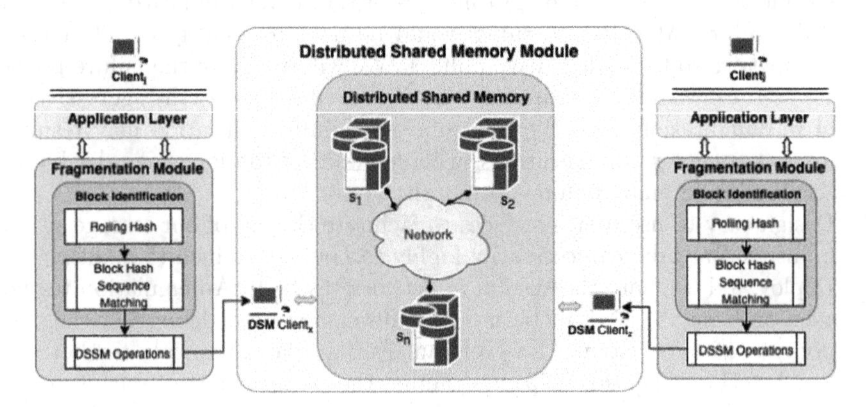

Fig. 1. The basic architecture of CoBFS

Basic Architecture Overview: The basic architecture of CoBFS, shown in Fig. 1, is composed of two main modules: (i) a Fragmentation Module (FM), and

(ii) a Distributed Shared Memory Module (DSMM). The asynchronous communication between layers is achieved by using DEALER and ROUTER sockets, from the ZeroMQ library [26]. In summary, the FM implements the fragmented object while the DSMM implements an interface to a shared memory service that allows operations on individual block objects. Following this architecture, clients can perform operations, passing commands through command-line interface. Subsequently, the FM uses the DSMM as an external service to execute these operations on the shared memory. To this respect, CoBFS is flexible enough to utilize any underlying distributed shared object algorithm.

File as a Fragmented Object: Each file f is a ***list of blocks*** with the first block being the ***genesis block*** b_{gen}, and each block having the id of its next block, whereas the last block has a null next value.

Fragmentation Module: The FM is the core concept of our implementation. Each client has a FM responsible for (*i*) fragmenting the file into blocks and identify modified or new blocks, and (*ii*) following a specific strategy to store and retrieve the file blocks from the R/W shared memory.

Update Operation: The update strategy of the FM is the most challenging part of our work. The FM uses a Block Identification (BI) module, which draws ideas from the RSYNC (Remote Sync) algorithm [24]. The BI includes three main modules, the *Block Division*, the *Block Matching* and *Block Updates.*

1. ***Block Division:*** Initially, the BI splits a given file f into data blocks based on its contents, using *rabin fingerprints* [21]. This rolling hashing algorithm performs content-based chunking by calculating and returning the fingerprints (block hashes) over a sliding window. The algorithm allows you to specify the minimum and maximum block sizes, avoiding blocks that are too small or too big. It ignores a minimum size of bytes after a block boundary is found and then starts scanning. However, if no block boundary occurs before the maximum block size, the window is treated as a block boundary. The algorithm guarantees that when a file is changed, only the hash of a modified block (and in the worst case its next one) is affected, but not the subsequent blocks.
   BI has to match each hash, generated by the rabin fingerprint from the previous step, to a block identifier.
2. ***Block Matching:*** At first, BI uses a string matching algorithm [25] to compare the current sequence of the hashes with the sequence of hashes computed in the previous file update. The string matching algorithm outputs a list of differences between the two sequences in the form of four *statuses* for all given entries: (*i*) equality, (*ii*) modified, (*iii*) inserted, (*iv*) deleted.
3. ***Block Updates:*** Based on the hash statuses, the blocks of the fragmented object are updated. In the case of equality, if a $hash_i = hash(b_j)$ then D_i is identified as the data of block b_j. In case of modification, an *update* operation is then performed to modify the data of b_j to D_i. If new hashes are inserted after the hash of block b_j, then an *update* operation is performed to create

the new blocks after b_j. The deleted one is treated as a modification that sets an empty value; thus, *no blocks are deleted.*

Read Operation: When the system receives a read request from a client, the FM issues a series of read operations on the file's blocks, starting from the genesis block and proceeding to the last block by following the next block ids. As blocks are retrieved, they are assembled in a file.

Read Optimization in DSMM: In the first phase, if a server has a smaller tag than the reader, it replies only with its tag. The reader performs the second phase only when it has a smaller tag than the one found in the first phase.

5 Preliminary Evaluation

We performed an experimental evaluation in the *Emulab* testbed [20], to compare the performance of CoBFS and of its counterpart that does not use the fragmentation module; we refer to this version as CoABD.

Experimental Setup: In our scenarios, we use three distinct sets of nodes, writers, readers and servers. Communication between the distributed nodes is via point-to-point bidirectional links implemented with a DropTail queue.

Performance Metrics: We measured performance by computing operational latency as the sum of communicational and computational delays. Additionally, the percentage of successful file update operations is calculated.

Scenarios: To evaluate the efficiency of the algorithms, we use several scenarios:

- **Scalability:** examine performance under various numbers of readers/writers
- **File Size:** examine performance when using different initial file sizes
- **Block Size**: examine performance under different block sizes (CoBFS only)

Readers and writers pick a random time between $[1..rInt]$ and $[1..wInt]$, respectively, to invoke their next operation. During all the experiments of each scenario, as the writers kept updating the file, its size increased.

Results: As a general observation, the efficiency of CoBFS is inversely affected by the number of block operations, while CoABD shows no flexibility regarding the size of the file.

Scalability: In Fig. 2(a), the update operation latency in CoBFS is always smaller than the one of CoABD, mainly because in any number of writers, each writer has to update only the affected blocks. Due to the higher percentage of successful file updates achieved by CoBFS, reads retrieve more data compared to reads in CoABD, which explains why it is slower than CoABD (Fig. 2(b)). Also, it would be interesting to examine whether the read block requests in CoBFS could be sent in parallel, reducing the overall communication delays.

File Size: As we can see in Fig. 2(c), the update latency of CoBFS remains at extremely low levels, although the file size increases. That is in contrast to the

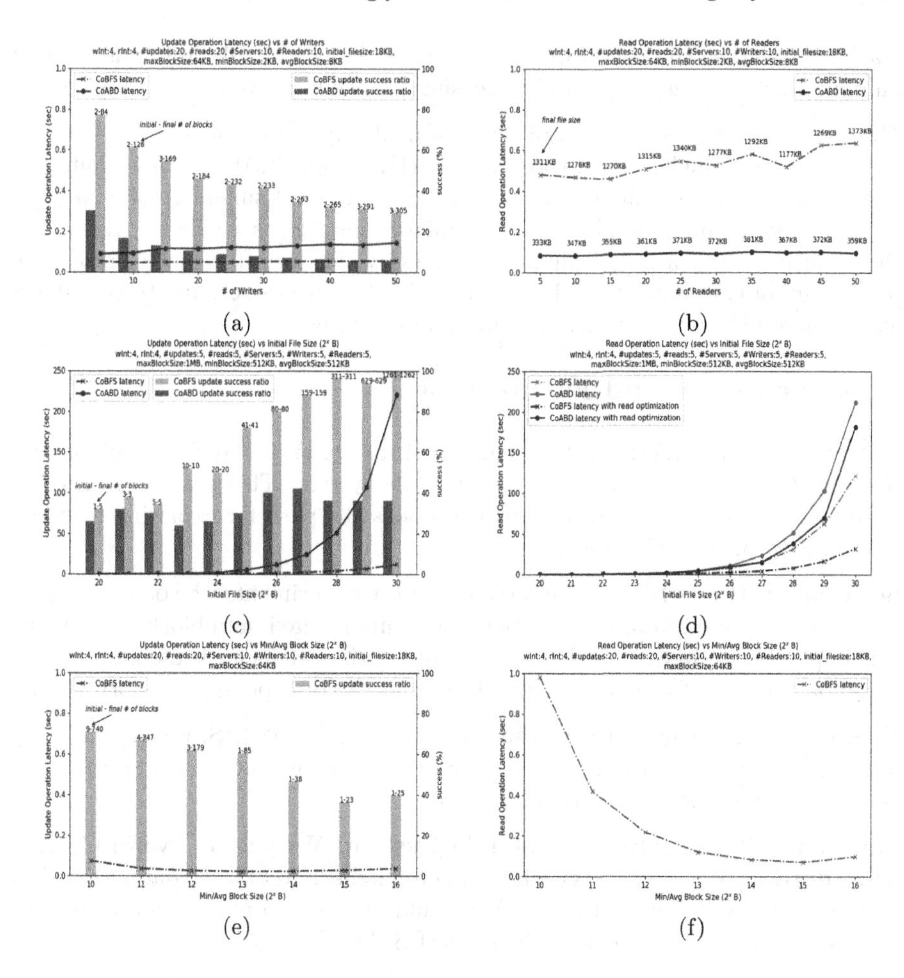

Fig. 2. Simulation results for algorithms CoABD and CoBFS.

CoABD update latency which appears to increase linearly with the file size, since it updates the whole file. The read latencies with and without the read optimization can be found in Fig. 2(d). The CoABD read latency increases sharply, even when using the read optimization. This is due to the fact that each time a new file version is discovered, CoABD sends the whole file. However, read optimization decreases significantly the CoBFS read latency, since it is more probable for a reader to already have the last version of some blocks.

Block Size: When smaller blocks are used, the update and read latencies reach their highest values and larger number of blocks (Figs. 2(e)(f)). As the minimum and average b_{sizes} increase, an update operation needs to add lower number of blocks. Similarly, smaller b_{sizes} require more read block operations to obtain the file's value. Therefore, further increase of b_{size} forces the decrease of the latencies, reaching a plateau in both graphs. This means that the emulation finds optimal minimum and average b_{sizes} and increasing it does not give better latencies.

Concurrency: The percentage of successful file updates achieved by CoBFS are significantly higher than those of CoABD (Fig. 2(a)). As the number of writers increases (and therefore concurrency), CoABD suffers greater number of unsuccessful updates, since it manipulates the file as a whole. Also, as is shown in Fig. 2(c), a larger number of blocks yields a better success rate. The probability of two writes to collide on a single block decreases, and thus CoBFS allows more file updates to succeed in all block updates.

6 Conclusions and Future Work

We investigated several strategies in order to build CoBFS, a *Robust* and *Strongly Consistent* prototype distributed file system. This system brings forward several optimization directions and opens the path for exploring new features which can boost its reliability.

Selection of Block Size: As observed from the experiments, the operation performance is affected from the selection of minimum/maximum block sizes. Thus, it is important to have a mechanism for tuning the values for these parameters, based on the size of the file, in order to obtain the best possible performance.

Fragmentation: Due to the modular architecture of CoBFS, we can integrate other fragmentation strategies, even at the level of the shared memory module (such as EC storage mentioned in Sect. 3).

Fully-Functioning Distributed File System: We plan to evolve CoBFS into a distributed storage service handling different kind of large data, as well as impose strong security guarantees. We would also like to provide an open API, in which people could integrate their own DSSMs.

References

1. Attiya, H.: Robust simulation of shared memory: 20 years after. Bull. EATCS **100**, 99–114 (2010)
2. Attiya, H., Bar-Noy, A., Dolev, D.: Sharing memory robustly in message-passing systems. J. ACM (JACM) **42**(1), 124–142 (1995)
3. Cadambe, V., Nicolaou, N., Konwar, K.M., et al.: ARES: adaptive, reconfigurable, erasure coded, atomic storage. In: Proceedings of ICDCS, pp. 2195–2205 (2018)
4. Carpen-Amarie, A.: BlobSeer as a data-storage facility for clouds: self- adaptation, integration, evaluation. Ph.D. thesis, ENS Cachan, Rennes, France (2012)
5. Dutta, P., Guerraoui, R., Levy, R., Chakraborty, A.: How fast can a distributed atomic read be? In: Proceedings of PODC, pp. 236–245 (2004)
6. Elbert, S.T., Kouzes, R.T., Anderson, G.A., Gorton, I., Gracio, D.K.: The changing paradigm of data-intensive computing. Computer **42**, 26–34 (2009)
7. Fan, R., Lynch, N.: Efficient replication of large data objects. In: Fich, F.E. (ed.) DISC 2003. LNCS, vol. 2848, pp. 75–91. Springer, Heidelberg (2003). https://doi.org/10.1007/978-3-540-39989-6_6

8. Fernández Anta, A., Georgiou, Ch., Nicolaou, N.: CoVerability: consistent versioning in asynchronous, fail-prone, message-passing environment. In: Proceedings of NCA, pp. 224–231 (2016)
9. Fernández Anta, A., Hadjistasi, Th., Georgiou, Ch., Nicolaou, N., Stavrakis, E., Trigeorgi, A.: Fragmented objects: boosting concurrency of shared large objects. In: Proceedings of SIROCCO (2021). To appear
10. Fernández Anta, A., Hadjistasi, Th., Nicolaou, N., Popa, A., Schwarzmann, A.A: Tractable low-delay atomic memory. Distrib. Comput. **34**, 33–58 (2020)
11. Georgiou, C., Hadjistasi, T., Nicolaou, N., Schwarzmann, A.A.: Unleashing and speeding up readers in atomic object implementations. In: Podelski, A., Taïani, F. (eds.) NETYS 2018. LNCS, vol. 11028, pp. 175–190. Springer, Cham (2019). https://doi.org/10.1007/978-3-030-05529-5_12
12. Georgiou, Ch., Nicolaou, N., Shvartsman, A.A.: Fault-tolerant semifast implementations of atomic read/write registers. J. Parallel Distrib. Comput. **69**(1), 62–79 (2009)
13. Ghemawat, S., Gobioff, H., Leung, S.: The Google file system. In: Proceedings of SOSP 2003, vol. 53, no. 1, pp. 79–81 (2003)
14. Hadjistasi, T., Nicolaou, N., Schwarzmann, A.A.: Oh-RAM! one and a half round atomic memory. In: El Abbadi, A., Garbinato, B. (eds.) NETYS 2017. LNCS, vol. 10299, pp. 117–132. Springer, Cham (2017). https://doi.org/10.1007/978-3-319-59647-1_10
15. Herlihy, M.P., Wing, J.M.: Linearizability: a correctness condition for concurrent objects. ACM Trans. Program. Lang. Syst. **12**(3), 463–492 (1990)
16. Lynch, N.A., Shvartsman, A.A.: Robust emulation of shared memory using dynamic quorum-acknowledged broadcasts. In: Proceedings of FTCS, pp. 272–281 (1997)
17. Viotti, P., Vukolić, M.: Consistency in non-transactional distributed storage systems. ACM Comput. Surv. **49**, 1–34 (2016)
18. Ansible Playbooks. https://www.ansible.com/overview/how-ansible-works
19. Dropbox. https://www.dropbox.com/
20. Emulab Network Testbed. https://www.emulab.net
21. Fingerprinting. http://www.xmailserver.org/rabin.pdf
22. HDFS. https://hadoop.apache.org/docs/r1.2.1/hdfs_design.html
23. Planetlab Network Testbed. https://www.planet-lab.eu
24. RSYNC. https://rsync.samba.org/tech_report/
25. String Matching Alg. https://xlinux.nist.gov/dads/HTML/ratcliffObershelp.html
26. ZeroMQ Messaging Library. https://zeromq.org

The Impact and Potential of Using Blockchain Enabled Smart Contracts in the Supply Chain Application Area

Samya Dhaiouir(✉)

University Paris-Saclay, University of Evry, IMT-BS, LITEM, 91025 Evry, France
Samya.dhaiouir@imt-bs.eu

Abstract. Blockchain potential in supply chain management (SCM) has increased considerably over the last few years, both in academia and industry. However, according to the literature, few researchers have tackled the real impact of blockchain in changing businesses and creating value. This research fully delved into an analysis of the SCM function with specific focus on measuring the potential of using a blockchain-based system in terms of enhancing effectiveness, trust and transparency. The main contributions of this research aim to address the main challenges of blockchain enabled smart contracts implementation in the field of SCM through a deep qualitative research that highlights the inconsistencies and misfits that are common in that application area.

Keywords: Blockchain · SCM · Impact · Trust · Transparency · Misfit

1 Introduction

Over the last few years, practitioners and researchers have significantly broadened their knowledge in different blockchain applications because of the rapid changes in the technological environment. Thus, blockchain has mainly been adopted in SCM application area for its ability to efficiently and effectively reorganize the organization's processes, and this has gone a long way to building some level of trust, traceability and transparency for all the stakeholders of the main system [10]. In fact, Failures in supply chain area could negatively affect all the stakeholders in terms of the lack of quality and trust [5]. In addition to the traditional challenges of generalized supply chain, there is a lack of understanding of the requirements and needs regarding the implementation of a blockchain system in such a complex application area, where participants are not known and/or trusted.

We tend to believe that this study will help businesses to understand their requirements and needs regarding the development of their blockchain-based applications. Indeed, not every blockchain platform is suitable for every network as every objective behind a blockchain project's implementation has a specific purpose [8]. As part of

Doctoral consortium

S. Cherfi et al. (Eds.): RCIS 2021, LNBIP 415, pp. 680–687, 2021.
https://doi.org/10.1007/978-3-030-75018-3_52

this research, it is crucial to have an insight into the criteria that would be instrumental in assessing or measuring the impact of the blockchain implementation in Supply Chain systems because highlighting what works and why in a technology is a must in terms of [19]. In fact, many businesses implement projects that could be sometimes very expensive with poor knowledge about their fit capability. However, the underlying challenge is no longer related only to the useless costs caused by the project's failure but to the long-term future of its technical and organizational performance. Therefore, technologies should be proven to 'work' before they are widely adopted to avoid unnecessary and unwanted bonuses. The need of a theoretical basis in our research work is of a major consideration [23] because it will enable us to measure the empirical impact of the blockchain implementation. In this thesis we will mainly use the Misfit theory [18] as a basis of evaluating the impact of blockchain implementation in an organization. The Misfit theory was first applied to the ERPs' implementation within an organization in order to define the deficiencies and the impositions resulting from the adoption of these enterprise systems (ESs) packages. We believe that a Misfit's application to our research area will bring some scientificity to our findings and enable us understand some complex phenomena.

Moreover, a today's recurrent issue in blockchain projects is to understand what works, what doesn't and why. It is important to evaluate the impact of this technology implementation especially in a field that requires specific requirements. The many previous initiatives to ensure full traceability come up with stakeholders' reluctance to share their information. Quite understandably, Stakeholders do not want to trust anymore, they want to be sure. This is where the role of Blockchain Technology comes into play. This technology encrypts the information and distributes it to the different actors in an open, unfalsifiable and transparent way [20].

2 State of the Art

Blockchain is an emerging technology that cleverly combines a set of well-known technologies such as: Cryptography, data storage and peer-to-peer networks. Given the significance of its industrial potential, blockchain is touted to disrupt not only the financial domain but also many other application areas [21]. However, blockchain technology is still considered as a threat by several researchers and practioners. The disruption caused by blockchain lies in the ability to remove exchange intermediaries without control but in a verifiable and reliable manner. However, many companies still scramble to understand the functionalities of this technology and how it can support and fit with their business models [14]. Thus, its potential remains to be tested and its impact to be evaluated mainly in supply chain application area. For this purpose, it is important to understand the functioning of this technology technically in terms of platforms, consensus, programing languages [8] and organizationally (Table 1).

Since 2015, numerous research projects at both national and international level have been looking at blockchain technology. As recent reviews of the literature in this field, much of the existing work is concerned with field of finance [3, 6]. In addition, the focus on technological issues is predominant, neglecting managerial issues such as the added value and governance in industrial applications [7, 16]. Questions of a managerial nature

Table 1. Blockchain platform criteria grid [8]

Technical features	
Scalability	**Transaction intensive**
	Time
Ledger type	**Permissioned**
	Pretensionless
Supported consensus mechanism	**PoW**
	PoS
	DPoS
	Pluggable framework
Supported Programming language	**Object-oriented language**
	Functional language
	Specifically designed language
	Procedural language
	Declarative language
Smart contracts functionality	**Yes**
	No

are thus defined as future research perspectives in a collective analysis of the challenges and opportunities of the blockchain for the management of business process [5].

Several related works aim to identify current studies and challenges in smart contract research for future research in different fields [1, 11, 13]. Nevertheless, some recent work examines the applicability of blockchain in supply chain, such as [2, 15, 24], Others explore the contribution of blockchain [4, 14], analyze its adoption [9, 12], or report case studies [17]. Finally, a quick search on the 'theses.fr' website shows that around thirty theses are currently conducted in France on the subject of blockchain, with in particular two theses which have just started and whose subject is related to supply chain management.

3 Research Objectives and Methodology

In this work, our research goal is to explore and assess the current perception regarding the impact of using blockchain technology in the supply chain domain. We further seek to better understand the potential role that Smart Contracts might play in mitigating the potential of the blockchain adoption in the supply chain domain. The concepts of trust and inalterability linked to the basic principle of transparency could be used to convince these actors that the blockchain remains a very reliable option in the industry. In other words, the blockchain can constitute a prime traceability system whose main objective is to improve trace products (whatever their nature) throughout the supply chain. It is in this context that lies the thesis proposal which can be defined through the following research questions:

1. What are the determinants of the adoption - and the non-adoption - of the blockchain in the enterprises?
2. To what extent does the adoption of blockchain impacts the ecosystems of the company, in particular its relations with customers, suppliers and the reconfiguration of the underlying processes?
3. What impact does the adoption of the blockchain hold within a firm, be it on its organizational structure, its business model, its IT architecture and information system?

These are preliminary main research questions that were defined based on the gaps and stakes identified in the literature review, taking account of the positioning in the ecosystem. These problem statements are raised with a particular focus on issues related to quality, security and governance of data, business processes and the information system (IS) of the organization. The research work will particularly focus on smart contracts and its use as a support of the customer-supplier relationship in an IS supported by a blockchain system.

Several empirical studies will be carried out during this thesis project to determine and measure the change at every organization's level before and after the implementation of this technology in order to collect qualitative data that will be rigorously analyzed. These analyzes and explanations will be based on appropriate theoretical frameworks, such as technology acceptance models, digital maturity models, misfits models or models of organizations transformation. Indeed, an experimental context will enable us to understand the fit between the system and its technological needs.

For this purpose, we adopt a qualitative research approach based on semi-directed interviews. Guided by the research goals and relying on the existing literature, we elaborated a questionnaire starting by the main open question: Could you tell me the story of your project? The main purpose behind starting by asking this open question is to give to the interviewee the freedom and space to answer and thus provide us much details and accurate information about the project implementation. Moreover, blockchain technology is very promising but still faces many challenges. It is for this reason that the method of case studies will also be used in this thesis. It will indeed enable us to breakdown the complex inconsistencies linked to this technology and further understand its intellectual and industrial aspects.

In order to justify and report our research results, we focus on a justification approach which is properly explained in the figure bellow [22]. In fact, we intend to use an empirical research cycle rather than a design cycle in order to solve the mentioned issues (Fig. 1).

According to [22], it is important de address these three questions in order to well justify our research steps;

- "Why would anyone use your design? There are many other designs,
- Why would anyone believe your answers? Opinions are cheap,
- Your report must have a logical structure"

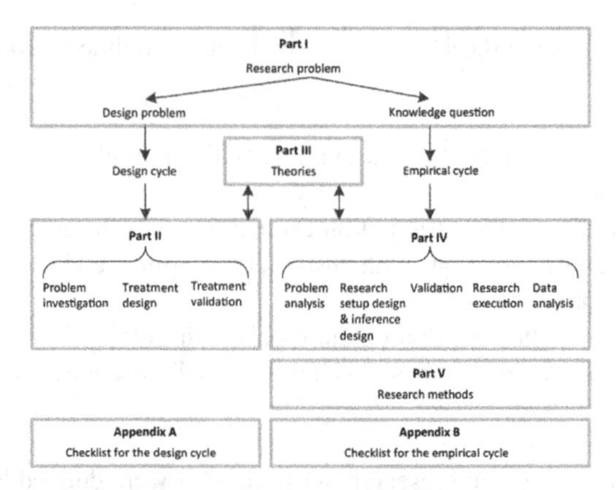

Fig. 1. Road map of the design science methodology [22]

In our case, we will focus on the second point, by trying to define three main knowledge oriented levels: The knowledge that will be produced by the project, the involved stakeholders and their goals, and the design that would solve their problem.

4 Results, Impacts and Benefit of the Research

The major results that will be obtained by achieving the objectives of this research are: The evaluation of the impact of using blockchain in SCM projects, the definition of the determinants of the adoption or non-adoption of the blockchain. Apart from the ability of providing a huge knowledge about the technical aspects of blockchain features (Smart contracts, consensus protocols, platforms, programming languages…) and of giving some choice criteria related to the blockchain platforms, this research proposal aim at also to determine the misfits that could occur during or after the implementation of blockchain project in SCM area and try to give some practical solution to overcome these misfits. The resiliency (the ability of having an automated solution- blockchain-enabled smart contracts - that is always upgraded to deal with new behaviors make them very powerful and resilient to any contextual change that may arise during a specific project phase) of blockchain technology in SCM could also be a major result of this research. Even if we never did mention it before during the proposal, we can recognize some first and preliminary findings that refer to resiliency and that would be validated in future work. Furthermore, scalability will be improved as well. Storage and time capacity is difficult to scale in situations where demand fluctuates especially in SCM. Moreover, the understanding of the real impact of blockchain technology by organizations stakeholders will allow multiple blockchain projects to be deployed when trust is still needed in that domain. All these challenges are more or less already present in our current research and should be proven with more qualitative studies.

Overall, this thesis will contribute to a new understanding of the digital transformation of companies in general and of the supply chain processes in particular, in the light of the emergence and adoption of the blockchain. More precisely, it goes all first to help identifying the factors likely to lead a business to adopt -or reject - the blockchain, especially from the point of view of the chain's quality of logistics and security. This potential result is of a great managerial utility for information systems officers and decision-makers in companies. Another important contribution is an analytical mapping of the potential impacts of blockchain on business processes and relationships with partners in the company's supply-chain. This mapping will contribute to a better understanding of the impact of blockchain and can constitute for CIOs the premises of a plan to the introduction of blockchain and its integration with the company's IS.

From a more academic point of view, the contributions of this research will take a conceptual form, descriptive and explanatory models of the phenomena relating to the use of blockchain technology in the company's IS (Misfit Theory). This research thus fits into the general issue of the digital transformation of industry and the emergence of the industry 4.0, with a focus on blockchain technology and "smart contracts" and its role in supply chains.

Appendix

In the table below we find, the mains ongoing and next projects that will lead to the proper conduct of this research project.

Research project	Details
Published research paper	A systematic literature review of Blockchain-enabled smart contracts: platforms, languages, consensus, applications and choice criteria Samya Dhaiouir, Saïd Assar https://www.springerprofessional.de/en/a-systematic-literature-review-of-blockchain-enabled-smart-contr/18116594
Ongoing research paper	• Papers: 1. Blockchain technology and Misfit Theory Samya Dhaiouir, Saïd Assar 2. Blockchain-enabled smart contracts: an organizational evaluation Samya Dhaiouir, Saïd Assar • Field study: Preliminary data collection in France
Future international projects	• International field study for data collection (Country and University to be defined) From September 2021

References

1. Alharby, M., van Moorsel, A.: Blockchain-based smart contracts: a systematic mapping study. In: Computer Science & Information Technology (CS & IT), pp. 125–140 (2017). https://doi.org/10.5121/csit.2017.71011

2. Bhalerao, S., et al.: Supply chain management using blockchain. In: 2019 International Conference on Intelligent Sustainable Systems (ICISS), pp. 456–459 (2019). https://doi.org/10.1109/ISS1.2019.8908031
3. Casino, F., et al.: A systematic literature review of blockchain-based applications: current status, classification and open issues. Telemat. Inform. **36**, 55–81 (2019). https://doi.org/10.1016/j.tele.2018.11.006
4. Chang, S.E., Chen, Y.: When blockchain meets supply chain: a systematic literature review on current development and potential applications. IEEE Access **8**, 62478–62494 (2020). https://doi.org/10.1109/ACCESS.2020.2983601
5. Chen, S., et al.: A blockchain-based supply chain quality management framework. In: 2017 IEEE 14th International Conference on e-Business Engineering (ICEBE), pp. 172–176 (2017). https://doi.org/10.1109/ICEBE.2017.34
6. Chen, Y., Bellavitis, C.: Blockchain disruption and decentralized finance: the rise of decentralized business models. J. Bus. Ventur. Insights **13**, e00151 (2020). https://doi.org/10.1016/j.jbvi.2019.e00151
7. Clack, C.D., et al.: Smart contract templates: foundations, design landscape and research directions. arXiv:1608.00771 [cs] (2017)
8. Dhaiouir, S., Assar, S.: A systematic literature review of blockchain-enabled smart contracts: platforms, languages, consensus, applications and choice criteria. In: Dalpiaz, F., Zdravkovic, J., Loucopoulos, P. (eds.) RCIS 2020. LNBIP, vol. 385, pp. 249–266. Springer, Cham (2020). https://doi.org/10.1007/978-3-030-50316-1_15
9. Fosso Wamba, S., et al.: Dynamics between blockchain adoption determinants and supply chain performance: an empirical investigation. Int. J. Prod. Econ. **229**, 107791 (2020). https://doi.org/10.1016/j.ijpe.2020.107791
10. Koirala, R.C., et al.: Supply chain using smart contract: a blockchain enabled model with traceability and ownership management. In: 2019 9th International Conference on Cloud Computing, Data Science Engineering (Confluence), pp. 538–544 (2019). https://doi.org/10.1109/CONFLUENCE.2019.8776900
11. Leka, E., et al.: Systematic literature review of blockchain applications: smart contracts. In: 2019 International Conference on Information Technologies (InfoTech), pp. 1–3 (2019). https://doi.org/10.1109/InfoTech.2019.8860872
12. Lisa, L., Mendy-Bilek, G.: Analyzing how blockchain responds to traceability for sustainable supply chain: an empirical study. HAL (2020)
13. Macrinici, D., et al.: Smart contract applications within blockchain technology: a systematic mapping study. Telemat. Inform. **35**(8), 2337–2354 (2018). https://doi.org/10.1016/j.tele.2018.10.004
14. Morkunas, V.J., et al.: How blockchain technologies impact your business model. Bus. Horiz. **62**(3), 295–306 (2019). https://doi.org/10.1016/j.bushor.2019.01.009
15. Paliwal, V., et al.: Blockchain technology for sustainable supply chain management: a systematic literature review and a classification framework. Sustainability **12**(18), 7638 (2020). https://doi.org/10.3390/su12187638
16. Parizi, R.M., et al.: Smart contract programming languages on blockchains: an empirical evaluation of usability and security. In: Chen, S., et al. (eds.) Blockchain – ICBC 2018, pp. 75–91. Springer, Cham (2018). https://doi.org/10.1007/978-3-319-94478-4_6
17. Queiroz, M.M., Fosso Wamba, S.: Blockchain adoption challenges in supply chain: an empirical investigation of the main drivers in India and the USA. Int. J. Inf. Manag. **46**, 70–82 (2019). https://doi.org/10.1016/j.ijinfomgt.2018.11.021
18. Strong, D.M., Volkoff, O.: Understanding organization—enterprise system fit: a path to theorizing the information technology artifact. MIS Quart. **34**(4), 731–756 (2010). https://doi.org/10.2307/25750703

19. Walshe, K.: Understanding what works—and why—in quality improvement: the need for theory-driven evaluation. Int. J. Qual. Health Care **19**(2), 57–59 (2007). https://doi.org/10.1093/intqhc/mzm004
20. Wan, P.K., et al.: Blockchain-enabled information sharing within a supply chain: a systematic literature review. IEEE Access **8**, 49645–49656 (2020). https://doi.org/10.1109/ACCESS.2020.2980142
21. Wang, S., et al.: An overview of smart contract: architecture, applications, and future trends. In: 2018 IEEE Intelligent Vehicles Symposium (IV), pp. 108–113 (2018). https://doi.org/10.1109/IVS.2018.8500488
22. Wieringa, R.J.: Design Science Methodology for Information Systems and Software Engineering. Springer, Heidelberg (2014). https://doi.org/10.1007/978-3-662-43839-8
23. Wilkins, S., et al.: The role of theory in the business/management PhD: how students may use theory to make an original contribution to knowledge. Int. J. Manag. Educ. **17**(3), 100316 (2019). https://doi.org/10.1016/j.ijme.2019.100316
24. Yousuf, S., Svetinovic, D.: Blockchain technology in supply chain management: preliminary study. In: 2019 Sixth International Conference on Internet of Things: Systems, Management and Security (IOTSMS), pp. 537–538 (2019). https://doi.org/10.1109/IOTSMS48152.2019.8939222

Tutorials and Research Projects

Supporting the Information Search and Discovery Process with the Bash-Shell

Andreas Schmidt[1,2(✉)]

[1] Karlsuhe Institute of Technology, Karlsruhe, Germany
andreas.schmidt@kit.edu
[2] University of Applied Sciences, Karlsruhe, Germany

Abstract. The bash shell contains a wealth of useful programs for examining, filtering, transforming and also analyzing data. In conjunction with the underlying filter and pipe architecture, powerful data transformations can be performed interactively and iteratively within a very short time, which can for example support the knowledge discovery process with further dedicated tools like mathematica, R, etc. In the tutorial presented here, the most useful command-line tools from the GNU coreutils and their interaction will be introduced on the basis of a continuous scenario and clarified by means of two in-depth practical exercises in which the participants have to convict a murderer using a series of available police documents - exciting!

Keywords: Filter and pipes · Shell programming · Data transformation

1 Introduction

The basis for all our data discovery processes is the actual data itself. Once we have identified valuable data and loaded it into an appropriate tool, like a relational database, the statistic program R, mathematica, or some other specialized tools to perform our analysis, the discovery process can start. However, until the data is in the system of choice, a number of tasks have to be completed:

1. The data must be considered relevant to our mission.
2. Often the entire data set is not relevant, but only a part of it that needs to be extracted.
3. The data format must be adapted accordingly before it can be imported into our analysis tool.
4. Other possible tasks include the automatic extraction of data from the word wide web, combining different data sources or enriching the data.

Some of these tasks can also be performed more or less comfortably with the dedicated analysis tool, but the question is whether there is no better way to perform these preparatory tasks. If, for example, the relevance of a data set needs to be checked for usefulness, this is ideally done before importing the (potentially huge) data set into our analytics tool. During this analysis, non-relevant data can be filtered out and a suitable transformation for the import can be carried out, so that the import and subsequent processing can take place on a already appropriately adapted data set.

S. Cherfi et al. (Eds.): RCIS 2021, LNBIP 415, pp. 691–693, 2021.
https://doi.org/10.1007/978-3-030-75018-3

The aim of this tutorial is to present the most useful tools from the GNU coreutils [1] like cat, grep, tr, sed, awk, comm, join, split, etc., and give an introduction on how they can be used together. So, for example, a wide number of queries which typically will be formulated with SQL, can also be performed using the tools mentioned before, as it will be shown in the tutorial. Even more interesting than the single components is the toolbox's underlying concept of the filter and pipe architecture. More complex programs are built iteratively from the available single components (so called filters) and allow an intuitive, iterative approach to prototype development. Another interesting point is that they are typically stream based and so, huge amounts of data can be processed, without running out of main-memory.

The tutorial will also include hands-on parts, in which the participants do a number of practical data-analysis and transformation tasks.

2 Learning Objectives

After completing the tutorial, the participants will be able to successfully create their own filter pipes for various tasks. They have internalized the idea of composing complex programs from small well defined components allows rapid prototyping, incremental iterations and easy experimentation.

3 Didactic Concept

We believe that a successful tutorial should not only teach theoretical knowledge, but also give the participants the opportunity to apply what they have learned in practice. For this reason, we have adapted the exciting command line oriented learning game "The Command Line Murders" [2] by Noah Veltman for the needs of the tutorial and send the participants on a murder hunt, where they have to analyze a large amount of police records with the previously learned tools in order to unmask the murderer.

4 Target Audience

Level: Intermediate - Participants should be familiar (or at least interested) using a shell like bash, csh, DOS-shell. A basic knowledge of Regular Expressions is helpful, but not necessarily required.

5 Materials to Be Distributed to the Attendees [3]

- Slideset
- Command refcard
- Practical exercises

References

1. GNU Core Utilities. https://en.wikipedia.org/wiki/GNU_Core_Utilities. Accessed 25 Mar 2021
2. Noah Veltman, N.: The Command Line Murders. https://github.com/veltman/clm\ystery#the-command-line-murders. Accessed 25 Mar 2021
3. Schmidt, A.: RCIS-2021 Tutorial Page. https://www.smiffy.de/RCIS-2021. Accessed 25 Mar 2021

Fractal Enterprise Model (FEM) and Its Usage for Facilitating Radical Change in Business Models

Ilia Bider[1,2(✉)] and Erik Perjons[1]

[1] DSV - Stockholm University, Stockholm, Sweden
{Ilia, perjons}@dsv. su. se
[2] ICS -University of Tartu, Tartu, Estonia

1 Tutorial Abstract

The situation caused by the COVID-19 pandemic has clearly demonstrated that the business environment of today is volatile and highly dynamic. A modern enterprise should be prepared to totally review its Business Model (BM) in order to survive and prosper in such a dynamic world. The goal of this tutorial is twofold. Firstly, it introduces a new type of enterprise modeling technique called Fractal Enterprise Model (FEM) [1]. Secondly, it illustrates how FEM can be used for radical Business Model Innovation (BMI), e.g. for designing a completely new BM [2, 3]. FEM expresses the relationships between the enterprise assets and its business processes. The innovation consists of finding a way of reconfiguring enterprise assets to produce new value for a new or the same group of customers. The idea corresponds to the Boyd's concept of *destruction* and *creation* [4].

As an example, Fig. 1 represents a radical BMI case related to the current pandemic. The example was presented in the interview with Nassim Taleb [5] in the following way: "A friend of mine owns a gym in California, and you see the heaviest hurt business is a gym okay. So instead of sitting down and praying and getting money from the government and crying, he started the business of equipping people with home trips and he made a fortune. So, you call him up if you want a home gym; he sets it up, sends you the material, the one, you know, uses zoom to train you".

The expected audience of the tutorial is academics and practitioners who are interested in practical usage of Enterprise Modelling and/or in organizational change in general, and radical change in Business Models (BMs) in particular. The tutorial is practically oriented, it requires acquaintance with how an enterprise or any other human organization functions, either from a theoretical or from the practical perspective (basic level is enough). General understanding of modeling (of any kind), especially modeling of business, or human-related activities is desirable.

The tutorial is planned as a workshop, where presentation is combined with work in small teams and general discussion. During the presentation, the basic notions of FEM are introduced using FEM toolkit [6], which the participants will be asked to download and install. Beside the example in Fig. 1, other examples will be used, in particular a case of transforming a manufacturer into software provider [7]. After the presentation,

S. Cherfi et al. (Eds.): RCIS 2021, LNBIP 415, pp. 694–696, 2021.
https://doi.org/10.1007/978-3-030-75018-3

the participants are split in small teams and go to break rooms in Zoom to complete an exercise based on a textual description of a business situation and a FEM of the current state of the business. They will be asked to invent a new business model based on transforming the existing FEM. After the exercise, the participants will discuss their findings in a common room.

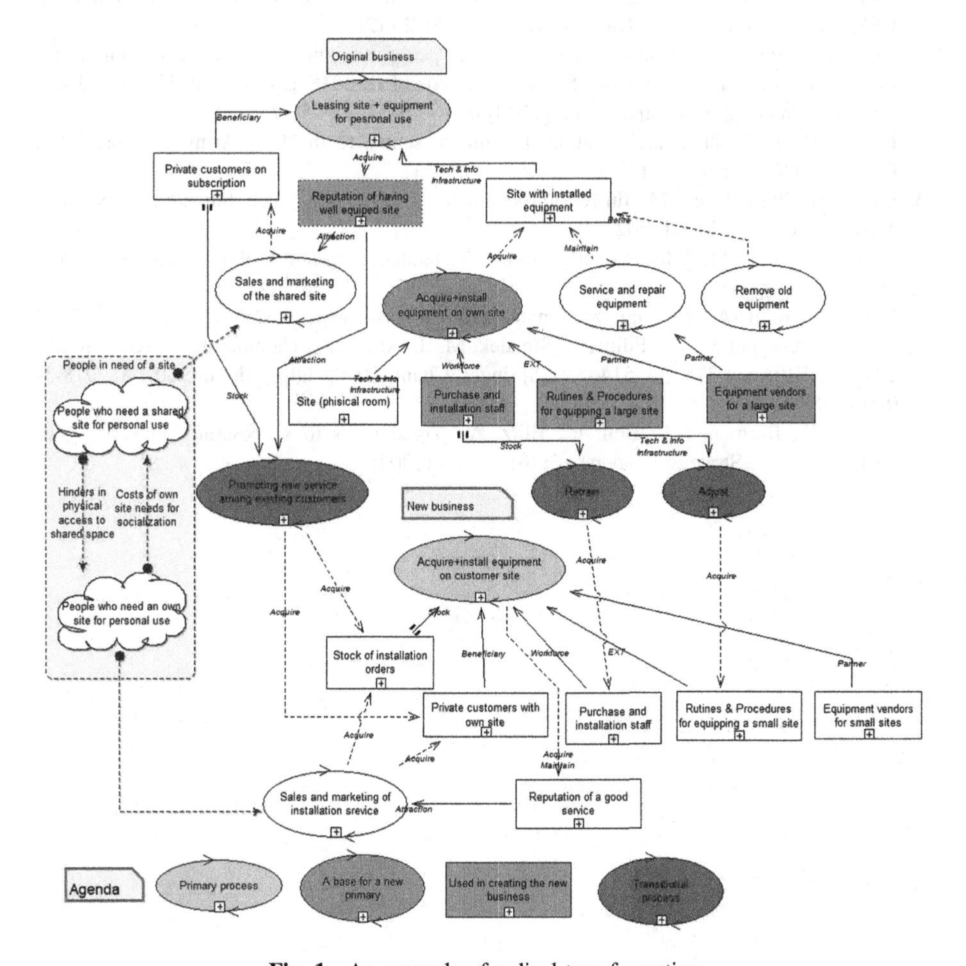

Fig. 1. An example of radical transformation

The expected outcome from the tutorial is as follows. The participants become acquainted with a new type of enterprise modeling, and a tool that supports creating models. They will be introduced to the concept of Industry level Business Model Innovation [8] that requires a radical change in what an enterprise does. They will learn how FEM can assist in generating hypothesis, assessing and planning radical change. We expect that the participants, after the tutorial, will be able to innovate the current BM of the organization for which they work.

References

1. Bider, I., Perjons, E., Elias, M., Johannesson, P.: A fractal enterprise model and its application for business development. Softw. Syst. Model. **16**(3), 663–689 (2016). https://doi.org/10.1007/s10270-016-0554-9
2. Bider, I., Perjons, E.: Using a fractal enterprise model for business model innovation. In: BPMDS 2017 RADAR, CEUR, vol. 1859, pp. 20–29 (2017)
3. Bider, I., Perjons, E.: Defining transformational patterns for business model innovation. In: Zdravkovic, J., Grabis, J., Nurcan, S., Stirna, J., (eds.) BIR 2018. LNBIP, vol. 330, pp. 81–95. Springer, Cham (2018). https://doi.org/10.1007/978-3-319-99951-7_6
4. Boyd, J.R.: Destruction and creation. Lecture presented to the U.S. Army Command and General Staff College (1976)
5. EnlightED 2020: Teresa Martín-Retorcillo and Nassim Nicholas Taleb. https://youtu.be/OuIi-Y3Pce4. Accessed March 2021
6. fractalmodel.org: FEM toolkit. https://www.fractalmodel.org/fem-toolkit/. Accessed March 2021
7. Bider, I., Lodhi, A.: Moving from manufacturing to software business: a business model transformation pattern. In: Filipe, J., Śmiałek, M., Brodsky, A., Hammoudi, S., (eds.) ICEIS 2019. LNBIP, vol. 378, pp. 514–530. Springer, Cham (2020). https://doi.org/10.1007/978-3-030-40783-4_25
8. Giesen, E., Berman, S.J., Bell, R., Blitz, A.: Three ways to successfully innovate your business model. Strategy Leadersh. **35**(6), 27–33 (2007)

Introduction to the Theory and Practice of Argument Analysis

Martín Pereira-Fariña[1(✉)] and Cesar Gonzalez-Perez[2]

[1] Department of Philosophy and Anthropology, Universidade de Santiago de Compostela, Pz. de Mazarelos s/n, 15782 Santiago de Compostela, Spain
martin.pereira@usc.es

[2] Institute of Heritage Sciences (Incipit) Spanish National Research Council (CSIC), Avda. de Vigo, s/n, 15705 Santiago de Compostela, Spain
cesar.gonzalez-perez@incipit.csic.es

Abstract. Argumentation is an essential part of society, both in everyday situations and in academic environments. People argue for defending their standpoints or for criticising viewpoints that they do not share. For these reasons, understanding how arguments are assembled, interpreted and, eventually, evaluated plays a major impact in our lives. However, analysing and understanding arguments is a challenging task, which requires processes of identifying and reconstructing reasoning expressed in natural language.

This tutorial aims to introduce attendees to the roots of the computationally supported analysis of arguments, a field that has been growing quickly over the past few years. It provides the fundamentals of what an argument is, how to identify them in natural language discourse and how they can be analysed by means the *IAT/ML* theory and the *LogosLink* software tool. The goal is not to simply identify what people think about a particular topic but to discover why they hold their views.

Keywords: Argumentation theory · Computational models of arguments · Discourse analysis · Argument analysis · Natural language

1 Introduction

Argument and debate constitute the cornerstones of civilised society and intellectual life, as it is an essential part of both activities. However, it is also one of the most challenging aspects of the computational analysis of discourse. Questions such as *What is your main standpoint? What are the reasons that support your claim? Are you disagreeing with my standpoint?* are at the core of argument analysis, and become crucial when we try to unpack the logical and argumentative structure of a text.

In this tutorial we will address the fundamentals of argumentation theory, introducing basic concepts in *IAT/ML* such as Speech Act theory, argumentative vs. non-argumentative text, argumentative discourse units, premise vs. conclusion, or claim vs. evidence. We will also present *LogosLink*, a software tool that implements some of these ideas and focuses on computational argumentation analysis. Through various group exercises, we will illustrate how real discourse can be analysed in this way.

S. Cherfi et al. (Eds.): RCIS 2021, LNBIP 415, pp. 697–698, 2021.
https://doi.org/10.1007/978-3-030-75018-3

2 Contents

This tutorial addresses the following learning objectives:

1. Fundamentals of argumentation theory and argument analysis, applying *IAT/ML* theoretical framework.
2. Introduction to *LogosLink* and argument analysis applying it.
3. Group exercises analysis different textual fragments applying *IAT/ML* by means of *LogosLink*.

3 Added Value of the Tutorial

Researchers and practitioners from different fields will benefit from this tutorial, ranging from information systems to teaching and education or design science. The tutorial is highly interdisciplinary, and it can be attractive for an audience from multiple different fields.

Major benefits for attendees include:

- Enhancing capabilities and skills for unpacking the deep structure of argumentative discourses and, as a consequence, attaining a better understanding.
- Learning a methodology for discourse analysis based on principles that are reproducible and more objective than using a qualitative and individual analysis.
- Acquiring advanced skills for extracting pragmatic and semantic knowledge from natural language, going further than a pure linguistic analysis.
- Enhancing personal skills for producing a more solid and cogent discourse.

There are additional benefits depending on the attendees' backgrounds:

- For those in information systems or software engineering: A procedure for identifying system requirements from natural language texts based on a detailed analysis of what is said and why it is said.
- For those in design science: Exploring and assessing the main reasons that are supporting why an artefact is as it is, or prescribing why an artefact should have certain properties.
- For those in conceptual modelling and ontologies: Assessing the relevance of the concepts in the model or candidate concepts based on discursive evidence.
- For those in teaching and education: A framework for evaluating students' understanding and reasoning capabilities about any topic; also, key strategies for building best arguments.
- For those in business process management: A tool for stakeholder opinion analysis based on reasons, i.e., why they argue in favour or against a specific idea.

Digital (R)evolution in Belgian Federal Government: An Open Governance Ecosystem for Big Data, Artificial Intelligence, and Blockchain (DIGI4FED)

Evrim Tan(✉) and Joep Crompvoets

KU Leuven Public Governance Institute, Leuven, Belgium
{evrim.tan, joep.crompvoets}@kuleuven.be

1 Summary of the Project

1.1 Objectives

Three contextual factors define the context by which DIGI4FED is influenced. The first factor is the growing attention for the potential impact of big data (BD), artificial intelligence (AI) and blockchain technology (BCT) on traditional government information processes. The second factor is the growing expectation of society from public administrations, to adopt new technological means to advance efficient and effective governance and public service delivery whilst ensuring the core democratic and moral values are not lost out of sight. The third factor concerns the Belgian federal administration itself. Previous research projects funded by Belgian federal government such as "FLEXPUB" and "PSI-CO" have demonstrated that the federal level has certain requirements and faces challenges concerning trust and equity embedded in digital tools, transparency of data and data use, the human dimension of digital judgments, technical difficulties, human and cultural factors, a gap between ambition and reality, and an imbalance between in- and outsourcing.

The main objective of DIGI4FED is to understand 'how (big) data can be used in the Belgian federal administration system to enable better public provision in the social security and taxation areas through new technologies such as AI and blockchain?'.

This main objective will be addressed by following subquestions:

- RQ1: How do technical, moral, legal and organisational conditions within the federal ecosystem influence current and future strategic needs of (big) data for the Belgian federal government?
- RQ2: What is the impact of (big) data, through the use of AI and BCT on the internal administrative decision- making processes, the role and independence of the executive decision-makers in federal public organisations?
- RQ3: What is the impact of (big) data, through the use of AI and BCT, on the external transparency of federal decision-making processes and the stakeholders and citizens' trust to the federal administrative system?

S. Cherfi et al. (Eds.): RCIS 2021, LNBIP 415, pp. 699–701, 2021.
https://doi.org/10.1007/978-3-030-75018-3

- RQ4: What technical and organisational modalities are required for the exploitation of (big) data within the federal administrative system to improve the effectiveness of public services without undermining accountability, moral values (e.g. ethics and equity to the public) and internal human competencies?

1.2 Expected Tangible Results

DIGI4FED aims to develop a proof of concept of a governance design in two specific federal areas: social security infringements and tax fraud. These policy areas concern two central policy domains of the federal administration, and they are relevant both for the executive and the judicial branches of the federal level, and for other stakeholders such as social security agencies, social partners and judiciary bodies.

The outcomes of this project will offer an improved insight in how the Belgian federal administration can adopt the new technologies such as BD, AI and BCT to effectively govern its internal and external administrative processes, the technical, judicial and ethical rules that should frame the administrative policies, and a basis for the establishment of policy guidelines for collection and usage of the big data in the federal government.

2 Summary of Current Project Results

DIGI4FED has started in June 2020, and most of the research is still in progress. A current research output of the project is a systematic decision-making heuristic to design of an open government data (OGD) governance model. This model will be used to develop the governance models in the selected policy domains to be tested by a focus group of stakeholders. The purpose of the tool is to systematically identify and

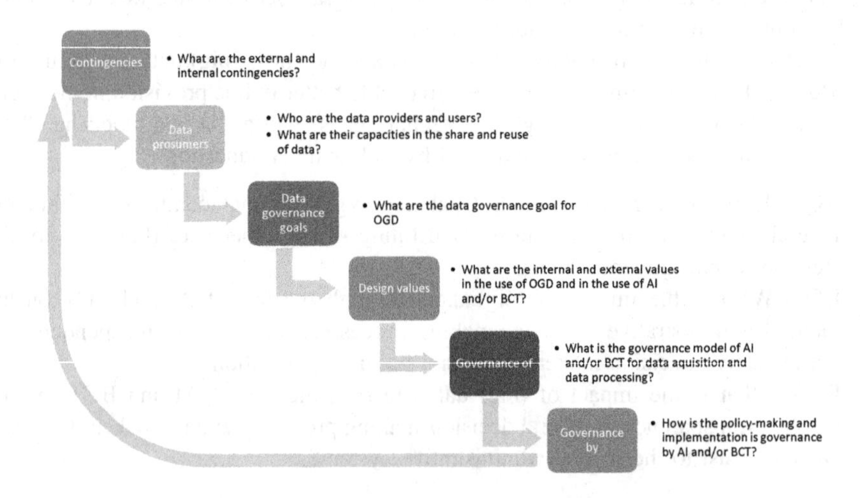

Fig. 1. The 6-step model in the OGD governance

analyze the interrelationships among multiple change factors on governance design, and to project the available design options based on the managerial, organizational, legal, technological, moral, and institutional variances in the OGD ecosystem (Fig. 1).

Integrating Public Displays with Other Participation Methods(UbiPart Project)

Antoine Clarinval(✉)

Namur Digital Institute, University of Namur, Namur, Belgium
antoine.clarinval@unamur.be

1 Research Objective

The emerging participative orientation of smart cities [4] has lead to the implementation of various participation methods to include citizens in decision-making [6]. They range from traditional such as workshops to innovative approaches supported by technology such as online platforms that allow citizens to submit ideas and vote for them with the expectation that the most popular ones will be implemented by the government. Recently, public displays (i.e. interfaces deployed in the public space to be accessible by any passerby [7]) have been used as participation method [2]. These devices possess qualities that are desirable in the context of citizen participation such as the ability to be interacted with by several citizens at a time, therefore fostering discussion [1], and their deployment in the urban space, thus being able to contextualize content that concerns its location [7]. Furthermore, public displays are exempt from a limitation faced by the other participation methods. With these, citizens have to make a step forward to have the opportunity to participate (e.g. login to an online platform, attend a scheduled meeting), implying that it is challenging to attract citizens who are not already engaged in participation. On the contrary, citizens encounter public displays without explicitly looking for them, and can thus be offered a direct opportunity to participate.

However, while comparing the advantages of participation methods is interesting, the reality is that citizen participation is implemented by several methods that need to be articulated together thoughtfully. While too many concurrent methods might overburden citizens and discourage them from participating altogether, combining methods can prove valuable. Such complementarity could consist in using the results of one method to fuel another (e.g. a civic hackathon fueled by citizens' input from an online platform and social media [5]), or in alleviating the limitations of one method with another (e.g. complete a consultation on social media with a mail consultation to reach citizens who are not on social media). Therefore, when proposing a new participation method, it is essential to study how it can integrate efficiently with the others. In other terms, what are the synergies between this method and the others already put in place that can add value? This question remains unstudied for public displays [2], and is the focus of the UbiPart Project.

S. Cherfi et al. (Eds.): RCIS 2021, LNBIP 415, pp. 702–704, 2021.
https://doi.org/10.1007/978-3-030-75018-3

2 Project Steps and Expected Outputs

The first step of the Ubipart project would be to study the literature to identify potential complementarities with public displays. For example, a study found that public displays can attract much more citizens than online platforms but are less suited to collect rich data [3], thus suggesting interesting complementarities with online platforms. This first step leads to the identification of candidate methods to be combined with public displays. Then, for each method, a public display prototype would be developed to have a testable implementation of the pair. To be complementary to an online platform, a public display, performing well at conveying information to a large audience and collecting simple data, could show a visual overview of the ideas on a public display and allow voting. The display would also serve as advertisement for the participation platform and redirect citizens interested to contribute a richer feedback, since public displays are not suited to collect detailed data. Finally, following the practices of research on public displays, the prototype would be evaluated through a field study [2]. This process, exemplified with the online participation method, can be repeated for each method identified early in the project.

The Ubipart project is still at an elaboration stage, this paper being the first attempt to formalize it. The project requires expertise in citizen participation, development, and user studies. In order to ensure that several prototypes can be developed in an iterative way, the project should employ two researchers over two years. Regarding its output, the Ubipart project aims at a twofold contribution. First, a contribution for research lies in the synergies identified on which other researchers can build. Second, the developed and tested public displays can be reused by governments and thus constitute contributions for practice.

References

1. Brignull, H., Rogers, Y.: Enticing people to interact with large public displays in public spaces. In: Proceedings of the 9th IFIP TC13 International Conference on Human-Computer Interaction, vol. 3, pp. 17–24 (2003)
2. Clarinval, A., Simonofski, A., Vanderose, B., Dumas, B.: Public displays and citizen participation: a systematic literature review and research agenda. Transforming Government: People, Process and Policy, ahead-of-print (ahead-of-print) (2020)
3. Goncalves, J., Hosio, S., Liu, Y., Kostakos, V.: Eliciting situated feedback: a comparison of paper, web forms and public displays. Displays **35**(1), 27–37 (2014)
4. Hollands, R.G.: Will the real smart city please stand up? Intelligent, progressive or entrepreneurial? City **12**(3), 303–320 (2008)
5. Simonofski, A., Amaral de Sousa, V., Clarinval, A., Vanderose, B.: Participation in Hackathons: a multi-methods view on motivators, demotivators and citizen participation. In: Dalpiaz, F., Zdravkovic, J., Loucopoulos, P. (eds.) RCIS 2020. LNBIP, vol. 385, pp. 229–246. Springer, Cham (2020). https://doi.org/10.1007/978-3-030-50316-1_14

6. Simonofski, A., Snoeck, M., Vanderose, B.: Co-creating e-government services: an empirical analysis of participation methods in Belgium. In: Rodriguez Bolivar, M.P. (ed.) Setting Foundations for the Creation of Public Value in Smart Cities. PAIT, vol. 35, pp. 225–245. Springer, Cham (2019). https://doi.org/10.1007/978-3-319-98953-2_9
7. Vande Moere, A., Hill, D.: Designing for the situated and public visualization of urban data. j. Urban Technol. **19**(2), 25–46 (2012)

AM3BIT: Multi-stakeholder Multi-modelling Multi-representation Development of IS

Monique Snoeck[1(✉)] and Jean Vanderdonckt[2]

[1] KU Leuven, Leuven, Belgium
monique.snoeck@kuleuven.be
[2] UCLouvain, Ottignies-Louvain-La-Neuve, Belgium
jean.vanderdonckt@uclouvain.be

1 Summary of the Project

1.1 Objectives

Architecting software requires considering multiple concerns simultaneously, and designing software using multiple views that need to be consistent and coherent. The specific expertise required for different aspects of information systems development has resulted in **isolated silos of expertise and knowledge**. Application development, business process management and user interface design have evolved in separate communities, each using their own modelling languages, but lacking integration with other disciplines. For example, task models used by UI designers are similar in nature to -yet not integrated with- Process Models used by business analysts. For successful software development, it thus is crucial to move **to an *integrative* multi-modelling approach**, covering a broad range of taxonomic domains while addressing needs for integration and transformations [1]. To foster communication with ***all*** relevant stakeholders, including non-developer profiles, additional more adequate ***representations*** tailored to the stakeholders' needs are required as well. The general Research Objective of this project is therefore developing an integrative multi-view MDE approach through the use of multiple integrated models (=multi-modelling), capable of addressing (at least) Business Process Modelling, Domain Modelling, Application development and UI Design. Covering these aspects in one integrated environment (even with a limited set of models) would be a true innovation. To cater for each stakeholder's capabilities and needs, multiple representations can be used for a single type of model (=multi-representation). The specific research objectives of the project are:

- RO1: Survey today's landscape of modelling languages in terms of frequency of use, by which stakeholders, along with their associated meta-models, the internal quality of these meta-models, and currently defined correspondences and consistency rules. Available surveys provide partial but incomplete pictures.
- RO2: The MMQEF [1] provides a framework to assess the quality of a set of modelling languages used in combination. For example, MMQEF allows evaluating

S. Cherfi et al. (Eds.): RCIS 2021, LNBIP 415, pp. 705–707, 2021.
https://doi.org/10.1007/978-3-030-75018-3

if a proposed MDE approach based on a combination of modelling languages covers all dimensions in a chosen reference taxonomy, and also offers adequate support for transformations, model integration, etc. MMQEF itself does not suggest a best combination. The goal of this project is to propose a minimal and sufficiently complete sets of IS modelling languages and their meta-models addressing domain modelling, application development, business process modelling and UI design, and to provide for integration and transformations.
- RO3: Define the appropriate representations per user of a model. Although current representations will be taken as a starting point, they typically lack suitable support for all types of stakeholders, thus creating a possible need for new representations as well. The goal is to choose amongst existing representations, possible optimizing them based on quality criteria depending on the stakeholder and the development stage, and -when needed- define additional representations.
- RO4: Develop a demonstrator to demonstrate the validity and usability of the developed integrated set of modelling languages.

1.2 Expected Tangible Results

The different steps of the projects are expected to yield the following results:

- A Targeted Literature (meta-)Survey (TLS) and an inventory of existing meta-models including an assessment of their internal quality, defined correspondences to other meta-models, including consistency or transformation rules.
- The development of a set of linked meta-models, each defining a modelling language that is used by specific stakeholders, and a set of correspondence rules that define how the different meta-model are interrelated.
- One or several concrete modelling language representations targeting specific stakeholder profiles based on stakeholder studies.
- A demonstrator: an integrated multi-model and multi-representation modelling tool

2 Summary of Current Project Results

This project can build on FENIkS, prior PhD research [2] that extended the MERODE modelling tools with a UI design tool based on UsiXML, hereby combining key research results from both teams. The feasibility of integrating MERODE-models with BPMN-models based on the Camunda BP Engine has been investigated and proven through master-thesis research [3].

References

1. Giraldo, F.D., España, S., Giraldo, W.J., Pastor, Ó.: Evaluating the quality of a set of modelling languages used in combination: a method and a tool. Inf. Syst. **77**, 48–70 (2018). https://doi.org/10.1016/j.is.2018.06.002

2. Ruiz, J., Serral, E., Snoeck, M.: Learning UI functional design principles through simulation with feedback. IEEE Trans. Learn. Technol. (2020). https://doi.org/10.1109/TLT.2020.3028596
3. Mohout, I., Leyse, T.: Enriching Business Process Simulation by integration with MERODE Prototype Applications. KU Leuven, (2020)

On the Development of Formative Tests to Improve Teaching Conceptual Business Process Modeling to Novice Higher Education Learners

Stephan Poelmans(✉), Monique Snoeck, and Pavani Vemuri

KU Leuven, Leuven, Belgium
{stephan.poelmans,monique.snoeck,pavani.vemuri}@kuleuven.be

1 Summary of the Project

1.1 Objectives

Modeling techniques and languages to support software development, such as BPMN or UML are essential in the educational fields of information systems, and software engineering [1, 2]. Proficient conceptual modeling often implies coping with versatility in open-ended problems, making it challenging for novice modelers.

Despite the increased attention in the literature, teaching conceptual modeling often still lacks a structured method and lecturers tend to develop their own experience-based approaches [1, 3, 4]. Tool support for syntactical and certain pragmatic errors exist, but do not address semantic errors, nor are embedded in a learning system. In the presented project, we address these gaps for process modelling by developing an evidence-based and systematic teaching approach for BPMN that incorporates an adaptive learning system with formative assessments, using appropriate educational tools.

Adaptive learning trajectories, containing several decision points to redirect students, seem useful to target a student population with varying backgrounds and competences [5]. Formative assessments are a possible information source. They have been proved to be effective in both student engagement and learning performance [6, 7] and can give insight into the learning progress and typical errors of learners. More formative tests can provide automated feedback and redirection, allowing to optimize teacher interventions, making them ideal learning activities for blended or online teaching, as well as teaching to large groups of students.

Based on the reasoning above, the research questions are stated as follows.

1. Does formative assessment generate an impact on students' learning outcomes and understanding in the field of business process modelling?
2. To what extent can formative tests be automated and integrated into a digital adaptive learning path to optimize teachers' intervention for feedback?

S. Cherfi et al. (Eds.): RCIS 2021, LNBIP 415, pp. 708–710, 2021.
https://doi.org/10.1007/978-3-030-75018-3

Providing meaningful formative assessments of students' responses to complex, open-ended problems in process modeling is challenging. The following gaps and ensuing principal research objectives are formulated:

In the literature, error types such as syntactical or semantical errors, and process quality metrics have been presented (e.g. [8]), but are often on a high level of abstraction. They need further scrutiny and refinement to be usable for automated feedback. RO1 thus targets classifying types of common errors sourced from a dataset of hundreds of BPMN models and from process quality metrics. RO2 targets the design of formative tests with (semi-)automated feedback and appropriated contents using the learning framework in [1]. Once developed, the formative tests for business students require validation, to be done in three study programs (RO3). The final RO (4) encompasses the design of a learning path with the incorporation of formative testing in an LMS (e.g. Blackboard) with the goal to optimize teacher interventions.

1.2 Expected Results

The project is intended as a 4-year PhD. The first milestone is a classification of errors in BPMN modelling, taught to students in business-oriented programs. Currently, three datasets containing several hundreds of BPMN models are available.

In a second milestone, the taxonomy is to be used to develop formative tests that can consist of quizzes and more engaging design exercises. Scheduling formative learning activities can be done within at least 3 courses in 2 business faculties. In the final mile-stone, formative testing with corresponding feedback should be automated to a maximum degree and incorporated into an adaptive learning path for BPMN that can be applied in a blended or online teaching approach.

Furthermore, developing an evidence-based, systematic, comprehensive modular teaching approach for BPMN will benefit students by helping the teaching community to identify and bridge gaps between the learning items used and expected learning outcomes. Teachers can adopt modules with different levels of difficulty into their own courses. Lastly, further research is also promising. With the developed taxonomies and tests, we can develop measuring instruments for the mastery on conceptual modeling concepts to be used in industry for training and certification purposes.

References

1. Bogdanova, D., Snoeck, M.: CaMeLOT: an educational framework for conceptual data modelling. Inf. Softw. Technol. **110**, 92–107 (2019)
2. Jung, R., Lehrer, C.: Guidelines for education in business and information systems engineering at tertiary institutions. Bus. Inf. Syst. Eng. **59**(3), 189–203 (2017). https://doi.org/10.1007/s12599-017-0473-5
3. Bogdanova, D., Snoeck, M.: Domain modelling in bloom: deciphering how we teach it. In: Poels, G., Gailly, F., Serral, E., Snoeck, M., (eds.) PoEM. LNBIP, vol. 305, pp. 3–17. Springer, Cham (2017). https://doi.org/10.1007/978-3-319-70241-4_1
4. Bogdanova, D., Snoeck, M.: Learning from errors: error-based exercises in domain modelling pedagogy. In: Buchmann, R.A., Karagiannis, D., Kirikova, M., (eds.) PoEM. LNBIP, vol. 335, pp. 321–334. Springer, Cham (2018). https://doi.org/10.1007/978-3-030-02302-7_20

5. Howard, L., Remenyi, Z., Pap, G.: Adaptive blended learning environments. In: 9th International Conference on Engineering Education, pp. 23–28 (2006)
6. Dalby, D., Swan, M.: Using digital technology to enhance formative assessment in mathematics classrooms. Br. J. Educ. Technol. **36**, 217–235 (2018)
7. Chen, Z., Jiao, J., Hu, K.: Formative assessment as an online instruction inter-vention. Int. J. Distance Educ. Technol. **19**(1), 50–65 (2020)
8. Claes, J., Vanderfeesten, I., Gailly, F., Grefen, P., Poels, G.: The Structured Process Modeling Method (SPMM) what is the best way for me to construct a process model? Decis. Support Syst. **100**, 57–76 (2017)

Chatbot Technologies for Digital Entrepreneurship Education of Adult Learners – CHAT2LEARN

Thomas Fotiadis[1](✉), Evangelia Vanezi[1], Mariana Petrova[2], Vitlena Vasileva[2], and George A. Papadopoulos[1]

[1] Department of Computer Science, University of Cyprus, Nicosia, Cyprus
{fotiadis.f.thomas, evanez01, george}@ucy.ac.cy
[2] School/Institute/Educational Centre, Nikanor Ltd., Sofia, Bulgaria
agency_nikanor@abv.bg
https://ec.europa.eu/programmes/erasmus-plus/projects/eplus-project-details/#project/2020-1-CY01-KA204-065974

1 Summary of the Project

The CHAT2LEARN project focuses on technology-enhanced learning, incorporating chatbot technologies and AI-based tools in adults' education. The project's innovativeness is to implement educational practices that will create unique and tailor-made educational experiences with tools, methodologies, and resources for teaching digital entrepreneurship and raise the awareness via chatbot-based development technologies and AI-based tools [1]. There has been increasing research effort and specialization in providing novel information and results for all the educational community exchanging learning experiences and good practices. The project's target groups include mainly economically active people and entrepreneurs, whose expectations are aimed to be met by implementing suitable educational tools, methodologies, and resources, to improve their knowledge. The project aims to promote best educational practices through the design of open-source and user-friendly software, applying principles of open pedagogy approaches and learner-centered models based on the technology. This will equip and encourage adult educators and training professionals to improve their awareness on chatbot and AI technologies and reveal opportunities for diversification of approaches that will support their training and teaching activities on entrepreneurship-related topics to involve their learners in educational procedures.

1.1 Objectives

The objectives of the project are to: (i) create opportunities for adult educators, trainers, entrepreneurs, and adult learners, in general to combine e-learning education and open pedagogy frameworks based on Technology Enhanced Learning, and (ii) enrich the self-learning opportunities of adult learners in the field of digital entrepreneurship by developing an inter-disciplinary training program based on chatbot technology. Moreover, the CHAT2LEARN project aims to improve the competencies of non-

S. Cherfi et al. (Eds.): RCIS 2021, LNBIP 415, pp. 711–712, 2021.
https://doi.org/10.1007/978-3-030-75018-3

formal and informal adult educators and training professionals by collecting the best practices and tools on technology-enhanced learning and creating a resource library (online teaching materials, online tests, quizzes, video lessons, animated videos, etc.). Furthermore, a methodology will be developed to incorporate chatbot technologies into the educational process and a handbook on creating and using the chatbot educational content for teaching entrepreneurship [1, 2].

1.2 Expected Tangible Results

CHAT2LEARN is an ongoing project just launched, that will follow a sequence of actions to achieve the objectives set and to have an expected impact. Beginning with gathering the best educational practices and tools on technology-enhanced learning, creating a resource library and developing a methodological procedure on incorporating the current technologies into the educational process are some of the project outcomes.

The developed chatbot learning environment in digital entrepreneurship, the resource library, the methodology, and handbook will give the target audience hands-on guidance and advice on how to apply technology-enhanced learning and chatbot technologies into the educational process. The developed training program based on chatbot technology with five lessons in digital entrepreneurship will benefit adult learners who want to improve their knowledge and competencies on how to develop their digital entrepreneurship endeavors. Besides, the program will support educators in their training activities on entrepreneurship-related topics. It will help them enrich the scope of AI-based tools they can use in their training and teaching activities.

New challenges are faced in front of adult learners, educators and training professionals as economically active people and entrepreneurs who need innovative educational practices that will create unique and tailor-made learning experiences. Furthermore, teachers, trainers and tutors need to adapt to this new reality and find new tools to meet the raised expectations of nowadays learners [1].

The expected results of the project completion are to increase the digital and professional competencies of adult educators and training professionals about the applications of AI-based tools and technology-enhanced learning into formal, non-formal, and informal adult education. Furthermore, the approach of applying the chatbot learning environment into daily practices, will increase the awareness and the skills in the field of digital entrepreneurship. In addition, the encouragement of using modern digital self-learning tools, will promote a network between adult education and training providers, universities, chambers of commerce and public bodies in a national and international level improving the educational process.

References

1. Soltanifar, M., Mathew H., Lutz G.: Digital Entrepreneurship: Impact on Business and Society. Springer Nature (2021). ISBN 978-3-030-53914-6 (eBook)
2. Feine, J., Morana S., Maedche A.: Designing interactive Chatbot development systems. In: Proceedings of the 41st International Conference on Information Systems (ICIS), pp. 1–18. AISel, India (2020)

Academic Research Creativity Archive (ARCA)

Massimo Mecella[1], Eleonora Bernasconi[1](✉), Miguel Ceriani[2], Clara Di Fazio[3], Maria Cristina Capanna[3], Roberto Marcucci[4], Erik Pender[4], and Fabio Petriccione[5]

[1] Sapienza Università di Roma - Department of Computer, Control, and Management Engineering, Rome, Italy
{mecella,bernasconi} @diag.uniroma1.it
[2] Università degli Studi di Bari Aldo Moro, Bari, Italy
miguel.ceriani@uniba.it
[3] Sapienza Università di Roma - Department of Science of Antiquities, Rome, Italy
{clara.difazio,cristina.capanna}@uniroma1.it
[4] L'Erma di Bretschneider, Rome, Italy
{roberto.marcucci,erik.pender}@lerma.it
[5] Aton Informatica, Rome, Italy
fabio.petriccione@atoninformatica.it
http://arca.diag.uniroma1.it:5000 - 2019-2020

1 Summary of the Project

The ARCA project was born from the cooperation between Sapienza University of Rome (operationally the Department of Computer, Control, and Management Engineering Antonio Ruberti and the Department of Sciences of Antiquity), the company Aton Informatica and the historic publishing house L'Erma di Bretschneider. ARCA project led to an application development that allows semantic search of a library's contents. The project regards the Digital Humanities research field and has favored the development of a system placed in a single market area and with few results produced so far (described in the related work of the paper [3], that is, it supports users in exploring topics and semantic connections of a catalog of documents. The project was launched in 2019 thanks to the Lazio Region's funding "Creativity 2020", as part of the Operational Program co-financed by the FESR, and aims to develop an innovative digital solution for advanced semantic and bibliographic searches.

1.1 Objectives

ARCA's objective is to create an integrated platform of editorial products and digital services to offer new methods and experiences of semantic and bibliographic research, renewing the traditional method of research by keywords.

This work has been partly supported by projects ARCA (POR FESR Lazio 2014–2020 - Avviso pubblico "Creatività 2020", domanda prot. n. A0128-2017-17189) and STORYBOOK (POR FESR Lazio 2014-2020 - Avviso Pubblico "Progetti di Innovazione Digitale", domanda prot. n. A0349-2020-34437).

S. Cherfi et al. (Eds.): RCIS 2021, LNBIP 415, pp. 713–714, 2021.
https://doi.org/10.1007/978-3-030-75018-3

1.2 Expected Tangible Result

The project regards the Digital Humanities research field. It provides to favour developing a system placed in a single market area with few results produced so far, namely that of research interfaces based on semantic technologies in the humanities. It supports researchers of humanities disciplines, and interested users, in exploring topics and semantic connections, of a catalogue of documents. One of the main competing platforms is Yewno Discover[1], from which Arca differs for the freedom and creativity with which the concepts of research can be explored and connected.

2 Summary of Current Project Results

ARCA has generated an integrated knowledge base, created through the use of Named Entity Recognition, Knowledge Graph (KG) and Linked Data. The application allows extracting from the text of a book the "entities", which are then connected to the KG Arca, which in turn is then integrated with other KGs, thus obtaining the construction of other semantic associations. The generated knowledge extraction and integration pipeline [2] expand the collection, qualitative and quantitative, of the available information, thus defining the book's reference context and expanding the knowledge horizon. A proof-of-concept of ARCA [1] is available online at http://arca.diag.uniroma1.it:5000[2].

The development took place in parallel with the evaluation carried out by a small focus group of six researchers in archaeology and history. The user-centred design helped to refine details and features of the system that improved its usefulness and usability. The user studies conducted so far confirm the amenability of the proposed system to domain experts who were able to perform non-trivial tasks of search and exploration, which would be more cumbersome to execute with the search tools they are used to. Feedback gathered from two user tests [3] suggests that the proposed exploration mechanism tends to amplify the user experience by offering opportunities for further study and discovery of sources, themes, and materials, which can enrich the research process with new ideas.

References

1. Bernasconi, E., et al.: F.: ARCA. Semantic exploration of a bookstore. In: AVI 2020, pp. 1–3. Association for Computing Machinery, New York (2020). Article 78
2. Ceriani, M., Bernasconi, E., Mecella, M.: A streamlined pipeline to enable the semantic exploration of a bookstore. In: Ceci, M., Ferilli, S., Poggi, A. (eds.) IRCDL 2020. CCIS, vol. 1177, pp. 75–81. Springer, Cham (2020). https://doi.org/10.1007/978-3-030-39905-4_8
3. Bernasconi, E., Ceriani, M., Mecella, M.: Exploring a text corpus via a knowledge graph. In: CEUR Workshop Proceedings, IRCDL2021. pp. 91–102 (2021)

[1] https://www.yewno.com/discover.

[2] Access with email address: *rcis2021@arca.com* and password: *rcis2021*.

DataCloud: Enabling the Big Data Pipelines on the Computing Continuum

Dumitru Roman[1], Nikolay Nikolov[1], Brian Elvesæter[1], Ahmet Soylu[2], Radu Prodan[3], Dragi Kimovski[3], Andrea Marrella[4](✉), Francesco Leotta[4], Dario Benvenuti[4], Mihhail Matskin[5], Giannis Ledakis[6], Anthony Simonet-Boulogne[7], Fernando Perales[8], Evgeny Kharlamov[9], Alexandre Ulisses[10], Arnor Solberg[11], and Raffaele Ceccarelli[12]

[1] SINTEF AS, Trondhei, Norway
[2] Oslo Metropolitan University, Oslo, Norway
[3] University of Klagenfurt, Klagenfurt, Austria
[4] Sapienza University of Rome, Rome, Italy
marrella@diag.uniroma1.it
[5] KTH Royal Institute of Technology, Stockholm, Sweden
[6] UBITECH, Athens, Greece
[7] iExec, Lyon, France
[8] JOT, Madrid, Spain
[9] Bosch Center for Artificial Intelligence, Renningen, Germany
[10] MOG, Lisbon, Portugal
[11] Tellu, Asker, Norway
[12] Ceramica Catalano, Fabrica di Roma, Italy

1 Summary of the Project

With the recent developments of Internet of Things (IoT) and cloud-based technologies, massive amounts of data are generated by heterogeneous sources and stored through dedicated cloud solutions. Often organizations generate much more data than they are able to interpret, and current Cloud Computing technologies cannot fully meet the requirements of the Big Data processing applications and their data transfer overheads [1] Many data are stored for compliance purposes only but not used and turned into value, thus becoming *Dark Data*, which are not only an untapped value, but also pose a risk for organizations [3].

To guarantee a better exploitation of Dark Data, the **DataCloud project**[1] aims to realize novel methods and tools for effective and efficient management of the Big Data Pipeline lifecycle encompassing the Computing Continuum.

Big Data pipelines are composite pipelines for processing data with non-trivial properties, commonly referred to as the Vs of Big Data (e.g., volume, velocity, value, etc.) [4]. Tapping their potential is a key aspect to leverage Dark Data, although it requires to go beyond the current approaches and frameworks for Big Data processing. In this respect, the concept of *Computing Continuum*

[1] DataCloud is a Research and Innovation project funded by the European Commission under the Horizon 2020 program (Grant number 101016835). The project runs for three years, between 2021–2023.

S. Cherfi et al. (Eds.): RCIS 2021, LNBIP 415, pp. 715–717, 2021.
https://doi.org/10.1007/978-3-030-75018-3

extends the traditional centralised Cloud Computing with Edge[2] and Fog[3] computing in order to ensure low latency pre-processing and filtering close to the data sources. This will prevent to overwhelm the centralised cloud data centres enabling new opportunities for supporting Big Data pipelines.

2 Objectives and Expected Results

The main objective of the project is to develop a software ecosystem for managing Big Data pipelines on the Computing Continuum. The ecosystem consists of new languages, methods and infrastructures for supporting Big Data pipelines on heterogeneous and untrusted resources. Six lifecycle phases are covered:

1. *Pipeline discovery* concerns discovering Big Data pipelines from various data sources.
2. *Pipeline definition* deals with specifying pipelines featuring an abstraction level suitable for pure data processing.
3. *Pipeline simulation* aims to evaluate the performance of individual steps to test and optimise deployments.
4. *Resource provisioning* is concerned about securely provisioning a set of (trusted and untrusted) resources.
5. *Pipeline deployment* is concerned with deployment of pipelines across the provisioned resources.
6. *Pipeline adaptation* deals with optimised run-time provisioning of computational resources.

The ecosystem separates the design-time from the run-time deployment of pipelines and complements modern serverless approaches [2]. A set of research challenges related to each pipeline phase will be tackled within the project, such as the advancement of process mining techniques to learn the structure of pipelines, the definition of proper DSLs for pipelines, novel approaches for pipeline containerisation and blockchain-based resource marketplaces, etc.

The expected impact of DataCloud is to lower the technological entry barriers for the incorporation of Big Data pipelines in organizations' workflows and make them accessible to a wider set of stakeholders regardless of the hardware infrastructure. To achieve this, DataCloud will validate its results through a strong selection of complementary business cases offered by four SMEs and a large company targeting higher mobile business revenues in smart marketing campaigns, reduced live streaming production costs of sport events, trustworthy eHealth patient data management, and reduced time to production and better analytics in Industry 4.0 manufacturing.

Acknowledgments. This work has been supported by the Horizon 2020 project DataCloud (Grant number 101016835).

[2] Edge Computing is a paradigm that brings computation and data storage closer to the location where it is needed to improve response times and save bandwidth.

[3] Fog Computing uses edge devices to carry out a substantial amount of computation, storage, and communication locally and routed over the Internet backbone.

References

1. Barika, M., Garg, S., Zomaya, A.Y., Wang, L., Moorsel, A.V., Ranjan, R.: Orchestrating big data analysis workflows in the cloud: research challenges, survey, and future directions. ACM Comput. Surv. (CSUR) **52**(5), 1–41 (2019)
2. Castro, P., Ishakian, V., Muthusamy, V., Slominski, A.: The rise of serverless computing. Commun. ACM **62**(12), (2019)
3. Gimpel, G.: Bringing dark data into the light: illuminating existing IoT data lost within your organization. Bus. Horiz. **63**(4), 519–530 (2020)
4. Plale, B., Kouper, I.: The centrality of data: data lifecycle and data pipelines. In: Data Analytics for Intelligent Transportation Systems, pp. 91–111. Elsevier (2017)

DIG-IT: Digital Education Initiatives and Timely Solutions

Evangelia Vanezi[1(✉)], Alexandros Yeratziotis[1], Christos Mettouris[1], George A. Papadopoulos[1], and Colla J. MacDonald[2]

[1] Department of Computer Science, University of Cyprus, Nicosia, Cyprus
{evanez01,ayerat01,mettour,george}@cs.ucy.ac.cy
[2] University of Malta, Msida, Malta
Colla.J.MacDonald@um.edu.ca
http://project-digit.eu/
Start Date: 01-09-2019, Duration: 36 months

1 Summary of the Project

In light of the Covid-19 crisis, which led to a substantial increase in the usage of digital learning environments, affecting many learners [2], DIG-IT is an ongoing project[1] aiming to support educational technologies. A contradiction inspired the project: even though we are living in an era of rapid technological changes able to generate new approaches to education bearing benefits [1], at the same time, academic staff still resist taking advantage of available technologies in their teaching. However, some EU universities offer robust online education, while others lag, offering few to zero online learning opportunities. DIG-IT aims to address the imbalance and inequity of digital education opportunities offered at EU universities. A preliminary literature review and needs analysis identified that the cost and time required to design or learn how to design online study units and resources are significant barriers in implementing digital education. The project deals with the need for convenient, accessible, continuing education in academia with a case study in the healthcare sector, having thousands of busy practitioners needing continuous education (CE) while ensuring patient safety.

DIG-IT partners offer diverse skills and expertise ranging from online learning experts, computer science researchers, and healthcare professionals. The partners were chosen with the consideration of expertise or need for expertise concerning knowledge and skills required to design, deliver and evaluate digital education; need and interest to enhance initiatives and investment in the use of technology in teaching; and previous success in academic outputs. Furthermore, industry partners were included that could facilitate pioneering new avenues to extend education opportunities and CE practice.

1.1 Objectives

DIG-IT overall objectives are: (i) to collaboratively design evidence-based methods to assist academic staff with adopting digital education practices, increasing

[1] Funded by the Erasmus+ programme of the European Union, Agreement Number: 2019-1-MT01-KA203-051171.

S. Cherfi et al. (Eds.): RCIS 2021, LNBIP 415, pp. 718–719, 2021.
https://doi.org/10.1007/978-3-030-75018-3

their knowledge and skills and the use of technology in teaching; and (ii) to create an inter-nations learning community of practice to collaboratively create, share and distribute innovative training and teaching resources to support academic staff by reducing time and cost required to design digital education products and processes.

1.2 Expected Tangible Result

The project has envisioned the following tangible results: 1. a digital education innovative *interactive framework* and companion evaluation toolkit as a quality standard in guiding the design, delivery and evaluation of effective online study units, supporting educational technologies; 2. *innovative and evidence-based methods* to assist university academic staff and health industry educators with adopting digital education practices into current curricula; 3. the two-phased delivery and evaluation of: (i) a *nine-module course* to support and motivate educators on how to design, deliver and evaluate digital education resources, and (ii) a *train-the-trainer* online course to develop digital education experts to support and promote digital education; 4. an *open access repository* and website providing access to free open digital education resources; 5. bilingual (English & Italian) digital healthcare education apps collaboratively designed and piloted in a hospital partner.

2 Summary of Current Project Results

At this point of the project, the team has delivered successfully the first round of the two envisioned courses: (i) the online course on how to design, deliver and evaluate digital study units; and (ii) the train-the-trainer online course. Additionally, the evaluation process of both courses was completed and the data were analysed. The results demonstrate positive outcomes and positive feedback. Moreover, the "*European Union Digital Education Quality Standard Framework and Companion Evaluation Toolkit*" aiming to guide the design, delivery and evaluation of effective online learning, was designed, and an interactive tool[2] was developed hosted in the DIG-IT web platform. In the same platform: (i) the "*ECG Interpretation for Nurses online course*" healthcare course was developed, and healthcare workers are currently piloting it gathering positive feedback; and (ii) an open-access resources repository was created and released to the public. The included resources will continue to be updated and enhanced throughout the project duration. All the above tools were developed using web technologies (HTML, CSS, Javascript, PHP).

References

1. Legon, R., Garrett, R.: Chloe 4: Navigating the mainstream. Quality Matters & Eduventures Survey of Chief Online Officers (2020)
2. McCarthy, N.: Covid-19's staggering impact on global education. In: World Economic Forum (2020)

[2] http://project-digit.eu/index.php/digital-education-quality-standards/.

Life-Cycle Modelling for Railway Infrastructure: Application to Autonomous Train Map

Nadia Chouchani[1(✉)], Sana Debbech[1], and Airy Magnien[2]

[1] IRT Railenium, 180 Rue Joseph Louis-Lagrange, 59300 Valenciennes, France
{nadia.chouchani,sana.debbech}@railenium.eu
[2] SNCF, 2 places aux Étoiles, 93200 Saint Denis, France
airy.magnien@sncf.fr

1 Introduction

A railway infrastructure model should be constantly updated with new versions to reflect the real-world objects life-cycle. In fact, the track assets are constantly changing, new tracks or lines could be extended and maintenance processes may cause updates. However, the current standards for infrastructure models, such as RailSystemModel (*RSM*) does not currently support life-cycle modelling and versioning. *RSM*, originally named *RailTopoModel* (*RTM*) [1], is developed by the International Union of Railways with the ambition to provide a systematic and standardized digital model of the whole railway system description, including topology, geographical positioning, geometry, scheduling, traffic management etc. This standard has been used as an infrastructure conceptual model for the autonomous train map development. In fact, as part of the Autonomous Freight Train project, we aim to design and develop the rail infrastructure map system which includes the description of the track topology and all the signaling assets and buildings. But to serve autonomous driving, we encountered the problem of modelling the life-cycle of the various objects of the infrastructure. It is a challenging subject in several domains and applications such as *CO2* emissions of aerial vehicles [2] and data transfer in transportation projects [3]. Our goal is to lay the foundation for a life-cycle model allowing to manage history and evolution of the rail assets over time in a simple and generic way. This model will be integrated to *RSM* as a standard for international usage, especially by the national society of French rails (*SNCF*) for the autonomous trains project.

2 Life-Cycle Modelling for Railway Infrastructure

Railway domain is critical and its systems design is a challenging and iterative task, thus rail assets change over time. How does a rail asset look at a specific

This research work contributes to the french collaborative project TFA (autonomous freight train), with SNCF, Alstom Transport, Hitachi Rail STS, Altran and Apsys. It was carried out in the framework of IRT Railenium, Valenciennes, France, and therefore was granted public funds within the scope of the French Program "Investissements d'Avenir".

S. Cherfi et al. (Eds.): RCIS 2021, LNBIP 415, pp. 720–721, 2021.
https://doi.org/10.1007/978-3-030-75018-3

point in time? How to manage its history and versions transitions? In this work, we propose to enrich the *RSM* standard to model different versions and transitions between them. For modelling of the semantic, topological, appearance and geometric changes of the various objects of the infrastructure, we will meet the following requirements:

- Represent several historical versions of objects;
- Allow multiple past representations of the same object;
- Exchange all versions in a single dataset.

In order to have a structured representation of the life-cycle process for railway infrastructure, we identified the following pertinent concepts (noted in italics). Every network entity is designed by *RSM::NamedResource* class. In order to represent a versionable object, *VersionableNamedResource* is introduced as a sub-type of the *RSM* class. It is associated to *RSM::ValidityPeriod*, an object lifetime representation; and to *Version* concept. A version, being a *VersionableNamedResource*, may aggregate other versions. The passage between versions is ensured by *VersionTransaction*, which groups all individual transactions acting on individual resource instances. *Transaction* could bear an attribute such as "add", "remove" or "keep". In addition, in order to manage the history or evolution over time, the transitions between the versions should be considered. These transitions represent changes in the state of all characteristics of an entity at a given time.

The proposed concepts can be used to describe the transformation of a subgraph of the railway network topology. The infrastructure transformations are indeed encountered when modelling the autonomous train map. Our proposal is an alternative to the most frequent versioning method, which consists in delegating versioning to the IT system that actually instantiates the model. By hosting the concept of "*version*" inside the conceptual model, we ensure highest integrity of data and secure its exchange. Semantics disambiguation is crucial and deserves an investigation by the integration of upper ontologies. For this purpose, we intend to propose an extended conceptual model of life-cycle founded on an upper ontology with a clear and well defined vocabulary.

References

1. Ciszewski, T., Nowakowski, W., Chrzan, M.: Railtopomodel and railml-data exchange standards in railway sector. Arch. Transp. Syst. Telemat. **10** (2017)
2. Figliozzi, M.A.: Lifecycle modeling and assessment of unmanned aerial vehicles (Drones) CO2e emissions. Transp. Res. Part D: Transp. Environ. **57**, 251–261 (2017)
3. Le, T., Le, C., David Jeong, H.: Lifecycle data modeling to support transferring project-oriented data to asset-oriented systems in transportation projects. J. Manage. Eng. **34**(4) (2018)

Author Index

Printed in the United States
by Baker & Taylor Publisher Services